MANTLE FIELDING'S

DICTIONARY

of

American Painters, Sculptors

and Engravers

With an Addendum
Containing Corrections and
Additional Material on the
Original Entries

Compiled by

JAMES F. CARR

JAMES F. CARR *Publisher*

New York 1965

PUBLISHED AND DISTRIBUTED BY

JAMES F. CARR *Publisher*
41 Fifth Avenue
New York 10003

COMPILER'S PREFACE
to the 1965 edition with
THE ADDENDUM

It would have been preferable to reset this entire work, integrating the corrections and additional material in their proper places, but the cost in both time and typesetting was prohibitive. Adding the new material in an Addendum, although not as convenient as a complete resetting, makes available a more accurate and dependable work.

There are no new entries in this present edition. The Addendum is entirely concerned with the corrections and additional material relating to the *existing* entries in the original work published in 1926. In using this new volume it will be necessary to refer to both the main work and the Addendum since the spelling of some names is corrected and any new information is added under the proper spelling and also because of several errors in alphabetizing in the original work.

In general when there are new dates cited in the addenda these are preferred over Fielding's dates. The sources for these new dates are always cited. When there are varying dates quoted from more than one later source, the date given in Groce & Wallace: *The New-York Historical Society's Dictionary of Artists in America 1564-1860* is preferred.

We are indebted to the Frick Art Reference Library, the library, Metropolitan Museum of Art, the New-York Historical Society and the New York Public Library for the use of their marked copies of the original edition of Mantle Fielding's *Dictionary*. These marked copies had many manuscript annotations and have proved invaluable in the compilation of the addenda. When the marked copies are cited they appear as: m.c. FARL (Frick Art Reference Library), m.c. Met (Metropolitan Museum of Art) etc. When there is more than one marked copy the 2nd and 3rd copies are listed as: m.c. FARL 2; m.c. Met 2 etc.

Jacqueline Mueller worked diligently checking and collating the corrections and additions and promptly went off to Europe to recuperate when the job was completed. James Nash typed and then retyped the copy with surprisingly few errors and then decided on the better life of a student at New York University.

As this goes to press work has begun on a new volume of short biographies of American Artists not included in this work or Groce & Wallace. Anyone who has suggestions for entries in this new work is invited to communicate with the compiler.

James F. Carr
New York, September 1965

AUTHOR'S PREFACE

It has been said that Art has no nationality. At the same time it is almost imperative that the collector or writer on subjects pertaining to American Art should have a dictionary of painters, sculptors and engravers who are now practicing their Art in the United States or who have done so in the past.

In the absence of any collected literature along these lines, which can be considered in the least a complete record, the author has sought to combine the previous compilations of the recognized authorities with his own catalogue of American Artists (a work of twenty years), producing a result by far the most comprehensive of its kind ever published.

Dunlap's History of the Arts in the United States served for years as a primary source of information for the student of early American Art. This book and Henry Tuckerman's Book of the Artist, together with several biographical dictionaries, have heretofore been almost the only available sources of published information on this interesting subject. Unfortunately, even taken collectively, they are far from complete. Nothing in the nature of a collected list of American Engravers and their work was known until the publication of Stauffer's and Fielding's volumes on American Engravers.

In the field of American Sculpture a similar condition existed until Lorado Taft's excellent work gave much needed information.

Paintings by many of the Early American Artists are still hard to identify, and in many cases the attributions are unreliable. For instance, many of the paintings of Joseph Badger (1708–1765) masqueraded for years as the work of Copley. Very good examples of Badger's painting can be seen at Bowdoin College, The Massachusetts Historical Society, and in many of the private collections in Boston and its vicinity, and yet one may look in vain for any mention of the name of Joseph Badger in Dunlap, Tuckerman, Bryan, or Appleton. This is only one case of many which exemplify the need and demand for a more accurate list not only of

v

the early American Artists, but of those who are working in the United States at the present time.

Perhaps only to a few will this volume give any idea of the amount of time and labor expended in its preparation, and the author does not claim that the following list of American Artists is even yet a satisfactory one, but he does maintain that it is the largest and most complete published up to the present time. Within its pages will be found the biographies and records of nearly eight thousand artists which the author sincerely hopes may prove of interest and value to those who are seeking information along the lines of American Art.

It is the desire of the author that any mistakes discovered may be made known to him for future correction, and that all authenticated additional information may be given him. He also makes his grateful acknowledgments to the many friends who have so courteously and generously helped him with information and material for the preparation of this book.

MANTLE FIELDING,
520 Walnut St.,
Philadelphia, Pa.

A

ABBATE, Paolo S. Sculptor. Born in Italy, 1884. Educated there and in the United States. Member of International Fine Arts Society. Works: Dante monument, Newburgh, N. Y., and at Providence, R. I. Bust collection in Newark, N. J. Bust of Enrico Caruso in New York. *Address,* 1931 Broadway, New York City.

ABBATT, Agnes Dean. Painter. Born 1847; died 1917. Elected member of National Academy, 1902. Studied Art at Cooper Union and the National Academy of Design. Painted in oils and water-colors, also wax modelling. She painted landscapes, coast scenes, and flowers. Medal at Cooper Union, and first prize in oil painting at San Antonio, Texas. *Address* was in New York.

ABBEY, Edwin. Painter, illustrator and mural decorator. Born in Philadelphia, 1852; died in London, 1911. He studied at the Penna. Academy of Fine Arts. His ''King Lear'' is at the Metropolitan Museum, N. Y., and his ''Quest of the Holy Grail'' at the Boston Public Library. His illustrations for Shakespeare's Works, Herrick's Poems, and She Stoops to Conquer are among his best known illustrations. Elected member of National Academy, 1902. See Life of Edwin Abbey, by E. V. Lucas. 2 vols. London.

ABBEY, Iva L. Painter. Born in Chester, Conn., in 1882. Pupil of Hale, Benson, and C. J. Martin. Member of Hartford Art Society. *Address,* Wilkes-Barre Institute, Wilkes-Barre, Penna.

ABBOTT, Anne Fuller. Painter. Born in Brandon, Vt. Pupil of William M. Chase and the National Academy of Design. *Address,* McLean Bldg., 1517 H Street, Washington, D. C.

ABBOTT, Eleanore P. Painter. Born at Lincoln, Maine, 1875; married Yarnall Abbott. Pupil of Penna. Academy of Fine Arts, Phila., and Simon and Cottet in Paris. *Address,* The Gladstone, 11th and Pine Sts., Philadelphia.

ABBOTT, Francis R. Painter. Pupil of the Penna. Academy of Fine Arts, and the Julian Academy in Paris. He was born in Philadelphia and was an Artist Member of the Art Club for twenty years. He died in Philadelphia in 1925.

ABBOTT, S. N. Painter. Born 1874. Pupil of Laurens and Constant. Well known by his illustrations. *Address,* 725 Lexington Ave., N. Y.

ABBOTT, W. H. Sculptor. *Address,* 46 Greenwich Ave., New York.

ABBOTT, Yarnall. Painter. Born in Philadelphia, 1870. Pupil of Thos. Anschutz at Penna. Academy of Fine Arts and Collin and Courtois in Paris. Exhibited at the Penna. Academy of the Fine Arts, 1924–25. *Address,* 1612 Latimer Street, Philadelphia, Pa.

ABDY, Rowena Meeks (Mrs.). Painter and illustrator. Born in Austria, 1887, of American parents. Came to San Francisco, California, and studied under Arthur F. Mathews. Awarded medal by California Museum of Art, 1920. Exhibited water-color ''Old Fashioned Room'' at Penna. Academy of Fine Arts, Phila., 1924. *Address,* 1050 Lombard Street, Russian Hill, San Francisco, California.

A'BECKET, Maria J. C. Landscape painter. Born in Portland, Maine. Studied in the White Mountains with Homer Martin in 1865, and in 1875–78 with William Hunt in Boston. She also spent a summer painting in France with Daubigny. She died in New York, September 6th, 1904. She exhibited in Boston, Baltimore, Philadelphia and Washington.

ABEL, Louise. Sculptor. Born at Mt. Healthy, Ohio, in 1894. Pupil of Barnhorn, Meakin, and Wessel. Exhibited portrait statuettes at the annual exhibition of the Penna. Academy of Fine Arts, 1924. *Address,* North Bend Road, Mt. Healthy, Ohio.

ABEL, M. Painter. Exhibited at Cincinnati Museum in 1925. *Address,* 939 Richmond Street, Cincinnati, Ohio.

ABERNETHIE. An early American Engraver of maps, Masonic prints and book plates who worked in Charleston, S. C., about 1780.

ABRAHAMSEN, Christian. Painter and illustrator. Born in Norway, 1887. Represented in Chicago Art Institute by ''Winter.''

ABRAMOVITZ, Albert. Painter. Member of Society of Independent Artists. *Address,* 336 East 17th Street, New York.

1

ABRAMS, Elanor. Painter. Born in Karns City, Pa. Pupil of Elliott Daingerfield and Henry B. Snell. *Address*, 10 East 9th Street, New York.

ABRAMS, Lucian. Painter. Born at Lawrence, Kansas. Pupil of Laurens, Constant, and Whistler in Paris. Member of Society of Independent Artists. Represented by "Sandy Bay," Dallas Art Association. *Address*, Lyme, Conn.

ABRAMSON, Rosalind. Painter and etcher. Born in Norfolk, Va., 1901. Pupil of Art Students' League of New York under Bridgman, Henri, Bellows, and DuMond. *Address*, 59 West 59th Street, New York, or 706 Riverside Drive, New York.

ACKERS, Charles. Sculptor. Born in 1835 near Hollis, Me. He went to Rome in 1855 to study art with his brother Benjamin Paul Ackers, also a sculptor. Charles Ackers died in New York in 1906.

ACKERSON, Floyd G. Painter. Born 1883 in Portage, Michigan. Pupil of Carnegie Art School. *Address*, 31 Rebecca Street, Wilkinsburg, Pa.

ACHERT, Fred. Painter. Member Cincinnati Art Club. *Address*, 10 East 3d Street, Cincinnati, Ohio.

ACHESON, Georgina Elliott. Miniature and water-color artist. Exhibited at the Penna. Academy of Fine Arts, Philadelphia, 1924–25. *Address*, Ardsley on Hudson, New York City.

ADAM, David Livingston. Portrait painter. Born in Glasgow, Scotland, in 1883; died in Chicago, Ill., 1924. He studied in Glasgow, Brussels, and the Art Institute of Chicago. He was a member of the Palette and Chisel Club, The Chicago Society of Artists, and the Alumni of the Art Institute of Chicago. In 1920 he was awarded a gold medal by the Palette and Chisel Club.

ADAM, Wilbur G. Painter. *Address*, 3033 Highland Ave., Cincinnati, Ohio.

ADAM, William. Painter, landscapes. Born in England, studied at Glasgow and Paris. *Address*, 450 Central Ave., Pacific Grove, California.

ADAMS, Charles P. Painter, landscapes. Born 1858, at Franklin, Mass. *Address*, 3935 Dalton Ave., Los Angeles, California.

ADAMS, Dunlap. Engraver. Working in Philadelphia in 1764. He engraved on gold, silver, copper and brass, and seems to have been more of a silversmith and die sinker than a copper-plate engraver. See announcement in "Pennsylvania Gazette" for September 6, 1764.

ADAMS, Herbert. Sculptor. Born 1856, in Concord, Vt. Studied at Mass. Institute of Technology, pupil of Mercie at Paris. Elected member of National Academy, 1899. His portrait statues are very fine; his William Cullen Bryant, in the park behind the Public Library, N. Y., the seated figures of Marshall and Ranney at the Cleveland Court House, and the McMillan Fountain, Washington, D. C., are among his best known works. His portrait busts of Miss DeFanti, Miss duPont, and his bas-relief of Choate at the Union League Club of N. Y. are also well known. *Address*, 131 West 11th St., New York.

ADAMS, J. Howard. Painter. Member of Providence Art Club. *Address*, 1217 Turks Head Bldg., Providence, R. I.

ADAMS, John Ottis. Painter, landscapes. Born 1851 at Amitz, Ind. Pupil of John Parker, London, and Loefftz in Munich. Among his works "Summer Afternoon" at Richmond, Ind. Also "The Road to Town," "The Pool" and "Late Autumn." *Address*, The Hermitage, Brookville, Ind.

ADAMS, John Wolcott. Born 1874, Worcester, Mass. Student of Art Mus., Boston; Art Students' League, New York. Began work in New York, 1899; illustrator of books, poems, etc., for Harper's, Scribner's, Century and other magazines. Illustrator: Hoosier Romance (by James Whitcomb Riley), 1910; known for drawings in connection with old songs, Colonial incidents, etc. *Address*, 360 West 22d Street, New York City.

ADAMS, Joseph Alexander. Born 1803; died 1880. An early American wood engraver, largely self-taught. He was elected an Associate member of the National Academy of Design in 1841. His Bible Illustrations are well known, his "Last Arrow" was engraved in 1837 for the New York Mirror. He also worked for the "Treasury of Knowledge" and other publications. See "History of Wood Engraving in America," by W. J. Linton.

ADAMS, K. Langhorne (Mrs.). Painter. Born Plainfield, New Jersey. Member of the Association of Women Painters and Sculptors, New York. Exhibited: "Gloss of Satin and Glimmer of Silk," "The Blue House." *Address*, 142 East 18th Street, New York.

ADAMS, Philip. Painter. Born 1881, in Honolulu. Pupil of Bridgman, Paxton, Hale, Benson, and Woodbury, in Boston. Member of Copley Society. *Address*, 1310 Massachusetts Ave., Washington, D. C.

ADAMS, Wayman. Portrait painter. Born September 23, 1883, Muncie, Ind. Student of John Herron Art Institute, Indianapolis, 1905–9, also studied in Italy, 1910, Spain, 1912. Awarded Thomas R. Proctor prize Nat. Acad. Design, New York. Elected Associate Member of National Academy. Among his portraits are Joseph Pennell, Samuel Rabston, Thomas R. Marshall, and Edward W. Redfield, the painter. *Address*, Sherwood Studios, 58 West 57th Street, New York City.

ADAMS, Winifred Brady (Mrs. John Ottis Adams). Painter. Born 1871 in Muncie, Ind. Studied in Philadelphia at Drexel Inst. Among her works, "Marigolds" at Art Inst. of Indianapolis, and several studies in still life painting. *Address*, The Hermitage, Brookville, Ind.

ADAMS, Woodhull. Painter. Exhibited oil painting, "At Miss Florence's," Penna. Academy of Fine Arts, Phila., 1924. *Address*, Lyme, Conn.

ADDAMS, Clifford. Painter and etcher. Exhibited miniatures at Exhibition Academy of Fine Arts for water-colors and miniatures, 1924–25. *Address*, London, England, and 71 Washington Square, New York.

ADDAMS, Inez (Mrs. Clifford Addams). Painter. *Address*, 71 Washington Square, New York.

ADNEY, Edwin Tappan. Artist and illustrator. Born at Athens, Ohio. Studied at Art Students' League, New York. Illustrated Harper's Weekly and Collier's Weekly.

ADOLPHE, Albert Jean. Painter and mural decorator. Born 1865 in Phila. Studied with Gerome and Whistler in Paris. *Address*, 2616 Montgomery Ave., Phila., Pa.

ADRIANCE, Minnie H. Painter. Member of Society of Independent Artists. *Address*, 51 East 53d Street, New York City.

AGATE, Alfred. Miniature painter. Brother of Frederick S. Agate. Born 1818 and died 1846. He received his instruction from the artist Thomas S. Cummings. Elected Associate Member of National Academy.

AGATE, Frederick S. Painter. Born 1807, in Sparta, West Chester Co., N. Y.; died in 1844. He first studied art with the engraver Rollinson, and later with John R. Smith and S. F. B. Morse. He painted an excellent portrait of Rollinson, also of the actor Forrest as "Metamora." He was elected an Associate of the National Academy of Design and an Academician in 1826.

AHL, Henry Hammond. Painter. Born at East Hartford, Conn., in 1869. Pupil of Alexander Wagner and Gerome. Among his works, "In the Shadow of the Cross" at Washington, D. C., "Sunset Glow" at Art Museum, Springfield, Mass., "Sunset Hour" at Portland, Maine, and "Sunset" at Worcester Art Museum. He has also done mural painting in Jamaica Plain, Boston, and in Providence, R. I. *Address*, 12 Harcourt Street, Boston, Mass.

AHRENS, Ellen Wetherald. Painter of portraits and miniatures. Born 1859, in Baltimore, Md. Member of Penna. Society of Miniature Painters. Awarded prizes at Penna. Academy of Fine Arts and Carnegie Institute, Pittsburgh. *Address*, Lansdowne, Pa.

AID, Geo. C. Miniature painter, etcher. Born 1872, in Quincy, Ill. Medal at St. Louis Exposition, 1904. Pupil of Laurens, and Benjamin, Constant, in Paris. *Address*, 3660 Blaine Ave., St. Louis, Mo.

AIKEN, Charles A. Mural painter. Born 1872 in Georgia, Vt. Pupil of Boston Museum of Fine Arts School. Exhibited water colors, Penna. Academy of Fine Arts, Phila., 1925. *Address*, 57 West 57th Street, New York.

AIKEN, Robert. Sculptor. He exhibited in 1920 the "Elizabeth Watrous Medal" at the Penna. Academy of Fine Arts, Phila. Elected member of National Academy, 1914. *Address*, 162 West 11th Street, New York.

AIKMAN, Walter Monteith. Artist. Born 1857, New York. Studied engraving in N. Y. under Frank French and J. G. Smithwick, drawing and painting under Boulanger and Lefebvre, Paris. Medal for engraving, Paris Expn., 1889, and Chicago Expn., 1893. Exhibited at Paris 1900; silver medal for original engravings on wood, Buffalo Expn., 1901. *Address*, 133 Macon Street, Brooklyn, N. Y.

AIMAN, Pearl. Painter. Exhibited "Fishing Pier, Provincetown," at Penna. Academy of Fine Arts, 1920. *Address*, East Willow Grove Ave., Chestnut Hill, Phila., Pa.

AITKEN, Peter. Wood engraver. Born June 16, 1858, Dundas, Can. Studied engraving under Timothy Cole several years, visited Europe 1887 and 1891, and studied in Paris 1895. Awarded medal, Chicago Expn., 1893, exhibited Paris Expn., 1900. *Address*, Hart Street, Brooklyn, N. Y.

AITKEN, Robert. Born 1734, in Scotland; died 1802, in Philadelphia. Aitken issued the Pennsylvania Magazine in 1776, and engraved the vignette on the title page after a design by Pierre E. duSimitiere, and a number of illustrations; among the latter were some of the first views of military operations in the revolution ever engraved.

AITKEN, Robert Ingersoll. Sculptor. Born 1878, at San Francisco. Studied Mark Hopkins Inst. of Art, San Francisco, and under Arthur F. Matthews and Douglas Tilden. Prof. sculpture, Mark Hopkins Inst. of Art (U. of Cal.), 1901–4. Among important works are busts of Mme. Modjeska, Douglas Tilden, Dr. J. L. York; monuments to William McKinley, at St. Helena, Cal., 1902, Berkeley, Cal., 1902; bust of Charles J. Dickman, Charles Rollo Peters, 1902; McKinley Monument, Golden Gate Park, San Francisco, 1903. Also designs of $50 gold coin issued by U. S. Govt. in commemoration of the expn. Burritt Memorial, New Britain, Conn. Helen Foster Barnet Prize, N. A. D.; Medal of Honor (gold) Architectural League, N. Y., for sculpture, 1915; silver medal for sculpture, Panama-Pacific Internat. Expn., 1915. Worked in Paris, 1904–7, Instr. Nat. Acad. Schools Sculpture Class. N. A. sec. Nat. Sculpture Soc. *Address,* 154 West 55th Street, New York City.

AKELEY, Carl Ethan. Sculptor. Born 1864, in Claredon, N. Y. Member of National Sculpture Society Works. Animal studies in Brooklyn Institute, and American Museum of Natural History.

AKERS, Benjamin Paul. Sculptor. Born 1825, in Westbrook, Me.; died 1861, in Phila., Pa. Was for some time a resident of Portland, Me., where he studied painting. In Boston, 1849, he was given lessons in plaster casting by Carew. After making several busts of a promising character, he made his first visit to Europe, visiting Florence, Italy, where he remained during the year 1852, and is said to have studied under Powers at that time. His second visit abroad was made in 1854. Among his works are: "Peace," "Una and the Lion," "Girl Pressing Grapes," "Isaiah," "Schiller's Diver," "Reindeer," "The Lost Pearl Diver," "St. Elizabeth of Hungary," "Milton," "Diana and Endymion"; portrait busts of Tilton, Longfellow, Samuel Appleton, Edward Everett, Prof. Cleveland, Gerrit Smith, Sam Houston, and Justice John McLean. According to some biographers, he was called Paul on account of his serious religious characteristics. He was also a frequent contributor on art subjects to the leading periodicals.

AKERS, Charles. Sculptor. Born in Maine, 1836. He also worked as a crayon portrait draughtsman. His studio was in New York, 1860–69. In 1875 he was working in Waterbury, Conn., and in 1879 he had returned to New York.

AKIN, Mrs. She is supposed to have been the wife of James Akin, and engraved membership certificates. Her work was done in Newburyport, Mass., in 1806–08.

AKIN, James. Born 1773, probably in South Carolina; died July 16, 1846, in Phila-

delphia. His earliest engraved work is found in Drayton's "Views of South Carolina," Charleston, S. C., 1802. In 1804 he was working in Salem, Mass.; in 1808 he returned to Phila., where he drew caricatures, and engraved book plates. He also published prints in connection with William Harrison, Jr.

AKIN, Louis. Painter. Was born 1868, in Portland, Me.; died 1913, in Flagstaff, Arizona. He studied in New York City under Chase and DuMond. His specialty was painting the life of the American Indian and the American Museum of Natural History in New York commissioned him to decorate their room devoted to Indians of the Southwest.

ALBEE, Percy F. Painter. Born 1883, in Bridgeport, Conn. Pupil of Penna. Academy of Fine Arts and Providence School of Design. *Address,* 235 Benefit Street, Providence, R. I.

ALBERT, Ernest. Painter. Born 1857, in Brooklyn, N. Y. Pupil of Brooklyn Art School. Elected associate National Academy of Design. *Address,* New Canaan, Conn.

ALBERT, E. Maxwell. Painter. Born 1890, in Chicago, Ill. Pupil of Art Students, League of New York. *Address,* New Canaan, N. Y.

ALBERTS, John B. Painter. Born 1886, at Louisville, Ky. Pupil of Cincinnati Art Academy.

ALBRECHT, C. J. Sculptor. State Museum, University of Washington, Seattle, Wash.

ALBRIGHT, Adam Emory. Artist. Born 1862, at Monroe, Wis. Student of Art Inst. of Chicago, 1881–3; Pa. Acad. Fine Arts, Philadelphia, 1883–6; Munich and Paris, 1887–8. Painter of Am. country children; has exhibited at many exhibitions, in America; represented at Chicago Expn., in 1893, and since in New York, Philadelphia, Boston, Washington, Chicago, Paris Salon. Mem. Soc. Western Artists, Fellowship of Pa. Acad. Fine Arts, Philadelphia, Chicago Soc. Artists (pres., 1915–16), Chicago Water Color Club (dir., ex-pres.), Chicago Acad. Design, Am. Water Color Soc., New York. Member Am. Federation of Arts. *Address,* Hubbard Woods, Ill.

ALBRIGHT, Gertrude P. (Mrs.). Painter. Born in England. Among her paintings, the "Portrait of an Actress," owned by the city of San Francisco, is the best known. Her *Address* is 737 Buena Vista Ave., San Francisco, Cal.

ALBRIGHT, Henry James. Painter and sculptor. Born 1887, in Albany, N. Y. Pupil of Wm. St. John Harper, John F. Carlson, and C. W. Hawthorne. *Address,* Albany, New York.

ALBRIGHT, H. Oliver. Painter. Born 1876 in Germany. Member of San Francisco Art Association. *Address*, 737 Buena Vista Ave., San Francisco, Cal.

ALBRIGHT, Ivan L. Painter. Exhibited in 1924 at Penna. Academy of Fine Arts. *Address*, New York City.

ALCOT, May. Painter. Born 1840 in Concord, Mass.; died 1879. Studied in Boston School of Design and abroad. Her professional life has been spent in Boston, London, and Paris. Her best known work is her still life compositions. She has exhibited in America and Europe.

ALDRICH, George Ames. Painter and etcher. Born 1872, in Worcester, Mass. Pupil of Julian and Colarossi Academies. *Address*, 155 East Ohio Street, Chicago, Ill.

ALEXANDER, Clifford. Painter, illustrator and teacher. Born 1870, in Springfield, Mass. Pupil of School of Boston Museum of Art. *Address*, 6 Upland Road, Faneuil Station, Brighton, Mass.

ALEXANDER, Cosmo. Scottish painter who visited this country in 1770 and remained in Newport, R. I., for a year or so, and then went to South Carolina and then to Edinburgh. He died shortly after reaching home. He painted portraits of Dr. William Hunter's family of Newport, and a number of his countrymen residing in this country. On his return to Scotland he took young Gilbert Stuart with him.

ALEXANDER, Francis. Born 1800 in Connecticut; presumed to have died in Italy in 1880. Began painting in water color, and studied under Alexander Robinson in New York. Later he went to Providence, and then opened his studio in Boston, where he had many sitters, the most famous being Daniel Webster, of whom he painted several excellent portraits. In 1831 he visited Europe, finally settling in Florence, where he remained until his death. Alexander wrote a short autobiography published in Dunlap's "History." He went to New York for a brief period in 1820 and again the following year for study. He then went to Boston with a letter to Gilbert Stuart from John Trumbull, where he advanced rapidly in his painting under Stuart's influence. In 1831 he first visited Italy. He did not in his final years continue his profession as an artist. He drew on stone the earliest attempts at portrait lithography in America. For full account see Boston Magazine, 1825. He painted Charles Dickens, Benjamin R. Curtis, John Odin, Baron Stow, Mrs. Fletcher Webster and Master Lord, and many others.

ALEXANDER, John W. Artist. Born 1856, in Allegheny City, Pa.; died in 1915 in New York City. Educated in the schools of his native city, he early manifested a talent for sketching and at sixteen went to New York, where he soon obtained employment with Harper & Brothers as an illustrator. In 1877 he went abroad and studied at the Munich Royal Gallery and later in Venice, Florence, Holland and Paris. On his return to this country in 1881 he won immediate recognition as a portrait painter, many eminent men, including Walt Whitman, Joseph Jefferson, Oliver Wendell Holmes, John Burroughs, Grover Cleveland and Robert Louis Stevenson, sitting for him. In 1891 he went to Europe for his health and during the course of his travels made a series of portraits of distinguished authors. Three of his portraits of women were accepted by the Paris Salon of 1893, marking the beginning of his international reputation and winning him election as an associate of the Société Nationale des Beaux Arts. He also achieved distinction in mural painting. The six decorative panels representing "The Evolution of the Book," which adorn the Congressional Library, were done by him in 1895. Later he painted the titanic series of murals surrounding the grand staircase of the Carnegie Institute, Pittsburgh, and in 1906 was engaged to do a series depicting "The Industrial Development of Pennsylvania" for the State Capitol, an assignment which he never completed. He was one of the most active members of the National Academy of Design, and its president from 1909 until shortly before his death. Among his paintings, "The Pot of Basil," painted in 1856, is owned by the Boston Museum of Fine Arts. "The Blue Bowl" is owned by the Rhode Island School of Design. His portrait of the Norwegian painter Thaulow is owned by the Penna. Fairmount Park, Wilstach Collection.

ALEXANDER, Mary L. Sculptor. Pupil of Duvenech, Bamhorn and Graffy. Represented in Cincinnati Art Academy. *Address*, Alexandra Bldg., Cincinnati, Ohio.

ALFANO, Vicenzo. Neapolitan sculptor. Exhibited in 1902 at the Sculpture Society in New York, "Cicerone."

ALGER, John. Painter. Born 1879 in Boston, Mass. Member of the Society of Independent Artists. *Address*, 210 East 17th Street, New York.

ALKE, Stephen. Painter. Exhibited landscapes in the annual exhibition of Cincinnati Museum, 1925. *Address*, New Richmond, Ohio.

ALLAIRE, Louise. Painter. Member of National Association of Women Painters and Sculptors. *Address*, 646 St. Marks Ave., Brooklyn, New York.

ALLAN, Mrs. Charles Beach. Painter. Born 1874 in Detroit, Mich. *Address*, 542 Park Ave., Kansas City, Mo.

ALLEN, Anne Huntington (Mrs. Thomas W. Allen). Painter. Born New York, 1858. Student, Cooper Institute, pupil of Wyatt Eaton, and Carolus Duran. *Address*, 230 Southern Ave., Mt. Auburn, Cincinnati, Ohio.

ALLEN, Charles Curtis. Painter. Born in 1886. Instructor in water color painting, Worcester Art Museum. Exhibited at Penna. Academy of Fine Arts, Philadelphia, 1925. *Address*, 41 Commouwealth Ave., Chestnut Hill, Mass.

ALLEN, Frank L. Painter. Born in Portland, Maine, in 1884. Pupil of Tarbell. *Address*, Pratt Inst., Brooklyn, N. Y.

ALLEN, Frederick W. Sculptor. Boston, Mass. Born Vermont, 1888. Exhibited ''Toreo'' at Penna. Academy of the Fine Arts, Philadelphia, 1924. Instructor, Museum of Fine Arts Schools, Boston. *Address*, 1126 Boyleston Street, Boston, Mass.

ALLEN, Gregory S. Sculptor. Born in Orange, N. J., 1884. Pupil of G. Borglum and H. N. Bushbrown.

ALLEN, Greta. Portrait painter. Born in Boston. Pupil of DeCamp Benson. Member of Copley Society. *Address*, 755 Boylston Street, Boston.

ALLEN, Harold A. Painter. Exhibited water colors at the Penna. Academy Exhibition 1925. *Address*, 142 Oakdale Ave., Pawtucket, R. I.

ALLEN, Joel. Engraver. Born 1755, at Farmington, Conn.; died 1825. He engraved plates for ''Maynard's'' edition of Josephus, pub. 1792.

ALLEN, Louise (Mrs. Hobbs). Sculptor. Born Lowell, Mass. Studied art, R. I. School of Design and Boston Museum Fine Arts. Exhibited at Penna. Academy Fine Arts; Nat. Academy, New York; Art Inst. Chicago; Albright Galleries, Buffalo; Museum Fine Arts, Providence, R. I.; represented in Cleveland Museum. Prin. works: World War Memorial, East Greenwich, R. I., World War Tablet. Gloucester, Mass.; memorial tablet Bancroft Hall, Annapolis, Md.; also ideal bronzes, portraits, etc. Mem. Nat. Assn. Women Painters and Sculptors, Copley Society (Boston), Providence Art Club. *Address*, 45 Charles Street, Boston, Mass.

ALLEN, Luther. Engraver. Born at Enfield, Conn., June 11, 1780; died at Ithaca, N. Y., Nov. 27, 1821. He was the son of Moses Allen of Enfield, Conn., a soldier in the Revolu-

tion. Luther Allen married Sally P. Abbe on November 17, 1802, and soon after that date removed to Ithaca, N. Y., where he is referred to as an engraver, portrait painter, and a musician of some ability. The only engravings of Luther Allen noted are a quarto mezzotint portrait of the Rev. Stephen Williams, D.D., a view of New Port, N. J., and a book-plate engraved by him, either for his father, Moses Allen, or for a brother by the same name.

ALLEN, Marion B. (Mrs. William A. Allen). Painter. Born in Boston, Mass., 1862. Pupil of Tarbell and Benson, at School of Boston Museum of Fine Arts. Specialty portraiture. *Address*, Fenway Studios, Boston, Mass.

ALLEN, Mary Coleman. Pasadena, California. Miniatures exhibited at Penna. Academy of Fine Arts, Philadelphia, 1924. Member of American Society of Miniature Painters. *Address*, 125 East 10th Street, New York City.

ALLEN, Sarah Lockhart. Miniature painter, also drew portraits in crayon. Born in Salem, Mass., in 1793. Died in 1877. In Felt's ''Annals of Salem'' there is the following note under the year 1820. ''Portraits of full size are executed by Miss Sarah Allen in crayons. She is a native of this City.''

ALLEN, Thomas. Born in St. Louis, 1849. Studied in France and Germany and exhibited at the Salon in Paris and the National Academy of Design in 1877. Awarded medals Boston and Buffalo. Among his paintings are ''Maplehurst at Noon,'' ''Toilers of the Plains,'' ''Upland Pastimes,'' and ''Moonlight Landscapes.'' The Boston Museum of Fine Arts owns his ''Portals of the Mission of San Jose, Texas.'' He was elected an Associate Member of the National Academy. Died 1924.

ALLEN, Willard. Painter. Born in Woodstock, N. Y., 1860. Pupil of Academy of Fine Arts, Philadelphia, Pa., under Chase and Carlesen. *Address*, Woodstock, New York.

ALLEN & GAW. Engravers who signed a ''Chart of Boston Harbor, Surveyed in 1817.'' It was published by John Melish in Philadelphia in 1819. The Gaw of the above firm was R. M. Gaw, who was employed by Peter Maverick of Newark, New Jersey, in 1829.

ALLERDICE, Samuel. Engraver. Was a pupil and later a partner of Robert Scot of Philadelphia. He engraved many copper-plates for book illustrations. Scot and Allerdice made many of the plates for Dobson's edition of Rees' Encyclopedia, published in Philadelphia, 1794–1803.

ALEXANDER, Mrs. Nina. Painter and illustrator. Born in Auburn, Kansas. Pupil of Penna. Academy of Fine Arts. Student under Chase, and under Henri and Brangwyn in London. *Address*, 1315 Clifton Street, Washington, D. C.

ALLIS, C. Harry. Painter. Exhibited "November in the Ozarks" at National Academy of Design, 1925. *Address*, Newcomb, Maetchin.

ALLSTON, Washington. Painter. A South Carolinian, born at Waccanaw, on November 5, 1779, was sent to Rhode Island as a child, his native climate not agreeing with him. He was educated at Harvard, and returned to South Carolina, where he painted some religious compositions. In 1801 he went with Malbone to England and studied under West at the Royal Academy. In the following year he exhibited three pictures at Somerset House and sold one of them. Three years later he accompanied Vanderlyn to France, reveling there in the art treasures Napoleon had accumulated from all Europe, and developing the richness of color that came to characterize many of his paintings. He visited Italy, came back to America and married, and again in 1811 returned to England, taking with him S. F. B. Morse as a pupil. After a few years he returned home, a success on both sides of the ocean. He died at Cambridge, Mass., July 9, 1843. His "Uriel in the Sun" and "Jacob's Dream" are owned in England. His best known paintings in the United States are "Jeremiah," "Belshazzar's Feast" and "Witch of Endor." Among his portraits, Wm. Ellery Channing; Sam'l T. Coleridge and his self-portrait are owned by the Boston Museum of Fine Arts. The "Dead Man Revived" is in the Penna. Academy of Fine Arts, Philadelphia. See "Life and Letters of Washington Allston, by Jared B. Flagg." Also see "Artist Biographies," Allston. (Boston 1879.)

ALTEN, Mathias J. Painter. Born in Germany 1871. Pupil of Constant, Laurens, and Whistler in Paris. Member of Grand Rapids, Mich., Art Association. *Address*, 1593 E. Fulton Street, Grand Rapids, Michigan.

ALTMANN, Aaron. Painter. Born San Francisco, Cal., 1872. Student of Constant, Laurens, and Gerome, Paris. *Address*, 2298 Green Street, San Francisco, California.

ALVAREZ, Mabel. Painter. Born in Hawaii. Pupil of Cahill and McBurney. Painter of still life subjects. *Address*, 2180 West 25th Street, Los Angeles, California.

AMANS, Jaques. Painter. Born in 1801, died in Paris in 1888. Painted portraits in New Orleans from 1828 till 1856. Amans is a forceful painter concerning whose work nothing is known except the portraits painted in New Orleans. His work compares favorably with the best portrait painters of to-day. *Address*, 1838, 163 Royal Street; 1840, 184 Royal Street; 1854–56, Bienville and Customhouse Streets.

AMATEIS, Edmond R. Sculptor. Born in Italy, 1897. *Address*, 126 East 75th Street, New York.

AMATEIS, Louis. Born in Turin, Italy, December 13, 1855; died in West Falls Church, Va., March 16, 1913. Educated in the schools of Turin, and a graduate of the Institute of Technology and the Academy of Fine Arts of Turin, where he was awarded a gold medal upon his graduation. His first sculptural work of importance was a bas-relief purchased by a committee of sculptors for the Art Gallery of Turin. In a competition he was awarded the commission for the sculptural decorations for the Palace of Fine Arts of Turin. In 1884 he came to the United States and became a naturalized citizen of this country. After living for some time in New York, removed to Washington, D. C., where he maintained a studio and executed many works of note. He was the founder of the School of Architecture and Fine Arts of the Columbian University, Washington, D. C., and a member of the National Sculpture Society. Among his works are many portraits busts, and the bronze doors in the Capitol, Washington, D. C.

AMENT, Robert S. Painter and etcher. Born in New York, 1879. Pupil of Ward, Chase and Henri. *Address*, 2380 Grand Avenue, New York City.

AMES, Daniel F. Flourished 1841–1852. New York miniature painter.

AMES, Ezra. 1768–1836. An American portrait painter of the later eighteenth and early nineteenth century. Little is known of his life excepting that he commenced work as a coach painter in Albany. Later he turned his attention to portrait painting, and gained recognition in 1812, by a portrait of Gov. Geo. Clinton, exhibited at the Penna. Academy of Fine Arts. For many years after this he painted in Albany and Western New York, painting most of the New York legislators. He also painted miniatures.

AMES, Frances (Mrs. Linwood P. Ames). Painter. Born Massina, N. Y., 1868. Pupil of Chase, New York, also studied in Paris, Specialty portraiture. *Address*, "The Twinpike," Fort Plain, New York.

AMES, Joseph Alexander. Portrait painter. Born at Roxburg, N. H., in 1816; died in New York City, 1872. Elected an Associate of National Academy of Design in 1869 and Academician 1870; had his studio in Boston, Baltimore and later in New York. He also studied in Rome. His best known work is "The Death of Webster," which has been engraved. His portraits of Prescott, Geo. Southward, Ristori, Gazzaniga, Felton and his portrait of Brady at the Metropolitan Museum.

AMES, Julius R. He was a son of Ezra Ames, the portrait and miniature painter. Julius Ames worked in Albany, New York, and flourished from 1834 to 1850.

AMES, May. Painter and teacher. Born in Cleveland, Ohio. *Address,* 9315 Miles Ave., Cleveland, Ohio.

AMES, Sarah Fisher. Sculptor. Born in Lewis, Delaware, 1817, and died in Washington, D. C., 1901. Studied Art in Boston, and Rome, Italy. She was the wife of Joseph Ames, portrait painter. She was personally acquainted with President Lincoln and her bust of him is considered excellent. Among her other portrait busts are General Grant and Ross Winans.

AMICK, Robert W. Painter and illustrator. Born in Canon City, Colo., in 1879. Pupil of Art Students' League, New York. *Address,* 63 Washington Square, New York.

AMEN, Will Rice. Painter. Exhibited water colors at the Penna. Academy of Fine Arts, Philadelphia, 1925. *Address,* 17 Gramercy Park, New York.

ANCORA, Pietro. He was an Italian painter and drawing-master who had an art school and gave instructions in drawing in Philadelphia early in 1800; he taught John Neagle to draw.

ANDERSON, Hendrik Christian. Sculptor. Born Bergen, Norway, 1872. Brought to United States in infancy, settling at Newport, R. I., 1873; studied art and architecture at Boston, Paris, Naples, Rome. Prin. works: "Fountain of Life," "Fountain of Immortality," "Jacob Wrestling with the Angel," "Study of an Athlete," etc.

ANDERSON, Martinus. Painter and illustrator. Born in Peru, Ind., 1878. Pupil of Herron Art Institute, Indianapolis. He has also done mural decorations in City Hospital, Indianapolis. *Address,* 135 West 44th Street, New York.

ANDERSON, Alexander. Born in New York City, April 21, 1775; died in Jersey City, N. J., April 18, 1870. Anderson early became interested in copperplate engraving and was self-taught; but, yielding to the wishes of his family, he studied medicine. and in 1796 was graduated from the Medical Department of Columbia College as an M.D. He was again engraving on copper in New York in 1797, and the next year he permanently abandoned medicine for the burin. He engraved a number of copperplates and attained very considerable proficiency in that branch of his art. But in 1820 Dr. Anderson became interested in the wood-engravings of Bewick and his followers, and he so much improved upon the work of his predecessors in this country that he is generally recognized as the Father of Wood-Engraving in the United States. His use of the "white line" in wood-engraving was peculiarly successful and effective. He made many pencil and wash drawings and painted portraits. The New York Historical Society has a small portrait painted by him in 1820. See Life and Works of Alexander Anderson by Frederick M. Burr, and a "Memorial of Alexander Anderson," by Benjamin J. Lossing.

ANDERSON, Abraham Archibald. Artist. Born in New Jersey, 1847. Studied painting under Cabanel, Bonnat, Cormon, Godin and Collin. Exhibited Paris Salon, Universal Expn., Paris, 1899, etc.; pictures: (portraits) Gen. O. O. Howard, Gov. Morgan, H. B. Claflin, Thomas A. Edison, Bishop Cleveland Coxe, Elihu Root, Charles Stewart Smith, John Wanamaker, etc., also "Morning after the Ball," "The Convalescent," "Neither Do I Condemn Thee," etc. *Address,* 80 West 40th Street, New York.

ANDERSON, Dorothy V. Painter. Born in Norway. Pupil of W. M. Chase. *Address,* 3130 Palmer Square, Chicago, Ill.

ANDERSON, Ellen G. Painter and illustrator. Born in Lexington, Va. Pupil of Charles Guerin; studied also in Paris. *Address,* 39 Charles Street, New York.

ANDERSON, Elmer G. Painter. Exhibited a "Landscape," at the Penna. Academy of Fine Arts, Philadelphia, 1920. *Address* 2545 North Chadwick Street, Philadelphia.

ANDERSON, Frederic A. Illustrator. Exhibited at the Penna. Academy of Fine Arts 1922. *Address,* 1520 Chestnut Street, Philadelphia.

ANDERSON, G. Adolph. Painter. Born Rochester, Minn., in 1877. Pupil of Robert Henri. Member of National Arts Club, New York. *Address,* 522 Franklin Ave., Ridgewood New Jersey.

ANDERSON, George M. Painter. His water color at Pas Christian was loaned the Cincinnati Museum, by Mrs. Larz Anderson for their 33d Annual Exhibition 1925.

ANDERSON, Helge. Painter. Boston Mass. Exhibited at Penna. Academy of the Fine Arts, Philadelphia, 1921. *Address,* 15 Huntingdon Ave., Boston, Mass.

ANDERSON, Hugh. Engraver. His name appears in the Philadelphia Directory from 1811 to 1824; he engraved a number of plate for S. F. Bradford's Philadelphia edition of the Edinburgh Encyclopedia. He also engraved portraits and book illustrations.

ANDERSON, Karl. Painter. Born in Oxford, Ohio, in 1874. Student of Chicago Art Institute and Colarossi Academy in Paris. Painted in Holland, Italy and Madrid. Elected member of National Academy of Design. Has also illustrated for many publications. Among his works, "The Idlers," "Sisters," "Apple Gatherers," and "The Heirloom." *Address,* Westport, Conn.

ANDERSON, Oscar. Painter. Born in Sweden in 1873. Pupil of Charles N. Flagg, Hartford. *Address,* 78 Rocky Neck Avenue, Gloucester, Mass.

ANDERSON, Peter Bernard. Sculptor. Born in Sweden in 1898. Pupil of J. K. Daniels. *Address,* 959 Lombard Street, St. Paul, Minn.

ANDERSON, Raymond H. Painter. Born at Bradford, Penna., in 1884. Pupil of Stevenson Art School. *Address,* R. D. No. 1, Saltsburg Road, Verona, Penna.

ANDERSON, Ronald. Painter and illustrator. Born at Lynn, Mass., in 1886. Student at Chicago Art Inst. Pupil of Eric Pape. *Address,* 54 West 37th Street, New York.

ANDERSON, Ruth A. (Mrs. Sam'l Temple). Painter. Born in Carlisle, Penna. Pupil of Penna. Academy of Fine Arts. Member of National Association of Women Painters and Sculptors, and the Fellowship of the Penna. Academy of Fine Arts. *Address,* 53 Charles Street, Boston, Mass.

ANDERSON, W. About 1855 this excellent engraver of portraits and landscapes was working for the engraving firm of C. A. Jewett & Co. of Cincinnati, Ohio. Much of his work will be found in the *Ladies' Repository,* published in that city.

ANDERTON, G. Engraver. Born in London about 1828, he was engraving in the United States as early as 1850. He was in the employ of J. M. Butler of Philadelphia and was a good engraver of portraits in both the stipple and mezzotint manner.

ANDREW, John. Wood engraver. Working in New York and Boston for the publishers during the last half of the nineteenth century.

ANDREW, Richard. Portrait painter. Exhibited at the Penna. Academy of Fine Arts, Philadelphia, 1921. Pupil of Laurens and Gerome in Paris. *Address,* Fenway Studios, Boston, Mass.

ANDREWS, Ambrose. Portrait painter in oils and miniature. From 1829 to 1831 he was in Troy, New York. He later moved to St. Louis and then to New York. He painted a portrait of Gen'l Sam. Houston.

ANDREWS, Eliphalet F. Painter. Born at Steubenville, Ohio, in 1835. Portrait and general painter; studied in Paris under Bonnat. Director of Corcoran Art School for twenty-five years. He painted several of the portraits now in the White House, including those of Martha Washington, Dolly Madison, Jefferson and others. He died in Washington, D. C., in 1915.

ANDREWS, Helen F. Painter. Born in Farmington, Conn., in 1872. Pupil of Art Students' League, New York. Student of Laurens and Constant in Paris. *Address,* Westover School, Middlebury, Conn.

ANDREWS, J. W. Painter. Born in Newtonville, Mass., in 1879. Pupil of DuMond, Hamilton, and DeCamp. *Address,* Yonkers, New York.

ANDREWS, Joseph. Engraver. Born in Hingham, Mass., 1806, he was apprenticed to Abel Bowen, a wood engraver of Boston, and learned copper plate engraving from Hoogland. In 1835 he went to London and studied under Goodyear, and in Paris he engraved the head of Franklin by Duplessis. Returning to the United States he engraved many fine portraits and did considerable work for the book publishers. His portrait of Washington after Stuart is one of his best plates; he also engraved "Plymouth Rock in 1620." He died in 1873. For a life of this engraver and a list of his work see *Pennsylvania Magazine* for 1908, "Joseph Andrews and His Engravings," by Mantle Fielding.

ANDREWS, Mrs. M. Minnigerode. Painter and illustrator. Born in Richmond, Va., 1869. Pupil of Andrews and Chase. Represented by portraits owned by University of Virginia. *Address,* 1232 Sixteenth Street, Washington, D. C.

ANGAROLA, Anthony. Painter. Born in Chicago, 1893. Minneapolis School of Art. He exhibited paintings at Academy of Fine Arts, Philadelphia, 1921, and Carnegie Institute, Pittsburgh, Pa. *Address,* 1318 Rosedale Avenue, Chicago, Ill.

ANGELA, Emilio. Sculptor. Born in Italy, 1889. Studied at Cooper Union, Art Students' League, National Academy of Design, and was pupil of A. A. Weinman Membership, National Sculpture Society, American Federation of Fine Arts. Works: "Goose Boy," "Barking Seals," "Boxer," "Goose Girl," "Baby Angela." *Address,* 558 Broome Street, New York City.

ANKENEY, John S. Painter. Born at Zenia, Ohio, in 1870. Pupil of Twachtman, Chase and Saint Gaudens; also studied in Paris. *Address,* 906 Conley Ave., Columbia, Mo.

ANNABLE, George O. Sculptor. Born about 1829. He had a studio in the Hoppin Building in Providence, and in 1850 cut a cameo portrait of Dr. Nathan B. Crocker, the rector of St. John's Church. The following account from the *Providence Journal* of January 18, 1851, gives us an idea of Annable's work and ambition: "With respect to the medallion heads and cameos by Mr. George O. Annable, of Providence, the committee heartily concur in the general expression of opinion. They are excellent; and considering the youth of the artist and the short time which has passed since his first work was produced—remarkably so." In 1852 cameos were exhibited by Annable and were described as "capital likenesses and finely executed." He received a silver medal, the highest premium, for portrait busts in marble and cameos. Besides the portraits of Dr. Chapin, Mr. Chapin, and Dr. Crocker, Annable cut a cameo likeness of James S. Lincoln, the portrait painter, who in exchange painted Annable's portrait. This cameo portrait of Lincoln is in the possession of Mrs. Joseph T. A. Eddy of Hingham. Annable's cameo portraits were cut in shell and were usually about an inch and a half tall.

ANNAN, Abel H. Painter. Member of Washington (D. C.) Watercolor Club. *Address,* Carnegie Studios, West 57th Street, New York.

ANNAN, Alice H. Painter. Born in New York. Member of Art Students' League, pupil of Snell, and Ben Foster. *Address,* Carnegie Studios, West 57th Street, New York City.

ANNELLI, Francesco. He painted historic compositions, portraits and miniatures. Very little of his work is known. He flourished in New York from 1841 to 1878.

ANNIN, William B. This engraver was a pupil of Abel Bowen of Boston; he was working for him in 1813. As early as 1823 he was associated with George Girdler Smith. The firm of Annin & Smith did a general engraving business and were for some time also engaged in lithography in Boston.

ANSBACHER, Jessie. Painter. Portrait of Miss Tait. Exhibited at Penna. Academy of Fine Arts, Philadelphia, 1921. Pupil of William Chase. *Address,* 1 West 81st Street, New York City.

ANSHUTZ, Thomas Pollock. Painter. Born Newport, Kentucky, October 5, 1851; died, Fort Washington, Pennsylvania, June 16, 1912. Painter and teacher. Pupil of National Academy of Design, Pennsylvania Academy of the Fine Arts and of Doucet and Bouguereau, Paris. Gold Medal of Honor, Pennsylvania Academy of the Fine Arts, Philadelphia, 1909. Lippincott Prize, Pennsylvania Academy of the Fine Arts, 1909. Member of Fellowship, and also of

Faculty, of Pennsylvania Academy of the Fine Arts; Philadelphia Watercolor Club; New York Watercolor Club. Elected an Associate Member of the National Academy of Design 1910. Represented in collection of the Penna. Academy of Fine Arts.

ANTHONY, Andrew Varick Stout. Artist. He was born in New York City in 1835, and studied drawing and engraving under the best teachers. Anthony was an original member of the American Water Color Society. His illustrations for the works of Whittier, Longfellow and Hawthorne are of considerable merit. He passed part of his professional life in New York and California, but settled in Boston in 1878. He died in 1906.

APEL, Charles P. Painter. Born in Brooklyn, New York, in 1857. Pupil of Chase and Mora. *Address,* 57 Eby Place, East Orange, New Jersey.

APEL, Mrs. Marie. Sculptor. Born in England, 1888. Member of National Association of Women Painters and Sculptors. Work: Langdon Memorial Augusta, Ga., and Hodges Memorial, St. Paul's, Baltimore, Md. *Address,* 3 Washington Square, New York.

APPLEGATE, Frank G. Sculptor. Born in Atlanta, Ill., in 1882. Studied under Frederick and Grafly and in Paris under Verlet. Exhibited water colors at Penna. Academy of Fine Arts, Philadelphia, 1925. *Address,* Santa Fe, New Mexico.

APPLETON, Eliza B. (Mrs. Everard Appleton). Sculptor. Born in 1882. Studied with M. Ezekiel in Rome. *Address,* 42 Pleasant Street, Rumford, R. I.

APPLETON, Thomas G. Art patron and painter. Born in Boston in 1812; died in 1884. He studied in America and England. He exhibited many paintings on his return from Egypt in Boston that attracted much attention. He was deeply interested in the Boston Museum of Fine Arts.

ARCHAMBAULT, A. Margaretta. Portrait and miniature painter. Born in Philadelphia. Pupil of Penna. Academy of Fine Arts, and Julian Academy. Painted miniature of Warren G. Harding, at White House, Washington. Also Mrs. Jasper O. Nicolls, Master William Jasper Nicolls, and Mrs. William I. Moseley. *Address,* 1714 Chestnut Street, Philadelphia.

ARCHER, James. Engraver. He did the majority of the large plates illustrating "Hinton's History of the United States" published in Boston in 1834.

ARENSBACH, Haral. Artist. Exhibited water color paintings at the Academy of Fine Arts in 1921-25. *Address,* 121 North 21st Street, Philadelphia, Pa.

ARMBUSTER, A. E. Scenic painter. Member of League of Columbus Artists. *Address*, 3102 North High Street, Columbus, Ohio.

ARMFIELD, Maxwell. Painter and illustrator. Born in England. Studied abroad. He has done mural painting, and illustrates for *Century* and other magazines. *Address*, 104 West 40th Street, New York City.

ARMS, John Taylor. Etcher. Born in Washington, D. C., in 1887. Trained as an architect, in 1919 he devoted himself to the graphic arts. His aquatints are most successful. See the "Print Connoisseur," Vol. 1, 1921, for Catalogue of his Work. *Address*, No. 9 Greenfield Hill, Fairfield, Conn.

ARMSTRONG, Arthur. 1798–1851. Portrait, landscape and historic painter. Born in Manor Township, Lancaster County. In 1820 he opened a studio in Marietta, Lancaster County, and there began his career as artist and teacher. In 1849 he opened a studio and gallery for exhibition of paintings in Mechanics' Institute, Lancaster, and later had a large studio on Orange Street, Lancaster, built by himself and with the second story fitted up as a gallery to exhibit paintings. He painted there some very large canvases, "Hamlet and Ophelia" and the "Assassination of Caesar." At some time in his career he resorted to "potboilers," painting signs and banners, and made and gilded frames. One silk banner which was painted for the Washington Fire Company of Louisville, Kentucky, represented the Washington Family under the portico of their mansion at Mount Vernon, with the Potomac dotted with sails seen in the background. He was a prolific painter, and while many of his works are in the vicinity of Lancaster, others are widely scattered.

ARMSTRONG, Barbara. Painter. Born in Bellaire, Ohio, 1896. Pupil of Hamilton E. Field. *Address*, Ogunquit, Maine.

ARMSTRONG, D. Maitland. Painter. He was an early member of the American Artists Society, founded in 1877, and elected an Associate Member in 1906 of the National Academy of Design. He died in 1918.

ARMSTRONG, Estelle M. Painter. Member of National Association of Women Painters and Sculptors and exhibited at 33d Annual (1924). *Address*, 603 Bloomfield Avenue, Nutley, N. J.

ARMSTRONG, Helen Maitland. Mural painter and designer. Born in Florence, Italy, 1869. Student of Art Students' League, New York. *Address*, Maitland Armstrong Co., 58 West 10th Street, New York.

ARMSTRONG, Samuel John. Painter and illustrator. Born Denver, Colorado, 1893. *Address*, Steilacoorn Lake, Pierce Co., Washington.

ARMSTRONG, Voyle N. Painter and illustrator. Born in Dobbin, West Virginia, in 1891. Pupil of Driveneck at Cincinnati Art Academy. *Address*, 717 North 1st Street, Bedford, Ind.

ARMSTRONG, William G. Engraver, portrait painter in water color, and portrait draughtsman. Born 1823, Montgomery Co., Pa. Lived in Philadelphia. Armstrong was a pupil of Longacre in Philadelphia, drew small portraits and finally became a line engraver. He engraved several portraits for Longacre's "National Portrait Gallery." He also devoted a large part of his professional life to bank-note engravings.

ARNOLD, Mrs. Clara Maxfield. Painter. Born East Providence, R. I. Member of Providence Art Club. Specialty flower and fruit paintings. *Address*, 22 Highland Avenue, East Providence, R. I.

ARNOLD, Harry. Painter. Born in England. Member of the Society of Independent Artists. *Address*, 208 Gillette Avenue, Waukeegan, Ill.

ARNOLD, John K. Portrait painter. Born in 1834; died in 1909. He painted the portraits of many prominent men of the state of Rhode Island.

ARPA, Jose. Painter. Exhibited water color painting at the Penna. Academy of the Fine Arts, Philadelphia, 1925. *Address*, 418 Oakland Street, San Antonio, Texas.

ARTER, Charles J. Painter. He died in Alliance, Ohio, in 1923. He had formerly had his studios in Venice, London and New York. He had painted many people of distinction and was decorated by the King and Queen of Italy for portraits he had made of them.

ARTHUR, Robert. Painter. Born in Philadelphia, 1850, he died in New York, 1914. His early work was mainly decorative, and his later work was largely marine painting. He was a close friend of Robert Louis Stevenson; his studio was at Ogunquit, Maine.

ARTHURS, Stanley. Mural painter. Born in Kenton, Del., 1877. Pupil of Howard Pyle. Among his works, "Landing of DeVries," at Delaware College, Newark, Delaware, "The Crusaders" at the State Capitol, Dover, Delaware. *Address*, 1305 Franklin Street, Wilmington, Delaware.

ASANGER, Jacob. Painter and etcher. Born in Bavaria in 1887. Member of Society of Independent Artists. *Address*, 12 East 15th Street, New York City.

ASHBROOK, Paul. Painter. He exhibited in oil, water color and etching at the Cincinnati Museum, 1925. *Address*, No. 2 Hedgerow Lane, Cincinnati, Ohio.

ASHLEY, Clifford W. Painter. Born in New Bedford, Mass. Pupil of Howard Pyle. Among his works, ''The Whaling Industry,'' ''Outfitting the Whaler.'' *Address*, 31 Eighth Street, New Bedford, Mass.

ASHLEY, William John. Born in England in 1868. He was successful as a landscape painter. He died at Mt. Vernon, N. Y., October, 1921, having lived and painted for the last ten years in this country.

ATHERTON, E. Miniature painter. Mentioned in the Boston directories for 1841–1842.

ATKINS, Albert Henry. Sculptor. Born Milwaukee, Wis. Studied at Cowles Art School, Boston, 1896–98; Academie Julien and Academie Colorossi, Paris, 1898–1900. Mem. faculty R. I. School of Design, Dept. of Sculpture, since 1909. Mem. Nat. Sculpture Soc., Architectural League of N. Y., Copley Society of Boston, American Art Assn. (Paris), Provident Art Club. Prin. works: Coppenhagen Memorial Fountain, City of Boston; Lapham Memorial, Milwaukee, Wis.; Architectural sculptures, Christ Church, Ansonia, Conn., All Saints Church, Dorchester, Mass.; also portraits, ideal sculptures, etc. Exhibited at Natl. Acad. Design (New York), Pa. Acad. Fine Arts, Philadelphia, Albright Galleries (Buffalo), Art Inst. (Milwaukee). *Address*, 162 West 11th Street, New York City.

ATKINS, Florence Elizabeth. Sculptor. Exhibited ''Frogs,'' ''Rabbit,'' at the Penna. Acad. of the Fine Arts, Philadelphia, 1921. *Address*, 1040 Bush Street, San Francisco, California.

ATKINSON, Leo F. Painter. Born at Sunnyside, Washington, in 1896. Pupil of Seattle Art Club. Mural paintings in Columbian Theatre, Baton Rouge, La., and American Theatre, Bellingham, Washington. Represented at Seattle Fine Arts Gallery. ''On Cedar Drive.'' *Address*, 1122 Thirty-sixth Street, Seattle, Washington.

ATROBUS, John. Painter. Died in Detroit, Michigan, October 18, 1908. He had lived in Chicago, and Washington, D. C.

ATWOOD, Jr. Was a map engraver working in Philadelphia about 1840.

ATWOOD, Jesse. Philadelphia portrait painter in 1860. He painted several portraits of President Lincoln.

ATWOOD, William E. Painter. Born at Killinoly, Conn. Member of National Arts Club, New York. *Address*, East Gloucester, Mass.

AUDUBON, John James. Born April 26, 1785, Haiti, West Indies; died January 27, 1851, New York City. The celebrated ornithologist and artist Audubon was the son of Captain Jean Audubon and a Creole woman named Rabin. He was legally adopted in France by both his father and his father's legal wife, Anne Moynet Audubon. He was in America from 1804 to 1805, visiting France in 1806. It was probably at this time that he received the instruction in drawing from Louis David of which he speaks in his ''Journal.'' In 1807 he returned to America. He traveled extensively in United States and Canada, making notes and drawings for his ''Birds of North America'' and ''Quadrupeds of North America.'' John James Audubon came to New York in August 1824, Sully having given him letters to Stuart, Allston and Trumbull. At this time Audubon met John Vanderlyn and stood to him for the figure of Vanderlyn's portrait of General Jackson. Audubon visited Meadville, Penna., in 1824, and while in that city painted several portraits. Late in 1824, he went to Louisiana. He remained in the South until May 1826, when he again started to Europe, landing at Liverpool on July 21. He was at once invited to show his drawings at the Royal Academy. He made several trips to the United States between 1829 and 1839. He died in New York, January 27, 1851. See ''Life of Audubon, Edited by his Widow,'' ''Audubon, the Naturalist,'' by F. H. Herrick; also *Scribner's* for March, 1893.

AUDUBON, Victor Gifford. Son of John J. Audubon, was born in 1809 and died in 1860. He was elected in 1846 an Academician of the National Academy in New York. His brother, J. W. Audubon, was elected an associate member of the National Academy in 1847; he died in 1862.

AUERBACH, Levy William. Painter and etcher. Exhibited at the Penna. Academy of Fine Arts, 1924. *Address*, 137 East 34th Street, New York.

AUGUR, Hezekiah. Born in New Hampshire in 1791, the son of a shoemaker. He was self-taught, his artistic studies being carried out in New Haven, Conn. His modeling and carving were excellent; his group ''Jephthah and his Daughter'' is in the Yale College Gallery. He died in New Haven, January 10, 1858.

AULT, George C. Painter. Born in Cleveland, Ohio, 1891. Member of Society of Independent Artists. *Address*, 11 Charles Street, New York, N. Y.

AUSTIN, Charles P. Painter. Born in Denver, Colo., 1883. Pupil of Twachtman in New York and Castelluche, Paris. *Address*, San Juan Capistrano, California.

AUSTRIAN, Ben. Painter. Died in Kempton, Penna., Dec. 9, 1921. He was self-taught and first achieved distinction in depicting barnyard subjects and later landscapes. He also had a studio at Palm Beach, Florida.

AVERY, Hope. Painter. Exhibited portrait of Mr. Baker, in 33d Annual Exhibition of National Association of Women Painters and Sculptors, 1924. *Address*, Pittsford, Vt.

AYLWARD, William J. Painter and illustrator. Born in Milwaukee, Wis., 1875. Pupil of Howard Pyle. Exhibited at the Paris Salon, 1924, and National Academy of Design, New York, 1925. *Address*, 51 West 10th Street, New York City.

AZADIGIAN, Manuel. Painter. Exhibited "Still Life" at Penna. Academy of the Fine Arts, Philadelphia, 1921. *Address*, 1834 North Darien Street, Philadelphia, Pa.

AZZI, Marius A. Sculptor. Exhibited statuettes at the Penna. Academy of the Fine Arts, Philadelphia, 1921. *Address*, 120 West 11th Street, New York.

B

B. S. P. Engraver. The initials "S. P. B." are signed to a heading of the fire insurance policy of "The Mutual Assurance Society against Fire in Virginia." There is no indication of date but the work would suggest about the year 1825.

B. W. These initials "W. B. 1825" are signed to a number of plates illustrating "Pug's Tour through Europe," published in Baltimore about 1826.

BARR, Stanfield Marion. Painter. Born in New York City. Pupil of Johansen and Henri. *Address*, 342 Madison Ave., New York City.

BABCOCK, Dean. Painter. Born in Canton, Ill., in 1888. Pupil of Robert Henri. Member of the Denver Artists' Association. *Address*, Long's Peak, Colorado.

BABCOCK, E(lizabeth) J(ones) (Mrs. J. W. Babcock II). Painter and illustrator. Born Keokuk, Iowa, 1887. Pupil of Duveneck and Chase. Member: National Academy Women Painters and Sculptors; Guild of Free Lance Artists. Illustrates for *Scribner's*, *Harper's*, etc. *Address*, 571 Park Ave., New York City.

BABCOCK, Richard. Mural painter. Born in Denmark, 1887. Member of Art Students' League, New York. *Address*, Woodland Road, Pittsburgh, Pa.

BABCOCK, William P. Painter. Born in Boston in 1826; died in 1899, in Bois d'Arcy, France. Studied under Conture in Paris. Boston Museum of Fine Arts have: "The Red Hat," "Susanna and the Elders," "Still Life," "Fish," "Landscape, with Figures."

BABOT, Amy W. Painter. Exhibited at Penna. Academy of Fine Arts, 1924. *Address*, 72 Chestnut St., Boston, Mass.

BABSON, R. Engraver of stipple portraits. About 1860 he was apparently in the employ of Joseph Andrews of Boston as we find plates signed "Eng'd at J. Andrews by R. Babson."

BACH, Florence J. Painter and sculptor. Born Buffalo, N. Y., 1887. Member of Art Students' League. Pupil of William M. Chase and Du Mond. *Address*, 1110 Elmwood Ave., Buffalo, N. Y.

BACHELER, Frances H. Painter. Born Lebanon, Conn., in 1889. Member of Hartford Art Club. *Address*, 39 Hopkins St., Hartford, Conn.

BACHER, Otto Henry. Painter, etcher, and illustrator. He was born in Cleveland, Ohio, in 1856. Pupil of Duveneck, in Cincinnati; and of Duvan, Boulanger, and Lefebvre in Paris. He spent some time with Whistler in Venice. He died in New York 1909, having received many honors and medals. He was an Associate of the National Academy of Design.

BACHMAN, Max. Sculptor. Died in New York City, 1921. He designed the allegorical figures of the continents for the Pulitzer Building in New York City.

BACON, Charles Roswell. Painter. Born in New York, 1868. Pupil of Constant, Lefebvre and Collin in Paris. Paintings in Union Trust Co., New York. He died in 1913.

BACON, George. An excellent music-engraver working in the city of Philadelphia about 1815. The firm was Bacon & Hart, and he was a near relative of the senior member of the firm.

BACON, Henry. Painter. Born in Haverhill, Massachusetts, 1839; died Cairo, Egypt, March 13, 1912. Painted in oils and water colors. Made a specialty of Egyptian subjects. Visited Paris in 1864, where he became a pupil of the École des Beaux Arts and of Cabanel; and in 1866–67 studied under Edouard Frere at Ecouen. Represented at the Corcoran Art Gallery by ''The Nile-Evening'' (water color) and in Boston Museum of Fine Arts by ''On Shipboard.''

BACON, Irving R. Painter. Born in Fitchburg, Mass., 1875. Pupil of William M. Chase. *Address*, Redford, Michigan.

BACON, Peggy. Painter. Born in Ridgfield, Conn. Pupil of James Lie. Member of Society of Independent Artists. *Address*, 152 West 55th Street, New York.

BADGER, James W. Miniature painter working in Boston from 1845 to 1846.

BADGER, John C. Crayon portrait draughtsman. He exhibited at the Pennsylvania Academy in 1855 and must not be confused with Joseph W. Badger who painted miniatures in New York from 1832 to 1838, nor with the two artists who painted portraits in Boston. Thomas Badger lived there from 1836 to 1859 and James W. Badger lived there from 1845 to 1846.

BADGER, Joseph W. Miniature painter, working in New York 1832–1838.

BADGER, Joseph. Painter. Born in Charleston, Mass. He died in Boston, and was an early colonial portrait painter of rather stiff and formal pictures. Of humble origin, he did mingle with the higher social life of Boston and his work was not as good as Copley, Smibert and Feke. An excellent life of Joseph Badger with a description of about a hundred of his portraits, written by Laurence Park and published by the Massachusetts Historical Society, Dec. 1917. His work is owned by Worcester Art Museum, Bowdoin College and is in many private collections in Boston.

BADGER, Thomas. Miniature painter, working in Boston from 1836 to 1859.

BAER, Herbert M. Painter and engraver. Born in New York, 1879. Honorable mention at Paris Salon 1905. *Address*, 655 Fifth Ave., New York.

BAER, Lilian. Sculptor. Was born in New York City, 1887. Student of Art Students' League, pupil of Jas. E. Fraser and K. H. Miller. Works: ''The Dance,'' ''Specialty Statuettes.'' *Address*, 601 Madison Ave., New York City.

BAER, William Jacob. Artist. Born at Cincinnati, Jan. 29, 1860. Pupil of Munich Royal Academy, 1880, receiving 4 medals and one of his works being purchased by the Directors for the Academy. Painted pictures in genre and portraits in oil and taught, 1885–92; then confined himself to miniature painting, of which art he is a pioneer of the modern school. Awarded 1st medal for miniatures and ideal paintings, New York, 1897; 1st class medals Paris Expn. Among his better known works in miniature are: ''Aurora,'' ''The Golden Hour,'' ''Summer,'' ''Daphne,'' ''Nymph,'' ''In Arcadia,'' ''Madonna with the Auburn Hair,'' ''Primavera.'' Treas. Am. Soc. of Miniature Painters; A. N. A. 1913. *Address*, West 59th Street, New York.

BAERE, Henry. Sculptor. Born in Germany in 1837, he came to the United States as a young man. Among his best known works is his statue of Beethoven in Central Park, General Fowler in Fort Green Park, and General Warren in Prospect Park, Brooklyn. He died in New York in 1908. He was a member of the National Sculpture Society.

BAILEY, C. Foster. Painter. Was awarded honorable mention Carnegie Institute, 1923.

BAILEY, Henry Lewis. Etcher. Member of Print Makers Society of California. *Address*, Mortgage Guarantee Bldg., Los Angeles, California.

BAILEY, Henry T. Illustrator. Born in Mass., 1865. Student of Mass. Normal Art School. *Address*, Cleveland School of Art, Cleveland.

BAILEY, Minnie M. Painter, illustrator. Born in Oberlin, Kans., in 1890. *Address*, 3908 Swiss Ave., Dallas, Tex.

BAILEY, Vernon Howe. Artist. Born in Camden, N. J., April 1, 1874. Student Pa. Mus. Sch. of Art, and Pa. Acad. Fine Arts, Philadelphia. Studied in London and Paris. Staff artist, *Philadelphia Times*, 1892–4; *Boston Herald*, 1894–01—spl. artist for latter at coronation of Edward VII; artist contbr. to *Graphic, Mail and Express*, London, 1902, and since to leading Am. mags., *The Studio* (London). Exhibited at Pa. Acad. Fine Arts, Philadelphia, 1891; Architectural League, New York, 1903–12. Represented in permanent collections, Detroit Mus. of Art, Minn. State Art Soc., St. Paul. Illustrator: ''Lady Baltimore,'' ''Charleston, the Place and Its People,'' ''The Story of Harvard,'' etc. Mem. Soc. of Illustrators. *Address*, The Players, 16 Gramercy Park, New York, N. Y.

BAILLY, Joseph A. Sculptor. Born in Paris in 1825; died 1883. Came to Philadelphia and followed his occupation of carving on wood and marble. Later became instructor at the Penna. Academy of Fine Arts. He produced a statue of Washington that was placed in front of the Philadelphia state-house (1869), also portrait busts of Gen. Grant and Gen. Meade.

BAINS, Ethel F. Betts. Painter. Exhibited at the Penna. Academy of Fine Arts, Philadelphia, 1922. *Address*, 104 Harvey Street, Germantown, Philadelphia.

BAISDEN, Frank. Painter. Exhibited at the Penna. Academy Annual Water Color Exhibition, Philadelphia, 1925. *Address*, Care of Penna. Academy of the Fine Arts, Philadelphia.

BAINBOROUGH. Miniature painter. An Englishman, who worked on portraits in 1830 at Shippenport.

BAKER, Bryant. Sculptor. Born in London, 1881. Among his works "Snowden Andrews Memorial" at Winchester, Va., "Edward Wright Memorial," Austin, Texas, and busts of President Wilson, Senator Lodge, Gen'l March, Gen'l Pershing, and Hon. Herbert Hoover. *Address*, 154 West 55th Street, New York City.

BAKER, Burtis. Painter. Exhibited 1921 at Penna. Academy of the Fine Arts, and in 1923 at Carnegie Inst. "Interior with Figure." *Address*, Fenway Studios, Boston, Mass.

BAKER, Charles. Painter. Born in 1844. He was the son of Charles Baker, one of the founders of the Art League. His home was in Brooklyn, N. Y., and he died at Hague, Lake George, N. Y., in 1906.

BAKER, Elizabeth G. Portrait painter. Born in 1860. Specializes in children's portraits in water color. Student of New York School of Art, and Penna. Academy of Fine Arts. Studied also in Rome, Florence, and Paris. *Address*, 24 Gramercy Park, New York.

BAKER, Ellen Kendall. Painter. Born in New York State; she lived for years in Buffalo, New York. She married Harry Thompson, the English artist, and exhibited in the Paris salons and at many exhibitions in this country. She died in 1913.

BAKER, Frederick Van Vliet. Artist. Born in New York, Nov. 6, 1876. Educated, Pratt Inst., Brooklyn, École des Beaux Arts, Colorossi, Paris. Instr. in life drawing, painting and composition, Pratt Inst. Exhibited in salons, Paris, 1901-2-3; also at Ghent, Vienna, Chicago, New York, etc. *Address*, 39 West 67th Street, New York.

BAKER, George A. Portrait painter. Born in New York City, 1821; died there 1880. His first portrait work was in miniature paint-ing, but he soon became an excellent portrait artist; he studied in Europe. Elected to the National Academy in 1851. Noted for his portraits of women and children. His portrait of the artist John F. Kensett is in the Metropolitan Museum, New York, and an Ideal Head in the Corcoran Gallery, Washington, D. C.

BAKER, George H. Painter. Born in Muncie, Ind., in 1878. *Address*, 605 Main St., Richmond, Ind.

BAKER, George O. Painter and illustrator. Born in Mexico, Mo., 1882. Pupil of Laurens, and Miller in Paris. *Address*, Care of Chas. E. Johnson, 941 Glengyle Place, Chicago.

BAKER, Horace. Wood engraver. Born in North Salem, N. Y., in 1833. He studied engraving in his brother's firm in Boston, of which he afterwards became a partner. For many years he was connected with the engraving department of *Harper's Magazine*. He died in 1918.

BAKER, I. H. A good engraver of stipple portraits working in Boston, about 1860.

BAKER, John. Engraver. He designed and etched in line a large plate of the "Battle of Bunker's Hill." About 1832, also two separate plates of "Washington Crossing the Delaware."

BAKER, Joseph E. Etcher and caricature illustrator. He was a native of Boston and drew many of the caricatures of the Civil War period.

BAKER, Miss M. K. Painter. Born in New Bedford, Mass. Specialty, figure painting and portraits. Exhibits at Boston Art Club and New York Academy of Design.

BAKER, Maria M. Painter. Born in Norfolk, Va., 1890. Pupil of Penna. Academy of Fine Arts and Corcoran Art Gallery. *Address*, 408 Raleigh Ave., Norfolk, Va.

BAKER, Martha S. Miniature painter. Born 1871. Also paints in oil and water color, and has done some mural work. Pupil of Chicago Art Institute. (Deceased.)

BAKER, Mary F. Painter. Born in New Orleans, La., in 1879. Student of Penna Academy of Fine Arts. *Address*, 2263 Carondelet Street, New Orleans, La.

BAKER, P(ercy) Bryant. Sculptor. Born in London, Eng., 1881. Graduated Royal Academy Arts, London, 1910. Executed bust and heroic statue of King Edward VII; bust of Prince Olav of Norway; also busts of many notable persons in Eng. Exhibited at Royal Academy, London (medals 1910), Paris Salon, Corcoran Art Gallery, Washington, etc. Member Royal Soc. British Sculptors. Came to United States 1915. *Address*, 100 Chestnut Street, Boston, Mass.

BAKER, Samuel B. Painter. Born in Boston, Mass., 1882. Pupil of Major, De Camp, and Edw. H. Barnard. Instructor at Corcoran Art Gallery, Washington, D. C.

BAKER, William Bliss. Painter. Died at about the age of thirty, but painted some excellent landscapes.

BAKER, William H. Painter. Born in 1825; died in Brooklyn, N. Y., May 29, 1875. He was brought up in mercantile pursuits in New Orleans; he devoted his spare time to the study of art and became a portrait and genre painter. He had a studio from 1853 to 1861 at 123 Canal Street; moved to New York in 1865, where he taught art and painted portraits and ideal subjects. He was a painstaking and conscientious artist. Among his works, "Cupid Disarmed," "Floral Offering," "Red Riding Hood," and "Morning Glories."

BAKOS, Joseph G. Painter and sculptor. Born Buffalo, N. Y., 1891. Pupil of J. E. Thompson. *Address*, Old Palace, Santa Fe, New Mexico.

BALANO, Paula H. (Mrs.). Painter and illustrator. Born in Germany, 1878. Pupil of Penna. Academy of Fine Arts under Chase and of Mucha in Paris. Awarded gold medal for her work in water color. *Address*, 54 Linden Ave., Lansdowne, Penna.

BALCH, Vistus. Engraver. Born in Williamstown, Mass., in 1799; he died at Johnstown, N. Y., in 1884. Balch worked in Utica, Albany, and New York; he engraved a number of book illustrations, and several plates for the *New York Mirror*. About 1825 Balch drew on stone a portrait of Dr. Samuel L. Mitchell, for Imbert, who was the pioneer lithographer of New York City.

BALCOM, Lowell L. Painter and illustrator. Born in Kansas City, Mo., 1887. Pupil of J. D. Patrick. *Address*, 136 65th Street, New York.

BALDAUGH, AMIE. Miniature painter. Exhibited the miniature of the "Washburn Children" at Miniature Exhibition, Penna. Academy of the Fine Arts, Philadelphia, 1924. *Address*, Los Angeles, California.

BALDRIDGE, Cyrus L. Illustrator. Born in Alton, N. Y., 1889. Pupil of Frank Holme. *Address*, Harmon-on-Hudson, N. Y.

BALDWIN, Burton Clarke. Illustrator. Born in Danville, Ill., 1891. Pupil of Chicago Academy of Fine Arts. *Address*, 805 Junior Terrace, Chicago, Ill.

BALDWIN, George. Painter. A native of Thompson, Conn., born about 1818. He received a common school education and went to Norwich where he studied portraiture. George Baldwin painted many portraits of men prominent in his native state of Connecticut.

BALDWIN, William. Flourished 1827–1846. New Orleans miniature painter.

BALFOUR, Mrs. Helen. Painter and illustrator. Born in England. Member of California Art Club. Illustrated "Sunset Highways." *Address*, 310 Mt. Washington Drive, Los Angeles, California.

BALINK, Hendricus C. Painter and etcher. Born in Holland in 1882. Member of Chicago Society of Artists.

BALL, Alice Worthington. Painter. Exhibited landscapes entitled "The Portuguese Hill" and "Gloucester" at Penna. Academy of the Fine Arts, Philadelphia, 1921. *Address*, West Monument Street, Baltimore, Md.

BALL, Caroline Peddle. Sculptor. Born in Terre Haute, Ind., 1869. Pupil of Augustus St. Gaudens and Kenyon Cox, New York. Honorable mention Paris Expn., 1900; sculptor of figure of "Victory" in quadriga on the U. S. bldg., at Paris Expn., 1900; memorial corbels, Grace Church, Brooklyn; memorial fountain, Auburn, N. Y. *Address*, Westfield, N. J.

BALL, L. Clarence. Landscape painter. Born in Ohio, 1858; he died at South Bend, Ind., in 1915. Member of Chicago Society of Artists. His specialty was landscapes with cattle and sheep.

BALL, Linn B. Painter and illustrator. Born in Milwaukee, Wis., in 1891. *Address*, 163 West 23d Street, New York.

BALL, Robert. Painter and illustrator. Born in Kansas City, Mo., in 1890. Pupil of Richard Miller in Paris. *Address*, 9 West 47th Street, New York.

BALL, Ruth N. Sculptor. Born in Madison, Wis. Pupil of Liberty Tadd in Philadelphia. Represented in City Art Museum, St. Louis. *Address*, Indian Arts Bldg., San Diego, California.

BALL, Thomas. Sculptor. Born near Boston in 1819. His art studies began with silhouette-cutting, miniature and portrait painting. After 1851 he devoted himself to sculpture. His prominent works are the Washington monument in Boston, Forrest as "Coriolanus," Emancipation Group, Washington. He died in 1911. For his life see "My Three Score Years and Ten," by Thomas Ball, Boston, 1891.

BALL, Thomas Watson. Painter. Born in New York City, 1863. Pupil of Art Students' League, New York. Studied with Beckwith and Mowbray. He has also done mural decorations. *Address*, Old Lynne, Conn.

BALLANTINE, Edward J. Painter. Born in Scotland in 1885. Member of the Society of Independent Artists. *Address*, 36 Grove Street, New York.

BALLIN, Hugo. Artist. Born New York, 1879. Studied at Art Students' League, New York, and in Rome and Florence. Awarded Scholarship Art Students' League; Shaw Prize Fund, 1905; Thomas B. Clarke Prize, 1906; Architectural League Medal, 1906 and 1907. Elected Associate Member of National Academy. Specialty, mural decorations. Works: executive chamber, Madison, Wis.; room in home of Oliver Gould Jennings, N. Y. City, and E. D. Brandegee of Boston; decorative pictures in many pvt. collections; also represented in National Museum, Washington, D. C.; Montclair Museum, N. J.; Ann Mary Memorial, R. I.; etc. *Address*, 662 Lexington Ave., New York.

BALLING. A painter of the Civil War, his "Heroes of the Republic," a group of twenty-seven Union generals on horseback, has been much praised.

BALLINGER, H(arry) R(ussell). Illustrator. Born in Port Townsend, Wash., 1892. Pupil Maurice Braun, Art Students' League of N. Y., and Harvey Dunn. Illustrations for *Cosmopolitan, Good Housekeeping, Saturday Evening Post, McClure's*, etc. *Address*, Studio, 1947 Broadway; Home, 15 West 67th Street, New York, N. Y.

BALLOU, P. IRVING. Painter. Exhibited water colors at the Penna. Academy of the Fine Arts, Philadelphia, 1925. *Address*, 1015 Prospect Place, Brooklyn, N. Y.

BANCROFT, Hester. Painter. Exhibited National Academy of Design, 1925. *Address*, Ithaca, New York.

BANCROFT, Milton H. Painter. Born at Newton, Mass., 1867. Student Mass. State Normal Art School, 1883–6; continued studies irregularly in Pa. Academy Fine Arts; Supt. Schools and instr. in Pa. Academy Fine Arts, 1892–4; studied in Colorossi, Delacluse and Julien Academies, Paris, 1894–9. Exhibited in Societe des Artists Francais, and in all large exhibitions of New York, Philadelphia, Boston, Washington and Chicago. Specialty, portraits; also executed mural decorations for Court of the Seasons, Panama-Pacific Expn., San Francisco. Instr. Mechanics Inst., New York. *Address*, 58 W. 57th Street, New York, N. Y.

BANNERMAN, J. Engraver. He produced two portraits of Franklin, one in line and the other in stipple, about 1800; they were published in the "Works of Franklin" and are rather crude in manner.

BANNERMAN, W. W. Engraver of book illustrations for the publishers in Baltimore, Md. He etched in rather a crude manner a series of full-length portraits of statesmen for the *United States Magazine and Democratic Review* in 1840–45.

BANNING, William J. Painter. Born at Lynne, Conn., in 1810. Pupil of National Academy under Sam'l Waldo. His specialty was portrait painting. He exhibited in the National Academy of Design in 1840 and 1841. He died in 1856.

BANNISTER, Eleanor C. Painter. Born in New York, N. Y. Pupil of Whittaker in Brooklyn; Constant and Lefebvre in Paris. Member: Brooklyn Society of Artists. Work: "Portrait of Rev. R. S. Storrs," Brooklyn Museum.

BANNISTER, E. M. Artist. Born in St. Andrews, New Brunswick, in 1833. He studied art at the Lowell Institute in Boston, and spent the greater part of his professional life there. In 1871 he removed to Providence, R. I. He has contributed regularly to the Boston Art Club exhibitions. His picture "Under the Oaks" was awarded a first-class medal at the centennial exhibition of 1876 in Philadelphia. He died in 1901.

BANNISTER, James. Engraver. Was born in England. He came to New York at an early age and was apprenticed in the engraving establishment of A. L. Dick in New York. He also became interested in bank-note work, but his chief production was portraits for book-illustrations.

BANVARD, John. Painter. Born in 1815 and died in 1891. Educated in New York schools. At an early age he supported himself with selling his pictures at New Orleans. He painted a panorama of the Mississippi River that was exhibited in this country and abroad. He also painted the picture from which the first chromo made in America was taken. It was entitled "The Orison" (New York, 1861).

B., J. W. These initials as "J. W. B. del. et sc." are signed to a quarto line print representing an engagement between the Georgia militia under Gen. John Floyd and a force of Creek Indians at Antossee, Ala.

BARBEE, Herbert. Sculptor, son of William R. Barbee the sculptor. He studied in Florence.

BARBEE, William R. Sculptor of Virginia. His famous "Fisher Girl" belonged to Mrs. A. T. Stuart of New York City.

BARBER, Charles E. Engraver. Born in London in 1840; he came to this country early in his career. In 1869 he was appointed assistant engraver in the United States Mint in Philadelphia. His best work is found in the medals struck for Presidents Garfield, Arthur, and the Great Seal of the United States. He died in Philadelphia in 1917.

BARBER, John Warner. Engraver. Born 1798 in Windsor, Vt., and died 1885. He was apprenticed to Abner Reed, who was then established as a bank-note engraver. Reed soon turned his attention to engraving historical scenes, both on copper and wood. Barber engraved on wood the illustrations for "Easy Lessons in Reading" and the "History of New England." His engraving establishment was in New Haven, Conn. See "Linton's Wood Engraving."

BARBER, William. Engraver. Born in London 1807; died in Philadelphia 1879. He started as a silver-plate engraver but soon entered the employ of the U. S. Mint in Philadelphia where he remained until his death.

BARBIERE-WALBONNE, Jacques Luc. Miniature painter. Born in France, 1769. He was sent to the United States by Louis XVI to paint a miniature of George Washington. He painted an original miniature for the King as well as a replica for himself. The artist delivered to the President his Majesty's present of the Badge of the Order of Saint-Esprit.

BARCLAY, Edith Lord. Painter. Exhibited "The May Basket" at 33d Annual of National Association of Women Painters and Sculptors. Address, 229 Williamsburg Ave., Brooklyn, N. Y.

BARCLAY, J. Edward. Painter. At one time occupied a studio in this city, during which time his portrait of Mr. S. H. Kauffman was painted from life. No biographical data at hand concerning this painter.

BARCLAY, McClelland. Painter, illustrator. Born St. Louis, Mo., 1891. Pupil of H. C. Ives, George R. Bridgman, Thomas Fogarty. Member: Art Students' League of New York; Chicago Art Club; Art Service League, Chicago. Awards: Navy poster prize, Committee on National Preparedness, 1917; first prize U. S. M. C. recruiting poster; first prize for allegorical painting of Commerce of Chicago from Chicago Association of Commerce.

BARHYDT, Jean K. (Mrs. George Weed Barhydt). Painter. Born Brooklyn, N. Y., 1868. Pupil of G. A. Thompson. Member: National Academy Women Painters and Sculptors; Conn. Association of Fine Arts. Address, The Belnord, 548 Orange Street, New Haven, Conn.

BARILE, Xavier J. Painter, illustrator, etcher. Born in Italy, 1891. Pupil of Chapman, Mora, Sloan, and Dodge. Member: Art Students' League of New York.

BARKER, Katherine. Painter. Born Pittsburgh, Pa., 1891. Pupil of Breckenridge, Anshutz, Carlson, Hale, Beaux, and Vonnoh. Member: Fellowship, Penna. Academy of Fine Arts. Address, The Avondale, 39th and Locust Streets, Philadelphia, Pa.

BARKER, M. Miniature painter, working in New York about 1820.

BARBER, William. Engraver of maps and script. He engraved the title-page to "Birch's Views of Philadelphia," published in 1800.

BARLOW, John Noble. Painter. Died in England, 1917. He was born there 1887. He was a member of the Providence Art Club, and is represented by three landscapes in the Rhode Island School of Design.

BARLOW, Myron. Born in 1873. Pupil of Art Institute Chicago, and Ecole des Beaux Arts in Paris. Exhibited in Salon. Member of the Paris American Artists' Association. Works: "Mother's Love," Penna. Academy of Fine Arts; "Pecheuse," Detroit Museum of Art. Address, 362 Woodland Ave., Detroit, Mich.

BARNARD, Edward Herbert. Painter. Born in Belmont, Mass., in 1865. Studied at Boston Museum of Fine Arts, and with Boulanger and Collin in Paris. Awarded many honorable mentions and medals. Address, 603 Belmont Street, Belmont, Mass.

BARNARD, Elinor M. (Mrs. Komroff). Painter. Born Kensington, London, England, 1872. Member: National Academy of Women Painters and Sculptors. Specialty, portraits in water color. Address, 601 Madison Ave., New York, N. Y.

BARNARD, George Grey. Sculptor. Born in Bellefonte, Pa., 1863. Studied at Art Institute of Chicago, Ecole Nationale des Beaux Arts, 1884-5-6-7. Exhibited in Paris Salon, 1894. Awarded Gold medal Paris Expn., 1900. Prof. Sculpture, Art Students' League, New York; Associate Member of National Academy. Works include: "Brotherly Love," "Norway," "Two Natures" (Metropolitan Museum, New York), "The God Pan" (in Central Park), "The Boy," group, "Brotherly Love in Norway," "The Hewer," "Urn of Life" (19 figures in marble), group, "Brotherhood in Suffering," "Despair and Hope," "Youth," "Mother and Angel," "Lone Woman," "Prodigal Son and Father," great group, "Adam and Eve," relief (22 ft. high), "Labor and Rest," "Christ," group of "Baptism," "Love and Labor," "The Brothers," family group of 4 figures; Pa. Capitol. *Address*, 454 Fort Washington Ave., New York, N. Y.

BARNARD, Josephine W. Painter. Born in Buffalo, N. Y., 1869. Pupil of Dow, Snell and Carlson. *Address*, 117 Waverly Place, N. Y., or 26 Middagh Street, Brooklyn, N. Y.

BARNARD, W. S. Engraver of book illustrations, working in New York about 1845. He was associated with A. L. Dick and was probably in his employ in his engraving establishment. Other engravings are signed "Tuthill & Barnard, Sc."

BARNES, Ernest Harrison. Landscape painter. Born Portland, N. Y., 1873. Exhibited at National Academy of Design, 1925. Pupil of Art Students' League, New York. *Address*, Detroit, Mich.

BARNES, Gertrude J. (Mrs.). Painter. Born at Tyngsboro, Mass., 1865. Pupil of Minneapolis School of Fine Arts. Specialty, landscapes. *Address*, 1812 Emerson Ave., Minneapolis, Minn.

BARNES, Hiram Putnam. Artist, illustrator. Born in Boston, 1857. Public school education; studied drawing and painting with Fernand Lungren and F. Childe Hassam. Began as engraver making designs for Waltham Watch Co., also engraved on wood; became illustrator for leading Boston publishers. Exhibited water colors Boston Art Club. *Address*, Waltham, Mass.

BARNES, John P. Painter. Exhibited pastels at the Annual Water Color Exhibition at the Penna. Academy of Fine Arts, Philadelphia, 1922. *Address*, 518 Parker Ave., Collingsdale, Penna.

BARNETT, Tom P. Painter. Exhibited oil painting entitled "Old Coal Pocket" at Penna. Academy of the Fine Arts, Philadelphia, 1921. Student of Paul Carnoyer. Born in St. Louis, Mo., in 1870. *Address*, Lindell Boulevard, St. Louis, Missouri.

BARNEY, Mrs. Alice Pike. Painter. Born Cincinnati, Ohio, in 1860. Pupil of Carolus Duran and Whistler. Represented by portraits of Whistler (used in illustrating) and of Natalie Barney, owned by the French Government. *Address*, Studio House, Washington, D. C.

BARNEY, J. Stewart. Landscape painter. He exhibited a collection of Scottish and American landscapes at the Ehrich Galleries, New York, in 1924. He died in New York City, Nov. 1925, in his 57th year.

BARNHORN, Clement J. Sculptor. Born in Cincinnati, Ohio, in 1857. Studied at Academie Julien in Paris. Salon Medals and honorable mention. Member of National Sculpture Society, Cincinnati Art Club. Works: Fountain figures, Hartford, Conn., and Prince George Hotel, New York; "Magdalen," Cincinnati Art Museum. *Address*, Art Museum, Cincinnati, Ohio.

BARNS, Cornelia. Painter and illustrator. Born in New York, 1888. Pupil of Twachtman and Chase. *Address*, Morgan Hill, California.

BARNUM, Emily K. Painter. Born in New York, 1874. Pupil of Vibet in Paris and Irving Wiles in New York. Member of Art Students' League, New York. Specialty is water colors. *Address*, Switzerland.

BARONE, Antonio. Painter. Member of Oakland Art Association, Oakland, Calif. Awarded Gold Medal, Philadelphia Art Club, 1917. Exhibited "Grazia" at the Carnegie Institute, 1920, and "Lady with Muff" at the Penna. Academy of the Fine Arts, 1921. *Address*, 771 Lexington Ave., New York City.

BARR, William. Painter and illustrator. Born in Scotland, 1867. Among his works "Paisley Cross," portrait of Provost Peter Eadie, and portrait of Thomas Boyle at City Hall, San Francisco. *Address*, 311 Lyon Street, San Francisco, Calif.

BARRALET, John James. Painter and engraver. Born in London, 1747. He died in Philadelphia, 1815. He painted portraits, engraved a few plates, painted landscapes in water color, and designed a number of plates for other engravers.

BARRATT, Thos. E. Miniature painter. Flourished 1837–1854, Philadelphia. May have been identical with or a relative to Edward Barratt, who painted miniatures in Dublin in 1790.

BARRATT, Watson. Illustrator and mural painter. Born in Salt Lake City, Utah, in 1884. Pupil of Howard Pyle and Henri. Represented by "Canton Street" in Corcoran Art Gallery, and mural painting in Burham Library, Art Institute, Chicago. *Address*, 330 West 39th St., New York.

BARRET, Laura A. Painter. Member: Society of Independent Artists, National Arts Club, 15 Gramercy Park, New York, N. Y.

BARRETT, Elizabeth Hunt (Mrs. Edward N. Barrett). Painter. Born New York, N. Y., 1863. Pupil of Nad. *Address*, Amherst, Va.

BARRIE, Erwin (S.). Painter. Born Canton, Ohio, 1886. Pupil A. I. C. Member: Chicago A. C.; Business Men's A. C. of Chicago. *Address*, 1188 Asbury Ave., Hubbard Woods, Ill.

BARRINGTON, Amy L. Painter. Member: National Academy of Women Painters and Sculptors. *Address,* 3089 Broadway, New York, N. Y.

BARRON. A little-known genre painter noted in Tuckerman's Book of the Artists.

BARRY, Charles A. A little-known portrait and genre painter. Among his best remembered work was "Motherless," "Evangeline," and a head of the poet Whittier. He flourished in Boston, 1851–1859.

BARRY, Edith C(leaves). Painter. Born in Boston, Mass. Studied in New York and France. Member: National Academy of Women Painters and Sculptors; Conn. Academy of Fine Arts; Society of Independent Artists; Art Students' League of New York.

BARRY, Gerard. Painter. Born in County Cork, Ireland, 1864. Began to study art at Paris, France, in 1885, at the Academie Julien, and studied under Le Febre, Boulanger, and Carolus Duran. Exhibited in the Paris Salons of 1885 and 1886, and at the Royal Academy, London, England, in 1887. Came to the United States in 1888, and after remaining for 18 months returned to study under Carmon. Returning to the United States, he has remained ever since, engaged in portrait painting, with the exception of occasional trips in Europe for vacation purposes.

BARRY, John J(oseph). Etcher. Born Hamilton, Ontario, Canada, 1885. Pupil of Ernest Haskell. Member: California Society of Etchers; Calif. Print-Makers. *Address,* Burton Arms Apts., 680 Witmer Street, Los Angeles, Calif.

BARSE, George Randolph, Jr. Artist. Born Detroit, 1861. Studied art at Ecole des Beaux Arts and Academie Julien, Paris, 1879–85; pupil of A. Cabanel, Boulanger and Lefebvre. Academy prize, Paris, France, 1882; New England prize, Boston, 1885; 1st prize Nat. Acad. Design, 1895; Academy of National Arts, 1898; National Academy, 1899. Member: Architectural League of New York. *Address,* Katonah, N. Y.

BARTHOLDI, Frederic Auguste. A French sculptor. Born in 1834. Known in this country from his gigantic statue of "Liberty Enlightening the World" on Bedloes Island in New York harbor. He was a commissioner in 1876 of the French government, at the Centennial Exposition in Philadelphia. His statue of "Lafayette Arriving in America" is in Union Square, New York.

BARTHOLOMEW, Edward Sheffield. Sculptor. Born in Connecticut in 1822. He studied in Italy. A collection of his work is in Hartford, Conn. His full-length statue of

Washington belonged to Noah Walker and his "Eve Repentant" to Jos. Harrison of Philadelphia. He died in Naples in 1858.

BARTLE, George P. Wood engraver. Born in 1853. He studied wood engraving with H. H. Nichols. Much of his best work was done for the *Century Magazine.* He died in 1918.

BARTLE, Sara N(orwood). Miniature painter. Born Washington, D. C. Pupil of Carroll Beckwith, Art Students' League of N. Y.; Art Students' League of Washington. *Address,* 2300 18th Street, Washington, D. C.

BARTLETT, Dana. Painter, illustrator, teacher. Born Ionia, Mich., 1878. Pupil of Art Students' League of New York and William M. Chase. Member: California Arts Club; California Women's Color Club; Print-Makers of California. *Address,* 231 South Spring Street, Los Angeles, California.

BARTLETT, Elizabeth M. P. Painter. Member: Society of Independent Artists. *Address,* 136 Hemenway Street, Boston, Mass.

BARTLETT, Frederic Clay. Artist. Born at Chicago, 1873. Educated, Harvard School, St. Paul's School, Concord, N. H., Royal Academy Art Munich, Germany, and studied art in Paris under Collin, Aman-Jean, Whistler, etc. Professionally engaged as artist in mural decorations; has done work in U. of Chicago, Second Presbyn. Church, University Club, Chicago, mural decorations in Council Chamber of Chicago City Hall. *Address,* The Players, 16 Gramercy Park, New York.

BARTLETT, Madeleine A. Painter. Born in Woburn. Pupil of Cowles Art School, and Henry H. Kitson. She has made a specialty of small bas-reliefs. Exhibited portraits at Penna. Academy of the Fine Arts, 1924. *Address,* Boyleston Street, Boston, Mass.

BARTLETT, Paul Wayland. Sculptor and painter. Born New Haven, Conn., 1865. Pupil Cavelier and Rodin. Represented by statue of General Joseph Warren in Boston, equestrian statue of Lafayette in Louvre, Paris, statue of Columbus in Washington. Elected member of National Academy of Design, 1917. Painting "The Pond above the Sea" at Carnegie Institute, 1923. Died in Paris in 1925.

BARTLETT, Truman H. Sculptor, teacher. Born Dorset, Vt., 1835. Pupil of Fremiet in Paris. Work: "Wells," bronze statue, Hartford, Conn.; "Benedict," cemetery monument, Waterbury, Conn.; "Clark," cemetery monument, Hartford, Conn.; many busts and statuettes. Writings: "Life of Dr. William Rimmer," "Physiognomy of Abraham Lincoln." He died in 1923.

BARTOL, E. H. (Miss). Painter. A disciple of William M. Hunt, who had her studio in Boston.

BARTON, Loren R. Painter and Etcher. Born Oxford, Mass. Member of California Art Club. Her dry point of Geo. Arliss as Disraeli, and her studies of the Spanish types of California are well known. *Address,* 993 South Wilton Place, Los Angeles, Calif.

BARTON, Ralph. Painter and illustrator. Born Kansas City, Mo., 1891. *Address,* 15 West 51st Street, New York.

BARTOO, Catherine R. Born Williamsport, Penna. Pupil of Henri and Mora. *Address,* 102 Oak Street, Binghamton, N. Y.

BASING, Charles. Painter. Born in Australia in 1865. Pupil of Bougnereau. Has executed museum decorations in Columbia College, New York, and Carnegie Institute, Pittsburgh. *Address,* 163 Clymer Street, Brooklyn, N. Y.

BASSETT, Reman. Exhibited at National Academy of Design, New York, 1925. *Address,* Dallas, Texas.

BASSETT, W. H. Engraver. His plates occur in ''The Poetical Works of John Trumbull,'' published in Hartford, Conn., in 1820, the designs being by E. Tisdale.

BATE, Rutledge. Painter. Exhibited portrait at Annual Exhibition of the National Academy of Design, 1925. *Address,* Brooklyn, N. Y.

BATEMAN, Charles. Painter. Born in Minneapolis in 1890. Pupil of Art Students' League of New York. *Address,* Woodstock, Ulster Co., N. Y.

BATEMAN, John. Sculptor. Born Cedarville, N. J., 1887. Studied at Penna. Academy of Fine Arts; also studied in Paris. Pupil of Charles Grafly. *Address,* 230 Park Ave., Haddonfield, N. J.

BATEMAN, William. Engraver on ''stone, steel, silver, and copper.'' Is known only from his advertisement in the *New York Mercury* for Dec. 1, 1774.

BATES, Bertha Day (Mrs.). Painter and illustrator. Pupil of Howard Pyle. Born in Philadelphia in 1875. *Address,* Chestnut Hill, Philadelphia.

BATES, Dewey. Painter. Born 1851. Specialized in landscape painting, portraiture, genre. He studied in Paris, under Gerome.

BATES, Earl Kenneth. Painter. Exhibited oil paintings ''The Waning Year'' and ''The Hills of Pennsylvania'' in the Penna.

Academy of the Fine Arts, Philadelphia, 1921, also 1924. He was born in Haverhill, Mass., in 1895. Pupil of Penna. Academy of Fine Arts. *Address,* North 21st Street, Philadelphia; Studio, Hopewell, N. J.

BATHER, George. Engraver. Born in England, he came to the United States in 1851. He was employed in book illustrating in New York by J. C. Buttre & Co. His son, George Bather, Jr., was employed by the same firm; he died in Brooklyn in 1890.

BATHER, W. T. An engraver of portraits in a mixed and rather mechanical manner, working in Chicago in 1897, and residing in Brooklyn, N. Y. He was probably a son of the engraver George Bather.

BATHURST, Clyde C. Sculptor. Born in Mount Union, Penna., 1883. Pupil of Grafly at Penna. Academy of Fine Arts. *Address,* 20th and Cherry Streets, Philadelphia.

BAUER, Theodor. Sculptor. He has exhibited at the National Sculpture Society in New York.

BAUER, William. Painter and illustrator. Born in St. Louis, Mo., in 1888. Awarded 1921 prize for landscapes. *Address,* 709 Pine Street, St. Louis, Mo.

BAUGHMAN, Mary B. Sculptor. Born in Richmond, Va. Pupil of Colarossi Academy. *Address,* 521 West Grace Street, Richmond, Virginia.

BAULCH, A. V. Engraver. Did some excellent line engraving for the Appletons of New York in 1869, after designs by F. O. C. Darley.

BAUM, Walter E. Painter and illustrator. Born in Penna., 1884. Pupil of Penna. Academy of Fine Arts. Exhibited at the Penna. Academy of Fine Arts, 1924. *Address,* Sellersville, Bucks County, Pa.

BAUMANN, Gustave. Engraver, painter. Born in Germany, 1881. Awarded gold medal for engraving at San Francisco, 1915. *Address,* 140 Canyon Road, Santa Fe, N. M.

BAUMBER, Julius H. Portrait painter. Born in Germany in 1848, he came to America in 1869, and died in Chicago in 1917.

BANS, Simon P. Painter. Born in Indianapolis in 1882. Pupil of Adams and Stark. *Address,* Union Trust Bldg., Indianapolis.

BAXTER, Bertha E. Painter. Exhibited oil paintings ''Evening Tide'' and ''Sails Drying'' at the Penna. Academy of the Fine Arts, 1921, Philadelphia, and ''Down by the Sea'' at National Academy, N. Y., 1925. *Address,* Gramercy Park, New York City.

3

BAXTER, Elijah, Jr. Painter. Born in Hyannis, Mass., 1849. Studied in the Antwerp Academy from 1871–73, after that his studio was in Providence, R. I. He paints chiefly landscapes with figures, and occasional fruit and flower pieces. He exhibited at the Boston Art Club and the Academy of Design in New York.

BAXTER, Martha W. Miniature painter. Born at Castleton, Vt., in 1869. Pupil of Penna. Academy of Fine Arts and Art Students' League of New York; also studied in Paris and Venice. Represented by "The Girl in Red," at Penna. Academy of Fine Arts in 1924. *Address*, Santa Barbara, Calif.

BAYARD, Clifford A. Painter. Member of the Associated Artists of Pittsburgh. He exhibited "The Road to Ripples," at the Carnegie Institute, Pittsburgh, Pa.

BAYLINSON, A. S. Painter. Born in Russia in 1882. Pupil of Robert Henri. Member of Society of Independent Artists. *Address*, 1947 Broadway, New York.

BAYLISS, Lillian. Miniature painter.

BAYLOS, Zelma. Painter and sculptor. Born in Hungary. Pupil of Will Low. Painted portrait of General Geo. R. Dyer, also "Spirit of Democracy" owned by the American Red Cross.

BAYMAN, Leo. Sculptor. Exhibited a portrait at the Penna. Academy of Fine Arts, Philadelphia, 1920. *Address*, 10 East 14th Street, New York.

BEACH, Chester. Sculptor. Born San Francisco, 1881. Member: National Academy 1924; National Sculpture Society; Architectural League of New York; American Numismatic Society. *Address*, 207 E. 17th Street, New York.

BEACHAM, Noble F. Painter. Exhibited water color at the Penna. Academy of the Fine Arts, Philadelphia, 1925. *Address*, Lansdowne, Penna.

BEAL, Gifford. Painter. Born in New York City, 1879. Pupil of William Chase, Du Mond, and Ranger. Elected Associate Member of National Academy 1908, and Academician 1914. Represented at Metropolitan Museum by "Mayfair" and "The Albany Boat"; at Chicago Institute by "A Puff of Smoke." Also at Syracuse Museum and San Francisco Art Institute. *Address*, 230 West 59th Street, New York.

BEAL, Reynolds. Painter. Born in New York City, 1867. Pupil of William Chase, and studied in Europe especially at Madrid. Elected Associate Member of National Academy, 1909; also member of New York Water Color Club. *Address*, Wilellyn, Newburgh, N. Y.

BEALES, Isaac B. Painter. Born Great Yarmouth, England, 1866. Pupil of E. J. Poynter, Woodhouse Stubbs. *Address*, 356 Harrison Ave., Hasbrouck Heights, N. J.

BEAN, Caroline Van Hook. Painter. Born Washington, D. C. Pupil of Harry Thompson, Paris; Chase, New York. Member: National Academy of Women Painters and Sculptors.

BEARD, Adelia Belle. Artist. Born Painesville, Ohio. Went to New York; studied drawing at Cooper Union and Art Students' League; portrait painting with Wyatt Eaton and William Chase. Taught classes in drawing and painting; exhibited at National Academy Design; illustrator books and magazines.

BEARD, Daniel C. Born in 1850. The fourth son of the artist James Henry Beard, like the rest of the family, became an artist. He has an extraordinary talent for allegory as applied to decoration, and introduces animals and natural objects in singularly quaint and suggestive combinations. *Address*, Flushing, L. I., New York.

BEARD, Frank. The third son of the artist James Henry Beard was a special artist for Harper & Bros. during the Civil War. He was for a time Professor of Fine Arts in Syracuse University. Born in Cincinnati in 1842, he died in Chicago in 1905.

BEARD, George. Miniature painter. Flourished 1840, Cincinnati, Ohio.

BEARD, Henry. The second son of the artist James Henry Beard. He painted genre subjects in oil and water colors and made designs for many of Prang's publications.

BEARD, James Henry. Painter. Born in 1814 in Buffalo, New York, died at Flushing, L. I. He lived in Cincinnati during the earlier part of his life at a time when he devoted himself almost exclusively to portrait painting. He is known to have made portraits of Henry Clay, and Presidents John Q. Adams, Taylor, and Wm. H. Harrison. He came to New York in 1846 and was one of the originators and charter members of the Century Club. In his later years he devoted his time chiefly to animal painting. In 1872 he was elected a full member of the New York School of Design.

BEARD, William Holbrook. Born in Painesville, Ohio, 1825. Began his career as a traveling portrait painter after some instruction from his elder brother, James H. Studio in Buffalo, N. Y., 1850. Went to Europe in 1857. Studied and practised in Dusseldorf, Switzerland, Italy and France. Settled in New York City, 1860. National Academy 1862. Died Feb.

20, 1900, in New York. Represented at Chicago Art Institute by ''The Bear's Temperance Question.''

BEATTY, John Wesley. Painter. Born Pittsburgh, Pa., 1851. Pupil of Royal Bavarian Academy, Munich. Has been represented at several exhibitions. Member of jury on painting, Columbian Exp., Chicago, 1893; National Advisory Board, Paris Exp., 1900; Fine Arts Committee Pan-American Exp., Buffalo, 1901; National Advisory Committee, St. Louis Exp., 1904; International Jury of Awards, Panama-Pacific International Exp., San Francisco, 1915. Member: Pittsburgh Art Society; Pittsburgh Photographers' Society; Royal Society of Arts, London. Painter and etcher. Director Department of Fine Arts, Carnegie Institute, Pittsburgh. Represented by ''Plymouth Hills,'' at National Gallery, Washington, D. C. *Address*, Richland Lane, Pittsburgh, Pa.

BEAU, John Anthony. Engraver and chaser. He was evidently a silver-plate engraver and advertised in the *New York Journal* for Dec. 13, 1770.

BEAULEY, William Jean. Painter. Born Joliet, Ill., 1874. Pupil of Henri and Maratta in New York; Yvon in Paris. Member: New York Arch. League; Philadelphia Art Club; Art Fund Society. Award: Arch. League prize awarded 1912.

BEAUMONT, Arthur. Painter. Born Bradford, Eng., 1879. Pupil of Bouguereau in Paris; Olsson in London. Member: Society of Independent Artists, United Scenic Artists' Association. Award: Gold medal, Julien Academy, Paris, 1905. *Address*, 112 Rhine Ave., Stapleton, N. Y.

BEAUMONT, Lilian A(dele). Painter. Born Jamaica Plain, Mass. Pupil of School of Boston Museum of Fine Arts under Benson, Tarbell and Philip Hale. Member Copley Society. Died 1922. *Address*, 23 Alveston Street, Jamaica Plain, Boston, Mass.

BEAUX, Cecilia. Artist. Born Philadelphia. Pupil of Wm. Sartain, the Julien School and the Lazar School, Paris. Awarded the Mary Smith Prize, Pa. Academy Fine Arts, 4 times; gold medal, Philadelphia Art Club; Dodge Prize National Academy of Design. Represented at Pa. Academy Fine Arts, Toledo Art Museum, Metropolitan Museum, New York, Brooks Memorial Gallery, Memphis, John Herron Art Institute, Indianapolis. Exhibited at Champs de Mars, 1896; National Academy, 1902; Societaire des Beaux Arts. Director of American Federation of Arts. *Address*, Gloucester, Mass.; (Dec.–May) 132 E. 19th Street, New York, N. Y.

BEBIE, W. Portrait painter, who flourished about 1845. His work is not well known;

an excellent portrait-group of a lady and her two daughters is in the Gallery of the Minneapolis Institute of Arts.

BECHER, Arthur E. Painter, pupil of Louis Mayer and Howard Pyle. Born in Germany, 1877. *Address*, Hopewell Junction, N. Y.

BECHDOLT, Jack. Painter. Exhibited water color at Annual Exhibition of Penna. Academy, 1922. *Address*, 404 West 20th Street, New York City, N. Y.

BECK. An American landscape painter, who died in 1814. He was the first painter who penetrated beyond the Alleghenies.

BECK, Carol H. Portrait painter. Born in Philadelphia in 1859. She was a pupil of Penna. Academy of Fine Arts; also studied in Dresden and Paris. Among her best known portraits are ''Governor Patterson'' for the State Capitol, and her brother, ''Hon James M. Beck.'' She died in 1908.

BECK, Augustus J. Painter. The Penna. Historical Soc. has several copies of portraits that were made by this artist from original pictures. Independence Hall also has several copies by this artist.

BECK, Minna McLeod. Painter. Born in Atlanta, Ga., 1878. Pupil of Arthur Dow in New York. *Address*, 121 Chestnut Street, Harrisburg, Penna.

BECK, Raphael. Painter, sculptor, and illustrator. Studied at Julien Academy in Paris. *Address*, 78 Delaware Ave., Buffalo, N. Y.

BECK, Walter. Mural painter. Born Dayton, Ohio, 1864. Studied in Munich. Work: Murals, City Hall, Cincinnati; Art Museum of Brooklyn; and National Gallery, Washington, D. C. *Address*, Millbrook, N. Y.

BECKER, Frederick. Painter. Born at Vermillion, S. D., in 1888. Pupil of H. Breckenridge and Daniel Garber. His paintings, the ''Gray Day'' and ''After the Shower,'' are in the Gallery of University of Oklahoma. *Address*, 511 East 7th Street, New York.

BECKER, Maurice. Painter and cartoonist. Born in Russia. Pupil of Robert Henri. *Address*, Tioga, Tioga County, Penna.

BECKINGTON, Alice. Painter. Born St. Louis, 1868. Studied Art Students' League, New York; Academie Julien, Paris; and with Charles Lazar, Paris. Has exhibited at Paris Salons, and Paris Expn., 1900, Society of American Artists; honorable mention, Buffalo Expn., 1901; bronze medal, St. Louis Expn., 1904. A founder and now president of American Society Miniature Painters. *Address*, 156 Carnegie Hall, New York.

BECKWITH, Arthur. Painter. Born in London in 1860, now living in San Francisco, California. Among his paintings "Sunlight and Shadow" is in Golden Gate Park Museum, and "Foggy Morning on the Coast" in San Francisco Gallery. *Address*, 438 Montgomery Block, San Francisco, California.

BECKWITH, Henry. Engraver. His best work is of animals after paintings by Landseer; he also engraved landscapes after American artists. He was working in New York 1842–43.

BECKWITH, James Carroll. Painter. Born Hannibal, Mo., 1852. Died 1817. Pupil of Carolus Duran and École des Beaux Arts in Paris. Honorable mention Paris Salon, 1887; bronze medal, Paris Exp., 1889; gold medal, Atlanta Exp., 1895; bronze medal, Paris Exp., 1900; gold medal, Charleston Exp., 1902; National Academy, 1894. Member: American Water Color Society; Art Students' League, New York; National Institute Arts and Letters. Specialty, portraits and genre pictures. Represented by "The Blacksmith" at National Museum, Washington, D. C. Portrait Mrs. R. H. McCurdy, Academy Exhibition, 1789. Portrait Capt. Jos. Lentilhon, Paris Salon, 1889. His works include "Judith" and the "Falconer" sent to the Paris Exposition of 1878.

BEDFORD, Henry E. Painter and sculptor. Born Brooklyn, 1860. *Address*, 2744 Broadway, New York.

BEDORE, Sidney. Sculptor. Born in Stephenson, Mich., 1883. Pupil of Beaux-Arts Institute of Design, New York. *Address*, Midway Studios, Chicago, Ill.

BEEBE, Dee. Painter. Member of National Association of Women Painters and Sculptors. *Address*, 18 Gramercy Park, New York.

BEECHER, Hilda. Painter. Exhibited at National Association of Women Painters and Sculptors, 1924. *Address*, 939 Eighth Ave., New York.

BEEK, Alice D. (Mrs.). Painter. Born in Providence, R. I., in 1876. Pupil of Puvis de Chavannes. *Address*, 1310 North 5th Street, Tacoma, Wash.

BEEKMAN, Henry R. Painter and etcher. Born in New York City, 1880. Pupil of Hawthorne, Bredin and Lathrop. He exhibited his etching "The Gallery" at the Penna. Academy of Fine Arts, Philadelphia, 1924. *Address*, 38 East 76th Street, New York.

BEERS, Alexander R. Painter. Born in Titusville, 1882. Student of Art Institute, Chicago. *Address*, Auditorium Theatre, Chicago.

BEEST, Albert Van. Born in Holland in 1820. In 1845 he came to New York, where he made a reputation as a marine painter and teacher. He lived mainly in Boston and New York. Among his pupils were William Bradford and R. Swain Gifford. He died in 1860.

BEHAR, Ely M. Painter. Exhibited water colors at the Penna. Academy of the Fine Arts, Philadelphia, 1925. *Address*, 880 West 181st Street, N. Y.

BELAUME, J. In 1825 this name as "J. Belume Sculpt." appears on a dry-point etching in New Orleans, on a print representing the triumphal arch erected to commemorate the visit of General Lafayette to New Orleans.

BELCHER, Hilda. Painter. Student New York School of Art. Born in Pittsford, Vt., 1881. She exhibited "The Easter Window" at Penna. Academy of the Fine Arts, Philadelphia, 1921. *Address*, 939 Eighth Ave., New York City.

BELCHER, Martha Wood. Painter, etcher, teacher. Born in England, 1844. Pupil of Cooper Institute, New York; Flugen, Lietzenmeyer, and Lindenschmidt in Munich. Member of National Association of Women Painters and Sculptors; New York Water Color Club Association. *Address*, Van Dyke Studios, 939 Eighth Ave., New York.

BELKNAP, Zedekiah. Painted portraits as early as 1810 in Massachusetts; he graduated from Dartmouth College in 1807, and died in Weathersfield, Vt.

BELL, Clara Louise. Painter. Born Newton Falls, Ohio, 1886. Pupil of Edith P. Stevenson, Cleveland School of Art, Art Students' League of New York. Award: Penton medal for miniature painting, Cleveland Museum, 1919. *Address*, 3226 Euclid Ave., Cleveland, Ohio.

BELL, Edward August. Painter. Born in New York, 1862. Pupil of National Academy of Design. Member of Art Students' League. His pictures are usually symbolic or decorative in theme and carried out by the youthful female figure. Elected an Associate Member of the National Academy of Design. *Address*, 226 West 59th Street, New York.

BELLEW, Frank Henry Temple. Illustrator for Harper Bros.; also drew caricatures for the magazines. In 1866 he issued a book on the "Art of Amusing." His son, F. P. W. Bellew ("Chip"), has illustrated for *Life*.

BELLOWS, Albert F. Born in Milbury, Mass., 1830. Studied in Paris and in Antwerp Royal Academy. Painted in England and Wales. Associate member of National Academy, 1859; National Academy, 1861. Died in

1883. "A Village Scene" (New England?), signed A. F. Bellows, 1876. Lent by W. T. Carrington, Art Institute, Chicago. "Forest Life," painted in 1860. Owned by New York Public Library.

BELLOWS, George Wesley. Painter. Born at Columbus, Ohio, in 1882. Died in 1924. Studied in New York School of Art, under Robert Henri. Elected an associate member of National Academy in 1908, and Academician in 1918. Among his works: "Riverfront," "Gramercy Park," "Ringside Seats," "Crucifixion," and many portraits. Represented in Metropolitan Museum, Penna. Academy of Fine Arts and Brooklyn Museum. He also executed many very excellent lithographs.

BELZONS, M. A French gentleman who painted miniatures in Charleston, S. C. He was the first instructor of Thomas Sully in 1799, whose sister he married. Dunlap notes "he was a very poor painter." He flourished about 1779 in Charleston, S. C.

BEMENT, Alon. Painter. Born Ashfield, Mass., 1878. Pupil of Boston Museum School; Bonnat and Constant in Paris; Naas School, Sweden; Ecole des Beaux Arts, Paris. Prof. of Fine Arts, Teachers Coll., Columbia University, since 1906. Instructor, College of City of New York. Director, Maryland Institute, Baltimore. *Address,* 210 West 59th Street, New York, N. Y., or care of Maryland Institute, Baltimore, Md.

BEMIS. Painter. Flourished about 1850. The Worcester Art Museum owns a "View in Worcester or Vicinity." Oil on canvas. Size 20 in. by 24 in.

BEMUS, Mrs. Mary B. Painter, teacher. Born Leicester, New York, 1849. Pupil of L. M. Wiles. *Address,* 401 S. Hope Street, Los Angeles, Calif., 2130 Emerson Ave., Santa Barbara, Calif.

BENBRIDGE, Henry. Portrait painter and miniature artist. Was born in Philadelphia, 1744, and as early as 1758 was painting pictures. In 1759 he was sent to Italy to study art with Battoni and Mengs. On his way to Italy he stopped in London long enough to paint portraits of Dr. Franklin (at Carnegie Institute) and Rev. Thomas Coombs. Benbridge painted many portraits in the South. He died in 1812. His work has frequently been attributed to Copley. He lived for years in Charleston, S. C.

BENDA, W(ladyslaw) T. Illustrator. Member: Arch. League, 1916; Players' Club, 1905. Mural Painter Award: silver medal, at Panama and Pacific Exposition. *Address,* 140 Wadsworth Ave., 1 Gramercy Park, New York, N. Y.

BENDER, Russell Thurston. Illustrator. Born in Chicago, 1895. Pupil of Chicago Academy of Fine Arts. Member: Palette and Chisel Club. *Address,* 333 South Dearborn Street; Home, 2717 Jackson Blvd., Chicago, Ill.

BENEDICT, J. B. Painter. Exhibited water color landscape at Annual Exhibition Penna. Academy of Fine Arts, 1922. *Address,* 1669 Broadway, Denver, Colorado.

BENEDUCE, Antimo. Painter. Exhibited water colors in annual exhibition of Water Colors, Penna. Academy of Fine Arts, Philadelphia, 1925. *Address,* 1959 East 73d Street, Cleveland, Ohio.

BENEKER, Gerrit A. Painter and illustrator. Born Grand Rapids, Mich., 1882. Pupil of John Vanderpoel and Frederick Richardson in Chicago; F. V. Du Mond, Henry Reuterdahl in New York; Charles W. Hawthorne in Provincetown. Member: Provincetown Art Association; Cleveland Art Students' Association. Award: New York Herald Easter prize, 1905; Scarab Club 3d prize, Detroit, 1916; Penton medal for industrial painting, Cleveland Museum, 1919. Represented in permanent collection of Provincetown Art Association, and Grand Rapids Central High School; Youngstown Museum of Art. Author of Victory Liberty Loan Poster, "Sure, We'll Finish the Job." *Address,* Provincetown, Mass.

BENJAMIN, Mrs. Lucile J. Painter. Born at Genesco, Ill., in 1876. Pupil of John Vanderpoel and Art Institute of Chicago. She painted under the name of Lucile Joullin. She died in San Francisco, Calif., 1924. Represented by the "Algerian Slave," in the Bohemian Club, San Francisco, Calif.

BENJAMIN, Samuel G. W. Marine painter. Born in 1837. Graduated from Williams College in 1859, became a member of Boston Art Club, which owns his painting "Daybreak off the Corbiere." He died in Burlington, Vt., in 1914.

BENN, Ben. Painter. Born in Russia, 1884. Pupil at National Academy of Design. His portrait of Judge J. Planken in Muncipal Court House, New York. *Address,* 244 East 23d Street, New York.

BENNETT, Belle. Sculptor. Born in New York City in 1900. She studied under Solon Borglum, and is now a student at the School of American Sculpture. *Address,* 152 East 63d Street, New York.

BENNETT, Emma D. (Mrs.). Sculptor. Born in New Bedford, Mass. Pupil of British Academy in Rome. *Address,* Cochituate, Mass.

BENNETT, Francis I. Painter. Born in Philadelphia, 1876. Pupil of Anshutz, Chase, and Henri. *Address,* 72 Whitford Ave., Nutley, N. J.

BENNETT, William James. Born in England, 1777, he died in New York, 1844. He came to that city in 1816 as a landscape painter in water color and an engraver in aquatint. He was elected an associate member of the National Academy of Design in 1827 and an Academician in 1828; for some years he was the curator of the Academy.

BENSELL, G. F. Portrait draughtsman in crayons. Flourished 1855–1868, Philadelphia.

BENSON, Eugene. Born in 1840. He was best known for his writing and was considered the best art critic in America. He was most successful in his portraits, elected to the Artists' Fund in 1861. In 1873 Mr. Benson went abroad for study and has since resided there. Among his works are ''Bazaar at Cairo,'' ''Slaves Tower,'' ''Reverie,'' ''Ariadne,'' and ''Strayed Maskers.''

BENSON, Frank W. Painter and etcher of portraits, interiors, birds and landscapes with figures; also teacher. Born, Salem, Massachusetts, 1862. Pupil of Boston Museum School; Boulanger and Lefebvre, in Paris. Temple Gold Medal, Penna. Academy of the Fine Arts, 1908; Harris Silver Medal, Art Institute of Chicago, 1909; Palmer Medal and prize, Art Institute of Chicago, 1910; Associate National Academy, 1897; National Academy, 1905; Ten American Painters; National Institute of Arts and Letters. Represented by ''My Daughter,'' in Corcoran Art Gallery. *Address*, 120 Riverway, Boston.

BENSON, Leslie L. Illustrator. Born at Mahone, N. S., 1885. Pupil of School of Boston Museum of Fine Arts. *Address*, 602 West 190th Street, New York.

BENTLEY, John W. Painter. Born in Patterson, N. J., in 1880. Pupil of Bridgeman, Du Mond, and Henri. *Address*, Woodstock, Ulster Co., N. Y.

BENTON, Henry S. Painter and illustrator. Born at Saratoga Springs in 1877. Student of Chicago Art Institute. *Address*, South Norwalk, Conn.

BENTON, Thomas H. Painter of landscapes and figures; also paints in water color. Exhibited at the Penna. Academy of Fine Arts, 1924. *Address*, 102 East 29th Street, New York.

BENZIGER, August. Portrait painter. Born at Einsiedein, Switzerland, 1867. Art Studies, Royal Academy, Vienna, Academie Julien and Ecole des Beaux Arts, Paris. Engaged as portrait painter, 1891; has painted portraits of Presidents McKinley, Roosevelt and Taft; of Popes Leo XIII and Benedict XV; President Diaz, Mexico; Sir Stuart Knill, Lord Mayor of London; Leon Bourgeois, Prime Minister of France; Presidents Hauser. Forrer and Deucher, of Switzerland; J. Pierpont Morgan, Robert S. Brookings, St. Louis, Charles F. Brooker, Charles M. Schwab; Cardinals Gibbons, Farley, and O'Connell, and many other notables, United States and abroad. *Address*, Villa Gutenberg, Brunnen, Switzerland; 140 W. 57th Street, New York, N. Y.

BERDANIER, Paul F. Painter. Born in Frackville, Penna., in 1879. Pupil of St. Louis School of Fine Arts. *Address*, 5877 Nina Place, St. Louis.

BERG, George Louis. Painter. Born at McGregor, Ia. Pupil of Art Students' League, New York. *Address*, Stony Creek, Conn.

BERGE, Edward. Sculptor. Born in Baltimore, 1876; he died there in 1924. He studied in Baltimore, and in Paris under Verlet and Rodin. He was a member of the National Sculpture Society. Represented by Watson Monument, Baltimore; ''Pieta,'' St. Patrick's Church, Washington; and the Gist Memorial, Charleston, S. C.

BERGER, C. F. Painter. His full-length portrait of President Polk with his hand extended is signed C. F. Berger (canvas 26 in. by 54 in.).

BERGLUND, Hilma L. G. Painter. Born Stillwater, Minn., 1886. Pupil St. Paul School of Art; Handicraft Guild, Minneapolis. Member: Artists' Society, St. Paul, Minn. *Address*, 1860 Feronia Ave., St. Paul, Minn.

BERKAN, Otto. Portrait painter. Born in 1832. He lived in Philadelphia for many years, many of his pictures being in the Catholic Cathedral of that city. He died in his studio at Passaic, N. J., in 1906.

BERMAN, Harry G. Painter in oils and water colors. Exhibited at the Penna. Academy of Fine Arts, 1924. *Address*, North 15th Street, Philadelphia.

BERNARD, Edward H. Painter. Born in Belmont, Mass., in 1855; died in 1909. Student of Boston Museum of Fine Arts.

BERNARD, Francisco. Nothing is known of this artist except that he painted portraits and landscapes of merit in New Orleans at intervals from 1848 until 1867, having a studio in the latter year at 146 Customhouse Street.

BERNATH, Sandor. Painter. Born in Hungary in 1892. Pupil of National Academy of Design. Member of New York Water Color Club. *Address*, 341 West 22d Street, New York.

BERNEKER, Louis F(rederick). Painter. Born Clinton, Mo. Pupil of St. Louis School of Fine Arts; Laurens in Paris. Member: New York Water Color Club, Allied Art Association. Represented in Dallas, Tex., Art Association. Instructor Mechanics Institute. *Address*, 53 East 59th Street, New York, N. Y.

BERNINGHAUS, Oscar E. Painter, illustrator. Born St. Louis, 1874. Pupil of St. Louis School of Fine Arts. Member: Salma Club and the Taos Students' Association. Awards: Dolph prize, St. Louis, 1907; share of Chicago Fine Arts Bldg. prize; Chamber of Commerce prize. Works: Two lunettes, Jefferson City, Mo., State Capitol Bldg.; "Winter in the West," City Art Museum, St. Louis; and in various libraries and schools. Specialty, Western subjects. *Address*, Clayton, Missouri.

BERNSTEIN, Theresa F. Painter. Born Philadelphia, Pa. Pupil of Philadelphia School of Design. National Academy of Women Painters and Sculptors; Eclectics; Plastic Club. Awards: Shillard gold medal for water colors; Plastic Club, 1915; National Academy Women Painters and Sculptors, 1916; National Art Club prize. *Address*, 39 West 67th Street, New York.

BERNSTROM, Victor. Wood engraver. Born in Sweden in 1845. Worked in London on the staff of the *Grafic*; he came to New York and became associated with the Harpers. He joined the Society of American Wood Engravers, and received a medal at the Columbian Exposition, Chicago, in 1893, and at the Pan-American and Buffalo Expositions. Later he devoted his time to landscapes in water colors. He died in 1907.

BERRYMAN, Clifford Kennedy. Illustrator. Born Versailles, Ky., 1869. Author "Cartoons of 58th House of Representatives"; originator of "Teddy Bear." On staff of Washington *Evening Star* since 1907. *Address*, 1754 Euclid St., N. W., Washington, D. C.

BERSON, Adolphe. Painter. Born San Francisco, Calif. Pupil of Lefebvre and Robert-Fleury in Paris. *Address*, 1037 Fillmore Street, San Francisco, Calif.

BERT, Charles H. Painter. Born in Milwaukee, Wis., 1873. Pupil of Cincinnati Art Academy, and Art Students' League of New York, also Julien Academy, Paris. *Address*, Lyme, Conn.

BERTHELSEN, Johann. Painter. Born in Copenhagen, Denmark, in 1883. *Address*, 611 North 7th Street, Manitowoc, Wis.

BERTSCH, Fred S. Designer. Born in Michigan in 1879. Pupil of A. I. C. Member: Palette and Chisel Club. *Address*, 15 East Huron Street; Home, 1629 Granville Ave., Chicago, Ill.

BEST, E. S. Engraver. Born in London in 1826, he came to this country about 1850 and received employment in J. M. Butler's publishing establishment in Philadelphia. His best engraved plate is "Washington at Valley Forge" after the painting by C. Scheussele.

BETTIS, Charles Hunter. Illustrator, designer. Born in Texas in 1891. Pupil of A. I. C. Member: Palette and Chisel, Chicago Arch., T Square, and Palette Clubs. *Address*, 127 North Dearborn Street; Home, 1429 Sherwin Ave., Chicago, Ill.

BETTS, Anna Whelan. Illustrator, painter, teacher. Born in Philadelphia. Pupil of Howard Pyle, and of Vonnoh. Member: Philadelphia Water Color Club. Award: bronze medal, P. P. Expn. Work: Illustrations in color for *Century*, *Harper's* and other magazines.

BETTS, E. C. Landscape painter. Born in Hillsdale, Mich., in 1856, he died in Denver, Colo., 1917. His best known painting was "The Valley of the Housatonic."

BETTS, Edwin D. Painter. Born in 1847. He was the father of Louis Betts, and several other members of the family are artists. His best known work is an idealized "Birth of Christ." He died in 1915.

BETTS, Louis. Portrait painter. Born in Little Rock, Ark., 1873. Pupil of his father, E. D. Betts, Sr., Wm. Chase; A. I. C. Member: Academy of National Arts, 1912; National Academy, 1915. Works: "William M. R. French" and "Apple Blossoms." Art Institute of Chicago. *Address*, 19th St., New York.

BEVERIDGE, Kuhne. Sculptor. Born Springfield, Ill., 1877. Pupil of William Rudolph O'Donovan, N. Y. Exhibited at National Academy of New York; Royal Academy London; Salon Champs de Mars, Paris; Paris Expn., 1900. Hon. mention, Paris, 1900.

BEWLEY, Murray P. Painter. Born Fort Worth, Tex., 1884. Pupil of A. I. C.; Chase, Beaux and Henri in New York. Member: Paris American Arts Association; Salma. C. Awards: Hon. mention, Paris Salon, 1910; first prize Salma. C., 1921. Works: "Buds," and "Portrait of Mrs. Percy V. Pennybacker," Ft. Worth (Tex.) Museum, and in the Pennsylvania Academy of the Fine Arts, Philadelphia.

BIAFORA, Enea. Sculptor. Born in Italy, 1892; came to New York in 1914. Exhibited at National Academy, New York, 1922.

BICKFORD, Nelson N. Painter. Specialty, animal painting. *Address*, New York City.

BICKNELL, Albian H. Painter. Born in 1837, he died at Malden, Maine, in 1915. He painted chiefly portraits and historical subjects. His portrait work included "Lincoln," "Webster," and "Horace Mann." Two of his historical paintings are "Lincoln at Gettysburg" and the "Battle of Lexington."

BICKNELL, Evelyn M. Painter. Born in New York. Specialty, water colors. *Address*, 18 West 27th Street, New York.

BICKNELL, Frank Alfred. Painter. Born Augusta, Me., 1866. Died in 1905. Pupil of Julien Academy in Paris under Bouguereau and Robert-Fleury. Academy of National Art; member American Art Association of Paris. Elected Associate Member of National Academy; National Arts Club, New York; Chicago Water Color Society. Specialty, landscapes. *Address*, Old Lyme, Conn.

BICKNELL, William H. Etcher. Born in Boston, Mass., 1860. Pupil of School of Boston Museum of Fine Arts. *Address*, Arlington Street, Winchester, Mass.

BIDDLE, George. Painter and sculptor. Born in Philadelphia in 1885. Student of Penna. Academy of Fine Arts and Julien Academy in Paris. Represented in Penna. Academy by "Tahitian Family." *Address*, Care of Morgan Harges, Paris.

BIERSTADT, Albert. Painter. Born Dusseldorf, Germany, 1830; died in New York, 1902. Landscape painter. Brought by his parents in 1831 to New Bedford, Mass., where his youth was spent. Began painting in oils in 1851; returned to Dusseldorf in 1853, and studied four years there and in Rome. On his return to the United States in 1857 he made a sketching tour in the Rocky Mountains, and from this and other visits to the West gathered materials for his most important pictures. He again visited Europe in 1867, 1878 and 1883. Elected National Academy, 1860. Legion of Honor, 1867. Medals: Austria, Germany, Bavaria and Belgium, and various orders. Represented in the Metropolitan Museum, New York, and Corcoran Art Gallery of Washington, D. C.

BIESEL, Charles. Painter. Born New York City, 1865. Member of the Art Club of Providence, R. I. *Address*, 30 East Ontario, Street, Chicago, Ill.

BIESEL, H. Fred. Painter and illustrator. Born in Philadelphia, 1903. Pupil of the Rhode Island School of Design. *Address*, 5249 Calumet Ave., Chicago.

BIESTER, Anthony. Portrait and landscape painter. Born in Germany in 1837; he came to America early in life; died at Madisonville, Ohio, in 1917. He was a member of the Cincinnati Art Club. He painted portraits of Archbishop Purcell and Bishop Henri, and decorations in St. John's Church, Lewisburg, Ky.

BIGELOW, Constance. Painter. Exhibited in Annual Water Color Exhibition, Penna. Academy of the Fine Arts, Philadelphia, 1925. *Address*, Provincetown, Mass.

BIGELOW, Daniel Folger. Landscape painter. Born in 1823. He was a friend of the portrait painter, G. P. A. Healy, and with him organized the Academy of Design; later it became the Art Institute of Chicago. He died in Chicago in 1910.

BIGELOW, Folger Allen. Painter. Born in Chicago in 1868, he died there in 1891.

BIGELOW, I. W. Portrait painter. His portrait of Miss Lillian Pullen, of White Plains, was painted about 1840, and was exhibited recently in New York.

BIGGS, Walter. Illustrator. Born in Elliston, Va. Pupil of Henri and Edw. Penfield.

BIGOT, T. F. Painter. Settled in New Orleans in 1816. Painted mostly landscapes; in 1841 he had a studio at 45 St. Philip Street, New Orleans.

BILL, Carroll. Painter. Exhibited water colors at the Annual Water Color Exhibitions, at Penna. Academy of Fine Arts, Philadelphia, 1922. *Address*, 132 Riverway, Boston, Mass.

BILLINGS, A. Engraver. His work was chiefly book-plates and some crude book-illustrating; his book-plate for Richard Varick, an officer in the Revolution, and Mayor of New York in 1801, is signed "A Billing, Sculpt."

BILLINGS, E. T. Portrait painter. Born in 1824; died 1893. He painted a portrait of Stephen Salisbury that is signed and dated 1885. Several of his paintings are owned by the Worcester Art Museum, Worcester, Mass.

BILLINGS, Joseph. Engraver, on silver plate; was also a silversmith and watchmaker. According to a proclamation of 1770 he was a forger and counterfeiter of bills of credit of the Province of Pennsylvania.

BILLINGS, Mary H. Painter. Born in Brooklyn, N. Y. Member of National Arts Club, N. Y. *Address*, 939 Eighth Ave., New York City, N. Y.

BILLINGS, T. E. Portrait painter.

BILOTTI, S. F. Sculptor. Born in Italy, 1879. Member of National Sculpture Society. Exhibited at the Penna. Academy of the Fine Arts, 1924. *Address*, New York City, No. 9 Macdougal Alley.

BINGHAM, Geo. Caleb. Portrait and genre painter. Born 1811 and died in 1879. Friend of Chester Harding, the artist. He went to Dusseldorf in 1857, and in 1877 was made professor of art in the University of Missouri at Columbia, Missouri.

BINNS, Elsie. Sculptor. Exhibited at Penna. Academy of Fine Arts, Philadelphia, 1924. *Address,* Alfred, N. Y.

BINON. Sculptor, who exercised his art in Boston in 1820. He was educated in France and studied art there. When in Boston he executed a bust of John Adams, of considerable merit; he was an early instructor of the sculptor, Horatio Greenough.

BIRCH. Engraver. In 1789 a portrait was published of ''Mr. Tho. Gurney'' signed ''Birch Sculp.'' It is well engraved in line; it occurs in an Essay on ''The System of Short Hand,'' written by Thomas Sarjeant.

BIRCH, B. Flourished 1784. Portrait draughtsman in crayons, seal engraver, and miniature painter. He inserted an advertisement in the *N. Y. Packet,* 1784, ''Likenesses are painted in crayon at one guinea each, with elegant oval, gilt frames included.'' By B. Birch from London.

BIRCH, Reginald B. Illustrator. Born in London, 1856; came to America, 1872. *Address,* Box 636, Dover, N. J.

BIRCH, Thomas. Artist. Was born in London in 1779, and emigrated to the United States in 1793. He established himself in Philadelphia about the year 1800, and commenced the painting of profile likenesses. A visit, made in a pilot-boat, to the capes of the Delaware, in the year 1807, turned his attention to marine views, in the delineation of which he acquired a high reputation. During the War of 1812, he executed a series of historical paintings, representing the naval victories of the United States. He also painted many landscapes, which are highly prized, particularly those representing snow scenes. His views of Philadelphia are excellent, and will perpetuate his fame as long as one of them remains preserved. He died in 1851, aged seventy-two years.

BIRCH, William. Born in Warwickshire, England, 1755; died in Philadelphia, 1834. Birch was an enamel painter and engraver; for a time he was working in Bristol, and in 1788–91 he was engraving prints and publishing them at Hampstead Heath, near London, and he was later living in London. In 1794 he came to Philadelphia with a letter of introduction from Benjamin West to the Hon. William Bingham, and in that city he painted landscapes in water colors and miniatures in enamel; among the latter were several portraits of Washington done after the Stuart head.

The earlier engraved work of Birch was executed in stipple and was much more finished than that published in this country. His one known portrait, that of Mrs. Robinson, engraved after a portrait by Sir Joshua Reynolds, belongs to this period and is an excellent piece of work. In 1791 he published in London a quarto volume entitled ''Delicies de la Grande Bretagne,'' a collection of views of places in the neighborhood of London, and well done in stipple.

His reputation as an American engraver is founded upon his Views of Philadelphia, drawn and engraved in 1798–1800 in connection with his son Thomas Birch, later well known as a landscape and marine painter. In 1808 he also issued a smaller series of plates showing the country seats of the United States. These views are now chiefly valued for their historical interest. His Philadelphia Views were republished by him in 1802, and again republished by Robert Desilon in 1841. Extracts from an unpublished autobiography of William Birch are published in Anne Hollingsworth Wharton's ''Heirlooms in Miniatures.''

BIRDSALL, Amos, Jr. Painter. Exhibited ''The Coast'' at the Penna. Academy of Fine Arts, Philadelphia, 1921. Born in New Jersey, 1865. *Address,* Melrose Park, Penna.

BIRGE, Mary Thompson (Mrs.). Painter. Born in New York, 1872. Pupil of Yale School of Fine Arts. *Address,* 1914 North Pennsylvania Street, Indianapolis, Ind.

BIRREN, Joseph P. Painter. Born in Chicago, studied in Philadelphia, New York, and Paris. Exhibited at the Penna. Academy of the Fine Arts, Philadelphia, 1924. *Address,* 49 Elm Street, Chicago, Ill.

BISBEE, John. Artist and lithographer. He is recorded by Dunlap as a good draughtsman.

BISBING, H. Singlewood. Painter. Born in 1849, he died in 1919. Exhibited in the Paris Salon, and at the Penna. Academy of Fine Arts, Philadelphia.

BISHOP. A little-known portrait and genre painter, working about 1850.

BISHOP, Hubert E. Painter and etcher. Born in Norwalk, Conn., in 1869. *Address,* 87 East Ave., Norwalk, Conn.

BISHOP, Richard E. Etcher. Graduated from Cornell University, studied at Graphic Sketch Club, and with Ernest D. Roth. Specialty, bird studies; his ''Canada Geese'' was awarded the Charles Lea prize, in Philadelphia, 1924. *Address,* Springback Lane, Mt. Airy, Penna.

BISHOP, Thomas. Miniature painter. Flourished 1753 and died 1833. He lived in London and Paris, and came to Philadelphia about 1811; he took a studio in Germantown and painted miniatures. One of his enamels of a Venus was much admired. He exhibited at the Penna. Academy in 1811.

BISPHAM, Henry Collins. Born in Philadelphia, 1841. He studied there with William T. Richards, and later with Otto Weber in Paris. He died in 1882. "The Lion Sultan," signed "H. C. Bispham Paris 1879," exhibited at the Salon, 1879, and Royal Academy, 1880, was presented in 1883 to Penna. Academy of Fine Arts, Philadelphia.

BISSELL, Edgar J. Painter. Born in Aurora, Ill., 1856. Studied in Boston, Mass., and with Boulanger and Lefebvre in Paris. *Address*, 3016 Bartold Ave., St. Louis, Mo.

BISTRAM, Emil J. Painter. Exhibited at Annual Exhibition of Academy of the Fine Arts, Philadelphia, 1925, of Miniatures and Water Colors. *Address*, 53 Greenwich Ave., New York City.

BISSELL, George Edwin. Sculptor. Born New Preston, Litchfield Co., Conn., 1839. Died in 1920. In marble business with his father and brother at Poughkeepsie, N. Y., 1866; studied art, Paris, Rome and Florence. Public monuments and statues: Soldiers' and Sailors' Monument, and statue Col. Chatfield, Waterbury, Conn.; portrait statue Gen. Horatio Gates on Saratoga Battle Monument; Chancellor John Watts and Col. Abraham de Peyster, New York; Abraham Lincoln, Edinburgh, Scotland; Chancellor James Kent, Congressional Library; bronze statues Admiral Farragut and Gen. Sherman; statue of Lincoln, Clermont, Ia.; marble bust and bronze statuette in Metropolitan Museum, New York.

BITTENBENDER, Ben. Painter. Exhibited "Twilight, Susquehanna Valley" at Annual Exhibition of National Academy of Design, New York, 1925. *Address*, Nescopeck, Penna.

BITTER Karl T. Sculptor. Born in Vienna in 1867 and died in 1915. He came to America in 1889. He was President of the National Sculpture Society at the time of his death. Among his works were statue of Gen'l Sigel, on Riverside Drive, N. Y.; panels in Trinity Church Gates, N. Y.; figures in Facade of Metropolitan Museum, New York; statue of Dr. William Pepper, Philadelphia; and the battle group for Dewey Arch, New York. See "Karl Bitter, A Biography," by Schevill, pub. in Chicago, Ill., 1917. Elected Associate Member of National Academy.

BITTINGER, Charles. Artist. Born Washington, 1879. Student Mass. Institute Tech.,

1897–99; Ecole des Beaux Arts, Paris, 1901–5. Has exhibited at Paris Salon; Societie Nationale des Beaux Arts; New York, Philadelphia, Washington, etc.; medal St. Louis Expn., 1904; 2d Hallgarten prize, National Academy Design, 1909; Clark prize, same, 1912; silver medal, San Francisco Expn., 1915; 1st prize, Duxbury Art Assn., 1919. Elected Associate Member of National Academy. *Address*, 1 West 81st Street, New York.

BIXBEE, William J. Painter, illustrator, and teacher. Born 1850, died 1921. He was secretary of the Boston Society of Water Color Artists. Designer of the seal of the City of Lynn. His painting of "Morning" has been exhibited.

BJORKMAN, Olaf. Sculptor of Scandinavian birth, living in New York. Among his best known works, "Beethoven," "The Titan," and heads of Lincoln, and Edgar Allen Poe. *Address*, New York.

BJURMAN, Andrew. Sculptor. Born in Sweden in 1876. Member of California Art Club. *Address*, 834 South Garfield Ave., Alhambra, California.

BLACK, Eleanor Simms (Mrs.). Painter. Born in Washington, D. C., 1872. Exhibited at the Penna. Academy of the Fine Arts, 1924. *Address*, 3732 Dawson Street, Pittsburgh, Pa.

BLACK, Mrs. Kate Eleanor. Painter. Born London, 1855. Pupil of Cincinnati Academy. Member: Cincinnati Woman's Art Club. Award: Bronze medal, Provincial Exhibition, New Westminster, British Columbia, Canada. *Address*, 4168 Forest Ave., South Norwood, Ohio.

BLACK, Mary C. W. (Mrs. Clarence A. Black). Painter. Born Poughkeepsie, N. Y. Pupil of W. L. Lathrop, Art Students' League of New York, Mora and Glenn Newell. Member: National Academy of Women Painters and Sculptors; California Art Club; National Art Club; Society of Independent Artists. *Address*, "El Cerrito," Santa Barbara, California.

BLACK, Norman I. Painter and illustrator. Born in Chelsea, Mass., 1883. Pupil of Eric Pape School, Boston; Julien Academy and Beaux Arts, Paris. *Address*, 414 West 154th Street, New York, N. Y.

BLACK, Mrs. Norman I. Painter. Born Providence, R. I., 1884. Pupil of Eric Pape School, Boston; Julien Academy in Paris; studied in Munich. Member: Providence Art Club. *Address*, 414 West 154th Street, New York.

BLACK, Olive P(arker). Painter. Born Cambridge, Mass., 1868. Pupil of H. Bolton Jones, Chase, Art Students' League of New

York, and National Academy of Design in New York. Member: National Academy of Women Painters and Sculptors. *Address*, 242 West 56th Street, New York.

BLACK, William Thurston. Flourished 1850–1851, Philadelphia and New York. Portrait painter and portrait draughtsman in pastel and crayon.

BLACKBURN, Joseph. He was born and trained in Great Britain, and painted in this country from 1754 to 1762. His portraits were painted in Bermuda in 1753. From 1754 to 1761 he was working in Boston. There are about eighty portraits by Blackburn in America, most of them signed. He painted a number of his figures ''knee-length'' with rather awkwardly posed legs. His portrait of Thomas Dering and his wife Mary are owned by the Metropolitan Museum. Theodore Atkinson, Jr., owned by the Rhode Island School of Design, and Col. Theodore Atkinson, owned by the Worcester Art Museum. The Boston Museum of Fine Arts own the portrait of Jonathan Simpson and his wife Margaret.

BLACKMAN, Carrie Horton (Mrs. George Blackman). Painter. Born Cincinnati, Ohio. Pupil of St. Louis School of Fine Arts; Chaplin in Paris. Specialty, children's portraits.

BLACKMAN, Walter. Painter. Born in New York. Studied in Paris under Gerome. Exhibited with the Society of American Painters in 1878 and in the Paris Salon of the same year.

BLACKMORE, Arthur E(dward). Painter. Born Bristol, England, 1854, and died in 1924. Pupil of South Kensington Museum, London. Member: Arts Aid Society; Art Fund Society; N. Y. Architectural League, 1914; Washington Art Club; and Society of Independent Artists. Has executed many mural decorations.

BLACKSHEAR, Anne. Painter, born in Augusta, Ga., in 1875. Pupil of Twachtman, Chase, Breckenridge and Garber. *Address*, Georgia State College.

BLACKSTONE, Harriet. Painter. Born New Hartford, N. Y. Pupil of Julien Academy in Paris; Chase Summer Schools; Pratt Institute, Brooklyn. Member: Chicago Society of Artists; American Women's Art Association, Paris. Represented in Vincennes Art Association; San Francisco Museum; National Gallery of Art, Washington.

BLAKE, Donald. Illustrator. Born Tampa, Fla., 1889. Pupil of Henry McCarter. Award: Cresson Traveling Scholarship. Member of Fellowship Penna. Academy of Fine Arts. *Address*, 244 West 14th Street, New York.

BLAKE, James Henry. Painter, illustrator and teacher. Born in Boston, Mass., 1845.

Pupil of Hollingsworth and Rimmer in Boston; Moore in Cambridge. President Cambridge Art Circle. Specialty, scientific subjects. *Address*, 117 Elm Street, West Somerville, Mass.

BLAKE, William W. Engraver of business buildings, working in New York in 1848; he then had his work rooms at 167 Broadway.

BLAKELOCK, Ralph. Landscape painter, the son of a physician, R. A. Blakelock, born in the city of New York in 1847, was intended by his parents to follow the medical profession, but his sympathy for music and painting caused him to work out his own destiny. He had no means of securing instruction in these arts, and a trip to the far western country, where he studied the Indians and, in his own self-taught way, attempted to depict them, constituted about all of his preliminary preparation for his career as a painter. His works are notable for rich, vibrating color. At the Academy, in 1899, he was awarded the First Hallgarten Prize, and in 1892 received an honorable mention at the Pennsylvania Academy. His picture ''From St. Ives to Lelant'' is in the permanent collection of the St. Louis Museum. His landscape work is well known; he was elected an Academician of the National Academy in 1916. He died in 1919, his mind having been affected for years. See his life, by Elliott Daingerfield, 1914.

BLANC, Anthony. French artist. He was for a time painting in Philadelphia, and is noted in the Directory shortly after 1800 as a ''Profile Portrait Painter.''

BLANCHARD, Mrs. Eliza H. Portrait and miniature painter. Flourished 1843–1846, Providence, R. I.

BLANCHARD, Washington. Miniature painter, Boston. His miniature of Wm. Ellery Channing was exhibited at the Boston Athenaeum in 1834. Also painted Alex. H. Everett, John C. Calhoun, Henry Clay, and Abram Aldrich. He flourished 1831–1843.

BLANCHING, C. This painter's name is signed to portraits of Revolutionary patriots at Independence Hall, Philadelphia.

BLANEY, Dwight. Painter. Exhibited at Penna. Academy of the Fine Arts, Philadelphia, 1921. Born in Brookline, Mass., 1865. He works in both oil and water colors. *Address*, 308 Fenway, Boston, Mass.

BLANKE, Esther. Painter. Born Chicago, Ill., 1882. Pupil of Chicago Art Inst., studied in London and Munich. Member: Chicago A. G.; Cordon Club. *Address*, 1200 Steinway Hall, 64 East Van Buren Street; Home, 418 Deming Place, Chicago, Ill.

BLANKE, Marie Elsa. Painter. Born in Chicago. Pupil of Chicago Art Inst., and studied in Munich and London. Member: Chicago Society of Artists; Chicago Art Club. Instructor in art, Lewis Institute, Chicago.

BLASHFIELD, Edwin Howland. Artist. Born New York, 1848. Studied Paris, 1867, under Leon Bonnat, also receiving advice from Gerome and Chapu; exhibited at Paris Salon, yearly, 1874–79, 1881, 1891, 1892; also several years at Royal Academy, London; returned to America, 1881; has exhibited genre pictures, portraits and decorations. Among his paintings are ''Christmas Bells'' and ''Angel with Flaming Sword.'' Decorated great Central Dome, Library of Congress; decorative panel, Bank of Pittsburgh. Elected member of National Academy in 1888. *Address,* Carnegie Hall, New York City.

BLASY, Alexander. Sculptor. Exhibited at Penna. Academy of Fine Arts, 1924. *Address,* 31 Bank Street, New York.

BLAUVELT, Charles F. Painter. Born in New York in 1824, he was elected an Academician of the National Academy in New York in 1859. He died in 1900. Represented in Wilstach Collection in Fairmount Park, Philadelphia.

BLEIL, Charles G. Painter and etcher. Born in San Francisco, 1893. Among his works ''Autumn Road'' and the ''Green House'' at California Artists' Gallery.

BLENNER, Carle Joan. Painter. Born Richmond, Va., 1864. Educated Marburg, Germany, and special course, Yale; 6 years at Julien Academy, Paris. Exhibited Paris Salon, 1887–8–9–91; Chicago Exposition, 1893; medal at Boston, 1891; Hallgarten Prize, National Academy of Design, 1899; represented at current exhibitions in New York since 1889; bronze medal St. Louis Expn., 1904. *Address,* 58 W. 57th Street, New York.

BLOCH, Albert. Painter. Born St. Louis, Mo., 1882. Studied in Munich. Painted portraits, and lectured on art. *Address,* Lawrence, Kans.

BLOCH, Julius T. Painter. Born in Germany, 1888. Studied at Penna. Academy of Fine Arts. Exhibited at Penna. Academy of Fine Arts, 1924. *Address,* 10 South 18th St., Philadelphia.

BLONDEL, Jacob D. Portrait painter. Born 1817 and died 1877. He was elected an Associate Member of the National Academy in 1854. His work was particularly remarkable for the free effect of his coloring.

BLONDHEIM, Adolphe W. Painter and etcher. Born in Maryland, 1888. Pupil of Maryland Institute, and Penna. Academy of Fine Arts. Represented in Chicago Art Institute, California Public Library, and State House, Mo. *Address,* Provincetown, Mass.

BLOOMER, H. Reynolds. Painter. Born in New York, studied in Paris, and exhibited in the Salon of 1877.

BLUM, Alex. A. Etcher and painter. He exhibited dry point etchings at the Penna. Academy of Fine Arts in the exhibition of 1924. *Address,* 1520 Chestnut Street, Philadelphia.

BLUM, Robert F. Painter, illustrator, and mural decorator. Born in Cincinnati, Ohio, in 1857, and died in New York City in 1903. He worked in oil and pastel and studied lithography and etching. He traveled in Europe and in Japan and did much illustrating. Blum painted many Japanese street scenes, his ''The Amega'' being in the Metropolitan Museum, N. Y. He also executed the long wall-panels for the old Mendelssohn Glee Club Hall in New York City. Elected Member of National Academy, 1893.

BLUME, Mrs. Melita. Landscape painter. Born in Germany. Pupil of Art Students' League of New York. *Address,* Brookhaven, L. I., N. Y.

BLUMENSCHEIN, Ernest L. Painter. Born at Pittsburgh, 1874. Pupil Art Students' League and Academy Julien, Paris; illustrator for *Century, Scribner's, McClure's, Harper's, American,* and other magazines and books. Chiefly engaged in portrait work. Elected Associate Member of the National Academy, 1910. *Address,* Taos, New Mexico.

BLUMENSCHEIN, Mrs. Mary S. G. Painter and sculptor. Born in New York; pupil of Herbert Adams in New York and Collin in Paris. Elected an Associate Member of National Academy of Design in 1913. *Address,* Taos, New Mexico.

BLUMENTHAL, M(oses) L(aurence). Illustrator and teacher. Born Wilmington, N. C., 1879. Pupil Pennsylvania Museum School, and studied in Munich. Member: Guild of Free Lance Artists; Philadelphia Sketch Club. Illustrates for *Saturday Evening Post, The Ladies' Home Journal, Collier's, McClure's, Scribner's,* etc.

BLYTH, Benjamin. Engraver and portrait draughtsman in pastel. Born 1746, Salem, Mass.; died after 1787. The son of Samuel Blyth. He was admitted to the Essex Lodge of Masons in Salem on March 1, 1781. In Felt's ''Annals of Salem'' under the date 1769, there is the following entry: ''Benjamin Blyth draws crayons at his father's house in the great street leading to Marblehead.'' He painted with great success in colored crayons. Many of his portraits are extant in the old families of New York. His only work as an engraver is found in a Mezzotint Allegorical Composition entitled ''Sacred to Liberty, or an Emblem of Ye Rising Glory of Ye American States'' signed ''Cole del-Blyth Fecit.'' On the portrait of Martha Washington engraved by John Norman his name appears ''B. Blyth del.''

BOARDMAN, Rosina C(ox). Miniature painter. Born New York City. Pupil of Alice Beckington, George Bridgman, Frank du Mond. Member: National Art Club; National Academy Women Painters and Sculptors. *Address,* ''Banburyholt,'' Huntington, N. Y.

BOBBS, Ruth Pratt. Painter. Born Indianapolis, Ind., 1884. Pupil of Wm. M. Chase. Member: National Art Club; National Academy Women Painters and Sculptors; Pen and Brush Club; Indiana Art Club. Work: ''The Spanish Shawl,'' Herron Art Institute, Indianapolis. *Address,* 10 Gramercy Park, New York.

BOCK, Charles Peter. Painter. Born in Germany, 1872. Pupil of Art Institute of Chicago; Simon in Paris. Member: Dallas Painters; Overland Landscape Outfit. Work: ''Where Sand and Water Meet,'' Dallas Public Library. *Address,* Manvel, Texas.

BOCK, Richard W. Sculptor. Born in Germany, 1865; came to America at age of five. Pupil of Schafer, Berlin Academy; Falguiere, Ecole des Beaux Arts, Paris. Work: Illinois State Soldiers' and Sailors' Monument at Shiloh; Lovejoy monument at Alton, Ill.; bronze group on Public Library at Indianapolis; Soldiers' Monument at Chickamauga, for Lancaster, Pa. *Address,* The Gnomes, River Forest, Ill.

BODMER, Karl. Painter and etcher. Born 1805 in Zurich, Switzerland. He traveled in America in 1832. He made water color sketches of his travels, also executed the copper plates in the atlas published in Maximilian's ''Journey through North America'' (1838–1842).

BOEBINGER, Charles William. Painter, illustrator, teacher. Born Cincinnati, Ohio, 1876. Pupil of Cincinnati Art Academy; Art Students' League of New York. Member: Western Drawing and Manual Teachers' Association. *Address,* Walnut and Central Parkway, Cincinnati, Ohio.

BOERICKE, Johanna M. Painter and sculptor. Born in Philadelphia in 1868. Pupil of Penna. Academy of Fine Arts, studied in Rome and Paris. *Address,* 5932 Overbrook Ave., Philadelphia.

BOGARDUS, James. Engraver and diesinker. Born 1800 in Catskill, N. Y. He was a skilful mechanic and invented a machine for producing bank-notes from separate dies. He died in 1874.

BOGARDUS, William. Engraver and miniature painter. He exhibited his miniatures in the National Academy in 1843.

BOGARDUS, Mrs. William. Miniature painter. Was born in 1804, and died in 1879. She exhibited portraits at the National Academy, New York, 1842 to 1846.

BOGDANOVE, A. J. Painter and teacher. Born Minsk, Russia, 1887. Pupil at National Academy under Maynard and F. C. Jones. Member: Society Independent Artist League of New York. Work: Mural decoration in Hebrew Sheltering Guardian Society, Pleasantville, N. Y.; two mural decorations in the Brooklyn Commercial High School. *Address,* 145 East 23d Street, New York, N. Y.

BOGER, Fred. Painter and illustrator. Born Baltimore, Md., 1857. Pupil of Frank Duveneck in Cincinnati. Member: Cincinnati Art Club. Work: ''Judge Alphonso Taft,'' Superior Court, Hamilton County, Ohio; portraits of George B. Cox and August Herrman at Blaine Club, Cincinnati, Ohio. *Address,* 2440 Jefferson Ave., S. Norwood, Ohio.

BOGERT, George Hirst. Landscape painter. Born New York in 1864. Pupil of the National Academy of Design; also studied in Paris. Elected an associate member of the National Academy in 1899; also member of the Society of American Artists. Represented at Metropolitan Museum, N. Y., by ''Moonlight,'' at Corcoran Art Gallery by ''Sunset,'' and at Brooklyn Institute by ''Dordrecht.'' He died at Montclair, N. J., in August 1923.

BOGGS, Frank M. Born in Springfield, Ohio, 1855, lives in Paris. Studied at the Ecole des Beaux Arts and under Gerome in Paris; ''A Rough Day, Harbor of Honfleur, France'' is owned by Boston Museum of Fine Arts.

BOGLE, James. Portrait painter. Born in South Carolina in 1817. He moved to New York in 1836, where he studied under Morse. He was elected an Associate of the National Academy in 1850, and an Academician in 1861. He painted many portraits in the south, Calhoun, Clay, Webster; his portraits of John Dix and Henry Raymond were among his later works. He died in 1873.

BOHM, Max. Painter. Born in Cleveland, Ohio, in 1868, he died in 1923. Student at Cleveland Art School and at the Louvre and at Academie Julien. Member of National Academy of Design. Represented in Metropolitan Museum, New York; Luxembourg,

Paris. Work: The mural decorations at the Court House, Cleveland, Ohio, and portrait of Gov. Lind, Capitol, St. Paul, Minn.

BOHNERT, Herbert. Painter and illustrator. Born Cleveland, Ohio, 1888. Pupil Cleveland School of Art. *Address*, 2258 Euclid Ave., Cleveland, O.

BOILEAU, Philip. Painter. Born in 1864, he died in New York in 1917. He lived in Baltimore for some years and painted many pictures of fashionable women.

BOIT, Edward Darley. Painter in water colors. Born in 1843, he graduated from Harvard in 1863 and died in Rome 1915. He was an intimate friend of John S. Sargent and held several joint water color exhibitions with him in Boston and New York. Represented in Boston Museum of Fine Arts by forty water color paintings.

BOIX, Richard. Painter. Exhibited in Philadelphia in 1921. *Address*, 49 West 8th Street, New York.

BOLANDER, KARL S. Painter. Born in Marion, Ohio, in 1893. Pupil of Dow and Walter Sargent. *Address*, 1026 West Berry Street, Fort Wayne, Ind.

BOLEN, J. G. This engraver's work is unknown except for an armorial book-plate of Charles M. Connolly, signed ''J. G. Bolen, 104 B'way.''

BOLMAN, Miss. Amateur miniature painter, flourished in Philadelphia about 1827. Exhibited miniature of Madame Murat, Penna. Academy, 1827.

BOLMER, M. de Forrest. Landscape painter. Born 1854, he died in 1910. His painting ''Cold and Gray'' was sold in auction at New York, 1923.

BOLTON, J. B. Engraver of letters and script. He was located in Boston, Mass., in 1841 and worked in connection with D. Kimberly.

BOLTON, Robert F. Painter. Born in New York City, 1901. Studied with Curran, Maynard and Bridgman. *Address*, 502 West 139th Street, New York.

BONA-PARTE: This fictitious signature appears on a crude portrait of James Madison. The portrait is printed from the plate of Benjamin Rush, engraved by James Akin; this is a case of the engraver Akin disclaiming his own work.

BONAR, T. Engraver of stipple portraits. About 1850 he was working for the Methodist Book Room. About the same time the firm of Bonar and Cummings were producing portraits for the *Methodist Magazine.*

BONE, Henry. An English miniaturist of note. Likely to have painted in America, as portraits of prominent Americans by him are known.

BONFIELD, George R. Marine and landscape painter. Born in England in 1802; came to Philadelphia as a youth and became a stone carver. Encouraged by Joseph Bonaparte of Bordentown, N. J., he turned his attention to painting, and became one of the leading marine painters of America. He was an early member of the Penna. Academy of Fine Arts; he died in Philadelphia in 1898. Represented in Wilstach Collection, Fairmount Park, Philadelphia.

BONHAM, Horace. Genre painter. Born West Manchester, Penna., 1835; died 1892. Pupil of Bonnat, in Paris. Represented by ''Nearing the issue at the Cockpit,'' at the Corcoran Gallery, Washington, D. C.

BONSALL, Elizabeth F. Painter. Born in Philadelphia in 1861. Pupil of Penna. Academy of Fine Arts, under Eakins and Howard Pyle. Studied in Paris under Collin and Courtois. Represented at Penna. Academy of Fine Arts by ''Hot Milk'' (purchased 1897). *Address*, 3430 Walnut Street, Philadelphia.

BONSALL, Mary W. Painter and illustrator. Has exhibited miniatures at the Penna. Academy of Fine Arts. Born at Fernwood, Penna. Pupil of Cecilia Beaux, Chase, and Vonnoh. *Address*, 3430 Walnut Street, Philadelphia.

BONTA, Elizabeth B. Painter. Born in Syracuse, N. Y. Received medal for water color, ''The Pale Moon,'' St. Paul Institute, 1916. *Address*, 290 Adelphi Street, Brooklyn, N. Y.

BOOG, Carle M. Painter. Born in Switzerland, 1877. Pupil of Art Students' League of New York and of Bonnat in Paris. *Address*, 206 Parkville Ave., Brooklyn, N. Y.

BOOGAR, Jr., William F. Sculptor. Born at Salem, N. J., 1893. Pupil of Penna Academy of Fine Arts. Exhibited at Penna. Academy of Fine Arts, Philadelphia. *Address*, Haddonfield, N. J.

BOONE, Cora. Painter. Exhibited water colors at Annual Exhibition of Water Colors, 1922, Penna. Academy of Fine Arts, Philadelphia. *Address*, Oakland, Calif.

BOOTH, Cameron. Painter. Exhibited at Penna. Academy of Fine Arts, 1924. *Address*, Minneapolis School of Art, Minneapolis, Minn.

BOOTH, Hanson. Painter and illustrator. Born at Noblesville, Ind., 1886. Pupil of Bridgman in New York. *Address*, Woodstock, Ulster County, N. Y.

BOOTH, James S. Painter and sculptor. Born in Detroit, Mich., 1888. He studied in Europe. Member of California Art Club. *Address*, 836 South El Molina Ave., Pasadena, Calif.

BOOTH, T. D. Engraver. Said to have been born in Albany, N. Y. He was for a time engaged in bank-note work, but is chiefly known for illustrating for the publishing firm of G. P. Putnam and Co. of New York.

BOOTT, Elizabeth. Painter. Born in Cambridge, Mass. She studied in Europe. Some of her paintings were exhibited in Boston in 1877, and in 1878 she exhibited "Head of a Tuscan Ox" and "Old Man Reading." At the National Academy Exhibition of 1886 she had "Hydrangeas" and "Old Woman Spinning."

BORDLEY. According to Dunlap, a painter of this name was working in Baltimore, Md., early in 1800.

BOARDMAN, Rosina C. Miniature painter. Exhibited miniatures at the Penna. Academy of the Fine Arts, 1924. *Address*, Huntington, N. Y.

BOREIN, Edward. Etcher of Western life. His work is well known for its truth as well as artistically. Borein cowboys and their mounts are true to the last strap and buckle. He is a member of the Print Makers' Society of California. *Address*, El Patio, Santa Barbara, Calif.

BORG, Carl O. Painter. Born in Sweden 1879. Member of California Art Club. Represented in University of California, and Golden Gate Museum. *Address*, Santa Barbara, Calif.

BORGLUM, Gutzon. Sculptor. Born in Idaho in 1867. Studied art in San Francisco, went to Paris, 1890. Exhibited as painter and sculptor in Paris Salon, and in London. In New York after 1902. He died there in 1918. Work: Apostles for Cathedral of St. John the Divine in N. Y. Sheridan monument, Washington. Head of Lincoln, in Capitol. Statue of Lincoln in Newark.

BORGLUM, Solon H. Sculptor. Born at Ogden, Utah, 1868; died at Stamford, Conn., 1922. Student of Cincinnati Art Academy, and of Fremiet and Puech in Paris. Elected an Associate of the National Academy of Design in 1911. Among his works, equestrian statue Gen'l Gordon at Atlanta, Ga. Soldiers' and Sailors' Monument, Danbury, Conn. Statues, "Inspiration" and "Aspiration." He also executed eight colossal portrait busts of Civil War Generals.

BORGORD, Martin. Painter and sculptor. Born Norway, 1869. Pupil of Laurens in Paris. Member: Allied Art Association; Paris American Art Association; St. Lucas Society, Amsterdam, Holland. Award: medal, Paris Salon, 1905. Work: "Laren Weaver," Carnegie Institute, Pittsburgh. *Address*, care of Salmagundi Club, 47 Fifth Ave., New York, N. Y.

BORIE, Adolphe. Artist. Born Philadelphia, 1877. Studied Penna. Academy of Fine Arts, Royal Academy, Munich, Bavaria. Awards: Carol Beck gold medal, Penna. Academy Fine Arts, 1910; silver medal, San Francisco Expn., 1915; Isaac N. Maynard prize, National Academy of Design, 1917; Academy of National Arts, 1917. Fellow, Penna. Academy of Fine Arts. Member: National Society Portrait Painters. *Address*, 4100 Pine Street, Philadelphia, Pa.

BORKMAN, Gustaf. Wood engraver. Born in Sweden, 1842; died in New York, 1921. Worked for the *Graphic, Harper's Weekly*, and for *Harper's Monthly*.

BORONDA, Lester D. Painter. Born in Nevada, 1886. Exhibited at the Penna. Academy of Fine Arts, 1924. *Address*, 131 Waverly Place, New York City.

BOSLEY, Frederick Andrew. Born at Lebanon, N. H., 1882. Pupil of the Museum of Fine Arts School, Boston. Represented by "The Dreamer." Signed "F. Bosley, 1911." Owned by Boston Museum of Fine Arts. *Address*, 162 Newbury Street, Boston.

BOSS, Homer. Painter. Exhibited at Philadelphia in 1921. *Address*, 37 West 16th St., New York.

BOSTON, Frederick J(ames). Painter. Born Bridgeport, Conn., 1855. Pupil of Whittaker in Brooklyn; Carolus Duran in Paris. Member: Brooklyn Society of Artists. *Address*, Carnegie Hall, New York City.

BOSTON, Joseph H. Painter. Born Bridgeport, Conn. Associate Member of the National Academy of Design and the Brooklyn Art Club, New York. Member of the Allied Artists of America, New York. Representation, Brooklyn Institute of Arts and Sciences, New York. *Address*, Carnegie Hall, N. Y.

BOSWORTH, Winifred. Painter and etcher. Born Elgin, Ill., 1885. Studied at Boston Museum of Fine Arts; Art Students' League of New York; Laurens in Paris; Eisengruber in Munich. Member: Chicago Water Color Club; Society of Independent Artists. *Address*, Woodland, Elgin, Ill.

BOTH, Armand. Painter and illustrator. Born in Portland, Maine, in 1881; died in New York, 1922. Studied in Boston, and with Laurens in Paris. Illustrator for magazines and books.

BOTKE, Cornelius. Painter. Born Leenwarden, Holland, 1887. Pupil of Chris. Lebrun. Member: Chicago Society of Artists. Awards: Fine Arts Bldg. Prize, 1918; Hon. mention for landscapes, American Exhibition, Chicago, 1921. Work: "The Golden Tree," Public School, Chicago; "The Last Snow," Oak Park High School; "Lifting Clouds," Public Library, Ponca City, Okla. For the past two years he has been etching in Holland, France, and Italy.

BOTKE, Mrs. Jessie Arms. Painter and illustrator. Born Chicago, Ill., 1883. Pupil of Johansen, Woodbury and Herter. Member: Chicago Society of Artists. Awards: Englewood Woman's Club prize, 1917; bronze medal, Peoria Society of Allied Arts, 1918; medal Chicago Society of Artists, 1919. Work: "White Swans," Municipal Gallery, Chicago; mural decoration for Ida Noyes' Hall, University of Chicago; "Geese," Chicago Art Institute. *Address,* Carmel-by-the-Sea, Calif.

BOTTUME, Geo. F. Painter. Born in Baltic, Conn., 1828, and died 1846; painted many portraits in the eastern part of the state. He lived for many years in Springfield, Mass.

BOUCHÉ, Louis. Painter and etcher. Born in New York, 1896. Pupil of Richard Miller, Simon, Menard and J. P. Laurens in Paris; Ossip Linde, Du Mond, Luis Mora in New York. *Address,* 2 West 47th Street, New York, N. Y.

BOUCHÉ, Marian Wright. Painter. Born New York, 1895. Pupil of Henry Matisse. Wait Kuhn. Member: Penguin Club, Society of Independent Artists. *Address,* care of Daniel Gallery, 2 West 47th Street, New York, N. Y.

BOUDIER. Engraver of portraits in the same style as St. Memin. He was evidently of French birth and probably was only in this country for a short time, as only one plate of his is known and that was engraved in Philadelphia.

BOUGHTON, George H. Painter. Born in England in 1834 he was brought to this country when 3 years old and lived for years in New York City. His specialty was landscapes. Boughton was elected a member of the National Academy of Design in 1871; he died in 1904. Represented at Boston Museum of Fine Arts by "Sea Breeze."

BOUGUEREAU, Elizabeth Gardinier. Born in Exeter, N. H., 1851. Studied in Paris and married her teacher, W. A. Bouguereau; she survived him, dying in 1922. Her specialty was ideal figure-pieces. She received a medal at the Philadelphia Centennial in 1876.

BOULTON, Joseph I. Sculptor. Born in Ft. Worth, Texas, 1896. Member of League of American Artists. Exhibited at the Penna. Academy of Fine Arts, Philadelphia, 1924. *Address,* 424 West 20th Street, New York City, N. Y.

BOUNETHEAU, Henry Brintnell. Miniature painter. Born 1797; died 1877. He painted a miniature of a descendant of the patriotic family of Manigault of South Carolina.

BOURDON. Portrait painter, flourishing about 1810, Pittsburgh, Pa. The artist James R. Lamden wrote to Dunlap that "Bourdon was a French refugee who painted small portraits in an indifferent manner."

BOURNE, Gertrude B. (Mrs.). Painter. Specialty, water colors. Member of National Association of Women Painters and Sculptors. *Address,* 130 Mt. Vernon Street, Boston.

BOUTELLE, De Witt Clinton. Painter. Born in Troy, 1820, and died 1884. He early came under the influence of Cole and Durand. After painting in New York and Philadelphia, he moved to Bethlehem, Penna. He painted a portrait of Asa Packer, presented to Lehigh University. He was elected an associate to the National Academy in 1853, and a member of the Pennsylvania Academy in 1862.

BOUTWOOD, Charles E. Painter. Born in England, naturalized in United States 1892.

BOUVÉ, E. W. Lithographer (of Bauvé and Sharp, who had their lithographic establishment at Graphic Court, Boston, Mass.). He printed many rare views of Boston, as well as the scarce, colored print representing *S. S. Britannia* leaving her dock, after being ice-bound in the severe winter of 1844. She was enabled to sail by cutting a channel in the ice one hundred feet wide and seven miles long to clear water.

BOWDITCH, Mary O. Sculptor. Exhibited at the Penna. Academy of Fine Arts, Philadelphia, 1920. *Address,* 16 Arlington Street, Boston, Mass.

BOWDOIN, Harriette. Painter and illustrator. Born in Mass. Pupil of Eilliott Dangerfield. *Address,* 1947 Broadway, N. Y.

BOWEN, Abel. Engraver. Born in Sand Lake Village, Greenbush, N. Y., 1790; died in Boston, 1850, according to an extended sketch of Abel Bowen prepared for the Bostonian Society, by the late Wm. H. Whitmore, and published in Boston, 1884. Bowen was engraving upon wood as early as 1811, and in August, 1812, he was in business as a printer in Boston. In 1816 Bowen published in Boston "The Naval Monument," illustrated by copper and woodcut views of naval combats, a number of which were engraved by Bowen himself. He was certainly engraving upon copper in 1817 in both line and stipple; in 1821 he was in business with Alexander McKensie, a copperplate printer, and in 1825 he published Shaw's "History of Boston," illustrated by very creditable full page views, mostly engraved upon copper, by Bowen. About this same time he drew upon stone the illustrations for an edition of the lectures of Sir Astley Paston Cooper, published by Pendleton, who established the first lithographic press in Boston.

Mr. W. G. Linton, in his "History of Wood Engraving in America," says that in 1834 Abel Bowen, in association with the wood-engravers Alonzo Hartwell and John C. Crossman, established the American Engraving and Printing Co. This company later became the "Boston Bewick Co.," the publishers of the *American Magazine*, a publication devoted to the encouragement of wood-engraving in America. The two volumes of this magazine contain about 500 woodcuts, generally coarse and crude in execution. In 1836 their printing establishment was burned down and the company failed. In the course of his business career Abel Bowen published a number of books.

BOWEN, Benjamin James. Painter. Born in Boston, 1859. Studied abroad, studio in Paris. Exhibited in the Salon, and in America.

BOWEN, Thomas. Portrait painter. He died in 1790.

BOWEN, Alexander. Painter. Born in New York in 1875. Pupil of Penna. Academy of Fine Arts. *Address*, Salmagundi Club, 45 Fifth Ave., New York.

BOWEN, John. Engraver of maps, and some rather crude stipple portraits and illustrations. He was working in Philadelphia 1810–19.

BOWERS, Edward. Portrait painter in oils, and crayon portrait draughtsman. He was working in Philadelphia in 1855–58.

BOWES, Joseph. Engraver in line and stipple. He was living in Philadelphia as early as 1796. His work appears in the *American Universal Magazine* and the *Monthly Magazine of Philadelphia*.

BOWES, Julian. Sculptor. Born in New York City in 1893. *Address*, 7 Macdougal Alley, N. Y.

BOWMAN, F. G. According to Dunlap a painter by this name was born in Pennsylvania and had a studio in Boston. He was said to have exhibited in the early days of the Boston Athenaeum, and was working in Maryland about 1800.

4

BOWNE, J. C. A line engraver of this name made a number of landscape plates for *Peterson's Magazine* of Philadelphia about 1854.

BOYD, Everett C. Painter. Exhibited a "Grey Day" at Cincinnati Museum, Annual Exhibition of 1925. *Address*, 1322 Arlington Street, Cincinnati, Ohio.

BOYD, John. Engraver of stipple portraits and book-illustrations for the Philadelphia publishers from 1811 to 1827.

BOYDEN, Dwight F. Landscape painter. Born in Boston, 1865. Pupil of Boulanger in Paris. Gold medal of Paris Salon, 1900. *Address*, Algonquin Club, Boston, Mass.

BOYLE, Charles W. Painter. Born in New Orleans, La. Pupil of Art Students' League of New York. Represented by "Afternoon Light" Delgado Museum, and "Oak on Bayou" New Orleans Art Association. (Deceased.)

BOYLE, Ferdinand Thomas Lee. Painter. Born in England 1820 and died 1906. He came to this country in childhood and studied painting under Inman. He settled in St. Louis in 1855, and organized the Western Academy of Art. In 1866 he came to New York, where he painted portraits of Chas. Dickens, Archbishop Hughes, Gen'l Grant (Union League Club of Brooklyn), Edgar Allan Poe and other celebrities. For many years he was professor at Brooklyn Institute of Art.

BOYLE, John J. Sculptor. Born in New York City, 1852. He began life as a stonecarver and studied at the Penna. Academy of Fine Arts. He was elected an Associate of the National Academy. Represented by the "Alarno" in Lincoln Park, Chicago, and "Plato" in the Library of Congress. In 1902 he removed to New York City, where he died.

BOYLE, Sarah Y. (Mrs.). Miniature painter. Born in Germantown, Pa. Studied at Drexel Institute. Pupil of Howard Pyle. Exhibited at the Penna. Academy of Fine Arts in 1924–25. *Address*, 94 South Munn Ave., Orange, N. J.

BOYNTON, George Rufus. Painter. Born at Pleasant Grove, Wis. Student National Academy Design (medalist), and Art Students' League, and under Walter Shirlaw, C. Y. Turner and J. G. Brown, New York. Portraits are hung in Union League Club; 7th Regt. Armory; 71st Regt. Armory; New York Yacht Club; Larchmont Yacht Club; U. S. District Court, etc. Has painted portraits of Gen. F. D. Grant, Gen. Alexander S. Webb, Gen. Stewart L. Woodford, Gen. James Grant Wilson. *Address*, 58 W. 57th Street, New York, N. Y.

BOYNTON, G. W. Engraver of maps, apparently located in Boston in 1842.

BRABAZON, Thomas. Painter. Member of the Connecticut Academy of Fine Arts, Hartford. *Address*, 21 Pavilion Street, Hartford, Conn.

BRACKEN, Clio Huntion (Mrs. William B.). Sculptor. Born in 1870, died in 1925. Pupil of Art Students' League, and of Rodin and Mac Monnies. Among her statues is ''General Fremont'' in California, and recently she executed a bust of General Pershing.

BRACKEN, Julia M. Sculptor. Miss Bracken is the leader of the women sculptors of the West. Her best known work ''Illinois Welcoming the Nations,'' a souvenir of the Columbian Exposition, stands in bronze in the capitol at Springfield, Ill.

BRACKET, Miss H. V. Engraver. Probably the earliest woman engraver in the United States. Her name appears on a large Bible plate of ''Ruth and Boaz,'' published in 1816.

BRACKETT, Edwin E. Sculptor. Born in Vassalboro, Maine, in 1819. He has confined himself for the most part to portrait busts, among which are ''President Harrison,'' ''W. C. Bryant,'' ''H. W. Longfellow,'' ''Charles Sumner,'' ''Wendell Phillips.'' His group of the ''Shipwrecked Mother'' is at Mount Auburn, and another of his groups was purchased by the Boston Athenaeum.

BRACKETT, Walter M. Born in 1823 and died in 1919. A native of Maine, he first painted portraits and fancy heads; he now makes a specialty of Game Fish.

BRACKMAN, Robert. Painter. He exhibited ''Life and Still-Life'' in Annual Exhibition of National Academy of Design, 1925. *Address*, 67 West 52d Street, New York.

BRACOUY, Leopold. Sculptor. Has exhibited in many exhibitions.

BRADBURG, C. Earl. Painter and illustrator. Born at North Bay, N. Y., 1888. Pupil of Laurens and Academie Julien, Paris. Exhibited at Penna. Academy of Fine Arts, Philadelphia, 1924. *Address*, 610 So. Prairie Street, Champaign, Ill.

BRADFIELD, Elizabeth P. (Mrs.). Sculptor. Exhibited at National Academy of Design, 1925. *Address*, Pontiac, Mich.

BRADFORD, William. American marine painter with specialty of Arctic scenes. Born in New Bedford, Mass., 1830. Self-taught but influenced by Van Beest, whose studio at Fairhaven he shared for two years. Accompanied several exploring expeditions towards the North Pole. Died 1892. ''Arctic Whaler Homeward Bound,'' signed ''Wm. Bradford, N. Y.,'' is in Chicago Art Institute.

BRADISH, A. Portrait painter. Born in Geneva, New York State. He is noted in Dunlap as ''Painting Portraits in Detroit.''

BRADLEY, Mrs. Susan H. Landscape painter. Born Boston, 1851. Pupil of Thayer, Edward Boit, Chase, and School of Boston Museum. Member: Philadelphia Water Color Club; Boston Water Color Club; New York Water Color Club; Society of Independent Artists. Represented in Herron Art Institute, Indianapolis. *Address*, 20 Brimmer Street, Boston, Mass.

BRADLEY, Will (William H.). Illustrator. Born Boston, Mass., 1868. Art director *Collier's Magazine, Metropolitan*, and *Century*.

BRADSHAW, G. A. Etcher. Member of Chicago Society of Etchers. *Address*, Trenton, N. J.

BRADSTREET, Edw. D. Painter. Born in Meriden, Conn., 1878; died there 1921. Member of Connecticut Academy of Fine Arts.

BRADT, Delphine. Painter. Exhibited flower-pieces at the Penna. Academy of Fine Arts, Philadelphia, 1924. *Address*, 1820 Spruce Street, Philadelphia.

BRADWAY, Florence D. Painter. Born in Philadelphia 1898. Exhibited at Penna. Academy of Fine Arts, Philadelphia, 1924. *Address*, Philadelphia Art Alliance Bldg.

BRAINARD, Mrs. Elizabeth H. Portrait painter. Born in Middleboro, and after studying in Boston went to Italy. On her return to this country she had her studio in New York and Boston. Several of her portraits are owned by Boston College; she died in Boston in 1905.

BRAMNICK, David. Painter. Born Kishineff, Russia, 1894. Pupil of the Penna. Academy of the Fine Arts, Philadelphia. Work in Graphic Sketch Club. *Address*, Mark Bldg., 721 Walnut St., Philadelphia, Pa.

BRANCH, Grove R. Painter, teacher. Instructor of Jewelry Department, School of the Worcester Museum; also at Commonwealth School of Art, Boothbay Harbor, Me. Director of Manual Arts, Worcester Academy. Member: Arts and Crafts Society of Boston. *Address*, 64 Fruit St., Worcester, Mass.

BRANCHARD, Emile (Peter). Painter. Born New York, N. Y. Member: Society of Independent Artists. *Address*, 61 South Washington Square, New York, N. Y.

BRANDEGEE, Robert B. Born in Berlin, Conn., 1848. He studied in Paris at the École des Beaux Arts. He painted portraits and landscapes, also executed a number of notable mural decorations. A fine portrait of the artist by Harold A. Geen was recently exhibited at Hartford, Conn. Mr. Brandegee died in 1922 at the age of 74.

BRANDT, Carl L. Born in Germany, 1831, he came to America in 1852. He painted portraits of John Jacob Astor, Mr. and Mrs. William Astor, and many other prominent people. Mr. Brandt also has done some work as a sculptor. He was elected a member of the National Academy of Design in 1872. He died in 1905.

BRANNAN, Sophie Marston. Painter. Born Mountain View, Cal. Pupil of Mark Hopkins Institute of Art, San Francisco; studied in Paris. Member: National Association of Women Painters and Sculptors. *Address*, 27 West 67th St., New York, N. Y.

BRANNAN, William Penn. He died in Cincinnati in 1866. He opened his studio there about 1840 and became known as a portrait painter of ability.

BRANNIGAN, Gladys (Mrs. Robt. A.). Painter. Born in Hingham, Mass. Pupil of Corcoran Art School, Washington, D. C. Member of National Association of Women Painters and Sculptors. Exhibited at Penna. Academy of Fine Arts, Philadelphia, 1924. *Address*, 145 West 55th St., New York City.

BRANSOM, Paul. Painter and illustrator. Born Washington, D. C., 1885. Member: Society of Illustrators, 1911; New York Zoological Society. Illustrated: "The Call of the Wild," "The Wind in the Willows," "Neighbors Unknown," "The Feet of the Furtive," "Hoof and Claw," "The Sandman's Forest," "The Sandman's Mountain," "Over Indian and Animal Trails," "More Kindred of the Wild," "The Secret Trails," "Children of the Wild," etc. *Address*, Green Lake P. O., Fulton Co., N. Y.

BRANSON, Lloyd. Painter. Born in 1861, he died in Knoxville, Tenn., in 1925.

BRASZ, Arnold F(ranz). Painter, sculptor, illustrator and etcher. Born in Polk County, Wis., 1888. Pupil of Minneapolis School of Fine Arts; Henri in New York. Member: Wis. "Painters and Sculptors." *Address*, 189 Main St., Oshkosh, Wis.

BRAUGHT, Ross E. Painter. Born in Carlisle, Pa., in 1898. Pupil of Penna. Academy of Fine Arts. Exhibited landscape, "Provincetown," at Penna Academy of Fine Arts, Philadelphia, 1924. *Address*, Carlisle, Penna.

BRAUN, Mrs. Cora Fischer. Painter. Born Jordon, Minn., 1885. Pupil of Garber, Hale, Joseph Pearson, Breckenridge, Chase, Blashfield and Beaux. Acting Associate Professor of Art, University of Nebraska; Acting Assistant Professor of Art, Ohio State University; Director, Dept. of Applied and Fine Arts, University of Tennessee. *Address*, Department of Fine and Applied Arts, University of Tennessee, Knoxville, Tenn.

BRAUN, M(aurice). Painter. Born Nagy Bittse, Hungary, 1877. Pupil of E. M. Ward, Maynard and Francis C. Jones at National Academy of Design in New York. Member: California Art Club. Represented in Municipal Collection, Phoenix, Ariz.; San Diego Museum. Awards: Hallgarten prize, National Academy of Design; gold medal, Panama-California Exp., San Diego, 1910; gold medal, Panama-California Int. Exp., San Diego, 1916. *Address*, Point Loma, California.

BRAUNER, Olaf. Painter. Born in Norway, 1869. Pupil of Benson and Tarbell in Boston; Professor of Painting at Cornell University since 1900. Portraits in Kimball Library, Randolph, Vt. Sculptor of "Dane Memorial" in Brookline, Mass. Painted altarpiece, Church of Our Saviour, Chicago, Ill. *Address*, Cornell University, Ithaca, N. Y.

BRAUNHOLD, Louis. Etcher. Member of Chicago Society of Etchers. *Address*, 35 North Dearborn St., Chicago, Ill.

BRAXTON, William E. Painter and illustrator. Born in Washington, D. C., 1878. Member of League of New York Artists, and Society of Independent Artists.

BRECK, George William. Artist. Born Washington, D. C., 1863, and died 1920. Studied Art Students' League, New York; first winner Lazarus Scholarship for study of mural painting (offered through Metropolitan Museum) and thereby became student of American Academy Fine Arts, Rome, Italy. Director Academy of Fine Arts, Rome. Located in New York, 1910. Mural decorations, University of Va.; Watertown, N. Y. Member: Century Club; Architectural League of New York; National Society of Mural Painters; Municipal Art Society.

BRECK, Joseph. Painter and illustrator. Awarded gold medal for painting, Minnesota State Art Society, 1916. *Address*, Metropolitan Museum of Art, New York.

BRECKENRIDGE, Hugh H(enry). Painter. Born Leesburg, 1870. Pupil of Penna. Academy of Fine Arts and of Bouguereau, Ferrier and Doucet in Paris. Member: New York Water Color Club; Philadelphia Water Color Club; Art Club of Philadelphia. In-

structor in Penna. Academy of Fine Arts since
1894. Member of Municipal Art Jury of Philadelphia. Awards: Hon. mention Paris Exp.,
1900; gold medal Fellowship P. A. F. A.,
1920, etc. Work: Portraits in University of
Pa. and in Art Club, Philadelphia. "Still
Life," San Francisco Art Museum; Court
House, Reading, Pa.; State Normal School,
West Chester, Pa., etc. Elected Associate
Member of National Academy of Design. *Address*, Fort Washington, Penna.

BREDIN, C. Painter and illustrator.
Pupil of Cincinnati Art Academy, and Cola-
rossi in Paris. *Address*, 5450 Delancey St.,
Philadelphia.

BREDIN, R. Sloan. Painter. Born in Butler Co., Pa., 1881. Pupil of Chase, Du Mond,
and Beckwith. Elected Associate of National
Academy. Among his works, "Midsummer"
and "By the River." *Address*, New Hope, Pa.

BREGLER, Charles. Painter and sculptor.
Born in Philadelphia. Studied at the Penna.
Academy of Fine Arts. Pupil of Thomas
Eakins. *Address*, 4935 North 11th St., Phil-
adelphia.

BREGY, Edith. Painter. Born in Philadelphia. Studied at Penna. Academy of Fine
Arts, pupil of Beaux and Carlsen. Represented
at Herron Art Inst., Indianapolis, Ind., by
"Pink Roses." Exhibited at Penna. Academy
of Fine Arts, Philadelphia, 1924. *Address*,
1627 Sansom St., Philadelphia, Pa.

BREHM, George. Illustrator. Born in
Indiana, 1878. Pupil of Twachtman and
Bridgman. *Address*, 15 West 67th St., New
York.

BREIN, John David. Sculptor. Born in
Servia in 1899. Exhibited at Penna. Academy
of Fine Arts, Philadelphia, 1924. *Address*, 4
East Ohio St., Chicago, Ill.

BREITMAYER, M. V. Etcher. Exhibited
etchings at the Annual Water Color Exhibition,
1922, Penna. Academy of Fine Arts, Philadelphia. *Address*, Pomona, New York.

BREMER, Anne. Painter and mural decorator. Born at San Francisco and died there
in 1923. Pupil of Art Students' League of
New York, and member of the San Francisco
Art Association. She is represented by mural
panels in many of the cities in California.

BRENNAN, Alfred Laurens. Painter and
illustrator. Born 1853; died in New York,
1921. He worked in pen and ink, and water
colors.

BRENNER, Victor D. Sculptor and medalist. Born in Russia in 1871; came to New
York 1890. Represented by medals in Metropolitan Museum, New York, and Luxembourg,
Paris. Died in 1924.

BRENNERMAN, George W. Painter and
illustrator. Born in New York in 1856. He
studied with Chase and Duveneck in Munich.
Landscapes and animals, especially horses in
action, were his favorite subjects. He died in
New York in 1906.

BRETT, Harold M. Painter and illustrator. Born Middleboro, Mass., 1880. Pupil
of Walter Appleton Clark, H. Siddons Mowbray,
and Howard Pyle. Member: Boston Art Club.
Address, Fenway Studios, 30 Ipswich St., Boston, Mass.

BREUER, Henry J. Landscape painter.
Born in Philadelphia in 1860. He has painted
many California views. *Address*, Lone Pine,
Inyo County, Calif.

BREUL, Harold G(uenther). Illustrator.
Born 1889. Pupil of Henry McCarter.
Awarded Cresson Scholarship, P. A. F. A. Il-
lustrates for *Collier's* and McGraw-Hill publica-
tions. *Address*, 57 West 10th St., New York
City, N. Y.

BREULL, Hugo. Painter. Born in Ger-
many, 1854. Pupil of William M. Chase in
New York, and of Boulanger and Lefebvre in
Paris. His studio was in Providence, R. I.
He died in 1910.

BREVOORT, James Renwick. Landscape
painter. Born in Westchester County, N. Y.,
in 1832. Studied with Thomas Cummings; also
sketched in England, Holland and Italy.
Elected an associate member of National Academy in 1861 and full member 1863. Among his
pictures "English Moor" (1882), "New England Scene," and "Morning in Early Winter."
He died in 1918.

BREWER, Adrian L(ouis). Painter. Born
St. Paul, Minn., 1891. Pupil of N. R. Brewer.
Member: Minneapolis Art Club. Awards:
Bronze medal St. Paul Institute, 1917; silver
medal for oils, St. Paul Institute, 1918. *Ad-
dress*, 448 River Blvd., St. Paul, Minn.

**BREWER, Alice Ham (Mrs. F. Layton
Brewer).** Miniature painter. Born Chicago,
Ill., 1872. Pupil Art Students' League of New
York; Art Institute of Chicago. *Address*, 241
Midland Ave., Montclair, N. J.

BREWER, Mary Locke. Painter. Studied
in Rome in 1911, under Signor Tanni, and later
in Paris under Henri, Martin and Ernest
Laurent. Among her best known pictures are
"The Lagoon" in Jackson Park, Chicago
"The Sun Dial," "The Seine Boat," and
"High and Dry."

BREWER, Nicholas Richard. Painter
Born in Olmstead County, Minn., 1857. Pupil
of D. W. Tryon and Charles Noel Flagg in
New York. Member: Chicago Society of
Artists, 1891. Represented in collection of por

traits of governors of Rhode Island, Wisconsin, South Dakota and Minnesota; state portrait collections of Maine, Iowa, North Dakota; Salmagundi Club, New York; Art Institute of Chicago. Now deceased.

BREWSTER, Anna Richards. Painter, illustrator and sculptor. Born Germantown, Pa., 1870. Pupil of Dennis Bunker and H. Siddons Mowbray in America; Constant and Laurens in Paris. Member: National Academy of Women Painters and Sculptors. Award: Dodge prize National Academy of Design, 1889. *Address*, Hartsdale, N. Y.

BREWSTER, Edmund. Philadelphia portrait painter, working there about 1818.

BREWSTER, Eugene V. Painter. Born Bayshore, N. Y., 1870. Self-taught. Salmagundi Club. *Address*, 175 Duffield St., Brooklyn, New York. Home, Roslyn, N. Y.

BREWSTER, George T(homas). Sculptor. Born Kingston, Mass., 1862. Pupil of Mass. State Normal Art School; Ecole des Beaux Arts, under Du Mond; and of Mercie in France. Member National Sculpture Society, 1898; Instructor R. I. School of Design, 1892–93. Instructor at Cooper Union since 1900. Work: Portraits of "Thomas R. Proctor," Utica, New York; "J. Carroll Beckwith," Library of New York University; "Robert E. Lee," for Hall of Fame, New York City; "J. S. Sherman," Utica, N. Y.; "Indiana," crowning statue at Indianapolis; "Hope," crowning statue, State House, Providence, R. I.; Mural portrait tablets of Judge Andrews and Judge Bischoff, Supreme Court, New York, N. Y. *Address*, Tottenville, Staten Island, N. Y.

BREWSTER, John. Portrait painter in oils and miniatures, flourishing in Boston about 1802. According to Dunlap "he was deaf and dumb since birth."

BRICHER, Alfred T. Marine painter. Born in Portsmouth, N. H., in 1837. He was elected an Associate Member of the National Academy of Design in 1879, also of the American Water Color Society. He died in Staten Island, N. Y., in 1908. He painted "Rocky Shore, Off Shelter Island," and "Grand Manan, Monhegan Island."

BRIDGES, Charles. An Englishman, painted in Virginia from 1730 to 1750. Most of the portraits in the South attributed to Sir Godfrey Kneller were by Bridges. He painted as late as 1750. Many of his portraits are extant and almost always, in case of women, may be known by a lock of hair resting on or in front of the shoulder. Bridges was trained in the British School, and shows by his work the influence of Lely and Kneller. The portrait of Mrs. John Page, in the collection at William and Mary College, is a good example of his art.

BRIDGES, Fidelia. Artist. Born in Salem, Mass., 1835. Removed to Brooklyn, 1854, and to Philadelphia, 1859, where she studied art under William T. Richards. Has painted and exhibited many noteworthy landscapes; earlier work principally in oil; later work mostly in water colors. Academy of National Arts, 1869. Member of American Water Color Society. Died in 1924.

BRIDGMAN, Frederic Arthur. Artist. Born at Tuskegee, Ala., 1847. Apprentice in American Bank Note Co., New York; meanwhile studied in Brooklyn Art School and National Academy of Design; pupil under J. L. Gerome at the Ecole des Beaux Arts, Paris; since then has had studio in Paris, occasionally visiting New York. Painter of figure, and of oriental and archaeological pictures. Elected member of National Academy in 1881. Represented at Corcoran Art Gallery of Washington, D. C., by "Procession of the Sacred Bull, Apis-Osiris." The Art Institute of Chicago has "Awaiting His Master," "Cafe in Cairo," "A Street in Algiers," and "The Neighbors." *Address*, 5 Impasse de Guelma, Paris, France.

BRIDGMAN, George B. Painter. Instructor at Art Students' League of New York. *Address*, 215 West 57th St., New York.

BRIDPORT, George. Painter. Brother of Hugh Bridport. He was associated with his brother as instructor in an Art School in Philadelphia in 1818. He also did the ceiling decorations in the old Hall of the House of Representatives in Washington burned by the British in 1814. He died in Havana, Cuba, in 1819.

BRIDPORT, Hugh. Painter and miniaturist. Born in London, 1794, and died Philadelphia, 1832. He was induced by Thomas Sully to come to this country in 1816. He opened a drawing-academy in 1817, in Philadelphia. He was one of the instructors of the deaf-mute lithographer, Albert Newsam. Bridport gained a great reputation in Philadelphia as a portrait painter. The Penna. Academy of Fine Arts has a collection of seven miniatures by Hugh Bridport; he also painted a number of oil portraits.

BRIDWELL, Harry L. Painter. Born in Leesburg, Ohio, in 1861. Member Cincinnati Art Club. *Address*, 287 McCormick Place, Cincinnati, Ohio.

BRIGHAM, William E. Painter and illustrator. Born North Attleboro, Mass., in 1885. Pupil Henry Hunt Clark and Denman Ross. *Address*, 460 Rochambeau Ave., Providence, R. I.

BRINDESI, Olympio. Sculptor. Born in Italy, 1897. Pupil of Chester Beach. Exhibited at Penna. Academy of Fine Arts, Philadelphia, 1924. *Address*, 207 East 17th St., New York City, N. Y.

BRINGHURST, Robert Porter. Sculptor. Born at Jerseyville, Ill., 1855. Studied at St. Louis School of Fine Arts and at Ecole des Beaux Arts, Paris; died 1925. Principal works: "Awakening Spring," Art Institute, Chicago; "Kiss of Immortality," destroyed at Portland Fair; statue of General Grant, City Hall Park, St. Louis; Minnesota's monument at Gettysburg; Pennsylvania's monument at Shiloh.

BRINKERHOFF, Robert M. Illustrator. Born in Toledo, Ohio, 1879. Pupil of Art Students' League, New York. Studied in Florence and Paris. *Address*, 50 West 67th St., New York.

BRINLEY, Daniel P. Landscape painter. Born in Newport, R. I., 1879. Pupil of Art Students' League of New York. *Address*, Dachet House, New Canaan, Conn.

BRINTON, Caroline P. (Mrs.). Born in Pennsylvania. Student at the Penna. Academy of Fine Arts. *Address*, Androssan Park, West Chester, Penna.

BRISTOL, John Bunyan. Painter. Born in Hillsdale, N. Y., 1826. Pupil of Henry Ary, in Hudson, N. Y. He became an Associate of the National Academy in 1861, and an Academician in 1875. His landscapes received medals in the Exhibitions at Philadelphia in 1876 and Paris in 1889. He died 1909.

BRITT, Ralph M. Painter. Born in Winchester, Ind., 1895. Pupil of William Forsyth. Works: "Melting Snow," "Wood Cutters," and "November Weather." *Address*, 456 West South St., Winchester, Ind.

BRITTON, James. Painter, illustrator and engraver. Born in Hartford, Conn., in 1878. Pupil of C. N. Flagg, and Geo. de F. Brush. Represented at Morgan Museum at Hartford, Conn., by portrait of William G. Bunce. *Address*, Holbein Studios, 107 West 13th St., New York City, N. Y.

BROBECK, Charles I. Born in Columbus, Ohio, in 1888. Pupil of Columbus Art School and Detroit School of Fine Arts. *Address*, 893 Locburn Ave., Columbus, Ohio.

BROCK, Emma L. Illustrator. Born in Fort Shaw, Mont., in 1886. Pupil of George Bridgman. *Address*, Fort Snelling, Minn.

BRODEAU, Anna Maria. Amateur miniature painter, wife of Dr. Thomton, whom she married in Philadelphia, 1790.

BRODHEAD, George H(amilton). Painter. Born in Boston, Mass., 1860. Member of Rochester Art Club. *Address*, 194 Harvard St., Rochester, N. Y.

BRODZKY, H(orace). Painter, illustrator and etcher. Born Melbourne, Australia, 1885. Studied in Melbourne and London. Member: Allied Artists' Association, London. *Address*, 141 East 27th St., New York, N. Y.

BROEDEL, Max. Illustrator. Born 1870, in Leipzig, Germany. Pupil of Leipzig Academy of Fine Arts. Associate professor of art as applied to medicine, Johns Hopkins University.

BROKAW, Irving. Painter. Born New York, N. Y., 1871. Pupil of Bouguereau, Ferrier, Julien Academy. *Address*, 522 Fifth Ave., New York, N. Y.

BROMWELL, Elizabeth Henrietta. Painter. Born in Charleston, Ill. Studied in Denver and Europe. Member: Denver Art Association. *Address*, 646 Williams Parkway, Denver, Colo.

BROOK, Alexander. Painter. Member: Society of Independent Artists. *Address*, care of Mrs. C. R. Bacon, Ridgfield, Conn.

BROOKE, Richard Norris. Artist. Born at Warrenton, Va., 1847; died 1920. Studied Pa. Academy of Fine Arts, and under Bonnat and Constant, Paris, France. Vice-principal Corcoran School of Art; President Society Washington Artists. Member: American Federation of Arts; Council Washington Society Fine Arts. Represented at Corcoran Art Gallery of Washington, D. C., by "A Pastoral Visit" and "Incoming Tide."

BROOKS. Engraver. He engraved the bookplate of Dr. J. Dove, of Richmond, Va., about 1800; he was probably a local silverplate engraver of the early American period.

BROOKS, A(lden) F(inney). Painter and sculptor. Born West Williamsfield, Ohio, 1840. Pupil of Edwin White in Chicago; Carolus-Duran in Paris. Member: Chicago Society of Artists. Works: "Boys Fishing," Union Club, Chicago; "Gen. George H. Thomas," and "Judge Kirk Hawes," Public Library, Chicago; "Gov. Jno. R. Tanner," Capitol, Springfield, Ill. *Address*, 4357 St. Lawrence Ave., Chicago, Ill.

BROOKS, Amy. Painter, illustrator. Born Boston, Mass. Pupil of Boston Museum School. Illustrates own books, such as "The Dorothy Dainty Books," "The Randy Books," and "At the Sign of the Three Birches." *Address*, 2 Colliston Road, Brookline, Mass.

BROOKS, Caroline Shawk. Sculptor and modeller. Born in Cincinnati, 1840. First known by her modelling in butter exhibited in Paris World's Fair, 1878. She subsequently opened her studio in New York and executed portrait marbles of Garfield, Geo. Eliot, Thomas Carlyle, and a portrait group of five figures representing "Mrs. Alicia Vanderbilt and Family."

BROOKS, Cora S(malley). Painter. Studied at Philadelphia School of Design for Women. *Address,* 524 Walnut St., Philadelphia, Pa.

BROOKS, Richard Edwin. Sculptor. Born in Braintree, Mass., 1865. Art instruction received in the studios of T. H. Bartlett, Boston, Mass., and Jean Paul Aubé and Antonin Injalbert, Paris. Among his works are: Busts of Gov. William E. Russell (bronze) and Col. Gardener Tufts (marble), Boston Statehouse; O. W. Holmes, 1897; and Gen. F. A. Walker, Boston Public Library. Awards: Honorable mention, Paris Salon, 1895. Is also represented by statues of Charles Carroll and John Hanson in Statuary Hall, Capitol Bldg., Washington, D. C. He died in 1919.

BROOKS, Isabel. Painter. Exhibited in Annual Water Color Exhibition at Penna. Academy of the Fine Arts, Philadelphia, 1925. *Address,* 1506 Park Ave., Baltimore, Md.

BROOKS, Samuel. Medallist, miniature, and profile painter, flourishing in Boston in 1790.

BROOME, Isaac. Sculptor. He was born in 1836, and died in 1922. He was a Canadian, and his best known work was his carving of Crawford's pediment on the Capitol at Washington, D. C.

BROUN, Aaron. Illustrator. Born London, England, 1895. Pupil New York School of Design, Beaux Arts Society. Member: American Bookplate, Society; Society of Poster Friends; Alliance. *Address,* Pocono Bldg., 229 4th Ave., New York City, N. Y.

BROWNING, Mrs. Miniature painter. Flourished about 1839, New York.

BROWERE, Alburtis D. O. Born in 1814 and died in 1887. Son of John Henri Isaac Browere, the artist who made the life-masks of Jefferson, Gilbert Stuart, and many other eminent Americans. He painted a profile likeness in water color of his father. He was a student of the National Academy; he later went to California and painted mining scenes.

BROWERE, John Henri Isaac. Sculptor. Born in New York City, 1792; died 1834. Pupil of Archibald Robertson. He also studied in Italy. On his return to America he modeled several busts, and perfected a method of making casts from the living model. These life-masks are faithful portraits. Browere painted pictures in addition to his modelling.

BROWN, Abby Mason. Miniature painter. Flourished 1800–1822. She painted a miniature portrait of C. F. Herreshoff, Newport, R. I.

BROWN, Agnes. Born at Newburyport, Mass. Wife of J. Appleton Brown. She paints in oil landscapes and flowers; also painted cats. She exhibits at the Boston Art Club.

BROWN, Alice Van Vechten. Painter. Born Hanover, N. H., 1862. Pupil of Art Students' League of New York. Professor of Art, Wellesley College, since 1897. Author with William Rankin of "Short History of Italian Painting."

BROWN, Arthur William. Illustrator. Member: Society of Illustrators, 1910. *Address,* 233 West 100th St., New York, N. Y.

BROWN, Benjamin. Engraver. The earliest known plate signed by B. Brown is an excellent stipple portrait of Sir Philip Francis, the frontispiece to "The Identity of Junius," by John Taylor, published in New York in 1812. A number of very good line illustrations to a botanical work, also published in New York, are signed "B. Brown Sc. New York." The New York directory for 1819 contains the name of "Benjamin Brown, engraver and printer of bookplates, maps, visiting-cards, etc., in the first style of elegance." The name only appears for this one year.

BROWN, Benjamin C. Landscape painter and etcher. Pupil of Paul Harney and John Fry, in St. Louis; Laurens and Benjamin Constant in Paris. Awards: Bronze medal for etching, Panama Pacific Exp., San Francisco, 1915. Represented in Oakland Art Gallery; Public Library, Pasadena, Calif.; British Museum; Smithsonian Institute, Washington, D. C. *Address,* 120 N. El Molino Ave., Pasadena, Calif.

BROWN, Bolton (Colt). Painter and etcher. Born Dresden, N. Y., 1865. Instructor, Cornell University; Head of Art Dept., Leland Stanford University. Work: "The Bather," National Arts Club, New York; "Monterey Fishing Village," Indianapolis Art Association; "Sifting Shadows" and "Farmhouse in Winter," Brooklyn Institute Museum; lithographs in Brooklyn Museum and New York Public Library. *Address,* National Arts Club, 15 Gramercy Park, New York, N. Y.

BROWN, Charles V. Portrait painter. Son of J. Henry Brown, born in Philadelphia in 1848. Pupil of Thos. Eakins, and Prof. Schussele, at the Pennsylvania Academy of Fine Arts. He has devoted himself especially to portrait painting in Philadelphia, where his professional life has been spent.

BROWN, Charlotte Harding (Mrs. James A. Brown). Illustrator. Born Newark, N. J., 1873. Pupil of Philadelphia School of Design for Women. *Address,* Smithtown, L. I., N. Y.

BROWN, Dorothy H. Painter. Member of Providence Art Club. *Address,* 69 Arlington Ave., Providence, R. I.

BROWN, Ethel P. Painter and illustrator. Born in Wilmington, Del. Pupil of Twachtman and Howard Pyle. Student at the Penna. Academy of Fine Arts. *Address,* Frederica, Delaware.

BROWN, Francis F. Painter. Born in Glassboro, N. J., in 1891. Represented in Richmond Art Gallery and Herron Art Institute. *Address,* 126 W. 7th St., Richmond, Va.

BROWN, G. Two portraits were exhibited at the Penna. Academy in 1847. They were miniatures by G. Brown and may be the work of the English artist by that name who exhibited at the Royal Academy from 1825 to 1839.

BROWN, George Bacon. Painter, born in Ogdensburg, N. Y., 1893. Pupil of Chicago Art Institute. Also painted mural decorations. He died in 1923.

BROWN, Frank. Painter. Exhibited in Annual Water Color Exhibition at Penna. Academy of the Fine Arts, Philadelphia, 1925. *Address,* 38 Rue de Provence, Paris, France.

BROWN, George L. Born in Boston, Mass., 1814; died at Malden, Mass., 1889. Brown was originally apprenticed to a wood-engraver, and woodcuts are found signed by him. He went abroad in 1853–55, studied in Rome and became a reputable painter of landscapes. The only work upon copper known to the compiler is a series of admirable etchings of views about Rome, executed from his own drawings and published in 1860. He returned to America in 1860 with a high reputation as a landscape painter. His view at Amalfi is in the Metropolitan Museum of New York. He was a pupil of Isabey in Paris.

BROWN, Glenn Madison. Painter and etcher. Born in Hartford, Conn., in 1876. Member of Art Students' League of New York, and Julien Academy, Paris. Pupil of Laurens and Colarossi.

BROWN, Grace E. Painter and illustrator. Born Beverly, Mass., in 1873. Pupil of Joseph De Camp. *Address,* Trinity Bldg., 168 Dartmouth St., Boston, Mass.

BROWN, Harold Haven. Artist. Born Malden, Mass., 1869. Studied École des Beaux Arts, Paris, under Gerome, and Academy Julien, Paris, under Laurens. Director of Art Museum, and teacher in School of Art, of The John Herron Art Institute, Indianapolis, since 1913.

BROWN, Harrison B. Marine painter. Born in Maine in 1831. His best known paint-

ings were of Casco Bay, Maine. He died in England, where he had been living for several years, in March, 1915.

BROWN, Harrison P. Painter. Born in Waterloo, Ind., 1889. Member of Indiana Art Club. *Address,* 42 Macomb St., Mt. Clemens, Michigan.

BROWN, Henry B. Born in Portland Maine, in 1839, and died 1860. He soon became successful as a landscape and marine painter with very little training or instruction. His best known picture is "On the Coast of Maine." He has exhibited in England and America.

BROWN, Henry I. Miniature painter. Flourished in Boston, 1844–1851.

BROWN, Henry Kirke. Sculptor. Born in 1814; died 1886. Beginning as a portrait painter, he early took up sculpture, and after five years' study in Italy, established himself in New York. Work: "Washington" in Union Square, N. Y.; "Lincoln" in Union Square, N. Y.; "General Scott" and "Nathaniel Greene," Stanton Square, Washington, D. C. Elected Member of National Academy in 1851.

BROWN, Horace. Painter. Born at Rockford, Ill., in 1876. Pupil of John Carlson and Johansen. Member of the Allied Artists of America. Exhibited landscapes at Penna. Academy of Fine Arts, Philadelphia, 1924, and at the Art Institute of Chicago. *Address,* Springfield, Vt.

BROWN, Howard V. Painter and illustrator. Born Lexington, Ky., 1878. Student of Art Students' League of New York. *Address,* 131 West 23d St., New York.

BROWN, Howell C. Etcher. Born Little Rock, Ark., 1880. Member of the California Society of Etchers. Specialty, western scenes of the Indian country; his "Edge of the Desert" is well known. *Address,* Molino Ave., Pasadena, Calif.

BROWN, Irene. Painter and sculptor. Born Hastings, Michigan. Pupil of William M. Chase. Member of National Association of Women Painters and Sculptors. *Address,* Rome, Italy.

BROWN, J. This name, as engraver, is signed to a Bibical plate published in New York about 1810, but nothing else of his work has been found.

BROWN, J. Appleton. Born in West Newbury, Mass., 1844, and died in 1902. He came to Boston in 1865, where he opened his first studio; in 1867 he went to Paris for study. Since then he has exhibited frequently in the

Salon in Paris, and has also had exhibitions of his landscape and figure work in this country. Several of his landscapes are in the collection of the Museum of Fine Arts in Boston. Elected Associate Member of National Academy in 1896.

BROWN, James Francis. Painter. Born at Niagara Falls, N. Y. Pupil of National Academy of Design, New York, and of Collin and Bouguereau in Paris. *Address*, 51 West 10th St., New York City, N. Y.

BROWN, John B. Painter. Elected Academician of National Academy in 1875. He died in 1909.

BROWN, John G. Genre painter. Born Durham, England, 1831; died New York City, 1913. Studied first at Newcastle-on-Tyne, then at Edinburgh Academy, and in 1853 at the schools of the National Academy of Design, New York. Elected Associate National Academy 1862, and to the National Academy in 1863. Represented in Metropolitan Museum, N. Y., and Corcoran Art Gallery, Washington, D. C.

BROWN, John Henry. Painter. Born in Lancaster, 1818. In 1836 he commenced the study of painting under Mr. Arthur Armstrong. In 1839 he went into business for himself in the same line as that followed by Mr. Armstrong, viz., portrait, historical, landscape, sign and fancy painting, to which he also added miniature painting on ivory. He followed the business as above until 1844, when he discontinued all other kinds of painting except miniature painting on ivory. In the fall of 1845 he removed to Philadelphia, where he continued to follow the choice of his profession until his death, 1891. He painted a miniature on ivory of Abraham Lincoln at Springfield, Ill., 1860, at the request of Judge John M. Read of Philadelphia. The miniature is in possession of Hon. Robert T. Lincoln.

BROWN, Laurence. According to the Selectmen's Records of the Town of Boston, July 31st, 1701, "Laurence Brown, a Limner, was granted admittance to this Towne."

BROWN, Lilian C. (Mrs.). Painter. Member of Art Students' League of New York. *Address*, 8 Ellsworth Terrace, Pittsburgh, Pa.

BROWN, Mather. Portrait painter. Born in Massachusetts, 1761, and died in 1831, was the son of a noted clock-maker. After painting a number of portraits in this country, he went to London to study under Benjamin West. His portraits are much in the manner of Gilbert Stuart and West. He was appointed portrait painter to the Duke of York, and painted George III and others of the Royal family. He is also said to have painted miniatures while in this country. His portraits are owned by the National Portrait Gallery, London, and in collections in America. Among his portraits are Mrs. James Madison, William V. Murray, John Howard, and his self-portrait owned by Mrs. Frederick L. Gay.

BROWN, ("Mysterious"). Miniature painter. Flourished in New York, 1812. He was an English artist who came to New York City, and drew chalk portraits and painted miniatures.

BROWN, Pamela V. Miniature painter. Exhibited portrait miniatures at Exhibition of Miniatures, Penna. Academy of Fine Arts, Philadelphia, 1922–25. *Address*, 51 West 12th St., New York City, N. Y., or Woodstock, New York.

BROWN, Roy. Landscape painter and illustrator. Born Decatur, Ill., 1879. Pupil of Art Students' League of New York; Rafaelli and Menard in Paris. Member: Academy of National Artists, etc. Work: "The Dunes," Art Institute of Chicago; "Landscape," Northwestern University, Evanston, Ill.; "Pines and Poplars," National Arts Club, New York. Elected Associate Member of National Academy. *Address*, 45 Washington Square, New York.

BROWN, Uriel. According to Dunlap, a portrait painter of that name was working in Salem, Mass., in 1805.

BROWN, Walter. A little known genre painter who exhibited several highly-finished small pictures of great elaborateness of detail. He is best known for his work in miniatures; he was the son of John Henry Brown, the Lancaster artist.

BROWN, Walter Francis. Painter, illustrator. Born Providence, R. I., 1853. Pupil of Gerome and Bonnat in Paris. Member: Providence Art Club. Work: "The Acropolis" and "The Parthenon," Hay Library, Providence. Illustrated "A Tramp Abroad," by Mark Twain, "Roger Williams," by Charles Miller. *Address*, Palazzo da Mula, San Vio 725, Venice, Italy.

BROWN, W(illiam) Alden. Landscape painter. Born Providence, 1877. Pupil of E. M. Bannister; R. I. School of Design. Member: Providence Art Club; Providence Water Color Club. Work: "Beside Still Waters," Penn and Pencil Club, Providence, R. I.; "The Oaks," Alpha Delta Psi Fraternity, R. I. State College, Kingston, R. I. *Address*, 120 Dora St., Providence, R. I.

BROWN, William Mason. Born in Troy, New York, 1830. Studied with local artist for several years when he removed to Newark, N. J., and there began landscape painting. Subsequently he painted still-life, in which branch he gained his reputation. "Fruit and Art Objects," signed "W. M. Brown," purchased 1889, Pa. Academy of Fine Arts.

BROWNBACK, Louis U. Painter, specialty landscapes and harbor scenes. Represented in Brooklyn Museum by "The Harbor." *Address,* 7 East 12th St., New York.

BROWNE, Belmore. Painter. Born Thomkinsville, S. I., New York, 1880. Pupil of Chase and Carroll Beckwith; under Julien in Paris. Member: Society of American Animal Painters and Sculptors.

BROWNE, Charles Francis. Painter. Born in 1859. Elected an Associate Member of National Academy in 1913. He died in 1920. His specialty was landscape painting. Instructor in Art Institute, Chicago.

BROWNE, Frances E. Painter. Member: Cincinnati Woman's Art Club. *Address,* 11 "The Westminster," Walnut Hills, Cincinnati, Ohio.

BROWNE, George Elmer. Born Gloucester, Mass., 1871. Studied at School of Drawing and Painting, Museum of Fine Arts, and Cowles Art School, Boston; Julien Academy, Paris, under Lefebvre and Robert-Fleury. Member: Artists' Fund Society; American Art Association, Paris. Associate member of National Academy of Design, New York. *Address,* 58 West 57th St., New York.

BROWNE, Harold Putnam. Painter. Born Danvers, Mass., 1894. Son of George Elmer Browne. Pupil of Caro-Delvaille at Colarossi Academy; of Jean Paul Laurens and Paul Albert Laurens at Julien Academy in Paris; Heymann at Munich; George Elmer Browne and F. Luis Mora in New York. Professor, School of Fine Arts, University of Kansas. *Address,* School of Fine Arts, University of Kansas, Lawrence, Kans.

BROWNE, Margaret Fitzhugh. Painter and illustrator. Born Boston, Mass., 1884. Pupil of Joseph De Camp. *Address,* Fenway Studios, Boston, Mass.

BROWNE, Matilda (Mrs. Frederick Van Wyck). Painter and teacher. Born in Newark, N. J., 1869. Pupil of C. M. Dewey, H. S. Bisbing and Julien Dupré. Member: National Academy Women Painters and Sculptors. Awards: Hon. mention, Columbian Exposition, Chicago. *Address,* 142 East 18th St., New York.

BROWNELL, Chas. De Wolf. Born in Providence, R. I., 1822. Studied in Hartford, Conn. In 1860 moved his studio to New York; studied abroad 1861 to 1867 and afterwards settled in Bristol, R. I. Painted many pictures of the Connecticut Valley. He has also painted in Cuba.

BROWNELL, Matilda A. Painter. Born New York. Pupil of Chase and MacMonnies. *Address,* 1110 Carnegie Studios; Home, 322 West 56th St., New York.

BROWNELL, Rowena P. Painter. Member Providence Art Club. *Address,* 368 Thayer St., Providence, R. I.

BROWNING, G. W(esley). Painter and illustrator. Born Salt Lake City, 1868. Member: Society Utah Artists. Awards: First prize for water color, Utah Art Institute. Illustrations on nature study. *Address,* 730 Third Ave., Salt Lake City, Utah.

BROWNLOW, C(harles). Painter. Born in England, 1863. Pupil of J. W. Whymper. *Address,* 435 Hansberry St., Philadelphia, Pa.

BROWNSCOMBE, Jennie (Augusta). Painter. Born Honesdale, Pa., 1850. Pupil of L. E. Wilmarth, N. A. D.; Henry Mosier in Paris. Work: "First Thanksgiving," Museum of Pilgrim Hall, Plymouth, Mass. Specialty, historical figure-subjects, many of which have been reproduced as etchings, etc.

BRUBAKER, Jay O. Painter and illustrator. Born in Dixon, Ill., 1875. Pupil of Bridgman and Julien. *Address,* 32 West 47th St., New York City.

BRUCE, Edward. Painter. Exhibited in the Cincinnati Museum Annual Exhibition of 1925. *Address,* Care of Scott & Fowles, New York.

BRUCKNER, C. W. Portrait painter. His portrait of Gen'l Robert E. Lee is signed and dated 1865. It was sold in auction in New York.

BRUEN, R. C. Engraver. He was apprenticed to Maverick and Durand, but, his mind becoming deranged, he was drowned in the Hudson River. He engraved book-illustrations, published by Wm. Durell of New York about 1820.

BRUESTLE, George M. Landscape painter. Born in New York, 1872. Pupil of Art Students' League, New York; also studied in Paris. Represented by "Afternoon Landscape," in Gibbes Museum, Charleston, S. C., and "Brown Hillside," Reading Museum, Pa. *Address,* 132 East 23d St., New York.

BRUFF, Charles Oliver. Bruff advertised in the *New York Mercury* of 1770, and possibly earlier, as a goldsmith and jeweler. In 1775 he added an engraving department to his business, then established at the sign of "The Teapot, Tankard & Ear-ring," between Maiden Lane and Crown Street, near the Fly Market; and he adds to his notice, "Where he engraves all sorts of arms, crests, cypher & fancies, in the neatest manner and greatest expedition, with heads of Lord Chatham, Shakespear, Milton, Newton, etc., with Mason's arms and all emblems of Liberty.''

BRULS, Michelson Godhart de. This man seems to have been the chief engraver doing business in New York in the period 1759–64; though Elish Gallaudet was engraving in that city as early as 1759. De Bruls, according to advertisements in the New York newspapers of this day, engraved book-plates, maps and views. The earliest of his work, and the only large plate seen by the compiler, is a very well-executed ''Plan of Niagara with the Adjacent Country, surrendered to the English Army under the Command of Sir Will'm Johnson, Bart., on the 28th of July 1759.'' This map contains a good coat of arms of Sir William Johnson, and is signed ''Engraved and published by Michelson Godhart de Bruls in New York, North America.''

The *New York Mercury,* for May 3, 1762, and succeeding numbers states that this plan and a companion plate were to be published by subscription by ''Michael de Bruls, Engraver and an Inhabitant of this City.'' The second plate was ''A plan of the Landing, Encampment and Attack against Fort Niagara, on Lake Ontario,—also the Engagement where the French Reinforcements were defeated.'' The advertisement goes on to say that these two plans were engraved ''on two large copperplates'' and ''would form a print 2 ft. 11 in. by 1 ft. 1 in. exclusive of margins.'' It is stated that ''they were almost ready for printings,'' and it is to be presumed that both plates were published, though the second plate is unknown. The price to be paid was eight shillings each, and they were to be delivered to subscribers before June 26, 1762.

Another ambitious work by de Bruls is noted in the *New York Mercury* of Oct. 1762. He then proposed to engrave and publish by subscription ''Two different Waterviews and two different Landviews of the flourishing City of New York.'' On March 5, 1759, ''Mr. Michael de Bruls, Engraver,'' was located at ''Mr. Furer, Silversmith, in French Church Street, New York,'' and he probably added to his scanty income by engraving on silver. He neatly engraved at least one book-plate.

BRUMBACK, Louise Upton (Mrs.). Painter. Born Rochester, New York. Pupil of William M. Chase. Member of National Association of Women Painters and Sculptors. *Address,* 118 East 19th St., New York.

BRUMIDI Constantino. Painter. Born in Rome, 1805. Died in Washington, D. C., in 1880. He came to this country in 1852, and soon thereafter declared his intention to become a citizen of the United States, obtaining his naturalization papers in the city of Washington. The rapid progress of the Capitol extension under the superintendency of Capt. Meigs suggested to him the idea that the solid construction of this national building required a superior style of decoration in real fresco, like the palaces of Augustus and Nero, the Baths of Titus and Livia at Rome, and the admired relics of the paintings at Herculaneum and Pompeii. At the first meeting with the said superintendent the latter accepted the service of Brumidi.

''The committee room on Agriculture, in the south wing of the Capitol, was painted in 1885 as the first specimen of real fresco introduced in America.''

BRUNDAGE, William Tyson. Painter. Born in New York, 1849. He was a pupil of Walter Shirlaw at the Art Students' League, New York. His specialty was marine subjects. He died in February, 1923.

BRUNNER, F. Sands. Illustrator. Born in Boyertown, Pa., in 1886. Pupil of Herman Deigendesch. *Address,* 6033 Webster St., Philadelphia, Pa.

BRUNTON, Richard. Engraver and die-sinker. He advertised in 1781 in the *American Journal and Daily Advertiser* of Providence, R. I. A memoir of Richard Brunton, by A. C. Bates, librarian of the Connecticut Historical Society at Hartford, states that he was imprisoned for making counterfeit money.

BRUSH, George de Forest. Painter. Born Shelbyville, Tennessee, 1855. Figure painter and painter of Indian subjects. Pupil of the National Academy of Design, and of Gerome in Paris. Awards: First Hallgarten Prize, National Academy of Design, 1888; Medal, Columbian Exposition, Chicago, 1893; Temple Gold Medal, Pennsylvania Academy of the Fine Arts, Philadelphia, 1897; Gold Medal, Paris Exposition, 1900. Elected Society of American Artists, 1880; Associate National Academy, 1888; National Academy, 1901. *Address,* Studio, New York and Dublin, N. H.

BRYANT, Everett L. Painter. Born in Galion, Ohio, in 1864. Pupil of Couture in Paris, Herkomer in London, and Anshutz, Chase and Breckenridge in Philadelphia. Member of the Penna. Academy of Fine Arts. Specialty, flower painting. *Address,* Care of Alley and Trask, 52 East 53d St., New York City.

BRYANT, Henry. Painter. Born in East Hartford, Conn., 1812. Painted portraits and landscapes; in 1837 he was elected an Associate Member of the National Academy of Design. He died in 1881.

BRYANT, Mrs. Maud D. Painter. Born in Wilmington, Del., in 1880. Studied at Penna. Academy of Fine Arts under Anshutz, Chase and Breckenridge; also at Colarossi Academy in Paris. *Address,* Hendricks, Penna.

BRYANT, Nanna Mathews (Mrs.) Sculptor. Exhibited at Academy of Fine Arts, Philadelphia, 1924. *Address*, 94 Beacon St., Boston, Mass.

BRYANT, Wallace. Portrait painter. Born in Boston, Mass. Pupil of Constant, Laureny, Robert-Fleury and Bouguereau in Paris. *Address*, Cosmos Club, Washington, D. C.

BUBERL, Casper. Sculptor. Member of the National Sculpture Society. He died some years ago.

BUCHANAN, Ella. Sculptor. Born in Canada. Member of the Chicago Society of Artists. Work: "Martha Baker Memorial," Chicago; "Pete" and "Dry Water Hole." *Address*, 1539 North Edgemont St., Los Angeles, Calif.

BUCK, Charles C. Painter and sculptor. Born in New York City. Pupil of Emil Carlsen. *Address*, 495 East 188th St., New York City.

BUCK, Emma G. Painter and sculptor. Member of Chicago Art Club. Born in Chicago, Ill., in 1888. Work: Wisconsin, Perry's Centennial Medal. *Address*, 1732 North Shore Ave., Chicago, Ill.

BUCK, William H. Painter. Born in Norway in 1840, died in New Orleans, 1888. He was a clerk in a cotton office before he became a professional painter. He studied under Clague and also in Boston; opened a studio as a professional painter in 1880 at 26 Carondelet St., New Orleans, where he remained until his death. He painted Louisiana landscapes with considerable force and feeling. Many of his paintings are highly meritorious, but some show carelessness in execution.

BUCKLIN, William S. Painter. Born in Phalanx, N. J., 1851. Member of Art Students' League, New York. Mural paintings in Library, Westminster, Mass. *Address*, Riverside, Conn.

BUDD, Charles Jay. Painter and illustrator. Born S. Schodack, Rensselaer County, N. Y., 1859. Pupil of P. A. F. A. under Eakins; Art Students' League of New York. Member: Philadelphia Sketch Club. Specialty, children's books.

BUDD, Katherine Cotheal. Painter and illustrator. Pupil of William M. Chase. *Address*, 527 Fifth Ave., New York, N. Y.

BUDDINGTON, Jonathan. According to Dunlap, an artist of this name was painting portraits in New York City about 1798 to 1812.

BUDELL, Ada. Painter and illustrator. Born Westfield, N. J., 1873. Pupil of Art Students' League of New York. Member: National Association of Women Painters and Sculptors. Illustrated numerous books for children. *Address*, 76 Washington Place, New York, N. Y.

BUDELL, Hortense. Painter. Exhibited at National Association of Women Painters and Sculptors in 1924. *Address*, 627 Fourth Ave., Westfield, N. J.

BUDWORTH, William S(ylvester). Painter. Born Brooklyn, N. Y., 1861. Self-taught. Awards: Silver medals, American Art Society, Philadelphia, 1902 and 1903. Work in Rochester Museum, N. Y. *Address*, 615 South Eighth Ave., Mt. Vernon, N. Y.

BUEHLER, Lytton (Briggs). Painter. Born Gettysburg, 1888. Pupil of P. A. F. A. Member: Fellowship P. A. F. A. Award: European traveling scholarship, P. A. F. A., 1908. Work: "Portrait Major Richardson" in Canandaigua, N. Y., Public Library. *Address*, 346 W. 58th St., New York, N. Y.

BUEHR, Karl Albert. Painter. Born in Germany. Studied in England, France and Holland. Pupil of Art Institute, Chicago. Awards: Bronze medal, St. Louis Exp., 1904; Hon. mention, Paris Salon, 1910; silver medal, Chicago Society of Artists, 1914. Associate Member of National Academy of Design. *Address*, 1727 Chase Ave., Chicago, Ill.

BUEHR, Mary G. Hess (Mrs. Karl Albert Buehr). Miniature painter. Born in Chicago, Ill. Studied in Holland and in France. Pupil of Art Institute, Chicago. *Address*, 1727 Chase Ave., Chicago, Ill.

BUELL, Abel. Engraver. Born in 1742 and died 1825. Engraver on silver plate and type metal. It is said he was imprisoned for having altered a Colonial note. He engraved a plan of Boston, published by Romans in 1775, and a diploma-plate for Yale College prior to 1775.

BUERGERNISS, Carl. Painter. Member: Fellowship Penna. Acad. of Fine Arts. *Address*, 2819 West Girard Ave., Philadelphia, Pa.

BUFFORD, James A. Engraver. About 1850 he engraved upon copper, and published a few views of Boston. Later he is listed as a lithographer with an office at No. 313 Washington St., Boston, Mass. His work was chiefly on the covers of sheet music.

BUFFUM, Katharine G. Illustrator. Born Providence, R. I., 1884. Pupil of P. A. F. A. Work: Illustrated "The Secret Kingdom," "Mother Goose in Silhouette," "Silhouettes to Cut in School," "Songs of Schooldays," etc. Specialty, silhouettes. Died December 1921.

BULL, Charles Livingston. Illustrator and painter. Born New York State, 1874. Pupil of Harvey Ellis and M. Louise Stowell. Member: New York Water Color Club; National Art Club. Specialty, wild animals. *Address*, Oradell, N. J.

BULL, Martin. Engraver. Born 1744 and died 1825. Engraver of early American book-plates. He was probably born in Farmington, Conn. Bull engraved the book-plate for the Monthly Library of Farmington, Conn.

BULLARD, Marion. Painter. Exhibited "The Apple Tree" at Penna. Academy of Fine Arts, Philadelphia, 1920. *Address*, Woodstock, New York.

BULLARD, O. A. An artist of that name was said to be painting pictures in New York, 1844–46.

BUMSTEAD, Ethel Quincy. Painter. Born London, England, 1873. Pupil of Boston Museum School, of Abbot Graves and of A. Buhler. Member: Copley Society, 1893. *Address*, 12 Berkeley St., Cambridge, Mass.

BUNCE, William Gedney. Born in Hartford, Conn., 1840, and died 1916. In 1863 he went to New York and studied under William Hart. In 1867 he sailed for Europe and is an artist resident of Paris. He is a member of the National Academy of Design, and is noted for his landscapes. Among his works are "Watch Hill, R. I.," "Sautucket, New England," and "Venetian Night."

BUNDY, John Elwood. Landscape painter. Born Guilford County, N. C., 1853. Awards: Holcomb prize, Herron Art Institute, 1917. Member Richmond Art Association. Work: "Blue Spring" and "Old Farm in Winter," Public Gallery, Richmond, Ind.; "Wane of Winter" and "Beech Woods in Winter," Art Association of Indianapolis. *Address*, 527 West Main St., Richmond, Ind.

BUNKER, Dennis M. Painter. Born in New York City in 1861, he died in Boston in 1890. Pupil of National Academy of Design in New York, and Herbert and Gerome in Paris. His specialty was portraying feminine charm in portrait and figure painting. The portrait of his wife is in the Metropolitan Museum, N. Y. "Jessica," painted in 1890, is owned by the Boston Museum of Fine Arts, and "The Mirror" by the Philadelphia Art Club.

BUNNER, Rudolph F. Painter and illustrator. Member: New York Water Color Club. *Address*, Ridgefield, Conn.; or Great Kills, S. I., New York.

BUNT. A little-known landscape painter, has only left a record of his name as painting landscapes.

BUONGIORNO, Donatus. Mural painter. Born Solofra, Italy, 1865. Pupil of Roil Institute of Fine Arts, Naples. Work: "Apotheosis of the Evangelist," in Church of St. Leonard of the Franciscan Fathers, Boston, Mass.; "St. Charles Borromeo," in Church of Sacred Heart, Boston; "Fall of the Angels," in Church of St. Peter, Boston. *Address*, Maddaloni, Caserta, Italy.

BURBANK, E(lbridge) A(yer). Painter. Born Harvard, Ill., 1858. Pupil of Academy of Design in Chicago; Paul Nauen in Munich. Since 1897 has made portraits of over 125 types of North American Indians. Represented in Field Museum and Newberry Library, Chicago, and Smithsonian Institute, Washington, D. C.

BURBANK, William Edwin. Painter. Born Boston, Mass., 1866. Pupil of Cowles Art School in Boston; Laurens and Constant in Paris. Died in 1922.

BURCHFIELD, Charles S. Painter. Born in Ohio in 1893. Pupil of Cleveland School of Art. *Address*, 459 Franklin St., Buffalo, N. Y.

BURD, Clara Miller. Painter and illustrator. Born in New York; studied there and in Paris. *Address*, 18 West 34th St., New York City.

BURDICK, Horace R. Portrait painter. Born in East Killingly, Conn., 1844. Pupil of Boston Museum of Art Schools. His portraits are in crayon and oil. Member of Boston Art Club. *Address*, 16 Park Ave., Malden, Mass.

BURGDORFF, Ferdinand. Painter. Born in Cleveland, Ohio, 1881. Student at Cleveland School of Art. Represented at Memorial Museum, San Francisco, by "Old Wharf."

BURGER, I., Jr. In the *New York Magazine* for May 1790, a plate of well-engraved music is signed "Burger Jun. Sc." This may have been a son or relative of the John Burger silversmith of New York, with whom Cornelius Tiebot served his apprenticeship about 1790. One of the plates is signed as "printed by I. Burger, Jun'r." This is probably the music engraver noted above.

BURGESS, Alice L. (Mrs.). Painter. Born in St. Louis, Mo., 1880. Pupil of W. M. Chase. *Address*, 1268 Quinnipiac Ave., New Haven, Conn.

BURGESS, Ida J. Painter. Born in Chicago, Ill. Pupil of Chase and Shirlaw in New York, and Mason in Paris. Has executed decorations and mural paintings. *Address*, Washington Square, New York.

BURGESS, Ruth Payne (Mrs. John W. Burgess). Artist. Born in Montpelier, Vt. Studied at Art Students' League, New York, and in Germany and Italy. Ex. Pres. of Art Students' League; Patron of Metropolitan Museum of Art, New York; member of Providence Water Color Club. Has painted portraits of Hon. A. B. Hepburn, Judge Pierson, Professor March, and Dr. Daniel Bliss. *Address*, Rhode Island Ave., Newport, R. I.

BURGIS, William. Engraver. His work was chiefly in line, though he did attempt mezzotint engraving. He was a publisher of American maps and views as early as 1717. Burgis also published views of the College at Cambridge, Mass., and of the New Dutch Church in New York.

BURINE. This name as "Burine sc." is signed to a large sheet of "shells," engraved for Reese's Encyclopedia published by S. F. Bradford of Philadelphia, 1805 to 1818.

BURKE, Frances. Painter. Resided in Richmond, Virginia. She made several copies of the Washington portrait painted by William Joseph Williams in 1792. It is owned by the Masonic Lodge of Alexandria, Va., and shows Washington in Masonic Dress. The copy of this picture in the Philadelphia Masonic Hall was made by Miss Burke from the original painting.

BURLEIGH, Charles C. Painter. Born in Pennsylvania in 1848, he lived in Plainfield, Conn., as a young man and later painted portraits at Northampton, Mass.

BURLEIGH, Sydney R. Born in Little Compton, R. I., 1853. Pupil of Laurens in Paris. Among his pictures, "Landscape," "Luxembourg Garden." *Address*, "Fleur-de-Lys," Providence, R. I.

BURLIN, Paul. Artist. Born in New York City, 1886. Studied New York, and London, England. Landscape, mural and figure painter; has spent much time in the Southwest; exhibited at Salon des Independents, Paris, and annual exhibitions in U. S. Associate member of Societé Internationale des Arts et Lettres, Salon d'Automne, Paris. *Address*, 106 West 57th St., New York City.

BURLIN, Richard. Miniature painter. Flourished 1845–1863, New York. He also painted small portraits in oils.

BURLING, Gilbert. Painter in oil and water colors. Born in 1843, he died in 1875. He excelled in the portrayal of game birds.

His last works exhibited in 1875, "Normandy Sketches," "Beach below East Hampton, L. I.," "Canadian Lake," and the "Old Harness-Maker."

BURLINGAME, Charles A. Painter and illustrator. Born at Bridgeport, Conn., 1860. Pupil of Edward Moran. *Address*, Nanuet, New York.

BURNAP, Daniel. Engraver. His chief work was on brass clockfaces. He was working in East Windsor, Conn., before 1800.

BURNHAM, Anita W. (Mrs.). Painter and etcher. Born in Brooklyn, N. Y., 1880. Pupil of W. M. Chase for painting, and Ralph Pearson for etching. *Address*, 1255 Asburg Ave., Hubbard Woods, Ill.

BURNHAM, Roger N. Sculptor. Born in Boston, Mass., in 1876. Work: Four colossal figures, City Hall Annex, Boston; panels on main doors, Forsyth Dental Infirmary for Children, Boston; "Uncle Remus" memorial tablet, Atlanta; medallion, "Johann Ernest Perabo," Boston Art Museum; Carrington Mason Memorial, Memphis; figure of Centaur, head of Athena and Tritons on Germanic Art Museum, Harvard. Instructor in School of Architecture, Harvard University, 1912 to 1917. *Address*, 5 Garden Terrace, Cambridge, Mass.

BURNSIDE, Cameron. Painter. Born in England, 1887. Studied in Paris. Paintings owned by French Government. Exhibited at the Penna. Academy of Fine Arts, Philadelphia, 1924. *Address*, 7637 Thirty-First St., Washington, D. C.

BURPEE, William P. Painter. Born in Rockland, Maine, in 1846. Represented in Boston Art Club, Springfield Museum, and Rockland Public Library. *Address*, 43 Park St., Rockland, Maine.

BURR, G(eorge) Brainard. Painter. Born Middletown, Conn. Pupil of Berlin and Munich Academies F. A.; Art Students' League of New York; Colarossi Academy in Paris. Member: Allied Art Association. *Address*, Old Lyme, Conn.

BURR, George Elbert. Etcher and water colorist. His plates for his etchings and aquatints are generally small and his work shows the miniaturist's precise delicacy. His late studies made in Arizona and New Mexico are of great interest. Mr. Burr was born in Cleveland, Ohio, and before going abroad made many illustrations for the Metropolitan Museum Collection. His home is in Denver, Colorado.

BURRAGE, Mildred G(iddings). Painter. Born Portland, Me., 1890. Pupil of Richard Miller. Member: International Art Union, Paris. *Address*, Kennebunkport, Me.

BURRELL, Mrs. Louise. Painter. Born London, England. Pupil of Herkomer. Member: California Art Club. *Address*, 1189 West Adams St., Los Angeles, Cal.

BURROUGHS, Bryson. Artist. Born Hyde Park, Mass., 1869. After general education, studied at Art Students' League, New York, where he won Chanler Scholarship, 1891; also studied in Paris and Florence. Engaged professionally as artist since 1889; silver medal, Buffalo Expn., 1901; Pittsburgh Expn., 1903; 3d prize, Worcester Expn., 1904; Curator of paintings, Metropolitan Museum Art, New York. Member: Association of National Artists. *Address*, Metropolitan Museum, New York City, N. Y.

BURROUGHS, Edith W. Sculptor. Born 1871 and died 1916. Pupil of Art Students' League, New York, also studied in Paris. She was elected an associate member of the National Academy in 1913. Her best known works are the busts of John La Farge, at the Metropolitan Museum of Art, and the "Fountain of Youth."

BURROWS, Harold L. Painter and etcher. Born in Salt Lake City in 1889. Pupil of Young and Henri. *Address*, 469 Fifth Ave., New York.

BURT, Beatrice Milliken. Miniature painter. Born New Bedford, Mass., 1893. Pupil of Delécluse and Mme. Laforge in Paris; Mrs. Lucia F. Fuller, Mrs. Elsie Dodge Pattee and Miss Welch in New York.

BURT, Charles. Born in Scotland 1823 and died 1892. He came to New York in 1836. He was employed for a time by A. L. Dick of that city, and engraved and etched a number of portraits and book illustrations. His later work was bank-note engraving. For some years he was one of the chief engravers for the Treasury Department at Washington, D. C. Several of his larger plates were made for the American Art Union in 1851-52.

BURT, Louis. Painter. Born in New York, N. Y., 1900. Pupil of Henri, George Bellows, John Sloan. Awards: Hon. mention, Mac-Dowell Club, 1916-17-18. *Address*, 3835 White Plains Ave., Bronx, New York, N. Y.

BURT, Mary Theodora. Painter. Born Philadelphia. Pupil of P. A. F. A.; Julien Academy in Paris. Member: Plastic Club, Philadelphia. *Address*, 1203 Walnut St., Philadelphia, Pa.

BURTIS, Mary E(lizabeth). Painter. Born Orange, N. J., 1878. Pupil of Mme. Christine Lumsden. Member: Society of Independent Artists. *Address*, 406 Clarendon Place, Orange, N. J.

BURTON, S(amuel) C(hatwood). Painter, sculptor, illustrator and etcher. Born Manchester, England, 1881. Pupil of Laurens in Paris; Lanteri in London. Member: Beachcombers' Club, Provincetown; Chicago Society of Etchers; Art Masters of England. Awards: Third prize for painting, 1917; second prize for painting, 1918; and bronze medal for etching, 1920, Minnesota State Fair; second prize for etching, Minneapolis Institute, 1921. Professor of painting and lecturer on art, University of Minnesota.

BUSBEE, Jacque. Painter. Born in Raleigh, N. C., in 1870. Student of National Academy of Design, and Art Students' League, New York. Painted a number of portraits; later became interested in pottery.

BUSCH, Clarence F. Painter. Exhibited "Nude," Annual Exhibition of the National Academy of Design, 1925. *Address*, 58 West 57th St., New York.

BUSENBARK, E. J. Painter. Member: Guild of Free Lance A. *Address*, 117 East 27th St., New York, N. Y.

BUSEY, Norval H. Painter. Born in Christiansburg, Va., 1845. Studied in Paris under Bouguereau. Member: Salma. Club. *Address*, 39 West 67th St., New York, N. Y.

BUSH, Agnes S(elene). Painter. Born Seattle, Washington. Pupil of Ella S. Bush and Paul Morgan Gustin. *Address*, 529 Belmont, North, Seattle, Washington.

BUSH, Ella Shepard. Miniature painter. Born Galesburg, Ill. Pupil of J. Alden Weir, Kenyon Cox, Robert Henri, Theodore W. Thayer. Member: Painters, Sculptors, Miniature Painters; Art Students' League of New York; California Art Club; Seattle Fine Arts Society. Award: Prize, Seattle Fine Arts Society, 1920.

BUSH, Joseph H. Painter. Born 1794 and died 1865. He was of German descent and was born at Frankfort, Ky. At seventeen he became a student of Thomas Sully in Philadelphia, and after two years opened his studio at Frankford, passing his winters at Natchez and New Orleans. He died in Lexington, Ky. He painted Gen'l Zachary Taylor, Gov. John Adair, Judge Thos. B. Monroe and Gen. Martin D. Hardin.

BUSH, Norton. Painter. Born in Rochester, N. Y., 1834. He became a student of Jasper F. Cropsey in New York. Among his works are "Lake Tahoe," "Summit of the Sierras," and "Lake Nicaragua." In 1874 he was elected a member of the San Francisco Art Association, and in 1878 a director.

BUSH-BROWN, Henry Kirke. Sculptor. Born Ogdensburg, N. Y., 1857. Studied art at National Academy of Design. Pupil of Henry Kirke Brown; studied art in Paris and Italy 1886–9. Prominent works: Equestrian statues Gen. G. G. Meade and Gen. John F. Reynolds, Gettysburg, Pa.; statues "Justinian," Appellate Court, New York; "Indian Buffalo Hunt," Chicago Expn., 1893; equestrian statue Gen. Anthony Wayne for Valley Forge, Pa.; memorial architecture, Stony Point, N. Y.; The Lincoln Memorial, Gettysburg, 1911; Union Soldiers' Monument, Charleston, W. Va., 1912; equestrian statue, Gen. John Sedgwick, Gettysburg, Pa. Member: National Sculpture Society, Architectural League. *Address*, 1729 G St., Washington, D. C.

BUSH-BROWN, Mrs. Margaret L. Portrait painter. Born in Philadelphia, 1857. Pupil of Penna. Academy of Fine Arts, and Julien Academy in Paris. Represented by portraits of Lincoln, Lee, and Professor Lesley. Also paints miniatures. *Address*, 1729 G St., Washington, D. C.

BUTENSKY, Jules L. Sculptor. Born in Russia, 1871. Pupil of Mercie and Boucher in Paris. Among his works are "Universal Peace" at the Metropolitan Museum, New York, "Exile" at the White House, Washington, D. C., and "Goliath," group at Hebrew Institute, Chicago, Ill. *Address*, Ramah, Romona, Rockland County, New York.

BUTLER. Engraver of Baltimore. A well-known engraving of a man and a lion signed "Butler Sc. Balto." was published prior to 1835.

BUTLER. A little-known genre painter, who lost an arm in the Civil War. He was painting in Rome in 1870.

BUTLER, Edward B. Painter. Born in Lewistown, Me., in 1853. Pupil of F. C. Peyraud. Member of Chicago Art Club. Among his works "Misty Morning," City of Chicago; "October Mist," Chicago Art League; "California Wheat," Los Angeles Museum; and Cleveland Museum of Art, "Early Springs." *Address*, 1608 Monroe Bldg., Chicago, Ill.

BUTLER, Edward Smith. Painter. Born in Cincinnati, 1848. Member of the Cincinnati Art Club. *Address*, 1001 Chapel St., Walnut Hill, Cincinnati, Ohio.

BUTLER, Frank. Painter. Exhibited in Annual Water Color Exhibition at Penna. Academy of the Fine Arts, Philadelphia, 1925. *Address*, Care of A. R. Thayer, 126 Moss Ave., Boston, Mass.

BUTLER, George Bernard. Portrait painter. Born in New York, 1838. Pupil of Thomas Hicks, and with Couture. Served in the Civil War. In 1873 he was elected a member of the National Academy, his last picture being shown there in 1907. Represented in the Metropolitan Museum by "The Gray Shawl." He died in 1907 at Orton Falls, N. Y.

BUTLER, Helen Sharpless (Mrs.). Painter. Born in West Chester, Pa. Pupil of Chase and Anshutz. Member of Fellowship of Penna. Academy of Fine Arts.

BUTLER, Howard Russell. Painter. Born New York. Honorable mention Paris Salon, 1886, medals Paris Expn., 1889. Elected Associate member of National Academy, 1898, and Academician, 1902. Member of New York Water Color Club. *Address*, Santa Barbara, California, and Princeton, N. J.

BUTLER, J. M. Engraver, or rather a publisher of prints, as there is no evidence that he engraved himself. He was active in Philadelphia about 1850.

BUTLER, M. Working in Boston 1821, he engraved in line five humorous copperplate illustrations for "The Songster's New Pocket Companion, etc.," published by T. Swan, Boston, 1821. This may be the same Butler who was working in Baltimore at a somewhat later date.

BUTLER, Mary. Painter. Born in Philadelphia. Pupil of Chase, Henri and Redfield. Member of Fellowship of Penna. Academy of Fine Arts, Philadelphia. Among her paintings "Goatfell Mountain," Penna. Academy of Fine Arts, Philadelphia; "Ogonquit Dunes," West Chester State Normal School; and "Maine Headlands," Williamsport High School. *Address*, 2127 Green St., Philadelphia, Pa.

BUTLER, Theodore E. Painter. Member of Society of Independent Artists. *Address*, 75 Washington Place, New York, N. Y.

BUTTERWORTH, A. H. He engraved the frontispiece and vignette title page for "The Life and Adventures of Robinson Crusoe," published by Silas Andrews, Hartford, N. J., about the year 1828.

BUTTON, Albert Prentice. Painter and illustrator. Born in Lowell, Mass., 1872. Pupil of Boston Art Club. *Address*, 44 Boyleston St., Boston, Mass.

BUTTRE, John Chester. Engraver. Born 1821 and died 1893. He did a little work in portrait painting, but soon became a line engraver of reputation, and established an extensive engraving business in New York.

BUZBY, Rosella T. Painter and illustrator. Born in Philadelphia in 1867. Pupil of Penna. Academy of Fine Arts. *Address*, Fuller Building, 10 South 18th St., Philadelphia, Pa.

BYE, Arthur E. Painter and teacher. Born in Philadelphia, 1885. Pupil of John Carlson; studied in Paris. Member of Art Alliance, Philadelphia. *Address*, Langhorne, Philadelphia.

BYER, Samuel. Painter. Born in Poland, 1886. Pupil of Art Institute of Chicago, Ill. *Address*, 439 South Halstead St., Chicago.

BYERS, Evelyn. Painter. Exhibited water colors at Penna. Academy of Fine Arts, Philadelphia, 1922. *Address*, 1102 Bagby St., Houston, Texas.

BYFIELD, N. Portrait painter. Born in Boston, 1677, and probably the son of Nathaniel and Deborah Byfield. He painted an excellent portrait of Richard Middleton which he signed and dated 1713.

BYRAM, Ralph Shaw. Painter and illustrator. Born in Philadelphia, 1881. Member of Philadelphia Sketch Club. *Address*, Lena and Church Lane, Germantown, Philadelphia.

BYRD, Henry. A portrait painter of some merit; lived in New Orleans in the 40's and 50's. He travelled through the country, painting portraits, but in 1867 he took up his abode in the vicinity of Hilary and Commercial Sts., New Orleans, where he continued to paint portraits until 1883, about the time of his death.

BYRNE, Ellen A(bert). Painter. Born Fort Moultrie, S. C., 1858. Pupil of Corcoran School of Art in Washington; William M. Chase; Simon and Menard in Paris. Member: Society of Washington Artists.

C

CADE, J. J. Engraver. Was born in Canada. He was a good engraver of portraits and worked for the New York publishers. In 1890 he was living in Brooklyn, N. Y.

CADMUS, Egbert. Painter. Exhibited at the Annual Exhibition of Water Colors at the Penna. Academy of the Fine Arts, Philadelphia, 1925. *Address*, 150 West 103d St., New York City.

CADMUS, Paul. Painter. Exhibited at the Annual Exhibition of Water Colors at the Penna. Academy of the Fine Arts, Philadelphia, 1925. *Address*, 150 West 103d St., New York City.

CADORIN, Ettore. Sculptor. Born in Italy in 1876. Member of National Sculptors' Society, New York. *Address*, 440 Riverside Drive, New York.

CADY, Mrs. Edwin A. Painter. Member: Providence Art Club; Providence Water Color Club. *Address*, Warren, R. I.

CADY, (Walter) Harrison. Illustrator. Born Gardner, Mass., 1877. Member: Salma. Club; Society of Illustrators, 1911. Illustrated "Rackety Packety," "Queen Silver Bell," "The Spring Cleaning," "The Cosy Lion," by Frances Hodgson Burnett, etc.; contributor to *Life, St. Nicholas, Saturday Evening Post, Country Gentleman, Ladies' Home Journal*, etc.

CAFARELLI, M. A. Painter. Member: Society Independent Artists. *Address*, 24 West 60th St., New York, N. Y.

CAFFERTY, James H. Painter. Born in 1819 and died in 1869. He began his professional life as a portrait painter, but his latter years were given for the most part to game-pieces and still life. He became an Academician National School of Design in 1853. His most notable paintings are "My Girl," "Brook Trout," and several studies of "Fish." With L. M. Wiles he painted the graveyard scene from Hamlet, a picture of great merit.

CAHILL, Arthur. Painter and illustrator. Born in San Francisco, 1879. Pupil of California Art School. Member: California Artists' Association; Bohemian Club, San Francisco. Work: "Governor Hiram Johnson of California," State Capitol, Cal.; "Congressman Kent of California," "Templeton Crocker" in Crocker Art Gallery, Sacramento; "Chief Justice Irwin," Bohemian Club, San Francisco. *Address*, San Anselmo, Cal.

CAHILL, William V. Painter. Born Syracuse, N. Y. Pupil of Howard Pyle. Member of Art Students' League of New York. Professor of drawing and painting, University of Kansas, 1918–19. Work: "Thoughts of the Sea," Museum of History, Science and Art,

Los Angeles; "Summer," Municipal Collection, Phoenix, Arizona. He died in Chicago, 1924.

CAIN. An American portrait painter who flourished about 1760 in Maryland.

CALDER, Alexander (Milne). Sculptor. Born Aberdeen, Scotland, 1846, and died 1923. Pupil of John Rhind in Edinburgh. Studied in England; came to United States in 1868. Pupil of P. A. F. A. under J. A. Bailly and Thomas Eakins. Work: Equestrian statue of Gen. George G. Meade in Fairmount Park, Philadelphia, Pa.; colossal statue of William Penn, and groups on City Hall, Philadelphia, Pa.

CALDER, Alexander Stirling. Sculptor. Born Philadelphia, Pa. Pupil of Penna. Academy of Fine Arts; Chapu and Faiguiere in Paris. Member: National Sculptors' Society. Elected Associate Member of the National Academy 1906, and Academician in 1913. Instructor at National Academy of Design. Work: "Fountain Energy," Philadelphia; "The Star," Herron Art Institute, Indianapolis; "Washington Group," Washington Arch, New York, N. Y.; Depew memorial fountain, Indianapolis, Ind.; "The Island," Viscaya, Fla. Represented in permanent collection, Pennsylvania Academy; St. Louis Museum of Art; Smithsonian Institute grounds, Washington, D. C.; Metropolitan Museum, New York, N. Y. *Address,* 11 East 14th St., New York, N. Y.

CALDER, Mrs. Josephine. Painter. Member: National Academy of Women Panters and Sculptors. *Address,* 1861 Parkwood Ave., Toledo, O.

CALDER, Ralph M(ilne). Painter, artist. Born Philadelphia, Pa., 1884. Pupil of Penna. Academy of Fine Arts. *Address,* Care Paul Chalfin, 597 Fifth Ave., New York, N. Y.

CALEWAERT, Louis H. S. Painter, etcher, sculptor. Born Detroit, Mich., 1894. Pupil Detroit School of Fine Arts under Wicker, and studied in Italy, Sicily, France and Belgium. Member: Chicago Society of Etchers. Work: Toledo Museum of Art. *Address,* 4316 Greenwood Ave., Chicago, Ill.

CALHOUN, Frederic D. Painter. Born Minneapolis, Minn., 1883. Pupil of Art Students' League of New York; Minneapolis School of Art. Member: Minneapolis Art Club.

CALIGA, Isaac H. Painter. Born in Indiana in 1857. Studied in Boston and abroad. Represented by portraits of H. F. Waters in New England Historical Society, and Marcus Waterman in New York Chamber

of Commerce. *Address,* 1422 Federal St., Salem, Mass.

CALKINS, Loring G. Etcher. Born in Chicago, 1881. Pupil of Vanderpoel. He has illustrated a number of books. *Address,* 24 Milk St., Boston, Mass.

CALLENDER, Benjamin. Engraver. Born in Boston, Mass., 1773, and died 1856. His engraved work chiefly consists of maps and charts. He was engraving for Boston publishers as early as 1796. Callender engraved some of the maps in the "American Gazetteer" by Jedediah Morse, Boston, 1897.

CALLENDER, Joseph. Born in Boston, Mass., 1751; died there 1821, and was buried in the Old Granary Burying Ground in Boston. He was the son of Eleazer Callender and Susanna Hiller. Joseph Callender was employed for some time as a die-sinker for the Massachusetts Mint. In association with Paul Revere he engraved a number of line-plates for the *Royal American Magazine,* published in Boston in 1774. His chief occupation, however, seemed to be the engraving of book-plates, bill-heads, and work of a similar character.

CALVERLY, Charles. Sculptor. Born in Albany, N. Y., 1833, and died 1914. Educated in Albany, N. Y., became Associate National Academy of Design in 1872, and a full member in 1875; has executed many groups and figures; is especially known by his portrait busts in bronze of Horace Greeley, John Brown, Peter Cooper, and Elias Howe.

CALVERT, Bertha W. Painter. Born in Nashville, Tenn., in 1885. Specialty, ivory miniatures. *Address,* Fourth Ave. and Union St., Nashville, Tenn.

CALVERT, E. Painter. Born in England, 1850. Has painted portraits in Mercer University, Macon, Ga., and Vanderbilt University, Lake Geneva, Wis. *Address,* 238 Fourth Ave., Nashville, Tenn.

CALVERT, Peter R. Painter. Born in England, 1855. Pupil of John Sowden. Specialty, ivory miniatures. *Address,* Fourth Ave. and Union St., Nashville, Tenn.

CALYO, Nicolino V. Painter. Born in 1799 and died 1884. Italian portrait and miniature painter. In 1837 he lived in New York with other refugees, among them Napoleon III. He died there (see *N. Y. Tribune,* Dec. 14, 1884).

CAMERON, Edgar S. Mural painter. Born in Ottawa, Ill., in 1862. Pupil of Chicago Academy of Design, and of Constant and Laurens in Paris. Work in Art Institute of Chicago, Supreme Court Library, Springfield, Ill. *Address,* 10 East Ohio St., Chicago, Ill.

CAMERON, J. Artist. Employed by the lithographic firm of Currier & Ives, of 125 Nassau St., New York. His specialty was hunting and sporting field scenes.

CAMERON, Marie G. (Mrs.). Painter. Born in France. Pupil of Laurens and Constant, and Art Institute of Chicago. *Address,* 10 East Ohio St., Chicago, Ill.

CAMERON, William R. Illustrator and etcher. Born in New York in 1893. Pupil of Meyer, Mackey and Griffin. *Address,* 545 New Call Bldg., San Francisco, Calif.

CAMFFERMAN, Peter M. Painter. Born in Holland, 1890. Pupil of Minneapolis School of Fine Arts. *Address,* Brackenwood, Langley, Wash.

CAMMEYER, W. Engraver, working in Albany, N. Y., about 1812. He engraved a number of book-illustrations.

CAMPBELL. An American portrait painter, said to have flourished about 1776. Washington writes at that date of a portrait painted of himself, but states that he never saw the artist.

CAMPBELL, Anna B. Miniature painter. Born in St. Louis, Mo., 1879. Pupil of Art Students' League of New York, and Corcoran Art Gallery, Washington, D. C. *Address,* 1977 Biltmore St., Washington, D. C.

CAMPBELL, Blendon R. Painter. Born in St. Louis, Mo., in 1872. Pupil of Constant and Laurens in Paris. Specialty in figures and landscapes, also paints portraits. *Address,* 147 West 4th St., New York City.

CAMPBELL, Edmund S. Painter. Born in Freehold, N. J. Member of Associated Artists of Pittsburgh. Exhibited water color paintings at Penna. Academy Fine Arts, 1922. *Address,* Care of Chicago Art Institute.

CAMPBELL, Floy. Painter and illustrator. Born in Kansas City, Mo. Pupil of Art Students' League of New York, and Simon Cottet in Paris. *Address,* 4026 East 67th St., Terrace, Kansas City, Mo.

CAMPBELL, Helena E. (Mrs.). Painter. Born at Eastman, Ga. Pupil of Chase School in New York. Her portrait of Rt. Rev. Frederick F. Reese, Bishop of Georgia, is owned by the Diocese of Georgia. *Address,* The Delaware, 520 West 122d St., New York.

CAMPBELL, Robert. Engraver, working in Philadelphia about 1806–1831.

CAMPBELL, Wands. Painter. Exhibited in the 1925 Annual Exhibition of the National Academy of Design. *Address,* Athens, Penna.

CANADE, George and Vincent. Painters. Exhibited in Philadelphia, 1921. *Address,* 1454 65th St., Brooklyn, N. Y.

CANDEE, Geo. Edward. Painter. Born in New Haven, Conn., 1838. Pupil of Joseph Kyle in New Haven, also studied in Italy. He painted landscapes and a few figure pieces.

CANNON, Beatrice. Painter. Born in Louisville, Ky., in 1875. Pupil of Art Institute of Chicago. *Address,* 1115 East 61st St., New York.

CANNON, Hugh. Sculptor. Born in Ireland, he settled in Philadelphia, and there did considerable modeling and carving.

CANTER, Albert M. Painter. Born at Norma, Salem County, N. J., 1892. Member of Fellowship of the Penna. Academy of Fine Arts, Philadelphia. Among his best known paintings are ''Virginia Road,'' and ''Landscape'' at the Graphic Sketch Club Gallery. *Address,* 721 Walnut St., Philadelphia, Pa.

CANTRALL, Harriet M. Painter. Born near Springfield, Ill. Pupil of Pratt Institute, Dow, Woodbury, Townsley, Poore, Van Laer. Member: Western Arts Association; St. Louis A. G.; Springfield Art Association. *Address,* 853 Grand Blvd., Springfield, Ill.

CAPELLANO, Antonio. An Italian sculptor, who according to Wyeth was a pupil of Canova. As early as 1815 he was in New York, going from that city to Baltimore, Md., at the request of Maxmillian Godefroy, the architect of the Battle Monument of that city. Previous to his engagement upon the Battle Monument he secured a commission for the execution of two panels in bas-relief upon the front of St. Paul's Church, of which Robert Cary Long was the architect. These two works, ''Moses with the Tables of the Law'' and ''Christ Breaking Bread,'' were executed for the sum of $1,000 and completed before his employment upon the Battle Monument. His employment upon the Battle Monument is evidenced by vouchers in the possession of the Maryland Historical Society. In September, 1817, Capellano, writing from Baltimore to James Madison at Montpelier, solicits a commission for a marble bust of James Madison, an arrangement which he was unable to complete. From the report of the Commissioner of Public Buildings for the year of 1827, it is found that Capellano was then employed as a sculptor at the Capitol at a salary of $1,500 per annum. By a proposal dated Washington, May 22, 1827, he offered to execute a colossal statue of Washington for the Washington Monument at Baltimore for $12,000. Rembrandt Peale in his Reminiscences refers to an acquaintance with Capellano while in Baltimore in 1815, and to meeting him in the Boboli Gardens in Florence in 1830. Capellano was at that time a resident of Florence.

CAPOLINO, Joseph. Painter and mural decorator. Student of Penna. Academy of Fine Arts, and winner of Stotesbury prize, 1924. *Address,* U. S. Marine Corps, Broad St. and Washington Ave., Philadelphia.

CARAVIA, Thalia Flora. Painter. Exhibited at Annual Exhibition of the National Academy of Design in 1925. *Address,* Paterson, N. J.

CARBEE, (Scott). Painter. Born Concord, Vt., 1860. Pupil of Hugo Breul in Providence; Bouguereau and Ferrier in Paris; Max Bohm in Florence. Member: Boston Art Club; Copley Society, 1902.

CARDELLI, Georgio. Sculptor and painter. Born in Italy, 1791, in 1816 he came to New York. About 1818 he was commissioned by Trumbull the artist to model busts of himself and wife, but they were unsatisfactory. He turned his attention to portrait painting and did considerable work in New England; his portraits were hard and lifeless. Cardelli worked for some time on the decorations for the Capitol in Washington, D. C.

CAREW, Mrs. Bertha. Painter. Born Springfield, Mass., 1878. Pupil of Blashfield, Mowbray and Chase in New York; Carlandi in Rome; Mme. Richarde in Paris. Member: National Academy Women Painters and Sculptors. *Address,* Care Kidder, Peabody Co., 17 Wall St., New York City.

CAREY, Henry. Contemporary American. "Landscape and Cattle." In a marshy pool, cattle are wading; trees to the right and low hills in the distance.

CAREY, Peyton. At the Exhibition of Early Engraving in America, held at the Museum of Fine Arts, Boston, 1904, a seal of the University of Georgia was shown. A note says that this seal was designed and cut by "Mr. Peyton Carey, a graduate of 1810."

CARIANI, Veraldo J. Painter. Born in Italy in 1891. Pupil of National Academy of Design, and Art Students' League of New York. *Address,* 148 Bemis Place, Springfield, Mass.

CARIATA, Giovanni. Sculptor. Born in Rome in 1865, he lived for some years in New York and died there in 1917. He made the bronze medallion presented to Gen'l Joffre.

CARIO, Michael. *The American Weekly Mercury,* Philadelphia, July 8–15, 1736, advertises the arrival from London of "Michael Cario, Jeweller." After detailing his various wares, in the form of rings, buttons for sleeves, snuff boxes, etc., he adds the following: "N. B. The said Michael Cario buys all sorts of old Diamonds, or any other Stones, and per-

forms all sorts of Engraving Work, either in Gold or Silver."

CARL, Katharine Augusta. Artist. Born at New Orleans. Studied art under Bouguereau and Gustave Courtois, Paris. Painted portrait of Empress Dowager of China; also "At the Mirror," "Cupid and Psyche," "Iris," etc. Member: Societe Nationale des Beaux Arts, Paris; International Society Women Painters, London. Member International Jury of Fine Arts, International Jury of Applied Arts, St. Louis Expn., 1904. Orders of Double Dragon and Manchu Flaming Pearl, China, etc.

CARLES, Arthur B. Painter. Member: Fellowship Penna. Academy of Fine Arts. Awards: Harris bronze medal ($300), Stotesbury prize, Penna. Academy of Fine Arts, 1919. Work: "An Actress as Cleopatra," Pennsylvania Academy of the Fine Arts. *Address,* 2007 Girard Ave., Philadelphia.

CARLES, Sarah. Painter. Exhibited at Penna. Academy of Fine Arts, Philadelphia, 1924. *Address,* 2007 Girard Ave., Philadelphia.

CARLETON, Clifford. Illustrator. Born Brooklyn, N. Y., 1867. Pupil of Art Students' League of New York under Mowbray. Member Society of Illustrators 1901. Illustrated: "Pembroke," by Julian Ralph; "Their Wedding Journey," by Howells. *Address,* 52 West 94th St., New York, N. Y.

CALHART, Genevieve Acee. Painter. Member: Society Independent Artists. *Address,* 131 Riverside Drive, New York, N. Y.

CARLIN, John. Born in Philadelphia, 1813. A deaf mute, graduate of the Penna. Institution for the Deaf and Dumb, 1825. Studied drawing under J. R. Smith and portrait painting under John Neagle; went to London, 1838, and made studies from the antiques in the British Museum; afterwards became a pupil of Paul Delaroche in Paris; returned to America, 1841, taking up his permanent residence in New York, and devoting himself to miniature painting for many years until interfered with by the progress of photography. After that his attention was turned to landscape and genre subjects, and the painting of portraits in oil. Loan Ex. Philadelphia, 1887.

CARLISLE, Mary Helen. Painter. Member National Academy of Painters and Sculptors. Award: McMillin prize, National Academy of Women Painters and Sculptors, 1914. *Address,* 24 West 40th St., New York, N. Y.

CARLSEN, Dines. Painter. Born in New York, N. Y., 1901. Pupil of Emil Carlsen. Award: Third Hallgarten prize, National Academy of Design, 1919. Elected an Associate Member of National Academy. Work: "The Brass Kettle," Corcoran Gallery of Art, Washington, D. C. *Address,* 43 East 59th St., New York, N. Y.

CARLSEN, Emil. Painter. Born in Copenhagen, Denmark, 1853; came to United States in 1872. Elected Associate Member of the National Academy, 1904; Academician, 1906. work: "The Open Sea" and "Still Life," Metropolitan Museum, New York; "Moonlight on the Kattegat," Albright Art Gallery, Buffalo; "Morning," Rhode Island School of Design, Providence; "The South Strand," National Gallery, Washington; "The Lazy Sea," Brooklyn Institute Museum; "Summer Clouds," Pennsylvania Academy of the Fine Arts, Philadelphia; "Moonlight on a Calm Sea," Corcoran Gallery of Art, Washington, D. C. *Address,* 43 East 59th St., New York, N. Y.

CARLSEN, John H. Painter and etcher. Born Arendal, Norway, 1875. Member: Palette and Chisel Club; Chicago Society of Artists. *Address,* 5230 West Congress St., Chicago, Ill.

CARLSON, Harry. Painter. Member: Society of Independent Artists. *Address,* 1909 59th St., Brooklyn, N. Y.

CARLSON, John F. Born in Sweden, 1875. Landscape painter; also teacher. Studied under American artists. Elected Associate National Academy, 1911, and Academician in 1925. New York Water Color Club; American Water Color Society; Salmagundi Club. Instructor, Woodstock School of Landscape Painting. *Address,* Woodstock, N. Y.

CARLSON, Margaret Goddard (Mrs. John Carlson). Painter. Born Plainsfield, N. J., 1882. Member: National Academy of Women Painters and Sculptors. *Address,* Woodstock, N. Y.

CARLSON, Mrs. Margaret Mitchell. Illustrator. Born Deming, Wash., 1892. *Address,* 393 Throckmorton Ave., Mill Valley, Calif.

CARMIENCKE, John Hermann. Painter. Born in Germany 1810 and died 1867. He came to America in 1848 and settled in Brooklyn. His paintings are faithful delineations of the forms of nature. He was an early member of the Brooklyn Academy and of the Artists' Fund Society of New York.

CARNALL, James L. Painter. Member of the Society of Independent Artists. *Address,* 80 Columbia Heights, Brooklyn, N. Y.

CARNELL, Althea J. Painter and illustrator. Member of the Plastic Club, Philadelphia. *Address,* 1907 North 7th St., Philadelphia.

CARPENTER, B. Carpenter was a line-engraver of landscapes and buildings, apparently working in Boston in 1855.

CARPENTER, Dudley S. Painter and illustrator. Born in Nashville, Tenn., 1880. Pupil of Art Students' League of New York, and of Julien Laurens and Constant in Paris. Member of Denver Art Association. *Address,* Mining Exchange Bldg., La Jolla, Calif.

CARPENTER, Ellen M. Born in Killingly, Conn., 1830. She visited Europe and studied in Paris under Lefebvre and Fleury. Amony her works are "The Yosemite Valley" and numerous portraits.

CARPENTER, Fletcher H. Painter. Born in Providence, R. I., in 1879. Member of Rochester Art Club. *Address,* 97 Middlesex Road, Rochester, N. Y.

CARPENTER, Francis Bicknell. Painter. Born in Homer, N. Y., 1830, and died in New York, 1900. In 1844 he became a pupil of Sanford Thayer at Syracuse, N. Y. In 1851 he removed to New York City and painted portraits of many prominent people: Lincoln, Fillmore, Greeley, Asa Packer, Lieut. Gov. Woodford, Ezra Cornell, Geo. Wm. Curtis, James Russell Lowell, Lewis Gass and many others. His most celebrated work "The Emancipation Proclamation" was exhibited in the large cities in 1864–65 and is now in the House of Representatives, Washington, D. C.

CARPENTER, Fred Green. Painter. Born Nashville, Tenn., 1882. Art study at St. Louis School of Fine Arts and later in Julien Academie, Paris. Pupil of Lucien Simon and Richard Miller. Instructor drawing and painting, St. Louis School Fine Arts. Represented in permanent collections of St. Louis City Art Museum, and John Herron Institute, Indianapolis, and Penna. Academy of Fine Arts. Honorable mention par droit, Salon des Artistes Francais, Paris, 1910; silver medal, Panama Expn., San Francisco, 1915. Member: Society Western Artists. *Address,* Washington University, St. Louis, Mo.

CARPENTER, Helen K. (Mrs.). Illustrator. Born in Philadelphia, 1881. Pupil of Penna. Academy of Fine Arts, under Chase, Breckenridge and Anshutz. *Address,* 75 West 55th St., New York.

CARPENTER, Horace T. Pupil of Penna. Academy of Fine Arts, and member of League of American Artists, New York. Portrait painter, and specializes on copies of early American historical pictures.

CARR, Alice R. Sculptor. Born in Roanoke, Va., 1899. Pupil of C. Stirling Calder. Member of Art Students' League of New York. *Address,* 934 State St., Santa Barbara, Calif.

CARR, Gene. Illustrator. Born in New York, 1881. Has been illustrator on staff of *New York World* and other papers since 1903. *Address*, "The World," New York City.

CARR, Michael C. Painter and engraver. Born in San Francisco, Calif., 1881. Pupil of Wilson Steer, Fredk. Brown and Gordon Craig. Awarded Slade Scholarship. *Address*, 711 Missouri Ave., Columbia, Mo.

CARRERE, John M. Died in 1914. Member of National Academy of Design, N. Y.

CARRIGAN, William L. Painter. Born San Francisco, Calif., 1868. Pupil of Emil Carlsen. *Address*, Falls Village, Conn.

CARROLL, John. Painter. Exhibited, Penna. Academy of Fine Arts, 1924. *Address*, Woodstock, New York.

CARSON, C. W. This man was a line-engraver of maps and vignettes, located in Albany, N. Y., in 1843.

CARSON, E. Francis. Painter. Born in Waltham, Mass., 1881. Member of Copley Society and Providence Water Color Club. *Address*, Craftsman Studio, 26 Lime St., Boston, Mass.

CARSPECKEN, George L. Painter. Born in Pittsburgh, Penna., 1884. Studied at Carnegie Institute, and abroad. Awarded first prize in 1902 at Worcester Art Museum. He died in 1905.

CARTER, Charles M. Painter. Born in Brookfield, Mass., in 1853. Student of Boston Art School and of European schools. *Address*, Care of C. R. Tuttle, 209 West Jackson Blvd., Chicago, Ill.

CARTER, Dennis Malone. Born in Ireland, 1827, and died 1881. He was accompanied by his parents to America in 1839. He painted portraits and historical pictures. He settled in New York City and was one of the original members of the Artists' Fund Society founded in 1859. He painted "Washington's Reception" (to Alex. Hamilton after his marriage to the daughter of Gen'l Schuyler) and numerous portraits.

CARTER, Mary M. (Mrs.). Miniature painter. Born in Philadelphia, 1864. Pupil of Carl Weber. *Address*, 2002 Spruce St., Philadelphia.

CARTOTTO, Ercole. Painter. Born in Italy in 1889. Pupil of Paxton, Hale, Benson and Tarbell in Boston. *Address*, 200 West 57th St., New York City.

CARTWRIGHT, Isabel Branson (Mrs.). Painter. Born Coatesville, Pa., 1885. Pupil

of Dangerfield, Snell and Frank Brangwyn. Awarded Art Club of Philadelphia Gold Medal for Water Colors, 1906. Exhibited at Penna. Academy of Fine Arts, Philadelphia, 1924. *Address*, 1823 Walnut St., Philadelphia.

CASARIN, Alexander. Painter and sculptor. Born in Mexico and educated in France. Studied with Messonier. Served in Franco-Prussian War. Became interested in sculpture and came to the United States. 'Specialty was portrait busts; his bust of President McKinley attracted considerable attention.

CASEAU, Charles H(enry). Painter, illustrator. Born Boston, Mass., 1880. Pupil of Boston Museum School of Fine Arts; Denman Ross. *Address*, 133 East 34th St., New York. N. Y.

CASELLAS, Fernando. Sculptor. He was born in Spain and came to this country in 1876. He designed a statue of Columbus and other decorations for the St. Louis Exposition. He was President of the American Sculpture Society. He was born in 1842 and died in New York, 1925.

CASER, Ettore. Painter and etcher. Born in Venice, 1880. Pupil of de Maria in Venice, he went to Boston, Mass., in 1908. Exhibited Penna. Academy of Fine Arts, 1924. *Address*, 1931 Broadway, New York, N. Y.

CASEY, F. De Sales. Illustrator. Member: Society of Illustrators. *Address*, Care of Life Publishing Co., 598 Madison Ave., New York, N. Y.

CASEY, J(ohn) J. Illustrator and painter. Born San Francisco, 1878. Pupil of Tarbell and Benson in Boston; Laurens, Julien and Lazar in Paris. *Address*, 278 West 11th St., New York, N. Y.

CASEY, Mrs. L. W. Painter. Member Society of Washington Artists. *Address*, Stoneleigh Court, Washington, D. C.

CASILAER, John W. Engraver and painter. Born in New York, 1811; died 1893. At the age of fifteen Casilaer was apprenticed to the engraver Peter Maverick, and after a time he became an excellent line engraver; his large plate of "A Sibyl," after the painting by Daniel Huntington, being an admirable example of pure line work. Having studied banknote engraving under Maverick and A. B. Durand, he was engaged in that business for some years, and about 1854 he became a member of the banknote engraving firm of Tappan, Carpenter, Casilaer & Co., of New York. But having become interested in painting in oil, and having studied painting in Europe in 1840 and in 1857, Casilaer became a landscape painter of reputation. He was an Associate of the National Academy in 1835, and a full Academician in 1851. The Metropolitan Museum owns his "View of the Catskills" painted 1891; and the Corcoran Gallery of Washington, D. C. owns his painting of "Lake George."

CASS, George N. For many years a resident of Boston. He studied with Inness and painted landscapes in oil and water colors. His pictures are generally owned in New England where they were popular. Among his works are "Evening on the Kennebeck River" and "A View in Medway, Mass." He died in Boston in 1882.

CASSATT, Mary. Figure painter and etcher. Born in Pennsylvania in 1855. Pupil of Pennsylvania Academy of the Fine Arts. Elected Associate of National Academy of Design, 1910; Legion of Honor, 1904. Miss Cassatt was associated with the modern French School of Monet, Renoir, Pissario and Degas. She has exhibited in the Paris Salon since 1872; her paintings are from child life, many of her groups being "Mother and Baby." Her work is represented in the principal American Museums.

CASSELL, John Harmon. Cartoonist. Born Nebraska City, Nebr., 1873. Pupil of Art Institute of Chicago. Member: Society of Illustrators, 1905. *Address*, "Evening World," Park Row, New York.

CASSIDY, I. D. Gerald. Painter and illustrator. Born Cincinnati, Ohio. Pupil of Cincinnati Academy; National Academy of Design of New York. Work: Decorations on Indian Arts Bldg., San Diego, Calif.; decorations "Last of the Indians," Hotel Gramatan, Bronxville, N. Y.; "Reflections" Freer Collection, Detroit, Mich. Represented in San Diego Museum, and Museum of New Mexico; Freer Collection, Washington, D. C. *Address*, 541 El Canimo del Canon, Santa Fe, N. M.

CASTELLO, Eugene. Painter. Born in Philadelphia, Pa., 1851. Pupil of Penna. Academy of the Fine Arts, under Eakins. Represented in Historical Society of Pennsylvania; University of Pennylvania. Correspondent, *American Art News, The Studio*, London

CASTLE, Montague. Painter. Member: Mural Painters. *Address*, 247 West 36th St., New York, N. Y.

CASTERTON, Mrs. Eda Nemoede. Miniature painter. Born Brillion, Wis., 1877. Pupil of Virginia Reynolds, Lawton S. Parker and Chicago Academy of Fine Arts. *Address*, Fine Arts Bldg., Chicago, Ill.

CATALANO, Guiseppi. Etcher. Member of Chicago Society of Etchers. *Address*, Chiesannova, Province of Trapani, Sicily.

CATLIN, George. Painter. Born in Wilkesbarre, Pa., in 1796; died in Jersey City, N. J., 1872. Catlin was noted for his portraits of American Indians. He lived and painted in Louisiana in the late 40's and early 50's. His collection of painting of Indians is now in the United States National Museum of Washington, D. C.

CATTON, Charles. Painter. Born in 1756 and died 1819. Painter of genre and still-life.

CAULDWELL, Leslie Giffen. Artist. Born in New York, 1861. Studied art in Julien Academy, Paris, 1884. Pupil of Boulanger, Lefebvre, Carolus-Durant. Had pictures admitted to Paris Salon, 1886 and 1888; also Paris Expn., 1889; Salon, Champs de Mars, 1890-1-2-3-4-5-6; also to Society British Artists, and Royal Academy, London. Exhibited at Liverpool and Berlin, and at National Academy Design, and Society of American Artists, New York; has since exhibited his paintings in various American cities and at World's Fair. Specialty, portraits in pastel. *Address*, 58 West 57th St., New York.

CAUSICI. An Italian who sculptured the "Washington" for the monument at Baltimore, and several subjects for Congress at Washington. He died in Havana. He modelled an equestrian statue of Washington at New York; it was erected in 1826.

CAVACOS, E(mmanuel). Sculptor and painter. Born Island of Kythera, Greece, 1885. Pupil of Ephraim Keyser in Baltimore; Jules Coutan and V. Peter in Paris. Member: Baltimore Water Color Club. Award: Rinehart Paris Scholarship. Work: "Aspiration," Enoch Pratt Free Library; "Penseur," Peabody Institute, Baltimore.

CAVANAGH, J. Albert. Painter. Member: Salma. Club. *Address*, 25 East 26th St., New York, N. Y.

CAVERLEY, Charles. Sculptor. Born in Albany, 1833. Pupil of E. D. Palmer in Albany. He was elected to the National Academy in 1871. He is represented in the Metropolitan Museum of New York by a bust of Robert Burns. He died in Essex Falls, N. J., in 1914.

CECERE, Gaetano. Sculptor. Born in New York, 1894. Awarded Scholarship 1920, American Academy in Rome. *Address*, 426 East 15th St., New York City.

CERRACCHI, Enrico Filiberto. Sculptor. Born in Italy, 1880; came to America in 1900, and settled at Houston, Texas. Principal works: Monument to John A. Wharton, State Capitol, Austin, Texas; "The American Doughboy" for Italian Government. *Address*, 705 Harold St., Houston, Texas.

CERRACCHI, Guiseppe. An Italian sculptor, who arrived in Philadelphia in 1791. He executed a bust of Washington, and also made portraits of Jefferson, Clinton, Hamilton, Jay Benson, and Paul Jones. His portrait painted in miniature by Trumbull is in Yale Museum. On returning to France he was guillotined for his conspiracies against Napoleon.

CHACE, Dorothea. Painter and sculptor. Born in Buffalo, N. Y., 1894. Member of Art Students' League of New York. *Address,* 108 Dorchester Road, Buffalo, N. Y.

CHADEAYNE, Robert O. Painter. Exhibited at the Penna. Academy of Fine Arts, Philadelphia, 1920. *Address,* Firthcliffe, New York.

CHADWICK, Arch. D. Painter. Born in Ovid, N. Y., in 1871. Scenic artist, also theatrical and motion-picture studio productions. *Address,* 945 Cliff St., Ithaca, N. Y.

CHADWICK, Charles Wesley. Engraver. Born Red-Hook-on-the-Hudson, N. Y., 1861. Studied wood-engraving under Frederick Juengling, William Miller. Work has appeared mostly in *Century Magazine* and *Scribner's Magazine;* now engaged in finishing and engraving half-tone plates. Exhibited at Paris Expn., 1900; bronze medal, Buffalo Expn., 1901; St. Louis Expn., 1904; silver medal, Panama Expn., San Francisco, 1915. Has lectured on wood-engraving. *Address,* 137 E. 150th St., New York.

CHADWICK, William. Painter. Exhibited at Penna. Academy of Fine Arts, 1924. *Address,* Blackhall, Lyme, Conn.

CHAFFEE, Oliver N. Painter. Born in Detroit, Mich., 1881. Pupil of Wm. M. Chase, Robt. Henri and Miller. *Address,* 141 East 21st St., New York City.

CHALFANT, J. D. Painter. Born in Pennsylvania, 1856. Pupil of Bouguereau and Lefebvre in Paris. *Address,* "Ashley," Wilmington, Del.

CHALFIN, Paul. Mural painter. Born in New York City, 1874. Awarded Lazarus Scholarship for mural painting, 1905. *Address,* 597 Fifth Ave., New York.

CHAMBERLAIN, Arthur B. Painter. Born in Canada in 1860. Member of Rochester Art Club. *Address,* 16 Gladstone St., Rochester, N. Y.

CHAMBERLAIN, Judith. Painter. Born in San Francisco, Calif., in 1893. Pupil of Max Weber. *Address,* 728 Montgomery St., San Francisco, Calif.

CHAMBERLIN, Edna W. Sculptor. Exhibited "The Muff" at the Penna. Academy of Fine Arts, Philadelphia, 1925. *Address,* Hobart Ave., Summit, New Jersey.

CHAMBERLIN, F. Tolles. Painter, sculptor, and etcher. Born in San Francisco, Calif., in 1873. Pupil of D. W. Tryon and George de Forrest Brush. Also executed mural paintings. *Address,* 223 South Catalina Ave., Pasadena, Calif.

CHAMBERS, C. B. Painter and illustrator. Born in St. Louis, Mo., 1883. Has painted the decorations and altar pieces in St. Ignatius Church, Chicago. Also portraits in Missouri Historical Society at St. Louis. *Address,* Carnegie Hall, New York City.

CHAMBERS, Charles E. Illustrator. Born in Ottumwa, Ind. Pupil of Art Institute, Chicago, and Art Students' League of New York. Illustrates for *Harper's Magazine. Address,* Waldo Ave., Riverdale-on-Hudson, N. Y.

CHAMBERS, Christine F. Painter. Exhibited at Penna. Academy of Fine Arts, Philadelphia, 1924. *Address,* 1530 Pine St., Philadelphia.

CHAMBERS, Hallie W. (Mrs.). Painter. Born in Louisville, Ky., in 1881. Pupil of Hugh Breckenridge. Specialty, still-life painting. *Address,* 100 East Main St., Louisville, Kentucky.

CHAMBERS, R. This engraver was doing some fairly good work, in both line and stipple, Washington, D. C., about 1820–26. His best work, noted by the writer, is a bust of Thomas Jefferson, in an oak-garlanded circle, heading a facsimile of a letter written by Jefferson to R. C. Weightman, Mayor of Baltimore. The letter is dated June 24, 1826, and the engraving seems from its inscription to be of contemporaneous date.

CHAMBERS, Robert William. Painter. Born in Brooklyn, 1865. Student in Julien Academy, Paris, 1886–93. First exhibited in Salon, 1889. Illustrator for *Life, Truth, Vogue,* etc. *Address,* 43 East 83d St., New York City.

CHAMPLAIN, Duane. Sculptor. Born in Black Mountain, North Carolina, in 1889. Student of Art Students' League of New York. *Address,* 509 West 161st St., New York.

CHAMPLIN, Ada B. Painter. Born in St. Louis, Mo. Pupil of Art Institute, Chicago, and Art Students' League, New York. *Address,* 640 Prospect Ave., Pasadena, Calif.

CHAMPNEY, Benjamin. Painter. Born in New Hampshire in 1817, he went to Boston and worked in Pendleton's lithographic establishment. He later studied in Europe, and on his return to this country turned his attention to landscape painting. He was president of the Boston Art Club, and died in 1907.

CHAMPNEY, James Wells ("Champ"). Painter. Born in Boston, in 1843. Pupil of Lowell Institute, he studied wood-engraving. In 1866 went to Europe studying in Paris and Antwerp. Returned and opened his studio in Boston. He paints genre subjects in oil and pastel. Elected an Associate Member of the National Academy in 1882. He died in 1903.

CHANDLER, George W. Etcher. Born in Milwaukee, Wis. Pupil of Julien Academy in Paris. His work is in the Petit-Palais, Paris, Victoria and Albert Museum, London, and Congressional Library, Washington, D. C.

CHANDLER, Helen C. Painter, illustrator and etcher. Born in Wellington, Kans., in 1881. Pupil of MacMonnies and Birge Harrison. Member of San Francisco Art Association. *Address*, 543 North Heliotrope Drive, Los Angeles, Calif.

CHANDLER, Robert W. Mural painter and designer. Exhibited at Cincinnati Museum in 1925. *Address*, 147 East 19th St., New York City.

CHANDLER, Winthrop. Painter. Born 1747 and died 1790. Early American portrait painter, who studied art in Boston. Several of his portraits are preserved in Woodstock and Thompson, Conn., and in Worcester and Petersham, Mass.

CHAPEL, Guy M. Painter. Born in Detroit in 1871. Pupil of Art Institute, Chicago. *Address*, 3919 North Kenneth Ave., Chicago, Ill.

CHAPIN, Archibald B. Illustrator and cartoonist. Born at Mt. Vernon, Ohio, in 1875. *Address*, 435 Clay Ave., Kirkwood, Mo.

CHAPIN, Henry. An artist of that name was said to be painting pictures in America, flourishing towards the last of the 18th or early 19th centuries.

CHAPIN, James O. Painter. Born in West Orange, New York, in 1887. Pupil of Antwerp Royal Academy, and Society of Independent Painters of America. *Address*, 232 West 14th St., New York City.

CHAPIN, Lucy C. Painter. Born Syracuse, N. Y., 1873. Pupil of Baschet, Merson, Collin and Prinet in Paris. Member: Graduates' Club, College of Fine Arts, Syracuse University. Work: Portrait of Chief Justices Ezekiel Whitman and Prentiss Mellen, in State Gallery, Capitol, Augusta, Me.; "Portrait of Bishop Eveland," Dickinson Seminary, Williamsport, Pa.

CHAPIN, William. Engraver. Born in Philadelphia, 1802; died there 1888. William Chapin was a lineal descendant of Deacon Samuel Chapin, who settled at Springfield, Conn., in 1642. In 1817 William Chapin was apprenticed to John Vallance of the engraving firm of Tanner, Vallance, Kearny & Co., of Philadelphia. He remained with this firm until 1822, when he purchased his freedom for $125, and then began business for himself as an engraver. In December of the same year he made a contract with the Baltimore publisher, Fielding Lucas, to engrave for him for the sum of $416 per annum or less than $35 per month, and in 1824 he accepted a similar engagement with a New York firm for $520 per year.

About 1827 Mr. Chapin turned his attention to projecting and engraving maps, and in time he established an extensive map business in New York. Chapin's large map of the United States is said to be the first map engraved upon steel in this country.

In 1838 Mr. Chapin became much interested in the education of the blind, and in 1840 he permanently abandoned engraving and map publishing to become the principal of an institution for the blind in Columbus, O., and in 1849 Mr. Chapin was elected principal of the Institution for the Blind in the city of Philadelphia, and to this work he devoted the remainder of his life.

For these notes upon Mr. Chapin the compiler is indebted to the courtesy of his son, John Basset Chapin, M.D., physician in charge of the Pennsylvania Hospital for the Insane in Philadelphia.

CHAPLIN, Christine (Mrs. Brush). Painter. Born in Bangor, Me., in 1842. Studied in London and Paris. Her specialty is painting wild flowers in water color.

CHAPLIN, James. Painter. *Address*, Care of Seattle Fine Arts Society, Seattle, Washington.

CHAPLIN, Margaret. Painter. Member: National Academy of Women Painters and Sculptors. *Address*, 346 West 22d St., New York, N. Y.

CHAPMAN, Carlton Theodore. Painter and illustrator. Born in New London, Ohio, in 1860. Student of National Academy, Art Students' League of New York and Julien Academy in Paris. Specialty, marines and landscapes. Represented in Brooklyn Institute by "Gloucester Harbor" and at Toledo Museum by "Rocky Coast." He died in 1925.

CHAPMAN, Charles S. Painter. Born in Morristown, N. Y., 1879. Pupil of Chase and W. Appleton Clark. Member: Salma. Club; Academy of National Artists. Elected an Associate Member of the National Academy. Awards: First Shaw prize, Salmagundi Club; Saltus gold medal, National Academy of Design. Work: "In the Deep Woods," Metropolitan Museum, New York. *Address*, Leonia, N. J.

CHAPMAN, Conrad Wise. Painter. Son of the artist John Gadsby Chapman, was born in Rome, and studied with his father. When the Civil War started he joined the Confederate troops and made many pictures of army life. After the war he lived in Virginia where he died. His painting of "Fort Sumter" is in Richmond, with a collection of his paintings of the war.

CHAPMAN, C. Durand. Painter. Born Irvington, N. J., 1856. Pupil of Wilmarth and J. G. Brown in New York; Cormon and Constant in Paris. *Address*, 3323 Wisconsin Ave., Washington, D. C.

CHAPMAN, Esther McCord. Painter. Member Washington Water Color Club. *Address*, 1600 Q St., Washington, D. C.

CHAPMAN, John Gadsby. Painter and engraver. Born in Alexandria, Va., 1808; died in Brooklyn 1890. Little of Mr. Chapman's early life is known other than that he studied art in Italy and in 1836 he opened a studio in New York. For some time thereafter he was largely employed by the Harper Bros. and by others as a designer for book-illustrations, as a wood-engraver, and an etcher after his own designs. He did not engrave upon copper in line or stipple. In 1848 Mr. Chapman returned to Italy and devoted himself entirely to painting, maintaining a studio in Rome until his death. Two of Mr. Chapman's sons, Conrad Wise and John Linton Chapman, were painters and artist etchers. Both of these sons were born in Rome. The first-named served in the Confederate Army throughout the Civil War, and died some years ago; the other was living in 1900. A daughter, Mary Chapman, married Count Cerovitch, one time private secretary to Victor Emanuel, late King of Italy. John Gadsby Chapman had his studio for several years in Washington, D. C., during which period he painted "The Baptism of Pocahontas" now in the rotunda of the Capitol.

CHAPMAN, Kenneth Milton. Painter. Born Ligonier, Ind., 1875. Pupil of Art Institute of Chicago; New York Art Students' League. Work: Three murals, Museum of New Mexico; illustrator of works on Natural Sciences; writer and lecturer on Indian Art. *Address*, Museum of New Mexico.

CHAPMAN, Minerva J. Painter. Born Altmar, N. Y., 1858. Pupil of Art Institute of Chicago, and Annie Shaw; Robert Fleury, Bouguereau, Courtois and Chas. Lazar in Paris. *Address*, 9 Rue Falguiere, Paris, France.

CHAPMAN, W. E. Painter. *Address*, 18 East 90th St., New York, N. Y.

CHARD, Louise Cable. Painter. Member: Society Independent Artists. *Address*, 54 Melrose Place, Montclair, N. J.

CHARD, Walter G. Sculptor. Born Buffalo, N. Y., 1880. Pupil of Charles Grafly; School of the Museum of Fine Arts, Boston; Beaux Arts Institute of Design. *Address*, Fenway Studios, Ipswich St., Boston, Mass.

CHARLES, H. He signed a number of crudely engraved copper-plates published in Philadelphia in 1810. As William Charles did not establish himself in Philadelphia until 1816, he can not be connected with him.

CHARLES, S. M. Miniature painter. 1836. Portrait, "Andrew Jackson" (miniature), signed "S. M. Charles."

CHARLES, William. Engraver. Died in Philadelphia, 1820. Mr. Lossing says that William Charles was a Scotchman who was compelled to hastily depart from Edinburgh to escape prosecution for caricaturing some of the dignitaries of that city. Dr. Anderson says Charles came to New York in 1801, and in 1807 he was established in this city as an engraver and publisher at "Charles Repository of Arts." The directories of Philadelphia locate him in that city from 1816 to 1820, inclusive; he was in business there as a copper-plate engraver, as a bookseller and as a publisher and stationer.

Charles engraved in line-stipple, and in aquatint, but he is best known by his series of caricatures, chiefly of events connected with the War of 1812, or with local politics. These war etchings were issued in 1813, in connection with S. Kennedy.

CHARMAN, Laura B. Sculptor. Member: Fellowship Penna. Academy of Fine Arts. *Address*, Magnolia, N. J.

CHARMAN, Montague. Painter. Exhibited water colors at Annual Exhibition of Water Colors at Penna. Academy of Fine Arts, Philadelphia, 1925. *Address*, 615 Walnut Ave. Syracuse, N. Y.

CHARON. This name is evidently fictitious; it appears on a stipple quarto plate, representing a hussar with a goose on his back in the background is a cottage with an American flag on a pole with people dancing.

CHARPENTIER, Auguste. A French American portrait painter. Born in Paris 1815, and died in Besancon in 1880. He was a pupil of Ingres, and exhibited in the Paris Salon of 1833. He lived and had his studio for many years in New Orleans, where he painted numerous fine portraits.

CHASE, Adelaide Cole (Mrs. William) Portrait painter. Born in Boston, 1868, daughter of the artist J. Foxcroft Cole. Pupil of Tarbell in Boston, and Carolus Duran in Paris. Elected an Associate of the National

Academy of Design, 1906. Represented by "The Violinist" in the Boston Museum of Fine Arts.

CHASE, Edward L. Illustrator. *Address*, Woodstock, N. Y.

CHASE, Ellen Wheeler. Painter. Born Faribault, Minn. Studied in Buffalo, New York City, Boston, under Tarbell, and Rene Menard and Lucien Simon, Paris. Member: Buffalo Society of Artists. *Address*, The Meyer Studios, 1110 Elmwood Ave., Buffalo, N. Y.

CHASE, Elsie Rowland (Mrs. Frederick S. Chase). Painter. Born Saratoga Springs, N. Y., 1863. Pupil of Yale School of Fine Arts. Member: Hartford Art Club; National Art Club; Society of Independent Artists. *Address*, 165 Grove St., Waterbury, Conn.

CHASE, Frank Swift. Painter. Born St. Louis, Mo., 1886. Member of Allied Association of Artists; Salma. Club. Work: "Morning Shadows," South Carolina Art Association, Charleston, S. C.

CHASE, Harry. Born in Woodstock, Vt., 1853, and died 1889. He studied at The Hague, and in Paris. On his return he opened his studio in New York. He was elected an associate of the National Academy in 1883. His principal work: "The Harbor of New York," at the Corcoran Art Gallery; "Low Tide," "Outbound Whaler," "The North River," and "Bringing the Fish Ashore."

CHASE, Jessie Kalmbach (Mrs. Wilfrid E. Chase). Landscape painter. Born Bailey's Harbor, Wis., 1879. Pupil of Art Institute of Chicago and Frederick Fursman. Member: Wisc. Painters and Sculptors.

CHASE, Joseph Cummings. Artist. Born Kents Hill, Me., 1878. Studied art at Pratt Institute, New York; Penna. Academy Fine Arts; Academie Julien, Paris, under Jean Paul Laurens. Exhibited in Paris Salon; won 1st and 2d prizes, Grunwaldt poster competition, Paris, 1904. Portrait painter. As war artist, painted at the front 142 portraits of officers of A. E. F., including General Pershing and staff; also many "Doughboys" who had been cited for extraordinary heroism in action, and several officers of the Allies, including Marshal Foch. *Address*, 222 West 23d St., New York, N. Y.

CHASE, Marion Monks. Painter. Born Boston, Mass. Pupil of G. L. Noyes. *Address*, 144 Brattle St., Cambridge, Mass.

CHASE, Sidney Marsh. Painter and illustrator. Born in Haverhill, Mass., 1877. Pupil of Tarbell, and Howard Pyle. *Address*, 4 Mt. Vernon St., Haverhill, Mass.

CHASE, Susan B. (Mrs.). Painter. Born in St. Louis, Mo. Pupil of H. B. Snell and R. E. James. *Address*, 1811 Riggs Place, Washington, D. C.

CHASE, Wendall W. Painter and etcher. Born in Foxcroft, Maine, in 1875. Pupil of Geo. L. Noyes and Hawthorne. *Address*, 9–A Park Square, Boston, Mass.

CHASE, William Merritt. Painter. Born at Franklin, Ind., in 1849. A pupil of B. F. Hayes, of Indianapolis, he was a local portrait painter for a time, but came east to study under J. O. Eaton and in the schools of the Academy in New York. In 1872 he went to Munich. His masters there were Alexander Wagner and Karl Von Piloty. His studies in the great art museums have never been given up, and his travels include sojourns in Spain, the Low Countries, France, England and Italy. Mr. Chase was for ten years president of the Society of American Artists, and has been most successful with his work in portraiture; his "Carmencita" and his "James McNeill Whistler" are owned by the Metropolitan Museum of New York. The Cleveland Museum owns "Alice in Her Grandmother's Gown" and his portrait of Miss Dora Wheeler. Elected a Member of the National Academy in 1890. Mr. Chase died in 1916.

CHATTERTON, Clarence K. Painter. Born at Newburgh, N. Y., 1880. Pupil of Henri, Case, and Miller. *Address*, Care of Vassar College, Poughkeepsie, N. Y.

CHENEY, Benjamin and Timothy. Engravers. These clock-makers of East Hartford, Conn., were working about 1781–1801, and their well-engraved brass clock-faces show very considerable skill in handling the burin. They are referred to by Mr. James Terry, in his "Ex Libris Leaflet, No. 4."

CHENEY, John. Engraver. Born at South Manchester, Conn., 1801; died there 1885. This unexcelled line-engraver of small heads and book illustrations was working as an engraver in Boston in 1829, and in 1833 he went to Europe to study art, supporting himself there by engraving for American publishers. Disheartened by the lack of encouragement for art in this country, he virtually abandoned engraving while he was still comparatively a young man. A life of John Cheney, by Ednah D. Cheney, was published in 1889; and a very complete check-list of the engraved work of both John and Seth W. Cheney has been compiled by the late Mr. S. R. Koehler, Boston, 1891. John Cheney also drew upon stone for some of the Boston lithographers.

CHENEY, Russell. Painter. Born in South Manchester, Conn., in 1881. Pupil of Kenyon Cox and William M. Chase. Trained at Art Students' League, New York, and Academie

Julien in Paris. Among his works, "Garden of the Gods," "Chartes," "Woodstock," "November," and the "Red Barns." He paints still-life as well as landscapes.

CHENEY, Seth Wells. Painter and engraver. Born at South Manchester, Conn., 1810; died in Boston, 1856. In 1829 S. W. Cheney joined his brother, John Cheney, in Boston, and with him learned to engrave. After working with a publishing firm in Brattleboro, Vt., for about a year, he accompanied John Cheney to Europe in 1833, and studied in Paris under Isabey, Delaroche, and other French masters. Seth W. Cheney returned home in 1834, and then spent several years in Ohio, with another brother, in an attempt at growing mulberry trees and rearing silk-worms. He again went to Europe in 1837 and resumed his art studies in France, Italy and Germany. In 1841 he opened a studio in Boston. He there began to draw portraits in crayon, which by their artistic merit earned him much-deserved fame, and to Seth W. Cheney belongs the credit of having been practically the first among American artists to effectively work in "black and white." The line-engravings of Seth W. Cheney are comparatively few in number. His life was written by Ednah D. Cheney, and published in Boston, 1881. A memorial exhibition of the work of John and Seth Wells Cheney at the Boston Museum in 1893 included 338 engravings, paintings, drawings and two or three objects of sculpture.

CHERRY, Emma R. (Mrs.). Painter. Born in Aurora, Ill., in 1859. Pupil of Art Students' League of New York, and Julien Academy of Paris. *Address*, 608 Fargo Ave., Houston, Tex.

CHERRY, Kathryn (Mrs.). Painter. Born Quincy, Ill., in 1880. Pupil of Hugh Breckenridge, and the St. Louis Art School. Specialty, landscapes. Exhibited, Penna. Academy of Fine Arts, 1924. *Address*, 4432 Washington Boulevard, St. Louis, Missouri.

CHESDEBIEN. Miniature painter. Flourished 1783 in Baltimore. See his announcement in *Maryland Gazette* and *Baltimore Advertiser*, November 7, 1783.

CHILD, Edwin Burrage. Painter. Born Gouverneur, N. Y., 1868. Studied art at Art Students' League, New York, 1891, and was a pupil of John La Farge. Asst. of John La Farge in glass work and mural painting for several years. Exhibited regularly in Society of American Artists, and National Academy of Design, and other important annual exhibitions. Illustrator of many articles in *Scribner's* and other periodicals and contributor to magazines. Recently engaged chiefly in portrait painting. *Address*, 42 West 93d St., New York, N. Y.

CHILD, Louis. Portrait painter, working in New York about 1800. His portrait of Micah Hawkins is inscribed on back of canvas, "Retouched from memory by Wm. S. Mount, 1856."

CHILD, Thomas. Early American portrait painter, noted by Dunlap as being in Boston in 1688.

CHILDS, Benjamin F. Wood engraver. Was born at Cambridge, 1814, and died 1863. In 1850 he became superintendent of engraving for the Tract Society. He engraved the illustrations after drawings by Darley for Irving's "Knickerbocker's History of New York," published by Wiley and Putnam of New York, in 1853.

CHILDS, Cephas G. Engraver. Born in Bucks Co., Penna., 1793; died in Philadelphia, 1871. Childs was taught to engrave by Gideon Fairman in Philadelphia, and as a "historical and landscape engraver" his name appears in the directories of that city from 1818 to 1845, inclusive. Probably his earliest signed work is to be found in S. F. Bradford's edition of the Edinburgh Encyclopedia.

Childs issued his "Views of Philadelphia" in 1826–33, many of these being engraved by himself. After a visit to Europe, he associated himself with the artist Henry Inman, under the firm name of Childs & Inman. This firm, which was in existence from 1831 to 1835, brought P. S. Duval from Europe and placed him at the head of the lithographic department; this added to their general engraving business. Inman drew upon the stone himself, and their deaf and dumb apprentice, Albert Newsam, executed some of his best work for the firm of Childs & Inman, and became the foremost lithographic artist of his day.

Cephas G. Childs was a very good engraver of portraits in stipple and landscape and vignettes in line, though his signed work is not very abundant. In 1822 the firm of Childs & Carpenter was publishing elaborately engraved business-cards and script work in Philadelphia.

About 1845 Childs abandoned engraving and interested himself in newspaper work in Philadelphia. Along with Walter Colton he was one of the editors of *The Commercial Herald*, John R. Walker being the publisher. He was afterward commercial editor of *The North American*, published by Thomas R. Newbold. Childs established the "Philadelphia Commercial List," and published that journal for many years at the corner of Dock Street and Bank Alley, Philadelphia.

Childs was a soldier in the War of 1812, and was long interested in the volunteer military organizations of Philadelphia. He was for a time captain of the Washington Grays, and was colonel of one of the militia regiments of his city.

CHILDS, Lillian E. Miniature painter. Born in Little Silver, N. J. Pupil of William M. Chase in New York and Art Institute of Chicago. *Address*, 85 Washington Place, New York City.

CHILTON, William B. Painter. Born in Washington, D. C., in 1856. Pupil of Art Students' League of Washington. *Address*, 1961 Biltmore St., Washington, D. C.

CHIQUET. Evidently a French engraver. His American work consists of a crudely executed plate of ''Perry's Victory.'' The date is about 1812.

CHISOHN, Mary B. Painter. Exhibited at National Association of Women Painters and Sculptors, 1924. *Address*, 1337 Lexington Ave., New York.

CHITTENDEN, Alice B. Painter. Born in Brockport, Maine, in 1860. Pupil of California School of Design. Painted portraits of Rt. Rev. William F. Nicholls, and six portraits for California Society of Pioneers. *Address*, 2230 Pacific Ave., San Francisco, Calif.

CHORLEY, John. Engraver. All that the writer has been able to discover about this man is that he was a fairly good line-engraver of portraits and book-illustrations, and was working in Boston as early as 1818. Upon a well-executed Bible print the name is signed ''I. P. Chorley Sc.''

CHOUINARD, Nelbert M. Painter and designer. Pupil of Batchelder, Ralph Johonnot and the Pratt Institute. *Address*, 2606 West 8th St., Los Angeles, Calif.

CHRISTY, Howard Chandler. Illustrator and portrait painter. Born in Morgan County, Ohio, 1873. He was employed as an illustrator on *Harper's* and *Scribner's* Magazines. He has recently devoted his time to painting portraits. Among his best known pictures is the portrait of Mrs. William Randolph Hearst of New York, and of Secretary of State Hughes. *Address*, 15 West 67th St., New York City.

CHUBB, T. Y. Engraver. About 1860 Chubb was an engraver of portraits in mezzotint and in a mixed manner. He worked for the book publishers. He is also said to have painted a few portraits and genre subjects.

CHUBBUCK, Thomas. Engraver of portraits and landscapes in line and stipple. He was located in Springfield, Mass.

CHURBUCK, Leander M. Painter. Born in Wareham, Mass., in 1861. Pupil of Boston Art Students' Association. His painting ''On the Cape Ann Shore'' is in the Municipal Gallery, Brockton, Mass. *Address*, 270 Green St., Brockton, Mass.

CHURCH, Angelica Schuyler. Sculptor. Born at Scarborough-on-Hudson, New York, 1878. Pupil of New York School of Design, and of Alphonse Mucha. Represented by statue of the Savior, in Calvary Church, N. Y., Mark Twain portrait-tablet, and ''The Rescue'' erected for New York City Police Department. *Address*, 212 Spring St., Ossining-on-Hudson, N. Y.

CHURCH, Charles F. Painter. Member of Chicago Society of Artists. *Address*, 9244 South Winchester Ave., Chicago, Ill.

CHURCH, Frederick Edwin. Painter. Born Hartford, Conn., 1826; died New York, 1900. Landscape painter. Pupil of Thomas Cole at Catskill, where he worked for several years before opening a studio in New York. Was elected a member of the National Academy of Design in 1849. Traveled in South America in 1853 and 1857; later visited Labrador and the West Indies, and in 1868 made his first trip through Europe, which also extended to Palestine. Received a second-class medal at the Paris Exposition, 1867. His best known work is ''The Falls of Niagara,'' owned by the Corcoran Gallery of Art; also the ''Aurora Borealis.''

CHURCH, Frederick Stuart. Painter. Born Grand Rapids, Mich., 1842; died 1923. Pupil of Chicago Academy of Design, L. E. Wilmarth, Walter Shirlaw, National Academy of Design and Art Students' League of New York. Silver medal, St. Louis Exp., 1904. Painter in oil and water color, illustrator and etcher. His pictures are generally of animal life or figures. National Academy, 1885. Member: American Water Color Society; New York Etching Club; Society of Illustrators, New York. Studio, New York. His painting ''Moonrise'' (a nude woman with auburn hair is partly seen through rolling green waves; back of her, in the water, is a crescent) is in the Metropolitan Museum, New York.

CHURCHILL, Alfred Vance. Painter. Born Oberlin, Ohio, 1864. Student Berlin, Leipzig, and Academie Julien, Paris, 1887–90; University of Paris, 1904–6. Director of art department and professor of fine arts, Ia. (now Grinnell) College. *Address*, 38 Franklin St., Northampton, Mass.

CHURCHILL, Francis G. Painter, illustrator and etcher. Born in New Orleans in 1876. Pupil of Cincinnati Academy. *Address*, Canal-Commercial Bldg., New Orleans, La.

CHURCHILL, Letha E. Painter. *Address*, 3919 Wyandotte St., Kansas City, Mo.

CHURCHILL, William W. Painter. Born in Jamaica Plains, Mass., in 1858, and lives in Boston. Pupil of Bonnat in Paris. ''Leisure'' (girl dressed in white), signed and dated 1910, is in Boston Museum of Fine Arts Collection. *Address*, Fenway Studios, Boston, Mass.

CHURCHMAN, E. Mendenhall. Painter. Born Brooklyn, N. Y. Pupil of Penna. Academy of Fine Arts, Tarbell and Benson in Boston. Member: Fellowship Penna. Academy of Fine Arts; Plastic Club; Society Independent Artists. *Address*, Union Lane, Brielle, N. J.

CIAMPAGILA, Cario. Painter. Born in Italy. Award: American Academy in Rome Scholarship, 1920. *Address*, Care of the American Academy in Rome, Rome, Italy; also 555 Newark St., Hoboken, N. J.

CIANI, Vittorio A. Sculptor. Born in Florence, Italy, 1858; died in Perth Amboy, N. J., 1908. At the age of 12 his family moved to Rome, where he entered the Royal Academy of Art, studying under Professor Mazzini, winning several prizes, and graduating with the privilege of entering the studio of the celebrated Monteverdi. In 1889 he married an American, and soon thereafter opened a studio in New York. Among his works are: Panels and fireplace for ''The Breakers,'' the Newport home of the Vanderbilts; group, ''Appollo, Tragedy and Comedy,'' proscenium arch, Pabst's Theatre, Milwaukee, Wisc.; reredos, The Lord's Supper, St. Bartholomew's Church, New York; Langdon Memorial, Grace Church, New York; Landing of the Pilgrims, Earle Hall, Columbia College, New York; portrait busts of Austin Corbin and George Clinton.

CIAVARRA, Pietro. Sculptor. Born in Philadelphia, 1891. Pupil of Charles Grafly, Guiseppe Donato, Charles T. Scott. Member: Fellowship Penna. Academy of Fine Arts. *Address*, 207 North 64th St., Philadelphia, Pa.

CICERI, Eugene. Painter, working in New Orleans about 1850.

CIMIOTTI, Gustave. Painter. Born in New York City, 1875. Studied at Art Students' League 1895-9, and with H. S. Mowbray, J. C. Beckwith, Kenyon Cox, New York; Julien Academy and Delecluse Academy 1900, and with Benjamin Constant, Paris. Exhibited at Society of American Artists, National Academy of Design, Corcoran Gallery, etc. Member: Salmagundi Club, Allied Artists of America. *Address*, 51 West 10th St., New York City, N. Y.

CLAGHORN, J. C. Painter. Born in Philadelphia, 1869. Pupil of Penna. Academy of Fine Arts. *Address*, 3115 Hiatt Place, N. W., Washington, D. C.

CLAGUE, Richard. Painter. Born in Louisiana in 1816; died in New Orleans, 1878. He studied with Ernest Hebert and at École des Beaux Arts, Paris. Clague has left us many landscapes portraying, in a poetic and forceful manner, street scenes in New Orleans, and Louisiana scenery.

CLAPP, William H. Painter and engraver. Born Montreal, Canada. Pupil of Jean Paul Laurens. Member: Royal Canadian Academy; Canadian Art Club; Pen and Pencil Club, Columbus, Ohio; Montreal Art Club; Oakland Artist Association. Work in Canadian National Gallery, Montreal Art Gallery, Oakland Art Gallery, and landscape owned by Ontario Provincial Government.

CLARK. As ''Clark Sculpt'' this man signed three very poorly executed copperplates of buildings in Lancaster, Pa. The work was done evidently between 1813 and 1820.

CLARK. Miniature artist, flourishing in Philadelphia, 1795. He died in 1800. Dunlap says that John Wesley Javis speaks of ''Clark, a miniature painter'' as living in Philadelphia during his school days.

CLARK, A. Engraver. Dunlap says that A. Clark was born at Cooperstown, N. Y., and about 1825 he, with Ralph Rawdon, were members of the firm of Rawdon, Clark & Co., general engravers of Albany, N. Y. In 1834 Clark was in business in New York City.

CLARK, Adele. Painter. Pupil of D. J. Connah, Kenneth Hayes Miller, Henri and Chase. Member Richmond Art Club. Work: ''Portrait of R. A. Dunlop,'' Richmond Chamber of Commerce.

CLARK, Allan. Sculptor. Born in Missoula, Mont., in 1896. Pupil of Polasek at Art Institute of Chicago. Member of National Sculpture Society, and Society of Independent Artists. Work: Bronze statue, ''The Antelope Dance''; Marble bust, ''Mme. Galli-Curci.'' *Address*, 436 West 24th St., New York.

CLARK, Alson Skinner. Painter and illustrator. Born in Chicago in 1856. Student of Chicago Art Institute. Pupil of Whistler and Mucha in Paris, and Chase in New York. Work: ''The Coffee House,'' ''The Bridge Builders,'' ''The Song of the Nightingale,'' and many lithographs.

CLARK, Alvin. Painter and engraver. He was born in Ashfield, Mass., 1804. He was an engraver and was employed for a short time in Boston, where he made water colors and India ink portraits. He also painted in Providence, R. I., New York and Fall River, Mass. In 1835 he commenced to make miniatures and large portraits. At forty years of age Clark became interested in telescopes and made the first achromatic lenses manufactured in this country. Alvin Clark died in Cambridge, Mass., 1864. He painted miniatures of his wife, his brother, also an engraver (Barnabus Clark), and Lucius M. Sargent; also a large portrait of his brother Barnabus.

CLARK, C. H. Painter. Pupil of Julien and Delecluse Academies in Paris. *Address*, 432 Baldwin St., Meadville, Pa.

CLARK, Eliot Candee. Painter. Born New York, 1883; self-taught. Represented in New York Water Color Club at 9, and in National Academy at 13 years of age; residence and travel abroad. Specialty, landscapes. Third Hallgarten prize, National Academy of Design, 1912. Academy of National Artists. Vice-President Allied Artists of America; New York Society of Painters. Member of New York Water Color Club; American Water Color Society; Academy of Fine Arts; Union Internationale des Beaux Arts et des Lettres. *Address,* Kent, Conn.

CLARK, Elsie S. (Mrs.). Painter. Born in Providence, R. I., 1881. Studied in Paris. *Address,* Rodin Studios, 200 West 57th St., New York City, N. Y.

CLARK, Freeman. Painter. Born in Holly Springs, Miss. Pupil of William M. Chase, and Wiles. Member of Art Students' League of New York. *Address,* 107 West 64th St., New York.

CLARK, Harriette A. Miniature painter. Born in Depere, Wisc., 1876. Pupil of Laurens and Blaschet in Paris. Has painted miniatures of Ex-President Diaz and Madame Diaz. *Address,* 27 West 67th St., New York City, N. Y.

CLARK, Herbert F. Painter and illustrator. Born Holyoke, Mass., 1876. Pupil of Rhode Island School of Design, Providence, R. I., and the School of the Corcoran Art Gallery, Washington, D. C. Specialty, landscapes. *Address,* 3034 R St., N. W., Washington, D. C.

CLARK, James. Engraver. In 1840, James Clark was an engraver of bank-notes, cards, etc., with an establishment at 67 Broadway, New York City.

CLARK, James L. Sculptor. Born in Providence, R. I., 1883. Pupil of Rhode Island School of Design. *Address,* 1160 Southern Bldg., Bronx, N. Y.

CLARK, Roy C. Landscape painter. Born in Sheffield, Mass., in 1889. Pupil of Edgar Nye. Member of Society of Independent Artists. *Address,* 734 Seventh St., N. E., Washington, D. C.

CLARK, Sarah L. Painter and illustrator. Born in Philadelphia, Pa. Pupil of Chase and Carlsen. Member of Fellowship of Penna. Academy of Fine Arts. Specialty, pathological and surgical drawings. *Address,* 523 Wilson Bldg., 15th and Chestnut Sts., Philadelphia.

CLARK, Mrs. Virginia Keep. Portrait painter. Born in New Orleans, 1878. Pupil of Beckwith and Howard Pyle. *Address,* 4 East 66th St., New York.

CLARK, Walter. Landscape painter. Born in Brooklyn, 1848. Pupil of Innes. He became an Associate of the National Academy in 1898 and an Academician in 1909. His specialty was landscape painting. Among his paintings were "In Early Leaf," and "Gloucester Harbor." He died in 1917.

CLARK, Walter Appleton. Illustrator. Born in Worcester, Mass., in 1876. Pupil of H. Siddons Mowbray and William M. Chase. He was connected with *Scribner's,* also an instructor at the Art Students' League. He received a silver medal for his illustrations for "Canterbury Tales." He died in 1906. Represented by painting "Aawkening of Helena Ritchie," at Worcester Art Museum.

CLARKE, Fred B. Painter. Pupil of Augustus Saint Gaudens. *Address,* 126 East 75th St., New York City.

CLARKE, John L. Painter. Exhibited, Penna. Academy of Fine Arts, Philadelphia, 1924. *Address,* Glacier Park, Montana.

CLARKE, Rene. Painter. Exhibited water colors at Penna. Academy of Fine Arts, Philadelphia, 1922. *Address,* 46 Bayley Ave., Yonkers, N. Y.

CLARKE, Thomas. Engraver. The name of this engraver in the stipple manner first appears in 1797, when he was engraving portraits and subject plates for the *American Universal Magazine* of Philadelphia, and illustrations for an edition of "Telemachus," published by David Longworth of New York. He was apparently in both cities in this year, as he signed his plates respectively, "T. Clarke, Sculp.," Philadelphia, 1797, and "engraved by Thos. Clarke, N. Y." Clarke was engraving in New York at least as late as 1800, but Dunlap says that he went South about this time, became deranged, and then committed suicide.

CLARKE, Thomas Shields. Sculptor and painter. Born 1860 in Pittsburgh, Penna. He died 1920 in New York. Studied painting and sculpture at École des Beaux Arts, Paris, and in Rome and Florence, for 11 years. Exhibited works and won many medals at London, Madrid, Berlin, Paris, Chicago Expn., and at Expn. of San Francisco and Atlanta, Ga. He executed many large works in bronze and marble for New York, San Francisco, Chicago and other cities. Pictures in Museums of Boston and Philadelphia. Academy of National Artists. Member: Royal Society of Arts, London; National Sculpture Society; Metropolitan Museum of Art; American Museum Natural History; Architectural League. Among his best known paintings is the "Night Market, Morocco," owned by the Philadelphia Art Club.

CLARKSON, Ralph Elmer. Portrait painter. Born at Amesbury, Mass., in 1861. Student of School of Boston Museum and pupil of Lefebvre and Boulanger in Paris. Elected an Associate Member of National Academy of Design in 1910. Represented in Art Institute of Chicago by "A Daughter of Armenia." *Address,* Studio, 410 South Michigan Ave., Chicago, Ill.

CLASSEN, William M. Engraver. This name is signed to a few well-engraved lineplates of buildings and book-illustrations as "Wm. M. Classen, Eng. No. 1 Murray St. Corner of B. Way" (New York). The apparent date of these plates is about 1840–50. On one plate seen, the name is signed "J. M. Classen Sc.," though the work seems to be the same.

CLAUS, May A. (Mrs.). Painter. Born at Berlin, N. Y., in 1882. Pupil of School of Boston Museum, and of W. A. G. Claus. Exhibited miniatures at Penna. Academy of Fine Arts, Philadelphia, 1922. *Address,* 410 Boylston St., Boston, Mass.

CLAUS, W. A. J. Portrait painter. Born in Germany, 1862. Pupil of Grundmann in Boston and Julien Academy in Paris. Among his paintings, "Old Pioneer" is owned by the Boston Art Club; "Gov. Greenhalge," State House, Boston; "Carl Faelten," "Dr. Eben Tourjee," "Dr. Stowell" and portraits of prominent natives painted in India 1884 to 1887. *Address,* 410 Boylston St., Boston, Mass.

CLAY, Edward W. Engraver. Born in Philadelphia, Pa., 1792; died in New York, 1857. Clay is said to have been a midshipman under Commodore Perry, but he later studied law and was admitted to the Philadelphia bar in 1825. He had, however, a decided leaning toward art; he drew some of the plates engraved for Childs' "Views of Philadelphia," and he drew upon stone for the lithographing firm of Childs & Inman. Clay was a merciless caricaturist, and some of his lampoons of fellow-citizens are said to have caused him much personal inconvenience. In the Philadelphia directories of 1835–36 his profession is given as "Artist." He engraved several fairly well-executed plates in the stipple manner, the best of these being a portrait of the Rev. Joseph Eastburn. His caricatures were etched.

CLAY, Mary F. R. Painter. Exhibited at Penna. Academy of Fine Arts, Philadelphia, 1924. *Address,* 1734 Pine St., Philadelphia.

CLAYPOOLE, James. Painter. Was the earliest native artist of Pennsylvania. He was born in Philadelphia, 1720, and died in the West Indies about 1796. He was the son of Joseph Claypoole of Philadelphia and his wife, Edith Ward. Joseph Claypoole was the First Warden of Christ Church, Philadelphia, and

was "Concerned in the promoting and assisting of the building of Christ Church, and contributed much toward it." Joseph Claypoole, the artist's father, was born in 1677, and died before May 3, 1744. He was the son of James Claypoole, friend of Penn, Patentee of Pennsylvania, and Register General of the Colony. The first James Claypoole was a wealthy merchant. His son Joseph, father of the artist, was also a man of wealth, as he was a large property owner in Philadelphia.

James Claypoole painted portraits in Philadelphia before 1750; little is known of his paintings, but he was the instructor of his nephew, Matthew Pratt, whose autobiographical notes state that he was apprenticed "To my uncle James Claypoole, limner and portrait painter in general" in 1749. His work shows that he was guided by a painter of no mean acquirements. Claypoole abandoned art for public life and was High Sheriff of Philadelphia during the Revolutionary War. His daughter, Elizabeth, married Timothy Matlack, the soldier and patriot of Philadelphia, whose portrait was painted by Charles Wilson Peale. His daughter Mary married James Peale, the artist, brother of Charles Willson Peale, and his cousin John Claypoole was the husband of the celebrated Betsy Ross.

There is a portrait inscribed on the back of the canvas "Margaret Allen drawn and colored by Claypoole, Philadelphia, 1746."

Charles Willson Peale, in a letter, mentions "James Claypoole," whose paintings he examined at his home in Philadelphia in 1762.

CLELAND, Thomas M. Painter. Born in New York in 1880. Painted altar-piece in Church of the Messiah, Glens Falls, N. Y. *Address,* 70 Fifth Ave., New York City, N. Y.

CLEMENS, Isaac. Engraver. The *New York Gazette,* 1776, contains the following advertisement: "Isaac Clemens, Engraver (who lately arrived with his Majesty's Fleet from Boston, in New England) informs the Gentlemen of the Navy and Army and the Public in general, that he now carries on the Engraving Business at his Shop near the French Church, in King St., New York."

This advertisement disappears in a very short time, and Mr. Clemens probably went back to England, as nothing more is known about him.

CLEMENT, Edward H. Painter. Born in Chelsea, Mass., 1843. Pupil of Boston Art Students' Association. He is now deceased.

CLEMENTS, Gabrielle De Veaux. Painter. Born Philadelphia, 1858. Pupil of Robert-Fleury and Bouguereau in Paris. Member: Fellowship Penna. Academy of Fine Arts. Work: Painting in St. Patrick's Church, Washington, D. C. Mural paintings, St. Paul's Chapel, Baltimore; St. Matthew's Church, Sparrow Point, Md. Etchings in National Museum, Washington, D. C.

CLEMENTS, George H. Painter. Member: New York Water Color Club. Born in Louisiana. Landscape and genre painter. He exhibited a portrait of Frank Duveneck at Cincinnati Museum in 1925. *Address,* 33 West 67th St., New York City, N. Y.

CLEMENTS, R. Thomson. Painter. Born in Washington, D. C., 1878. Pupil of E. F. Andrews in Washnigton; F. Luis Mora and Thomas Fogarty in New York. Member: National Art Club. *Address,* 107 East 59th St., New York, N. Y.

CLEPHANE, Lewis. Painter. Born Washington, D. C., 1869. Pupil of Birge Harrison; Alexander Robinson in Holland. Member: Society of Washington Artists; Washington Water Color Club; Washington Art Club; Society of Independent Artists. *Address,* 1115 I St.; 1225 K St., Washington, D. C.

CLEVENGER, Shobal V. Sculptor. Born near Middleton, Ohio, in 1812. Largely self-taught, he executed many busts of prominent men, and was enabled to go abroad for study. His death occurred in 1843 when he was thirty-one, on a homeward voyage. His work was known for its fidelity to nature and his skill with the chisel.

CLIME, Winfield Scott. Painter. Born Philadelphia, 1881. Pupil of Drexel Institute, Philadelphia; Corcoran Art School, Washington. Member: Society Washington Artists; Washington Water Color Club; Washington Art Club.

CLINEDINST, B. West. Painter. Born Woodstock, Va., 1860. Studied at École des Beaux Arts, Paris. Pupil of Cabanel and Bonnat. Specialty, genre pictures and portraits; illustrator of books. Painted portraits of Theodore Roosevelt, Admiral Peary, Gen. Curtis Lee, Edward Echols, Gen. E. W. Nichols. Elected Member of the National Academy of Design, 1898. *Address,* Pawling, N. Y.

CLONNEY, James Goodwyn. Genre and miniature artist. Born in England, 1812, and died 1867. He started painting miniatures in New York, 1834, and exhibited at the National Academy, 1841–1852. He was elected an Associate Member of the National Academy in 1867.

CLOPATH, Henriette. Painter. Born in Switzerland. Award: Gold medal, University of Okla., 1916. Writer and lecturer on modern painting. *Address,* Chalet Art Studio.

CLOSSON, William Baxter Palmer. Painter and engraver. Born Thetford, Vt., 1848. Pupil of Lowell Institute; traveled in Europe. Followed engraving on wood, 1872–94; since then has painted in pastel and oil. Awards for wood engraving: Gold, silver and bronze

medals; silver medal, Paris Expn., 1889; medal, Columbian Expn., Chicago. Member: Boston Art Club; Copley Society; Society Washington Artists; Union Internationale des Beaux Arts et des Lettres. See "History of Wood Engraving in America," by W. J. Linton. *Address,* Newton, Mass.

CLOVER, Lewis P. Born in New York, 1819, and died 1896. He studied painting and engraving under Asher B. Durand. He had his studio for some years in New York and Baltimore. Later he entered the church and afterward the priesthood. Among his paintings are "The Rejected Picture," "The Idle Man," and "The Phrenologist."

CLOVER, Philip. Portrait painter. Born in 1842. He was formerly of Columbus, Ohio, but painted many Chicago politicians. His "Fatima" was exhibited all over the country, and "The Criminal" was also of the sensational class. He died in 1905.

CLUSMANN, William. Painter. Born North Laporte, Ind., 1859. Pupil of Benczur at Royal Academy in Munich. Member: Chicago Society of Artists; Chicago Water Color Club. Awards: Hon. mention, Stuttgart, Germany, 1885.

CLUTE, Beulah Mitchell (Mrs. Walter Marshall Clute). Painter. Born Rushville, Ill. Pupil of Art Students' League of New York; Art Institute of Chicago. Member: Artists' Guild, Chicago; Art Institute of Chicago Alumni Association. Specialty, bookplates. *Address,* 2614 Channing Way, Berkeley, Calif.

CLUTE, Walter M. Painter and illustrator. Born in Schenectady, New York, 1870. He was a pupil of the Art Students' League of New York, and of Constant and Laurens in Paris. He received the 1910 prize of Art Institute of Chicago, and was vice-president of the Society of Western Artists at the time of his death in 1915.

CLYMER, Edwin Swift. Painter. Born Cincinnati, Ohio, 1871. Pupil of Penna. Academy of Fine Arts. Member: Fellowship Penna. Academy of Fine Arts; Philadelphia Sketch Club; Philadelphia Water Color Club. Work: in Reading, Pa., Museum of Art.

CLYMER, James Floyd. Painter. Exhibited, Penna. Academy of Fine Arts, 1924, Philadelphia. *Address,* Provincetown, Mass.

COALE, Griffith B. Painter. Born Baltimore, Md., 1890. Studied with M. Heymann, Munich; Richard Miller and Laparra in Paris, and in Italy and Spain. Work: "Portrait of Cardinal Mercer," Maryland Historical Society. *Address,* 241 West Biddle St., Baltimore, Md.

COAN, Helen E. Painter. Born Byron, N. Y. Pupil of Art Students' League of New York; Frederick Freer and William E. Chase. Member: California Art Club. Award: Medals for oil and water color, Alaska-Yukon-Pacific Exposition, Seattle, 1909; medal and diploma, San Diego Exp., 1915. *Address,* 204 North Burlington Ave., Los Angeles, Calif.

COAST, Oscar R. Painter. Born Salem, Ohio, 1851. Studied in Paris and Rome. Specialty, landscapes. *Address,* Santa Barbara, Calif.

COBB, Cyrus, Portrait painter. Born at Malden, Mass., 1834. His career for about twenty years was identical with that of his twin brother, Darius Cobb. He painted portraits of Rev. A. P. Peabody, Dr. Appleton and others, but devoted himself to the law, which was his profession. He died in 1905.

COBB, Darius. Painter. Born in Malden, Mass., 1834. Twin brother of Cyrus Cobb with whom he studied and worked until 1870. Their professional life was spent near Boston. Darius Cobb painted many portraits, some landscapes and figure pieces; he also cut several busts in marble. He was a frequent lecturer on art subjects in Boston and elsewhere. He died in 1919.

COBB, G. A book-plate engraver working about 1800, but without indication of place. He was most probably an American, as the only plate signed by him is of the pictorial type, with an American eagle bearing an oval frame, once containing a name, now carefully erased; there is a scratchy landscape at the base.

COCHRAN, Allen D. Painter. Born in Cincinnati, Ohio, 1888. Pupil of Kenyon Cox and Birge Harrison. *Address,* Woodstock, N. Y.

COCHRANE, Constance. Painter. Exhibited at National Association of Women Painters and Sculptors, New York, 1924. *Address,* 7103 Penna. Ave., Bywood, Penna.

COCKCROFT, Edith V. (Mrs.). Painter. Born in Brooklyn, N. Y., 1881. Member of National Association of Women Painters and Sculptors. *Address,* 17 East 39th St., New York City.

COCKRELL, Dura (Mrs.). Painter. Pupil of William M. Chase. Born at Liscomb, Iowa, in 1877. *Address,* Fort Worth, Texas.

CODEZO, T h o m a s. Spanish-American painter. Born in Havana in 1839. Studied in Paris with Henri Regnault. He came to the United States in 1869; his work is generally in oil, but many of his portraits are in crayon. His last work was a life-size crayon portrait of William Orton, in the office of the Western Union Telegraph Company.

CODMAN, Edwin E. Painter. Member of Providence Art Club. *Address,* 166 Ontario St., Providence, R. I.

COE, Ethel L. Painter and illustrator. Born in Chicago, Ill. Pupil of Art Institute. *Address,* Care of Art Institute, Chicago, Ill.

COFFEE. An English sculptor noted in Dunlap as modelling small portrait-busts of merit. He resided in Charleston.

COFFEE, Will. Painter. Exhibited water colors at Annual Exhibition of Water Colors at Penna. Academy of Fine Arts, Philadelphia, 1925. *Address,* 729 Walnut St., Philadelphia.

COFFIN, George Albert. Marine painter. He was born 1856, and died 1922.

COFFIN, Sarah T. (Mrs.). Painter. Born in Vassalboro, Me., 1844. Pupil of R. Swain Gifford and Frank Duveneck. *Address,* Chestnut Hill, Mass.

COFFIN, William Anderson. Landscape and figure painter. Born in Allegheny, Penna., in 1855. Studied in New York and Paris. Elected an Associate Member of the National Academy of Design in 1898, and National Academy in 1912. Represented in Collection of Metropolitan Museum, New York, and National Collection at Washington, D. C. He died in New York City, 1925, at the age of 70.

COFFIN, W. Haskell. Painter. Studied at Corcoran Art School, Washington, D. C., and in Paris. *Address,* 80 West 40th St., New York City.

COGDELL, John Stephano. Sculptor and painter. Born in Charleston, S. C., in 1778. He was largely self-taught, but received some help from Washington Allston, and studied abroad. About 1820 to 1850 he modelled a few busts of distinguished Americans.

COGSWELL, William. Painter. Born in Fabius, N. Y., 1819. He died in Pasadena, Calif., 1903. He was practically self-taught as a portrait painter. He resided at times in New York, Philadelphia, Chicago, St. Louis, and California. His list of portraits include: Presidents Lincoln, Grant and McKinley. His "President Grant and Family" is now in the National Gallery, and the portraits of Gen'l Grant and Salmon P. Chase are in the Capitol, Washington, D. C.

COHEN, Isabel. Painter. Exhibited at National Association of Women Painters and Sculptors, New York, 1924. *Address,* 81 Irving Place, New York.

COHEN, Katherine M. Sculptor and painter. Born in Philadelphia, 1859. Pupil of Penna. Academy of Fine Arts, Art Students'

League of New York, under Augustus Saint Gaudens, and of Mercie in Paris. Among her best known works: Statue of General Beaver, bronze of Abraham Lincoln, "Dawn of Thought," and "Vision of Rabbi Ben Ezra." She died in Philadelphia in 1924.

COHEN, Lewis. Painter. American. Born 1858 in London; died 1915 in New York. Pupil of Alphonse Legros, J. Watson Nicholl, and A. S. Cope. Elected an Associate Member of the National Academy. He painted "Puente San Martin, Toledo." (The bridge extends diagonally across the picture; the city in sunlight is shown on the farther bank and the foreground is in shadow.)

COHEN, Nessa. Sculptor. Born in New York City. Pupil of James S. Fraser. Among her work "Sunrise," Havana, Cuba, and groups of Indians of the Southwestern United States. Exhibited, Penna. Academy of Fine Arts, Philadelphia, 1924. *Address*, 1143 Lexington Ave., New York City.

COHILL, Charles. A portrait painter of fair ability, who was painting in 1838. A painting of a Shakespearean character was shown in Philadelphia at Barr & Co. in 1923. It was inscribed on the back of the canvas "Charles Cohill, 1838."

COLBURN, Eleanor R. (Mrs.). Painter. Born in Dayton, Ohio, in 1866. Pupil of Art Institute of Chicago. Among her paintings "An Offshore Wind" is owned by the Chicago Art Institute. *Address*, 3028 Michigan Ave., Chicago, Ill.

COLBY, George W. Painter and illustrator. Exhibited at the Penna. Academy of Fine Arts, Philadelphia, 1922, pastel, "Study of a Woodcock." *Address*, 25 Cedar St., Malden, Mass.

COLBY, Josephine W. (Mrs.). Painter. Born in New York City, 1862. Pupil of Will Low and John W. Alexander. She is represented in the Gallery of the Penna. Academy of Fine Arts and the Manchester Art Gallery, England. *Address*, "The Tamaracks," Andover, New Jersey.

COLE, Alphaeus P. Painter. Born Jersey City, N. J., in 1876. Pupil of Constant and Laurens in Paris. Member of the Conn. Academy of Fine Arts, Hartford. *Address*, 33 West 67th St., New York.

COLE, Annie Elizabeth (Mrs. Myron Asa Cole). Painter. Born Providence, R. I., 1880. Pupil of Henry W. Moser, Edgar Nye, and Bertha E. Perrie. Member: Washington Water Color Club.

COLE, C. O. Portrait painter. He was working in New Orleans, La., about 1835.

COLE, Emily Beckwith. Sculptor. Born New London, Conn., 1896. Pupil of Louis Gudebrod. *Address*, 220 Beacon St., Hartford, Conn.

COLE, George Townsend. Painter. Born in California. Pupil of Bonnat in Paris. *Address*, 1103 El Centro Ave., Los Angeles, Calif.

COLE, J. Foxcroft. Painter. Born in Maine, 1837, he died in Boston, 1892. He studied abroad and was a pupil of Charles Jacque in 1867. He exhibited in the Salon, 1866–67–73–74, and the Royal Academy of 1875. His landscapes show the quiet repose of nature, and are of decided merit. The Boston Museum of Fine Arts owns several of his paintings.

COLE, Jacques Moyse Dupré. Afterwards known as Moses D. Cole. Was born in France, in 1783. He came to Newburyport, Mass., from the West Indies with his father in 1795, and on the death of his father he took the name of Moses Dupre Cole. He remained in Newburyport where he painted many portraits.

COLE, Mrs. Jessie (Duncan) Savage. Painter. Born Pass Christian, Miss., 1858. Pupil of Wyatt Eaton; John La Farge. *Address*, 81 Wickes Ave., Nepperham, Yonkers, N. Y.

COLE, Joseph Greenleaf. Painter. He was a son of Moses D. Cole, and was born in Newburyport in 1803. After studying with his father a few years, he established himself in Boston where he died in 1858. He painted many portraits, one of the best being that of Geo. R. T. Hewes, belonging to the Bostonian Society, and hanging for years in the Old State House, Boston.

COLE, Thomas. Landscape painter. Born in England in 1801. Died 1848, near Catskill, N. Y. In 1819 his father, James Cole, emigrated to America and settled in Ohio where he studied the rudiments of his art; later he studied abroad but lived the greater part of his life in New York City. Elected Member of National Academy in 1826. He is represented by the "Catskill" in the Metropolitan Museum, New York, and in the Corcoran Museum, Washington, by "The Departure and the Return."

COLE, Thomas Casilear. Painter. Born Staatsburgh-on-Hudson, N. Y., 1888. Pupil of Tarbell, Benson and Hale in Boston; Julien Academy under Baschet and Laurens in Paris. *Address*, 154 West 55th St., New York, N. Y.

COLE, Timothy. Wood-engraver. Born London, England, 1852. Burned out by Chicago fire of 1871; returned to New York penniless; entered employment of *Century Magazine* (then Scribner's); went to Europe to engrave the Old Masters, 1883; finished 1st Italian series 1892; Dutch and Flemish series, 1896; English series, 1900; Spanish series, 1907; French series, 1910; engraved "Old Italian Masters." Honorable mention, Society of Sculptors, Painters and Engravers, London; National Academy, 1908. Member: American Academy Arts and Letters; honorable mention, Brotherhood of Engravers of Chicago. Represented in Carnegie Institute, Pittsburgh, and City Art Museum, St. Louis; Chicago Art Institute; Metropolitan Museum; Boston Art Museum; Washington National Gallery, etc. *Address*, Ferris Lane, Poughkeepsie, New York.

COLEMAN, Charles Caryl. Painter. Born in 1840 in Buffalo, N. Y. He studied with W. H. Beard. Went to Europe for study in 1859, and returned for three years during the Civil War. Since 1865 he has lived abroad, painting in London, Paris, and Italy, and is considered one of America's foremost water colorists. Elected an Associate Member of National Academy. Represented in Boston Museum of Fine Arts, Brooklyn Institute, and his "An Artist's Studio," with portrait of Vedder, was owned in New York City. His studio is Villa Narcissus, Island of Capri, Italy.

COLEMAN, Glenn O. Painter. Born Springfield, Ohio, 1887. Pupil of Henri and Chase. Member: Society of Independent Artists. *Address*, 154 East Park St., Long Beach, N. Y.

COLEMAN, Ralph P. Illustrator. Born Philadelphia, 1892. Pupil of Philadelphia School of Industrial Art. Illustrated "The Man with Three Names," and "Drums of Jeopardy," by McGrath; "Nobody's Man" by Oppenheim, etc., and illustrates for many magazines.

COLEMAN, Samuel. Painter. Born in Portland, Maine, 1832. He moved to New York and became a pupil of Asher B. Durand. He studied in France and Spain. He became an associate member of the National Academy in 1860, and a full member in 1862. He was a founder of the American Society of Painters in Water Colors. Among his works are "Bay of Gibraltar," "Market Day in Brittany," and "The Arab Burying-Ground."

COLES, Ann Cadwallader. Painter. Born Columbia, S. C., 1882. Pupil of C. A. Whipple, A. V. Tack and F. Luis Mora. Member: Society of Independent Artists. Work: "Gen. M. C. Butler," Confederate Museum, Richmond, Va. *Address*, 164 Waverly Place, New York, N. Y.

COLES, John, Jr. Son of John Coles, heraldic painter, was a student with Frothingham under Gilbert Stuart. He painted portraits from 1807 to 1820 in Boston. His portraits are well drawn, good in color, but without style or arrangement. His pictures are always on panels with lead color background.

COLL, Joseph Clement. Illustrator. Exhibited at Penn. Academy of Fine Arts, 1922. Pen and Ink Drawings. (Deceased.)

COLLARD, W. Line-engraver of portraits, working for the magazines about 1840–45.

COLLAS, Louis A. Painter. Nothing could be found regarding the life and work of this artist except that he painted miniatures and larger portraits in oil of a superior quality, in and about New Orleans, from 1820 till 1828. He is listed in the directory, 1822, as "portrait and miniature painter, 44 St. Peter Street." Nothing is recorded of him after 1828. His miniature of "Miss Ewing" was painted in 1818, and is owned in Charleston, S. C.

COLLES, Gertrude. Painter. Born Morristown, N. J., 1869. Pupil of Laurens in Paris; George de Forest Brush and B. R. Fitz in New York. Work: "Former Senator Jacob Miller," State House, Trenton, N. J. *Address*, 939 Eighth Ave., New York, N. Y.

COLLES, J. Profile miniature painter. Flourished 1778–1780, New York. His advertisement is recorded in the *New York Gazette* for May 10, 1780.

COLLIER, Charles M. Marine painter. Born at Hampton, Va., in 1836. Died in New York, 1909.

COLLINS, Alfred Q. Painter. Born at Portland, Maine, in 1855, died at Cambridge, Mass., in 1903. Represented at the Metropolitan Museum, New York, by "The Artist's Wife," and at the Boston Museum by an unfinished portrait of Thomas B. Clarke.

COLLINS, Marjorie S. Miniature painter. Exhibited portrait miniatures at Penna. Academy of Fine Arts, Philadelphia, 1922. *Address*, 701 Nottingham Road, Wilmington, Del.

COLLOW, Jean. Painter. She exhibited water colors in Cincinnati Museum in 1925. *Address*, Art Academy, Cincinnati.

COLLVER, Ethel Blanchard (Mrs. Leon Collver). Painter. Born Boston, Mass. Pupil of Tarbell, Benson, and Hale in Boston; Academie, Colarossi, Naudin, Guerin, in Paris. Member: Copley Society, 1901. *Address*, Fenway Studios, 125 Commonwealth Ave., Boston, Mass.

COLMAN, R. Clarkson. Painter. Born Elgin, Ill., 1884. Studied in Chicago and with Laurens and Julien in Paris. Represented in Public Library, Ajo, Arizona; Public Library, Waco, Texas; Santa Monica Woman's Club. *Address*, Studio-by-the-Sea., Laguna Beach, Calif.

COLMAN, Samuel. Painter in oils and water colors. He was born in Portland, Me., in 1832. Studied with Asher B. Durand; in 1860 he went to Paris and later to Spain and Italy. In 1854 opened his studio in New York, and in 1864 was elected a member of the National School of Design, and was a founder of Society of American Artists. He died 1920. Represented in Metropolitan Museum and Chicago Art Institute.

COLSON, Frank V. Painter, illustrator and etcher. Born in Boston, 1894. Pupil of Benson and Paxton. Member of Boston Society of Etchers. *Address,* 198 Dartmouth St., Boston.

COLT, Morgan. Painter. Born in Summit, N. J., 1876. Member of Rochester Art Club. *Address,* New Hope, Penna.

COLTMAN, Ora. Painter and sculptor. Born in Shelby, Ohio, 1860. Member of Art Students' League and Julien Academy of Paris. *Address,* 10714 Deering Ave., Cleveland, Ohio.

COLTON, Mary R. Painter. Born in Louisville, Ky., 1889. Pupil of Eliot Dangerfield. Exhibited water colors at Penna. Academy of Fine Arts, 1922. *Address,* Wister Road, Ardmore, Pa.

COLWELL, Elizabeth. Illustrator and etcher. Born in Michigan, 1881. Pupil of Olson-Nordfeldt in Chicago. Represented in Print Department of Chicago Art Institute. *Address,* 1373 East 57th St., Chicago, Ill.

COLYER, Vincent. Painter. Born in 1825 and died 1888. In 1849 he was elected an associate of the National Academy. Before the Rebellion he painted ''Freedom's Martyr,'' representing the burial of Barber by John Brown. He also painted a number of Indian pictures from sketches he had made in the West during his visits among them. He was born in New York, but lived most of his life in Connecticut.

COMAN, Charlotte Buell. Painter, landscapes. Born at Waterville, N. Y., 1833. Pupil of James Brevoort in New York, and Vernier in Paris. Elected an Associate Member of National Academy of Design in 1910. Represented in Metropolitan Museum, New York, and National Gallery, Washington, D. C. She died in New York in 1924.

COMEGYS, Geo. H. Painter. Born in Maryland. Died in the Penna. Hospital for the Insane, in Philadelphia. He was a pupil of Neagle and member of Board of the Artists' Fund Society in 1845. ''The Ghost Story'' (canvas 17 in. by 17 in.), ''Little Plunderers'' (canvas 17 in. by 20 in.), Penna. Academy of Fine Arts.

COMINS, Alice R. Painter. Exhibited at National Association of Women Painters and Sculptors, New York, 1924. *Address,* Cape Neddick, Me.

COMINS, Eben F. Painter (portraits). Born in Boston, Mass. Pupil of ''Beaux Arts,'' Paris, and Denman Ross in Boston. Exhibition at the Ehrich Galleries, New York. *Address,* 203 Fenway Studios, 30 Ipswich St., Boston, and Washington, D. C.

COMSTOCK, Enos B. Painter and illustrator. Born in Milwaukee in 1879. Has illustrated a number of children's books. *Address,* 178 Highwood Ave., Leonia, N. J.

COMSTOCK, Frances B. Painter, sculptor, and illustrator. Born in Elyria, Ohio, in 1881. Pupil of Gari Melchers and John Vanderpoel. *Address,* 178 Highwood Ave., Leonia, N. J.

CONANT, Alban Jasper. Painter. Born Chelsea, 1821; died 1914. Painted portraits of Lincoln, Sherman, Anderson at Sumter; judges of Ct. of Appeals and Supreme Ct. of U. S., and cabinet secretaries; 4 portraits of Henry Ward Beecher, Dr. James McCosh, Bishop H. C. Potter, ''Burial of De Soto,'' etc. Author: ''Footprints of Vanished Races in the Mississippi Valley,'' ''My Acquaintance with Abraham Lincoln,'' etc.

CONANT, Marjorie. Painter. Born in Boston, 1885. Pupil of Hale Benson and Tarbell. Exhibited at Penna. Academy of Fine Arts, Philadelphia, 1924. *Address,* 129 East 10th St., New York City.

CONARD, Grace D. Painter. Born in Dixon, Ill., 1885. Pupil of Chicago Art Institute. *Address,* Art Institute of Chicago.

CONARROE, George W. Born in 1803 and died 1882. He was a portrait painter of decided merit, who flourished in Philadelphia about 1825. A self-portrait of the artist is owned by the Penna. Historical Society in Philadelphia. In 1829 he exhibited paintings in the Pennsylvania Academy of Fine Arts. At that time he was living in Salem, N. J. He lived after that in Philadelphia, where he died in 1882.

CONE, Joseph. Engraver in both stipple and in line, was chiefly engaged upon portrait work. He is said to have been a brother of the Rev. Spencer H. Cone, who came from New Jersey to Philadelphia, in 1802, to accept a position as a teacher in Doctor Abercrombie's Academy. Joseph Cone possibly came with him to study engraving. In any event, Joseph Cone was engraving over his own name in Philadelphia, 1814–19, inclusive. In the period 1820–24 he was engraving prints and publishing them in Baltimore, Md. He also worked for Boston publishers, and in 1829–30 his name reappears in the Philadelphia directories as an "Engraver."

CONGDON, Adairene Vose (Mrs.). Painter. Born in New York City. Pupil of Art Students' League of New York. Represented in Petit Palace, Paris, Library of Congress, and New York Public Library. *Address*, Villa Vose Studios, Campbell, N. Y.

CONGDON, Thomas R. Painter and etcher. Born in Addison, N. Y., in 1862. Pupil of Art Students' League of New York, also studied in Paris. Represented by prints in Library of Congress, New York Public Library, and Boston Art Club. He died in 1917.

CONKLING, Mabel (Mrs.). Sculptor. Born in Boothbay, Me., in 1871. Studied in Paris under Bouguereau and Collin until 1899. In 1900 she studied sculpture under MacMonnies. Work: "The Lotus Girl," "Song of the Sea," and portrait reliefs of Dr. Geo. Alexander, Mrs. James A. Garland, and Hope Garland. *Address*, 22 West 9th St., New York.

CONKLING, Paul. Sculptor. Born in New York City, 1871. Pupil of MacMonnies. His specialty is portraiture. *Address*, 5 McDougal Alley, New York.

CONLEY, Sarah W. Painter, sculptor, and illustrator. Born in Nashville, Tenn., 1861. Pupil of Bouguereau, Julien and Bridgman in Paris, and of Ferrari in Rome. *Address*, 2104 West End Ave., Nashville, Tenn.

CONLON, George. Sculptor. Born in Maryland. Pupil of Injalbert and Bartlett in Paris. *Address*, 1230 St. Paul St., Baltimore, Md.

CONN, James. Engraver and writing-master at Elizabethtown, N. J., advertises in 1771 his "intention to teach writing, arithmetic, mathematics, geography," etc., and adds to his notice the following: "Furthermore, the said Conn at leisure hours, engraves Shop Bills, Bills of Parcels, Bills of Exchange, or any Kind of Writing for the Rolling-Press, in the neatest Manner."

CONNAWAY, Jay. Painter. Born at Liberty, Ind., 1893. Pupil of Chase in New York. Studied in Paris. *Address*, 1649 North Alabama St., Indianapolis, Ind.

CONNELL, Edwin D. Painter. Born New York, N. Y., 1859. Pupil of Bouguereau, Robert-Fleury and Julien Dupré in Paris. Awards: Honorable mention, Paris Salon, 1899; medal, second class, Orleans Expn., 1905. Work: "Cattle," Toledo Museum of Art. *Address*, 56 Rue de Sevres, Clamart, France.

CONNELLY, Eugene L. Painter. Member Pittsburgh Academy of Artists. *Address*, Davis Theatre, Pittsburgh, Pa.

CONNELLY, Marc. Illustrator. Member: Society of Illustrators. *Address*, 159½ East 83d St., New York, N. Y.

CONNELLY, Pierce Francis. Born in southern city, 1840. He was taken to England as a child. He studied painting in France, and sculpture in Italy. In 1876 he visited the United States, and exhibited in the Centennial at Philadelphia.

CONNER, Jerome. Sculptor. Born in Ireland, 1875. Self-taught. Member: Society of Washington Artists. *Address*, 322 North Carolina Ave., S. E., Washington, D. C.

CONNER, J. R. Painter. Born Radnor, Pa. Pupil of Penna. Academy of Fine Arts. Work: "The Fisherman," Pennsylvania Academy of the Fine Arts, Philadelphia; "Under the North Light," Des Moines Association of Fine Arts; "A Cottage Interior," California Club, Los Angeles. *Address*, Bryn Athyn, Pa.

CONNER, Charles. Landscape painter. Born in Richmond, Ind., in 1857. His best known canvas was "Wet Night in February," shown at St. Louis Exposition. He died in 1905.

CONNOR, Jerome. Sculptor. Exhibited study for Bishop Huntington Tablet, at the Penna. Academy of Fine Arts, Philadelphia, 1920. *Address*, 322 North Carolina Ave., Washington, D. C.

CONNY, John (or Cony). Engraver. Was a prominent gold- and silversmith, of Boston, at least as early as 1700. The MSS. Archives of Massachusetts, under date of March 12, 1702–3, note the indebtedness of the Colony "To John Conny for graving 3 Plates for Bills of Credit," and on Nov. 26, 1706, the same records shows that, to prevent counterfeiting, the plate for the bills was to be provided with "Eight blazons and put on by the engraver." This Massachusetts currency of 1702 included little more than the engraved script and the seal of the Colony, and the earlier bills of 1690 approach it so closely in general design and execution, especially in the character of the decoration at the top of the note, that there is a strong possibility that both plates were made by the same man. If this assumption were correct, John Conny would be the first American engraver upon copper on record.

CONRADS, Carl H. Sculptor. Born in Germany, 1839, came to New York in 1860. He served in the Union Army. Among his works are statues of Alexander Hamilton, Central Park; "Gen'l Thayer," West Point;

and "Daniel Webster" for the Capitol at Washington. He has resided in Hartford, Conn., since 1866.

CONREY, Lee F. Illustrator. Born St. Louis, Mo., 1883. Pupil of St. Louis School of Fine Arts. Member: Society of Illustrators. Illustrations for *Cosmopolitan, McClure's, Munsey's* Magazines.

CONROW, Wilford S. Painter. Born South Orange, N. J., 1880. Pupil of Jean-Paul Laurens. Work: "Portrait of Cephas Brainerd," New York City; "Portrait of Henry Clay Cameron," Whig Hall, Princeton University, Princeton. Mural painting of George Washington, National Gallery of Art, Washington, D. C. *Address*, 30 East 57th St., New York, N. Y.

CONROY, George I. Painter. Member: Salma. Club. *Address*, 793 Gravesend Ave., Brooklyn, N. Y.

CONSTANT, Marjorie. Painter. Exhibited at National Association of Women Painters and Sculptors, New York, 1924. *Address*, Duxbury, Mass.

CONVERSE, Lilly S. Painter. Born Petrograd, 1888. Pupil of Kenneth Hayes Miller. *Address*, Rue Desbordes, Valmore, Paris, France.

CONWAY, John Severinus. Painter and sculptor. Born at Dayton, Ohio, in 1852. Pupil of Conrad Diehl, Jules Lefebvre and Boulanger in Paris. Work: Mural decorations in Chamber of Commerce, Milwaukee. Sculptor for Soldiers' Monument, Milwaukee. *Address*, Tenafly, New Jersey, P. O. 231.

CONWAY, William John. Painter and sculptor. Born St. Paul, 1872. Pupil of Colarossi Academy under Collin, Courtois and Prinet in Paris. Member: Whistler Club; Art Workers' Guild; Minnesota State Art Society; Artists' Society, St. Paul Institute. *Address*, 1394 Lincoln Ave., St. Paul, Minn.

COOK, Charles B. Painter. Exhibited "Mountain Building" at the Penna. Academy of Fine Arts, 1924. *Address*, Woodstock, New York.

COOK, Daniel. Painter. Born Cincinnati, 1872. Pupil of Nicholas Gysis, Cincinnati Art Academy. Member: Munich Art Club; Cincinnati Art Club. Instructor at University of Cincinnati. Work: "A Rainy Day," University of Cincinnati; mural decorations, Cincinnati Music Hall. *Address*, 104 Saunders St., Cincinnati, Ohio.

COOK, I. Vernon (Mrs. Jerome Cook). Painter. Born Brooklyn, N. Y. Pupil of Art Students' League of New York and Chase;

Blanche and Simon in Paris. Member: National Academy Women Painters and Sculptors. *Address*, 39 West 67th St., New York, N. Y.

COOK, John A. Painter. Born Gloucester, Mass., 1870. Pupil of DeCamp, E. L. Major and Douglas Volk. Member: Society of Independent Artists. *Address*, 8 Highland St., Gloucester, Mass.

COOK, May Elizabeth. Sculptor. Born in Chillicothe, Ohio, 1881. Pupil of Paul Bartlett; École des Beaux Arts and Colarossi Academy in Paris. Member: Columbus League of Artists. Represented in Carnegie Library, Columbus, Ohio; Ohio State University, Columbus. *Address*, 1550 Clifton Ave., Columbus, Ohio.

COOK, T. B. Engraver. In 1809–16 T. B. Cook was engraving portraits in stipple for Wm. Durell and other book publishers of New York.

COOK-SMITH, Jean Beman. Painter and sculptor. Born in New York, 1865. Pupil of Art Institute of Chicago; Chase. Studied in Holland, France and Italy. Member: National Academy of Women Painters and Sculptors. Work: "The Maya Frieze," San Diego Museum, Calif. *Address*, Jamaica, Long Island, New York.

COOKE, Abigail W. Painter. Pupil of Rhode Island School of Design. Member of Providence Art Club. *Address*, 15 Pitman St., Providence, R. I.

COOKE, Charles H. Painter. Born in Toledo, Ohio. Pupil of Art Institute of Chicago. *Address*, 1841 Kenilworth Ave., Chicago, Ill.

COOKE, Edna. Illustrator. Born in Philadelphia, 1891. Pupil of Breckenridge and McCarter at the Penna. Academy of Fine Arts. *Address*, Care of 235 South 11th St., Philadelphia.

COOKE, Jessie D. Painter and illustrator. Born in Atchison, Kans., 1872. Pupil of Art Institute of Chicago. *Address*, 1841 Kenilworth Ave., Chicago, Ill.

COOKE, George. Engraver. It is difficult to locate the engraver of this name, or to decide whether some of the plates so signed were executed in England or in the United States. The American artist and portrait-painter, George Cooke, was born in St. Mary County, Md., 1793. He studied art in Europe in 1826–30, and established himself in New York on his return to this country. It is not known that this man ever attempted to engrave, and the plates signed by George Cooke as "engraver" are too well done to be ascribed to any 'prentice hand.

COOKE, Joseph. Engraver. In the *Pennsylvania Gazette*, Philadelphia, 1789, Joseph Cooke advertises himself as goldsmith, jeweler and hair-worker. He closes by announcing, "Church, State or County Seals, Coats of Arms, and all manner of Engraving on steel, silver, gold or metal, executed in the best manner and at the lowest prices."

COOKINS, James. Artist. Born in Terre Haute, Ind., 1825. After study abroad he opened his studio in Cincinnati in 1861. He finally settled in Chicago, Ill. He had marked talent as a landscape painter.

COOKMAN, Charles Edwin. Painter. Born in Columbus, Ohio, in 1856; died in 1913.

COLLIDGE, Bertha. Miniature painter. Born in Lynn, Mass., 1880. Pupil of School of Boston Museum of Fine Arts under Tarbell and Benson. *Address*, 133 East 40th St., New York City, N. Y.

COLLIDGE, John. Painter and illustrator. Born in Pennsylvania, 1882. Pupil of Chase and Anshutz. *Address*, 826 California Bldg., Los Angeles, Calif.

COLLIDGE, Montfort. Painter. Born in Brooklyn, New York, in 1888. Pupil of Robert Henri. *Address*, 126 Pennsylvania St., Brooklyn, New York.

COONSMAN, Nancy. Sculptor. Born at St. Louis, 1888. Pupil of Zolnay and Grafly. *Address*, 6171 Delmar Blvd., St. Louis, Mo.

COOPER, Alice. Sculptor. Born in Denver, Colo. Among her best known works, "Summer Breeze," "Dancing Fawn," and "Frog Girl."

COOPER, B. Z. Painter. Exhibited water colors at Penna. Academy of the Fine Arts, Philadelphia, 1922. *Address*, 1947 Broadway, New York.

COOPER, Colin Campbell. Painter. Born Philadelphia. Studied Penna. Academy of the Fine Arts, Philadelphia, Julien Academie and other art schools, Paris; spent much time in Europe painting figure and architectural subjects. Specialty, views in American and European cities and "sky-scrapers"; represented in Art Museum, Cincinnati; Boston Art Club; St. Louis Museum; Pennsylvania Academy of Fine Arts; Philadelphia Art Club; Memorial Art Gallery, Rochester, N. Y. Awards: Gold medal, Art Club, Philadelphia, 1905; Lippincott prize, Penna. Academy, 1919; National Academy. Member: American Water Color Society; New York Society Painters; Fellowship Pa. Academy Fine Arts. Clubs: Water Color, Art (Philadelphia), Lotos (New York). *Address*, Santa Barbara, Calif.

COOPER, Elizabeth. Sculptor. Born in Dayton, Ohio, 1901. She makes a specialty of animals. *Address*, Stamford, Conn.

COOPER, Emma Lampert (Mrs. Colin Campbell Cooper). Painter. Born Nunda, N. Y. Began study of art New York, Cooper Union, and Art Students' League, and with Miss Agnes D. Abbatt in water colors; later went abroad several times for study in Paris and to sketch in Holland, Italy, etc. Member: N. Y. Water Color Club; American Water Color Society; National Association Women Painters and Sculptors; New York Society of Painters; (pres.) Women's Art Association of Canada; Philadelphia Water Color Club. Died 1920.

COOPER, F. G. Illustrator. Born at McMimville, Ore., 1883. Has illustrated books and magazines, also designed posters. *Address*, 425 Tremont Ave., Westfield, N. J.

COOPER, James. Miniature painter. Flourished in Philadelphia, 1855. He exhibited at the Penna. Academy in 1855.

COOPER, Margaret M. Painter. Born in Terryville, Conn., 1874. Exhibited "Hambury Cove" at Annual Exhibition of National Academy of Design 1925. *Address*, New Britain, Conn.

COOPER, Peregrine F. Painter. He worked in oil portraits, miniatures, also drawing in pastels. He flourished in Philadelphia from 1840 to 1890. In 1863 he published a book on miniature painting. He exhibited for a number of years at the Pennsylvania Academy of the Fine Arts, Philadelphia.

COOPER, Peter. Painter. Nothing is known of this painter beyond the fact that he painted a view of Philadelphia, and the following item from the records of the "Philadelphia City Council" reads: "Peter Cooper, painter, was admitted a freeman of the city in May 1717."

COOPER, W. Painter. Flourished 1835.

COOTES, F. Graham. Painter and illustrator. Born at Staunton, 1879. Pupil of Robert Henri. *Address*, 1947 Broadway, New York.

COPELAND, Alfred Bryant. Painter. Born in Boston, 1840. He studied abroad and on returning to this country he became professor in the University of St. Louis. He later opened his studio in Paris, exhibited in the Salon, and sent a collection of his paintings to Boston. He died in 1909.

COPELAND, Charles. Painter. Born Thomaston, Me., 1858. Engaged as illustrator and painter in water color; exhibited at Society American Artists; Penna. Academy Fine

Arts; Boston Art Club, etc. Member: Boston Art Club, Boston Society Water Color Painters. *Address*, 110 Tremont St., Boston, Mass.

COPELAND, Joseph F. Painter. Born at St. Louis, Mo., 1872. Instructor at Penna. Museum of Industrial Art. *Address*, 320 South Broad St., Philadelphia.

COPELAND, M. B. Portrait painter. Born in El Paso, Texas. Pupil of Kenyon Cox in New York, and Shannon in London. His studio is in Paris.

COPLEY, John Singleton. Portrait painter. Born in Boston, 1737; died in London, 1815. This famous American portrait painter was the stepson of the English portrait painter and mezzotint engraver Peter Pelham, who died in Boston in 1851. On May 22, 1748, his first wife having died, Pelham married Mary Singleton Copley, the widow of Richard Copley and the mother of the subject of this sketch.

John Singleton Copley doubtless received instructions from his stepfather in both portrait painting and in engraving. As evidence of the latter statement there exists a small but creditably executed mezzotint plate of the Rev. Mr. William Welsted of Boston in New England. This plate is signed "J. S. Copley pinxt. et fecit." William Welsted died 1753, and this plate was probably engraved soon after this date. He sent over to London, for exhibition at the Royal Academy in 1760, a picture of "The Boy and the Flying Squirrel." In 1775 after a successful career as a portrait painter in Boston he established himself in London. His masterpieces, "The Death of Lord Chatham" and "The Death of Major Pierson," are both in the National Academy. See "Life of John Singleton Copley," by Martha B. Amory; "Life and List of Some of the Works of John Singleton Copley," by Augustus T. Perkins. Also "The Life and Works of John Singleton Copley," by Frank W. Bayley. The Boston Museum of Fine Arts owns his portraits of Samuel Adams, Gen'l Jos. Warren, Mrs. Warren, John Quincy Adams, and "Watson and the Shark."

COPPEDGE, Mrs. Fern. Painter. Born Decatur, Ill., 1888. Pupil of William M. Chase, John Carlsen, and Art Students' League of New York; Art Institute of Chicago; Penna. Academy of the Fine Arts. Member: National Academy Women Painters and Sculptors. Work: "The Thaw," Detroit Institute of Art; "Winter on the Schuylkill," Pennsylvania State Capitol. *Address*, 4011 Baltimore Ave., Philadelphia, Pa.

COPPINI, Pompeo. Sculptor. Born Florence, 1870. Pupil of Augusto Rivalta in Florence; came to America in 1896; citizen of United States since 1901. Represented in the United States by 29 public monuments, 16 portrait statues, and about 75 portrait busts, and

in Mexico City by the Washington Statue, gift from Americans to Mexico. *Address*, 7444 Blackstone Ave., Chicago, Ill.

CORAM, Thomas. Artist. He was born in Bristol, England, 1756, and died 1812. He came to Charleston, S. C., at an early age. He was a self-taught artist and attempted engraving (see "Stauffer's American Engravers"). Tuckerman speaks of him in his "Book of the Artists" as a "Portrait Painter of Charleston, S. C."

CORBETT, Gail Sherman (Mrs. Harvey Wiley Corbett). Sculptor. Born in Syracuse, N. Y. Pupil of Augustus Saint Gaudens. Awards: Honorable mention for sculpture, and bronze medal for medals, Panama Pacific Expn. Work: "Hamilton White Memorial" and "Kirkpatrick Fountain," Syracuse, N. Y.; bronze doors, Auditorium and Municipal Building, Springfield, Mass.; Springfield medal, Boston Museum. *Address*, 443 West 21st St., New York City, N. Y.

CORNE, Michaele Felice. Italian marine and portrait painter in oil. Born in 1712 and died 1832. He also drew portraits in India ink, several being in the Essex Institute at Salem, Mass. During the War of 1812 he painted a series of naval engagements.

CORNER, Thomas C. Painter. Born Baltimore, Md., 1865. Pupil of Weir and Cox in New York; Lefebvre and Constant in Paris. Member: Charcoal Club. Represented in Virginia State Library, Richmond, by portrait of Gov. F. W. Mackey Holliday, painted in 1897.

CORNETT, Robert F. Painter. Born in Lafayette, La., 1867. Pupil of Corcoran Art School. *Address*, 1221 15th St., N.W., Washington, D. C.

CORNISH. A portrait of Charles Paxton, signed "Cornish," is in the collection of the American Antiquarian Society at Worcester, Mass.

CORNOYER, Paul. Painter. Born St. Louis, Mo., 1864; died 1923. Pupil of Lefebvre, Constant and Louis Blanc in Paris. Work: "After the Rain," Brooklyn Institute Museum; "Madison Square," Art Association, Dallas, Tex.; St. Louis Art Museum; "Rainy Day, Columbus Circle," Newark Art Association.

CORNWELL, Dean. Illustrator. Born Louisville, Ky., 1892. Pupil of Harvey Dunn. Member: Society of Illustrators. Illustrated: "Torrent," "Kindred of the Dust," "River's End," "Valley of Silent Men," "Fine the Woman," etc. *Address*, 1931 Broadway, New York, N. Y.

CORNWELL, Martha J. Sculptor and painter. Born West Chester, 1869. Studied at Philadelphia School of Design, and Art Students' League of New York; and with Saint Gaudens, H. Siddons Mowbray and Geo. deForest Brush. Member: Art Students' emy of Fine Arts. Specialty, portrait bronzes. Exhibited at Penna. Academy of Fine Arts, Philadelphia, 1924. She is now deceased.

CORNWELL, William Caryl. Painter. Born Lyons, N. Y., 1851. Pupil of Lefebvre, Boulanger, and Julien Academy, Paris. Member: National Art Club. Inventor of Cornwell luminos. *Address*, 26 East 8th St., New York City, N. Y.

CORSON, Katherine Langdon (Mrs. Walter Heilner Corson). Landscape painter and illustrator. Born Rochdale, England. Pupil of Emil Carlsen, H. Bolton Jones and F. C. Jones in New York. Member: National Academy of Women Painters and Sculptors: Fellowship Penna. Academy of Fine Arts; Plastic Club. Award: Medal, Atlanta Expn., 1895. Work: ''Across the Cove,'' Hamilton Club.

CORTRIGHT, Hazel Packer. Painter. Member: Plastic Club. *Address*, St. Martin's, Philadelphia, Pa.; Saunderstown, R. I.

CORWAINE, Aaron H. Born in Kentucky in 1802; died in Philadelphia in 1830. He studied with Thomas Sully, and for a time had a studio in Philadelphia and later in Cincinnati. He visited England for study but soon returned to America in ill health. He died at the early age of twenty-eight.

CORWIN, Charles Abel. Painter. Born Newburgh, N. Y., 1857. Pupil of Frank Duveneck. Member: Chicago Society of Artists. Work in Piedmont Gallery, Berkeley, Calif. *Address*, 45 Fifth Ave., New York, N. Y.

CORY, Kate T. Painter. Born in Illinois. Pupil of Cooper Union and Art Students' League of New York. Member: National Academy Women Painters and Sculptors; Society of Independent Artists. Represented by collection of pictures in the Smithsonian Institute, Washington, D. C. *Address*, Prescott, Ariz.

COSTA, Hector. Sculptor. Exhibited ''Lion Cubs'' at Annual Exhibition of National Academy, 1925. *Address*, 238 East 86th St., New York.

COSTAGGINI, Filippo. Painter. Born in Rome, Italy, 1837; died at Upper Falls, Baltimore County, Md., 1907. Began his artistic career in Rome, where he won distinction as an historical painter. He came to America in 1870 and engaged in the painting of historical and religious pictures, as well as portraits, among his notable portraits being one of the late Senator Justin S. Morrill, of Vermont. His works can be found in the large cathedrals and churches of the United States, especially in New York, Philadelphia, and Baltimore. He was given the commission to complete the historical frieze in the Rotunda of the Capitol representing American History, commenced by Constantino Brumidi. The work of Costaggini began at the three Indians in the group, representing Penn's Treaty, and continued the historical events in chronological order to the period of the Discovery of Gold in California, this being two thirds of the frieze. He died before completing the work.

COSTELLO, Val. Painter. Member of California Art Club. *Address*, 518 West 54th St., Los Angeles, Calif.

COSTIGAN, Ida. Sculptor. Born in Germany in 1894. Exhibited Penna. Academy of Fine Arts, Philadelphia, 1924. *Address*, Orangeburg, N. Y.

COSTIGAN, John E. Painter. Member: New York Water Color Club. *Address*, Orangeburg, N. Y.

COTHARIN, Kate Leah. Painter. Born Detroit, Mich., 1866. Pupil of J. M. Dennis in Detroit. Specialty, pastel landscape in miniature.

COTTON, John W. Painter, etcher, and illustrator. Born in Canada. Student of Art Institute of Chicago, and E. H. Wilson in London. Honorable mention for his etchings. His views in New Mexico are well known and were exhibited at the Print Makers' Society of California. *Address*, 1137 San Rafael Ave., Glendale, California.

COTTON, William. Portrait painter. Born Newport, R. I., 1880. Studied Cowles Art School, Boston, under Andreas Anderson and Joseph De Camp, also Julien Academy, Paris, under Jean Paul Laurens. Has exhibited at National Academy of Design, New York; Corcoran Art Gallery, Washington; Art Institute, Chicago; Penna. Academy of Fine Arts; St. Louis Art Museum; Carnegie Institute, Pittsburgh; etc. First Hallgarten prize, National Academy of Design, 1907. Has painted portraits of Honorable Willard Bartlett, George Barr McCutcheon, Harrison Rhodes, Miss Chrystal Herne; mural paintings in the Capitol Theatre, N. Y.; represented in the exhibition of American Artists at Luxembourg Museum, at the invitation of the French Gov't, Academy of National Artists; a founder National Association Portrait Painters. Member: Newport Art Association. *Address*, 132 East 19th St., New York City, N. Y.

COUARD, Alexander P. Painter. Born in New York City, 1891. Pupil of George Bridgman and F. V. DuMond. *Address*, R. D. 42, Norwalk, Conn.

COUDERT, Amalia K. Miniature painter. Born 1876. Painted King Edward, Czar and Czarina, Cecil Rhodes, and many of the English aristocracy.

COULON, George D. Portrait painter, who had a studio at 103 Condé Street in 1850, and continued to paint in New Orleans for fifty years, with studios in various parts of the city. His last residence, given shortly before his demise, was at 1536 North Claiborne St., in 1904.

COULTER, Mary R. (Mrs.). Painter and etcher. Born in Newport, Ky. Pupil of Cincinnati Art Academy under Duveneck. *Address,* 628 Montgomery St., San Francisco, Calif.

COUPER, B. King (Mrs.). Painter and sculptor. Born in Augusta, Ga., in 1867. Pupil of Chase and Dangerfield. *Address,* Pine St., Spartansburg, S. C.

COUPER, William. Sculptor. Born at Norfolk, Va., 1853. Began art studies in Cooper Institute, New York; entered Royal Academy, Munich, 1874, for study of drawing and anatomy; went to Florence, 1875, entered studio of Thomas Ball. Lived in Italy 22 years. Settled at New York 1897. Specialty, ideal works, portrait statues, busts and bas-reliefs. Member jury for acceptance of works of art sent from Italy to Chicago Expn., 1893, and other Expns. in this country; now retired. *Address,* 105 Upper Mountain Ave., Montclair, N. J.

COUSE, Eanger Irving. Painter. Born in Saginaw, Mich., 1866. Pupil of the National Academy of Design in New York, Robert-Fleury, and École des Beaux Arts in Paris. Elected member of the National Academy of Design, 1911. Specialty, painting American Indians. *Address,* 58 West 57th St., New York.

COUTTS, Gordon. Painter. Born in Scotland, 1880. Pupil of Lefebvre in Paris. *Address,* 406 Pacific Ave., Piedmont, California.

COUTURIER, Henri. Portrait painter. He is said to have painted a portrait of Frederick Philipse (owner of Philipse manor, Yonkers) in New Orange in 1674. He resided for some years in Delaware, where he became councillor or Burgomaster of the Province. He died in 1684. Some of his portraits are signed by the monogram of the artist.

COVELL, Margaret. A little known portrait and genre painter, now deceased.

COVERT, John. Painter. Exhibited "Resurrection" and "Temptation of St. Anthony" at Exhibition of "Paintings Showing the Later Tendencies in Art," at the Penna. Academy of Fine Arts, 1921. *Address,* 15 West 29th St., New York City.

COVEY, Arthur S. Etcher and painter. Born in Bloomington, Ill., 1877. Pupil of Frank Brangwyn, and has etchings in Library of Congress. Also executed mural decorations. *Address,* 163 West 23d St., New York City.

COWAN, Sarah E. Miniature painter. Exhibited portrait miniatures at the Penna. Academy of Fine Arts, Philadelphia, 1922. *Address,* 125 East 10th St., New York City.

COWELL, Joseph G. Painter. Born Peoria, Ill., 1886. Pupil of Bridgman, DuMond, Tarbell, and Benson; Laurens in Paris. Member: Boston Art Club. Murals in St. Mary's Cathedral, Universalist Church, Peoria, Ill.; theatre, Holyoke, Mass.; theatres in Boston. Stained glass windows, St. Mary's Cathedral, Peoria, Ill. *Address,* 221 Columbus Ave., Boston, Mass.

COWLES, Edith V. Painter and illustrator. Born Farmington, Conn., 1874. Pupil of John T. Niemeyer; Bruneau and Mme. Laforge in Paris. Illustrated: "House of Seven Gables," by Hawthorne; "Old Virginia," by Thomas Nelson Page; "Friendship," by Emerson. Has five stained glass windows in St. Michael's Church, Brooklyn. Director of Craft Work at the "Lighthouse for the Blind." *Address,* 152 West 57th St., New York, N. Y.

COWLES, Genevieve A. Painter and illustrator. Born Farmington, Conn., 1871. Pupil of Niemeyer at Yale Art School; Robert B. Brandegee at Farmington. Specialty, mural decorations and stained glass windows. Work: "Charge to St. Peter," Chapel of Conn. State Prison (wax mural). *Address,* 152 West 57th St., New York, N. Y.

COWLES, Mildred. Painter. Born in Farmington, Conn., 1876. Pupil of Yale Art School. *Address,* 102 West 57th St., New York, N. Y.

COWLES, Russell. Painter. Born Algona, Ia., 1887. Member of National Art Club. Mural paintings. Award: American Academy in Rome Fellowship, 1915–1920. *Address,* 44 Gramercy Park, New York, N. Y.

COX, Albert Scott. Painter and illustrator. Born Randolph, Me., 1863. Studied at Academy, Paris. Painter of figures and landscapes; has done much illustrating and many caricatures.

COX, Allyn. Painter. Born New York, N. Y., 1896. Pupil of his father, Kenyon Cox; National Academy of Design; George Bridgman. Awarded Fellowship American Academy in Rome 1916. Work: Overmantel in Public Library, Windsor, Vt., *Address,* 130 East 67th St., New York, N. Y.

COX, Charles Brinton. Sculptor. Born in Philadelphia. His modeling of animals shows beauty and power. He died in 1905.

COX, Dorothy E. Painter. Exhibited at Penna. Academy of Fine Arts, Philadelphia, 1924. *Address*, 107 South Front St., Harrisburg, Penna.

COX, George J. Sculptor. Exhibited "The Zodiac" at Annual Exhibition of National Academy of Design, 1925, New York. *Address*, 509 West 121st St., New York.

COX, James. Artist. Born in England, 1751, and died 1834. He came to this country as a young man and settled in Philadelphia where he was the fashionable drawing-master for many years. He collected over 5,000 volumes on the fine arts which he sold to the Library Co. of Philadelphia; he did much to advance the arts in that city. He excelled in flower painting.

COX, Kenyon. Painter. Born Warren, Ohio, 1856. Pupil of Carolus Duran and Gerome in Paris. Second Hallgarten prize, National Academy of Design, 1889. Temple silver medal, Pa. Academy of Fine Arts, 1891; medal of honor for mural paintings, N. Y. Architectural League, 1909; Isidor medal, National Academy of Design, 1910. National Academy, 1903. Member: Mural Painters; National Institute and American Academy of Arts and Letters. Specialty, portraits, figure pieces, mural decoration; also illustrator, teacher and writer. He died in 1919.

COX, Louise (Howland King). Painter. Born San Francisco, Calif., 1865. Pupil of National Academy of Design and Art Students' League, New York. Third Hallgarten prize, National Academy of Design, 1896. *Address*, 130 East 67th St., New York.

COX, Palmer. Illustrator. Born in Quebec, Canada, in 1840. In 1875 he settled in New York, where he followed his artistic and literary pursuits. His illustrated work was well known. Died in 1924.

COX-McCORMACK, Nancy, Mrs. Sculptor. Born Nashville, Tenn., 1885. Principal works: "Harmony," original in private collection of C. S. Scotten, Chicago; copy in Nashville Art Museum; Carmack Memorial, heroic figure of Edward W. Carmack, on Capitol grounds, Nashville, Tenn.; bust of William H. Mitchell, banker, Chicago; also various statues, portraits of children, etc. Member: Western Society Sculptors. *Address*, Lake Shore Drive and Ontario St., Chicago, Ill.

COXE, R. Cleveland. Painter and engraver. Born Baltimore, Md., 1855. Pupil of Bonnat and Gerome in Paris. *Address*, 1320 Fifth Ave., Seattle, Wash.

COY, Anna. Painter. Born Rockford, Ill. Pupil of Chase, F. V. DuMond, Henri and Alexander Robinson. Gallery director, Rockford Art Guild. *Address*, 118 Main St., Rockford, Ill.

COY, C. Lynn. Sculptor. Born Chicago, Ill., 1889. Pupil of Artists' Institute of Chicago. *Address*, 245 West North Ave., Chicago, Ill.

COYLE. According to Dunlap an excellent scene painter and designer; came to New York from England. He died in New York City in 1824.

COYLE, James. Painter. He was elected a member of National Academy of Design, New York, in 1826. He died in New York City in 1828.

COYNE, William. Painter, illustrator, and engraver. Born New York, 1896. Pupil of John Sloan. Member: Society of Independent Artists; Society of New York Artists; Beaux Arts Institute. Illustrations for *New York Evening Post, New York Call, The Bookman*.

CRAIG, Anna Belle. Painter. Born 1878, in Pittsburgh, Pa. Pupil of Art Students' League of New York, Chase, Shirlaw, Henry G. Keller, Martin G. Borgard, and Howard Pyle. Member: Pittsburgh Artist Association. Illustrates in *Harper's, St. Nicholas, Metropolitan*, and books for children. *Address*, 6202 Walnut St., Pittsburgh, Pa.

CRAIG, Charles. Painter. Born on farm, Morgan County, Ohio, 1846. Educated Penna. Academy of Fine Arts, Philadelphia. Painter of Indians, cowboys, plains and mountains; has exhibited at American Water Color Society, New York; Denver, 1883; Minneapolis Expn., 1886–8; St. Louis, 1889; Omaha, 1894–6. Honorable mention Western Artists' Association. Represented by Indian paintings in many fine private collections in U. S. and abroad. *Address*, Colorado Springs, Colo.

CRAIG, Isaac Eugene. Painter. Born near Pittsburgh, in 1830. After studying art in Philadelphia he went to Paris. He returned to this country in 1855, but returned to Europe some ten years later. He painted a portrait of Joel T. Hart, the Kentucky sculptor, and some striking views of Venice.

CRAIG, Thomas Bigelow. Painter. Born in Philadelphia, 1849; died in New York, 1924. Exhibited at Pennsylvania Academy of Fine Arts, and National Academy of Design. Represented at the Boston Art Club and Pennsylvania Academy of Fine Arts. Elected Associate Member of the National Academy.

CRAIG, William. Born in Dublin, Ireland, 1829; in 1863 he settled in this country. He was one of the original members of the American Society of Water Color Painters. He was drowned in Lake George, N. Y. Among his paintings "Mount Washington," "Hudson River, near West Point" and many landscapes of peculiar transparency in coloring. He died in 1875.

CRAM, Allan G. Painter, illustrator and engraver. Born Washington, D. C., 1886. Pupil of Woodbury, Chase and Shurtleff. *Address*, Care of Marblehead P. O., Mass.

CRAMER, Florence Ballin. Painter. Born Brooklyn, N. Y. Pupil of DuMond, Brush and Harrison. Member: National Academy of Women Painters and Sculptors. *Address*, 163 East 72d St., New York, N. Y.

CRAMER, Konrad. Painter and engraver. Pupil of Bolton Brown; also studied in Europe. Director of Woodstock School of Applied Art. *Address*, 163 East 72d St., New York, N. Y.

CRAMPTON, Rollin McN. Painter and illustrator. Born in New Haven, Conn., in 1886. Pupil of Yale Art School and Thomas Benton. *Address*, 52 West 36th St., New York City.

CRANCH, Caroline A. Painter. Daughter of Christopher P. Cranch, and pupil of her father and the Cooper Institute in New York, under William Hunt. Specialty, figurepieces. *Address*, Cambridge, Mass.

CRANCH, Christopher Pearse. Painter. Born in Alexandria, Va., in 1813. He studied abroad, returned to New York and in 1864 was elected a member of the National Academy. He later moved to Cambridge, Mass. Among his paintings are "Washington Oak, at Newburg, N. Y."; "Venice," and "Forest of Fontainebleau." Represented in the Boston Museum of Fine Arts. He died in Cambridge, Mass., in 1892.

CRANCH, John. Portrait painter. Born in Washington, D. C., in 1807; he died in Urbana, Ohio, in 1891. Student of King, Harding, and Sully, he commenced painting portraits in Washington, D. C., in 1829. In 1830 he studied in Italy, and in 1834 returned to this country, where he painted many portraits and original compositions. He was elected an Associate of the National Academy in 1853. He was the brother of Christopher Pearse Cranch.

CRANE, Ann (Mrs. Bruce). Painter. Born in New York City. Pupil of Twachtman in New York and of Merson in Paris. *Address*, Arcade, Bronxville, N. Y.

CRANE, Frederick. Painter of mountain scenery. Born in Bloomfield, N. J., in 1847. He was awarded the bronze medal in 1904 of the St. Louis Exposition. He died in New York City in 1915. Represented in Worcester Art Museum by "London from the Thames."

CRANE, Robert Bruce. Painter. Born in New York, 1857. Studied painting under A. H. Wyant. Specialty, American landscapes. He was elected member of the National Academy of Design in 1902. He received the Webb Prize at the Society of American Artists in 1897. *Address*, Bronxville, New York.

CRASKE, Leonard. Sculptor. Born in London, 1882, he came to America in 1910 and made his home in Boston and Gloucester. *Address*, 22 St. Botolph Studios, Boston.

CRAWFORD, Arthur R. Painter. Born in Marilla, Mich., in 1885. Pupil of Chicago Academy of Fine Arts under Reynolds and Henderson. Member of Art Students' League of Chicago. *Address*, 2028 Lincoln St., Evanston, Ill.

CRAWFORD, Brenetta H. (Mrs. Earl S.). Painter and illustrator. Born in Toledo, Ohio, in 1875. Pupil of Art Students' League of New York and Colarossi and Carmen Academies in Paris. Specialty, portrait painting. *Address*, *Address*, "The Enclosure," Nutley, N. J.

CRAWFORD, Earl Stetson. Painter. Born Philadelphia, Pa., 1877. Studied at School of Industrial Art, Philadelphia, Pa.; Penna. Academy of Fine Arts; Delacluse and Julien Academies; Ecole Nationale des Beaux Arts, Paris; also in Munich, London, Rome, Florence and Venice. Connected with School of Applied Design for Women, New York, 1912–17. Portrait painter and mural decorator, also designer of stained glass windows in various churches; mural work in U. S. govt. bldgs., San Francisco. Fellow of Society American Illustrators; Member of National Association Portrait Painters. *Address*, "The Enclosure," Nutley, N. J.

CRAWFORD, Esther M. Painter. Born in Atlanta, Ga., 1872. Pupil of Whistler, Dow, and Beck. Member of San Francisco Art Association. *Address*, 716 North Avenue 66, Los Angeles, Calif.

CRAWFORD, Thomas. Sculptor. Born of Irish parentage in New York, 1813. In 1835 he went to Rome, and studied with Thorwaldsen. He died in New York City in 1857. His best known works are the bronze doors and work on the Capitol at Washington, D. C.; the equestrian statue of Washington at Richmond, Va.; and his statue of Adam and Eve. His son was Frances Marion Crawford, the well-known author.

CRAWLEY, Ida J. Painter. Born in London County, Tenn., in 1867. Pupil of Corcoran Art School, Washington, D. C., and of Massi in Paris. *Address*, 31 Park Ave., Asheville, N. C.

CRAWLEY, John. Painter. Born in England, 1784, he was brought over to this country by his parents when very young and settled at Newark, N. J. He studied with the artist Savage. Crawley painted portraits at Philadelphia and exhibited at the first opening of the Penna. Academy of Fine Arts.

CRAWLEY, John (Jr.). Draughtsman. Son of the artist is recorded in Dunlap's "History of Art" as an excellent draughtsman, much interested in Lithography. He was engaged at Endicott's and Swett's lithographic establishment and executed some beautiful specimens of work on the title pages of the music of that day.

CREIFELDS, Richard. Portrait painter. Portrait of Chas. A. Schieren by Creifelds owned by City of New York. *Address*, 2231 Broadway, N. Y.

CRENIER, Henri. Sculptor. Born in Paris, 1873. Member of National Sculpture Society of New York. His "Boy and Turtle" is at Metropolitan Museum, N. Y. The pediments and caryatides of City Hall, San Francisco, Calif., are also his work. *Address*, Shore Acres, Mamaroneck.

CRESSON, Margaret French. Sculptor. Born in Concord, Mass., 1889. Studied with her father Daniel Chester French. Exhibited, Penna. Academy of Fine Arts, Philadelphia, 1924. *Address*, 12 West 8th St., New York.

CRIMI, Alfred. Painter. Exhibited at the Annual Exhibition of the National Academy of Design, 1925. *Address*, 1962 Pilgrim Ave., New York.

CRISP, Arthur. Painter. Born Hamilton, Ont., 1881. Pupil of Bryson Burroughs and F. V. DuMond. First Hallgarten prize, National Academy of Design, 1916. Decorations, Belasco Theatre, and The Playhouse, N. Y. "British Recruiting on Boston Common," for Canadian War Memorials; "Commons Reading Room," House of Parliament, Can.; picture presented to Prince of Wales. Director of mural painting, Beaux Arts School of Design, 1917. Member: National Society Mural Painters; Architectural League of New York; American Water Color Society; New York Water Color Club; Allied Artists of America; Associate Member of National Academy. *Address*, 308 East 51st St., New York.

CRISSEY, Thomas Henry. Painter. Born Stamford, Conn., 1875. Pupil of George Bridgman, Walter Florian, Edward Dufner. Member: Society of Independent Artists; New York Society of Artists. *Address*, Powers St., New Canaan, Conn.

CRITCHER, Catherine Carter. Painter. Born in Westmoreland County, Va. Pupil of Richard Miller and Charles Hoffbauer in Paris. *Address*, 3 St. Mathews Alley, Washington, D. C.

CRITTENDEN, Elizabeth C. Painter. Exhibited at National Association of Women Painters and Sculptors, New York, 1924. *Address*, 76 North 30th St., Flushing, L. I.

CROASDALE, E. Portrait painter. He painted a portrait of Abraham Lincoln, and on the back of the canvas is inscribed "Painted by E. Croasdale, and retouched by S. J. Ferris, 1863."

CROCKER, J. Denison. Landscape and portrait painter. He was born in Salem, Conn., in 1823. With the exception of some instruction from Charles Lanman, he was self-taught.

CROCKER, Marion E. Painter. Born Boston, Mass. Pupil of Tarbell in Boston; Kenyon Cox in New York; Constant and Laurens in Paris; George Hitchcock in Holland. *Address*, 136 Cypress St., Brookline, Mass.

CROCKER, Martha E. Painter. Exhibited, Penna. Academy of Fine Arts, Philadelphia, 1924. *Address*, 107 Fenway Studios, Boston, Mass.

CROCKER, W. H. Painter. Born in New York City, 1856. Pupil of Robert Vonnoh and Charles Rosen. *Address*, 50 Hamilton Terrace, New York, N. Y.

CROM, Lillian Hobbes. Painter. Member: Fellowship Penna. Academy of Fine Arts. *Address*, Schwenksville, Pa.

CRON, Nina N. (Mrs.). Miniature painter. Exhibited at Annual Miniature Exhibition, Penna. Academy of Fine Arts, Philadelphia, 1925. *Address*, 3302 McKinley St., Washington, D. C.

CRONENWETT, Clare. Engraver. *Address*, 641 O'Farrell St., San Francisco, Calif.

CROOKS, Forrest C. Illustrator. Born Goshen, Ind., 1893. Pupil of George Sotter and Arthur Sparks. Illustrates for *Scribner's*, *Pictorial Review*, *Collier's Weekly*, *Woman's Home Companion*, *Century*. *Address*, Carversville, Pa.

CROOME, William. Wood engraver; was a pupil of Bowen's. He illustrated a number of books. Later in life he gave his time to designing bank-notes. He is also said to have been a very good painter in water-colors. See "History of Wood Engraving in America," by W. J. Linton.

CROPSEY, Jasper F. Painter. American. Born 1823 at Rossville, L. I., New York; died 1900 at Hastings-on-Hudson, N. Y. Pupil of

National Academy of Design in New York City; traveled in Europe. At first an architect; later painted landscapes, chiefly Hudson River scenery. He painted a landscape (open country with rocks and cattle in the immediate foreground and trees at the left; farm lands and a glimpse of a river in the distance; misty atmosphere) owned by the Metropolitan Museum, New York. Elected member of National Academy in 1851.

CROSBY, Katharine V. R. Sculptor. Born Colorado Springs, Colo., 1897. Pupil of Jess M. Lawson. Member: National Academy of Women Painters and Sculptors; Society of Independent Artists. *Address*, 103 East 75th St., New York, N. Y.

CROSBY, Raymond Moreau. Illustrator. Born Grand Rapids, Mich., 1877. Studied in Italy and France. *Address*, 252 Boylston St., Boston, Mass.

CROSS, A. B. This engraver of landscapes was a pupil of A. L. Dick in 1840. He is said to have abandoned engraving early in his life for some other business.

CROSS, Amy. Painter. Born Milwaukee, Wis., 1856. Pupil of Cooper Institute, R. Swain Gifford, William Sartain and Art Students' League of New York; Hague Academy in Holland under Jacob Maris and Albert Neuhuys; Julian Academy in Paris. Member: New York Water Color Club. *Address*, Hotel Grenoble, 7th Ave. and 56th St., New York, N. Y.

CROSS, Anson K. Painter. Born Lawrence, Mass., 1862. Pupil of Mass. Normal Art School. Member: Boston Art Club; Copley Society. Member of Faculty, Boston Museum School, since 1891. *Address*, Ashland, Mass.

CROSS, P. F. Engraver. Born in Sheffield, England; died in Philadelphia in 1856. Cross was a die-sinker and served in that capacity in the Mint of England before he came to Philadelphia about 1845, and became an assistant to James B. Longacre, chief engraver of the U. S. mint. Cross engraved the adverse of the Ingraham medal.

CROSS, Sally. Painter. Born Lawrence, Mass. Pupil of De Camp and Ross Turner in Boston. Member: Penna. Society of Miniature Painters; New York Water Color Club. *Address*, 120 Riverway, Boston, Mass.

CROSSMAN, Abner. Painter. Born St. Johnsbury, Vt., 1847. Pupil of William Hart in New York; F. W. Moody in London. Member: Chicago Water Color Club. *Address*, 658 Woodland Park, Chicago, Ill.

CROSSMAN, William H. Painter and engraver. Born New York, 1896. Pupil of Henri, Lie, Bridgman and Hawthorne. Member: Art Students' League of New York. Work: mural painting, "Brig," in Harvey School, New York City. *Address*, 39 West 67th St., New York, N. Y.

CROUCH, Emily H. Painter. Member: Providence Water Color Club. *Address*, 102 George St., Providence, R. I.

CROWELL, Margaret. Illustrator, painter and sculptor. Born in Philadelphia, Pa. Pupil of Penna. Academy of Fine Arts. Member: Fellowship Penna. Academy of Fine Arts. *Address*, Avondale, Pa.

CROWNINSHIELD, Frederic. Painter. Born Boston, 1845, and died 1918. Studied art, France and Italy. Specialty, mural painting and stained glass windows; also landscape in oils and water colors. Instructor of drawing and painting, Museum of Fine Arts, Boston, 1879–85. Director American Academy in Rome. Academy of National Arts. Member: National Society Mural Painters; National Institute Arts and Letters. The Boston Museum of Fine Arts own his "Perugia" painted 1911, "Taormina," 1913, and "Capri Cliff," 1916. Elected Associate Member of National Academy in 1905.

CRUMB, Charles P. Sculptor. Born in Bloomfield, Mo., 1874. Pupil of Barnard, Taft, and Grafly. Exhibited, Penna. Academy of Fine Arts, Philadelphia, 1924. *Address*, 721 Walnut St., Philadelphia.

CRUMMER, Mary Worthington. Painter. Exhibited water colors at the Penna. Academy of Fine Arts, Philadelphia, 1922. *Address*, 302 Suffolk St., Guilford, Baltimore, Md.

CRUMBLING, Wayne K. Painter. Exhibited at Penna. Academy of Fine Arts, Philadelphia, 1920. *Address*, Wrightville, Penna.

CRUNELLE, Leonard. Sculptor. Born in France, 1872. Pupil of Art Institute, Chicago. Represented by "Squirrel Boy" at the Art Institute, Chicago. *Address*, Studio 6016 Ellis Ave., Chicago, Ill.

CUCUEL, Edward. Painter and illustrator. Born in San Francisco, Calif., in 1875. Pupil of Constant, Laurens, and Gerome in Paris. Studio in Paris.

CULBERTSON, Linn. Painter. Born in Princeton, Ia., in 1890. *Address*, 1131 Twenty-second St., Des Moines, Ia.

CULIN, Alice Mumford (Mrs. Stewart Culin). Painter. Born in Philadelphia in 1875. Studied in Paris and France, 1897–1900; Spain, 1901–2. Exhibited at the Salon, Paris, 1900; Ville de Yant, 1901; Earl's Court, London, 1902; National Academy of Design;

Penna. Academy of Fine Art, Philadelphia. *Address*, 296 Sterling Place, Brooklyn, New York.

CUMING, B. L. Painter. Exhibited at the Annual Exhibition of the National Academy of Design, 1925. *Address*, 166 Remsen St., Brooklyn, N. Y.

CUMMING, Charles A. Painter. Born in Illinois. Pupil of Boulanger and Lefebvre in Paris. Specialty, portraits; has also executed mural paintings in the Polk County Court House. *Address*, City Library, Des Moines, Iowa.

CUMMINGS, Melvin Earl. Sculptor. Born Salt Lake City, Utah, 1876. Student of Mark Hopkins Art Institute, San Francisco; pupil of Douglas Tilden. Executed numerous statues in and around San Francisco, notably 11-ft. statue of Robert Burns, Golden Gate Park; also Conservatory Fountain; National Monument to Commodore Sloat, Monterey, Cal., etc. Instructor of modeling, University of California, 1904. Member: San Francisco Art Association. *Address*, 3966 Clay St., San Francisco.

CUMMINGS, Thomas Seir. Painter. Born in Bath, England, 1804, he came to America at an early age and became one of the most successful miniature painters in the country. He was one of the founders of the National Academy in 1826 and an early vice-president. Among his many beautiful portraits are those of Miss O'Bryan, Mrs. Cummings, Henry Inman and Mr. Hatch. He died in Connecticut in 1894.

CUNEO, Rinaldo. Painter. Born in California in 1877. Member of San Francisco Art Association. He is represented in the San Francisco Academy of Fine Arts by "Belle Vue France." *Address*, Ross, Martin County, Calif.

CUPRIEN, Frank W. Painter. Born in Brooklyn, N. Y., in 1871. Studied in Leipzig and Paris; pupil of Carl Weber in Philadelphia. Represented in Vecchio Gallery, Leipzig, by painting "Homeward Bound." *Address*, The Viking Studio, Laguna Beach, Calif.

CURRAN, Charles Courtney. Painter. Born at Hartford, Ky., 1861. Studied at Cincinnati School of Design; National Academy of Design; Art Students' League, New York; and Academie Julien, Paris. Elected member of the National Academy in 1904. *Address*, 39 West 67th St., New York.

CURRIER, C. B. Painter and illustrator. Born at Marietta, Ohio, in 1868. Pupil of Julian Academy, Paris. *Address*, 1754 North Alexandria Ave., Hollywood, Calif.

CURRIER, Charles. Lithographer. Brother of Nathaniel (of Currier & Ives, 1862–1901), had a lithographic establishment for years at 33 Spruce St., New York City. He did a large amount of work on the sheet music illustrations of the day.

CURRIER, J. Frank. Painter. Born in 1843, died in 1909. He is represented in the permanent collection in Herron Art Gallery, Ind., and the St. Louis Museum. He studied in Munich, and in 1878 sent to the Society of American Artists "A Bohemian Beggar," and two landscapes.

CURRIER, Nathaniel. Lithographer. Was born 1838, and died in 1862. The firm of Currier and Ives, 1862–1901, issued for years lithographic portraits, views and pictorial records of sporting events and other happenings. For a number of years in the fifties and sixties the work on the lithographic stone quite crowded out the wood block. As might be expected in such a large commercial lithographing establishment, the Currier productions were often vulgar in subject and crude in execution, but some very beautiful prints did come from his presses. The shooting, fishing and racing prints were in some cases most interesting and decorative, and furnish us today with a pictured idea of American sports of the period which is of great interest to the modern sportsman

CURRIER, Walter B. Painter and engraver. Born in Springfield, Mass., in 1879. Pupil of Kenyon Cox. Represented by the "Sunset Glow," "The Phantom," "Dalton Canyon." *Address*, Box 490, R. D., San Gabriel, Calif.

CURTIS, Calvin. Painter. Born in Stratford, Conn., 1822. He began his studies under Daniel Huntington in 1841, also working at the Academy of Design. His work was largely portrait painting. In a limited degree he extended his work to landscapes.

CURTIS, Constance. Painter. Born Washington. Pupil of Art Students' League of New York, and William M. Chase. Exhibited Paris Expn., 1900; St. Louis Expn., 1904. Pres. Art Workers' Club for Women. Member: Art Students' League; Women Painters and Sculptors. *Address*, 1199 Park Ave., New York.

CURTIS, Elizabeth. Painter. Born in New York, N. Y. Pupil of Twachtman and Chase. *Address*, 399 Park Ave., New York, N. Y.

CURTIS, George. Painter. Born at Southampton, England, in 1859. Pupil of Legros; Benjamin Constant. Member: Society of Independent Artists. Represented in Musée de Melun; large mural paintings in the Church Villemomble. *Address*, 5 West 16th St., New York.

CURTIS, Ida Maynard. Painter. Born Lewisburg, Pa., 1860. Pupil of Hawthorne, Ross, Maynard, Simon, Jolley. Member: Copley Society; California Art Club; Provincetown Artists' Association. *Address*, Care, Back Bay Branch of Old Colony Trust Co., Boston, Mass.

CURTIS, Nathaniel Cortlandt. Painter and lithographer. Born Southport, N. C., 1881. Pupil of William R. Ware. Member: Arts and Crafts Club of N. O. Designed buildings for Alabama Polytechnic Institute, Auburn, Ala. *Address*, 706 Title Guaranty Bldg., New Orleans.

CURTIS, Sidney. Painter. Member: Salmagundi Club. *Address*, 112 Hicks St., Brooklyn, New York, N. Y.

CURTIS, William Fuller. Painter. Born at Staten Island, New York, 1873. Studied under Rolshoven, and Jules Lefebvre and Robert-Fleury at Julien Academy. Work: Panels for church of St. Michael, and Cosmos Club, Washington, D. C. *Address*, 331 West 76th St., New York.

CUSHING, Howard Gardiner. Portrait painter. Born in Boston, 1869, and died in New York in 1915. He studied for five years in Paris at the Julien Academy; was also pupil of Laurens and Constant. Represented at Metropolitan Museum, New York, by portrait of Mrs. Ethel Cushing. He exhibited "A Woman in White," "Woman in Silver Dress," and "Sunlight." He also painted a series of murals for Mrs. H. P. Whitney's studio, on Long Island. Elected Associate Member of National Academy in 1906.

CUSHMAN, Alice. Landscape painter. Born Philadelphia, 1854. Pupil of National Academy of Design in New York; Ross Turner in Boston. Member: Philadelphia Water Color Club; National Academy of Women Painters and Sculptors; Fellowship Penna. Academy of Fine Arts Association. Specialty, water colors. *Address*, 919 Pine St., Philadelphia, Pa.

CUSHMAN, George H. Engraver and painter. Born at Windham, Conn., 1814, died in Jersey City, N. J., 1876. Cushman was a pupil of Asaph Willard, the Hartford engraver, and he became an admirable line-engraver of landscapes and book illustrations. He was chiefly known as a miniature painter of high rank, though he did not do much work professionally. He was also a fine water colorist in every department, these water colors, like his miniatures, being remarkable for purity and simplicity of character.

CUSHMAN, Thomas Hastings. Born at Albany, N. Y., in 1815, he died there in 1841. He was apprenticed in the engraving establishment of A. L. Dick in New York. He is well known as a bank-note engraver.

CURTIS, Eleanor Parke. Painter. Born Washington, D. C., 1897. Pupil of Corcoran Art School. Member: Washington Water Color Club. *Address*, 626 East Capitol St., Washington, D. C.

CUTLER, Carl Gordon. Painter. Born Newtonville, Mass., 1873. Pupil of Constant and Laurens in Paris. Member: Boston Art Club; Copley Society. *Address*, Fenway Studios, Boston, Mass.

CUTLER, Jervis. Engraver. Born in Martha's Vineyard, Mass., 1768; died at Evansville, Ind., 1846. In 1812 he engraved, on copper, illustrations for a book, including the earliest view of Cincinnati.

D

DABO, Leon. Landscape and mural painter. Born at Detroit, Mich., 1868. Studied in France and Italy. Represented by "Moose Park," Luxembourg Museum, Paris; "The Cloud," Metropolitan Museum, New York; "Hudson in Winter," Boston Museum of Fine Arts. *Address*, 28 West 63d St., Manhattan, New York.

DABO, Theodore Scott. Painter. Born New Orleans, La., 1877. Painting in Ecole des Arts Decoratifs and Ecole des Beaux Arts, Paris; has traveled extensively and studied painting independently. Ceased painting 1890, owing to irreconcilable views of teachers and his own ideas; studied natural law and optics, and made discoveries in atmosphere, luminosity and vibration that have since made his paintings quoted; returned to New York 1900, and entered various exhibitions; subsequently, exhibitions at London, Paris and elsewhere. *Address*, Billancourt (Seine), France.

DABOUR, John. Artist. Born in Smyrna, Asia, in 1837. Pupil of Academy of Fine Arts in Paris. Fifteen years of his professional life was spent in the United States painting portraits which are found in the principal cities in the United States, but chiefly in Baltimore, Md. Among his most prominent sitters were Archbishop Spaulding, Senator Cameron, Senator Davis and Governor Groome of Maryland. He died in New York in 1905.

DAGGETT, Alfred. Line engraver of portraits, and bank-note vignettes, was the uncle and the first preceptor of the American artist J. F. Kensett. Daggett was born in New Haven, Conn., 1799, and died there 1872. He was a member of the engraving firms of Daggett & Ely, and Daggett, Hinman & Co. The work signed by these firm names, however, is usually executed in stipple.

DAGGETT, Maud. Sculptor. Born in Kansas City, Mo. Pupil of Lorado Taft. Has designed and executed fountains at Hotel Raymond, Pasadena, and Memorial Fountain, "Castelar St. Creche." *Address,* 530 South Orange Grove Ave., Pasadena, Calif.

DAHLER, Warren. Painter. Born in Helena, Mont., 1887. Pupil of New York School of Art. Has executed several mural paintings. *Address,* 625 West 127th St., New York.

DAHLGREEN, Charles W. Landscape painter and etcher. Pupil of Art Institute of Chicago. Represented in Library of Congress and New York Public Library. *Address,* 409 North Cuyler Ave., Chicago, Ill.

DAINGERFIELD, Elliott. Painter. Born at Harpers Ferry, Va. Studied in New York and Europe. Elected member of the National Academy of Design in 1906. "My Lady Rhododendron," "Madonna and Child," and "Christ in the Wilderness" are his principal works. *Address,* 222 West 59th St., New York.

DAINTY, S. This man was engraving landscapes in a mixed manner, about 1840, in Philadelphia. John Dainty was a copperplate printer in Philadelphia, working as early as 1817, and this S. Dainty may have been his son.

DALAND, Katharine M. Illustrator. Born in Boston, Mass., 1883. Has illustrated "Lyrics of Eliza," and many other books.

DALLAM, Elizabeth F. Painter. Born in Philadelphia in 1879. Pupil of Anshutz and Breckenridge at Penna. Academy of Fine Arts, Philadelphia. *Address,* 2224 Pine St., Philadelphia.

DALLIN, Cyrus E. Sculptor. Born in Springville, Utah, 1861. He studied in 1889 in Paris: pupil of Chapu and Dampt. He worked with Rosa Bonheur during the time Buffalo Bill and his Indians were in Paris. Since then he has been awarded many medals for his statues of the American Indian. Elected an Associate Member of National Academy. Principal works "Signal of Peace" in Lincoln Park, Chicago; statue of "Massasoit" at Plymouth, Mass., and "The Cavalryman," Hanover, Pa. *Address,* Arlington Heights, Boston.

DALTON, E. Miniature painter, who flourished 1827. Philadelphia.

DALY, Matt A. Painter. Born in Cincinnati, Ohio, in 1860. Pupil of Duveneck. Member of the Cincinnati Art Club. *Address,* 4166 Forest Ave., Norwood, Ohio.

DAMIANKES, Cleo. Painter and etcher. Born in California. Member of Chicago Society of Etchers. Has also executed mural decorations at Berkeley High School Auditorium. *Address,* 327 Lennox Ave., Oakland, Calif.

DAMMAT, William T. Painter. Born at New York, 1853. Pupil of Munich Academy, and Munkacsy. Represented by "The Woman in Red" and "The Contrabandist" in the Luxembourg Museum, Paris; "A Quartette," Metropolitan Museum, New York; "Eva Haviland," Boston Museum. *Address,* 45 Avenue de Villiers, Paris.

DAMROSCH, Helen T. Painter and illustrator. Born in New York City, 1893. Pupil of George De Forrest Brush. *Address,* 154 West 55th St., New York.

DANA, Charles E. Painter. Specialty, water colors. Born in Pennslyvania in 1843, he received the gold medal of the Philadelphia Art Club for his water colors in 1891. He died in Philadelphia in 1924.

DANA, William Parsons Winchester. Painter. Born Boston, 1833. Went to sea in early life; studied art Ecole des Beaux Arts, and under Le Poittevin, Paris, 1854–62. Had studio in New York 1862–70, residing abroad since 1870. Member of Academy of National Artists 1862; National Academy 1863. Paints marine, landscape and figure pictures. Received medals at Paris International Expn., 1878 and 1889; 1st prize marine painting at Penna. Academy of Fine Arts 1881. *Address,* 57 Onslow Gardens, London, S.W., Eng.

DANBY, J. "Paulson's Advertiser," Philadelphia, May 29, 1822, contains the advertisement of "J. Danby, Engraver in General, from London." This notice says that he engraves on "Gold, Silver, Copper, Brass, Wood, etc. in a superior manner," but no signed work by Danby is known to the compiler.

DANDO, S. M. Painter. Born in Odell, Ill., 1873. Pupil of William L. Judson in California. Member of California Art Club. *Address,* 126 Brooks Ave., Calif.

DANFORTH, Mosely Isaac. Engraver. Born in Hartford, Conn., in 1800; died in New York in 1862. In 1818 Danforth was an apprentice to Asaph Willard of The Graphic Company, of Hartford, and he became a meritorious line-engraver of portraits and bank-note vignettes. He established himself in business in New Haven in 1821, but soon after removed to New York. Danforth was one of the founders of the Drawing Association of 1825, and of the National Academy of Design in 1826.

Danforth went to London in 1827 and remained there about ten years, and some of his largest and best plates were engraved in that city. Upon his return to New York he became interested in bank-note engraving as a business. He was a member of the firm of Danforth, Underwood & Co. about 1850; about 1858 this firm was merged into the American Banknote Co., and he was vice-president of the latter company at the time of his death.

While abroad in 1827 he began to study art at the Royal Academy in London. He was chiefly successful as a painter in water colors, and some of his sketches became very popular and brought high prices.

DANIEL, William Swift. Painter. Born in San Francisco in 1865. Pupil of Laurens in Paris. Member of California Art Club. *Address*, 2620 Manitou Ave., Los Angeles, Calif.

DANIELE, Franceso. Painter. Exhibited water colors in Annual Exhibition at Penna. Academy of Fine Arts, Philadelphia, 1925. *Address*, 2021 Randon Road, Cleveland, Ohio.

DANIELS, J. B. Painter. Born New York, N. Y., 1846. Pupil of Lindsay. Member: Cincinnati Art Club. *Address*, 619 Walnut St., Cincinnati, Ohio.

DARBY, Henry F. An American portrait painter, born about 1831. From 1853 to 1859 he resided in New York and Brooklyn, and painted portraits exhibited at the National Academy of Design. His grief at the loss of his wife in 1859 caused him to abandon his profession, and live in England. His last exhibited portraits were "Henry Clay" and "John Calhoun," and these paintings are in the Capitol at Washington, D. C.

DARBY, J. G. This name, as engraver, is signed to a view of Niagara Falls, and to a map of the region about the falls, both published in Buffalo, N. Y., in 1838.

DARLEY, Edward H. Philadelphia portrait painter, and a brother of F. O. C. Darley the illustrator. He painted a portrait of the poet, Edgar Allen Poe.

DARLEY, Felix O. C. Illustrator and draughtsman. Born in Philadelphia 1822 and died 1888. He soon became known as an accomplished pen and ink artist; his fine drawings in outline for Irving, Cooper and other authors place him in the front rank of the illustrators. Darley traveled in Europe and made many sketches and drawings, also a few compositions in color.

DARLEY (Sully), Jane Cooper. Born in 1807, and died in 1877. She was the daughter of Thos. Sully, and married W. H. W. Darley. She painted a number of portraits before and after her marriage. In the register of paintings noted by her father, he mentions "finishing several paintings begun by Jane." (See "Life and Works of Thomas Sully," by Biddle & Fielding.)

DARLEY, John Clarendon. Portrait painter, exhibiting in Philadelphia between 1830 and 1840. Represented in loan exhibition of Penna. Academy in 1887.

DARLING, Jay Norwood (J. N. Ding). Illustrator. Born Norwood, Mich., 1876. Member: National Art Club. Cartoonist for *Des Moines Register* and *New York Tribune*. *Address*, 2320 Terrace Road, Des Moines, Ia.

DARRAGH, Marian R. A. Miniature painter. Exhibited at the Annual Miniature Exhibition of the Penna. Academy of Fine Arts, Philadelphia, 1925. *Address*, 1830 Manning St., Philadelphia, Pa.,

DARRAH, Mrs. S. T. Painter. A native of Pennsylvania, her professional life was spent in Boston. She painted landscapes and marines. Among her paintings are "Rocks at Manchester, Mass." and "Gathering Kelp." She died in Boston in 1881.

DASBURG, Andrew. Painter. Exhibited "Landscape" and "Village Street" at "Exhibition of Paintings showing the Later Tendencies in Art," Penna. Academy of Fine Arts, Philadelphia, 1921. *Address*, 72 Washington Square, New York City.

D'ASCENZO, Nicola. Painter. Born Torricella, Italy, 1871. Pupil of Mariani and Jacovacci in Rome. Member: Fellowship, Penna. Academy of Fine Arts. Work: Stained glass, Chapel of the Intercession, New York; mural decoration, Municipal Building, Springfield, Mass.; stained glass, Washington Memorial Chapel, Valley Forge; mosaic frieze, Cooper Library, Camden, N. J. Specialty, mural decoration and stained glass. *Address*, 1602 Summer St., Philadelphia.

DAUGHERTY, James (Henry). Painter, illustrator and engraver. Born Asheville, N. C., 1886. Pupil of Frank Brangwyn; also Penna. Academy of Fine Arts. Member: Mural Painters; Modern Artists of America; New York

Architectural League. Work: Murals in State Theatre, Cleveland; decoration in Safety Institute, New York; recruiting posters for U. S. Navy. *Address*, 59 South Washington Square, New York, N. Y.

DAVENPORT, E. Fairfax. Painter. Born in Kansas City, 1884. Pupil of Collin, Laurens and Ecole des Beaux Arts in Paris. *Address*, 220 Olive St., Kansas City, Mo.

DAVENPORT, Henry. Painter. Born Boston, Mass., 1882. Pupil of Ecole des Beaux Arts, Dechenaud, Charles Hawthorne, George Elmer Browne. Member: Paint and Clay Club; Society of Independent Artists. Assistant professor, History of Art, Yale School of Fine Arts. *Address*, 114 East 84th St., New York.

DAVEY, Randall. Painter. Born Kansas City, Mo., in 1887. Member: Portrait Painters; Society of Independent Artists. Awards: Second Hallgarten prize. Work: ''Flowers'' and ''Portrait of a Young Lady,'' Art Institute of Chicago; ''Old Sea Captain,'' Corcoran Gallery, Washington, D. C.

DAVIDSON, Clara D. (Mrs. Simpson). Painter. Exhibited at the National Association of Women Painters and Sculptors, New York, 1924. *Address*, 3 Park St., Norwalk, Conn.

DAVIDSON, George. Painter. Born Butka, Russian Poland, 1889. Pupil of F. C. Jones and Douglas Volk. Award: ''American Academy in Rome'' Scholarship, 1913–1916. *Address*, 11 East 14th St., New York, N. Y.

DAVIDSON, Harry. Wood engraver. Born in Philadelphia in 1857, he went to New York in 1878 and entered the employ of the Century Company. He died in New York City in 1924.

DAVIDSON, Jo. Sculptor. Born in New York in 1883. Designed U. S. War Industries badge; designed heroic group for French Gov't to commemorate first victory of the Marne; made bust of President Wilson, 1916; selected to make bronze busts of leaders of the Allies. *Address*, 23 Macdougal Alley, New York, N. Y.

DAVIDSON, Oscar L. Painter. Born in 1875; died in Indianapolis, Ind., in 1922. He was a member of Society of Indiana Artists, and of the Indiana Illustrators' Club. He made a specialty of reproducing historic ships.

DAVIES, Arthur B. Painter. Born at Utica, New York, in 1862. He studied in the Art Institute of Chicago, and in New York. Specialty, landscapes with figures. Represented in Metropolitan Museum and Chicago Institute. *Address*, 53 West 39th St., New York.

DAVIES, Charles William. Engraver. Born at Whitesboro, N. Y., 1854; living in 1901. Davies learned to engrave upon copper and steel in Utica, N. Y., was in partnership with his preceptor for two years, and then went into business for himself in Syracuse, N. Y. He was burned out after a short time; and after working at his business in various places, in 1881 he established himself in Minneapolis, Minn., as the pioneer engraver of that city. No signed work of this engraver is known to the writer.

DAVIESS, Maria T. Painter. Born in Harrodsburg, Ky., 1872. Pupil of Blanche, Mucha, and Delecluse. Member of the Nashville Art Club. Died 1924 at Acklen Ave., Nashville, Tenn.

DAVIS, Cecil Clark. Painter. Born Chicago, Ill., in 1877. Member of Chicago Art Club. Specialty, portrait painting. *Address*, 7 West 51st St., New York, or Marion, Mass.

DAVIS, Charles Harold. Painter. Born at Amesbury, Mass., 1856. Pupil of Otto Grundmann in Boston, and of Boulanger and Lefebvre in Paris. Elected Member of National Academy, 1906. Specialty, landscapes. Represented by ''Evening'' and ''August,'' at the Metropolitan Museum, New York; ''Twilight,'' at Art Institute of Chicago. Also represented at Pennsylvania Academy of Fine Arts; Museum of Fine Arts, Boston. *Address*, Mystic, Conn.

DAVIS, Charles Henry. Lanscape painter. Born in Cambridge, Mass., 1845; died Dec. 21, 1921. Exhibited ''Noonday Clouds'' at the Penna. Academy of Fine Arts, Philadelphia, 1914.

DAVIS, Charles P. Painter and illustrator. Born in Iowa City, Ia. Pupil of Chase and Beckwith in New York, and Bouguereau in Paris. Curator of City Art Museum, St. Louis, Mo., since 1914.

DAVIS, Cornelia Cassady. Painter. Born 1870, died 1920. Pupil of Cincinnati Art Academy. She is represented in London by her portrait of President Wm. McKinley. She also painted pictures of American Indian life.

DAVIS Hallie. Painter. Exhibited at the Pennsylvania Academy of Fine Arts in 1924. *Address*, 1620 Summer St., Philadelphia, Pa.

DAVIS, J. P. Wood engraver. His work appeared in the *American Art Review* and *Harper's Monthly*. Among his best engravings is ''Eager for the Fray'' after Shirlaw. See ''History of Wood Engraving in America'' by W. J. Linton. He was one of the founders of the Society of American Wood Engravers. He was born in 1832, and died in 1910, and was the last Secretary of the Society of American Wood Engravers.

DAVIS, Leonard M. Landscape painter. Born in Winchendon, Mass., 1864. Pupil of Art Students' League of New York, and Julien Academy, Paris, under Laurens, Lefebvre, and Benjamin Constant. Among his paintings the "Charm of the Yukon" is in Washington, State Art Museum; and the "Aurora Borealis" in the Museum of New Mexico.

DAVIS, Stuart. Painter and illustrator. Born in Philadelphia, 1892. Pupil of Robert Henri. Member of the Society of Independent Artists. *Address*, Whitney Studio Club, 4th St., New York City.

DAVIS, Warren B. Painter. Awards: Inness prize 1905; Evans prize 1906; Isidor prize 1911. *Address*, 7 East 42d St., New York City.

DAVIS, William S. Marine painter. Born at Orient, L. I., New York, 1884. Also well known by his etchings and block prints. *Address*, Orient, Long Island, N. Y.

DAVIS, W. Triplett. Painter and illustrator. Born Washington, D. C. Pupil of Corcoran Gallery School of Arts, and of Lucien Powell. Member: Society Washington Artists. *Address*, 3521 13th St., N.W., Washington, D. C.

DAVISSON, H. G. Painter. Born in Randolph County, Indiana, 1866. Pupil of Penna. Academy of Fine Arts; Corcoran School of Art in Washington; Art Students' League of New York. Studied three years in Europe. Director Fort Wayne School of Art, 1911–17. *Address*, Fort Wayne, Ind.

DAVOL, Joseph B. Painter. Born Chicago, Ill., 1864. Pupil of Benjamin Constant and Laurens in Paris. Member: Fellowship, Penna. Academy Fine Arts. Died in 1923.

DAWES, Edwin M. Painter. Born Boone, Ia., 1872. Self-taught. Member: California Art Club. Awards: Honorable mention 1909, Minn. State Art Soc.; bronze medal, St. Paul Institute of Art, 1915. Work: "By the River," State Art Society, St. Paul, Minn.; "Dawn in Sweet Grass Mountains," Public Library, Owatonna, Minn.; "Channel to the Mills," Minneapolis Institute. *Address*, Reno, Nev.

DAWES, H. M. Book-plate engraver. Was probably a member of the Massachusetts family of that name. He engraved a book-plate for Rev. Wm. Emerson (1769–1811), the father of Ralph Waldo Emerson. Dawes must thus have been working prior to 1811.

DAWKINS, Henry. Henry Dawkins was one of the earlier engravers in the American Colonies, and in a document of record he describes himself as an "engraver and silversmith." He was located in New York as early as 1754, when he engraved a book-plate for Burnet, an attorney of that city, and in 1775 Dawkins advertises in the *New York Mercury* that he had left Anthony Lamb, with whom he had lately lived, and "has now set up his business opposite the Merchants Coffee House in New York, where he engraves in all sorts of metal." Dawkins then seems to have gone to Philadelphia, as he was working with James Turner in that city in 1758, and in 1761 he engraved the title-page and music for "Urania," a music-book published by James Lyon, A.B., in Philadelphia. He remained in Philadelphia until 1774, when he returned to New York.

According to the "American Archives," edited by Peter Force, Dawkins was arrested in May, 1776, somewhere in the vicinity of New York, and was charged with engraving, printing and issuing counterfeit Continental, Connecticut and Massachusetts paper money. He was put into prison and in the trial ensuing he confessed that he engraved the plates, but he implicated the Tory "Rivington, the printer," in the enterprise. It appeared from the evidence that Dawkins had been previously imprisoned in New York for a similar crime.

As an engraver, Dawkins was chiefly occupied in the production of book-plates, bill-heads, map ornamentation, etc. This work is executed in line and is fairly good. His large plate of Nassau Hall, at Princeton, is probably his best work, and his one known portrait plate is that of Benjamin Lay, an eccentric Quaker of Philadelphia. The latter plate is atrociously drawn and poorly engraved.

DAWLEY, Herbert M. Sculptor. Born Chillicothe, O., 1880. Pupil of Buffalo Society of Artists. Award: Fellowship prize 1915, Buffalo Society of Artists. *Address*, Chatham, N. J.

DAWSON, Arthur. Painter. Born in England in 1857, he studied at South Kensington Schools; in 1857 he came to this country. He was a founder of the Chicago Society of Artists. He had charge of the restoration of the pictures belonging to the Public Library, New York, and the United States Military Academy at West Point, New York. He died at Richmond, Va., in 1922.

DAWSON, George Walter. Painter. Born Andover, Mass., 1870. Pupil of Mass. Normal Art School in Boston; Penna. Academy of Fine Arts. Member: Philadelphia Water Color Club. Professor of drawing at University of Penna. Specialty, landscapes and flowers. *Address*, Department of Architecture, University of Pennsylvania.

DAWSON-WATSON. Painter and engraver. Born London, England, 1864; came to U. S. in 1893; settled in St. Louis, 1904. Pupil of Mark Fisher in London; Carolus Duran, Charltran, Collin, Aimé Morot and Leon Glaize in Paris. Work: "Light Breeze," painting; also mezzotint, City Art Museum, St. Louis; "The Open Book," decorative panel, Wichita High School; "Rainbow in Winter," Central High School and Barr Branch Library, St. Louis; Oakland (Cal.) Museum; Library, Houston, Tex.; "The Wheatfield," Springfield, Ill. *Address,* San Antonio, Tex.

DAY, Francis. Painter. Born at Le Roy, New York, 1863. Studied at Art Students' League, New York, and Ecole des Beaux Arts, Paris. Elected Associate Member of the National Academy of Design. Work: "Patience"; represented at Art Museum of Montclair, New Jersey, by "Fairland." *Address,* Lanesboro, Mass.

DEAKIN, Edwin. Painter. Born in England in 1840. He came to America, and settled in Berkeley, Calif. His specialty has been the Spanish Missions.

DEAN, Elizabeth M. Painter. Born Cambridge, Mass. Pupil of Ludovici in London, and Lazar in Paris; Duveneck and H. D. Murphy in Boston. Member: Copley Society, 1896. *Address,* 107 Winthrop St., Roxbury, Mass.

DEAN, Grace R. Painter. Exhibited water colors at the Penna. Academy of Fine Arts, Philadelphia, 1922. *Address,* 1064 Oakwood Ave., Toledo, Ohio.

DEAN, J. Ernest. Etcher. Exhibited at Philadelphia Water Color Exhibition, 1922. *Address,* 1064 Oakwood Ave., Toledo, Ohio.

DEANE, Lillian Reubena. Miniature painter. Born Chicago, 1881. Pupil of Art Institute of Chicago; and of J. Wellington Reynolds and Virginia S. Reynolds. *Address,* 1446 Stanley Ave., Los Angeles, Calif.

DEARBORN. In Dunlap's History he records that the artist Lambdin stated that "Dearborn is the first portrait painter of whom I can gain any knowledge as having practiced in the west." There are several of his portraits in Pittsburgh, painted from 1807 to 1810.

DEARBORN, Nathaniel. Engraver. Born in New England, 1786. Died in South Roadway, Mass., 1852. Nathaniel was the son of Benjamin Dearborn, a man of some scientific attainments. At an early age he was apprenticed to Abel Bowen, in Boston, to learn wood engraving; and in 1814 Dearborn was in business for himself as an engraver on wood, with an office on School Street, Boston. He also engraved upon copper, in the stipple manner, a few portraits and views, of little merit.

Dearborn published several books: among them "The American Text-Book for making Letters"; "Boston Notions" (1848); "Reminiscences of Boston and a Guide through the City and its Environs" (1851); and a "Guide through Mount Auburn."

DEARTH, Henry Golden. Painter. Born in Bristol, R. I., 1864. He spent most of his professional life in Paris. He painted landscapes and figures. Is represented at Metropolitan Museum by "Cornelia"; "The Old Church at Montreuil" is in the National Galery at Washington, D. C., and the "Black Hat" at Art Institute, Indianapolis. Elected an Associate of the National Academy of Design, 1902; Academician in 1906. He died in New York City March 27, 1918.

DEAS, Charles. Painter. Born in Philadelphia in 1818; grandson of Ralph Izard. Visits to the Penna. Academy, and Sully's painting-room fostered his artistic propensities. He was also a great sportsman and traveled among the Indians, his best known work being his painting of Indian character. In his late years his mind became deranged. Elected Associate Member of the National Academy of Design in 1829. He died in 1867.

DE BEET, Cornelius. Painted a number of landscapes in Baltimore, Md., in 1812; he also painted fruit and flower pieces.

DE BEUKELAER, Mrs. Laura Halliday. Sculptor. Born Cincinnati, Ohio, 1885. Pupil of Cincinnati Art Academy; St. Louis School of Fine Arts. Member: Cincinnati Woman's Art Club. Work: State Normal School, Geneseo, N. Y.; Washburn College, Topeka, Kan. *Address,* 1346 College Ave., Topeka, Kan.

DE BOYEDON, O. H. Sculptor. Exhibited at the Pennsylvania Academy of Fine Arts, Philadelphia, in 1924. *Address,* Montrose, Winchester County, New York.

DE BREHAN, Marchioness. Miniature painter. The Marchioness De Brehan was the sister of Count de Moustier, French minister to the United States. She visited Mount Vernon in 1788 with her brother, and painted several profile miniatures of George Washington and Nelly Custis.

DE CAMP, Joseph Rodefer. Painter. Born at Cincinnati, Ohio, 1858. Pupil of Duveneck at Cincinnati Academy; Royal Academy in Munich; Florence, and Italy. Died in 1923. Represented in Wilstach Collection, Philadelphia, by "The New Gown"; Cincinnati Museum, by "Woman Drying her Hair"; Portrait of "Dr. Horace Howard Furness" at Pennsylvania Academy of Fine Arts; Portrait of "Frank Duveneck" at Cincinnati Museum; "Daniel Merriman" at Worcester Museum.

DECKER, Mrs. E. Bennett. Miniature painter. Born in Washington, D. C., 1869. Pupil of William H. Whittemore. Made microscopic drawings for Smithsonian Institute. *Address*, 2106 O St., Washington, D. C.

DECKER, Joseph. Painter. Born in Germany, 1853; came to United States in 1867. Studied in the schools of the National Academy of Design and abroad. He died in Brooklyn, N. Y., in 1924.

DE CORDOBA, Mathilde. Painter and etcher. Born in New York City. Pupil of Whittenmore, Cox, and Mowbray in New York, and Aman-Jean in Paris. Represented by prints in Luxembourg, Paris, and Library of Congress, Washington, D. C. *Address*, "The Rembrandt," 152 West 57th St., New York.

DEELEY, S. Engraver. All that is known to the writer of this man is that he engraved in line, a fairly well-executed plate showing "The New Hampshire Granite Ledge, at Concord, N. H." The plate is signed "C. Deeley Sc., Boston." The apparent date is about 1835-40.

DE FOE, Mrs. Ethellyn B. Miniature painter. Born in New York. Pupil of Whittemore and Mowbray in New York. *Address*, 250 West 88th St., New York.

DE FOREST, Lockwood. Painter. Born at New York, 1850. Studied art with Herman Corrode, Rome, 1869; Frederic E. Church and James M. Hart, 1870; in Egypt, Syria and Greece, 1875-6; Greece and Egypt, 1877-8; India, 1881-2. Founded workshops at Ahemedabad, India, for the revival of wood carving, 1881; exhibited by special request at the 1st Indian Exhibition, Lahore, 1882, the principal carvings being purchased for the India Museum at S. Kensington, London. Medals for best carving, Colonial Exhibition, London, 1886; Chicago, 1893. Elected Member of Academy of National Artists, 1891; National Academy, 1898. Specialty, landscape painting. *Address*, Santa Barbara, Calif.

DE FRANCA, Manuel J. Painter. One of the original members of the Artists' Fund Society of Philadelphia; member of its Council 1835-6; Controller 1837. Painted portrait of Mrs. Sartain (John) in 1836.

DE FRANCISCI, Anthony. Sculptor. Born in Italy in 1887. Pupil of George T. Brewster. *Address*, 24 West 60th St., New York, N. Y.

DE GROOT, Adriaan M. Portrait painter. Born in Holland in 1870. His portrait of Col. Roosevelt is owned by *The Outlook*, New York. *Address*, 92 Fifth Ave., New York.

DE HASS, M. F. H. Marine painter. Born in Rotterdam in 1832. He came to New York, and during the Civil War painted several naval actions for Admiral Farragut. He was elected a member of the National Academy in 1867; he died in 1895. His "Rapids above Niagara" was exhibited at the Paris Exposition of 1878.

DE HAVEN, Frank. Painter. Born at Bluffton, Ind., 1856. Pupil of George H. Smillie in New York. Specialty, landscapes. Elected an Associate of the National Academy of Design in 1902; Academician in 1920. Represented in National Gallery, Washington; Brooklyn Museum of Arts and Sciences. *Address*, 257 West 86th St., New York.

DEIGENDESCH, Herman F. A painter, etcher and teacher. He was born in Philadelphia in 1858, and was a pupil of the Munich Academy. For many years he was an instructor at the School of Industrial Art in Philadelphia. He was a member of the Philadelphia Society of Etchers. Represented at Independence Hall, Philadelphia, by his copy of the portrait of "John Hart" by Copley. He died at Southampton, Penna., May 9, 1921.

DEIKE, Clara L. Painter. Born in Detroit, Mich., in 1881. Pupil of H. H. Breckenridge. *Address*, 1309 West 111th St., Cleveland, Ohio.

DE KAY, Helena (Mrs. R. Watson Gilder). She has exhibited since 1874 flower-pieces and decorative panels at the National Academy of Design. In 1878 she exhibited the "Young Mother" and "The Last Arrow" (figurepiece).

DE KRUIF, Henri G. Painter and etcher. Born in Grand Rapids, Mich. Pupil of Gifford Beal and Luis Mora. *Address*, Cypress and Magnolia Aves., Los Angeles, Calif.

DE KRYZANOVSKY, Roman. Painter. Born Balta, Russia, 1885. Pupil of E. Renard, E. Tournes and P. Gouzguet. Member: Scarab Club, Detroit. Work: "Kismet," Detroit Institute of Arts. *Address*, 48 Adams Ave., West Detroit, Mich.

DE LAMOTTE, Caroline J. (Mrs. Octave John de Lamotte). Painter. Born Pikesville, Md., 1889. Pupil of C. Y. Turner, Ephraim Keyser, Charles H. Webb. Work: In M. E. Church, Le Compte, La. *Address*, McNary, La.

DE LAND Clyde Osmer. Illustrator and painter. Born Union City, Pa., 1872. Pupil of Drexel Institute under Howard Pyle, in

Philadelphia. Work: Painting, "First American Flag," City of Somerville, Mass.; "First Continental Congress," Carpenters' Hall, Philadelphia; illustrated, "The Count's Snuff-Box," etc. *Address*, 22 N. St. Bernard St., Philadelphia, Pa.

DELANEY, J. E. This man was a line-engraver of portraits and landscape, working for the magazines about 1850.

DELANOY, Abraham, Jr. Painter. Born in New York, probably in 1740, and died in the same city about 1786. He visited England about 1766 to 1769, and was instructed for a time by West. There is a reference to his being in London, in a letter from Charles Willson Peale, published in John Sartain's "Reminiscences of a Very Old Man," where he mentions going with West in 1769, to the rooms of Mr. Delanoy, who expected soon to "return to his native place, New York." One of the students in the painting by Pratt, "The American School," is supposed to be Abraham Delanoy. Dunlap mentions several portraits of members of the Beekman family by this painter, and he himself remembered the man from 1780 to 1783 in "the sear and yellow leaf both of life and fortune; consumptive and poor, his only employment being sign-painting." In 1772 he painted a portrait of Peter Livingston (1737–1794).

DELBOS, Julius. Painter. Exhibited at National Academy of Design, New York, 1925.

DELLEKER, George. With the profession of "engraver" appended, this name appears in the Philadelphia directories for 1817–24, inclusive. He was possibly engraving in that city earlier than the first-named date, as we find portraits of naval heroes of the War of 1812 executed by him, and evidently intended for popular distribution. He was later associated with the engraver G. H. Young, under the firm name of Delleker & Young, in the general engraving business in Philadelphia.

DELLENBAUGH, Frederick Samuel. Painter. Born in McConnelsville, Ohio, 1853. Pupil of Carolus Duran and Academie Julien, Paris. Engaged in art and literary pursuits; librarian American Geographical Society, 1909–11; artist and topographer with Major Powell's 2d expedition down Colorado River 1871–3; with Harriman expedition to Alaska and Siberia 1899; voyages to Iceland, Spitzbergen, Norway, West Indies and S. A. 1906; several personal expeditions to the Southwest in early days.

DELNOCE, Luigi. Engraver. Born in Italy; died in New York about 1888. Delnoce was an admirable engraver of book-illustrations, appearing in New York publications of 1855–60; but he was chiefly engaged in bank-note work.

DE LUCE, Percival. Painter. Born New York, 1847, and died 1914. Pupil of Antwerp Academy, Joseph Portaels, Brussels; Bonnat, Paris. Specialty, portrait and genre painting; exhibited at all principal exhibitions, especially in New York. Silver medal, S. C. Inter-State Expn.; Academy of National Artists. Member: American Water Color Society, Artists' Fund Society, S. C.

DEL MAR, Francesca. Painter. Born Washington, D. C. Pupil of Collin Fleury and Bouguereau in Paris; Rolshoven in London. Work: Mural decorations at Caroline Rest (hospital), Hartsdale, N. Y.; paintings of New Zealand and South Sea Islands for the American Museum of Natural History. *Address*, 39 West 67th St., New York, N. Y.

DEL MUE, M. Painter. Born in Paris, France, 1878. Member: San Francisco Artist Association. Award: Silver medal, Panama-Pacific Expn., San Francisco, 1915. Work: "Late Afternoon in the Sierras," Comparative Museum of Art, San Francisco. *Address*, 563 South 41st Ave., San Francisco, Calif.

DEL PIATTA, Begni. Sculptor. Exhibited at the Pennsylvania Academy of Fine Arts, Philadelphia, in 1924. *Address*, 125 West 11th St., New York.

DE MAINE, Harry. Painter. Born Liverpool, England, 1880. Pupil of Castellucho in Paris; F. V. Burridge in London. Member: Salmagundi Club. *Address*, 160 West 13th St., New York, N. Y.

DE MANCE, Henri. Painter. Born Hamburg, Germany, 1871. Pupil of Lenbach. Member: Society of Independent Artists; League of New York Artists. Work: "Portrait of a Man," "Grapes of the Hudson," Schiller Museum, Marbach. *Address*, 332 East 69th St., New York, N. Y.

DE MAR, John L. Illustrator. Born in Philadelphia, 1865. Cartoonist on *Philadelphia Record* since 1903. *Address*, 1954 N. 31st St., Philadelphia, Pa.

DEMETRIOS, George. Sculptor. Exhibited at the Pennsylvania Academy of Fine Arts, Philadelphia, in 1924. *Address*, 4 Harcourt St., Boston, Mass.

DE MILHAU, Zella. Etcher. Pupil of Art Students' League, New York; Arthur Dow and Wm. Chase. *Address*, 234 Stuyvesant Square, New York.

DEMILLIERE. Portrait painter in oils and miniatures, flourished in New York, 1796.

DEMING, Adelaide. Landscape painter. Born Litchfield, Conn., 1864. Pupil of Art Students' League of New York; Pratt Institute; Chase, Lathrop and Snell. Member: National Academy of Women Painters and Sculptors. Represented in Litchfield Public Library. *Address*, Litchfield, Conn.

DEMING, E. W. Painter and sculptor. Born Ashland, Ohio, in 1860. Pupil of Art Students' League of New York; Lefebvre and Boulanger in Paris. Specialty, Indian and animal subjects. Work: Two mural paintings, Morris High School, New York City; "Braddock's Defeat" and "Discovery of Wisconsin," mural decorations, Wis. Historical Society, Madison, Wis.; "The Fight" and "Mutual Surprise," two bronzes, Metropolitan Museum, New York; "The Watering Place," "Pueblo Buffalo Dance," and "Sioux War Dance," Art Museum, Montclair, N. J.; "Mourning Brave," National Museum, Washington, D. C. *Address*, Cosmos Club, Washington, D. C.

DEMUTH, Charles. Painter. Exhibited "In Vaudeville," "Aucassin and Nicolette," at the "Exhibition of Paintings Showing Later Tendencies in Art," 1921, at Penna. Academy of Fine Arts. *Address*, 2 West 47th St., New York, and Lancaster, Penna.

DE NESTI, Adolfo. Sculptor. Exhibited "Dancing Faun" at Penna. Academy of Fine Arts, 1914. *Address*, 3919 Irving St., Philadelphia.

DENGLER, Frank. Sculptor. Born in Cincinnati, Ohio, in 1853. He studied abroad, and on his return to this country was for a time instructor in modelling in the Boston Museum. He resigned in 1877, and removed to Covington, Ky., and afterwards to Cincinnati. Among his works are "Azzo and Melda," and an ideal head of "America," and several portrait busts.

DENMAN, Herbert. Painter. Born in New York in 1855. Student at the Art Students' League, New York, and with Carolus Duran in Paris. His "Trio" received Honorable Mention at the Paris Salon of 1886. He decorated Mr. Fred. Vanderbilt's Ball Room. He died in California in 1903.

DENNING, Charlotte. Miniature painter. Flourished about 1834, Plattsburg, New York.

DENNIS, Charles W. Painter. Born New Bedford, 1898. Pupil of Harold Brett, Howard E. Smith, Frederick Bosley. Member: Society of Independent Artists; League of New York Artists. *Address*, 323 Cottage St., New Bedford, Mass.

DENNISON, George Austin. Painter and sculptor. Born in New Boston, Illinois, 1873. Exhibited sculptured enamels in the Louvre Museum, Paris. *Address*, Cathedral Oaks, Alma, Calif.

DENNY, Milo B. Painter. Born Waubeek, Ia., 1887. Pupil of Art Institute of Chicago; Art Students' League of New York. *Address*, 1000 Cherry St., Grand Rapids, Mich.

DENSLOW, Dorothea H. Sculptor. Born in New York City, 1900. Pupil of H. C. Denslow. *Address*, 3 Summer St., Hartford, Conn.

DE PEYSTER, Gerard Beekman. Several portraits of the De Peyster family are in the collection of the New York Historical Society, and are painted by Gerard Beekman De Peyster.

DERCUM, Elizabeth. Painter. Exhibited at the Pennsylvania Academy of Fine Arts, Philadelphia, in 1924. *Address*, 1719 Walnut St., Philadelphia.

DE ROSE, Anthony Lewis. Painter. Born in New York City in 1803. He studied under J. R. Smith, and was an early student at the National Academy School. He was elected an Academician in 1833, his specialty being portraiture and historical composition. He died in New York in 1836.

DERRICK, William R. Painter. Born in San Francisco. Pupil of Bonnat, Boulanger, and Lefebvre, in Paris. Also known for his work in water colors. Elected an Associate Member of National Academy of Design, New York. Represented by painting in National Gallery, Washington, D. C. *Address*, 58 West 57th St., New York.

DERUJINSKY, Gleb. Sculptor. Born in Russia in 1888, he studied in Paris. In 1919 he came to this country and opened his studio in New York where he has done a great many portraits; his busts of Lilian Gish, Mrs. Henry Hammond and Theodore Roosevelt have attracted much attention.

DESCH, Frank H. Painter and illustrator. Born in Philadelphia. Pupil of Wm. M. Chase and Hawthorne. *Address*, 222 West 23d St., New York.

DESSAR, Louis Paul. Painter. Born at Indianapolis, Ind., in 1867. Pupil of the National Academy of Design, New York; Bouguereau, and Robert-Fleury, Paris; and École des Beaux Arts, Paris. Specialty, landscapes. Elected member of the National Academy of Design in 1900. Represented at National Gallery, Washington, by the "Return to the Fold" and the "Watering Place"; the Metropolitan Museum of New York by "The Wood Cart." *Address*, 342 West 21st St., New York.

DESVARREUX–LARPENTEUR, James. Painter. Born in Baltimore, Md., 1847. Pupil of Van Marcke, and École des Beaux Arts in Paris. Specialty, landscapes with cattle or sheep.

DETHLOFF, Peter Hans. Painter. Born in Germany, 1869. Executed mural decorations. *Address*, 130 South 9th St., East Salt Lake City, Utah.

DETWILLER, F. K. Painter, etcher and illustrator. Born in Easton, Pa., 1882. Pupil of École des Beaux Arts. Awarded Shaw prize for his etchings. *Address*, Studio, Carnegie Hall, 56th and 7th Ave., New York City.

DE VEAUX, Jacques Martial. Born in 1825 and died 1891. Painted portraits.

DE VEAUX, James. Born in Charleston, S. C., in 1812. In 1829 he visited Philadelphia and received help and instruction from Henry Inman and Thomas Sully. In 1836 he visited Europe for study, returning to America in 1838 where he painted many portraits, his portrait of his friend Col. John S. Manning, of South Carolina, painted in Clarendon. S. C., about 1839, being one of his best. He died in Rome 1844. (See life of James De Veaux in ''Artists of America'' by C. E. Lester, New York, 1846.)

DEVILLE, J. Portrait painter who had a studio about 1840 to 1855, at 66 Saint Ann St., New Orleans.

DEVINE, Bernard. Painter. Born in Portland, Me., in 1884. Pupil of Bridgman in New York and Laurens in Paris. Member of the Paris American Artists' Association. *Address*, Williard, Maine.

DE VOLL, F. Usher. Painter. Born in Providence, R. I., in 1873. Pupil of Rhode Island School of Design and Henri in Paris. Among his best known works, ''Autumn Landscape'' and ''Spring'' in Providence, R. I.; ''Winter in New England'' at Delago Museum, New Orleans. Specialty, landscape painting. *Address*, Providence, Rhode Island.

DE WENTWORTH, Cecile. Painter. See Wentworth, Cecile De.

DEWEY, Charles Melville. Painter. Born at Lowville, N. Y., 1849. Pupil of Carolus Duran, Paris, 1876–7. Specialty, landscapes. Represented in Corcoran and National Galleries, Washington; Art Institute, Brooklyn; Albright Gallery, Buffalo. Elected member of National Academy in 1907. National Institute Arts and Letters. *Address*, 222 West 23d St., New York.

DEWEY, Charles S. Painter. Born in Cadiz, Ohio, in 1880. Member of Chicago Society of Artists. *Address*, 2708 Lake View Ave., Chicago.

DEWEY, Julia H. (Mrs. Charles M.). Painter and illustrator. Born in Batavia, N. Y. Member of National Association of Women Painters and Sculptors. *Address*, 222 West 23d St., New York City, N. Y.

DEWEY, S. Silhouettist and miniature painter. Flourished 1800–1810 in Baltimore. There was a Silas Dewey, a portrait painter, in Baltimore, 1814–1815.

DEWING, Francis. Engraver. A Boston newspaper heralds the arrival of this early American engraver in New England as follows: ''Boston, July 30th, 1716. Lately arrived from London, Francis Dewing, who Engraveth and Printeth Copper Plates, Likewise Coats of Arms and Cyphers on Silver Plate. He likewise Cuts neatly in wood and Printeth Callicoes.'' In 1722, Dewing engraved and printed a large map of ''The Town of Boston in New England, By John Bonner, 1722, Aetatis Suae 60.'' The plate is signed as ''Engraven and Printed by Fra. Dewing, Boston N. E. 1722. Sold by Captain John Bonner and William Price, against ye Town House where may be had all sorts of Prints, Mapps etc.''

DEWING, Maria Oakey. Painter. Born at New York, 1845. Studied at National Academy, New York, and under John LaFarge and Thomas Couture. Specialties are figures, flower pieces and portraits. *Address*, 12 West 8th St., New York City.

DEWING, Thomas W. Painter. Born Boston, 1851. Pupil of Boulanger and Lefebvre in Paris. Elected Associate Member of the National Academy, 1887; National Academy, 1888. Work: ''Summer,'' National Gallery, Washington; ''The Recitation'' and ''Lady in Green and Gray,'' Art Institute, Chicago; ''The Letter,'' ''Tobit and the Angel,'' and ''Girl at Desk,'' Metropolitan Museum, New York; ''Lady with a Mask,'' Corcoran Gallery, Washington, D. C.; ''Lady with a Macaw,'' Fine Arts Academy, Buffalo; ''Lady in Gold,'' Brooklyn Institute Museum; ''Lady in Black and Rose,'' Carnegie Institute, Pittsburgh; ''A Musician,'' Luxembourg Museum, Paris. *Address*, 12 West 8th St., New York, N. Y.

DE WITT, Jerome Pennington. Painter and illustrator. Born Newark, N. J., 1885. Pupil of Pratt Institute under Prellwitz, Beck, Moschcowitz and Paddock. Member: League of New York Artists. *Address*, Clinton Studios, 253 West 42d St., New York, N. Y.

DE WOLF, Wallace L. Painter and engraver. Born Chicago, Ill., 1854. Self-taught. Member: Art Institute of Chicago; Chicago Society of Artists; Municipal Art League; Chicago Society of Engravers. Work: ''Lake Louise,'' Springfield Art Association; ''Coast Scene, Santa Barbara,'' Union League Club, Chicago; ''Hermit Range, Glacier, B. C.,'' South Park Commission.

DEXTER, Henry. Sculptor. Born New York State in 1806. Died in Cambridge, Mass., 1876. Among his portrait busts are those of Charles Dickens, Longfellow, Agassiz, Henry Wilson and Anson Burlingame. His statues include "The Backwoodsman," "The Cushing Children," "Gen'l Jos. Warren at Bunker Hill" and "Nymph of the Ocean."

DEXTER, Mary L. Painter. Member: Society Independent Artists. *Address*, 526 Astor St., Milwaukee, Wis.

DEYOUNG, H. A. Landscape painter. Born Chicago, Ill., 1893. Pupil of Art Institute of Chicago; F. de Forrest Schook. Member: Palette and Chisel Club. *Address*, 59 East Van Buren St., Chicago, Ill.

DE ZAYAS, Marius. Portrait painter. Exhibited at the "Exhibition of Paintings Showing the Later Tendencies in Art," at the Penna. Academy of Fine Arts, Philadelphia, 1921. *Address*, 549 Fifth Ave., New York City.

DICK, Alexander L. Engraver. Born in Scotland about 1805. Dick was a pupil of Robert Scott, a reputable engraver of Edinburgh; he came to the United States in 1833 and in time established an extensive engraving business in New York City. While Dick doubtless did some engraving himself, he was the employer of many engravers, and as all plates issuing from his place bore his name, it is practically impossible to identify his individual work.

DICK, G. R. Painter. Born in New York, N. Y., 1889. Pupil of George Bridgman. *Address*, 818 Madison Ave., New York, N. Y.

DICK, James T. Artist. Born in 1834 and died 1868. He was the son of A. L. Dick the engraver. James T. Dick was one of the originators of the Brooklyn Art School, and a founder of the Academy of Design. Among his best efforts are "Cooling Off," "Leap-Frog" and "At Mischief."

DICKINSON, Anson. Portrait painter in oils and miniatures. Born in Litchfield, Conn., in 1780. He was a brother of the artist Daniel Dickinson. In 1811 he was considered the best miniature painter in New York; in 1818 he went to Canada, and in 1840 settled in New Haven, Conn. He worked for a time in Boston, but led a wandering and irregular life. He died in 1847 at New Haven, Conn.

DICKINSON, Daniel. Painter. Born in 1795 and died after 1840. He was a portrait painter in oils and miniatures, and was a contemporary of Jocelyn in New Haven, Conn. He moved to Philadelphia in 1820 and in 1830 he started painting in oils. He was a brother of Anson Dickinson. He exhibited six miniatures at the Penna. Academy 1827–1831, several being after paintings by Sully.

DICKINSON, Preston. Painter. Exhibited at the Pennsylvania Academy of Fine Arts, Philadelphia, in 1924. *Address*, Care of Daniel Gallery, 2 West 47th St., New York.

DICKINSON, Sidney Edward. Painter. Born Wallingford, Conn., 1890. Portrait and figure painter. Pupil of George Bridgman and William M. Chase, at Art Students' League, and Douglas Volk, at National Academy of Design, New York City. Elected an Associate Member of the National Academy. Principal works: "Self-portrait" at the Corcoran Gallery, Washington, D. C.; "Unrest" at Chicago Art Institute, and "The Black Cape" at City Art Museum, St. Louis. *Address*, 112 West 54th St., New York City.

DICKMAN, Charles J. Painter. Born Demmin, Germany, 1863. Pupil of Laurens and Constant in Paris. Mural decoration in Syndicate Bldg., Oakland, Calif. *Address*, 628 Montgomery St., San Francisco, Calif.

DICKSON, H. E. Painter. Exhibited water colors at the Annual Exhibition of Water Colors at the Penna. Academy, Philadelphia, 1925. *Address*, 240 Pugh St., State College, Penna.

DIEDERICH, (Wilhelm) Hunt. Sculptor. Born Hungary, 1884. Member Salon d'Automme, Paris. *Address*, 8 East 85th St., New York, N. Y.

DIEDRICKSEN, Theodore, Jr. Illustrator and etcher. Pupil of Yale School of Fine Arts; Baschet and Gervais in Paris. Instructor in Drawing, Yale School of Fine Arts, New Haven, Conn. *Address*, 343 York St., New Haven, Conn.

DIELMAN, Ernest B. Painter. Born New York City, 1893. Pupil of Volk. *Address*, 154 West 55th St., New York City, N. Y.

DIELMAN, Frederick. Painter. Born Hanover, Germany, 1847; came to United States in childhood. Studied art under Diez at Royal Academy, Munich; opened studio in New York, 1876; illustrator and figure painter; designer of mosaic panels "Law" and "History" in Congressional Library, and of large mosaic, "Thrift," Albany Savings Bank. Elected member of National Academy, 1883; president of National Academy of Design, 1889–1909. *Address*, 41 West 10th St., New York, N. Y.

DIETERICH, Louis P. Portrait painter. Born in Germany, 1842. *Address*, 347 North Charles St., Baltimore, Md.

DIETERICH, Waldemar Franklin. Portrait painter and illustrator. Born Baltimore, 1876. Pupil of Constant and Laurens. *Address*, 347 North Charles St., Baltimore, Md.

DIETSCH, C. Percival. Sculptor. Born in New York City, 1881. Member of American Academy in Rome. Among his works, "Besso Memorial" at Rome, and the "Athlete" at Peabody Institute, Baltimore, Md. *Address*, Saybrook, Conn.

DI BONA, Antonio. Sculptor. Exhibited at the Penna. Academy of Fine Arts, Philadelphia, in 1924. *Address*, 126 Dartmouth St., Boston, Mass.

DI FILIPPO, Antonio. Sculptor. Exhibited at the Pennsylvania Academy of Fine Arts, Philadelphia, in 1924. *Address*, 126 East 75th St., New York.

DILLAYE, Blanche. Painter. Born at Syracuse, New York. Studied art at Penna. Academy of Fine Arts, and in Paris; etching with Stephan Parrish. Has exhibited in Paris Salons, in England, and in all principal exhibitions of America; silver medals for etchings. Represented in art collection of Syracuse Museum of Fine Arts, and University of Syracuse; gold medal for water color, National Conservation Expn., Knoxville, Tenn. *Address*, 1726 Chestnut St., Philadelphia, Pa.

DIX, Charles T. Artist. Born in Albany in 1838, died in Rome 1873. Served on his father's staff in the Civil War. Later he won a name for his marine and landscape painting. In 1866–7 he exhibited at the Royal Academy, London. His "Sunset at Capri" is a spirited study of sea and shore.

DIX, Eulabee. Miniature painter. Born in Greenfield, Ill., in 1879. Pupil of St. Louis School of Fine Arts. *Address*, 57 West 75th St., New York.

DIXEY, George. Sculptor. Son of John Dixey, an English sculptor; was born in Philadelphia and studied under his father. He executed "Theseus Finding his Father's Sword," "Saint Paul in the Island of Malta," and "Theseus and the Wild Boar."

DIXEY, John. Sculptor. An Irishman; settled in Philadelphia towards the close of the eighteenth century, and did some modelling and stone cutting. His "Hercules and Hydra" and "Ganymede" were much admired. The figures of "Justice" on the New York City Hall are by him.

DIXEY, John V. Sculptor and painter. The youngest son of the English sculptor was born in Philadelphia and received instruction from his father. In 1819 he modelled "St. John writing the Revelations." He also painted several landscapes in oil that were exhibited at the gallery of the National Academy of Design.

DIXON, Francis S. Painter. Exhibited at Annual Exhibition of Academy of Design, New York, 1925. Born in New York, 1879. *Address*, 11 East 68th St., New York.

DIXON, (Lafayette) Maynard. Painter. Born Fresno, Calif., 1875. Began in newspaper work, San Francisco; made illustrations for numerous volumes of western fiction, and for leading magazines; represented in many private galleries, New York, Chicago, San Francisco and elsewhere. Paintings and mural work restricted to western life and scenes, almost exclusively. Member: Architectural League; Society of Illustrators; Society of Mural Painters (New York); San Francisco Art Association. *Address*, 728 Montgomery St., San Francisco.

DODD, Mark D. Painter and etcher. Born in St. Louis, Mo., 1888. Pupil of Art Students' League of New York. *Address*, 106 Columbus Heights, Brooklyn, N. Y.

DODD, Samuel. Engraver. Born in Bloomfield, N. J., 1797; he died in 1862. He was little known. The only signed plate of Samuel Dodd is a portrait of "Washington in Uniform" (Hart, 690) signed "S. Dodd Set. New Ark." The plate was probably engraved about 1820.

DODGE, Chester L. Painter and illustrator. Born in Salem, Me., in 1880. Studied at Rhode Island School of Design and Art Students' League of N. Y. *Address*, 7 Thomas St., Providence, R. I.

DODGE, Frances F. (Mrs.). Painter. Born in Lansing, Mich., in 1878. Pupil of Duveneck and Meakin. *Address*, Care of Fairbanks, Morse & Co., St. Paul, Minn.

DODGE, John Wood. Miniature painter. Born 1807 and died 1893. His portrait miniature of General Jackson executed in 1842 was engraved for the postage stamp of 1863. He was elected an associate member of the National Academy of Design in 1832.

DODGE, Ozias. Painter and etcher. Born in Morristown, Vt., in 1868. Pupil of Yale School of Fine Arts, and under Gerome in Paris. Represented by etchings in Congressional Library, Art Institute Chicago, and New York Public Library. He died in 1925.

DODGE, William De Leftwich. Mural painter. Born at Liberty, Va., 1867. Studied at École des Beaux Arts in Paris and in Munich. Principal works: Administration Building, Chicago, and panels in Library of Congress. *Address*, 51 West 10th St., New York.

DODSON, Richard W. Engraver. Born at Cambridge, Md., 1812; died at Cape May, N. J., 1867. Dodson was an excellent line-engraver of portraits and book-illustrations. He was a pupil of the Philadelphia engraver James B. Longacre, and he made some of the best portraits in the National Portrait Gallery, published by Longacre & Herring. Dodson is said to have abandoned engraving for another business in 1845.

DODSON, Sarah Paxton Ball. Landscape and figure painter. Born Philadelphia, Pa., 1847; died Brighton, England, 1906. Pupil of M. Schussele, in Philadelphia; later in Paris, of Evariste Vital Luminais and Jules Lefebvre; also criticisms by Boutet de Monvel. Was an exhibitor at the Paris Salon.

DOELGER, Frank J. Painter. Member: Society of Independent Artists. *Address*, 430 Irving Ave., Brooklyn, N. Y.

DOHERTY, Mrs. Lillian C. Painter. Pupil of Corcoran School of Art, Washington, D. C.; Rhoda H. Nicholis; C. W. Hawthorne; also studied in Europe. Member: Washington Society of Artists. *Address*, 12 Rhode Island Ave., N.W., Washington, D. C.

DOKE, Sallie George (Mrs. Fred Doke). Painter. Born Keachie, La. Pupil of Cincinnati Academy and Chicago Academy of Fine Arts. Member: Society of Independent Artists. Award: Gold medal at Dallas, 1916. *Address*, Lometa, Texas.

DOLINSKY, Nathan. Painter. Born in Russia, 1889. Pupil of National Academy of Design. Member: Salmagundi Club; New York Architectural League; Mural Painters. *Address*, 709 Willoughby Ave., Brooklyn, N. Y.

DOLPH, John Henry. Painter. Born 1835. Elected a Member of the National Academy in 1898. He died in 1903. Represented at Penna. Academy of Fine Arts by his portrait of the artist, Charles Loring Elliott. His specialty was the painting of cats and dogs.

DOMVILLE, Paul. Painter. Exhibited water colors at the Penna. Academy of Fine Arts, Philadelphia, 1922. *Address*, 1720 Delancey St., Philadelphia.

DONAHEY, James H. Illustrator. Born West Chester, Ohio, 1875. Pupil of Cleveland School of Art. Member: Cleveland Artists' Association. *Address*, "Plain Dealer," Cleveland, Ohio.

DONAHEY, William. Painter. Born in West Chester, Ohio, 1883. Artist for children's papers, magazines, and books. *Address*, 2331 Cleveland Ave., Chicago, Ill.

DONAHUE, William Howard. Painter. Born New York City, 1881. Pupil of Henry R.

Poore, E. L. Warner, F. A. Bicknell. Member: Brooklyn Society of Artists; Washington Art Club. *Address*, Nanuet, Rockland County, N. Y.

DONALDSON, Alice Willets. Painter and illustrator. Born in Illinois, 1885. Pupil of Cincinnati Academy. Member: Alumni Pa. Museum School of Industrial Arts; New York Water Color Club. Work: Colored frontispieces and covers for "Touring Great Britain," and "The Book of New York," by Robert Shackleton. *Address*, 313 West 20th St., New York, N. Y.

DONATO, Giuseppe. Sculptor. Born Maida, Province of Catanzaro, 1881. Came to America, 1892, graduated Philadelphia Public Industrial Art School, 1897; studied under Charles Grafly, Pa. Academy of Fine Arts, 1897–1903; drawing under Wm. M. Chase, Thomas P. Anshuts, Hugh H. Breckenridge; anatomy under Dr. George McClellan; studied modelling and architecture, Pa. Museum Industrial Art; entered École des Beaux Arts, Paris, 1903; studied Academy Julien under Angelbert; Academy Colarossi, Paris, under Messieurs Gouquiet and Roland; private student under Auguste Rodin. Exhibited Grand Salon, Paris; Academy of Fine Arts and Art Club, Philadelphia; Art Institute Chicago; National Academy of Design, New York; National Sculpture Society Exhibition, Baltimore; San Francisco Expn., etc. Represented in permanent exhibition, Pa. Academy of Fine Arts, Philadelphia; Conversation Hall, City Hall, Philadelphia; St. John's R. C. Church, Philadelphia; "Dance of Eternal Spring," Harrisburg, Pa.; American Academy of Music. Member: Fellowship, Pa. Academy of Fine Arts; National Sculpture Society. *Address*, 716 Walnut St., Philadelphia.

DONEY, T. Engraver. This capital engraver of portraits in mezzotint came to Canada from France, and after working for some time in Illinois and Ohio, he established himself in business in New York about 1845. Doney engraved a number of meritorious portrait plates for the *Democratic Review* and other New York and Philadelphia periodicals.

DONIPHAN, Dorsey. Painter. Born in Washington, D. C., in 1897. Pupil of Tarbell and Meryman. *Address*, 1624 H St., N.W., Washington, D. C.

DONLEVY, Alice H. Painter and illustrator. Born Manchester, England, 1846. Pupil of Women's Art School of Cooper Union, New York. *Address*, 308 East 173d St., Bronx, New York, N. Y.

DONLON, Louis J. Painter. Member: Conn. Academy of Fine Arts. *Address*, Care of Connecticut Academy of the Fine Arts, 904 Main St., Hartford, Conn.

DONLY, Eva Brook. Painter. Born Simcoe, Ontario, Canada, 1867. Pupil of F. M. Bellsmith and John Ward Stimson. Member: New York Water Color Club; National Art Club; National Academy of Women Painters and Sculptors. Work: "Arrival of U-Boat Deutschland at Norfolk, Va.," owned by United States Government; "Elba Beach, Bermuda," "Beach, Lake Erie," National Gallery, Washington, D. C. *Address*, 115 East 27th St., New York, N. Y.

DONOGHUE, John. Sculptor. Born in Chicago in 1853. Pupil of Academy of Design; also studied in Paris. Principal work: "Young Sophocles" (1885), "Hunting Nymph" (1886), and "St. Paul," at Congressional Library, Washington, D. C. His death by his own hand in July 1903 closed his career.

DONOHO, Gaines Ruger. Landscape painter. Born in Church Hill, Miss., in 1857. He died in New York City, 1916. Pupil of Art Students' League in New York; also studied in Paris. Represented in Brooklyn Institute Museum by "La Marcellerie."

DONOHUE, William H. Painter. He exhibited at Annual Exhibition, Academy of Design, New York, 1925. *Address*, Nanuet, New York.

DOOLITTLE, Amos. Engraver. Born in Cheshire, Conn., 1754; died at New Haven, Conn., 1832. Originally an apprentice to a silversmith, Doolittle early learned to engrave upon metal. In 1775 he joined the Revolutionary army at Cambridge and served through that campaign. His artist friend Ralph Earle made some rather curious drawings of the engagement at Lexington and Concord, and these Doolittle engraved on copper and published in New Haven in 1775. They are very roughly engraved, but interesting historically, and highly prized. Doolittle engraved a considerable number of portraits, views, Bible illustrations, book-plates, etc., all executed in line, and including a small view of the Battle of Lexington done very late in his life, in connection with Mr. Barber. His work, at the best, possesses little other than historical interest.

Mr. Barber credits Doolittle with engraving the first historical plates done in America. Mr. Barber overlooked Paul Revere's plate of the Boston Massacre, published in 1770, and Romans' "Exact View of the Late Battle at Charleston," which was published in Philadelphia in September 1775, or about three months before the appearance of Doolittle's views of Lexington and Concord.

DOOLITTLE, Edwin S. Painter. Born in Albany, 1843. He had a studio in 1867 in New York; in 1868 he went to Europe for study. In 1869 he painted his "Shadow of a Great Rock in a Weary Land." His paintings comprise landscapes and marine subjects. Mr. Doolittle also executed illustrations for books, and has designed book-covers. He died in 1900.

DOOLITTLE, Harold L. Etcher. Born in Pasadena, Calif., in 1883. *Address*, 127 North Catalina Ave., Pasadena, Calif.

DOOLITTLE & MUNSON. Engravers. This firm was engraving portraits, bank-notes, etc., in 1842, in Cincinnati, Ohio. The second member of this firm may have been S. B. Munson, living, earlier, in New Haven. Some good line work of about this period, signed "A. Doolittle Sc.," may be the work of the first member of this firm. The work referred to is too well done to have been engraved by Amos Doolittle, of New Haven, and this latter Amos died in 1832.

A view of the engraving establishment of Doolittle & Munson is to be found in a work entitled "Cincinnati in 1842," published in that city. The sign shown calls them "bank-note engravers."

DOOLITTLE, Samuel. Engraver. A "Goodwin" book-plate, signed "S. D. Sct. 1804," is assigned to this name in the descriptive catalogue of the late exhibition of early American engravings held under the auspices of the Museum of Fine Arts, in Boston.

DOONER, Emilie L. Painter. Born in Philadelphia in 1877. Pupil of Penna. Academy of Fine Arts; also studied abroad. *Address*, 1822 Chestnut St., Philadelphia.

DORAN, Robert C. Painter and etcher. Born Dallas, Tex., 1889. Pupil of Kenneth Hayes Miller in New York. *Address*, 304 West 52d St., New York, N. Y.

DORSEY, John Syng. Born in Philadelphia, 1783; died there, 1818. This eminent American surgeon published, in 1813, his "Elements of Surgery," "with plates by John Syng Dorsey, M.D." These plates are etched and sometimes finished in stipple; they are excellently done. Dr. Dorsey also etched several good book-plates.

DOSKOW, Israel. Painter and illustrator. Born in Russia, 1881. Pupil of Penna. Academy of Fine Arts. Member: Society of Illustrators. *Address*, 452 Fifth Ave., New York, N. Y.

DOTY & JONES. This firm, about 1830, was engraving portraits in stipple.

DOUGAL, W. H. Engraver. Born in New Haven, Conn., about 1808; was living in Washington, D. C., in 1853. Mr. Alfred Jones says that his name was originally Macdougal, and he was so known for a time, but for some reason he later dropped the "Mac." He was a good engraver of landscapes and portraits, the latter being executed in a mixed manner. In 1853 he was in the employ of the U. S. Treasury Department at Washington, D. C.

DOUGHERTY, Louis R. Sculptor. Born Philadelphia, 1874. Pupil of Penna. Academy of Fine Arts, and Drexel Institute. Member: The Scumblers, Philadelphia; Fellowship Penna. Academy of Fine Arts. *Address*, 27 Norwood Ave., Stapleton, N. Y.

DOUGHERTY, Parke C. Painter. Born Philadelphia, Pa., 1867. Pupil of Penna. Academy of Fine Arts; Julien Academy in Paris. Member: Art Club, Philadelphia; Fellowship Penna. Academy of Fine Arts, 1916. *Address*, 49 Boulevard du Montparnasse, Paris, France.

DOUGHERTY, Paul. Marine painter. Born Brooklyn, New York, 1877; studied also in Paris, London, Florence, Venice and Munich. Elected Associate Member of the National Academy, 1906; National Academy, 1907; National Institute of Arts and Letters; American Water Color Society, New York. *Address*, 7 West 43d St., New York.

DOUGHTY, Thomas. Landscape painter. Born in Philadelphia, 1793; died in New York, 1856. Self-taught. Represented at the Metropolitan Museum by "On the Hudson" and "A River Glimpse."

DOUGLAS. An American portrait painter of whom little is known. He painted a portrait of Judge Henry A. Moore, owned by the city of New York, and now in the old City Hall. He is often spoken of as "Georgia Goulas."

DOUGLAS, Walter. Painter. Born in Cincinnati, Ohio, in 1868. Pupil of Wm. M. Chase, and National Academy of Design. Represented by "In the Shade," at the Art Association, Dallas, Tex. Specialty, poultry painting. *Address*, 264 West 19th St., New York City.

DOULL, Mary Allison. Miniature painter. Born in Canada. Pupil of National Academy of Design, New York, and Julien Academy, Paris. *Address*, 18 East 9th St., New York City.

DOVE, Arthur G. Painter. Exhibited at the "Exhibition of Paintings Showing the Later Tendencies in Art," at the Penna. Academy of Fine Arts, Philadelphia, 1921. *Address*, Westport, Conn.

DOW, Arthur Wesley. Painter. Born 1857, in Ipswich, Mass. Studied art in Boston and at Paris. Pupil of Boulanger and Lefebvre. Pictures in Salon, Paris, 1886–7. Instructor of Art, Pratt Institute, Brooklyn, 1895–1904; instructor of Composition at Art

Students' League, New York, 1897–1903. Member: Society of Independent Artists; American Federation Arts. Died in 1922.

DOWNES, John I. Landscape painter. Born in Derby, Conn., in 1861. Pupil of Yale School of Fine Arts, and J. Alden Weir. Member of Conn. Academy of Fine Arts. *Address*, 254 Laurence St., New Haven, Conn.

DOYLE, Alexander. Sculptor. Born in Steubenville, Ohio, 1857, and died in 1922. He went to Italy with his family to reside when 9 years of age. Studied sculpture in Florence and Rome. Returned to the United States in 1878. Among his works are: Bronze equestrian statue of Gen. Albert Sidney Johnston; bronze statue of Gen. Robert E. Lee; marble statue of Margaret Haugherty (known as "The Bread Giver"), for New Orleans, La.; National Revolutionary Monument, Yorktown, Va.; bronze statue of Gen. Philip Schuyler, Saratoga, N. Y.; marble statue of Gen. Garfield, Cleveland, Ohio; bronze statue of Gen. James R. Steedman, Toledo, Ohio; marble statue of Senator Benjamin H. Hill, Atlanta, Ga.; bronze statue of Horace Greeley, New York; bronze statue and monument to Henry W. Grady, Atlanta, Ga.; and statues of Benton, Blair, and Kenna, in Statuary Hall, Capitol.

DOYLE, Margaret Byron. She was a daughter of W. M. S. Doyle, and became the wife of John Chorley the engraver. She painted many excellent portraits in Boston between 1820 and 1830.

DOYLE, William M. S. Portrait painter. Born in Boston, Mass., in 1796. Was the son of a British army officer who was stationed there. He associated as a young man with Daniel Bowen the silhouettist, at the "Bunch of Grapes Tavern," and in 1805 the Boston directory states he was a "miniature painter." He died in 1828 and at that time was proprietor of the Columbian Museum in Boston. Among his portraits are those of Gov. Caleb Strong, Isaiah Thomas and John Adams.

DRADDY, John G. Sculptor. Born in 1833. He executed many notable church altars including the August Daly altar, and the "Coleman Memorial" in St. Patrick's Cathedral, New York City. He died in Italy, 1904.

DRAKE, Will H. Painter and illustrator. Born in New York, 1856. Pupil of Julien Academy under Constant and Doucet. Elected Associate Member of National Academy, 1902. Specialty, animals. *Address*, 362 West 9th St., Los Angeles, Calif.

DRAPER, John. Engraver. The directories of Philadelphia contain the name of "John Draper, engraver," continuously from

1801 to 1845. Dunlap says that Draper was an apprentice with Robert Scot, of Philadelphia, and was living in 1833. Draper was engraving for Dobson's edition of Rees' Encyclopedia in 1794–1803, and in 1810 he was a member of the bank-note engraving firm of Murray, Draper, Fairman & Co. In 1835 the firm of Draper, Underwood, Bald & Spencer was engraving bank-notes in Philadelphia and New York, and in 1838 Draper, Tappan, Longacre & Co. had similar establishments in these cities. That there was a younger Draper is shown by the existence, as late as 1860, of the bank-note engraving firms of Draper & Co., and Draper, Welsh & Co., both working in Philadelphia. Aside from the encyclopedia work referred to, no plates have been found signed by John Draper alone, as engraver.

DRAYTON, Grace G. (Mrs.). Illustrator. Born in Philadelphia, 1877. Member of Fellowship of Penna. Academy of Fine Arts. Specialty, illustrations and posters of children. *Address*, 830 Park Ave., New York.

DRAYTON, J. Engraver of landscape in aquatint, and an expert print colorist. At least as early as 1820 he was working in Philadelphia. He was later employed for some years as a draftsman in one of the Government departments in Washington. Drayton engraved a few book illustrations in line.

DREIFOOS, Byron G. Painter and illustrator. Born in Philadelphia, 1890. *Address*, 17 West Kinney St., Newark, N. J.

DRESHER, A. Dresher was a landscape engraver of little merit, working in New York about 1860.

DREYFOUS, Florence. Painter. Born in New York, N. Y. Pupil of Robert Henri. *Address*, 315 West 99th St., New York, N. Y.

DREXEL, Francis M. Painter and banker. Born in Dornbirn, Austrian Tyrol, 1792; died in Philadelphia, 1863. After studying art in Italy he found his native country in the possession of Napoleon and, to escape conscription, went to Switzerland and in 1817 sailed for America, settling in Philadelphia. Here he achieved success as a portrait painter, taking up his residence at the southwest corner of Sixth and Chestnut Streets, where he established his studio. After several years, hearing that South America offered a profitable field for an ambitious artist, he sailed for Valparaiso. On his return home he brought with him a large collection of curiosities for Peale's Museum, then in the State House. Having accumulated some capital, he decided to settle down and become a broker, in order to open a career for his sons. In this field he made an auspicious beginning in Louisville, Ky., but on his wife's desire to return to Philadelphia,

he opened an office on Third Street, below Market, on January 1, 1838, the beginning of the noted house of Drexel & Co.

DREYFUS, Isidora C. Miniature painter. Exhibited at Annual Exhibition of Miniatures at Penna. Academy of Fine Arts, Philadelphia, 1925. *Address*, 221 Constance Ave., Santa Barbara, Calif.

DREYFUSS, Albert. Sculptor. Born New York, N. Y., 1880. Pupil of George Gray Barnard. Member: Society of Independent Artists; League of New York Artists. Work: Arsenal Park Memorial, Pittsburgh, Pa. *Address*, 232 West 14th St., New York, N. Y.

DRIER, Katharine S. Painter. Born in Brooklyn, N. Y., in 1877. Pupil of Walter Shirlaw. *Address*, 88 Central Park, N. Y.

DROGSETH, Einstein Olaf. Painter. Exhibited ''Rough Country'' at Penna. Academy of Fine Arts, 1920. *Address*, 190 Beniteau Ave., Detroit, Michigan.

DRUCEZ. Flourished in New York about 1805. According to Dunlap he was ''a Flemming.''

DRURY, Hope Curtis (Mrs. William H. Drury). Painter. Born Pawtucket, R. I., 1889. Pupil of R. I. School of Design. Member: Providence Art Club; Providence Water Color Club.

DRURY, J. H. Painter. Born at Georgetown, D. C., in 1816. A follower of the French school, and pupil of Thomas Couture of Paris. He was a member of the Chicago Academy of Design, and spent the better part of his professional life in that city.

DRURY, William H. Marine painter. Born Fitchburg, Mass., 1888. Pupil of R. I. School of Design; Tarbell and Woodbury. Member: Providence Art Club. *Address*, Paradise Road, Newport, R. I.

DRYDEN, Helen. Illustrator. Born Baltimore, Md., 1887. Pupil of Penna. Academy of Fine Arts. Member: Society of Independent Artists; Society of Illustrators. Designs covers for magazines, posters, stage costumes and scenery. *Address*, 9 East 10th St., New York, N. Y.

DRYSDALE, Alexander John. Painter and illustrator. Born Marietta, Ga., 1870. Pupil of Paul Poincy in New Orleans; Art Students' League of New York; also under Curran and Du Mond. Member: Arts and Crafts Club of New Orleans. Represented in Delgado Museum, New Orleans. *Address*, 1301 Burgundy St., New Orleans, La.

DU BOIS, Guy Pene. Painter. Born Brooklyn, N. Y., 1884. Pupil of Chase, Du Mond and Henri. *Address*, Care Montross Gallery, 550 5th Ave., New York, N. Y.

DU BOIS, Guy Rene. Painter. Exhibited at the Pennsylvania Academy of Fine Arts, Philadelphia, in 1924. *Address*, 430 Lafayette St., New York.

DUBOIS, Charles E. Landscape painter. Born in New York, 1847. He studied in Paris; also painted in Venice and Rome. Among his paintings, ''Willows at East Hampton'' and ''Palisades, Hudson River,'' were exhibited at the Philadelphia Exposition. His ''Evening at East Hampton'' was in the Exhibition of Soceity of American Artists in 1878. He died in 1885.

DUBOURJAL, Savinien Edme. Painter in oils and miniatures. He was born in Paris, 1795, and died there in 1853. Pupil of Girodet. He exhibited at the Salon in 1814. In 1846 he was working in Boston, and in 1847 to 1850 he was in New York, where he exhibited frequently at the National Academy of Design Exhibitions. He was a friend of the artist G. P. A. Healy; see the ''Life of Healy'' by Healy's daughter.

DUBUFE, Claud Marie. French portrait painter, who had his studio in New Orleans, La., about 1837, and painted portraits of many of the members of the old French families of Louisiana. Born in Paris, 1790, he studied under David. He died in 1864. His portraits painted when in the United States are remarkable for their forceful character and their firm, strong modeling.

DU BRAU, Gertrude M. Painter. Born in Germany in 1889. Pupil of Maryland Institute, Baltimore. Mural paintings in Masonic Temple and City Hall, Cumberland, Maryland. *Address*, Piedmont Ave., Cumberland, Md.

DUCHÉ, Thomas Spence. Born in Philadelphia in 1763. He went to England and studied painting under Benjamin West, and while there he painted the portrait of Bishop Seabury now at Trinity College, Hartford, Conn. He also painted a portrait of Bishop Provost, which is owned by the New York Historical Society. He died in England in 1790.

DUCLORY, Lepelitier. Portrait painter; a creole of Martinique, West Indies. He came to New Orleans in the first half of the nineteenth century, and remained there about ten years, painting portraits.

DUDENSING, F. Valentine. Painter. Born in San Francisco, Calif., 1901. Member: Society of Independent Artists. *Address*, 116 East 19th St., New York, N. Y.

DUDENSING, R. Engraver of portraits and landscape, in stipple and in line. Came to the United States from Germany about 1857. About 1880 he established a book publishing house in New York which is still in existence. He died in 1899 during a visit to the old home in Germany.

DUDLEY, Frank V. Painter. Born Delavan, Wis. Studied at Chicago Art Institute. Member: Union Internationale des Beaux Arts et des Lettres, Paris. Represented in Chicago Art Institute collection; Municipal collection of Owatona, Minn.; collection of Cedar Rapids Art Association; Public School collections of St. Louis and Chicago. *Address*, 6356 Greenwood Ave., Chicago, Ill.

DUER, Douglas. Painter. Member: Society of Illustrators. *Address*, 51 West 10th St., New York, N. Y.

DUESBERG, Otto. Painter. Member: Society of Independent Artists. *Address*, 10 Eldert St., Brooklyn, N. Y.

DUFFIELD, Edward. Engraver, and a clock and watch-maker of Philadelphia. Born 1730, and died 1805. He was also a die-sinker and engraver of medals. He engraved the silver medal presented to Col. John Armstrong, in 1756, as a memorial of the destruction of the Indian village of Kittanning by Armstrong; he also made the dies for the medals prepared in 1762 for distribution among the Indians, by The Friendly Association for the Preservation of Peace among the Indians. The dies for this latter medal cost 15£; they were cut upon punches fixed in a socket, and the impression was made by the stroke of a sledge-hammer.

DUFFY. A little known painter of portraiture and genre subjects.

DUFFY, Richard H. Sculptor. Born New York, N. Y., 1881. Pupil of Art Students' League of New York; Mercie in Paris. *Address*, 9 East 55th St., New York, N. Y.

DUFNER, Edward. Painter. Born Buffalo, N. Y., 1872. Pupil of Art Students' League of Buffalo and New York, under James McNeil Whistler; Paris and Academy Julien under Laurens. Awards: Wanamaker prize, Paris, 1899. Represented in Buffalo Fine Arts Academy; William M. Chase collection in National Academy; National Arts Club; Lotos Club, New York; Milwaukee Art Society. Elected an Associate Member National Academy of Design in 1910. *Address*, 939 8th Ave., New York.

DUGGAN, Peter Paul. Painter. Born in Ireland. He came to America in 1810, and settled in New York, where he taught in the

New York Academy. He drew a head of Washington Allston for the American Art Union Medal. He later left America and went to England, and finally to Paris, where he died in 1861.

DUGGAR, Mrs. Marie R. Sculptor. She died in St. Louis, Mo., in 1922. She made a specialty of bas-relief portraits of children.

DULL, John J. Painter. Born Philadelphia, Pa., 1862. Pupil of Penna. Academy of Fine Arts. Member: Fellowship Penna. Academy of Fine Arts; Philadelphia Sketch Club. Award: Gold medal, Plastic Club, 1903. *Address*, 1524 Chestnut St., Philadelphia, Pa.

DUMMER, Jeremiah. Portrait painter. A noted goldsmith and engraver of Boston in the seventeenth century; son of Richard and Frances Curr Dummer of Newbury, and the father of William Dummer, acting governor of Massachusetts from 1723 to 1728. Jeremiah Dummer was born in 1645, and died in 1718. The portraits of himself and his wife are the property of direct descendants of the heirs of Samuel Dummer of Wilmington, Mass. On the back of the self-portrait of Jeremiah Dummer is inscribed: ''Jeremiah Dummer pinx. Del in Anno 1691. Mei Effigles, Aetat 46.''

DUMMETT, Laura Dow. Painter. Born Allegheny, Pa., 1856. Pupil of Pittsburgh School of Design for Women; Julien Academy and Desgoffe in Paris. Member: Pittsburgh Artists' Association. *Address*, 867 North 66th St., Overbrook, Philadelphia, Pa.

DU MOND, Frank Vincent. Painter. Born at Rochester, N. Y., 1865. Pupil of Boulanger, Lefebvre and Benjamin-Constant, Paris. Member: Society of Mural Painters; Architectural League; Artists' Fund. Member of International Jury of Awards, Panama Expn., 1915. Elected member of National Academy, 1906. *Address*, 27 West 67th St., New York.

DU MOND, Helen S. (Mrs.). Miniature painter. Born in Portland, Ore., 1872. *Address*, 109 East 10th St., New York.

DUNBAR, Harold C. Painter and illustrator. Born in Brockton, Mass., 1882. Pupil of De Camp and Tarbell, and of Colarossi in Paris. Among his paintings ''Spring Evening'' at Boston Art Club; portrait of Gov. Woodbury at State House, Vermont; and portrait of Chief Justice Watson at Supreme Court, Vermont. *Address*, Chatham, Mass.

DUNBAR, Ulric Stonewall Jackson. Sculptor. Born London, Ont., 1862. Professionally engaged as sculptor since 1880. Has received medals and diplomas; executed over 150 portrait busts, principally of prominent men, for U. S. Capitol and Corcoran Gallery of Art, Washington; bronze statue of late Gov. Alex. R. Shepherd for front of new Municipal Bldg., Washington. *Address*, 1517 H St., N.W., Washington, D. C.

DUNBIER, Augustus William. Painter. Born in Osceola, Nebr., 1888. Student of Chicago Art Institute. *Address*, 1617 Wirt St., Omaha, Nebr.

DUNCAN, Frederick A. Painter. Born at Texarkana, Ark., 1881. Pupil of Art Students' League of New York. *Address*, 1 West 67th St., New York.

DUNCAN, Walter Jack. Illustrator. Born Indianapolis, Ind., 1881. Student of Art Students' League of New York. Pupil of John Twachtman. Began with *Century Magazine*, 1903; sent to England by *Scribner's*, 1905; became connected with *McClure's*, 1907; with *Harper's*, 1912–13. Illustrated books by Booth Tarkington, Robert C. Holliday, Christopher Morley, etc. *Address*, 7 East 8th St., New York, N. Y.

DUNDAS, Verde Van V. Sculptor. Born in Marlin, Tex., 1865. Pupil of Lorado Taft. Member of the Chicago Art League. *Address*, 630 Orchestra Hall, Chicago, Ill.

DUNKERLEY, Joseph. Miniature painter, who flourished 1784 and 1785 in Boston, Mass. He advertised in the *Independent Chronicle*, Boston, December 1784, saying that he ''Still carries on his Profession of Painting in Miniatures at his house in the North Square.''

DUNLAP, Helena. Painter. Born in Los Angeles, Calif. Pupil of Penna. Academy of Fine Arts, Philadelphia, and Simon in Paris. Studio in Paris. *Address*, South Windsor Bldg., Los Angeles, Calif.

DUNLAP, Mary S. Born in Ohio, now resides in Pasadena, Calif.

DUNLAP, William. Painter and engraver. Born in Perth Amboy, N. J., in 1766. He died in New York in 1839. In 1784 Dunlap went to London to study art with Benjamin West, and as early as 1783 he had made a crayon portrait from life of George Washington. He engraved a portrait of the actor Wignell in the character of Darby. He painted a number of portraits, settled in New York, and was elected president of the National Academy of Design. The Metropolitan Museum owns his portraits of Mr. and Mrs. John A. Conant. He was the author of the ''History of the Arts of Design, in the United States'' (1834).

DUNLAP, Zoe F. Miniature painter. Born in Cincinnati, Ohio, 1872. Pupil of Cincinnati Academy; also studied in Paris. *Address*, Dunlap Villa, 2210 Upland Place, Cincinnati, Ohio.

DUNN, Alan C. Painter. Born in Belmar, N. J., in 1900. Pupil of National Academy of Design; also studied in France. *Address,* 418 West 144th St., New York.

DUNN, E. B. Painter and sculptor. Born Rochester, N. Y., 1859. Pupil of Hiram Powers in sculpture, and in painting of Wiles. *Address,* 435 West 119th St., New York.

DUNNEL, E. G. Engraver. He was a student in the National Academy of Design, in New York, in 1837, and in that year he secured the third prize for drawing. He became a good engraver of landscape and book illustrations, and in 1847 he was in the employ of Rawdon, Wright & Hatch, an engraving firm of New York. Soon after this latter date he is said to have abandoned engraving for the pulpit.

DUNNEL, William N. This clever engraver in line and stipple was one of the many pupils of A. L. Dick, of New York. Dunnel was engraving for the magazines about 1845, but he contracted bad habits and disappeared.

DUNSMORE, John Ward. Painter. Born near Cincinnati, Ohio, 1856. Pupil of Couture in Paris. Member: New York Architectural League, 1903. Associate Member of National Academy. Work: "Macbeth," Ohio Mechanics' Institute, Cincinnati; "All's Fair in Love and War," Lassell Seminary, Auburndale, Mass.; represented in collection of Salmagundi Club, New York, N. Y. Specialties, historical subjects and portraits. *Address,* 96 Fifth Ave., New York, N. Y.

DUNTON, W. Herbert. Painter. Born in Maine 1878, his sketches of cowboys in the West became well known. His painting "The Cattle Buyer" was shown in Venice in 1924. His pictures are of the woods and plains, and of hunting and fishing in the West.

DUPHINEY, Wilfred I. Painter. Born Central Falls, R. I., 1884. Pupil of W. C. Loring and Albert F. Schmitt. Member: Providence Art Club. Work: Portrait of Bishop Hickey in Providence, R. I.; portrait Ex-Mayor John Lamay, Central Falls, R. I.; illustrations for magazines. *Address,* Fleur-de-lis Bldg., 7 Thomas St., Providence, R. I.

DUQUE, Francis. Painter. Born in 1832. Studied in Paris and Rome. He came to the United States about 1865 and became a popular portrait painter. He died in New York City in 1915.

DURAND, Asher Brown. Engraver and painter. Born in Jefferson, N. J., 1796; died in South Orange, N. J., 1886. Durand's father was a watchmaker and in his father's shop he acquired some knowledge of the elementary

processes of engraving. In 1812 he was apprenticed to the engraver Peter Maverick, and in 1817 he became a partner of his preceptor, under the firm name of Maverick & Durand. The reputation of Asher B. Durand as an engraver in pure line was established by his large plate of the "Declaration of Independence," after the painting by John Trumbull. His "Musidora," engraved in 1825, was also one of his important plates of this period, and his portrait work has never been surpassed in excellence by an American engraver. For a time he was interested in the business of bank-note engraving in 1825, in connection with his brother Cyrus Durand, and in the same year he was a member of the firm of Durand, Perkins & Co.

About 1836, A. B. Durand abandoned engraving for the brush and palette, and he soon became as famous as a painter of landscapes as he had been as an engraver; and to this branch of art he devoted the remainder of his life. In 1895 the Grolier Club, of New York, published a very full check-list of the engraved work of Asher B. Durand. He was a charter member and very active in the affairs of the National Academy and was president from 1845 to 1861. His biography was written by John Durand. Durand painted the portraits of Edward Everett, Gouverneur Kemble, Christian Gobrecht, and many other prominent men. The New York Historical Society has a set of the early Presidents painted by Durand from originals by Gilbert Stuart. The Metropolitan Museum owns his "Judgment of Gog" and five of his landscapes. Durand has been called the "Father of American Landscape Painting."

DURAND, Cyrus. Engraver. Born in Jefferson, N. J., 1787; died at Irvington, N. J., 1868. He was the elder brother of Asher B. Durand. In 1814 Cyrus Durand was in business as a silversmith in Newark, N. J. He was a most ingenious mechanic, and among his earlier inventions was a machine constructed for Peter Maverick, then of Newark, for ruling straight and wavy lines in connection with bank-note work. This was the first of a long series of improvements and inventions intended for use in the production of bank-notes, and Cyrus Durand is credited with having made the first American geometrical lathe. Though not an engraver himself, Cyrus Durand devoted his life to the invention and perfection of machinery used in bank-note work, and his services were so important in this connection that his name can not be omitted from the present record.

DURAND, John. Engraver. Two well-engraved vignettes on the title-pages of the works of William Cowper and Thomas Gray, published in New York by R. & W. A. Bartow, but undated, are signed "Engraved by J. Durand." In answer to a query, Mr. John Durand, of

Nice, Italy, and son of Asher B. Durand, writes that these vignettes were engraved by John Durand, a younger brother of A. B. Durand, who died about 1820, aged twenty-eight years. Mr. Durand says that his father always maintained that his brother John was the most talented member of the family at the time of his death.

DURAND, Theodore. Durand was a script engraver, working in New York in 1835.

DURAND, William. This nephew of A. B. Durand was a man of very considerable mechanical ability. He was engraving for note work in New York in 1850.

DURANT, J. Waldo. Portrait painter. Born in the West Indies in 1774; died in Philadelphia in 1832. The Worcester Art Museum owns a portrait of John Waldo, signed by Durant and dated 1791.

DURKEE, Helen Winslow. Miniature painter. Born New York, N. Y. Pupil of Art Students' League of New York; Chase, Du Mond and Mora. Member: National Academy of Women Painters and Sculptors. Award: C. D. Smith Memorial prize, Baltimore Water Color Club. *Address*, 124 West 72d St., New York, N. Y.

DURRIE, George H. Painter. Born in New Haven, Conn., 1820. He was a pupil of Jocelyn, and painted portraits, but was better known for his farm-scenes. He died in 1863. The Yale Art School owns his "Winter in the Country."

DURRIE, John. Painter. In 1818 John Durrie was born in Hartford, Conn. He passed most of his life at New Haven, Conn., and painted landscapes and a few portraits.

DUSHINSKY, Joseph. Painter. Exhibited at Annual Exhibition of Water Colors at the Penna. Academy of Fine Arts, Philadelphia, 1925. *Address*, 64 East 88th St., New York City.

DU SIMITIÈRE, Pierre Eugene. Artist, antiquary and naturalist. Born in Geneva, Switzerland, about 1736, and died in Philadelphia in 1784. In 1768 he was elected a member of the American Philosophical Society, and in 1777 one of the curators of the society. He designed the vignette for the title page of Aitkin's *Pennsylvania Magazine* in 1775, and the frontispiece for the *United States Magazine* in 1779. He painted portraits in oils and miniature, also maps and views. See "Memoir of Du Simitière" in the *Pennsylvania Magazine*. His collection of manuscripts, drawings, and broadsides is in the Philadelphia Library Co., Philadelphia.

DUSTIN, Silas S. Landscape painter. Born Richfield, Ohio. Pupil of National Academy of Design, and William M. Chase. Member: Art Fund Society; League of New York Artists. *Address*, Wright St., Westport, Conn.

DUTCH, George Sheldon. Painter. Born Chelsea, Mass., 1891. Pupil of Mass. Normal Art School under Major and DeCamp. Member: College Association of Artists. *Address*, 1501 Barnard Ave., Nashville, Tenn.

DUTHIE, James. He was born in England and was there taught to engrave. Duthie was engraving book-illustrations on steel in New York in 1850–55. Some of his best line work appears in the illustrations of an edition of Cooper's works, published in New York in 1860.

DUVAL, Ambrose. Flourished 1827 to 1830 in New Orleans, La., as a miniature painter. His miniature of Gov. William C. C. Claiborne of Louisiana has often been reproduced and copied. It is signed "A. Duval." He also painted Lelande de Ferrier.

DUVAL, P. S. Lithographer. He was first in the employ of Cephas G. Childs in Philadelphia, and afterwards became his successor. In 1850 his firm executed the title for "Godey's"; their card read "P. S. Duval's Lithographic & Color Printing Establishment."

DUMLER, M. G. Painter. Born Cincinnati, Ohio, 1868. Pupil of Edward H. Potthast, M. Rettig, and R. Busebaum. Member: Cincinnati Art Club. *Address*, 19 West 8th St., Cincinnati, Ohio.

DUMLER, M. G. Painter. Exhibited landscape "Autumn" at Cincinnati Museum, 1925. *Address*, 1607 Dexter Ave., Cincinnati.

DUVENECK, Frank. Painter, sculptor, etcher and teacher. He was born at Covington, Ky., in 1848, and received his early training at a monastery near Pittsburgh. He also studied in Munich. He was made a National Academician in 1906, and was a member of the Society of American Artists of New York, Cincinnati Art Club, and the National Institute of Arts and Letters. He died 1919. Represented at the Cincinnati Museum Association; Art Association of Indianapolis; Pennsylvania Academy of Fine Arts, Philadelphia; National Gallery of Art, Washington, D. C.

DUVIVIER AND SON. Portrait painters, flourishing in Philadelphia about 1796. Their advertisement in Claypoole's "American Daily Advertiser," Philadelphia, is as follows: "Academy of Drawing and Painting, Duvivier & Son, No. 12 Strawberry St., between Second & Third Sts., Near Market, Philadelphia."

DUYCKINCK, Evert 1st. Portrait painter, who came to New Amsterdam in 1638 from Holland. He is described as a limner, painter, glazier and burner of glass. Born in 1621, he died in 1702. In 1693 he painted the portrait of Stephanus Van Cortland, Mayor of New York City in 1677.

DUYCKINCK, Evert 3d. Portrait painter. Born in 1677 and died in 1727. He painted in 1725 the portrait of his cousin Ann Sinclair Crommelin. He is also said to have painted a portrait of Lieut.-Governor William Stoughton. The Duyckincks were the most important family of painters in Colonial America.

DUYCKINCK, Gerardus. Portrait painter. Born 1695; died 1742. He was the son of Gerret Duyckinck. He was admitted as a freeman of the city in 1731, and there described as a limner.

DUYCKINCK, Gerret. Portrait painter of the early Dutch families in New York State. Born 1660; died about 1710. He painted Anne Van Cortland, who married Stephen de Lancey in 1700. The portrait is signed and dated "Gt. Duyckinck, 1699."

DWIGGINS, W. A. Illustrator. Born Martinsville, Ohio, 1880. Member: Boston Society of Printers; Boston Art Club. *Address,* 384A Boylston St., Boston, Mass.

DWIGHT, Julia S. Painter. Born Hadley, Mass., 1870. Pupil of Tryon and Tarbell in Boston; Brush in New York. *Address,* 1651 Beacon St., Brookline, Mass.

DWIGHT, Mabel. Painter. Exhibited at National Academy of Design, New York, 1925. *Address,* 220 West 14th St., New York.

DYE, Clarkson. Painter. Born San Francisco, Calif., 1869. Pupil of Virgil Williams, Burridge, Michelson, etc. Work: Mural decorations in Cathedral of Los Angeles, Durango, Mexico; Grand Opera House, Waco, Tex. *Address,* 2595 Union St., San Francisco, Calif.

DYER, Mrs. Agnes S. Painter. Born San Antonio, Tex., 1887. Pupil of Julian Onderdonk, Arthur Dow, John Carlson and Art Students' League of New York. *Address,* 483 North Grove St., East Orange, N. J.

DYER, Charles Gifford. Painter. Born in Chicago, 1846. Graduated from U. S. Naval Academy and served in Civil War, but resigned, from ill health, and studied art in Paris. Among his works, "St. Mark's, Venice," "Venice at Birth of Day," and "Among the Domes of St. Mark's."

DYER, H. Anthony. Landscape painter, chiefly in water colors. Born in Providence, R. I., in 1872. Studied art in France, Holland, and Italy. Member of the Providence Art Club, and President of the Providence Water Color Club. Lecturer on Art. Represented in permanent exhibition of the Corcoran Art Gallery by "The Road that Leads them Home" (water color). *Address,* Providence, R. I.

DYER, H. W. Painter and illustrator. Born Portland, Me., 1871. Pupil of Chas. L. Fox in Portland; Frank W. Benson and Ross Turner in Boston; Voltz Preissig, and Art Students' League of New York. Member: Society of Independent Artists. *Address,* 483 North Grove St., East Orange, N. J.

E

EAKINS, Thomas. Painter. Born in Philadelphia, 1844; died there, 1916. Studied in the École des Beaux Arts under Gerome and the sculptor Du Mond. After returning to America, he taught in life classes, lectured as a demonstrator of anatomy, and became professor of painting, and director of schools of the Pennsylvania Academy of the Fine Arts. He also taught and lectured in New York, Brooklyn and Washington. Besides portraits, he painted many pictures of early American domestic life, sporting scenes and incidents in the lives of fishermen and cowboys. Among the more familiar of his works are his large composition portraits of Dr. D. Hayes Agnew and Professor Gross in their clinics; "William Rush Carving an Allegorical Figure of the Schuylkill," and "The Cruxifixion," the latter hanging in Overbrook Seminary. He also assisted his pupil, Samuel Murray, in modelling the figures of the prophets which adorn the Witherspoon Building; modelled two reliefs for the Trenton Battle monument, and the horses ridden by Grant and Lincoln on the Soldiers' and Sailors' monument at Brooklyn. His paintings won awards. Elected member of the National Academy in 1902. A memorial exhibition of the works of Thomas

Eakins was held at the Penna. Academy of the Fine Arts, 1917–1918, and about one hundred and fifty of his paintings were catalogued.

EAKINS, Mrs. Thomas. Mrs. Eakins copied and restored Sully's portrait of Dr. Philip Syng Physick at the University in 1889.

EARHART, John Franklin. Landscape painter. Born in Ohio, 1853. Member: Cincinnati Art Club. *Address,* Perin Bldg., Cincinnati, Ohio.

EARL, Ralph. Painter of portraits and historical scenes. Born in Leicester, Mass., 1751. He was the author of "Four Scenes of the Battle of Lexington," and was present at the famous march. Amos Doolittle later engraved the subjects. After the war he went to London, where he studied with Benjamin West. He returned to America in 1786. He died of intemperance in Bolton, Conn., in 1801. (Also signed "Earle.")

EARL, Ralph E. Painter. Son of Ralph Earl, the well-known portrait painter, who died in 1801. Ralph Jr. was born in England, 1788, while his father was studying art in that country, and came to the United States with him when he was a child. He studied first with his father, and then went to London in 1809, where he continued his art studies, and to Paris in 1814. He returned from Europe in 1815, arriving in Georgia, from which place he went to Tennessee, where he married Miss Caffery, a niece of General Andrew Jackson. He painted in New Orleans and died there in 1837. He was buried at the "Hermitage."

EARL (or EARLE), Thomas. A little-known American painter who lived at Cherry Valley, Mass. Born 1737, and died 1819. He was a cousin of Ralph Earl, the artist, gun-maker, and soldier of the Revolutionary War. He painted portraits in Connecticut in 1775 and in Charleston, S. C., in 1792. His full-length portrait of Dr. Dwight and his wife are in Copley's manner with black shadows.

EARLE, Augustus. Artist, and son of James Earle, was admitted as a student at the Royal Academy in 1793. From 1815 to 1832 he travelled in North and South America. When in New York he spent his time with Thomas Cummings the well-known painter of miniatures.

EARLE, Elinor. Painter. Born in Philadelphia. Pupil of Penna. Academy of Fine Arts. Awarded Smith prize, 1902, and medal, St. Louis Exposition, 1904.

EARLE, J. All that is known of this man is that he was engraving portraits in Philadelphia in 1876, in connection with James R. Rice.

EARLE, James. Painter. Born in Mass., 1761; died in Charleston, S. C., 1796. Brother of Ralph Earle. He painted portraits in Charleston, and died suddenly of yellow fever. His portrait of Charles Pinckney is owned by the Worcester Art Museum.

EARLE, Lawrence Carmichael. A painter. Born New York City, 1845; died at his home at Grand Rapids, 1921. He studied in Munich, Florence and Rome. He was an Associate of the National Academy of Design, and a member of the American Water Color Society; Artists' Fund Society; Art Institute of Chicago (honorary); and the New York Water Color Club. He was represented in the Art Institute of Chicago, and in the Chicago National Bank. He made a specialty of portraits.

EASTMAN, Seth. Painter. Born in Brunswick, Maine, 1808. He entered the Military Academy at West Point, and graduated in 1831, and taught drawing there from 1833–40. He was afterwards stationed with his regiment in the Western states where he became greatly interested in the Indians. Nine paintings of Indian life, and 17 paintings of U. S. forts are in the Capitol Bldg., Washington, D. C. He died in 1875.

EASTMAN, William J. Painter. Born in 1888. Member of Cleveland Society of Artists. *Address,* 1868 East 82d St., Cleveland, Ohio.

EATON, Charles Frederick. Painter. Born at Providence, R. I., 1842. Lived in Europe until 1886; settled at Santa Barbara, 1886; occupied in painting, wood carving and landscape architecture; made rare collection of antique carved furniture and tapestries; known as earnest worker in and advocate of the Arts and Crafts movement in America. *Address,* Santa Barbara, Calif.

EATON, Charles Harry. Painter. Born in 1850, and died 1901. First exhibited at National Academy of Design, N. Y. Gold medal at the Philadelphia Art Club, 1900, exhibiting "The Willows." Elected an Associate Member of the National Academy of Design in 1893. He exhibited "The Willows" at the Paris Exposition in 1889, and at the World's Fair, Chicago, in 1893.

EATON, Charles Warren. Painter. Born Albany, N. Y., 1857. Pupil of National Academy Design, and Art Students' League, New York. Exhibited, Royal Academy, and Grosvenor Gallery, London; Paris Expn., 1900. Received Inness gold medal, National Academy of Design, 1904; gold medal, Paris Salon, 1906; silver medal, Buenos Aires, 1910. Elected Associate Member of National Academy. Member: American Water Color Society; New York Water Color Club. *Address,* Bloomfield, N. J.

EATON, Hugh McD. Painter and illustrator. Born in Brooklyn, N. Y., in 1865. Pupil of Cox and Chase. Specialty, illustrations and lead block prints. Died 1924 at Halsey St., Brooklyn, N. Y.

EATON, Joseph Oriel. Painter. Born in Licking Co., Ohio, in 1829. Genre and portrait painter in oil and water colors. He was an Associate of the National Academy, and a member of the Society of Painters in Water Colors. He visited Europe in 1873. Exhibited at National Academy in 1868, "View on Hudson." He died in New York in 1875.

EATON, Margaret F. (Mrs. Hugh M. Eaton). Painter. Born in England, 1871. Pupil of Art Students' League of New York, under Cox and Mowbray. Member of New York Water Color Club. *Address*, 339 Halsey St., Brooklyn, N. Y.

EATON, Wyatt. Painter. Born Philipsburg, Canada, 1849; died Newport, R. I., 1896. Figure and portrait painter. Pupil of J. O. Eaton, the National Academy of Design, and later of Gerome at the École des Beaux Arts. He was the first secretary of the Society of American Artists. He painted "Ariadne," and is represented at the Boston Museum of Fine Arts by "Mother and Child."

EBBELS, Victoria. Painter. Born in Hasbrouck Heights, N. J., in 1900. Pupil of George Luks and Robert Henri. Member of the Society of Independent Artists. *Address*, 1213 Carrier St., Denton, Texas.

EBERHARD, Robert G. Sculptor. Born in Switzerland, in 1884. Pupil of Rodin. Work: War Memorial Tablets, White Plain, N. Y. Instructor in sculpture at Yale University, New Haven, Conn. *Address*, 154 West 55th St., New York.

EBERLE, Abastenia St. Leger. Sculptor. Born Webster City, Ia., 1878. Studied modeling at Canton, Ohio, under Frank Vogan; Art Students' League, New York, under C. Y. Harvey, Kenyon Cox and George Grey Barnard. Has exhibited in leading cities of America and Europe. Represented in Metropolitan Museum, New York; Worcester, Mass., Art Museum; Newark, N. J.; Peabody Institute, Baltimore; Carnegie Institute, Pittsburgh; Detroit Museum, etc. Member: National Sculpture Society, and Associate Member of National Academy. He received H. F. Barnett prize at National Academy, New York, in 1910. *Address*, 204½ West 13th St., New York.

EBERT, Charles H. Painter. Born in Wisconsin in 1872. Pupil of Art Students' League of New York, and Julien Academy in Paris. *Address*, Lyme, Conn.

EBERT, Mary R. (Mrs.). Painter. Born in Titusville, Pa., 1873. Pupil of Art Students' League of New York, also of Twachtman and Hunt. *Address*, Lyme, Conn.

ECHERT, Florence. Painter. Born in Cincinnati, Ohio. Pupil of Wm. M. Chase. *Address*, The Valencia, St. George St., St. Augustine, Florida.

ECKFORD, Jessiejo. Painter. Born in Dallas, Tex., 1895. Member of Dallas Art Association, and Society of Independent Artists. *Address*, 4403 Gaston Ave., Dallas, Texas.

ECKSTEIN, John. Was a portrait painter, a modeler in clay, and an engraver of portraits executed in a somewhat curious stipple manner. In the proposals for publishing his engraving of a "Representation of a Monument of General Washington," he is referred to as "Formerly historical painter and statuary to the King of Prussia." His name appears in the Philadelphia directories of 1796–97 as "Limner and Statuary," and again in 1805–06; from 1811 to 1816 his occupation is given as "Engraver," and at intervals in this period he appears as "A merchant." He was painting and engraving as late as 1822.

Eckstein's few portrait plates are inscribed as "Painted and Engraved by John Eckstein," and they are executed in a combination of stipple and roulette work, hard in effect. In 1806 he modeled a statue of Washington for a proposed monument, and in the same year he issued proposals for, and engraved for the Society of the Cincinnatus, the plate noted above. In 1809 he engraved illustrations for an edition of Freneau's poems, published by Lydia R. Bailey, of Philadelphia.

This engraver, though a German, should not be confounded with Johannes Eckstein, a German portrait painter and excellent engraver in mezzotinto, who died in London in 1798.

EDDY, Henry B. Illustrator. Born in New York in 1872. Member of the Society of Illustrators of New York. *Address*, 2 Duane St., New York City.

EDDY, Henry S. Painter. Born in Rahway, N. J., 1878. Pupil of Volk, Cox, and Twachtman. Represented in Milwaukee Art Institute by "In from the Nets." *Address*, Springfield Road, Westfield, N. J.

EDDY, Isaac. Engraver. Born in Weathersfield, Vt., 1777, died in 1847. He engraved some crude plates for the "First Vermont Edition of a Bible," published at Windsor, Vt., by Merifield & Cochran. He is mentioned as an engraver, or possibly as a land-surveyor. Sometime in his engraver's career he appears to have been connected with Pendleton's engraving establishment in Boston.

EDDY, James. Engraver. Born in 1806, was living in Providence, R. I., 1881. He was a good engraver of portraits in the stipple manner, and was working as early as 1827 to 1830 in Boston.

EDDY, O. T. Engraver. A folio map of New Hampshire with an inset view of Bellows Falls engraved in line is signed "O. T. Eddy, engraver, Walpole (N. H.) Aug. 1817."

EDDY, Sarah J. Sculptor. Exhibited portrait bust of Samuel S. Fleisher, at the Penna. Academy of Fine Arts, Philadelphia, 1914. *Address*, Bristol Ferry, R. I.

EDERHEIMER, Richard. Portrait painter. Born Frankfort, Germany, 1878. Member: League of New York Artists; Society of Independent Artists. *Address*, 18 East 57th St., New York.

EDHOLM, C. L. Painter and illustrator. Born Omaha, 1879. Pupil of Ludwig Herterich in Munich. Member: League of New York Artists; Whitney Studio Club. *Address*, 10 Larchmont Ave., Larchmont, N. Y.

EDMOND, Elizabeth. Sculptor. Exhibited at the Penna. Academy of Fine Arts, Philadelphia, 1914. Died June 22, 1918.

EDMONDS, Esther. Painter. Born in New York City, 1888. Daughter of A. Edmonds, a painter of rare ability. She first commenced her art studies with her father, following this instruction by courses of study at Cooper Union and the Art Students' League of New York, graduating with honor from these schools. After completing her studies she became associated with her father, assisting in his work. In 1910 her father opened a studio in Columbia, S. C., where Miss Edmonds continued to work with him. Since the death of her father she has continued her profession of a portrait painter, and has painted many portraits of prominent men.

EDMONDS, Francis W. Painter. Born in Hudson, N. Y., in 1806. He was a clever genre painter, but had little art education. He was a cashier in a New York bank and employed his leisure in painting. He was elected a member of the National Academy in 1840. He died in 1863.

EDMONDSON, William J. Painter. Born Norwalk, Ohio, 1868. Pupil of Vonnoh in Philadelphia; Aman-Jean and Lefebvre in Paris. Member: Fellowship, Penna. Academy of Fine Arts. Work: represented in Delgado Art Museum, New Orleans; Cleveland Museum; Chamber of Commerce, Cleveland; Fellowship, Penna. Academy of Fine Arts, Philadelphia; State House, Columbus, Ohio. *Address*, 2362 Euclid Ave., Cleveland, Ohio.

EDROP, Arthur N. Painter and illustrator. Born Birmingham, England, 1884. Pupil of Whittaker in Boston. Member: Association of Artists of Philadelphia. Contributor to *Life, Judge*, etc. *Address*, 1630 Sansom St., Philadelphia.

EDSTROM, David. Sculptor. Born at Hvetlanda, Sweden, 1873. Graduated Polytechnical School, Stockholm, Sweden, 1896; Royal Academy of Fine Arts, Stockholm, 1899; studied Florence, Italy, 1900–2; in Paris, France, with Injalbert, 1905. Came to United States with parents, 1880. Started for Europe to study art at twenty-one. Has made portrait busts of many noted personages, including Crown Prince and Princess of Sweden; Princess Patricia of Connaught; Dr. Ludvig Loostrom, director of National Gallery, Stockholm; Ellen Key; etc. Psychology sculptures: "Fear," "Pride," "Envy," "Caliban," "The Cry of Poverty," etc. Silver medal, St. Louis Expn., 1904. *Address*, 33 W. 67th St., New York, N. Y.

EDWARDS, Edward B. Painter and illustrator. Born Columbia, Pa., 1873. Studied in Paris and Munich. Member: New York Architectural League, 1892. *Address*, 127 West 12th St., New York, N. Y.

EDWARDS, George Wharton. Painter. Born at Fairhaven, Conn. Studied at Antwerp and Paris. Work: Mural decoration, "Henrik Hudson," U. S. Military Academy; illustrated Austin Dobson's "Sun Dial," "Old English Ballads," "The Last Leaf," by O. W. Holmes, etc. Author of "Alsace-Lorraine," "Vanished Halls and Cathedrals of France," "Holland of Today," "Belgium, Old and New," etc. *Address*, 331 Madison Ave., New York.

EDWARDS, H. C. Painter and illustrator. Born Philadelphia, Pa., 1868. Pupil of Adelphi College, Brooklyn, under J. B. Whittaker; Art Students' League of New York under Mowbray. Member: Brooklyn Society of Artists. Illustrated "The Gun Brand," "Blackwater Bayou," etc. Died in 1922.

EDWARDS, Kate Flournoy. Portrait painter. Born in Marshallville, Ga., 1877. Daughter of Joseph Asbury and Emma Miller Edwards. Pupil of Art Institute of Chicago, under Frederick Warren Freer. She has painted portraits of many prominent people of the South, and of many residing in the vicinity of Chicago. Portrait of Philip P. Barbour, property of United States Govt.; Senator A. S. Clay, at Georgia State Capitol. *Address*, 35 East 4th St., Atlanta, Ga.

EDWARDS, Robert. Painter and illustrator. Born Buffalo, N. Y., 1879. Pupil of Art Students' League of Buffalo; Art Students' League of New York; Chase School; Eric Pape School, and Cowles School in Boston. Member:

Society of Illustrators, 1910. Illustrated "The Lovers of Sana," "Eve's Second Husband," "The Wiving of Lance Cleveridge." Composer of "The Song Book of Robert Edwards." Editor of "Mr. Quill."

EDWARDS, S. Arent. Engraver. Born in 1862 in Somersetshire, England; living in New York in 1905. Mr. Edwards was a student at the Kensington Art School in 1877–81, and was then taught to engrave in mezzotint by Appleton, Josey & Alais, of London. He first exhibited examples of his engraving in the Royal Academy in 1885.

In 1890 Mr. Edwards came to the United States and established himself in New York, and made book illustrations, portraits, and subject plates. He very successfully revived the art of printing in colors from mezzotinto plates, and deservedly achieved a reputation. His color plates are issued absolutely without touching up with water colors, as it is too often the custom in prints of this description.

EDWARDS, Thomas. Flourished 1822–1856 in Boston, Mass. Silhouettist, and portrait painter in oils and miniatures. He was a frequent exhibitor in the early years of the Boston Athenaeum, and also contributed drawings to the first lithographic press in Boston, established in 1825 by the Pendleton Brothers.

EDWIN, David. Engraver. Born in Bath, England, in 1776. He was a son of John Edwin, an English actor. David Edwin was apprenticed to a Dutch engraver named Jossi, who was residing in England, but who finally returned to Holland, taking Edwin with him. After a short time Edwin disagreed with his master, and, disliking the country, shipped as a sailor on board a vessel bound from Amsterdam to Philadelphia, where he arrived in 1797. He speedily found a friend and employer in T. B. Freeman, for whom he engraved the title-page for a selection of "Scotch Airs," made by Benjamin Carr, of which Freeman was the publisher. For some years subsequently he was engaged as an assistant to Edward Savage. He is said to have encountered great obstacles from lack of tools, from the poor quality of obtainable plates, and from rude printing, and, in overcoming them, he totally changed his style and mode of working. His talent as an engraver of portraits soon brought him constant employment, and for upwards of thirty years he was the most prolific workman in America. Failing health and overwork impaired his sight, and about 1830 he was compelled to cease work. In 1835 he became treasurer of the newly formed "Artists' Fund Society of Philadelphia," and about the same time received a bequest from a friend which rendered his last years comfortable. He died in 1841. These details are all drawn from a biographical sketch published in "Catalogue of the Engraved Work of David Edwin," by Mantle Fielding, Philadelphia, 1905. In this work 263 of his engravings are described. His engravings are in stipple, and beautifully finished. Among his best known plates are Thomas McKean, Thomas Jefferson, Dolly Madison, and a number of General Washington.

EGGELING, Herman. Painter and illustrator. Born in New York, 1884. Pupil of Bridgman and Sloan. *Address*, 106 Pleasant Ave., Tuckahoe, N. Y.

EGGLESTON, Benjamin. Painter. Born in Goodhue County, Minn., 1867. Pupil of Minneapolis School of Fine Arts under Douglas Volk. *Address*, 164 East 22d St., Brooklyn, New York.

EHNINGER, John W. Painter. Born in New York in 1827. He studied abroad and afterwards painted a number of genre studies of American life. His best known paintings are "New England Farmyard," "Yankee Pedler," "Lady Jane Grey." He also produced illustrations in outline and a series of etchings. Elected a member of the National Academy in 1860. Died in 1889.

EICHHOLTZ, Jacob. Painter. Born of an old family, of German origin, in Lancaster, Penna., in 1776. He was an expert coppersmith, but early developed a talent for portrait drawing. Early in the century he was aided by visiting artists, and when Thos. Sully visited Lancaster, on the eve of his departure for Europe, 1809, he left Eichholtz his "half-worn brushes," and directed him to the instruction of Gilbert Stuart, at Boston. As a specimen of his work at that time he took with him his best known portrait, that of Nicholas Biddle, with the U. S. Bank in the background. On his return, he settled in Philadelphia as a professional portrait painter, remaining there for ten years. Following the style of Sully and Stuart, he painted more than 250 portraits and some landscapes and historical groups, between 1810 and the time of his death, 1842. Twice married, he left many descendants. Among his subjects and sitters were Chief Justices Marshall and Gibson; Governors Shulze, Porter and Ritner; Attorneys General Elder, Franklin and Champneys; Nicholas Biddle and many of the foremost people of his day in Philadelphia, Baltimore, Harrisburg and Lancaster. (For extended notice see W. U. Hensel's monograph and catalogue of Eichholtz's works.)

EILERS, Emma. Painter. Born in New York. Pupil of Art Students' League, under Cox, in New York. Member of Fellowship of Penna. Academy of Fine Arts. *Address*, 751 St. Marks Ave., Brooklyn, New York.

EISENLOHR, E. G. Painter. Born in Cincinnati, Ohio, 1872. Pupil of R. J. Onderdonk. *Address*, 324 Eads Ave., Station A, Dallas, Tex.

ELAND, John S. Painter and etcher. Pupil of Sargeant. Illustrator of children's books. Born in England, 1872. *Address*, Rodin Studios, 200 West 57th St., New York City.

ELDER, Arthur J. Painter and etcher. Born in England in 1874. *Address*, Nutley, New Jersey.

ELDER, John A. Painter of portraits and battle subjects. Born Fredericksburg, Va., 1833; died there, 1895. In his early youth he was a cameo carver. Pupil of the Dusseldorf Academy and of Emanuel Leutze. Won prize at Dusseldorf Academy. He painted portraits of General Robert Edward Lee and General T. J. Jackson.

ELDRED, L. D. Marine artist and etcher. Was born in Fairhaven, Mass. He studied in Julien Studio in Paris. On his return to this country he opened his studio in Boston, where his work has been much sought after.

ELDRIDGE. A line engraving of a residence, "Hickory Grove," is signed as "Drawn by J. Collins, Engraved by Eldrige." It is a good work and appears in "The Miscellaneous Writings of Samuel J. Smith, of Burlington, N. J.," Philadelphia, 1836.

ELDRIDGE, C. W. Miniature painter. Born in New London, Conn., in 1811. He lived for years in Hartford, Conn. He also painted many miniatures in the south. He was a member for years of the old firm of miniature painters, Parker & Eldridge.

ELKINS, Henry Arthur. Painter. Born in Vershire, Vt., in 1847. He removed to Chicago in 1856 and taught himself to paint. Among his pictures are "Mount Shasta," "New Eldorado," and the "Crown of the Continent." Died in 1884.

ELLERHUSEN, Ilric H. Sculptor. Born in Germany, 1879; came to America, 1894. Pupil of Lorado Taft and Karl Bitter. Well known for his designing of medals, also for "Schwab Memorial Fountain" on Yale University Campus. *Address*, 51 West 10th St., New York City.

ELLICOTT, Henry Jackson. Sculptor. Born in Anne Arundel County, Md., 1847; died in Washington, D. C., 1901. Studied drawing at the National Academy of Design; also studied under Brumidi, Powell, and Leutze.

ELLIOT, George. A little-known American portrait painter born in 1776; he died in 1852. His portrait of Mr. Van Dusen, of Connecticut, was signed. He was said to have been an Academician, but the published lists of the National Academy of Design do not note his name.

ELLIOTT, Benjamin F. Landscape and portrait painter. Born in Middletown, Conn., in 1829; died there in 1870. He painted many portraits for Kellogg Brothers, in Hartford. He died in 1870.

ELLIOTT, Charles Loring. Portrait painter. Born at Scipio, N. Y., in 1812. He came to New York City about 1834, and became the pupil of John Trumbull. In 1846 he was elected a member of the National Academy of Design. He was said to have painted more than seven hundred portraits of prominent men of his time. His portraits are in all the prominent galleries. He died in Albany, N. Y., in 1868.

ELLIOTT, Elizabeth Shippen Green (Mrs.). Illustrator and painter of children. Born in Philadelphia; student of Penna. Academy of Fine Arts and Howard Pyle. *Address*, Cresheim Road, Germantown, Philadelphia.

ELLIOTT, John. Painter. Born in England, 1858. Student in Julien's Academy. Pupil of Carolus Duran, Paris; José di Villegas at Rome. Subjects, chiefly portraits and mural decorations, some of the more notable in America being "The Vintage," frieze and ceiling in house of Mrs. Potter Palmer, Chicago; "The Triumph of Time," ceiling decoration in Boston Public Library; "Diana of the Tides," mural painting in new National Museum, Washington. Represented in permanent collection of Metropolitan Museum of Art, New York; Old State House, Boston; collection of H. M. the Dowager Queen of Italy.

ELLIS, Edmund L. Painter and etcher. Born in Omaha, Nebr., in 1872. *Address*, 21 East 40th St., New York.

ELLIS, Edwin M. This engraver of portraits and landscape, working both in stipple and in line, was in business in Philadelphia in 1844.

ELLIS, George B. In 1821 Ellis was a pupil of the Philadelphia engraver Francis Kearny, and in 1825–37, inclusive, he was in business for himself in the same city. His name disappears from the Philadelphia directories in 1838.

Ellis first attracted attention as an engraver by his excellent copies of English engravings, made by him for an edition of "Ivanhoe." He produced some very good portraits, but his best work is found among his small "Annual" plates.

ELLIS, Fremont F. Painter and etcher. Born in Virginia City, Mont., in 1897. Pupil of Art Students' League of New York. Member: California Art Club. *Address*, Caminio del Monte Sol, Santa Fé, N. M.

ELLIS, Harriet. Miniature painter. Exhibited portrait miniatures at the Penna. Academy of Fine Arts, Philadelphia, 1922. *Address,* 138 Sherman St., Springfield, Mass.

ELLIS, Joseph B. Sculptor. Born in North Scituate, Mass., in 1890. Pupil of Albert H. Munsell. *Address,* 431 Fourth Ave., Pittsburgh, Pa.

ELLIS, Salathiel. Flourished 1845–46, New York. A painter of cameo likenesses.

ELLIS, W. H. Was a good line-engraver of landscape and book illustrations. His work appears in Philadelphia publications of 1845–47.

ELLSWORTH, James S. Miniature painter. Born in Windsor, Conn., 1802, and died 1874. He moved to the West, and died in Pittsburgh, Penna., in destitute circumstances. He painted ''A Wounded Grecian Racer,'' and made several copies of Gilbert Stuart's full-length portrait of Washington; one being in the Wadsworth Gallery.

ELMORE, Mrs. Elizabeth Tinker. Painter. Exhibited at National Association of Women Painters and Sculptors, New York, 1924. *Address,* 2 West 67th St., New York.

ELOUIS, Jean Pierre Henri, or, as he called himself in this country, Henry Elouis, was born in Caen, France, 1755, and died there, 1843. He studied art under the French painter, Jean Barnard Restout, going to London in 1783. He exhibited at the Royal Academy in 1785, 1786, 1787, and at the beginning of the French Revolution emigrated to America, settling in Baltimore. Charles Wilson Peale met him in 1791 at Annapolis, and calling him ''Mr. Louis,'' mentions that ''he paints in a new stile,'' querying ''if this gentleman so cried up will do better than Mr. Pine, whose reputation was equally cried up.'' In 1792 Elouis removed to Philadelphia and his name appears in the Directories for 1793 as ''limner, 201 Mulberry St.'' He remained in Philadelphia until 1799, during which period he gave instruction in drawing to Eleanor Custis and painted miniatures of Washington and of Mrs. Washington. Elouis, travelling over the United States, Mexico, and South America, returned in 1807 to France. His portraits are noted for their simplicity and directness.

ELWELL, Francis Edwin. Sculptor. Born in Concord, Mass., in 1858; he died in Darien, Conn., 1922. He was a pupil of Daniel French, and also studied in Paris. Among his works ''Dickens and Little Nell,'' in Philadelphia; ''The Flag'' at Vicksburg, Miss.; Equestrian statue of General Hancock at Gettysburg, Pa.; and ''The New Life'' at the Penna. Academy of Fine Arts, Philadelphia.

ELWELL, John H. Painter, sculptor and illustrator. Born Marblehead, Mass., 1878. Pupil of Vesper L. George; Reuben Carpenter. *Address,* 30 Bromfield St., Boston, Mass.

ELY, A. Ely engraved the script title-page, the music, and a curious ''musical'' vignette for ''The Songster's Assistant, etc.,'' by T. Swan, Suffield, Conn.; printed by Swan and Ely. The work is undated, but seemingly belongs to the first decade of the last century. The only copy known is in the Watkinson Library, of Hartford, Conn.

EMERSON, Arthur W. Painter, illustrator and etcher. Born Honolulu, Hawaii, 1885. Pupil of John C. Johansen. Member of Art Students' League of New York. *Address,* 176 Waverly Place, New York, N. Y.

EMERSON, C. Illustrator and painter. Member: Society of Illustrators, 1912; Boston Art Club. Died in 1922.

EMERSON, Edith. Painter. Born in Oxford, 1888. Pupil of Art Institute of Chicago; Penna. Academy of Fine Arts; and pupil of Violet Oakley. Member: Fellowship, Penna. Academy of Fine Arts; Philadelphia Print Club; Philadelphia Art Alliance. Work: Mural decorations in the Little Theatre, Philadelphia; Roosevelt memorial window, Temple Keneseth Israel, Philadelphia, Pa. *Address,* Allen Lane, Philadelphia, Pa.

EMERSON, W. C. Painter. Member: Chicago Society of Artists; Chicago Water Color Club; New York Water Color Club. *Address,* 109 West 84th St., New York, N. Y.

EMERTON, James H. Illustrator. Born in Salem, Mass., 1847. *Address,* Fenway Studios, 30 Ipswich St., Boston, Mass.

EMMES, Thomas. The earliest known attempt of a portrait engraved upon copper by an American engraver is the work of Thomas Emmes, of Boston. This is a portrait of the Rev. Increase Mather, and appears as a frontispiece to ''The Blessed Hope, etc.,'' published in Boston, New England, 1701, by Timothy Green for Nicholas Boone. The plate itself is a very rough attempt at a copy of a London portrait engraved either by Sturt or by Robert White, and is little more than scratched upon the copper in nearly straight lines; it has a strongly cross-hatched background. The plate is signed ''Tho. Emmes Sculp. Sold by Nicholas Boone 1701.''

EMMET, Leslie. Painter. Exhibited at the National Association of Women Painters and Sculptors, New York, 1924. *Address,* Salisbury, Conn.

EMMET, Lydia Field. Miniature painter and illustrator. Born at New Rochelle, N. Y., in 1866. Pupil of Bouguereau and Fleury, Paris, and William Chase, MacMonnies, Mowbray, Cox and Reid, in New York. Awarded: Medal, Chicago Exposition, 1893; Philadelphia Prize, Penna. Academy of Fine Arts, 1915; Corcoran Popular prize, 1917; Maynard prize, National Academy of Design, 1918. Elected Associate Member of the National Academy of Design in 1909; Academician in 1911. *Address*, 535 Park Ave., New York.

EMMONS, Alexander H. Portrait painter. Was born in East Haddam, Conn., in 1816. He painted in oil, and executed numerous miniatures. In 1843 he opened his studio in Hartford; his only absence for any length of time from this country was an extended trip through Europe to study the work of the old masters. He finally settled in Norwich, Conn., where he died in 1879.

EMMONS, Mrs. C. S. Painter. Born Kingfield, Me., 1858. Pupil of Enneking and Alice Beckington. *Address*, 21 Bennington St., Newton, Mass.

EMMONS, Dorothy Stanley. Painter. Born Roxbury, Mass., 1891. Pupil of Woodbury, J. G. Browne, G. A. Thompson and G. L. Noyes. *Address*, 21 Bennington St., Newton, Mass.

EMMONS, Nathaniel. Born in Boston, 1704. A little-known American painter of considerable merit. He painted a portrait of Judge Sewall (engraved by Pelton), William Clarke, Andrew Oliver and Rev. John Lowell (painted 1728). He died in 1740.

ENDRES, Louis J. Painter. Exhibited at Cincinnati Art Museum in 1925. *Address*, 4206 Ballard Ave., Cincinnati.

ENGEL, Richard Drum. Painter. Born Washington, D. C., 1886. Member: Washington Art Club; Society of Washington Artists. *Address*, 1634 3d St., Washington, D. C.

ENGELMANN, C. F. Engraver. An elaborate, curiously designed, and crudely engraved Birth and Baptismal Certificate, published about 1814, is signed ''Eng. and sold by C. F. Engelmann on Pennsmount near Reading, Pa.'' The design follows closely similar work emanating from the community of Seventh Day Baptists, at Ephrata, Lancaster Co., Pa., which is in the vicinity of Reading.

ENGLE, H. L. Landscape painter. Born Richmond, Ind., 1870. Pupil of Art Institute of Chicago. Member: Palette and Chisel Club; Chicago Society of Artists. Award: Palette and Chisel Club prize, 1917. Work: ''Old Lyme Road,'' purchased by Chicago Art Commission, 1914; ''Laurel Blossoms,'' Long Beach (Calif.) Public Library.

ENGLER, Arthur. Engraver. Born Jersey City, 1885. Pupil of Francis Clarke. *Address*, 150 Nassau St., New York, N. Y.

ENGLISH, Frank F. Painter. Born in Louisville, Ky., in 1854. Pupil of Penna. Academy of Fine Arts; he also studied in England. *Address*, Point Pleasant, Bucks County, Penna.

ENGLISH, Mabel B. P. (Mrs.). Painter. Born in Hartford, Conn., 1861. Pupil of Chase and D. W. Tryon. *Address*, 210 Fern St., Hartford, Conn.

ENNEKING, John Jos. Painter. Born in Ohio, in 1841. He came to Boston in 1865. In 1872 he went abroad for study, and afterwards returned to this country and settled in Boston. His landscapes and cattle pictures have decided merit. His ''Hillside'' is in the Boston Museum of Fine Arts, and ''Autumn in New England'' is owned by the Worcester Art Museum.

ENNEKING, Joseph E. Painter. Born in Hyde Park, Mass. Pupil of De Camp, Benson, and Tarbell. *Address*, 17 Webster Square, Hyde Park, Mass.

ENNIS, George Pearse. Painter. Born in St. Louis, Mo., 1884. Pupil of William Chase. He was also a designer of stained glass. Exhibited at Exhibition of the Penna. Academy of the Fine Arts, Philadelphia, 1924. *Address*, 58 West 57th St., New York.

ENTZING-MILLER, T. M. This man was a designer for engravers, and an engraver of portraits in line. He did good work and was located in Philadelphia and in New York in 1850-55.

ERICKSON, Carl Olaf. Painter. Exhibited at the Pennsylvania Academy of Fine Arts, Philadelphia, in 1924. *Address*, 3702 Herndon St., Chicago, Ill.

ERICSON, David. Painter. Born in Sweden in 1870. He was brought to this country in 1875. He was a pupil of Chase and the Art Students' League, and later with Whistler in Paris. He has executed a series of mural paintings of American Historical Subjects. *Address*, 48 Commercial St., Provincetown, Mass.

ERSKIN, Harold P. Sculptor. Pupil of the Beaux Arts in Paris, 1907-12. *Address*, 251 E. 61st St., New York City.

ERTZ, Edward. Painter, illustrator and etcher. Born in Canfield, Ill. Pupil of Lefebvre, Constant and Delance in Paris. His paintings are in many of the English Galleries, and his etchings in the Library of Congress, Washington, D. C. *Address*, Pulborough, Sussex, England.

ESKRIDGE, Robert Lee. Painter and etcher. Born in Phyllysburg, Pa., in 1891. Pupil of Chicago Academy of Fine Arts and Brooklyn Society of Etchers. *Address*, Coronada Beach, Calif.

ESSIG, George E. Painter and illustrator. Born in Philadelphia, 1838. Pupil of Edward Moran, and James Hamilton. Student at Penna. Academy of Fine Arts, Philadelphia. Specialty, marines. *Address*, Ventnor, Atlantic City, N. J.

ESTÉ, Florence. Painter. Her water colors won the Penna. Academy of the Fine Arts prize, 1925. *Address*, Paris, France.

ETTER, David Rent. Born in Philadelphia, 1807; he lived there until his death. He was interested in the city and state politics. An artist of fair ability, best known for his copies of Gilbert Stuart's paintings. The city of Philadelphia owns his copy of the Stuart-Washington ''Lansdowne'' portrait.

ETTL, John. Sculptor. Born in Hungary in 1872. Represented in New York State Arsenal by ''Abraham Lincoln,'' and ''Chief Oratam,'' Bergen Co. Historical Society. *Address*, 180 13th Ave., New York, N. Y.

ETTL, Alex. J. Sculptor. Born at Fort Lee, N. J., 1898. Pupil of his father, John Ettl, and Robert Aitken. Designed a number of memorials. *Address*, 180 13th Ave., New York, N. Y.

EUWER, Anthony Henderson. Illustrator. Born in Allegheny, Penna., in 1877. Illustrated many American and English periodicals and papers. *Address*, 508 Aspen Road, Portland, Oregon.

EVANS, De Scott. Born in Wayne Co., Ind., 1847. He studied in Paris, and returned to Cleveland and became instructor and co-director in the Academy of Fine Arts there. He is especially skillful in painting draperies. He painted numerous portraits, and among his genre paintings are ''The First Snow-Storm,'' ''Grandma's Visitors,'' and ''Day before the Wedding.'' He died in 1898.

EVANS, Edwin. Painter. Born in Utah in 1860. Pupil of Laurens and Constant in Paris. *Address*, University of Utah, Salt Lake City, Utah.

EVANS, Elizabeth H. Painter. Exhibited at National Association of Women Painters and Sculptors. *Address*, 204 Clay St., Baltimore, Md.

EVANS, Grace. Painter and illustrator. Born Pittston, Pa., 1877. Pupil of Penna. Academy of Fine Arts under Chase, Anshutz and Breckenridge; Drexel Institute. Member: Phila. Art Alliance; Fellowship, Penna. Academy of Fine Arts. Work: Portrait of Dr. Francis March, March High School, Easton, Pa. *Address*, 930 Presser Bldg., Philadelphia, Pa.

EVANS, Jessie Benton. Painter. Born in Ohio. Pupil of Art Institute of Chicago. Member: Chicago Society of Artists; Chicago Art Club. *Address*, 1517 East 61st St., Chicago, Ill.

EVANS, John T. Flourished in 1809, in Philadelphia, as a landscape and miniature painter. He exhibited his miniatures and water colors at the Penna. Academy of the Fine Arts.

EVANS, John William. Artist engraver. Born in Brooklyn, 1855. Pupil of P. R. B. Pierson. Exhibited Chicago Expn., 1893; Paris Expn., 1900; also in London, Berlin, Vienna, Munich and New York. Bronze medal, Buffalo Expn., 1901; St. Louis Expn., 1904; silver medal, Panama P. I. Expn., 1915. *Address*, 633 St. Marks Ave., Brooklyn, New York.

EVANS, Ray O. Illustrator. Born in Columbus, Ohio, 1887. Made illustrations for daily papers and *Puck*. *Address, The Columbus Dispatch*, Columbus, Ohio.

EVANS, Rudulph. Sculptor. Born Washington, D. C. Pupil of Falguiere and Rodin. Member of Academy of National Artists 1919; Associate of National Academy. Work: Statue acquired by French Government for Luxembourg; ''The Golden Hour,'' Metropolitan Museum, New York. *Address*, 71 Washington Place, New York, N. Y.

EVANS, W. G. A map designed to illustrate the geography of the heavens is fantastically designed by E. H. Burnett, and is engraved by W. G. Evans. It was published at Hartford, Conn., in 1835.

EVENS, T. A. A good line map of Cincinnati published in 1838 is signed as ''Drawn & Engraved by T. A. Evans.''

EVERDELL. This name as ''Everdell Sct. 1816'' is signed to a business card, in line and script. It is an advertisement of the business of ''Elijah Lewis, Saddle, Harness & Trunk Maker,'' New York, 1816.

EVERETT, Herbert Edward. Sculptor. Born Worcester, Mass. Pupil of Boston Museum School; Julien Academy in Paris. Member: Philadelphia Water Color Club. *Address*, 1632 Latimer St., Philadelphia, Pa.

EVERETT, Raymond. Painter and sculptor. Born in Englishtown, N. J., in 1885. Pupil of Howard Pyle and J. L. Smith. Professor of drawing and painting at University of Texas. *Address*, 917 West 31st St., Austin, Texas.

EVERS, Ivar Eils. Painter. Born in Sweden, 1866. Pupil of Napoleon Caesar in Sweden; De Camp in Boston; Twachtman in New York. Member: Society of Independent Artists. *Address*, Tillson, Ulster County, New York.

EVERS, John. Miniaturist and painter of theatre scenery. Born in 1797 and died 1884. He was a founder of the National Academy of Design.

EXILIOUS, John G. This reputable line-engraver of landscape and buildings was working in Philadelphia in 1810–14. He was, in 1810, one of the founders of the Society of Artists, in Philadelphia, but nothing more is known about him. His largest and best plate is a view of the Pennsylvania Hospital, engraved in 1814 after his own drawings.

EYRE, Louisa. Sculptor. Born Newport, R. I., 1872. Pupil of Augustus Saint Gaudens. Member: Fellowship, Penna. Academy of Fine Arts; Phila. Alliance. Work: Tablet to Gen. George Sykes for Memorial Hall, West Point, N. Y. *Address*, 1003 Spruce St., Philadelphia, Penna.

EZEKIEL, Moses. Sculptor. Born Richmond, Va., 1844. Graduated Va. Military Institute, 1866; studied anatomy at Medical College of Va.; removed to Cincinnati, 1868; visited Berlin, Germany, 1869, where he studied at Royal Academy of Art, and under Prof. Albert Wolf. Admitted into Society of Artists, Berlin, on the merits of his colossal bust of Washington, and was first foreigner to win the Michael Beer prize. The Jewish order, "Sons of the Covenant," commissioned him, in 1874, to execute a marble group representing "Religious Liberty," for Centennial Exhibition, now in Fairmount Park, Philadelphia. Among his productions are busts of Liszt, Cardinal Hohenlohe, Eve, Homer, David, Judith; "Christ in the Tomb"; statue of Mrs. Andrew D. White for Cornell University; "Faith," Cemetery, Rome; "Madonna," for Church, Tivoli; "Apollo and Mercury," in Berlin, etc. Died 1917.

F

FABER, L. E. Painter and etcher. Born in 1855 in Philadelphia; studied at Penna. Academy of the Fine Arts. Painted portraits and miniatures. He died in 1913.

FABIAN, Lydia Dunham. Painter. Born Charlotte, Mich., 1867. Pupil of the Art Students' League of New York; Art Institute of Chicago. *Address*, 3918 Lake Park Ave., Chicago, Ill.

FAGNANI, Joseph. Born in Naples, 1819; died in New York, 1873. He came to America in 1851, and lived in New York. His painting of the "Nine Muses," now in the Metropolitan Museum of Art, New York, attracted much attention as well known American beauties had served as models.

FAIG, Mrs. Frances Wiley. Painter. Pupil of Duveneck, Grover, and Hawthorne. Member: Cincinnati Woman's Art Club. Work: Mural decorations in Engineering Library, University of Cincinnati. *Address*, 3345 Whitfield Ave., Clifton, Cincinnati, Ohio.

FAIR, Robert. Painter. Born in Ireland in 1847, he came to America in 1876 and established himself in New York City. He later moved to Philadelphia and painted several pictures of note, some of which gained places in the Pennsylvania Academy of Fine Arts. He died in 1907.

FAIRBANKS, Avard Tenneson. Sculptor. Born Provo, Utah, 1897. Pupil of James E. Fraser; Beaux Arts in Paris, under Injalbert. Work: "The Indian," "The Pioneer," Salt Lake City Public Schools; monument, "The Blessing of Joseph," and fountain in honor of Hawaiian motherhood, Laie, H. I.; "Doughboy of Idaho." *Address*, University of Oregon, Eugene, Ore.

FAIRBANKS, Frank P. Painter. Born Boston, 1875. Pupil of Tarbell and De Camp in Boston. Member: (Vice-Pres.) New York Architectural League, 1913; (Sec.) Soc. Mural Painters; Players' Club. Awards: Sears prize and Paige traveling scholarship from the Boston Museum of Fine Arts. Instructor in painting, Cooper Union. *Address*, 15 Vanderbilt Ave., New York, N. Y.

FAIRBANKS, John B. Painter. Born Payson, Utah, 1855. Pupil of Constant, Lefebvre and Laurens in Paris. Member: Society of Utah Artists; Association of Artists Salt

Lake City. Awards: First prize Utah State Fair, 1899. *Address*, 1111 Whitlock Ave., Salt Lake City, Utah.

FAIRBANKS, J. Leo. Painter, etcher and teacher. Pupil of Julien Academy, Paris. Member: Associated Artists of Salt Lake City; Utah Art Institute. Designed and assisted in executing sculpture frieze on Mormon Temple, Hawaii. Director of Art in public schools of Salt Lake City. *Address*, 1228 Byran Ave., Salt Lake City, Utah.

FAIRCHILD, Charles Willard. Illustrator. Born in Marinetto, Wis., in 1886. Pupil of Chicago Academy of Fine Arts; Art Students' League of New York. *Address*, 26 Franklin Court, Garden City, New York.

FAIRCHILD, Louis. Engraver. Born in Farmington, Conn., in 1800; was living in New York in 1840. Fairchild learned to engrave with Asaph Willard, in New Haven, and became an etcher and line-engraver of landscape. He also painted portraits in miniature, and is said to have excelled in that branch of art, though he did little work as a painter.

FAIRCHILD, Max. Painter. Exhibited at the National Association of Women Painters and Sculptors, New York, 1924. *Address*, 58 West 57th St., New York.

FAIRCHILD, May (Mrs. C. N.). Miniature painter. Born Boston, Mass. Member of Art Students' League of New York, and is an instructor in miniature painting. *Address*, 58 West 57th St., New York, N. Y.

FAIRFAX, D. R. Portrait painter, who flourished early in the nineteenth century. The collection of paintings at Independence Hall, Philadelphia, has a portrait of Johnston Blakeley, 1781–1814, painted by D. R. Fairfax.

FAIRMAN, David. A brother of Gideon Fairman. He is mentioned as an engraver, though none of his work has been found. David was born in 1782 and died in Philadelphia, 1815. His obituary refers to him as ''A respectable Artist.''

FAIRMAN, Gideon. Engraver. Born in Newtown, Conn., in 1774. Died in Philadelphia, 1827. In 1796 he opened an office in Albany as an engraver, and in 1810 he removed to Philadelphia and became a member of the bank-note engraving firm of Murray, Draper, Fairman & Co. Later he entered into partnership with Cephas G. Childs about 1824, and in 1826 he was a member of the firm of Fairman, Draper, Underwood & Co.

FAIRMAN, Richard. Born in 1788. Died in Philadelphia, 1821. Mr. C. Gobrecht says that Richard was a brother of Gideon Fairman,

and in 1820 he was working in the establishment of the latter engraver. He was engraving subject plates in line in Philadelphia as early as 1812.

FALCONER, John M. Born in Scotland, 1820, and died 1903. He came to America in 1836, and became an honorary member of the National Academy in 1856. He has made numerous paintings in oil and water colors, besides etching on copper, many plates from his own works, and the designs of other artists.

FALLS, Charles Buckles. Illustrator. Born at Fort Wayne, Ind., in 1874. Known as designer and artist. Member of the Society of Illustrators, and the Society of Mural Decorators. *Address*, 2 East 23d St., New York.

FALLS, De Witt C. Painter and illustrator. Born in New York, 1864. Pupil of Walter Satterlee. Specialty, military subjects and portraits. *Address*, 16 East 60th St., New York.

FANNING, Ralph. Painter. Exhibited water colors at Exhibition of Penna. Academy of Fine Arts, Philadelphia, 1922. *Address*, 206 Sixteenth Ave., Columbus, Ohio.

FANNING, Solomon. Painter. Born in Preston, Conn., in 1807. In 1833 he went to New York and studied portrait painting, and in 1840 he settled in Norwich, Conn., where he practised his profession. His portraits are said to have been good likenesses.

FANSHAW, Samuel R. Miniature painter. Born 1814; died 1888. He exhibited at the National Academy from 1841 to 1847. He was elected an Associate of the Academy in 1881.

FARINA, Pasquale. Painter. Born in Naples, Italy, 1864. Member of Fellowship of Penna. Academy of Fine Arts. Specialty, restoration and care of paintings. *Address*, Art Alliance Bldg., Walnut St., Philadelphia.

FARIS, Ben H. Illustrator and painter. Born at St. Clairsville, Ohio, 1862. Pupil of Cincinnati Art Academy. Illustrator for papers and magazines. *Address*, The Primrose Bldg., Cincinnati, Ohio.

FARJEON, Elliot E. Portrait painter. Born in New York. Studied at the National Academy of Design, and Art Students' League of New York; with Bouguereau, Robert Fleury and Lefebvre in Paris. *Address*, 418 Penn Ave., Pittsburgh, Pa.

FARLEY, Richard Blossom. Portrait and landscape painter. Born Poultney, Vermont, 1875. Pupil of Whistler, Chase and Cecilia Beaux. Awards: Fellowship Prize, Pennsylvania Academy of the Fine Arts, Philadelphia, 1912; Gold medal, Philadelphia Art Club, 1912. Member of Philadelphia Sketch Club;

Allied Artists of America. Represented by his painting ''Fog,'' at the Corcoran Art Gallery. *Address*, New Hope, Penna.

FARLOW, Harry. Painter. Born in Chicago, Ill., 1882. Pupil of Duveneck, Benson and Tarbell. Specialty, portraits. Represented in Hunter College; Yale Club; Board of Education, New York; Neff College, Philadelphia. *Address*, Hotel Chelsea, 222 West 23d St., New York.

FARMER, Birgitta N. Miniature painter. Exhibited portrait miniatures at the Penna. Academy of Fine Arts, Philadelphia, 1922. *Address*, 912 North Alvord St., Syracuse, N. Y.

FARMER, John. Engraver. Born in Half Moon, Saratoga County, N. Y., 1798; died in Detroit, Mich., 1859. Farmer was educated near Albany, N. Y., and taught school in that city. In 1821 he removed to Michigan, became a surveyor, and drew the first published map of Michigan. He afterward published a number of maps of Michigan, Wisconsin, Lake Superior, Detroit, etc. It is stated that he engraved most of these maps himself. John Farmer held many important city offices in Detroit.

FARNDON, Walter. Painter. Born in England in 1876. Pupil of National Academy of Design. *Address*, Douglaston, Long Island, N. Y.

FARNHAM, Sally James. Sculptor. Exhibited at Annual Exhibition, National Academy of Design, New York, 1925. *Address*, 57 West 57th St., New York, N. Y.

FARNSWORTH, Jerry. Painter. Born in Dalton, Ga., in 1895. Pupil of C. W. Hawthorn. Exhibited at National Academy of Design in 1925. Awarded the Third Hallgarten Prize. *Address*, 57 Lawton St., New Rochelle, New York.

FARNUM, Herbert C. Painter. Born in Gloucester, R. I., in 1866. Pupil of Rhode Island School of Design, and Julien Academy in Paris. His ''Flood Tide'' is in permanent collection of Rhode Island School of Design. *Address*, 23 Waterman St., Providence, R. I.

FARNUNG, Helen M. Painter and etcher. Born in Jersey City, N. J., in 1896. Pupil of Art Students' League, New York. *Address*, 413 West 147th St., New York.

FARNY, Henry. Born in Alsace, 1847. He came to this country in 1853, and later lived in Cincinnati. In 1867 he worked for Harper Bros. in New York, illustrating their publications; he visited Europe, and in Rome met Regnault, who gave him employment. He returned to America in 1870, and died in New York City in 1916.

FARRAR, Henry. Etcher and painter in oil and water colors. Born 1843. He attained distinction as a landscape painter. His principal works are ''On the East River,'' ''November Day,'' ''A Hot Day.'' He is a member of the New York Etching Club and the American Society of Painters in Water Colors.

FARRAR, Thomas Charles. Painter. Born in England, 1838. He came to America in 1858, and served in the Union Army during the Civil War. He was the brother of Henry Farrar. Among his works exhibited at the National Academy in New York are ''Twilight on the Hudson,'' ''Sunset,'' and ''Coming through the Lock.'' He is now deceased.

FARRELL, Katherine L. (Mrs.). Painter and etcher. Born in Philadelphia. Pupil of Penna. Academy of Fine Arts. *Address*, 330 South 43d St., Philadelphia.

FARRINGTON, Katherine. Painter in St. Paul, Minn., in 1877. Pupil of De Camp, and Art Students' League of New York. *Address*, 483 Field Point Road, Greenwich, Conn.

FASSETT, Mrs. Cornelia A. Painter. Born in 1831, and died 1898. Daughter of Judge Strong. Studied abroad under Meissonier, and removed to Washington, D. C., in 1875. Her large portrait of the Supreme Justices of 1876 was exhibited at the Centennial. She painted many portraits of men and women in public life of Washington. She had eight children. Several of her paintings are in the Capitol Bldg., Washington, D. C.

FASSETT, Truman E. Painter. Born Elmira, N. Y., 1885. Pupil of Boston Museum. Work: ''Reflections.'' *Address*, 58 West 57th St., New York.

FAULKNER, Barry. Artist. Born Keene, N. H., 1881. Studied at Art Students' League, New York, and American Academy, Rome; also with George de Forest Brush and Abbott H. Thayer. Association of Architectural League, New York. Member: Mural Painters' Society; American Academy, Rome. Work: Mural decorations in the house of Mrs. H. Harrison, Arden, N. Y.; Panels in Wash. Irving High School, N. Y. Pictorial maps in Cunard Building, N. Y. *Address*, 11 Macdougal Alley, New York.

FAULKNER, Herbert Waldron. Painter, illustrator and engraver. Born at Stamford, Conn., in 1860. Studied at the Art Students' League, N. Y., and École des Beaux Arts, Paris, France. Represented at the Dallas (Tex.) Art Association by ''Gondolier's Kitchen''; at St. Louis Museum, by ''Palace on Grand Canal.'' *Address*, Washington, Conn.

FAUST, Dorbert C. Painter. Exhibited a water color at Cincinnati Museum, 1925. *Address,* 552 Mt. Vernon Road, Newark, Ohio.

FAWCETT, George. Illustrator and etcher. Born in England in 1877. Member of Chicago Society of Etchers. *Address,* 333 7th Ave., New York.

FAXON, William Bailey. Painter. Born in Hartford, Conn. Elected Associate Member of the National Academy of Design in 1906. *Address,* 7 West 43d St., New York.

FAY, Nellie. Painter. Born Eureka, Calif., 1870. Pupil of Arthur F. Mathews and Emil Carlsen. *Address,* 1612 Washington St., San Francisco, Calif.

FECHIN, Nicolai. Painter. Exhibited at Annual Exhibition of National Academy of Design, 1925. *Address,* 2 West 67th St., New York.

FEHRER, Oscar. Portrait painter. Born New York City in 1872. Studied in New York, Paris and Munich. Member: National Art Club. Represented in Memorial Hall, City Library, Lowell, Mass. *Address,* 347 West 87th St., New York, N. Y.

FEKE, Robert. Early American portrait painter. Was born at Oyster Bay, Long Island. He married Eleanor Cozzens in 1742 at Newport, R. I. He is known to have worked there as well as at Boston, New York, and Philadelphia. The earliest date on his painting is 1741, and the latest is only seven years afterwards, 1748. He is said to have made several sea trips and to have been captured and taken to Spain. Feke went to Bermuda for his health and died there in 1750. His portraits are in Harvard University and the Redwood Library, Newport, R. I. His portraits of the Bowdoins are owned by Bowdoin College, Brunswick, Maine. The Rhode Island School of Design has his "Pamela Andrews," and the Cleveland Museum owns his portrait of Charles Apthorp. Robert Feke's own portrait and that of his wife are in the possession of his descendants in Providence, R. I.

FELCH. This name is signed to some poorly executed landscape work published in 1855, with no indication of place.

FELDMAN, Baruch M. Painter. Born in Russia, 1885. Pupil of Anshutz. Member: Fellowship, Penna. Academy of Fine Arts. *Address,* 320 Harmony St., Philadelphia, Pa.

FELKER, Ruth Kate (Mrs. W. D. Thomas). Painter and illustrator. Born in St. Louis, Mo., in 1889. Studied at St. Louis School of Fine Arts; Art Students' League,

New York, and in Europe. Work: Mural decorations in St. John's Hospital, St. Louis. Represented at the St. Louis Art Gallery. *Address,* 6949 Mitchell Ave., St. Louis, Mo.

FELLOWS, A. P. Painter and etcher. Pupil of School of Industrial Art, and of Drexel Institute, Philadelphia. Member: Philadelphia Society of Etchers; Philadelphia Sketch Club. *Address,* 119 East 47th St., New York.

FELLOWS, Cornelia Faber (Mrs. A. P. Fellows). Portrait painter. Born Philadelphia. Pupil of Penna. Academy of Fine Arts, and Drexel Institute. Member: Fellowship, Penna. Academy of Fine Arts; Plastic Club. *Address,* 3203 Summer St., Philadelphia, Pa.

FELTON, Robert. Engraver, and one of the early American die-sinkers, according to the Colonial Records of Pennsylvania. At a meeting of the Governor's Council, held in Philadelphia, 1663, Charles Pickering and others were accused of coining silver "in imitation of Spanish pieces with too great an alloy of copper in it." From the minutes of the trial it appears that Robert Felton testified that he "made the Seals and the bills, viz—the Spanish Bills." He further speaks of the "Stamping of New Bills" and "Striking on the Stamp"; and he says he worked several weeks in "Cutting the Seals."

FENDERSON, Annie M. Miniature painter. Born Spartansburg, Pa. Member: National Academy of Women Painters and Sculptors. *Address,* 144 West 23d St., New York N. Y.

FENN, Harry. Painter, illustrator and engraver. He was born in England in 1845, and died 1911. In 1864 he came to America. He was a founder of the American Water Color Society, the Society of Illustrators, and the Salmagundi Club.

FENTON, Beatrice. Sculptor. Born Philadelphia, Pa., 1887. Pupil of School of Industrial Art, Philadelphia, and Penna. Academy of Fine Arts. Awards: Stewardson Sculpture prize, Penna. Academy of Fine Arts, 1908; Cresson traveling scholarship, Penna. Academy of Fine Arts, 1909 and 1910. Represented in permanent collection, Philadelphia Art Club. *Address,* 1523 Chestnut St., Philadelphia.

FENTON, Hallie Champlin (Mrs. Warden Fenton). Painter. Born St. Louis, Mo., 1880. Pupil of Art Institute of Chicago; Blanche in Paris; National Academy of Design. Member: National Academy of Women Painters and Sculptors. *Address,* Bronxville, N. Y.

9

FENTON, John William. Painter. Born Conewango Valley, 1875. Pupil of New York School of Fine and Applied Art; Cullen Yates and Howard Giles. *Address*, 11 Clove Road, New Rochelle, N. Y.

FERG, Frank X. Painter. Member: Penna. Academy of Fine Arts. *Address*, 6026 Webster St., Philadelphia, Pa.

FERGUSON, Alice Lowe (Mrs. H. G. Ferguson). Painter. Born Washington, D. C. Pupil of Corcoran School in Washington; also of Hawthorne. Member: Washington Water Color Club; Washington Art Club; Society of Independent Artists. Address, 2330 California St., Washington, D. C.

FERGUSON, Duncan. A little known painter of portraits and genre subjects. Born in New York; son of John Ferguson, Esq., at one time mayor of the city. He was a student at the School of the National Academy. He flourished about 1834.

FERGUSON, Edward L. Engraver. Born in Illinois, in 1859. He lived in New York, his specialty being steel engraving. He died in New York City in 1915.

FERGUSON, Eleanor M. Sculptor. Born in Hartford, Conn., in 1876. Pupil of C. N. Flagg; student of the New York Art Students' League. *Address*, 123 Vernon St., Hartford, Conn.

FERGUSON, Elizabeth F. Illustrator. Born in Omaha, Nebr., 1884. Pupil of Penna. Academy of Fine Arts. *Address*, 1039 Fine Arts Bldg., Chicago, Ill.

FERGUSON, Henry. Painter. Elected an Associate Member of the National Academy in 1884. He died in 1911. His painting ''In Venice'' was exhibited in the Centennial of the National Academy in 1925.

FERGUSON, Lillian Prest. Painter. Born in Windsor, Ontario, Canada, in 1871. Pupil of Julien Academy, Paris. *Address*, Laguna Beach, Calif.

FERGUSON, Nancy M. Painter. Member of Fellowship of Penna. Academy of Fine Arts, Philadelphia. *Address*, 524 Walnut St., Philadelphia.

FERGUSON, William H. Etcher. Exhibited at the Annual Exhibition of Water Colors at the Penna. Academy of Fine Arts, Philadelphia, 1925. *Address*, Perkiomen Ave., Reading, Penna.

FERNBACH, Agnes B. Etcher. Born in New York City, 1879. Pupil of Art Sutdents' League, New York. *Address*, 48 St. Nicholas Place, N. Y.

FERNOW, Bernice P. (Mrs.). Miniature painter. Born in Jersey City, N. J., 1881. Pupil of Olaf Brunner. Member of Art Students' League of New York. *Address*, 432 Lafayette Place, Milwaukee, Wis.

FERRARI, Febo. Sculptor. Born in Italy, 1865. Member of New Haven Paint and Clay Club. *Address*, 96 Williams St., New Haven, Conn.

FERRER, Vera L. Miniature painter. Born in New York in 1895. Member of National Association of Women Painters and Sculptors. *Address*, 193 Washington Ave., Brooklyn, N. Y.

FERRIS, Bernice B. (Mrs). Painter. Born in Astoria, Ill., 1882. Pupil of Chicago Art Institute. *Address*, 1002 B St., S.W., Washington, D. C.

FERRIS, Edyth. Painter. Exhibited at the Pennsylvania Academy of Fine Arts, Philadelphia, in 1924. *Address*, 3733 Locust St., Philadelphia.

FERRIS, Jean Leon Gerome. Painter. Born in Philadelphia, 1863. Studied under S. J. Ferris and Christian Schuessele, in Philadelphia, 1878–83; at Academie Julien, Paris, under W. Bouguereau, 1884; private pupil of J. L. Gerome; South Kensington Museum, London, 1888. Has devoted attention since 1900 to production of series of paintings of American history, covering period from 1492–1865; in 1917 the city of Philadelphia built a gallery in Congress Hall for accommodation of the entire collection (numbering over 50 subjects), where they now hang. He has made a special study of early types of American vehicles and ordnance, models of same being now in Congress Hall Museum, Philadelphia, and data filed with National Museum, Washington, and New York Historical Society. *Address*, 8 North 50th St., Philadelphia.

FERRIS, Stephen J. Portrait painter. Born in Plattsburg, N. Y., in 1835. He received the Fortuny prize for the best portrait of the artist in Rome, 1876. He painted about 2000 portraits and made a number of etchings. He died in Philadelphia in 1915.

FERRIS, Stephen, Jr. Etcher and crayon portrait draughtsman. Flourished 1857–1860, Philadelphia. He was a close friend of the engraver John Sartain of Philadelphia.

FERRISS, Hugh. Illustrator and etcher. Born in St. Louis, Mo., in 1889. Member of League of American Artists. Work appears in *Harper's*, *Century*, and *Arts and Decoration*. *Address*, 101 Park Ave., New York.

FERRY, Isabella H. Painter. Born in Williamsburgh, Mass. Pupil of Tryon, Henri and Bouguereau. *Address*, Skye Studio, Boothbay Harbor, Me.

FETERS or PETERS, W. T. A crudely done stippled portrait of the Rev. John Davenport, of Connecticut, is signed "W. T. Feters," though this may be a mistake of the letter-engraver for Peters. The plate has no indication of its origin, and the only reasons for ascribing it to an American are the poor quality of the work and the fact that the subject is American. The date of publication is probably about 1820.

FETTE, Henry G. Portrait painter in oils and miniature. Flourished in Boston, 1842–71.

FIELD, E. Loyal. Landscape painter. Was born in 1856 and died in 1914. He also painted in water color.

FIELD, Hamilton Easter. Painter and etcher. Born in Brooklyn, 1873; died there, 1922. Pupil in Paris of Gerome, Gollin, Courtois, Fantin-Latour, and Lucien Simon. He was also an art editor, writer and teacher.

FIELD, Louise B. (Mrs.). Painter. Born in Boston. Pupil of William Morris Hunt. Member of Boston Water Color Club. *Address* 32 Cottage St., Wellesley, Mass.

FIELD, M. (Mrs.). Painter. Born in Stoughton, Mass., 1864. Pupil of Art Institute, Chicago. *Address*, 4826 Kimbark Ave., Chicago, Ill.

FIELD, Robert. Portrait painter and engraver. Is said to have been born in Gloucester, England; he died at Jamaica, in 1819. William Dunlap says that Field came to New York about 1793. He tells little else, other than that he went to Halifax, after painting very good miniatures in Boston, Philadelphia, Baltimore, and New York.

Field was in Philadelphia, 1795, and on August 1st of the same year he published his portrait of Washington in New York City. While in the United States he engraved stipple portraits of Washington, Jefferson, Hamilton and Shakespeare; but he was chiefly occupied in painting miniatures. Among the latter may be mentioned those of Washington and Jefferson, after Stuart, and of Charles Carroll of Carrollton, both of the latter engraved by Longacre and William Cliffton, and of J. E. Harwood, engraved by Edwin. Dunlap mentions his portraits of Mrs. Allen, of Boston, and Mrs. Thornton, of Washington, D. C.

About 1808 Robert Field removed to Halifax, Nova Scotia, and he seemingly remained there until 1816, painting portraits; he there engraved at least one large plate, a full-length portrait of Governor-General Sir John Coape

Sherbrooke, published in Halifax in 1816. He painted this portrait, and several Governors for the Government House in Halifax.

Mr. Harry Peirs, curator of the Provincial Museum of Halifax, writes that in addition to those mentioned, there are a number of Field's portraits in that city. He notes the portrait of Bishop Charles Ingles, now in the National Gallery in London, and portraits of Adam Dechezean, John Lawson, Michael Wallace, and William Bowie, all citizens of Halifax. He probably returned to England for a short period, as Algernon Graves, in his "Dictionary of Artists," mentions R. Field as "a portrait painter of Halifax, N. S." He probably went from London to Jamaica, and died there, as stated, in 1819.

An interesting letter of Robert Field is preserved among the "Dreer Manuscripts" in the Pennsylvania Historical Society. It is addressed to Robert Gilmor, Jr., of Baltimore, and is dated in Philadelphia, 1795. In this letter Field refers to the Robertson portrait of Washington which he afterward engraved. He says that "This miniature of the President is as good a likeness and as fine a piece of painting as I ever saw"; and goes on to say that he had engaged to engrave it of the same size "with some ornaments to surround and make it more interesting." But as Mr. Robertson proposed to go to India, he declined the large plate and proposed to sell the miniature to Field for $1,000.

FIELDING, Mantle. Architect, designer and author of books relating to painting and engraving. Born in New York, 1865. Member of Philadelphia Art Club, and Penna. Academy of Fine Arts. Author of "American Engravers," and "Gilbert Stuart, and his portraits of Washington." *Address*, 520 Walnut St., Philadelphia, Pa.

FILMER, John. Engraver and book illustrator.

FINCH, Elinor G. Miniature painter. Exhibited portrait miniatures at the Penna. Academy of the Fine Arts, Philadelphia, 1922. *Address*, 22 Terrace Park, Spokane, Washington.

FINCKEN, James H. Engraver and etcher; has excepted some excellent bookplates.

FINCKEN, James H. Painter and etcher. Born in England, 1860. Member of the Philadelphia Sketch Club. *Address*, 1012 Walnut St., Philadelphia.

FINK, Denman. Painter and illustrator. Born in Springdale, Penna., Aug. 1880. Pupil of Benson and Hale. Illustrates for *Harper's*, *Scribner's*, and *Century*, also for books and other publications. *Address*, Haworth, N. J.

FINK, Frederick. Born at Little Falls, N. Y., in 1817. Genre and portrait painter. Studied under Morse. The subjects of the few pictures he lived to execute are "An Artist's Studio," "The Shipwrecked Mariner," "The Young Thieves," "A Negro Woodsawyer," and a portrait of W. S. Parker, painted when the artist was eighteen years old. Fink died in 1849.

FINKELNBURG, Augusta. Painter. Born in Fountain City, Wis. Pupil of Chicago Art Institute; Pratt Institute, Brooklyn; also studied in France and England. Represented by two pictures in San Francisco Art Museum. *Address*, 5035 Alabama Ave., St. Louis, Mo.

FINN, Henry J. Actor, author and miniature painter. Born 1782 and died 1840. Painted miniatures in Boston, 1833.

FIRESTONE, I. L. Painter and illustrator. Born in Austria-Hungary, 1894. Pupil of Carnegie Institute of Technology and Stevenson Art School, Pittsburgh; Art Students' League of New York. Member: Pittsburgh Artists' Association. *Address*, 549 Riverside Drive, Pittsburgh, Pa.

FISCHER, Anton Otto. Illustrator. Born at Munich, Bavaria, Germany, in 1882. Student of Julien Academy, Paris. Came to America in 1903. Member of the Society of Illustrators. *Address*, Shandaken, Ulster County, New York.

FISCHER, H. Painter. Member: Society of Independent Artists. *Address*, 48 West 90th St., New York, N. Y.

FISCHER, J. F. Work: Portrait of Albert Pike, born in 1809 and died 1891. American lawyer, author, and Confederate commissioner appointed to treat with the Indians. Half length to left, long white locks and white beard. Size 29½ in. x 23½ in. Signed "J. F. Fischer." Sold American Art Association, N. Y., Dec., 1921.

FISCHER, Mary Ellen Sigsbee (Mrs. Anton O. Fischer). Illustrator. Born New Orleans, 1876. Member: Society of Illustrators, 1912. *Address*, Bushnellville, Greene County, N. Y.

FISHER, Alvin. American portrait and genre painter. Born in Massachusetts, 1792, and died 1863. In 1825 he visited Europe for study and travel. He established his studio in Boston, where he painted many portraits. One of his best works is a portrait of Spurzheim painted after death, from recollection, in 1832.

FISHER, Anna S. Painter. Member: Academy of National Artists, National Academy of Women Painters and Sculptors, and Associate Member of National Academy. Award: National Art Club prize, National

Academy of Women Painters and Sculptors. Work: "The Orange Bowl," National Academy of Design, New York, N. Y., and "Reflections." *Address*, 939 Eighth Ave., New York, N. Y.

FISHER, Bud. Cartoonist. Born in 1885. *Address*, 258 Riverside Drive, New York.

FISHER, Emily Kohler. Painter. Member: Fellowship, Penna. Academy of Fine Arts. *Address*, Manheim Apartments, Queen Lane, Germantown, Philadelphia.

FISHER, Flavius J. Portrait painter. Born in 1832. He studied in Philadelphia; also abroad. In Washington he painted portraits of many prominent people; also some landscapes. He died in 1905.

FISHER, George V. Painter. Member: Society of Independent Artists. *Address*, 858 52d St., New York, N. Y.

FISHER, H. Melville. Painter. Born in Brooklyn in 1878. Pupil of Whistler, Laurens, and Constant in Paris. He is a brother of Harrison Fisher. *Address*, 344 West 28th St., New York City.

FISHER, Harrison. Illustrator. Born in Brooklyn, N. Y., in 1875. He studied in San Francisco, drawing from the works of his father. Member of the Chicago Institute of 1911. He has illustrated many books and magazines, as well as numerous posters. *Address*, 80 West 40th St., New York City.

FISHER, Hugh Antoine. Landscape painter. Died in 1916 in California. He was the father of the illustrator Harrison Fisher.

FISHER, Irma. Exhibited water colors at the Exhibition of the Penna. Academy of Fine Arts, 1925, in Philadelphia. *Address*, 7621 Star Ave., Cleveland, Ohio.

FISHER, John. The Journals of the Continental Congress, under date of June 26, 1773, note—"that there is due to John Fisher, for re-newing two copper-plates for loan-office certificates, and making two letters in the device of the thirty dollar bills, 20 dollars."

FISHER, J. J. Crayon portrait draughtsman. Flourished 1850, Petersburg, Virginia.

FISHER, Vaudrey. Painter. Born Staffordshire, England, 1889. Pupil of von Herkomer; Castellucho; Brangwyn. *Address*, 1730 Broadway, New York, N. Y.

FISHER, William Edgar. Illustrator. Born Wellsville, N. Y., 1872. Pupil of Art Institute of Chicago; Cornell University. Specialty, book-plate designs. *Address*, 52 East 19th St., New York, N. Y.

FISHER, William Mark. Landscape painter. Born in Boston, 1841. Studied at the Lowell Institute, Boston, and in Paris. He was elected an Associate of the Royal Academy in 1913. He died in 1923. Represented at Boston Museum of Fine Arts by ''Road to Menil,'' painted in 1869.

FISK, Edward. Landscape painter. Exhibited at the ''Exhibition of Paintings Showing the Later Tendencies in Art,'' at the Penna. Academy of the Fine Arts, Philadelphia, 1921. *Address*, Care of Daniel Galleries, New York City.

FISKE, Charles A. Painter. Born in Maine, 1837, he graduated from Dartmouth College, and lived in New York City, and exhibited at the National Academy of Design. He died in 1915.

FISKE, Gertrude. Painter and etcher. Born in Boston, Mass., 1879. Pupil of Tarbell, Hale and Benson. Elected an Associate Member of the National Academy of Design. Has exhibited paintings in the exhibitions of the National Academy and Carnegie Institute. *Address*, 132 Riverway, Boston, Mass.

FISKEN, Jessie. Painter. Born in Row, Scotland, 1860. Pupil of Glasgow School of Art. *Address*, 1607 Minot Ave., Seattle, Wash.

FITCH, Benjamin Herbert. Painter. Born Lyons, N. Y., 1873. Self-taught. Member: Rochester Art Club; Rochester Society of Artists. *Address*, 217 West 33d St., Philadelphia, Penna.

FITCH, John. Engraver. Born in South Windsor, Conn., 1743; died in Bardstown, Ky., 1798. John Fitch, also inventor of the steamboat, received a common school education and was apprenticed to a clock-maker at an early age. After some service in the Revolutionary War as a gunsmith, in 1780, he was appointed a deputy-surveyor by the State of Virginia.

In 1785 Fitch made a map of the northwest country for the use of explorers, basing his work upon the maps of Hutchins and Morrow and his own explorations. This map he crudely engraved upon copper, hammered out and prepared by himself, and he printed the maps upon a press of his own manufacture. According to his advertisement in the *Pennsylvania Packet* of 1785, Fitch sold this map for ''A French crown,'' and he apparently disposed of a considerable number of impressions, as his biographers state that with $800 thus raised he formed a steamboat company in 1787, and commenced building a 60-ton boat.

FITCH, John Lee. Born in Hartford, Conn., 1836; died in 1895. He studied abroad, and spent his professional life in Hartford and New York City. He was an Associate of the National Academy and Treasurer of the Artists' Fund Society of New York. Among his works are ''In the Woods''; ''Gill Brook Willows on the Croton''; ''Near Carmel, N. Y.''

FITLER, William C. Painter. Specialty, landscapes in water color. His studio is in New York.

FITSCH, Eugene C. Painter. Born Alsace, France, 1892. Pupil of Mahonri Young; Frank V. DuMond. *Address*, 253 West 42d St., New York.

FITTS, Clara Atwood. Illustrator. Born Worcester, Mass., 1874. Pupil of School of the Boston Museum of Fine Arts. Work: Altar piece, consisting of three panels, St. John's Church, Roxbury, Mass. Illustrates books for children and for *St. Nicholas*, etc. *Address*, 40 Linwood St., Roxbury, Mass.

FITZ, Benjamin Rutherford. Painter. Born in 1855 in New York. Pupil of National Academy and Art Students' League from 1877 to 1881; studied in Munich under Loefftz and returned to America in 1884. He died in New York in 1891. He was a member of the Society of American Artists and is represented in the Metropolitan Museum, New York.

FITZ, Grace Randolph. Painter and sculptor. She was a pupil of Alden Weir and Augustus Saint Gaudens. She died in New York, Jan., 1917.

FITZGERALD, Pitt L. Painter and illustrator. Born in 1893. Pupil of Penna. Academy of Fine Arts, and of N. C. Wyeth. *Address*, Chads Ford, Penna.

FITZGERALD, Harrington. Landscape painter. Born in Philadelphia, 1847. Pupil of Fortuny and Gerome in Paris. Represented by four panels in State Capitol, Harrisburg, Pa., subject, ''Valley Forge''; in the National Gallery, Washington, D. C., by ''The Wreck''; and in the Penna. Museum by ''On the Shore.'' *Address*, 716 Walnut St., Philadelphia.

FITZPATRICK, Daniel R. Cartoonist. Born at Superior, Wis., 1891. Pupil of Art Institute of Chicago. *Address*, Post-Dispatch Bldg., St. Louis, Mo.

FITZPATRICK, John C. Painter and illustrator. Born in Washington, D. C., in 1876. Pupil of Art Students' League, New York. *Address*, 212 First St., S.E., Washington, D. C.

FJELKE, Paul. Sculptor. Born Minneapolis, Minn., 1892. Pupil of Lorado Taft. His works include the ''Lincoln Monument'' in Norway, the ''Pioneers' Memorial'' at Council Bluffs, and the ''Downersberger Memorial,'' McKinley Park, Chicago. *Address*, 333 Fourth Ave., New York, N. Y.

FLACK, Arthur W. Painter. Born in San Francisco, 1878. Pupil of Rochester Fine Arts Institute; also studied in London and Paris. *Address,* Atlas Building, Rochester, N. Y.

FLAGG, Charles Noel. Portrait painter. Born in Brooklyn, 1848; he died in Hartford, Conn., 1916. He studied for years in Paris. His principal portraits were of Mark Twain, Charles Dudley Warner, and a series of seven governors of Connecticut. He was elected an Associate of the National Academy in 1908.

FLAGG, Geo. W. Painter. Nephew of Washington Allston, born in New Haven, Conn., 1816, he spent his childhood in South Carolina. In 1830 he proceeded to Boston and soon afterwards commenced his career as a portrait painter. He was assisted by Luman Reed, patron of art and artists, and many of his works are to be found in the Reed collection (New York Historical Society). In 1851 he was elected a member of the National Academy of New York. Represented at the New York Historical Society by the "Wood-chopper's Boy," "Match Girl," "Lady and Parrot," and "The Nun." He died in 1897.

FLAGG, Henry C. Marine painter. Nephew of Washington Allston, and brother of George W. Flagg, was born in New Haven, Conn., in 1812. He painted many marines and later joined the United States Navy.

FLAGG, H. Peabody. Painter. Born in Somerville, Mass., 1859. Pupil of Carolus Duran in Paris. Represented by historical paintings in Flower Memorial Library, Watertown, N. Y. *Address,* 26 East 23d St., New York.

FLAGG, James Montgomery. Painter. Born Pelham Manor, Westchester County, N. Y., 1877. Student of Art Students' League, New York, four years; Herkomer's Art School, Bushey, England; and also under Victor Marec in Paris. Became illustrator for *St. Nicholas* Magazine, 1890; has been drawing for *Judge* and *Life* since 1892; illustrator for various other magazines. Painted portraits in Paris, also in St. Louis and New York. Exhibited portraits at Paris Salon; also portraits in oil and water color in National Academy of Design and New York Water Color Club.

FLAGG, Jared B. A younger brother of Geo. W. Flagg, the artist, was born in New Haven, Conn., 1820. He studied with his brother and also received some instruction from his uncle, Washington Allston. He afterwards became a minister in the Episcopal Church. He painted many portraits and was active in the work of the Yale Art Gallery at New Haven. Elected a Member of the National Academy of New York in 1849. He died in 1899.

FLAGG, Josiah. Charles E. Goodspeed, of Boston, notes the following book as containing 70 pages of copper-plate music engraved by Josiah Flagg—"Sixteen Anthems, collected from Tan'sur Williams, Knapp, Ashworth & Stephenson, etc. Engraved and printed by Josiah Flagg, and sold by him at his house near the Old North Meeting House and at his shop in Fish Street. Also by the Booksellers in Boston, New England."

FLAGG, Josiah (Jr.). Flourished in Boston about 1783. He advertised in the *Boston Gazette,* Feb. 10, 1783. "Copying of Miniature Painting in Hair."

FLAGG, Montague. Painter. Born in 1842 in Hartford, Conn.; died 1915 in New York City. Pupil of Jacquesson de la Chevreuse in Paris. Most of his professional life was spent in New York. Elected a member of the National Academy in 1910. He painted "Portrait of My Wife." The figure is seen to the waist; the hair is parted and drawn over the ears; she wears a simple black dress, slightly open at the throat. Painting now owned by the Metropolitan Museum of Art, New York.

FLANAGAN, John F. Sculptor. Born Newark, N. J. Pupil of École des Beaux Arts, Paris. Awarded various medals and prizes, École des Beaux Arts. Executed Monumental Clock, Library of Congress, Washington; large tinted marble relief, "Aphrodite," Knickerbocker Hotel, New York; bronze memorial portrait, Samuel Pierpont Langley, Smithsonian Institute, Washington, D. C.; Bulkeley memorial, bronze and marble, Aetna Life Institute Co., Hartford, Conn.; other large works in the round, and relief; various portrait busts and heads in the round portrait plaquettes, and commemorative medals, including the medal which celebrated the visit of the Prince of Wales. Represented in medal collections of the Musee du Luxembourg, Paris; Museum of Ghent, Belgium; Carnegie Institute, Pittsburgh, Pa. Elected Associate Member of the National Academy of Design in 1915. *Address,* 1931 Broadway, New York City.

FLEISHBEIN, F. Portrait painter, who came to New Orleans in 1833. He had a studio at 135 Condé Street, New Orleans, from 1840 to 1860.

FLEISHER, Lillian B. Painter. Exhibited at the Pennsylvania Academy of Fine Arts, Philadelphia, in 1924. *Address,* 237 Wyncote Road, Jenkintown, Penna.

FLEMING, Henry S. Illustrator, painter and sculptor. Born in Philadelphia, 1863. Pupil of Lefebvre and Benjamin Constant in Paris. *Address,* 44 West 47th St., New York.

FLEMMING, Jean R. (Mrs.). Painter. Born in Charleston, S. C., in 1874. Pupil of

FLETCHER, Calvin. Painter and sculptor. Born in Utah, 1882. Pupil of Pratt Institute; also studied in London and Paris, and did mural paintings at Logan, Utah. *Address*, 166 South 4th St., East Logan, Utah.

FLETCHER, Godfrey B. Painter. Born at Watsonville, Calif., 1888. Pupil of Armin Hansen. Frequently worked in water color. Died in 1923 at Watsonville, Calif.

FLEURY, Albert. Mural painter. Born in France, 1848. Member of Chicago Water Color Club. *Address*, 1133 North Dearborn St., Chicago, Ill.

FLISHER, Edith M. Painter. Born in Nashville, Tenn. Pupil of Penna. Academy of Fine Arts. Represented in State Capitol by portrait of Gov. Thomas Rye. *Address*, Church St., Belmont Heights, Tenn.

FLOET, Lydia. Painter. Exhibited at National Association of Women Painters and Sculptors, New York, 1925. *Address*, Wilton, Conn.

FLORANCE, Eustace Lee. Painter. Born in Philadelphia. Member: St. Botolph Club. *Address*, 1090 Washington St., Dorchester, Mass.

FLORENTINO-VALLÉ, Maude Richmond. Painter and illustrator. Pupil of Art Students' League of New York, under Cox, Chase, Brush and Beckwith; Academie Julien under Lefebvre, Constant and Beaury-Sorel, in Paris. *Address*, 1136–1140 Corona St., Denver, Colo.

FLORIAN, Walter. Painter. Born 1878 in New York City; died there, 1909. Pupil of Metropolitan Museum Art School under Twachtman and Herbert Morgan; Art Students' League of New York; Julien and Colarossi in Paris. He painted Jozef Israels, Dutch painter, life size; seated figure, with palette and brushes held in his left hand; a characteristic pose, painted in Israel's studio. Signed: "Walter Florian." It is owned by the Metropolitan Museum, New York.

FLORIMONT, Austin. Portrait draughtsman in crayon, and miniature painter. Flourished in Philadelphia, 1781.

FLOWER, Sherwood. Painter. Born Oakwood, Cecil County, Md., 1878. *Address*, Evesham Ave., Baltimore, Md.

FOGARTY, Thomas. Illustrator. Born New York, 1873. Pupil of Art Students' League of New York. Member: Society of Illustrators. Illustrated "The Making of an American," by Riis; "On Fortune's Road," by Will Payne, etc. *Address*, 38 East 22d St., New York, N. Y.

Elliott Dangerfield, John Carlsen and F. S. Church. *Address*, Talbot Building, Norfolk, Va.

FOLAWN, Thomas Jefferson. Painter. Born Youngstown, Ohio, 1876. Pupil of C. Sanborn Miles. Member: Denver Art Association; Brush and Pencil Club, St. Louis. *Address*, 1809 Marine St., Boulder, Colo.

FOLEY, Margaret. Sculptor. Biographers differ as to where Margaret Foley, or Margaret E. Foley, as she is sometimes called, was born. Some give her birthplace as Vermont, while others place it in New Hampshire. She was apparently largely self-instructed in her artistic work.

Mrs. Clements says of her: "At length she made some reputation in Boston, where she cut portrait and ideal heads in cameo. She then went to Rome." Some of her works were exhibited at the Centennial Exposition at Philadelphia in 1876. Tuckerman wrote of her that she "achieves new and constant success in her relievos." Her medallions of William and Mary Howitt, of Longfellow, and of William Cullen Bryant, and her ideal statues of Cleopatra, of Excelsior, and of Jeremiah are considered to be the best specimens of her cameo work.

The cameo portrait of William Cullen Bryant, which is now in the New York Historical Society, is said to be the one cut by Margaret Foley. She died in 1877 at the home of Mr. and Mrs. Howitt, at Menan in the Austrian Tyrol.

FOLGER, L. Portraits signed "L. Folger" are found in the southern states; one known to the author was so signed, and dated 1837.

FOLINSBEE, John Fulton. Landscape painter. Born in Buffalo, New York, 1892. Studied with Birge Harrison, John F. Carlson, and DuMond. Awarded the third Hallgarten prize, National Academy of Design, 1916; Richard S. Greenough Prize, Newport, R. I., 1917; Corcoran bronze medal in 1921; first Hallgarten prize, National Academy of Design in 1923. Represented in the Syracuse Museum and the Corcoran Gallery, Washington. Elected Associate Member of the National Academy of Design in 1919. *Address*, New Hope, Penna.

FOLSOM, Mrs. C. A. Flourished in New York, 1837–1838, painting miniatures.

FOLWELL, Samuel. Born about 1765; died in Philadelphia, 1813. Folwell probably came from New England, as he engraved book-plates in 1792 for residents of New Hampshire. In 1798 he came to Philadelphia as a miniature painter, a cutter of silhouettes, and a "worker in hair"; he also conducted a school in that city for a time. Very few examples of the engraved work of Folwell have been seen, and his two portraits are executed in a combination of aquatint and stipple which is rather pleasing in effect, though showing an unpracticed hand. His studio in the year 1795 was at No. 2 Laetitia Court, Philadelphia, and he exhibited portraits the same year at the "Columbianum" in Philadelphia. The Pennsylvania Historical Society owns a profile portrait of George Washington which is inscribed "S. Folwell, Pinxt. 1795." It is said to have been taken from life on a public occasion, the President being unaware of the fact. It is drawn on paper and solidly painted in India ink, with certain lights touched in, and, as declared at the time, is certainly a most spirited and correct likeness. It was reproduced on wood and published in Watson's "Annals and Occurrences of New York City and State in the Olden Time," 1846.

FON, W. W. Painter. Exhibited water colors at Exhibition at Penna. Academy of Fine Arts, Philadelphia, 1922. *Address,* Care of Penna. Academy of Fine Arts, Philadelphia.

FOOTE, Mary. Painter and illustrator. Member: National Academy of Women Painters and Sculptors. Work: "Portrait of an Old Lady," Art Institute of Chicago. *Address,* 3 Washington Square, North, New York, N. Y.

FOOTE, Mary Hallock (Mrs. Arthur De Wint Foote). Painter and engraver. Born in Milton, N. Y., in 1847, where she has since lived. Studied at the Cooper Institute, and with William J. Linton, the wood engraver. Many of her illustrations were published by Scribner & Co. The Worcester Art Museum owns a pencil drawing, "Spring Whistles."

FOOTE, Will Howe. Painter. Born Grand Rapids, 1874. Studied Art Institute of Chicago; Art Students' League of New York; Julien Academy of Paris, under Jean Paul Laurens and Benjamin Constant. Instructor, Art Students' League, 1902–6. Elected Associate Member of the National Academy of Design in 1910. *Address,* Old Lyme, Conn.

FORBELL, Charles. Illustrator. Member: Salmagundi Club. *Address,* 116 Nassau St., New York, N. Y.

FORBES, Edwin. Painter and etcher. Was born in New York, 1839. At first he devoted himself to animal painting. During the Civil War he was a special artist of Frank Leslie's Illustrated Newspaper. His studio was in Brooklyn, and since 1878 he has devoted himself to landscape and cattle pictures. In 1877 he was elected an Honorary Member of the London Etching Club. He died in 1895.

FORBES, Helen K. Painter and etcher. Born in San Francisco, Calif., 1891. Pupil of

San Francisco Artists' Association, and A. Hansen. *Address,* 426 Palo Alto Ave., Palo Alto, Calif.

FORBES, Lionel C. V. Painter. Born in Australia in 1898. Member of California Water Color Society. *Address,* Los Angeles, Calif.

FORD, J. W. Neilson. Painter. Pupil of Léonce Rabillon in Paris; Hugh Hewell in New York; B. West Clinedinst in Philadelphia; J. W. Jackson in England; Lippish in Berlin. *Address,* 1124 Calvert St., Baltimore, Md.

FORESMAN, Alice Carter. Miniature painter. Member: National Academy of Women Painters and Sculptors. *Address,* 2117 Eighth Ave., Seattle, Wash.

FORINGER, A. E. Mural painter and illustrator. Born Kaylor, Armstrong County, Pa., 1878. Pupil of H. S. Stevenson in Pittsburgh; Blashfield and Mowbray in New York. Work: Eleven panels, Council Chamber, City Hall, Yonkers, N. Y.; baptistery and organ walls, Church of the Savior, Philadelphia; panels, County Court House, Mercer, Pa.; House of Representatives, Utah State Capitol; bank-note designer for European and Canadian banks; Red Cross War posters, "The Greatest Mother in the World." *Address,* 15 West 67th St., New York, N. Y.

FORKNER, Edgar. Painter. Born Richmond, Ind. Pupil of C. Beckwith; Irving Wiles; F. DuMond; Art Students' League of New York. *Address,* 2615 East Cherry St., Seattle, Wash.

FORREST, Ion B. Engraver and painter. Born in Aberdeenshire, Scotland, about 1814; died in Hudson County, N. J., in 1870. Forrest was an apprentice to the London engraver Thomas Fry, and he remained in the employ of Fry until he was induced, in 1837, to come to Philadelphia to engrave for the National Portrait Gallery. He later turned his attention to miniature painting.

Forrest was a good engraver of portraits in the stipple manner; but some of his best work is found in the form of small fancy heads and vignettes.

FORSTER. Lithographer, of the firm of Kimmel & Forster, executed a number of lithographs of the Civil War period.

FORSYTH, William. Painter. Born Hamilton County, Ohio. Studied Indiana School of Art; Royal Academy of Artists, Munich, Bavaria, Germany. Instructor in life classes, John Herron Art Institute, Indianapolis. Work: "Autumn at Vernon," "The Constitutional Elm-Corydon," "Close of a Summer Day," and "Still Life," Art Association,

Indianapolis; "Autumn Roadside," Public Gallery, Richmond, Ind. *Address*, 15 South Emerson Avenue, Indianapolis, Ind.

FORSYTHE, (Victor) Clyde. Painter and illustrator. Born Orange, Calif., 1885. Pupil of L. E. Garden Macleod; Vincent DuMond. Member: Southern California Art Club. Author of poster used in 5th Victory Liberty Loan, "And They Thought We Couldn't Fight." *Address*, 40 Prospect St., New Rochelle, N. Y.

FORTUNE, E. C. (Miss). Painter. Born in California, 1885, studied in London. Member of San Francisco Art Association. *Address*, Edinburgh, Scotland.

FOSDICK, Gertrude C. (Mrs.). Painter. Born in Virginia, 1862. Pupil of Julien Academy in Paris. *Address*, 33 West 67th St., New York City.

FOSDICK, James William. Painter. Born at Charlestown, Mass., 1858. Studied in school of Boston Museum Fine Arts; studied drawing and painting, Paris, 1881–8, under Boulanger, Lefebvre, Colin and others. Mural painter; founder of art of fire etching in America. Decorations in homes of the Goulds, Havemeyers, Lewisohns, etc.; also Pa. Academy of Fine Arts, St. Louis Museum, etc. Principal work: "The Glorification Adoration of St. Jeanne d'Arc," National Gallery of Fine Arts, Washington. Grand gold medal for mural decoration. "The Field of the Cloth of Gold," Atlanta Expn. Sec. National Society of Mural Painters. Member: Architectural League of New York. President of American Alumni of Julien Academy, Paris. *Address*, 33 West 67th St., New York.

FOSSETTE, H. Was an engraver of landscape, working in New York about 1850, after drawings by A. Dick.

FOSTER, Ben. Landscape painter and art writer. Born North Anson, Maine, 1852. Student of Abbott H. Thayer in New York; Morot and Merson in Paris. Awards: Carnegie prize, National Academy of Design, New York, 1906; Inness gold medal, National Academy of Design, 1909. Elected Society of American Artists, 1897; Associate, National Academy, 1901; National Academy, 1904; New York Water Color Club; American Water Color Society, New York; Century Association; National Institute of Arts and Letters. *Address*, 119 East 19th St., New York.

FOSTER, C. Was a designer and banknote engraver located in Cincinnati, Ohio, in 1841.

FOSTER, Charles. Painter. Born in North Anson, Me., 1850. Pupil of Cabanel in Paris. *Address*, Farmington, Conn.

FOSTER, John. Born in Dorchester, Mass., 1648; died in Boston, 1681. In 1667 Foster was graduated from Harvard College; in 1675 he established the first printing office in Boston, New England. Foster was the first engraver of a portrait in this country, of whom we have any record. This is a wood-block portrait of the Rev. Richard Mather, and one of the three known impressions has written upon it, in an almost contemporaneous hand, "Johannes Foster, Sculpt." This particular impression was found in the New York Public Library, as the frontispiece to a life of Richard Mather published in Cambridge, New England, in 1670. Another copy of this portrait, framed, is in the possession of the Massachusetts Historical Society. It has the name of Richard Mather printed upon it in type, but has no indication of the engraver. Dr. Samuel A. Green, of the Massachusetts Historical Society, has made a close study of Foster as the possible engraver of this portrait. Foster is also credited with having engraved the rude woodcut map of New England issued with Rev. W. Hubbard's narrative of the troubles with the Indians in New England, published by John Foster in Boston in 1677.

FOSTER, Ralph L. Illustrator. Born in Providence, R. I., 1881. Pupil of Rhode Island School of Design. *Address*, 268 President Ave., Providence, R. I.

FOSTER, Will. Painter. Exhibited at Annual Exhibition of National Academy of Design, 1925. *Address*, 15 West 67th St., New York.

FOURNIER, Alexia Jean. Landscape painter. Born St. Paul, Minn., 1865. Studied under Douglas Volk; pupil of Julien Academy, Paris, under J. P. Laurens, Benjamin Constant, Henri Harpignies. Represented in Pa. Historical Bldg.; Minn. State Historical Society, St. Paul; Vanderbilt University, Nashville; Congressional Library Print Dept.; Minneapolis Publishing Gallery; Detroit Art Museum, etc. Painted 20 pictures entitled "The Haunts and Homes of the Barbizon Masters." *Address*, East Aurora, New York.

FOWLE, E. A. This man was a landscape engraver, working in line in Boston in 1843, and in New York a little later.

FOWLER. Philadelphia portrait painter, living in Germantown about 1860. Painted a portrait of Miss Anna Howell of Philadelphia about 1860.

FOWLER, Carlton C. Painter. Born in New York, 1877. Pupil of Academie Julien, Paris. *Address*, Colonial Studios, New York City.

FOWLER, Frank. Portrait painter. Born in 1852 and died 1910. Studied at École des Beaux Arts. Member of Society of American Artists, and National Academy of Design, 1899. He exhibited a portrait at the Society of American Artists in New York in 1878; he has also done some work in fresco.

FOWLER, T. T. Portrait painter, working in New Orleans from about 1830 to 1850. His studio was at No. 10 St. Charles St., New Orleans.

FOX, Gilbert. According to Wm. Dunlap, Fox was born in England about 1776. He was apprenticed to the London engraver, Thomas Medland, and was induced to come to Philadelphia in 1795 by James Trenchard. Fox engraved a few portraits and book illustrations for Philadelphia publishers and later became a teacher of drawing in a ladies' academy in that city. Dunlap says that he eloped with one of his pupils, lost his position, and then went upon the stage; and the Philadelphia directory of 1798 contains his name as "A Comedian." It was for Gilbert Fox that Joseph Hopkinson wrote "Hail Columbia," and Fox sang it for the first time at his benefit, in 1798.

FOX, Margaret M. T. (Mrs. George). Painter, illustrator and etcher. Born in 1857. Pupil of Peter Moran and Anshutz. Illustrated many books. *Address,* Silver Spring P. O., Maryland.

FRANCE, Jesse L. Painter and illustrator. Born in Cincinnati, Ohio. Pupil of Carolus-Duran, Paris. *Address,* 78 Pearl St., New Haven, Conn.

FRANCIS, George. Painter. Was born in Hartford, Conn., in 1790, and died there in 1873. He studied drawing under Benjamin West, and coloring with Washington Allston. His father was a carriage builder and he had to carry on the business after his father's death. He designed the ornamental work for sleighs and carriages, and occasionally painted a portrait or landscape.

FRANCIS, John F. Painter. Born about 1810. Practised portrait painting in Schuylkill County, and elsewhere; came to Philadelphia and devoted himself to painting fruit pieces, many of which were sold from the exhibition rooms of the Art Union, between 1844–1850. Died in Montgomery County, 1885. He painted a portrait in 1838 of William R. Smith of Philadelphia, which was exhibited in the Loan Ex. at Penna. Academy of Fine Arts in 1887.

FRANCIS, Vida Hunt. Illustrator. Born in Philadelphia in 1892. Illustrated "Bible of Amethens," "Cathedrals and Cloisters of the South of France," etc. *Address,* Hillside School, Norwalk, Conn.

FRANCISCO, J. Bond. Painter. Born Cincinnati, Ohio, 1863. Pupil of Fechner in Berlin; Nauen Schule in Munich; Bouguereau, Robert-Fleury and Coutois in Paris. Member: Laguna Beach Association, California. *Address,* 1401 Albany St., Los Angeles, Calif.

FRANK, Gerald A. Painter. Born Chicago, 1888. Pupil of Reynolds and Ufer in Chicago; Hawthorne, Webster and Nordfeldt in Provincetown, Mass. Member: Chicago Society of Artists; Chicago Art Club. Represented in Art Institute of Chicago. *Address,* Tree Studio Bldg., Chicago, Ill.

FRANKENSTEIN, John. Sculptor, who worked in Cincinnati about a generation ago. A number of casts show masterly handling of the clay.

FRANKLIN, Dwight. Painter and sculptor. Born New York, N. Y., 1888. Member: American Association of Museums. Work represented in American Museum of Natural History; Newark Public Library; Metropolitan Museum; Children's Museum, Brooklyn; Cleveland Museum; University of Illinois; French War Museum. Specialty, miniature groups for museums, usually of historical nature. *Address,* Care of "The Coffee House," 54 West 45th St., New York.

FRANTZ, Marshall. Illustrator. Born Kief, Russia, 1890. Pupil of Walter Everett. Member: Philadelphia Graphic Sketch Club. Has illustrated for *Saturday Evening Post, McClure's,* etc. *Address,* 49 West 37th St., New York, N. Y.

FRANZEN, August. Portrait painter. Born Norrkoping, Sweden, 1863. Member: Academy of National Artists, 1906; National Academy, 1920. Work: "Yellow Jessamine," Brooklyn Institute Museum; "William H. Taft," Yale University. *Address,* 222 West 59th St., New York.

FRANZONI. The brothers Carlo and Giuseppe were both born in Italy about 1780 and died in Washington, D. C. They are represented by sculptures in the Capitol at Washington, D. C. The Franzoni brothers are interred in Oak Hill Cemetery, Washington.

FRASER, Charles. Portrait painter in miniature and oils. Born 1782, Charleston, S. C.; died there 1860. He entered Charleston College about 1792, graduated in 1798, studied in a law office until 1800, and then devoted himself for a time to art, probably encouraged by the example of his friend Malbone. He lived in Charleston almost all his life except for a few visits to Boston, New York, and Columbia, South Carolina. In 1857 his friends and admirers formed an exhibition of more than three hundred examples of his work. (See the excellent illustrated article by Miss Alice R. H. Smith in "Art in America," 1915, and "Early American Portrait Painters in Miniature," by Bolton.)

FRASER, James E. Sculptor. Born in Winona, Minn., 1876. Studied at Chicago Art Institute, and at École des Beaux Arts, Julien Academy, Colarossi's, Paris. Won first prize for best work in sculpture offered by American Art Association of Paris, 1898. Executed first bust made from life of ex-President Roosevelt, 1908, now in Senate corridor, Washington, D. C., and bust of Col. Roosevelt, 1910, to be placed in public library, Oshkosh, Wis. A group of medals, exhibited at the International Exposition, Brussels, 1910, were bought the same year by the Belgian Government for the Musée at Gand, Belgium. Represented in Metropolitan Art Museum, New York City. Instructor in sculpture, Art Students' League, New York City. Important works: Monument to John Hay, Cleveland, Ohio; relief portrait of Morris K. Jessup, Museum of Natural History, New York City; fountain, country residence of the late E. H. Harriman, Arden, N. Y.; statue of Alexander Hamilton, at Treasury Building, Washington, D. C.; also many medals, and the nickel five cent piece for the United States Government. *Address*, 3 MacDougal Alley, New York City.

FRASER, Laua G. Sculptor. Born in Chicago, Ill., 1889. Studied at Art Students' League. Member of National Sculpture Society, and an Associate Member of the National Academy of Design. Specialty, animals in low reliefs, and statues, medals, etc. *Address*, 3 MacDougal Alley, New York.

FRASER, Malcolm. Illustrator. Born Montreal, Canada, 1868. Pupil of Art Students' League of New York, under Wyatt Eaton; Julien Academy in Paris, under Boulanger and Lefebvre. Illustrated "Richard Carvel," "Caleb West," etc. *Address*, Care of Salmagundi Club, 45 Fifth Ave., New York, N. Y.

FRAZEE, John. Sculptor. Born in Rahway, N. J., 1790; died in Crompton Mills, R. I., 1852. He was apprenticed as a lad to a country bricklayer, William Lawrence. His first work with the chisel was in carving his employer's name upon the tablet of a bridge, constructed by Lawrence over Rahway River at Bridgetown, in 1808. In 1814 he formed a partnership with a former apprentice, and established a stonecutting business at New Brunswick. In 1818 he removed to New York, and with his brother William opened a marble shop in Greenwich Street. From that time until 1825 the work of making tombstones and mantels seems to have been his school of art instruction. His portrait bust of John Wells, old St. Paul's Church, Broadway, New York,

is probably the first marble bust made in this country by a native American. Several busts were executed by Frazee in 1834, seven of which are in the Boston Athenaeum.

FRAZER, Oliver. Painter. Born in Fayette County, Kentucky, 1808, and died at his home near Lexington, 1864. He was the son of Alexander Frazer, an Irish patriot. The father dying while Oliver was very young, an uncle, Robert Frazer, assumed charge of his education. He early showed signs of great artistic talent, and his uncle placed him under the tuition of Kentucky's great artist, Matthew H. Jouett. Later he was sent to Philadelphia and studied under Thomas Sully. After his course in Philadelphia, he spent four years studying in Europe, attending the art schools of Paris, Florence, Berlin and London. Returning to America, he opened a studio in Lexington. Frazer devoted himself principally to portrait painting, his group-portrait of his wife and children, and portraits of Col. W. R. McKee, Chief Justice George Robertson, M. T. Scott, Joel T. Hart, the famous sculptor, and Henry Clay being among his works. His portrait of Clay has been considered by many critics as the finest portrait of the Great Commoner ever made.

FRAZIER. Nothing known of him except that he flourished about 1763, in Norfolk, Va., and painted a number of portraits.

FRAZIER, John R. Painter. Born Stonington, Conn., 1889. Pupil of R. I. School of Design, and C. W. Hawthorne. Member: Providence Art Club. Award: Phila. Water Color Club prize, 1920. *Address*, Rhode Island School of Design, Providence, R. I.

FRAZIER, Kenneth. Artist. Born Paris, France, 1867. Art studies at Julien Academy; pupil of Lefebvre and Constant. Professionally engaged as artist since 1889. Elected Associate Member of the National Academy. *Address*, 7 West 43d St., New York.

FRECHETTE, M. M. Painter. Born Ottawa, Canada, 1884. Pupil of Kenyon Cox, Charles Hawthorne; Mme. LaFarge in Paris. Member: Union Internationale des Beaux Arts et des Lettres. Work: Ten historical portraits for Chateau Frontenac, Quebec. *Address*, 67 Somerset St., West Ottawa, Canada.

FREDERICK, Edmund. Illustrator. Born Philadelphia, Pa., 1870. Studied at Penna. Academy of Fine Arts. Member: Society of Illustrators, 1910. Worked in New York for the *World* and *The Morning American*. Illustrated books by Elinor Glyn, Robert W. Chambers, Joseph C. Lincoln, etc.

FREDERICK, Frank F. Painter. Born Methuen, Mass., 1866. Pupil of Mass. Normal

Art School; Royal College of Art, London; Trenton School of Industrial Arts. Director, Trenton School of Industrial Arts.

FREDERICK, John L. Frederick was an engraver of buildings and book illustrations, in business in Philadelphia from 1818 until 1845. As he was engraving for Collins' Quarto Bible, published in New York in 1816, it is probable that he came from that city to Philadelphia. His one known portrait, that of the Rev. Joseph Eastburn, is an attempt in stipple, and is poorly done. He is said to have died in Philadelphia in 1800–81.

FREDERICKS, Alfred. Wood engraver and illustrator of books.

FREEDLANDER, Arthur R. Painter. Born in New York. Pupil of Twachtman and Mowbray in New York, and Cormon in Paris. *Address*, 220 West 59th St., New York.

FREEDLEY, Elizabeth C. Painter. Exhibited at Annual Exhibition of Penna. Academy of Fine Arts, Philadelphia, 1924, and at National Association of Women Painters and Sculptors. *Address*, New Hope, Penna.

FREEDMAN, Ruth. Painter. Born in Chicago, Ill., 1899. Pupil of Chicago Academy of Fine Arts. *Address*, Seattle, Wash., 1001 Seaboard Bldg.

FREELAND, Anna C. Painter. Born in 1837; died in 1911. She painted figure and historical scenes; her "William the Conqueror" is signed and dated "1886," and is owned by the Worcester Art Museum.

FREELON, Allan R. Painter. Born in Philadelphia, 1895. Member of Alumni Association of Penna. Museum School of Art. *Address*, 774 South 15th St., Philadelphia.

FREEMAN. Well-engraved line-plates so signed are found in a quarto Bible published in New York in 1816; but nothing more is known by which to identify the man.

FREEMAN, E. O. This good line-engraver of historical subjects was working for Boston publishers about 1850.

FREEMAN, Florence. Sculptor. Born in Boston, Mass., 1836. After study with Richard Greenough, she went abroad and studied with Hiram Powers. She has executed several bas-reliefs of Dante, and many portrait busts.

FREEMAN, George. Miniature painter. Born at Spring Hill, Conn., in 1787. In 1813 he went abroad for study and remained in London and Paris for twenty-four years. He painted on ivory and porcelain, and was honored by being allowed to paint Queen Victoria and Prince Albert, from life. He returned in 1837 and died in Hartford, Conn., in 1868. He painted miniatures of President Tyler, Mrs. Sigourney, Mr. and Mrs. Nicholas Biddle, Mr. and Mrs. James Brown, and Mrs. J. W. Wallace.

FREEMAN, Mrs. H. A. L. Sculptor. Wife of the artist James E. Freeman. Born in 1826. For many years she had her studio in Rome. A "Group of Children," also the "Culprit Fay," of Drake's poem, were modelled with skill by Mrs. Freeman.

FREEMAN, James Edward. Painter. Born in Nova Scotia in 1808. He was brought to the United States in 1810. He studied in New York City and entered the School of the National Academy. He afterward studied abroad, and had his studio in Rome. His best known paintings are "The Beggars," "Italian Peasant Girl," "The Bad Shoe," "Girl and Dog on the Campagna," and "The Mother and Child." His self-portrait was shown in the Centennial Exhibition of the National Academy of Design, New York, 1925. Elected a Member of the National Academy in 1833. He died in 1884.

FREEMAN, Marion. Painter. Exhibited at National Academy of Design, 1925. *Address*, 123 Waverly Place, New York.

FREEMAN, W. H. Very little is known about this engraver or his work beyond the fact that he was a fairly good engraver of line plates, and worked for New York and Baltimore publishers in 1815 and 1816. In Mr. Stauffer's work he notes that Freeman engraved a number of plates for a quarto Bible that was published in New York in 1816. Freeman also engraved "The Washington Monument at Baltimore," which was published by John Horace Pratt in 1815, in the scarce little publication giving an account of the laying of the corner stone of the Washington Monument.

FREER, Frederick W. Painter. Born in Chicago in 1849; died there in 1908. He was elected an Associate Member of the National Academy of Design, and a member of the American Water Color Society. He was president of the Chicago Academy of Design.

FRENCH, Daniel Chester. Sculptor. Born Exeter, N. H., 1850. Studied under Dr. William Rimmer, Boston; Thomas Ball, Florence. Had studio in Washington; Boston and Concord, Mass.; in New York since 1887. Among his best known works are "The Minute Man of Concord," at Concord, Mass.; a statue of Gen. Cass, in the Capitol at Washington; statue of Rufus Choate, Boston Court House; John Harvard, at Cambridge, Mass.; Thomas Starr King statue; "Dr. Gallaudet and His First Deaf-Mute Pupil." Medal of honor, Paris Exposition, 1900. Elected to National Academy in 1902. Trustee of Metropolitan Museum of Art. Member: National Sculpture Society; Architectural League; American Academy of Arts and Letters; Fellow of American Academy of Arts and Sciences. Chevalier, Legion of Honor, France. *Address*, 125 West 11th St., New York, N. Y.

FRENCH, Edwin Davis. Engraver. Born in North Attleborough, Mass., in 1851. In 1869 he began engraving on silver with the Whiting Manufacturing Co., and he went with that establishment, when it removed its works, to New York in 1876. Mr. French studied drawing and painting at the Art Students' League of New York, under William Sartain in 1883–86; he was later on the board of control of that organization until 1891, serving as president in 1890–91.

In 1894 Mr. French began the designing and engraving of book-plates and similar work on copper, and in this branch of the art he has achieved a well-deserved reputation. Since 1894 he has designed and engraved 245 book-plates, chiefly for private owners; but he also made many for clubs and public institutions. Among the latter may be noted the beautiful plates designed and engraved for the Grolier Club, Union League, and Metropolitan Museum of Art of New York; Dean Hoffman Library, etc. For the Society of Iconophiles he engraved their first publication, a series of views of historical New York buildings, and he has also made a number of title-pages and certificate plates. In 1897 Mr. French moved his studio to Saranac Lake. He died there in 1906.

FRENCH, Frank. Painter and engraver. Born at London, New Hampshire, in 1850. Medal at the Chicago Exposition, 1893, and at the Buffalo Exposition, 1901. Specialty, portrait painting. Elected Associate Member of the National Academy of Design. *Address*, Manchester, N. H.

FRERICHS, William C. A. Painter. Born in Germany in 1829, he afterward came to New York. In 1854 he became instructor in various art schools. He died in 1905.

FREY, Grace Eggers. Sculptor. Exhibited a portrait in the Cincinnati Museum in 1925. *Address*, 1801 E. Rich St., Columbus, Ohio.

FRIEDLANDER, Leo. Sculptor. Born in New York City, 1889. Pupil of Art Students' League of New York. Work: Sculptures on Washington Memorial Arch, Valley Forge, Penna. *Address*, 71 Woodside St., Stamford, Conn., or 637 Madison Ave., N. Y.

FRIES, Charles Arthur. Painter and illustrator. Born in Hillsboro, Ohio, 1854. Pupil of Cincinnati Art Academy. *Address*, 28 Broadway, San Diego, Calif.

FRIESEKE, Frederick Carl. Painter. Born at Owosso, Mich., 1874. Pupil of Art Institute of Chicago; Art Students' League of New York; Julien Academy and Whistler School, Paris. Pictures in Gallerie-Modern, Venice; Luxembourg Gallerie, Paris; Modern Gallery, Odessa, Russia; Telfair Gallery, Savannah, Ga.; Art Institute of Chicago, 1912; Metropolitan Museum. Elected Member of National Academy of Design, 1914. *Address*, Care Macbeth Galleries, New York City, N. Y.

FRISHMUTH, Harriet W. Sculptor. Born Philadelphia, 1880. Pupil of Rodin and Injalbert in Paris; Gutzon Borglum in New York. Member: National Sculptors' Society; National Academy of Women Painters and Sculptors. *Address*, 152 East 36th St., New York, N. Y.

FRITZ, Henry E. Painter and etcher. Born in Germany in 1875. Pupil of Geo. Bridgman, Robert Blum and Arthur Dow. Exhibited at National Academy of Design, and awarded gold medal. *Address*, 4 Poplar Ave., Chester Park, Pelham, N. Y.

FROELICH, Paul. Painter. Exhibited at Annual Exhibition of Penna. Academy of Fine Arts, Philadelphia, 1924, and Water Color Exhibition, 1925. *Address*, 1703 Tioga St., Philadelphia.

FROLICH, Finn H. Sculptor. Born in Norway in 1868. Pupil of Saint Gaudens and D. C. French. Designed monuments to James Hill, Edward Grig, and Jack London. *Address*, Wilcox Ave., Hollywood, Calif.

FROMEN, Agnes Valborg. Sculptor. Born Waldermasvik, Sweden, 1868. Pupil of Art Institute of Chicago under Lorado Taft. Member: Chicago Society of Artists; Art Institute of Chicago Alumni. Award: Prize, Municipal Art League of Chicago, 1912. Work: "The Spring," Art Institute of Chicago; "Bust of Washington Irving," Washington Irving School, Bloomington, Ill.; memorial fountain in Englewood High School; memorial tablet in Hyde Park Church of Christ, Chicago. *Address*, 6016 Ellis Ave., Chicago, Ill.

FROMKES, Maurice. Portrait painter. Born in Russia, 1872, and brought to America in 1880. Studied in Cooper Union and National Academy of Design. Traveled in Italy, and painted Cardinal Merry de Val, and Maurice Renaud, in Thais. He also painted Mrs. Armour of Chicago. *Address*, 51 West 10th St., New York.

FROMUTH, Charles Henry. Painter. Born in Philadelphia, 1861. Pupil of Thomas Eakins, 1880–84; Penna. Academy of Fine Arts, Philadelphia. Associate Member, Société Nationale des Beaux Arts, Paris. Member:

London Pastel Society. *Address,* Concarneau, France.

FROST, Anna. Painter and lithographer. Born in Brooklyn, N. Y. Pupil of Hawthorne and Breckenridge. *Address,* 152 Henry St., Brooklyn, N. Y.

FROST, Arthur B. Born in Philadelphia, 1851, he early turned his attention to illustrating. In 1877 he went to England and returned in 1878, preferring American life and atmosphere.

FROST, John. Painter and illustrator. Born Philadelphia, 1890. Pupil of A. B. Frost. Member: California Art Club. *Address,* 284 Madeline Drive.

FROTHINGHAM, James. Portrait painter. Born in Charleston, Mass., 1786, he began life as a coach painter; later he received some instructions from Gilbert Stuart and finally became his pupil. Frothingham painted portraits in Boston, Salem, New York and Brooklyn. Elected Member of National Academy of Design in 1831. He died in 1864. His copies of Start's "Washington" are excellent, and his original portraits have fine coloring at times, resembling his master's work in color and composition. A number of his portraits are owned by the City of New York, and hang in the Old Court House.

FROTHINGHAM, Sarah C. Miniature painter. Born in 1821 and died 1861. Daughter of James Frothingham, N. A. She exhibited at the National Academy, 1838–1842.

FRUEH, (Alfred J.). Painter and illustrator. Born Lima, Ohio, 1880. Member: Society of Independent Artists.

FRY, Mrs. Georgia Timken. A painter, and wife of the painter John H. Fry. She was born in St. Louis in 1864, and was a pupil of Harry Thompson, Aimé Morot, Schenck and Cazin in Paris. She was a member of the National Association of Women Painters and Sculptors; Society of New York Artists; Society of Women Artists. She is represented by "Return of the Flock," at the Boston Art Club. She made a specialty of landscapes with sheep. She died in China in 1921.

FRY, John Henning. Born in Indiana; studied in Paris and Rome. *Address,* 200 West 57th St., New York City.

FRY, Sherry Edmundson. Sculptor. Born Creston, Ia., 1879. Studied at Art Institute of Chicago, 1900; Julien Academy, Paris, France, 1902; École des Beaux Arts, Paris, 1903; Florence, Italy, 1904; pupil of Frederick MacMonnies, Barrias, Verlet, and Lorado Taft. Traveled and studied in Italy, Greece and Ger-

many, 1908–11; honorable mention, Salon, Paris, 1906; gold medal, 1907. Elected Associate Member of the National Academy of Design, New York, in 1914. Work: "Statue of Indian Chief," Iowa; "The Turtle," Worcester, Mass.; etc. *Address,* Century Club, 7 West 43d St., New York.

FUCHS, Emil. Painter, sculptor and etcher. Born in Vienna in 1886. Represented in Metropolitan Museum, Cleveland Museum, and designer of medal for Hudson-Fulton Exhibition. *Address,* 80 West 40th St., New York.

FUECHSEL, Herman. Painter. Born in Germany, 1833, he came to America in 1858, and was a member of the Artists' Fund Society of New York. He died in 1915.

FUERTES, Louis Agassiz. Painter. Born at Ithaca, N. Y., 1874. Painter of birds since 1896. Illustrated: "Birding on a Broncho," 1896; "Citizen Bird," 1897; "Songbirds and Water Fowl," 1897; "Birdcraft Birds of the Rockies," 1902; "Handbook of Birds of Western United States"; "Coues' Key to North American Birds," 1903; "Handbook of Birds of Eastern United States"; plates for "Report of N. Y. State Game, Forest and Fish Commission"; "Birds of New York"; several series in *National Geographic Magazines.* Permanent work: Habitat groups, American Museum Natural History, New York; 25 decorative panels for F. F. Brewster, New Haven, Conn.; birds of New York at State Museum, Albany. *Address,* Cornell Heights, Ithaca, N. Y.

FULLER, George. Born at Deerfield, Mass., 1822. Studied in Boston, New York, London and Continental Europe. First became known as a portrait painter. Elected Associate of the National Academy of Design, 1857. Original Member of Society of American Artists. Died in Boston, 1884. Since his death the exhibition of his later works has placed him in the front rank of American colorists and painters of original inspiration. He painted "Fedalma" (the Spanish gypsy), "Nydia" (the blind girl in Bulwer's "Last Days of Pompeii"); also represented at Corcoran Gallery, Washington, by "Lorette."

FULLER, Henry Brown. Painter. Born Deerfield, Mass., 1867. Studied art at Cowles Art School; Art Students' League; and School of Raphael Colin, Paris. Painter of subject pictures and decorations; best known works: "Illusions"; "Life Disarming Death." Bronze medal, Buffalo Expn., 1901; Carnegie prize, National Academy of Design, 1908. Elected Associate Member of National Academy of Design. Invented mellowtint etching, 1919. *Address,* Cambridge, Mass.

FULLER, Lucia Fairchild. Miniature painter. Born in Boston, 1872, and died 1924.

Pupil of Art Students' League of New York under William M. Chase and H. Siddons Mowbray. Engaged professionally as painter since 1889, chiefly doing miniatures. Bronze medal, Paris Expn., 1900; silver medal, Buffalo Expn., 1901. Member: American Society of Miniature Painters; Penna. Society of Miniature Painters; New York Water Color Club, etc.

FULLER, Ralph B. Painter and illustrator. Born in Michigan in 1890. Humorous illustrator for *Life* and other magazines. *Address*, 170 Ames Ave., Leonia, N. Y.

FULLER, Richard Henry. Painter. Born at Bradford, N. H., in 1822, he was chiefly self-taught. He died in 1871 at Chelsea, Mass. He is represented in the Boston Museum of Fine Arts by his painting ''Near Chelsea,'' painted in 1847.

FULTON, Agnes. Painter and sculptor. Born in Yonkers, N. Y., in 1898. Pupil of Dow and Martin. *Address*, Saratoga Springs, New York.

FULTON, Cyrus J. Painter. Born in Colorado in 1873. Pupil of Wentz and Schroff. *Address*, 1192 Jefferson St., Eugene, Ore.

FULTON, Robert. Artist, inventor, successful introducer of the steamboat; born in Little Britain township, Lancaster County, Pa., in 1765; died in New York, February, 1815. Coming to Philadelphia as a portrait painter in 1782, within four years he earned enough money to establish his widowed mother on a small farm clear of debt. He then went to London to study under Benjamin West for several years, afterward establishing himself in Devonshire under the patronage of men of wealth. In 1794 he became a member of the family of Joel Barlow, author of ''The Columbiad,'' in Paris, where he painted the first panorama exhibited in the French capital. In 1797 he began experiments in submarine navigation and torpedo warfare. As early as 1803 he had, with the financial assistance of Chancellor Livingston, launched a steamboat on the Seine, which immediately sank, though a partial success later achieved, encouraged him to build the famous ''Clermont,'' which, in 1807, set out on her historic voyage to Albany. (See Dickinson's ''Life of Fulton'' for list of his portrait painting and miniatures.)

FUNK, Wilhelm Heinrich. Painter. Born Hanover, Germany, 1866. Studied at Art Students' League of New York, and in museums of Spain, Holland, France, Italy and Germany. Came to America 1885; first attracted attention by a pen-portrait of Edwin Booth, the actor. He became the pen and ink artist on the staff of the *New York Herald;* also contributed to *Scribner's Magazine, Century, Harper's, Judge* and *Truth;* he now devotes his attention to

portrait painting. *Address*, 80 West 40th St., New York.

FURLONG, Charles Wellington. Painter. Born Cambridge, Mass., 1874. Graduated Mass. Normal Art School, 1895; course at Arts, Paris; Academie Julien under Bouguereau Cornell and Harvard; studied École des Beaux and Laurens. Instructor of drawing and painting; head of art department, summer session, Cornell University. Illustrated ''Bailey's Cyclopedia of Horticulture'' and other books. Discovered in Tripoli Harbor, 1904, wreck of U. S. Frigate, ''Philadelphia,'' sunk by Lt. Decatur in 1804. *Address*, Back Bay, Boston, Mass.

FURNASS, John Mason. Painter and engraver. Born in 1763; died at Dedham, Mass., 1804. He was the nephew of the engraver Nathaniel Hurd, who bequeathed him his engraving tools. Furnass engraved book-plates and certificates for the Massachusetts Loan Society. In 1785 he was painting portraits in Boston, and in 1834 the Boston Athenaeum exhibited two copies by him of paintings by Teniers. He painted two portraits of John Vinal, the old schoolmaster of Boston.

FURNESS, William Henry, Jr. Born in Philadelphia, 1827; died in 1867. Son of Rev. William H. Furness. He drew many excellent portraits in crayon, and later on painted a number of portraits of well-known Philadelphians, in oil. His work in crayon stood next to Cheney. He painted Charles Sumner, Lucretia Mott, Rev. Dr. Barnes, Hamilton Wilde, Mrs. Lathrop and Miss Emerson.

FURSMAN, Frederick. Painter and Director of Summer School of Painting, Sagatuck, Mich.

FURSMAN, Frederick F. Painter. Member of Chicago Society of Artists. Represented in Museum of Art, Toledo, by ''In the Garden.'' *Address*, 4465 North Kildare Ave., Chicago, Ill.

FURST, Moritz. Born at Boesing, Hungary, 1782, he was living in New York in 1834. Furst was an engraver of dies for coins and medals. In 1807 Mr. Joseph Clay, U. S. Consul at Leghorn, induced Furst to come to the United States, as die-sinker in the U. S. Mint at Philadelphia; in this capacity he engraved the dies for a large number of Congress medals awarded to military and naval heroes of the War of 1812. Furst was also engaged at the same time in general business, as he advertises in 1808 as an ''Engraver of Seals and Dye-Sinker on Steel and other metals,'' and asks for the patronage of the citizens of Philadelphia. He was in business as an ''Engraver on Steel'' in Philadelphia as late as September, 1820.

G

G. L. The initials of this unknown engraver, which appear upon a reversed copy of a caricature originally etched by William Charles, of Philadelphia, and also signed as ''L. G. Sculpt.'' to a map of Sacketts Harbour, by Patrick May, published and sold by Patrick May in Bristol, Conn. This map is copyrighted in 1815 indicating the date of the work.

GABAY, Esperanza. Painter. Exhibited at the National Association of Women Painters and Sculptors, New York, 1924. *Address,* 136 West 91st St., New York.

GAERTNER, Carl F. Painter. Exhibited at Annual Exhibition of Penna. Academy of Fine Arts, Philadelphia, 1924. *Address,* 10312 Westchester Ave., Cleveland, Ohio.

GAG, Wanda H. Illustrator. Born in New Ulm, Minn., in 1893. Pupil of Art Students' League, New York. Awarded New York prize, and honorable mention, Minnesota State Art Society. *Address,* 236 North Washington St., New Ulm, Minn.

GAGE, G. W. Painter and illustrator. Born in Laurence, Mass., in 1887. Pupil of Hale, Benson and Pyle. *Address,* 64 Poplar St., Brooklyn, N. Y.

GAGE, Robert M. Sculptor. His bronze statue of Lincoln stands in the State House Grounds, Topeka. *Address,* 1031 Filmore Ave., Topeka, Kan.

GAINS. Nothing is known of this painter, except that the portrait of Rev. James Honyman, pastor of Trinity Church, Newport, R. I., from 1704 to 1750, was engraved by Samuel Oakey of Newport in 1774. The engraving records the portrait as being painted by ''Gains,'' probably a local artist. The picture hangs in the vestry of Old Trinity Church, Newport, R. I.

GALE, Charles F. Painter. Born in Columbus, Ohio, in 1874; died in 1920.

GALE, Walter R. Painter and illustrator. Born in Kent County, Md., in 1878. Pupil of Maryland Institute. *Address,* Baltimore City College, Baltimore, Md.

GALLAGHER. An Irishman who painted portraits in Philadelphia about 1800; he also painted signs and other pictures. In 1807 he was employed in New York as a scene painter by Thomas A. Cooper, but he was not a success. In 1798 he painted a standard for the First Philadelphia Volunteer Cavalry, commanded by Capt. McKean.

GALLAGHER, Sears. Painter. Born in Boston, Mass., 1869. Pupil of Tomaso Juglaris, Boston; Jean Paul Laurens and Benjamin Constant, Paris. Exhibited in the Salon, Paris, the most important exhibitions in America, and the Paris Expn., 1900. Member: Boston Society Water Color Painters; Chicago Society Etchers; California Society of Etchers; Boston Art Club; Brooklyn Society Etchers. Etchings in Boston Museum of Fine Arts; Art Institute of Chicago; New York Public Library; the Library of Congress, Washington, D. C. *Address,* 755 Boylston St., Boston, Mass.

GALLAND, John. The name of John Galland, ''engraver,'' appears in the Philadelphia directories for 1796–1817, inclusive. He engraved in the stipple manner and with little effect. Probably his most ambitious work is a large portrait of Washington done after a similar plate by David Edwin. A number of portraits and historical plates executed by Galland are to be found in a history of France published by James Stewart, Philadelphia, 1796–97.

GALLAUDET, Edward. Born in Hartford, Conn., 1809; died there, 1847. He was the son of Peter Wallace Gallaudet, merchant. Edward Gallaudet was probably apprenticed to one of the several engraving establishments in Hartford; he then worked in Boston with John Cheney. Gallaudet was a reputable line-engraver, his best work appearing in the Annuals of 1835–40. A miniature portrait of Edward Gallaudet is in the possession of his nephew, Mr. E. M. Gallaudet, principal of the Gallaudet College for the Deaf and Dumb, at Washington, D. C.

GALLAUDET, Elisha. Born in New Rochelle, N. Y., about 1730; was living in 1800. Elisha Gallaudet was the second son of Dr. Peter Gallaudet. As early as 1759 Gallaudet was in business in New York as an engraver, as is shown in an advertisement in the *New York Mercury* of March 5, 1759. In this issue appear proposals for printing by subscription, ''Six Representations of Warriors who are in the Service of their Majesties, the King of Great Britain and the King of Prussia. Designed after life with a Description as expressed in the Proposals.'' Besides some early book-plates the only known engraving by Elisha Gallaudet is a portrait of the Rev. George Whitfield, issued as a frontispiece to a ''Life of Whitfield,'' published by Hodge & Shober, New York, 1774. This plate is very poorly engraved, and is evidently a copy from an English print. In the list of subscribers to this book is the name of ''Elisha Gallaudet, engraver, New York.''

GALLISON, Henry H. Landscape painter. Born in Boston in 1850. Studied in Paris, pupil of Bonnefoy. Represented in Boston Museum of Fine Arts by "The Golden Haze" and "The Morning Shadow." He died in Cambridge, Mass., in 1910.

GALT, Alexander. Sculptor. Born in Norfolk, Va., 1827; died in Richmond, 1863. He studied abroad. Among his works are many portrait busts, his Jefferson Davis being made from actual measurements.

GALT, Charles F. Painter. Born St. Louis, 1884. Pupil of St. Louis School of Fine Arts and of Richard Miller. *Address,* 4021 Washington Ave., St. Louis, Mo.

GAMBERLING, Grace Thorp. Painter. Exhibited at the Pennsylvania Academy of Fine Arts, Philadelphia, in 1924. *Address,* Cynwyd, Penna.

GAMBLE, John Marshall. Painter. Born Morristown, N. J., 1863. Pupil of San Francisco School of Design; Academie Julien, Laurens and Constant in Paris. Represented in Museum of Art, Auckland, N. Z.; Park Museum, San Francisco. *Address,* 813½ State St., Santa Barbara, Calif.

GAMBLE, Roy C. Painter. Born 1887. Pupil of Detroit Fine Arts Academy; Art Students' League of New York; of Julien in Paris. Member: Scarab Club. Award: Second Hopkins prize for painting, Scarab Club. Work represented in Pennsylvania Academy of the Fine Arts; "Freckles," Detroit Art Institute. *Address,* 83 Fort St., West, Detroit, Mich.

GAMMELL, R. H. Ives. Painter. Born Providence, R. I., 1893. Pupil of William M. Paxton. Member: Providence Art Club; Provincetown Academy of Artists. *Address,* 480 Boylston St., Boston, Mass.

GANDOLFI, Mauro. Engraver. Born in Bologna, Italy, in 1771; died there in 1834. This master engraver in line, and a pupil of the famous Giuseppe Longhi, was probably the first of the really prominent European engravers to visit the United States professionally, although he never engraved here. Dunlap tells us that he came to the United States under a contract to engrave for $4,000 Col. Trumbull's large plate of the "Declaration of Independence."

GANIERE, George Étienne, Sculptor. Born Chicago, Ill. Pupil of Art Institute of Chicago. Work: "Lincoln" at Lincoln Memorial School, Webster City, Ia., and at Burlington, Wis.; "Lincoln Memorial," Starved Rock, State Park, Ill.; Dr. Frank W. Gunsaulus Memorial, Chicago. Former instructor in Sculpture Department, Chicago Art Institute. *Address,* 6016 Ellis Ave., Chicago, Ill.

GANO, Katharine V. Painter. Born in Cincinnati in 1884. Pupil of Duveneck. *Address,* Southern Railway Bldg., Cincinnati, Ohio.

GARBER, Daniel. Painter. Born N. Manchester, Ind., 1880. Studied at Cincinnati Art Academy and Penna. Academy of Fine Arts. Member: Faculty, Penna. Academy of Fine Arts, 1909. Represented in permanent collections of Art Institute of Chicago; Cincinnati Museum; Corcoran Gallery of Art, Washington, D. C.; Mary Brown Memorial, Providence, R. I.; University of Mo.; Institute of Fine Arts, St. Paul, Minn.; St. Louis Museum; Carnegie Institute, Pittsburgh. Elected Member of National Academy of Design, 1913. *Address,* 1819 Green St., Philadelphia.

GARCIA, J. Torres. Painter. Exhibited at the Penna. Academy of Fine Arts, 1921, at "Exhibition of Paintings Showing the Later Tendencies in Art." *Address,* 4 West 29th St., New York.

GARDEN, Francis. Engraver. The *Boston Evening Post,* 1745, contains the following advertisement: "Francis Garden, engraver from London, engraves in the newest Manner and at the cheapest Rates, Coats-of-Arms, Crests or Cyphers on Gold, Silver, Pewter or Copper. To be heard of at Mr. Caverly's Distiller, at the South End of Boston." "N. B. He will wait on any Person, in Town or Country, to do their work at their own House, if desired; also copperplate printing performed by him." No work of any kind signed by Garden is known to the writer.

GARDIN, Laura (Mrs. James E. Fraser). Sculptor. Born in Chicago, Ill., 1889. Pupil of James E. Fraser. Member: National Sculptors' Society; National Academy of Women Painters and Sculptors. Awards: Helen Foster Barnett prize, National Academy of Design, 1916; Shaw memorial prize, National Academy of Design, 1919. *Address,* 3 MacDougal Alley, New York, N. Y.

GARDINER, Eliza D. Painter and engraver. Born in Providence, R. I., 1871. Pupil of Rhode Island School of Design. Member: Providence Art Club; Providence Water Color Club; Society of Independent Artists. Represented in Detroit Institute, Springfield Public Library, and Philadelphia Print Club. *Address,* 2139 Broad St., Providence, R. I.

GARDNER, Elizabeth Jane. See Bouguereau.

GARDNER, Gertrude G. Painter. Born Palo Alto County, Ia., 1878. Pupil of Henry B. Snell. *Address,* 171 Union St., Flushing, New York.

10

GARNER, Charles S., Jr. Painter. Exhibited at Annual Exhibition of the Penna. Academy of Fine Arts, Philadelphia, 1924. *Address*, 320 Harmony St., Philadelphia.

GARNER, Frances C. Painter. Exhibited at the Water Color Exhibition of the Penna. Academy of the Fine Arts, Philadelphia, 1925. *Address*, 320 Harmony St., Philadelphia.

GARNSEY, Elmer Ellsworth. Painter. Born at Holmdell, N. J., 1862. Pupil of the Cooper Institute, Art Students' League, George W. Maynard, and Francis Lathrop, New York. Decorations in: Library of Congress; Boston Public Library. *Address*, Prospect Hill, White Plains, New York.

GARRETSON, Albert M. Painter and illustrator. Born in Buffalo, N. Y., 1877. Pupil of Laurens in Paris. *Address*, 53 Jackson Ave., Long Island City, New York.

GARRETT, Anne Shapleigh. Painter. Exhibited at the Pennsylvania Academy of Fine Arts, Philadelphia, in 1924. *Address*, 1609 Broome Street, Wilmington, Del.

GARRETT, Clara P. (Mrs.). Sculptor. Born in Pittsburgh, Pa. Pupil of St. Louis School of Fine Arts and École des Beaux Arts, Paris. Represented in Metropolitan Museum by "Boy Teasing Turtle"; City of St. Louis by "McKinley"; Eugene Field School, St. Louis, by frieze "Children at Play." *Address*, Bayside, Long Island, New York.

GARRETT, Edmund Henry. Painter, illustrator and etcher. Born in Albany, N. Y., 1853. Studied at Academie Julien, Paris; pupil of Jean Paul Laurens, Boulanger and Lefebvre, Paris. Medal at Boston, 1890. Exhibitor at Paris Salon and principal exhibitions in America. *Address*, 142 Berkeley St., Boston, Mass.

GARRETT, J. W. B. Portraits, signed "J. W. B. Garrett," are found in the southern states; one known to the author was so signed, and dated 1852.

GARRETT, Theresa A. Etcher. Born 1884; member of Chicago Society of Etchers. *Address*, 410 South Michigan Ave., Chicago, Ill.

GARRISON, Robert. Sculptor. Born in Fort Dodge, Ia., 1895. Pupil of Penna. Academy of Fine Arts, and Gutzon Borglum. *Address*, Chappell House, Denver, Conn.

GARVEY, Joseph M. Painter. Born in New York, 1877. Pupil of William M. Chase. Member of Society of Independent Artists. *Address*, Alpine, N. J.

GARY, Louisa M. Miniature painter. Exhibited a portrait miniature at the Penna. Academy of Fine Arts, Philadelphia, 1922. *Address*, Catonsville, Maryland.

GASPARD, Leon. Painter. Born Vitebsk, Russia, 1882. Studied at Academie Julien, Paris, France. Came to U. S. 1916. Exhibited in cities of Belgium; Salon d'Artistes Française; Salon d'Autumn, Paris; also in New York, Philadelphia, Chicago, New Orleans, etc. Awarded gold medal, National Academy, Russia. Honorable mention, Salon Française. Clubs: Russian (Moscow), Salmagundi, New York. *Address*, 108 West 57th St., New York.

GATTER, Otto J. Painter and illustrator. Born in Philadelphia, 1892. Pupil of Penna. Academy of Fine Arts. Illustrates for *Scribner's, Cosmopolitan* and *McClure's. Address*, 1530 Wallace St., Philadelphia.

GAUGENGIGL, Ignatz Marcel. Painter. Born Passau, Bavaria, 1855. Studied at Academy of Fine Arts, Munich, 1878. Came to U. S., 1880, and since then has had a studio in Boston. Received gold medal at New Orleans Exposition. Member: Council for School of Boston Museum of Fine Arts. Represented at the Metropolitan Museum by "A Difficult Question." Associate Member of National Academy of Design. *Address*, 5 Otis Place, Boston, Mass.

GAUK, James. The New York directories for 1799–1804 contain this name as "Engraver." No work signed by Gauk is known to the writer.

GAUL, Arrah L. (Mrs.). Painter. Member of American Water Color Society. *Address*, 34 South 16th St., Philadelphia, Pa.

GAUL, Gilbert. Painter. Born in Jersey City, N. J., in 1855. He was a pupil of J. G. Brown, of the National Academy. He has made a close study of all that pertains to a soldier's career, and his academic training, his keen insight, and his feeling for dramatic composition have done the rest. "Charging the Battery" and "Wounded to the Rear" are among the best of his episodic compositions, and these stirring pictures have equally interesting, if less animated companion pieces in a host of subjects wherein are depicted the excitement and the picturesque features of army life. Many of these are scenes on the plains of the Far West. For "Charging the Battery" Mr. Gaul was awarded a medal at the Paris Exposition of 1889. In 1882 he was elected National Academician. He died in 1919.

GAULEY, Robert David. Painter. Born Carnaveigh County, Monaghan, Ireland, 1875; known to be with parents in 1884. Studied with Denman W. Ross, Cambridge, Mass.; Edmund Tarbell and Frank Benson, Museum of Fine Arts, Boston; Bouguereau and Ferrier, Julien Academy, Paris. Elected Associate Member of the National Academy, 1908. *Address*, Watertown, Mass.

GAUSTA, H. Painter. Born in Norway, 1854. Pupil of Royal Academy of Munich. Member: Minneapolis Art League. *Address*, 1706 Elliott Ave., Minneapolis, Minn.

GAVIN, H. A fairly well-executed line frontispiece to Marmontel's ''Belisarius'' is signed ''H. Gavin, Sculp.'' The work itself was published at Newburyport, in 1796, for Thomas and Andrews, of Boston, Mass. No other example of Gavin's work has been seen by the compiler.

GAVIT, John E. Engraver. Born in New York, 1817; died at Stockbridge, Mass., 1874. Gavit learned his business in Albany, N. Y., and he there established an engraving, printing and lithographing establishment. He later became especially interested in bank-note work, and in 1855 he assisted in organizing the American Bank Note Co., in New York. After serving as secretary for a time, he was elected president of that company, in 1866, and held the office until his death.

GAW, R. M. This engraver was probably in the employ of Peter Maverick in Newark, N. J., in 1829. He engraved in line portraits and architectural work.

GAY, Edward. Painter. Born Dublin, Ireland, 1837. He came to America in 1848; began to study art under Lessing and Schirmer at Carlsruhe, Germany. Specialty, landscapes. He received the Metropolitan prize for the picture ''Broad Acres,'' presented to the Metropolitan Museum of Art, New York; later works are: ''Washed by the Sea,'' ''Atlantis,'' ''The Suburbs,'' in Tewksberry Collection. New York; ''Where Sea and Meadow Meet,'' Governor's Mansion, Albany, N. Y. Elected Associate Member National Academy, 1868; National Academy, 1907. *Address*, 434 South 2d Ave., Mt. Vernon, New York.

GAY, George Howell. Painter. Born Milwaukee, 1858. Pupil of Paul Brown and Henry A. Elkins in Chicago. Settled in New York in 1889. Specialty, marines and landscapes. *Address*, 100 Kraft Ave., Bronxville, N. Y.

GAY, Walter. Painter. Born Hingham, Mass., 1856. He began to paint flower subjects in 1873; went to Paris, 1876, to study art. Pupil of Bonnat and Constant. Exhibitor at Paris Salon; painted the large picture ''Benedicite,'' now in Museum at Amiens, France; ''Las Cigarreras,'' in the Luxembourg, Paris, also pictures in London, Metropolitan Museum of Art, New York, and Museum of Fine Arts, Boston. *Address*, 11 Rue de Université, Paris, France.

GAY, Winckworth Allan. Landscape painter. Born in West Hingham, Mass., in 1821. He studied under Robert W. Weir, and later in Paris. He is represented by landscapes in the Boston Museum. He was a brother of the artist Walter Gay. He died in 1910.

GAYLOR, (Samuel) Wood. Painter and etcher. Born Stamford, Conn., in 1883. Pupil of National Academy of Design. Member: Penguins; Modern Artists of America. *Address*, 142 West 127th St., New York, N. Y.

GEARHART, Frances H. Etcher. *Address*, 18 West California St., Pasadena, Calif.

GEDDENS, George. Painter. Born in Bedford, England, in 1845. By profession an actor, he practiced painting in his leisure hours. He studied in California, and at the National Academy schools in New York. His studio was in New York City. Among his works, ''Twilight'' was exhibited at the National Academy in 1878, and ''Noontide'' and ''Eventide'' at the Brooklyn Art Association.

GEER, Grace Woodbridge. Portrait painter. Born in Boston, 1854. Pupil of Mass. Normal Art School, F. H. Tompkins, Triscott, Tarbell, Vonnoh and Lowell Institute. Represented by portrait at International Institute for Girls, Madrid, Spain; Girls' High School, Boston. *Address*, 12 Pinckney St., Boston, Mass.

GEERLINGS, Gerald K. Exhibited water colors at the Exhibition of Water Colors at the Penna. Academy of Fine Arts, Philadelphia, 1925. *Address*, 148 Central Ave., Flushing, Long Island, N. Y.

GELERT, Johannes S. Sculptor. Born in Denmark, 1852; came to the United States in 1887, and died in New York City, 1923. He was a member of the National Sculpture Society. Represented by Haymarket Monument, Chicago; Gen'l Grant in Galena, Ill.; in the Art Institute, Chicago, and museums in Denmark.

GENDROT, Felix A. Painter and sculptor. Born in Cambridge, Mass., 1866. Studied at Julien Academy under Laurens and Constant, and sculpture with Puech and Verlet. *Address*, Buena Vista St., Roxbury, Mass.

GENIN, John. Born in France, 1830; died in New Orleans, 1895. He had a studio as portrait, historical and genre painter at 150 Canal Street in 1876; he resided and painted in New Orleans for the next twenty years, and at the time of his death had a studio at 233 Royal Street.

GENIN, Sylvester. Born in Ohio, 1822, and with comparatively little training he evinced a remarkable talent for composition. His painting of historical art had a spirited style which would have led him to permanent triumphs, but his death occurred at the age of twenty-eight, in 1850.

GENTH, Lillian. Painter. Born Philadelphia, Pa. Pupil of School of Design for Women under Elliott Daingerfield; Whistler in Paris. Elected Associate Member of the National Academy, 1908; Fellowship, Penna. Academy of Fine Arts. Work: ''Depth of the Woods'' and ''Adagio,'' National Gallery, Washington, D. C.; ''Springtime,'' Metropolitan Museum, New York; ''The Lark,'' Engineers' Club, New York; ''The Bird Song,'' Carnegie Institute, Pittsburgh; ''Pastoral,'' Brooklyn Institute of Arts and Sciences; ''Venice'' and ''In Normandy,'' Philadelphia Art Club, Philadelphia. *Address,* 108 West 57th St., New York.

GEORGE, Vesper L. Painter. Born in Boston, 1865. Pupil of Constant and Lefebvre in Paris. *Address,* 120 Riverway, Boston.

GERE, Nellie H. Landscape painter. Born Norwich, Conn. Member of Chicago Art Students' League. *Address,* 123 South Virgil Ave., Los Angeles, Calif.

GERHARDT, Karl. Sculptor. Born in Boston, Mass., 1853. He was largely self-taught, but was sent to Paris to study art. He afterward exhibited in the Salon; has executed portrait busts of many prominent men, and statues of Gen'l Putnam at Brooklyn, Nathan Hale at Hartford, Conn., and Gen'l Gouveneur K. Warren at Gettysburg, Penna.

GERITZ, Frank. Painter and etcher. Born in Hungary, 1895. Specialty, block printing. *Address,* 238 West First St., Los Angeles, Calif.

GERLACH, Gustave. Sculptor. Pupil of Karl Bitter, and sculptor of the colossal personification of ''Minnesota.''

GERMAN, John D. Miniature painter. Flourished in New York in 1837.

GERBER, Robert G. Painter. Born in France in 1867. Painted portrait of Pope Pius X in the Vatican, Rome. *Address,* St. Benedict and Kickapoo Sts., Shawnee, Okla.

GERRY, Samuel L. Portrait painter in oils and miniatures. Born in 1813. He was President of the Boston Art Club in 1858. Among his works are ''The Old Man of the Mountain,'' ''The Artist's Dream,'' and ''Bridal Tour of Priscilla and John Alden.'' He died 1891 at Roxbury, Mass.

GERSTENHEIM, Louis. Painter. Born in Poland, 1890. Pupil of National Academy

of Design. Member of the Society of Independent Artists. *Address,* 344 East 57th St., New York.

GERSTLE, Miriam A. Painter and illustrator. Born in San Francisco in 1868. Member of San Francisco Artists' Association. *Address,* 2360 Washington St., San Francisco.

GERSTLE, William L. Painter. Born in San Francisco, 1868. Pupil of Art Students' League of New York and San Francisco Artists' Association. *Address,* 617 Montgomery St., San Francisco, Calif.

GEST, Joseph H. Painter. Born in Cincinnati in 1859. Director of Cincinnati Museum. *Address,* Art Museum, Cincinnati.

GETCHELL, Edith L. Etcher. Born in Bristol, Pa. Pupil of Penna. Academy of Fine Arts. Her etchings are in the Library of Congress, Boston Museum of Fine Arts, Worcester Art Museum, and Walters Collection, Baltimore, Md. *Address,* 6 Linden St., Worcester, Mass.

GETTIER, G. Wilmer. Painter. Born in Baltimore, Md., 1877. Studied in Baltimore, Md., and Munich. *Address,* 855 North Howard St., Baltimore, Md.

GETZ, Peter. He was a silversmith and jeweler of Lancaster, Pa., in the last quarter of the eighteenth century. He was a ''self-taught mechanic of singular ability,'' says Wm. Barton in his life of David Rittenhouse. In 1792 Getz was a candidate for the position of Chief Coiner and Engraver to the newly organized mint in Philadelphia, but the place was given to the engraver Robert Scott.

GIBBS, George. Painter and illustrator. Born in New Orleans, La., 1870. Pupil of Corcoran School of Art. *Address,* 1520 Chestnut St., Philadelphia, Pa.

GIBSON, Charles Dana. Illustrator and painter. Born in 1867. Many of his drawings have appeared in *Life,* with which publication he has been connected for years. *Address,* Carnegie Studios, New York.

GIBSON, Thomas. Nothing is known of this artist, except the notice of his death published in the *Morning Star* of New York City of December 27th, 1811: Thomas Gibson, painter, died December 23, 1811.''

GIBSON, William Hamilton. Artist and illustrator. Born in Sandy Hook, Conn., 1850. He worked on the ''Art Journal'' and ''Picturesque America.'' He was a member of the New York Water Color Society, and exhibited his work after 1872. He died in 1896.

GICHNER, Joanna E. Sculptor. Born in Baltimore in 1899. Pupil of Grafly. *Address,* 1516 Madison Ave., Baltimore, Md.

GIDDINGS, Albert F. Painter and etcher. Born in Brenham, Tex., 1883. Pupil of Art Institute of Chicago; Frederick W. Freer. Decoration in Wendell Phillips High School, Chicago. *Address,* Hotel Del Prado, 1400 East 59th St., Chicago, Ill.

GIDDINGS Frank A. Painter and etcher. Born Hartford, Conn., 1882. Pupil of Chase. Member: Conn. Academy of Fine Arts. *Address,* 74 Webster St., Hartford, Conn.

GIDEON, Sam'l E. Painter. Born in Louisville, Ky., 1875. Pupil of Ross Turner, Gorguet. *Address,* University of Texas, Austin, Tex.

GIEBERICH, O. H. Painter. Born New York City, 1886. Pupil of Bridgman, Cox, Mora, DuMond and Hawthorne. *Address,* Care of Hawthorne Art School, Provincetown, Mass.

GIES, Joseph W. Painter. Born Detroit. Pupil of Bouguereau and Robert-Fleury in Paris; Royal Academy in Munich. Work: "Lady in Pink" and "Portrait of Robert Hopkins," Detroit Institute. *Address,* 14 West Adams Ave., Detroit, Mich.

GIESE, Augustus F. Painter. Member: Society of Independent Artists. *Address,* 1852 Jerome Ave., New York, N. Y.

GIFFEN, Lillian. Painter. Born New Orleans, La. *Address,* 1004 North Charles St., Baltimore, Md.

GIFFORD, Frances Eliot. Painter. Born New Bedford, Mass., 1844. Received art education in Cooper Institute, New York, and in Boston, under S. L. Gerry. Painter of birds with landscapes; also magazine illustrator.

GIFFORD, Robert Swain. Landscape painter and etcher. Born at Island of Naushon, Mass., 1840; died New York, 1905. He learned the rudiments of his art from Albert Van Beest, a Dutch marine painter at New Bedford, Mass. Moved to Boston in 1864 and two years later settled in New York. First exhibited in 1864 at the National Academy of Design, of which he was elected an Associate in 1867, and an Academician in 1878. Traveled extensively, painting in Oregon and California in 1869, and later in Europe, Algiers, and Egypt. Mr. Gifford was a member of the Society of American Artists; American Water Color Society; National Arts Club; Society of London Painters; Royal Society of Painters and Etchers, London. He painted "Near the Ocean," and is represented at the Corcoran Gallery by "October on Massachusetts Coast."

GIFFORD, (Sanford R.). Painter. Born at Greenfield, N. Y., 1823. Graduate of Brown University, 1842. Pupil of J. R. Smith and the National Academy of Design, New York. Elected National Academician, 1854. Studied in Paris and Rome, 1855 to 1857; traveled also in Italy, Greece, Syria, Egypt and through the Rocky Mountains. Died in New York, 1880. He was one of the first American painters to depart from the conventions of the old school and create a broader and higher style. He painted "The Villa Malta," "Sunset on the Lake," "Near Palermo"; and he is represented at the Corcoran Gallery, Washington, D. C., by "Ruins of the Parthenon."

GIGNOUX, F. Regis. Landscape and historical painter. Born in France in 1816. He came to America in 1844. Elected National Academician in 1851. His best known landscapes are "Niagara Falls," "Virginia in Indian Summer," "Mount Washington," and "Spring." He died in 1882.

GIHON, Albert Dakin. Painter. Born Portsmouth, N. H., 1876. Pupil of Thomas Eakins, Philadelphia; Benjamin Constant, Jean Paul Laurens, Gerome, A. T. G. Motley, and École des Arts Decoratifs in Paris. Exhibited, Paris Expn., 1900; also exhibited at the old and new Salons, Paris; the Royal Academy, London, and by special invitation, at Society of American Artists, New York, and the Penna. Academy Fine Arts, Philadelphia. He has had an art school in Paris since 1898, and landscape classes in the country in summer. Represented in various public and private collections in U. S. and abroad. Special exhibition of pictures at Corcoran Gallery, Washington, D. C., 1917. Picture "Soir D'Automne," accepted by French Govt. for American section at Luxembourg Gallery, Paris, 1919. *Address,* 59 Avenue de Saxe, Paris, France.

GIHON, Clarence Montfort. Painter. Born Philadelphia, 1871. Pupil of Chase and Cox in New York; Laurens and Constant in Paris. *Address,* 51 Boulevard St., Jacques, Paris, France.

GILBERT, Arthur Hill. Painter. Exhibited in National Academy of Design, 1925. *Address,* Los Angeles, Calif.

GILBERT, Caroline. Designer and etcher. Born Pardeeville, Wis., in 1864. Pupil of Art Students' League of New York. Member: St. Paul Institute Artists' Society. *Address,* Mechanic Arts High School, St. Paul, Minn.

GILBERT, Charles Allan. Illustrator, painter. Born Hartford, Conn., 1873. Pupil of Art Students' League of New York; Constant and Laurens in Paris. Illustrated "Women of Fiction"; "A Message from

Mars.'' *Address*, 251 East 61st St., New York, N. Y.

GILBERT, Grove Sheldon. Born in Clinton, N. Y., 1805. In 1834 he settled in Rochester, N. Y. He devoted himself to portraiture. In 1848 he was elected an honorary member of the National Academy of Design of New York. He died in 1885.

GILBERT, Sarah. Painter of flowers and several figure pieces. She was a student of the Cooper Institute, and for years had her studio in New Haven, Conn., and exhibited at the New Haven Art Building.

GILCHRIST, W. Wallace. Painter. Born 1879. Studied at Penna. Academy of Fine Arts, and in Munich, Paris and London. Awards: Third Hallgarten prize, National Academy of Design, 1908; gold medal, Washington, D. C., Society Artists, 1914. Work: ''The Model's Rest,'' at Cincinnati Museum. *Address*, Brunswick, Me.

GILDEMEISTER, Charles. Lithographer. Signed a ''View of the Narrows'' and a ''View of the Hudson River, from Fort Lee.'' Published by Seitz in 1851.

GILDER, Robert F. Painter. Born Flushing, N. Y., 1856. Pupil of August Will in New York. Work: ''Where Rolls the Broad Missouri,'' University Club, Omaha; ''Sunshine and Shadow,'' Omaha Friends of Art Association; ''Winter Morning,'' St. Paul Institute; ''Desert Clouds,'' Philip Payne Memorial, Amherst College; ''Arizona Desert'' and ''San Gabriel Canyon, California,'' Omaha Public Library. *Address*, World Herald Bldg., Omaha, Nebraska.

GILES, Charles T. Born in New York, 1827; living in Brooklyn, N. Y., in 1900. This reputable line-engraver of landscape and historical subjects began work in New York, in 1847, and was practising his profession as late as 1898.

GILES, Howard. Painter and illustrator. Born Brooklyn, N. Y., 1876. Pupil of Art Students' League of New York, under Mowbray. Elected Associate Member of the National Academy. Represented in Pennsylvania Academy of the Fine Arts; Chicago Art Institute. *Address*, 35 West 14th St., New York, N. Y.

GILKISON, Mrs. A. H. Painter. Member: Pittsburgh Artists' Association. *Address*, 226 West Swissvale Ave., Pittsburgh, Pa.

GILL, Paul L. Landscape painter. Exhibited water colors at Exhibition at the Penna. Academy of Fine Arts, Philadelphia, 1922. *Address*, 260 South 17th St., Philadelphia.

GILLAM, F. Victor and T. Bernard. Illustrators for *Harper's Weekly* and other papers and magazines. They were born in England, but came to this country and settled in New York. Their work suggests the work of Tenniel.

GILLESPIE, George. Painter. Member: Pittsburgh Artists' Association. *Address*, 711 Penn Ave., Pittsburgh, Pa.

GILLESPIE, Jessie. Illustrator. Born Brooklyn, N. Y. Pupil of Penna. Academy of Fine Arts. Member: Plastic Club. *Address*, 5909 Wayne Ave., Germantown, Philadelphia.

GILLESPIE, W. Engraving on steel in Pittsburgh, Pa., about 1845, he made a line map of Pittsburgh and vicinity, ''Designating the portion destroyed by fire April 10th, 1845.'' It is signed as ''Eng'd by W. Gillespie.''

GILLIAM, Marguerite Hubbard. Painter. Born Boulder, Colo., 1894. Pupil of Edwin H. Blashfield; Emil Carlsen; John Sloan; Hugh H. Breckenridge. Member of Fellowship, Penna. Academy of Fine Arts. *Address*, 1216 20th St., Boulder, Colo.

GILLINGHAM, Edwin. A map of Boston and its vicinity, made from an actual survey by John G. Hales, is signed ''Edwin Gillingham Sc.''

GILMAN, J. W. He engraved the music and words in ''The American Harmony, or Royal Melody Complete, etc.,'' in two volumes, by ''A. William Tan'sur, Senior, Musico Theorico,'' and by ''A. Williams, Teacher of Psalmody in London.'' The book was ''Printed and Sold by Daniel Bayley, at his House next Door to St. Paul's Church, Newbury-Port, 1771.'' A study of the ''Gilman Genealogy'' leads the writer to assume that this engraver was John Ward Gilman, born in Exeter, Mass., 1741, who died in the same place, 1823. There is no record of the career of John Ward Gilman, other than that he was postmaster of Exeter for forty years.

GILMORE, Ada. Painter and wood engraver. Born in Kalamazoo, Mich., 1882. Studied with Henri in New York; Art Institute of Chicago; and in Paris. Work: ''Parasols,'' purchased by Municipal Art Commission, Chicago. *Address*, Provincetown, Mass.

GILPIN, Charles Armour. Painter. Born Cumberland, Md., 1867. Work: ''Relic of 1824,'' owned by ''Hundred Friends of Pittsburgh Art.'' *Address*, 5818 Alder St., Pittsburgh, Pa.

GIMBER, Stephen H. Engraver and lithographer. Born in England in 1810, he there learned to engrave, but was working at his profession in New York as early as 1830; in 1832–33 his name is associated on plates with that of A. L. Dick of that city. His name is found in the New York directories until 1842, when he probably removed to Philadelphia, as he was in business in the latter city, as an engraver and lithographer, after 1856. Gimber was a good portrait engraver in stipple and mezzotint, and his early subject plates are in line; he also drew portraits upon stone, and printed miniatures. He died in Philadelphia in 1862.

GIMBREDE, Joseph Napoleon. Born at West Point, N. Y., in 1820. He was a son of Thomas Gimbrede and learned to engrave with his uncle, J. F. E. Prud'homme. J. N. Gimbrede was in business as an engraver in New York in 1841–45, producing portraits and subject plates. He was later a stationer with an establishment under the Metropolitan Hotel, 588 Broadway, New York.

GIMBREDE, Thomas. Engraver. Born in France in 1781; died at West Point, N. Y., 1832. Gimbrede came to the United States in 1802 as a miniature painter; but he was engraving some excellent portraits in the stipple manner for the New York publishers John Low and William Durell, as early as 1810. In 1816 he had an office at 201 Broadway, New York, and he furnished a considerable amount of work for the Philadelphia magazines, *The Port Folio* and *The Analectic*. On January 5, 1819, Thomas Gimbrede was appointed drawing-master at the Military Academy at West Point, and he remained in that position until his death. He continued to engrave, however, until late in life, as we find portrait plates engraved and published by him in 1831. He was a brother-in-law of J. F. E. Prud'homme, also an engraver of portraits in stipple.

GIMENO, Patricio. Painter. Born in Peru, S. A., 1865. Member of Oklahoma Art League. *Address*, 807 Jenkins Ave., Norman, Okla.

GINTHER, Walter K. Painter and etcher. Born Winona, Minn., in 1894. *Address*, 407 East 7th St., Winona, Minn.

GIRARDET, P. A well-engraved line and stipple plate was published in New York in 1857 and entitled "Winter Scene in Broadway." The plate is signed as engraved by "P. Girardet" from a painting by H. Sebron. As this is the only plate by this engraver known to the writer he can not say that the work was executed in the United States. The names of the engraver and painter are French, and though the scene is laid in New York, the plate may have been made abroad.

GIRARDIN, Frank J. Landscape painter. Born in Kentucky, 1856. Pupil of Cincinnati Art Academy. Represented by "The Hillside"

and "Lingering Snow" in Public Gallery, Richmond, Ind. *Address*, Redondo Beach, Calif.

GIRAULT. Miniature painter. Flourishing 1798 in New York.

GIRSCH, Frederick. Born in Germany, 1821; died in Mt. Vernon, N. Y., 1895. Left an orphan at an early age, young Girsch was forced to assist in the support of his mother and four sisters. Having received some instruction in painting from a local artist, one Carl Seeger, he earned some money by portrait painting, and his portrait of a Princess attracted such general attention that a sufficient sum was raised by subscription to enable him to pursue his art studies at the Royal Academy of Darmstadt.

Mr. Girsch finally settled in New York, and having in the course of his art studies learned to etch and to engrave in line, the first work executed by him in this country was done for the then *New Yorker Criminal Zeitung.* As was then the custom, this publication issued "premium" engravings, and Mr. Girsch engraved two of these—"Die Helden der Revolution" and "Niagara Falls." He rapidly improved in the quality of his line work and made a number of portraits for the publishers of New York City.

It was, however, as a bank-note engraver that Mr. Girsch did his best work and achieved a reputation. Mr. Girsch engraved the "De Soto Discovering the Mississippi" on the back of one of the early bank-notes; the head of "Liberty" on the fractional currency, and the portrait of Washington on a similar note.

At the age of seventy-three years Mr. Girsch engraved, in etching and in line, a large plate entitled "Grandma's Toast," which is an excellent piece of work; but another plate, "The Gypsy Girl," executed for "his own pleasure," about the same time, is in pure line, and is probably as meritorious a plate as was ever engraved by him.

GLACKENS, William J. Painter and illustrator. Born in Philadelphia in 1870. Pupil of Penna. Academy of Fine Arts; also studied abroad. Elected an Associate Member of National Academy of Design in 1906. *Address*, 10 West 9th St., New York.

GLADDING, K. C. Several rather poorly engraved "Rewards of Merit" are signed "K. C. Gladding Sc." There is no indication of the place of origin, other than that the plates are undoubtedly American. Judging from the "bank-note" ornamentation the date of the plates is about 1825–30.

GLAMAN, Mrs. F. F. Painter. Born in St. Louis, Mo., 1873. Pupil of Art Institute, Chicago. Specialty, animal subjects. *Address*, 2850 Lexington St., Chicago, Ill.

GLASS, James W. Painter. Born in 1825. He became a student of Huntington, and afterwards painted in England for a number of years. He died in New York City. He was particularly successful in his drawing of horses, and an equestrian portrait of the Duke of Wellington brought him first into prominence. He died in 1857.

GLEESON, Adele S. (Mrs.). Sculptor. Born in St. Louis, Mo., 1883. Student of St. Louis School of Fine Arts. *Address,* 115 Edwin Ave., Kirkwood, Mo.

GLEESON, Joseph Michael. Painter. Born in Dracut, Mass., 1861. Went to Munich to study art, 1885, and afterward made many trips to Europe, studying in France and Italy. Settled in New York as painter and illustrator of animal life. Writer about animal life for magazines. *Address,* Newfoundland, N. J.

GLENNY, Alice Russell (Mrs.). Painter and sculptor. Born in Detroit, Mich., 1858. Pupil of Chase in New York, and Boulanger in Paris. *Address,* 1150 Amherst St., Buffalo, New York.

GLOVER, DeWitt Clinton. Born in De-Ruyter, Madison County, N. Y., in 1817; died there 1836. He was the son of Daniel and Rhoda (Gage) Glover and the brother of D. Lloyd and Lloyd Glover. He early attempted engraving on wood and steel and to perfect himself in the art he entered the office of J. & W. Casilear in New York, where he made rapid progress; but he died at the age of nineteen.

GLOVER, D. L. Glover was an engraver of portraits and subjects, in line and in stipple. He was located in New York in 1850–55.

GLOVER, Lloyd. Engraver. Born in De-Ruyter, Madison County, N. Y., in 1825; he was living in 1859. He was the son of Daniel Glover, and the brother of D. Lloyd Glover, also an engraver. Lloyd Glover was taught to engrave under a Boston master and for several years he was the head of the New England branch of the Bank Note Engraving firm of "Danforth, Wright & Co." of New York. He finally abandoned engraving for commercial pursuits, residing at Lynn, Mass. He was said to be a man of decided literary and artistic attainments.

GOATER, John. Illustrator and engraver. He worked on the *Illustrated American News.*

GOBRECHT, Christian. Born in Hanover, York County, Pa., 1785; died in Philadelphia, 1844. Gobrecht was apprenticed to a clockmaker of Manheim, Lancaster County, Pa. He learned engraving and die-sinking, and as early as 1810 he engraved a creditable portrait of Washington for J. Kingston's "New American

Biographical Dictionary," published in Baltimore. About 1811 he removed to Philadelphia, and while especially engaged in sinking dies for medals and other work of that nature, he furnished a few good portrait plates for the publishers of that city. Among his better known dies may be mentioned the Franklin Institute medal of 1825, after a design by Thomas Sully; a portrait medal of Charles Willson Peale; the Seal of St. Peter's Church, Philadelphia. In 1836 Mr. Gobrecht was appointed draughtsman and die-sinker to the U. S. Mint in Philadelphia, and he designed and made the dies for the dollar of 1836. In 1840 he succeeded William Kneass as chief engraver to the Mint, and held this office until his death in 1844. The dies made by Mr. Gobrecht are justly esteemed for the artistic excellence of the work put upon them. Christian Gobrecht was the original inventor of the medal-ruling machine, a device whereby medals, etc., could be engraved directly from the relief face, and a plate thus prepared for reproduction upon paper.

GODDARD, Ralph Bartlett. Sculptor. Born Meadville, Pa., 1861. He was educated at the National Academy of Design; Art Students' League of New York; Academie Julien, Paris. His early years were devoted to the execution of many bronze bas-relief portraits of noted men, including a series of 12 of the foremost authors and poets of modern English literature; he made a specialty of portrait busts. The statue, the "Premiere Epreuve," now in the Detroit Museum of Fine Arts, was exhibited in Paris Salon, 1897; he completed for Robert Hoe the bronze heroic statue of "Gutenberg" erected at Grand and Sheriff Sts., New York; finished ideal statue, "Invictus," 1890. Member: National Sculpture Society. *Address,* Madison, Conn.

GODEFROID, F. All that we can find regarding this artist is that he was the father of another artist of that name. In 1807 he painted a portrait of merit of M. Fortin, master of a Masonic Lodge, which is now in the Louisiana State Museum. In 1809 he had a studio in South Burgundy Street, near Canal Street, New Orleans.

GODEFROY, Louis. Nothing is known regarding this artist except that we find him in the New Orleans directory of 1824 as "a painter, with his studio at 139 Tehoupitoulas street," and in 1830 at "31 Poydras, corner of Tehoupitoulas street."

GODWIN, Abraham. Engraver. Born in what is now Paterson, N. J., 1763; died there in 1835. Enlisted in a New York regiment as fife major, and he served until the close of the Revolutionary War. At this time Godwin became an apprentice to A. Billings, an indifferent engraver of book-plates, etc., located in New York. As an engraver Godwin apparently issued but few signed plates, and his work is akin to that of his master in quality.

GOETSCH, Gustav F. Painter and etcher. Born in Minneapolis, 1877. Pupil of Chase and Beckwith in New York and Julien in Paris. *Address,* 20 Elm Ave., Glendale, Mo.

GOFF, Sudduth. Painter. Born in Eminence, Ky., in 1887. Pupil of Benson and Hale. *Address,* 441 West 2d St., Lexington, Kentucky.

GOHL, Edward Heinrich. Painter. Born in Harrisburg, Pa., 1862. Pupil of Constant, Laurens, Bashet and Schommer in Paris. *Address,* Pearson Bldg., Auburn, N. Y.

GOLDBECK, W. D. Painter, sculptor and etcher. Born in St. Louis, Mo., 1882. Award: Cahn honorable mention, Art Institute of Chicago, 1911. Died in 1925.

GOLDBERG, Reuben Lucius. Illustrator. Born in San Francisco, 1883. Cartoonist on *Evening Mail* since 1907. *Address,* "Evening Mail," 25 City Hall Place, New York, N. Y.

GOLDIE, James L. Painter. Born in Dorchester, Mass., in 1892. Member of Conn. Academy of Fine Arts, Springfield, Mass. *Address,* 284 Oakland St., Springfield, Mass.

GOLDSBOROUGH, Mrs. N. Cox. Died in 1923. She painted a number of portraits and exhibited at the Paris Salons.

GOLDSWORTHY, Emelia M. Painter. Born in Platteville, Wis., 1869. Pupil of Art Institute of Chicago, and of Otis Art Institute, Los Angeles, Calif. *Address,* Art Director, Western States Normal School, Kalamazoo, Mich.

GOLDTHWAIT, G. H. This man, apparently a bank-note engraver, was working in Boston in 1842. There is a "Miniature County Map of the United States, Drawn, Engraved and Published by G. H. Goldthwait, Boston 1842." The map is embellished with a border of small views of public buildings, natural scenery, etc.

GOLDTHWAITE, Anne. Painter and etcher. Born in Montgomery, Ala. Pupil of National Academy of Design under Mielatz in New York; Academie Moderne in Paris. Member: National Academy of Women Painters and Sculptors; New York Water Color Club. Award: prize, National Academy of Women Painters and Sculptors. Work: In Library of Congress, Washington, D. C. *Address,* 35 West 10th St., New York, N. Y.

GOLTZ, Walter. Painter. Born Buffalo, N. Y., 1875. Pupil of Mowbray and Birge Harrison. *Address,* Woodstock, N. Y.

GONZALES, Boyer. Painter. Born Houston, Tex., 1867. Pupil of Wm. J. Whittemore in New York; Walter Lansel in Boston; Art Students' League at Woodstock, N. Y.; studied in Holland, Paris and Florence; painted with Winslow Homer. Represented in Galveston Art League; Municipal Schools of Galveston; Delgado Museum, New Orleans, La. *Address,* 3327 Avenue O, Galveston, Tex.

GOODALL, Albert Gallatin. Engraver. Born in Montgomery, Ala., 1826; died in New York, 1887. In 1844 he went to Havana and there learned copperplate engraving. He removed to Philadelphia in 1848, commenced to engrave bank-notes on steel, and later connected himself with the New York company, which became in time the American Bank Note Co. Goodall was president of this conmpany for the last twelve years of his life.

GOODELMAN, Aaron J. Sculptor, illustrator and etcher. Born in Russia in 1890. *Address,* 25 East 14th St., New York.

GOODING, William C. Portrait painter. In the *Ontario Messenger,* published in Canandaigua, N. Y., 1815, Mr. William C. Gooding advertised to do "Portrait and Miniature Painting."

GOODMAN, Charles. Engraver. Born in Philadelphia about 1790; died there in 1830. Goodman was a pupil of David Edwin, and a good engraver in the stipple manner. When he had learned his business he and his fellow apprentice, Robert Piggot, founded the firm of Goodman & Piggot and produced a considerable number of portraits, etc., in Philadelphia.

GOODMAN, Walter. Painter. Born in England in 1838. He resided in Cuba for five years. He was in the United States in 1870. He devoted himself to portrait painting, and also did illustrating.

GOODRICH, J. H. Painter. Born Colon, St. Joseph County, Mich., 1878. Pupil of Gies in Detroit; Freer in Chicago. *Address,* 2119 24th Ave., North Nashville, Tenn.

GOODRIDGE, Sarah. Miniature artist. Was born in Massachusetts in 1788. She early showed a love of art, but did not have the means to study. Miss Goodrich was largely self-taught and it was not till about 1812 that she went to Boston and began painting miniatures; here she was introduced to Gilbert Stuart, who gave her the only real instruction that she ever received. Her miniature of Stuart is in the Metropolitan Museum, New York; others of her miniatures are owned by the Boston Museum and Mr. Herbert Pratt of New York. A memoir of Sarah Goodridge will be found in Mason's "Life and Works of Gilbert Stuart." She died in 1853.

GOODWIN, Alice H. (Mrs.). Painter. Born in Hartford, Conn., 1893. Pupil of Emil Carlsen. Member of Fellowship of Penna. Academy of Fine Arts, Philadelphia. *Address,* 3927 Locust St., Philadelphia.

GOODWIN, Arthur Clifton. Painter and illustrator. Born in Portsmouth, N. H., 1866. Exhibited at Annual Exhibition of Penna. Academy of Fine Arts, Philadelphia, 1924. *Address,* 139 West 54th St., New York.

GOODWIN, Frances M. Sculptor. Born in Newcastle, Ind. She commenced her art study at Indianapolis, Ind., and studied later at the Chicago Art Institute, where she became interested in modeling, and abandoned her intention of becoming a painter for the study of sculpture. She studied at the Art Students' League, New York, with D. C. French as instructor. Except as stated she was self-taught. Among her works are: Statue representing Indiana, for Columbian Exposition; bronze bust of Capt. Everett, Riverhead Cemetery, New York; marble bust of Schuyler Colfax, Senate gallery; bust of "Robert Dale Owen" for the statehouse at Indianapolis, Ind.

GOODWIN, Gilberta D. Painter. Born in Burlington, Vt., 1888. Pupil of John F. Weir; Edwin Taylor; G. A. Thompson; Hayes Miller. *Address,* 847 East Blvd., Weehawken, N. J.

GOODWIN, Helen M. Miniature painter. Born in Newcastle, Ind. Pupil of Collin and Courtois in Paris. *Address,* 320 South Main St., Newcastle, Ind.

GOODWIN, Philip R. Painter and illustrator. Born in Norwich, Conn., 1882. Pupil of R. I. School of Design; Howard Pyle; Art Students' League of New York. *Address,* Grove and Louis Sts., Mamaroneck, N. Y.

GORDON, Frederick Charles. Painter. Born at Cobourg, Ont., 1856; died in 1924. Studied at Art Students' League, New York, and Julien and Colarossi Academies, Paris. Began work 1882, at Toronto, Can., and came to U. S. in 1886; painter of portraits, landscapes, genre, etc., but during recent years he has devoted his attention chiefly to decorative drawings for publications.

GORDON, Leon. Sculptor. Born Bonsor, Russia, 1888. Pupil of Art Institute of Chicago; Art Students' League of New York. *Address,* 80 West 40th St., New York, N. Y.

GORE, Thomas H. Painter and designer. Born in Baltimore, Md., 1863. Studied with Duveneck. Member: Cincinnati Art Club. *Address,* 211 Pleasant St., Covington, Ky.

GORSON, Aaron Harry. Painter. Born in Russia, in 1872. He came to America in 1889.

Pupil of Penna. Academy of Fine Arts; Julien Academy, Constant and Laurens in Paris. Specialty, views of factories. *Address,* 6 West 28th St., New York City.

GOSHORN, John T. Painter. Born near Independence, Ia., 1870. Pupil of Art Institute of Chicago, and Smith Art Academy. *Address,* 512 Washington Bank Bldg., Pittsburgh, Pa.

GOSS, John. Painter and illustrator. Born at Lewiston, Me., in 1886. *Address,* 384A, Boyleston St., Boston, Mass.

GOSSELIN, Lucien H. Sculptor. Born in Whitefield, N. H., 1883. Pupil of Verlet, Bouchard and Landowski. *Address,* Paris, France.

GOTHELF, Louis. Painter. Born in Russia, 1901. Pupil of National Academy of Design, New York. *Address,* 322 Beacon St., Toledo, Ohio.

GOTTHOLD, Florence W. (Mrs.). Painter. Born in Uhrichsville, Ohio, 1858. Pupil of H. Siddons Mowbray. *Address,* Carnegie Studios, New York.

GOTTWALD, Frederick C. Painter. Born in 1860. Pupil of Art Students' League, New York. Represented in Cleveland Museum by "The Umbrian Valley, Italy." *Address,* 2031 East 100th St., Cleveland, Ohio.

GOULD, Carl Frelinghuysen. Painter. Born in New York in 1873. Pupil of William Sartain, and École des Beaux Arts, Paris. *Address,* 710 Hoge Building, Seattle, Washington.

GOULD, Thomas R. Sculptor. Born in Boston in 1818. He studied with Seth Cheney. His two colossal heads of "Christ" and "Satan" were exhibited at the Boston Athenaeum in 1863. His most celebrated statue was the "West Wind"; among his portrait busts were those of Emerson, Seth Cheney, and the elder Booth. He died in 1881.

GOULD, Walter. Born in Philadelphia in 1829, he studied under J. R. Smith and Thomas Sully. He became a member of the Artists' Fund Society of Phila. His subjects are generally oriental, a reminiscence of his travels in Egypt and Asia. He visited Constantinople and painted pictures of many important persons there.

GOVE, Elma Mary. Portrait draughtsman in crayons. She was working in New York in 1851–55.

GRABACH, John R. Painter and sculptor. Born in Newark, N. J., 1886. Pupil of Art Students' League of New York. Awarded Peabody prize at Art Institute of Chicago, 1924. *Address*, 900 South Grove St., Irvington, N. J.

GRAF, Carl C. Painter. Born in 1890. Pupil of Herron Art Institute. *Address*, 43 Union Trust Bldg., Indianapolis, Ind.

GRAFLY, Charles. Sculptor. Born in Philadelphia, 1862. Pupil of Penna. Academy of Fine Arts, and Chapu and Dampt, Paris. Member of International Jury of Awards, St. Louis Expn., 1904; Instructor in Sculpture, Penna. Academy of Fine Arts, since 1892. Represented in permanent collections of Penna. Academy of Fine Arts; Detroit Art Museum; St. Louis Museum; Carnegie Institute, Pittsburgh; Boston Museum. Member of Municipal Art Jury, Philadelphia National Academy, 1906. Member: National Institute Arts and Letters; National Sculpture Society; Architectural League; Philadelphia Art Club. Executed much notable work in busts, life size; colossal figures and portrait and ideal figures, and groups, largely in bronze. George D. Widener gold medal, 1913; Watrous gold medal, National Academy, 1918. *Address*, 20th and Cherry Sts., Philadelphia, Pa.

GRAFTON, Robert W. Painter. Born in Chicago, Ill., 1876. Pupil of Art Institute of Chicago; Julien Academy in Paris; also studied in Holland and England. Has executed some excellent mural panels. *Address*, 131 West 2d St., Michigan City, Ind.

GRAHAM, A. W. Engraver. Born in England, he studied engraving under Henry Meyer, a well-known London engraver. He came to the United States about 1832, and in 1834 he engraved some excellent views for the *New York Mirror*. He engraved a few portraits at a later date; but his best work is to be found in the small plates executed for the "Annuals" of 1835-40. Graham was located in Philadelphia in 1838-40, and in 1844-45, according to the directories of that city; he was living in New York as late as 1869.

GRAHAM, Elizabeth. Miniature painter. Exhibited at the Penna. Academy of Fine Arts, Philadelphia, 1925. *Address*, 240 Fulton St., Brooklyn, New York.

GRAHAM, George. Of this clever engraver in mezzotint and in stipple, little more is known than that he was seemingly located in Philadelphia in 1797, and was working for New York publishers in 1804. He designed and apparently engraved a frontispiece for the "Proceedings of the Society of the Cincinnati," published in Boston in 1812, and he was again engraving in Philadelphia in 1813. A. G. Graham is referred to in "Nagler's Lexicon" as an "engraver in the stipple manner," but this man was publishing prints in London in 1799.

GRAHAM, P. Purdon. This name, as engraver, is signed to a well-executed line-engraving of Cadwallader Colden, after a portrait painted by Matthew Pratt, and belonging to the Chamber of Commerce of New York. The work was probably done about 1870-75, but nothing more is known about the engraver.

GRAHAM, Miss Payson. Sculptor and illustrator. Member of Art Students' League of New York. *Address*, 251 West 81st St., New York.

GRAHAM, Robert A. Painter. Born in Brooklyn, N. Y., 1873. Pupil of Art Students' League of New York. *Address*, 1931 Broadway, New York.

GRAHAM, William. Born in New York, but has spent many years in Rome. Paints generally Roman and Venetian landscapes. "Outside the Porto del Popolo, Rome," (signed) "W. Graham, 1874, Rome," exhibited at Penna. Academy of Fine Arts.

GRANDIN, Elizabeth. Painter. Born in Hamden, N. J. Pupil of Henri and Dow, and Guerin in Paris. *Address*, 154 Carnegie Hall, New York.

GRANER, Luis. Portrait, genre and landscape painter of great versatility. Born in Barcelona, Spain, 1867. Came to America in 1910, and lived and painted in New Orleans from 1914 to 1922, at intervals, and therefore can be classed as an American painter. Received medals at Barcelona, Madrid, Berlin, Paris, and in many other places. In 1904 he was made a member of the "Societie Nationale des Beaux Arts," France. Represented in art museums, Madrid and Barcelona, Spain; Brussels, Belgium; Bordeaux, France; Berlin, Germany; and in the National Museums of Brazil, Chile, Argentina and Uruguay, and in the Papal gallery, Rome. His work possesses those qualities of technique, color, simplicity and dignity which place him in the front rank of painters.

GRANGER, Caroline Gibbons. Painter. Exhibited at the Penna. Academy of Fine Arts, Philadelphia, in 1924. *Address*, 1016 South Forty-sixth St., Philadelphia, Pa.

GRANT, Catherine. Painter. Exhibited at the Pennsylvania Academy of Fine Arts, Philadelphia, in 1924. *Address*, Bellwood, Penna.

GRANT, Charles Henry. Marine painter. Born at Oswego, N. Y., 1866. Studied at National Academy of Design, New York; San Francisco Art Institute. Exhibited in leading cities; also San Francisco Expn., 1915; principal works: "Will the Anchors Hold?"; "Ship Off the Starboard Bow"; "Nearing Port"; "At the Mercy of Neptune"; "Under Sealed Orders"; "The Arrival of the Atlantic Battle

Ship Fleet at the Golden Gate, 1908.'' *Address,* The Bohemian Club, San Francisco, Calif.

GRANT, Clement Rollins. Painter. Born in Freeport, Me., 1849. Studied abroad, and on his return to this country established his studio in Boston and became a member of the Boston Art Club. His specialty is landscape and portrait work. Among his paintings are ''Amy Wentworth,'' ''Marguerita,'' and a ''Normandy Fisherman.''

GRANT, Frederic M. Painter, illustrator and etcher. Born Sibley, Iowa, 1886. Pupil of Chase, Miller, Vanderpoel and Jonas Lie. *Address,* 139 East Ontario St., Chicago, Ill.

GRANT, Gordon. Painter and illustrator. Born San Francisco, Calif., 1875. Pupil of Heatherley's and Lambeth's Schools in London. *Address,* 137 East 66th St., New York.

GRANT, Isaac H. Painter. Member: Conn. Academy of Fine Arts. *Address,* 10 Olds Place, Hartford, Conn.

GRANT, J. A little known portrait painter who was working in Philadelphia in 1829.

GRANT, J. Jeffrey. Painter. Exhibited at Annual Exhibition of Penna. Academy of Fine Arts, Philadelphia, 1924, and awarded Cahn prize at Chicago Art Institute, 1924. *Address,* 21 East Van Buren St., Chicago, Ill.

GRANT, Lawrence W. Painter. Born Cleveland, Ohio, 1886. Pupil of Chase in New York; Laurens and Lefebvre in Paris. *Address,* Studio Arcade, Bronxville, N. Y.

GRANVILLE-SMITH, W. Painter. (See Smith, W(alter) Granville.)

GRAVES, Abbott Fuller. Painter. Born Weymouth, Mass., 1859. Studied in 1888 under Georges Jeannin, Paris; pupil of Cormon 3 yrs. Has received various prizes in the U. S. and Europe; has done notable decorative work and executed much approved work in flower and figure paintings. *Address,* Kennebunkport, Maine.

GRAVES, Elizabeth Evans. Painter. Exhibited at National Association of Women Painters and Sculptors, New York, 1924. *Address,* 3705 Harrison St., Chevy Chase, Md.

GRAY, Charles A. Painter. Born in Iowa in 1857. Connected with Art Department of *Chicago Herald* and *Tribune.* He painted portraits of Presidents McKinley and Garfield, Eugene Field, Opie Read and many others. His portraits of J. Warren Keifer and M. G. Kerr are in the Capitol Bldg., Washington.

GRAY, Henry Peters. Painter. Born in New York in 1819. He began his art studies under Daniel Huntington, P. N. A., in 1839. He went to Europe in 1840, and fell under the magic spell of the old masters, whose secrets he endeavored to find out by much patient study and experiment. On his return in 1842 he was elected a National Academician, and later on, from 1869 to 1871, he held the office of president of that association. Painting portraits in New York, with an occasional figure picture, occupied the greater part of his artistic career, and ''The Origin of Our Flag'' was one of the last of his exhibits at the Academy. This was shown in 1875. His work shows his sound academic study, and his color is reminiscent of the golden tone of Titian or Correggio. Many of his portraits were of cabinet size. He died in New York in 1877.

GRAY, Kathryn. Painter. Born in Jefferson County, Kans., 1881. Pupil of Weber; Art Students' League of New York; and La Forge in Paris. *Address,* 939 Eighth Ave., New York, N. Y.

GRAY, Mary. Painter. Exhibited at National Academy of Design, New York, 1925. *Address,* 59 West 9th St., New York.

GRAY, Percy. Painter. Born in San Francisco, 1869. Studied in San Francisco and New York. *Address,* 628 Montgomery St., San Francisco, Calif.

GRAY, W. F. Painter. Born Philadelphia, Pa., 1866. Pupil of Penna. Museum and Penna. Academy of Fine Arts. *Address,* 10 South 18th St., Philadelphia, Pa.

GRAY & TODD. This firm was engraving diagrams and script-work in Philadelphia, in 1817.

GRAYDON, Alexander. Author, soldier and limner. Born in Bristol, Pa., 1752, and died 1818. He served in the Revolution, was taken prisoner, was exchanged, and received the appointment of Captain from Congress for raising recruits for the army. In 1811 he published ''Memoirs of a Life, chiefly passed in Penna. within the Last Sixty Years.'' In this he notes his love of drawing and painting. He is known to have copied Stuart's portrait of Washington, painted on glass, similar to those done in China about 1800, but not as well painted.

GRAYHAM, William. Painter. Born in 1832, and died in 1911. His ''Rainy Day in Venice'' is signed ''W. Grayham, Venezia 1885.''

GRAYSON, Clifford Prevost. Painter. Born in Philadelphia, 1857. Pupil of Gerome, École des Beaux Arts, Paris. Represented in the permanent collections of Corcoran Art Gallery, Washington, and Chicago Art Institute. *Address*, Century Association, 7 West 43d St., New York.

GREACEN, Edmund. Painter. Born in New York, 1877. Pupil of Chase and Du Mond in New York; studied in Europe. Award: Shaw purchase prize, Salmagundi Club, 1921. Elected Associate Member of National Academy. *Address*, 142 East 18th St., New York.

GREASON, William. Painter. Born in Canada in 1884. Pupil of Penna. Academy of Fine Arts; and Julien Academy, Paris. *Address*, 1504 Broadway, East Detroit, Mich.

GREATH. Miniature painter from Sweden who visited Philadelphia and, according to Chas. W. Peale, "painted for his own amusement."

GREATOREX, Eleanor. Painter. Born in New York City, 1854. She devotes her time to painting and illustration. Her flower painting has been frequently exhibited.

GREATOREX, Eliza. Painter. Born in Ireland in 1820, she came to America in 1836. Pupil of James and William Hart in New York. In 1869 she was elected an Associate of the National Academy, being the first woman to receive that recognition. Her work was in oils, and she also illustrated a number of publications. She died in 1897.

GREATOREX, Kathleen Honora. Painter. Born Hoboken, N. J., 1851. Studied art in New York, Rome and Munich. Besides decorative work and book-illustration, she has done much work in painting flower pieces, etc., which she has exhibited in the Paris Salon and elsewhere. Honorable mention, Paris Salon; gold medals, Philadelphia, Chicago and Atlanta Expns. Among her flower pieces she has exhibited the panels "Thistles" and "Corn" and "Hollyhocks."

GREAVES, William A. Painter. Born in Watertown, N. Y., 1847, he died in 1900. He studied under Thomas Le Clair, and was a student at the Cooper Institute of New York City. He resided at Utica, N. Y., for several years and in 1873 removed to Warrentown. He painted portraits of S. J. Randall, G. A. Grow, Matthew S. Quay, Gov. Fenton, and Gov. Beaver. His portraits of Randall and Grow are in the Capitol Bldg., Washington, D. C.

GREBEL, Alphonse. Painter. Member: Society of Independent Artists. *Address*, 174 St. Nicholas Ave., New York, N. Y.

GRECO, Daniel. Painter. Member: Pittsburgh Artists' Association. *Address*, 608 Fifth Ave.. New Kensington, Pa.

GREEN. An English portrait painter, who arrived in the Colonies about 1750 and painted portraits from then until towards 1785.

GREEN, Bernard I. Painter and etcher. Born Swerzen, Russia, in 1886. Pupil of Douglas Volk, Francis Jones, Edgar M. Ward and Pressig. Work: "Girl Reading," Museum of Oakland, Calif. *Address*, 1058 South Boulevard, The Bronx, New York, N. Y.

GREEN, Elizabeth Shippen. (See Mrs. Huger Elliott.)

GREEN, Mrs. Erik H. Painter. Member: Providence Art Club. *Address*, Oldtown, North Attleboro, Mass.

GREEN, Frank Russell. Genre painter. Born in Chicago, 1859. Studied art at Academie Julien, under Boulanger and Lefebvre, and under Collin and Courtois, Paris, France. Elected Associate Member of the National Academy. Member: American Water Color Society; New York Water Color Club. *Address*, Salmagundi Club, 47 5th Ave., New York City.

GREEN, Fred Stuart. Painter. Born in North Stonington, Conn., 1876. Pupil of Rhode Island School of Design. Member of Providence Water Color Club. *Address*, "Ye Hollie Studio," Westerly, R. I.

GREEN, Harold. Painter. Born in Montreal, Canada, 1883. Pupil of Flagg and Brandagee. *Address*, 284 Asylum St., Hartford, Conn.

GREEN, Hiram H. Painter, illustrator and etcher. Born in New York State in 1865. Pupil of Mowbray, Cox and Bridgman. *Address*, Fort Erie, Ontario, Canada.

GREEN, Mildred C. Painter and illustrator. Born in Paris in 1874. Pupil of Bridgman, Hitchcock and Dufner. *Address*, Fort Erie, Ontario, Canada.

GREENBERG, Maurice. Illustrator. Born in Milwaukee, Wis., in 1893. Pupil of Wisconsin School of Art. *Address*, 608 South Dearborn St., Chicago, Ill.

GREENBERG, Morris. Etcher. Pupil of Birge Harrison and Maynard. Member of Brooklyn Society of Etchers. *Address*, 563 Howard Ave., Brooklyn, N. Y.

GREENE, Albert V. Painter. Born Jamaica, L. I., in 1887. Pupil of Corcoran Art Gallery and Penna. Academy of Fine Arts. *Address*, 223 North 11th St., Philadelphia, Pa.

GREENE, A. Van Nesse. Painter. Exhibited water colors and pastels at Exhibition of the Penna. Academy of Fine Arts, Philadelphia, 1922. *Address*, Penna. Academy of Fine Arts, Philadelphia.

GREENE, E. D. E. Painter. He was elected National Academician of Design, New York, 1858. He painted several beautiful female portraits, some of them ideal, and remarkable for exquisite finish. He died in 1879.

GREENFIELD, E. J. Forrest. Painter. Born in England in 1866. Member of Society of Independent Artists. *Address*, Point Pleasant, N. J.

GREENING, Harry C. Illustrator and cartoon artist. Born in Titusville, Pa., in 1876. Pupil of Art Students' League of New York. *Address*, 350 Madison Avenue, N. Y.

GREENLEAF, Benjamin. A painter of portraits who was working in New England about 1817.

GREENLEAF, Richard C. Painter. Born in Germany in 1887. Pupil of Collin, Courtois, Simon and Menard in Paris. *Address*, Lawrence, L. I., N. Y.

GREENMAN, Frances C. (Mrs.). Painter. Born in Aberdeen, S. D., 1890. Pupil of Chase and Benson. Received gold medal at Corcoran Gallery, and first award for portraits. *Address*, 2212 Pleasant Ave., Minneapolis, Minn.

GREENOUGH, Horatio. Sculptor. Born in 1805, and died in 1852. He made the design used afterwards for the construction of the Bunker Hill Monument; his colossal statue of "Washington" stands in front of the National Capitol.

GREENOUGH, John. A little known portrait painter who worked about 1840. He painted some excellent portraits. Was born in 1801 and died in Paris in November, 1852.

GREENOUGH, Richard S. Sculptor. Born in Jamaica Plain, Mass., in 1819. He was a younger brother of Horatio Greenough and worked for some years in Paris. Greenough had a studio in Newport, R. I. His statue of Benjamin Franklin is in City Hall Square, New York; and his "Boy and Eagle" is in the Boston Athenaeum. He died in 1905.

GREENWOOD, Ethan Allen. Painter. Born in 1779 and died 1856. He studied under Edward Savage and finally settled in Boston, and succeeded Savage in the ownership of the New England Museum. Greenwood frequently signed and dated his portraits "Greenwood Pinx 18." His portrait of Isaiah Thomas is reproduced in Goodspeed's edition of "Dunlap."

GREENWOOD, John. Painter and engraver. Born in Boston, New England, in 1727; died at Margate, England, 1792. Greenwood was a son of Samuel Greenwood of Boston and a nephew of Prof. Isaac Greenwood, of Harvard College.

In 1752 he went to Surinam, seemingly in a clerical capacity, and from there he went to Holland. In Holland he learned to engrave in the mezzotint manner. In 1763 he established himself in London as a painter and engraver of portraits.

Greenwood is sometimes referred to as an early American engraver, but there is no evidence that he ever practiced that art in this country. The portrait of Thomas Prince, engraved by Pelham in Boston in 1750, was painted by John Greenwood. In 1760 he engraved in mezzotint a beautiful portrait of himself. Greenwood's American portraits were all painted before 1752. His portrait of Benjamin Pickman of Salem, Mass., is dated 1749. His own portrait was engraved by Pether.

GREENWOOD, Joseph H. Painter. Born in Spencer, Mass., 1857. Pupil of R. Swain Gifford in New York. Represented by "Autumn," Worcester Art Museum. *Address*, 2 Woodbine St., Worcester, Mass.

GREER, Blanche. Painter and illustrator. Born at Eldora, Iowa, 1884. Pupil of Chase and Collins, and the Penna. Academy of Fine Arts. *Address*, 1840 Mintwood Place, Washington, D. C.

GREGORI, Luigi. Born in Italy, 1819. He came to the United States in 1874 and was made Art Director of the Art Department of the University of Notre Dame, Indiana. Historical and portrait painter; he has also been successful in fresco work and miniatures.

GREGORY. This name, as "Gregory Sc" is signed to a very crude line bible print, illustrating "Zachariah's Vision." As this print was found loose, there is no indication of place or date, though the apparent date is within the first quarter of the last century.

GREGORY, Eliot. Painter and sculptor. Born in New York in 1854. He entered Yale, studied in Rome and Paris and has exhibited both painting and sculpture in the Paris Salon. His pictures include "Soubrette," "Children," "Coquetterie," and portraits of Gen'l Cullum, Admiral Baldwin, and Ada Rehan. He died in 1915.

GREGORY, Frank M. Born in Mansfield, Tioga County, Pa., 1848. He studied at the National Academy of Design in 1871, and subsequently studied at the Art Students' League, and with Walter Shirlaw. He has done work in etching and design. In 1888 he illustrated "Faust."

GREGORY, John. Sculptor. Born in London in 1879. Pupil of Art Students' League of New York; later studied at the Beaux Arts, Paris. Sculptor of "Sir Launcelot," "The Eustis Memorial," at the Corcoran Art Gallery, Washington, D. C. *Address*, 126 East 38th St., New York City.

GREGSON, Marie E. (Mrs.). Painter. Born in New York City, 1886. Pupil of Twachtman and Cox. Member of National Association of Women Painters and Sculptors. *Address*, Bell Ave. and Rocky Hill Road, Bayside, Long Island, N. Y.

GREIMS, Mary Hearn (Mrs. Herbert S. Greims). Painter. Born in New York. Pupil of Cooper Union, and George Smillie in New York; Philadelphia School of Design for Women; Penna. Academy of Fine Arts, Philadelphia. Member of the Fellowship of the Penna. Academy of Fine Arts, and National Academy of Women Painters and Sculptors. *Address*, Ridgefield.

GREINER, Christopher. Portrait painter in oils and miniatures, flourishing in Philadelphia in 1837. Died in 1864. Portrait of "Daniel Billmeyer" is owned by the Historical Society of Penna.

GRENHAGEN, Merton. Portrait painter. Born near Oshkosh, Wis. Pupil of Chase in Philadelphia and Laurens in Paris. *Address*, Oshkosh, Wis.

GRIDLEY, Enoch G. This engraver in both stipple and line was in business in New York in 1803–05 inclusive, and at a later date he was working for Philadelphia publishers. The latest date on any of his plates noted by the compiler is 1818.

GRIFFIN, Thomas B. Landscape painter.

GRIFFIN, Walter. Landscape painter. Born in Portland, Me., 1861. Studied at Boston Museum of Fine Arts; Art Students' League of New York; in Paris, France. Pupil of R. Collin and Jean Paul Laurens. He lived principally in France, 1887–1915, making occasional visits to U. S. He was art instructor and director of School of Art Society of Hartford, Conn. Represented in Memorial Art Gallery, Rochester, N. Y.; Albright Art Gallery, Buffalo, and in many private collections. Elected Associate Member of the National Academy, and member of American Artists' Association, Paris. *Address*, Portland, Me.

GRIFFING, Martin. Painter of colored profiles. Born in 1784, and died in 1859. He worked in Massachusetts, Vermont, and New York.

GRIFFITH, C. Beatrice B. (Mrs. C. F. Griffith). Sculptor. Born Hoylake, Cheshire, Eng., 1890. Pupil of Giuseppe Donato. Work: Marble portrait of "Edith Wynne Mathison," Bennett School, Millbrook, Conn.; marble portrait, "President Ewing," Lahore Union College, Lahore, India; portrait of Howard B. French in College of Pharmacy, Philadelphia. *Address*, 1830 South Rittenhouse Square, Philadelphia, Pa.

GRIFFITH, Conway. Painter. Member of Laguna Beach Art Association. His specialty was marine and desert scenes. He died at Laguna Beach, Calif., in 1924.

GRIFFITH, Lois Oscar. Landscape painter and etcher. Born in Greencastle, Ind., 1875. Pupil of Frank Reaugh; St. Louis School of Fine Arts; Art Institute of Chicago; also studied in New York and Paris. Represented in Union League Club of Chicago, "Winter," Chicago Commission purchase; Delgado Museum, New Orleans, La.; Oakland (Calif.) Museum. *Address*, 1702 Auditorium Tower, Chicago, Ill.

GRIFFITH, W. A. Painter. Born Lawrence, Kans., 1866. Pupil of St. Louis School of Fine Arts; Lefebvre and Constant in Paris. *Address*, Laguna Beach, Calif.

GRIFFITHS, Elsa Churchill. Miniature painter. *Address*, 1114 9th Ave., West, Seattle, Washington.

GRIGWARE, Edward T. Painter and illustrator. Born in Caseville, Mich., 1889. Pupil of Chicago Academy of Fine Arts. *Address*, 1204 Century Bldg., 202 State St., Oak Park, Illinois.

GRIMALDI, William. Miniature painter. Born in England, 1750; died in London in 1830. He worked in Paris from 1777–85, and in London, 1786–1824, exhibiting yearly. He is said to have visited the United States about 1794, but it is doubtful if he ever came to this country. A portrait of George Washington in military uniform somewhat similar to the Trumbull type, signed "Grimaldi," was recently sold in Philadelphia.

GRIMES, Frances. Sculptor. Born in Braceville, Ohio, in 1869. Pupil of Pratt Institute in Brooklyn. Member: National Sculpture Society; National Academy of Women Painters and Sculptors. Work: Overmantel, Washington Irving High School, New York City; "Girl by Pool" and "Boy with Duck," Toledo Museum of Art. Bust of Bishop Potter, Grace Church, N. Y. *Address*, 229 East 48th St., New York, N. Y.

GRIMES, John. Painter. Born at Lexington, Ky., 1799. He studied under Matthew Harris Jouett, who painted his portrait, now owned by the Metropolitan Museum. Grimes painted for some time in Nashville, Tenn. He painted a portrait of Charles Wetherill owned in Germantown, and copied by Thomas Sully about 1853. He died in 1837.

GRINAGER, Alexander. Painter. Born in Minneapolis, Minn. Pupil of Royal Academy, Copenhagen, Denmark; Laurens and Constant in Paris; studied also in Norway, Italy and Sicily. *Address*, Mohegan Heights, Tuckahoe, N. Y.

GRISWOLD, Carrie. Painter. Born in Hartford, Conn. Studied under Leutze in New York City. She was a skilful copyist. She died in Florida.

GRISWOLD, Casimir Clayton. Painter. Born in Delaware, Ohio, 1834; died in 1918. He studied wood engraving in Cincinnati, but removed to New York in 1850. He received some instruction in painting from a brother and in 1857 exhibited his first picture at the National Academy of Design. Specialty, landscapes and coast scenes. He lived in Rome, Italy, 1872–86. Elected Associate Member of the National Academy in 1866; National Academy in 1867. He was one of the original members of the Artists' Fund Society. His best pictures were "December," exhibited in 1864; "A Winter Morning," 1865; "The Last of the Ice," 1866.

GROLL, Albert Lorey. Landscape painter. Born in New York in 1868. Studied in London and in Munich. Elected Member of National Academy, 1910. Represented in Metropolitan Museum; Boston Museum of Fine Arts; Corcoran Art Gallery; National Gallery, Washington, D. C. *Address*, 222 West 59th St., New York.

GROOM, Emily. Painter. Born in Wayland, Mass., 1876. Pupil of Art Institute of Chicago; Brangwyn in London. Member: National Academy of Women Painters and Sculptors. Work: "Hillside, November," St. Paul Institute, and in Milwaukee Art Institute. *Address*, Genesee Depot, Cambridge Ave., Milwaukee, Wis.

GROOME, Esther M. Painter and etcher. Born York County, Pa. Pupil of Fuchs, Castaigne, William M. Chase, Henri and Cecilia Beaux. Member: Fellowship, Penna. Academy of Fine Arts. *Address*, Library Bldg., State Normal School, West Chester, Pa.

GROOMRICH, William. An English landscape painter, who came to this country about 1800. He settled first in New York and later in Baltimore. He painted a view from Harlem Heights and other views around New York. He exhibited in 1811 at Philadelphia with the Society of Artists, giving his address as Baltimore.

GROOMS, Reginald. Painter. He painted "The Road to the River." *Address*, 3092 Madison Road, Oakley, Cincinnati.

GROPPER, William. Painter and illustrator. Born in New York in 1897. Pupil of Henri and Bellows. Illustrated "Chinese White"; "Diary of a Physician." *Address*, 149 West 14th St., New York.

GROSBECK, Dan Sayre. Painter and illustrator. *Address*, Care of Foster and Kleiser, 287 Valencia St., San Francisco, California.

GROSH, Peter Lehn. Born near Mechanicsville, Lancaster County, Pa., in 1798. Lived at same village, where he was a general utility artist and painter, as well as fruit and flower grower, until 1857. Painted a number of portraits, most of which were produced between 1820 and 1835. He was a versatile man, practically self-taught, though with much native ability in striking a likeness. He died at Petersburg, 1859. He painted Mr. and Mrs. John Beck; Peter and Samuel Grosh; Mrs. Samuel Grosh; "King and Jester"; etc.

GROSS, Albert R. Painter. Member: Charcoal Club. *Address*, 1230 St. Paul St., Baltimore, Md.

GROSS, J. This reputable engraver of portraits in stipple was working for the "National Portrait Gallery," published in 1834; he was probably one of the group of engravers brought to Philadelphia by James B. Longacre. J. D. Gross was engraving portraits in mezzotint about the same time, but the work is so inferior in execution to the stipple work of J. Gross that it must be executed by another man.

GROSS, Mrs. Juliet White. Painter. Born in Philadelphia, Pa., 1882. Pupil of Philadelphia School of Design; Penna. Academy of Fine Arts. Member: Fellowship, Penna. Academy of Fine Arts. *Address*, 232 De Lancey Place, Philadelphia.

GROSS, Oscar. Painter. Born in Vienna, Austria, in 1870. Pupil of Imperial Royal Academy of Fine Arts, Vienna. Studied in Munich and Paris. Work: "Dreams of Future," Chicago Municipal Commission Purchase.

GROSS, Richard. Painter. Was born in Munich in 1848, but taken to America as a child. Pupil of National Academy in New York. Among his important pictures was a portrait of "William Chambers," "Old Nuremberg," "The Savant," and "The Lady of Shalott."

GROSS, Sydney. Exhibited water colors in 1925 at the Annual Exhibition of Water Colors at the Penna. Academy of Fine Arts, Philadelphia. *Address*, 3335 North 17th St., Philadelphia.

GROSSMAN, Edwin Booth. Painter. Born in Boston, Mass., 1887. Pupil of Chase and Richard Miller. Member of Society of Independent Artists. *Address*, 133 East 21st St., New York.

GROSSMAN, Joseph B. Painter. Born in Russia, 1888. Pupil of Penna. Academy of Fine Arts. *Address*, 1523 Chestnut St., Philadelphia.

GROSVENOR, Thelma C. Illustrator. Born in Richmond, Va., 1891. Student of New York Artist Students' League and St. John's Wood School, London, England. Illustrations for *Harper's, Century, McClure's* and *Saturday Evening Post. Address*, 128 East 61st St., New York.

GROVE, Shelton Gilbert. Painter. Born in Clinton, N. Y., 1805; died in Rochester, 1885. Studied medicine, but gave it up for painting, his work being mostly portraiture.

GROVER, Oliver Dennett. Painter. Born Earlville, Ill., 1861. Student of University of Chicago; studied painting at Royal Academy, Munich; Duveneck School, Florence, Italy; and in Paris. Received first Yerkes prize for painting "Thy Will Be Done," Chicago, 1892; executed mural decorations, Branford, Conn., Memorial Library, 1897; Blackstone Memorial Library, Chicago, 1903. His pictures are in many public collections. Elected Associate Member of the National Academy, 1913. *Address*, 9 E. Ontario St., Chicago, Ill.

GROVES, Hannah C. Painter. Born in Camden, N. J., in 1868. Pupil of William M. Chase and School of Design, Philadelphia. *Address*, Pressor Bldg., Chestnut St., Philadelphia.

GRUB, Henry. Painter and sculptor. Born in Baltimore, Md., 1884. Pupil of Maynard, Ward and Bridgman. Member: New York Society of Independent Artists. *Address*, 53 Greenwich Ave., New York.

GRUELLE, Richard B. Landscape painter. Born in 1851. Among his best known paintings are "The Passing Storm" at Indianapolis Public Library; "A Gloucester Inlet" at the Herron Art Institute; "In Verdure Clad" at Public Gallery, Richmond, Ind. He died in Indianapolis in 1915.

GRUENBERG, Ruth. Painter. Exhibited at the Penna. Academy of Fine Arts, 1922. (Water colors.) *Address*, 3211 Oxford St., Philadelphia.

GRUGER, Frederic R. Illustrator. Born in Philadelphia in 1871. Studied at the Pennsylvania Academy of Fine Arts. *Address*, 57 West 57th St., New York.

GRUNEWALD, Gustavus. Painter. A Pennsylvania German artist who was painting landscapes in Bethlehem, Penna., in 1832.

GRUPPE, Charles Paul. Painter. Born Picton, Canada, 1860. Studied art in Holland. Represented in Library, Rouen, France; St. Louis Museum; Maryland Institute, Baltimore; and in numerous private galleries. *Address*, 58 West 57th St., New York.

GRUPPE, Emile A. Painter and illustrator. Born in Rochester, N. Y., 1896. Pupil of Bridgman and Carlsen, and the Art Students' League of New York. *Address*, 158 Manhattan Ave., New York.

GRUPPE, Karl H. Sculptor and painter. Born in Rochester, N. Y., 1893. Pupil of Karl Bitter the sculptor. He has modeled numerous figures and memorial tablets. *Address*, 141 Sixth Ave., New York.

GSCHWINDT, R. He painted some excellent portraits in New Orleans in 1859 and 1860, having a studio at 82 Camp Street. No date could be found regarding his birth or death.

GUARINA, Salvator Anthony. Painter and etcher. Born in Sicily, Italy. Pupil of Whittaker and Blum, and member of the Washington Art Club. *Address*, Care of Salmagundi Club, New York.

GUDEBROD, Louis Albert. Sculptor. Born in Middletown, Conn., in 1872. Studied at Art Students' League under Mary Lawrence and Augustus St. Gaudens, and in Paris, 1898–1900, under Jean Dampt and Augustus St. Gaudens. Executed portrait statue of Sieur de la Salle for St. Louis Expn.; monument on site of Andersonville Prison for State of N. Y., 1910; silver design, "Spirit of the West" (awarded gold medal). Member: National Sculpture Society. *Address*, 69 Silver St., Meriden, Conn.

GUE, David John. Portrait, landscape and marine painter. Born in Farmington, N. Y., 1836. He painted the portraits of Grant, Lincoln and Beecher. He died in Brooklyn, N. Y., in 1917.

GUERIN, Jules. Painter. Born in St. Louis, Mo., in 1866. He studied with Benjamin Constant and Jean Paul Laurens in Paris. Elected an Associate Member of the National Academy, New York. Executed the decorations in the Lincoln Memorial, and Pennsylvania Railroad Station, New York. *Address*, 24 Gramercy Park, New York.

GUERNSEY, Eleanor Louise. Sculptor. Born in Terre Haute, Ind., 1878. Pupil of Art Institute of Chicago. Member: Art Students' League of Chicago; Ind. Sculptors' Society.

Address, James Milliken University, Decatur, Illinois.

GUGLIELMO, Victor. Sculptor. Born in Italy. He has assisted Frank Happersburger in his work in San Francisco.

GUILLETT, Madame J. French miniature painter who flourished in New York, 1839–1842. She also painted many miniatures in Virginia.

GUINNESS, Mrs. Benjamin. Painter. Member: National Academy of Women Painters and Sculptors.

GUINZBERG, Frederic Victor. Painter and sculptor. Born in New York, 1897. Member: Society of Independent Artists. Studied at Art Students' League, and in France and Italy. *Address*, Chappaqua, N. Y.

GUISLAIN, J. M. Painter. Born in Louvain, Belgium, 1882. *Address*, 725 West 172d St., New York, N. Y.

GULLAGER, Christian. Born in 1762, and died in 1826. He painted excellent portraits in Boston from 1789 to nearly the day of his death. He painted a portrait of President Washington, also one of Geo. Richards Minot, Col. John May, Rev. James Freeman, Dr. Eliakin Morse, David West, Rev. Ebenezer Morse and Benjamin Goldthwait. His portraits are signed "Gullager."

GULLEDGE, Josephine. Painter. Member: Washington Water Color Club. *Address*, Fairmount Seminary, Washington, D. C.

GULLIVER, Mary. Painter. Born Norwich, Conn., 1860. Pupil of Boston Museum of Fine Arts School, under Grundmann, Vonnoh and Crowninshield; Whistler, Collin, Delance, Callot, Lazar and Prinet in Paris. *Address*, 1101 Orange Ave., Eustis, Florida.

GUNN, Archie. Painter, illustrator and etcher. Born Taunton, Somersetshire, England, 1863. Pupil of Archibald Gunn; P. Calderon in London. *Address*, 120 West 49th St., New York, N. Y.

GUNN, Edwin. Painter. Member: Salmagundi Club, New York. *Address*, 252 Mt. Hope Ave., New York, N. Y.

GUSSOW, Bernard. Painter. Born in Russia, 1880. Pupil of Bonnat in Paris. Member: Society of Independent Artists; Modern Artists of America. *Address*, 54 Charles St., New York, N. Y.

GUTHERS, Carl. Painter. Born in Switzerland in 1844. He came to America in 1851. His art training was received in America, and in 1868 he went to Paris. His work was mural, portrait, and genre subjects. Many of his portraits are in the Minnesota State Capitol. His mural paintings in the Library of Congress, Washington, D. C., are excellent. He died in 1907, in Washington, D. C.

GUTMANN, Bernhard. Illustrator and painter. Born in Hamburg, Germany, 1869. Studied in Dusseldorf and Karlsruhe, Germany, and in Paris. *Address*, Silvermine (R. F. D. No. 43), New Canaan, Conn.

GUY, Francis. Born in 1760 and died in 1820. Painted landscapes in Baltimore and Philadelphia about 1800. He was originally a tailor, and was self-taught. His style was crude and harsh. He exhibited a number of drawings and paintings at the Exhibition in 1811 of the Society of Artists in Philadelphia. About 1817 he returned to Brooklyn, N. Y., where he died.

GUY, Seymour J. Painter. Born in England, 1824. He came to America in 1854 and settled in New York. Pupil of Ambrosino Jerome in London. He was elected a member of the National Academy of Design in 1865. His portrait of the artist Chas. Loring Elliott (1868) is in the Metropolitan Museum. He has painted many scenes and incidents drawn from childlife, among them "The Good Sister," "The Little Stranger," and "The Little Orange Girl." He died in 1910.

GUYSI, Alice V. Painter. Born Cincinnati, Ohio. Pupil of Colarossi Academy, and of Harry Thompson in Paris. *Address*, 209 Longfellow Ave., Detroit, Mich.

GUYSI, Jeannette. Painter. Born Cincinnati, Ohio. Pupil of Colarossi Academy and of Harry Thompson in Paris. *Address*, 209 Longfellow Ave., Detroit, Mich.

GYBERSON, Indiana. Painter. Studied with Chase on Long Island, also studied in Paris, and while working on a picture for the Salon in 1912, nearly lost her sight from getting paint in her eyes. Her studio is now in Chicago, where she paints when her eyesight allows her.

GYER, E. H., Jr. Painter and illustrator. Born in Tacoma, Wash., in 1900. Pupil of O. Z. Heuston. *Address*, 5811 Junett St., Tacoma, Wash.

GUSTIN, Paul Morgan. Painter. Born in Fort Vancouver, Washington, in 1886. *Address*, 1115 35th St., Seattle, Wash.

H

HAAG, C. Miniature painter, who flourished in New York about 1848, and exhibited at the National Academy, New York.

HAAG, Charles. Sculptor. Born in Norrkoping, Sweden, 1867. Pupil of Junghaenel Ziegler, and Injalbert. Work: "Cornerstone of the Castle," in Winnetka; "Accord," Metropolitan Museum, New York; series of fountains, among them the "American Fountain," at Johnstown, Pa. Sculptor of symbolic and poetic art.

HACK, Gwendolyn Dunlevy Kelley (Mrs. Charles Hack). Painter. Born in Columbus, Ohio, in 1877. Educated in Art Students' League of New York; in Paris studied under Mesdames Debillement and Gallet. Specialties, miniatures on ivory, pastels, bas-reliefs etc.; painted portraits on ivory, Queen of Italy, 1895, and received decoration; exhibited paintings in Paris Salon; National Academy of Design; Chicago Art Institute; Cincinnati Art Museum and in other cities; also in Nashville and Omaha expositions. *Address,* 12 West 93d St., New York.

HACKETT, Grace E. Painter and illustrator. Born in Boston in 1874. Pupil of Mass. Normal Art School in Boston; H. B. Snell in Europe. *Address,* 297 Newbury St., Boston, Mass.

HADEN, Elmer S. Painter. Born in United States. Pupil of Flameng in Paris. *Address,* Nyack, N. Y.

HADLEY, Mary Hamilton. Painter. *Address,* 355 Willow St., New Haven, Conn.

HADLEY, Paul. Painter and designer. Born in Indianapolis, Ind. Pupil of Penna. Museum, Philadelphia. Member: Indiana Art Club. Work: Decoration in Eagle's Club, Indianapolis, Ind.; design for Indiana flag, accepted by the legislature, 1917. *Address,* 44 Union Trust Bldg., Indianapolis, Ind.

HAGEN, Louise. Painter. Born in Chicago, Ill., 1888. Pupil of Henri and Jonas Lie. *Address,* 130 West 57th St., New York.

HAGENDORN, Max. Painter. Born in Germany, 1870. *Address,* Bullard St., Sharon, Mass.

HAGER, Luther George. Illustrator and cartoonist. Born in Terre Haute, Ind., in 1885. *Address,* 655 Empire Building, Seattle, Wash.

HAGGIN, Ben Ali. Portrait and figure painter. Associate Member of the National Academy. His charming portrait of Miss Kitty Gordon is now famous, and his portrait of Mary Garden as Thais sold for $25,000. It is in the painting of the nude that he has had his greatest success. *Address,* 875 Madison Ave., New York.

HAGUE, Maurice Stewart. Painter. Born in Richmond, Ohio, in 1862. He studied medicine 3 years, but abandoned it for art. Followed portrait painting and modeling until 1895, then took up landscape painting. Represented in private collections in New York, Baltimore, Buffalo, Pittsburgh, Cleveland, Rochester and Columbus, Ohio, Gallery of Fine Arts. Exhibited at Boston, St. Louis, Minneapolis, Buffalo, Cleveland and Columbus. *Address,* 1470 Fair Avenue, Columbus, Ohio.

HAHN, Mrs. N. C. Sculptor. Born in St. Louis, Mo., in 1892. Pupil of Zolnay and Grafly. *Address,* 6171 Delmar Blvd., St. Louis, Mo.

HAHS, Philip B. Painter. Born in Reading, Penna., in 1853. He commenced preparing for a business career in Philadelphia, but employed his leisure in artistic experiments, and about 1872 he joined the Philadelphia Sketch Club. Here Mr. Hahs went on with his studies and also continued to receive instruction from Mr. Thomas Eakins. Mr. Hahs was considered almost unrivalled in technique. He was a regular contributor to the exhibitions, until at the Exhibition of the Philadelphia Society of Artists in 1881, in which he was represented by a landscape and four genre paintings, he was recognized as the foremost among the young artists of his period. About this time he was attacked by a severe illness, terminating, after some months, in his death, which occurred in Philadelphia, 1882.

HAIDT, John Valentine. Born in Germany in 1700. He emigrated to America and joined the Moravian Church. A gallery of his portraits and several other pictures are still preserved at Bethlehem, Penna. He died in 1780.

HAILMAN, Johanna K. W. (Mrs. James Hailman). Painter. Born in Pittsburgh in 1871. Member of the National Association of Women Painters and Sculptors. *Address,* 7010 Penn Ave., Pittsburgh, Pa.

HAINES, Bowen Aylesworth. Painter and illustrator. Born in Canada in 1858. *Address,* 402 Hayward Building, Rochester, N. Y.

HAINES, D. Engraver of business cards, etc., working in Philadelphia about 1820.

HAINES, Marie B. Painter and illustrator. Born in Cincinnati, Ohio, 1885. Among her best known works are a portrait of Dr. F. B. Clark, and ''The Path,'' at State College, Tex. *Address,* 368 Peachtree St., Atlanta, Ga.

HAINES, William. This excellent engraver of portraits in the stipple manner was born in 1778. He came from England to Philadelphia in 1802. He opened a studio at No. 178 Spruce St., and advertised that he painted portraits in water colors ''in a style entirely new in the United States,'' and his work of this description proves that Haines was a master of this branch of his art. He produced a number of good portrait plates for American publishers, and he also drew for other engravers. Haines returned to England about 1809, as his name disappears from the Philadelphia directory of 1810, and a subject plate engraved by ''W. Haines'' was published in London in 1809. He died in 1848.

HAKE, Otto E. Painter and illustrator. Born in Germany in 1876. Pupil of Art Institute, Chicago, and Matisse in Paris. *Address,* 29 Quince St., Chicago, Ill.

HALBERG, Charles Edw. Painter. Born in Sweden in 1855. Member of Chicago Society of Artists. *Address,* 1114 North Parkside Ave., Austin, Ill.

HALBERT, A. Engraver. He was a nephew of J. F. E. Prud'homme and was probably a pupil of that engraver. In 1835 he was working for the Harper Bros. in New York, and in 1838 he was in the employ of the engraving firm of Rawdon, Wright & Hatch, of the same city. Halbert was a good line engraver of portraits and vignettes; as his signed plates are very few in number he was probably chiefly engaged in bank-note work.

HALBERT, Samuel. Painter. Exhibited paintings at the Academy of Fine Arts, Philadelphia, 1921, in ''Exhibition of Paintings Showing the Later Tendencies in Art.'' *Address,* 128 West 85th St., New York.

HALE, Ellen Day. Born in Worcester, Mass., in 1855. Studied with Dr. Rimmer, Wm. Morris Hunt, and at the Academie Julien in Paris. She removed from Boston to Washington in 1904. Her portrait of John G. Carlisle is in the Capitol Bldg., Washington, D. C. *Address,* 1748 N. St., Washington, D. C.

HALE, Lilian Westcott (Mrs. Philip L. Hale). Portrait painter. Born in Hartford,

Conn., in 1881. Pupil of Tarbell and Chase. Member: Conn. Academy of Fine Arts; Concord Artists' Academy. Award: gold medal and medal of honor, Panama Pacific Exposition, San Francisco, 1915; gold medal, Philadelphia Art Club, 1919. Represented in the collection of the Penna. Academy of the Fine Arts and the Pennsylvania Club. *Address,* Dedham, Mass.

HALE, Mary P. (Mrs.). Painter and sculptor. Born in Kingston, R. I., 1862. Pupil of Rhode Island School of Design, and of Chase and Saint Gaudens. *Address,* 45 Middle St., Gloucester, Mass.

HALE, Philip L. Painter. Born in Boston in 1865. Son of Rev. Edw. Everett Hale. Studied under J. Alden Weir in New York and at Julien Academy, Paris. Elected an Associate Member of the National Academy of Design. *Address,* Fenway Studios, Boston, Mass.

HALE, Robert. Painter and etcher. Born in Chicago, Ill., 1876. *Address,* 670 Portland Ave., St. Paul, Minn.

HALE, Susan. Painter. Born in Boston, 1838. Specialty, landscape painting in water colors. She has exhibited a series of pictures of the White Mountains.

HALL, Anne. Miniature painter. Born in Pomfret, Conn., in 1792. When very young she received some instruction in miniature painting from S. King of Newport, who at one time had given lessons in oil painting to Washington Allston; she afterward studied painting in oil with Alexander Robertson in New York, but finally devoted herself to miniature painting. She was an exhibitor at the National Academy of Design in New York, and elected Academician in 1833. Among her best known works are a portrait of a Greek girl, which has been engraved, and a group representing Mrs. Dr. Jay with her infant child. She died in 1863.

HALL, Alfred Bryan. Engraver. Born in Stepney, London, England, in 1842. She was living in New York in 1900. A. B. Hall was a son of H. B. Hall, Sr., and came to New York in 1851. After serving an apprenticeship of seven years with his father, he worked as an engraver with J. C. Buttre, H. Wright Smith, A. H. Ritchie and George E. Perine, all of New York. He was later a member of the firms of H. B. Hall & Sons, and H. B. Hall Sons, until his retirement in 1899.

HALL, Alice. Engraver. Born at Halloway, London, England, 1847. She was living in New York in 1900. She was a daughter of H. B. Hall, Sr., and while still young she evinced very considerable talent in drawing and etching. She etched portraits of Washington, after Stuart and Trumbull, among her other works.

HALL, Charles Bryan. Engraver. Born in Camden Town, London, in 1840. C. B. Hall was the second son of H. B. Hall, Sr., and he came to New York in April, 1851, and commenced his studies under his father. In 1885 he was apprenticed to James Duthie, a landscape engraver then living in Morrisania, N. Y. After working about five years with George E. Perine, of New York, he started in business for himself as an engraver of portraits. He died in 1896.

HALL, E. W. A little known landscape painter working about 1840.

HALL, Mrs. Frances Devereux. Painter and sculptor. Born in New Orleans, La. Pupil of Sophie Newcomb College, New Orleans; and of John Twachtman, Howard Pyle and Charles Grafly. Member: Philadelphia Art Alliance. *Address,* "Springside," Chestnut Hill, Philadelphia, Pa.

HALL, Florence S. Painter. Born in Grand Rapids, Mich. Pupil of Art Institute of Chicago, and of Johansen. Member: Chicago Art Students' League. *Address,* 63 West Ontario St., Chicago, Ill.

HALL, Frederick Garrison. Etcher. Trained as an architect, he has besides become a brilliant and forceful etcher. His plates have a direct expression that show his early training, and his etching of the Boston Public Library has all the architectural detail of the building fully recorded. He has also done some very good book plates. (See "The Print Connoisseur," Vol. 1, 1921.) *Address,* 132 Riverway, Boston, Mass.

HALL, George Henry. Painter. Born in Boston in 1825. He was largely self-taught and began painting in 1842. Elected member of National Academy in 1868. Represented by "Self-portrait," in Brooklyn Museum, painted in 1845; "The Roman Wine Cart," in Boston Museum of Fine Arts, painted in 1851. He died in 1913.

HALL, George R. Engraver. Born in London, England, in 1818. He was a brother of H. B. Hall, Sr. George R. Hall commenced engraving under the tuition of his brother, and then worked in London and in Leipsic. He came to New York in 1854, and was first employed by Rawdon, Wright, Hatch & Co., and was later engraving over his own name for the Putnams and other New York publishers.

HALL, Henry Bryan. Engraver. Born in London, England, in 1808; died at Morrisania, N. Y., 1884. Hall was a pupil of the London

engravers Benjamin Smith and Henry Meyer, and he was later employed by H. T. Ryall, historical engraver to the Queen, to execute the portrait work in the large plate of "The Coronation of Victoria," after the painting by Sir George Hayter. Mr. Hall came to New York in 1850, and soon established a very extensive business as an engraver and publisher of portraits. He had very considerable ability as a portrait painter, and while in London he painted a portrait of Napoleon III, among others; among his portraits painted in the United States are those of Thomas Sully and C. L. Elliott. He painted miniatures on ivory, and etched a large number of portraits of men prominent in the Colonial and Revolutionary history of this country for a private club of New York, and for Philadelphia collectors. He made the drawings in pencil and wash for Dr. Thomas Addis Emmett's series of privately printed "Club" portraits of the signers of the "Declaration of Independence" and of other Revolutionary characters which he also engraved.

HALL, Henry Brayn, Jr. Engraver. Born in Camden Town, London, England. He was living in New York in 1900. He came to New York with his father in 1850 and served his apprenticeship with his father. In 1858 he went to London and worked under Charles Knight for about one year, and then returned and established himself in the engraving business in New York. He engraved many portraits of generals and officers of the Civil War, and also a number of historical plates, but retired from business in 1899. Among his larger plates are "The Death of Lincoln," and subjects after the paintings of J. G. Brown and other American artists.

HALL, John H. Wood engraver. Was born at Cooperstown, N. Y. He was self-taught except for a few lessons from Dr. Anderson. He began to engrave about 1826 and in 1840 he illustrated the "Manual of Ornithology," which contains some of his best work. (See "The History of Wood Engraving in America," by W. J. Linton.)

HALL, Peter. Engraver. Born in Birmingham, England, in 1828; died in Brooklyn, N. Y., in 1895. Mr. Hall came to the United States in 1849 and learned to engrave in the New York establishment of the American Bank Note Company. His special work was banknote script engraving, in which he excelled. In 1886 he went into business in New York as a bank-note engraver; later the firm became Kihn & Hall, and is still in existence as "Kihn Brothers." His son, Charles A. Hall, is now in the employ of the Bureau of Printing and Engraving, at Washington, D. C. A well-executed stipple portrait of Washington, after the portrait by Mrs. E. Sharpless, is signed as "Engraved by P. Hall" and appears as a frontispiece to the "Memoirs of Thaddeus Kosci-usko."

HALL, Thomas. Painter. Born in Sweden in 1883. Pupil of Freer; Wolcott; Reynolds. Member: Society of Independent Artists; Swedish Society, Chicago; Scandinavian-American Society, New York. *Address*, Holbein Studio, 63 West Ontario St., Chicago, Ill.

HALLETT, Hendricks A. Painter. He was born at Charlestown, Mass., in 1847, and studied in Antwerp and Paris. He was well known for his pictures of various types of ships and of notable events. He was a member of the Boston Society of Water Color Painters. He was awarded a bronze medal at the Massachusetts Charitable Mechanics' Association, Boston, 1892. He died in Boston in 1921.

HALLIDAY, Mary H. Painter. She was a pupil of William M. Chase and studied for years abroad. *Address*, Santa Monica, Calif.

HALLOWELL, George Hawley. Born in Boston in 1871. He studied architecture and painting. His early work was making copies of the old Italian Masters. His specialty is landscapes, and he is fond of logging scenes and the woods. In 1906 he studied abroad. He works in both oil and water colors. Pupil of F. W. Benson; E. C. Tarbell; and H. B. Warren. Studio, Boston, Mass. Represented in the Boston Museum of Fine Arts. *Address*, 229 Park Ave., Arlington Heights, Mass.

HALLOWELL, Robert. Illustrator. Born in Denver, Colo., in 1886. *Address*, 421 West 21st St., New York.

HALPERT, S. Painter. Exhibited at Penna. Academy of Fine Arts, Philadelphia, 1924. *Address*, 21 West 46th St., New York.

HALPIN, Frederick. Engraver. Born in Worcester, England, in 1805. He was the pupil of his father, an engraver for one of the Staffordshire potteries. About 1827 Frederick Halpin was located in London, engraving historical subjects and portraits. He came to New York about 1842, and for a time was in the employ of Alfred Jones in that city. He was a good engraver of portraits and book illustrations in stipple. His name is sometimes signed to prints as "F. W. Halpin."

HALPIN, John. Engraver. He was a brother of Frederick Halpin, and was engraving in St. Petersburg, Russia, before he reached the United States, by way of Halifax. About 1850 John Halpin was engraving landscapes and a few portraits for New York publishers. Some few years later he was employed by the Ladies' Repository and the Methodist Book Concern, both of Cincinnati, Ohio.

HALSALL, William Formby. Painter. Born in Kirkdale, England, in 1841; died in 1919. At the age of 12 he went to sea in the ship "Ocean Rover," of Portsmouth, N. H., and followed the sea for seven years. He was in the United States Navy during part of the Civil War, and afterwards learned the trade of fresco painting. He was a student in the Massachusetts Institute of Technology, class 1874. Since 1877 he has painted the following marine pictures: "First Fight of Ironclads, Monitor and Merrimac"; "The Mayflower" (Memorial Hall, Plymouth, Mass.); "Niagara Falls"; "Sheeted Ghost"; "The Winter Passage"; and "When Sleep Falleth on Men."

HAMANN, Charles F. Sculptor. Member of National Sculpture Society.

HAMBIDGE, Jay. Painter and illustrator. Born in 1867; he died in New York City, 1924. Pupil of the Art Students' League in New York and of William M. Chase. He was the discoverer of dynamic symmetry.

HAMILTON, Edward W. D. Painter. Born in 1862. He painted "Canal, Venice." (owned by the Boston Museum of Fine Arts).

HAMILTON, Hamilton. Painter. Born in England, 1847. He began his career as a portrait painter at Buffalo, N. Y., in 1872; specialty now, landscapes. Elected Associate Member of the National Academy in 1886; National Academy, 1889. Member of American Water Color Soc. Represented at the Fine Arts Academy, Buffalo, N. Y., by "The Valley of Fountains" and "Sunset After the Storm." *Address*, Norwalk, Conn.

HAMILTON, J. M. C. Painter. His work is said to be similar to that of Alfred Stevens.

HAMILTON, James. Marine and landscape painter. Born in Ireland in 1819; he died in Philadelphia in 1878. He was particularly successful in his marine views. He also painted several views of Niagara Falls which attracted much attention.

HAMILTON, John McClure. Painter. Born in Philadelphia in 1853. Studied at Penna. Academy of Fine Arts; Royal Academy, Antwerp; Jerome Atelier, Beaux Arts, Paris; settled in London, 1878. Specialty, portraits and pastels. Principal works: "Gladstone at Hawarden," Richard Vaux, Cardinal Manning, George Meredith, and Henry Thouron (in Penna. Academy of Fine Arts). Honorable mention, Paris Salon; gold medals, Buffalo, St. Louis, Penna. Academy, etc. Member: Council of Royal Society of Portrait Painters; Pastel Society. He was Pres. of the Fellowship of the Penna. Academy of Fine Arts. *Address*, Hermitage, Kingston-on-Thames, England.

HAMILTON, Norah. Etcher. Born in Fort Wayne, Ind., in 1873. Pupil of Cox in New York and Whistler in Paris. Member of Chicago Society of Etchers. *Address*, 62 Washington Square, N. Y.

HAMILTON, Wilbur Dean. Painter and illustrator. Born in Somerfield, Ohio, in 1864. Pupil of École des Beaux Arts in Paris. Member of Guild of Boston Artists. His painting, "Beacon St., Boston," is owned by the Rhode Island School of Design. *Address*, Trinity Court, Dartmouth St., Boston.

HAMLIN, Genevieve. Sculptor. Specialty, animals in low relief. Exhibited in National Academy of Design in 1925. *Address*, 39 Claremont Ave., New York.

HAMLIN, William. Engraver. Born in Providence, R. I., 1772; died there in 1869. Mr. Hamlin established himself in business as a manufacturer and repairer of sextants, quadrants, and such other nautical and mathematical instruments as were used by the navigator.

As engraving upon metal was part of his business he began experimenting upon copper, and his business card of a later date adds to his business proper, that of "Engraving & Copperplate Printing."

As an engraver Mr. Hamlin made his own tools and worked practically without instruction. His plates show a somewhat weak mixture of mezzotint and stipple, frequently worked over with the roulette. Good impressions of his plates, however, show that he made the best of his limited opportunities.

Mr. Hamlin saw Gen. Washington, on one of his visits to the Eastern States, and the impression made upon the engraver was so strong that his most important plates have Washington for their subject. Considering the Savage portrait as the best likeness, he followed that artist in his several portraits of Washington; but he also held Houdon's bust in high esteem and in his ninety-first year he engraved Washington after that sculptor. This was his last plate.

HAMM, Phineas Eldridge. Engraver. Born in Philadelphia in 1799; he died there in 1861. Hamm was probably the pupil of a Philadelphia engraver and in 1825–27 he was in business as an engraver in that city. While he usually worked in line, he engraved a few good portraits in stipple.

HAMMER, Trygve. Sculptor. Born in Norway in 1878. Pupil of Art Students' League of New York, National Academy of Design, and Society of Independent Artists. *Address*, 1931 Broadway, New York.

HAMMERSMITH, Paul. Etcher. Born in Naperville, Ill., in 1857. Member of the Chicago Society of Etchers. Represented by etchings in New York Public Library and Newark

Library. *Address*, 116 Michigan Ave., Milwaukee, Wis.

HAMMITT, Clawson S. Painter. Born in Wilmington, Del., in 1857. Pupil of Eakins and Chase in Philadelphia, and Constant and Lefebvre in Paris. Among his portraits are those of James Latimer and Henry Latimer in the U. S. Capitol, others in State House, Dover, Del., and State College, Newark, Delaware. *Address*, 12th and Jefferson Sts., Wilmington, Del.

HAMMOND, Arthur J. Painter. Born at Vernon, Conn., in 1875. Pupil of Pape, Woodbury, and Noyes. Member of the Conn. Academy of Fine Arts. *Address*, 424 Humphrey St., Swampscott, Mass.

HAMMOND, J. T. A good line engraver of landscapes and subject plates in 1839. In that year he was employed in Philadelphia, but later he seems to have removed to St. Louis, Mo.

HAMMOND, Richard Henry. Painter. Born in Cincinnati, Ohio, in 1854. Pupil of Noble, Weber and Duveneck. Member of Cincinnati Art Club. *Address*, 806 Barr St., Cincinnati, Ohio.

HANCOCK, Joseph Lane. Landscape painter. Born in Chicago, Ill., in 1864. Pupil of Art Institute, Chicago. He died in 1925.

HANCOCK, Nathaniel. Miniature painter and engraver. He was working in Boston from 1790 to 1802. In 1805 he moved to Salem, Mass. His miniature of Colonel William Raymond Lee is in the collection at the Essex Institute, Salem, Mass.

HANCOCK, Walker. Sculptor. Born in St. Louis, Mo., in 1901. Studied at Penna. Academy of Fine Arts. Work: Portraits, "Janet Shields" and "James W. Walker"; also modelled "Sea-Weed" fountain figure. *Address*, 4332 McPherson Ave., St. Louis, Missouri.

HANDLEY, Montague. Sculptor. His work includes busts of "Diana," "Bacchus," and "Flora."

HANEY, James Parton. Painter. Born in New York in 1869. Pupil of Bell, DuMond and Mucha. Studied with Woodbury. Became art director and teacher. He died in 1923.

HANKS, Jervis F. Born in New York state in 1799. He removed with his family to Wheeling, West Va., in 1817, and found employment there in painting signs. In 1823 he visited Philadelphia, and made some experiments in portrait painting which he continued on his return to Virginia. In 1827 he was in New York and when he could not gain sufficient employment painting portraits he returned to his sign painting.

HANKS, O. G. Engraver. Born in Troy, N. Y., in 1838. He studied engraving in the establishment of Rawdon, Wright & Hatch, in New York. He was a capital line engraver, both of portraits and landscapes, and was chiefly employed by the bank-note companies. He died about 1865.

HANLEY, W. H. Portrait draughtsman in crayon. He is known to have been working in Boston from 1850 to 1856.

HANNA, Thomas K. Painter and illustrator. Born in Kansas City, Mo., in 1872. Pupil of Art Students' League of New York. *Address,* Caldwell, N. J.

HANNAFORD, Alice Ide (Mrs.). Sculptor. Born in Baltimore, Md., in 1888. Pupil of Fraser, and Art Students' League of New York. The Brooklyn Institute Museum owns her ''Wigwam Dance.'' *Address,* 1900 Dupont Ave., South Minneapolis, Minn.

HANNY, William F. Cartoonist. Born in Burlington, Ia., in 1882. *Address,* Pioneer Press, St. Paul, Minn.

HANSELL, George H. Portrait painter in oils and miniatures, who flourished 1844–1857 in New York. In 1844 he exhibited a ''Miniature of a Little Girl'' at the National Academy of Design in New York.

HANSEN, Armin. Etcher, well known for his rendering of sea and water craft. He was awarded the gold medal for his etching ''The Sardine Barge'' at the International Exhibition of the Print Makers' Society of California. Member of California Society of Etchers. He has also painted marines and coast scenes. *Address,* Studio at Monterey, Calif.

HANSEN, Armin Carl. Painter and etcher. Born in San Francisco, Calif., in 1886. Pupil of Mathews; Grethe at Royal Academy, Stuttgart, Germany. Member: San Francisco Art Association; California Society of Etchers. Awards: prize, International Exposition, Brussels, 1910; silver medal, Panama-Pacific Exposition, 1915; gold medals for drawing and painting, San Francisco Art Association, 1919; first Hallgarten prize, National Academy of Design, 1920. Represented in Memorial Museum, San Francisco; Los Angeles Museum of History, Science and Art; Palace of Fine Arts, San Francisco. *Address,* 716 Pacific St., Monterey, Calif.

HANSEN, Hans Peter. Painter. Born in Denmark in 1881. Member: Kunst Gewerbe Verein. Award: Mention, collaborative competition, New York Architectural League, 1915. Instructor in Art Students' League, New York. *Address,* 467 West 159th St., New York, N. Y.

HANSON, Henry T. Painter and illustrator. Born in Chicago, Ill., in 1888. Pupil of DuMond, Bridgman, Snell and John Carlsen. *Address,* 225 West 39th St., New York, N. Y.

HAPGOOD, Alice Hathaway. Painter and illustrator. Born in Hartford, Conn., in 1893. Pupil of Breckenridge and Emil Carlsen. *Address,* 3927 Locust St., Philadelphia, Pa.

HAPPERSBURGER, Frank. Sculptor. His work is better known on the Pacific coast than in the east. His statue of ''Garfield'' was made in Europe.

HARBESON, Georgiana (Newcomb) Brown (Mrs. John F. Harbeson). Painter and illustrator. Born New Haven, Conn., in 1894. Pupil of Hugh Breckenridge; Joseph T. Pearson, Jr.; Daniel Garber; Violet Oakley. Member: Fellowship, Penna. Academy of Fine Arts; Philadelphia Art Alliance; Plastic Club of Philadelphia. *Address,* 5301 Knox St., Germantown, Pa.

HARDENBERGH, H. Elizabeth R(utledge). Painter. Born in New Brunswick, N. J. Pupil of H. B. Snell and Mrs. E. M. Scott. Member: National Academy of Women Painters and Sculptors; New York Water Color Club. *Address,* 939 Eighth Ave., New York, N. Y.

HARDIE, Robert Gordon. Painter. Born in Brattleboro, Vt., in 1854. Studied at Cooper Institute, and National Academy of Design, New York; with Gerome in Paris. Elected to Society of American Artists in 1897. His portrait of Miss Harriet S. Walker (painted in 1900) is in the Walker Art Gallery, Bowdoin College, Brunswick, Me. He died in Brattleboro, Vt., in 1904.

HARDING, Chester. Born at Conway, Mass., in 1792. He began life as a peddler in Western New York, painted signs in Pennsylvania, and finally, although entirely self-taught, became a fashionable portrait painter. He lived at various times in St. Louis, Philadelphia, and Boston; he went to London and painted the poet Rogers, the historian Alison, and several members of the Royal Family. Among his American portraits are one of Daniel Webster, owned by the Bar Association of New York; John Randolph, in the Corcoran Gallery, Washington; Charles Carroll of Carrollton. Elected Honorary Member of National Academy in 1828. He died in 1866. (See ''Autobiography of Chester Harding, Artist,'' edited by his daughter Margaret E. White, Boston, 1890.)

HARDING, George. Painter and illustrator. Born in Philadelphia in 1882. Studied in the Pennsylvania Academy of the Fine Arts, and with Howard Pyle, and independently, abroad. He has travelled extensively in foreign countries, and is the author of travel articles, and the illustrator of fictional and descriptive work in *Harper's* and other magazines. He was assigned by the United States War Department to duty as artist with the American Expeditionary Forces in 1918 and 1919. He has executed mural decorations in banks, hotels and theatres. Fellow of the Royal Geographic Society. Member of National Society of Mural Painters; Architectural League of New York; The Society of Illustrators; The Philadelphia Water Color Club. Instructor in illustration at Penna. Academy of Fine Arts. *Address,* 10 South 18th St., Philadelphia, Pa.

HARDING, J. L. Portrait painter working in New England about 1825. His portrait of Mrs. John Lovett is signed "J. L. Harding, 1837" and is owned in Woodstock, Conn.

HARDWICK, Alice R. (Mrs. Melbourne H. Hardwick). Painter. Born in Chicago in 1876. Pupil of DuMond, Birge Harrison, Melbourne H. Hardwick; Art Students' League of New York; studied in Holland and Belgium. Member: Concord Artists' Association; Society of Independent Artists; Copley Society. *Address,* 486 Boylston St., Boston, Mass.

HARDWICK, Melbourne H. Painter. Born in Nova Scotia in 1857. He died in Waverley, Mass., in 1916. He was a pupil of Triscott, Luyton and Blummers. Represented in Boston Museum of Fine Arts by "Midsummer."

HARDY, Anna E. Painter. Born in Bangor, Me., in 1839. Pupil of George Jeanin in Paris; Abbott H. Thayer in Dublin, N. H. Specialty, flower painting. *Address,* South Orrington, Me.

HARDY, Mrs. Beulah Greenough. Painter. Born in Providence, R. I. Pupil of Collin, Merson, Courtois and Virginia Reynolds in Paris; studied also in Boston and London. Member: Society of Miniaturists, London; Plastic Club; and Philadelphia Art Alliance, Philadelphia. *Address,* Pelham Court, Mt. Airy, Philadelphia, Pa.

HARDY, Charles. Illustrator. Born in England in 1888. Pupil of E. P. Kinsella. Member: Guild of Free Lance Association. *Address,* 27 East 22d St., New York, N. Y.

HARDY, Jeremiah. Painter. Born in 1800. Pupil of S. F. B. Morse. He painted a portrait of Cyrus Hamlin (seen in profile to left, wearing spectacles), owned by Boston Museum of Fine Arts. He died in 1888.

HARDY, Walter Manly. Painter and illustrator. Born at Brewer, Maine, in 1877. Pupil of Lazar in Paris; Blum, Brush, Cox, Clark and Bridgman in New York. *Address,* 159 Wilson St., Brewer, Me.

HARE, J. Knowles. Illustrator. Born in Montclair, N. J., in 1882. Designer of covers for *Saturday Evening Post, American Magazine,* etc. *Address,* 27 East 27th St., New York, N. Y.

HARER, Frederick W. Etcher. Born in Blossburg, Pa., 1880. Pupil of Penna. Academy of Fine Arts under Anshutz and Chase. Member: Chicago Society of Etchers; Fellowship, Penna. Academy of Fine Arts. Represented in Pennsylvania Academy of Fine Arts. *Address,* 319 Walnut St., Philadelphia, Pa.

HARGENS, Charles. Painter. He exhibited water colors at the Penna. Academy of Fine Arts Water Color Exhibition, Philadelphia, 1925. *Address,* 303 Walnut St., Philadelphia, Penna.

HARHBERGER, Mrs. Florence E. Smith. Painter and illustrator. Born in Freetown, Cortland County, N. Y., 1863. Pupil of Art Students' League and Cooper Union in New York. *Address,* 223 West Fayette St., Syracuse, N. Y.

HARKINS, Robert. Miniature painter of Brooklyn, N. Y. He flourished about 1841.

HARLAND, Mary. Painter. Born in England in 1863. Studied in London and Paris. Member of California Society of Miniature Painters. *Address,* 1323 Fourteenth St., Santa Monica, Calif.

HARLAND, Thomas. Book plate engraver, located for a time in Norwich, Conn.

HARLES, Victor J. Painter. Born in St. Louis, Mo., in 1894. Pupil of St. Louis School of Fine Arts. *Address,* Hanley Road and Canton Ave., Clayton, Mo.

HARLEY, Charles Richard. Sculptor. Born in Philadelphia in 1864. Educated at Spring Garden Institute; Penna. Academy of Fine Arts; in Paris at École Nationale des Arts Decorative, Academie Julien, École des Beaux Arts, and under Dampt and Aube; also in New York under St. Gaudens and Martiny; and in Rome and Florence. Professionally engaged as sculptor since 1895. Medal, Buffalo Exposition, 1901. *Address,* 709 West 169th St., New York.

HARLOW, Harry M. S. Painter. Born in Haverhill, Mass., in 1882. Has executed mural decorations in many churches in New York and Boston. Specialty, illumination. *Address,* 47 Fourth Ave., Haverhill, Mass.

HARLOW, Louis R. Water color artist and etcher. Born in Wareham, Mass. In 1880 he opened his studio in Boston. Since that time he has been much sought after by publishers of fine books, his illustrations having color and brilliancy.

HARMON, Evelyn S. Miniature painter. Exhibited in Penna. Academy of Fine Arts, Philadelphia, 1925. *Address,* 40 Carlton St., Brookline, Mass.

HARNETT, William M. Painter of still life.

HARNISCH, Albert E. Sculptor. Born in Philadelphia, 1843. Pupil of Jos. A. Bailly. He has executed the Calhoun Monument and the Barclay family group. He has also made a specialty of portrait busts; he studied at the Pennsylvania Academy of Fine Arts and later went to Italy for study, residing for eight years in Rome.

HARPER, Edith W. Painter. Exhibited at Cincinnati Museum in 1925. *Address,* 2119 Alpine Place, Cincinnati, Ohio.

HARPER, Marian D. Miniature painter. Studied at Art Institute of Chicago and in Paris. *Address,* 847 Grove St., Glencoe, Ill.

HARPER, William St. John. Painter, etcher and illustrator. He was born at Rhinebeck, N. Y., in 1851, and first studied in the schools of the National Academy under Professor Wilmarth. Later he was a pupil of William M. Chase and Walter Shirlaw in New York and of MM. Munkacsy and Bonnat in Paris. Mr. Harper was president of the Art Students' League in 1881 and is an Associate of the National Academy. He is a Member of the New York Etching Club. In 1892 he was awarded the Clarke Prize at the Academy for his picture called "Autumn." He died in 1910.

HARRIS, Alexandrina R. Miniature painter. Born in Scotland in 1886. Pupil of American School of Miniature Painters. *Address,* 1 Sidney Place, Brooklyn, N. Y.

HARRIS, Charles X. Painter. Born in Maine in 1856. Pupil of Cabanel in Paris. His portraits are in Memorial Hall, Philadelphia, and the Lambs' Club, N. Y. *Address,* 356 Mountain Road, West Hoboken, N. Y.

HARRIS, James. A line engraving of a Madonna, well executed and published about 1850, is signed "Ja's Harris, Engraver, 58 Nassau Street, New York." No other plates of this engraver have been seen.

HARRIS, J. T. Portrait painter. He exhibited at the Boston Athenaeum in 1833, "A Portrait of a Gentleman."

HARRIS, Marion D. Painter. Exhibited water colors at Annual Exhibition of Water Colors, Penna. Academy of Fine Arts, Philadelphia, 1925. *Address,* 920 Madison Ave., Wilmington, Del.

HARRIS, Samuel. Engraver. Born in Boston, Mass., in 1783. He was drowned in the Charles River while bathing, on July 7, 1810. "The Polyanthos," Boston, 1812, published a memoir of Samuel Harris, and from this we learn that he was apprenticed at an early age to his relative, the Boston engraver, Samuel Hill, and the first portrait executed by Harris appeared in "The Polyanthos" for 1806. As an engraver Harris worked in both line and in stipple and his plates possess some merit and show great promise.

HARRIS, William L. Mural painter. Born in New York in 1870, he died at Lake George, N. Y., in 1924. Studied art at Art Students' League, New York, and in Paris at Academie Julien. Worked on decorations for Congressional Library, Washington, D. C., and collaborated with Francis Lathrop in decorating St. Bartholomew's Church, New York. He also lectured on art subjects. Designed decorations for Church of the Paulist Fathers, New York.

HARRISON, Catherine Norris. Painter. (See Patterson, Catherine Norris.)

HARRISON, Charles. Engraver. In 1840 he was working as a letter engraver in New York; in 1900 he was still employed in this capacity by the American Bank Note Co. of New York.

HARRISON, Charles P. Engraver. Born in England in 1783, he was the son of Wm. Harrison, Sr., and was brought to Philadelphia by his father in 1794. He was probably a pupil of his father in engraving. From 1806 until 1819 he was in business in Philadelphia as a copperplate printer, but in 1820–22 Harrison combined "engraving" with his printing establishment. In 1823 he was in business in New York; he remained there until 1850 and probably later.

There is some very good line work signed by C. P. Harrison, but his stipple portrait work is inferior in execution. He also attempted portrait painting with very indifferent success.

Charles P. Harrison was the father of Gabriel Harrison, the actor and author, born in Philadelphia in 1818.

HARRISON, David R. This bank-note engraver was for many years in the employ of the American Bank Note Co., and he continued to engrave until he was nearly ninety years of age.

HARRISON, Henry. Painter. Born in England in 1844. He came to America with his parents when six years old and studied under

Danl. Huntington and LeClear. He has painted many portraits. His picture of Jonathan Dayton is in the Capitol Building at Washington, D. C. He died in 1923.

HARRISON, J. P. Engraver. He is known as the first engraver who practised west of the Alleghenies. He was established in Pittsburgh, Penna., in 1817.

HARRISON, (L.) Birge. Painter. Born in Philadelphia in 1854. Pupil of Cabanel in Paris. Elected an Associate Member of the National Academy of Design, New York, in 1902, and to full membership in 1910. Represented by "The Mirror," in Wilstach Collection, Philadelphia; "Glimpse of St. Laurence" at Penna. Academy of Fine Arts; at the Luxembourg Gallery, Paris. *Address,* Woodstock, N. Y.

HARRISON, Richard. The name of "Richard Harrison, Engraver" appears in the Philadelphia directories in 1820–22 inclusive, together with that of Richard G. Harrison, noted below. Previous to that time, or in 1814, he was engraving line frontispieces, etc., for F. Lucas & J. Cushing, publishers of Baltimore, Maryland.

HARRISON, Richard G. This line engraver was probably one of the "several sons" of Wm. Harrison, Sr., who came to Philadelphia in 1794. R. G. Harrison was engraving for the "Port Folio" in 1814 and possibly earlier than that for S. F. Bradford's Philadelphia edition of the "Edinburgh Encyclopedia" of 1805–18. After 1822 he is called "bank-note engraver" in the Philadelphia directories and in this capacity his name appears there continuously until 1845.

HARRISON, Richard G., Jr. This younger R. G. Harrison was a mezzotint engraver working in Philadelphia about 1860–65, chiefly upon portraits.

HARRISON, Samuel. Engraver. Westcott, in his "History of Philadelphia," says that Samuel Harrison was a son of William Harrison and that he was a pupil in engraving with his father before 1810, and died on July 18, 1818, aged twenty-nine years. The only example of his work seen is a good line map of Lake Ontario and Western New York, engraved in 1809.

HARRISON, Thomas Alexander. Landscape and marine painter. Born in Philadelphia in 1853. Pupil of Penna. Academy of Fine Arts, and École des Beaux Arts, Paris. Elected Member of National Academy in 1901. Represented in Luxembourg, Paris; Penna. Academy of Fine Arts, Philadelphia; Corcoran Art Gallery, Washington, D. C. *Address,* Woodstock, N. Y.

HARRISON, William. Engraver. Born in England; died in Philadelphia, 1803. William Harrison is said to have been a grandson of John Harrison the inventor of the chronometer. He learned to engrave in London and was for a time in the employ of the Bank of England; he also engraved maps for the East India Company.

In 1794 Wm. Harrison came to Philadelphia "with several sons" under an engagement to engrave for the Bank of Pennsylvania. He remained there until his death.

HARRISON, William, Jr. Engraver. This son of William Harrison was engraving in line in Philadelphia as early as 1797, signing himself "W. Harrison, Junior Sculp't." As an engraver his name appears in the Philadelphia directories for 1802–19 inclusive. He was a good portrait engraver in line and also worked in stipple. Very little of his signed work is seen and he was probably chiefly employed by the bank-note engraving companies.

HARRISON, William F. This excellent letter engraver was in the employ of New York bank-note companies 1831–40.

HARRITON, Abraham. Painter and etcher. Born in Bucharest, Roumania, 1893. Pupil of J. W. Maynard and C. F. Mielatz. Member: Society of Independent Artists. Represented in Oakland (Cal.) Public Museum.

HARSHE, Robert Bartholow. Painter and etcher. Born in Salisbury, Mo., in 1879. Studied at the Art Institute of Chicago; Art Students' League, New York; in Paris and London. Represented at the Luxembourg Museum, Paris (etchings). *Address,* 2764 Hampton Court, Chicago, Ill.

HART, Alfred. Painter. Born in Norwich, Conn., 1816, in 1848 he moved to Hartford, Conn., and later to the West.

HART, George O. Painter and etcher. Born in Cairo, Ill., in 1868. Represented in collection of New York Public Library and Metropolitan Museum. *Address,* Coytesville, New York.

HART, James McDougal. Landscape painter. Born in Kilmarnock, Scotland, in 1828. He was brought to America in 1831 and apprenticed to a coach painter. In 1851 he went to Dusseldorff, Germany, for a year's study and returning home he settled in New York City. Elected Associate of National Academy in 1857 and National Academy in 1859. Represented at Corcoran Art Gallery, Washington, D. C., by "The Drove at the Ford." He died in 1901.

HART, Joel T. Sculptor. Born in Clark County, Ky. He went abroad for study and spent much of his life in Florence, Italy. He executed several statues of Henry Clay and busts of many prominent men. He died in 1877.

HART, John Francis. Cartoonist. He was born in Germantown, Philadelphia, in 1867. *Address*, 169 Hansberry Street, Germantown, Philadelphia.

HART, Leon. Painter. Exhibited at ''Exhibition of Paintings Showing Later Tendencies in Art,'' Philadelphia, 1921. *Address*, 311 West 24th St., New York City.

HART, Letitia Bennett. Painter. Born in New York in 1867. Studied at National Academy of Design; pupil of James M. Hart and Edgar M. Ward. Painter of figure pictures and portraits. Exhibited at National Academy of Design, 1885; awarded Dodge prize for best picture painted by a woman, National Academy of Design, 1898; this picture was entitled ''The Keepsake.'' Other prominent pictures are ''Unwinding the Skein,'' ''In Silk Attire,'' ''The Bride's Bouquet.'' *Address*, 94 1st Pl., Brooklyn, New York.

HART, William H. Painter. Born in Fishkill-on-Hudson, N. Y., 1863. Pupil of Art Students' League and J. Alden Weir in New York; Boulanger and Lefebvre in Paris. Member: Salmagundi Club. *Address*, 133 East 66th St., New York.

HART, William M. Painter. Born at Paisley, Scotland, in 1823; died at Mt. Vernon, N. Y., in 1894. Specialty, landscapes with cattle. Represented at the Metropolitan Museum by ''Scene at Napanock'' and ''Seashore Morning.'' Elected to National Academy, 1858.

HARTING, G. W. Illustrator and painter. Born in Little Falls, Minn., 1877. Pupil of Henri, Chase, Mora, Miller and Koehler. Member: Society of Illustrators, 1912; Salmagundi Club, 1917. Illustrations in following magazines: *McClure's, Harper's, Vogue, House and Garden*, etc. *Address*, 51 West 10th St., New York, N. Y.

HARTLEY, Jonathan S. Sculptor. Born in Albany, N. Y., in 1845. He studied in New England and later in Paris and Italy. His first teacher was Erastus D. Palmer, one of the early American sculptors. He married the daughter of the painter George Inness. He was elected to the National Academy in 1891 and died in New York City in 1912.

HARTLEY, Marsden. Painter. He exhibited in Philadelphia, 1921, at ''Exhibition of Paintings Showing the Later Tendencies in Art'' (Penna. Academy of Fine Arts). *Address*, Care of Daniels Gallery, 2 West 47th St., New York.

HARTMAN, Reber S. Painter. He exhibited water colors at the Penna. Academy of Fine Arts, Philadelphia, 1925. *Address*, 1316 Spring Garden St., Philadelphia, Penna.

HARTMAN, C. Hartman was a very clever line-engraver of portraits, working about 1850–55 for J. C. Buttre and other New York print publishers.

HARTMAN, C. Bertram. Painter. Born in Junction City, Kans., 1882. Studied at Art Institute of Chicago; Royal Academy, Munich; and in Paris. *Address*, Care of the Montross Gallery, 550 Fifth Ave., New York.

HARTMAN, Sydney K. Painter and illustrator. Born in Germany in 1863. Pupil of Laurens and Benjamin Constant in Paris. *Address*, 13 West 30th St., New York, N. Y.

HARTRATH, Lucie. Painter. Born in Boston, Mass. Studied with A. Rixens, Paris, France; student of Art Institute of Chicago, 1896; with Raphael Collin, Paris; with Angelo Jank, Munich, 1906. Head of Department of Drawing and Painting, Rockford, Ill., College. He established his studio in Chicago in 1908. Exhibited at Paris Salon, 1901, and at the St. Louis Exposition and in other large American cities. Awarded: Butler Purchase Prize, 1911; Young Fortnightly Prize; Rosenwald Purchase Prize; Clyde Carr Landscape Prize (all Art Institute of Chicago). Member: Western Society of Artists; Chicago Society of Artists; Chicago Water Color Club; Kunstlerinnen Verein, Munich. *Address*, 4 East Ohio St., Chicago, Ill.

HARTSON, Walter C. Painter. Born in Wyoming, Ia., in 1866. Member: New York Water Color Club; Society of Independent Artists. Awards: Bronze medal and honorable mention, Atlanta Exposition, 1895; third Hallgarten prize, National Academy of Design, 1898; first landscape prize, Osborne competition, 1904. *Address*, Wassaic, Dutchess County, New York.

HARTWELL, Alonzo. Portrait painter in oils, and crayon portrait draughtsman. Born 1805 in Littleton, Massachusetts; died Waltham, Mass., 1873. Hartwell moved to Boston in 1822, and was apprenticed to a wood engraver and practised that art professionally from 1826 to 1851. In the latter year he started painting portraits in oils.

HARTWELL, George K. Painter and illustrator. Born in Fitchburg, Mass., 1891. Working for *Century* and *Scribner's*. *Address*, 556 West 180th St., New York.

HARTWELL, Kenneth. Painter. Exhibited water colors at the Penna. Academy of Fine Arts, Philadelphia, 1925. *Address*, 518 Fort Washington Ave., New York City.

HARTWICH, Herman. Painter. Born in New York in 1853. He received his first instruction in drawing and painting from his father; studied in Royal Academy, Munich, in 1877; received medal there; pupil of Profs. Diez and Loefftz. Specialty, figure, landscapes, portraits, animals, etc.; has painted many subjects in Upper Bacaria in the Tyrol. Made short stays in Paris and Holland, and was painting portraits in the United States, 1893–96.

HARVARD. Portrait painter, flourishing about 1771.

HARVEY, Eli. Sculptor. Born in Ogden, Ohio, in 1860. He studied sculpture and painting at the Academy of Fine Arts, Cincinnati, Ohio. Member of National Sculpture Society and American Art Association. Specialty, animals. Work: Sculpture for New York Zoological Park; Recumbent Lions for Eton Mausoleum, Toronto, Canada; portraits of Senator Savage, Ohio; Gov. Anderson, Ky. *Address,* 191 Waverly Place, N. Y.

HARVEY, George. Painter of landscapes and miniatures, flourishing 1837 to 1840. In 1836 he painted a miniature from life of Daniel Webster in the Senate Chamber, Washington, District of Columbia.

HARVEY, Paul. Painter. Born in Chicago, Ill. Pupil of Art Institute, Chicago. Member of Boston Art Club and represented there by ''The Cedars.'' *Address,* Santa Barbara, Calif.

HARWOOD, Burt S. Painter. Born in Iowa in 1897. His specialty was painting the Indians of Taos, New Mexico, where he died in 1924.

HASELTINE, James Henry. Sculptor. Born in Philadelphia in 1833. He studied in Paris and Rome. Served in the United States Army in Civil War. He executed statue of ''America Honoring Her Fallen Brave,'' owned by Philadelphia Union League Club. He also did portraits of Longfellow, Read, Gen'l Sheridan and Gen'l Merritt.

HASELTINE, W. Stanley. Born in 1835; died 1900. Studied in Philadelphia under Weber. Elected an Academician of National Academy of Design, 1861. He had a studio in Rome, and exhibited at the ''Centennial,'' in Philadelphia, 1876.

HASKELL, Ernest. Etcher and illustrator. His etchings of the woods and the country towns of Maine are most picturesque. Work: ''The Idle Cove,'' ''Kennebec Homestead,'' ''The Dead Pine,'' ''Phippsburg.''

HASLER, William N. Landscape painter. Born in Washington, D. C., in 1865. Pupil of Art Students' League of New York. *Address,* Hillside Ave., Caldwell, N. J.

HASSAM, Childe. Painter. Born in Boston in 1859. Studied art in Boston, and under Boulanger and Lefebvre, Paris. Awards: Bronze medal, Paris Exposition, 1889; gold medal, Munich, 1892; Society of American Artists, 1895; prize, Boston Art Club, 1896; medal, Carnegie Institute, Pittsburgh, 1898; Temple gold medal, Penna. Academy of Fine Arts, 1899. Represented in permanent collections of Penna. Academy of Fine Arts; Carnegie Institute, Pittsburgh; Cincinnati Museum; Buffalo Fine Arts Academy; Boston Art Club; Rhode Island School of Design; Art Club of Erie; Corcoran Gallery, Washington, D. C.; Metropolitan Museum of Art, New York; Walters Gallery, Baltimore. Elected member of National Academy, 1906. Member: Ten American Painters, New York; Societé Nationale des Beaux Arts, Paris; The Secession, Munich; American Water Color Society; National Institute of Arts and Letters. *Address,* 130 West 57th St., New York.

HASSELBUSCH, Louis. Painter. Born in Philadelphia in 1863. Pupil of Penna. Academy of Fine Arts; Academie Julien under Constant and Lefebvre, in Paris; Royal Academy in Munich. Member: Philadelphia Sketch Club. Specialty, portraits. *Address,* 1026 Arch St., Philadelphia, Pa.

HASWELL, Ernest Bruce. Sculptor. Born in Kentucky in 1887. Pupil of Barnhorn; Meakin; Dubois. Member: Cincinnati Art Club. Work: ''Spinoza,'' bas-relief; Hebrew Union College and Spinoza House, The Hague; ''Northcott Memorial,'' Springfield, Ill.; Cincinnati Museum; Cincinnati MacDowell Society; Rookwood Pottery; St. Coleman's Church, Cleveland. *Address,* 148 East 4th St., Cincinnati, Ohio.

HATCH, Emily Nichols. Painter. Born in Newport, R. I. Pupil of John Ward Stimson, Chase and Hawthorne. Member: National Academy of Women Painters and Sculptors. Represented in National Museum, Washington, D. C. *Address,* 62 Washington Square, New York, N. Y.

HATCH, George W. Engraver. Born about 1805, in western New York; died at Dobbs Ferry, N. Y., in 1867. Hatch was one of the first students in the National Academy of Design in 1826, and for a time he was a pupil of A. B. Durand. He was a good line engraver, and in 1830 he was designing and engraving bank-note vignettes in Albany and in New York City. While he engraved portraits, landscape plates and subject plates for the ''Annuals,'' his signed work is not plentiful.

A large and well-engraved portrait of Washington Irving, published in the *New York Mirror* in 1832, is signed "Engraved by Hatch & Smillie."

HATCH, L. J. He was a bank-note engraver in the employ of the Treasury Department, at Washington, D. C., about 1875.

HATFIELD, Joseph Henry. Painter. Born near Kingston, Canada, in 1863. Pupil of Constant, Doucet and Lefebvre in Paris. Awards: Silver medal, Mass. Charitable Mechanics Association, Boston, 1892; second Hallgarten prize, National Academy of Design, 1896. Work in Boston Art Club. *Address*, Canton Junction, Mass.

HATHAWAY, J. Miniature painter. Flourishing in Boston about 1833. He exhibited a miniature of a lady at the Boston Athenaeum in 1833.

HATHAWAY, Dr. R. Porrtait artist. He was working in New England in 1793. The lithograph portrait of Col. Briggs Alden is inscribed "Dr. R. Hathaway, del 1793."

HAUPT, Erik G. Painter. Born in Cassel, Germany, in 1891. Pupil of Laurens and Richard Miller in Paris. *Address*, Care of the Charcoal Club, 1230 St. Paul St., Baltimore, Md.

HAUSHALTER, George M. Painter. Born in Portland, Me., in 1862. Pupil of Julien Academy and École des Beaux Arts. Member: Rochester Art Club. Work: Decorations in St. Andrew's and St. Philip's Church, Rochester, N. Y.

HAVELL, Robert, Jr. In 1839 the English engraver, Robt. Havell, Jr., arrived in America; his work was well known in "Audubon's Birds of America." He settled on the Hudson soon after his arrival, and died in Tarrytown in 1878. In 1848 he published his engraving of "West Point from Fort Putnam" after a painting by himself. He also engraved a "View of the City of Hartford," and a number of views of other American Cities. An excellent sketch of Robert Havell and Robert Havell, Jr., by Geo. A. Williams, will be found in *The Print-Collector's Quarterly*, Vol. 6, No. 3, 1916.

HAVILAND, John. An English artist and architect who was in Philadelphia soon after 1800. He designed a number of buildings, and started a school for drawing in 1818 with Hugh Bridport, the miniature painter.

HAWEIS, Stephen. Painter and etcher. Born in London, England. Pupil of Alphonse Mucha and Eugéne Carriere in Paris. Work: Mural decorations in War Memorial Chapel of St. Francis Xavier, Nassau, Stone Ridge Church, New York; painted windows in St. Anselm's Church, Bronx, N. Y.; paintings in Detroit Institute and Toledo Museum. *Address*, Nassau, N. P., Bahama Islands, B. W. I.

HAWKINS, Cornelius H. Portrait and landscape painter. Born near Tupelo, Miss., in 1861. Studied in St. Louis School of Fine Arts; in New York, under William Chase. He is represented in the Louisiana State Museum at New Orleans, and the Alabama State Capitol.

HAWKINS, Edward M. Painter. Born in New York in 1877. Pupil of Whistler, Cazin, Monet and Beardsle. Works owned by Queen of Roumania, King of Serbia and the late King Leopold of Belgium. *Address*, 120 East State St., Ithaca, N. Y.

HAWKS, Rachel M. Sculptor. Born in Port Deposit, Md., in 1879. Pupil of Maryland Institute; Rinehart School of Sculpture, under Ephraim Keyser and Charles Pike. Member: Handicraft Club of Baltimore; Maryland Int. Alumni. Work: Bust of Dr. Basil Gildersleeve, Johns Hopkins University, Baltimore. Specialty, mural decorations in relief. *Address*, Ruxton, Baltimore County, Md.

HAWLEY, Carl T. Painter, illustrator and etcher. Born in Montrose, Penna., 1885. Pupil of Art Students' League of New York, and Julien Academy in Paris. *Address*, 615 Walnut St., Syracuse, N. Y.

HAWLEY, Margaret Foote. Miniature painter. Member: American Society of Miniature Painters; Penna. Society of Miniature Painters. Award: Medal of honor, Penna. Academy of Fine Arts, 1918. Work: In Metropolitan Museum, New York.

HAWTHORNE, Charles Webster. Born in Maine in 1872. Painter and teacher. Pupil of National Academy of Design, and Art Students' League, New York; Wm. M. Chase at Shinnecock, Long Island. Awards: First Hallgarten prize, National Academy of Design, 1904; second Hallgarten prize, National Academy of Design, 1906; honorable mention, Carnegie Institute, Pittsburgh, 1908; Clarke prize, National Academy of Design, 1911; Isidor medal, National Academy of Design, 1914; Temple gold medal, Pennsylvania Academy of the Fine Arts, 1915. Elected Associate Member of National Academy, 1908; National Academician in 1911. He painted "A Fisherman's Wife" and "The Trousseau." *Address*, 280 West 4th St., New York.

HAWTHORNE, Marion G. (Mrs. C. W.). Born in Joliet, Ill. Pupil of Chicago Art Institute. Member of National Association of Women Painters and Sculptors. *Address*, Care of Macbeth Gallery, New York, N. Y.

HAY, De Witt Clinton. Engraver. Born in or near Saratoga, N. Y. In 1850 he was an apprentice with Rawdon, Wright, Hatch & Smillie, in New York. He devoted himself to bank-note engraving as a member of the firm of Wellstood, Hanks, Hay & Whiting, of New York.

No plates signed by Hay as engraver have been seen by the compiler; but Mr. Alfred Jones says that Hay engraved the small Annual plate of "The Oaken Bucket," after the painting by Frederick S. Agate; this plate is signed by his employers, Rawdon, Hatch & Smillie.

HAY, William. This line engraver of buildings and subjects was working in Philadelphia from 1819 to 1824.

HAY, William H. Engraver. This name is signed to plates found in C. G. Childs' "Views of Philadelphia," published in 1828. Both this man and the William Hay noted above were line engravers of similar subjects and about contemporaneous. There is enough difference in their style of work, however, to encourage the belief that they were different men.

HAYDEN, Charles H. Landscape painter. Born in Plymouth, Mass., in 1856; died in Belmont, Massachusetts, in 1901. Pupil of the Boston Museum School; also of Boulanger, Lefebvre and R. Collin, in Paris. Awards: Honorable mention, Paris Exposition, 1889; Jordon prize, Boston, 1895; silver medal, Atlanta Exposition, 1895; bronze medal, Paris Exposition, 1900. Member of Boston Water Color Society. Represented by "The Poplars, Chatham, Massachusetts" at the Corcoran Art Gallery, and "Turkey Pasture," owned by Boston Museum of Fine Arts.

HAYDEN, Edward Parker. Landscape painter. Died in Haydenville, Mass., Feb. 7, 1922.

HAYDEN, Ella Frances. Landscape painter. Born in Boston in 1860. Pupil of National Academy of Design, also studied in Paris. *Address,* 160 Tabor Ave., Providence, R. I.

HAYS, Austin. Sculptor. Born in New York City in 1869. He was the son of the late William J. Hays, and a brother of William J. Hays, the landscape painter. Elected Associate Member of the National Academy. His work was exhibited at the Petit Salon, Paris, and the National Academy of Design, New York.

HAYS, George A. Landscape painter. Born in Greenville, N. H. Member of the Providence Art Club. Specialty, landscapes with cattle. *Address,* 19 College St., Providence, Rhode Island.

HAYS, Henry. This book-plate engraver was an Englishman working in London as early as 1820 at 168 Regent Street. While working on book-plates, Fenshaw says that Hays was located in New York in 1830–55. American book-plates signed by him are found.

HAYS, William Jacob. Animal painter. Born in New York in 1830; died in 1875. He was a pupil of J. R. Smith. Elected an Associate Member of the National Academy of Design in 1852. Represented in Corcoran Art Gallery of Washington, D. C., by "head" of a Bull-Dog.

HAYS, William Jacob. Painter. Born in 1872 at Catskill, N. Y. Student of National Academy of Design and Julien Academy, Paris. Has exhibited at National Academy of Design and in the Pennsylvania Academy of Fine Arts exhibitions. *Address,* Millbrook, N. Y.

HAYWARD, Alfred. Painter. Student at Penna. Academy of Fine Arts. *Address,* 200 South 15th St., Philadelphia.

HAYWOOD, Mary C. Painter. Born in Philadelphia in 1898. Pupil of Breckenridge. Represented in the Penna. Academy of Fine Arts by a portrait. *Address,* Care of Art Alliance, Philadelphia.

HAZARD, Arthur M. Painter. Born in North Bridgewater, Mass., in 1872. Pupil of Boston Museum of Fine Arts and of Henri Blanc in Paris. Specialty, portraits and mural decorations. Work to be found in Boston State House and Court House in Baltimore.

HAZELL, Frank. Painter and illustrator. Born in 1883. Pupil of Art Students' League of New York and of Alphonse Mucha. *Address,* 130 East 31st St., New York.

HAZELTON, I. B. Painter and illustrator. Born in Boston in 1875. Pupil of Tarbell and Benson. *Address,* 2 East 23d St., Nutley, New Jersey.

HAZELTON, Mary B. Painter. Born in Milton, Mass. Pupil of Edmund C. Tarbell. *Address,* Fenway Studios, Boston.

HAZEN, Bessie E. Painter. Pupil of Columbia University, New York. Etches and works in water color. *Address,* Care of the University of California (Southern Branch).

HAZLITT, John. Born in England in 1767. He painted portraits in Hingham, Mass., and was working in Salem, Mass., in 1782 painting both miniatures and large portraits in oil. In 1785 he conducted an Art School in Boston. He was of English birth and returned to England in 1787. He died in 1837.

HAZZARD, Sara. Painter. Member: National Academy of Women Painters and Sculptors; Penna. Society of Miniature Painters. *Address*, 29 East 29th St., New York, N. Y.

HEADE, Martin Johnson. Born in Bucks County, Penna. He began his career as a portrait painter, studied in Italy, traveled in the west and then settled in Boston as a landscape painter. His studio was later moved to New York. His best known works are "Off the California Coast" and his South American scenes.

HEALY, G. P. A. Portrait painter. Born in Boston, 1813; died in Chicago in 1894. Began studies in Paris in 1836. Went to Chicago about 1858 where he was given a farm of 50 acres which eventually came into the city limits and which he sold for a large price. With his family he went to Europe and remained a long time in Rome. His portraits of distinguished people are numerous. He painted many portraits in Chicago and Washington and for Louis Philippe. He was an honorary member of the National Academy of Design. (See "Reminiscences of a Portrait Painter," by George P. A. Healy.)

HEATH, Howard P. Painter and illustrator. Born in Boulder, Colo., in 1879. Pupil of Art Institute of Chicago; Art Students' League of New York; Frank Nankivell. Member: Society of Illustrators, 1911; New York Water Color Club. *Address*, 294 West 11th St., New York.

HEATON, Augustus. Painter. Born in Philadelphia in 1844. He studied in the Penna. Academy of Fine Arts under P. F. Rothermel and in Paris under Bonnat. He has painted many portraits and historical compositions. His "The Recall of Columbus" is in the U. S. Capitol, Washington, D. C. The Union League of Philadelphia owns "Washington's First Mission," and his pictures were used on postage stamps and coins. *Address*, West Palm Beach, Florida.

HEBER, Carl Augustus. Sculptor. Born in Stuttgart, Germany, in 1874. Pupil of Taft in Chicago. Member: National Sculpture Society. Awards: Bronze medal, St. Louis Exposition, 1904; bronze medal, Panama-Pacific Exposition, San Francisco, 1915. Work: "Pastoral," Art Institute, Chicago, Ill.; "Champlain Memorial," Crown Point, N. Y.; "Schiller Monument," Plattsburg, N. Y.; "Benjamin Franklin," Princeton University. *Address*, 51 West 10th St., New York, N. Y.

HECHT, Victor D. Painter. Born in Paris, France, in 1873. Pupil of Art Students' League of New York; Lefebvre and Robert-Fleury in Paris. Member: Nat. Association of Portrait Painters.

HECKMAN, Albert W. Painter and etcher. Born in Meadville, Pa., in 1893. Pupil of Arthur Dow. *Address*, 525 West 120th St., New York.

HEERMAN, Norbert. Painter. Born in Frankfort-on-the-Main, Germany, in 1891. Pupil of Reynolds in Chicago; Fleury in Paris; Corinth in Berlin; Duveneck in Cincinnati. Member: Cincinnati Art Club; Colorado Springs Artists' Society. Work: "The Continental Divide" (mural), Evanston School, Cincinnati; "Cameron's Cone, Colorado," Hughes High School, Cincinnati. Author of "Frank Duveneck," a biography. *Address*, Ralston Galleries, 4 East 46th St., New York.

HEIDEMANS, Henri. Miniature painter, who flourished in New York about 1841–42.

HEIL, Charles Emile. Painter and illustrator. Born in Boston in 1870. Studied in Boston and Paris. Member: Boston Water Color Club; Society of Independent Artists. Awards: Gold medal for water color, Panama-Pacific Exposition, San Francisco, 1915. Represented in Worcester, Mass., Art Museum; Malden, Mass., Public Library. *Address*, 1215 Grand Concourse, New York, N. Y.

HEIMER, J. L. Marine painter. He was known for his many excellent paintings of ships.

HEINTZELMAN, Arthur William. Painter and etcher. Born in Newark, N. J., in 1891. Pupil of Rhode Island School of Design; also studied in Holland, France, Belgium, Spain, England and Scotland. Member: Chicago Society of Etchers; Providence Art Club. Etchings in Metropolitan Museum, New York; Chicago Art Institution; New York Public Library; Detroit Institute of Arts; Library of Congress, Washington, D. C., etc. *Address*, Care of Frederick Keppel & Co., New York, N.Y.

HEINZ, Charles L. Painter. Born in Shelbyville, Ill., in 1885. Pupil of R. M. Root; St. Louis School of Fine Arts; Chicago Academy of Fine Arts. Awards: Ten first and seven second prizes at Indiana State Fair, Indianapolis; two second prizes, State Fair, Springfield, Ill. *Address*, Shelbyville, Ill.

HEINZMANN, Samilla L. Jameson. Painter, sculptor and illustrator. Born in Indianapolis, Ind., in 1881. Pupil of Chicago Art Institute; Detroit Fine Arts Academy; De Lug in Vienna. Member: Society of Independent Artists; League of New York Artists. *Address*, The Willow Bridge Studio, 28 Terrace Ave., Princess Bay, New York.

HEITLAND, Wilmot E. Painter. Born in Superior, Wis., in 1893. Pupil of Penna. Academy of Fine Arts. *Address*, 27 Grace Court, Brooklyn, N. Y.

HEKKING, William M. Painter and illustrator. Born in Chelsea, Wis., in 1885. Pupil of Laurens. Member: College Art Association; Wilmington Society of Painters. Work: Decorations in Natural History Museum, State University of Kansas, Lawrence. *Address*, 219 East 11th St., Kansas City, Mo.

HELCK, C. P. Painter. Exhibited at National Academy of Design, New York, in 1925. *Address*, 256 West 55th St., New York.

HELLER, Eugenie M. Painter and sculptor. Pupil of Alden Weir in New York and of Whistler in Paris. *Address*, 502 West 113th St., New York.

HELMICK, Howard. Painter, etcher and illustrator. Born in Zanesville, Ohio, in 1845. Studied in Paris and London. Member of British Artists and Royal Society of Painters and Etchers. He was a professor of art at Georgetown University. He died at Georgetown in 1907.

HELWIG, Arthur. Painter. He exhibited the "Black Canyon, Colorado," at the exhibition held at the Cincinnati Museum in 1925. *Address*, 323 Elland Circle, Cincinnati, Ohio.

HEMING, Arthur. Painter and illustrator. Born in Paris, Ont., in 1870. Studied at Art Students' League under Frank Brangwyn. Illustrator of many books on animal and wild life. Represented by three pictures in Canadian National Gallery. Member of Society of Illustrators. *Address*, 72 Madison Ave., Toronto, Canada.

HENDERSON, A. Elizabeth. Miniature painter. Born in Ashland, Ky., in 1873. Pupil of Art Students' League of New York. *Address*, 79 Hamilton Place, N. Y.

HENDERSON, Helen Weston. Painter. Born in Philadelphia in 1874. Studied at Penna. Academy of Fine Arts, 1892–97; Academie Colarossi, Paris. Art and music editor of Philadelphia *North American*, 1900–04; art editor Philadelphia *Inquirer*, 1904–09.

HENDERSON, William Penhallow. Painter. Born in Medford, Mass., in 1879. Studied at Boston Museum of Fine Arts; winner of "Paige" traveling scholarship. Painted Joliet and Marquette mural decorations for Joliet Township High School, Cook County, Ill., 1907; represented in the Art Institute of Chicago and in private collections. His work includes mural decorations, portraits and landscapes, pastels and lithographs.

HENGLE, Walter Vanden. Painter. Exhibited water colors at the Penna. Academy of Fine Arts, Philadelphia, 1925. *Address*, 2095 North 63d St., Philadelphia.

HENNESSY, William J. Painter. Born in 1839. Entered the National Academy in 1856, and was elected an Academician in 1861. He went to London in 1870. Genre painting and illustrating were his chief interests. Among his works, "On the Sands," "Autumn," "The Votive Offering," "Flowers of May." He died in 1900.

HENNINGS, E. Martin. Painter. He won 1925 prize at Penna. Academy of Fine Arts, with "Announcements" (purchased by the Academy). Specialty, Indian and Western scenes. *Address*, 4 East Ohio St., Chicago, Ill.

HENRI, Pierre. Miniature painter, who flourished in Philadelphia about 1790–1812. He painted Mrs. Beaumont in the character of "The Grecian Daughter," Penna. Academy, 1811.

HENRI, Robert. Painter. Born in Cincinnati in 1865. Studied at Penna. Academy of Fine Arts, Philadelphia, 1886–88; Academie Julien and École des Beaux Arts, Paris, 1888–91. He studied without instruction for years, in France, Spain and Italy. His picture "La Neige" was purchased from the Salon, 1899, by the French Govt. for the Luxembourg Gallery; represented in permanent collections of Carnegie Institute, Pittsburgh; Art Institute, Chicago; Columbus, Ohio, Fine Arts Gallery; New Orleans Art Association; City of Spartanburg, S. C.; Dallas Art Association; Penna. Academy of Fine Arts; Brooklyn Museum of Arts and Sciences; Art Institute, Kansas City; Carolina Art Association, Charleston, S. C.; Metropolitan Museum of New York; San Francisco Institute. *Address*, 10 Gramercy Park, N. Y.

HENRY, Albert P. Sculptor. Born in Versailles, Ky., in 1836; died in 1872. His first art work was commenced when, but a mere boy, he carved from a block of marble an ambitious group, comprising an Indian girl holding a dove while a wolf creeps up to snatch the bird from her grasp. He occupied his leisure time in modelling small portrait busts, and, casting them in iron, used them as weights to keep doors open. At the breaking out of the Civil War, young Henry recruited a company of the Fifteenth Kentucky Cavalry. In a skirmish near Fort Henry he was captured by the enemy and taken to Libby Prison. While in prison he devoted much of his time to carving upon the bones of oxen used for making soup. He managed to smuggle from the prison, in a wooden box with a false bottom, some of these carvings; among them "The Prisoner's Dream," showing the interior of a cell, an armed sentry at the door, while the prisoner is sleeping on the floor. Following the close of the war he was appointed consul at Anconia, Italy. Prior to his leaving the United States he had executed his bust of Henry Clay, now in the Capitol at Washington, and a bust of Abraham Lincoln from life, now in the Custom House, in Louisville, Ky. While in Italy, he spent considerable time in Florence, where he studied art under Powers and Joel T. Hart. His most ambitious production is an ideal bust of Genevieve. He also made a bust of Senator Guthrie, of Kentucky, and a bust of Senator Garrett Davis.

HENRY, Colonel, of Kentucky. He modelled a most creditable bust of Lincoln, now in the United States Court Room of Louisville, Ky.

HENRY (Edward L.). Born in Charleston, S. C., in 1841. Pupil of Penna. Academy of Fine Arts, and of Gleyre in Paris. Lived in Paris, Rome, and Florence from 1800 to 1863. Sketched and studied with the armies in Virginia during the Civil War. Elected National Academician in 1869. His special gift lay in the line of American genre, and he painted scenes from real life with a keen eye for character and much quiet humor. He is represented in the Metropolitan Museum in New York, and the Corcoran Art Gallery, Washington, D. C. He died in New York City in 1919.

HENRY, John. The name of "John Henry, Engraver," appears in the Philadelphia directory for the one year of 1793, and he was engraving well-executed business cards in that city. In 1818 he was working for Baltimore publishers, and in 1828 he was engraving the illustrations for Madame Mothe Guion's "Die Heilige Liebe Gottes," published in Lancaster, Pa. He may have been some connection of William Henry of Lancaster, Member of the Continental Congress and prominent in Revolutionary affairs in that section; in support of this suggestion we find that a John Henry was a pupil at the Franklin College, in Lancaster, in 1787.

HENSCHE, Henry. Painter. He exhibited in the Annual Exhibition, 1925, of the National Academy of Design, New York. *Address*, 50 East 86th St., New York.

HENTZ, N. M. Engraver. A large and very well executed etching of an "American Alligator" appears in Vol. 11 of the *Transactions of the American Philosophical Society*, Philadelphia, 1825. This plate is signed "N. M. Hentz Del. & Sculp." and illustrates an article by Hentz on the American alligator presented to the society on July 21, 1820.

HENWOOD, Mary R. Miniature painter. She exhibited at the Penna. Academy of Fine Arts, Philadelphia, in 1925. *Address*, 3219 West Penn St., Philadelphia.

HEPBURN, Nina Maria. Painter. She exhibited water colors at the Penna. Academy of Fine Arts, Philadelphia, in 1925. *Address*, Freehold, N. J.

HERBERT, Lawrence. Engraver. The *Pennsylvania Gazette*, in 1748, contains the following advertisement: "Engraving on Gold, Silver, Copper or Pewter, done by Lawrence Herbert, from London, at Philip Syng's, Goldsmith, in Front Street."
In 1751 Herbert apparently left Philadelphia, as on August 1st of that year he requests persons having any demands upon him to present them at the home of Peter David, in Second Street, Philadelphia.

HERDLE, George Linton. Painter. Born in Rochester, in 1868. Studied in Holland and in Paris. Member: Rochester Art Club; Rochester Municipal Art Commission. Director, Memorial Art Gallery of Rochester University. *Address*, 47 Clinton Ave., Rochester, N. Y.

HERGESHEIMER, Ella S. Painter. Born in Allentown, Pa. Pupil of Penna. Academy of Fine Arts under Cecilia Beaux and Chase; Prinet and Mucha in Paris; also studied in Italy and Spain. Member: Fellowship of Penna. Academy of Fine Arts. Awarded traveling scholarship, Penna. Academy of Fine Arts. Director of art schools in Tennessee and Kentucky. *Address*, 803½ Broad St., Nashville, Tenn.

HERING, Elsie Ward (Mrs. Henry Hering). Sculptor. Born in Howard County, Mo.; died in New York, 1923. Studied in Denver, Colo. Pupil of Augustus Saint Gaudens. Member: Denver Art Club. Work: Schermerhorn memorial font in Chapel of Our Savior, Denver, Colo.; W. C. T. U. drinking fountain, St. Louis Museum.

HERING, Henry. Sculptor. Born in New York City in 1874. Pupil of Art Students' League, New York, 1894–98; École des Beaux Arts and Colarossi Academy, Paris, France, 1900–01. Principal works: Civil War Memorial, Yale University; Robert Collier Memorial, Church of Messiah, New York; Huntington Wolcott Jackson Memorial, Crerar Library, Chicago, and Princeton University; (portrait busts) Augustus St. Gaudens; Bishop Ethelbert Talbott; (portrait reliefs) Stephen Olin, Rhinebeck, N. Y.; Mrs. Tracy Dows and son; also executed fountains, statuettes, etc.; sculpture for Field Museum of Natural History, Chicago, 1916, 1917. Member: National Sculpture Society. *Address*, 4 West 33d St., New York, N. Y.

HERMAN, Leonora Owsley. Painter and etcher. Born in Chicago in 1893. Pupil of Simon, Menard, Hellen, Leon in Paris. Member: Philadelphia Alliance; Fellowship, **Penna.** Academy of Fine Arts. *Address*, 1521 Pine Street, Philadelphia, Pa.

HERMANN, Max. Painter. Specialty, cattle and sheep. Member of "Society of Animal Painters and Sculptors of America."

HEROLD, Don. Illustrator. Born in Bloomfield, Ind., in 1889. *Address*, Bronxville, New York.

HERRICK, Henry W. Miniature painter, who flourished in Nashville, Tenn., about 1843; he was also a wood engraver.

HERRICK, Margaret Cox. Painter. Born in San Francisco, Calif., in 1865. Pupil of Carlsen, Fred Yates and Mary C. Richardson. Member: San Francisco Artists' Association. Work: Lunette in Y. W. C. A., Oakland, Calif. *Address*, 312 Pacific Ave., Piedmont, Calif.

HERRING, Frederick William. Son of the artist James Herring, he was born in New York City in 1821, and studied art with his father and Henry Inman and devoted his attention to portrait painting.

HERRING, James. Portrait painter and engraver who was born in London, England, in 1794. His father emigrated to the United States in 1804 and settled in New York. He associated himself with James Longacre in publishing the "National Portrait Gallery." He painted a number of portraits and had a studio in Chatham Square, New York. He died in 1867.

HERTER, Adele (Mrs. Albert). Painter. Born in New York. Pupil of Courtois, Bouguereau and Robert-Fleury in Paris. Member: National Academy of Women Painters and Sculptors. Awards: Honorable mention, Pan-American Exposition, Buffalo, 1901; bronze medal, St. Louis Exposition, 1904. *Address*, 130 East 67th St., New York, N. Y.

HERTER, Albert. Painter. Born in New York in 1871. Pupil of Carroll Beckwith, New York; J. P. Laurens and Cormon, Paris. Specialty, mural decorations. Honorable mention, Paris Salon, 1890; medal, Atlanta Exposition, 1895; Lippincott prize, 1897. Elected Associate Member of the National Academy. Member: American Water Color Society; Society of Mural Painters; Architectural League, New York; New York Water Color Club. *Address*, East Hampton, L. I., and Santa Barbara, Calif.

HERTER, Christine. Painter. Born in Irvington-on-Hudson, N. Y., 1890. Pupil of Sergeant Kendall. Member: New York Water Color Club; National Academy of Women Painters and Sculptors; Newport Artists' Association. Award: Second Hallgarten prize,

National Academy of Design, 1916. *Address*, 30 East 68th St., New York, N. Y.

HERTHEL, Alice. Painter. Born in St. Louis, Mo. Pupil of St. Louis School of Fine Arts; Simon and Anglada-Camarasa in Paris. Member: Society of Ancients, St. Louis, Mo. *Address*, 3841 Flora Blvd., St. Louis, Mo.

HERVIER, Auguste. Miniature painter, flourishing in the United States about 1827–1858.

HERVIEUE, Augustin Jean. Painter. Born near Paris, France, in 1794. He studied in England with Sir Thomas Lawrence. He painted "The Landing of Lafayette," and a portrait of Robert Owen which is owned by the Ohio Historical Society. Exhibited at the Royal Academy, London, 1819 and 1858.

HERZBERG, Robert A. Painter and etcher. Born in Germany in 1886. Pupil of Vanderpoel, Mucha and Kenyon Cox. *Address*, 2036 Woodward Ave., Mich.

HERZEL, Paul. Sculptor, painter and illustrator. Born in Silesia in 1880. Pupil of St. Louis School of Fine Arts; Beaux Arts Institute of Design, New York. Member: National Sculptors' Society. Awards: Mrs. H. P. Whitney "Struggle" prize, 1915; Barnett prize, National Academy of Design, 1913. *Address*, 126 East 75th St., New York, N. Y.

HERZOG, Lewis. Painter. Born in Philadelphia, Pa., in 1868. Studied in London, Rome, Berlin, Dusseldorf, Munich and Venice. Member: Art Club, Philadelphia; National Arts Club, New York. *Address*, 80 West 40th St., New York, N. Y.

HESS, Harold W. Painter. Exhibited water colors at the Penna. Academy of Fine Arts, Philadelphia, 1925. *Address*, 346 South Smedley St., Philadelphia.

HESSELIUS, Gustavus. Swedish artist. Born in 1682. He arrived in America (1711) near Wilmington, Del. He painted an altarpiece of the "Last Supper" for the parish Church of St. Barnabas, Prince George's County, Md., in 1721. He was the first organ builder in America. He also painted a number of portraits. The Cleveland Art Museum owns the portraits of Judge William Smith of New York, and his first wife Mary Het. (Signed and dated "G. H. 1729.") He died in 1755.

HESSELIUS, John. Painter. Born in 1728. He was the son of Gustavus Hesselius, the Swedish artist, and nephew of Samuel Hesselius, the Swedish missionary. He settled in Maryland, and in 1763 he married Mary, only child of Col. Richard Young of Annapolis,

Md. His earliest portraits were painted in Philadelphia in 1750; he afterwards painted many portraits in Maryland. He was an early instructor of Charles Willson Peale.

HETZEL, George. Painter. Born in Alsace in 1826. He studied at Dusseldorf, and lived and painted for years at Pittsburgh, Pa. Represented in Wilstach Collection, Fairmount Park, Philadelphia. He died in Pittsburgh in 1906.

HEURRMANN, Magda. Painter and illustrator. Born in Galesburg, Ill. Member of Chicago Art Club. *Address*, Fine Arts Building, Chicago, Ill.

HEUSTIS, Louise L. Portrait painter. Born in Mobile, Ala. Pupil of Art Students' League of New York under Chase, and of the Julien Academy in Paris. *Address*, 230 West 59th St., New York, N. Y.

HEWINS, Philip. Portrait painter. Born in Blue Hill, Me., in 1806. In 1834 he established his studio in Hartford, Conn., where he lived till his death in 1850. His portraits were pronounced good likenesses.

HEWITT. This engraver was working for the ''Port Folio'' and other Philadelphia magazines about 1820. He was an engraver of landscapes in line.
J. Hewitt is noted as an engraver of music, published in New York, but without indication of date.

HEWITT, Edwin H. Painter. Born in Red Wing, Minn., in 1874. Director of Minneapolis Art Institute. *Address*, 716 4th Ave., Minneapolis, Minn.

HEWITT, William K. Portrait painter. Born in New Jersey in 1818. He commenced exhibiting at the Penna. Academy of Fine Arts about 1847. He painted many excellent portraits of Philadelphians of his day. He died in Philadelphia in 1892.

HEWLETT, James Monroe. Mural painter. Born in Laurence, L. I., N. Y., in 1868. Work: Represented in Carnegie Technical School and Columbia University Club. *Address*, 2 West 45th St., New York, N. Y.

HEYLER, Mary Pemberton Ginther. Painter and author. Born in Philadelphia, Pa. Studied at School of Design, Philadelphia, and Penna. Academy of Fine Arts. Painter of landscapes and figures. She has exhibited at Penna. Academy of Fine Arts; Art Club, Philadelphia, etc.; also private exhibitions of oil, water color and charcoal. Designed stained glass windows: ''Peter and John at the Tomb,'' St. John's P. E. Church, Suffolk, Va.; ''John on Patmos,'' Church of the Restoration, Philadelphia, etc. *Address*, Buckingham, Pa.

HIBBARD, Aldro T. Painter. Born in Falmouth, Mass., in 1886. Pupil of De Camp, Major and Tarbell. Elected Associate Member of the National Academy of Design. Represented in the Boston Museum of Fine Arts by ''Winter Days.'' *Address*, 90 Somerset St., Belmont, Mass.; Main St., Rockport, Mass.

HIBBARD, Frederick C. Sculptor. Born in Canton, Mo., in 1881. Pupil of Art Institute of Chicago under Taft. Work: ''The Virginian,'' at Winchester, Va.; Genl. Grant, Vicksburg, Miss.; and Genl. H. W. Lawton, Ft. Wayne, Ind. *Address*, 923 East 60th St., Chicago, Ill.

HICKOX, Anna L. Painter. Exhibited water colors at the Annual Water Color Exhibition at the Penna. Academy of Fine Arts, Philadelphia, in 1925. *Address*, 1901 Pine St., Philadelphia.

HICKS, Thomas. Painter. Born in Newton, Bucks County, Pa., in 1823; died in 1890. Began painting at the age of 15. Studied in the Penna. Academy of Fine Arts, Philadelphia, Pa., and the Academy of Design, New York. His first important picture, the ''Death of Abel,'' was exhibited in 1841. In 1845 he sailed for Europe, and painted in London, Florence, Rome and Paris. In Paris he was a pupil of Couture. In 1849 he returned to New York and entered upon a successful career as a portrait painter. Among his works are: Portraits of Dr. Kane, Henry Ward Beecher, William C. Bryant, T. Addison Richards, Bayard Taylor, Oliver Wendell Holmes, Henry W. Longfellow, Harriet Beecher Stowe, Daniel Wesley Middleton in the Capitol, at Washington; Mrs. Hicks (wife of the artist) in Metropolitan Museum, New York. He was elected a member of the National Academy in 1851. His portrait of Abraham Lincoln is known from the engraving only.

HIGGINS, Eugene. Painter and etcher. Born in Kansas City, Mo., in 1874. Pupil of St. Louis Art Schools, and he studied later in Paris. Elected Associate Member of the National Academy. He portrays poverty, and types of dissolute and ruined humanity. *Address*, 360 West 22d St., New York, N. Y.

HIGGINS, (W.) Victor. Painter. Born in Shelbyville, Ind., in 1884. Pupil of Academy of Fine Arts in Chicago; Rene Menard and Lucien Simon in Paris; Hans von Hyeck in Munich. Member: Chicago Palette and Chisel Club; Taos Society of Artists. Awards: Gold medal, Palette and Chisel Club, 1914; Altman prize, National Academy of Design, 1918. Work: ''Moorland Piper,'' Terre Haute Art Association; ''Moorland Gorse and Bracken,'' Municipal Gallery, Chicago; mural decorations in Englewood Theatre, Chicago; ''The Bread Jar,'' City of Chicago; ''A Shrine to St. Anthony,'' collection of Des Moines Association of Fine Arts, etc. Instructor in Chicago Academy of Fine Arts. *Address*, Taos, New Mexico.

HIGHWOOD, C. Painter. He painted a portrait of Henry Clay (1777–1852); half length, seated; body to left; arms folded in front; large collar and cravat. Size 29½ by 39½ inches. Painted from life in New York in 1850. Signed ''C. Highwood.'' Sold by American Art Association, New York, December, 1921.

HILDEBRANDT, Cornelia (Ellis). Painter. Born in Eau Claire, Wis. Pupil of Chicago Art Institute; Augustus Koopman and Virginia Reynolds in Paris. Member: National Academy of Women Painters and Sculptors. *Address*, 39 West 67th St., New York, N. Y.

HILDEBRANDT, Howard L. Painter. Born in Allegheny, Pa., in 1872. Pupil of École des Beaux Arts under Constant and Laurens in Paris; National Academy of Design in New York. Associate Member of National Academy. Work: ''Cleaning Fish,'' John Herron Art Institute, Indianapolis; represented in Lotos Club, New York; Butler Art Institute, Youngstown, Ohio. *Address*, 306 East 51st St., New York, N. Y.

HILDER, G. Howard. Painter and illustrator. Born in London, England, in 1868. Pupil of Bouguereau, Ferrier, Dagnan-Bouveret, De la Gandara and Jacque in Paris; De Bock in Amsterdam. Member: St. Lucas Society, Amsterdam, Holland; Newport Artists' Association. *Address*, Charleston, S. C.

HILDRETH, Susan W. Painter. Born in Cambridge, Mass. Pupil of Ross Turner; Art Students' League of New York. *Address*, 425 West 118th St., New York, N. Y.

HILL, A. T. Painter. Born in New York in 1868. Pupil of Brooklyn Institute Art School; chiefly self-taught; studied works of George Inness. Work: ''The Dunes–Amagansett,'' and ''The Marshes—Amagansett,'' Museum of the Brooklyn Institute; ''After a Storm,'' National Gallery, Washington, D. C.; ''Low Tide—Amagansett,'' National Arts Club, New York. *Address*, 33 West 67th St., New York, N. Y.

HILL, Clara. Sculptor. Born in Massachusetts. Pupil of Augustus Saint Gaudens; Julien Academy under Puech, and Colarossi Academy under Injalbert, in Paris. *Address*, Arts Club, 2017 I St., Washington, D. C.

HILL, James. In 1803 James Hill engraved some crude Bible illustrations published in Charlestown, Mass. He also engraved a large plate of the ''Resurrection of a Pious Family,'' after the painting by the English clergyman, Rev. William Peters. This was published in Boston, without date; but the copy of this print sold in the Clark sale, Boston, 1901, shows a watermark of ''1792'' in the paper, though this paper may be older than the impression. It is executed in stipple, and a large plate of the same subject was engraved by Thomas Clarke and published in New York in 1797.

HILL, James Jerome II. Painter. Born in 1905. Member: Society of Independent Artists. *Address*, 260 Summit Ave., St. Paul, Minn.

HILL, John. Engraver. Born in London in 1770; died at West Nyack, N. Y., in 1850. John Hill engraved in aquatint a considerable number of plates published in London, the best of these being a series of views after the paintings of J. M. W. Turner, Loutherberg, and others. Hill came to New York in the summer of 1816, but soon removed to Philadelphia, and remained there until 1824. He lived in New York from 1824 until 1839. The first plates executed in the United States by Hill were his small magazine plates of Haddrill's Point and York Springs, Pa. He later issued his American drawing-books, with colored plates; but his best work is found in ''The Landscape Album,'' a series of large aquatint plates of American scenery, after the paintings by Joshua Shaw, and published by Hill and Shaw in Philadelphia in 1820. His ''Hudson River Port Folio'' is an equally good series of still larger plates; these views on the Hudson were aquatinted by Hill after paintings by W. G. Wall. One of his last plates was a large view of Broadway, New York, published in 1836. He seems to have retired from active work soon after this date.

HILL, J. W. In Dunlap's ''History of the Arts'' he is recorded as painting landscapes in New York.

HILL, John Henry. Engraver. Son of J. W. Hill, was born in 1839. He is an etcher of landscape.

HILL, John William. Born in England in 1812. He died in this country in 1879. He worked in aquatint and lithography. Later he painted landscapes in water color and achieved considerable reputation; he also drew upon stone for the lithographers.

HILL, Pamela E. Miniature painter. Born in 1803; died in 1860. Exhibited at a number of the Boston Athenaeum Exhibitions. She painted miniatures of Mrs. Joel Thayer, Miss L. B. Vose, Rev. Mr. Sharp, Rev. Mr. Croswell, and Miss Walsingham. Her studio in 1834 was at 28 Somerset St., Boston.

HILL, Pearl L. Painter. Born in Lock Haven, Pa, in 1884. Pupil of Penna. Museum and School of Industrial Art. Member: Plastic Club; Fellowship, Penna. Academy of Fine Arts; Philadelphia Art Alliance. *Address*, 10 South 18th St., Philadelphia, Pa.

HILL, R. Jerome. Painter. Born in Austin, Texas. Pupil of Art Students' League of New York, and of Kunz-Meyer. Member: Dallas Artists' Association; Texas Art League; Dallas Art Club. *Address*, 1802½ Elm St., Dallas, Texas.

HILL, Samuel. Engraver. As early as 1789 Samuel Hill was engraving in Boston, and he made many portraits and engraved early American views for the *Massachusetts Magazine*, published in that city. In 1803 Hill engraved some Bible plates for the New York publisher, William Durell. In *Russell's Gazette*, Boston, 1794, Samuel Hill advertises as "engraver and copperplate printer, with a shop at No. 2 Cornhill."

HILL, Sara B. Etcher. Born in Danbury, Conn. Pupil of Alphaeus Cole. Member: American Bookplate Society; Bookworkers Guild. *Address*, 135 East 66th St., New York, N. Y.

HILL, S. W. A little known landscape painter, who also painted fruit-pieces.

HILL, Thomas. Painter. Born in England in 1829, he came to the United States in 1840 and settled in Taunton, Mass. He later removed to Philadelphia and studied in the life class of the Penna. Academy of Fine Arts. He studied in Paris in 1866 and in 1867 opened his studio in Boston. He soon moved to San Francisco. Among his works: "Yosemite Valley"; "Danner Lake"; "The Heart of the Sierras"; "The Yellowstone Cañon." He died in 1908.

HILLARD, William H. Painter. He died in Washington, D. C., in 1905. Among his best known paintings were "The Fight above the Clouds" and a portrait of President Garfield.

HILLBOM, Henrik. Painter. Born in Sweden in 1863. Pupil of Lefebvre and Constant. Member: Conn. Association of Fine Arts. Silver designer with Wallace Mfg. Co. since 1899. *Address*, Wallingford, Conn.

HILLER, J., Jr. Engraver. A close copy of the Joseph Wright etching of Washington is signed "J. Hiller Ju'r Sculp. 1794." This Hiller portrait has only appeared on the back of playing cards and the few copies known all come from New England.

It is possible that this J. Hiller, Jr., was Joseph Hiller, Jr., son of Major Joseph Hiller, an officer in the Revolution and the collector of customs at Salem, Mass., in 1789–1802. The younger Hiller was born in Salem, June 21, 1777, and the "Cleveland Genealogy" says

that he was lost overboard from a ship off the Cape of Good Hope in 1795.

HILLER, Lejaren A. Illustrator and painter. Born in Milwaukee, Wis., in 1880. Pupil of Art Institute, Chicago, Ill. *Address*, 322 West 28th St., New York.

HILLES, Carrie P. Miniature painter. Exhibited at the Penna. Academy of Fine Arts, Philadelphia, in 1925. *Address*, 238 Allen Lane, Germantown, Philadelphia.

HILLIARD, William Henry. Painter. Born in Auburn, N. Y., in 1836. He studied art in New York City; also studied abroad, and on his return to this country established his studio in Boston. Landscapes and marine views are his specialty, and among his best known works are views of Maine, the White Mountains and the Atlantic Coast, including "Castle Rock"; "Wind against Tide"; "Allatoona Pass, Ga."

HILLS, A. A. Painter. Born in Ravenna, Ohio. Pupil of Art Institute of Chicago; Cooper Union; of Julien in Paris. Member: California Art Club; Laguna Beach Artists' Association. *Address*, Laguna Beach, Calif.

HILLS, J. H. This line-engraver was working at his profession in Burlington, Vt., about 1845–50. Though his plates possess considerable merit, his lack of business ability interfered with his success and he abandoned engraving.

HILLS, Laura Coombs. Miniature painter. Born in Newburyport, Mass., in 1859. Pupil of Helen M. Knowlton, Cowles Art School and Art Students' League, New York. Medal, Art Interchange, 1895; Paris Exposition, 1900; medal of honor, Panama, P. I., Exposition, 1915; 1st award of medal of honor, Penna. Society of Miniature Painters, 1916. Elected Associate Member of the National Academy. Member: Woman's Art Club; American Society of Miniature Painters; Water Color Club. *Address*, 66 Chestnut St., Boston, Mass.

HILLYER, William. Portrait painter in oils and miniatures, flourishing in New York 1834–1861. Member of the firm of Miller & Hillyer.

HINCHMAN, Margaret S. Painter. Exhibited water colors at the Annual Exhibition of Water Colors at the Penna. Academy of Fine Arts, Philadelphia, 1925. *Address*, 3635 Chestnut St., Philadelphia.

HINCKLEY, Robert. Painter. Born in 1835. Studied art in Paris 1864 to 1884 and has had a studio in Washington, D. C., since 1884, where he has painted 350 portraits of eminent Americans. He also was the instructor of the portrait class at the Corcoran Art School for six years. His portraits of Chas. F. Crisp and John E. Rutledge are in the Capitol Building, Washington, D. C.

HINCKLEY, Thomas Hewes. Born in Milton, Mass., 1813. He early devoted himself to animal painting. In 1851 he went abroad to study the work of Sir Edwin Landseer and the Flemish masters. He painted two pictures of dogs and game in 1858, which were exhibited at the Royal Academy. Among his early works were a few portraits and landscapes. He died in 1896.

HINE, Charles. Painter. Born in Bethany, Conn., in 1827. Studied with Jared B. Flagg. His work was largely figure-pieces, and his masterpiece was a nude figure, "Sleep." He died in New Haven in 1871.

HINGSTON. Line-engraver of bill-heads and work of that description, apparently working in Georgetown, near Washington, D. C., as he signs his plates "Hingston ft., G. Town." One of his plates is a bill-head for the City Hotel of Alexandria, Va. The work appears to belong to the first quarter of the last century.

HINMAN, D. C. This capital engraver of portraits in stipple was working about 1830–35, both over his own name and as a member of the firm of Daggett, Hinman & Co., of New Haven, Conn.

HINSCHELWOOD, Robert. Engraver. Born in Edinburgh in 1812. He came to the United States about 1835 and was employed as a landscape engraver by the Harpers and other New York publishers. He also worked for the Ladies' Repository, of Cincinnati, about 1855, and was later, for a long time, in the employ of the Continental Bank Note Co. of New York.

Hinschelwood married a sister of James Smillie and many of his landscape plates are engraved after Smillie's drawings.

HINSDALE, Richard. Landscape and genre painter. Born in Hartford, Conn., in 1825. He died early in life, when his work was beginning to show great promise.

HINTERMEISTER, Henry. Painter and illustrator. Born in New York in 1897. Member of New York Water Color Club. *Address,* 4622 Fourteenth Ave., Brooklyn, N. Y.

HINTON, Charles Louis. Painter and sculptor. Born in Ithaca, N. Y., in 1869. Studied art at National Academy of Design, New York; also in the Julien Academy and the École des Beaux Arts, Paris. Teacher of drawing in the National Academy of Design since 1901; also of Woman's Art School of Cooper Union since 1903. He has exhibited paintings and small bronzes in numerous ex-

hibitions in N. Y. City; painted life-size mural painting for Orphans' Court, City Court House, Wilkes-Barre, Pa. Elected an Associate Member of the National Academy. *Address,* Bronxville, N. Y.

HINTON, Mrs. Howard. Sculptor. Pupil of Lant Thompson. She was born in 1834 and died in New York City.

HIRAMOTO, Masaji. Sculptor. Exhibited at Penna. Academy Ex. in 1924. *Address,* 102 West 103d St., New York.

HIRSCHBERG, Carl. Painter and illustrator. Born in Germany in 1854. Pupil of Art Students' League; also studied in Paris. Specialty, figure painter of genre. Founder of Salmagundi Club. Died in 1923.

HIRSH, Alice Y. Painter. Exhibited at the 33d Annual Exhibition of National Association of Women Painters and Sculptors, New York. *Address,* 51 West 10th St., New York.

HIRST, Claude R. (Mrs.). Painter. Born in Cincinnati, Ohio. *Address,* 65 West 11th St., New York.

HITCHCOCK, Geo. Painter. Born in 1850. Studied painting in Paris. Exhibited "Tulip-Growing," Paris Salon, 1887. He was fond of painting subjects and places in Holland. Elected an Associate Member of the National Academy. He died in 1913.

HITCHCOCK, Lucius W. Painter and illustrator. Born in West Williamsfield, Ohio, in 1868. Pupil of Art Students' League of New York; Constant, Laurens and Colarossi Academy in Paris. *Address,* Point Park, New Rochelle, N. Y.

HITE, George H. Miniature painter; flourished 1839–61 in New York.

HITTELL, Charles J. Painter. Born in San Francisco, 1861. Studied in San Francisco School of Design, 1881–83; Royal Academy of Fine Arts, Munich, 1884–88; Academie Julien, Paris, 1892–93. Since 1893 he has been engaged in painting Western American subjects, figures and landscapes. His landscapes are in the American Museum of Natural History, New York; and in the Museum of Vertebrate Zoology, Berkeley, Calif. *Address,* San José, Santa Clara County, Calif.

HITTLE, Margaret A. Painter, illustrator and etcher. Born in 1886. Pupil of Art Institute of Chicago. Has executed mural panels in several schools in Chicago, Ill. *Address,* 55 Arlington Place, Chicago, Ill.

HOARD, Margaret. Sculptor. Born in Iowa. Pupil of Art Students' League of New York. Represented in Metropolitan Museum of New York.

HOBART, Clark. Painter and etcher. Born in Illinois. Pupil of Art Students' League, New York; also studied in Paris. *Address*, 1371 Post St., San Francisco, Calif.

HOBART, Elijah. Engraver. Born in England; was killed in battle during the Civil War of 1861–63. As early as 1845 Hobart was engraving in Albany and in New York. He was a good line-engraver of portraits and was at one time, apparently, in the employ of Joseph Andrews, as we find plates engraved by Hobart under the "direction" of that engraver. The most ambitious work of this engraver found by the writer is a folio line-plate of "The Landing of the Pilgrims," dedicated to the Pilgrims Society of Plymouth and published by Hobart in 1850, apparently in Boston, Mass.

HOBER, Arthur. Painter. Born in New York City, 1854. Studied in Art Students' League under Beckwith and later in Paris under Gerome. He contributed to many exhibitions and in 1909 was elected an Associate of the National Academy of Design. He died in 1915.

HODGE, Mrs. Helen F. Painter. Born in Topeka, Kan. Pupil of Corcoran School of Art in Washington. Awards: Five first prizes, Kansas State Fair. *Address*, 714 Kansas Ave., Topeka, Kan.

HOECKNER, Carl. Painter. Born in Munich, Germany, in 1883. Studied in Hamburg and Cologne. Member: Chicago Society of Artists. "Cor Ardens." *Address*, 63 West Ontario St., Chicago, Ill.

HOFFBAUER, Charles. Painter. Born in Paris, France, 1875. Pupil of Gustave Moreau, F. Flameng and Cormon in Paris. Member: Societe Internationale; New York Architectural League, 1912. Work: "Les Gueux," Museum of Rouen; "The Roof Garden," Carnegie Institute, Pittsburgh; "Revolte de Flamands," Memorial Hall, Phila.; "Coin de Bataille," Luxembourg, Paris; "Sur les Toits," National Gallery, Sydney, N. S. Wales; mural decorations in Confederate Memorial Hall, Richmond, Va. *Address*, The Players' Club, 16 Gramercy Park, New York, N. Y.

HOFFMAN, Gustave Adolph. Painter and etcher. Born in Brandenburg, Germany, 1869. Pupil of National Academy of Design and Royal Academy of Fine Arts, Munich. Represented by a series of etchings in the National Gallery, Berlin; Royal Gallery, Munich; National Gallery, Leipzig; Art Gallery, Frankfort; British Museum, London; Lenox Library,

New York City; Capitol, Hartford; Superior Court, Rockville, Conn. *Address*, 5 Laurel St., Rockville, Conn.

HOFFMAN, Harry Leslie. Painter. Born in Cressona, Pa. Studied at Julien Academy, Paris, and under Du Mond in New York. Represented at Boston Art Club; Art Institute of Chicago; Museum at Memphis, Tennessee. *Address*, 50 West 67th St., New York, N. Y.

HOFFMAN, Malvina. Sculptor and painter. Born in New York City, 1887. Pupil of Rodin in Paris; Gutzon Borglum in New York. Member: National Institute of Social Sciences; Three Arts Club, New York; National Academy of Women Painters and Sculptors. Work: "Russian Bacchanale," Luxembourg Museum, Paris; "Head of Modern Crusader," Metropolitan Museum of Art, New York; "Pavlowa Gavotte," Detroit Institute; "Modern Crusader," Art Institute of Chicago. *Address*, 157 East 35th St., New York, N. Y.

HOFFMAN, Wilmer. Sculptor. Exhibited at Penna. Academy of Fine Arts in 1924. *Address*, 219 South 17th St., Philadelphia.

HOFFMANN, Arnold. Landscape painter. Exhibited at Annual Exhibition of National Academy of Design, 1925. *Address*, West New York, N. J.

HOFFMANN, Maximilian A. Sculptor and painter. Born in Trier, Germany, in 1888. Pupil of Milwaukee Art Students' League; Royal Academy, Munich. Member: Chicago Society of Artists. He died in 1922.

HOFFY, Alfred. Portrait painter, crayon portrait draughtsman and lithographer. Hoffy exhibited at the Pennsylvania Academy for a number of years and was working in Philadelphia, 1840–52.

HOFSTETTER, W. A. Painter. Exhibited at the Annual Exhibition of Water Colors at the Penna. Academy of Fine Arts, 1925. *Address*, Glenside, Penna.

HOFTRUP, J. Lars. Painter. Exhibited at Penna. Academy of Fine Arts in 1924. *Address*, 400 West 57th St., New York, N. Y.

HOLBERG, Richard A. Painter. Exhibited water colors at the Annual Water Color Exhibition at the Penna. Academy of Fine Arts, Philadelphia, 1925. *Address*, Rockport, Mass.

HOLDEN, Cora. Mural painter. Born in New England. Pupil of Massachusetts Normal Art School and Cleveland School of Art; she has studied in Europe. Her murals are in the Federal Reserve Bank of Cleveland and Goodyear Hall, Akron, Ohio. *Address*, Cleveland Museum of Art.

HOLLAND, F. Raymond. Painter. Born in Pittsburgh, Pa., in 1886. Pupil of Art Students' League of New York. Member: Society of Independent Artists; Silvermine Group; Conn. Society of Artists; Pittsburgh Artists' Association. Award: Second prize, Pittsburgh Artists' Association, 1916. Work: "Marsh House," Darien, Conn. *Address*, 627 Madison Ave., New York, N. Y.

HOLLAND, John Joseph. Scene-painter. Born in London in 1776, he came to Philadelphia in 1796 and worked at the Chestnut Street Theatre. He also painted landscapes in water colors; in 1797 he drew a view of Philadelphia which was engraved by Gilbert Fox.

HOLLAND, Thomas. Landscape artist working in New York about 1800. He exhibited in Philadelphia at the Society of Artists Exhibition in 1811.

HOLLINGSWORTH, Geo. Born in Milton, Mass., in 1813. He painted a portrait of Captain Fisher of Milton (owned by the Boston Museum of Fine Arts). He died in 1892.

HOLLISTER, Antoinette B. Sculptor. Born in Chicago, Ill., in 1873. Pupil of Art Institute of Chicago; Injalbert and Rodin in Paris. Member: Chicago Society of Artists. Shaffer prize for sculpture, Art Institute of Chicago, Chicago, 1919. *Address*, Foster Hall, University of Chicago, Chicago, Ill.

HOLLOWAY, Edward Stratton. Painter. Born in Ashland, N. Y. Studied art at Penna. Academy of Fine Arts, Philadelphia. Specialty, marines and landscapes. Decorative designer, particularly of book covers and decorations. *Address*, Care of J. B. Lippincott Co., Philadelphia.

HOLLYER, Samuel. Engraver. Born in London in 1826; died in New York City in 1919. Mr. Hollyer was a pupil of the Findens in London. He came to the United States in 1851; but he twice returned to England for periods of two and six years, and finally settled in this country in 1866. Besides engraving, Mr. Hollyer was engaged here at different times in lithography, photography and the publishing business.

He was an excellent engraver in both line and in stipple and has produced a large number of portraits, landscapes and historical subjects. Among his larger and best plates are "The Flaw in the Title," "Charles Dickens in His Study" and "The Gleaner."

HOLM, Victor S. Sculptor. Born in Copenhagen, Denmark, in 1876, he came to America in 1890; pupil of Lorado Taft, Chicago; Art Institute of Chicago, 1894–98; Art Students' League, New York. Instructor in sculpture and lecturer on history of art, St. Louis School of Fine Arts (Washington University) since 1909. Principal works: Missouri State Monument at Vicksburg, Miss.; Halsey C. Ives Memorial in City Art Museum, St. Louis; Barnes Memorial, Barnes Hosp., St. Louis; Gov. Thomas Carlin Monument, Carrollton, Ill.; Luman Parker Monument, Rolla, Mo.; The Crucifixion and the Papal Trophy, St. Pious Church, St. Louis. Member: National Sculpture Society; St. Louis Artists' Guild; St. Louis Art League; Washington University Faculty Club, etc. *Address*, School of Fine Arts, Washington University, St. Louis, Mo.

HOLMAN, Louis Arthur. Illustrator. Born at Summerside, P. E. I., in 1866. Illustrated "Boston, the Place and the People," in 1903, "Boston Common" in 1910; contributor also to *Scribner's*, *Century*, *Printing Art*, etc. *Address*, 9A Ashburn Place, Boston, Mass.

HOLMES, William H. Painter. Born in Harrison County, Ohio, 1846. Self-taught. Awards: First Corcoran prize, Washington Water Color Club, 1900; Parson's prize, Washington Water Color Club, 1902. Member: Washington Water Color Club; Society of Washington Artists; Curator, National Gallery of Art; Geologist and Archaeologist of Smithsonian Institution. Represented at Corcoran Gallery by "Mid-summer" painted in 1907.

HOLSLAG, Edward J. Painter and mural designer. Born in Buffalo, N. Y., in 1870. Pupil of National Academy of Design, and of John La Farge. He exhibited portraits and landscapes at the Chicago Art Institute, and is represented by murals in the Congressional Library, Washington, D. C., and in many banks, theatres and public buildings. He died in De Kalb, Ill., in 1924. He was formerly president of the Palette and Chisel Club.

HOLSMAN, Elizabeth Tuttle. Painter and sculptor. Born in Brownville, Nebr., in 1873. Pupil of Art Institute of Chicago. He painted portraits of David Rankin and Joseph Addison Thompson; executed bas-reliefs of Dr. Beesey, Dean Reese and Lieut. Alexander McCornick. *Address*, 1224 East 57th St., Chicago, Ill.

HOLT, Samuel. Miniature painter. Born in Meriden, Conn., in 1801. He lived in Hartford for many years.

HOLYLAND, C. I. Engraver. He engraved on copper in New York in 1834. The only plate known is an allegorical frontispiece to "A Defense of Particular Redemption—In four letters to a Baptist Minister," New York, 1834. He signed his work "C. I. Holyland Sc."

HOLYOKE. A little known genre painter of some talent.

HOLZER, J. A. Mural painter and sculptor. Born in Berne, Switzerland, in 1858. Pupil of Fournier and Bernard in Paris. His mural, "Homer," is at Princeton University, Princeton, N. J. *Address*, 182 East 72d St., New York, N. Y.

HOMAN, S. V. Miniature painter, flourishing in Boston in 1844.

HOMER, Winslow. This noted landscape, marine and genre painter was born in Boston in 1836; died at Scarboro, Me., in 1910. Beginning work for a lithographer when nineteen years old, he took up painting and illustrating two years later. He came to New York in 1859, and for a short time studied at the National Academy of Design and with Frederick Rondel. He was sent by Harper & Brothers to make war paintings in 1861; he subsequently painted many pictures of negro life, and a visit to the Adirondack mountains inspired him to paint camping scenes with mountain guides. Later he traveled in England and France. He is best known by his pictures of the Maine coast, where for many years he lived the life of a recluse at Scarboro. He was elected an Associate of the National Academy in 1864, and an Academician the following year, and was a member of the American Water Color Society and the National Institute of Arts and Letters.

HONIG, George H. Portrait painter and sculptor. Born in Rockport, Ind., in 1881. Pupil of National Academy of Design. He designed and executed many war memorials. *Address*, 315 Mercantile Bank Bldg., Evansville, Ind.

HONORE, Paul. Painter, illustrator and etcher. Born in Pennsylvania in 1885. Pupil of Brangwyn and Wicker. Member: Scarab Club; Association for Culture, New York; Fine and Industrial Art Guild. *Address*, 4729 Fourth Ave., Detroit, Mich.

HOOGLAND, William. He was an admirable engraver in both line and stipple. He appears in New York about 1815 as the designer and engraver of vignettes. In 1826 he was working with Abel Bowen in Boston, and among his pupils there were John Cheney and Joseph Andrews. In 1841 he was again located in business in New York. Hoogland was one of the early American bank-note engravers.

HOOKER, Margaret Huntington. Painter. Born in Rochester, N. Y., in 1869. Studied in Art Students' League and Metropolitan Schools of New York; also studied in Paris and London. Taught art in Normal School, Cortland, N. Y., 1893–94; illustrated for *New York Tribune*, 1897; now teaching arts and crafts in Paris.

HOOKER, William. As early as 1805 Hooker was engraving in Philadelphia, and in 1810 he was one of the organizers of the Philadelphia Society of Artists. In 1816 he removed to New York and his name appears in the directories of that city until 1840. His occupation is generally given as "Engraver," but he also appears as "map-publisher" and as "instrument maker and chart-seller to the U. S. Navy." The "New Pocket Plan of New York," of 1817, is "Drawn, engraved, published and sold" by Hooker. He engraved a few portraits in stipple, and subject plates in line, but he seems to have been chiefly employed in map engraving.

HOOPER, Mrs. Annie Blakeslee. Painter and illustrator. Born in California. Pupil of San Francisco Art School; Art Students' League of New York, and Charles Melville Dewey. Member: New York Water Color Club. *Address*, 200 Fifth Ave., New York, N. Y.

HOOPER, Edward. Born in England in 1829; died in Brooklyn, 1870. He was an engraver and was for many years a member of the firm of Bobbett and Hooper, wood-engravers. Mr. Hooper produced several water colors remarkable for their accuracy of drawing and harmony of color. He was one of the originators of the American Water Color Society.

HOOPER, Will Phillip. Painter and illustrator. Born in Biddeford, Me. Pupil of Benjamin Fitz and of Art Students' League, New York; Mass. Normal Art School, Boston. Member: New York Water Color Club; Salmagundi Club. *Address*, 200 Fifth Ave., New York, N. Y.

HOPE, James. Painter. Born in England in 1818, he accompanied his father to Canada; after the death of his parent he removed to Fair Haven, Vt., and became interested in art. In 1853 he opened his studio in New York and was elected an Associate of the National Academy. His pictures include "The Army of the Potomac," "Rainbow Falls," "The Gem of the Forest," and the "Forest Glen." He died in 1892.

HOPE, John W. Sculptor. Exhibited at National Academy of Design in 1925. Specialty, animals. *Address*, 65 Gun Hill Road, N. Y.

HOPE, Thomas W. Portrait and miniature painter, flourishing 1839–45 in New York.

HOPKIN, Robt. Painter. Born in Scotland, 1832, he went with his parents when eleven years old to Detroit, Mich., where he grew up and became the head of the art interests of that city. His best work consists of landscape and marine painting. He died in 1909.

HOPKINS, C. E. Painter and etcher. Born in Cincinnati, Ohio, in 1886. Pupil of Newotany and Barnhorn. Member: Cincinnati Art Club. *Address*, 3525 Trimble Ave., Evanston, Cincinnati, Ohio.

HOPKINS, Daniel. Engraver. This man engraved the music and words for "The Rudiments of Music," etc. The book is dated in 1783, and it was published in Cheshire, Conn.

HOPKINS, Edna Boles (Mrs. James R. Hopkins). Engraver. Born in Michigan. Member: Societé Internationale des Graveurs en Couleurs; Societé Internationale des Graveurs sur Bois; Societé Nationale des Beaux Arts in Paris. Work: In Library of Congress, Washington, D. C.; Walker Art Gallery, Liverpool; National Museum, Stockholm; Bibliotheque d'Art et Archaeologie, Paris; Cincinnati Art Museum; Detroit Institute of Arts. *Address*, 55 rue de Dantzig, Paris, France.

HOPKINS, James R. Painter. Born in Irwin, Ohio, in 1877. Studied at Art Academy of Cincinnati; also in Paris; then traveled around the world, studying art in Japan, China, Ceylon, Egypt, Italy, etc.; painted in Paris 1904–14. Member of Faculty (drawing and painting) Art Academy of Cincinnati since 1914. Awards: Walter Lippincott prize, Penna. Academy of Fine Arts, 1908. Elected Associate Member of the National Academy. Represented in Memorial Hall Museum, Philadelphia, Pa.; Cincinnati Museum Association; Atlanta Art Association; Art Institute of Chicago. *Address*, Columbus, Ohio.

HOPKINS, Mark. Sculptor. Born in Williamstown, Mass., in 1881. Pupil of Frederick MacMonnies. Member: Societé des Artistes Français; Union Internationale des Beaux Arts. *Address*, Giverny-par-Vernon, Eure, France.

HOPKINSON, Charles Sydney. Portrait painter. Born in Cambridge, Mass., in 1860. He studied in New York and in Paris. He was commanded by the National Art Community in 1919 to paint portraits of war celebrities. Represented at Harvard University; National Gallery of Art, Washington, D. C.; the Rhode Island School of Design. *Address*, Fenway Studios, 30 Ipswich Street, Boston, Mass.

HOPKINSON, Francis. Painter and lawyer, signer of the Declaration of Independence, was born in 1737. He drew and painted several portraits. He died in 1791.

HOPPE, Leslie F. Designer. Born in Jerseyville, Ill., in 1889. Pupil of Chicago Academy of Fine Arts and Art Institute of Chicago. Member: Palette and Chisel Club. *Address*, 415 South Claremont Ave., Chicago, Illinois.

HOPPER, Edward. Painter, illustrator and etcher. Born in Nyack, N. Y., in 1882. Pupil of Henri, Hayes Miller and Chase. Represented in California State Library. *Address*, 3 Washington Square, North, New York, N. Y.

HOPPIN, AUGUSTUS. Painter and wood engraver. Born in Providence, R. I., in 1828. He illustrated and engraved for many publications.

HOPPIN, Howard. Painter. Member of Providence Art Club. *Address*, 32 Westminster St., Providence, R. I.

HOPPIN, Thomas Frederick. Born in Providence, R. I., in 1816. Studied in Philadelphia and later in Paris under Delaroche. On his return to this country he opened his studio in New York. He has produced statues in plaster, stained glass designs, also many etchings and illustrations of American life and history. The American Art Union in 1848 and 1850 published two of his etchings.

HOPSON, William Fowler. Illustrator and engraver. Born in Watertown, Conn., in 1849. Pupil of L. Sanford, New Haven, and J. D. Felter, New York. Exhibited at Paris Exposition in 1900. Specialty, engraving and designing book-plates. *Address*, 730 Whitney Ave., New Haven, Conn.

HOPWOOD. A mixed copper-plate engraving is signed "Hopwood Sc." The title is "A Winter Piece"; it shows a snow scene with cottage in right background, tree in left; in the center of foreground is a man with a stick in his right hand standing by a horse with a pannier. This print was published in 1803 by J. Nicholdson, Halifax.

HORNE, Laura Trevitte. Painter. Born in Dalton, Ga., in 1891. Pupil of John Carlsen; Francis Jones; Van Dearing Perrine. Member: Newport Artists' Association. *Address*, Woodstock, N. Y.

HORNE, Nellie Mathes. Painter. Born at Eliot, Me., in 1870. Studied art with N. D. Tenney. Painted portraits of Ed. Everett Hale, Hon. Frank Jones and others. *Address*, The Dewey, Washington, D. C.

HORNER, T. About 1844 Horner was living at Sing Sing, N. Y., and he there engraved a large "View of New York from Brooklyn," published by W. Neale of New York.

HORNLY, Lester George. Painter and etcher. Born in Lowell, Mass., in 1882. Student of School of Design, Providence, R. I.; also studied in Paris under Jean Paul Laurens and other masters. Represented by etchings in New York and Boston Public Libraries; Congressional Library; South Kensington Museum, London. *Address*, 9A Park St., Boston, Mass.

HORSFALL, R. Bruce. Painter. Born in Clinton, Ia., in 1869. Studied at Cincinnati Art Academy, 1886–89; gained European scholarship and studied at Art Academy, Munich, and in Paris, France. Has exhibited at Chicago, Ill., since 1886; and at Midwinter Exposition, San Francisco. Made scientific illustrations for American Museum of Natural History, New York, 1898–1901; illustrated ''Land Mammals of the Western Hemisphere,'' 1912–13; also many books of birds, etc. Permanently represented by 12 backgrounds for Habitat Groups, American Museum of Natural History, New York. *Address*, Box 80, R. 6, Portland, Ore.

HORTER, Earl. Painter, illustrator and etcher. Member of the Society of Illustrators, 1910. His etchings of the streets and industries of the large cities show picturesque qualities of a high order. Work: ''Smelters—Pittsburgh''; ''Madison Square, New York''; and ''Old Creole Quarters, New Orleans.'' *Address*, 4920 Parkside Ave., Philadelphia, Pa.

HORTON. This engraver is simply mentioned in Mr. Stauffer's volume as engraving portraits and views in 1830–35 for Philadelphia and Baltimore publishers. He probably came from Providence, R. I. He engraved a business card of the Roger Williams Hotel in that city, and the card says that this house was ''formerly kept by Mr. Horton,'' but whether the former innkeeper was the engraver himself, or a relative, is uncertain. Horton was certainly engraving for Providence book publishers as early as 1823. In that year he engraved ten copper plates illustrating a ''Complete System of Stenography,'' by J. Dodge.

HORTON, Harriet H. Portrait and miniature painter. Represented by portraits in Minnesota Historical Society. She died in 1922.

HORTON, William S. Painter. Born in Grand Rapids, Mich., in 1865. Pupil of Art Students' League and National Academy of Design, New York; Laurens and Julien Academy in Paris. Represented in Luxembourg Museum by ''Good Friday in Seville,'' also in Brooklyn Museum, New York. *Address*, Studio in Paris.

HOSKIN, Robert. Wood engraver. Born in Brooklyn, N. Y., in 1842. He studied at the Brooklyn Institute where he received the Graham medal. In 1883 he received the gold medal of the Paris Salon for engraving. He has done considerable engraving for the magazines in this country. His best known engraving is ''Cromwell Visiting Milton.''

HOSMER, Harriet. Sculptor. Born in Watertown, Mass., in 1831. Studied in Lenox and Boston. In 1852 she went to Europe with her friend Charlotte Cushman and studied in

Rome. Her principal statues were: ''Puck,'' ''Beatrice Cenci,'' ''Zenobia,'' ''Sleeping Faun,'' and a statue of Thomas H. Benton cast in bronze for Lafayette Park, St. Louis.

HOSTATER, Robert B. Painter. Born in San Francisco. He has lived and studied for the past twenty-five years in Paris. Exhibited at the Salon.

HOTCHKISS. A little known landscape painter who worked much of his time in Italy. He painted views of ''Mount Aetna'' and ''Colosseum by Moonlight.''

HOTCHKISS, Wales. Painter. Born in Bethany, Conn., in 1826. Pupil of George W. Flagg in New Haven. He painted many portraits in oils, but his forte was in water color. He lived in Northampton for years.

HOUDON, Jean Antoine. French sculptor, who came to this country in 1785. He was commissioned by the State of Virginia to execute a statue of Washington. He also made busts of Franklin, Lafayette, Thomas Jefferson, Robert Fulton, Joel Barlow and John Paul Jones. (See ''Memoirs of Life and Works of Houdon,'' by Biddle & Hart, Philadelphia, 1911.)

HOULTON, J. A poorly designed and roughly engraved heading to a certificate of the Charitable Marine Society, of Baltimore, is signed ''J. Houlton Sculp't.'' As the certificate is filled out in 1797, it must have been engraved prior to that date. The design shows Columbia handing a book to a sailor; ship in full sail; lighthouse, etc., in the background. The plate is further signed ''F. Kemelmeyer Delin't.''

HOUSE, James. According to Dunlap House painted a number of portraits in Philadelphia, but gave up art and entered the United States Army. He was known as Colonel House in 1814.

HOUSE, James, Jr. Painter. Exhibited water colors at the Annual Exhibition of Water Colors at the Penna. Academy of Fine Arts, Philadelphia, in 1925. *Address*, 1635 Race St., Philadelphia.

HOUSE, T. He was a bank-note engraver, chiefly employed in Boston. He engraved a few portraits for book publishers and he seemed to be working as early as 1836. He died about 1865. It is said that his full name was Timothy House.

HOUSTON, F. C. Lyons. Painter. Born in 1867. Studied in Paris under Lefebvre and Boulanger. Painted a portrait of Ethel Barrymore. He died in 1906.

HOUSTON, H. H. He was one of the earliest good stipple-engravers of portraits who worked in the United States. He probably came here from Ireland as the *Hibernian Magazine,* of Dublin, contains portraits very similar in execution to his known work and signed "H. Houston."

Houston appears in Philadelphia in 1796 and as his latest dated work was done in 1798, his stay here was a comparatively short one. He engraved two separate plates of John Adams, and portraits of Washington; Rittenhouse; Kemble as Richard III; Kosciusko, etc.

The first state of the John Adams plate published in Philadelphia in 1797 is lettered "H. H. Houston, Sculp't."

HOVENDEN, Martha M. Painter. Exhibited at Annual Exhibition of Penna. Academy of Fine Arts, 1924. *Address,* Plymouth Meeting, Penna.

HOVENDEN, Thomas. Painter. Born in 1840 in Dunmanway, County Cork, Ireland; died 1895 at Plymouth Meeting, Penna. Studied at the Cork School of Design. Came to New York in 1863 and entered the school of the National Academy of Design; studied in Paris under Cabanel. He painted "Jerusalem the Golden," "Last Moments of John Brown," and "A Brittany Image Seller." Elected Member of the National Academy in 1882.

HOVEY, Otis. Painter. Dunlap mentions him as a youthful genius. He made several copies of paintings that possessed merit. Born in Massachusetts in 1788 he moved to Oxford, State of New York. He painted a few portraits but was not successful.

HOWARD, Cecil De Blaquiere. Sculptor. Born in Canada in 1888. At the age of thirteen he started working at the Art School, Buffalo, N. Y. He has done many portraits and animal studies. He is fond of working directly in stone and marble.

HOWARD, Clara F. Miniature painter. Born in Poughkeepsie, N. Y. Pupil of National Academy of Design and Art Students' League, New York. *Address,* 20 Gramercy Park, New York.

HOWARD, Edith L. Painter. Born at Bellows Falls, Vt. Pupil of Daingerfield and Snell. *Address,* 19 West 8th St., New York, N. Y.

HOWARD, Eloise. Painter. Exhibited "Summer" (decorative panel) at 33d Annual Exhibition of National Association of Women Painters and Sculptors. *Address,* Woodstock, New York.

HOWARD, Marion. Landscape painter. Born in Roxbury, Mass. Pupil of Tarbell, Benson and Hale. *Address,* 1517 H St., Washington, D. C.

HOWE, Arthur V. Painter. Born in 1860. Specialty, landscape painting. Died in 1925.

HOWE, William H. Painter. Born at Ravenna, Ohio, in 1846. He began the study of art in 1880 at the Royal Academy of Dusseldorf, Germany, and after working there two years went to Paris. Here he studied with Otto de Thoren and F. de Vuillefroy and had a picture accepted at the Salon of 1883. For ten years thereafter he was a successful exhibitor at the Salon and other European exhibitions. Returning to the United States, he was elected a National Academician in 1897 and a Member of the Society of American Artists in 1899. At the Paris Exposition of 1889 he was awarded a medal of the second class. At London in 1890 he received a gold medal, and in the same year the Temple Gold Medal at the Pennsylvania Academy of Fine Arts, Philadelphia, Pa., and a gold medal at Boston. A medal was awarded to him at the Chicago World's Fair in 1893, a gold medal at San Francisco in 1894, and a gold medal at Atlanta in 1895. He is an Officier d'Academie and a Chevalier of the Legion of Honor, both by decree of the French Government. He has pictures in the permanent collections of the St. Louis Museum of Fine Arts and in the Cleveland Museum.

HOWE, Z. This name, as "Z. Howe Sc't," is signed to a poorly engraved figure of a man used as a frontispiece to "A New Collection of Sacred Harmony, etc.," by Oliver Brownson, Simsbury, Conn., 1797. The music in this collection is also doubtless engraved by Howe.

HOWELL, Felicie Waldo. Painter. Born in Honolulu in 1897. Pupil of Corcoran Art School and Henry B. Snell. Elected an Associate Member of the National Academy. She is represented in the Corcoran Art Gallery, Washington, D. C. *Address,* 58 West 57th St., New York, N. Y.

HOWES, Samuel P. Portrait and miniature painter, who flourished 1829–35 in Boston. He exhibited a portrait of S. Baker in 1833 at the Boston Athenaeum.

HOWITT, John Newton. Painter and illustrator. Born in White Plains, N. Y., in 1885. Pupil of Art Students' League of New York. Member: Society of Illustrators; Guild of Free Lance Artists; League of New York Artists. *Address,* 147 West 23d St., New York.

HOWLAND, Alfred Cornelius. Painter. Born in Walpole, N. H., in 1838; died in Pasadena, Calif., in 1909. Studied art in Boston and New York and was a pupil of the Royal Academy and of Albert Flamm in Dusseldorf, and of Emile Lambinet in Paris. He became an Associate of the National Academy of Design in 1874 and an Academician in 1882. He was a regular exhibitor in New York and his works were frequently seen in Paris and Munich. His studio, during the winter, was in New York, while his summer home was "The Roof Tree," Williamstown, Mass. He painted "Friendly Neighbors" and "The Old Windmill."

HOWLAND, Mrs. Anna Goodhart. Painter. Born in Atchison, Kans., 1871. Pupil of J. H. Moser. Member: Washington Water Color Club. *Address,* 1429 Belmont St., Washington, D. C.

HOWLAND, Edith. Sculptor. Born in Auburn, N. Y. Pupil of Gustave Michel in Paris, and of Augustus Saint Gaudens. Member: Art Students' League of New York; National Academy of Women Painters and Sculptors. Award: Honorable mention, Paris Salon, 1913. Represented in Metropolitan Museum by marble group "Between Yesterday and Tomorrow."

HOWLAND, George. Painter. Born in New York in 1865. Pupil of Benjamin-Constant, Laurens and Collin in Paris. Awards: Honorable mention, Paris Salon, 1914; silver medal, Paris Salon, 1921. Member: Chevalier of the Legion of Honor of France. *Address,* 29 Quai Voltaire, Paris, France.

HOWS, John Augustus. Painter. Born in New York City, he graduated from Columbia in 1852. He studied art and in 1862 was elected an Associate Member of the National Academy. He has been successful as a wood-engraver and illustrator. Among his paintings are "An Adirondack Lake," Sanctuary of St. Alban's Church, N. Y., and "Paul Smiths, St. Regis." He died in 1874.

HOXTE, Vinner Ream. Sculptor. Born in Madison, Wis., in 1847, and died in Washington, 1914. She studied under Bonnat in Paris and with Majolilin in Rome. Her statues of Abraham Lincoln, in the rotunda of the Capitol, Washington, D. C., and Admiral Farragut, standing in Farragut Square, Washington, were executed under commissions from Congress. Among her other productions were many portrait busts and medallions of prominent Americans and foreigners, and a number of ideal statues.

HOYT, Albert G. Painter. Born in Sandwich, N. H., in 1800; died in 1856. He studied in France and Italy and on his return to this country settled in Boston where he painted many portraits. He was the first President of the Boston Art Club. His full length portrait of Daniel Webster is owned by the Union League Club of New York.

HOYT, Edith. Painter. Born in West Point, N. Y. Pupil of Charles Woodbury. *Address,* 1301 21st St., N. W., Washington, D. C.

HUBARD, William J. Portrait painter. Born in Warwick, England, in 1807; died in Richmond, Virginia, 1862. Had assistance and advice of Robert W. Weir and Thomas Sully. Exhibited at the National Academy of Design, 1834. At one time he painted portraits in Baltimore. Represented by Portrait of John C. Calhoun in Corcoran Gallery, Washington, D. C.

HUBBARD, C. D. Painter and illustrator. Born in Newark, N. J., in 1876. Pupil of Kenyon Cox and John H. Niemeyer. Member: Guild of Free Lance Artists. *Address,* 37 Park St., Guilford, Conn.

HUBBARD, Frank McKinney. Caricaturist. Born at Bellefontaine, Ohio. Employed as caricaturist on *Indianapolis News* since 1891. *Address,* Indianapolis News, Indianapolis, Indiana.

HUBBARD, Mary W. Painter. Born in Springfield, Mass., in 1871. Pupil of Art Students' League of New York; Constant in Paris. Member: National Academy of Women Painters and Sculptors; New York Water Color Club. *Address,* 142 East 40th St., New York, N. Y.

HUBBARD, Platt. Painter. Born in Columbus, Ohio, in 1889. Pupil of Robert Henri; has also studied in Paris. *Address,* Old Lyme, Conn.

HUBBARD, Richard W. Painter. Born in Middletown, Conn., in 1817. American landscape painter, Lake George and the Connecticut River are his favorite scenes. In 1858 he was elected a member of the National Academy. Among his paintings are "High Peak"; "North Conway"; "Vermont Hills"; "The Adirondacks"; "Early Autumn." He died in 1888.

HUBBARD, Whitney M. Painter. Born in Middletown, Conn., in 1875. Pupil of F. V. Du Mond. Member: Conn. Society of Artists; Brooklyn Water Color Club; Conn. Academy of Fine Arts. *Address,* 511 First St., Greenport, N. Y.

HUBBELL, Henry Salem. Painter. Born in Paoli, Kans., in 1870. Pupil of Art Institute of Chicago; also studied in Paris with Jean Paul Laurens, Raphael Collin and Whistler; studied for a while in Madrid, Spain. As a painter he made his debut at the Paris Salon, 1901, with a large picture, "The Bargain"; other pictures: "The Return"; "The Poet" (bought by Wm. M. Chase); "The Brasses" (now in Wilstach Collection, Memorial Hall Museum, Philadelphia); "Child and Cat" (bought by French Govt.); "Larkspurs" (bought by French Govt.); also has painted various portraits. Honorable mention, Paris Salon; medal, Paris Salon. Member: Paris Society of American Painters; Societé Internationale de Peinture et de Sculpture, Paris; National Association of Portrait Painters. Elected Associate Member of the National Academy. Now head of School of Painting and Decoration, Carnegie Institute of Tech., Pittsburgh, Pa. *Address*, Carnegie Institute of Technology, Pittsburgh, Pa., or Miami Beach, Florida.

HUDNUT, Alexander M. Painter. Born in Princeton, N. J. Member: Century Association; New York Water Color Club. *Address*, 5 Nassau St., New York, N. Y.

HUDNUT, Joseph. Painter. Member of the Salmagundi Club of New York. *Address*, 44 West 10th St., New York.

HUDSON, Charles W. Painter. Born in Boston in 1871. Pupil of Boston Museum School under Grundmann, Tarbell and Benson. Member: Boston Water Color Club; New York Water Color Club. *Address*, 13 Hilton St., Hyde Park, Boston, Mass.

HUDSON, Elmer F. Marine painter. Born in Boston in 1862. Member: Boston Art Club; Copley Society, 1895. *Address*, Gramatan Court, Bronxville, New York.

HUDSON, Eric. Painter. Exhibited at Annual Exhibition of National Academy of Design, New York, 1925. Specialty, marine and shipping subjects. *Address*, 1 Gramercy Park, New York, or Care of Ferargil Galleries, N. Y.

HUDSON, Julien. Painter. Born in New Orleans. Studied art in Paris. Had a studio from 1837 to 1844, the year of his death, at 120 Baronne St., New Orleans.

HUDSON, William, Jr. Portrait and miniature artist, flourishing in Boston, 1829–1855.

HUDSPETH, R. N. Painter. Born in Caledonia, Ontario, Canada, 1862. Pupil of Academie Julien under Bouguereau, Ferrier, Bashet and Doucet. Work: Portrait miniature owned by Lord Milner, England; vase owned by H. R. H. Queen Mary of England. *Address*, 49 Thoreau St., Concord, Mass.

HUELSE, Carl. Sculptor. Exhibited at Annual Exhibition of National Academy of Design, New York, 1925. *Address*, Philadelphia, Penna.

HUESTIS, Joseph W. Painter. Member of Society of Independent Artists. *Address*, 564 Jefferson Ave., Brooklyn, New York.

HUEY, Florence Greene. Miniature painter. Exhibited at the Penna. Academy of Fine Arts, Philadelphia, 1925. *Address*, Ruxton, Baltimore County, Maryland.

HUF, Karl. Painter and illustrator. Born in Philadelphia in 1887. Pupil of Penna. Academy of Fine Arts, and of Chase and Breckenridge. *Address*, 16th and Locust Sts., Philadelphia.

HUGHES, Ball Robt. Sculptor. Born in England in 1806, where he studied and received the silver medal of the Royal Academy. He came to the United States in 1829 and settled first in New York and later in Dorchester, Mass. He modeled the groups, "Little Nell," "Uncle Toby and the Widow Wadman," preserved in plaster at the Boston Athenaeum. His life-size high-relief of Bishop Hobart of New York is in the vestry of Trinity Church, New York. He died in 1868.

HUGHES, Daisy M. Painter. Born in California in 1883. Pupil of Macleod, Johonnot, and Townsley. *Address*, 1941 South Union Ave., Los Angeles, Calif.

HULBERT, Charles Allen. Painter. Student of Penna. Academy of Fine Arts, and School of Metropolitan Museum of Fine Arts. His portrait of Edward Lazansky is in the Capitol, Albany, N. Y. *Address*, South Egremont, Mass.

HULBERT, K. A. (Mrs. Chas. A.). Painter. Exhibited in 33d Annual Exhibition of National Association of Women Painters and Sculptors. *Address*, South Egremont, Mass.

HULL, Mrs. Marie A. Painter and illustrator. Born in 1890 at Summit, Miss. Pupil of Penna. Academy of Fine Arts and Broadmoor Art Academy. *Address*, 222 North St., Jackson, Miss.

HUMPHREY, David W. Painter and illustrator. Born in Elkhorn, Wis., in 1872. Pupil of Art Institute of Chicago; of Julien Academy, Paris; studied with Whistler in Paris. *Address*, 259 West 23d St., New York.

HUMPHREY, Elizabeth B. Painter. Born in Hopedale, Mass., about 1850. She was a pupil at the Cooper School of Design and of Worthington Whittredge. Her professional life has been devoted chiefly to designing illustrations. She made some excellent sketches and paintings during a trip to California. Her illustrations include landscapes, still-life and figures.

HUMPHREYS, Albert. Painter and sculptor. Born near Cincinnati, Ohio. Pupil of Gerome and Alexander Harrison in Paris. Represented by paintings in Detroit Institute of

Arts and Boston Public Library. Represented by sculptures in National Gallery of Art, Washington, D. C., and Children's Fountain, South Manchester, Conn. *Address*, 96 Fifth Ave., New York.

HUMPHREYS, F. Capitol engraver of portraits and subject plates in both mezzotint and in line. He was employed in 1850–58 by the Methodist Book Concern, of Cincinnati, Ohio.

HUMPHREYS, Marie C. Miniature painter, who exhibited in Europe and America. She was born in Deerfield, Mass., in 1867, and was the daughter of J. Wells Champney, well known for his art works. She died at New Rochelle, N. Y., in 1906.

HUMPHRISS, Charles H. Sculptor. Born in England in 1867. Exhibited at New York Academy of Design; Philadelphia Academy of Fine Arts. Member of National Association of Sculptors, New York. Work: "Indians Appeal to Manitou"; "Indian Sundial." *Address*, 162 East 35th St., New York.

HUMPHRYS, William. Engraver. Mr. Baker, in his "American Engravers," says that William Humphrys was born in Dublin in 1794 and died in Genoa, Italy, 1865. He adds that he learned to engrave with George Murray in Philadelphia; went to England in 1823; returned to this country in 1843 and in 1845 again went abroad to remain there for the rest of his life. Mr. Baker credits him with numerous small "Annual" plates, but says that he was principally engaged in bank-note engraving.

HUNT, Clyde Du V. Sculptor. Born in Scotland in 1861. Student of Mass. Institute of Technology, Boston. Represented in Metropolitan Museum of Art, New York, by marble statue, "Nirvana." *Address*, Weathersfield, Vermont.

HUNT, Leigh. Etcher. Born in Galena, Ill., in 1853. Pupil of Henry Farrer. *Address*, 600 West 14th St., New York.

HUNT, Samuel Valentine. Engraver. Born in Norwich, England, in 1803; died at Bay Ridge, N. Y., in 1893. Mr. Baker says that Hunt was originally a taxidermist and was a self-taught artist and engraver. He came to the United States in 1834 and was then an excellent line-engraver of landscape. He worked for New York and Cincinnati publishing houses.

HUNT, Thomas L. Painter. Exhibited at Penna. Academy of Fine Arts Annual Exhibition of 1924. *Address*, Laguna Beach, Cal.

HUNT, Una C. (Mrs.). Painter and illustrator. Born in Cincinnati, Ohio, in 1876. Pupil of Boston Museum of Fine Arts School. *Address*, 5 Chelsea Square, New York City.

HUNT, William Morris. Painter. Born in Brattleboro, Vt., in 1824; died, Isles of Shoals, N. H., 1879. Studied at Dusseldorf; pupil of Couture in Paris; influenced by Millet and the Barbizon School. In 1862 he settled in Boston where he spent most of his life. He painted many portraits of noted persons, was the author of many original sketches of types of Parisian life, and is well known by his mural paintings in the State Capitol at Albany, N. Y. Represented at the Metropolitan Museum, New York, by a "Landscape" and "Girl at a Fountain"; at Washington by "The Spouting Whale."

HUNTER, Evangeline D. Miniature painter. Exhibited at the Penna. Academy of Fine Arts, Philadelphia, 1925. *Address*, 4205 Sansom St., Philadelphia, Pa.

HUNTER, John Young. Painter. Exhibited water colors at the Annual Water Color Exhibition of the Penna. Academy of Fine Arts, Philadelphia, 1925. *Address*, 58 West 57th St., New York.

HUNTER, Lizbeth C. Painter. Born in California in 1868. Pupil of Henry B. Snell. Member of National Association of Women Painters and Sculptors. *Address*, 50 West 67th St., New York City.

HUNTINGTON, Anna H. (Mrs.). Sculptor. Born in Cambridge, Mass., in 1876. Pupil of Borglum. Represented by bronzes in the Metropolitan Museum, New York, and in the Carnegie and Cleveland Museums. Elected Member of National Academy, 1922. *Address*, 1083 Fifth Ave., New York.

HUNTINGTON, Daniel. Portrait and genre painter. Born in New York in 1816; died in New York, 1906. Pupil of Professor Samuel F. B. Morse, 1835, and later of Inman; also of G. P. Ferrero in Rome. Elected Associate of the National Academy, 1839; National Academy, 1840; President of National Academy, 1862–1869 and 1877–1891; Vice-President of the Metropolitan Museum of Art, New York, 1870–1903.

HUNTINGTON, Eleazer. Engraver. Born in 1789, he resided at Hartford, Conn., and was the son of Nathaniel Gilbert and Betsy (Tucker) Huntington. In 1825 he published at Hartford "The American Penman Etc.," written and engraved by Eleazer Huntington. In 1828 he engraved, in line, maps, diagrams and a series of small American Views for a school atlas, published in New York. He engraved a fairly well executed portrait of himself.

HUNTLEY, Samantha L. Portrait painter. Pupil of École des Beaux Arts and Academie Julien, Paris. Among her best known portraits are those of Col. Lamont, Col. Wm. Vilas, Gov. Higgins of New York, and of John J. Glennon, Catholic Archbishop of St. Louis. *Address*, Kinderhook, New York.

HURD, E. A line-engraver of buildings, etc., working about 1840. His work possesses very little merit and the compiler has been unable to locate him.

HURD, Nathaniel. Engraver. Born in Boston, Mass., 1730; died there in 1777. Nathaniel Hurd advertised his business as follows: "Nathaniel Hurd Informs his Customers he has remov'd his shop from MacCarty's corner, on the Exchange, to the Back Part of the opposite Brick Building where Mr. Ezekiel Pirce Kept his Office. Where he continues to do all sorts of Goldsmith's Work. Likewise engraves in Gold, Silver, Copper, Brass and Steel, in the neatest, Manner, and at reasonable Rates." But Hurd was engraving upon copper at an earlier date than this, as a bookplate of Thomas Dering is noted as engraved by Hurd in 1749. In 1762 he engraved a rare caricature portrait of Dr. Seth Hudson, a notorious character, and in 1764, a portrait of Rev. Joseph Sewall. With these exceptions, and that of a Masonic notice engraved about 1764, numerous book-plates constitute the known engravings of Nathaniel Hurd.

The only early published record of Hurd is found in *The New England Magazine*, Vol. III, Boston, 1832. This article is illustrated by a lithographic portrait of Hurd, said to have been made from a mezzotint engraved by "a man by the name of Jennings," after a painting by J. S. Copley, then (1832) in the possession of a descendant living in Medford, Mass.

HURLEY, Edward Timothy. Painter and etcher. Born in Cincinnati, Ohio, in 1869. Studied in Cincinnati Art Academy with Frank Duveneck. Has exhibited at Carnegie Institute, Pittsburgh; Art Institute of Chicago; National Arts Club, New York; Herron Institute, Indianapolis; Cincinnati Museum, etc.; represented in permanent collections of Cincinnati Museum; British Museum, London; New York Pub. Library; Congressional Library; Detroit Museum of Art; Toledo Art Museum; Richmond Art Association, etc. Gold medal, St. Louis Exposition, 1904. Especially known for numerous etchings of Cincinnati and vicinity. Has given illustrated lectures and practical demonstrations in etching. Member: MacDowell Society, Cincinnati; Duveneck Society of Painters; Cincinnati Art Club. Illustrator of "The Town of the Beautiful River," 1915; "For Old Acquaintance"; "Bridges and Byways." *Address*, Care Rookwood Pottery, Cincinnati, Ohio.

HURRY, Mrs. Lucy Washington. Painter. Born in Hagerstown, Md., in 1884. Pupil of Art Students' League of New York under Kenyon Cox; Marshall Fry; Fayette Barnum. Member: New York Water Color Club, and National Academy of Women Painters and Sculptors. *Address*, 60 Greenwich St., Hempstead, N. Y.

HURST, L. E. Painter and illustrator. Born in Avon, Ohio, 1883. Pupil of Cleveland School of Art, F. C. Gottwald and of H. G. Keller. Specialty, botanical illustrating. *Address*, Avon, Lorain County, Ohio.

HURTT, Arthur R. Painter and illustrator. Born in Wisconsin, 1861. Pupil of Douglas Volk. Member: California Art Club. Award: Bronze medal, Pan-Cal. Exposition, San Diego, 1915. Painter of stage scenery, murals and panoramas. *Address*, 1518 Mohawk St., Los Angeles, Cal.

HUSTON, William. Painter. Exhibited in a New York Gallery his "Afternoon in Great South Bay." Signed "Wm. Huston, 1880."

HUTAF, August W. Painter and illustrator. Born in Hoboken, N. J., in 1879. Pupil of W. D. Streetor. Member: American Numismatic Society; Society of Illustrators. Specialty, posters, book covers and decorations. Author of poster "The Spirit of the Fighting Tanks," 5th Liberty Loan. *Address*, 1 31st St., Wood-Cliff-on-Hudson, N. J.

HUTCHENS, Frank Townsend. Painter. Born in Canandaigua, N. Y. Studied at Art Students' League of New York, Academie Colarossi and Academie Julien, Paris, France. Exhibited at Royal Academy, London; Paris Salon; Amsterdam Internationale Exposition; National Academy of Design, New York; Pa. Academy of Fine Arts; Art Institute of Chicago; Corcoran Gallery, Washington, D. C. Awarded: Silver medal, Paris. Work: Represented in permanent exhibition in Toledo Museum; John Herron Art Institute; West Point Museum; Capitol at Albany, N. Y.; Erie Museum; Contemporary Exhibition, Baltimore, Md., etc. Member: American Water Color Society; New York Water Color Society. *Address*, 48 Barrow Street, New York; or Norwalk, Conn.

HUTCHINS, John E. Painter. Born in Wyoming, Pa., in 1891. *Address*, 709 Putnam Ave., Brooklyn, New York, N. Y.

HUTCHINS, Will. Painter. Born in Westchester, Conn., in 1878. Pupil of Yale School of Fine Arts; Laurens in Paris. *Address*, Deerfield, Mass.

HUTCHINSON, Allen. Painter. Exhibited at Annual Exhibition of National Academy, 1925, New York. *Address*, 4666 Broadway, New York.

HUTCHISON, Mrs. Ellen Wales. Painter. Born in East Hartford, Conn., in 1868. Pupil of C. E. Porter; Geo. Thomson. Member: Conn. Academy of Fine Arts.

HUTCHISON, F. Painter. Born in Montreal, Canada. Pupil of Jean Paul Laurens; Benjamin-Constant. Elected Associate Member of National Academy. *Address*, 45 East 59th St., New York City.

HUTSON, Charles Woodward. Painter. Born in 1840, in McPhersonville, S. C. Member: Arts and Crafts Club, New Orleans; Southern States Art League. Specialty, landscape, portrait and genre. Represented in Louisiana State Museum.

HUTSON, Ethel. Landscape painter. Born in 1872. Studied under Mrs. J. P. McAuley, Galveston, Tex.; at Pratt Institute, Brooklyn, N. Y.; National Academy of Design, N. Y.; Newcomb Art School, New Orleans, La.; Cooper Institute, New York; Art Students' League, New York. Member: Art Association of New Orleans; Artists' Guild; Arts and Crafts Club, New Orleans, La.; Southern States Art League.

HUTT, Henry. Illustrator. Born in Chicago, Ill., in 1875. Pupil of Chicago Art Institute. His studio is now in New York City and he has illustrated for the leading magazines and periodicals.

HUTT, John. Engraver. In Rivington's *New York Gazette* for 1774, we find the following: "John Hutt, Engraver in general, from London, at Mr. Hewitt's directly opposite the Merchants' Coffee House, in Dock Street, New York. Engraves—Coats of Arms, Crests, Seals and Cyphers, Bills of Exchange, Bills of Lading, Shop Bills, Bills of Parcels, Card Plates, etc. Architecture, Frontispieces, Doorplates, Compliment Cards, Plate Dog-Collars, Etc., Stamps, etc. Gentlemen disposed to employ him may depend on the utmost neatness and dispatch."
The only examples of Hutt's work known to the compiler are some book-plates and a few

diagrams engraved in connection with John Norman and published in Philadelphia in 1775.

HUTTON, Isaac and George. Engravers. This firm of jewelers and silversmiths, of Albany, N. Y., working about 1796, made dies for seals; one for the Union University, at Schenectady, N. Y. But as this firm employed engravers, among them Gideon Fairman (about 1795–), the actual work was probably done by some one in their employ.

HUTTON, J. A fairly well-engraved line plate of a battle scene is signed "J. Hutton, Sc't Alb'y." The print was apparently made about 1825–30, but no other work by Hutton is known.

HUTTY, Alfred H. Painter. Born in Grand Haven, Mich., in 1877. Pupil of St. Louis School of Fine Arts; Art Students' League of New York, under Chase and Birge Harrison. Member: Woodstock Artists' Association; Carolina Art Association. Represented in Gibbes Memorial Art Gallery, Charleston, S. C. Director of School of Art of Carolina Art Association.

HYDE, Helen. Painter and etcher. Born in Lima, N. Y., in 1863. Member of the Chicago, also California, Society of Etchers. Represented in Library of Congress, Washington; New York Public Library; Boston Museum. She died in Pasadena, Calif., in 1919.

HYDE, Russell Taber. Painter, etcher and illustrator. Born at Waltham, Mass., in 1888. Pupil of Laurens, Bachet and Richer. *Address*, 159 Summer St., Waltham, Mass.

HYDE, William Henry. Painter. Born in New York in 1858. Studied painting in Paris under Boulanger, Lefebvre, Deucet and Harrison. Elected Associate Member of the National Academy, 1900. *Address*, 829 Park Avenue, New York.

HYETT, Will J. Painter. Born in Cheltenham, England, in 1876. Pupil of Sir Alfred East. Member: Pittsburgh Artists' Association; Pittsburgh Architectural Club. Awards: Bronze medal, Panama-Pacific Exposition, San Francisco, 1915; third honor, Pittsburgh Artists' Association, 1917. *Address*, Care of Gillespie Galleries, 422 Wood St., Pittsburgh, Pa.

I

ILLIAN, George J. Illustrator. Born in Milwaukee, Wis., 1894. Member of Art Students' League of New York. *Address*, 21 East 38th St., New York.

ILLMAN, Thomas. Born in England. He was engraving in London in 1824, and about six years later he came to New York, and at once formed the engraving firm of Illman & Pilbrow. He worked in stipple and in mezzotint, and was a good engraver. Illman Sons, about 1845, engraved portraits for both New York and Philadelphia publishers.

IMBERT, Anthony. Lithographer. A French naval officer. He was the proprietor of the first lithographic establishment in New York. He was located at 79 Murray St., and in 1831 he had removed to 104 Broadway.

INGERLE, Rudolph F. Painter. Born in Germany in 1879. Member of Chicago Society of Artists. Represented in Municipal Art Gallery, Chicago, Ill., by "After the Storm." *Address*, 28 S. Wabash Ave., Chicago, Ill.

INGERSOLL, Anna. Painter. Exhibited at the Penna. Academy of Fine Arts in 1924. *Address*, 1815 Walnut St., Philadelphia.

INGERSOLL, Emma K. H. (Mrs.). Painter. Born in Chicago in 1878. She was awarded bronze medal for miniatures in 1904. *Address*, Chestertown, Md.

INGHAM, Charles Cromwell. Painter. Born in Dublin. He studied in the Academy there and obtained a prize for "The Death of Cleopatra"; settled in New York in 1817; was one of the founders of the National Academy of Design and its Vice-President 1845–50. Died in 1863. His best known picture is "The White Plume," which was beautifully engraved by A. B. Durand. Among his well-known portraits are those of Edwin Forrest, Lafayette, De Witt Clinton, Gulian C. Verplank and Catharine M. Sedgwick. He was particularly happy in his portraits of women and children.

INGHAM, Elizabeth H. (Mrs.). Painter and illustrator. Born in Easton, Pa. Pupil of Penna. Academy of Fine Arts and of Whistler in Paris. *Address*, E. Palisade Ave., Englewood, N. J.

INGLIS, John J. Painter and illustrator. He was born in Ireland and studied in London. *Address*, 144 North Union St., Rochester, N. Y.

INGRAHAM, George H. Etcher. Born in New Bedford, Mass., in 1870. *Address*, 1127 Guardian Bldg., Cleveland, Ohio.

INMAN, Henry. Portrait, genre and landscape painter. Born in 1801 in Utica, N. Y. Studied under John Wesley Jarvis in New York City. He went to Europe in 1845, remaining about a year. He painted Wordsworth, Macaulay, Dr. Thomas Chalmers and others. Among his sitters in this country were many distinguished men, whose portraits are preserved in public collections in Boston, New York, Philadelphia and elsewhere. He was, between 1831 and 1835, associated with Col. Cephas G. Childs in a lithographic printing and publishing business carried on in this city, and was a Director of the Penna. Academy of Fine Arts in 1834. His portrait of Chief Justice Marshall has been lithographed by A. Newsam and engraved by A. B. Durand. He was vice-president of the National Academy from 1820 to 1830 and again from 1838 to 1844. From 1831 to 1835 he lived at Mt. Holly, New Jersey, and in Philadelphia. In 1843 his health broke and he sailed for England. The voyage and the change revived him but upon his return late in 1845 he again fell ill and died the following year. Tuckerman gives a long account of Inman in his "Book of Artists."

INMAN, J. O'Brien. Painter. Son of Henry Inman. As a young man he painted portraits in the Western States; later he removed his studio to New York. In 1866 he went to Europe and opened his studio in Rome. He was elected an Associate of the National Academy of Design in 1865. He died in 1896.

INNESS, George. Landscape painter. Born in Newburg, N. Y., in 1825. The career of this the greatest American landscape painter was brought to an end by his sudden death in Scotland in 1894, while he was on a trip abroad undertaken for the recuperation of his health, impaired by unceasing hard work. Except for some elementary instruction in his youth in Newark, N. J., and a few months' study under Regis Gignoux in New York, he received no academic art education. He found out for himself by a long course of patient study from Nature out of doors, how best to express his ideals on canvas. His work is distinctly divided into two periods, the first covering the years during which, in conscientious, analytical fashion, he painted scenes in this country, Italy and other parts of Europe; the second embracing the time from about 1878 to his death, during which he became more and more a synthesist. In this latter period he painted passing effects with such power, individuality and beauty of color and composition as to place his work among that of the greatest artists of the nineteenth century. There are points of similarity in his development and that of two great Frenchmen, Corot and Rousseau. Both had more academical training than Inness, but both, in their landscape work, went through the analytical stages that mark the earlier pictures of Inness. The landscapes of George Inness show the same sort of grasp as those of the two masters mentioned above, the same intensity of purpose, the same general conception of nature, and they possess a great quality of tone, and an unusual depth and variety of color. His pictures are in the principal galleries and his ''Georgia Pines'' is in the William T. Evans Collection. In 1868 he was elected to the National Academy.

INNESS, George, Jr. Painter. Born in Paris, France, in 1854. He was a pupil of his father in Rome, Italy; studied one year in Paris. Lived in Boston and New York, where he occupied a studio with his father (1878). He resided with his family in Montclair, N. J., after 1880, but had a studio in Paris; exhibited annually at Paris Salon; honorable mention, Paris Salon, 1896, and gold medal, 1900. Officer Academie des Beaux Arts, Paris, 1902. Elected Associate Member of the National Academy, 1895; National Academy, 1899. Art signature always ''Inness, Jr.'' Author of ''Life and Letters of George Inness,'' 1917. His painting ''Shepherd and Sheep'' is in the Metropolitan Museum. *Address*, Care of Century Co., 353 Fourth Ave., New York.

INUKAI, Kyohei. Painter. Exhibited ''Self-Portrait'' at Annual Exhibitions, 1925, of National Academy of Design and Penna. Academy of Fine Arts, Philadelphia. *Address*, 200 West 57th St., New York.

INVERNIZZI, Prosper. Painter. Exhibited at Penna. Academy of Fine Arts in 1924. *Address*, 500 West 178th St., New York.

IORIO, Adrin. Painter and illustrator. Born in New York in 1879. *Address*, 6 Newbury St., Boston, Mass.

IPSEN, Ernest L. Portrait painter. Born in Malden, Mass., in 1869. Pupil of School of Boston Museum and of Royal Academy at Copenhagen. Elected Member of the National Academy in 1924. Exhibited portrait of Edwin H. Blashfield, N. A., in the Centennial Exhibition of National Academy of Design, 1925. Represented in Chicago Art Institute. *Address*, 119 East 19th St., New York, N. Y.

IRELAND, Leroy. Painter. Born in Philadelphia in 1889. Pupil of Penna. Academy of Fine Arts. Represented by ''God of

the Snake Dance'' in Dallas Art Association. *Address*, 53 East 59th St., New York.

IRISH, Margaret H. (Mrs.). Painter. Born in 1878. Pupil of St. Louis School of Fine Arts. *Address*, Webster Grove, St. Louis, Missouri.

IRVINE, Wilson H. Landscape painter. Born in Byron, Ill., in 1869. Pupil of Chicago Art Institute where he is represented by his paintings, ''The Road'' and ''Autumn.'' *Address*, Lyme, Conn.

IRVING, John Beaufain. Painter. Born in Charleston, S. C., in 1825, he died in New York City in 1877. He studied in Charleston and in 1851 he went to Europe and studied with Leutz. On his return he had a studio in Charleston and later in New York. Elected an Associate of the National Academy and an Academician in 1872. His portraits and historical subjects are spirited and rich in color, he also painted genre subjects.

IRWIN, Benoni. Painter. Born in 1840 at Newmarket, Canada; died in 1896 at South Coventry, Conn. Pupil of the National Academy of Design in New York; Carolus Duran in Paris. Represented at the Metropolitan Museum, New York, by a life-size bust portrait of Charles H. Farnham. Represented at the Corcoran Art Gallery, Washington, D. C., by a portrait of Edward C. Messer.

ISHAM, Ralph. A portrait and landscape painter. Born about 1820 in Connecticut. He was connected with the Wadsworth Athenaeum Gallery when it was first opened. He died early in life.

ISHAM, Samuel. Painter. Born in New York in 1855; died in Easthampton, Long Island, N. Y., 1914. Pupil of Julien Academy, Paris, under Jacquesson de la Chevreuse, Boulanger and Lefebvre. He exhibited at Paris Salons and in most of the larger American exhibitions. He was a member of the jury of the Pan-American Exposition, Buffalo, 1901, and received a silver medal at the St. Louis Exposition, 1904. He was elected an Associate of the National Academy in 1900 and an Academician in 1906, and also held membership in the New York Water Color Club; New York Architectural League; the National Institute of Arts and Letters. He was the author of ''A History of American Painting,'' 1905.

ISRAEL, Nathan. Painter. Born in Brooklyn, New York, in 1895. Pupil of Max Weber; K. H. Miller; B. Robinson. Member: Art Students' League of New York; Society of Independent Artists. *Address*, 15 Kossuth Place, Brooklyn, N. Y.

IVES, Chauncey B. Sculptor. Born in Connecticut in 1812, he has had a studio for years in Rome. His best known statues are "Pandora," "Rebecca," "Bacchante," and his statues of Roger Sherman and Jonathan Trumbull are in the Capitol at Washington, D. C.

IVES, Halsey C. Landscape painter. Born in 1847 in New York State. He taught in St. Louis and became director of the Museum of Fine Arts. He received medals for his landscapes. He died in England in 1911.

IVES, Neil McDowell. Painter. Born St. Louis, Mo., in 1890. Pupil of Du Mond, Carlsen and Dasburg. *Address*, Woodstock, N. Y.

IVES, Percy. Portrait painter. Born in Detroit, Mich., in 1864. Studied at Penna. Academy of Fine Arts and in Paris, France. Exhibited in Paris, New York, Boston, Philadelphia, Cincinnati, Chicago, etc.; painted portrait of Grover Cleveland, Sec. of War Alger, Postmaster-General Dickinson, etc. Received honorable mention, Buffalo Exposition, 1901; member of Jury of Admission, Art Department, St. Louis Exposition, 1904. Member: Detroit Museum of Art; Society of Western Artists; Fine Arts Society, Detroit; Archaeology Institute of America. *Address*, 502 Cass Ave., Detroit, Mich.

IZOR, Estelle Peele. Painter. Pupil of Forsyth and Steel in Indianapolis; Freer and Vanderpoel in Chicago; Chase and Herter in New York; H. D. Murphy in Boston. Member: Indianapolis Art Club. *Address*, "The Wellington," West Michigan St., Indianapolis, Ind.

J

JACKMAN, W. G. Engraver. He was born in England and came to the United States about 1841. He established himself in business in New York and was largely employed by the Harpers, Putnams and Appletons, publishers of that city. He was a very good engraver of portraits and subject plates, in both line and stipple; he also did some portrait work in mezzotint for Harper & Bros.

JACKSON. A very poorly engraved line plate is so signed, as engraver. The plate represents "Capt. William Mason in the Magazine of Fort Niagara, Sept., 1826."

JACKSON, Annie Hurlburt. Miniature painter. Born in 1877. Pupil of Eric Pape; Murphy; Woodbury. Member: Penna. Society of Miniature Painters; American Society of Miniature Painters. *Address*, 329 Tappan St., Brookline, Mass.

JACKSON, Charles Akerman. Painter. Born in Jamaica Plain, Mass., in 1857. Pupil of John Arnold. Among important portraits painted by him are: Honorable Rog< Wolcott, Bishop Brooks, Dr. A. J. Gordon, Dr. Alexander McKenzie, Mayors Frank E. Olney and E. D. McGuinness, for Providence City Hall. *Address*, American Art Society, Boston, Mass.

JACKSON, Chevalier. Illustrator and lithographer. Born in Pittsburgh, Pa., in 1865. Pupil of A. Bryan Wall. Member: Pittsburgh Artists' Association. *Address*, Schwenksville, Penna.

JACKSON, Edwin W. Miniature painter, flourishing in 1846–47, New York.

JACKSON, Elbert McGran. Illustrator. Member: Guild of Free Lance Association. Illustrates for *Saturday Evening Post*. *Address*, 116 East 66th St., New York, N. Y.

JACKSON, Hazel Brill. Sculptor. Exhibited at Penna. Academy of Fine Arts in 1924. *Address*, 219 Homer St., Newton Center, Mass.

JACKSON, John Adams. Sculptor and crayon portrait draughtsman. Was born at Bath, Maine, in 1825, and died in 1879. He was a pupil of the engraver D. C. Johnson and in 1851 he started making portrait busts. He received instruction in Paris under Suisse and later opened his studio in New York. His busts of Rev. Dr. Beecher and of Rev. Dr. Bethune, and his statue of Dr. Kane received great praise.

JACKSON, John Edwin. Painter. Born in Nashville, Tenn., in 1875. Pupil of National Academy of Design and Art Students' League of New York. Specialty, New York street scenes; was also illustrator for Scribner, Harper, and Century Co. *Address*, 135 West 12th St., New York City.

JACKSON, (Miss) Lesley. Painter. Born in Rochester, Minn. Member: Society of Washington Artists; Washington Water Color Club; Washington Society of Fine Arts; National Academy of Women Painters and Sculptors; New York Water Color Club. Award: Second Corcoran prize, Washington Water Color Club, 1905. Address, ''The Concord,'' Washington. D. C.

JACKSON, Martin J. Painter. Born in Newburgh, N. Y., in 1872. Pupil of Cooper Union and National Academy of Design under Edgar M. Ward in New York; Comelli in London; also studied in Paris, Brussels and Antwerp. Address, Bradbury Bldg., Los Angeles, Calif.

JACKSON, Mrs. May Howard. Sculptor. Born in Philadelphia, Pa., in 1877. Pupil of Penna. Academy of Fine Arts. Work: ''William P. Price,'' St. Thomas' Church, Philadelphia; ''Paul Lawrence Dunbar,'' Dunbar High School, Washington, D. C.; ''William H. Lewis,'' ex-Assistant Attorney General; ''Kelly Miller,'' Howard University, Washington, D. C. Address, 1816 16th St., Washington, D. C.

JACOBS, Michel. Portrait painter and sculptor. Born in Montreal, Canada, in 1877. Pupil of Laurens in Paris; of E. M. Ward at National Academy of Design. Member: Salmagundi Club. Work: ''Portrait of Senator Underwood'' and ''Portrait of Champ Clark'' in the Capitol, Washington, D. C. Address, 58 West 57th St., New York, N. Y.

JACOBSEN, Norman. Painter. Born at Cokeville, Wyo., in 1884. Student of Art Institute of Chicago, 1905; Lewis Institute, Chicago, 1906–07; New York School of Art, 1908.

JACOBSON, Oscar B. Painter. Born in Sweden in 1882. Pupil of Birger; Sandzen; Weir; Neimeyer. Work: ''Prayer for Rain,'' McPherson Art Gallery, Kansas; ''Voices of the Past,'' Bethany Art Gallery, Lindsborg, Kansas; ''Portrait of Gov. Williams,'' State Capitol, Oklahoma City, Okla.; ''Rio Grande,'' Hayes Normal School. Represented in collection of the University of Oklahoma, Norman. Address, University of Oklahoma, Okla.

JACOBY, Helen Eaton. Painter and illustrator. Born in Indianapolis, Ind. Pupil of Otto Stark in Indianapolis; Pratt Institute of Brooklyn. Member: Indiana Artists' Club. Address, 859 East 58th St., Indianapolis, Ind.

JAEGERS, Albert. Sculptor. Born in Germany in 1868. He was brought to America in 1882. Engaged as sculptor since 1890; died in 1925. Among his works, statuary for Fine Arts Building, St. Louis; Custom House, New York; the Von Steuben statue in Washington, D. C.; also many tablets and busts.

JAEGERS, Augustine. Sculptor. Born in Germany in 1878. He was brought to America in 1882. Pupil of Art Students' League, and National Academy of Design, of New York. Among his works, ''Frey Memorial'' in New York, and statues at San Francisco Exposition. Address, 182 Eighth Ave., Long Island, N. Y.

JAMES. Dunlap speaks of Mr. James as a native of New York, and that he was painting there shortly after 1800. He afterwards worked in Quebec.

JAMES, Alexander R. Painter. Born in Cambridge, Mass., in 1890. Pupil of Boston Museum of Fine Arts, and Abbott Thayer. Represented in Boston Museum of Fine Arts by portrait of ''Prof. William James'' and ''Portrait of a Girl.'' Address, Dublin, N. H.

JAMES, Alice A. S. (Mrs.). Painter and illustrator. Born in Ohio in 1870. Exhibited in Philadelphia, Chicago, Washington and in the Paris Salon. Illustrator for Harper's and Century Magazines. Address, Urbana, Ohio.

JAMES, Esther M. Miniature painter. Born in Brookline, Mass., in 1885. Pupil of Hale and Benson. Address, 16 Strathmore Road, Brookline, Mass.

JAMES, John Wells. Painter. Born in Brooklyn, N. Y., in 1873. Pupil of James Knox. Exhibited in 1925 at National Academy of Design, New York. Address, 1239 Dean St., Brooklyn, N. Y.

JAMES, William. Painter. Born in Cambridge, Mass., in 1882. Pupil of Benson and Tarbell. Address, Riverway Studios, Boston.

JAMESON, Arthur E. Illustrator. Born in England in 1872. Pupil of Art Students' League of New York. Address, 282 West 4th St., New York, N. Y.

JAMESON, John S. Painter. Born in Hartford, Conn., in 1842. He died in the Civil War at Andersonville Prison in 1864. He was a member of the Artists' Fund Society, and gave promise of great future excellence.

JAMESON, Minor S. Landscape painter. Exhibited in 1925 in National Academy of Design, New York. Address, Chevy Chase, Md.

JAMIESON. Dunlap speaks of Mr. Jamieson as being a very ingenious artist in cameos, in New York.

JANSSON, Alfred. Painter. Born in Sweden in 1863. Studied in Paris. Member of Chicago Society of Artists. Awarded: landscape prize, 1914, Chicago Art Institute. Address, 1851 Byron St., Chicago, Ill.

JANVIER, A. W. Crayon-portrait draughtsman. He was doing portrait work in Philadelphia about 1858.

JANVIER, Catharine Ann (Mrs.). Painter. Born in Philadelphia. Her early life was passed in China; studied in the Penna. Academy of Fine Arts and Art Students' League, New York. Pictures: "Geoffrey Rudel and the Countess of Tripoli"; "The Princess Badroulbadour"; "Daniel at Prayer"; "The Violinist," etc. Member: Art Students' League; Fine Arts Society of New York. Died Dec. 12th, 1923.

JAQUES, Bertha E. (Mrs.). Etcher. Born in Covington, Ohio. Pupil of Chicago Art Institute. Represented by work in New York Public Library and Congressional Library, Washington, D. C. *Address*, 4316 Greenwood Ave., Chicago, Ill.

JARVIS, C. A little known painter of portraiture and genre subjects.

JARVIS, John Wesley. Painter and engraver. Born in England in 1780. A nephew of John Wesley. He was brought to Philadelphia when but five years old, and there educated; spent much of his time out of school with Pratt, Paul, Clark and other painters then working in a humble way. He met Gilbert Stuart, who "occasionally employed Paul to letter a book" in one of his pictures; was apprenticed to Edward Savage, to learn engraving, of whom he spoke most unfavorably, and with him removed to New York. He learned to draw and engrave from D. Edwin, who was employed by Savage on his first arrival in this country; finally commenced engraving on his own account, but having seen Martin, a crayon artist, just arrived from England, very successful, adopted portrait painting as his profession. He met with success, but was extravagant, irascible and eccentric He made several trips South, taking Henry Inman with him as assistant on his first trip to New Orleans, where he finished six portraits a week. This was probably in 1833. It was after this that he painted his most important works, the full-length portrait of military and naval heroes for the City of New York. He died in extreme poverty in 1839. While Jarvis was in New York he published the prints of other engravers, notably those of Robert R. Livingston, published in 1804 and engraved by George Graham.

JAY, Cecil (Mrs.). Miniature painter and portrait painter in oil. Member of New York Water Color Club.

JEFFERSON, Joseph. Painter and actor. Born in Philadelphia in 1829; died at Palm Beach, Florida, in 1905. He painted "The Coast of Maine" and "Massachusetts Bay."

JEMNE, Mrs. Elsa L. Painter and illustrator. Born in St. Paul, Minn., in 1888. Pupil of Penna. Academy of Fine Arts. *Address*, 212 Mt. Curve Blvd., St. Paul, Minn.

JENCKES, Joseph. Born in England in 1602, he emigrated to America in 1642. He was an inventor and die-sinker. He was employed by the Lynn Iron Works to make the dies for the "pine-tree shilling." He built the first American fire-engine. He died in 1683.

JENKINS, Mrs. Hannah T. Painter. Born in Philadelphia. Pupil of Penna. Academy of Fine Arts. *Address*, Pomona College, Claremont, Calif.

JENKINS, Mattle M. Miniature painter and illustrator. Born in Whitman, Mass., in 1867. *Address*, 704 Washington St., Whitman, Mass.

JENKS, Phoebe Pickering. Portrait painter. Born in Portsmouth, N. H., in 1847. She came to Boston to live when sixteen and made it her home. Her best portraits have been of women. Among her many sitters were Mrs. Ellis L. Mott and daughter, Mrs. S. A. Bigelow, Mrs. Harrison Gardiner, Mrs. C. C. Walworth, Mrs. Edward Taylor, Mrs. Henry Lancaster, and a large portrait of the two Lovering boys. She died in 1907.

JENNEWEIN, Carl P. Painter and sculptor. Member of American Academy, Rome, and New York Architectural League. Represented in Metropolitan Museum, New York, by "Cupid and Gazelle," and by "Portrait of a Child" at the Corcoran Gallery, Washington, D. C. *Address*, 560 West 26th St., New York.

JENNEY, Edgar W. Painter and mural decorator. Born in New Bedford, Mass., in 1869. Pupil of Major in Boston, and Laurens in Paris. Mural panels in Wisconsin State Capitol, and Hibernia Bank, New Orleans, La. *Address*, 15 West 38th St., New York.

JENNINGS, Samuel. Painter. Native of Philadelphia. In 1792 he painted a large and imposing allegorical picture which he presented to the Philadelphia Library, called "The Genius of America Encouraging the Emancipation of the Blacks." Jennings went to London, and Dunlap says that he was there in 1794.

JENNINGS, William. Portrait painter. One of his pictures is signed and dated 1774.

JENNYS, J. Wm. Painter. He painted portraits of Col. and Mrs. Constant Storrs, which are dated 1802 and owned by John F. Lewis, Philadelphia.

JENNYS, Richard, Jr. Engraver. A well-executed mezzotint portrait of the Rev. Jonathan Mayhew is signed by Richard Jennys, Jr., as engraver. It was published in Boston about 1774 and was "Printed and Sold by Nat. Hurd, Engraver, on ye Exchange."

JENSEN, Holger W. Painter. Born in Denmark in 1880. Pupil of Chicago Art Institute. *Address*, 257 North Oakland Ave., River Forrest, Ill.

JENSEN, Thomas M. Portrait painter. Born in Denmark in 1831. He came to this country in 1870. He painted many of the portraits of the New York judges which are now in the Kings County Court House and the City Hall of New York City. Among his best known portraits were those of Roswell C. Brainard; Michael McGoldrick; and Hamilton W. Robinson. He died in 1916.

JEROME, Elizabeth Gilbert. Painter. Born in New Haven, Conn. Studied in the National Academy, New York, under E. Leutze. She exhibited in the National Academy in 1866, and excelled in ideal figure painting.

JEROME, Irene Elizabeth. Painter and illustrator. Born in New York state in 1858, and with the exception of a few lessons was self-taught in art. In 1882 she exhibited eighteen sketches of Colorado which had decided merit. Among her work was considerable illustrating for books and other publications.

JETTEL, Eugene. Painter (Austrian). Born in 1845 in Johnsdorf; died in 1901 at Trieste. He painted "A Marsh in North Holland" which was exhibited in this country.

JEWETT, Charles A. Engraver. Born in Lancaster, Mass., in 1816; died in New York in 1878. This good line-engraver of subject plates was engraving in New York in 1838. He later removed to Cincinnati, Ohio, and about 1853 he was conducting an extensive engraving business in that city. In 1860 he was again located in New York.

JEWETT, Frederic S. A marine painter. Born in 1819; died in 1864. He moved to the West Indies when 22, and visited Europe, but lived most of his life in his native state Connecticut. One of his best paintings is in the Wadsworth Athenaeum.

JEWETT, Maude S. (Mrs. Edward H.). Sculptor. Born in Englewood, N. J., in 1873. Pupil of Art Students' League of New York. Member: National Academy of Women Painters and Sculptors. Work: "Fountain" in Cleveland Museum. *Address*, 245 East 61st St., New York, N. Y.

JEWETT, William. Portrait painter. Born in East Haddam, Conn., in 1795. He was apprenticed to a coach maker, and when eighteen years of age he met Samuel Waldo, and going to New York with him he formed the partnership of Waldo & Jewett, with whom he collaborated in painting many excellent portraits of prominent men. He was elected an associate member of the National Academy of Design in 1847. He died in 1874 at Bayonne, New Jersey.

JEWETT, William S. Portrait painter. Born in South Dover, N. Y., in 1812. He came to New York City as a very young man and studied at the Schools of the National Academy of Design. In 1845 he was elected an Associate Member. He sailed in 1849 from New York for San Francisco where he resided for years and painted a number of pictures, and prospected for gold. He died in 1873.

JIROUCH, Frank L. Painter and sculptor. Born in Cleveland, Ohio, in 1876. Pupil of Matzon; Ludikie; Grafly; Garber; Pearson. Member: Cleveland Art Club. Work: Bronze relief in Church of Lady of Lourdes; "Christ and Angels" (stone), St. Colman's Church; "Diana of Ephesus," Union National Bank; Chapman Memorial, Cleveland Ball Park; Altar of Sacrifice, Cleveland; Fitzsimons bronze tablet, Paris. *Address*, 4821 Superior Ave., Cleveland, Ohio.

JOCELYN, Nathaniel. Portrait painter and engraver. Born in New Haven, Conn., in 1796; died there in 1881. Nathaniel Jocelyn was the son of a watchmaker. At the age of eighteen years he was apprenticed to an engraver, and when he was twenty-one he entered into partnership with Tisdale, Danforth and Willard, in the Hartford Graphic and Bank-Note Engraving Company; he later, with Mr. Danforth, virtually founded the National Bank-Note Engraving Company.

Dissatisfied with engraving, Jocelyn gave it up in 1820 and became a painter of portraits, and exhibited at the National Academy in 1826. He went abroad with S. F. B. Morse in 1829-30, and became a meritorious portrait painter. He was made an Academician of the National Academy on May 13, 1846.

JOCELYN, Simeon S. Engraver and painter. Born in New Haven, Conn., in 1799; died in Tarrytown, N. Y., 1879. S. S. Jocelyn was engraving line portraits in New Haven, after drawings by N. Jocelyn, as early as 1824, and in 1827 the engraving firm of N. & S. S. Jocelyn was in business in that city. S. S. Jocelyn and S. B. Muson were also associated as engravers. He also painted miniatures and oils. The latter part of his life was passed in New Haven, Conn.

JOHANSEN, John C. Portrait painter. Born in Copenhagen, Denmark, in 1876. He was brought to America in infancy. He was a pupil of the Art Institute of Chicago; Academie Julien, Paris, France; of Duveneck, at Art Students' League, New York, in 1912. Represented in National Gallery, Santiago, Chile; Art Institute, Chicago; Penna. Academy of Fine Arts, Philadelphia, Pa.; National Museum of Art, Washington, D. C.; National Academy of Design, New York; University of Wisconsin; University of Chicago. He was elected a member of the National Academy in 1915. *Address*, 12 West 9th St., New York City.

JOHN, Francis Coates. Painter. Born in Baltimore in 1857. Studied at École des Beaux Arts in Paris, under Yvon, Lehmann, Boulanger and Lefebvre. He has had a studio in New York since 1882. Specialty, figure painting. He won Clarke prize, National Academy of Design. Elected member of the National Academy in 1894. Member: National Institute of Arts and Letters; American Water Color Society; Architectural League; Society Mural Painters; American Federation of Arts. *Address*, 33 W. 67th St., New York.

JOHNS, Clarence M. Painter. Born in Pittsburgh, Penna., in 1843. Pupil of Penna. Academy of Fine Arts, and later studied in Paris. He was widely known for his animal pictures. He served for years on the jury of awards for the Carnegie Art Exhibitions at Pittsburgh. He died in 1925.

JOHNSON, Mrs. Adelaide. Sculptor. Born in Plymouth, Ill. Pupil of Monteverde and Fabi Altini in Rome. Work: Portrait-bust of Susan B. Anthony, Metropolitan Museum, New York. *Address*, 128 Piccadilly, London, England.

JOHNSON, Belle. Sculptor. Exhibited at Penna. Academy of Fine Arts, Philadelphia, in 1925. *Address*, 200 Claremont Ave., N. Y.

JOHNSON, Burt W. Sculptor. Born in Flint, Ohio, in 1890. Pupil of Louis Saint Gaudens; J. E. Fraser; Robert Aitken; George Bridgman. Member: Laguna Beach Artists' Association. Work: "Spanish Music Fountain" and "Greek Tablet," Pomona College, Claremont, California; panel, "Christ," St. Francis Hospital, La Crosse, Wis.; memorial fountain, Huntington Park, California; Pomona Valley memorial monument, Pomona, California; E. N. Dimick statue, West Palm Beach, Calif. *Address*, 86 Grove St., Flushing, N. Y.

JOHNSON, Clarence R. Painter. Exhibited in 1925 his "Lumberville Lock" at the Annual Exhibition of the National Academy of Design, New York, and was awarded the first Hallgarten prize. *Address*, Lumberville, Penna.

JOHNSON, (Miss) Content. Painter. Born in Bloomington, Ill. Pupil of Julien Academy under Constant and Laurens, in Paris; New York School of Art, under Chase. *Address*, 200 West 57th St., New York, N. Y.

JOHNSON, Cordelia. Painter. Born in Omaha, in 1871. Pupil of J. Laurie Wallace. Member: Omaha Art Guild. *Address*, 2346 South 34th St., Omaha, Neb.

JOHNSON, David. Painter. Born in New York in 1827. At the beginning of his artistic career he received a few lessons from J. F. Cropsey. He has studied the works of the great European masters of landscape painting, but his professional life has been passed entirely in New York, and he has never been abroad. He was elected a National Academician in 1861, and was one of the founders of the Artists' Fund Society. At the Centennial Exhibition at Philadelphia in 1876 he exhibited "Scenery on the Housatonic," "Old Man of the Mountains," and "A Brook Study, Orange County, N. Y.," and received one of the first awards. His pictures are notable for fine color and excellent drawing. He died in 1908.

JOHNSON, David G. Painter and line-engraver of portraits and views of little merit, who was working in New York in 1831–35, and again in 1845.

JOHNSON, Eastman. Genre and portrait painter. Born in Lovell, Me., in 1824; died in New York in 1906. He studied in Dusseldorf, Rome, Paris and The Hague, and settled in New York in 1860, becoming a member of the National Academy of Design in the same year. He was the son of Philip C. Johnson, Secretary of State for Maine. He worked in a lithographic establishment in Boston in 1840 and after a year went to Augusta, Maine, where he commenced making portraits in black crayon. He also visited Newport. In 1845 the family moved to Washington, D. C., and young Johnson drew many crayon portraits, working in the Senate Committee Rooms at the Capitol. In 1858 he moved to New York where he remained the rest of his life except for a period spent in Boston and in visits to Europe in 1885, 1891 and 1897.

JOHNSON, Edyth A. B. Miniature painter. Exhibited at the Penna. Academy of Fine Arts, Philadelphia, in 1925. *Address*, Hamilton Court, Philadelphia.

JOHNSON, Frank Edward. Painter. Born in Norwich, Conn., in 1873. Pupil of Laurens and Constant in Paris. Member: Washington Water Color Club. *Address*, 3038 N St., Washington, D. C.

JOHNSON, Frank Tenney. Painter and illustrator. Born in Big Grove, Ia., in 1874. Pupil of Lorenz, Heinie and Henri. Represented in National Gallery, Washington, D. C., and Dallas Art Association. *Address,* 48 Charles St., New York, N. Y.

JOHNSON, G. M. Sculptor. Born in New York City in 1882. Pupil of Hermon McNeil and Gutzon Borglum. Member: National Sculpture Society; National Academy of Women Painters and Sculptors. Specialty, animals. *Address,* 145 Trenchard St., Yonkers, N. Y.

JOHNSON, Harry L. Miniature painter. Member: Penna. Society of Miniature Painters; American Society of Miniature Painters. *Address,* Swarthmore, Pa.

JOHNSON, Henrietta. Portrait draughtsman in pastels. Noted in ''Art and Artists in Provincial South Carolina'' published in the Charleston ''Year Book'' for 1899. Her portraits are of men and women, famous in the early life of South Carolina. She died in Charleston in 1728.

JOHNSON, Herbert. Illustrator. Born in Sutton, Nebr., in 1878. Member: Society of Illustrators, 1913. Cartoonist for various magazines. *Address,* 518 Walnut St., Philadelphia.

JOHNSON, Horace C. Portrait painter. Born in Oxford, Conn., in 1824. He was a student of the National Academy, also of the English Life Schools. He settled in Waterbury, Conn. Among his pictures are the ''Roman Mother,'' ''Rebecca at the Well,'' and ''Italian Girls at the Fountain.''

JOHNSON, Jeanne Payne (Mrs. Louis C.). Painter. Born near Danville, Ohio, in 1887. Pupil of Art Students' League of New York; of Mme. La Farge, Richard Miller and Lucien Simon in Paris. Member: Brooklyn Miniature Society. *Address,* 39 Remsen St., Brooklyn, New York, N. Y.

JOHNSON, Jeanne P. Miniature painter. Exhibited at the Penna. Academy of Fine Arts, 1925. *Address,* 39 Remsen St., Brooklyn, New York.

JOHNSON, Joseph Hoffman. Portrait painter. Born in 1821; died in 1890. He painted several portraits for the City of New York.

JOHNSON, Marshall. Painter. Born in Boston. Pupil of Lowell Institute. Painter of the United States Frigate, ''Constitution.''

JOHNSON, Marie R. Painter. Born in Flemington, N. J., in 1861. Pupil of Chase in New York; studied in Paris under Girardot

and Courtois. *Address,* 255 South Fair Oaks Ave., Pasadena, Calif.

JOHNSON, Mrs. Mary Ann. Painter. She excelled in still-life subjects. She died in New London, Conn., where much of her best painting was done.

JOHNSON, Samuel Frost. Painter. Born in New York City in 1835. He studied in the life schools of the National Academy and afterwards in the Academies of Brussels and Paris. He painted for some time in London, and on his return to this country accepted a professorship in the Metropolitan Museum. His works include ''Les Pommes'' shown at the Salon in 1869; ''Moorland Landscape''; portraits of Cardinal McCloskey and Lady Helen Blackwood.

JOHNSON, Thomas. Wood-engraver. He engraved a series of portraits of musicians in 1878.

JOHNSON, W. T. Engraved subject-plates for *Sartain's Magazine* about 1850.

JOHNSTON, David Claypoole. Engraver. Born in Philadelphia in 1797; died at Dorchester, Mass., 1865. In 1815 Johnston was a pupil of the Philadelphia engraver Francis Kearney, and in 1819 he was in business for himself etching caricatures of Philadelphia celebrities. The complaints of some of his victims finally became so loud that the publishers and print-sellers declined to handle his plates.

Johnston engraved a few good portraits in stipple and some line illustrations for the Boston publishers, and he also drew upon stone for lithographers. He is best known, however, by his annual publication of ''Scraps,'' first issued in 1830. This Annual was usually made up of four to six sheets, each containing from nine to twelve small etched caricatures of local, social, or political significance, all designed and etched by Johnston. The character and general excellence of these etchings gained for Johnston the name of ''The American Cruikshank.''

JOHNSTON, Henrietta. Portrait painter. He is said to have signed and dated portraits in 1755.

JOHNSTON, John. Painter. Born in Boston in 1752; died in 1818. He was the son of Thomas Johnston, who kept a shop in Brattle Street, where he sold colors, made charts, painted coats of arms, and engraved portraits, music plates, etc. John Johnson had military service in the Revolution, reaching the rank of Major, and was an original member of the ''Cincinnati.'' He painted many portraits of public men of Massachusetts, and his pictures, although deficient in drawing, possessed talent.

JOHNSTON, John Bernard. Landscape painter. Born in Boston in 1847. He was a pupil of William Morris Hunt, and died in 1886. Represented in Boson Museum of Fine Arts by "Landscape with Cattle."

JOHNSTON, Mary V. Painter. Born in Cuba in 1865. Pupil of Robert Henri. *Address,* Riverdale, Maryland.

JOHNSTON, Thomas. Engraver. Born in Boston, Mass., in 1708; died there 1767, and was buried in King's Chapel burying ground. The *Boston Evening Post* (1767) says: "Last Friday Morning, died here Mr. Thomas Johnston, Japanner, Painter and Engraver, after a short illness, being seized with an Apoplectic Fit a few days before."

Johnston was a fairly good engraver of maps, buildings, book-plates, sheet music, etc., and he was also a heraldic painter. His plan of Boston, signed as "Engraven by Thos. Johnson, Boston, N. E.," is dedicated "to His Excellency William Burnet, by the publisher, William Burgis." He was also an organ builder of some reputation in his day. Among his eleven children were William and John, both portrait painters. His engravings are listed in Stauffer's and Fielding's books on American Engraving.

JOHNSTON, Thomas Murphy. Portrait draughtsman in crayons. The latter part of his life he lived in Dorchester. He was the son of David C. Johnston, and was working in Boston, Mass., in 1856–1868.

JOHNSTONE, John Humphreys. Painter. Born in New York in 1857. Pupil of John La Farge in New York, and of Lefebvre and Doucet in Paris. His paintings are in the Luxembourg in Paris; Wilstach Gallery, Philadelphia; Carnegie Institute, Pittsburgh. *Address,* Paris, France.

JOINER, Harvey. Painter. Born in Charlestown, Ind., in 1852. Member of Louisville Artists' League. Specialty, Kentucky beechwoods. *Address,* 405 Equitable Bldg., Louisville, Ky.

JONES, A. L. Plates so signed are really engraved by W. S. Lawrence, an apprentice to Alfred Jones, and were finished by Mr. Jones. A further notice of Lawrence will be found in its proper place.

JONES, Albertus E. Painter. Born in South Windsor, Conn., in 1882. Pupil of Charles Noel Flagg. *Address,* 93 Niles St., Hartford, Conn.

JONES, Alfred. Engraver. Born in Liverpool, England, in 1819; accidentally killed in New York in 1900. Mr. Jones came to the United States as a very young man and in 1834 he was apprenticed to the engraving firm of Rawdon, Wright, Hatch & Edson, of Albany, N. Y. He later studied at the National Academy of Design, in New York, and in 1839 he was awarded the first prize in drawing. Mr. Jones was made an Academician of the National Academy in 1851.

About 1841 Alfred Jones began engraving over his own name, and in 1843 he engraved in line his first large plate, "The Farmers' Nooning," after the painting by W. S. Mount; this plate was executed for the American Art Union. As a line-engraver Mr. Jones had few, if any, superiors in this country, and his large plate of "The Image Breaker," published by the American Art Union in 1850, is deservedly recognized as one of the best engravings ever produced in the United States. Among other fine examples of his work published by the Art Union are "Mexican News" (1851), "The New Scholar" (1850), and "The Capture of Major André." Mr. Jones continued to engrave with undiminished skill up to the time of his death; his late portraits of Washington, A. B. Durand and Thomas Carlyle being admirable examples of a combination of line work with etching.

JONES, Bayard. Illustrator. Born in Rome, Ga., in 1869. Pupil of Laurens and Constant in Paris. *Address,* 40 West 28th St., New York.

JONES, Benjamin. Engraver. Located in Philadelphia in 1798–1815, inclusive. He engraved in line subject-plates possessing little merit, and Dunlap says that he was living in 1833.

JONES, Carminta de Solms. Painter. Exhibited in Penna. Academy of Fine Arts, Philadelphia, 1925. *Address,* 1822 Chestnut St., Philadelphia.

JONES, Fitzedward. This good engraver of subject-plates and portraits in mezzotint and in stipple was originally a printer in Carlisle, Pa. It is not known where or when he learned to engrave, but in 1854 he was in business in Cincinnati, Ohio, as a "practical portrait, historical and landscape engraver, and Plain and color printer," according to his business-card. He also worked for many years for the Western Methodist Book Concern, of Cincinnati.

JONES, Grace Church. Painter. Born in West Falls, N. Y. Pupil of Gaspard, Calot, and of the Colarossi Academy in Paris. *Address,* 118 Sherman St., Denver, Colo.

JONES, Hugh Bolton. Painter. He was born in Baltimore in 1848, and began his art studies in that city. He went to France in the seventies, and became a member of the artist colony at Pont Aven, in Brittany. Many good pictures from his easel date from that period. Later on he travelled in Spain and in Northern Africa, but for ten or fifteen years he found all his subjects in the United States, whether in picturesque fields and forests of New Jersey, or along the Massachusetts coast. He was elected a National Academician in 1833, and is a member of the Society of American Artists, and the American Water Color Society. Mr. Jones has a studio in New York, but, like many of our landscape painters, spends more months of the year in the country than in town. *Address*, 33 West 67th St., New York.

JONES, Leon Foster. Painter. Born in Manchester, N. H., in 1871. Pupil of Cowles Art School in Boston, under Major and De Camp. Represented in Boston Museum of Art. *Address*, Port Jefferson, L. I.

JONES, R. S. A line-engraver working in Boston in 1873.

JONES, Seth C. Painter and illustrator. Born in Rochester, N. Y., in 1853. Pupil of Wm. H. Holmes and Thomas Moran. *Address*, Municipal Bldg., 435 East Main St., Rochester, N. Y.

JONES, S. K. Born in Clinton, Conn., in 1825. After 1861 he painted in New Haven, his specialty being portraits.

JONES, Thomas. Painter. Exhibited at the Penna. Academy, Philadelphia, in 1924. *Address*, 5113 Chester Ave., Philadelphia, Pa.

JONES, Thomas D. Sculptor. But little is known of him except from letters written by him in October and November, 1857, to Honorable Lewis Cass and Capt. Meigs. The letters refer to a bust of the Honorable Lewis Cass executed nine years previous to this time. He also refers to a bust of Honorable John C. Breckenridge, on which he was then engaged, and to the fact that he himself was a western sculptor. In November, 1857, he resided in Cincinnati, Ohio. He was elected an Associate Member of the National Academy in 1853. He died in 1881.

JONES, William Foster. An American portrait painter working in Philadelphia about 1850. He also painted miniatures, several being signed and dated 1847–1849.

JONES, William R. Engraver of portraits in the stipple manner. Born in the United States. He first appears in Philadelphia in 1810, when he was an Associate of the Society of Artists of the United States, organized in Philadelphia in that year. As an engraver his name appears in the directories of Philadelphia in 1811–24, inclusive.

JONGERS, Alphonse. Portrait painter. Born in France in 1872. Pupil of École des Beaux Arts; also studied in Spain. He came to America in 1897 and was elected Associate Member of the National Academy in 1906. Among his works are a portrait of William T. Evans at National Gallery, Washington, and of Louise and Arthur Hearn at the Metropolitan Museum, N. Y. *Address*, 200 West 57th St., New York.

JONSON, C. Raymond. Painter. Born in Chariton, Ia., in 1891. Pupil of W. J. Reynolds. Member: "Cor Ardens." Work: "The Bur Reed" (a decoration), City of Chicago; "Irony," University of Oklahoma, Norman; "Mountain Vista," Mississippi Art Association, Jackson, Miss. *Address*, 19 East Pearson St., Chicago, Ill.

JORDAN, David W. Landscape painter. Born in Harrisburg, Pa., in 1859. Pupil of Penna. Academy of Fine Arts under Schussele and Eakins. Member: Art Club of Philadelphia; Philadelphia Sketch Club; Fellowship, Penna. Academy of Fine Arts. *Address*, 19 West Ashmead Place, Germantown, Philadelphia, Pa.

JORDAN, Henry. Born in England. Came to the United States about 1836, and was for a time in the employ of Alfred Jones, in New York City. Jordan was a good line-engraver of landscape, and was later a member of the engraving firm of Jordan & Halpin. He returned to England for a time, but ultimately settled in the United States.

JORDAN, Mildred C. Miniature painter. Born in Portland, Me. Pupil of Yale School of Fine Arts. Member: New Haven Paint and Clay Club. *Address*, 129 Whalley Ave., New Haven, Conn.

JOSEPH, Adelyn L. Sculptor and illustrator. Born in Chicago in 1895. Pupil of Mulligan and Polasek. Member: Chicago Society of Artists; Society of Women Sculptors. *Address*, 4334 Drexel Blvd., Chicago, Ill.

JOSEPH, Joan A. Sculptor. Exhibited "The Art Student" at the Academy of Fine Arts, Philadelphia, 1924. *Address*, 4320 Drexel Boulevard, Chicago, Ill.

JOSEPH, Isaac A. Miniature and landscape painter. Pupil of Art Students' League of New York, and of Leon Bonnat in Paris. Awarded honorable mention, Paris Exposition of 1900. *Address*, 924 West End Ave., New York, N. Y.

JOUETT, Matthew Harris. Portrait painter. Born in Mercer County, Ky.; died at Louisville, Ky., in 1827. After studying with Gilbert Stuart in Boston, he returned to Lexington, Ky., and there painted many portraits. He also worked in Natchez, Louisville, and New Orleans. About 350 portraits have been recorded as painted by him. He is represented in the Metropolitan Museum of New York by his portrait of John Grimes.

JOULLIN, Amedée (Miss). Painter. Born in San Francisco in 1862. Studied there and in France. Her specialty was Indian pictures. She is represented in many art galleries in California. She died in San Francisco in 1917.

JOULLIN, Lucile. See Benjamin, Mrs. L. J.

JUDKINS, Miss E. M. Portrait artist in crayons, who worked in New England about 1847.

JUDSON, Alice. Painter. Born in Beacon, N. Y. Pupil of Art Students' League of New York, and of J. H. Twachtman. Member: National Academy of Women Painters and Sculptors. Work: Over-mantle decoration, Administration Bldg., Matteawan State Hospital, Beacon, N. Y. *Address,* 58 West 57th St., New York, N. Y.

JUDSON, Almira. Painter. Born in Milwaukee, Wis. Pupil of Woman's Academy, Munich; Colarossi in Paris; Henri in New York. Member: San Francisco Artists' Association. *Address,* 123 Edgewood Ave., San Francisco, Calif.

JUDSON, Mrs. Minnie Lee. Painter. Born in Milford, Conn., in 1866. Pupil of Yale School of Fine Arts. Member: Conn. Academy of Fine Arts. *Address,* Main St., Stratford, Conn.

JUDSON, William Lees. Painter. Born in Manchester, England, in 1842. Came to America in 1852. Pupil of J. B. Irving in New York, and of Boulanger and Lefebvre in Paris. *Address,* 212 Thorne St., Los Angeles, Calif.

JUENGLING, Frederick. Engraver and painter. Born in New York City in 1846. He

studied art there and attained high rank as an engraver. He was a founder of the American Society of Wood-Engravers. He received honorable mention at the Paris Salon. Among his works are "The Professor," engraved after Duveneck, "The Voice of the Sea." His paintings include "The Intruder," "Westward Bound," and "In the Street." He died in 1889.

JUERGENS, Alfred. Painter. Born in Chicago in 1866. Pupil of Chicago Academy of Design, and of the Munich Royal Academy. Has exhibited paintings in principal exhibitions, and has mural paintings in many churches. *Address,* 213 South Grove Ave., Oak Park, Ill.

JULIO, E. B. D. Fabrino. Painter. Born in the Island of St. Helena, of an Italian father and a Scotch mother, in 1843. He died in Georgia in 1879. Specialty, portraits, genre and landscape. Julio came to the United States in 1861, and to New Orleans in the latter part of the "60's," where he resided the greater part of the time during the remainder of his life, except the year 1872, which he spent in Paris as a student of Leon Bonnat. His "Diana," "Harvest Scene," and several Louisiana landscapes were exhibited at the Centennial at Philadelphia in 1876.

JUNGE, Carl S. Painter and illustrator. Born in Stockton, Calif., in 1880. Pupil of School of Art in London; Julien Academy in Paris. Awards: Prizes, 1916, 1917 and 1921 from American Bookplate Society. *Address,* 143 South Harvey Ave., Oak Park, Ill.

JUSZKO, J. Sculptor. Exhibited "Portrait Bust," in 1925, in Annual Exhibition of the National Academy of Design, New York. *Address,* 59 East 59th St., New York.

JUSTICE, Joseph. Engraver. In 1804 Justice was working in New York in connection with Scoles, and the directories of Philadelphia locate him in that city as an engraver from 1810 until 1833. His plates show an ineffective combination of etching and stipple work, poorly done.

K

KAELIN, Charles Salis. Painter. Born in Cincinnati in 1858. Pupil of Cincinnati Art School; Art Students' League of New York; Cincinnati Museum Association. Exhibited at Paris Exposition, 1900. Member: Society Western Artists; Cincinnati Art Club. *Address,* Rockport, Mass.

KAHILL, Joseph B. Portrait painter. Born in 1882. Studied in Paris. Member of Portland Society of Artists. Represented in Walker Art Gallery of Bowdoin College, Maine. *Address,* 562 Congress St., Portland, Me.

KAHILL, Victor. Sculptor. Exhibited "A Study," at the Penna. Academy of Fine Arts, Philadelphia, 1924. *Address,* 3610 Spring Garden St., Philadelphia.

KAHLER, Carl. Painter. Exhibited at Philadelphia, 1921, Academy of Fine Arts, Exhibition of "Paintings Showing the Later Tendencies in Art." *Address,* 49 West 8th St., New York City.

KAHN, Isaac. Painter. Born in Cincinnati, Ohio, in 1883. Pupil of Duveneck and Lindsay. Member of Cincinnati Art Club. *Address,* 2426 Reading Road, Cincinnati, Ohio.

KAISER, August. Painter, illustrator and etcher. Born in Germany in 1889. *Address,* 111 East 35th St., New York.

KAJIWARA, Takuma. Painter. Exhibited in 1925 in Annual Exhibition of National Academy of Design, New York. *Address,* 750 Century Bldg., St. Louis, Mo.

KALDENBERG, Frederick Robert. Sculptor. Born in New York in 1855; died 1923. Self-taught in art. Took up carving in meerschaum at ten years of age, and at fourteen commenced ivory carving, being the first native American to do this work. Some of his productions were in the possession of the late Russian Emperor, the King of Belgium and the Presidents of Venezuela and Mexico, and among the relics of Gen. U. S. Grant; also in the gallery of George W. Vanderbilt, the Smithsonian Institution, and the palace of Li Hung Chang, etc.

KALLEM, Morris J. Painter. Exhibited portraits at Annual Exhibition, 1925, of National Academy of Design, New York. *Address,* 1916 Grand Concourse, New York.

KAMP, Glinten. Painter. Exhibited water colors at the Penna. Academy of Fine Arts,

1925. *Address,* 19 East 16th St., New York City.

KAMPF, Mrs. Malissa Q. Painter. Born in Philadelphia in 1867. Pupil of Chase and Carolus Duran. *Address,* 200 Rodney St., Brooklyn, N. Y.

KANTOR, Morris. Painter. Born in Russia in 1896. Exhibited in Philadelphia, 1921, at the Penna. Academy of Fine Arts at the "Exhibition Showing the Later Tendencies in Art." Pupil of Homer Boss. *Address,* 1947 Broadway, New York City.

KAPPES, Carl. Painter. *Address,* 410 Monroe St., Toledo, Ohio.

KAPPES, Walter. Painter of Negro Life.

KARASA, Ilona. Painter. Born at Budapest in 1896. Member: Salons of America. *Address,* 27 West 8th St., New York.

KARFIOL, Bernard. Painter. Born in Brooklyn, N. Y., in 1886. Pupil of Laurens in Paris. *Address,* Ridgefield, N. J.

KARFUNKLE, David. Painter, sculptor and etcher. Born in Austria. Pupil of National Academy of Design, New York. *Address,* 13 East 14th St., New York City.

KARST, John. Wood engraver. Born in Germany in 1836; died in De Bruce, N. Y., in 1922, having lived his entire professional life in this country.

KASE, Paul G. Painter. Born in Reading, Penna., in 1896. Pupil of Breckenridge and Penna. Academy of Fine Arts. *Address,* 30 North 8th St., Reading, Pa.

KASSLER, Charles (Jr.). Painter. Exhibited Water Colors at the Penna. Academy of Fine Arts, Philadelphia, 1925. *Address,* 1756 Vine St., Denver, Colo.

KATO, Kentaro. Painter. Born in Japan in 1889. Won second Hallgarten prize, National Academy of Design, 1920. *Address,* 680 Fifth Ave., New York.

KATOAKA, Genjiro. Painter. Born in Japan in 1867. Came to America and studied with Twachtman in New York. Member of New York Water Color Club. *Address,* Tokio, Japan.

KATZIEFF, Julius D. Painter and etcher. Born in 1892. Pupil of Boston Museum of Art and Penna. Academy of Fine Arts. *Address*, 126 Dartmouth St., Boston, Mass.

KAUFMAN, Jean F. Painter, sculptor and etcher. Born in Switzerland in 1870. Pupil of Gerome. His portrait of Hon. Asa Bird Gardiner is in the War Department, Washington, D. C.; mural decorations in Monumental Church, Richmond, Va.; monumental bronze bust, Poughkeepsie, N. Y. *Address*, 1208 Carnegie Hall, New York.

KAUFMAN, Theodore. Painter. Born in Nelson, Hanover, in 1814. He studied abroad, and returning to this country fought in the National Army during the Civil War. Subsequently he resided in Boston. His works include "Genl. Sherman near the Watchfire," "On to Liberty," "Farragut in the Rigging."

KAUFMANN, Ferdinand. Painter. Born in Germany in 1864. Pupil of Laurens, Constant and Bouguereau in Paris. Member of Pittsburgh Art Association. *Address*, 9 Wood St., Pittsburgh, Penna.

KAULA, Lee L. (Mrs.). Painter. Born in Erie, Penna. Pupil of Dewey in New York and Aman Jean in Paris. *Address*, 311 Fenway Studios, Boston.

KAULA, William J. Landscape painter. Born in Boston in 1871. Pupil of Cowles Art School in Boston, and Collin in Paris. *Address*, 311 Fenway Studios, Boston, Mass.

KAVANAUGH, Katharine (Mrs. William V. Cahill). Painter. Born in Falmouth, Ky., in 1890. Pupil of Wm. V. Cahill. *Address*, 2625 Polk St., San Francisco, Calif.

KAWACHI, J. B. Painter. Born in Toyoaka Tajima, Japan, in 1885. Studied in Japan. *Address*, 170 Fifth Ave., New York, N. Y.

KAWAMURA, Gozo. Sculptor. Born in Japan in 1886. Studied in Boston and New York. Pupil and assistant of MacMonnies. Specialty, portrait busts and animal studies. *Address*, 5 West 16th St., New York.

KAY, Gertrude A. Illustrator. Born in 1884. Pupil of Howard Pyle. She began illustrating work in Philadelphia in 1903. Member of Plastic Club, Philadelphia. *Address*, 133 S. Union St., Alliance, Ohio.

KAYE, Mrs. Elizabeth Gutman. Painter. Born in Baltimore, Md., in 1887. Pupil of S. Edwin Whiteman, Hugh Breckenridge and H. B. Snell. *Address*, 856 Park Ave., Baltimore, Md.

KEANE, Theodore J. Painter. Born in San Francisco in 1880. Pupil of California School of Design and Art Institute of Chicago. Specialty, animal paintings. Formerly director of Minneapolis Society of Fine Arts, and dean of School of the Chicago Art Institute. *Address*, 5027 Dorchester Ave., Chicago, Ill.

KEASBEY, Henry T. Painter. Born in Philadelphia in 1882. Pupil of Herkomer and Brangwyn. *Address*, Hotel Chelsea, West 23d St., New York.

KEARNY, Francis. Engraver. Born in Perth Amboy, N. J., about 1780. Kearny is said to have been a nephew of Commodore James Lawrence, and Westcott, in his "History of Philadelphia," says that he learned drawing with Archibald and Alexander Robertson, and engraving with Peter R. Maverick, in New York City. Kearny was in business in New York in 1798–1801, as an engraver. In 1810 he appeared in Philadelphia and remained there continuously until 1833.

Kearny founded his fame as an engraver upon a faithful copy of "The Last Supper," after Raphael Morghen. He did considerable work in line, stipple, and aquatint for the magazines, "Annuals," and book publishers, and in 1820–23 he was interested in banknote work as a member of the firm of Tanner, Vallance, Kearny & Co., of Philadelphia.

KEAST, Susette S. Painter. Born in Philadelphia in 1892. Pupil of Breckenridge, Anshutz and Chase. Member of Fellowship of Penna. Academy of Fine Arts. *Address*, 1928 Rittenhouse Square, Philadelphia.

KECK, Charles. Sculptor. Member of National Sculpture Association. Represented by "Stonewall Jackson," Charlottesville, Va.; "Booker Washington" at Tuskegee, Ala. Elected Associate Member of National Academy. *Address*, 40 West 10th St., New York.

KEELER, Burton. Painter. Born in Philadelphia in 1886. Pupil of Penna. Academy of Fine Arts. Awards: Cresson Traveling Scholarship, Penna. Academy of Fine Arts, 1911 and 1912. *Address*, 224 West 11th St., New York.

KEELER, Charles B. Painter and etcher. Born in Cedar Rapids, Ia., in 1882. Pupil of Art Institute of Chicago; of Johansen, Stevens and Nordfeldt. *Address*, Fin del Viaje, Glendora, Los Angeles Co., Calif.

KEELER, (Louis Bertrand) Rolston. Painter. Born in New York in 1882. Pupil of National Academy of Design. *Address*, Sammis Ave., Huntington, Suffolk County, N. Y.

KEENAN, William. This etcher of portraits, and line-engraver of vignettes and subject-plates, was working for the magazine and book publishers of Philadelphia in 1830–33. He then apparently located himself in business in Charleston, S. C., as we find an aquatint view of Charleston, engraved by Keenan and published by him at "132 King St., Charleston, S. C.," and other plates executed for book publishers in that city, in 1835. Some of these latter plates are inscribed as "Drawn, Engraved and Printed by W. Keenan."

KEENER, Anna E. Painter. Born in Flagler, Colo., in 1895. Awarded medal for wood engraving. *Address*, 9th and Minnesota Ave., Kansas City, Kans.

KEFFER, Frances. Painter. Born in Des Moines, Ia., in 1881. Pupil of Pratt Institute; Alex. Robinson; Frank Brangwyn; Ossip Linde. Member: National Academy of Women Painters and Sculptors; Nanuet Painters; League of New York Artists. *Address*, Hillsdale, N. J.

KEHRER, F. A. Illustrator. Member: Pen and Pencil Club, Columbus. *Address*, 24 W. Maynard Ave., Columbus, Ohio.

KEISTER, Roy C. Illustrator. Born in Ohio in 1886. Pupil of Art Institute of Chicago. *Address*, 1909 Republic Bldg., Chicago, Ill.

KEITH, Dora W. (Mrs.). Portrait painter and illustrator. Born in Jamaica, L. I., in 1857. Pupil of William Chase; also studied in Paris. Elected Associate Member of National Academy in 1906. Painted portraits of Saml. L. Clemens, Charles Dudley Warner and Col. John Hay. *Address*, 3 West 67th St., New York.

KEITH, William. Landscape and portrait painter. Born in Scotland in 1839; died in California in 1911. Pupil of Achenbach and Carl Marr. Represented in Corcoran Art Gallery by Portrait of Irving M. Scott, builder of ships for the United States Navy.

KELLER, Arthur I. Painter and illustrator. Born in 1867; died in 1924. Pupil of National Academy of Design; also studied in Munich. Member of American Water Color Society and New York Water Color Club. He is represented by a painting "The Mass," in the Munich Academy.

KELLER, Clyde Leon. Painter. Born in Salem, Ore., in 1872. Studied in London. Represented by "After the Shower," "California Marshes" and "Columbia River." *Address*, 450 Washington St., Portland, Ore.

KELLER, Henry G. Painter. Born in Cleveland, Ohio, in 1870. Studied in Munich. Represented in Cleveland Museum by "In the Sand Pit." *Address*, 1381 Addison Road, Cleveland, Ohio.

KELLOG, Miner K. Painter. Born in Cincinnati, Ohio, he has long resided abroad. He painted a portrait of General Scott, in the City Hall, New York, also a replica of the head. During a visit to this country he sold many excellent examples of his work. He has also painted miniatures.

KELLOGG, Edmund P. Painter and illustrator. Born in Chicago, Ill. Pupil of Chase and Duveneck. Student at Art Institute of Chicago. *Address*, 3839 Lake Park Ave., Chicago.

KELLOGG, J. G. Engraver of portraits in line, working in New Haven, Conn., about 1850. He was born in Tolland, Conn., in 1805, and died in Hartford, Conn., in 1873.

KELLY, J. This engraver in 1851 had an office at 141 Fulton St., New York City. He engraved portraits in a mixed manner.

KELLY, James Edward. Sculptor. Born in New York in 1855. Studied art at National Academy of Design; studied wood engraving in 1871. Illustrated for *Scribner's, St. Nicholas, Harper's*, etc., until 1881; since then he has worked exclusively as a sculptor. Prominent works: Monmouth Battle Monument, including Molly Pitcher, 1885; Paul Revere, 1882; 6th New York Cavalry, Gettysburg, 1890; equestrian figures of Gen. Sherman, Col. Roosevelt at San Juan Hill; busts from life of Admiral Dewey, Admiral Sampson, Lt. Hobson, Admiral C. E. Clark, President Roosevelt, and Count Rochambeau at Southington, Conn. War memorial to soldiers and sailors, Kingston, N. Y., 1919. Was one of the founders of the Art Students' League. *Address*, 318 West 57th St., New York.

KELLY, J. Reading. Portrait painter. Born in New York in 1873. Pupil of National Academy of Design. *Address*, 56 West 95th St., New York.

KELLY, Thomas. Born in Ireland about 1795; died in the almshouse in New York City about 1841. The professional career of this very good engraver in line and in stipple is difficult to trace. He was working for Boston publishers in 1823, but was in Philadelphia in 1831–33, and in New York in 1834–35. Kelly was associated for a short time with Joseph Andrews, in Boston. Besides his portraits he engraved a considerable number of good plates for the "Annuals" and magazines. Later in life he contracted bad habits and died as stated above.

KELMAN, Benjamin. Painter and illustrator. Born in 1890. Pupil of Penna. Academy of Fine Arts and National Academy of Design. *Address*, 1692 Park Ave., New York City, N. Y.

KEMBLE, Edward W. Illustrator. Born in Sacramento, Calif., in 1861. Specialty, negro subjects. *Address*, Care of Leslie's Weekly, New York.

KEMEYS, Edward. Born in Savannah, Ga., in 1843. He studied in New York and later in Paris. He has made a specialty of the wild animals of the American continent. His "Fight between Buffalo and Wolves" was exhibited in the Salon of 1878. Among his works: "Panther and Deer," "Coyote and Raven"; he has also made the colossal head of a Buffalo for the Pacific railroad station at St. Louis. A collection of some fifty of his small bronzes are at the National Gallery in Washington, D. C. He died at Georgetown Heights, Washington, D. C., in 1907.

KEMMELMYER. An artist by that name made a sketch from life of Washington on Oct. 2d, 1894, when the latter was reviewing the Western troops at Cumberland, Md.

KEMP, Oliver. Painter and illustrator. Born in Trenton, N. J., in 1882. Pupil of Howard Pyle, Chase and Gerome. Illustrating for *Scribner's, Century* and *Saturday Evening Post. Address*, 116 West 39th St., New York.

KEMPER, Ruby W. Painter. Born in Cincinnati, Ohio, in 1883. Pupil of W. H. Fry and Frank Duveneck. *Address*, Milford, Ohio.

KEMPTON, Elmira. Painter. Born in Richmond, Ind., in 1892. Member of the Indiana Artists' Club. *Address*, 916 Main St., Richmond, Ind.

KENDALL, Beatrice. Painter. Born in New York City in 1902. Pupil of Yale School of Fine Arts. *Address*, 58 Trumbull St., New Haven, Conn.

KENDALL, Elizabeth. Painter, sculptor and illustrator. Born in 1896. Pupil of Yale School of Fine Arts. *Address*, 58 Trumbull St., New Haven, Conn.

KENDALL, Kate. Painter, of Cleveland, Ohio. Exhibited water colors at the Penna. Academy of Fine Arts. Deceased 1915.

KENDALL, Margaret. Painter. Born, Staten Island, N. Y., in 1871. Pupil of J. Alden Weir, Julius Rolshoven and Sergeant Kendall. Exhibited, Penna. Academy of Fine Arts, 1898–1902; Society of American Artists, 1898–1902; Minneapolis, 1900; Paris Exposition, 1900; Society Miniature Painters, 1901–4; Society of Miniature Painters. *Address*, Simsbury, Conn.

KENDALL, Mrs. Marie B. Painter. Born in 1885. Pupil of Chase. Member of California Art Club. *Address*, 2122 Perkins Ave., Long Branch, Calif.

KENDALL, W. Sergeant. Painter. Born in 1869. Pupil of Art Students' League; Penna. Academy of Fine Arts. Pupil of Merson in Paris. Elected an Associate Member of National Academy in 1903, and National Academy in 1905. Director of Yale School of the Fine Arts. Represented by paintings in Metropolitan Museum of New York, and National Gallery in Washington, D. C. *Address*, Hot Springs, Va.

KENNEDY, James. Engraver in line and stipple. In 1797 he was working for the New York publisher, John Low. He remained in that city until 1812, and then went to Philadelphia, as he was later employed by the publishers S. F. Bradford and T. W. Freeman, both of that city.

KENNEDY, Laurence. Painter. Born in Pittsburgh, Pa., in 1880. Pupil of Art Institute of Chicago. *Address*, 30 North Michigan Blvd., Chicago, Ill.

KENNEDY, S. Engraver. Working in Philadelphia in 1813 with William Charles, who was best known by his series of caricatures of the War of 1812.

KENNEDY, Samuel J. Painter. Born in Mt. Pleasant, Mich., in 1877. Pupil of Henri Martin. Work: "Young Genius," Mt. Pleasant Public Gallery; "The Marshes," Library of Michigan Agricultural College. *Address*, 4 East Ohio St., Chicago, Ill.

KENNEL, Louis. Painter. Born in North Bergen, N. J., in 1886. Pupil of George Bridgman; Wm. H. Lippincot; Charles Graham; Ernest Gros. *Address*, 741 Monroe St., New Durham, N. J.

KENSETT, John Frederick. Born in Cheshire, Conn., in 1818; died in New York City in 1872. In 1840 he went to England to study art, and during his five years' stay in that country he partially supported himself by engraving. Kensett continued his studies in Rome and returned to the United States in 1848. He opened a studio in New York and established a reputation as a painter of landscape. In 1850 he sent a painting to the Royal Academy for exhibition, which was highly praised. He was elected a National Academician in 1849. He is represented in the Metropolitan Museum by his painting "Lake George," also a number of landscapes painted in 1871. He is considered one of the most distinguished landscape painters of the last generation.

KENSETT, Thomas. Engraver. In 1812 Thomas Kensett was a member of the engrav-

14

ing and print-publishing firm of Shelton & Kensett, located at Cheshire, Conn. As evidence that he was an engraver himself, we have a well-executed map of Upper and Lower Canada, published in 1812, and signed "Kensett Sculp. Cheshire, Conn't." Another large plate entitled "Brother Jonathan's Soliloquy on the Times" is signed "Kennsett, Paint. et Sculp."

Mr. H. W. French, in his "Art and Artists in Connecticut," says that Thomas Kensett came from England to Cheshire in 1812, and had previously been an engraver at Hampton Court, in England, and Mr. James Terry says that he was born in England in 1786 and died in 1829.

KENT, Ada Howe. Painter. Born in Rochester, N. Y. Pupil of Brush, Abbott Thayer and Whistler. Member: New York Water Color Club. *Address,* 29 Atkinson St., Rochester, N. Y.

KENT, Rockwell. Painter. Born in 1882. Pupil of William Chase, Robert Henri and Abbott Thayer. Represented by "Marine" in Metropolitan Museum, New York. *Address,* Arlington, Vt.

KENYON, Henry R. Painter. Work: "Landscape, Holland," "November Twilight" and "Venice," Rhode Island School of Design, Providence. *Address,* Ipswich, Mass.

KEPLINGER, Lorna Miller. Miniature painter. Exhibited at the Penna. Academy of Fine Arts, 1925. *Address,* Bethesda, Md.

KEPPLER, George. Sculptor. Born in Germany in 1856. He came to America, and lives in Providence, R. I. *Address,* 58 Wesleyan Ave., Providence, R. I.

KEPPLER, Joseph. Illustrator and caricaturist. Born in Vienna in 1838. He came to America about 1868. In 1873 he was in New York as a cartoonist for *Frank Leslie's Weekly.* He also was successful with lithography. He died in New York in 1894.

KERNAN, F. G. This man was an engraver of portraits, in a mixed style, located in New York in 1870.

KERNS, Fannie M. Painter and illustrator. Born in Los Angeles, Calif. Pupil of Arthur Dow; Frank Ingerson; Ralph Johnnot. *Address,* 916 Grattan St., Los Angeles, Calif.

KERR, Irene Waite. Painter. Born Pauls Valley, Okla., 1873. Pupil of Walcott, Clarkson, William M. Chase, James Fraser, Du Mond and F. L. Mora. *Address,* 144 East 14th St., Oklahoma City, Okla.

KERSHAW, J. M. This engraver of buildings, etc., was working in St. Louis, Mo., in 1850.

KETCHAM, Austin. Painter. Born in 1898. Pupil of Art Institute of Chicago. Specialty, portraits. *Address,* Kansas City, Mo.

KETCHAM, Susan M. Painter. Born in Indianapolis, Ind. Pupil of Art Students' League of New York, under Chase and Bell. Member: National Academy of Women Painters and Sculptors. Work: "A Young Student"; "Beatrix"; "The Restless Sea, Ogunquit, Me.," Herron Art Institute, Indianapolis. *Address,* 1010 Carnegie Hall, New York, N. Y.

KETTEN, Maurice. Illustrator. *Address,* 50 West 67th St., New York, N. Y.

KETTERER, Gustav. Painter. Member: Philadelphia Art Club. *Address,* 1502 Walnut St., Philadelphia, Pa.

KEUHNE, Max. Painter. Born in New York, 1880. Pupil of Kenneth Hayes Miller, Chase and Henri. *Address,* 18 Bank St., New York, N. Y.

KEY, F. C. The firm of F. C. Key & Sons, of No. 123 Arch St., Philadelphia, was engaged in die-sinking and embossing, about 1850. A fairly well-executed head of Millard Fillmore was published by this firm. It is embossed on white paper, surrounded by an oval in gold, with the name and publisher also printed in gold.

KEY, John Ross. Painter. Born in Baltimore, Md., 1837. Studied in Paris. Studio in Chicago and Boston. Principal paintings: "Marblehead Beach"; "Newport"; "Golden Gate, San Francisco." He has also been successful in his work in black and white. He died in Baltimore in 1920.

KEY, Mabel. Painter. Born in Paris, France, 1874, of American parents. Awards: Honorable mention for water color, St. Paul Institute, 1915; silver medal, St. Paul Institute, 1916; silver medal, Wisconsin Painters and Sculptors. Instructor in Milwaukee Art Institute. *Address,* Fullerton Parkway, Chicago, Ill.

KEY, William H. Engraver. Born in Brooklyn, N. Y.; was living in 1892. From 1864 until 1892 and possibly later, Key was an assistant engraver for the U. S. Mint at Philadelphia. Key engraved the dies for the Kane Expedition medal, and a medal for Archbishop Wood.

KEYS, Harry J. Illustrator. Member: Pen and Pencil Club, Columbus. *Address,* "Columbus Citizen," Columbus, Ohio.

KEYSER, Ephraim. Sculptor. Born in Baltimore in 1850. Pupil of Royal Academy, Munich, and in Berlin. Represented by statue of Maj.-Gen. Baron de Kalb; marble statue, "Psyche," at Cincinnati Art Museum; busts of Sidney Lanier and Cardinal Gibbons. *Address*, 2408 Linden Ave., Baltimore, Md.

KEYSER, Ernest Wise. Sculptor. Born in Baltimore, Md., in 1874. Pupil of Maryland Institute; Art Students' League of New York; Julien Academy of Paris. Work: "Enoch Pratt Memorial"; Admiral Schley statue at Annapolis; "Sir Galahad" for Harper Memorial, Ottawa, Canada. *Address*, 59 West 12th St., New York.

KIBBEY, Ilah M. Painter and illustrator. Born in Genver, Ohio, in 1888. Pupil of Breckenridge and Snell. *Address*, 3424 Bell St., Kansas City, Mo.

KIDDER, Frank Howard. Painter. Born in Litchfield, Conn., in 1886. Pupil of Kenneth Hayes Miller and Denys Wortman. *Address*, 210 South Main St., New Canaan, Conn.

KIDDER, J. The "Polyanthos," Boston, June, 1813, refers editorially to an aquatint, "View on Boston Common," contained in that number, and says it is "a specimen of the talents of Master J. Kidder, a youth of Boston, and also his first essay in aquatinta." Kidder's few plates, all in aquatint, represent views in and about Boston. Kidder designed plates engraved by Abel Bowen about 1823.

KIEFER, Sam P. Painter. Member: Pen and Pencil Club, Columbus, O. *Address*, 147 West Maynard Ave., Columbus, Ohio.

KILM, Wilfred Langdon. Painter. Born in Brooklyn, N. Y., in 1898. Pupil of Art Students' League, New York. Specialty, painting of American Indians. *Address*, 46 West 85th St., New York.

KILBURN (or KILBRUNN), Laurence. Painter. He arrived from London in 1754, and advertised in the New York papers soliciting business. There are a number of portraits in New York by Kilburn which show him to have had some skill as a portrait painter; a bunch of flowers at the breast, or a flower held in the hand were several of the characteristics of his style. He died in 1775. (See portrait of Mrs. Philip Schuyler, at New York Historical Society.)

KILENYI, Julio. Sculptor and medalist. Born in Hungary. Represented in Metropolitan Museum of Art; Cleveland Museum of Art; Boston Museum of Fine Arts; Massachusetts Historical Society. *Address*, 20 East 90th St., New York.

KILBRUNN, L. Painter. According to Dunlap. (See Kilburn.)

KILPATRICK, Aaron Edward. Landscape painter. Born in Canada in 1872. Pupil of William Wendt. Elected Associate Member of the National Academy. Came to the United States. Represented in San Francisco and Cleveland Museums. *Address*, 5199 Ellenwood Drive, Los Angeles, Calif.

KIMBALL, Isabel M. Sculptor. Pupil of of Herbert Adams. Represented by Winona Fountain, in Central Park, Winona, Minn.; Richards Tablet at Vassar College; the War Memorial Tablet for Essex Co. *Address*, 290 Adelphia St., Brooklyn, N. Y.

KIMBALL, Alonzo Myron. Painter and illustrator. Born in Green Bay, Wisc., in 1874; died in Evanston, Ill., in 1923. He was a pupil of the Art Students' League, New York, and of the Julien Academy, Paris, under Lefebvre and Whistler. He was a member of the Society of Illustrators, 1911.

KIMBALL, Isabel Moore. Sculptor. Exhibited at National Association of Women Painters and Sculptors, New York, 1924. *Address*, 246 Fulton St., Brooklyn, N. Y.

KIMBALL, Katharine. Etcher and illustrator. Born in New Hampshire. Pupil of Art Students' League of New York. Represented in Victoria and Albert Museum, London; New York Public Library; Library of Congress, Washington; Boston Museum of Fine Arts.

KIMBERLY, Cora Draper (Mrs. Samuel A. Kimberly). Painter. Born in St. Louis, Mo. Pupil of Hawthorne; Vanderpoel; Messer. *Address*, 2112 O St., N.W., Washington, D. C.

KIMBERLY, Denison. Engraver and painter. Born in Guilford, Conn., in 1814. Kimberly was a fellow-student with George H. Cushman in the engraving establishment of Asaph Willard, and as a line-engraver of portraits he achieved considerable success. He was working in 1830 for S. Walker, the Boston publisher, and was later connected with the Franklin Print Company, of Boston. In 1858 Kimberly abandoned engraving for painting; he studied in Boston, and in 1862 he opened studios in Hartford and in Manchester. He was chiefly engaged in portrait work, producing good likenesses, strong and free in outline, yet remarkably soft in feature. The portrait of his friend Seth W. Cheney is one of his best works.

KIMBERLY, James H. Miniature artist, flourishing 1841–43, in New York.

KIMMEL, P. K. Engraver of vignettes and portraits working in New York about 1850, and was later a member of the engraving firm of Capewell & Kimmel, of the same city. There was also an engraving firm of Kimmel & Foster.

KINDLER, Alice Riddle (Mrs.). Painter. Born in Germantown, Philadelphia, in 1892. Student of Penna. Academy of Fine Arts, Philadelphia. *Address,* Mt. Airy, Philadelphia.

KING, Albert F. Painter. Born in Pittsburgh, Pa., in 1854. Painted portraits in the Duquesne Club, Pittsburgh. He was largely self-taught. *Address,* 605 McCance Bldg., Pittsburgh, Pa.

KING, Charles Bird. Born in Newport, R. I., in 1785. He first studied with Edward Savage, and in 1805 he went to London where he continued his studies. He returned in 1812, had a studio in Philadelphia, and in 1816 removed to Washington, D. C. He died in Washington in 1862, leaving a number of his pictures and several thousand dollars to the Redwood Library of Newport, R. I. His portrait of John C. Calhoun is in the Corcoran Art Gallery, Washington, D. C.

KING, Charles B. Painter and etcher. Born in California in 1869. Pupil of Laurens in Paris, and of Brangwyn in London. Represented in New York Public Library, and Library of Congress, Washington, D. C. *Address,* 814 Jefferson Ave., Detroit, Mich.

KING, Emma B. Painter. Born in Indianapolis. Pupil of Cox; Beckwith; Chase, and of the Art Students' League of New York. *Address,* 2118 North Talbot St., Indianapolis, Ind.

KING, Francis Scott. Painter. Born in Auburn, Me., in 1850. Designer and engraver on copper. Designer of ''Libris'' of the printer's devil; designed the ''Sylvester'' bronze tablet for Johns Hopkins University; also seal for The Rockefeller Institute for Med. Research, New York; designed and engraved copper plates for ''The Boston Port Bills,'' published by Grolier Club, New York; designed and engraved on copper numerous important plates for the Society of Iconophiles, New York. Member: Society of American Wood Engravers. *Address,* 106 South 7th St., Newark, N. J.

KING, Frank S. Engraver. Well known as a wood engraver, and later turned to copper plate engraving. He executed a series of wood engravings after the work of Burne-Jones.

KING, G. B. This line-engraver produced some portraits and book illustrations of little merit for the New York publishers of 1830-34.

KING, Gertrude. Painter. Exhibited water colors at the Penna. Academy of the Fine Arts, Philadelphia, 1925. *Address,* 24 Winsor Place, Bloomfield, N. J.

KING, Hamilton. Painter and illustrator. Born in Lewiston, Me., in 1871. Pupil of Julien Academy in Paris. Member: Society of Illustrators. *Address,* 200 West 57th St., New York, N. Y.

KING, James. Painter, etcher and engraver. Born in New York in 1852. Pupil of Art Students' League, New York; also of École des Beaux Arts under Gerome. He died at Montclair, N. J., in 1925. He made a specialty of portraits and marine views.

KING, James S. Engraver. The ''Ladies Repository,'' published in Cincinnati in 1852, contains some good line subject-plates signed by James S. King as engraver.

KING, John. Portrait painter of the Civil War period. (See his portrait of Gen. Henry Lee, Gov. of Virginia.)

KING, John C. Sculptor. Born in Scotland in 1806; died in Boston in 1882. He modeled busts of many public men and made cameo likenesses. He resided in New Orleans, La., and later in Boston, Mass. Among his best known busts are: ''Daniel Webster,'' ''John Quincy Adams,'' ''Louis Agassiz'' and ''Emerson.''

KING, Paul. Landscape painter. Born in Buffalo, N. Y., in 1867. Pupil of Art Students' League, New York; also studied in France and Holland. Awards: First Altman prize at National Academy of Design. Elected an Associate Member in 1919. Represented in Philadelphia Art Club and Youngstown Butler Art Institute. *Address,* Stony Brook, L. I. New York.

KING, Marion. Sculptor. Exhibited at Penna. Academy of the Fine Arts, Philadelphia, 1924. *Address,* 11 Lantern Lane, Philadelphia.

KING, Saml. Portrait painter in oils and miniature. Born in 1749 in Newport, R. I. He painted a miniature of Rev. Ezra Stiles, President of Yale University in 1770, and a portrait in oil in 1771. In the winter of 1771-72 he was painting in Salem, Mass. In 1780 King made a copy of Peale's portrait of Washington, belonging to John Hancock, which was sent to France. King had as pupils, Stuart, Allston, Malabone and Charles B. King. He died in 1819.

KING, Virginia M. (Mrs.). Sculptor. Born in Norfolk, Va., 1879. Pupil of Salon Borglum and of Harriet Frishmuth. *Address,* Keokuk St., Chevy Chase, Washington, D. C.

KINGSBURG, Edward R. Painter. Born in Boston, Mass. Pupil of School of Boston Museum of Fine Arts; also studied. in Paris. Mural painting in Charlestown, Mass., High School. *Address*, 24 St. Botolph St., Boston, Mass.

KINGSLEY, Eldridge. Wood engraver and painter. Born in 1842; died in New York in 1918. Pupil of Cooper Institute of New York. Awarded gold medal at the Paris Exposition of 1889. Many examples of his work are in the Print Department of the New York Public Library. He was a member of the Society of American Wood Engravers.

KINNEY, B. H. Sculptor. His bust of Isaiah Thomas is owned in Worcester, Mass.

KINNEY, Margaret West (Mrs. Troy Kinney). Illustrator. Born in Peoria, Ill., in 1872. Pupil of Art Students' League of New York; Julien Academy in Paris under Robert-Fleury, Collin, Merson and Lefebvre. Member: American Society of Illustrators, 1912. *Address*, 154 East 38th St., New York, N. Y.

KINNEY, Troy. Artist and etcher. Born in Kansas City, Mo., in 1871. Studied art in the Yale School of Fine Arts and in the Chicago Art Institute. He has specialized in etchings of dancers. (See the Print Connoisseur, Vol. 1, 1921, for catalogue of his etchings and dry points.)

KINSELLA, James. Painter. Born in New York in 1857; died in 1923. Pupil of National Academy of Design; École des Beaux Arts in Paris. Member: National Art Club. Work: "Seven O'Clock from Manasquan," Museum of Newark, N. J., Technical School.

KINSEY, Alberta. Painter. Native of West Milton, Ohio, and studied art in the Cincinnati Art Academy and in the Chicago Art School. Instructor of art in Lebanon University, Lebanon, Ohio. Member: Women's Art Club, Cincinnati; Art Association, and Arts and Crafts Club, New Orleans. Architectural work, and landscapes in oil and water colors. Represented in Cincinnati Art Museum and in the Delgado Museum.

KINSEY, Helen Fairchild. Painter and illustrator. Pupil of Chase, Anshutz, Breckenridge and Grafly. Member of Fellowship of Penna. Academy of Fine Arts. *Address*, 1301 Spring Garden St., Philadelphia.

KINSEY, Nathaniel, Jr. Engraver. In 1854–55 this good landscape engraver was employed by the Western Methodist Book Concern, of Cincinnati, Ohio.

KINSMAN-WATERS, Ray. Painter. Born in Columbus, Ohio, in 1887. Pupil of Columbus Art School. Awarded prize for water colors, 1923. *Address*, 380 East Town St., Columbus, Ohio.

KIRALFY, Verona A. Portrait painter. Born in New York City in 1893. Pupil of Chase and of Art Students' League of New York. Member of Pittsburgh Art Association. *Address*, 3d and Wood Sts., Pittsburgh, Penna.

KIRK, John. Engraver. Born in England; died in the United States about 1862. Kirk came to the United States about 1841, and was largely employed by the publishers G. P. Putnam, and by A. B. Hall and other New York engravers. He did some admirable work in line.

KIRK, Marie Louise. Painter and illustrator. Born in Philadelphia. Student of Philadelphia School of Design and of the Penna. Academy of Fine Arts. Received the Mary Smith prize at the Penna. Academy of Fine Arts in 1894.

KIRKHAM, Mrs. Charlotte B. Miniature painter. Exhibited at the Penna. Academy of Fine Arts, 1925. *Address*, 62 Harrison Ave., Springfield, Mass.

KIRKPATRICK, Frank Le Brun. Painter. Exhibited water colors at the Penna. Academy of Fine Arts, Philadelphia. Died in 1917.

KIRKPATRICK, William A. B. Painter. Exhibited "Day's Work" at the Penna. Academy of Fine Arts, Philadelphia, 1924. *Address*, 206 Fenway Studio, Boston, Mass.

KIRSHNER, Raphael. Painter and illustrator. Born in Vienna in 1876; died in New York City in 1917. He painted a series of prominent American women.

KISSACK, R. A. Painter. Born in St. Louis, Mo., in 1876. Pupil of St. Louis School of Fine Arts; also studied in Paris. *Address*, 411 Algonquin Place, Webster Grove, Mo.

KITCHELL, Joseph Gray. Painter and writer. Born in Cincinnati, O., in 1862. Photographic editor of *Quarterly Illustrator*. In 1900 he produced the Kitchell "Composite Madonna," a merging of the most important madonnas painted by the great masters during 300 years, which attracted wide attention in America and Europe. In 1915 he invented and patented a new method of reproducing pictures known as "Sub-Chromatic Art," examples of which were accepted by the Metropolitan Museum; National Academy of Design; Congressional Library; British Museum; Bibliotheque Nationale, Paris, etc. *Address*, Mountain Lakes, N. J.

KITSON, Henry Hudson. Sculptor. Born in Hudersfield, England, in 1865. Pupil of Bonnaissieux; École des Beaux Arts, Paris. Executed monument to Mayor Doyle, Providence, R. I.; Hayes Memorial Fountain, Providence; "The Minute Man," at Lexington, Mass.; statues of Gen. N. P. Banks and Patrick A. Collins, Boston. *Address*, St. Botolph Studios, 4 Harcourt St., Boston, Mass.

KITSON, Samuel James. Sculptor. Born in England in 1848, he came to America in 1878, having studied in Italy. He produced such work as the "Sheridan Monument" and the portrait of Gov. Greenhalge in the State House at Boston. He died in New York in 1906.

KITSON, Theo. Alice Ruggles (Mrs. H. H.). Sculptor. Born in Brookline, Mass., in 1871. Pupil of H. H. Kitson and Dagnan-Bouveret, Paris. Exhibited at Paris Exposition in 1889; Soc. of American Artists; National Academy of Design, New York; Penna. Academy of Fine Arts, Philadelphia; Boston Art Club; Museum of Fine Arts, Boston; Art Institute of Chicago; medal, St. Louis Exposition, 1904. Member of National Sculpture Society. *Address*, Framingham, Mass.

KLAGES, Frank H. Painter and illustrator. Born in Philadelphia in 1892. Pupil of Penna. Academy of Fine Arts. *Address*, 2027 North 31st St., Philadelphia.

KLAGSTAD, August. Painter. Born in Norway in 1866. Pupil of Art Institute, Chicago. *Address*, 305 West Broadway, Minn.

KLAR, Walter H. Painter. Pupil of National Academy of Design. Member of Pittsburgh Artists' Association. *Address*, University of Pittsburgh.

KLAUDER, Alice. Portrait painter. Born in San Diego, Calif., in 1871. Pupil of Chase and Henri. *Address*, Care of San Diego Museum, San Diego, Calif.

KLAUDER, Mary. Sculptor. Exhibited "A Study" at the Penna. Academy of the Fine Arts, Philadelphia, 1914. *Address*, Bala, Penna.

KLEIN, Isidore. Painter and etcher. Born in Russia in 1897. Pupil of National Academy of Design. *Address*, 123 East 22d St., New York.

KLEIN, Nathan. Painter. Exhibited in 1925, at Annual Exhibition of National Academy of Design, New York. *Address*, 1841 61st St., Brooklyn, N. Y.

KLEMINGER, A. F. Painter. Born in Chicago in 1865. Pupil of Henri Martin. Member of Chicago Society of Artists. *Address*, 4164 Lake Park Ave., Chicago, Ill.

KLEPPER, Frank. Painter and etcher. Born in Texas in 1890. Pupil of Art Institute of Chicago. Studied in Paris, under Harry Lachman. *Address*, 405 West Davis St., McKinney, Texas.

KLEPPER, Max Francis. Painter. Born in Germany in 1861. Came to America in 1876 and settled in Toledo, Ohio. Established himself in New York, working on magazine illustration. He also specialized in animal pictures. He died in Brooklyn, N. Y., in 1907.

KLIME, George T. Painter and illustrator. Born in Baltimore, Md., in 1874. Pupil of S. E. Whitman. *Address*, 407 Matthews St., Columbia, Mo.

KLINE, Hibbard Van Buren. Painter and illustrator. Born in 1895. Pupil of Art Students' League, under Chase and Mora. *Address*, Leonia, N. J.

KLINE, William Fair. Figure and mural painter. Born in Columbia, S. C., in 1870. the Swan." *Address*, 244 West 14th St., New York, and of Julien Academy, Paris. Elected an Associate Member of the National Academy. Important pictures, "Her Tribute," "The Flight into Egypt," and "Leda and the Swan." *Address*, 244 West 14th St., New York City.

KLOPPER, Zanwill D. Painter and illustrator. Born in Russia in 1870. Pupil of Julien Academy in Paris. Specialty, anatomical drawings. Represented by "Immaculate Conception," and mural decorations in "St. Mary's of the Woods." *Address*, 1642 West Division St., Chicago, Ill.

KLOTZ, Isidore E. Painter. Exhibited "The Rose Bower" at the Penna. Academy of Fine Arts, Philadelphia, 1925. *Address*, East Gloucester, Mass.

KLUMPKE, Anna Elizabeth. Painter. Born in San Francisco, Calif., in 1856. Pupil of Fleury and Bouguereau. Represented by "In the Wash-House," signed A. E. Klumpke, Paris, 1888, Paris Salon, 1888, Temple medal. (Presented by the Artist to Penna. Academy of Fine Arts, 1890.) *Address*, 12 Rue Rosa Bonheur, Thomery Seine-et-Marne, France.

KLUTH, Robert. A marine and landscape painter. Born in Germany in 1854. He came to America at the age of seven years. He studied art in America, Germany and Norway. He was one of the founders of the Brooklyn Society of Artists. Many of his paintings of Norwegian fjords were purchased by Andrew Carnegie, for public libraries. He died in Brooklyn, New York, in September, 1921.

KNAPP, C. W. Painter. Born in Philadelphia in 1823; he died there in 1900.

KNAUBER, Alma H. Painter. Born in Cincinnati, Ohio, in 1893. Pupil of Duveneck. Member of Cincinnati Artists' League. *Address*, Ohio State University, Cincinnati, Ohio.

KNEASS, William. Engraver. Born in Lancaster, Pa., in 1781; died in Philadelphia in 1840. It is not known with whom Kneass learned to engrave, but he worked continuously in Philadelphia as an engraver from 1805 to the time of his death. On Jan. 29, 1824, he was appointed engraver and diesinker at the U. S. Mint, succeeding Robert Scot. His work is usually in line, though he produced some good aquatint views. He was a member of the firm of Kneass & Dellaker, general engravers.

KNEELAND. Sculptor. His spirited basrelief of a "Trotting Horse" is owned in Washington, D. C.

KNIFFIN, Herbert R. Painter and art director. Studied at National Academy of Design, New York. *Address*, 5 West 65th St., New York.

KNIGHT, Charles. Miniature painter, flourishing in Philadelphia 1811–1816. He exhibited at Exhibition of Society of Artists, Philadelphia, 1811.

KNIGHT, Charles Robert. Painter and sculptor. Born in Brooklyn in 1874. Studied art in Metropolitan Museum and Art Students' League of New York. Specialty, animals and birds. Illustrator for magazines, and painted and made models of fossil creatures for U. S. Govt., Carnegie Museum and American Museum of Natural History; executed series of large mural paintings (prehistoric men and animals) for American Museum of Natural History, etc., N. Y. *Address*, 27 West 67th St., New York, N. Y.

KNIGHT, Clayton. Painter and illustrator. Born in Rochester, N. Y., in 1891. Pupil of Von der Lancken, Henri and Bellows. Member: Guild of Free Lance Association. Illustrates for magazines. *Address*, 36 East 29th St., New York, N. Y.

KNIGHT, D. Ridgway. Painter. Born in Philadelphia in 1839; died in France in 1924. Pupil of Penna. Academy of Fine Arts, and of Meissonier in Paris. Officer of the Legion of Honor of France. He is represented in the Penna. Academy of Fine Arts by "Hailing the Ferry," and in Brooklyn Institute Museum by "The Shepherdess."

KNIGHT, E. H. Engraver. Born in Brooklyn, N. Y., in 1853. He died there in 1896. In 1867 E. H. Knight studied engraving with H. B. Hall; he was then in the employ of H. B. Hall & Sons, and was later a partner in this firm. As an engraver, his individuality was lost in the signed work of the firm, but his name appears on a fine portrait of Charles Dickens.

KNIGHT, L. Aston. Landscape painter. Born in Paris, France. Studied art under his father and with Jules Lefebvre and Robert Fleury, Paris. Represented in Luxembourg, Museum, Paris; art galleries of Toledo, Ohio; Rochester, N. Y.; Newark, N. J., etc. *Address*, 147 Rue de la Pompe, Paris, France.

KNIGHT, T. Engraver. In 1856, and possibly earlier, Knight was a partner of George Girdler Smith, of Boston, along with W. H. Tappan, the firm name being Smith, Knight & Tappan. His name is signed to some very good portraits executed in both line and stipple.

KNOPF, Nellie Augusta. Painter. Born in Chicago in 1875. Pupil of Art Institute of Chicago under Vanderpoel and Freer; also of Charles H. Woodbury; John F. Carlson. Member: Jacksonville Art Association; Art Institute of Chicago Alumni; College Art Association. Director of School of Fine Arts, Illinois Woman's College. Represented in John H. Vanderpoel memorial collection. *Address*, Illinois Woman's College, Jacksonville, Ill.

KNOWLES, Elizabeth McG. Painter. Exhibited at 33d Annual Exhibition of National Association of Women Painters and Sculptors. *Address*, 19 East 49th St., New York City.

KNOWLES, F. McGillvray. Painter and illustrator. Born in Syracuse, N. Y., in 1860. Studied in England, France, Canada and the United States. Awards: Honorable mention, Pan-American Exposition, Buffalo, 1901; medal, Louisiana Purchase Exposition, St. Louis, 1904; medal, Panama-Pacific Exposition, San Francisco, 1915. Represented in National Galleries of Ottawa and Toronto. *Address*, 340 West 57th St., New York.

KNOWLTON, Helen Mary. Born in Littleton, Mass., in 1832. Pupil of William M. Hunt, she opened a studio in Boston in 1867. She has exhibited many charcoal sketches as well as landscapes and portraits in oil. Some of her most effective work is in charcoal. She has also published "Talks on Art," of William M. Hunt. The Boston Museum of Fine Arts own her "Haystacks." She died in 1918.

KNOX, James. Painter. Born in Glasgow, Scotland, in 1866. Pupil of Joseph H. Boston. Work: "First Attack of the Tanks," U. S. National Museum, Washington, D. C. *Address*, 54 Seventh Ave., Brooklyn, New York, N. Y.

KNOX, Susan Ricker. Painter. Born in Portsmouth, N. H. Studied in Philadelphia, New York and in Europe. Member: National Art Club; Pen and Brush; National Academy of Women Painters and Sculptors. Specialty, portraits. *Address*, 119 East 19th St., New York.

KOEHLER, P. R. Landscape painter. Exhibited "Early Evening" in New York.

KOEHLER, Robert. Painter. Born in Hamburg, Germany, in 1850; died in 1917. He was brought to the United States in 1854. Studied at Milwaukee, Wis., and there learned lithography which he practiced in Pittsburgh, Pa., and in New York; studied drawing in night classes at National Academy of Design; studied painting in Munich. Began to exhibit at National Academy in 1877; organized the American department of the art exhibition, Munich, 1883 and 1888; director of Minneapolis School of Fine Arts since 1893. Principal paintings: "Holiday Occupation"; "Her Only Support"; "The Socialist"; "The Strike"; "Violet"; "Judgment of Paris"; "Love's Secret"; "The Family Bible"; "Father and Son"; "Salve Luna." Member: Society of Western Artists; Minneapolis Society of Fine Arts; Minneapolis Art League; City Art Commission, Minn.; State Art Society.

KOEHLER, Sylvester R. Painter. Born in Germany in 1837; died at Littleton, N. H., on Sept. 10th, 1900.

KOEVOETS, H. & C. This firm was engraving and publishing portraits in New York about 1870.

KOHN, Irma. Landscape painter. Born in Rock Island, Ill. Represented in Toledo Museum and Penna. Academy of Fine Arts, Philadelphia.

KOLLOCK, Mary. Painter. Born in Norfolk, Va., in 1840. She studied at the Academy of Fine Arts, Philadelphia. Later she spent a year in Paris at the Julien School. She was a member of the Art Students' League, and exhibited at the National Academy of Design, N. Y. Among her works: "A November Day"; "Glimpse of the Catskills"; "Midsummer in the Mountains," which was exhibited in 1876 at the "Centennial," Philadelphia, Pa.

KONTI, Isidore. Sculptor. Born in Vienna, Austria, in 1862. After a stay in Rome he returned to Vienna and came to the U. S. in 1890. He worked for the Chicago Exposition and has since executed much decorative monumental and ideal work, including group, "West Indies," for the colonnade of the Dewey Arch, and "The East and North River," for the same arch; groups for Temple of Music; group of playing children for Court of Fountains; large group symbolizing "The Despotic Age," at the Esplanade, Pan-American Exposition, Buffalo; groups, "Pan and Cupid," "Awakening of Spring," "Inspiration" and "Orpheus," exhibited in various exhibitions; the marble fountain, "Brook," at Greystone, Yonkers, N. Y.; also group, "Progress," for Mfrs. Bldg., and two grand cascade fountains, the Atlantic and Pacific Oceans (consisting of over 20 different groups), at St. Louis Exposition. Elected Associate Member of the National Academy, 1906; National Academy in 1909. Member: Council National Sculpture Society; Architectural League of New York. *Address*, 314 Riverdale Ave., Yonkers, N. Y.

KOOPMAN, Augustus. Painter and etcher. Born in Charleston, S. C., in 1869. Studied at the Penna. Academy of Fine Arts and later in Paris. Represented in Philadelphia Art Club by "The Old Troubadour"; his dry-points and etchings are in the Congressional and New York Public Libraries. He died in 1914.

KOOPMAN, John R. Painter. Exhibited water colors at the Penna. Academy of Fine Arts, Philadelphia, 1925. *Address*, 257 West 86th St., New York City.

KOPMAN, Benjamin D. Painter. Born in New York. Member of the Allied Artists of America, New York. Represented in Brooklyn Institute of Arts and Sciences; Penna. Academy of Fine Arts, Philadelphia. "Portrait of a Young Man" at Penna. Academy of Fine Arts. *Address*, 8 East 15th St., New York.

KOPMAN, Katharine. Native of New Orleans. Studied under Molinary, Newcomb School of Art, and with Dodge Macknight. Instructor of drawing and design, Newcomb High School; Newcomb School of Art; supervisor of art, Alexandria Grammar Schools, Alexandria, La. Specialty, landscapes.

KORBEL, Mario J. Sculptor. Born in Russia in 1882. Studied in Munich and Paris. Represented by Dancing Group, at Cleveland Museum; "Andante," Metropolitan Museum, N. Y.; "Minerva," University of Havana; the McPhee Memorial Monument, Denver, Colo. *Address*, Care of Gorham, 36th St. and 5th Ave., New York.

KORNHAUSER, David E. Painter. Studied at Penna. Academy of Fine Arts. Represented at Penna. Academy of Fine Arts by "Along the Schuylkill River."

KOSCIUSKO, Tadeusz A. B. A Polish soldier who fought in the American Revolution, was born in 1746 and died in 1817. He drew a portrait of General Gates and several of the other Revolutionary soldiers.

KOSH, A. E. Born in Germany in 1838; died in this country in 1897. Kosh was an engraver of landscape and subject-plates for the magazines, and came to the United States in 1868.

KOST, Frederick W. Landscape painter. Born in New York in 1861. Student of National Academy of Design, N. Y., and studied later in Paris and Munich. Elected National Academician in 1906. Received honorable mention at Paris Exhibition, 1900. Represented at Penna. Academy of Fine Arts, Philadelphia, and in the Brooklyn Institute. He died at Brookhaven, L. I., in 1923.

KRAFFT, Carl R. Painter. Born in Reading, Ohio, in 1884. Member: Artists' Guild; Chicago Society of Artists: The Cliff Dwellers, Chicago; Society of Ozark Painters. Representation: City of Chicago Collection and Municipal Art League, Chicago; Peoria Society of Allied Arts, Peoria, Ill. *Address*, 220 South Michigan Ave., Chicago.

KRAMER, Scheire B. Portrait painter. His portrait of William L. Strong, Mayor of New York, is in the City Hall. It is signed and dated 1898.

KRAUS, Robert. Sculptor. Deceased. He was the sculptor for the Crispus Attucks monument.

KREHBIEL, Albert H. Painter. Born in Chicago, Ill. Pupil of Art Institute of Chicago and of Frederick Richardson; Laurens in Paris. Member: Chicago Society of Artists; Chicago Water Color Club; Cliff Dwellers. Instructor, Art Institute of Chicago. Work: Mural decorations for Supreme Court, Springfield, Ill. *Address*, Park Ridge, Chicago, Ill.

KRETZINGER, Clara Josephine. Painter. Born in Chicago. Pupil of Art Institute of Chicago; Chicago Academy of Fine Arts; studied under Lefebvre, Robert-Fleury, Laurens, Congdon and Richard Miller in Paris. Member: Chicago Society of Artists; Chicago Art Club. Award: Honorable mention, Paris Salon. Represented in Beloit Art Museum. *Address*, Lyme, Conn.

KRIEGHOFF, W. G. Painter. Born in Philadelphia in 1875. Pupil of Chase. Member: Philadelphia Art Alliance; Philadelphia Sketch Club. *Address*, Care of The Art Alliance, 1823 Walnut St., Philadelphia, Pa.

KRIMMEL, John Lewis. Portrait and genre painter. Born in 1787 in Wurtemberg, Germany. He came to this country in 1810 to join his brother who was a merchant of Philadelphia. Disliking trade, he continued the course he had begun in Germany, and painted small portraits. In 1812, he exhibited at the Pennsylvania Academy of Fine Arts a picture of Centre Square, Philadelphia, containing numerous small figures, and painted many other works of like character, two of which are owned by the Pennsylvania Academy. He was President of the Society of American Artists. He was drowned in Wissahickon Creek, Philadelphia, in 1821.

KROLL, Leon. Painter. Born in New York City in 1884. Studied at Art Students' League and in the National Academy of Design, New York, and under Jean Paul Laurens, Paris, France. Portrait, landscape, genre and still-life artist; represented in permanent collections of Penna. Academy of Fine Arts; Detroit Museum; Los Angeles Museum; Art Institute of Chicago; National Academy of Design; and in many private collections. Awarded Logan medal, Art Institute of Chicago, 1919; medals, San Francisco and Panama-Pacific expositions; Porter prize, Salmagundi Club, 1912. Member: Society of American Painters, Sculptors and Engravers; New York Society of Etchers; Society of Independent Artists. Elected Associate Member of National Academy of Design. *Address*, Art Institute, Chicago.

KRONBERG, Louis. Painter. Born in Boston in 1872. Studied art at Museum of Fine Arts, Boston; Art Students' League, New York; Academie Julien, Paris. Instructor, portrait class, Copley Society, Boston; silver medal, Mass. Charitable Mechanics' Association; and Longfellow traveling scholarship. Exhibited at Paris Exposition, 1900. Represented permanently at Penna. Academy of Fine Arts, Philadelphia, by the painting entitled "Behind the Footlights"; also in Mrs. J. L. Gardner's and F. Gair Macomber's collections; also represented in permanent collections of the Metropolitan Museum of Art, New York; Museum of Fine Arts, Boston; John Herron Art Institute, Indianapolis. Member: Boston Art Club; Copley Society; London Pastel Society; silver medal, Panama Exposition, 1915. *Address*, Boston Art Club, Boston.

KRUELL, Gustav. Wood engraver. Born in Germany in 1843. He organized the American Wood Engravers' Society, of which he was president. He received many honorable mentions and medals for his work. His engraved portraits include those of Darwin, Wm. Lloyd Garrison and Lincoln. He published "A Portfolio of National Portraits." He died in California in 1907. (See "History of Wood Engraving," by W. J. Linton.)

KUHN, Harry P. Painter. Born in Zurich, Switzerland, in 1862. Award: Gold medal, Louisiana Purchase Exposition, St. Louis, 1904. *Address*, Colt Bldg., Paterson, N. J.

KUHN, Robert J. Sculptor. Exhibited at National Academy of Design, 1925. *Address,* Richmond Hill, N. Y.

KUHN, Walt. Painter. Exhibited in Philadelphia, 1921, at "Exhibition of Paintings Showing the Later Tendencies in Art," Penna. Academy of Fine Arts. *Address,* 11 East 13th St., New York City.

KUNIYOSHI, Yasuo. Painter. Born in Okayama, Japan. Pupil of Kenneth Hayes Miller.

KUNTZE, Edward J. Born in Prussia in 1826. He came to New York in 1852, and in 1869 was elected an Associate of the National Academy. Among his works are statuettes of Irving, Lincoln, and a statue of "Psyche" and one of "Puck." He also exhibited three etchings at the National Academy in 1868.

KUPFER, R. Engraver. Line-engravings of some merit, published in New York magazines about 1865, after drawings by Thos. Nast and other American designers, are so signed. Among other prints engraved by Kupfer is a folio plate of a view of New York, published in 1867.

KURTZ, Wilbur G. Painter and illustrator. Born in Oakland, Ill. Pupil of Art Institute of Chicago. Member: Atlanta Artists'

Association. Represented in Atlanta Woman's Club. *Address,* 141 East North Ave., Atlanta, Ga.

KURTZ, William. Painter. Born in 1833; died in Far Rockaway, N. Y., in 1904.

KURTZWORTH, Harry M. Painter. Born in Detroit, Mich., in 1887. Pupil of Detroit Academy of Fine Arts. *Address,* Kansas City Art Institute, Kansas City, Mo.

KURZ, Louis. Mural painter and one of the founders of the Chicago Art Institute. He was born in Austria in 1834, and came to America in 1848. He fought for the North in the Civil War, and he was a personal friend of Lincoln. His sketches of the Civil War were the first to be issued after the close of the conflict. He died in Chicago, Ill., March 21, 1921.

KUTCHIN, Lou. Painter. Exhibited water colors at the Penna. Academy of Fine Arts, Philadelphia, 1925. *Address,* 2038 Spruce St., Philadelphia.

KYLE, Joseph. Painter. Born in 1815. His work was portraiture, genre subjects and still-life. In 1849 he was elected an Associate Member of the National Academy of Design. He died in 1863. His painting, "A Family Group," is owned by the Academy of Fine Arts, Elgin, Illinois.

L

LABATUT. Miniature painter, flourishing the latter part of the eighteenth century. He was a Frenchman, and Washington employed him to paint a large miniature as a gift for Genl. Chas. C. Pinckney, 1782.

LACHAISE, Gaston. Painter. Exhibited in Philadelphia in 1921 at Penna. Academy of Fine Arts in the "Exhibition Showing the Later Tendencies in Art." *Address,* 77 Washington Place, New York City.

LACHENMEYER, Paul N. Sculptor. Member of the National Sculpture Society.

LACHMAN, Harry B. Painter. Born at La Salle, Ill., in 1886. Studied in France. Member of the Legion of Honor. Represented

in Chicago Art Institute by "Old Church." Studio in France.

LADD, Anna Coleman (Mrs. Maynard Ladd). Sculptor and author. Born in Philadelphia in 1878. Studied in Paris and Rome; was for twenty years under Profs. Ferrari and Gallori; also studied with Charles Grafly, in America. Exhibited in Paris Salon; National Sculpture Society; National Academy of Design; Art Institute of Chicago; Art Museum, Boston; etc. First special exhibition 40 bronzes, Gorham's, New York, 1913; 2d, Corcoran Art Gallery, Washington; 3d, Penna. Academy of Fine Arts; bronzes in Fenway Court, Palazzo Borghese and other collections. Honorable mention, Panama, P. I. Exposition. *Address,* 270 Clarendon St., Boston, Mass.

LADD, Laura D. S. Painter. Exhibited at 33d Annual Exhibition of National Association of Women Painters and Sculptors. *Address*, 508 South 41st Street, Philadelphia, Pa.

LAESSLE, Albert. Sculptor. Born in Philadelphia, Pa., in 1877. Graduate of Penna. Academy of Fine Arts, 1901; studied with Charles Grafly, Philadelphia, and with Michel Bequine, Paris, 1904–7. Awarded Stewardson prize, 1902; Cresson traveling scholarship, 1904–7. Won George D. Widener memorial gold medal, Penna. Academy of Fine Arts, 1918. Represented in permanent collections of Penna. Academy of Fine Arts; Philadelphia Art Club; Metropolitan Museum, New York; Carnegie Institute, Pittsburgh; Peabody Institute, Baltimore. The bronze, "Billy," was purchased by Fairmount Park Art Common, Philadelphia, in 1917. Member: National Sculpture Society; Fellowship of Penna. Academy of Fine Arts. *Address*, 1662 Summer St., Philadelphia, Penna.

LA FARGE, Bancel. Painter of figures and landscapes; also of mural decorations, and a designer of stained glass windows and mosaics. Member: National Institute of Arts and Letters; New York Water Color Club; Society of Mural Painters. *Address*, "Edgehill," Mt. Carmel, Conn.

LA FARGE, Jean. Miniature painter. Father of the late artist John La Farge. He was a French refugee from Santo Domingo, and came to New York and painted miniatures in the early part of the nineteenth century.

LA FARGE, John. Landscape and figure painter, decorator, glass painter and sculptor. Born in 1835 in New York; died 1910 in Providence, R. I. Pupil of William M. Hunt in Boston, and Couture in Paris. Elected member of National Academy, 1869. Represented in Metropolitan Museum, New York, and Boston Museum of Fine Arts. (See "American Painting and its Tradition," by John C. Van Dyke.)

LA FAVOR, Will. Sculptor. Exhibited "Herr Meisner," at the Penna. Academy of the Fine Arts, Philadelphia, 1914. *Address*, Washington Park Field House, Pittsburgh, Penna.

LA FONTAINE, Rachel Adelaide. Painter and author. Born in Zonnemaine, Holland, 1845. Took course at Art Students' League, New York; afterward studied under Charles Melville Dewey, J. H. Beard, Sr., and Harry Chase, New York. Traveled in England, France and Holland, 1878. Specialty, sundowns and marines. First exhibited in National Academy of Design, 1885. He has illustrated several de luxe editions. *Address*, Care Thomas Whittaker, Inc., New York.

LAHEY, Richard F. Painter. Exhibited water colors at the Penna. Academy of Fine Arts, Philadelphia, 1925. *Address*, 2695 Boulevard, Jersey City, N. J.

LAKEMAN, N. Painter. He painted quite a number of portraits, many of them in Salem, Mass., about 1820.

LAKEY, Emily Jane. Painter. Born at Quincy, N. J., in 1837. She studied art in Ohio and Tennessee, and has exhibited at Chicago, and in the National Academy. In 1877 she studied in Paris under Emile Van Marcke. Her best known paintings are the "Leader of the Herd" and "An Anxious Mother."

LALANNE, Mary E. Miniature painter, flourishing in Boston, 1833. Exhibited several miniatures at the Boston Athenaeum in 1833.

LAMAR, Julian. Portrait painter. Exhibited at the Annual Exhibition of Penna. Academy of Fine Arts, 1924. *Address*, National Arts Club, New York City.

LAMB, Anthony. Engraver. The *New York Mercury*, of Dec. 1, 1760, contains the following advertisement: "Maps, Plans, Coats of Arms, Shop Bills, Monthly Returns and other Engraving neatly done on Silver, Copper, etc., with Care and Dispatch, and all sort of Copper Plate Printing done in the best manner and at Reasonable Rates, at Anthony Lamb's, at Sir Isaac Newton's Head, New York"

LAMB, Charles R. Painter. Executed mural and decorative work; was also designer of stained glass and religious art work. Born in New York. He was a pupil of the Art Students' League. *Address*, 23 Sixth Ave., New York.

LAMB, Ella Condie. Painter. Born in New York. Studied in New York under William M. Chase, Walter Shirlaw and C. Y. Turner; in England under Hubert Herkomar, R. A.; in Paris under R. Collin. Specialty, portrait and decorative painting and miniatures; important examples of mural work: "The Open Book," Governor Flower Memorial Library, Watertown, N. Y.; "Governor Baldwin memorial," St. John's Church, Detroit; the "Sage" memorial figures of Science and Arts, Cornell University; "Russell Memorial," Wellesley College; "Hobart Memorial," Briarly School, New York. Member: National Arts Club; Art Students' League, N. Y.; National Society of Mural Painters. *Address*, 360 W. 22d St., New York.

LAMB, Frederick Stymetz. Painter. Born in New York in 1863. Brother of Charles Rollinson Lamb. Student of Art Sutdents' League, New York; pupil of Lefebvre, Boulanger and M. Millet in Paris. Honorable mention, Chicago Exposition, 1893; gold medal, Atlanta Exposition, 1895; received gold medal from French Govt. Member: National Society of Mural Painters; National Art Club; Art Students' League. *Address*, 23 6th Ave., New York.

LAMB, F. Mortimer. Landscape painter. Born in Middleboro, Mass., in 1861. Pupil of Massachusetts Normal Art School; School of Boston Museum of Fine Arts; Julien Academy in Paris. Work: Memorial corridor, City Hall, Brockton, Mass.; "The Good Samaritan," Universalist Church, Stoughton, Mass.; "Spring," Chicataubut Club, Stoughton, Mass.; two landscapes in Christian Science Students' Library, Brookline, Mass. *Address*, Stoughton, Mass.

LAMB, John. A New York silversmith. In the "Mercury" of 1756, he advertises "Engraving in gold, silver, copper and other materials, by John Lamb."

LAMBDIN, George C. Painter. Son of James R. Lambdin. He was born in Philadelphia in 1830. He painted portraits, but was better known for his flower painting, his flower pieces and roses being much sought after at the time. He was elected a National Academician of the National Academy of Design in 1868. He died in Germantown, Philadelphia, in 1896.

LAMBDIN, James R. Painter. Born in Pittsburgh, 1807. He came to Philadelphia in 1823 to study painting, working under E. Miles for six months, and afterwards under Sully for a year. Returned to Pittsburgh, where, about 1828, he established a Museum and Gallery of the Fine Arts, the first public exhibition of works of art in the West. About four years later he removed with his collection to Louisville. He lived in Philadelphia after 1838, in which year he was made Corresponding Secretary of the Artists' Fund Society. He was Vice-President of the same Society, 1840–43; Corresponding Secretary again in 1844; President in 1845–67. He painted many portraits in Washington, including several of the Presidents, one of Webster and one of Chief Justice Marshall. He was an active officer of the Pennsylvania Academy of the Fine Arts. He died in Philadelphia, 1889.

LAMBERT, Gertrude A. Painter. Born in South Bethlehem, Pa., in 1885. Pupil of Philadelphia School of Design for Women, and of the Penna. Academy of Fine Arts. Work: "The Little Market, Baveno," Pennsylvania Academy of the Fine Arts. Instructor in water color, Philadelphia School of Design for Women, 1910-11. *Address*, 12 East 15th St., South Bethlehem, Pa.

LAMONT, Daniel G. Historical painter and portrait painter in oils and miniatures, flourishing in New York, 1846–47.

LANDEAU, Sandor L. Painter. Born in Hungary in 1864. Pupil of Laurens and Constant in Paris. *Address*, Care of Paul Foinet, 21 Rue Brea, Paris, France.

LANDER, Louisa. Sculptor. Born in Salem, Mass., in 1826. Began her art career by modelling likenesses of members of her family; went to Rome, 1855, and studied under Thomas Crawford. Among her first notable works were figures of marble, "Today" and "Galatea." Among her later works are: a bust of Gov. Gore, of Mass.; bust of Hawthorne; statues of "Virginia Dare"; "Undine"; "Virginia"; "Evangeline"; "Elizabeth"; "The Exile of Siberia"; "Ceres Mourning for Proserpine"; "A Sylph Alighting"; "The Captive Pioneer"; also many portrait busts. *Address*, 1608 19th St., Washington, D. C.

LANE, Susan Minot. Painter. Born in Cambridge, Mass., in 1832. She was a pupil of William Morris Hunt. She is represented by a painting in the Boston Museum of Fine Arts. She died in 1893, in Cambridge, Mass.

LANE, Thomas H. Painter. He was born in 1814, and died in 1900, at Elizabeth, N. J.

LANG, Charles M. Painter and sculptor. Born in Albany, N. Y., in 1860. Pupil of John Benzer and of Prof. Lofftz. Work: "Gov. David B. Hill," "Gov. Roswell P. Flower," City of Albany; "Hugo Flagg Cook," Capitol, Albany, N. Y.; Judges Parker and Henton, Court House, Albany, N. Y. *Address*, Miller Bldg., Studio, 1931 Broadway, New York, N. Y.

LANG, George S. Engraver. Born in Chester County, Pa., in 1799; living in Delaware County, Pa., in 1833. Mr. Baker says that Lang was a pupil of George Murray, the Philadelphia engraver, in 1815, and that he abandoned engraving early in life. The Philadelphia directories, however, contain his name as "engraver" until 1833, and as his signed work is scarce, he was probably employed in bank-note work. He was a good line-engraver.

LANG, Louis. Painter. Born in Germany in 1812. He came to America in 1838, and settled in Philadelphia. He was elected a National Academician in 1852, and was a member of the Artists' Fund Society. His work was portraits and historical scenes. Work: "Maid of Saragossa," "Blind Nydia" and "Romeo and Juliet" in the Century Club, New York. He died in 1893.

LANGERFELDT, Theodore O. Painter. Born in Germany in 1841. He came to Boston, Mass., in 1868. He paints chiefly in water colors, and one of his architectural paintings was awarded a prize at the Centennial Exhibition in Philadelphia in 1876.

LANGLEY, Sarah. Painter. Exhibited at the "Exhibition of Paintings Showing the Later Tendencies in Art," Penna. Academy of Fine Arts, Philadelphia, 1921. *Address*, 218 Narberth Ave., Narberth, Penna.

LANGTON, Berenice Frances (Mrs. Daniel W. Langton). Sculptor. Pupil of Augustus Saint Gaudens in New York; Rodin in Paris. Member: National Academy of Women Painters and Sculptors. Award: Bronze medal, St. Louis Exposition, 1904. *Address*, 165 West 82d St., New York, N. Y.

LANKES, Julius. Painter and etcher. Born in Buffalo, N. Y., in 1884. Pupil of Hale, Fosbery and Paxton. *Address*, Orchard Ave., Gardenville, N. Y.

LANMAN, Charles. Painter. Born in 1819. He was elected an Associate Member of the National Academy in 1847. His largest picture, "View of Filziyama," was purchased by the Japanese government. He died in 1895.

LANSIL, Walter F. Born in Bangor, Maine, in 1846. He early became familiar with ships and the sea. He studied abroad and on his return to this country set up his studio in Boston, where he has become well known in his style of painting. Among his works: "Crossing the Georges" and "View of Charlestown, with Shipping."

LARNED, Marguerite Y. Painter. Exhibited at 33d Annual Exhibition of National Association of Women Painters and Sculptors. *Address*, 6 East 12th St., New York City.

LARSEN, Charles P. Painter and etcher. Born in Philadelphia in 1892. Pupil of Penna. Academy of Fine Arts. Member of Chicago Art Institute, and represented in their permanent collection. *Address*, 17 East 14th St., New York.

LARSH, Theodora. Miniature painter. Born in Crawfordville, Ind. Pupil of Art Students' League of New York. Member of Chicago Society of Miniature Painters. *Address*, Netherlands Hotel, 5th Ave., New York City.

LATHROP, Elinor L. Painter and sculptor. Born in Hartford, Conn., 1899. Pupil of Hale, Logan and Jones. *Address*, 96 Niles St., Hartford, Conn.

LATHROP, Francis. Painter. Born in 1849. He was educated in New York City and in Germany. He exhibited at the Society of American Artists in 1878, portraits of Ross R. and Thomas Winans. He has devoted himself chiefly to mural painting, and designing of stained glass. He has executed wall paintings at Bowdoin College Chapel; Metropolitan Opera House, New York; and decorations for Trinity Church, Boston. Elected an Associate Member of the National Academy in 1906, three years before his death. He was also a member of the Society of American Artists. He died in New York, 1909.

LATHROP, Gertrude K. Sculptor. Born in Albany, N. Y., in 1896. She studied under Solon H. Borglum. Exhibited at National Academy of Design, 1925. *Address*, Albany, N. Y.

LATHROP, Ida P. (Mrs.). Painter. Born in Troy, N. Y., in 1859. Paints portraits, landscapes and still-life. *Address*, 151 South Allen St., Albany, N. Y.

LATHROP, William Langson. Landscape painter. Born in Warren, Ill., in 1859. Self-taught in art. Winner of W. T. Evans prize; Webb prize; gold medal, Philadelphia Art Club; 3d prize, Worcester, Mass.; 3d prize, Carnegie Institute, Pittsburgh. Represented in permanent collections at Carnegie Institute; Albright Gallery, Buffalo; Minneapolis Art Museum; Metropolitan Museum of Art, New York; National Gallery, Washington. Member of New York Water Color Club. *Address*, New Hope, Bucks County, Pa.

LATILLA, Eugenio. Painter. He lived in Italy for years, but later moved his studio to New York. His portraits were excellent; he painted many of the most eminent American clergymen. Latilla taught for some years in the School of Design in New York.

LAUBER, Joseph. Painter and sculptor. Born in Westphalia, Germany, in 1855, and came to the United States at the age of 9. He studied sculpture with Karl Muller; drawing and painting at Art Students' League, New York, under Shirlaw and Chase. He was assistant to John La Farge, then traveled abroad for observation and study. He began his career as sculptor about 1878; assisted John La Farge in sculptural decorations of Cornelius Vanderbilt's house, 1882; painted a number of pictures abroad, but became more identified with mural arts. He has a number of paintings in the Church of the Ascension, New York. Produced numerous etchings, 1887–94. Head of department of mural decorations and design, Md. Institute of Art, Baltimore, 1912–16; instructor, figure drawing and composition, School of Architecture at Columbia University, since 1917. Member: National Society of Mural Painters; Architectural League. *Address*, 280 E. 162d St., New York, N. Y.

LAUNITZ, Robert E. Sculptor. Born in Russia in 1806. In 1830 he came to America and was elected a member of the National Academy in 1833. Among his productions are the Pulaski monument in Savannah, Ga.; the Battle monument in Frankfort, Ky.; the monument to General George H. Thomas in Troy, N. Y. He was connected in his work with the sculptor John Frazee in New York. He died in 1870.

LAURENT. A little known genre painter who worked in America with some success.

LAURENT, Robert. Sculptor. Born in France, 1890. Member: Brooklyn Society of Art; Modern Artists of America. *Address,* 106 Columbia Heights, Brooklyn, N. Y.

LAURIE, Alexander. Painter. Born in New York City in 1828. Studied at the National Academy of Design, and later in Paris. He painted many portraits of the Generals who served in the Civil War. He died at Lafayette, Ind., in 1917.

LAUTER, Flora. Painter. Born in New York in 1874. Pupil of Henri, Chase and Mora in New York. *Address,* 12 East 9th St., New York.

LAUTZ, William. Sculptor. Born in Germany in 1838. He came to the United States in 1854 and settled in Buffalo, N. Y. Some of his work is in the Buffalo Historical Society Building. He died in 1915.

LAUX, August. Painter. Born in the Rhine Pfaiz, Bavaria, in 1847; died in Brooklyn, N. Y., 1921. Removed with his parents to New York in 1863, and studied at the National Academy of Design. Exhibited in spring of 1870 at National Academy, and became notable for decorative work, but since 1880 has given his attention to genre and still-life pictures.

LAVALLE, John. Painter. Exhibited at National Academy of Design in 1925. *Address,* Boston, Mass.

LAVALLEY, J. Painter. Born at Rouse Point, N. Y., in 1858. Member: Springfield Art League. Work: "Birth of Springfield," owned by the City of Springfield. Represented in Springfield Art Museum. *Address,* 317 Main St., 101 Allen St., Springfield, Mass.

LAVIGNE. Engraver. The few known plates signed by Lavigne are well executed in stipple, and appear in the "Polyanthos," published in Boston in 1814.

LAW, Margaret Moffet. Painter. Born in Spartanburg, S. C. Pupil of Chase, Henri, Mora and Hawthorne. Work: "Feeding Chickens," Kennedy Library, Spartanburg, S. C.; "Wayside Chat," Converse College, S. C. *Address,* 13 East Read St., Baltimore, Md.

LAWFORD, Charles. Painter. Member: Attic Club, Minneapolis; Minneapolis Art League. *Address,* Los Angeles, Calif.

LAWLESS, Carl. Painter. Born in Illinois, 1894. Exhibited at National Academy of Design, 1925. Pupil of Penna. Academy of the Fine Arts. *Address,* Stony Run, Penna.

LAWLOR, George W. Painter. Born in Chelsea, Mass., in 1848. Pupil of Julien and Colarossi Academies, and at École des Beaux Arts, Paris. Member: Boston Art Club. *Address,* Studio Bldg., 110 Tremont St., Boston, Mass.

LAWMAN, Jasper Holman. Landscape and portrait painter. Born in Cleveland, Ohio, in 1825. Studied abroad. He has painted many of the leading families in Western Pennsylvania. He died in Pittsburgh, Penna., in 1906.

LAWRENCE, Charles B. Painter. Born in Bordentown, N. J. He removed to Philadelphia about 1813. He was a pupil of Rembrandt Peale, and is said also to have studied with Stuart. He finally abandoned art for commerce. His portrait of José Francisco Correa de Serra, the distinguished Portuguese botanist, is owned by the American Philosophical Society, Philadelphia. He also paintd some landscapes which Dunlap says were without merit.

LAWRENCE (or LAURENCE) Samuel. Portrait painter. Born in England in 1812. He died there in 1844. In 1854 he was living in the United States, where he painted or drew the portraits of a number of prominent men.

LAWRENCE, Wm. R. Painter. Born in 1829. His paintings were all of a peculiarly imaginative tendency, but most carefully drawn. There are two in the Wadsworth Gallery in Hartford, Conn.: "The Royal Children" and "Napoleon at Waterloo." He spent his entire life in Hartford, Conn., and died there in 1856.

LAWRENCE, W. S. This landscape engraver was an apprentice with Alfred Jones in 1840, and in 1846 he was engraving over his own name for New York publishers. Plates signed "A. L. Jones" were executed by Lawrence when an apprentice with Jones, and were finished by the latter.

LAWRIE, Alexander, Jr. Portrait painter, engraver and crayon portrait draughtsman. Born in New York City in 1828. He exhibited a crayon portrait of Thomas Sully at the Pennsylvania Academy in 1854. He studied both at the National Academy and at the Pennsylvania Academy of Fine Arts. Later he was a pupil of Leutze in Dusseldorf, and of Picot in Paris. Appleton's "Cyclopaedia" notes that "He has made upward of a thousand crayon heads, including likenesses of Richard H. Stoddard and Thomas Buchanan Read." Among his best portraits in oil is the likeness of Judge Sutherland, painted for the New York Bar Association. He also painted landscapes. In 1866 he was elected an Associate Member of the National Academy of Design. He died after 1870.

LAWRIE, Lee O. Sculptor. Born in 1877. Pupil of Saint Gaudens and Martiny. Instructor in sculpture, Harvard University, 1910–12; Yale University, 1908–18. Member: National Sculpture Society. Work: Decorations in United States Military Academy, West Point; Church of St. Vincent Ferrer, and reredos of St. Thomas' Church, New York; Harkness Memorial Tower and Archway, Yale University. *Address*, 1923 Lexington Ave., New York.

LAWSON, Adelaide J. Painter. Born in New York, N. Y., in 1890. Pupil of Kenneth Hayes Miller. Member: Society of Independent Artists. *Address*, 209 West 97th St., New York, N. Y.

LAWSON, Alexander. Engraver. Born in Ravenstruthers, Lanarkshire, Scotland, in 1773; died in Philadelphia, 1846. An extended memoir of Alexander Lawson was read before the Pennsylvania Historical Society, in 1878, by the late Townsend Ward and from this paper the following brief sketch is compiled.

Alexander Lawson was left an orphan at the age of fifteen years and was cared for by an elder brother residing in Liverpool. As he sympathized deeply with the Revolutionary movement in France, in 1793, Lawson determined to seek his future in that country, and as he could not obtain a direct passage from England, he sailed for the United States, expecting to return on a French vessel.

He landed at Baltimore on July 14, 1794, and was so well pleased with the social and political conditions existing in this country that he changed his plans and concluded to cast in his lot with the Americans. He went to Philadelphia, and as he seemed to have some knowledge of engraving, he first found employment with the engravers "Thackara & Vallance." Some time after this he commenced business for himself, and first attracted attention by his admirable plates for an edition of Thomson's "Seasons." In 1798 Lawson met his fellow-countryman Alexander Wilson, and a firm and lasting friendship resulted. Lawson engraved the best plates in Wilson's famous Ornithology, the first volume of which was issued in 1808, and also those in its continuation, by Charles Lucien Bonaparte.

LAWSON, Ernest. Landscape painter. Born in California, 1873. He spent several years in France. Awards: Silver medal, St. Louis Exposition, 1904; Sesnan medal, Penn-

sylvania Academy of the Fine Arts, 1907; gold medal, American Art Society, Philadelphia, 1907; First Hallgarten prize, National Academy, 1908. Elected Associate of National Academy, 1908; Academician, 1917; also member of American Painters and Sculptors, New York. Represented by "Boat-House, Winter, Harlem River," at the Corcoran Gallery, Washington, D. C.

LAWSON, Helen E. Engraver. This daughter of Alexander Lawson made the drawings for her father's illustrations in the works of Prof. Haldeman and Dr. Binney, and she also engraved several plates of birds for a publication of about 1830. She showed decided talent in this work.

LAWSON, Jess M. Sculptor. Born in Edinburgh, Scotland, 1885. Member: National Sculpture Society; National Academy of Women Painters and Sculptors. Awards: Helen Foster Barnett prize, National Academy of Design, 1918; Widener gold medal, Penna. Academy of Fine Arts, 1919. *Address*, 120 Lexington Ave., New York, N. Y.

LAWSON, Katharine S. Sculptor. Born in Indianapolis, Ind., 1885. Pupil of Lorado Taft; Herman A. MacNeil. Member: National Academy of Painters and Sculptors. Award: Shaw prize, National Academy of Design, 1921. *Address*, "Lone Pine Studio," Westport, Conn.

LAWSON, Oscar A. Engraver. Born in Philadelphia in 1813; died there 1854. This son of Alexander Lawson was probably a pupil of his father, and he became an accomplished line-engraver. He furnished a number of small plates for the "Annuals"; but about 1840 he entered the service of the U. S. Coast Survey, at Washington, as a chart engraver, and he remained there until failing health compelled him to resign in 1851.

LAWSON, Thomas B. Painter. Born in Newburyport, Mass., in 1807. He drew from the Antique in the National Academy of Design, N. Y., for six months in 1831; returned to Newburyport, and commenced painting portraits in 1832. In 1844 he painted a portrait of Daniel Webster. Lawson died in 1888.

LAY, Oliver Ingraham. Painter. Born in New York City in 1845. He died there in 1890. He studied at the Cooper Institute, and the National Academy, and was also a pupil of Thomas Hicks. Elected an Associate Member of the National Academy in 1876. He painted many portraits, and some genre subjects. His copy of Stuart's portrait of Chief Justice John Jay is owned by the New York Historical Society.

LAYBOURNE–JENSEN, (Lars Peter). Painter and sculptor. Born in Copenhagen, Denmark, in 1888. Pupil of Danish Academy. Member: Society of Independent Artists. *Address*, 211 Locust St., Roselle Park, N. J.

LAZARD, Mrs. Alice A. Painter. Born in New Orleans, La., in 1893. Pupil of Charles Sneed Williams and of the Art Institute of Chicago. Member: Springfield, Ill., Artists' Association; Art Club of Chicago; Art Institute of Chicago Alumni Association. *Address*, Klaubers, Louisville, Ky.

LAZARUS, Jacob H. Portrait painter. Born in New York City in 1822; he died there in 1891. He studied portraiture with Henry Inman, whose portrait he painted; it was given by the artist's widow to the Metropolitan Museum, N. Y. He also painted miniatures and the one he painted of Chas. A. May was exhibited at the Centennial of the National Academy in 1925. He was elected an Associate Member of the National Academy of Design in 1849.

LAZZELL, Blanche. Painter and etcher. Born in Maidsville, Monongalia County, Va. Pupil of Charles Guerin; William Schumacher. Member: Society of Independent Artists; Provincetown Printers; Provincetown Artists' Association. Works: Wood block-prints, "The Violet Jug," Detroit Art Institute; "Tulips," "The Monongahela," "Trees" and "Fishing Boat," W. Va. University Library. *Address*, Provincetown, Mass.

LEACH, Bernard. Painter and etcher. Born in Hong Kong, China, 1887. Pupil of Slade School of London and of Frank Brangwyn. Member: Chicago Society of Etchers. *Address*, Care of Dr. W. E. Hoyle, Crowland, Liandaff, Cardiff, Wales.

LEACH, Samuel. Engraver. The *Pennsylvania Gazette* of Dec. 1741 advertises that "Samuel Leach, from London, performs all sorts of Engraving, such as Coats of Arms, Crests, Cyphers, Letters and Sc., on Gold, Silver or Copper. Also engraving of all kinds for Silversmiths. N. B. The said Leach may be heard of at Mr. Samuel Hazard's, Merchant, opposite the Baptist Meeting House, in Second Street, or at Andrew Farrels, Tanner, in Chestnut St., Philadelphia."

LEAKE, Gerald. Painter. Exhibited at National Academy of Design, New York, 1925. *Address*, 46 Washington Square, New York.

LEARNED, Arthur Garfield. Etcher and painter. Born in Chelsea, Mass., 1872. Studied in Paris, 1907–8. Illustrated various books for Boston publishers; drawings for *Life, Ladies' Home Journal, St. Nicholas, Town and Country, Harper's Magazine*, etc. Exhibited dry portraits in New York, Philadelphia, Worcester, Boston; produced etchings of Edgar Allan Poe, Tennyson, Grieg, MacDowell, John Alexander, Paul Helleu, Grace George and many others. Member: Chicago Society of Etchers; California Society of Etchers. *Address*, 36 Gramercy Park, New York.

LEAVITT, W. H. Painted portraits in New Orleans in 1904, and afterwards had a studio at 622 Commercial Place.

LeBLANC, E. M. de Hoa. Painter. Born in New Orleans, La. Studied in Newcomb School of Art; under Dr. Ross, Harvard University; Art Institute, Chicago, Ill.; under J. C. Johanse. Medal, Art Association of New Orleans. Teacher of Art, New Orleans Public High Schools; Supervisor of Drawing, New Orleans Elementary Schools. Paints portraits, marines and landscapes. *Address*, New Orleans, La.

LE CASTRO, A. Miniature painter. A miniature painted on ivory of a gentleman evidently of the southern states is signed "A. Le Castro."

LE CLEAR, Thomas. Portrait painter. Born in Owego, New York, 1818; died in 1882. He was elected a member of the National Academy, 1863. He is represented by a portrait of "William Page," in the Corcoran Gallery, Washington, D. C.

LE COUNT & HAMMOND. Engravers. Well-engraved landscape plates published in 1840 are thus signed. The second member of the firm was probably J. T. Hammond, who was in business as an engraver in Philadelphia in 1839.

LEDDEL, Joseph, Jr. Engraver. The *New York Weekly Post Boy*, in 1752, contains the advertisement of Joseph Leddel, Jr., for the sale of all manner of pewterwork. At the end of this advertisement he says that "He also engraves on Steel, Iron, Gold, Silver, Copper, Brass, Pewter, Ivory or Turtle Shell, in a neat manner very reasonably."

LE DUC, Arthur C. Painter. Born in Washington, D. C., in 1892. Pupil of John Sloan, and of Academie Julien, Paris. *Address*, 617 Lexington Ave., New York.

LEE, Arthur. Sculptor. Awarded the George D. Widener Memorial gold medal, 1924, at Penna. Academy of the Fine Arts. *Address*, 5 Mac Dougal Alley, N. Y.

LEE, Bertha S. Painter. Born in San Francisco, Calif., 1873. Studied in New York and abroad. Represented in Del Monte Art Gallery by "Monterey Coast," and in Golden

Gate Park Museum, San Francisco, by "In the Gloaming." *Address*, 2744 Steiner St., San Francisco, Calif.

LEE, Homer. Engraver. Born in Mansfield, Ohio, in 1855. He was the son of John Lee, an engraver, and received some instruction from his father in this art. He was later regularly apprenticed to a steel-engraver in New York City, but his master having failed before the expiration of his apprenticeship, he began business for himself as Homer Lee & Co. He was successful, and in 1881 he founded the Homer Lee Bank Note Co. of New York. Later he was vice-president and director of the Franklin-Lee Bank Note Co., of the same city. Mr. Lee studied art in Canada and in Europe, and received honorable mention for one of his paintings at the Vienna Exposition of 1873. He also received honorable mention in the Paris Exhibition of 1900, and the bronze medal at the Charleston Exposition, 1902. He died 1923.

LEEPER, Vera B. Painter. Born in Denver, Colo., in 1893. Pupil of Boston Museum School; also studied abroad. *Address*, 6 Morningside Ave., New York City.

LEGGETT, R. This good line-engraver of landscapes was working about 1870 and signed plates from "No. 4 John St., New York."

LEHMAN, George. Painter and engraver. Born in Lancaster County, Pa.; died in Philadelphia in 1870. About 1829 Lehman painted, engraved in aquatint, and hand-colored a series of admirable views of Pennsylvania towns. He also aquatinted a number of smaller plates and drew for engravers. In 1835–37 he was in the lithographing business in Philadelphia, and was later a member of the print publishing firm of Lehman & Baldwin, of the same city. In 1830 he painted a number of landscapes in Philadelphia.

LEICH, Chester. Painter and etcher. Born in Evansville, Ind., in 1889. Member of Chicago Society of Etchers and Brooklyn Society of Etchers. *Address*, 315 Mercantile Bldg., Evansville, Ind.

LEIGH, William Robinson. Portrait and figure painter. Born in West Virginia in 1866. Pupil of Maryland Institute and of the Royal Academy, Munich, Bavaria. *Address*, 61 Poplar Street, Brooklyn, N. Y.

LEIGHTON, Scott. Animal painter. Born in Auburn, Maine. His best work is as a painter of horses. Mr. Leighton's horses are always technically good in drawing. He was a member of the "Art Club" of Boston. His death occurred in an insane asylum in 1898.

15

LEISENRING, Mathilde Muedon (Mrs. L. M.). Portrait painter. Born in Washington, D. C. Pupil of Art Students' League of New York and of Washington; also of Laurens, Constant and Henner in Paris. Member: Society of Washington Artists; Washington Water Color Club; Washington Art Club. *Address*, 1777 Church St., Washington, D. C.

LEITH-ROSS, Harry. Painter. Born in Mauritius, 1886. Pupil of Birge Harrison and J. F. Carlsen; of Laurens in Paris. Member: Conn. Academy of Fine Arts; Allied Artists' Association. Awards: Charles Noel Flagg prize, Conn. Academy of Fine Arts, 1921; 2d prize, Duxbury, Mass., Artists' Association, 1921. *Address*, Woodstock, Ulster County, N. Y.

LEITNER, L. Painter and illustrator. Born in Delphos, Ohio, 1873. Pupil of J. B. Whittaker, Henry Prelwitz, Joseph Boston and F. V. Du Mond. Member: Society of Independent Artists; League of New York Artists. *Address*, 10 Beekman Place, New York, N. Y.

LELAND, Henry. Painter. Born in Walpole, Mass., in 1850. His early death was the result of an accident. In 1876 he exhibited the portrait of Mlle. D'Alembert at the Paris Salon, and in 1877 "A Chevalier of the Time of Henry III" and "An Italian Girl." He died in 1877.

LEMET, L. Engraver. He was a close follower of the methods of St. Memin, producing portraits by the same means, and identical in appearance and size. He was located in Philadelphia in 1804.

LEMOS, Pedro J. Etcher, painter and illustrator. Born in Austin, Nev., 1882. Award: Honorable mention for etching. Director of Museum of Fine Arts, Leland Stanford University. *Address*, Museum of Fine Arts, Leland Stanford Junior University, Stanford University, Calif.

LENEY, William Satchwell. Engraver. Born in London, England, 1769; died at Longue Pointe, near Montreal, Canada, 1831. Leney was of Scotch descent. He is said to have been a pupil of the well-known English engraver Peltro W. Tompkins, and Leney's work bears evidence of a careful training in the art of stipple-engraving. About 1805 Leney was induced to come to the United States; he settled in New York and seems to have had abundant employment. One of Leney's early plates executed in this country is that of "Moses in the Bulrushes," done for Collins' Bible published in 1807; for this plate he is said to have received a gold medal.

L'ENGLE, Lucy. Painter. Born in New York in 1899. Member: Society of Independent Artists. *Address*, 144 East 19th St., New York, N. Y.

L'ENGLE, W. J., Jr. Painter. Born in Jacksonville, Fla., in 1884. Pupil of Richard Miller; J. P. Laurens; Collin; Louis Biloul. Member: Society of Independent Artists; Provincetown Artists' Association. *Address*, 144 East 19th St., New York, N. Y.

LENSKI, Lois. Painter. Exhibited water colors at the Penna. Academy of Fine Arts, Philadelphia, 1925. *Address*, 971 Split Rock Road, Pelham Manor, N. Y.

LENTELLI, Leo. Painter and sculptor. Born in Bologna, Italy, 1879. Member: National Sculptor, Society, 1907. Work: Figure of the Saviour and sixteen angels for the reredos of the Cathedral of Saint John the Divine, New York; group over entrance of Mission Branch Library, San Francisco; five figures for façade of San Francisco Public Library. Former instructor of sculpture, California School of Fine Arts; instructor of drawing, Art Students' League of New York. *Address*, 51 West 10th St., New York, N. Y.

LENZ, Alfred. Sculptor. Born in Wisconsin in 1872. Specialty, bronze statuettes. Member of National Sculpture Society.

LENZ, Oscar. Sculptor. Born in Providence, R. I., in 1874. Studied under Saint Gaudens in New York and under Saulievre in Paris. After his return to this country he executed the Colonial Group at Charleston, S. C., and some of the groups in the Pennsylvania Railroad Station in New York. He died in 1912.

LEONARD, George H. Landscape painter. Born in Boston in 1869. Pupil of Gerome, Bouguereau and Aman-Jean in Paris. Member: Boston Art Club. *Address*, 71 Rue Boissonade, Paris, France.

LEONARD, William J. Painter. Born in Hinsdale, N. H., in 1869. Pupil of Laurens and Constant in Paris. *Address*, Norwell, Mass.

LEPELLETIER. Engraver. Maps and plans published by T. C. Fay, of New York, in 1814, are signed "Lepelletier, Sculpt., New York."

LEPPERT, Rudolph E. Illustrator. Born in New York City, 1872. Pupil of G. deF. Brush and C. deGrimm. *Address*, 354 Fourth Ave., New York, N. Y.

LE ROY, Anita. Born in Philadelphia. She studied at the Penna. Academy of Fine Arts. Specializes in Dutch scenes.

LESLIE, Anne. Portrait artist. Sister of the artist Charles Robert Leslie. She showed ocnsiderable artistic talent. In 1822 she copied several portraits, and drew original crayon portraits of her friends. She also copied a number of her brother's paintings; her copy of the "Duchess and Sancho," exhibited at the Penna. Academy of the Fine Arts in Philadelphia in 1847, was admirably executed.

LESLIE, Charles Robert. Born in London, England, of American parents in 1794; brought by his parents to Philadelphia in 1800, and apprenticed to Bradford & Inskeep, booksellers, but developed a taste for art, as evinced by three early water color sketches of noted actors in character, now hanging in the print room of the Penna. Academy of Fine Arts. These drawings so interested his employer Mr. Bradford that he obtained subscriptions for sending young Leslie to London. Mr. Bradford was at that time a Director of the Academy, and at a special meeting of the Board held in 1811 he introduced the following resolutions, which were adopted: "Resolved, that this Academy, having examined the drawings produced at the exhibition by Master Leslie, are of the opinion that such rare talents evinced so early in life, give promise of great celebrity and usefulness, if fostered by the smiles of public patronage."

Leslie arrived in London, Dec. 1811, and studied at the Royal Academy and with West and Allston. He was elected to the Royal Academy in 1826. He was appointed in 1833 Professor of Drawing at the U. S. Military Academy at West Point, N. Y. He returned to London and died there in 1859. His works include "Uncle Toby and the Widow," "Anne Page and Master Slender," and "The Murder cf Rutland by Clifford," owned by the Penna. Academy of Fine Arts, Philadelphia.

LESLIE, Eliza. Authoress and artist, and sister of Charles Robert Leslie. Was born in Philadelphia, 1787; died in Gloucester, N. J., in 1858. She made a few crayon portraits.

LESSHAFFT, Franz. Painter. Born in Berlin, Germany, 1862. Pupil of Royal Academy of Fine Arts, Berlin, under Anton V. Werner, Thumann and Meyerheim. Member: Philadelphia Sketch Club; Fellowship, Penna. Academy of Fine Arts; Society of Independent Artists; Philadelphia Art Club. Award: Honorable mention, Berlin, for water colors. *Address*, 1020 Chestnut St., Philadelphia, Pa.

LESTER, William H. Illustrator and etcher. Born in Valparaiso, Chili, S. A., 1885. Pupil of Art Institute of Chicago. Member: Chicago Society of Etchers; Brooklyn Society of Etchers. *Address*, 121 South Hill St., Los Angeles, Calif.

LESUEUR, Alexander Charles. Born at Havre de Grace, France, 1778; died there in

1846. In 1815 he came to Philadelphia on the invitation of William Maclure, the geologist, and he assisted Maclure in a study of American Zoology. He finally settled in Philadelphia and taught drawing and painting, and he became a prominent member of the American Philosophical Society, and of the Academy of Natural Sciences.

The *Journal* of the Academy of Natural Sciences for 1818 contains a number of plates illustrating papers upon natural history beautifully etched by Lesueur. He returned to France in 1837 and was for a time curator of the Museum of Natural History at Havre.

LEUSCH, Franziska A. Painter. Born in Philadelphia, Pa. Pupil of Fred Wagner. Instructor in Philadelphia Normal School. *Address*, 114 Wharton Ave., Glenside, Pa.

LEUTZE, Emanuel. German historical painter. He was born in the village of Emingen, near Reutlingen, in Wurtemburg, in 1816. He went as a child to Philadelphia, where he was instructed by John A. Smith, a portrait painter. In 1841 he returned to Europe and pursued his studies at Dusseldorf under Lessing; but as he did not hold with the views of that academy, he established an atelier of his own. In 1842 he visited Munich, Venice and Rome, and returned to Dusseldorf, in 1845, and there executed a considerable number of paintings. He obtained in 1850 the gold medal at Berlin for his "Washington Crossing the Delaware," now in the Kunsthalle at Bremen. (Replica at the Metropolitan Museum, New York.) After having been in America in 1851, and again in 1859, he established himself there in 1863, and died in Washington, D. C., in 1868.

LEVER, Hayley. Painter. Born in Adelaide, South Australia, 1876. Studied in Paris, London and New York. Awards: Honorable mention, Carnegie Institute, Pittsburgh, 1913; silver medal, National Art Club, 1914; Carnegie prize, National Academy of Design, 1914; gold medal, Panama-Pacific International Exposition, San Francisco, 1915. Member: Royal British Artists, London; Royal Institute of Oil Painters, London; Royal West of England Academy; National Academy of Design, New York (life). Represented at Corcoran Gallery, Washington, D. C., by "Dawn." *Address*, 253 West 42d St., New York.

LEVI, Julian C. Painter and etcher. Born in New York in 1874. Exhibited in Paris Salon, 1904. *Address*, 105 West 40th St., New York.

LEVITT, Joel J. Painter. Exhibited at National Academy of Design, 1925. *Address*, 6 West 28th St., New York.

LEVY, Alexander O. Artist. Born in Bonn, Germany, in 1881. He was brought to America at the age of three years. At eight he won his first laurels as an artist in a newspaper competition in Cincinnati, and at twelve he was working under Duveneck in that city, and at fifteen participated in the Spanish-American War as a newspaper artist. His later youth he spent as a designer, lithographer and illustrator. In this period he studied drawing under William M. Chase and Robert Henri, and painting under Ossip Linde. *Address*, 41 Berkeley Place, Buffalo, N. Y.

LEVY, Beatrice S. Painter and etcher. Born in Chicago in 1892. Her etchigs are well known in many exhibitions. *Address*, 1540 East 57th St., Chicago, Ill.

LEVY, William Auerbach. Painter and etcher. Born in Brest-Litovsk, Russia, in 1889. Studied at National Academy of Design, and Academie Julien, Paris. Represented in permanent collection of Carnegie Institute, Pittsburgh; Art Institute, Chicago; Art Museum, Boston; Public Library, New York, and in important private collections. Awarded Mooney traveling scholarship, 1911; 1st prize, Chicago Society of Etchers, 1914; bronze medal, San Francisco Exposition, 1915. Instructor of etching, National Academy of Design, and in the Educational Alliance, New York. Member: Painters-Gravers of America; Chicago Society of Etchers. *Address*, 230 East 15th St., New York, N. Y.

LEWIS, Arthur A. Painter, etcher, engraver and illustrator. Born in Mobile, Ala., in 1873. Pupil of George Bridgman in Buffalo, and of Gerome in Paris. His work is in the New York Public Library, Brooklyn Institute Museum and in the Chicago Art Institute. *Address*, Southington, Conn.

LEWIS, David. Portrait painter. In 1805 he had his studio at 2 Tremont St., Boston, Mass.

LEWIS, Edmond Darch. Landscape painter; he has also painted marine views. Born in 1837, and lived in Philadelphia. Tuckerman mentions his paintings as having decided merit. Among his works are "Queen of the Antilles," "Fairmount Park," "Bass Rocks, after a Storm" and "Casino at Narragansett Pier." He died in 1910.

LEWIS, Edmonia. Sculptor. Born near Albany, N. Y., in 1845. She was part Indian by birth. Her work shows considerable ideality and talent, and her chief patronage was from abroad. She also executed portrait busts of Henry W. Longfellow, Charles Summer, John Brown and Abraham Lincoln.

LEWIS, J. This engraver signs his name "J. Lewis Sculpt." to several maps illustrating a bible published by S. Etheridge, of Charlestown, Mass., 1813. The same man probably engraved the book-plate of Dr. Peter Middleton, who died in New York in 1781. This plate bears evidence of American origin and would thus locate Lewis in New York at a considerably earlier date than that above mentioned.

LEWIS, J. O. This engraver in the stipple manner first appears in books published in Philadelphia in 1815. As he engraved the portrait of Lewis Cass, as secretary of war under President Jackson, he must have been engraving in 1831.

There is no record of such an engraver in the Philadelphia directories, and in the New York directory the nearest approach to this name is "Joseph Lewis, engraver and seal-cutter" in 1816-23. Lewis probably spent some time in the western country, as he published in Philadelphia, in 1835, "The North American Aboriginal Portfolio," a collection of lithographic portraits of Indians; some of these are inscribed as "Painted from life by J. O. Lewis, at Detroit, 1833." His engraving of Commodore Decatur full-length, standing on deck of ship, after G. Strickland, is a creditable piece of stipple engraving.

LEWIS, Josephine M. Painter. Born in New Haven, Conn., in 1865. Pupil of John F. Weir and of Frederick MacMonnies. *Address*, Carnegie Studio, 154 West 57th St., New York.

LEWIS, Phillips F. Painter. Born in Oakland, Calif., in 1892. Pupil of California School of Arts and Crafts and of Armin C. Hansen. Member: San Francisco Artists' Association; Oakland Artists' Association. *Address*, 843 Sixth Ave., Oakland, Calif.

LEWIS, W. He painted portraits in Salem, Mass., in 1812. His work appeared frequently in the early exhibitions at the Boston Athenaeum.

LEWIS, Yardley. The following appeared in the *Boston Weekly Journal* of Dec. 13, 1737: "Yardley Lewis of London, late from Ireland, dwelt lately in widow Howard's house near the north market place. Draws family pictures by the Life, also surveys and draws maps."

LEYENDECKER, Frank X. Painter and illustrator. Born in Germany in 1877. He came to America in 1883. Studied at Chicago Art Institute and Julien Academy; pupil of Laurens and Constant. He was also a designer and painter of stained glass windows. He died in 1924.

LEYENDECKER, Joseph Christian. Painter. Born in Montabour, Germany, in 1874. Studied at Art Institute of Chicago and Academie Julien, Paris. Exhibited at Salon, Champ de Mars, Paris, 1897. Draws for magazines. *Address*, 80 West 40th St., New York.

LICHTENAUER, J. Mortimer. Portrait and mural painter. Born in New York in 1876. Pupil of Mowbray in New York; of Merson and Laurens in Paris. Member: Mural Painters; Art Students' League of New York. Award: President's prize, New York Architectural League, 1903 and 1907. Work: Proscenium Arch, Frazee Theatre, New York; "Portrait of Gen. Julius Stahêl"; "Portrait of Gen. Palmer Pierce"; National Museum of Art, Washington. *Address*, 30 West 59th St., New York, N. Y.

LIE, Jonas. Landscape and marine painter. Born in Norway in 1880, he came to America when thirteen years old and settled in Plainfield, N. J. Pupil of National Academy of Design, and of the Art Students' League of New York. Elected Associate Member of National Academy in 1912. He has painted a series of pictures of Panama Canal. Represented in Metropolitan Museum by "The Conquerors"; in Detroit Institute by "Culebra Cut"; in Boston Museum by "The Fisherman's Return." *Address*, 58 West 57th St., New York.

LIMERICK, James Arthur. Painter and sculptor. Born in Philadelphia in 1870. Pupil of Anshutz and Grafly. *Address*, 960 North Howard St., Baltimore, Md.

LINCOLN, James Sullivan. Born in Taunton, Mass., in 1811. He came to Providence, R. I., at the age of ten and was apprenticed to an engraver. At 17 he chose the profession of portrait painting and established his studio at Providence. He became the first president of the Providence Art Club, and died in 1888.

LINDE, Ossip L. Painter. Born in Chicago. Pupil of the Art Institute of Chicago; of Laurens in Paris. Member: Allied Artists' Association. Awards: Honorable mention, Paris Salon, 1907; third class medal, Paris Salon, 1910. Represented in Oakland, California, Museum. *Address*, Care of Guaranty Trust Co., 1 Rue des Italiens, Paris, France.

LINDENMUTH, Tod. Painter and etcher. Born in Allentown, Pa., in 1885. Pupil of Henri, Webster and Browne. Member: Providence Artists' Association. Work: "Mending Nets" and "Provincetown Wharf," Toledo Museum; "Garden Near the Dunes," Pennsylvania State College Museum; "The Runway," Rochester Memorial Art Gallery; also represented in the New York Public Library. *Address*, 26 North 6th St., Allentown, Pa.

LINDER, C. Bennett. Painter. Exhibited portrait in National Academy of Design, 1925. *Address*, Carnegie Hall, New York.

LINDER, Henry. Sculptor. Exhibitor at the National Sculpture Society, of busts, and the sitting figures "Music" and "Spring." Address, New York City.

LINDIN, Carl. Painter. Born in Sweden in 1869. Pupil of Laurens, Constant and Aman-Jean in Paris. Award: First prize, Swedish Club, Chicago. Work: decorations in Hull House, Chicago, Ill. *Address*, Woodstock, Ulster County, N. Y.

LINDING, Herman M. Painter and sculptor. Born in Sweden in 1880. Pupil of Callmander, Carl Wilhelmson, and of Colarossi. Member: Society of Independent Artists; Whitney Studio Club; Alliance. *Address*, 154 East 64th St., New York, N. Y.

LINDNEUX, Robert O. Painter. Born in New York, N. Y., in 1871. Studied in Dusseldorf, Germany. Member: Denver Artists' Association. Specialty, animals. *Address*, 2939 East Colfax Ave., Denver, Colo.

LINDSLEY, E. E. Painter and illustrator. Born in New Rochelle, N. Y., in 1858. Pupil of W. Chase; John Weir; C. Ferrari. Member: National Association of Women Painters and Sculptors. *Address*, 23 Chatsworth Ave., Larchmont, N. Y.

LINEN, George. Painter. Born in Scotland in 1802. He was a student of the Royal Scottish Academy in Edinburgh. In 1843 he settled in New York, and painted portraits in oil, of a small size. He died in New York in 1888.

LINFORD, Charles. Landscape painter. Born in Pittsburgh, Penna., in 1846, he died in 1897. His painting "Lowland Woods" is owned by the Penna. Academy of Fine Arts, Philadelphia.

LINK, B. Lillian. Sculptor. Born in New York. Pupil of Mrs. Charles Sprague-Smith, George Grey Barnard and of Herbert Adams. *Address*, 260 West 76th St., New York, N. Y.

LINSON, Corwin K. Painter and illustrator. Born in Brooklyn, N. Y., in 1864. Pupil of Gerome and Laurens in Paris. Illustrates for *Century*, *Scribner's* and *Cosmopolitan*. *Address*, Atlantic Highlands, N. J.

LINTON, Frank B. Painter. Born in Philadelphia in 1871. Pupil of Gerome, Constant, Bonnat and Laurens in Paris. *Address*, 1707 Chestnut St., Philadelphia.

LINTON, William J. Wood engraver, designer and water color painter. Born in England in 1812. He came to the United States in 1867. He was elected a member of the National Academy of Design in 1882; was also author of "History of Wood Engraving in America." He died in 1897. Member of Society of Painters in Water Colors.

LION, Jules. Lithographer. He opened a studio in New Orleans in 1839, bringing with him the first daguerreotype outfit used in that city. He had exhibited in the Salon, Paris, 1831 and 1836. He remained in New Orleans making lithograph portraits of the leading statesmen of the South until 1865, after which no record of him is found.

LIPPERT, Leon. Painter. Born in Germany in 1863. Pupil of Cincinnati Art Academy under Duveneck; also studied abroad. *Address*, 631 Main St., Cincinnati, Ohio.

LIPPINCOTT, Margarette. Painter. Born in Philadelphia in 1862. Student of the Penna. Academy of Fine Arts, Philadelphia. Her specialty was flower painting.

LIPPINCOTT, William Henry. Painter. Born in Philadelphia in 1849; died in New York, 1920. Began study of art in Penna. Academy of Fine Arts; became designer of illustrations, later, scenic artist; was a pupil of Leon Bonnat, 1874, remaining in Paris 8 years, and regularly exhibiting at Paris Salons. He returned to the U. S., 1882; established a studio in New York. He was a professor of painting, National Academy of Design. Painted portraits, figure compositions and landscapes; was a regular contributor to American art exhibitions. "The Duck's Breakfast," "Love's Ambush," and "Pleasant Reflections" are his most important pictures. Elected Associate Member of the National Academy, 1884; National Academy, 1896. Member: American Water Color Society; Society of American Etchers; Century Association.

LITTLE, Arthur. Painter. Exhibited at National Academy of Design, 1925. *Address*, 27 West 67th St., New York.

LITTLE, Gertrude L. Miniature painter. Exhibited at the Penna. Academy of Fine Arts, Philadelphia, 1925. *Address*, 4417 Prospect Ave., Hollywood, Calif.

LITTLE, J. Wesley. Landscape painter. Born in Sullivan County, Pa., in 1867; died in 1923. Studied at National Academy of Design, New York, 1888–94, and with Leonard Ochtman; went abroad for travel and study 1899–1900 and 1905. He has exhibited at the St. Louis Exposition; Penna. Academy of Fine Arts; Art Club, Philadelphia; American Water Color Society; New York Water Color Club; Art Institute of Chicago; Washington Water Color Club; International Exhibition, Montevideo, 1911; Panama, P. I., Exposition, etc. Silver medal, American Art Society, 1901. Member: Philadelphia, Washington and Chicago water color clubs; Philadelphia Sketch Club.

LITTLE, Philip. Painter. Born in Swampscott, Mass., 1857. Studied at Art School of Museum of Fine Arts, Boston, 1881–82. Exhibited in all leading art museums in U. S.; Paris Salon, 1912, etc. Honorable mention, Art Institute, Chicago, 1912; silver medal, Panama, P. I., Exposition, 1915. Curator of Fine Arts, Essex Institute. Represented in permanent collections of Essex Institute, Salem, Mass.; Walker Memorial, Brunswick, Me.; Penna. Academy of Fine Arts, Philadelphia; Minneapolis Institute; Milwaukee Art Association; Nashville Art Association; Dubuque Art Association. Life member of Portland Society of Arts; National Art Club, N. Y. Member of Chicago Society of Etchers and of Boston Society of Etchers. *Address,* 10 Chestnut St., Salem, Mass.

LITZINGER, Dorothea M. (Mrs.). Painter and etcher. Born in Cambria County, Penna., in 1889; died in 1925. Pupil of National Academy of Design. Illustrated for "County Life in America"; well known for her flower painting.

LIVERMORE, Mrs. Miniature painter; flourished 1847 to 1848 in Boston, Mass.

LIVINGSTON, Harriet. Amateur miniature painter. She became the wife of Robert Fulton, 1808, and painted a miniature of her father, Walter Livingston, reproduced in C. W. Bowen's "Centennial of the Inauguration of Washington."

LLOYD, Sara A. W. (Mrs.). Painter. Pupil of Swain Gifford, Volk and Chase in New York. Among her paintings are "Sunshine and Shadow" and portraits of W. J. Morehead, John Jones, and Miss Slade. *Address,* Hamilton, N. Y.

LOBER, George J. Sculptor. Born in Chicago, Ill., in 1891. Pupil of Calder and Borglum. Represented in Corcoran Gallery, Washington, D. C. *Address,* 6 East 15th St., New York.

LOCK, Alice G. Painter. Exhibited "The Crusader's Beat" at the 33d Annual Exhibition of National Association of Women Painters and Sculptors. *Address,* 288 Ryerson St., Brooklyn, New York.

LOCKE, Alexander S. Mural painter. Born in New York, 1860. Pupil of John La Farge. Member: New York Architectural League, 1894; Mural Painters; National Art Club. *Address,* 103 Pineapple St., Brooklyn, New York.

LOCKE, Charles W. Painter, illustrator and etcher. Born in Cincinnati, Ohio, in 1899. Pupil of Art Academy of Cincinnati. *Address,* Care of Traxel Galleries, Norwood, Ohio.

LOCKINGTON, Walter P. Painter. Born in 1857; died in Philadelphia, 1905.

LOCKMAN, De Witt M. Portrait painter. Elected a member of the National Academy of Design in 1921. Awards: Silver medal, Panama-Pacific Exposition, San Francisco, 1915; Lippincott prize, Penna. Academy of Fine Arts, 1918. *Address,* 58 West 57th St., New York, N. Y.

LOCKWOOD, Wilton (Robt.). Portrait painter. Born in Wilton, Conn., in 1861. He was also known for his flower painting. Pupil of John La Farge; also studied for ten years in Paris. Elected Associate Member of the National Academy in 1906 and Academician, 1912. He died in Brookline, Mass., in 1914. His portrait of John La Farge is in the Boston Museum of Fine Arts; his flower piece "Peonies" is owned by the Corcoran Art Gallery of Washington, D. C.

LOEB, Dorothy. Painter and etcher. Born in Bavaria in 1887, of American parents. Pupil of Art Institute of Chicago; T. W. Stevens; Hawthorne; also studied in Paris and Munich. Decorations in Lane Technical High School, and Smith Public School, Chicago, Ill. *Address,* 4346 North Hermitage Ave., Chicago, Ill.

LOEB, Louis. Painter. Born in Cleveland, Ohio, in 1866. He studied in Paris under Gerome. Elected a member of the National Academy in 1906. Specialty, figure painting. He was a member of the Society of American Artists. He died in 1909.

LOEBL, Florence Weinberg. Painter. Born in New York in 1894. Pupil of Kenneth Hayes Miller. Member: Society of Independent Artists; League of New York Artists. *Address,* 135 West 79th St., New York, N. Y.

LOEWENGUTH, Frederick M. Painter. Born in Rochester, N. Y., in 1887. Studied in London and Paris. Member: Rochester Art Club. *Address,* 401 Powers Bldg., Rochester, N. Y.

LOGAN, Robert Fulton. Painter and etcher. Born in Lauder, Manitoba, Canada. Pupil of Boston School of the Museum of Fine Arts. Member: Chicago Society of Etchers. Work: "Spanish Iris," Art Society of Hartford; "Les Molineaux-Billancourt," Luxembourg Museum, Paris. Assistant Director of Atelier of Painting, Bellevue Art Training Centre, 1919. *Address,* Villa Adrien, Route Des Gardes, Meudon, Seine et Oise, France.

LONDONER, A. Painter. Born in Lexington, Mo., in 1878. Pupil of Robert Henri and of John Sloan. Member: Art Students' League of New York; Society of Independent Artists; League of New York Artists. *Address*, 1947 Broadway, New York.

LONG, Adelaide Husted (Mrs. George T.). Painter. Born in New York. Pupil of Art Students' League of New York; also of John Twachtman, Ernest Knaufft and George T. Collins; of Anglade in Paris. Member: National Art Club. *Address*, 57 North Broadway, White Plains, N. Y.

LONG, Ellis B. Painter and sculptor. Born in Baltimore, Md., in 1874. Pupil of André Castaigne and of E. S. Whiteman in Baltimore; of Cox, Mowbray, Saint Gaudens and D. C. French in New York. *Address*, 127 Richmond St., Baltimore, Md.

LONGACRE, James Barton. Engraver. Born in Delaware County, Pa., in 1794; died in Philadelphia in 1869. Longacre was taught to engrave by George Murray, in Philadelphia. His earliest work was done for S. F. Bradford's Encyclopedia, but he first attracted attention by his admirable large plate of Andrew Jackson, after the portrait by Thomas Sully, published in Philadelphia in 1820. He soon found abundant employment in engraving portraits in the stipple manner, many of them done after his own drawings from life.

About 1830, in connection with James Herring, Longacre conceived the idea of publishing "The American Portrait Gallery," a series of biographical sketches of statesmen, military and naval heroes. These were to be illustrated by portraits, and Longacre engraved a number of these himself and drew the originals for other engravers; taken as a whole it was the best series of portraits engraved in the United States up to that time.

The large plates of Longacre are remarkable for their faithfulness as portraits, and for the beauty of their execution. The majority of them are done in the stipple manner; but his large plate of Charles Carroll, after the painting by Chester Harding, proves him to have been an accomplished line-engraver. In 1844 Mr. Longacre was appointed engraver to the U. S. Mint, succeeding C. Gobrecht, and he held that position until his death. Longacre painted, in oil, many of the originals of the engraved portraits; they are cabinet size and carefully painted.

LONGACRE, Lydia E. Miniature painter. Born in New York in 1870. Pupil of Art Students' League of New York, under Chase and Mowbray; of Whistler in Paris. Member: American Society of Miniature Painters; Pa. Society of Miniature Painters; National Association of Women Painters and Sculptors. *Address*, 27 West 67th St., New York.

LONGFELLOW, Ernest Wadsworth. Painter. Born in Cambridge, Mass., in 1845; died in Boston, 1921. Studied art in Paris under Hebert Bonnat and Couture. His best known landscapes and compositions are: "Misty Morning"; "The Choice of Youth"; "Italian Pifferari"; "Morning on the Aegean"; "The Matterhorn"; "Evening on the Nile"; "First Love"; Portrait of H. W. Longfellow, etc.; "Marine" (signed "Ernest Longfellow 1875") is owned by the Boston Museum of Fine Arts.

LONGMAN, Evelyn B. Sculptor. Born in Winchester, Ohio, in 1874. Pupil of Art Institute of Chicago under Taft; of French in New York. Member: National Sculpture Society, 1906. Elected Associate Member of the National Academy, 1909; National Academy, 1919. Awards: French gold medal, Art Institute of Chicago, 1920; Widener gold medal, Penna. Academy of Fine Arts, 1921. Work: Bronze doors of Chapel, U. S. Naval Academy, Annapolis; bronze doors of Library, Wellesley College, Wellesley, Mass.; "Torso" and "Victory," Metropolitan Museum, New York; "Victory" and "Electricity," Toledo Museum; also represented in Chicago Art Institute; City Art Museum, St. Louis; Cincinnati Museum of Art; Cleveland Museum; Herron Art Institute, Indianapolis. *Address*, Windsor, Conn.

LONGPRE, Paul De. Painter. Born in France in 1855, he came to the United States in 1890, and died in Hollywood, Los Angeles, Calif., in 1911. His specialty was floral painting, and his first exhibition in New York in 1896 was composed entirely of floral subjects.

LOOMIS, Chester. Painter. Born near Syracuse, N. Y., in 1852; died in Englewood, N. J., in 1924. Portrait and landscape painter. Pupil of Harry Thompson and Bonnat in Paris. He was elected an Associate Member of the National Academy in 1906. He also executed several mural paintings.

LOOP, Henry A. Distinguished portrait and figure painter. He was born in Connecticut in 1831. He studied with Henry Peters Gray; also with Couture in Paris. One of his best portraits was that of Judge Skinner of Buffalo. In 1861 he was elected to the National Academy, and in 1863 to the Century Club. He died in 1895, at Lake George, N. Y.

LOOP, Mrs. Henry A. Portrait painter. She was a sister of Judge Lynde Harrison, and was born in 1840 in New Haven, Conn. She was a pupil of Henry A. Loop whom she married about 1865. In 1875 she was elected an Associate Member of the National Academy of Design. Her specialty was portraits of children, and her studio was in New York City, where she died in 1909.

LOPEZ, Charles A. Sculptor. Born in Mexico in 1869. He came to New York when a youth and studied with Ward of New York, and afterwards at the École des Beaux Arts in Paris. Awarded first prize for McKinley Monument, Philadelphia. He was elected in 1906 an Associate of the National Academy, but died in the same year.

LORD, Caroline. Painter. Born in Cincinnati in 1860. Pupil of Cincinnati Art School and of the Julien Academy, Paris. Represented in Cincinnati Museum by ''First Communion'' and ''Old Woman.'' *Address*, 975 East McMillan St., Cincinnati.

LORD, Harriet. Painter and etcher. Born in Orange, N. J., in 1879. Pupil of Tarbell, Benson and De Camp. *Address*, 208 East 68th St., New York.

LORD, James Brown. Painter. Born in 1859. He died in 1902.

LORD, Phoebe G. Born in 1797; died in 1875. Miniature painter in water color. She later became Mrs. P. G. L. Noyes.

LORENZ, Richard. Painter. Born in Germany in 1858. He came to this country as a young man. In 1905 he was awarded the ''Osborne prize.'' He was a member of the Society of Western Artists. Among his works were: ''A Critical Moment''; ''Burial on the Plains''; ''Plowing in Saxony.'' He died in Milwaukee, Wisc., in 1915.

LORENZANI, Arthur E. Sculptor. Born in Italy in 1885. Member: National Sculpture Society. *Address*, 232 W. 14th St., New York.

LORING, Charles Greeley. Painter. Born in 1828. He died in 1902.

LORING, Francis William. Painter. Born in Boston, Mass., in 1838. He studied in Europe and died in Meran, Austria, in 1905. His painting ''The Bridge of Chioggia'' is dated 1886, and is owned by the Boston Museum of Fine Arts.

LORING, William Cushing. Painter. Born in Newton Center, Mass., in 1879. Studied in New York, Boston, London and Paris. Exhibited portrait of ''Miss Whitten,'' in Carnegie Institute, Pittsburgh, and is represented in the Rhode Island School of Design. *Address*, Kirkside, Wayland, Mass.

LOSSING, Benson J. Illustrator. Born in Beekman, N. Y., in 1813. He made numerous drawings for illustrating his ''Field Book of the Revolution.'' He died in Dover Plains, N. Y., in 1891. (See ''Biographical Notice'' of Lossing, prepared for the Worcester Society of Antiquity in 1892.)

LOTARE, Carl. Painter. Died in 1924. Painter of American Indian subjects; he also did some mural painting.

LOUD, Mrs. H. C. Crayon portrait draughtsman who was working in Philadelphia about 1850.

LOVE, G. Engraver. This name as engraver is appended to a very poor frontispiece to Watts' ''Divine Songs,'' published in Philadelphia in 1807 by L. Johnson.

LOVEGROVE, Stanley D. Painter. Exhibited water colors at the Penna. Academy of Fine Arts, Philadelphia, 1925. *Address*, 1600 Wallace St., Philadelphia.

LOVELL, Katherine A. Painter. Exhibited at the 33d Annual Exhibition of the National Association of Women Painters and Sculptors. *Address*, 260 Cumberland St., New York.

LOVETT, Robert. According to *Poulson's Advertiser*, Lovett was an engraver upon metal and stone, located in Philadelphia in 1816–22, inclusive. He was principally engaged in engraving seals and dies. He removed to New York about 1825, but returned to Philadelphia in after years.

LOVETT-LORSKI, Boris. Sculptor. Born in Russia in 1891. *Address*, Layton Art School, Milwaukee.

LOVETT, William. Portrait and miniature painter of Boston, Mass. Born in 1773. His work was excellent, as shown by his miniature of Rev. John Clarke owned by the Essex Institute of Salem, Mass. He died in 1801.

LOW, Mary Fairchild. Painter. Born in New Haven, Conn. She studied in School of Fine Arts, St. Louis; Academie Julien, Paris; and with Carolus-Duran. Awarded medal, Chicago Exposition, 1893; bronze medal, Paris Exposition, 1900. Elected Associate Member of the National Academy; member of Woman's International Art Club, London. *Address*, Bronxville, New York.

LOW, Will H. Painter. Born in Albany, N. Y., in 1853, and after accumulating means by working for the illustrated periodicals in New York, he went to Europe in 1873. He studied for a time in the atelier of M. Gerome, but joined the Carolus-Duran atelier, where he found the master's instruction more in line with his own artistic sympathies, and remained a pupil there until 1877. He had meanwhile exhibited pictures at the Salon. Returning to New York, he was one of the founders of the Society of American Artists in 1878. In 1890 he was elected a National Academician. Portraits and such subject pictures as the beautiful classical composition "The Portrait," with an occasional nude figure notable for graceful drawing and tender color, constituted his principal work for several years, but later on he gave much time to mural painting. Mr. Low is widely known as an illustrator through his beautiful drawings for the editions de luxe of Keats' "Lamia" and "Sonnets," and enjoys a literary reputation from his contributions to the magazines on art topics. *Address*, Lawrence Park, Bronxville, N. Y.

LOWE, R. This man was working as a commercial engraver on copper in 1851, his office being at 104 Broadway, N. Y. He engraved diplomas, etc.

LOWELL, Orson. Painter and illustrator. Born in Wyoming, Ia., in 1871. Pupil of Vanderpoel and Grover at Art Institute of Chicago. Member: Society of Illustrators, 1901; Guild of Free Lance Artists; New Rochelle Artists' Association. Work: Drawings in Cincinnati Museum; La Crosse (Wisc.) Artists' Association; Maryland Institute, Baltimore; Mechanics' Institute, Rochester. *Address*, Astor Trust Bldg., 5th Ave., New York.

LOWENHEIM, F. Illustrator. Born in Berlin, Germany. Pupil of Kunst-Schule, Berlin; Art Institute of Chicago. Member: Society of Illustrators, 1911. *Address*, 303 Fifth Ave., New York, N. Y.

LOWNES, Caleb. Engraver. The *Pennsylvania Magazine*, Philadelphia, 1775, contains a fairly well-engraved line plate of a "New Plan of Boston Harbour," signed C. Lownes, Sculp.
This Caleb Lownes was a die-sinker and seal-cutter in business in Philadelphia, and was a prominent citizen of that city. In 1779, according to the Minutes of the Supreme Executive Council, he was paid £75 for cutting a seal for the Pennsylvania Board of Admiralty.

LUCAS, Albert P. Painter and sculptor. Born in Jersey City, N. J. Pupil of Hebert, Boulanger, Dagnan-Bouvert and Courtois in Paris. Elected Associate Member of the National Academy; Societé Nationale des Beaux Arts, Paris. Work: "October Breezes," National Gallery, Washington; "Ecstasy," marble figure, Metropolitan Museum, New York. *Address*, 1947 Broadway, New York, N. Y.

LUCAS, Jean W. Painter. Born in North Hagerstown, Md., in 1873. Pupil of Henri Daingerfield and Whittemore. Member: National Association of Women Painters and Sculptors; Penna. Society of Miniature Painters. Award: Honorable mention for miniatures, Panama-Pacific Exposition, San Fran-

cisco, 1915. *Address*, 418 Potomac Ave., Hagerstown, Md.

LUCE, Mrs. Laura H. Landscape painter. Born in Salem, N. Y., in 1845. Pupil of A. H. Wyant; C. B. Coman; H. B. Snell in New York. Member: National Academy of Women Painters and Sculptors. *Address*, 120 E. Main St., Titusville, Pa.

LUCE, Mrs. Marie Huxford. Painter. Born in Skaneateles, N. Y. Pupil of J. S. H. Keever in Holland; of Mr. and Mrs. Charles H. Woodbury in Boston. Member: New York Water Color Club; National Academy of Women Painters and Sculptors. *Address*, Skaneateles, N. Y.

LUDOVICI, Alice E. Miniature painter. Born in Dresden, Germany, in 1872. Of Italian and English descent. Pupil of Julius Ludovici in New York. Member: California Society of Miniature Painters. *Address*, 167 North Orange Grove Ave., Pasadena, Calif.

LUINI, Constant. Sculptor. Exhibited at Annual Exhibition of National Academy of Design, New York, 1925. *Address*, 3745 94th St., New York.

LUKEMAN, H. Augustus. Sculptor. Born in Richmond, Va., in 1872. Pupil of Launt Thompson and D. C. French in New York; École des Beaux Arts in Paris, under Falguiere. Elected Associate Member of the National Academy, 1909. Awarded bronze medal, St. Louis Exposition, 1904. Work: "McKinley," Adams, Mass., and Dayton, O.; "Manu," Appellate Court, New York; four figures for Royal Bank Bldg., Montreal; four figures, Brooklyn Institute Museum; Columbus Custom House; "Prof. Joseph Henry," Princeton University; "Kit Carson," Trinidad, Colo.; Straus Memorial, New York, 1915; U. S. Grant Memorial, San Diego, Calif.; "Franklin Pierce," Concord, N. H.; "Soldiers' Memorial," Red Hook Park, Brooklyn, N. Y. *Address*, 68 West 56th St., New York, N. Y.

LUKS, George. Painter. Born in Williamsport, Pa., in 1867. Pupil of Penna. Academy of Fine Arts and of the Dusseldorf Academy; also studied in Paris and London. *Address*, 141 East 57th St., New York, N. Y.

LUM, Mrs. Bertha. Painter and etcher. Born in Iowa. Pupil of Art Institute of Chicago; of Frank Holme and Anna Weston. Member: Calif. Society of Etchers; Asiatic Society of Japan; Alumni Art Institute of Chicago. Awarded: Silver medal, Panama-Pacific Exposition, San Francisco, 1915. Specialty, wood block prints. *Address*, 136 St. Anne Alley, Chinatown, San Francisco, Calif.

LUMSDON, Mrs. E. Christine. Painter. Born in Brooklyn, N. Y. Pupil of Carolus-

Duran, Henry Mosier, Childe Hassam and George de Forest Brush. Member: National Association of Women Painters and Sculptors; Society of Independent Artists. *Address*, Carnegie Studio, 154 West 57th St., New York, N. Y.

LUMIS, Harriet R. (Mrs. Fred W. Lumis). Painter. Born in Salem, Conn., in 1870. Pupil of Willis S. Adams; Leonard Ochtman; New York Summer School of Art; Hugh Breckenridge. Member: Conn. Academy of Fine Arts; Springfield Art League; Philadelphia Art Alliance. *Address*, 28 Bedford Road, Springfield, Mass.

LUND, Theodore. Miniature painter; flourished in New York, 1841–1844.

LUNDBERG, A. F. Painter. Exhibited "Lawn Party" at the Penna. Academy of the Fine Arts, Philadelphia, 1914. *Address*, 48 North Grant Ave., Columbus, Ohio.

LUNDBORG, Florence. Painter and illustrator. Born in San Francisco, Calif. Studied at Mark Hopkins Institute of Art; also in Paris and Italy. Painted mural panels for California Bldg., at Panama-Pacific Exposition. *Address*, Studio, Paris, France.

LUNDGREN, Martin. Mural painter. Born in Sweden in 1871. Pupil of Art Institute of Chicago. *Address*, 5242 Bernard St., Chicago, Ill.

LUNGREN, Ferdinand Harvey. Painter. Born in Toledo, Ohio, in 1857. He came to New York to study art at an early age. His best known painting was "Shadows on the Snow." He has also made many illustrations for the magazines.

LUPTON, Mrs. According to Dunlap, in his "History of the Arts," a Mrs. Lupton modelled and presented a bust of Governor Throop to the National Academy of Design.

LYBRAND, J. Engraver. About 1820, J. Lybrand neatly engraved in line a view of the Gilpin paper-mill, on Brandywine Creek, Pa., after a drawing by B. K. Fox. Possibly a little earlier than this he was engraving in connection with R. Campbell, of Philadelphia; these latter plates were also in line, but very simple in character.

LYMAN, Joseph. Painter. Born in Ohio in 1843. He visited Europe for study, and on his return to New York was elected an Associate Member of the National Academy of Design (1866). His most important paintings are "Summer Night," "Moonlight," "Sunset on the Maine Coast," and "Waiting for the Tide." He died in 1913.

LYMAN, S. S. Born in Massachusetts in 1813. He first painted portraits, and later landscapes. He worked largely in Hartford, Conn.

LYNCH, Anna. Miniature painter. Born in Elgin, Ill. He painted portraits of Joseph E. Gary and Arba E. Waterman. *Address*, 9 Tree Studio Bldg., Chicago, Ill.

LYND, J. Norman. Illustrator. Born in Northwood, Logan County, Ohio, in 1878. Member: Society of Illustrators, 1913. *Address*, New York Herald, New York, N. Y.

LYNN, Mrs. Katherine N. Painter. Exhibited at the 33d Annual Exhibition of National Association of Women Painters and Sculptors. *Address*, Nantucket, Mass.

M

M. (J.) AE: 14 Sculp. 1758. This early American engraver can not be identified by the compiler. The only evidence of his existence is a small quarto portrait of Frederick III of Prussia, "folded and inserted" in the New York Almanac for 1759; New York: Printed and Sold by Hugh Gaine at the Bible and Crown in Hanover Square. This print may be described as follows: Exceedingly rude line work with an attempt at stipple in the face. Vignette; half length in uniform, standing to right, face front, right hand on hip, left hand on hilt of sword resting on point; muzzle of cannon in right base. Inscription: "J. M. AE 14 sculp 1758 Frederick the Third The Great King of Prussia, Sold by J. Turner in Arch Street, Philadelphia."

MAAS, Jacob. Engraver. The only mention found of Jacob Maas is in connection with the engraving and sale of "Lafayette and Washington Badges" in 1824. The Philadelphia newspapers of that year contain conditions of sale of "their plates"; and this notice is signed jointly by "J. L. Frederick and Jacob Maas, Engravers."

MACAULEY, Charles R. Illustrator. Born in Canton, Ohio, in 1871. Executes cartoons and illustrations in the leading publications. *Address*, 82 West 12th St., New York.

MAC CAMERON, Robert Lee. Painter. Born in Chicago in 1866; died in New York in 1912. Figure and portrait painter. Pupil of Gerome and Collin in Paris. Awards: Honorable mention, Paris Salon, 1904; Third Class medal, Paris Salon, 1908; Legion of Honor, 1912. Elected Associate of the National Academy, 1910. Member: Paris Society of American Painters; International Society of Painters, Sculptors and Gravers, London; National Society of Portrait Painters, New York. Represented by ''Groupe D'Amis,'' painted 1907, and ''The Daughter's Return,'' at the Metropolitan Museum in New York.

MAC CORD, Mary. Painter. Exhibited water colors at Penna. Academy of Fine Arts, Philadelphia, 1925. Member of New York· Water Color Club. *Address*, 458 John St., Bridgeport, Conn.

MAC CORD, Charles William. Painter. Born in Allegheny City, Pa., in 1852. Self-taught. Work: ''Light on the Hills,'' Bridgeport Public Library; ''The Last Ray,'' Sea Side Club, Bridgeport. He died in 1923.

MAC CHESNEY, Clara Taggart. Painter. Born in Brownsville, Calif. Pupil of Virgil Williams, San Francisco; H. S. Mowbray and J. C. Beckwith of New York; also of Courtois and Girardot at Colarossi School, Paris, France. Exhibited, Paris Salon, 1896, 1898; Paris Exposition, 1900; bronze medal, Buffalo Exposition, 1901; St. Louis Exposition, 1904. Member: New York Water Color Club. *Address*, 15 W. 67th St., New York.

MAC DERMOTT, Stewart S. Painter. Exhibited at Annual Exhibition of National Academy of Design, New York, 1925. *Address*, 51 West 10th St., New York.

MAC DONALD, Arthur N. Engraver. Born in Attleboro, Mass., in 1866. Member: American Bookplate Society, 1919. Awards: Two first prizes, American Bookplate Society, 1919.

MAC DONALD, F. E. Painter and illustrator. Born in Kansas City, Mo., in 1896. Pupil of Roland Thomas, G. V. Millett, and of J. D. Patrick. *Address*, 4420 Norledge Place, Kansas City, Mo.

MAC DONALD, Harold L. Born in Manitowoc, Wisc., in 1861. He was a pupil of Boulanger and of Lefebvre in Paris. For many years he has been a resident of Washington, D. C., where he has maintained a high standard as a portrait painter; his portrait of

William Griffith is in the Capitol, Washington, D. C.

MAC DONALD, James Wilson Alexander. Sculptor. Born in Steubenville, Ohio. He started his art studies in 1840, and in 1849 went to New York. Among his busts are those of John Van Buren and Charles O'Connor. He was the possessor of Houdon's original model of Washington from which he made several bronze busts. He also painted a few portraits and landscapes.

MAC DONALL, Angus. Painter and illustrator. Born in St. Louis in 1876. Illustrator and cartoonist for *Life; Scribner's; American; Red Cross Magazine; Ladies' Home Journal; Harper's*. *Address*, Westport, Conn.

MAC DOWELL, Susan Hannah. Painter. Born in Philadelphia in 1851. Student at Pennsylvania Academy of Fine Arts. Pupil of Prof. C. Schussele and of Thomas Eakins. Her paintings are largely portraits, and are generally owned in Philadelphia where her professional life was spent.

MAC EWEN, Walter. Painter. Born in Chicago in 1860. Genre painter. Pupil of Cormon and of Robert-Fleury in Paris. Awards: Honorable mention, Paris Salon, 1886; silver medal, Paris Exposition, 1889; first class gold medal, Berlin, 1891; Lippincott prize, Penna. Academy of the Fine Arts, 1902; Harris prize, Chicago, 1902; gold medal, St. Louis Exposition, 1904; first medal, Liege Exposition, 1905. Elected Associate of National Academy, 1903. Member: Paris Society of American Painters; National Institute of Arts and Letters. Represented by ''An Ancester'' at the Corcoran Art Gallery, Washington, D. C. *Address*, Care of Century Association, 7 West 43d St., New York City.

MACFARLAN, Christina. Painter. Born in Philadelphia. He was a pupil of Chase and Breckenridge at Penna. Academy of Fine Arts. *Address*, Studio, 1805 Chestnut St., Philadelphia.

MACGILVARY, Norwood Hodge. Painter. Born in Bangkok, Siam, in 1874. Pupil of Davidson College; Mark Hopkins Institute, San Francisco; Myron Barlow; also of Laurens in Paris. Member: New York Water Color Club; Providence Water Color Club; Providence Art Club; New York Architectural League; Brooklyn Society of Etchers. Work: ''Twilight after Rain,'' National Gallery, Washington, D. C. *Address*, 4341 Andover Terrace, Pittsburgh, Pa.

MAC GINNIS, Henry R. Painter. Born in Martinsville, Ind., in 1875. Pupil of J. O. Adams and T. C. Steele, Indiana; also of Collin and Courtois in Paris. Award: Honorable mention, Royal Academy, Munich. Work: Mural painting, Memorial Room, Gregory School, Trenton, N. J. *Address,* School of Industrial Arts, State and Willow Sts., Trenton, N. J.

MAC INTOSH, Marion T. Painter. Born in Belfast, Ireland. Pupil of Heinrich Knirr and Henry B. Snell. Member: Philadelphia Art Alliance; Plastic Club, Philadelphia, Pa. *Address,* 291 Nassau St., Princeton, N. J.

MACK. Miniature painter, flourishing in 1834, in New York.

MACKALL, R. McGill. Painter and etcher. Born in Baltimore, Md., in 1889. Pupil of Laurens and of Miller in Paris. Has executed mural decorations. *Address,* The Charcoal Club, 1230 St. Paul St., Baltimore, Md.

MAC KAY, Edwin Murray. Painter. Born in Detroit, Mich. Pupil of Laurens, Blanche and Kenyon Cox. Member: Conn. Society of Artists. Work: Portraits of "Ex-Gov. Sleeper," Mich. State Capitol Bldg.; "Justice Ostrander," Mich. Supreme Court, Lansing, Mich. Drawings in New York Public Library. *Address,* 241 East Euclid Ave., Detroit, Mich.

MACKAY, William A. Mural painter and illustrator. Born in Philadelphia in 1878. Pupil of Constant and Laurens in Paris. Represented in Congressional Library and Freer Gallery, Washington, D. C. *Address,* 345 East 33d St., New York.

MACKENSIE, E. This accomplished engraver of portraits in the stipple manner came from England in 1833–34 to engrave for the "National Portrait Gallery." He remained in the United States, and was later employed in doing portrait work for the Methodist Book Concern, of New York.

MACKENZIE, Roderick. Painter, sculptor, illustrator and etcher. Born in England in 1865. Pupil of Constant, Laurens, Jules Lefebvre and of the École Nationale des Beaux Arts. *Address,* Art Studio School, Dauphin St., Mobile, Ala.

MACKINTOSH, Miss S. B. Miniature painter; flourished in Philadelphia in 1850.

MAC KILLOP, William. Painter. Born in Philadelphia. Pupil of St. Louis School of Fine Arts and of Laurens in Paris. Member of Allied Artists of America. *Address,* 938 Eighth Ave., New York.

MACKLOW, J. Engraver. A well-engraved portrait of Martha Washington, after the painting by Woolaston, is signed by this man about 1835; it is further inscribed as

"Engraved expressly for the Christian Family Annual."

MACKNIGHT, Dodge. Painter. Born in Providence, R. I., in 1860. Pupil of Cormon in Paris. Specialty, water colors, Fogg Museum, Cambridge, Mass., and in Gardiner collection, Boston, Mass. *Address,* East Sandwich, Mass.

MACKUBIN, Florence. Portrait and miniature painter. Born in 1866. She studied in France and Italy. Her portraits include "Gov. Lloyd Lowndes," Prof. Basil Gildersleeve and Prof. Marshall Elliott. Her miniatures are in the Walters Art Gallery, Baltimore. She died in Baltimore, Md., in 1918.

MAC LAUGHLIN, Donald Shaw. Etcher and painter. Born in Boston in 1876. Awarded medals for etchings. *Address,* 569 Fifth Ave., New York.

MAC LELLAN, Charles A. Painter and illustrator. Born in Canada in 1885. Pupil of Art Institute of Chicago and of Howard Pyle. *Address,* 1305 Franklin St., Wilmington, Del.

MAC LEOD, Alexander. Painter and etcher. Born in Canada in 1888. Member of the California Society of Etchers. *Address,* 638 Montgomery St., San Francisco, Calif.

MAC MONNIES, Frederick. Sculptor. Born in Brooklyn in 1863. Admitted to the studio of Augustus Saint Gaudens in 1880; worked four years studying at night in life classes of the Academy of Design and Art Students' League, New York; completed art education abroad at Munich and in the atelier of Falguiere in the École des Beaux Arts. Received 1st prize, National Academy of Design, 1884; École des Beaux Arts, Paris, 1886–87. Established his own studio in Paris, 1887. Honorable mention 1st figure, "Diana," Paris Salon; 2d medal, Salon, for statues of Nathan Hale, New York, and J. S. T. Stranahan, Brooklyn. Elected to National Academy in 1906. Member: American Academy of Arts and Letters; National Sculpture Society. Work: Three life-size bronze angels, St. Paul's Church, New York, 1899; Nathan Hale, City Hall Park, New York, 1891; James Samuel Thomas Stranahan, Prospect Park, Brooklyn; statue of Shakespeare, Congressional Library, 1898; army and navy groups of Soldiers and Sailors Arch, Prospect Park, Brooklyn, 1900; two groups of horses, Prospect Park, Brooklyn; equestrian statue of General Slocum, Brooklyn, 1900; equestrian statuette of Theodore Roosevelt, 1905; equestrian statue of General G. B. McClellan, Washington, 1906. *Address,* 20 W. 10th St., New York, N. Y.

MAC NEIL, Carol Brooks. Sculptor. Born in Chicago in 1871. Pupil of Art Institute and of Lorado Taft, Chicago, and of MacMonnies and Injalbert, Paris. Exhibited at Chicago Exposition, 1893; Paris Salons, 1894–95–1900; honorable mention, Paris Exposition, 1900; bronze medal, St. Louis Exposition, 1900; bronze medal, St. Louis Exposition, 1904. Member: National Sculpture Society; Society of Women Painters and Sculptors. *Address,* College Point, L. I., N. Y.

MAC NEIL, Hermon Atkins. Sculptor. Born in Chelsea, Mass., in 1866. Instructor at Art Institute of Chicago. Executed mural paintings at Chicago, Paris, Buffalo and St. Louis Expositions. Sculptor of McKinley Memorial, Columbus, Ohio; General Washington on Washington Arch, New York; has also made rather a specialty of Indian subjects. Elected Member of National Academy of Design in 1906. Member of National Sculpture Society. *Address,* College Point, L. I., N. Y.

MACOMBER, Mary L. Painter. Born in Fall River, Mass., in 1861. Student of Boston Museum Art School, and pupil of Duveneck. Member of the Boston Guild of Artists. She died in Boston in 1916.

MAC RAE, Elmer L. Painter. Born in New York in 1875. Pupil of Art Students' League of New York under Twachtman, Beckwith, Blum and Mowbray. Member: New York Water Color Club; American Painters and Sculptors; Pastelists; Greenwich Society of Artists. *Address,* Care of Montross Gallery, 550 Fifth Ave., New York.

MAC RAE, Emma Fordyce. Painter. Born in Vienna, Austria, in 1887. Pupil of Luis Mora; Robert Reid; Kenneth Hayes Miller. *Address,* 12 West 69th St., New York.

MACRUM, George H. Painter. Pupil of Art Students' League of New York. He is represented in the Penna. Academy of Fine Arts by "The Pile Driver"; in the Canadian National Gallery, Toronto, Canada, by "The Pardon on the Mountain." *Address,* 1302 Pacific St., Brooklyn, New York.

MACSOUD, Nicolas S. Miniature painter. Exhibited at the Penna. Academy of Fine Arts, Philadelphia, 1925. *Address,* 170 Fifth Ave., New York City.

MACY, Harriet. Painter. Born in Des Moines, Iowa. Pupil of Art Students' League, New York. *Address,* 1321 Twenty-eighth St., Des Moines, Ia.

MACY, William Starbuck. Born in New Bedford, Mass., in 1853. He studied art at the National Academy, New York, and at Munich. His best work represents familiar New England effects. He had studios in New York and New Bedford. Among his works

are "Edge of the Forest," "Winter Sunset," and "The Old Mill." He died in 1916.

MADEIRA, Clara N. Painter. Exhibited water colors at the Penna. Academy of Fine Arts, Philadelphia, 1925. *Address,* 2300 Pine St., Philadelphia, Pa.

MADSEN, Otto. Painter and illustrator. Born in Germany in 1882. He came to America as a young man, and has painted mural decorations in churches and office buildings in California. *Address,* 1700 East 15th St., Kansas City, Mo.

MAESCH, Ferdinand. Painter. Born in Germany in 1865. Studied in Germany and France. Represented in Surrogate Court, Kings County, N. Y., by portrait of Herbert T. Ketcham. He died in 1925.

MAGEE, James C. Landscape painter. Born in Brooklyn in 1846. Pupil of Penna. Academy of Fine Arts and of Chase in New York and of Robert Henri in Paris. He died in 1924. Represented in the Johnson collection in Philadelphia and the Lord Richmond collection, London.

MAGENIS, H. Portrait painter. He worked in Philadelphia in 1818.

MAGER, Gus. Painter. Exhibited at Penna. Academy of Fine Arts, Philadelphia, 1921, at "Exhibition of Paintings Showing Later Tendencies in Art." *Address,* 108 Glen Ave., Wyoming, N. J.

MAGIE, Mrs. Gertrude. Painter. Studied with Chase, and at Colarossi's studio in Paris. Specialty is portraiture. She has exhibited at the National Academy and elsewhere. *Address,* Princeton, N. J.

MAGONIGLE, Edith (Mrs.). Mural painter. Born in Brooklyn, N. Y., in 1877. She painted the frieze on the Administration Building, Essex Co., Newark, N. J. *Address,* 829 Park Ave., New York City.

MAGONIGLE, H. Van Buren. Painter. Born in New Jersey in 1867. Pupil of Vaux. Among his works: "Purple and Gold" and "Pattern in Violet and Gold." Elected an Associate Member of the National Academy. *Address,* 101 Park Ave., New York City.

MAGRATH, William. Born in Ireland in 1838. He came to America in youth. Member of National Academy of Design. He established his studio in Washington, D. C. Among his works are "Irish Peasantry," "Courtyard with Donkey," and the "Irish Interior." He died in 1918.

MAHIER, Edith. Painter. Born in Baton Rouge, La. Pupil of New York School of Fine Arts. Teaching in Department of Art, University of Oklahoma, Norman, Okla.

MAHONY, Felix. Painter and illustrator. Born in New York, N. Y. Pupil of Steinlen in Paris. Member: Washington Art Club; Beachcombers; Provincetown Artists' Association. Director of National School of Fine and Applied Art, Washington, D. C. *Address,* Conn. Ave. and M St., Washington, D. C.

MAIN, William. Engraver. Born in New York City. He practiced engraving there between 1821 and 1833. According to Wm. Dunlap, Main, as a young man, was taken to Italy by Mauro Gandolfi, who came to this country, in 1817, under contract to engrave Col. Trumbull's "Declaration of Independence." Gandolfi broke his contract and returned home the same year, and took Main with him under promise of teaching him engraving. For some reason not stated, Main was abandoned in Florence, and he then applied to Morghen and was admitted, and spent three years in the studio of that great master. This statement of Dunlap is supported by the fact that the peculiar engraving table brought by Main from Florence was for many years in the possession of James Smillie, in New York, and was always known among engravers as the "Morghen table."

In 1820 William Main returned to New York full of enthusiasm for his art. He eventually found employment and engraved a few portraits and book illustrations. William Main was one of the founders of the National Academy of Design in 1826; and he was a member of the class of engravers which included Durand, Danforth, Peter Maverick and C. C. Wright. He seems to have left New York in 1833, and died in 1876.

MAJOR, Ernest L. Painter. Born in Washington, D. C., in 1864. Pupil of Art Students' League of New York and of Boulanger and Lefebvre in Paris. Member: Boston Art Club. Instructor in Mass. Normal Art School, Boston. *Address,* Fenway Studios, Boston, Mass.

MAJOR, James Parsons. Engraver. Born at Frome, Somersetshire, England, in 1818; died at Somerville, N. J., 1900. Mr. Major came to the United States as a bank-note engraver in 1830. He resided in Brooklyn until 1872, and for over fifty-five years was in charge of the engraving and modeling department of what is now the American Bank-Note Co., of New York.

MAKIELSKI, Leon A. Painter. Born in Morris Run, Pa. Pupil of Art Institute of Chicago; Julien Academy, and Grande Chaumiere Academy in Paris. Award: The John

Quincy Adams travelling scholarship, Art Institute of Chicago. *Address,* 5 Geddes Ave., Ann Arbor, Mich.

MALBONE, Edward G. Miniature painter. Born in Newport, R. I., in 1777; received some instruction from a local scene painter, and painted in his sixteenth year a portrait of considerable merit; established himself in Boston as a miniature painter when about nineteen and formed a close friendship with Washington Allston; he afterward opened studios successively in New York and Philadelphia; in consequence of failing health, he removed with Allston, in the winter of 1800, to Charleston, S. C., where some of his best works were produced; he accompanied Allston to London in May 1801, and while there painted his largest and most celebrated miniature, "The Hours," now in the Providence Athenaeum—a group of three beautiful young girls representing the Past, the Present, and the Future. On returning to this country, Mr. Malbone chose Charleston for his permanent residence, visiting the North periodically. In 1806, his health still failing, he sought relief in Jamaica, and finding none, started home, but died on reaching Savannah, on his way to Newport, May 7, 1807. Malbone was the foremost American miniature painter. He also occasionally painted in oils and drew pastel portraits. One hundred and fifty-seven miniatures by him are listed in "Early American Portrait Painters in Miniature," by Theodore Bolton, N. Y., 1921.

MALCOM, James Peller. Engraver. Born in Philadelphia in 1767; died in England in 1815. Malcom began to engrave in Philadelphia prior to 1786, as he designed and engraved the frontispiece of the "Lyric Works of Horace" by John Parke, Philadelphia, 1786. Under the patronage of the Rev. Jacob Duche, Thomas Willing and other prominent citizens of Philadelphia, he was sent to England to study art, and he says in a memoir published in 1805 that he attended the Royal Academy course for three years. He did considerable engraving for English magazines during this time.

In 1792–93 he returned to Philadelphia, but finding little encouragement there for his art, he went back to England and resumed work for the *Gentleman's Magazine* and other English periodicals.

There is some confusion as to the spelling of his name. As an engraver and upon his earlier prints he signed his name Malcom; but as an author and upon his later prints he used the signature of "James Peller Malcolm F. A. S."

MALCOM, Thalia W. (Mrs. Donald C.). Painter. Born in New York City in 1883. Pupil of Randall Davey and Albert André. *Address,* 114 East 66th St., New York.

MALHAUPT, Frederick J. Painter. Exhibited at National Academy of Design, New York, 1925. *Address*, Gloucester, Mass.

MALLISON, Euphame C. Painter. Born in Baltimore, Md., in 1895. *Address*, Dobbs Ferry, N. Y.

MALLONEE, Miss Jo. Painter. Born in Stockton, N. Y., in 1892. Pupil of G. Bridgman. Member: Art Students' League of New York; League of New York Artists. *Address*, 39 West 39th St., New York, N. Y.

MALM, Gustav M. Painter and illustrator. Born in Svarttorp, Sweden, in 1869. Studied in Sweden. Member: Smoky Hill Art Club. Author and illustrator of "Charlie Johnson," a study of the Swedish emigrant. *Address*, Malm Studio, Lindsborg, Kan.

MALONE, Laetitia Herr (Mrs. John E.). Painter and illustrator. Born in Lancaster, Pa., in 1881. Pupil of Chase, Mora, Beaux, Anshutz and McCarter at Penna. Academy of Fine Arts. Member: Penna. Academy of Fine Arts; Philadelphia Art Alliance. *Address* Lancaster, Pa.

MANDL, A. Painter. Born in Munich in 1894. Pupil of Daniel Garber and LeRoy Ireland. Member: Fellowship, Penna. Academy of Fine Arts.

MANGRAVITE, Poppino J. Painter. Born in Italy in 1896. He came to New York as a youth and studied art in Brooklyn. *Address*, 9 East 59th St., New York.

MANIGAULT, E. Middleton. Painter. Born in London, Ontario, Can., in 1887. Pupil of Kenneth Hayes Miller. *Address*, 130 West 57th St., New York, N. Y.

MANLEY, Thomas R. Etcher and painter. Born in Buffalo, New York, in 1853. Pupil of Penna. Academy of Fine Arts. Member: National Art Club; New York Water Color Club. Award: Bronze medal for etchings, St. Louis Exposition, 1904. Work: Represented in Montclair Art Association, and in the Yale Club, New York. *Address*, 38 St. Luke's Place, Montclair, N. J.

MANLY, John. The only evidence of this man as an engraver is found in an etched portrait of Washington, executed after 1789. Manly is said to have been a die-sinker, and apparently flourished about 1800.

In an advertisement in the *Freeman's Journal*, Philadelphia, 1790, "an Artist" proposes "a subscription for a medal of George Washington." Subscriptions were received at Wilmington by Peter Rynberg, and in Philadelphia by J. Manly, "in the care of Robert Patton, Postmaster." This would indicate that Manly

was then in Philadelphia—if he were not the "artist" referred to. In 1772 he was painting portraits in Virginia, but they are crude and of little merit.

MANN, Jack. Painter. Exhibited at National Academy of Design, New York, in 1925. *Address*, 15 East 14th St., New York.

MANN, Parker. Painter. Born in Rochester, N. Y., in 1852. Studied at École des Beaux Arts, Paris. Engaged as landscape painter in Washington most of the time from 1887–98; in New York, 1899–1906. Spent several years painting in England, France, Holland, Switzerland, Italy and Spain. He died on Dec. 15th, 1918.

MANNHEIM, Jean. Painter. Born in Krenznach, Germany, 1862. Pupil of École Delecluse, Paris; Academy of Colarossi; London School of Art. Exhibited in Salon, Paris; National Academy, New York. Gold medal, Seattle Expostion; gold and silver medals, San Diego Exposition, 1915. *Address*, 500 Arroyo Drive, Pasadena, Calif.

MANOIR, Irving K. Painter and illustrator. Born in Chicago, Ill., in 1891. Pupil of Wellington Reynolds, H. M. Walcott, and of the Art Institute of Chicago. Member: Chicago Society of Artists; Chicago Art Club. Work: "Blue Hills," in Joliet, Ill., Public Library; mural decoration in Vincennes, Ind., High School. Teacher at Chicago Art Institute. *Address*, 4 East Ohio St.; 821 North Trumbull Ave., Chicago, Ill.

MANON, Estelle Ream. Painter. Born in Lincoln, Ill., in 1884. Pupil of William M. Chase and Charles W. Hawthorne. Member: St. Joseph Art League; Oklahoma Art League. Head of art department, Oklahoma City High School. *Address*, 716½ Tely St., St. Joseph, Mo.

MANSFIELD, Blanche McManus (Mrs. Francis Miltoun). Illustrator and painter. Born in East Feliciana, La., 1870. Studied in Paris. Specialty, book and periodical illustration. Author of "The American Woman Abroad," "Our French Cousins," etc. *Address*, 9 Rue Falguiere, Paris, France.

MANSFIELD, Louise B. Painter and illustrator. Born in Le Roy, N. Y., in 1876. Pupil of Art Students' League of New York. Member: National Association of Women Painters and Sculptors; Brooklyn Society of Artists; Brooklyn Water Color Club; Art Students' League of New York. *Address*, 368 Hancock St., Brooklyn, N. Y.

MANSHIP, Paul. Sculptor. Born in St. Paul, Minn., in 1885. Member: National Sculpture Society, 1912. Elected Associate Member of the National Academy, 1914; National Academy, 1916. Awards: American Academy in Rome scholarship 1909–12; Widener gold medal, Penna. Academy of Fine Arts, 1914. Work: "Centaur and Nymph," Metropolitan Museum, New York; "The Duck Girl" (bronze fountain), Fairmount Park, Philadelphia; "Centaur and Dryad" and "Flight of Night," Detroit Institute of Arts; "Indian and Pronghorn Antelope" and "Dancing Girl and Fawns," Art Institute of Chicago; "Dancer and Gazelles," Cleveland Museum; Luxembourg, Paris; also Corcoran Gallery of Art, Washington, D. C.; designer of Civic Forum medal; J. P. Morgan Memorial, Metropolitan Museum of Art. *Address*, 42 Washington Mews, New York, N. Y.

MANY, Alexis B. Painter. Born in Indianapolis, Ind., in 1879. Member of Washington Society of Artists. *Address*, 826 Connecticut Ave., Washington, D. C.

MAPES, James Jay. Amateur miniature painter. Born in 1806. He is noted by William Dunlap in his "History of the Arts of Design." From 1835 to 1838 he was "Professor of Chemistry and Natural Philosophy of Colors," at the National Academy. He died in 1866.

MARAFFI, Luigi. Sculptor. Born in Italy in 1891. Pupil of Grafly. Executed bronze portrait of E. T. Stotesbury in Drexel Bank, Philadelphia. *Address*, 1311 Christian St., Philadelphia.

MARAS, M. French miniature artist who flourished in New York from 1800 to 1802; he later went to Constantinople and became painter to the Sultan.

MARBLE, John Nelson. Painter. Born in 1855. He studied in France and Italy. He painted portraits of Bishop Phillips Brooks, Judge Henry E. Howland and Mary Baker Eddy. He died in Woodstock, Vt., in 1918.

MARCHANT, B. The only engravings known by Marchant are line illustrations in "The Narrative of Capt. James Riley," published in New York in 1816.

MARCHANT, Edward D. Born in Edgartown, Mass., in 1806. He painted portraits in Philadelphia and New York for many years. He also resided in Nashville, Tenn. He settled in Phila. in 1845. He first exhibited in 1829 at the National Academy of Design. He was a member of the Union League Club of Phila. where several of his portraits are owned. He died in Asbury Park, New Jersey, in 1887. In 1833 he was elected an Associate Member of the National Academy.

MARCHANT, G. W. Engraver. He was working in Albany in 1834.

MARCUS, Peter. Painter and etcher. Born in New York City in 1889. Pupil of École des Beaux Arts in Paris. *Address*, 30 West 59th St., New York City.

MARE, John. Portrait painter. He is recorded in the city of New York as a "Limner." He painted the portrait of Robert Monckton, Governor of New York in 1761; he signed his portrait of John Ketelas "Jno. Mare Pinxt, 1767." Three other portraits painted by him in 1766, 1767 and 1768 have been identified.

MARE, John De. Engraver. Born in Belgium, he belonged to a noble and ancient family, and was himself a highly cultivated man. It is not known where he learned to engrave; but he appeared in New York about 1850, and engraved in line a few admirable book illustrations. He is said to have returned to Europe about 1861.

MARGULIES, Pauline. Sculptor. Born in New York in 1895. Pupil of Eberle, Brewster and Fraser. *Address*, Cooper Hall, 20 East 7th St., New York City.

MARIE-TERESA, (Sister). Painter. Born in Stillwater, Minn., in 1877. Pupil of New York School of Art, and of Robert Henri; also studied in Florence, Italy. *Address*, College of St. Catharine, St. Paul, Minn.

MARIN, John. Painter and etcher. Born in Rutherford, N. J., in 1875. Pupil of Penna. Academy of Fine Arts. Represented by "Mills of Meaux," owned by the French Government, "Falling Leaves," in San Francisco Art Museum. *Address*, 291 Fifth Ave., New York.

MARK, Louis. Painter. Born in Hungary in 1867. Pupil of Bouguereau and Robert-Fleury. Represented in Buffalo Fine Arts Academy. *Address*, 130 West 57th St., New York.

MARKS, William. Illustrator, of Calumet, Mich., died Sept. 7, 1906.

MARKHAM, Charlotte H. Painter. Born in Wisconsin in 1892; pupil of Art Institute of Chicago. *Address*, 704 Marshall St., Milwaukee, Wis.

MARKHAM, Marion E. Painter. Born in Syracuse, N. Y., in 1875. Pupil of Chase. Represented by "Girl in Red" and "Portrait of a child," at Syracuse Museum of Fine Arts. *Address*, 430 La Fayette St., New York.

MARR, Carl. Painter and illustrator. Born in Milwaukee, Wis., in 1858. Studied abroad. Represented by "Dusk," Museum of Art, Toledo, "Gossip" and "The Mystery of Life," Metropolitan Museum, New York. *Address*, Royal Academy, Munich, Bavaria.

MARS, Ethel. Painter and engraver. Born in Sprinfield, Ill. Specialty, colored woodblock prints. *Address*, Paris, France.

MARSAC, Harvey. This name appears as an ''engraver'' in the New York Directory for 1834. As no work signed by him has been found by the compiler, it can not be positively stated that he engraved on copper.

MARSCHENER, Arthur A. Painter and etcher. Born in Detroit, Mich., in 1884. Pupil of J. P. Wicker. Member: Chicago Society of Etchers. *Address*, 1720 Field Ave., Detroit, Mich.

MARSH, Mrs. Alice Randall. Miniature painter. Born in Coldwater, Mich. Pupil of Art Institute of Chicago; also of Merson, Collin, Whistler and MacMonnies in Paris. Member: American Society of Miniature Painters. *Address*, Nutley, New Rochelle, N. Y.

MARSH, Charles H. Painter and etcher. Born in Magnolia, Ia., in 1885. Pupil of W. V. Cahill, Guy Rose, Clarence Hinckle, and of the Stickney Memorial School of Pasadena. Member: California Art Club; Laguna Beach Artists' Association. *Address*, Care of College of Fine Arts, University of Redlands, Redlands, Calif.

MARSH, Fred Dana. Painter. Born in Chicago, Ill., in 1872. Student of Chicago Art Institute. Elected Associate of National Academy. Has executed many mural paintings. *Address*, Wykagyi Park, New Rochelle, N. Y.

MARSH, Henry. Wood engraver. His work appeared in ''The Riverside Magazine'' published by Hurd & Houghton. He also executed the splendidly engraved wood-cuts of insects in Harris' ''Insects Injurious to Vegetation.'' This work of patience, and requiring remarkable eyesight, shows also true artistic skill, and evidences the great talent of the engraver.

MARSH, Mary E. Painter. Born in Cincinnati, Ohio. Pupil of Birger and Sandzen, Chicago Academy of Fine Arts; also of Cincinnati Art Academy. Member: California Art Club; Laguna Beach Art Association. Assistant Art Curator, Los Angeles Museum, Calif. *Address*, 1089½ W. 35th Place, Los Angeles, Calif.

MARSH, William R. Was engraving vignettes, advertising cards, etc., in New York, from 1833–43.

MARSHALL. In Judge Marshall's ''Life of George Washington,'' published by C. P. Wayne, Philadelphia, 1804–07, one of the illustrative maps is signed ''Marshall Sct.'' This map represents the relative positions of the American and British forces prior to the Battle of White Plains, Oct. 28, 1776.

16

MARSHALL, Frank H. Painter. Born in England in 1866. Pupil of Art Students' League of New York; Chase School, New York; Julien Academy in Paris, under Laurens; also studied in Madrid and London. *Address*, P. O. Box 418, Jamestown, N. Y.

MARSHALL, Frank W. Painter and illustrator. Born in Providence, R. I., in 1866. Pupil of R. I. School of Design; Julien Academy, Paris. Member: Providence Art Club; Providence Water Color Club. Instructor of drawing at Rhode Island School of Design; art editor for Providence Journal. *Address*, 652 Angell St., Providence, R. I.

MARSHALL, Thomas W. Landscape and genre painter. Born in 1850, he died in 1874. Exhibited at National Academy, 1871, ''Near Bellows Falls.'' His work showed much promise.

MARSHALL, William Edgar. Painter and engraver. Born in New York in 1837; died in New York, 1906. Employed by the American Bank Note Company in 1858, but subsequently painted portraits in oil and engraved large portraits in line. He settled in Boston, but in 1864–66 traveled in Europe, residing chiefly in Paris, where he exhibited in the Salons of 1865 and 1866. Established a studio in New York in 1866. Among his more noteworthy achievements have been engravings after Stuart's ''Washington'' and Da Vinci's portrait of Christ; his heroic ideal painting of Christ, which he also engraved; also engravings of many distinguished persons, including Lincoln, Longfellow, Cooper, Beecher, Grant, Sherman, Blaine, Hancock, Garfield, Harrison, McKinley, and Roosevelt, most of which were reproduced from oil paintings by himself. Represented at the National Gallery, in Washington, D. C., by his portrait of Henry Wadsworth Longfellow, and self-portrait at the age of 23.

MARSIGLIA, Gerlando. Portrait painter. Born in Italy in 1792, he arrived in New York about 1817. In 1826 he was elected a member of the National Academy of Design. His copy of the portrait of General Von Steuben after Robert Edge Pine is owned by the City of New York. He died in 1850.

MARSTON, J. B. Portrait painter, who worked in Boston in 1807. His portrait of Gov. Caleb Strong is in the Massachusetts Historical Society.

MARTIN. Portrait draughtsman in crayons. Martin was an Englishman who came from Sheffield to New York about 1797. Although his work was poor it was in steady demand, and he worked there until 1808.

MARTIN, Charles. Portrait painter. He flourished about 1850, in Bristol, Rhode Island. In 1851 he exhibited at the National Academy in New York.

MARTIN, D. He engraved at least one portrait, and also some of the maps found in *The Monthly Military Repository*, published by G. Smith, New York, 1796. These are maps of military operations during the Revolution.

MARTIN, E. In 1826 this man was engraving buildings, etc., for Cincinnati publishers.

MARTIN, Edna M. Painter. Born in Seekonk, Mass., in 1896. Pupil of Rhode Island School of Design. *Address*, 227 Fall River Ave., Seekonk, Mass.

MARTIN, Homer D. Painter. Born in Albany, N. Y., in 1836. He studied painting with William Hart, at the National Academy. In 1875 he was elected a National Academician, and in 1878 was one of the founders of the Society of American Artists. His early work followed the conventional lines of the Hudson River School, and he was the first to break away from mannerisms and artificiality, becoming, in a sense, the first American impressionist. Martin's landscapes are invariably fine in ensemble, and are generally sober and subdued in color. They are full of genuine sentiment, and impress the spectator by the charm of their poetic naturalism. His noted works, such as "Normandy Trees," "Adirondack Scenery," "River Scene" (Metropolitan Museum, New York) and "Old Church in Normandy," are among the most individual productions of American Art, and his work as a whole occupies a place by itself owing to its intrinsic beauty and admirable personal quality. He died in 1897.

MARTIN, J. B. Engraver. Several stipple portraits, fairly well engraved, and published in Richmond, Va., in 1822, are signed "Engraved by J. B. Martin, Richm'd."
Martin claimed to be an artist; and he drew upon stone a good quarto portrait of John Randolph, of Roanoke. This lithograph was printed by Cephas G. Childs, but is signed as "Drawn on Stone & Published by J. B. Martin, Richm'd."

MARTIN, Robert. In 1860 this man produced some excellent line illustrations for Cooper's works, published in New York.

MARTIN, William A. K. Marine painter. Born in Philadelphia in 1817. He studied painting abroad, and portraiture under John Neagle, in Philadelphia. The Wilstach Collection in Fairmount Park owns his picture "Bruce Defending the Path at Delrey." He painted many of the old "men-of-war" of the U. S. Navy. He died in Philadelphia in 1867.

MARTINEZ, Xavier. Painter and etcher. Born in Mexico in 1874. Pupil of Mark Hopkins Institute in San Francisco, and of Gerome

in Paris. *Address*, 816 Scenic Ave., Piedmont, Calif.

MARTINO, Michel. Sculptor. Born in Alvignano, Casserta, Italy, in 1889. Pupil of Lee Lawrie and H. Kitson. Award: English Fellowship prize of Yale University. Work: "Landing of Pilgrims," "Battle of Lexington," Strong School, New Haven; White Plains High School Memorial Tablet. *Address*, 1931 Broadway, New York, N. Y.

MARTINY, Philip. Sculptor. Born in Alsace, then France, in 1858; he came to America in the early eighties. Pupil of Eugene Dock in France; Augustus Saint Gaudens in United States. Elected Associate Member of National Academy 1902. Member: New York Architectural League. Work: Doors for St. Bartholomew's Church, New York; McKinley Monument, Springfield, Mass.; Soldiers and Sailors Monument, Jersey City, N. J.; portrait statue of ex-Vice-President G. A. Hobart, Paterson, N. J.; sculpture in Hall of Records, New York; two groups in Chamber of Commerce, New York. *Address*, 400 West 23d St., New York, N. Y.

MARULIS, Athan. Painter. Born in Athens, Greece, in 1889. Pupil of Manos; Paul M. Gustin; Yasushi Tanaka. Member: Seattle Fine Arts Society. *Address*, 211 Fourth Ave., North Seattle, Wash.

MARWEDE, Richard L. Painter. Born in New York, N. Y., in 1884. Pupil of Art Students' League of New York. Member: Art Students' League of New York; Art Alliance of America. *Address*, 976 Anderson Ave., New York, N. Y.

MASE, C. C. Landscape painter. Born in Matteawan, N. Y. Pupil of J. H. Twachtman. Member: Conn. Academy of Fine Arts; National Association of Women Painters and Sculptors. *Address*, 396 Genesee St., Utica, N. Y.

MASON, Abraham John. English engraver. Born in 1794. He was best known for his wood engraving. He came to this country with his family in 1829, and settled in New York, and the following year he was elected an Associate of the National Academy of Design, and professor of wood engraving; he also lectured on this subject in Boston. Mason finding his occupation unprofitable returned to London in 1839. He died in England.

MASON, Alva. Engraver. About 1819 the firm of W. & A. Mason advertised as "Engravers of brass ornaments for book-binding etc.; charter and Patent Medicine Seals, Embossing plates and Brass Engraving for Typographical Printing." Their establishment was located at No. 15 South 4th St., Philadelphia. It is not known that this firm did any copperplate engraving.

MASON, C. D. Sculptor. Born in France in 1830; came to New York in 1860. He worked in New York, Philadelphia, and in Chicago. He died in 1915.

MASON, Eleanor. Miniature painter. Exhibited at the Penna. Academy of Fine Arts, Philadelphia, 1925. *Address*, 871 Beacon St., Boston, Mass.

MASON, D. H. The Philadelphia directories of 1805–18 contain the name of D. H. Mason, "music-engraver." In 1816 he executed vignettes for the bank-note engraving firm of Murray, Draper, Fairman Co., of the same city, and in 1830 Mason signed a certificate as "Architect and Engraver."

MASON, George. Limner and crayon portrait draughtsman. He inserted an advertisement in the Boston *Chronicle* for June, 1768, stating that he drew "portraits in crayon for two guineas each."

MASON, John. Painter and designer. Born in New York, N. Y., in 1868. Pupil of Julien Academy in Paris under Laurens. Award: Bronze medal, Paris Exposition, 1889. Work: Decoration of dining room of Harmonic Club, New York; "Portrait of Admiral Dewey" and "Portrait of Major S. Ellis Briggs" in Armory, New York City. *Address*, 1502 North 17th St., Philadelphia, Pa.

MASON, Jonathan, Jr. Portrait painter, who lived in Mt. Vernon St., Boston. Exhibited portraits and figure subjects 1828–34 at the Boston Athenaeum, among them his own portrait.

MASON, Mary Stoddert. Sculptor. Born in Jackson, Tenn. Principal works, "Pilgrim Mother," "The Spirit of the New Era," and "Woman Triumphant." *Address*, Elmsford, Westchester County, N. Y.

MASON, Mary Stuard (Mrs.). Painter. Born in Zanesville, Ohio, in 1886. Pupil of Penna. Academy of Fine Arts, under Chase and Breckenridge. *Address*, 8233 Seminole Ave., Chestnut Hill, Philadelphia.

MASON, Maud M. Painter. Born in Russellville, Ky., in 1867. Pupil of Chase, Dow and Snell in New York and of Brangwyn in London. *Address*, 18 East 9th St., New York.

MASON, Robt. L. Illustrator. Born in Knoxville, Tenn., in 1874. Pupil of Howard Pyle, and illustrator for *Harper's. Address*, 230 East Church Ave., Knoxville, Tenn.

MASON, R. M. Painter. Exhibited at Annual Exhibition of the Penna. Academy of Fine Arts, Philadelphia, 1924. *Address*, Batavia, New York.

MASON, (W.) Sanford. Painter, engraver and copyist. He was working in Philadelphia about 1865. He made several copies of "The Washington Family, at Mount Vernon" after the painting by Savage.

MASON, William A. Painter and instructor. Born in Cambridge, Mass., in 1855; died in Philadelphia in 1920. Director of art education in the public schools of Philadelphia.

MASON, William G. This line-engraver of buildings, etc., was located in Philadelphia in 1822–45, except during the years 1823–29. He made the illustrations for Joshua Shaw's "U. S. Architecture," and for other publications by the same author. Judging from the excellence of line vignettes done by Mason for billheads, etc., he was probably chiefly engaged in bank-note work.

MASSON, Emile. Crayon portrait draughtsman who was working in Boston, Mass., 1852–1856.

MAST, Josephine. Painter. Exhibited water colors at the Penna. Academy of Fine Arts, Philadelphia, 1925. *Address*, 140 Halsey St., Brooklyn, New York.

MASTERS, Frank B. Illustrator. Born in Watertown, Mass., in 1873. Pupil of Howard Pyle. *Address*, 1 Morris Crescent, Yonkers, N. Y.

MATHEWS, Arthur Frank. Painter. Born in Wisconsin in 1860. Studied under Gustave Boulanger in Paris. He reorganized the Calif. School of Design (San Francisco Art Association) and continued as director until April, 1906. Exhibited at Paris Exposition; Paris Salons; Chicago Exposition, 1893; San Francisco Exposition, 1915. Principal work: 12 panels in State Capitol, Sacramento; Oakland Library; Lane Library, and Children's Hospital, San Francisco, etc. Honorable member of Art Association of San Francisco and of the Athenian Club. *Address*, 670 Fell St., San Francisco, Calif.

MATHEWS, Ferdinand S. Painter and illustrator. Born in New Brighton, N. Y., in 1854. Pupil of Cooper Institute, N. Y. Specialty, water colors, flowers, landscape and illumination. *Address*, 17 Frost St., Cambridge, Mass.

MATHEWS, Mrs. L. K. Painter and illustrator. Born in San Francisco, Calif., in 1872. Pupil of Whistler. *Address*, 670 Fell St., San Francisco.

MATHEWSON, Frank C. Painter. Born in Barrington, R. I., in 1862. Pupil of Laurens in Paris. Represented by "Ogunquit Pastures," at Rhode Island School of Design,

Providence, R. I., and "The Weisser Thurm," at Boston Art Club. *Address,* 29 Waterman St., Providence, R. I.

MATHUS, Henry. Lithographer. Member of the Providence Water Color Club. *Address,* 39 Henry St., Edgewood, Providence, R. I.

MATTERSON, Tomkins H. Born in Peterborough, N. Y., in 1813. In 1839 he began to paint portraits of merit, and was brought into notice by his "Spirit of '76" purchased by the American Art Union. His work was chiefly portraiture and historical painting. He became an Associate Member of the National Academy of Design in 1847. He died in 1884.

MATTHEWS, Anna L. Sculptor and painter. Born in Chicago, Ill. Pupil of the Chicago Art Institute, and of Simon and Garrido in Paris. *Address,* 6016 Ellis Ave., Chicago.

MATTHEWS, George Bagby. Painter. Born in Tappahannock, Va., in 1857. Studied art abroad, 1880–83; pupil of Carolus Duran, Paris. Among his historical paintings are "Lee and His Generals," "The Crucifixion," "Jefferson Davis," "John Paul Jones," "Stonewall Jackson," "Lee," "Daughter of the Confederacy," "Gen. Tyler," "Patrick Henry," General Joe Wheeler," "Colonel John S. Mosby," "Battle of the Merrimac with the Monitor," "Last of the Wooden Navy." *Address,* Washington, D. C.

MATTHEWS, William. Portrait painter. Born in Bristol, England, in 1821, he died in Washington, D. C., in 1905.

MATTHEWS, William F. Painter. Born in St. Louis, Mo., in 1878. Pupil of St. Louis School of Fine Arts. *Address,* 643 West 215th St., New York.

MATTOCKS, Muriel. Painter and illustrator. Born in Hastings, Nebr. Pupil of M. C. Carr, John S. Ankeney, Birger Sandzen and of the Art Institute of Chicago. *Address,* 4106 Lark St., San Diego, Calif.

MATZAL, Leopold C. Painter. Exhibited at the Annual Exhibition of the National Academy of Design, 1925. *Address,* Hoboken, N. J.

MATZEN, Herman N. Sculptor. Born in Denmark in 1861. Pupil of Munich and Berlin Academies of Fine Art. Member: National Sculptors' Society; National Art Club; Cleveland Society of Artists. Work: "War" and "Peace," Indianapolis Soldiers and Sailors Monument; "Schiller Monument," Detroit; "Law" and "Justice," Akron, Ohio, County Court House; "Wagner Monument," Cleveland; Burke Mausoleum; "Moses" and "Gregory," Cleveland Court House. *Address,* Cleveland School of Art, Cleveland, Ohio.

MATZKE, Albert. Painter and illustrator. Born in Indianapolis, Ind., in 1882. Pupil of Art Students' League of New York under Du Mond and George Bridgman. *Address,* 244 West 14th St., New York, N. Y.

MAUCH, Max. Sculptor. He has exhibited at the National Sculpture Society, New York. He died in Chicago, Ill., in 1864.

MAUNSBACH, Hans E. Painter. Born in Sweden in 1890. He has painted portraits in America. *Address,* 156 East 39th St., New York.

MAURER, Alfred H. Painter. Born in New York City in 1868. Pupil of National Academy of Design; he also studied in Paris. Represented in Memorial Hall, Philadelphia, by "The Peacock." *Address,* 404 West 43d St., New York.

MAURER, Louis. Painter, who lived in New York and worked for Currier & Ives. His specialty was sporting and racing prints. He was a great admirer of a horse, and has handed down to us today all the celebrated racing horses of his time.

MAURY, Cornelia Field. Painter. Born in New Orleans, La. Pupil of St. Louis School of Fine Arts; Julien Academy in Paris. Represented in City Art Museum and Public Library, St. Louis. *Address,* 5815 Pennsylvania Ave., St. Louis, Mo.

MAURER, Alfred H. Painter. Born in New York in 1868. Pupil of National Academy of Design under Ward; also studied in Paris. Represented in Memorial Hall Museum, Philadelphia, Pa. *Address,* 404 West 43d St., New York, N. Y.

MAUVAIS, A. Portrait painter in oil and miniatures, flourishing in 1776 in Savannah, Georgia. An excellent example of his work is the miniature of Maj. John Gedney Clark (1737–1784), a British Army officer, which is in the collection of the Essex Institute, Salem, Mass.

MAVERICK, Maria A. and Emily. Engravers. These two daughters of Peter Maverick, of New York, separately engraved several admirable stipple illustrations for an edition of Shakespere, published about 1830.

Ann Maverick, a daughter of Dr. Alexander Anderson and the wife of Andrew Maverick, was a capital wood-engraver at a somewhat later period.

Two other members of the Maverick family, Octavia and Catherine, were engaged in art work; the first named was a teacher of drawing in the Packard Institute, of Brooklyn; the other held a similar position in Madame Willard's School, in Troy, N. Y.

MAVERICK, Peter. Engraver. Born in New York in 1780; died there in 1831. Peter Maverick was the son and pupil of Peter Rushton Maverick, one of the early engravers of New York. In 1802 Peter Maverick was in business in New York as an engraver; but at a later period he removed to Newark, N. J., where he was the preceptor, and in 1817 the partner, of A. B. Durand. Maverick returned to New York and there conducted an extensive establishment as a general engraver and copperplate printer, and to this business he finally added lithography. Peter Maverick was one of the founders of the National Academy of Design in 1826, and the "Historic Annals of the Academy" refer to him as excelling in "letter engraving and bank-note work." A portrait of Peter Maverick is in existence painted by John Neagle.

MAVERICK, Peter, Jr. All that is known of this man is that he was a son of Peter Maverick, and the New York directories for 1832–45 give his occupation as "engraver and lithographer."

MAVERICK, Peter Rushton. Engraver. Born in New York in 1755: died in Newark, N. J., 1811. Peter Rushton Maverick was probably originally a silversmith and he advertised in the New York papers of the day that he was in the engraving, seal sinking, and copperplate printing business, and also engraved the tea table ware.

As an engraver on copper his work was generally poor in execution, his best work being book-plates. In 1788 he represented the engravers of his city in the Federal Procession of that year. Peter R. Maverick had three sons—Samuel, Andrew and Peter. Samuel and Peter were also engravers and plate printers, and Andrew published prints in connection with Cornelius Tiebout.

MAVERICK, Samuel. This name is signed as engraver to book illustrations published in New York in 1824. The New York directories call Samuel Maverick a "copperplate printer," in 1805, and in 1819–37 the occupation becomes "Engraver and Copperplate printer." The name appears in these directories until 1847.

MAXON, Charles. The New York directory for 1833 contains this name as "engraver." No copperplate is known so signed.

MAXWELL, Guida B. Painter. Born in Philadelphia in 1896. Pupil of Fred Wagner. Member: Plastic Club; Philadelphia Art Alliance. *Address*, 180 Manheim St., Germantown, Philadelphia, Pa.

MAY, Beulah. Sculptor. Born in Hiawatha, Kans., in 1883. Pupil of Lorado Taft; Wm. Chase; Charles Grafly. Member: Calif. Art Club; West Coast Arts Society. *Address*, Fruit and Mabury Sts., Santa Ana, Calif.

MAY, Edward Harrison. Painter. Born in England in 1824, he came to America as a boy of ten. He studied under Daniel Huntington, and his early work met with fair success in New York in the days of the Art Union. He studied abroad, and came back to America for visits, and finally died in Paris. The Union League Club of New York owns several of his portraits. He died in 1887.

MAY, Phil. Painter and illustrator. He was born in 1864, and died in 1903. He illustrated many books, magazines and other publications in New York.

MAYER, Bela. Painter. Exhibited at the Annual Exhibition of National Academy of Design, 1925. *Address*, 366 Fifth Ave., New York.

MAYER, Constant. Painter. Born in France in 1832. He studied under Cogniet, and came to New York in 1857. He was elected an Associate of the National Academy in 1866; he was also a member of the American Art Union. Mr. Mayer was best known for his genre pictures but he has painted portraits of Gen'l Grant, Gen'l Sherman and many other prominent men. He died in 1911.

MAYER, Frank Blackwell. Painter. Born in Baltimore, Maryland, in 1827; died in 1899. Portrait and genre painter. Pupil of Alfred Miller in Baltimore, and of Gleyre and Brion in Paris. Painted in Paris, 1864–69. Medal and Diploma, Philadelphia, 1876; Medal of Maryland Institute. Represented by "Leisure and Labor," at the Corcoran Gallery.

MAYER, H. Caricaturist. Born at Worms-on-Rhine, Germany, in 1868. He was the son of a London merchant, and came to the United States in 1886. Work: "Impressions of the Passing Show," New York *Times*; editor-in-chief of *Puck*. Contributor to many weeklies in the United States and Europe; originator of "Travelaughs" for moving pictures. *Address*, 15 West 67th St., New York, N. Y.

MAYER, Kasper. Sculptor. Member of National Sculpture Society of New York.

MAYER, Louis. Painter and sculptor. Born in Milwaukee in 1869. Pupil of Max Thedy in Weimar; Paul Hoecker in Munich; Constant and Laurens in Paris. Member: International Society Art League; Wisconsin Painters and Sculptors. Work represented in State Historical collections at Des Moines, Iowa, and Madison, Wis.; Public Library, Burlington, Iowa; Springer Collection, National Museum, Washington, D. C.; Milwaukee Art Institute, Wisconsin. *Address*, 253 West 42d St., New York, N. Y.

MAYFIELD, Robert B. Painter and etcher. Born in Carlinville, Ill., in 1869. Pupil of St. Louis School of Fine Arts, and Julien Academy in Paris. Represented by ''In the Studio'' and ''The Giant Oak'' at the Delgado Museum, New Orleans, La.

MAYHEW, Nell B. Painter and etcher. Born in Astoria, Ill., in 1875. Pupil of University of Illinois, and of the Chicago Art Institute. *Address*, 5016 Aldoma St., Los Angeles, Calif.

MAYNARD, George Willoughby. Painter. Born in Washington in 1843; died in 1923. Studied at Royal Academy of Fine Arts, Antwerp. Had a studio in Paris in 1878, but later located in New York. Member: National Academy in 1885; American Water Color Society; Society of American Artists.

MAYNARD, Richard Field. Painter. Born in Chicago in 1875. Studied at Art Students' League, New York, and New York School of Art, 1898–1902. His specialty is portrait painting. Awards: First prize, Cowles Art School, 1898; scholarship, Art Students' League, 1899. Exhibited, Society of American Artists; New York Water Color Club; National Academy of Design; American Water Color Society; Phila. Water Color Club; Corcoran Art Gallery, Washington, D. C.; Art Institute, Chicago; National Federation of Arts and Panama Exposition. Member: New York Society of Painters; Allied Artists America; New York Water Color Club. *Address*, 33 West 67th St., New York.

MAYOR, Mrs. Harriet H. Sculptor. Born in Salem, Mass., in 1868. Pupil of Henry H. Kitson and Dennis Bunker in Boston. Specialty, portraits. She is represented at the Princeton University Museum.

MAYR, Christian. Painter. Born in Germany, he was painting portraits and figure pieces in New York in 1840. He was elected a member of the National Academy of Design in 1849, and died in New York City in 1850. His painting ''Reading the News'' is in the permanent collection of the National Academy, and was exhibited in their Centennial Exhibition of 1925.

MAZUR, Wladyslaw. Sculptor. Born in Poland in 1874. Pupil of Academy of Fine Arts at Vienna. *Address*, 1070 Central Ave., Cincinnati, Ohio.

MAZZANOVICH, Lawrence. Landscape painter. Born at sea off the coast of California in 1871. Studied at Art Institute of Chicago and Art Students' League of New York; also studeied abroad near Fontainebleau, Paris. Exhibited in Beaux Arts, 1906, and in Chicago, New York and Boston since 1910; represented in permanent collections of Art Institute of Chicago; Hackley Museum, Muskegon, Mich.; in many private collections. *Address*, Westport, Conn.

MC AULIFFE, James J. Painter. Born in St. Johns, N. F., in 1848. He studied in the Boston Art School, and made a specialty of religious and marine subjects. His ''Ecce Homo'' and seventy-five life-size figures are in the Roman Catholic Cathedral in St. John, New Brunswick. He is also represented by ''The Constitution'' in the Parlin Library, Everett. He died at Medford, Mass., in 1921.

MC BURNEY, James E. Painter and illustrator. Born in Lore City, Ohio, in 1868. Studied with Arthur W. Dow, Howard Pyle, Charles H. Davis; also in Paris. Work: ''The Mission Period'' and ''The Spanish Period,'' Southern California Counties' Commission, San Diego, Calif. *Address*, 609 Fine Arts Building, Chicago, Ill.

MC CABE, E. This engraver of vignettes was seemingly working in New York about 1855.

MC CAIG, Mrs. Flora T. Painter. Born in Royalton, N. Y., in 1856. Pupil of Penna. Academy of Fine Arts, and of Carroll Beckwith. Work: ''A Mothers' Meeting,'' Women's Union, Buffalo, N. Y.; mural paintings in Genesee Hotel, Buffalo, N. Y. *Address*, 5122 Kenmore Ave., Chicago, Ill.

MC CARTAN, Edward. Sculptor. Pupil of Art Students' League of New York; École des Beaux Arts, in Paris. Member: National Sculpture Society. Elected Member of the National Academy of Design in 1925. Represented in Fine Arts Academy, Buffalo; Metropolitan Museum, New York; City Art Museum, St. Louis. *Address*, 225 East 67th St., New York, N. Y.

MC CARTER, Henry. Painter and illustrator. Born in Norristown, Pa., in 1865. Educated at Norristown, Philadelphia, Pa., and in Paris, France, under Thos. Eakins, the late Puvis de Chavannes, Alexander Harrison, Rixens and Leon Bonnat. Illustrator for *Scribner's, Century, Collier's* and other magazines. Instructor of Penna. Academy of Fine Arts, Philadelphia; Art Students' League, New York. *Address*, Penna. Academy of Fine Arts, Philadelphia, Pa.

MC CARTHY. A line-engraver of portraits, in the employ of J. C. Buttre, New York, in 1860–65.

MC CARTHY, C. J. Illustrator. Born in Rochester, N. Y., in 1887. Pupil of F. Luis Mora and F. R. Gruger. *Address*, 143 East 21st St., New York, N. Y.

MC CARTHY, Helen K. Painter. Born in Poland, Ohio, in 1884. Pupil of Phila. School of Design. Member: Plastic Club; Alumni of Penna. School of Design; International Society

Art League; National Association of Women Painters and Sculptors. *Address*, 1716 Chestnut St., Philadelphia, Pa.

MC CLELLAND, D. In 1850 this name appears on a map of the City of Washington, signed as "Eng. and pub. by D. McClelland, Washington, 1850."

MC CLUSKEY, William. Some very well-executed subject plates, signed by "Wm. Mc Cluskey" as engraver, were published in *The New Mirror*, New York, about 1845.

MC COMAS, Francis. Painter. Born in Fingal, Tasmania, in 1874. Member of the jury, Panama-Pacific International Exposition, 1915. Member: Philadelphia Water Color Club. Two mural decorations in the Del Monte Lodge, Pebble Beach, California; also represented in the Metropolitan Museum of Art, New York; Park Museum of San Francisco, and Portland Art Society. *Address*, Monterey, Calif.

MC COMB, Marie Louise. Painter. Exhibited water colors at the Penna. Academy of Fine Arts, Philadelphia, 1925. *Address*, 2009 Mount Vernon St., Philadelphia.

MC CORD, George Herbert. Painter. Born in New York in 1849. He first exhibited at the National Academy in 1870. Among his most important works are "Sunnyside" (home of Washington Irving); "Cave of the Winds, Niagara"; "The Genesee Valley." Elected an Associate of the National Academy in 1880. He died in New York in 1909.

MC CORMACK, Nancy. Sculptor. (See Cox-McCormack.)

MC CORMICK, Howard. Painter, illustrator and engraver. Born in Indiana in 1875. He illustrated with wood engravings numerous magazines. *Address*, Leonia, N. J.

MC COUCH, D. W. Painter. Exhibited at Penna. Academy of Fine Arts, Philadelphia, 1921; represented in "Exhibition of Paintings Showing the Later Tendencies in Art." *Address*, St. Martin's Lane, Chestnut Hill, Philadelphia.

MC CREA, S. Harkness. Landscape painter. Born in Palatine, Cook County, Ill., in 1867. Studied in San Francisco, Chicago, New York, Paris and Munich. *Address*, Scraggycrag, Darien, Conn.

MC CREERY, Franc Root (Mrs. E. A.). Painter. Born in Dodge City, Kans. Pupil of Students' School of Art, Denver, Colo.; Art Institute of Chicago; Buffalo Society of Arttists. *Address*, 15 Elmview Place, Buffalo, N. Y.

MC CUTCHEON, John T. Caricaturist. Born near South Raub, Tippecanoe County, Ind., in 1870. Pupil of Ernest Knaufft in New York. Member: Society of Illustrators, 1911. On staff of Chicago *Tribune* since 1903; correspondent during Spanish War. Author, "Stories of Filipino Warfare," "Bird Center Cartoons," etc. *Address*, Care of The Chicago Tribune, 1018 Fine Arts Building, Chicago, Ill.

MC DONALD, Ann H. Painter. Exhibited at Penna. Academy of Fine Arts, Philadelphia, 1924. *Address*, Seminole Ave., Chestnut Hill, Philadelphia.

MC DOUGAL, John A. Miniature painter, flourishing 1836–81 in New York and Newark.

MC ENTEE, Jervis. Painter. Born in Rondout, N. Y., in 1828; died in 1890. Specialty, landscapes. Studied with F. E. Church. Elected Associate Member of the National Academy, 1860; National Academy, 1861. Represented by "Eastern Sky at Sunset," at Corcoran Art Gallery, Washington, D. C.

MC EWEN, Katherine. Painter. Born in England, but lived most of her time in Detroit. She has painted landscapes in Arizona and Alaska. She is a member of the National Association of Women Painters and Sculptors.

MC EWEN, Walter. Painter and mural decorator. Born in Chicago. Pupil of Cormon and Robert-Fleury, Paris. Represented by paintings in Penna. Academy of Fine Arts; Corcoran Art Gallery, Washington; mural work in Congressional Library, Washington, D. C. *Address*, Century Club, New York City.

MC EWEN, William. A little known landscape painter, a friend and pupil of George Inness.

MC FEE, Henry L. Painter. Exhibited at Penna. Academy of Fine Arts, Phila., 1921; also in "Exhibition of Paintings Showing the Later Tendencies in Art." *Address*, Care of Daniels Gallery, 2 West 47th St., New York.

MC GIBBON, James. He was a portrait painter and worked in Boston, Mass., in 1801.

MC GILLIVRAY, F. H. Painter. Born in Whitby, Ontario, Can., in 1864. Pupil of Simon and Menard in Paris. Member: International Art Union, Paris; National Academy of Women Painters and Sculptors; Ontario Society of Artists. Work: "Afterglow" and "Stack in Winter," owned by the Canadian Government. *Address*, 202 Frank St., Ottawa, Can.

MC GOFFIN, John. Engraver. Born in Philadelphia in 1813; he was living in 1883.

McGoffin was an excellent line-engraver of landscape and subject plates. He was a pupil of James W. Steel, of Philadelphia, and was in the employ of that engraver in 1834. Mr. Baker says that he painted miniatures for some years, but he evidently continued to engrave, and was working at least as late as 1876.

MC ILHENNEY, Charles M. Painter. Born in Philadelphia in 1858. Studied at the Penna. Academy of Fine Arts in 1877. He established his studio in New York City. Among his pictures are "A Gray Summer Noon," "The Old Old Story," and "The Passing Storm." Elected an Associate Member of the National Academy in 1892. He died in 1904.

MC INTIRE, Katherine Angela. Painter and etcher. Born near Richmond, Va., in 1880. Pupil of Chase, Alice Beckington, George Bridgman in New York; also of Mme. La Forge in Paris. *Address*, 160 Waverly Place, New York, N. Y.

MC KAY. Painter. No work is known of this portrait painter but his painting of John Bush (1755–1816) and that of Abigail Bush (1765–1810) which are signed "Mc Kay," and belong to the American Antiquarian Society of Worcester, Mass.

MC KENZIE, R. Tait. Sculptor. Born in Ontario, Canada, in 1867. Lecturer on artistic anatomy and physical training. Principal statues, "Youthful Franklin," "George Whitefield," "The Sprinter," and the "Victory Memorial," Cambridge, England. *Address*, Care of University of Penna., Philadelphia.

MC KERNAN, Frank. Painter and illustrator. Born in Philadelphia in 1861. Pupil of Penna. Academy of Fine Arts, and of Howard Pyle. *Address*, Studio, 524 Walnut St., Philadelphia.

MC KINSTRY, Grace E. Portrait painter and sculptor. Born in Fredonia, N. Y. Pupil of Art Students' League of New York, and of the Julien Academy, Paris. *Address*, 228 West 72d St., New York.

MC LAIN, Mary. Miniature painter. Exhibited at the Penna. Academy of Fine Arts, Philadelphia, 1925. *Address*, 111 East 56th St., New York.

MC LANE, M. Jean (Mrs. John C. Johansen). Portrait painter. Born in Chicago in 1878. Graduated from Art Institute of Chicago in 1897, with honors and prizes. Awards: Hallgarten prize, 1913, National Academy of Design; Walter Lippincott prize, Penna. Academy of Fine Arts, 1913; silver medal, Panama P. I. Exposition, 1915. Represented in private galleries throughout U. S.; in Museum of Art,

Syracuse, N. Y.; Art Institute, Chicago; San Antonio Art Museum; Toledo Museum of Art; etc. Elected Associate Member of the National Academy; also member of the International Art League, Paris; MacDowell Club, New York; National Association of Portrait Painters. *Address*, 12 West 9th St., New York, N. Y.

MC LAUGHLIN, Charles J. Painter. Born in Covington, Ky., in 1888. Pupil of Cincinnati Art Academy and of Frank Duveneck. *Address*, 321 Front St., Covington, Ky.

MC LAUGHLIN, Mary Louise. Painter. Born in Cincinnati. She began making porcelain called Losanti ware in 1898; exhibited first in Paris Exposition, 1900; silver medal for decorative metal work, Paris Exposition, 1889; honorable mention for china painting, Chicago Exposition. Honorable member of Cincinnati Woman's Club. Member: Woman's Art Club; National League of Mural Painters. *Address*, 4011 Sherwood Ave., Annsby Place, Cincinnati, Ohio.

MC LEARY. Sculptor. Exhibited at the National Association of Women Painters and Sculptors, New York, 1924. *Address*, 7 Macdougal Alley, New York.

MC LELLAN, H. B. About 1860 this stipple-engraver of portraits was located in Boston, Mass.

MC LELLAN, Ralph. Painter and etcher. Born in Texas in 1884. Pupil of Hale, Tarbell, and Benson, in Boston. *Address*, Penna. Industrial Art School, Philadelphia.

MC MANUS, James G. Painter. Born in Hartford, Conn., in 1882. Pupil of Flagg and Brandegee. Represented by portraits of Alfred E. Burr, Dr. Geo. C. Bailey, and paintings in Hartford Art Museum. *Address*, 86 Pratt St., Hartford, Conn.

MC MEIN, Miss N. M. Painter and illustrator. Born in Quincy, Ill., in 1889. Pupil of Chicago Art Institute. *Address*, 226 Fifth Ave., New York.

MC MILLAN, Mary. Miniature painter. Exhibited at the Penna. Academy of Fine Arts, Philadelphia, in 1925. *Address*, 941 James St., Syracuse, New York.

MC MILLEN, Mildred. Wood-engraver. Born in Chicago, Ill., in 1884. Studied in Chicago, New York and Paris. Represented in the National Museum of Canada; Ottawa and New York Public Libraries. *Address*, 3 Central St., Provincetown, Mass.

MC NAIR, William. Painter. Exhibited at Annual Exhibition of the National Academy of Design, New York, in 1925. *Address*, 5 East 79th St., New York.

MC NULTY, William C. Painter. Exhibited water colors at the Penna. Academy of Fine Arts, Philadelphia, 1925. *Address*, 404 West 20th St., New York City.

MC PHERSON, W. J. Flourished in Boston, 1846–47, as a miniature painter.

MC RAE, John C. This artist engraved portraits and subject plates, in both line and stipple, for New York publishers in 1855. He executed several large and excellent subject plates for framing, and was working in 1880.

A portrait of John Wesley, in mezzotint, and published by Harper & Brother, New York, is signed "Mc Rae sc." While inferior in execution to his other work, this may have been engraved by John C. Mc Rae.

MC RICKARD, James P. Painter. Born in 1872. Pupil of Art Students' League of New York; Douglas Volk and George De Forest Brush. Member: Society of Independent Artists; League of New York Artists. *Address*, Third St., Bayside, L. I., N. Y.

MEADE, Larkin G. (or MEAD). Sculptor. Born in New Hampshire in 1835. He studied under Henry Kirke Brown. His statue of Ethan Allen is in Washington, D. C., and his statue of Abraham Lincoln is in Springfield, Ill. In 1878 he resided in Washington, D. C., and assisted the commission in the completion of the Washington Monument. He died in Florence, Italy, in 1910.

MEADOWS, C. This engraver of portraits and buildings signed himself thus at Windsor, Vt. He was working about 1850–55.

MEADOWS, R. M. A very well-executed stipple portrait of Edward Jenner, M.D., was engraved by R. M. Meadows and published in the *Analectic Magazine* for 1817. Meadows also engraved a portrait of F. Asbury for an American publication, but it is not certain that either of these plates was necessarily engraved in the United States.

Nagler, in his Kunstler-Lexicon, refers to a Robert Meadows who flourished in the first quarter of the last century and engraved for the Shakspere Gallery, of London.

MEAGHER, M. T. Painter and sculptor. Born in New York City. Pupil of National Academy of Design, and of Chase, Beckwith, and R. Swain Gifford in New York; he also studied in Paris and Antwerp. Artist to the Department of Anthropology, American Museum of Natural History and New York Ophthalmic College. *Address*, 939 Eighth Ave., New York, N. Y.

MEAKIN, Lewis Henry. Landscape painter. Born in England; died in Boston, 1917. He came to this country as a child; studied art in Europe, and taught in Cincinnati. He is represented at the Cincinnati Museum. He was elected an Associate Member of the National Academy of Design in 1913.

MEANCE. French miniature painter, flourishing in New York, 1795. Portrait of N. G. Dufief, engraved by Edwin. (See Fielding, Edwin Catalogue, No. 60.)

MEARS, Helen Farnsworth. Sculptor. Born in Oshkosh, Wis., in 1878. Studied in New York and Paris. First success "Genius of Wisconsin," exhibited at Chicago Exposition, 1893; executed "The Fountain of Life," 1904; marble statue of Frances E. Willard, 1905, placed in the Capitol, Washington; portrait bust of George Rogers Clark; also bust of William L. G. Morton, M.D., placed in Smithsonian Institution; portrait reliefs of Augustus St. Gaudens, Louis Collier Wilcox and Edward A. McDowell. She died in New York in 1916.

MEARS, Henrietta D. Painter and etcher. Born in Milwaukee, Wis., in 1877. Pupil of Art Students' League of New York, and of Hawthorne and Pape. *Address*, 16 Park Drive, Brookline, Mass.

MEDAIRY & BANNERMAN. This firm was engraving portraits and book-plates in Baltimore, Md., in 1828–29. The second member of the firm was doubtless W. W. Bannerman, already referred to.

MEDARY, Annie Hampton. Miniature painter. Exhibited at the Penna. Academy of the Fine Arts, Philadelphia, 1925. *Address*, 115 High St., Taunton, Mass.

MEEDER, Philip. Wood engraver. Born in Alsace, France, he came to the United States as a boy. He was associated with the wood-engraver Frederick Y. Chubb, under the firm name of Meeder and Chubb. He died in New York City in 1913.

MEEKER, Joseph R. Landscape painter. Born in Newark, N. J., in 1827. He has shown a special interest in southern scenery. Among his paintings are "The Indian Chief"; "Louisiana Bayou"; "The Lotos Eaters."

MEEKS, Eugene. Born in New York in 1843. He has spent much of his time abroad. Among his works are: "Gondola Party, Venice" and the "Halt at the Golden Lion."

MEER, John. He is included in Dunlap's list of artists and is described as an enamel painter. He was also a bank-note engraver.

MEESER, Lillian B. (Mrs. Spenser B.). Painter. Born in Ridley Park, Pa., in 1864. Pupil of Penna. Academy of Fine Arts; Art Students' League of New York; Worcester Art Museum. Member: Fellowship, Penna.

Academy of Fine Arts; Plastic Club, Philadelphia; Art Alliance. *Address*, Crozer Campus, Chester, Pa.

MÈGE, Violette. Painter and sculptor. Born in Alger, French Algiers, in 1889. Pupil of Georges Rochegrosse, École Nationale des Beaux Arts, Academie Julien, J. P. Laurens and Humbert, in Paris. *Address*, 119 West 87th St., New York, N. Y.

MEINSHAUSEN, George F. Painter, illustrator and wood-engraver. Born in Germany in 1855. Pupil of Cincinnati Art Academy. Represented by water colors and engravings in Carnegie Institute; also in Library of Congress and the New York Public Library. *Address*, 4617 Station Ave., Norwood, Ohio.

MEIERHANS, Joseph. Painter. Born in Switzerland in 1890. Pupil of A. N. Lindenmuth and of John Sloan. Member: League of New York Artists; Society of Independent Artists; Art Students' League of New York. *Address*, 4924 Eleventh Ave., Brooklyn, N. Y.

MEISSNER, Alfred. Portrait painter and illustrator. Born in Chicago in 1877. Pupil of Art Institute of Chicago. *Address*, 3057 North Christiana Ave., Chicago, Ill.

MELCHER, Mrs. Bertha Corbett. Illustrator and painter. Born in Denver, Colo., in 1872. Pupil of Volk in Menneapolis; Pyle at Drexel Institute, Philadelphia. Specialty, miniatures and illustrations for children's books. *Address*, Topanga, Calif.

MELCHERS, Gari. Painter. Born in Detroit, Mich., in 1860. Studied abroad. Elected an Associate Member of the National Academy in 1904, and an Academician in 1906. Gold medal, Penna. Academy of Fine Arts, 1896, and at Corcoran Art Gallery, 1910. Represented at Luxembourg Museum, Paris; Corcoran Art Gallery, Washington; Penna. Academy of Fine Arts; Metropolitan Museum of New York; National Gallery, Washington, D. C. *Address*, 80 West 40th St., New York.

MELIODON, Jules André. Sculptor. Born in France in 1867. Studied in Paris under Falguiere, Fremiet and Message. Represented by the "Explorer Lesueur" at Museum of Natural History, Paris. *Address*, Lincoln Park, N. J.

MELLON, Eleanor M. Sculptor. Born in Philadelphia in 1894. Studied at Art Students' League, and with Edward McCartan. *Address*, 903 Park Ave., New York.

MELLOR, Margaret W. Painter. Exhibited water colors at the Penna. Academy of Fine Arts, Philadelphia, 1925. *Address*, 5203 McKean Ave., Germantown, Philadelphia.

MELTZER, Arthur. Painter. Exhibited at Annual Exhibition of the National Academy of Design, New York, 1925. *Address*, Stony Run, Penna.

MELVILL, Mrs. Antonia. Portrait painter. Born in Berlin, Germany, in 1875. She came to America in 1894. Studied in London under W. P. Frith at the Heatherley School of Art. Work: "Portrait of Bishop J. H. Johnson," Good Samaritan Hospital, Los Angeles; "Portrait of Mrs. Dollard," Capitol at Pierre, S. D. *Address*, 424 Music-Art Studio Building Room, Los Angeles, Calif.

MENDENHALL, Emma. Landscape painter. Born in Cincinnati. Pupil of Cincinnati Art Academy under Nowottny and Duveneck; Julien Academy in Paris; summer school under Mrs. Rhoda Holmes Nicholls, Woodbury and Snell. Member: Woman's Art Club; National Association of Women Painters and Sculptors. *Address*, 2629 Moorman Ave., Cincinnati, Ohio.

MENG, John. American portrait painter. Born about 1734 in Germantown, Philadelphia, he died in the West Indies in 1854. A few of his paintings are preserved in the old Germantown families and in the Penna. Historical Society of Philadelphia.

MENTE, Charles. Painter and illustrator. Born in New York. Pupil of Gabl and Loefftz in Munich. Member: Chicago Water Color Club. *Address*, Congers, N. Y.

MENTEL, Lillian. Painter and illustrator. Born in Cincinnati, Ohio, in 1882. Pupil of Cincinnati Art Academy and Pratt Institute. Member: Cincinnati Woman's Art Club. *Address*, 2893 Romana Place, Oakley, Cincinnati, Ohio.

MENZLER-PEYTON, Bertha S. (Mrs. Alfred). Landscape painter. Born in Chicago, Ill. Pupil of Art Institute of Chicago; of Merson, Collin and Aman-Jean in Paris. Member: Chicago Society of Artists; Chicago Water Color Club; National Academy of Women Painters and Sculptors; New York Water Color Club. Work in Union League Club, Chicago; West End Woman's Club, Chicago; Evanston, Ill., Woman's Club; mural decorations in Fine Arts Building, Chicago. Specialty, Western scenery. *Address*, 33 West 67th St., New York N. Y.

MERCER, Geneva. Sculptor. Born in Jefferson, Ala., in 1889. Pupil of G. Moretti. Work: Statue of Rev. James L. Robertson; "Soldiers Memorial" at Bronxville, N. Y. *Address*, 4029 Bigelow Blvd., Pittsburgh, Pa.

MERCER, William. Portrait painter in oils and miniatures, who flourished in 1773–1850, Philadelphia. He was the deaf mute son of Gen'l Mercer (not nephew as stated by Dunlap). Pupil of Charles Willson Peale, he became an excellent portrait painter.

MERCHANT, G. W. A well-engraved plan of the floor of the Senate chamber, at Albany, N. Y., is signed "G. W. Merchant Engr. & Pub." The plan is used as a frontispiece to the "Legislative Manual of the State of New York, 1834," and it was published at Albany in that year.

MERINGTON, Ruth. Painter. Born in London, England. Pupil of National Academy of Design and Art Students' League of New York, under Edgar M. Ward, Bruce Crane and Birge Harrison; of Julien Academy in Paris under Constant. *Address,* 1 Wallace St., Newark, N. J.

MERO, Lee. Illustrator. Born in Ortonville, Minn., in 1885. Pupil of Robert Koehler in Minneapolis; Robert Henri in New York. Specialty, advertising art and decorative illustration. *Address,* Care of Charles Daniel Frey, 104 Michigan Ave., South, Chicago, Ill.

MERRELS, Mrs. Gray P. Miniature painter. Born in Topeka, Kans., in 1884. Pupil of Art Students' League of New York. Member of Brooklyn Society of Miniature Painters. *Address,* 248 Oxford St., Hartford, Conn.

MERRILL, Frank T. Painter. Born in Boston in 1848. He studied art at the Lowell Institute, and at the Boston Museum of Fine Arts; he also studied in France and England. His water colors are free in wash and color, and he has also been very successful with his etchings. Merrill's work has been used extensively for illustrating and may be found in Thackeray's "Mahogany Tree" and in Irving's "Rip Van Winkle."

MERRILL, Hiram C. Painter and woodengraver. Born in Boston, Mass., 1866. Pupil of Art Students' League and of Douglas Volk. Represented in Carnegie Institute, Pittsburgh, Penna. *Address,* 522 West 134th St., New York.

MERRILL, Katherine. Etcher. Born in Milwaukee, Wis., in 1876. Pupil of Chicago Art Institute and of Brangwyn in London. Represented in Library of Congress, Washington, D. C. *Address,* 415 West 23d St., New York.

MERRIMAN, Helen B. (Mrs.). Painter. Born in Boston in 1844. Pupil of William Hunt. Member of Boston Water Color Club. *Address,* 73 Bay State Road, Boston, Mass.

MERRITT, Anna Lea (Mrs. Henry). Painter. Born in Philadelphia in 1844. Studied painting privately. Diploma and medals, Centennial Exhibition in 1876; Chicago Exhibition; honorable mention, British Sect., Paris,

1889; represented in permanent collections at the Chantrey Collection in National Gallery of British Art; Penna. Academy of Fine Arts; portrait of Mr. J. R. Lowell in Memorial Hall, Harvard University; constant exhibitor since 1871 at the Royal Academy, London, including many portraits and subjects such as "Eve Repentant" and "Love Locked Out," "Merry Maids," "I Will Give You Rest," "Piping Shepherd," etc.; also mural decorations. She was also well known as an etcher.

MERTON, Owen. Painter. Exhibited at "Exhibition of Paintings Showing Later Tendencies in Art," Penna. Academy of Fine Arts, Philadelphia, 1921. *Address,* 57 Hillside Ave., Flushing, Long Island.

MERYMAN, Richard S. Portrait painter. Born in Boston, 1882. Pupil of Thayer and Tarbell. Exhibited portrait of Josephus Daniels at Philadelphia in Penna. Academy of Fine Arts Exhibition, 1924. *Address,* Care of Corcoran Art Gallery, Washington, D. C.

METCALF, Eliar. Painter. Born in Franklin, Mass. in 1785; died in 1834. He studied under Samuel Waldo. Metcalf resided and painted portraits in New Orleans, 1818–1823; they were considered excellent. He appears in the 1822 New Orleans directory as "portrait and miniature painter, 25 Magazine Street, above Common." In Sept. 1817 *The New York Commercial Advertiser* notes as follows: "E. Metcalf, Portrait and Miniature Painter having recovered his health has returned to the city and resumed the exercise of his profession at No. 152, Broadway." He painted an excellent portrait of the artist Asher B. Durand, now in the New York Historical Society.

METCALF, Willard Leroy. Painter. Born in Lowell, Mass., in 1858; died in New York in 1925. Pupil of George L. Brown in Boston, and of Boulanger and Lefebvre in Paris. Honorable mention, Paris Salon, 1888; medal, Columbian Exposition Chicago, 1893; Temple gold medal, Penna. Academy of Fine Arts, 1904; gold medal and first prize, Corcoran Gallery of Art, Washington, 1907; Harris medal and prize, Art Institute of Chicago, 1910. Represented by "The Birches" and "My Pastoral," Boston Museum of Fine Arts, Boston, Mass.; also "May Night" at the Corcoran Art Gallery.

METEYARD, Thomas Buford. Painter. Born at Rock Island, Ill., in 1865. Studied in Europe, and exhibited pictures at Paris Salon, Chicago Exposition, Society of American Artists, New York, Penna. Academy of Philadelphia, St. Louis Exposition, 1904, and other exhibitions in U. S. Decorator for "Songs from Vagabondia" (by Bliss Carman and

Richard Hovey) and numerous other books. *Address*, Moses Hill Farm, Fernhurst, Sussex England.

MEURER, Charles A. Painter. Born in Germany, 1865. Pupil of Julien Academy, Paris. Specialty, still-life; also sheep and cattle painting. *Address*, Terrace Park, Ohio.

MEYENBERG, John C. Sculptor. Born in Tell City, Ind., in 1860. Pupil of Cincinnati Art Academy under Thomas S. Noble; Beaux-Arts in Paris under Jules Thomas. Member: Cincinnati Art Club. Work: "Egbert Memorial," Fort Thomas, Ky.; "Pediment," Covington, Ky., Carnegie Library; "Aunt Lou Memorial," Linden Grove Cemetery; Theodore F. Hallam bust, Court House, Covington, Ky.; "Nancy Hanks," Lincoln Park entrance, State of Indiana; "Benn Pitman Memorial," Cincinnati Public Library. *Address*, 127 East 3d St., Cincinnati, Ohio.

MEYER, Alvin. Sculptor. Born in Bartlett, Ill., in 1892. Pupil of Charles Grafly. Member: Charcoal Club. Award: Cresson Traveling Scholarship of the Penna. Academy of Fine Arts. *Address*, 1606 Cherry St., Philadelphia, Pa.

MEYER, Christian. Landscape painter. Born in Germany in 1838, he came to this country as a young man. His paintings were shown at exhibitions of the Society of American Artists and at the National Academy of Design. He died in Brooklyn, N. Y., in 1907.

MEYER, Enno. Painter, sculptor and illustrator. Born in Cincinnati in 1874. Pupil of Duveneck. Member: Cincinnati Art Club. Specialty, animals. *Address*, 972 McMillan St., Cincinnati, Ohio.

MEYER, Ernest. Painter. Born at Rothenberg, Germany, in 1863. Pupil of Chase; Twachtman; Ward; Du Mond; Turner. Member of Conn. Academy of Fine Arts. *Address*, Tylerville, Conn.

MEYER, George Bernhard. Miniature painter. Member: Charcoal Club. *Address*, 6 East Pleasant St., Baltimore, Md.

MEYER, Henry Hoppner. Stipple engraver and portrait painter in oils and miniatures. Born in England in 1783. In 1830 he came to New York and engraved portraits and painted miniatures. Among his miniatures he painted one of President Jackson in 1833. He also engraved several plates for Longacre & Herring's "National Portrait Gallery," 1834. He died in 1847.

MEYER, Herbert. Painter and illustrator. Born in New York, N. Y., in 1882. Pupil of Art Students' League of New York; of Twachtman and Du Mond. Member: Society of Illustrators. *Address*, 867 West 181st St., New York, N. Y.

MEYERCORD, Grace E. Miniature painter. Exhibited at the Penna. Academy of Fine Arts, Philadelphia, 1925. *Address*, 329 West 84th St., New York.

MEYEROWITZ, William. Painter. Exhibited at Annual Exhibition of National Academy of Design, New York, 1925. He was born in Russia in 1887. *Address*, 39 West 67th St., New York.

MEYLAN, Paul J. Illustrator and painter. Born in Canton of Vaud, Switzerland, in 1882. Pupil of National Academy of Design in New York. Member: Society of Illustrators, 1907. Illustrated: "Two Faces," by Marie Van Vorst; "The Poor Lady," by Mary E. Wilkins Freeman; "Sarolta," by Agnes and Egerton Castle; "Come Out of the Kitchen" and "Ladies Must Live," by Alice Duer Miller; "The Unexpected," by Elizabeth Jordan, etc. *Address*, 140 Wadsworth Ave., New York, N. Y.

MEYNER, Walter. Painter. Exhibited at National Academy of Design, 1925. *Address*, 150 Nassau St., New York.

MEYRICK, Richard. The *American Weekly Mercury*, Philadelphia, No. 516, 1729, contains the following advertisement:

"Richard Meyrick, Engraver, removed from the Lock and Key in Chesnut Street to the Widow Walker's, in Front-Street Phila."

Meyrick was probably an engraver for silversmiths.

MEYROWITZ, Jenny Delony Rice. Painter of portraits and miniatures. Born in Washington, Hempstead County, Ark. Studied at Cincinnati Art Academy, and took Med. School course in "Artistic Anatomy," St. Louis School of Fine Arts; pupil of Julien, Delaunee and Delecluse studios, Paris. Studio in New York, 1900. Art Instructor, Va. Female Institute, Roanoke, Va., 1893–94; Norfolk, Va., College; Director of Art, State University of Ark., 1907–09. Exhibited at National Academy of Design, New York Water Color Club, National Arts Club, Woman's Art Club, Miniature societies of New York, Boston and Phila., etc. Has painted portraits of Jefferson Davis; Mrs. Jefferson Davis; George G. William, pres. Chemical National Bank, New York; Mrs. Hetty Green; Dr. George Taylor Stewart, etc. Member: Society of Women Painters and Sculptors. *Address*, 140 West 57th St., New York.

MEYVIS, Alme Leon. Painter. Born in St. Gilles-Waes, Belgium, 1877. Pupil of Mechanics Institute, Rochester; Royal Academy, The Hague. Member: Rochester Art Club. Work represented in Modern Museum, The Hague, Holland; Sibley Hall Library, Rochester. *Address*, 22 Centennial Building, East Rochester, N. Y.

MICKS, J. Rumsey. Illustrator. Born in Baltimore, Md., in 1886. Pupil of Henry McCarter. Illustrations for *Everybody's, Scribner's, Harper's, Red Book*. *Address*, 57 West 10th St., New York, N. Y.

MIDDLETON, Stanley. Painter. Born in Brooklyn, N. Y., in 1852. Pupil of Jaxquesson de la Chevreuse, Harpignies, Constant and Dagnan-Bouveret at Julien Academy in Paris. Member: Artists' Fund Society. Work Portrait of Honorable Lynn Boyd, the Capitol, Washington, D. C.; "Normandy Fish Wife," Hamilton Club, Brooklyn; "Portrait of George H. Daniels," Lotos Club, New York; portraits of Dr. Weisse, Dr. Starr and Dr. Satterlee, New York College of Dentistry. *Address*, 1 West 67th St., New York, N. Y.

MIDDLETON, Thomas. Engraver. Born on the family estate of Fanclure, S. C., in 1797; died in Charleston, S. C., in 1863. He was the third son of the Honorable Thos. Middleton of Charleston, S. C. In the Middleton Records he is referred to as a man of taste and knowledge in art and an amateur painter of considerable talent.

MIELATZ, Charles F. W. Etcher and painter. Born in Germany in 1864. Pupil of Chicago School of Design. Elected an Associate Member of the National Academy in 1906. Died in 1919.

MIELZINER, Leo. Portrait painter. Born in New York City in 1869. Studied at Cincinnati Art Academy; École des Beaux Arts, Paris. Pupil of Academie Julien and Colarossi, Paris; with Kroyer, Copenhagen. Instructor at Art Students' League, New York, 1913–15; writer and lecturer on art. Represented in the Metropolitan Museum, New York, and Boston Art Museum. *Address*, 79 West 12th St., New York, N. Y.

MIFFLIN, J. H. Miniature painter, who flourished in New York, 1840–42. He is said to have painted portraits in Philadelphia in 1832.

MIGNOT, Louis Remy. Painter. Born in Charleston, S. C., in 1831. The son of a Baltimore confectioner, he studied in Holland and opened his studio in New York about 1855, as a landscape painter. He went to South America with Frederick E. Church and painted tropical scenes. Elected National Academician in 1859. He died in London in 1870; after his death a collection of his paintings was exhibited there.

MILBOURNE, C. English scene-painter, who was brought from London in 1793 by Wignell for the Chestnut Street Theatre. He

painted some scenes of Philadelphia—"View of Arch St. Wharf With Boats Sailing on the Delaware"; also a view, "Third and Market Sts, Phila," both remarkable for their excellence.

MILES, Edward. Miniature painter and portrait artist in crayons. Was born in England in 1752. He was employed by Sir Joshua Reynolds to make miniature copies of his portraits. He exhibited in the Royal Academy in 1775–79. In 1807 he settled in Philadelphia, where he died in 1828. The directory entries list him both as a portrait painter and drawing teacher.

MILIONE, Louis. Sculptor. Born in Italy, 1884; came to this country as a youth and studied at the Penna. Academy of Fine Arts, under Charles Grafly. *Address*, 121 South 24th St., Philadelphia.

MILLAR, Addison T. Painter and etcher. Born in Ohio in 1860. Pupil of Chase in New York and of Constant in Paris. He is represented by paintings in Rhode Island School of Design, and in the Detroit Museum of Art. His etchings are in the New York Public Library and Congressional Library, Washington, D. C. He was killed in an automobile accident in 1913.

MILLER, Alfred J. Painter. Born in Baltimore in 1810. Studied first under Sully; viisited Europe in 1833, studying in Paris, Rome and Florence. He accompanied Sir William Drummond Stewart, a Scotch Baronet, to the Rocky Mountains in 1837, making a series of sketches which were the groundwork of the very interesting gallery of pictures now in Murthley Castle. These pictures were reproduced in water colors for W. T. Walters, of Baltimore. Miller died in 1874.

MILLER, Burr C. Sculptor. Exhibited portrait bust at Penna. Academy of Fine Arts, Philadelphia, 1914. *Address*, Franklin St., Wilkes-Barre, Penna.

MILLER, Charles Henry. Landscape painter. Born in New York, 1842; died in 1922. He first exhibited at the National Academy of Design in 1860; was elected an Associate in 1873, and an Academician, 1875. Gold medal at Philadelphia, 1876; also exhibited in Boston and New Orleans exhibitions. Represented in Metropolitan Museum by "Sunset, East Hampton"; also by paintings in the Brooklyn Museum, and the Rhode Island School of Design.

MILLER, Eleazer Hutchinson. Painter. Born in Shepherdstown, W. Va., in 1831; died in 1921. Painter in oils and water colors; also etcher and illustrator. Visited Europe in 1875. Lived and worked in Washington after 1848. He was one of the organizers of the old Washington Art Club, and also aided in the organization of the Society of Washington Artists, of which he was three times the president. He was an etcher of prominence. Represented at Corcoran Art Gallery by "Moonrise and Twilight" (water color), painted in 1907.

MILLER (or MILER), George M. A foreign sculptor and modeller, who came to this country towards the latter part of the eighteenth century. He made busts of C. W. Peale, Bishop White, Commodore Bainbridge, Mrs. Madison, Mrs. Jerome Bonaparte, and in 1798, of Washington. He was a member of the Penna. Academy of Fine Arts and the Columbian Society of Arts. He died in 1818.

MILLER, Godfrey. Miniature painter, who flourished in New York, 1841–87.

MILLER, J. Maxwell. Sculptor. Born in Baltimore in 1877. Studied in Maryland Institute; School of Art and Design; Rinehart School of Sculpture; Charcoal Club; winner Rinehart scholarship to Paris; pupil of Academie Julien, Paris; also of Verlet, in 1902–04. Honorable mention, Salon des Artistes Francais, Paris, 1902; silver medal, St. Louis Exposition, 1904; Officer d'Academie Francaise, 1912; honorable mention for medals, Panama Exposition, 1915. Member: National Sculpture Society. Represented at Penna. Academy of Fine Arts by portrait of "Cardinal Gibbons"; in Metropolitan Museum by "Ishmael"; also by Monument to the Confederate women of Maryland. *Address*, 1335 Greenmount Ave., Baltimore, Md.

MILLER, Kate Reno. Painter. Pupil of Cincinnati Art Academy. Member: Cincinnati Woman's Art Club. Instructor in Cincinnati Art Academy. *Address*, Art Academy, Cincinnati, Ohio.

MILLER, Kenneth Hayes. Painter. Born in Kenwood, N. Y. in 1876. Pupil of Art Students' League of New York under William Chase and Mowbray. *Address*, 408 West 23d St., New York.

MILLER, Mildred B. Painter. Exhibited at the Penna. Academy of Fine Arts, Philadelphia, 1924. *Address*, 4533 Pine St., Philadelphia.

MILLER, Minnie M. Painter. Exhibited flower painting at the Academy of Fine Arts, Philadelphia, 1921. *Address*, 1521 Lehigh Ave., Philadelphia.

MILLER, Richard E. Painter. Born in St. Louis, Mo., in 1875; has lived in Paris. Pupil of St. Louis School of Fine Arts, and of Constant and Laurens, in Paris. Represented in the Luxembourg; Rhode Island School of Design; Metropolitan Museum of New York. Elected Member of the National Academy of

Design, 1915. *Address*, Care of Macbeth Galleries, New York.

MILLER, William. Sculptor, of Providence, Rhode Island. He executed a series of large medallions of distinguished native citizens, civil and military.

MILLER, William. Engraver. Born in New York in 1850, of German parents; died in 1923. Started engraving on wood at Frank Leslie's publishing house, 1868; studied drawing, etc., in Germany, 1871–73; associated with Frederick Juengling, 1877–89. Exhibited in New York; Munich Salon; Paris Exposition, 1900. Medal, Chicago Exposition, 1893; Buffalo Exposition, 1901.

MILLER, William Henry. Portrait painter. Born in Philadelphia, Pa., in 1854. Pupil of Penna. Academy of Fine Arts under Eakins. Member: Fellowship of Penna. Academy of Fine Arts; Philadelphia Sketch Club. Instructor of drawing, Episcopal Academy, Philadelphia. *Address*, 102 West Montgomery Ave., Ardmore, Pa.

MILLER, William H. Miniature painter, who flourished about 1846–47, New York.

MILLESON, Royal Hill. Landscape painter. Born in Batavia, Ohio, in 1849. Member: Chicago Society of Artists; Boston Art Club. Work: "Mt. Hood, Oregon," Herron Art Institute, Indianapolis. Author, "The Artist's Point of View." *Address*, 2336 Osgood St., Chicago, Ill.

MILLET, Francis Davis. Painter. Born in 1846; died in 1912. Graduated at Howard University, 1869. Awarded medal at Royal Academy of Antwerp. He was elected a National Academician in 1885, and served one or two terms as vice-president. His painting "At the Inn" was exhibited at the Centennial Exhibition of the National Academy of Design in 1925.

MILLET, Geraldine B. (Mme. Francois). Painter. Born in America. Pupil of Wyatt Eaton in New York; of Carolus-Duran, Kerson, and Alfred Stevens in Paris. *Address*, Barbizon, France.

MILLET, Louis J. Mural painter. Born in New York; died there in 1923. Pupil of École des Beaux Arts in Paris. Member: Chicago Society of Artists; Chicago Architectural Club; Municipal Art League of Chicago.

MILLETT, G. Van. Painter. Born in Kansas City, Mo., in 1864. Pupil of Royal Academy of Fine Arts in Munich, under Gysis and Loefftz. Award: Silver medal, Munich Academy. Represented in Kansas City Public Gallery and City Hall, Kansas City. *Address*, 520 Studio Building, Kansas City, Mo.

MILLMORE, Joseph. Sculptor. Born in Ireland in 1842; brother of Martin Millmore. He worked with his brother on the memorial to the Union dead in Mount Auburn Cemetery, Cambridge, Mass. He died in 1886.

MILLMORE, Martin. Sculptor. Born in 1845. He entered the studio of Thomas Ball in Charlestown in 1860. He soon took a studio and modeled busts of Longfellow and Sumner, also executed marble statues for Horticultural Hall, Boston. Millmore executed a bust of George Ticknor for the Public Library, Boston; also busts of C. O. Whitmore, General Thayer, and an ideal bust of "Miranda." He died in 1883.

MILLS, Clark. Sculptor. Born in 1815. He lived in Charleston, S. C., where he discovered a method of taking casts from the living face. He executed busts of a number of eminent South Carolinians. He designed the Jackson monuments in Washington and New Orleans; also designed a scene in the battle of Princeton with a statue of Washington; this was dedicated in Washington, D. C., on Feb. 22, 1860. He died in 1883.

MILLS, Theodore Augustus. Sculptor. Born in Charleston, S. C., in 1839. Eldest son of Clark and Eliza S. Mills. During his boyhood he pursued modeling as an amusement, without regular instruction, until 1860, when he entered the Royal Art Academy of Munich as a pupil, receiving a prize for his composition, "Penelope Presenting the Bow of Ulysses to the Suitors"; this is said to be the only instance where a prize was conferred by this academy upon an American. Returned to the United States and commenced work in the studio of his father Clark Mills, then engaged in making a model for a proposed memorial in Washington to President Lincoln; was afterwards employed by the National Museum, Washington, and later at the Carnegie Institute, Pittsburgh. He died in 1916.

MILLS, Thomas Henry. Painter, illustrator and etcher. Born in Hartford, Conn., in 1877. Pupil of Kenyon Cox and of W. M. Chase. *Address*, Bass Rocks, Gloucester, Mass.

MILNE, David B. Painter and illustrator. Born in Paisley, Ontario, Canada, in 1882. Pupil of Art Students' League of New York, under Du Mond, Reuterdahl and Bridgman. Member: New York Water Color Club; Phila. Water Color Club. Award: Siver medal, Panama-Pacific Exposition, San Francisco, 1915. Represented in Canadian War Memorials Collections, Ottawa, Canada. *Address*, Boston Corners, Columbia County, N. Y.

MILNE, May Frances. Painter. Born in Brooklyn, N. Y., in 1894. *Address*, Boston Corners, Columbia County, N. Y.

MILSOM, E. Grace. Painter. Born in Buffalo, N. Y., in 1868. Studied with Bischoff and in Europe. Member: Buffalo Society of Artists. Represented in Albright Art Gallery, Buffalo. *Address*, 60 Ashland Ave., Buffalo, N. Y.

MINER, Fred R. Painter. Born in New London, Conn., in 1876. Pupil of Art Students' League of New York; also of William Wendt. Member: California Art Club; Laguna Beach Artists' Association; Society of Independent Artists. Award: Bronze medal, Panama-California Exposition, San Diego, 1915. *Address*, 2202 West 25th St., Los Angeles, Calif.

MINER, Georgia Watson (Mrs. Lewis H.). Painter. Born in Springfield, Ill., in 1876. Pupil of C. A. Herbert and Dawson-Watson. Award: Illinois State Centennial medals, 1918, for best painting and work in ceramics. *Address*, 1717 South 6th St., Springfield, Ill.

MINOR, Anne (B.) Rogers. Painter. Born in East Lyme, Conn., in 1865. Pupil of Robert C. Minor. *Address*, Waterford, Conn.

MINOR, Robert C. Painter. Born in New York in 1840; died in Waterford, Conn., in 1904. Landscape painter. Pupil of Van Luppen in Antwerp; and of Diaz and Boulanger in Paris. Awards: Honorable mention, Paris Exposition, 1900; silver medal, Pan-American Exposition, Buffalo, 1901. Elected to National Academy, 1897; Society of Landscape Painters. Represented at Corcoran Art Gallery, Washington, D. C., by "Eventide."

MIRANDA, Fernando. Sculptor. Exhibited at National Sculpture Society, New York.

MITCHELL, Alfred. Painter. Born in York, Pa., in 1888. Pupil of Garber and Pearson at Penna. Academy of Fine Arts. Represented at Reading Museum, Reading, Pa., by "Mission Valley," California.

MITCHELL, Arthur. Painter. Born in Gillespie, Ill., in 1864. Pupil of St. Louis School of Fine Arts. *Address*, 4211 Castleman Ave., St. Louis, Mo.

MITCHELL, E. Engraver. Fenshaw, in his work on book-plates, says that this English book-plate engraver was working in the U. S. in 1790. American book-plates so signed are found.

MITCHELL, Gurnsey. Sculptor, who died in Rochester, N. Y., in 1921. He was a graduate of the École des Beaux Arts in Paris. Among his best known works are the statue of Martin B. Anderson, former president of the University of Rochester; "Aurora"; "The Young Botanist"; "David and Goliath."

MITCHELL, Harvey. Portrait painter. His work was rather poor. He was painting in 1830 at Charleston, S. C.

MITCHELL, John. Painter. Born in 1811; died in 1866. His work was largely done in Hartford and in New London. He painted with a bold free hand, but unfortunately was strongly addicted to liquor.

MITCHELL, Laura M. D. Miniature painter. Born in Canada in 1883. Pupil of Bridgman, Cox and Beckington at Art Students' League of New York. She is Sec.-Treas. of the Society of Miniature Painters of America. *Address,* 307 South 4th St., Alhambra, Calif.

MIX, Florence. Painter of portraits and landscapes. She was born in Hartford, Conn., in 1881 and died in 1922.

MODJESKA, Marylka H. Etcher. Born in Chicago, Ill., in 1893. Pupil of Art Institute of Chicago and of George Senseney. Member: Chicago Society of Etchers; Alumni Art Institute of Chicago; Provincetown Artists' Association. *Address,* University Sta., Tucson, Ariz.

MOELLER, Gustave. Painter. Born in Wisconsin in 1881. Studied in Milwaukee, New York, Paris and Munich. *Address,* 1039 Third St., Milwaukee, Wisc.

MOELLER, Louis Charles. Painter. Born in New York in 1855. Specialty, genre subjects. Pupil of National Academy of Design, New York; of Dietz and Duveneck in Munich. Award: First Hallgarten prize, National Academy of Design, 1884. Elected Associate, National Academy, 1894; National Academy, 1895. Represented at Corcoran Art Gallery, Washington, D. C., by painting "Disagreement." *Address,* Edenwald, Wakefield, N. Y.

MOELLER, Selma. Miniature painter. Born in New York in 1880. Pupil of Art Students' League under Cox and Chase; also studied under Lucia Fairchild Fuller and Alice Beckington for miniatures. *Address,* 823 West End Ave., New York.

MOFFAT, J. A fairly well-engraved line portrait of Robert Burns is signed as "Eng'd on Steel by J. Moffat." This print was published by Wm. Pearson, New York, 1830–35; but it is possibly the work of a Scotch engraver and the plate was brought over here for publication.

MOFFETT, Ross E. Painter. Born in Clearfield, Ia., in 1888. Student of Art Institute of Chicago; Art Students' League, New York; also of Charles W. Hawthorne. Landscape and figure painter, and etcher. Exhibited in annual exhibitions at Penna. Academy of Fine Arts; Corcoran Art Gallery, Washington, D. C.; Philadelphia Art Club; Art Institute of Chicago; City Art Museum, St. Louis; John Herron Art Institute, Indianapolis; Brooklyn Society of Etchers. Represented in permanent collections of Penna. Academy of Fine Arts. Winner of Norman Wait Harris silver medal awarded by Institute of Chicago for painting "The Old Fisherman," 1918. *Address,* Provincetown, Mass.

MOFFITT, John M. Sculptor. Born in England in 1837. He came to the United States as a youth. He designed the figures that represent the four ages of man at the entrance to Greenwood Cemetery, the reredos in the Packer Memorial Church, and many altars in the principal churches of New York. He died in 1887.

MOISE, Theodore Sydney. Portrait painter. Born in Charleston, S. C., in 1806. He died in 1883. In 1850 his studio was at 51 Canal St., New Orleans, and he painted many portraits in Louisiana. He painted a standing portrait of Henry Clay now owned by the Metropolitan Gallery of New York.

MOLAND. In 1839 this name as "Moland Sc." is signed to fairly well-engraved script and sheet music, published in Philadelphia, by George Willing.

MOLARSKY, Abraham. Painter. Born in Russia in 1879. Pupil of Chase in Philadelphia and of the Penna. Academy of Fine Arts. *Address,* 62 High St., Nutley, N. J.

MOLARSKY, Maurice. Painter. Born in Kieff, Russia, in 1885. Studied at School of Industrial Art and at the Penna. Academy of Fine Arts, Philadelphia; also in France and England. Awards: Cresson scholarship, Penna. Academy of Fine Arts; honorable mention, Philadelphia Art Club; Fellowship prize, Penna. Academy of Fine Arts; silver medal, Panama-Pacific Exposition, San Francisco, 1915; gold medal, Art Club of Philadelphia. *Address,* Philadelphia, Pa.

MOLINARY, Marie Seebold (Mrs. Andres). Painter. Born in New Orleans, La., in 1876. Pupil of William Chase and A. Molinary. Work in Delgado Museum, New Orleans. *Address,* 2322 Canal St., New Orleans, La.

MOLINEUX. Engraver. In 1831 there was published by Luke Loomis & Co., of Pittsburg, Pa., a German work entitled "The Life and Works of Johann Friedrich Oberlin," with an introduction by Prof. S. S. Schmucker, of the Theological Seminary at Gettysburg, Pa. The frontispiece to this book is an engraved silhouette of Oberlin, signed "Molineux Sc. Pitt." This same Molineux engraved upon copper for this work a fairly well-executed portrait of Louise Schepler, and views of the residences of Oberlin and some of his fellow-workers. No other examples of the engraved work of Molineux are known to the compiler.

MOMBERGER, William. Painter. Born in Germany in 1829. He came to the United States in 1848. He painted several landscapes, but gave much of his time to illustrating.

MONACHISE, N. Painter. Nothing is known of his work except that he painted historical pieces and portraits, and that his studio was at 98 Locust St., Philadelphia.

MONAGHAN, Gertrude. Mural painter. Born in West Chester, Pa. Pupil of School of Design for Women; Penna. Academy of Fine Arts. Member: Plastic Club; Fellowship, Penna. Academy of Fine Arts. *Address,* 3309 Baring St., Philadelphia, Pa.

MONKS, John Austin Sands. Painter. Born in Cold Spring-on-Hudson, N. Y., in 1850; died in 1917. Studied wood engraving and etching in 1869. Pupil in painting of George Inness, 1875. Engaged in art work after 1874. His specialty was painting sheep. Member: Copley Society, Boston. Clubs: Salmagundi, New York Etching, Boston Art.

MONTAGUE, Harriotte Lee Taliaferro (Mrs. Jefry). Painter. Pupil of George de Forest Brush and Twachtman in New York; of Angelo Yank, Fehr, Hummel and Knurr in Munich; Simon in Paris. Member: Richmond Art Club. Work: "Portrait of Capt. Sallie Tompkins," Richmond Art Club; portrait in D. A. R. Hall, Washington, D. C. Represented in Confederate Museum and the State Library in Richmond; also in Westmoreland, Va., Court House. *Address,* 1609 Hanover Ave., Richmond, Va.

MONTANA, Pietro. Painter. Exhibited at National Academy, New York, 1925. *Address,* 28 East 14th St., New York.

MONTGOMERY, Alfred. Painter. His specialty was depicting farm life. He was born in 1857 and died in 1922.

MONTGOMERY, R. Engraver. The only example of the work of this engraver seen by the writer is a book-plate of James Giles, signed "R. Montgomery, Sculp." The plate is armorial, with a cannon and American flag introduced into the decoration, and it is crude enough in execution to have been the work of some apprentice or local engraver. Some collectors of "ex libris" assert that the engraver of the plate was Gen. Richard Montgomery, who was killed at Quebec in 1775. This book-plate was probably engraved by Robert Montgomery, who advertises in the *New York Packet* in 1783, as "Watch-Maker, Clock Maker and Engraver."

MOONEY, Edward L. Painter. Born in New York City in 1813. He began his art studies at the Academy of Design. He became a pupil of Henry Inman, and copied much of his work; later he studied with William Page. He has painted many excellent portraits of prominent men; his picture of Gov. Wm. H. Seward is in the State House in Albany and he has painted several of the Mayors of New York City, now in the City Hall. He died in 1887.

MOORE, Benson B. Painter and illustrator. Born in Washington, D. C., in 1882. Pupil of Corcoran School of Art, Washington. Member: Washington Society of Artists; Washington Water Color Club; Washington Landscape Club. *Address,* The "Oneida," 147 R St., N.E., Washington, D. C.

MOORE, C. H. Residence in Catskill, New York; has done some landscape work of decided merit.

MOORE, Cecil Gresham. Painter and illustrator. Born in Kingston, Ontario, Canada, in 1880. Pupil of the Rochester Athenaeum & Mechanics Institution. Member: Rochester Art Club. Work: Mural decorations in Powers Hotel, Rochester. *Address,* 126 Plymouth Ave., Rochester, N. Y.

MOORE, Edwin A. Painter. Born in Hartford, Conn., in 1858. He was a son of Nelson A. Moore, and has follwoed his father's profession of painting. *Address,* 901 West Lane, Kensington, Conn.

MOORE, Ellen Maria. Miniature painter. Born in Kensington, Conn. Pupil of Art Students' League of New York; also of Mary Elmer and I. A. Josephi. *Address,* Kensington, Conn.

MOORE, Frank M. Painter. Born in Taunton, Somersetshire, England, in 1877. Pupil of John Finnie, Liverpool. Member: New York Water Color Club. *Address,* 939 Eighth Ave., New York, N. Y.

MOORE, (Harry) Humphrey. Painter. Born in New York, N. Y., in 1844. Pupil of Bail in New Haven; S. Waugh in Philadelphia; École des Beaux Arts in Paris, under Gerome, Boulanger and Yvon. Member: Rochester Art Club. His work is principally Moorish, Spanish, and Japanese subjects. *Address,* 75 Rue de Courcelles, Paris, France.

MOORE, Isaac W. Engraver, who was engraving good line portraits and historical plates in 1831–33, for Philadelphia periodicals.

MOORE, Mrs. Lou Wall. Sculptor. Member: Chicago Society of Artists. Award: Bronze medal, St. Louis Exposition, 1904. *Address*, 5476 Ridgewood Court, Chicago, Ill.

MOORE, Nelson A. Born in Connecticut in 1824. He studied with Cummings, and later with Daniel Huntington. His pastoral scenes show great merit; "The Genius of Liberty" was also considered a great success.

MOORE, T. This stipple-engraver of portraits signs himself on one of his plates "T. Moore (successor to Pendleton) Boston."

MORA, Domingo. Sculptor, who has exhibited at National Sculpture Society, New York.

MORA, F. Luis. Painter. Born in Montevideo, Uruguay, S. A., in 1874. Studied art in the School of Drawing and Painting, Museum of Fine Arts, Boston; Art Students' League, New York. Beginning about 1892 he did illustrating work for all the leading magazines and periodicals. His first important commission was a large decorative panel for the main reading hall, Lynn (Mass.) Public Library, 1900; represented in all most important art exhibitions in America since 1894; painted decorations for Mo. State Bldg., St. Louis Exposition, 1904; also mural decorations for Orpheum Theatre, Los Angeles, Calif. Represented in permanent collections of Boston Art Club; Lotos Club, New York; Art Gallery, Oakland, Calif.; Columbia University; State Gallery, Dallas, Tex.; Art Association Gallery, Lafayette, Ind.; Lynn, Mass., Public Library; Youngstown. Elected Member of the National Academy, 1906; also member of Municipal Art Society; New York Water Color Club; Architectural League; Society of Illustrators; American Water Color Society; Art Students' League of New York. *Address*, Gaylordsville, Conn.

MORA, Joseph J. Painter and sculptor. Born in Montevideo, Uruguay, in 1876. Pupil of Art Students' League of New York. *Address*, Mountain View, Calif.

MORAHAN, Eugene. Sculptor. Born in Brooklyn, N. Y., in 1869. Pupil of Augustus Saint Gaudens. Member: National Sculpture Society. Work: Alfred Gwynne Vanderbilt memorial fountain, Newport, R. I.; Elks Memorial, Buffalo; Soldiers and Sailors Memorial, Carroll Park, Brooklyn, N. Y. *Address*, 1931 Broadway, Manhattan, New York, N. Y.

MORAN, Edward. Painter. Born in England in 1829. Lived in New York and Philadelphia. Member: Penna. Academy of Fine Arts. Exhibited in Philadelphia in 1853. Painted fishermen at their toil or water scenes and vessels. Represented in Wilstach collection, Fairmount Park, Philadelphia. He died in 1901.

MORAN, (Edward) Percy. Painter. Born in Philadelphia in 1862. Studied art under his father, and with his uncle, S. J. Ferris, Philadelphia. Pupil of National Academy of Design, New York; also studied in London and Paris. Award: First Hallgarten prize, National Academy of Design, 1886; 1st gold medal, American Art Association, 1888. Frequent exhibitor in important exhibitions; also represented in well-known collections. Specialty, colonial subjects. Member: American Water Color Society. Principal paintings: "A Corner of the Studio," 1882; "The Wood-Cutter's Daughter," 1882; "The Duet," 1884; "Afternoon Tea," 1885; "The Miller's Daughter," 1886; "Divided Attention," 1886; "The Dancing Lesson," 1887; "The Rehearsal for the Ball," 1887.

MORAN, (John) Leon. Painter. Born in Philadelphia in 1864. Studied art under his father; at the National Academy of Design, New York; also in London and Paris; returned to the U. S. in 1879 and established a studio in New York in 1883. He was a frequent exhibitor at the National Academy of Design, New York, and elsewhere; gold medal, Philadelphia, Art Club; gold medal, American Art Society. Principal paintings: "Waylaid," 1885; "An Interrupted Conspiracy," 1886; "An Amateur," 1887; "The Duel," 1887; "An Idyl," 1888; "Eel Fishing," 1888; "Intercepted Dispatches"; "Madonna and Child"; "Between Two Fires." *Address*, Plainfield, N. J.

MORAN, Mary Nimmo (Mrs. Thomas). Etcher. Her plates as a rule are bold and direct and are marked by energetic emphasis. Her work stands high among the women etchers in this country.

MORAN, Peter. Painter and etcher. Born in Bolton, Lancashire, England, in 1842; died in 1915. Studied with his brothers Thomas and Edward Moran; also in England, in 1863. Member: The Art Club of Philadelphia. Pres. of the Society of Etchers. His paintings are principally of landscapes and animal subjects.

MORAN, Thomas. Painter and etcher. Born in Lancashire, England, in 1837, but was brought to the United States when a boy of seven. He began his art career as a wood engraver in Philadelphia and in his hours of leisure taught himself to paint in water color and afterwards in oils. His brother, Edward Moran, gave him the benefits of the instruction he had himself received. In 1862 Thomas Moran went to England and made a study of the masters in the National Gallery, receiving a strong impression from the work of J. Turner.

In 1872 Mr. Moran established himself permanently in New York. He spent his summers at his country home at Easthampton, L. I. He was elected a National Academician in 1884, and was a member of the Pennsylvania Academy of Fine Arts; the Artists' Fund Society; the American Water Color Society; the New York Etching Club; Society of American Etchers. The subjects of his pictures were taken from one or another of the places he visited and studied, now Venice, now the Yellowstone Park, now Niagara, and now the luxuriant meadows of Kent and Sussex, or the quiet villages and pastures of Long Island. As a water color painter and as an etcher his skill and fertility of invention were equally notable.

MORANGES. Miniature painter, who flourished in Baltimore, 1795.

MORAS, Ferdinand. Engraver. Born in Germany in 1821, he studied lithography at Elberfeld. He established one of the first lithographic plants in this country, and was the first lithographer to attempt color printing with this process of engraving. In 1844 Thomas Moran became apprenticed to Moras in Philadelphia. In 1882 he published a book of poems of which he was the author, illustrator and engraver. He died in 1908.

MOREIN, J. A. Portrait painter in oils and miniatures, who flourished in New York in 1841–42.

MORETTI, Giuseppe. Italian sculptor, who came to New York and exhibited at the National Sculpture Society.

MORGAN, Alexander C. Painter. Born in Sandusky, Ohio, in 1849. Member: Artists' Fund Society. *Address*, 134 West 73d St., New York, N. Y.

MORGAN, Franklin T. Painter, etcher and illustrator. Born in Brooklyn, N. Y., in 1883. Pupil of Bridgman and Carlsen. *Address*, Moylan, Rose Valley, Penna.

MORGAN, George T. Engraver. Born in Birmingham, England, in 1845; living in Philadelphia in 1892. Morgan studied at the art school in Birmingham and won a national scholarship in the South Kensington Art School, where he was a student for two years. He came to the United States, and in 1875 he was made an assistant engraver in the U. S. Mint in Philadelphia, and remained there a number of years. He designed and executed the dies for the once famous "Bland Dollar."

MORGAN, Louis. American landscape painter. Born in 1814; died in 1852.

MORGAN, Matthew Somerville. Painter. Born in London in 1839. He came to the United States in 1870 and worked in New York in 1880. He went to Cincinnati, and in 1883 founded there the Morgan Art Pottery Co. and the Art Students' League. He painted a series of large panoramic pictures of the battles in the Civil War, which were exhibited in Cincinnati in 1886. His studio was in New York, and he died there in 1890.

MORGAN, Theodore J. Painter and wood-engraver. Born in Cincinnati. He studied at the Cincinnati Art School, and applied himself to wood engraving. In 1916 he gave up engraving for painting, and settled on Cape Cod where he has painted the harbor and sea. He has exhibited at the Penna. Academy of Fine Arts, Philadelphia. *Address*, 98 Commercial St., Provincetown, Mass.

MORGAN, Wallace. Illustrator. Born in New York. Student of National Academy of Design. Employed as illustrator on New York papers; also as book illustrator.

MORGAN, William. Born in London, England, in 1826. He came to this country in early life. He received his training in the schools of the National Academy of which he became an Associate in 1865. His works include "Emancipation"; "The Legend"; "Song without Words"; "Motherhood"; "Summer"; "Blowing Bubbles." He died in 1900.

MORIN, J. F. Engraver of maps, business-cards, etc., who was working in New York in 1825–31, as shown by dates of publication on his few signed plates. In 1825 he engraved in connection with S. Maverick, and was then apparently in the employ of that engraver and copperplate printer. In 1831 Morin engraved a good map of New York City for "The Traveller's Guide through the State of New York," published in New York in that year.

MORO, Paolo. Painter. Exhibited at National Academy of Design, New York, 1925. *Address*, 2104 Vyse Avenue.

MORRELL, Imogene Robinson. Painter. Born in Attleboro, Mass.; died in Washington, D. C., in 1908. Studied art under Gamphausen, and in Paris under Couture. Resided in Paris for several years and enjoyed the friendship of Meissonier, Bouguereau and other prominent artists of France. On her second visit to Paris she was accompanied by Elizabeth Jane Gardner, who became a pupil and later the wife of W. A. Bouguereau. Mrs. Morrell's work was recognized by medals at the Mechanics' Institute in Boston and at the Centennial Exposition in Philadelphia. Among her important pictures are: "First Battle between the Puritans and the Indians," "Washington and His Staff Welcoming a Provision Train," and "David before Saul."

MORRIS, Paul W. Sculptor. Born in Du Quoin, Ill., in 1865. He studied with Saint Gaudens, and under D. C. French in New York. He died in New York City in 1916.

MORRISON, Zaidee. Painter and illustrator. Born in Skowhegan, Me. Pupil of J. H. Twachtman; F. V. Du Mond; W. M. Chase; R. H. Nicholls. Member: Art Students' League of New York; New York Water Color Club. Work in Mary Lyon Room, Mount Holyoke College, Mass.; Colby University, Waterville, Me.; magazine covers for *Life*, *Judge*, posters, etc. *Address*, 152 West 57th St., New York, N. Y.

MORROW, Julie. Painter. Born in New York, N. Y. Pupil of Jonas Lie and C. W. Hawthorne. Member: National Association of Women Painters and Sculptors; Provincetown Artists' Association; League of New York Artists. *Address*, 101 West 85th St., New York, N. Y.

MORSE, Anne Goddard. Painter and illustrator. Born in Providence, R. I., in 1854. Pupil of Mass. Normal Art School; Art Students' League of New York; of Wyatt Eaton in New York; with John La Farge for stained glass. Member: Providence Water Color Club. *Address*, Care of Dr. C. C. Simmons, P. O. Box 235, North Scituate, Mass.

MORSE, Edward Lind. Painter and writer. Born in Poughkeepsie, N. Y., in 1857; died in New York, 1923. Studied at Royal Academy Art, Berlin, 1884–88; Grand Ducal Academy of Art, Weimar, Germany, 1888–91; Julien Academy, Paris, 1891–92. Exhibited in Paris Salon, 1893; held exhibitions at National Academy of Design; Society of American Artists, etc.; special exhibitions of work in Washington, New York, Chicago, St. Louis, etc. Member: American Federation of Arts.

MORSE, Henry D. Painter. Born in Boston in 1826, where he continued to live. He had no regular instruction in art and was not considered a professional artist; still in his leisure hours for many years he painted pictures, generally of animals, that met with a ready sale in Boston. He was a member of the Boston Art Club.

MORSE, Hazen. Engraver. In the *New England Palladium* of July 20, 1824, "Hazen Morse, Engraver," announces that he has removed from No. 6 Congress Street to Congress Square, "a few doors south of the Exchange Coffee House," and he there "continues the business of Copper Plate engraving, in its various branches." Copperplate printing was also done at the same place. For a time Hazen was in the employ of the Boston engraving firm of Annin & Smith. According to the advertisement quoted above he seems to have been chiefly engaged in engraving doorplates, brass

numbers for doors, coffin-plates, stencil-plates, etc. The only signed copperplate known to the writer is the "Carey" book-plate inscribed "H. Morse Sc."

MORSE, Mary Minns. Painter. Born in Dorchester, Mass., in 1859. Pupil of Ross Turner and Louis Ritter in Boston; of George Hitchcock in Holland. Member: Boston Water Color Club; Copley Society. Specialty, landscape and marines in water colors. *Address*, 211 Savin Hill Ave., Boston, Mass.

MORSE, Nathaniel. Engraver. The following death notice is found in *The Boston Gazette, or Weekly Journal*, Boston, June 21, 1748: "Last Friday (June 17) died here Mr. Nathaniel Morse, an ingenious engraver, whose corpse was decently inter'd last Lord's Day Evening."

The only engraving by Nathaniel Morse found by the compiler is a portrait of Rev. Matthew Henry, rudely engraved in line after a print by George Vertue. This portrait is the frontispiece to "The Communicant's Companion, etc.," by Matthew Henry, published in "Boston in New England, re-printed for T. Phillips at the Stationer's Arms, next to Mr. Dolbear, the Braziers, 1731."

The Mass. Archives contain a copy of a bill of 1735, showing that Morse was paid for engraving and printing a plate for Massachusetts paper money. This bill is signed "Nat Mors," as is the engraving of Matthew Henry referred to above.

MORSE, Sadie May. Painter. Born in Lexington, Mass., in 1873. Pupil of Mass. Normal Art School, Boston; also studied one year in Italy. Member: Hingham Arts and Crafts Society. Educational director under Federal Board for Vocational Education. *Address*, 11 Hancock Ave., Lexington, Mass.

MORSE, Samuel Finley Breese. Inventor, figure and portrait painter and sculptor. Born in Charlestown, Mass., in 1791; died in New York City in 1872. He was graduated from Yale in 1810; became a pupil of Washington Allston whom he accompanied the following year to London, where he studied under Benj. West. Returned to America in 1815 and painted portraits in Boston, Mass.; Concord, N. H.; in Charleston, S. C. Settled in New York in 1823, where, in 1826, he became one of the original founders of the National Academy of Design, and its first President, serving from 1827–45 and again, 1861–62. Among his most important paintings is the full-length portrait of Lafayette in the New York City Hall, and the large picture of the old "House of Representatives by Candle Light," now in the Corcoran Gallery of Art, in Washington, D. C. His model of a "Dying Hercules," made to assist him in painting a picture of this subject which was exhibited in 1813 at the Royal Academy, was awarded a gold medal the same year by the Adelphia Society of Arts.

He abandoned art as a profession in 1839, devoting the balance of his life to perfecting his invention of the telegraph. See life of Samuel Finley Breese Morse, by Edward Morse.

MORSE & TUTTLE. In 1840 this firm was engraving maps in Boston, Mass., and the Morse of the firm was probably Hazen Morse.

MORTON, Christina (Mrs. Benjamin A.). Painter. Born in Dardanelle, Ark. Member: Allied Artists' Association; National Academy of Women Painters and Sculptors. *Address*, 27 West 67th St., New York, N. Y.

MORTON, John Ludlow. Painter. He was a native of New York, and a son of General Morton. His best known painting was a historical scene from Scott's "Ivanhoe." He was elected an Academician in 1831. He died in New York in 1871, having been active all his life from his student days in the National Academy of Design.

MORTON, Mrs. Josephine A. Painter. Born in Boston, Mass., in 1854. Pupil of Eakins; of Laurens and Constant in Paris. Member: Newport Artists' Association; Society of Independent Artists. *Address*, 144 Main St., Williamstown, Mass.

MOSCHCOWITZ, Paul. Painter. Born in Hungary in 1875, he came to New York in 1890. Specialty, portraiture and mural painting. Elected an Associate Member of National Academy of Design. *Address*, 42 West 39th St., New York.

MOSELEY, Helen E. Painter. Exhibited at 33d Annual Exhibition of National Association of Women Painters and Sculptors, "Gloucester Moors." *Address*, Grand Rapids, Mich.

MOSER, James Henry. Painter. Born in Whitby, Ontario, Canada, in 1854; died in Washington, District of Columbia, in 1913. Landscape painter in oils and water colors. Pupil of John H. Witt and Charles H. Davis. Awards: medal, Atlanta Exposition, 1895; first Corcoran prize, Washington Water Color Club, 1900; bronze medal, Charleston Exposition, 1902, etc. Represented at the Corcoran Art Gallery, Washington, D. C., by "Winter Sunshine" (water color), painted in 1895; "The Mountain Road" (water color), painted in 1904.

MOSES, Thomas G. Landscape painter. Born in Liverpool, England, in 1856. Pupil of Art Institute of Chicago, and of R. M. Shurtleff. Member: Palette and Chisel Club; Chicago Society of Artists; California Art Club. *Address*, 417 South Clinton St., Chicago, Ill.

MOSLER, Henry. Painter. Born in New York in 1841; died in 1920. Figure and genre painter. Pupil of James H. Beard in Cincinnati; Mucke and Kindler in Dusseldorf; Hebert in Paris; Wagner in Munich. Awards: medal, Royal Academy, Munich, 1874; honorable mention, Paris Salon, 1879. Represented at the Corcoran Art Gallery by "Saying Grace," painted in 1897.

MOSS, Ella A. Painter. Born in New Orleans in 1844. Studied in Europe, and opened her studio in New York. She painted many portraits of prominent people and exhibited in the National Academy in 1878.

MOTE, Alden. Portrait and landscape painter. He was born in West Milton, Ohio, in 1840, and after 1880 lived in Richmond, Ind. Represented by a portrait of Daniel G. Reid in the Reid Memorial Hospital at Richmond, Ind.

MOTE, W. H. This English portrait-engraver did a large amount of work in London in the first half of the century. He engraved portraits of Charles Carroll, of Carrollton, Epes Sargent, and other Americans, and subject plates engraved by him were used in American publications; but no evidence has been found by the compiler that Mote ever actually engraved in this country. The plates mentioned were probably brought over here for publication.

MOTLEY, Eleanor W. Painter. Exhibited water colors at the Penna. Academy of Fine Arts, Philadelphia, 1925. *Address*, 22 Commonwealth Ave., Boston, Mass.

MOTT-SMITH, Mae (Mrs. Small). Painter and sculptor, also miniature painter. Born in 1879. Pupil of Colarossi Academy, Paris. Exhibited sculpture, "A Berber Woman" at National Academy of Design, 1925. *Address*, 17 West 47th St., New York.

MOTTET, Jeanie Gallup (Mrs. Henry). Painter. Born in Providence, R. I., in 1864. Pupil of Chase, Richard E. Miller, E. Ambrose Webster. Member: National Academy of Women Painters and Sculptors; Provincetown Artists' Association. Curator of painting, Museum of French Art, New York, N. Y. *Address*, 47 West 20th St., New York, N. Y.

MOTTRAM, C. Engraver. A fine line-engraving, signed by C. Mottram as engraver, represents a view of the city of New York from the Brooklyn shore. It is made from a drawing executed by J. W. Hill, New York, 1855, and was published in New York in the same year. John William Hill was the son of John Hill, the aquatint-engraver, who came to the United States in 1816 and died here in 1850. No other work has been seen signed by C. Mottram.

MOTZ-LOWDON, Elsie. Painter. Born in Waco, Texas. Pupil of Art Students' League of New York; American School of Miniature Painters. Member: National Academy of Women Painters and Sculptors. *Address*, 105 East 17th St., New York, N. Y.

MOULD, J. B. This name is signed as engraver to good stipple portraits published in New York about 1830, but as the portraits are those of foreigners it is possible that these plates were imported.

MOULTHROP, Reuben. Portrait painter. Born in 1763. He also modelled in wax. He died in East Haven, Conn., in 1814. His portraits of Ezra Stiles and Jonathan Edwards are good examples of his work.

MOULTON, Claxton B. Painter. Exhibited "Portrait of a Boy" at Penna. Academy of Fine Arts, Philadelphia, 1921. *Address*, 172 Townsend St., Boston, Mass.

MOUNT, Henry Smith. Painter. Born in 1802. He was a brother of Wm. S. and Shephard Alonzo. He was elected an Associate Member of the National Academy in 1832 and exhibited frequently. He died in 1841.

MOUNT, (Shepard) Alonzo. Painter, brother of W. S. Mount. Born in 1804; died in 1868. He was a distinguished portrait painter. Became an Associate of the National Academy, 1831, and Academician in 1842. He painted portraits of Martin Van Buren and other distinguished statesmen.

MOUNT, William Sidney. Painter. Born in Setauket, L. I., in 1807. Pupil of the National Academy of Design, he had a studio in New York for nearly forty years. He did not exhibit often at the Academy, his pictures having a very popular market. He was elected a Member of the National Academy of Design, and died in 1868. Represented in Metropolitan Museum of Art, and in the National Gallery, Washington, D. C.

MOUNTFORT, Arnold. Painter. Born in Eggbaston, England, in 1873. Pupil of Birmingham Municipal School of Art, England. *Address*, Sherwood Studios, 58 West 57th St., New York, N. Y.

MOWBRAY, H. Siddons. Painter. Born in Alexandria, Egypt, in 1858; brought to United States in 1859. Studied painting under Bonnat, Paris, 1878; in New York after 1878. Principal works: "A Lady in Black"; "Evening Breeze"; "Le Destin"; etc.; mural decorations in residences of F. W. Vanderbilt, C. P. Huntington, J. Pierpont Morgan, Appellate Ct. House, and University Club Library, New York; residence of Larz Anderson, Washington; Federal Court Room, Cleveland.

Elected member of the National Academy, 1891. *Address*, Washington, Conn.

MOWBRAY-CLARKE, John F. Sculptor. Born in 1863. Pupil of Lambeth School, London. Represented in Metropolitan Museum, New York. *Address*, 53 East 44th St., New York.

MOYNIHAN, Frederick. Sculptor, who has made rather a specialty of military figures of the Civil War period.

MOZIER, Joseph. Sculptor. Born in Burlington, Vt., in 1812; died at Faids, Switzerland, in 1870. He first entered a mercantile business in New York, but retired from that in 1845, in order to devote himself to art. He studied sculpture for several years in Florence, and then went to Rome, where he spent the greater part of his professional career. Among his best works are "Esther," the "Wept of Wish-ton-Wish," "Tacite," and "Truth," the "White Lady of Avenel," "The Peri," "Pocahontas," "Prodigal Son," "Rizpah," and "Il Penseroso" in marble; the latter was transferred from the Capitol in 1888 to the National Gallery, Washington, D. C.

MUELLER, Alexander. Painter. Born in Milwaukee, Wisc., in 1872. Studied in Milwaukee and in Germany. *Address*, School of Fine Arts, State Normal School, Milwaukee.

MUGFORD, William. Portrait painter. The Peabody Museum of Salem, Mass., owns a crayon portrait by William Mugford.

MUHLHOFER, Elizabeth. Painter. Exhibited water colors at the Penna. Academy of Fine Arts, Philadelphia, 1925. *Address*, 130 Eleventh St., Washington, D. C.

MULHAUPT, Frederick J. Painter. Born in Rockport, Mo., in 1871. Pupil of Art Academy, Kansas City, and of Paris Schools. *Address*, 57 East 59th St., New York.

MULLEN, Richard. Wood engraver. Born in Germany in 1849. He came to this country when a boy and was educated at the Cooper Union, and at the National Academy of Design. He illustrated many of the early New York magazines with wood cuts until his work was replaced by the photo-engraving process. He died in Brooklyn in 1915.

MULLER, H. Dunlap notes him as a landscape painter, working in New York in 1828.

MULLER, Olga Popoff. Sculptor. Exhibited at the National Association of Women Painters and Sculptors, 1924. *Address*, 121 Jamaica Ave., Flushing, Long Island, N. Y.

MULLER-URY, Adolfo. Portrait painter. Born in Airolo, Switzerland, in 1864. Pupil of

Deschwanden, Switzerland, then of the Munich Academy; in Paris he was a pupil of Cabanel in 1881. He came to America in 1886. At Rome he painted portraits of Cardinals Hergenrother, Hohenlohe, Pope Pius X, Cardinal Merry del Val, and of Bishop Kennedy in 1907; also many religious pictures. He painted in New York portraits of President McKinley; General Grant; Senator and Mrs. Depew; Senator Hanna; J. Pierpont Morgan; James J. Hill; also one of Cardinal Mercier, when visiting the U. S., for the Catholic University, Washington. *Address*, 33 West 67th St., New York.

MULLIGAN, Charles J. Sculptor. Born in Ireland in 1866. He came to America as a boy and worked with a stone cutter near Chicago. Studied at Chicago Art Institute, and later under Falguiere, in Paris. Among his statues are ''The Three Sisters,'' at Springfield, Illinois; Lincoln, known as ''The Rail Splitter,'' and a statue of Col. Finnerty. He died in 1916.

MULLIKEN, Jonathan. Engraver. Born in Newburyport, Mass., in 1746; died there June 1782. The only known copper-plate engraving by Mulliken is a very close copy of Paul Revere's ''Massacre'' plate, though there is no indication of the date of production. He was probably a self-taught engraver, producing some of his own metal clock faces, an accomplishment not rare among the early clockmakers.

MULVANEY, John. Painter. Born in 1844, he came to this country when he was twenty. He specialized in painting Western, Indian, and army life; he was best known for his ''Custer's Last Rally.'' He also painted many portraits, one of his last being that of Bishop Mc Donnell of Brooklyn. He died in New York in 1906.

MUMFORD, Edward William. Engraver. Son of Thomas Howland Mumford (1789–1825), cashier of the Merchants' Bank of Newport, R. I. In 1835–40 Mumford was engraving landscapes and subject plates for Philadelphia publishers.

MUNDAY, Rosemary. Painter. Exhibited at the Penna. Academy of Fine Arts, Philadelphia, 1914. *Address*, Norway, Maine.

MUNDY, Ethel Frances. Painter. Born in Syracuse, N. Y. Student of Art Students' League, New York; also of Rochester Mechanics' Institute. Pupil of Amy M. Sacker, Boston. With the aid of a chemist she discovered a new composition for use in wax portraiture, and revived the art of wax portraiture which was known in Europe for 500 years, until lost in the eighteenth century. Associate of the Royal Society of Miniature Painters of England. *Address*, 121 College Place, Syracuse, N. Y.

MUNGER, Anne Wells (Mrs. W. L. C.). Landscape painter. Born in Springfield, Mass., in 1862. Pupil of Philip Hale, Woodbury and De Camp in Boston; of Brush in New York. Specialty, landscape painting. *Address*, Sign of the Pine, South Wellfleet, Mass.

MUNGER, Caroline. Miniature painter. Born in 1808. She was the daughter of George Munger. In 1831 she married Horace Wasburn, and exhibited miniatures at the National Academy of New York in 1841. She died in 1892.

MUNGER, George. Engraver. Born at Guilford, Conn., in 1783; died in 1824. Munger was a miniature painter of some merit, and the firm of N. & S. S. Jocelyn engraved plates after portraits painted by him. In 1816, N. Jocelyn and G. Munger, of New Haven, Conn., published a large aquatint view of the Island of St. Helena. This plate is signed ''G. Munger, Sculp.''; but it is the only example of his engraved work found.

Munger was some relation of Anson Dickinson, the miniature painter, also born in Connecticut. Two of Munger's daughters became artists.

MUNN, George F. Artist. Born in Utica, N. Y., in 1852. Studied in the National Academy, N. Y., and later in England in the studio of George F. Watts. He has exhibited in many of the galleries.

MUNN, Marguerite C. Painter. Exhibited at Penna. Academy of Fine Arts, Phila., in Society of Artists; National Association of Women Painters and Sculptors. *Address*, 1842 Sixteenth St., Washington, D. C.

MUNRO, Albert A. Painter and etcher. Born in Hoboken, N. J., in 1868. *Address*, Springfield, L. I., N. Y.

MUNROE, Marjory. Painter. Born in New York, N. Y., in 1891. Pupil of Frank Du Mond, E. Percy Moran, and of Geo. Elmer Browne. *Address*, 12 East 30th St., New York, N. Y.

MUNROE, Sarah Sewell. Painter. Born in Brooklyn, N. Y. Member of Washington Society of Artists; National Association of Women Painters and Sculptors; Washington Art Club; Washington Water Color Club. Awards: Second Corcoran prize, Washington Water Color Club; honorable mention, Society of Washington Artists, 1921. *Address*, 1903 N St., Washington, D. C.

MUNSELL, Albert Henry. Portrait painter. Born in Boston in 1858. Student of École des Beaux Arts in Paris. Exhibited at Paris Salon, 1886–87–88; also in Boston, New York,

Chicago and Pittsburgh. Instructor in Mass. Normal Art School after 1881; lecturer on artistic anatomy and color composition. He patented new instruments for color measurement, and invented a system of pigment colors, which has been introduced in schools of Boston, New York, Baltimore, Mexico City, etc. Author: Color Notation, 1905; Atlas of the Color System, 1910. *Address*, 221 Columbus Ave., Boston.

MUNSELL, W. A. O. Painter. Born in Cold Water, Ohio, in 1866. *Address*, 416 Stimson Bldg., Los Angeles, Pasadena, Calif.

MUNSON, Lucius. Painter. Born in New Haven, Conn., in 1796. In 1820 he visited South Carolina and painted many portraits, and had hopes of being able to study in Europe, but sickness prevented and he died in Turks Island, in 1823.

MUNSON, Samuel B. Engraver. Born in Connecticut in 1806; died in Cincinnati, Ohio, in 1880. In 1830–35 Munson was engraving in New Haven in conjunction with S. S. Jocelyn of that town, but about 1836 he removed to Cincinnati, Ohio, and was a member of the banknote engraving firm of Doolittle & Munson of that city. For a time he was associated with G. K. Stillman in engraving and publishing prints.

MUNZIG, G. C. Portrait painter. Born in Boston in 1850. His specialty was portraits in crayon. Member of the Boston Art Club. He has exhibited in Philadelphia, New York, Cleveland and Boston.

MURDOCH, Dora Louise. Painter. Born in New Haven, Conn., in 1857. Pupil of Courtois, Rixen and Boutet de Monvel in Paris. Member: Baltimore Water Color Club; New York Water Color Club. Award: Purnell prize, Baltimore Water Color Club, 1903. *Address*, 245 West Biddle St., Baltimore, Md.

MURDOCH, Florence. Painter. Member: Cincinnati Woman's Art Club. *Address*, 2448 Maplewood Ave., Mt. Auburn, Ohio.

MURDOCH, Frank C. Painter. Member: Pittsburgh Artists' Association. *Address*, 5709 Woodmont St., Pittsburgh, Pa.

MURPHY. A crudely engraved line frontispiece, representing ''Wisdom,'' is signed ''Murphy sculp.'' This plate was published in New York in 1807. The design shows Minerva armed with spear and shield standing in center, with a flying Cupid and palm tree to left and a lamb at her feet. No other example of Murphy's work has been seen.

MURPHY, Ada C. Painter and illustrator. Pupil of Cooper Union and of Douglas Volk in New York. Member: National Association of Women Painters and Sculptors; National Art Club. Awards: Hallgarten prize, National Academy of Design, 1894. *Address*, 222 West 23d St., New York, N. Y.

MURPHY, H. Dudley. Painter and illustrator. Born in Marlboro, Mass., in 1867. Pupil of Boston Museum School; of Laurens in Paris. Member: Copley Society, 1886; Boston Water Color Club; New York Water Color Club. Awards: Silver medal for portrait and bronze medal for water color, St. Louis Exposition, 1904; silver medal for oil painting and silver medal for water colors, Panama-Pacific Exposition, San Francisco, 1915. Work: ''Mt. Monadnock,'' Art Institute of Chicago; ''The Opal Sunset,'' Art Association, Nashville, Tenn.; ''Murano'' and ''Still Life,'' Albright Art Gallery, Buffalo, New York; ''Moro Castle, San Juan,'' Dallas, Tex., Museum of Fine Arts. *Address*, Lexington, Mass.

MURPHY, John Francis. Landscape painter. Born in Oswego, N. Y., in 1853. He was largely self-taught. He first exhibited at the National Academy of Design in New York in 1876. He won many prizes, medals, and honors for his work in landscapes and his paintings are said to rank with Inness, Wyant and Homer Martin and are included in most of the prominent collections in America. He was elected a member of the National Academy in 1887. His studio was for years in New York. He died in 1921.

MURPHY, John J. A. Painter. Member: Guild of Free Lance Association. *Address*, 21 Greenwich Ave., New York, N. Y.

MURPHY, L. M. Painter. Member: California Art Club. *Address*, 115½ North Main St., Los Angeles, Calif.

MURPHY, Mrs. Minnie B. Hall. Painter. Born in Denver, Colo., in 1863. Pupil of Art Students' League of New York; Art Institute of Chicago; of Henry Read in Denver. Member: Denver Artists' Association. *Address*, 805 Gaylord St., Denver, Colo.

MURPHY, Nelly Littlehale (Mrs. H. Dudley). Painter and illustrator. Born in Stockton, Calif., in 1867. Pupil of Museum of Fine Arts, Boston. Member: Copley Society. *Address*, East Lexington, Mass.

MURPHY, Michael Thomas. Sculptor. Born in Bantry, County Cork, Ireland, in 1867. Apprenticed as marble carver in Cork; studied in School of Art, Cork, and later at Royal College of Art, London; also in Paris and Italy. Came to United States in 1912. Specializes in portraits and figure subjects in relief. Exhibited at Art Institute Chicago, 1918. Principal works: Busts of Most Rev. George W. Mundelein and of the late Dr. John B. Murphy, of Chicago; ''Aaron Blessing the Israelites,''

4th Presbyterian Church, Lincoln Parkway, Chicago; heroic size figures representing an athlete and a student, University of Michigan, Ann Arbor; etc. Member Art Workers' Guild, Artists' Annuity Fund, London; Chicago Society of Artists. *Address*, 4 E. Ohio St., Chicago.

MURPHY, William D. Painter. Born in Madison County, Ala., in 1834. In 1863 he received his first art education from William Cooper, a portrait painter, of Nashville, Tenn. Married Harriet Anderson, a pupil of Lorenz and William Morgan, in 1887. Since that time Mr. and Mrs. Murphy have been continuously engaged in portrait painting, their work being conducted jointly. The list of works from their studio contains the portraits of many eminent public men, including those of President Lincoln, President McKinley (now in the White House), President Roosevelt, Admiral Dewey, Admiral Schley, and other well-known public men.

MURRAY, George. Engraver. Born in Scotland; died in Philadelphia in 1822. Dunlap says that Murray was a pupil of the well-known English engraver Anker Smith, and he was certainly engraving portraits, etc., in London in 1796. Murray appears in Philadelphia in 1800, coming to that city from one of the Southern States. He was prominent in the Philadelphia Society of Artists in 1810, and in 1810–11 he organized the banknote and general engraving firm of Murray, Draper, Fairman & Co.

MURRAY, Grace H. (Mrs. Archibald Gordon). Painter. Born in New York in 1872. Pupil of Bouguereau and Gabriel Ferrier. Paints portraits and miniatures. *Address*, 129 East 56th St., New York, N. Y.

MURRAY, John. In Rivington's *Royal Gazette*, in 1776, we find the following: "John Murray, in the 57th Regiment from Edinburgh, engraves all manner of silver-plate, seals, coats of arms, etc." He may or may not have engraved on copper.

MURRAY, Samuel. Sculptor. Born in Philadelphia in 1870. Pupil of Thomas Eakins. Awards: Gold medal, Art Club of Phila., 1894; silver medal, St. Louis Exposition, 1904. Work: "Prophets," Witherspoon Bldg., Philadelphia; statues of "Commodore Barry" and "Joseph Leidy"; State monument, Gettysburg, Pa.; Corby statue, Notre Dame University, Notre Dame, Ind.; portrait, Dr. J. C. Wilson, Jefferson Medical College, Philadelphia. *Address*, 3326 Lancaster Ave., Philadelphia, Pa.

MUSGRAVE, A. F. Painter. Born in Brighton, England, in 1880. Pupil of Stanhope Forbes, Newlyn School of Art, London. Member: Santa Fé Artists' Society. *Address*, 3241 Thirty-eighth St., Santa Fé, N. M.

MUSSELMAN-CARR. Sculptor. Born in Georgetown, Ky., in 1880. Pupil of Bourdelle; Art Students' League of New York; Cincinnati Art School. Work: "Fountain," Kansas City, Roslyn, L. I., N. Y. *Address*, Stuyvesant Alley, New York, N. Y.

MUSSER, B. Illustrator and etcher. Born in Chicago, Ill., in 1885. Pupil of Robert Henri. Member: Art Directors' Club. Work: "Interior," Santa Fé Museum, N. M. *Address*, 392 Fifth Ave., Elmhurst, N. Y.

MYERS, Ethel. Sculptor. Exhibited at National Academy, New York, 1925. *Address*, 57 East 59th St., New York.

MYERS, Datus E. Painter. Born in Jefferson, Ore., in 1879. Pupil of Art Institute of Chicago. *Address*, 1549 East 57th St., Chicago, Ill.

MYERS, Jerome. Painter. Born in Petersburg, Va., in 1867. Pupil of Cooper Union, and of Art Students' League of New York. Elected Associate Member of National Academy of Design and exhibited there in 1925. Awards: Bronze medal, St. Louis Exposition, 1904; Clarke prize, National Academy of Design, 1919. Specialty, New York street scenes. Work: "The Night Mission," Metropolitan Museum, New York. *Address*, 57 East 59th St., New York.

MYERS, O. Irwin. Painter and illustrator. Born in Bananza, Nebr., in 1888. Pupil of Art Institute of Chicago and of Chicago Academy of Fine Arts. Member: Chicago Society of Artists; Chicago Art Club; Chicago Society of Independent Artists; Alumni Art Institute of Chicago. *Address*, Studio Bldg., 4 East Ohio St., Chicago, Ill.

MYRICK, Katherine S. (Mrs. H. M.). Miniature painter. Member of American Society of Miniature Painters; National Association of Women Painters and Sculptors. *Address*, Pelham Manor, N. Y.

N

NADELMAN, E. Sculptor. Exhibited "The Adolescent" at the Penna. Academy of the Fine Arts, Philadelphia, 1921. *Address*, 6 East 46th St., New York.

NAEGELE, Charles Frederick. Painter. Born in Knoxville, Tenn., in 1857. Pupil of William Sartain, William M. Chase, and of C. Myles Collier. Gold medal, Mechanics Fair, Boston, 1900; silver medal, Charleston Exposition, 1902. Member: Artists' Fund Society; National Arts Club, N. Y.; Atlanta Art Association. Specialty, portraits. Studio, New York. Represented by "Mother Love" in National Gallery, Washington, D. C. *Address*, Marietta, Georgia.

NAGEL, Elizabeth and Edward. Painters. Exhibited in Phila., 1921, at "Exhibition of Paintings Showing the Later Tendencies in Art," Penna. Academy of Fine Arts. *Address*, 77 Washington Place, New York City.

NAGEL, Herman F. Painter. Born in Newark, N. J., in 1876. Pupil of National Academy of Design. Member: Society of Independent Artists. *Address*, 23 Pennington St., Newark, N. J.

NAGLER, Edith K. Painter. Exhibited at National Academy of Design, New York, 1925. *Address*, Spuyten Duyvil, New York.

NAGLER, Fred. Painter. Exhibited at National Academy of the Fine Arts, Philadelphia, 1926. *Address*, Spuyten Duyvil, N. Y.

NAHL, Perham W. Painter. Born in San Francisco, Calif., 1869. Represented in many California galleries. Studied in Paris and Munich. *Address*, 6043 Harwood Ave., Oakland, Calif.

NANKIVELL, Frank Arthur. Painter. Born in Maldon, Victoria, Australia, 1869. Studied art in Japan, 1891–94; in San Francisco, 1894–96. Published and illustrated fortnightly magazine *Chic*, and made drawings for San Francisco *Call*, *Examiner*, and *Chronicle*; moved to New York in 1896, and illustrated daily papers; joined staff of *Puck*, May, 1896, as cartoonist and caricaturist. He also studied portrait painting in New York and London; now occupied as painter, illustrator and etcher for *Ladies' Home Journal*. Member of Association of American Painters and Sculptors. *Address*, 33 West 14th St., New York.

NASH, Willard A. Painter and etcher. Born in Philadelphia. Pupil of John P. Wicker. *Address*, Care of Detroit Institute, Detroit, Mich.

NASON, Gertrude. Painter. Exhibited "The Ivory Gown" at the Penna. Academy of Fine Arts, Philadelphia, 1921. *Address*, 102 Fenway Studios, Boston, Mass.

NAST, Thomas. Painter. Born in 1840 at Landau, Bavaria; died 1902 at Guayaquil, Ecuador, where he was the American Consul-General. Lived chiefly in New York, and was famous as a caricaturist. His head of Christ painted in 1900 is in the Metropolitan Museum of New York.

NAUMAN, Fred R. Painter and etcher. Born in St. Louis in 1892. Awarded prize for landscapes at St. Louis Exposition in 1919. *Address*, 7th and Pine Sts., St. Louis, Mo.

NAVE, Royston. Painter. Exhibited "Norma" at the Penna. Academy of Fine Arts, Philadelphia, 1921. *Address*, 146 West 59th St., New York.

NEAGLE, James. Engraver, who died in Philadelphia, in 1822, "aged 53 years." The directories of Philadelphia contain his name for 1820–22, inclusive, as an "engraver." In 1819 he was engraving in Philadelphia, and a few well-executed portraits bear his name. His signed work is very scarce and he was possibly chiefly engaged in banknote work.

NEAGLE, John. Portrait painter. Born in Boston in 1796; died in Philadelphia in 1865. Born of Philadelphia parents during their temporary residence in Boston, he was educated in Philadelphia, his instruction including a few months' instruction under Pietro Ancora, a drawing-teacher. Apprenticed to an ambitious coach painter who took some lessons from Bass Otis, he himself was inspired to do likewise, and later had the benefit of two months' guidance by Otis, all the instruction he ever had from a professional artist. In 1818 he set up for himself as a portrait painter, removing to Lexington, Ky. But after two years spent there and at other points in the Mississippi Valley, he returned to Philadelphia and soon married a daughter of Thomas Sully, the celebrated artist. Here he made his first decided success with a portrait of the Rev. Dr. Joseph Pilmore, one of the pioneers of Philadelphia Methodism. His masterpiece, however, is generally conceded to be a full-length of Patrick Lyon, the noted blacksmith, at his forge, which has long hung in the galleries of the Academy of the Fine Arts. Others of his long list of portraits may be seen at the Union League, the University of Pennsylvania, the Philadelphia Library and the rooms of the Phila. Law Association. Several years before his death he suffered a stroke of paralysis, from the effects of which he never recovered. He was one of the founders, and for eight years the president, of the Artist's Fund Society. An exhibition of his work was held at the Penna. Academy of Fine Arts in 1925. The Catalogue included a life or Memoir of the artist and a description of about 200 of his paintings, written by Mantle Fielding. John Neagle was elected an Honorary Member of the National Academy of Design in 1828.

NEAGLE, John B. Engraver. Born in England about 1796; died in Philadelphia in 1866. J. B. Neagle is said to have been the son of the English engraver John Neagle, born in 1760, and he was probably a pupil of his father. He came to Philadelphia when quite young, as he engraved, in 1815–18, a portrait of Dr. Caspar Wistar for "Delaplaine's Gallery."

NEAL, David. Painter, Born at Lowell, Mass., in 1838; died in 1915. He went to Europe in 1862; studied in Paris and Munich. He painted numerous historical romantic works, including "Mary Stuart and Riccio," "Oliver Cromwell Visits John Milton," "Nuns at Prayer," "James Watt in the Crypt," "Retour de Chasse," etc. His later work was portraiture, including portraits of Adolph Sutro; Rev. Mark Hopkins; Judge Hoffman of Calif.; D. O. Mills; Teackle Wallis; Misses Gladys and Beatrice Mills (daughters of Ogden Mills); Prof. Henry Green; Whitelaw Reid, etc.

NEAL, Grace Pruden. Sculptor. Exhibited at the Penna. Academy of Fine Arts, Philadelphia, 1924. *Address*, Studio, 1931 Broadway, New York.

NEANDROSS, Sigurd. Sculptor. Born in Norway in 1871. Pupil of Cooper Union, New York. Works: Statues of Genl. Geo. Washington, at Pottsville, Pa., and Chauncey M. Depew, at Peekskill, N. Y.

NEEBE, Minnie Harms. Painter. Born in Chicago, Ill., in 1873. Pupil of Hawthorne, Browne, Webster, Reynolds, Ufer. Member of Chicago Society of Artists. *Address*, 1320 Clybourn Ave., Chicago, Ill.

NEEDHAM, Charles Austin. Landscape painter. Born in Buffalo, N. Y., in 1844; died in 1923. Pupil of Art Students' League, and of August Will of New York. Honorable mention and medal, Atlanta International Exposition, 1895; honorable mention, New York State Agricultural Exposition, Syracuse, 1898. Represented in St. Louis Museum of Fine Arts, and in Annual Exhibition of American Water Color Society, 1906–7–8. Member: American Water Color Society; New York Water Color Club.

NEGUS, Caroline. Portrait painter in crayon and miniatures, working in Boston,

Mass., 1844–56. She shared a studio with her cousin, the artist George Fuller.

NEHLIG, Victor. Painter. Born in Paris in 1830. Pupil of Cogniet. He came to the United States in 1856, having resided for some time in Cuba. He settled in New York where he was elected an Associate Member of the National Academy in 1863, and an Academician in 1870. Many of his works are historical subjects; his "The Cavalry Charge" is in the New York Historical Society. Among his best known paintings are "Battle of Antietam," "Waiting for the Enemy," "Gertrude of Wyoming," and "The Artist's Dream."

NEILL, Frances Isabel. Painter and etcher. Born in Warren, Pa. Studied in New York, Boston and Paris. Member: National Association of Women Painters and Sculptors; Baltimore Water Color Club. *Address*, 939 Eighth Ave., New York, N. Y.

NEILL, John R. Illustrator. Member: Salmagundi Club. *Address*, 36 East 28th St., New York, N. Y.

NEILSON, Raymond P. R. Painter. Born in New York. Pupil of Chase, and studied in Paris with Laurens, Simon and Miller. Awarded silver medal at San Francisco, Calif., in 1915. Elected Associate Member of National Academy. His painting "Le Chapeau Noir" is owned by the French Government. *Address*, 140 West 57th St., New York.

NELL, (Miss) Tony. Painter and illustrator. Born in Washington, D. C. Pupil of Chase; Du Mond; Students' School of Art, Denver. Member of New York Water Color Club and Chicago Water Color Club. Awards: Beal prize, New York Water Color Club, 1910; Harriet Brooks Jones prize, Baltimore Water Color Club, 1921. *Address*, 2 Riverview Terrace, New York, N. Y.

NELL, William. Painter. Exhibited a landscape at the Penna. Academy of Fine Arts, Philadelphia, 1921. *Address*, 106 South Troy Ave., Ventnor, N. J.

NELSON. Dunlap records in his sketch of Chester Harding a primitive portrait painter of that name who painted signs. Nelson had painted on his own sign a copy of Sir Joshua Reynolds' "Infant Artists." He painted portraits of Harding and his wife for $10 each, but refused to give the former any information about his method of working.

NELSON, George L. Painter. Born in 1887. Pupil of National Academy, N. Y., and of Laurens in Paris. Painted portraits now in New York Hospital. *Address*, 15 West 67th St., New York.

NESBIT, Robert H. Landscape painter. Elected an Associate Member of the National Academy of Design. His painting "The Hurrying River," owned by the Telfair Academy of Savannah, Ga., was exhibited at the Centennial Exhibition of the National Academy, 1925. *Address*, South Kent, Conn.

NESEMAN, Enno. Painter. Born in Maysville, Calif., in 1861. Pupil of Alfred Hart. Member: Society of Independent Artists. Work: "The First Discovery of Gold in California at Sutter's Mill," De Young Memorial Museum, San Francisco, California. *Address*, 1635 Euclid Ave., Berkeley, Calif.

NESMITH, J. H. Engraver. In 1805–18 this line-engraver was making illustrations for the encyclopedia published by S. F. Bradford, of Philadelphia. In 1824 his name as engraver is associated with that of J. B. Longacre, and in 1828 Nesmith was working for New Haven publishers.

NETTLETON, Walter. Landscape painter. Born in New Haven, Conn., in 1861. Pupil of Yale School of Fine Arts; of Boulanger and Lefebvre in Paris. Elected Associate Member of the National Academy, 1905. Work: "December Sunshine," Yale Art Museum, New Haven; "A January Morning," Museum of Art, New Britain, Conn.; "The Beloved Physician," Jackson Library, Stockbridge, Mass.; "Waldesdämmerung," Vassar College Art Gallery. *Address*, Stockbridge, Mass.

NEUBAUER, Frederick August. Landscape painter and illustrator. Born in Cincinnati, 1855. Pupil of Cincinnati Art Academy. Member: Cincinnati Art Club. *Address*, 22 Hulbert Block, Sixth and Vine Sts., Cincinnati, Ohio.

NEUHAUS, Eugen. Painter. Born in Barmen, Germany, in 1879. Pupil of Royal Art School, Kassel; Institute of Applied Art, Berlin. Member: San Francisco Artists' Association. *Address*, 2922 Derby St., Berkeley, Calif.

NEUHAUSER, Marguerite Phillips (Mrs. Roy L. Neuhauser). Painter. Born in North Arlington, Va., in 1888. Pupil of Bertha Perrie; George Noyes; Corcoran School of Art. Member: Society of Washington Artists; Washington Art Club. *Address*, 1707 21st St., Washington, D. C.

NEVIN, Blanch. Sculptor. Born in 1841 in Mercersburg, Penna. She studied art in Philadelphia, and later in Italy. She has executed many portrait busts, and her statue of Peter Muhlenberg is in the Capitol in Washington, D. C. She died in 1925.

NEWCOMB, D. This name as engraver appears upon vignettes on the title-page of books published in Boston, in 1820. Judging from his work, Newcomb was probably one of the banknote engravers then in business in Boston.

NEWCOMBE, Geo. W. Painter. Born in England in 1799. He came to New York in 1829 and became a successful painter of portraits in oils and miniatures. He was elected an Associate Member of the National Academy in 1832. He died in New York in 1845.

NEWELL, George Glenn. Painter. Born in Berrien County, Mich., in 1870. Pupil of National Academy of Design, under Ward; also of Teachers' College, N. Y., under Will S. Robinson. Member: American Water Color Society; National Arts Club, New York. Specialty, cattle. Studio, Dover Plains, N. Y. "Mists of the Morning" (signed and dated 1910) is in the Corcoran Art Gallery, Washington, D. C. *Address*, Carnegie Studios, New York City.

NEWELL, Hugh. Born in Ireland in 1830. He came to this country as a youth and resided for eight years in Pittsburgh, Penna., removing to Baltimore, where he became connected with the Maryland Institute and the Johns Hopkins University. He was a member of the American Water Color Society. Among his pictures are "The Country Musician," "The Cottage Window," "In the Sugar Camp" and "Woods in Winter."

NEWELL, Peter S. Illustrator. Born in Illinois in 1862. Pupil of Art Students' League of New York. He died in Little Neck, L. I., in 1924. Most of his work was done for the Harpers publishing firm.

NEWHALL, Donald V. Painter and illustrator. Born in England in 1890. Pupil of Penna. Academy of Fine Arts. *Address*, 140 West 57th St., New York.

NEWHALL, Harriot B. Painter and etcher. Born in 1874 in Topeka, Kans. Pupil of Benson, Ross and Hawthorne. *Address*, Studio Bldg., 82 Chestnut St., Boston, Mass.

NEWMAN, Allen George. Sculptor. Born in New York in 1875. Pupil of National Academy of Design, New York, and studio of J. Q. A. Ward. Principal works: Bronze group, "Triumph of Peace," Atlanta, Ga.; "The Hiker," Spanish-American War Soldier, Providence, R. I.; marble figures, "Night and Day," Harriman Bank, New York; Henry Hudson monument erected by Colonial Dames of America, 72d St. and Riverside Drive, New York; Gen. Philip Sheridan monument, Scranton, Pa.; also numerous other statues and busts. *Address*, 1947 Broadway, New York, N. Y.

NEWMAN, Anna Mary. Painter and illustrator. Born in Richmond, Ind. Pupil of Art Institute of Chicago. Represented by portraits of Chester T. Lane and Judge Erwin. *Address*, 25 North 16th St., Richmond, Ind.

NEWMAN, B. P. Newman was a very good engraver of landscape, working in New York in 1860.

NEWMAN, Carl. Painter. Exhibited in Philadelphia in 1921, in ''Exhibition of Paintings Showing the Later Tendencies in Art,'' Penna. Academy of Fine Arts. *Address*, Beth Ayres, Penna.

NEWMAN, Henry. Portrait painter. Born in 1843. Dealer in artists' supplies. He lived in Philadelphia for over fifty years. He died in 1921.

NEWMAN, Henry R. Painter. Born in New York City about 1833. He had his studio in New York state in 1861–69, and after that in Florence, Italy. He is noted for his water color painting of architectural subjects, landscapes and flower pieces. He was a friend of John Ruskin.

NEWMAN, Robert L. Painter. Born in Richmond, Va. In 1827, aged eleven, he went with his parents to Tennessee. As a youth he read much about art, and in 1850 went to Europe with the intention of studying at Dusseldorf, but having stopped in Paris, he entered the atelier of Thomas Couture. After returning to Tennessee he made a second trip to Paris in 1854, and formed the acquaintance of William M. Hunt, who introduced him to Jean Francois Millet. In 1882 and subsequently he made several trips to Barbizon, and his work shows the influence of the group of masters who made that modest village a household word. He has been called the American Diaz on account of his poetic coloring.

NEWMAN, Willie Betty (Mrs.). Painter. Born in Murfreesboro, Tenn., in 1864. Studied at Cincinnati Art School under T. S. Noble; later in Paris, with Benjamin Constant, J. P. Laurens and Bouguereau. First exhibited in the Salon in 1891; also in Salons of 1893 to 1900 (honorable mention); at Paris Exposition, 1900. Principal works: ''La Neuvaine''; ''Le Pain Benit''; ''En Penitence''; ''Foolish Virgin''; ''An Instant Repose''; ''La Fille du Marin''; also portrait of Vice-President Sherman and others.

NEWPORT, J. W. Miniature painter, who flourished in Philadelphia, 1846–47, and exhibited at the Penna. Academy in 1847.

NEWSAM, Albert. Lithographer. Born, deaf and dumb, in 1809, at Steubenville, Ohio; died near Wilmington, Del., in 1864. Newsam was the son of a boatman and was left an orphan at an early age. His natural artistic bent was cultivated by placing him under the tuition of the artists George Catlin and Hugh Bridport.

In 1827 Newsam was apprenticed to Cephas G. Childs to be taught engraving, and two examples of copperplate engraving are known to the compiler signed ''A. Newsam, sc. Deaf & Dumb, Childs dir.'' These are two good stipple-engravings of ''Anna'' and ''Queen Dido,'' published in the *Casket* of Philadelphia. A catalogue of the ''Lithograph Portraits of Albert Newsam'' was written by Danl. Stauffer and published in the *Pennsylvania Magazine of History and Biography*, Oct. 1900–Jan. 1901, and April 1901.

NEWTON, Edith W. Painter. Exhibited at the 33d Annual Exhibition of the National Association of Women Painters and Sculptors. *Address*, New Milford, Conn.

NEWTON, Francis. Painter. Born in Lake George, N. Y., in 1873. Pupil of Howard Pyle in Wilmington, Del.; of Art Students' League and Chase School, New York; Drexel Institute, Philadelphia; Colarossi Academy in Paris. Member: New York Architectural League, 1911; Mural Painters; New York Municipal Artists' Society; League of New York Artists.

NEWTON, Gilbert Stuart. Portrait painter. Born in 1795 in Halifax, Nova Scotia; died in 1835 in Chelsea, England. He was the nephew of Gilbert Stuart and studied for a while under his uncle but proved a very unteachable pupil. He went to France and England and arrived in London in company with C. R. Lelie in 1817. Dunlap in his ''History of the Arts of Design'' gives an extended account of Newton, and quotes Washington Irving's recollections of the artist.

NEY, Elizabeth. Sculptor. Born in Westphalia, and patronized by the ''mad king'' Ludwig II of Bavaria. She left her home for political reasons, and settled in Texas soon after the Civil War. Her memorial to Genl. Albert Sidney Johnson for the cemetery at Austin, Texas, is very fine.

NEYLAND, Harry. Painter. Born in Erie, Pa., in 1877. Pupil of Art Students' League of New York, and of schools in Paris. *Address*, 391 Country St., New Bedford, Mass.

NICHOLDSON, J. D. Engraver. As ''J. D. Nicholdson sc'' this name is signed to line work done for an encyclopedia published by E. Lucas, Jr., Baltimore, Md. The date is about 1830.

NICHOLLS, Burr H. Painter. Born in 1848. He studied with Sellstedt in Buffalo, and with Carolus-Duran in Paris. Represented at Penna. Academy of Fine Arts by ''Effect of

Sunlight''; at Peabody Institute, Baltimore, by ''Hunting Up a Quotation''; in Fine Arts Academy, Buffalo, by ''A Group of Fowls.'' He died in 1915.

NICHOLLS, Josephine L. Painter. Born in Ontario, 1865. Pupil of Mowbray and Bridgman. *Address,* 188 Franklin St., Buffalo, N. Y.

NICHOLLS, Rhoda Holmes. Painter. Born in Coventry, England. Student at Bloomsbury School of Art, London; won Queen's scholarship. Was a member of Societa degli Aquarellisti and Circolo Artistico, Rome. Exhibited in Rome, Turin, Munich, Royal Academy, London, and in many American exhibitions. Took medals in Prize Fund, New York, Boston, Atlanta, Nashville, Charleston, and in the West Indies; also in Interstate expositions, Chicago, Buffalo and St. Louis. Member: American Society of Miniature Painters; American Water Color Society; Woman's Art Association of Can.; Art Students' League, N. Y. *Address,* Colonial Studio, 39 W. 67th St., New York.

NICHOLS, Edward W. Painter. Born in 1819. He was elected an Associate Member of the National Academy in 1861. He specialized in portrait painting. He died in 1871.

NICHOLS, Frederick B. Engraver. Born in Bridgeport, Conn., in 1824; he was living there in 1906. Mr. Nichols learned to engrave with the New York firm of Rawdon, Wright, Hatch & Smillie, the latter being his chief instructor. He then went into business for himself, and about 1846 he published ''Nichols Illustrated New York,'' with views engraved by himself. In 1848 he invented a process for relief-engraving. Mr. Nichols was a good landscape engraver and did considerable work for the New York publishers, but in 1858 he abandoned engraving with the intention of promoting certain inventions of his own.

NICHOLS, Harley De Witt. Landscape painter. Born in 1859. He has made illustrations for *Harper's* and *Century* Magazines. *Address,* 189 Montague St., Brooklyn, N. Y.

NICHOLS, Henry Hobart. Painter. Born in Washington, D. C., in 1869. Pupil of Howard Helmick and Art Students' League in Washington; of Julien Academy and Castellucho in Paris. Awards: Second Corcoran prize, 1901; Parsons prize, 1904; first Corcoran prize, 1906. Member: Society of Washington Artists; Washington Water Color Club; New York Water Color Club. Specialty, landscapes and illustrations. Represented by ''Moonrise at Ogunquit,'' at Corcoran Art Gallery, Washington, D. C. *Address,* Lawrence Park, Bronxville, New York.

NICHOLS, John W. Etcher. Born in Keokuk, Iowa, in 1881. Pupil of Charles A. Cumming. *Address,* 819 Carnegie Hall, New York, N. Y.

NICHOLS, Peggy (Martin). Painter and sculptor. Born in Atchison, Kans., in 1884. Pupil of Cecilia Beaux and Chase. Member: California Art Club. *Address,* 517 South Coronado St., Los Angeles, Calif.

NICHOLS, Spencer Baird. Painter. Born in Washington, D. C., in 1875. Pupil of Corcoran Gallery Art School, and of Art Students' League, Washington; also pupil of Howard Helmich. He then taught illustrating at the Art Students' League, Washington, then joined the Tiffany Studios, New York, in 1911, as a designer of windows and mosaics. He painted a portrait of Andrew Stephenson for the U. S. Govt., now in House of Representatives; mural decorations, Central Presby'n Church, N. Y. City; is also a book illustrator. Awarded 3d Corcoran prize, Society of Washington Artists, 1901. Member: Washington Water Color Club; Society of Washington Artists; New York Water Color Club. Elected Associate Member of the National Academy of Design. *Address,* Kent, Conn.

NICOLL, James Craig. Marine painter and etcher. Born in 1847, he died in Norwalk, Conn., 1918. Elected an Associate of the National Academy of Design, 1880, and an Academician, 1885. He worked with M. F. H. de Haas, and is represented by ''Squally Weather'' in the Metropolitan Museum of New York. He was awarded many mentions and medals for his marine painting and etchings, and his water colors were well known; among those exhibited were ''On the Gulf of St. Lawrence,'' ''Off Portland Harbor'' and ''Stormy Day at Block Island.''

NICOLOSI, Joseph. Painter and sculptor. Born in Italy in 1893. Pupil of Beaux Arts Institute of Design. *Address,* 3 East 14th St., New York, N. Y.

NICOLSON, Edith Reynaud (Mrs. H. W. Nicolson). Illustrator. Born in Mount Vernon, N. Y., in 1896. Pupil of New York School of Applied Design for Women. *Address,* 4 Parmley Place, Summit, N. J.

NIEDECKEN, George Mann. Mural painter. Born in Milwaukee, Wisc., in 1878. Pupil of Mucha, Robert-Fleury, Lefebvre and Laurens in Paris. Member: Society of Milwaukee Artists. *Address,* 436 Milwaukee St., Milwaukee, Wisc.

NIEHAUS, Charles Henry. Sculptor. Born in Cincinnati, Ohio, in 1855. In early life he followed wood engraving, stonecutting and carving in marble. He studied art in the McMicken School of Design, Cincinnati,

Ohio, and in the Royal Academy of Munich, receiving conspicuous awards in both institutions. He lived for some time in Rome. A member of the Council of the National Sculpture Society, since 1885 he has resided in the city of New York. Among his works are statues of Hooker and Davenport, New York; carved wood tympanums, Library of Congress, Washington; statues of Moses and Gibbons, Library of Congress, Washington; Hahnemann Memorial, Washington, D. C.; statues of Lincoln and Farragut, Muskegon, Mich.; statues of Garfield, Allen, Morton, and Ingalls, Statuary Hall, United States Capitol; and a portrait bust of Daniel Tompkins, in the gallery of the United States Senate. Elected a member of the National Academy of Design.

NIELSON, Harry A. Painter. Born in Slagelse, Denmark, in 1881. Pupil of Art Institute of Chicago; Jean Manheim. Member: California Art Club. *Address*, 701 California Terrace, Pasadena, Calif.

NIEMEYER, John Henry. Painter. Born in Bremen, Germany, in 1839. He came to the United States in 1843; studied in Paris under L. Jacquesson de la Chevreuse, Jean Leon Gerome, and at École des Beaux Arts. Painter of portraits and landscapes; Street prof. drawing, Yale School of Fine Arts, 1871–1908. Elected Associate Member of the National Academy. *Address*, 251 Laurence St., New Haven, Conn.

NIEPOLD, Frank. Painter. Born in Frederick, Md., in 1890. Pupil of Corcoran School of Art, Washington. Member: Washington Art Club; Society of Washington Artists. *Address*, 913 F St., Washington, D. C.

NIGHT, Edward W. Painter. Born in Auburn, N. Y., in 1872. *Address*, 105 Cook St., East Onondaga, Syracuse, N. Y.

NISBET, Robert H. Painter. Born in Providence, R. I., in 1879. Pupil of R. I. School of Design; Art Students' League of New York. Member: Elected Associate Member of the National Academy, 1920; also member of Allied Artists' Association. Awards: Dunham prize, Conn. Academy of Fine Arts, 1913; third Hallgarten prize, National Academy of Design, 1915. Work: "Eve of St. John," National Art Club, New York; "Earliest Spring," R. I. School of Design, Providence; "The Emerald Robe," Mahoning Institute of Art, Youngstown, Ohio. *Address*, South Kent, Conn.

NITZSCHE, Elsa Koenig. Portrait painter. Born in Philadelphia, Pa., in 1880. Student of Penna. Academy of Fine Arts; also graduate of Woman's School of Design; studied in France, Germany, Switzerland and Italy; also 8 years, under Bougeret and other eminent teachers. Has exhibited in principal exhibitions in America and abroad; honorable mention, Paris Salon; represented in many American and several foreign collections. *Address*, 441 Carpenter Lane, Germantown, Philadelphia, Pa.

NIVEN, Frank R. Painter and illustrator. Born in Rochester, N. Y., in 1888. Pupil of S. C. Jones. Member: Rochester Art Club. *Address*, 402 Municipal Bldg., Rochester, N. Y.

NOBLE, ——————. Painter. He has delineated the American negro in many of his paintings. His picture of John Brown on his way from prison to the gallows, embracing the negro children, is well known. His painting of the "Slave Mart" attracted much attention in the days of the Civil War and was exhibited in Boston and at the Capitol in Washington, D. C.

NOBLE, John. Painter. Born in Wichita, Kans., in 1874. Studied at Cincinnati Academy, U. S.; Julien Academy in Paris (Jean Paul Laurens); Beaux Arts, Paris; Colarossi, Paris. Member of American Art Association; Allied Artists, London. He is represented in many private collections in Paris; London; Buenos Aires; the United States; Germany. Director of the Provincetown Art Association. He painted Governor Fergusson's portrait for Oklahoma State Capitol. Elected Associate Member of the National Academy. *Address*, 230 East 15th St., New York City.

NOBLE, W. Clark. Painter and sculptor. Pupil of Pierce and Greenough; also studied in London. Represented by Soldiers' and Sailors' Monument, Newport, R. I.; memorial to Phillips Brooks, New York; portrait bust, Gen'l Potter, Chamber of Commerce, New York. *Address*, 739 Boyleston St., Boston, Mass.

NOCOUET, Paul Ange. Belgian sculptor. Born in Brussels in 1877. He came to America in 1903. His bronze "American Football" brought him recognition; it was presented to Columbia University. He received many awards. He died in 1906 in a balloon accident. The Belgian and French governments ordered casts made of his work here.

NOGUCHI, Isamy. Sculptor. Exhibited at Penna. Academy of Fine Arts, Philadelphia, 1926. *Address*, 127 University Place, New York.

NOLL, Arthur Howard. Engraver. Born in Caldwell, N. J., in 1855. Specialty, bookplate engraving. *Address*, 608 Woodlaun St., Memphis, Tenn.

NORCROSS, Eleanor. Painter. Born in Massachusetts. Pupil of William M. Chase in New York; studied with Alfred Stevens in

Paris. She died in Paris in 1923, and a memorial exhibition of her painting was held in the Louvre by the French Government. Her studio had been in Paris for more than thirty years.

NORDELL, Carl J. Painter. He has exhibited at the Penna. Academy of the Fine Arts, "The Call of Autumn." He is also known for his etchings, winning the Shaw prize for the best etching at the Salmagundi Club Exhibition, 1923. *Address*, Fenway Studios, Boston, Mass.

NORDFELDT, Bror J. O. Painter, etcher and engraver. Born in Sweden in 1878. Pupil of Herter in New York; Laurens in Paris; Fletcher in England. His etchings and engravings are represented in the Chicago Art Institute, New York Public Library and in many Museums abroad. *Address*, Santa Fé, New Mexico.

NORMAN, Mrs. Da Loria. Painter. Born in Leavenworth, Kans., in 1872. Studied abroad. Represented in New York Public Library. *Address*, Crags Studio, Lyme, Conn.

NORMAN, John. Engraver. According to the *New England Palladium and Commercial Advertiser*, in 1817, John Norman died in Boston in 1817 "aged 69 years." That he was an Englishman is shown by his advertisement in the *Pennsylvania Journal* of May 11, 1774, which probably notes his first appearance in this country.

As an engraver Norman's earlier work was exceedingly crude, and a number of his plates are more or less modified copies of English originals. Some few of his later plates show decided improvement. His chief claim to fame is the fact that he was probably the first engraver in America to attempt a portrait of Washington, about 1779. William Dunlap's assertion that Norman was a pupil of Sir Godfrey Kneller is met by the fact that Sir Godfrey died in 1723, many years before Norman was born.

NORRIS, Walter S. Painter. Exhibited "The Silver Cataract" at the Penna. Academy of Fine Arts, Philadelphia, 1921. *Address*, 1716 Chestnut St., Philadelphia.

NORSTAD, Magnus. Painter. Born in Norway in 1884. Pupil of National School of Design in New York. Represented in St. Paul Institute by "The City on the Hill." *Address*, Valhalla, New York.

NORTHCOTE, Stafford Mantle. Wood engraver. Born in Brooklyn, N. Y., in 1869. Studied engraving with Heineman, and painting under Boyle at the Brooklyn Art Institute. *Address*, 283 Carlton Ave., Brooklyn, New York.

NORTON, Clara Mamre. Painter. Exhibited water colors at the Penna. Academy of the Fine Arts, Philadelphia, 1925. *Address*, 49 Woodland St., Bristol, Conn.

NORTON, Elizabeth. Painter and sculptor. Born in Chicago, Ill., in 1887. Pupil of Art Institute of Chicago; Art Students' League of New York. Member: Alliance. Work: Wall Fountain in Detroit Athletic Club. *Address*, 353 Lowell Ave., Calif.

NORTON, Helen G. Painter. Born in Portsmouth, Ohio, in 1882. Pupil of Mills College; also of Jean Manheim. Member: California Art Club. *Address*, Laguna Beach, Calif.

NORTON, William Edward. Painter. Born in Boston in 1843; died in New York in 1916. Pupil of Lowell Institute, Boston; also of George Inness; of Jacquesson, de la Chevreuse, and A. Vollon, Paris. Awarded 3 gold medals in America; honorable mention, Paris Salon, 1895. Exhibited at Paris Exposition, 1900; regular exhibitor at the Royal Academy, London; also exhibited in Philadelphia; Chicago, and St. Louis expositions, etc. Awarded Osborne prize for marine painting, 1905, and again in 1906.

NOTHERMAN, G. Engraver. A Harrison campaign badge issued in Baltimore in 1840 is signed as "Drawn & Eng. by G. Notherman, Jr." The work is well done in line. The badge was done by "Notherman & Mettee, Balt."

NOTMAN, Howard. Painter. Born in Brooklyn in 1881. Pupil of Constantin Herzberg; Brooklyn Polytechnic Institute. Member: Brooklyn Society of Artists; Society of Independent Artists. *Address*, 136 Joralemon St., Brooklyn, New York, N. Y.

NOURSE, Elizabeth. Painter. Born in Cincinnati, Ohio, in 1860. Pupil of Art Academy in Cincinnati, and of Boulanger, Lefebvre, Carolus-Duran and Henner in Paris. Awards: Medal, Columbian Exposition, Chicago, 1893; gold medal, Panama-Pacific International Exposition, San Francisco, 1915. Member: Societie Nationale des Beaux Arts, Paris; Paris American Women's Art Association; New York Woman's Art Club. Studio, Paris, France. *Address*, 80 Rue d'Assas, Paris, France.

NOVANI, Guilio. Sculptor. Born in Massa-Carrara, Italy, in 1889. Pupil of Academy of Massa-Carrara and Beaux Arts Institute in New York. Work: Stimson Memorial; Medallions of Rev. Talbot and M. Ackerman. *Address*, 1347 Intervale Ave., New York, N. Y.

NOVELLI, James. Sculptor. Born in Italy in 1885. He came to New York in 1890.

Studied abroad in 1908. Work: "Rock of Ages," Durham, N. C.; bronze busts of Thos. Stewart, Julius Berger and Irving Green; also numerous busts in terra-cotta.

NOYES, Bertha. Painter. Exhibited "Katherine" at the 33d Annual Exhibition of the National Association of Women Painters and Sculptors, N. Y. *Address*, 614 Nineteenth St., Washington, D. C.

NOYES, George L. Painter. Born in Canada. Pupil of Courtois, Rixen, Le Blanc and Delance in Paris. Member: Boston Art Club. Award: Silver medal, Panama-Pacific Exposition, San Francisco, 1915. Work: "Gloucester Wharves," Museum of Fine Arts, Boston; "New Hampshire Hills," Des Moines Art Museum; "Road to Lisbon," Utah State Museum. *Address*, 100 Revere St., Boston, Mass.

NOYES, Josiah. Engraver, working in 1799. He engraved a copper plate for the Social Friends' Library of Dartmouth College, as a book-plate.

NUDERSCHER, Frank. Painter, illustrator and etcher. Born in St. Louis, Mo., in 1880. Self-taught. Member: Artists' Guild. Work: Mississippi River Scenes, in Chamber of Commerce, St. Louis, Mo. *Address*, 1909 Locust St., St. Louis, Mo.

NUNAMAKER, K. R. Landscape painter. Exhibited at National Academy of Design, New York, 1925. *Address*, Center Bridge, Penna.

NUNN, Evylena. Painter. Born in Mayfield, Kans., in 1888. Pupil of Art Students' League of New York; Berkshire Summer School of Art; of A. A. Hills; School of Art and Design of Pomona College; also studied in Japan. Member: California Art Club; Laguna Artists' Association. *Address*, 802 North Ross St., Santa Ana, Calif.

NUNN, Frederic. Painter. Born in Philadelphia in 1879. Pupil of Penna. Academy of Fine Arts under Anshutz, Breckenridge, Chase and Cecilia Beaux. Member: Fellowship, Penna. Academy of Fine Arts; Sketch Club; Phila. Art Alliance; Phila. Water Color Club. Represented in the collection of the Fellowship of the Pennsylvania Academy of the Fine Arts,

Philadelphia. *Address*, 320 Harmony St., Philadelphia, Pa.

NUSE, Roy C. Painter. Born in Springfield, Ohio, in 1885. Pupil of Duveneck; Cincinnati Art Academy; Penna. Academy of Fine Arts. Member: Fellowship, Penna. Academy of Fine Arts; League of New York Artists; Phila. Art Alliance. Awards: Cresson European scholarship, Penna. Academy of Fine Arts, 1918; second Cresson, first Toppan, and first Thouran prize, Penna. Academy of Fine Arts. *Address*, Rushland, Penna.

NUTTING, Benjamin F. Portrait painter. Working in Boston, 1826–84; he also drew on stone for the lithographers.

NUYTTENS, J. P. Painter and etcher. Born in Antwerp in 1880. Studied at Antwerp Royal Academy; École des Beaux Arts in Paris, and in Brussels. Awards: Bronze medal from Queen of Belgium, 1918; Chevalier of the Order of Leopold II. Member: Cliff Dwellers, Chicago; Alumni Art Institute of Chicago. Work represented in Chicago Art Institute; White House, Washington; Royal Palace, Brussels, Belgium; State House, Springfield, Ill. *Address*, 19 East Pearson St., Chicago, Ill.

NYE, E. Portrait painter. Advertised as a "Portrait Painter," in the *Rural Visitor*, Burlington, N. J., March 25th, 1811.

NYE, Edgar. Painter. Born in Richmond, Va., in 1879. Pupil of Corcoran Gallery of Art, Washington, and of John Noble Barlow, England. Member: Washington Society of Artists; Washington Water Color Club. Work: Picture in Plymouth Gallery, England. *Address*, 75 Bryant St., Washington, D. C.

NYE, Elmer L. Etcher. Born in St. Paul, Minn., in 1888. Member: Minneapolis Attic Club. Award: First prize poster, Minn. Society of Artists. *Address*, Grand Fords, Santa Fé, N. M.

NYHOLM, Arvid F. Painter. Born in Sweden. Pupil of Anders Zorn, and of Colarossi Academy in Paris. Represented by "Captain John Ericson," National Gallery, Washington, D. C., and "General Whipple," West Point Academy. *Address*, 4 East Ohio St., Chicago, Ill.

O

OAKEY, Maria R. (See Dewing, Mrs. T. W.)

OAKLEY, F. F. About 1860 Oakley was engraving vignettes in line, and probably banknote work, at 204 Washington St., Boston. His work is very good, though very few signed plates have been seen.

OAKLEY, George. Painter. He was elected an Associate Member of the National Academy in 1827. He died in 1869.

OAKLEY, Thornton. Painter and illustrator. Born in Pittsburgh, Pa., in 1881. Pupil of Howard Pyle in Wilmington, Del. He has worked in lithography, and is represented in the New York Public Library, Philadelphia Free Library, and in many other collections. *Address*, 905 Clinton St., Phila.

OAKLEY, Violet. Mural painter. Born in New York, 1874; pupil of Art Students' League, New York, under Cecilia Beaux; Pa. Academy of Fine Arts, under Howard Pyle; pupil of Aman Jean, Collin and Lazar in Paris, France. Designer of the mural decorations in the governor's reception room, State Capitol, Harrisburg, Pa.; series entitled ''Founding of the State of Liberty Spiritual''; also a series of 9 panels in Senate chamber entitled ''Creation and Preservation of the Union.'' *Address*, ''Cogslea,'' Allen Lane, Philadelphia, Pa.

OBERHARDT, William. Illustrator, who specializes in portraiture. He studied at the National Academy of Design, and took a postgraduate course in Munich. His heads show the force and power of a dextrous hand and a discerning eye. Working in all mediums he has found charcoal and the lithographic crayon best suited to his requirements. *Address*, 11 East 14th St., New York.

OBERTEUFFER, George. Painter. Born in Philadelphia in 1878. Pupil of Chase and Anshutz. Represented in Brooklyn Museum, Phillips Gallery at Washington, and by ''Winter'' owned by the French Government. *Address*, New Hope, Penna.

OBERTEUFFER, Henriette A. Painter. Born in France in 1878. Her painting of still-life is owned by the French Government. *Address*, Care of State Normal School, Milwaukee, Wisconsin.

O'BRIEN, John. Painter. Born in 1834, he died at Galveston, Tex., on Dec. 20th, 1904.

O'BRIEN, R. This portrait engraver worked for many years for the New York engraver A. H. Ritchie.

O'BRIEN, Seumas. Sculptor and writer. Born in Glenbrook, Co. Cork, Ireland, in 1880. Instructor in art, Cork School of Art, Mt. St. Joseph's Monastery (Cork); Queenstown Tech. School; Metropolitan School of Art (Dublin) until 1912; Abbey Theatre dramatist and lecturer, 1913–17; exhibited at Royal Hibernian Academy. Awarded silver medal (sculpture) by Bd. of Edn., London, 1912. Came to U. S. in 1913. *Address*, 117 W. 90th St., New York, N. Y.

O'CALLAHAN, Clinton. Painter. Born in New England. He studied in Provincetown under Chas. W. Hawthorne. Also studied four years in Paris under Charles Guerin.

OCHTMAN, Dorothy. Painter. Exhibited at National Academy of Design, New York, 1925. *Address*, Cos Cob, Conn.

OCHTMAN, Leonard. Landscape painter. Born in Zonnemain, Holland, in 1854. Leonard Ochtman was brought to the United States in his boyhood, and grew up in Albany, N. Y., where he made his first essays in landscape painting. He is self-taught, and first exhibited at the National Academy in 1882, to which he has been a regular contributor ever since, as well as to the Society of American Artists, of which body he is a member. He is a member of the National Academy and also of the American Water Color Society; the New York Water Color Club, and the Society of Landscape Painters. He has received prizes and medals at the Brooklyn Art Club in 1892; the World's Fair at Chicago, 1893; the Philadelphia Art Club, gold medal, 1894; also prizes in Boston. He is well represented in private and public collections throughout the country. *Address*, Cos Cob, Conn.

OCHTMAN, Mina Funda (Mrs. Leonard). Painter. Born in Laconia, N. H., in 1862; died in 1924. She was a member of the American Water Color Society and the National Association of Women Painters and Sculptors. Her pictures have been shown in exhibitions throughout the country.

O'CONNOR, Andrew, Jr. Sculptor. Born in Worcester, Mass., in 1874. Pupil of his father; also of D. C. French in New York. Elected Associate Member of the National Academy, 1919. Awards: Bronze medal, Pan-American Exposition, Buffalo, 1901; second class medal, Paris Salon, 1906. Work: ''Meditation," Art Association, Indianapolis; work purchased by French Government; "Adam and Eve" (marble), Corcoran Art Gallery, Washington, D. C.; Lincoln statue, State House Grounds, Springfield, Ill.; Santa Fortunata, Springfield, Ill., Art Association. *Address,* Worcester, Mass.

O'CONNOR, Henry M. Painter and etcher. Born in Brookline, Mass., in 1891. Pupil of Mass. Normal Art School and Boston Museum School. Member: Boston Society of Etchers; Copley Society; Chicago Society of Etchers. *Address,* 58 Putnam Ave., Cambridge, Mass.

ODDIE, Walter M. Landscape painter. He was elected an Associate Member of the National Academy of Design in 1833. He died in 1865.

O'DONOVAN, William Rudolph. Sculptor. Born in Preston County, Va., in 1844. Self-taught in art. He established a studio in New York and has executed many important portrait busts and bas-reliefs, including: Wm. Page, National Academy, which was presented to the National Academy of Design; Arthur Quartly, National Academy; Thomas Elkins, National Academy; Edmund Clarence Stedman; busts of Walt Whitman and Gen. Joseph Wheeler; equestrian statues of Lincoln and Grant for Soldiers' and Sailors' Arch, Prospect Park, Brooklyn; reliefs for Oriskany battle monument; statue of Archbishop Hughes, St. John's College, Fordham; memorial tablet to Bayard Taylor, Cornell University; a statue to the captors of Major André, Tarrytown, N. Y. He was one of the four founders of the famous Title Club; also a member of the Hudson-Fulton Commission. Elected Associate Member of the National Academy, 1878. Member: Society of American Sculptors; Architectural League. He died in 1920.

OERTEL, Johannes Adam. Engraver. Born in Furth, near Nuremberg, Germany, in 1823. Oertel was apprenticed to J. M. E. Muller, a well-known engraver of Nuremberg; but as a result of the German revolution of 1848 he came to America and settled in Newark, N. J. He at first tried painting and then resorted to engraving, doing much work for the banknote companies. He finally attained success with his pictures of army life done from studies made in Virginia during the Civil War. He was rector of a number of churches at various times and was professor in an art school in St. Louis for two years. All of this time he was busy painting especially in the line of Christian art, and at carving church decorations. About 1857 he assisted in decorating the Capitol at Washington.

OF, George F. Painter. Born in New York, N. Y., in 1876. Pupil of Art Students' League of New York; Weinhold in Munich; Delecluse Academy in Paris. Member: Society of Independent Artists; Modern Artists of America. *Address,* 2794 Morris Ave., New York, N. Y.

OFFICER, Thos. S. Miniature painter. Born in Carlisle, Penna., in 1820. He had his studio in New Orleans, Philadelphia and New York, but passed the last years of his life in California. His work is remarkable for crisp, fresh color and artistic delicacy. He died in 1860.

OGDEN, Henry A. Illustrator. Born in Philadelphia, Pa., in 1856. Pupil of National Academy of Design; Art Students' League of New York. Member: Society of Illustrators, 1911. Work: Collection of uniforms of the United States Army, 1775–1906, made by order of Quarter-Master General's Department. Author and illustrator of "The Boy's Book of Famous Regiments," etc. Specialty, military and historical subjects. *Address,* 709 Times Bldg., New York, N. Y.

OGDEN, Lyman Garfield. Painter and illustrator. Born in Walton, N. Y., in 1882. Pupil of Thomas Anshutz; Robert Henri. *Address,* East St., Walton, N. Y.

OGILVIE, Clifton. Painter. Born in New York City, 1836. He studied painting under James Hart. He went abroad for four years and on his return was elected an Associate Member of the National Academy. He has since exhibited "Among the Adirondacks," "The Mountain Brook," "Lake Como." His landscape work has decided merit. He died in 1900.

O'HARA, Miss. Miniature painter, who flourished, 1834, in New York.

O'HARA, Eliot. Painter. Exhibited water colors at the Penna. Academy of the Fine Arts, Philadelphia, 1925. *Address,* 44 Greenwood Lane, Waltham, Mass.

O'KEEFFE, Georgia. Painter. Exhibited at Phila., 1921, in "Exhibition of Paintings Showing Later Tendencies in Art." *Address,* 60 East 65th St., New York.

O'KELLY, Aloysius. Painter. Born in Dublin, Ireland, in 1853. Pupil of Bonnat and Gerome at École des Beaux Arts in Paris. Member: New York Water Color Club. *Address,* 402 Clermont Ave., Brooklyn, N. Y.

OKEY, Samuel. Engraver. John Chaloner Smith, in his "British Mezzotints," says that Samuel Okey, an engraver in mezzotint, was awarded premiums in 1765 and 1767, by the London Society of Arts, presumedly for his engravings.
Soon after the date mentioned Samuel Okey must have sailed for America. In 1773, 74 and

75 he was engraving and publishing portraits in mezzotint in Newport, R. I., his business partner being Charles Reak.

OLINSKY, Ivan Gregorewitch. Mural painter. Born in Southern Russia in 1878. He came to America in 1891; studied at the National Academy of Design, New York, in 1893–98; in France and Italy, 1908–11. He has been in New York most of the time since 1893; assistant to John La Farge, 1900–08; member faculty of National Academy of Design since 1912. Awarded Thomas B. Clarke prize, National Academy of Design, 1914. Elected Associate Member of the National Academy, 1914, and an Academician in 1919. Member of the Architectural League of New York; Artists' Aid Society; Association of Mural Painters. *Address,* 27 West 67th St., New York.

OLIVER, Jean Nutting. Miniature painter. Born in Lynn, Mass. Pupil of Boston Museum School; C. H. Woodbury; Philip Hale. Member: Copley Society, 1883; National Academy of Women Painters and Sculptors; Conn. Academy of Fine Arts; Concord Artists' Association; Provincetown Artists' Association. Awards: Hudson prize, Penna. Academy of Fine Arts, 1916; "People's Prize," Boston Women Painters' Exhibition, 1917. *Address,* Fenway Studios, 30 Ipswich St., Boston, Mass.

OLIVER, Myron A. Painter. Born in Fulton, Kans., in 1891. Pupil of Chase; Du Mond. Member: Art Students' League of New York Artists. *Address,* 106 Main St., Monterey, Calif.

OLSEN, Harry E. Painter. Exhibited water colors at the Penna. Academy of the Fine Arts, Philadelphia, 1925. *Address,* 2 Glenada Place, New York.

OLSON, Albert Byron. Painter. Born in Montrose, Colo., in 1885. Pupil of Penna. Academy of Fine Arts under Chase, Anshutz and McCarter. Member: Denver Artists' Association. Represented in collection of Denver Art Association; St. Mark's Church, Denver. *Address,* 25 East 18th St., Denver, Colo.

OLSON, Carl G. T. Painter. Exhibited at the Penna. Academy of Fine Arts, Philadelphia, 1924. *Address,* 60 Pine St., Belmont, Mass.

OLSON, J. Olaf. Painter. Exhibited at National Academy of Design, New York, 1925. *Address,* 144 Bleecker St., New York.

ONDERDONK, Julian. Painter. Born in 1882; died in San Antonio in 1922. Pupil of Chase, Henri, and of his father R. J. Onderdonk. Represented by "Springtime," Dallas Art Association, and "Morning Sunlight" in the San Antonio Art League.

ONDERDONK, Robt. J. Painter, who was born in Baltimore, Md., in 1853. He studied under Chase and Wyant in New York. Specialty, flower painting. He died in San Antonio, Texas, in 1917.

O'NEILL, John A. Engraver. Born in New Jersey. He worked chiefly in the city of New York, engraving portraits and historical subjects. During the Cleveland administration, O'Neill was chief engraver to the Treasury Department at Washington, D. C. In 1876 he was mayor of Hoboken, N. J.

O'NEILL, R. E. Painter. Born in Trenton, N. J., in 1893. Pupil of A. W. Dow; Lachman; Angel Zarrago, and of C. H. Martin. Member: Society of Independent Artists. *Address,* 331 Johnston Ave., Trenton, N. J.

ONTHANK, Nathan B. Portrait painter, who flourished in Boston from 1850 to 1879. The Gallery in Independence Hall, Philadelphia, has a copy of the portrait of Samuel Adams by Copley that was painted by Onthank.

OPERTI, Albert (Jasper Ludwig Roccabigliera). Painter. Born in Turin, Italy, in 1852. He became artist, caricaturist, and scenic artist in New York theatres. Studied Arctic history; made 2 voyages to Arctic regions with Comdr. R. E. Peary, U. S. N.; painted historical pictures, "Rescue of the Greeley Party" and "Farthest North," for army and navy depts., Washington; also "The Schwatka Search," "Finding De Long in the Lena Delta (Jeannette)"; "Dr. Kane"; portrait of Comdr. Peary; mural paintings in American Museum of Natural History, New York, and in the Pittsfield, Mass., Museum. *Address,* American Museum of Natural History, New York, N. Y.

OPPER, Frederick Burr. Painter. Born in Madison, Lake County, Ohio, in 1857. On art staff *Frank Leslie's,* 3 years; an artist on *Puck* Staff, 18 years; severed connection with *Puck* to accept offer from *Hearst's New York Journal,* May, 1899; illustrator for Bill Nye, Mark Twain, Hobart (Dinkelspiel), Dunne (Dooley), etc. *Address,* 62 Circuit Rd., New Rochelle, N. Y.

OPPER, Laura. Portrait painter. Studied at National Academy of Design under Chase and Beckwith; also studied abroad. Member of Art Students' League, New York. She died in New York City in 1924.

ORD, Joseph Biays. Portrait painter. Born in 1805; also well known in Philadelphia as a fruit painter. He was a member of the first Council of the Artists' Fund Society in 1835. His portrait of his father, the ornithologist, is owned by the Academy of Natural Sciences. He died in Philadelphia in 1865.

ORDWAY, Alfred. Painter. Born in 1819. Resident of Boston and founder of the Boston Art Club in 1854. His specialty was landscape painting. Among his best known works were "On the Charles River," "Newton Lower Falls," and "Arline." He died in 1897.

ORGAN, Marjorie (Mrs. Robt. Henri). Caricaturist. Born in New York, 1886. Pupil of Danl. McCarthy and Robt. Henri. He illustrates for many New York papers. *Address,* 10 Gramercy Place, New York.

ORMSBY, Waterman Lilly. Engraver. Born in Hampton, Windham County, Conn., in 1809; died in Brooklyn, N. Y., in 1883. Ormsby was a student in the National Academy of Design in 1829, and though his preceptor in engraving is unknown, he was engraving over his own name in Albany, N. Y., at an early date; he was also engraving for Carter, Andrew & Co., of Lancaster, Mass. Being of a decided mechanical turn of mind he invented a ruling-machine, a transferpress, and a "grammagraph," a device for engraving on steel, directly from medals and medallions.

ORR, Alfred Everitt. Painter and illustrator. Born in New York in 1886. Pupil of New York Art Students' League; W. M. Chase; the Royal Academy, London. Author of poster "For Home and Country" (5th Liberty Loan). *Address,* 14 West 72d St., New York.

ORR, Frances Morris. Painter. Born in Springfield, Mo., in 1880. Pupil of G. A. Thompson. *Address,* Woodland Road, Sewickley, Penna.

ORR, John William. Wood engraver, who was born in Ireland in 1815. He was brought to this country as a child. He studied engraving on wood in New York, and later established there the most important engraving business in that section of the country. He produced the frontispieces for Harper's Illustrated Shakespeare. He died in New York, 1887.

ORR, Louis. Painter and etcher. Born in Hartford, Conn., in 1879. Pupil of Laurens in Paris. Executed mural decorations in State Bank, Hartford, Conn. Etchings now in the Luxembourg, Paris, and in the New York Public Library. *Address,* 5 Rue Mazarine, Paris, France.

ORTMAN, F. Augustus. Painter. Specialty, landscapes.

ORWIG, Louise. Painter and illustrator. Born in Mifflinburg, Penna. Pupil of Penna. Academy of Fine Arts; also of Wm. Chase. *Address,* City Library, Des Moines, Iowa.

OSBORN, M. This stipple-engraver of portraits was working in Baltimore, Md., in 1812. In 1820 Osborn was located in Philadelphia.

OSBORN, Milo. In 1836 this very clever line-engraver of portraits and landscape was employed in New York. He was later working for Philadelphia magazines. One of his contemporaries says that he became dissipated and disappeared.

OSGOOD, Charles. Portrait painter. Born in Salem, Mass., in 1809. In 1827 he opened his studio in Boston, and in 1828 he returned to Salem where he lived until his death. His portraits hang in the historical societies in Boston, Worcester and the Peabody Museum of Salem.

OSGOOD, Harry H. Painter and etcher. Born in Illinois, 1875. Pupil of Julien and Colarossi Academies in Paris. *Address,* 1538 East 57th St., New York.

OSGOOD, S. S. Portrait painter. Born in Boston in 1808. Studied art in Europe, and settled in New York. The New York Historical Society owns a number of his portraits. He is said to have died in California in 1885.

OSNIS, Benedict A. Portrait painter. Born in Russia in 1872. Pupil of Penna. Academy of Fine Arts. *Address,* The Art Club, Philadelphia.

OSTHAUS, Edmund. Painter. Born at Hildesheim, Germany, in 1858. Pupil of Andreas Muller, Peter Jansen, E. V. Gebhardt, E. Deger and C. Kroner. He came to the United States in 1883; called to Toledo, Ohio, as principal of the Toledo Academy of Fine Arts, 1886; this school was later abandoned; he now devotes his entire time to pictures; paints principally pictures of shooting and fishing, hunters and dogs being the general subjects. *Address,* 27 Bedford Road, Summit, N. J.

OSTRANDER, P. This man was a landscape engraver working in New York, and later in Cincinnati, Ohio, from 1850–55.

OSTRANDER, William C. Painter. Born in New York, 1858. Pupil of Karl Hecker and Murphy. Member of Artists' Fund Society. *Address,* Pittsfield, Mass.

OSTROWSKY, Sam. Painter. Born in Russia in 1885. Pupil of Laurens and of the Julien Academy in Paris. *Address,* 1868 South Central Park Ave., New York.

OTIS, Amy. Portrait and miniature painter. Born in Sherwood, N. Y. She also paints in landscape. Studied at Penna. Academy of Fine Arts and at the Colarossi Academy, Paris. *Address,* Care of Wheaton College, Norton, Mass.

OTIS, Bass. Painter and engraver, maker of the first lithograph in the United States. Born in New England in 1784; died in Philadelphia in 1861. Apprenticed as a youth to a scythemaker, it is not known from whom he gleaned instruction in art, but in 1808 he was painting portraits in New York and four years later settled in Philadelphia. His well-known portrait of President Jefferson was engraved for Delaplaine's "Portrait Gallery" and many other celebrities sat for him. One of his best works is a portrait of himself, painted shortly before his death. In 1815 he invented the perspective protractor, which was well received by his co-workers in art, and in 1819, for the July issue of the *Analectic Magazine,* he produced the first lithograph in this country. The design was made on a stone brought from Munich and he did the printing himself. Only one composition from his brush is known—a large interior of a smithy, possibly the one in which he served his apprenticeship. This was first exhibited at the Pennsylvania Academy of the Fine Arts in 1819, and was afterwards presented to that institution. In 1815 he painted a delightful portrait of John Neagle, at the age of nineteen, who worked in his atelier.

OTIS, Sam D. Illustrator and etcher. Born in Sherwood, N. Y., in 1889. Pupil of H. McCarter. *Address,* 112 Waverly Place, New York.

OTTER, Thomas. Painter who resided in Philadelphia. Represented by his picture "Moonlight," painted in 1860, in the Wilstach Collection, Fairmount Park, Philadelphia.

OURDAN, Joseph James Prosper. Engraver. Born in Marseilles, France, in 1803; died in Washington, D. C., in 1874. Jos. J. P. Ourdan came to New York in 1821; removed later to Philadelphia, and having learned to engrave through instruction by his son, Joseph P. Ourdan, he became an expert letter engraver. In this capacity he was employed by the United States Treasury Department, at Washington, from 1866 until his death.

OURDAN, Joseph Prosper. Engraver. Born in New York City in 1828; died in Washington, D. C., in 1881. Joseph P. Ourdan was the son of the above, and served his apprenticeship as an engraver with W. L. Ormsby, of New York. Over his own name he engraved in line some good portraits and illustrative works for the book publishers, and the firm of Packard & Ourdan produced portraits in mezzotint; but he early became interested in banknote work and was in the employ of the Continental and the National banknote companies, of New York, and of the American Bank Note Company, of Philadelphia.

OURDAN, Vincent Le Comte. Engraver. Born in Brooklyn, N. Y., in 1855. He served his apprenticeship as an engraver with the Columbian Bank-Note Company, of Washington, D. C., from 1875 to 1878; for some time he was employed in the Bureau of Engraving and Printing, and then returned to the Columbian Company and was with the latter until it went out of business. In 1882 Mr. Ourdan went to the United States Hydrographic Office, in Washington, and there created the Mechanical Engraving Department.

OUREN, Karl. Painter. Born in Norway in 1882. Studied in Copenhagen and at the Art Institute of Chicago. Member: Palette and Chisel Club. Award: Gold medal, Palette and Chisel Club, 1919. *Address,* 1536 North Kedzie Ave., Chicago, Ill.

OURLAC, Jean Nicolas. Painter. Born in New Orleans, La., in 1789; died in 1821. The subjects of his paintings are mostly taken from American scenery.

OUTBANK, Nahum B. Painter, who lived in Boston from 1856–79. He painted portraits of John Brown, Wendell Phillips, and others of his friends.

OUTCAULT, Richard F. Comic illustrator. Born in Lancaster, Ohio, in 1863. On staff of the *New York Journal* since 1905. Created the "Yellow Kid" and "Buster Brown." Member: Salmagundi Club. *Address,* 245 Madison Ave., Flushing, L. I. New York.

OVERBECK, Mary Frances. Painter. Born in Cambridge City, Ind., in 1878. Pupil of Arthur Dow at Columbia University, New York. Member: Cincinnati Woman's Art Club; Indiana Artists' Club. *Address,* Cambridge City, Ind.

OWEN, Mrs. Esther S. D. Painter. Born in Boston, Mass., in 1843. Pupil of Votin, Geary and Tuckerman. Member: Conn. Academy of Fine Arts. Represented in Worcester Art Museum. *Address,* 40 Willard St., Hartford, Conn.

P

PACH, Walter. Painter. Born in New York in 1883. Pupil of Leigh Hunt, Chase and Henri in New York. Member: Society of Independent Artists, Paris. *Address*, 13 East 14th St., New York, N. Y.

PACKARD, Mabel. Miniature painter. Born in Iowa. Pupil of Art Institute of Chicago; Colarossi Academy in Paris. Member: Chicago Society of Artists. Award: Bronze medal, St. Louis Exposition, 1904. *Address*, 2031 Berkshire Ave., South Pasadena, Calif.

PACKER, Frank H. Sculptor. Pupil of Martiny and Saint Gaudens. He was the sculptor of "Nebraska."

PADDOCK, Ethel Louise. Painter. Born in New York City in 1887. Pupil of New York School of Art, and of Henri. Member: Society of Independent Artists; National Academy of Women Painters and Sculptors. *Address*, 12 East 15th St., New York, N. Y.

PADDOCK, Josephine. Painter. Exhibited at the Penna. Academy of Fine Arts, Philadelphia, 1914. Portraits, "Miss Trelawney" and "The Sealskin Muffs." *Address*, 130 West 57th St., New York City.

PADDOCK, Willard D. Sculptor and painter. Born in Brooklyn, N. Y., in 1873. Pupil of Herbert Adams in New York; Pratt Institute in Brooklyn; Courtois and Girardot in Paris. Member: Salmagundi Club, 1904; National Sculpture Society, 1915; Art Aid Society; Allied Artists' Association; Washington Art Club; Century Association; Guild of New York Artists. Elected Associate Member of the National Academy. *Address*, South Kent, Conn.

PAEFF, Bashka. Sculptor. Born in Minsk, Russia, in 1893. Pupil of Bela Pratt. Member: Boston Society of Artists. Work: Portraits in bas-reliefs of William Dixon Weaver, Jane Addams, Oliver Wendell Holmes, Louis D. Brandeis and Sherman Whipple; also portrait busts, statuettes and animal studies. *Address*, 45 River St., Boston, Mass.

PAGE, Marie D. (Mrs. Calvin G.). Portrait painter. Born in Boston. Pupil of School of the Boston Museum of Fine Arts. Member: Copley Society, 1890; International Society; Art League; Newport Artists' Association. Awards: Bronze medal, Panama-Pacific Exposition, San Francisco, 1915; Bok prize, Penna. Academy of Fine Arts, 1916; Shaw Memorial prize, National Academy of Design, 1916; first prize and honorable mention, Duxbury Artists'

Association, 1920. *Address*, 128 Marlborough St., Boston, Mass.

PAGE, Walter Gilman. Painter. Born in Boston. Pupil of Boston Museum School; of Boulanger and Lefebvre in Paris. Member: Copley Society; Mass. State Art Commission. Work: "A Head," Toledo Museum of Art; portraits now in Massachusetts State House; Portland (Me.) City Hall; Bowdoin College; Maine Historical Society; Colby College, Maine; Vermont State House; Worcester Public Library, etc. Chairman, State Art Commission, Mass. *Address*, 310 Fenway Studios, 30 Ipswich St., Boston, Mass.

PAGE, William. Painter. Born in Albany, N. Y., in 1811. He removed with his family to New York City in 1820 and entered the law office of Frederick De Peyster when quite a young man, but soon devoted himself entirely to art, studying under Professor Morse, and in the Schools of the National Academy. He painted portraits in Albany, 1828–29, returned to New York, and, later, opened a studio in Boston, where he remained until he went to Europe. He was for many years considered the leading American portrait painter in Rome. Elected a member of the National Academy in 1836, and delivered lectures to the Academy students which were highly esteemed. Among his earlier works are a "Holy Family," belonging to the Boston Athenaeum, a portrait of Governor Marcy, in the City Hall, New York, and "The Infancy of Henry IV." His exhibits in the National Academy include "Antique Timbrel Player," 1871; "Farragut's Triumphant Entry into Mobile Bay," 1872; "Shakespeare," 1874; "Shakespeare, from the German Death Mask," 1876. He was much impressed with the death mask of Shakespeare and wrote several articles in support of its authenticity. He painted a head of "Christ" which attracted much attention, because of the deep religious sentiment it expressed. A number of Page's pictures were on exhibition in New York in the winter of 1877, including his "Shakespeares" and his celebrated "Venus," painted in Rome, 1859, and exhibited in London and other cities including Philadelphia. The Penna. Academy has an interesting genre painting by Page, of excellent qualities, but in curious condition as to color—it being possibly one of the experiments in color which the artist was reputed to be fond of trying. He died at his home on Long Island in 1885.

PAGES, Jules. Painter. Born in San Francisco, Calif., in 1867. Pupil of Constant, Lefebvre and Robert-Fleury in Paris. Awards: Honorable mention, Paris Salon, 1895; second medal, Paris Salon; Knight of the Legion of Honor, 1910. He was instructor at the Julien Academy night class after 1902; life class since 1907. Member: International Society of Paris Sculptors and Painters. Represented in Museum of Pau, France; Museum of Toulouse, France; the Luxembourg, Paris; Golden Gate Park Museum and Art Institute, San Francisco; Municipal Art Gallery, Oakland, Calif. *Address*, 42 Rue Fontaine, Paris, France.

PAGON, Katherine W. Dunn (Mrs. William W.). Painter. Member: Fellowship, Penna. Academy of Fine Arts. *Address*, 114 St. John's Road, Roland Park, Md.

PAINE, Richard G. Sculptor. Born in Charleston, S. C., in 1875. Pupil of Amateis and Kemeys. *Address*, East Falls Church, Va.

PALL, Augustin G. Painter. Member: Chicago Society of Artists. *Address*, 19 East Pearson St., Chicago, Ill.

PALLISON. A landscape painter, noted in Tuckerman's ''American Artist Life.''

PALMER, Adelaide. Painter. Born in Oxford, N. H. Pupil of John J. Enneking in Boston and of G. H. Bartlett. Member: Copley Society in 1893.

PALMER, E. V. (See Elizabeth Palmer Bradfield.)

PALMER, Erastus Dow. Sculptor. Born in 1817 in Pompey, Onondaga County, N. Y. He first executed cameo portraits and finally undertook real sculpture. All his knowledge was acquired in America, and it was not until he had become famous that he visited Europe. Among his best known works are ''The Indian Girl''; ''White Captive''; ''Morning and Evening.'' He died in Albany, N. Y., in 1904.

PALMER, Frances F. (Mrs.). Painter, who lived in Brooklyn, New York, and worked for Currier & Ives. Her specialty was sporting scenes, and her lithographs were also published by Nathaniel Currier.

PALMER, Mrs. Fredrikke S. Painter. Born in Norway. Staff artist for *Woman's Journal*. *Address*, 221 Everit St., New Haven, Conn.

PALMER, J. A number of large and fairly well-executed Bible illustrations, published in New York in 1826, are signed ''J. Palmer, Sc.''

PALMER, Lucia A. Painter. Born in Dryden, N. Y. Prize winner in Paris Exposition, 1900. Member: Woman's National Press Association, Washington. *Address*, Park Hill-on-Hudson, New York.

PALMER, Pauline. Painter. Born in McHenry, Ill. Studied at Institute of Chicago and in Paris with Collin, Prinet, Courtois and Simon. Exhibited Paris Salon, 1903-4-5-6, 11; Naples Esposizione de Belle Arti., 1911; also in the principal cities of the United States. Represented in permanent collection of the Art Institute of Chicago; Muncie (Ind.) Art Association; also in various clubs. *Address*, 4 East Ohio St., Chicago, Ill.

PALMER, Walter Launt. Painter. Born in Albany, N. Y., in 1854. Studied art with F. E. Church, Hudson, N. Y., 1870-2, and in Paris, 1873-4, 1876-7, under Carolus-Duran. Specialist as painter of winter scenes. Awarded 2d Hallgarten prize, National Academy of Design, 1887; medal, Chicago Exposition, 1893; gold medal, Art Club, Phila., 1894; Evans prize, American Water Color Society, 1895; 1st prize, Boston Art Club, 1895. Elected Associate Member of National Academy, 1877, and Academician, 1897. *Address*, 5 Lafayette St., Albany, N. Y.

PANCOAST, Henry B., Jr. Painter. Exhibited ''Landscape'' at the Penna. Academy of Fine Arts, Philadelphia, 1924. *Address*, 2201 Chestnut St., Philadelphia.

PANCOAST, Morris Hall. Painter. Born in Salem, N. J., 1877. Pupil of Penna. Academy of Fine Arts and of Laurens in Paris. *Address*, 12 East 8th St., New York.

PANDICK, John. Painter. Exhibited at Philadelphia, 1921, in ''Exhibition of Paintings Showing Later Tendencies in Art.'' *Address*, Fanwood, N. J.

PAOLO, Cartaino S. Sculptor. Born in Italy in 1882. Pupil of American Academy in Rome. Work: Bust of Ex-Gov. MacCall in Boston State House; Cardinal O'Connell in Boston Cathedral; marble memorial in Cathedral of St. John the Divine, New York. *Address*, 80 Washington Square, New York City.

PAPE, Eric. Painter. Born in San Francisco, 1870. Art education in Paris under Boulanger, Lefebvre, Constant, Doucet, Blanc and Delance, and at École des Beaux Arts under Gerome and Laurens. He has lived in England, France, Germany, Mexico and Egypt. Instructor in Cowles Art School, Boston, 1897; founded in 1898, and was the director and head instructor of the Eric Pape School of Art until 1913. Exhibited 22 pictures at the Paris Salon; Chicago Exposition, 1893; Munich Kunst Austellung, 1897; 120 paintings, Omaha Exposition, 1899; Paris Exposition, 1900; 100 paintings and drawings, Buffalo Exposition, 1901; St. Louis Exposition, 1904; etc. Illustrated many important works. Member: Society of Arts; Honorable Council, N. British

Academy; Atlantic Union; United Arts Club, London. *Address*, Manchester, Mass.

PAPE, Mrs. Eric (Mrs. Alice M.). Painter, deceased 1911.

PAPPRILL, Henry. This engraver in aquatint produced at least two very large plates. One shows New York as seen from Governor's Island; the other is a most interesting and detailed view over the city from the steeple of St. Paul's Church. The first was engraved from a sketch made by F. Catherwood, and the other from a drawing by J. W. Hill. These plates were published in New York in 1849, and the view from St. Paul's steeple was reissued in 1855 with many changes in the buildings shown. There were also several editions of the other plate.

PAQUET, Anthony C. Engraver. Born in Hamburg, Germany, in 1814; died in 1882. Paquet came to the United States in 1848 and found employment here as a die-sinker. From 1857 until 1864 he was assistant engraver of the U. S. Mint in Philadelphia. Among others he engraved the dies for medals of Buchanan, Everett, Grant, and Johnson.

PARADISE, John. Painter. Born in New Jersey in 1783. He became a member of the National Academy of Design upon its formation in 1826. He painted many portraits of Methodist divines, his drawings being correct, but his ability as an artist not very high. He died in New York City in 1834. His son John W. Paradise was an admirable engraver of portraits.

PARADISE, John Wesley. Engraver. Born in New Jersey in 1809; died in New York in 1862. John W. Paradise was the son of John Paradise, an American portrait-painter who was born in 1783 and died in 1834. The son was a pupil of A. B. Durand and in time became an admirable line-engraver of portraits. He was one of the founders of the National Academy in 1826. Later in life John W. Paradise was chiefly employed as a banknote engraver, and he was working in this branch of his profession up to the time of his death.

PARAMINO, John F. Sculptor. Born in Boston, 1889. Pupil of Saint Gaudens and of Bela L. Pratt. *Address*, 295 Huntington Ave., Boston, Mass.

PARCELL, Malcolm S. Painter and etcher. Born in 1896. Pupil of Carnegie School of Fine Arts. Awarded the 1919 Medal by National Academy of Design. *Address*, Casino Bldg., Washington, Penna.

PARIS, Walter. Painter. Born in England in 1842. Specialty, water color painting He died in Washington, D. C., in 1906.

PARIS, William Francklyn. Mural painter. Born in New York. Pupil of Art Students' League of New York; Julien Academy in Paris. *Address*, 53 West 39th St., New York, N. Y.

PARISSEN, Otto. A silversmith and engraver on silver, he also designed the ornaments on the silverware he made. He was a native of Prussia and resided in New York City. His son painted miniatures.

PARISSEN, Philip. Miniature painter, who flourished in 1798–1812 in New York. He was the son of a silversmith who came from Prussia.

PARISSEN, William D. Miniature painter, who flourished in 1819–32 in New York.

PARK, Asa. Portrait painter, who flourished about 1800, and died in 1827.

PARKER, A. B. (Mrs. Neilson T. Parker). Painter. Member: National Academy of Women Painters and Sculptors; National Art Club. *Address*, Woodstock, N. Y.

PARKER, Charles H. Engraver. Born in Salem, Mass., about 1795; died in Philadelphia in 1819. Parker was a pupil of Gideon Fairman. He worked in Europe for a time, and about 1812 he was in business as an engraver in Philadelphia. He is referred to as the "best engraver of script, maps and ornament of his time." He was the engraver of the beautiful script on the title-page of the *Analectic Magazine*, of Philadelphia, and did considerable work of this character.

PARKER, Cora. Painter and illustrator, Born in Kentucky. Pupil of Cincinnati Art School; Julien Academy in Paris. Work: "Blue Waters of Gloucester," Kansas City, Mo., Art Club; "Prune Orchard, California," Nebraska Art Association, Lincoln. Custodian, Art Gallery, Bruce Museum, Greenwich, Conn. *Address*, Greenwich, Conn.

PARKER, Cushman. Illustrator. Born in Boston, Mass., in 1881. Pupil of Laurens and Carl Marr. Member: Society of Illustrators. Designer of covers for *Saturday Evening Post*, and for *McCall's*, *Collier's*, etc. *Address*, Woodstock, Ulster County, N. Y.

PARKER, Edgar. Born in Mass. in 1840. He spent his professional life in Boston. Three of his portraits are in Faneuil Hall (Sumner-Wilson & Winslow); Whittier gave him sittings in 1875. He painted "Embarkation of the Pilgrims," after Weir.

PARKER, Emma Alice. Painter and illustrator. Born in Gardner, Mass., in 1876. Pupil of Sydney R. Burleigh, Robert Henri, F. V. Du Mond and of H. R. Poore. Member: Providence Water Color Club. *Address*, 42 College St., Providence, R. I.

PARKER, George. Engraver. Born in England, he was engraving excellent stipple portraits in London in 1832. He came to the United States about 1834, to work for Longacre & Herring on ''The National Portrait Gallery'' plates, and he seems to have remained continuously in this country until his death, which occurred about 1868. Parker engraved a considerable number of good portraits.

PARKER, Harry H. Mural painter and sculptor. Born in Phiadelphia in 1869. Studied at Penna. Academy of Fine Arts. Died in 1917.

PARKER, John Adams. Painter. Born in New York City, 1829. He was elected an Associate Member of the National Academy in 1869. Mountain scenery has claimed his attention, and the Adirondacks, Catskills, and White Mountains have furnished him subjects for most of his pictures.

PARKER, John F. Painter and sculptor. Born in New York City in 1884. Pupil of Henri in New York; also studied in England and with Laurens and Steinlen in Paris. Member: Alliance. Award: Whitney prize, Labor Competition. He directed a pageant for the City History Club, New York, 1916; also the Westfield 200th Anniversary Pageant, etc. Represented in National Gallery, Wash., D. C. *Address*, 401 Convent Ave., New York, N. Y.

PARKER, Lawton S. Portrait painter. Born in Fairfield, Mich., in 1868. Pupil of Gerome, Laurens, Constant, Besnard and Whistler in Paris; of Chase in New York. Instructor in St. Louis School of Fine Arts, 1892; director of fine arts, Beloit College, 1893; president, New York School of Art, 1898–99; director of Parker Academy, Paris, 1900; nonresident professor, Art Institute of Chicago, 1902; later, president. *Address*, 2 Rue Brea, Paris, France.

PARKER, Stephen H. Portrait painter. Born in 1852. He was a friend of John Sargent and a fellow-pupil in Paris. He made his home for years in New York City, but lived in Italy and France for the last thirteen years of his life, and did little or no painting. He died in Italy in 1925.

PARKER, Thomas H. Miniature painter. Born in Sag Harbor, Long Island, in 1801. He studied under Rogers in New York, and later removed to Hartford, Conn., where he became most popular in his profession; he was painting there in 1829. He died in 1851.

PARKHURST, Anita (Mrs. Willcox). Painter and illustrator. Born in Chicago in 1892. Pupil of Art Institute of Chicago.

Member: Guild of Free Lance Artists; Society of Illustrators. He made illustrations for *Saturday Evening Post, Collier's*, etc. *Address*, 412 West 20th St., New York, N. Y.

PARKHURST, C. E. Illustrator. Born in Toledo, Ohio, in 1885. Pupil of Vanderpoel, Freer and Armstrong. Member: New York Architectural League. Awards: Three honorable mentions, Art Institute of Chicago, 1906. *Address*, 63 East 59th St., New York, N. Y.

PARKHURST, Thomas Shrewsbury. Landscape painter and illustrator. Born in Manchester, England, in 1853; he died in 1923. Self-taught. Member: Toledo Tile Club; National Art Club. Work: ''October Skies'' and ''The Spirit of the Maumee,'' Toledo Museum of Art; ''Landscape,'' Grand Rapids Art Association; ''Chariot of the Sky,'' Oakland, California, Art Museum; represented in Lima, Ohio, Art League; Des Moines, Ia., Art Club; Oklahoma Art League.

PARKMAN. A landscape painter noted in Tuckerman's ''American Artist Life.''

PARKYNS, George Isham. This English artist and designer for engravers came to Philadelphia about 1795. His only known print is a large and good aquatint view of Mount Vernon. He is said to have been employed by T. B. Freeman, the Philadelphia publisher of books and prints.

PARRISH, Clara Weaver (Mrs. Wm. P.). Painter and etcher. Born in Selma, Ala. Pupil of Art Students' League of New York, under Chase, Mowbray, Cox and J. Alden Weir; under Collin in Paris. Member: New York Water Color Club; National Academy of Women Painters and Sculptors; National Art Club. Awards: Watrous prize, N. Y. Women's Art Club, 1902 and 1913; silver medal, Appalachian Exposition, Knoxville, 1910; silver medal, Panama-Pacific Exposition, San Francisco, 1915. Died in New York, 1925.

PARRISH, Maxfield. Illustrator and painter. Born in Philadelphia, Pa., in 1870; son of Stephen Parrish. Pupil of Penna. Academy of Fine Arts and of Howard Pyle. Member: Associate Member of the National Academy, 1905; National Academy in 1906; Fellowship, Penna. Academy of Fine Arts; National Institute of Art League; Union International des Beaux Arts et des Lettres. Awards: Honorable mention, Paris Exposition, 1900; silver medal for drawings, Pan-American Exposition, Buffalo, 1901; Beck prize, Phila. Water Color Club, 1908; gold medal, New York Architectural League, 1917. *Address*, Windsor, Vt.

PARRISH, Stephen. Painter and etcher. Born in Philadelphia in 1846. Engaged in mercantile pursuits till the age of 31; he then applied himself to art, studying a year under a local teacher; he took up etching and produced his first plate in 1879; has exhibited in New York, Boston, Philadelphia, London, Liverpool, Munich, Paris, Vienna and Dresden. Member: New York Etching Club; Royal Society of Painters and Etchers, London. *Address*, Windsor, Vt.

PARROTT, William S. Painter of Western scenery. Born in Missouri. He went West in 1847, and died at Goldendale, Washington, in 1915.

PARSELL, Abraham. Miniature painter, who flourished in New York 1825–47.

PARSELL, J. H. Miniature painter, who flourished in 1846–47 in New York.

PARSHALL, De Witt. Painter. Born in Buffalo, N. Y., in 1864. He studied at Academie Julien and Academie Cormon in Paris,. 1886–92; also with T. Alexander Harrison. Specialty, landscapes. Represented in Metropolitan Museum, New York; Toledo, Ohio; also in Worcester, Mass., and Syracuse, N. Y., museums. Member, jury awards, Penna. Academy of Fine Arts, and National Academy of Design, 1909. National Academy, 1917. Member: Society of Painters of the Far West; International Society of Arts and Letters; Allied Artists of America. Clubs: Century (trustee); National Arts (life); Lotos (life); Sleepy Hollow Country, MacDowell, New York; Santa Barbara Country; California Art. *Address*, Santa Barbara, Calif.

PARSHALL, Douglass Ewell. Painter. Born in New York in 1899. Pupil of De Witt Parshall. Represented by "Marine" in Syracuse Museum. *Address*, Santa Barbara, Calif.

PARSONS, Charles. Born in England in 1821; died in 1910. He came to this country at an early age. He painted in oil and water color, besides having learned the art of lithography. He was elected an Associate Member of the National Academy of Design, and of the New York Water Color Society.

PARSONS, Edith B. (Mrs.). Sculptor. Born in Houston, Va., in 1878. Pupil of Art Students' League of New York, under French and Barnard. Specialty, fountains. *Address*, 13 Van Dam St., New York.

PARTINGTON, Richard L. Painter. Born in England in 1868. Member of San Francisco Art Association. *Address*, 1713 Sansom St., Philadelphia.

PARTON, Arthur. Landscape painter. He was born at Hudson, N. Y., in 1842, and studied in Philadelphia under William T. Richards. In 1869 he visited Europe and obtained some effective studies of Scotch and English scenery. He was elected a National Academician in 1884, and is a member of the American Water Color Society. Represented in the Metropolitan Museum; also exhibited in Paris, in 1889. He died in 1914.

PARTON, Ernest. Painter. Born in Hudson, N. Y., in 1845. He has studied in England, and has exhibited his landscapes at the Royal Academy and in the National Academy of Design in New York. Among his paintings are "The Silent Pool"; "Silver and Gold"; "Falling Leaves"; his picture "Waning of the Year" is in the South Kensington Museum, London.

PARTON, Henry Woodbridge. Painter. Born in Hudson, N. Y., in 1858; like his brother Ernest he has devoted himself to painting without any regular art-instruction. He has lived in Paris and London, and exhibited at the Royal Academy. Became an Associate Member of the National Academy of Design, and exhibited at its annual exhibition of 1925. *Address*, 119 East 19th St., New York.

PARTRIDGE, Joseph. Painter. He painted a portrait of Rev. Stephen Gano of Providence, R. I., which was engraved and published by Pekenino in 1822.

PARTRIDGE, Roi. Etcher. Born in Centralia, Wash., in 1888. Pupil of National Academy of Design in New York, and of Chicago Society of Etchers. Represented in New York Public Library; Library of Congress; Carnegie Institute, Chicago. *Address*, 4540 Evelyn St., Oakland, Calif.

PARTRIDGE, William Ordway. Sculptor. Born in Paris, France, in 1861. Art education in Rome, Florence, Paris. Lecturer on fine arts, Columbia University, 1897–1903; lecturer before National Social Science Association, Concord School of Philosophy, Brooklyn Institute, etc. Works include: Statue of Shakespeare, Lincoln Park, Chicago; Kauffmann Memorial, Washington, D. C.; Pulitzer Memorial, Woodlawn, N. Y.; bronze statue of Alexander Hamilton, Brooklyn; bronze statue same, Columbia University; bronze statue of Thomas Jefferson, Columbia University; bust of R. E. Peary, Bowdoin College, Me.; "Whittier," Boston Public Library; equestrian statue of General Grant, Grant Square, Brooklyn. *Address*, Republican Club, 54 West 40th St., New York, N. Y.

PASCIN, Jules. Painter, who exhibited in Philadelphia, 1921, in "Exhibition of Paintings Showing the Later Tendencies in Art." *Address*, Care of Daniel Galleries, New York City.

PASZTHORY, Arpad. Painter of "A Negro Newsboy"; standing, three-quarter length; wall background. Sold in New York Auction.

PATIGIAN, Haig. Sculptor. Born in City of Van, Armenia, in 1876. Studied sculpture with Alix Marquet, Paris, France, 1906–07. Member: International Jury of Awards, Panama P. I. Exposition, 1915. Principal works: McKinley Monument, Arcata, Cal., 1905; "Ancient History," Salon des Artistes Francais, 1907; "Guardian Angel," Dolbeer Mausoleum, San Francisco, Cal.; Rowell Monument, Fresno, Cal.; figures of "Invention," "Imagination," "Steam Power," "Electrical Power." Member: National Sculpture Society; American Federation Arts; Societé des Artistes Francais. *Address*, 923 Polk St., San Francisco, Calif.

PATTEE, Elsie D. Painter and illustrator. Born in Chelsea, Mass., in 1876. Pupil of Julien Academy in Paris. *Address*, 154 West 57th St., New York.

PATTERSON, Ambrose. Painter. Born in Australia. *Address*, 917 Seneca St., Seattle, Wash.

PATTERSON, Catherine Norris. Miniature painter. Born in Philadelphia. Studied at the Penna. Academy of Fine Arts, Phila. She has exhibited at the Penna. Academy of Fine Arts Exhibitions and in other places. *Address*, 2200 St. James Place, Philadelphia, Pa.

PATTERSON, Charles R. Marine painter. Born in England in 1878. Exhibited "A Ship of Yesterday" at the Penna. Academy of Fine Arts, Philadelphia, 1924. *Address*, 119 East 19th St., New York.

PATTERSON, Howard A. Painter. Born in Philadelphia, Pa., in 1891. Pupil of Philadelphia Industrial Art School; Penna. Academy of Fine Arts. Member: Fellowship, Penna. Academy of Fine Arts; Philadelphia Sketch Club; Society of Independent Artists. Work: "Lines and Patches," Fellowship of the Pennsylvania Academy of the Fine Arts, Philadelphia. *Address*, 514 Walnut St., Philadelphia, Pa.

PATTERSON, Margaret (Jordon). Painter and illustrator. Born in Soerabaija, Java. Pupil of Pratt Institute under Arthur Dow in Brooklyn; of Charles H. Woodbury in Boston; of Castellucho in Paris. Member: Boston Society of Etchers; Boston Water Color Club; Copley Society, 1900; Philadelphia Water Color Club; National Academy of Women Painters and Sculptors. Award: Honorable mention for etching, Panama-Pacific Exposition, San Francisco, 1915. Work: "Basque Fishing Boats," Museum of Fine Arts, Boston. Represented in Oakland, California Art Museum. Director of art department, Dana Hall School, Wellesley, Mass. *Address*, Trinity Court, Boston, Mass.

PATTERSON, Rebecca Burd Peale. Painter. Born in Philadelphia, Pa. Pupil of Penna. Museum and of the School of Industrial Art, Philadelphia. Also of Rebecca Van Trump and W. J. Whittemore, New York. Member: Penna. Society of Miniature Painters. *Address*, 5522 Morris St., Germantown, Philadelphia, Pa.

PATTISON, James William. Painter. Born in Boston in 1844; died in 1915. Painter of figures, domestic animals, landscapes, marines, etc.; exhibitor at Paris Salon, 1879–81; at National Academy, New York, for many years; at American Water Color Society, New York, 15 years; Penna. Academy of Fine Arts; at Art Institute of Chicago, many times; Chicago Exposition, 1893; St. Louis Exposition, 1904; also medal at Boston, 1882; was a constant exhibitor at art galleries all over the country. Director of School of Fine Arts, Jacksonville, Ill., 1884–96; faculty lecturer on the collections, Art Institute of Chicago after 1896; editor, Fine Arts Journal, Chicago, in 1910. Ex-pres., Chicago Society of Artists; member of the Municipal Art League of Chicago; also of Society of Western Artists.

PATTON, Elizabeth. Painter. Exhibited "Landscape" at the Penna. Academy of the Fine Arts, 1926. *Address*, 1522 Chestnut St., Philadelphia, Pa.

PATTON, Katharine. Painter. Born in Philadelphia. Pupil of Cox, Hawthorne and Snell in New York; of Frank Brangwyn in London. Member: National Academy of Women Painters and Sculptors; Philadelphia Water Color Club; Fellowship, Penna. Academy of Fine Arts; Plastic Club; Philadelphia Alliance. Awards: Silver medal, Knoxville, Tenn., Exposition, 1913; prize for landscape, National Association of Women Painters and Sculptors, 1918. Work: "The Maple Woods," Pennsylvania Academy of the Fine Arts; "Wood Interior," Fellowship, Pennsylvania Academy of the Fine Arts, Philadelphia; "Through the Old Window Screen," Southern High School, Philadelphia, Pa. *Address*, 1522 Chestnut St., Philadelphia, Pa.

PATTON, Katherine Maxey. Painter. Award: Mary Smith prize, Penna. Academy of Fine Arts, 1921. *Address*, 718 Southwest St., Wheaton, Ill.

PATTY, W. A. Painter. Born in New Hartford, Conn., in 1884. Pupil of Charles Noel Flagg; Robt. B. Brandegee; Edgar M. Ward. Member: Brooklyn Society of Artists; Society of Independent Artists; Brooklyn Water Color Club; League of New York Artists. *Address*, 1454 Seventy-eighth St., Brooklyn, New York, N. Y.

PAUL, Charles R. Illustrator. Born in Indiana, Pa., in 1888. Pupil of Anshutz, Chase and McCarter. Member: Philadelphia Sketch Club. *Address,* 17th St. and the Parkway, Philadelphia, Pa.

PAUL, E. Engraver. The only known print engraved by this man is a large and excellent mezzotint portrait of Henry Clay, published by R. A. Bachia, New York, 1855. This print is signed "Eng'd by E. Paul."

PAUL, Horace A. Painter, who exhibited at the Penna. Academy of Fine Arts, Philadelphia, 1924. *Address,* 2160 North Van Pelt St., Philadelphia.

PAUL, Jeremiah. Painted portraits from 1791 to about 1820, when he died, in Missouri. His studio was No. 35 South Fourth St., Philadelphia. Work: Portrait of Mrs. Rachel West Clarkson; bust, wears cap tied under chin, arms crossed in lap. Owned by Worcester Art Museum. Portrait of Tench Coxe; bust to left. Owned by Brinton Coxe, Philadelphia.

PAULDING, John. Sculptor. Born in Dark County, Ohio, in 1873. Pupil of Art Institute of Chicago. Member: Alumni Art Institute; Chicago Society of Artists; Cliff Dwellers. *Address,* 1200 Steinway Hall, Chicago, Ill.

PAULUS, Francis Petrus. Painter and etcher. Born in Detroit, Mich., in 1862. Pupil of Penna. Academy of Fine Arts; Royal Academy in Munich under Loefftz; École des Beaux Arts in Paris under Bonnat. Member: Chicago Society of Etchers; National Art Club; La Gravure Originale en Noir; Societé International des Beaux Arts et des Lettres. Work: "Alley in Bruges," Herron Art Institute, Indianapolis; "Low Tide," "Fish Market," "Shimmering Sea," "Old Bridge, Bruges," and set of etchings, Detroit Institute. Etchings in New York Public Library; Library of Congress, Washington, D. C.; Oakland, Calif., Museum. *Address,* Bruges, Belgium.

PAXON, Edgar Samuel. Illustrator and painter. Born in East Hamburg, N. Y., in 1852. Specialty, Indians and American pioneers. Work: Eight murals in Missoula County Court House; six murals in Montana Capitol; "Custer's Last Fight," exhibited in many cities. *Address,* 611 Stephens Ave., Missoula, Mont.

PAXSON, Ethel (Mrs. Clement Esmond). Painter and illustrator. Born in Meriden, Conn., in 1885. Pupil of Chase, Poore, and Penna. Academy of Fine Arts. *Address,* Kew Gardens, L. I., New York.

PAXTON, Mrs. Elizabeth Okle. Painter. Born in Providence, R. I. Pupil of W. M.

Paxton. Award: Silver medal, Panama-Pacific Exposition, San Francisco, 1915. *Address,* 132 Riverway, Boston, Mass.

PAXTON, W. A. Painter. Member: California Art Club. *Address,* 955 Edgeware Road, Los Angeles, Calif.

PAXTON, William M. Painter. Born in Baltimore, Md., in 1869. Pupil of Dennis Bunker in Boston, and of Gerome in Paris. Elected an Associate Member of the National Academy, 1917. Represented in Metropolitan Museum; Penna. Academy of Fine Arts; Corcoran Art Gallery. *Address,* 132 Riverway Studios, Boston, Mass.

PAYNE, Edgar. Painter. Born in Washborn, Mo., in 1882. Pupil of Art Institute of Chicago; chiefly self-taught. Member: Palette and Chisel Club; Chicago Society of Artists; International Society of Arts and Letters; California Art Club. *Address,* 867 North Dearborn St., Chicago, Ill.

PEABODY, Amelia. Sculptor, who exhibited at the Penna. Academy of the Fine Arts, Philadelphia, 1924. *Address,* 120 Commonwealth Ave., Boston, Mass.

PEABODY, Evelyn. Sculptor, who exhibited at the Penna. Academy of the Fine Arts, Philadelphia, 1924. *Address,* 1620 Summer St., Philadelphia.

PEABODY, M. M. Engraver. The earliest plate by this engraver, seen by the compiler, is a very large and crudely executed engraving of "The Unjust Sentence of the Jews against Jesus Christ the Saviour of the World." This print was engraved and published in 1823, without noting the place of publication; but in 1835 M. M. Peabody was located in Utica, N. Y., where he engraved maps in line, and general book illustrations in stipple. A few portraits, signed "M. Peabody," were probably the work of the above.

PEACOCK. An early New England portrait painter, of whom little is known. The American Antiquarian Society of Worcester, Mass., have two portraits of John and Mrs. Charles Bush which are attributed to "Peacock."

PEALE, Anna Claypoole. Painter. Daughter of James Peale. She was born in 1791, and died in 1878. She painted still-life subjects, and later took to miniature painting. She painted Gen. Lallemand, President James Monroe, Maj.-Gen. Jackson, and Commodore Bainbridge.

PEALE, Charles Willson. Painter and engraver. Born in Charlestown, Md., in 1741; died in Philadelphia in 1827. Peale is said to have been apprenticed to a saddler in Annapolis, Md., but he went to Boston to study art, and in 1768–69 he is credited with having received some instruction from J. S. Copley in that city. About this time he went to London with letters to Benjamin West and received some encouragement from him. In London Peale learned to paint miniatures, to engrave in mezzotint, to mold in wax, and to work in plaster.

He returned to Annapolis, but was in Philadelphia in 1775 and at once took an active part in the Revolution and in State politics. He was a captain of volunteers at the Battle of Trenton, and represented Philadelphia in the Pennsylvania Legislature of 1779. While in the army, and afterward, Peale painted the portraits of a great number of men prominent at the time in military affairs, besides doing much work in ordinary portraiture. He painted a number of portraits of General George Washington.

Peale was deeply interested in the study of natural history; and the finding of the remains of a "mammoth" in Ulster County, N. Y., practically induced him to establish in Philadelphia his once famous Museum and Art Gallery, opened to the public in 1802. To this institution he devoted the remainder of his life.

The accommodations in the American Philosophical Society Building proving inadequate, Peale made application to the Legislature of Pennsylvania for the use of the State House (Independence Hall), and in 1802 the whole of the second floor was granted to him, where he placed his portrait gallery of distinguished people, painted chiefly by himself and his son Rembrandt, together with his museum collections.

As early as 1794, Peale made an attempt to establish in Philadelphia an association for the encouragement of the fine arts; the society which he formed was called "The Columbianum," which was short lived.

In 1805 his ambition for an Academy to promote the Fine Arts was at last realized. A group of influential citizens formed an association which in 1806 was chartered, "The Pennsylvania Academy of the Fine Arts." Peale was not only influential in founding the Academy but he lived to contribute to seventeen of its annual exhibitions.

Charles Willson Peale's portraiture is characterized by the excellent likenesses he obtained of his subjects. His style is free, easy and at all times harmonious. There is no lack of charm either as to color or as to the arrangement of his subjects, unless it be in his early and late works. The former, the artist himself severely criticized, because he believed that through the use of improper pigments there was a loss of color in his flesh tints. In his late works the harshness which is sometimes noted, and an entirely different palette almost making one question whether Peale ever painted certain portraits attributed to him, were due

to the fact that after his son Rembrandt's return from Paris in 1805, he gave his father considerable instruction in the methods of the French school which he himself had studied there. We always see in Peale's sitters a certain vivacity of expression which is most pleasing.

His technique was founded on solid craftsmanship and his ability to depict the real character of his subject is being more and more recognized by students of history.

As for the artist himself, he was a mild and benevolent man, an untiring worker in everything that he ever undertook. There is but little doubt that, had he devoted his entire time to his art alone, he would have attained the very highest honors in the fine arts. As it is, there is a permanent place for him in art annals.

Married three times, he was blessed with a large family of sons and daughters, many of whom were also artists, named after illustrious characters, chiefly painters of former decades. The most noted of them was Rembrandt. The artist died in Philadelphia, 1827, at the age of eighty-five. In 1923, a Memorial Exhibition of Peale's work was held at the Penna. Academy of Fine Arts. (See Catalogue for list of his portraits.)

PEALE, James. Younger brother of Charles Willson Peale, was born at Chestertown, Md., in 1749. As a youth he lived with his brother and learned the trade of chaisemaker.

At about the time Charles Willson Peale returned from London and chiefly due to his instruction and influence, James Peale gave up his trade to become a painter. He devoted some attention to portraiture, executed some landscapes, and even attempted some historical composition, but it is as a miniature painter that he is best known.

During the Revolutionary War, James Peale, like his brother Charles, served as an officer in the Continental Army under Washington, first as an Ensign in the Maryland Battalion, Colonel Smallwood commanding, in 1776; then as a First Lieutenant of the First Battalion of Maryland Regulars, Colonel John H. Staul commanding, in 1777, being later (1778) promoted to a captaincy in the First Maryland Regiment of the Continental Line.

He was a good soldier and bore an enviable military record.

James Peale painted two portraits of Washington, one of which is owned by the City of Philadelphia and hangs in the National Portrait Gallery at Independence Hall; the other is owned by the New York Historical Society.

Most of his lifetime was spent in Philadelphia, though he worked and resided for a time in the Southern States.

He was married and had six children, all but one of whom were girls. Of these children James, Jr., Anna and Sarah were painters.

He was a member of the Maryland Society of the Cincinnati.

James Peale died in Philadelphia in 1831.

PEALE, James, Jr. Marine painter. He was the son of James Peale, who was born in 1749 and died, 1831. He exhibited paintings of the sea in the early Philadelphia exhibitions. His sisters were also painters.

PEALE, Maria. Daughter of James Peale. She commenced painting still-life subjects about 1810. It does not appear that she attempted portrait painting.

PEALE, Miss Mary Jean. Painter. Born in 1826. She was the daughter of Rubens Peale and a granddaughter of Charles Willson Peale. She died in Pottsville, Pa., in 1902.

PEALE, Raphaelle. Portrait, miniature and still-life painter. He was a son of Charles Willson Peale and was born in 1774. In 1801 he advertises as a portrait painter with his studio at No. 28 Powel St., Philadelphia. He died in 1825.

PEALE, Rembrandt. Son of Charles Willson Peale, was born in Bucks County, Penna., in 1778.

His father began giving him instruction in art at a very early age, and in his memoirs he tells us that his "first recollections were with a paint brush."

Passing over the years in which he received his early art education, we find that at the age of seventeen he obtained a sitting, with the aid of his father, from George Washington. This portrait from life, however, is not the familiar Rembrandt Peale portrait of Washington, a composite head known as the Porthole portrait, of which he made many copies. The original composition was painted in 1823.

About the year 1795, Charles Willson Peale retired from portrait painting, and as his successor, recommended to the public, his son. The younger Peale, however, did not meet with the success anticipated, and left Philadelphia for Charleston, S. C., to commence his career as an artist.

In 1801, he went to England to study, as had his father, under the distinguished Benjamin West. During his course of instruction under West, he painted a few portraits, and then on account of ill health he decided to abandon art for agricultural pursuits, returning to America with that object in view.

To his surprise, when he reached the United States he found his services as a paniter greatly in demand, and in 1804 he established himself in Philadelphia, where he showed marked improvement in his style.

In 1807, he again went abroad, living some time in Paris, where he painted many portraits of eminent Frenchmen. Three of his best examples of this period are his portraits of Jacques Louis David, Dominique Vivant Denou,

and Jean Antoine Houdon, now owned by The Pennsylvania Academy of the Fine Arts.

After his return to Philadelphia he painted his most important work, the large picture of "The Court of Death."

Rembrandt Peale's next accomplishment was the establishment of a Museum and Gallery of Paintings in the City of Baltimore. He remained there nine years, where he painted many portraits.

In 1829, he made his last trip abroad, going to France and Italy.

Beside painting, Peale made many lithographic drawings, a process which he was among the first of American artists to use.

Rembrandt Peale was at his best as a portrait painter in 1807 and 1809. His portraits executed during this period may be favorably compared with those of his father. He portrayed his subjects with the same animation and character as did the elder Peale.

His later portraits, for the most part, do not show that he worked under the same inspiration, however, many of them lacking in charm, and in some instances bearing a dry, searching, and pedantic expression. His style appeared to have become mechanical, although he always maintained an admirable sense of color proportions, rich, effective and true to life.

In 1834, he moved to New York to live, returning later to Philadelphia, where he passed the remainder of his life. He was one of the founders of The Pennsylvania Academy of the Fine Arts. He was one of the original members of the National Academy of Design.

On October 3, 1860, he died in Philadelphia, ending a long and successful career.

In 1923 a Memorial Exhibition of Peale's work was held at the Penna. Academy of Fine Arts. (See Catalogue for list of his portraits.)

PEALE, Rubens. Son of Charles Willson Peale. He painted in an indifferent manner.

PEALE, Sarah M. Daughter of James Peale, commenced painting fruit and still-life subjects about 1816, and later took to portrait painting. In 1820 she painted a portrait of the Rev. William Ward, and in 1822 of Commodore Bainbridge. In 1825, Lafayette accorded her four sittings. Miss Peale was born in 1800 and died in 1885; she painted in Philadelphia, and later in Baltimore and Washington.

PEALE, Titian. Born in 1800; died in 1885. He was best known as a student of natural history, and in his artistic labors he has devoted himself to animal life. He executed most of the plates for Charles L. Bonaparte's work on "American Ornithology." He has also exhibited water color drawings of animals in the Penna. Academy of the Fine Arts. He was a son of the artist Charles Willson Peale.

PEARCE, Charles Sprague. Painter. Born in Boston in 1851; died in 1914 in Paris,

France. Studied under Bonnat, Paris. Awards: Silver medals, Boston, 1878, 1881; gold medal, 1884, for best figure picture, Penna. Academy of Fine Arts, 1881; Temple gold medal, 1885; honorable mention, Paris Salon, 1881. Elected Associate Member of the National Academy of Design. Represented in Chicago Art Institute by "The Beheading of John the Baptist."

PEARCE, Edgar L. Painter and etcher. Born in 1885. Pupil of Chase and Weir. Represented in Penna. Academy of Fine Arts; National Academy of Design, New York; Carnegie Institute of Pittsburgh. *Address*, 3620 Washington Blvd., St. Louis, Mo.

PEARSON, Edwin. Painter and sculptor. Exhibited portrait bust at Pennsylvania Academy of Fine Arts. *Address*, Crystal Lake, Ill.

PEARSON, Joseph O. Painter and engraver. He served in the Civil War, and lived in Brooklyn for twenty years, and died in Little Falls, N. J., in 1917. Specialty, title pages and covers for music.

PEARSON, Joseph T., Jr. Painter. Born in Germantown, Philadelphia, in 1876. Studied in the Pennsylvania Academy of the Fine Arts and under J. Alden Weir. Awards: Fellowship prize, the Pennsylvania Academy of the Fine Arts, 1910; second Hallgarten prize, National Academy of Design, New York, 1911; honorable mention, Carnegie Institute, Pittsburgh, 1911; Inness gold medal, National Academy of Design, New York, 1915; Temple gold medal, the Pennsylvania Academy of the Fine Arts, 1916; Edward T. Stotesbury prize, the Pennsylvania Academy of the Fine Arts, 1916; Carol H. Beck gold medal, the Pennsylvania Academy of the Fine Arts, 1917; Potter Palmer gold medal, Chicago Art Institute, Chicago, 1918. Elected an Associate Member of the National Academy. *Address*, Huntington Valley, Penna.

PEARSON, Marguerite S. Painter, who exhibited at the National Academy of Design, New York, 1925; Penna. Academy of Fine Arts. *Address*, Somerville, Mass.

PEARSON, Ralph M. Etcher. Born in Angus, Ia., in 1883. Pupil of Art Institute of Chicago; of Brooklyn and California societies of etchers. Represented in New York Public Library, Library of Congress and Chicago Museum of Fine Arts. *Address*, Ranches of Taos, New Mexico.

PEASE, C. W. Miniature painter, who flourished in Providence, R. I., in 1844.

PEASE, Ernest Sherman. Painter in water colors. A son of the engraver J. I. Pease. Born in Philadelphia in 1846. His specialty is painting birds and animals.

PEASE, Joseph Ives. Engraver. Born in Norfolk, Conn., in 1809; died at Twin Lakes, near Salisbury, Conn., in 1883. In his early youth Pease showed very considerable mechanical ability, and among other things he designed and built a power-loom and also invented a propeller for boats. He finally became an apprentice with the Hartford engraver Oliver Pelton, and remained with him until 1830. In 1835 Pease located himself in Philadelphia and engraved portraits for the National Portrait Gallery and did a considerable amount of work for the "Annuals"; these small plates are the best examples of his skill as an engraver in line. In 1848 he went to Stockbridge, Mass., and finally settled on the farm where he died. He practically devoted the later portion of his life to banknote engraving and crayon portraits.

PEASE, Richard H. Engraver. Born in Norfolk, Conn., in 1813, he was living in 1869. He was a brother of Joseph Ives Pease, engraver.

R. H. Pease apparently began business as a wood engraver in Albany, N. Y., though he also engraved in a rather labored manner upon copper. He furnished many illustrations for publications of the state of New York.

PEASLEY, A. M. A map engraver working at Newburyport, Mass., in 1804. Examples of his work are to be found in "The American Coast Pilot," by Capt. Lawrence Furlong, printed for Ed. M. Blount, Boston. He also engraved at least one portrait—that of Sauvin—executed in line combined with roulette work.

PEBBLES, Frank M. Painter. Born in Wyoming, N. Y., in 1839. Pupil of National Academy of Design, and of G. A. P. Healy in Chicago. *Address*, 1160 Bay St., Alameda, Calif.

PECK, Anna M. Painter and illustrator. Born in Piermont, N. Y., in 1884. Pupil of Robert Henri and of Irving R. Wiles. Specialty, illustrating children's books. *Address*, 164 Waverly Place, N. Y.

PECK, Natalie. Painter. Born in Jersey City, N. J., in 1886. Represented in Penna. Academy of Fine Arts by painting, "Storm Clouds." *Address*, 50 Sixth Ave., New York.

PECK, Orin. Painter. Born in Delaware County, N. Y., in 1860. He was in charge of the artistic work planned for the ranch of W. R. Hearst in northern California, and had painted several portraits of the Hearst family. He was awarded a gold medal at the Columbian Exposition, Chicago, 1893, for his "Scene in the Garden of the Santa Barbara Mission." He died in Los Angeles, Calif. January 20, 1921.

PECKHAM. A landscape painter noted in Tuckerman's "American Artist Life."

PECKHAM, Robert. Portrait painter. Born in Petersham, Mass., in 1785. He traveled mostly in the country districts of New England, but established himself for a while in Boston. Most of his portraits are flat, hard and stiff. Peckham painted John Greenleaf Whittier in 1833.

PECKHAM, Rosa F. Nothing is known of this artist except that in the Phillips Academy, Exeter, N. H., there is a portrait of Rev. Aug. Woodbury, which is signed "Rosa F. Peckham."

PEDRETTI, Humberts. Sculptor. Exhibited at Penna. Academy of Fine Arts, Philadelphia, 1926. *Address,* Hollywood, Calif.

PEELE, John Thomas. Painter. Born in England in 1822, he came to this country as a child. He settled in New York, and in 1846 was elected an Associate Member of the National Academy. He painted portraits and genre subjects. Among his works are "Children of the Woods" (147), "Highland Supper," "The Village School" and "The Birds' Nest."

PEETS, Orville H. Painter and etcher. Born in Cleveland, Ohio, in 1884. Pupil of Baschet and Laurens, Paris. *Address,* Woodstock, N. Y.

PEIRCE, H. Winthrop. Painter. Born in Boston in 1850. He studied art at the Lowell Institute and the Boston Museum of Fine Arts. In 1881 he went to Paris and studied under Bouguereau, and his work was well hung at the Salon of 1882. He returned to Boston. Among his best works are "Old Houses, Warwick"; "Valley of the Wye"; "Sister Cecilia"; "High Tide in the Marshes." Mr. Peirce is a member of the "Paint and Clay Club," of Boston.

PEIRCE, Thomas Mitchell. Painter. Born in Grand Rapids, Mich., in 1864. *Address,* Bartholdi Building, Madison Square, New York.

PEIRCE, Waldo. Painter. He exhibited "La Sevilliana" at the Penna. Academy of Fine Arts in Philadelphia, 1915. *Address,* Hotel Ansonia, New York City.

PEIRSON, Alden. Painter. Born in Baltimore in 1873. Began his work in Baltimore, 1894; art manager of the *American Magazine* since 1912; are manager of the Caxton Advertising Co. *Address,* 64 East 34th St., New York, N. Y.

PEIXOTTO, George Da Maduro. Painter. Born in Cleveland, Ohio. Pupil of Meissonier and Munkacsy. Member: Societé des Artistes

Francais. Awards: Silver medal, Royal Academy, Dresden. *Address,* Waldorf-Astoria Hotel, New York, N. Y.

PEIXOTTO, Ernest C. Illustrator and painter. Born in San Francisco, Calif., in 1869. Pupil of Constant, Lefebvre and Doucet in Paris. Member: Associate Member of the National Academy, 1909; Mural Painters; New York Architectural League, 1911; Society of Illustrators, 1906. Award: Honorable mention, Paris Salon, 1921. Work: Scenes from "La Morte d'Arthur" in Library of Henry A. Everett, near Cleveland, Ohio; illustrations for Roosevelt's "Life of Cromwell." Author: "By Italian Seas"; "Romantic California"; "Our Hispanic Southwest"; "The American Front," etc. Official artist, American Expeditionary Forces, 1918. Director, Atelier of Painting, A. E. F. Art Training Center, Bellevue, France, 1919. Director, Department of Mural Painting, Beaux Arts Institute, New York. *Address,* 137 East 66th St., New York, N. Y.

PEIXOTTO, Mrs. Ernest. Painter. Born in San Francisco. Pupil of San Francisco Artists' Association, and of Delecluse. Member: National Academy of Women Painters and Sculptors. *Address,* 137 East 66th St., New York, N. Y.

PEKENINO, Michele. Engraver, who appears to have been in New York in 1820, and his latest prints are dated in 1822, so that his stay here was a comparatively short one; though he engraved about thirty plates while in the United States. He was located in Philadelphia in 1821–22. That he was an intimate friend of A. B. Durand is shown by each having engraved the other's portrait and adding very friendly inscriptions, but Dunlap's story that Durand taught Pekenino to engrave is very dubious, to say the least. Durand was a line-engraver; and Pekenino's portrait of Durand, done evidently soon after his arrival in New York, is executed in stipple and is a most excellent piece of work, showing the touch of a master rather than that of an apprentice.

PELHAM, Henry. Engraver. Born in Boston in 1749; accidentally drowned in Ireland in 1806. Henry Pelham was the son of Peter Pelham and of his second wife, Mary Singleton Copley; he was thus the half-brother of John Singleton Copley.

The late Wm. H. Whitmore says that Henry Pelham certainly engraved a picture of "The Finding of Moses," but he neither describes the print nor does he give his authority. The late Paul Leicester Ford also prints a letter of March 29, 1770, from H. Pelham to "Mr. Paul Revere," in which he says: "When I heard that you was cutting a plate of the late Murder, I thought it impossible as I knew you was not capable of doing it unless you copied it from mine, etc." In another letter to Charles Pelham written May 1, 1770, Henry Pelham says: "Inclosed I send you two of my prints of the late Massacre."

No such prints by Pelham are known. But several water color copies of the Massacre picture have been preserved, which are exactly the same in design as the Revere plate, but much superior to it as to details and in the expression of the faces. Some claim that these water colors are the work of Henry Pelham, and are the "prints" referred to, and that Revere used one of these as the original of his plate, and hence the complaint of Pelham to Revere.

PELHAM, Peter. Portrait painter and engraver. Born in England about 1684, he came to Boston with his wife and family in 1726. In 1734, he married his second wife, and a child was born in Newport. In 1748, he married again, the widow of Richard Copley, whose son John Singleton Copley, then eleven years of age, was destined to become celebrated as a portrait painter, and must have acquired the rudiments of art from his step-father. In the Antiquarian Society at Worcester is the portrait painted by Peter Pelham of the Rev. Increase Mather, who died in 1728. He painted other portraits that are known, and was the earliest engraver in America. His works in mezzotint are highly esteemed, a number of which are engraved from portraits by Smibert. He was buried in Boston in 1751.

PELTON, Oliver. Engraver. Born in Portland, Conn., in 1798; died at East Hartford, Conn., in 1882. He was first a pupil and then a partner of Abner Reed, in Hartford. In 1827 he was established in business as an engraver in Boston, and in 1836 the firm of Pelton & Terry was engraving banknotes in the same city. His son, Edward B. Pelton, was born in Boston in 1840, and was later a publisher in New York. Oliver Pelton was a fairly good line engraver of portraits and worked at his profession up to within a few years of his death. He also engraved a number of small subject-plates for the "Annuals."

PELTON, Agnes. Painter. Born in Stuttgart, Germany, of American parents, in 1881. Pupil of Pratt Institute, under Dow; of W. L. Lathrop and Hamilton E. Field; also studied in Rome. Member: National Academy of Women Painters and Sculptors. *Address,* 160 West 13th St., New York, N. Y.

PELL, Ella Ferris. Painter, sculptor and illustrator. Born in St. Louis, Mo., in 1846. Pupil of Cooper Union in New York under Rimmer; under Laurens, Ferdinand Humbert and Gaston St. Pierre in Paris. Work: "Salome," painting owned by Boston Art Club; "Andromeda," heroic statue. *Address,* Beacon, N. Y.

PEMBER, Ada Humphrey. Painter. Born in Shopiere, Wisc., in 1859. Pupil of W. M. Clute and F. Fursman. Member: Janesville Art League; Wisconsin Painters and Sculptors. *Address,* 103 Jackson St., Janesville, Wisconsin.

PEMBROOKE, Theo. K. Landscape painter. Born in Elizabeth, N. J., in 1865; died in New York, 1917.

PENFIELD, Edward. Illustrator and painter. Born in Brooklyn, N. Y., in 1866. Pupil of Art Students' League of New York. Member: Society of Illustrators, 1901. Specialty, posters and cover designs. Author and illustrator of "Holland Sketches" and "Spanish Sketches"; decorations for Rochester Country Club. He died in 1925.

PENDLETON, John. Lithographer. Born in New York State. While traveling in France he became interested in lithographs and studied the art under the best masters in Paris. On returning to America, he settled in Boston with his brother, a copperplate printer, and there they established a lithographing establishment about 1825.

PENFOLD, Frank C. Born in Buffalo, N. Y. Received honorable mention in Paris Salon, 1889, for his painting, "Stormy Weather, North Sea."

PENMAN, Edith. Painter. Member of National Association of Women Painters and Sculptors. Exhibited in Annual Exhibition, 1923–24. *Address,* 939 Eighth Ave., New York.

PENNELL, Joseph. Etcher, lithographer, illustrator and author. Born in Philadelphia, Penna., in 1860. Pupil of Penna. Academy of Fine Arts, and Penna. School of Industrial Art. Awards: 1st class gold medal, Paris Exposition, 1900; Dresden, 1902; Grand Prix, St. Louis Exposition, 1904; gold medal, Liege, 1905; Grand Prix, Milan, 1906; Barcelona, 1907; Brussels, 1910; Diplome d'Honneur, Amsterdam, 1912; 2 medals, London, 1913; Florence, 1914; commemorative medal same, 1915. Represented in the Luxembourg, and in the collection of the city of Paris; also in Cabinet des Estamps (France); Uffizi Gallery (Florence); British Museum; S. Kensington Museum; Guildhall Gallery, London, and in many state and municipal collections in Europe and the United States; Library of Congress, Washington; Penna. Academy, Phila.; Carnegie Institute, Pittsburgh. Elected Associate Member of the National Academy in 1907, and an Academician in 1909. Author of "Lithography and Lithographers," 1900; "The Authorized Life of J. McN. Whistler" (with Mrs. Pennell), 1910. Pictures of War Work in America, 1918; he has also illustrated a great number of books; contributor to the leading magazines. *Address,* Century Club, New York, N. Y.

PENNEY, L. P. Miniature painter, who flourished in Boston, 1845.

PENNIMAN, H. A. F. Painter. Born in New York, N. Y., in 1882. Pupil of Twachtman, Beckwith, S. E. Whiteman, Everett L. Bryant and Anshutz; also studied in Germany. Member: Society of Independent Artists. *Address*, 609 Cathedral St., Baltimore, Md.

PENNIMAN, John Ritto. Painter, who lived and worked for many years in Roxbury, Mass. He was married in Boston in 1805. He painted a well-executed picture of the Boston Common and other views in and about Boston.

PENNINGTON, Harper. Painter. Born in Newport, R. I., in 1854. Pupil of Gerome at the École des Beaux Arts, and of Carolus-Duran and Whistler, 1874–86, during which period he also spent some time in Italy.

PENNOYER, A. Sheldon. Painter. Born in Oakland, Calif., in 1888. Pupil of École des Beaux Arts, Academies Julien and Grande Chaumiere, and of Rene Menard and Lucien Simon in Paris; of Giuseppe Casciaro and Carlandi in Italy; Penna. Academy of Fine Arts. Member: National Art Club; San Francisco Artists' Association. *Address*, 152 West 55th St., New York, N. Y.

PEPPER, Charles Hovey. Painter. Born in Waterville, Me., in 1864. Pupil of Chase in New York; Constant, Laurens and Aman-Jean in Paris. Member: New York Water Color Club; Boston Water Color Club; Copley Society, 1900; Boston Art Club; St. Botolph Club. *Address*, Fenway Studios, 30 Ipswich St., Boston, Mass.

PERARD, Victor Semon. Painter. Born in Paris, France, in 1870. Studied art at École des Beaux Arts, Paris, under Gerome; also in the Art Students' League, New York, Illustrator for *Harper's Magazine, Scribner's Magazine*. Instructor in Cooper Institute. *Address*, 78 West 55th St., New York.

PERCIVAL, Edwin. Born in Kensington, Conn., in 1793. In 1830 he went to Hartford, to study art. He was gifted but very eccentric. His drawing was good and the coloring of his pictures pleasing. He excelled in ideal sketches; the ''Three Daughters of Job'' was his best known work. He spent some years in Albany, and died of depressing melancholy, starving to death.

PERCY, Isabelle (Mrs. Geo. West). Illustrator and etcher. Born in California in 1882. Pupil of Dow and Snell in New York, and of Brangwyn in London. *Address*, 17 East 11th St., New York.

PERERA, Gino. Sculptor and painter. Born in Italy in 1872. Pupil of Boston Mu-

seum of Fine Arts. *Address*, 382 Commonwealth Ave., Boston, Mass.

PERINE, George Edward. Engraver. Born in South Orange, Essex County, N. J., in 1837; died in Brooklyn, N. Y., in 1885. Mr. Perine was of Huguenot and Dutch descent, his ancestors having settled on Staten Island and in Ulster County prior to the Revolution. On May 25, 1852, he commenced engraving under Thomas Doney, of New York, and in 1856–58 he was with W. W. Rice, an excellent line and bank-note engraver of Scotch Plains. During this time and before he was nineteen years old, he engraved in mezzotint his large plate of ''The Signing of the Compact in the Cabin of the Mayflower.'' In 1858–60 Mr. Perine was in the employ of New York engravers, and in the latter year he began engraving on his own account and established, in time, an extensive and very successful business in New York City. Portrait engraving formed the chief part of his work; and while he employed many engravers in his establishment he is said to have finished every plate himself.

PERKINS, Miss. Portrait draughtsman in pastel. She was a sister of Dr. Perkins. Portraits in pastel (probably by Miss Perkins) of Caleb Perkins, Lucy Perkins, and Sarah Perkins are owned by the Connecticut Historical Society. She was working in Connecticut about 1790.

PERKINS, Charles C. Born in Boston in 1823. President of the Boston Art Club, 1871. Honorary life member of the Metropolitan Art Museum of New York. Though not a professional artist he drew and etched the plates to illustrate a number of the books on art and artists of which he was the author.

PERKINS, E. G. A line portrait of no particular merit, published by Samuel W. Wheeler, of Providence, R. I., in 1831, is signed ''E. G. Perkins, Sc.''

PERKINS, Granville. Born in Baltimore, Md., in 1830. He studied in Philadelphia under James Hamilton. He devoted himself to scene painting and illustrating. He was a member of the Water Color Society, and exhibited frequently at the National Academy of Design.

PERKINS, Jacob. Born in Newburyport, Mass., in 1776; died in London, England, in 1849. Perkins is not known to have been, himself, an engraver upon copperplate, but his influence upon the development of bank-note engraving was so marked that he deserves mention among engravers. As a silversmith in his native town he made the dies for the Massachusetts copper coinage of 1787, and he was early prominent as an inventor of machines for various purposes. In 1810 he found means for the important substitution of steel for copper plates in engraving bank-notes, thus greatly prolonging the life of the plate.

PERKINS, John U. Painter. Born in Washington, D. C., in 1875. Pupil of Chase. Member of Society of Washington Artists. *Address,* 815 A St., N. E., Washington, D. C.

PERKINS, Joseph. Engraver. Born in Unity, N. H., in 1788; died in New York City in 1842. Joseph Perkins graduated from Williams College in 1814; in 1818 he went to Philadelphia and there learned script engraving. He established himself in business in that city, but in 1825 he removed to New York and with A. B. Durand he became a member of the bank-note engraving firm of Durand, Perkins & Co.

PERKINS, Mary Smith (Mrs.). Painter. Born in Philadelpia. Pupil of Penna. Academy of Fine Arts. Represented in City Hall, Philadelphia, by portrait of James L. Miles. *Address,* Lumberville, Penna.

PERKINS, Willard. Painter, who exhibited water colors at the Penna. Academy of the Fine Arts, Philadelphia, 1925. *Address,* 4902 Forbes St., Pittsburgh, Penna.

PEROT, Anna Lovering. Painter, who exhibited at the Penna. Academy of the Fine Arts, Philadelphia, 1924. *Address,* Fort Washington, Pennsylvania.

PEROT, James. Engraver. He was one of the Huguenot settlers of New Rochelle, N. Y., and was a silversmith of that place, and later of Bermuda and Philadelphia. He was a brother-in-law of Robert Elliston of New York. He was probably the founder of the Perot family in Philadelphia, and the father of Elliston Perot, a prominent merchant of Philadelphia, about 1790. A Chippendale bookplate of James Perot with a wide engraved border is said to have been engraved by Perot himself.

PERRETT, Galen J. Illustrator. Born in Chicago in 1875. Pupil of Chicago Art Institute and of the Julien Academy, Paris. *Address,* 51 West 10th St., New York City, N. Y.

PERRINE, Van Dearing. Painter. Born in Garnett, Kans., in 1869; self-taught in America. Exhibited at Paris Exposition, 1902. Received honorable mention, Carnegie Institute, 1903; silver medal, Panama-Pacific Exposition, 1915. Now devoting his attention to development of "color music." Member: Prometheans; Society of American Painters, Sculptors and Gravers. Elected Associate Member of the National Academy of Design. *Address,* 42 Prospect Ave., Maplewood, N. J.

PERRY, Clara Fairchild. Painter. Member of the National Association of Women Painters and Sculptors, New York. Exhibited at 33d Annual Exhibition, N. Y. *Address,* 56 Cambridge Place, Brooklyn, N. Y.

PERRY, Clara G. Sculptor, who exhibited a portrait bust at the Penna. Academy of Fine Arts in Philadelphia, 1915. . *Address,* 344 Boylston St., Boston.

PERRY, Edith Weir (Mrs.). Miniature painter. Born in New Haven, Conn., 1875. Wife of Rt. Rev. James deWolf Perry, of Rhode Island. *Address,* Bishops' House, Providence, R. I.

PERRY, Enoch Wood. Painter. Born in Boston, Mass., in 1831; died in New York in 1915. Perry came to New Orleans in 1848; went to Europe and studied in Dusseldorf and Paris, 1852 and 1853; then to Rome and Venice, 1856 to 1858, returning to the United States in the latter year. In 1860 he had a studio at 108 St. Charles Street, New Orleans. At this time he painted the splendid life-size portrait of United States Senator John Slidell, now in the Louisiana State Museum. In 1861 he painted Jefferson Davis, using the map of the Confederate States as a background. Perry then traveled extensively and was a famous international portrait painter, having painted many of the great men of his time. Among his important figure compositions is "Signing the Ordinance of the Secession of Louisiana," painted in 1861. In 1865 he settled in New York where he remained till his death in 1915. He was elected an Associate Member of the National Academy of Design in 1868, and full Academician in 1869; he was also a member of the American Water Color Society.

PERRY, Oswald. Sculptor. He has exhibited in Chicago and Cincinnati.

PERRY, Ione. Painter. Born in New York City in 1839. Student of the Cooper Institute, and pupil of Henry Loop. Among her best known paintings are "Hypatia," "Romola," "Consuelo" and "Elsa, at the Coming of Lohengrin."

PERRY, John D. Sculptor. Born in Swanton, Va., in 1845. He lived in New York, 1869–70, but passed the rest of his professional life in Italy and Boston. He made many portrait busts, and his statuette of Sumner was highly praised.

PERRY, Lilla Cabot. Painter and author. Born in Boston. Studied painting in Boston and in Paris at Julien's and Colarossi's studios in 1887, and later. Her first pictures were exhibited at the Paris Salon, 1889; silver medal, Mass. Mechanics' Association, 1893;

bronze medal, St. Louis Exposition, 1904; bronze medal, Panama Pacific Exposition, 1915. *Address*, Fenway Studios, Boston, Mass.

PERRY, Raymond. Painter and illustrator. Born in Stirling, Ill., in 1876. Pupil of Art Institute, Chicago. *Address*, 144 East 34th St., New York.

PERRY, Roland Hinton. Sculptor and painter. Born in New York in 1870. Entered École des Beaux Arts, 1890. Studied at Academie Julien and Academie Delecleuse, Paris, 1890–94. Principal works: Bas-reliefs of Sibyls, Library of Congress, 1895; Fountain of Neptune, same, 1897; Cain, 1892; Death of Sigurd, 1898; paintings in Detroit Museum of Art; The Valkyrie, painting, 1899; The Lion in Love, sculpture, 1899; spandrels on Dewey Arch, New York, 1899; lions for Conn. Ave. Bridge, Washington, 1908; memorial, New York State, Andersonville, Ga., 1910; equestrian statue of Gen. John B. Castleman, of Louisville, Ky.; statue of Gen. Curtis for Ogdensburg, N. Y., and Gen. Wadsworth, Gettysburg; soldier monument to 38th Inf. ("The Rock of the Marne") for Syracuse, N. Y., 1919–20. Painting portraits since 1916. Member of National Sculpture Society. *Address*, 51 West 10th St., New York, N. Y.

PERRY, Walter Scott. Painter and sculptor. Born in Stoneham, Mass. Pupil of Langerfeldt, Higgins and Pierre Millet; also of Mass. Normal Art School. Member: National Art Club; Art Alliance; Eastern Artists' Association. Supervisor of drawing and art education, public schools, Fall River, Mass., 1875–79; and Worcester, Mass., 1879–87. Director, School of Fine and Applied Arts, Pratt Institute, since 1887. Author of "Egypt, the Land of the Temple Builders"; "With Azir Girges in Egypt"; text-books on art education. *Address*, 56 Cambridge Place, Brooklyn, New York.

PERRY, W. A. Painter. Born in Wasepi, Mich. Pupil of San Francisco School of Art and of W. V. Cahill and John Rich. *Address*, 6172 Chabot Road, Oakland, Calif.

PERSICO, Gennarino. Miniature painter. He was the brother of Lugi Persico, the sculptor. He came from Naples. See "Lancaster Historical Society Papers." Exhibited at the Penna. Academy, 1827.

PESCHERET, Leon R. Designer, who studied in London, and at the Art Institute of Chicago. Member: Palette and Chisel Club. *Address*, 64 East Van Buren St., Chicago, Ill.

PETERS, C. F. Illustrator and etcher. Born in Kristiania, Norway, in 1882. Work: Cartoons in *Life;* illustrations in *Scribner's,*

Harper's and *Century. Address*, 412 East 50th St. New York, N. Y.

PETERS, Charles Rollo. Painter. Born in California in 1862. Pupil of Virgil Williams in San Francisco; École des Beaux Arts under Gerome, and of Boulanger and Lefebvre in Paris. Member: Lotos Club; Salmagundi Club, 1901. Awards: Bronze medal, Pan-American Exposition, Buffalo, 1901; silver medal, St. Louis Exposition, 1904. *Address*, Monterey, Calif.

PETERS, Clinton. Painter and illustrator. Born in Baltimore in 1865. Pupil of École des Beaux Arts under Gerome and of Lefebvre, Boulanger and Collin in Paris. Award: Bronze medal, Paris Exposition, 1889. Founder and principal instructor, Clinton Peters Art Classes, New York. *Address*, Studio 606, 1947 Broadway, New York.

PETERSEN, John Erik Christian. Painter. Born in Denmark in 1839; died in Boston, Mass., in 1874. In 1864 he settled in this country and opened his studio in Boston, and devoted himself mainly to marine painting. His work is strong and effective. Among his paintings are "After the Collision," "Making Sail after the Gale," and "The Phantom Ship."

PETERSEN, Martin. Painter. Born in Denmark in 1870. Pupil of National Academy of Design. Member: New York Water Color Club; Salmagundi Club, 1906. *Address*, 437 West 59th St., New York, N. Y.

PETERSON, C. American marine painter.

PETERSON, Elsa Kirpal. Sculptor. Born in New York, N. Y., in 1891. Pupil of Edith Woodman Burroughs and of J. E. Fraser. Member of Art Students' League of New York. *Address*, 67 Hillside Ave., Flushing, N. Y.

PETERSON, Jane. Painter. Born in Elgin, Ill. Pupil of Brangwyn, Blanche and Sorolla. Member: National Association of Women Painters and Sculptors; Washington Water Color Club; Conn. Academy of Fine Arts. Awards: Water color prize, Girls' Art Club, Paris; honorable mention, Conn. Academy of Fine Arts, 1916; honorable mention, National Association of Women Painters and Sculptors, 1919. Work: "Glimpse of the Grand Canal," Art Association, Grand Rapids, Mich.; represented in Girls' Art Club, Paris; Brooklyn Athletic Club. Instructor at Art Students' League, 1914–19. *Address*, 58 West 57th St., New York.

PETREMONT, Clarice Marie. Painter and illustrator. Born in Brooklyn, New York. Pupil of Marshall Fry and of Paul Cornoyer. Member of Bridgeport Art League. *Address*, Shelton, Conn.

PETTICOLAS, Edward F. Portrait painter in oils and miniatures. He practiced in Richmond, Va., in 1805-34, after studying with Thomas Sully in Phila. His portrait of John Buchanan is owned by the Virginia State Library, Richmond, Va. A miniature of Elihu Etting, signed on front "E. F. Petticolas 1799," was presented in 1886 by Mr. Etting to the Penna. Academy of Fine Arts.

PETTICOLAS, Philip A. Miniature painter, who was born in 1760. He painted for years in Richmond, Virginia, and died there in 1843. It is claimed that Washington gave him sittings for a miniature in Philadelphia in 1796. He also made several miniatures of Washington from Gilbert Stuart's first portrait.

PEUGEOT, George. Painter and illustrator. Born in Buffalo, N. Y., in 1869. Pupil of Peter Gowans. Member: Buffalo Society of Artists. *Address*, 693 Main St., Buffalo, N. Y.

PEW, Gertrude L. Miniature painter, who exhibited at the Penna. Academy of Fine Arts, Philadelphia, 1925. *Address*, 48 East 49th St., New York.

PEYRAUD, Frank C. Painter. Born in Bulle, Switzerland, in 1858. Pupil of Art Institute of Chicago; of École des Beaux Arts, and of Bonnat, Frieburg, in Paris. Member: Chicago Society of Artists; Chicago Water Color Club. Awards: Fortnightly prize, Art Institute of Chicago, 1899; Butler prize, Art Institute of Chicago, 1912. Work in: Union League Club, Chicago; Art Institute of Chicago. *Address*, 1608 Monroe Building, Highland Park, Ill.

PEYTON, Alfred Conway. Painter and illustrator. Born in Dera Doon, British India, in 1875. Pupil of South Kensington Schools, London, England. Member: New York Water Color Club. Awarded silver medal at Bombay, B. I. *Address*, 33 West 67th St., New York, N. Y.

PEYTON, Ann Moon (Mrs. Philip B.). Painter and illustrator. Born in Charlottesville, Va., in 1891. Pupil of George Bellows. *Address*, 3804 Locust St., Philadelphia, Pa.

PEYTON, Bertha M. Landscape painter, who exhibited in National Academy of Design, 1924. *Address*, 33 West 67th St., New York.

PFEIFFER, Fritz W. Painter and illustrator. Born in Adams County, Pa., in 1889. Pupil of Penna. Academy of the Fine Arts. *Address*, 69 Wisconsin St., Milwaukee, Wis.

PFEIFFER, Harry R. Painter. Born in Hanover, Pa., in 1875. Pupil of Art Students' League, New York; Penna. Academy of the Fine Arts, Philadelphia, Pa. *Address*, 539 West King St., York, Pa.

PFEIFFER, Heinrich. Painter, who exhibited water colors at the Penna. Academy of the Fine Arts, Philadelphia, 1925. *Address*, Provincetown, Mass.

PFEIFFER, Justus. Painter, who exhibited in Philadelphia, 1921, in "Exhibition of Paintings Showing the Later Tendencies of Art." *Address*, Care of Preston Dickinson, Long Island, New York.

PHELAN, Harold L. Painter. Born in New York in 1881. *Address*, 67 West 67th St., New York City.

PHELPS, Edith Catlin. Painter and etcher. Born in New York City in 1875. Pupil of Julien in Paris. Member of Conn. Association of Fine Arts. *Address*, 161 East 74th St., New York City.

PHELPS, Helen Watson. Painter. Born in Attleboro, Mass. Studied at the Academie Julien, Paris, also with Raphael Collin. She has exhibited paintings in the Paris Salon; New York Academy of Design; Society of American Artists; Penna. Academy of Fine Arts. Honorable mention, Buffalo Exposition, 1901; Woman's Art Club prize, 1909; Watrous figure prize, Association of Women Painters and Sculptors, 1914. Member: Association of Women Painters and Sculptors; Pen and Brush Club; Society of Painters. *Address*, 58 West 57th St., New York.

PHELPS, W. P. Painter. Born in New Hampshire, he began life as a sign painter in Lowell, Mass. He was sent abroad for study and on his return he exhibited his paintings "Morning," "Evening," and "Forest Scene near Munich" at the National Academy in New York in 1878.

PHILBRICK, Otis. Painter, who exhibited water colors at the Penna. Academy of the Fine Arts, Phiadelphia, 1925. *Address*, Winchester, Mass.

PHILLIBROWNE, Thomas. Engraver. Born in London and who was said to have been a pupil of the Findens in that city. He was engraving admirable portraits in pure line in London in 1834, and came to the United States prior to 1851, as in that year he engraved a full-length portrait of Louis Kossuth for Boston publishers. Mr. Alfred Jones says that Phillibrowne was a very eccentric character, peculiar in appearance, and he claimed that his personal friend Hablot Knight Brown, or "Phiz," had used him as a model for the familiar "Mr. Pickwick" in his original illustrations to that story of Dickens.

PHILLIPS, Bert G. Painter and illustrator. Born in Hudson, New York, in 1868. Pupil of Art Students' League of New York, and of Constant and Laurens in Paris. Specialty, Indian subjects. Work: Mural decorations in Court House, Des Moines, Iowa. *Address*, Taos, Taos County, New Mexico.

PHILLIPS, Charles. This excellent engraver of portraits in stipple was located in New York in 1842, and was an Englishman by birth. Very little work is signed by him, and it is said that he went into the employ of the Government at Washington, D. C.

PHILLIPS, C. Holmead. Painter, who exhibited at the Penna. Academy of Fine Arts, Philadelphia, 1926. *Address*, 58 West 57th St., New York.

PHILLIPS, J. Campbell. Portrait painter. Born in New York in 1873. Studied at Metropolitan Museum of Art Schools; Art Students' League; also in studio of William Merritt Chase, New York. Began as illustrator for magazines, later making a specialty of negro life. He exhibited an oil painting in the National Academy, 1892, and has since often exhibited there; also in other leading cities of the United States. Isidor portrait prize, Salmagundi Club, 1914; Corcoran Gallery purchase fund, 1914; "The First Born"; competition portrait of Mayor William J. Gaynor, for City Hall, New York, 1914. Member of American Sculpture Society. *Address*, Carnegie Hall Studios, New York.

PHILLIPS, John Henry. Etcher. Born in Wisconsin in 1876. He has executed mural decorations in theatres. *Address*, 681 Fifth Ave., New York.

PHILLIPS, S. G. Painter, who exhibited the "Little Nude" at the Penna. Academy of the Fine Arts, Philadelphia, 1921. *Address*, 1520 Chestnut St., Philadelphia.

PHOENIX, Lauros M. Mural painter. Born in Chicago, 1885. Pupil of Art Institute, Chicago. He has executed many mural decorations in large commercial buildings and theatres. *Address*, 64 Burlington Lane, New Rochelle, N. Y.

PIAZZONI, Gottardo. Painter and etcher. Born in Switzerland in 1872. Pupil of Julien Academy in Paris. Member of San Francisco Art Association. *Address*, 712 Montgomery St., San Francisco, Calif.

PICART, B. This apparently fictitious signature, either as designer or engraver, is signed to a large and poorly engraved plate published by H. D. Robinson, New York, seemingly about 1800. The print is entitled "Church and State," and is a caricature dealing with the doctrines of Thomas Paine.

PICCIRILLI, Attilio. Sculptor. Born in Italy in 1866, and who came to the United States in 1888. Elected Associate Member of National Academy. Represented by "Mac Donough Monument," New Orleans; "Maine Memorial," in New York; "Dancing Faun" and "Head of Boy," in Buffalo Academy of Fine Arts. *Address*, 467 East 142d St., New York.

PICCIRILLI, Furio. Sculptor. Born in Massa, Italy, in 1868. Pupil of Accademia San Luca, Rome. He came to the United States in 1888. Associate Member of the National Academy; National Sculpture Society, 1907; New York Architectural League, 1914. Awards: Honorable mention, Pan-American Exposition, Buffalo, 1901; silver medal, St. Louis Exposition, 1904; silver medal, Panama-Pacific Exposition, San Francisco, 1915. *Address*, 467 East 142d St., New York.

PICKNELL, George W. Painter. Born in Springfield, Vt., in 1864. Pupil of Lefebvre and Constant. Member: Salmagundi Club. Work: "Stock Yard in Winter," Detroit Institute of Arts. *Address*, R. F. D. 43, Norwalk, Conn.

PICKNELL, William Lamb. Painter. Born in Massachusetts in 1853; died in Marblehead, Massachusetts, in 1897. Landscape painter. Pupil of George Inness in Rome, and of Gerome in Paris; painted in Brittany for several years under Robert Wylie. Awarded honorable mention, Paris Salon, 1880. Member Society of American Artists; elected Associate Member of National Academy of Design; Society of British Artists. Represented by "The Road to Concarneau," painted in 1880, in the Corcoran Art Gallery, Washington.

PIERCE, Anna Harriet. Painter and illustrator. Born in South Britain, Conn., in 1880. Pupil of F. C. Jones; George Maynard; Mora; K. H. Miller; John F. Weir; Niemeyer; E. C. Taylor. *Address*, 42 Edgewood Ave., New Haven, Conn.

PIERCE, Charles Franklin. Painter. Born in New Hampshire in 1844; died in Brookline, Mass., in 1920. Specialty, landscapes. Member of Boston Art Club and Boston Water Color Society.

PIERPONT, Benjamin, Jr. Pierpont engraved upon copper the music and words of "The Singing Master's Assistant; or Key to Practical Music. By William Billings, Author of the New England Psalm-Singer, etc. Boston, (New England), Printed by Draper and Folsom, 1778."

This singing-book is an oblong quarto, and on the last page of music the engraver signs himself thus: "Engrav'd by Benj. Pierpont Junr. Roxbury, 1778."

PIETERSZ, Bertus. Painter. Born in Amsterdam, Holland, in 1869. Studied in Rotterdam, and under Harry W. Ranger. Member: League of New York Artists. Work: "Campanile," Springfield, Mass. *Address*, Hancock, New Hampshire.

PIETZ, Adam. Sculptor and medalist. Born in Offenbach, Germany, in 1873. Studied at Penna. Academy of Fine Arts; Art Institute of Chicago, and in Germany. Member: Phila. Sketch Club; Fellowship, Penna. Academy of Fine Arts; American Numismatic Society; New York Numismatic Society. Work represented in Chicago Art Institute; Memorial Hall, Philadelphia; in American Numismatic Society; Navy Yard, Phila., Administration Building; Houston Club, University of Penna.; Philadelphia Sketch Club. *Address*, 512 West Clapier St., Germantown, Philadelphia, Pa.

PIGALLE. Rough line engravings signed "Pigalle" are found with other plates evidently engraved by Scoles for the same work. The date is about 1800.

PIGOTT, Frank E. Painter. Member: Rochester Art Club. *Address*, Care of Steck and Spelrein Lithographic Company, 65 West Houston St., New York, N. Y.

PILLARS, Charles Adrian. Sculptor. Born in Rantoul, Ill., in 1870. Pupil and assistant of Lorado Taft for 9 years; student life classes, Art Institute of Chicago. Engaged upon colossal sculpture for Chicago Exposition 18 months, 1891–92, under Daniel French and E. C. Potter—"The Republic," 60 feet in height, which stood in the Grand Basin, and the equestrian group of Columbus Quadrigae surmounting the arch of the Peristyle. Executed bronze doors for Leland Stanford Museum, Cal.; Bryan memorial, in bronze, for battleship Florida; replica Renaissance Fountain in bronze and marble, for Dillon memorial, Jacksonville, Fla.; also numerous portrait busts and medallions. Settled in Jacksonville, 1894. *Address*, Herkimer Building, Jacksonville, Fla.

PINE, Robert Edge. Painter. Born in London in 1742, son of John Pine, the engraver. He gained the premium of the Society for the Encouragement of Arts, etc., for the best historical design in 1760, and again 1762. Established himself as a portrait painter and went to Bath in 1772, and remained there until 1779. Made an exhibition in London, 1782, of a collection of pictures painted by himself in illustration of scenes in Shakespeare. He came to this country in 1783, bringing his family, and taking up his residence in Philadelphia. He painted Washington at Mt. Vernon in 1785, belonging now to J. Carson Brevoort, Esq., of New York. The Honorable Joseph Hopkinson, second President of the Academy, writing to Mr. Dunlap in 1833, says: "I remember his arrival in this country. He brought letters of introduction to my father, whose portrait was the first he painted in America. It is now in my possession . . . it bears the date of 1785, and is now as fresh in color as it was on the day it was painted. . . . Robert Morris, who patronized him, built a house in Eighth Street suitable to his objects. I remember a large picture in his gallery, of Medea murdering her children, and several others, some from Shakespeare—'Prospero and Miranda,' in 'The Tempest,' I particularly recollect. Many of his pictures are scattered about in Virginia, where he went occasionally to paint portraits. . . . P. S. He brought with him a plaster cast of the Venus, which was kept shut up in a case, and only shown to persons who particularly wished to see it, as the manners of our country at that time would not tolerate the public exhibition of such a figure." He died in Philadelphia in 1788. Rembrandt Peale in his "Reminiscences" mentions seeing him in London. In Philadelphia he painted the "Congress Voting Independence," to which Edward Savage later added. This was painted in the "Congress Chamber in the State House," the same room in which the scene portrayed took place, and the painting is of great documentary value.

PINKOVITZ, H. A. Painter, who exhibited "Anna Perry" at the Penna. Academy of Fine Arts, Philadelphia, 1921. *Address*, 721 Walnut St., Philadelphia.

PITMAN, Sophia L. Painter. Born in Providence, R. I. Member: Providence Art Club; Providence Water Color Club; Copley Society. *Address*, Moses Brown School, 156 Pitman St., Providence, R. I.

PITZ, Henry C. Painter, who exhibited water colors at the Penna. Academy of Fine Arts, Philadelphia, 1925. *Address*, 3712 Woodland Ave., Drexel Hill, Pa.

PLACE, Mrs. Vera Clark. Painter. Born in Minneapolis, Minn., in 1890. Pupil of Chase, Dufner, Richard Miller, and of Antonio de la Gandere. Member: Attic Club, Minneapolis; Alumni, Minneapolis School of Art; Minneapolis Society of Fine Arts. Awards: First and second prizes, Minnesota State Art Exhibit. *Address*, 621 Kenwood Parkway, Minneapolis, Minn.

PLACKETT, Ebenezer. Portrait and figure painter. Born in Wisconsin, 1844, he settled in New Milford in 1871.

PLANTOU, Mrs. Portrait painter in oils and miniatures; also historical painter. She painted portraits in Washington, D. C., about 1820. In 1821 she moved to Philadelphia. Her portrait of Bishop Conwell, painted in 1825, is well known from the engraving.

PLASCHKE, Paul A. Painter and illustrator. Born in Berlin, Germany, in 1878. Pupil of Cooper Union and of the Art Students' League of New York. Member: Society of Independent Artists; Louisville Art League; Palette and Chisel Club, Chicago. Work represented in Chicago Art Institute; St. Louis City Art Museum; John Herron Art Institute, Indianapolis, Ind. *Address*, Care of Louisville Times, Louisville, Ky.

PLASSMAN, Ernst. Sculptor. Born in Westphalia in 1823. He came to New York in 1853 where the following year he opened "Plassman's School of Art," which he carried on until his death. He executed many models, carvings and sculptures; his statue of Franklin is in Printing-House Square, N. Y., and his figure of "Tammany" is on Tammany Hall, N. Y. He died in New York City in 1877.

PLATT, Alethea Hill. Painter. Born in Scarsdale, N. Y. Pupil of Art Students' League of New York; Delecluse Academy in Paris. Member: National Association of Women Painters and Sculptors. Awards: First prize for water color, New York Woman's Art Club, 1903; first prize, Minnesota Art Association, Faribault, 1909. Work: "Old World Work Shop," Public Library, Faribault, Minn.; "An Old Garden," Anderson (Ind.) Art Gallery; portrait of Judge Lewis C. Platt, Court House, White Plains, New York. *Address*, 939 Eighth Ave., New York, N. Y.

PLATT, Charles A. Painter and etcher. Born in New York City in 1861. He studied art in the National Academy, and in Paris under Boulanger and Lefebvre. He is best known for his etchings, but he has also worked in oil and water color, exhibiting in the Salon and in the National Academy of Design, N. Y. *Address*, 101 Park Ave., New York City.

PLATT, H. Engraver. A well-executed stipple portrait of Samuel Thomson, botanist, is prefixed to his "New Guide to Health, Boston, 1832." This plate is simply signed "H. Platt," and while this signature is assumed to be that of the engraver, it may also indicate the painter. No other engraved work of Platt is known to the compiler.

PLEADWELL, Amy M. Painter. Born in Taunton, Mass., in 1875. Pupil of Mass. Normal Art School, Boston, and of Colarossi Academy in Paris. *Address*, 82 Chestnut St., Boston, Mass.

PLOCHER, Jacob J. This landscape engraver died in Philadelphia in 1820. From 1815 to 1818 Plocher had an engraving establishment in that city in the Shakespeare Building, but before this date he did considerable work for the encyclopedia published by S. F. Bradford, Philadelphia, 1808–11. He engraved at least one meritorious large plate, a view of the "Upper Ferry Bridge Over the Schuylkill River, Philadelphia."

PLOWMAN, George Taylor. Illustrator and etcher. Born in Le Sueur, Minn. Pupil of Douglas Volk and of Eric Pape; also studied in London and Paris. Represented by etchings in Boston Museum of Fine Arts, New York Public Library, and in the Library of Congress, Washington, D. C. *Address*, 99 Garden St., Cambridge, Mass.

PLUMB, Henry G. Painter. Born in Sherburne in 1847. Pupil of National Academy of Design, New York, and of Gerome in Paris. *Address*, 149 East 39th St., New York City.

PLUMMER, Ethel Mc C. (Mrs.). Painter. Born in Brooklyn. Pupil of Henri and Mora. Illustrator for *Vanity Fair, Life* and *Shadowland*. *Address*, 112 West 11th St., New York.

PODOLSKY, Henry. Sculptor. Exhibited "The Old Rabbi" at the Penna. Academy of Fine Arts, Philadelphia, 1921. *Address*, 1335 Greenmount Ave., Baltimore, Md.

POGANY, William A. Painter, sculptor, illustrator and etcher. Born in Hungary in 1882. *Address*, 145 West 55th St., New York.

POGANY, Willy (William Andrew). Illustrator and mural painter. Born in Szeged, Hungary, in 1882. Studied in Munich and Paris. Awards: Gold medals, Budapest; Leipzig; Panama-Pacific Exposition, 1915. Illustrator of more than 60 books. Member: Dodge & Pogany, Inc., theatrical producers and managers. *Address*, 54 Cooper Square, New York.

POINCY, P. Painter. Born in New Orleans in 1833; died in New Orleans in 1909. Poincy studied at the École des Beaux Arts, Paris, and at Julien's Academy, Paris. He was a portrait and genre painter of merit, and his street scenes are well executed, full of poetry and charm. As a teacher and painter he had much to do with furthering interest in local art.

POLASEK, Albin. Sculptor. Born in Frenstat, Moravia, in 1879. Studied art at Penna. Academy of Fine Arts; American Academy in Rome. Head of the department of sculpture, Art Institute, Chicago, since 1916. Has exhibited in Rome, Paris, Philadelphia, New York and Chicago. Awarded Prix de Rome, American Academy in Rome, 1910; honorable mention, Paris Salon, 1913; Widener gold medal, Penna. Academy of Fine Arts, 1914; silver medal, San Francisco Exposition, 1915; Logan medal, Art Institute, Chicago, 1917. Work represented in permanent exhibition at Penna. Academy of Fine Arts; Metropolitan Museum, New York; Art Institute of Chicago; Detroit Museum. Member: National Sculpture Society; Western Society of Sculptors; Architectural League of New York; Chicago Society of Artists; Alumni Association of Fellowship of American Academy in Rome. *Address*, Art Institute of Chicago, Ill.

POLK, Charles Peale. Painter. Born in 1767. He was the son of Charles Willson Peale's sister Elizabeth Digby Peale who married Capt. Robt. Polk of Virginia. At the age of 18 young Polk went to live with his artist uncle in Philadelphia. He painted portraits of General Washington, Rochambeau, and other noted men of the American Revolution, and at one time held office under the Government. He died in 1822.

POLK, George. Portrait painter. The collection of paintings at Independence Hall in Philadelphia has a portrait of Rev. George Duffield painted by George Polk.

POLLEY, Frederick. Painter and etcher. Born in Union City, Ind., in 1875. Pupil of Corcoran Art School, Washington, D. C. *Address*, 371 South Emerson St., Indianapolis, Ind.

POLLOCK, Courtenay. Sculptor, who exhibited at the Penna. Academy of the Fine Arts, Philadelphia, 1915. *Address*, "The Schuyler," 57 West 45th St., New York City.

POLLOCK, T. Engraver. In 1839 Pollock was engraving portraits in line in Providence, R. I. He was later apparently a member of the New York engraving firm of Pollock & Doty.

POMAREDE, Leon. Portrait painter. He opened a studio in New Orleans in 1837.

POOKE, Marion L. Painter and illustrator. Born in Natic, Mass. *Address*, Fenway Studios, Boston, Mass.

POOLE, Abram. Painter. Born in Chicago, Ill., in 1882. Studied art at the Royal Academy, Munich, 1905–12; pupil of Lucien Simon, Paris, 1912–15. Unmarried. Exhibited at Royal Academy, Munich; Paris Salon; Carnegie Institute, Pittsburgh; Art Institute, Chicago. Awarded bronze and silver medals, Royal Academy, Munich. Represented in Art Institute, Chicago. *Address*, 134 East 47th St., New York, N. Y.

POOLE, Bert. Painter and illustrator. Born in Brocton, Mass. Specialty, panoramic views in color. *Address*, 298 Edgehill Road, East Milton, Mass.

POOLE, Frederic Victor. Painter and illustrator. Born in England. Represented by portrait of President Lowden at Toronto University. Illustrates for magazines. *Address*, 65 East Elm St., Chicago, Ill.

POOLE, H. Nelson. Painter, illustrator and etcher. Born in Haddonfield, N. J., in 1885. Pupil of Penna. Academy of the Fine Arts. Member of California Society of Etchers, and of Chicago Society of Etchers. *Address*, 712 Montgomery St., San Francisco, Calif.

POOR, Henry V. Painter. Born in Kansas in 1888. Pupil of Slade School and of Walter Sickert in London; Julien Academy in Paris. Member of San Francisco Society of Artists; California Art Club. Award: Walter purchase prize, San Francisco Artists' Association, 1918. *Address*, Pamona, Rockland County, N. Y.

POOR, Henry Warren. Painter. Born in Boston, Mass., in 1863. Pupil of Mass. Normal Art School; also studied in Paris. Member: Boston Art Club. *Address*, Boston Normal School, Mass.

POORE, Henry R. Painter and illustrator. Born in Newark, N. J., in 1859. Pupil of Peter Moran and of the Penna. Academy of the Fine Arts in Philadelphia; National Academy of Design in New York; Luminais and Bouguereau in Paris. Elected Associate Member of the National Academy of Design in 1888. Awards: First prize, American Art Association; second Hallgarten prize, National Academy of Design, 1888; bronze medal, Pan-American Exposition, Buffalo. Work: "Night of the Nativity," Fine Arts Academy, Buffalo; "The Shore," City Museum, St. Louis; "In the Meadow," Art Association, Indianapolis; "Old English Stag Hound," Worcester Museum. Author: "Pictorial Composition"; "The Pictorial Figure"; "The Conception of Art." *Address*, 61 Ridge St., Orange, N. J.

POPE, Alexander. Painter and sculptor. Born in Boston in 1849. Member: Copley Society, 1893; Boston Art Club. Published "Upland Game Birds and Water Fowl of the United States." At the beginning of his career he painted and modeled animals; after 1912 he was chiefly a portrait painter. He died in 1924.

POPE, Mrs. Marion Holden. Painter and etcher. Born in San Francisco, California. Pupil of A. Mathews and Whistler. Member: San Francisco Artists' Association; California Society of Etchers. Work: Three mural decorations in the Carnegie Library, Oakland, Calif. *Address*, 854 Walker Ave., Oakland, Calif.

POPE, William Frederick. Sculptor. Born in 1865. He lived for a time in Boston, Mass. He died in Paris, 1906.

PORTER, Benjamin Curtis. Portrait painter. Born in Melrose, Mass., in 1845; died in New York in 1908. Pupil of Dr. Rimmer and of A. H. Bicknell, in Boston; also studied in Europe. Awards: Bronze medal, Paris Exposition, 1900; silver medal, Pan-American Exposition, Buffalo, 1901; silver medal, St. Louis Exposition, 1904. Elected Associate Member of National Academy, 1878; National Academy in 1880; Society of American Artists; National Sculpture Society; National Institute of Arts and Letters.

PORTER, Bruce. Mural painter and sculptor. Born in San Francisco in 1865. Studied in San Francisco, England and France. Member: American Painters and Sculptors. Award: Chevalier Legion of Honor of France. Work: Designed ''Stevenson Memorial,'' San Francisco; stained glass and mural paintings in churches and public buildings of California. Author: ''The Arts in California,'' etc. *Address*, 944 Chestnut St., San Francisco, Calif.

PORTER, James T. Sculptor. Born in Tientsin, China, in 1883. Pupil of Robert Aitkin. Member: Art Students' League of New York. Work: ''Portrait-bust of James W. Porter,'' ''Portrait-relief of my Mother,'' owned by Beloit College, Wisc. *Address*, 412 East 37th St., New York, N. Y.

PORTER, J. T. In 1815 this mediocre line-engraver of historical plates signed himself as of Middletown, Conn. The only plates to be found are in the ''Narrative of John R. Jewett,'' etc., published by Loomis & Richards, Middletown, Conn., in 1815.

PORTER, John S. Miniature painter in Boston, Mass., in 1832–1833.

PORTER, M. K. Miniature painter. Born in Batavia, Ill., in 1865. Pupil of Volk; also of Art Students' League of Washington, D. C. Member: Washington Water Color Club; Washington Art Club. *Address*, 1761 Q St., Washington, D. C.

PORTER, Raymond A. Sculptor. Born in Hermon, N. Y., in 1883. Member: Copley Society. Work: Memorial to President Tyler, Richmond, Va.; statue, ''The Green Mountain Boy,'' Rutland, Vt.; Victory Memorial, Salem, Mass.; World War Memorial, Commonwealth Armory, Boston, Mass. *Address*, Massachusetts Normal Art School, Boston.

PORTER, Mrs. S. C. Painter. Born in Hartford, Conn. Studied in art schools in New York and Paris. She exhibited in the Paris Salon of 1875 her ''Head of a Girl'';

it was also exhibited at the Centennial Exhibition in Philadelphia.

PORTNOFF, Alexander. Sculptor. Born in Russia in 1887. Pupil of Charles Grafly, Penna. Academy of Fine Arts. Member: Fellowship, Penna. Academy of Fine Arts; Graphic Sketch Club of Philadelphia. Awards: Cresson European scholarship, Penna. Academy of Fine Arts, 1912 and 1913; honorable mention, Panama-Pacific Exposition, San Francisco, 1915. Work: Busts of Prof. Alonzo Brown, Prof. Chas. La Wall and J. D. Toloff. *Address*, 703 Walnut St., Philadelphia, Pa.

POSSELWHITE, George W. Engraver. Born in England about 1822. He was living in New York in 1899. Posselwhite was an admirable engraver of landscape and subject plates. He came to the United States about 1850 and was largely employed in New York and Philadelphia.

POST, Charles Johnson. Painter and journalist. Born in New York in 1873. Since 1893 engaged as artist-journalist and editorial writer with the *Associated Press, New York Daily News, Recorder, World, Journal, Herald* and *Globe*. Illustrated for *American, New York Times, Philadelphia Inquirer,* the *Century Magazine, Pearson's, Cosmopolitan, Harper's Weekly, Harper's Magazine, Everybody's* and *Outing*.

POST, May Audubon. Painter and illustrator. Born in New York City. Pupil of Penna. Academy of Fine Arts under Chase, Beaux, Grafly and Breckenridge; of Drexel Institute under Howard Pyle; of Lucien Simon in Paris. Member: Fellowship, Penna. Academy of Fine Arts. Award: Traveling scholarships, Penna. Academy of Fine Arts; gold medal, Art Club of Philadelphia, 1903. *Address*, 4446 Sansom St., Philadelphia, Pa.

POST, W. Merritt. Painter. Born in Brooklyn in 1856. Pupil of Art Students' League, New York. Landscape painter, 1882– Honorable mention, Buffalo Exposition, 1901. Elected Associate Member of the National Academy, 1910. Member: American Water Color Society; N. Y. Water Color Club; Artists' Fund Society. Specialty, landscapes. *Address*, Bantam, Conn.

POTTER, Edward Clark. Sculptor. Born in New London, Conn., in 1857; died in 1923. Studied sculpture under Mercei and Fremo, Paris. Collaborated with D. C. French in sculpture for Chicago Exposition, 1892–93; executed equestrian statues of Grant at Philadelphia, 1894; one of Washington, at Paris, 1898; Hooker, at Boston, 1904; Derens, at Worcester, Mass., 1905; Slocum; at Gettysburg; De Soto, at St. Louis Exposition, 1904; also statues in Fulton Library, Washington.

Elected to National Academy of Design, 1906. Member: National Institute of Arts and Letters; National Sculpture Society; Architectural League.

POTTER, Harry S. Illustrator. Born in Detroit, Mich., in 1870. Pupil of Constant, Laurens and Simon in Paris. *Address*, 539 West 112th St., New York City.

POTTER, Lewis. Sculptor. "The Snake Charmer" attracted favorable comment at the Pan-American Exposition, while his busts "A Tunisian Jewess" and "A Young Bedouin" are highly praised.

POTTER, Mary K. Painter and writer on art. Pupil of Metropolitan Museum and of the Art Students' League of New York; also of the Julien Academy, Paris. *Address*, 184 Boylston St., Boston.

POTTER, Nathan D. Painter and sculptor. Born in Enfield, Mass., in 1893. Pupil of French. Represented by figures on the Greenwich Trust Co., Greenwich, Conn., and on the Ohio Gas Co. Building of Cleveland, Ohio. *Address*, 149 Sixth Ave., New York City.

POTTER, William J. Painter. Born in Bellport, Penna., in 1883. Pupil of Penna. Academy of Fine Arts and of Siebert of London. *Address*, Broadmoor, Colorado Springs, Colo.

POTTHAST, Edward Henry. Painter. Born in Cincinnati, Ohio, in 1857. Student in Cincinnati, Munich and Paris. Elected member of National Academy of New York in 1906. Represented in Art Museums in Cincinnati, Chicago, Brooklyn, and Buffalo, N. Y. *Address*, 222 Central Park, South, New York City.

POTTS, William S. Engraver. Born in New Jersey; died in St. Louis in 1852. In 1824 Potts was an engraver in a New York office, working with William Chapin, but he later studied for the ministry and became a prominent Presbyterian clergyman, and in 1837 was president of the Marion College.

POTTS, William Sherman. Portrait painter who paints miniatures. Born in Milburn, N. J., in 1876. Pupil of Penna. Academy of Fine Arts and of Laurens and Constant in Paris. *Address*, 45 East 59th St., New York.

POUPARD, James. Engraver, who advertised in the *Pennsylvania Gazette*, Philadelphia, in 1772. The earliest engraving by Poupard of which we have any note is mentioned in the *Gazette* of June 29, 1774. James Humphreys, Jr., announces the publication of "The Search after Happiness, a Pastoral Drama, by Miss More (embellished with an elegant Copperplate Frontispiece, engraved by James Poupard, of this City)." This print has not been

seen by the compiler. In 1775 Poupard engraved the portrait of Dr. Goldsmith for the *Pennsylvania Magazine;* in 1788–89 he was engraving diagrams, etc., for the *Transactions of the American Philosophical Society;* and as a "seal and die engraver" his name appears continuously in the Philadelphia directories for 1793–1807, inclusive. Poupard then removed to New York, and was engraving on wood for New York publishers in 1814. A fairly well-executed portrait of John Wesley may be ascribed to this latter period.

POUSETTE-DART, Nath. J. Painter, sculptor and etcher. Born in St. Paul, Minn., in 1886. Pupil of Penna. Academy of the Fine Arts. *Address*, Valhalla, N. Y.

POWELL, Arthur J. E. Painter. Born in Vanwert, Ohio, in 1864. Pupil of San Francisco School of Design and Julien Academy, Paris. Associate Member of the National Academy. *Address*, 59 East 59th St., New York.

POWELL, Caroline A. Wood engraver. Born in Ireland. Pupil of W. J. Linton and Timothy Cole. Represented in Boston Museum of Fine Arts, New York Public Library, and Carnegie Institute, Pittsburgh. *Address*, 121 West Carrillo St., Santa Barbara, Calif.

POWELL, Lucien Whiting. Painter. Born in Virginia in 1846. Landscape painter in oils and water colors. Pupil of the Pennsylvania Academy of the Fine Arts; of West London School of Art, under Fitz; also studied in National Gallery, London; under Leon Bonnat, in Paris. Awarded Parsons prize, Society of Washington Artists, 1903. Member of Society of Washington Artists and of the Washington Water Color Club. "The Afterglow, Grand Canyon, Arizona" (water color) is in the Corcoran Art Gallery, Washington, D. C. *Address*, Purcellville, Va.

POWELL, William Henry. Portrait and historical painter. Born in Ohio, 1824; died in New York in 1879. Represented in the Capitol, Washington, D. C., by "De Soto Discovering the Mississippi River" and by the "Battle of Lake Erie." A replica of this picture is in the State Capitol of Ohio. In the painting of his "Battle of Lake Erie" persons then employed about the Capitol were used as models. For many years he occupied a studio in New York. His "Landing of the Pilgrims" was purchased by Marshall O. Roberts, and his portraits of Gen. McClellan and Maj. Anderson are in the City Hall, New York.

POWERS, Hiram. Sculptor. Born in Vermont on a farm in 1805. He early acquired knowledge of modelling. In 1835 he went to Washington, and two years later he established himself in Florence, Italy. His work consists of busts of prominent men, statues of Adams, Jackson, Webster, Calhoun, Longfellow, Gen. Sheridan, etc., and his best known achievement "The Greek Slave." He died in 1873.

POWERS, Longworth. Sculptor. Son of Hiram Powers, who resided in Florence, Italy, for many years and died there in 1904.

POWERS, Marion (Mrs. W. A. Kirkpatrick). Painter. Born in London, England of American parents. Pupil of Garrido in Paris. Member: National Academy of Women Painters and Sculptors. Awards: Lippincott prize, Penna. Academy of Fine Arts, 1907; silver medal, Buenos Aires Exposition, 1910; gold medal, Panama-Pacific Exposition, San Francisco, 1915. Work: "Tresors," in Luxembourg, Paris, bought from Salon in 1904; mural decoration for Canadian Pacific Railway at Vancouver, B. C. *Address*, Fenway Studios, 30 Ipswich St., Boston, Mass.

POWERS, Preston. Portrait painter and sculptor. Son of Hiram Powers. Born in Florence in 1843. He has practiced his profession in Boston, Mass., Washington, D. C., and in Portland, Me. His life-bust of Whittier is in the Library at Haverhill, Mass.

PRADOS, Madame. Miniature portrait painter, working in New Orleans about 1800.

PRAHAR, Renee. Sculptor. Born in New York City in 1880. Studied in Paris under Bourdelle. Represented in Metropolitan Museum, New York, by "Russian Dancer." *Address*, 45 Christopher St., New York.

PRATT, Bela Lyon. Sculptor. Born in Norwich, Conn., in 1867. Studied with Saint Gaudens, Chase and Cox in New York, and in Paris with Falguiere. He died in Boston in 1917. Represented by statue of Nathan Hale at Yale University; "The Seasons" in the Congressional Library, Washington, and many war monuments and memorials.

PRATT, Henry Cheeves. Landscape painter. Born in 1803 and died in 1880. He also painted a bust-portrait of Longfellow.

PRATT, Matthew. Painter. Born in Philadelphia in 1734. He was the son of Henry Pratt (goldsmith), a friend of Doctor Franklin and one of his famous Junto. His mother's brother, James Claypole, "limner and painter in general," had the distinction, until recently, of being the earliest native-born American artist (1720) recorded, and it was he who gave his nephew the first instruction he received in art, "from whom," to use Pratt's language, "I learned all the different branches of painting from ten years of age." The earliest work of his apparently is the portrait of his father's friend, Franklin, painted circa 1756, now in the Manor House collection at Yonkers, New York, which is also the earliest known portrait of the philosopher. In the summer of 1764, Pratt sailed for London, having under his protection his kinswoman, the fiancée of Benjamin West, who a few months later Pratt gave in marriage to the future President of the Royal Academy of Arts in London. For two and a half years Pratt lived in the household of West and was West's first student. It was during this period that he painted the picture of "The American School"—West's painting-room, now in the Metropolitan Museum of Art, New York, and portraits of West and Mrs. West in the Pennsylvania Academy of Fine Arts, Philadelphia.

Matthew Pratt died in 1805, and was buried in Christ Chrch burying ground at 5th and Arch Streets, Philadelphia. He was the father of Henry Pratt, who built the famous "yellow mansion" which stood at Broad and Walnut Streets, Philadelphia, for so many years, and he was the progenitor of many families of prominence in that city. He also painted a full-length portrait of Cadwalader Colden belonging to the New York Chamber of Commerce, for that body in 1772, at a cost of thirty-seven pounds. The Spring Garden Institute of Philadelphia owned at one time a full-length portrait of Gov. James Hamilton, painted by Pratt, but it has been lost for years.

PRATT, Philip H. Painter and illustrator. Born in Kansas City, Mo., in 1888. Pupil of St. Louis School of Fine Arts; Philadelphia Industrial Art School; South Kensington Museum, London. Work: Twelve mural panels for Wisconsin State Capitol. *Address*, School of Fine and Applied Arts, Pratt Institute, Brooklyn, N. Y.

PRATT, Robert M. Portrait and genre painter. Born in Binghamton, N. Y., in 1811. He was a pupil of Morse and Ingham. He also painted a number of miniatures. The New York Historical Society owns his portraits of Richard Hildreth and Nicholas Triest. He died in New York City in 1888.

PRELLWITZ, Edith Mitchill (Mrs. Henry). Painter. Born in South Orange, N. J., in 1865. Pupil of Art Students' League under Brush and Cox; Julien Academy in Paris under Bouguereau, Robert-Fleury and Courtois. Elected Associate Member of the National Academy of Design, 1906; New York Woman's Art Club. Awards: Second Hallgarten prize, National Academy of Design, 1894; Dodge prize, National Academy of Design, 1895; medal, Atlanta Exposition, 1895; bronze medal, Pan-American Exposition, Buffalo, 1901. *Address*, Peconic, L. I., N. Y.

PRELLWITZ, Henry. Painter. Born in New York in 1865. Pupil of T. W. Dewing and Art Students' League in New York; Julien Academy in Paris. Elected Associate Member of National Academy, 1906, and an Academician in 1912. Awards: Third Hallgarten prize, National Academy of Design, 1893; bronze medal, Pan-American Exposition, Buffalo, 1901; silver medal, St. Louis Exposition, 1904; Clarke prize, National Academy of Design, 1907. *Address*, Peconic, L. I., N. Y.

PRENDERGAST, Charles E. Sculptor and etcher. Born in Boston, Mass., in 1868. Member: Copley Society; Society of Independent Artists. *Address*, 50 Washington Square, New York, N. Y.

PRENDERGAST, Maurice B. Painter. Born in Boston in 1861; died in New York in 1924. Pupil of Julien, Laurens and Blanc in Paris. Awarded medal at Buffalo Exposition in 1901, and at Corcoran Art Gallery, Washington, D. C., in 1923, for his "Landscape with Figures."

PRESCOTT, Katharine T. Sculptor. Born at Biddeford, Me. Pupil of E. Boyd, Boston, and of F. E. Elwell, New York. Member: Boston Art Students' Association; Copley Society, Boston. Has exhibited at Art Institute, Chicago; National Sculpture Society; National Academy of Design, New York; Penna. Academy of Fine Arts, Philadelphia; Boston Art Club. *Address*, 59 5th Ave., New York.

PRESTON, James. Landscape painter, who exhibited at the Penna. Academy of Fine Arts in Philadelphia, 1915. *Address*, 22 West 9th St., New York.

PRESTON, Mary Wilson (Mrs. James M.). Illustrator. Born in New York in 1873. Pupil of Art Students' League of New York, and of the National Academy of Design; also of Whistler School in Paris. Member: Society of Illustrators, 1904. Award: Bronze medal, Panama-Pacific Exposition, San Francisco, 1915. *Address*, 22 West 9th St., New York, N. Y.

PRICE, Edith Ballinger. Painter and illustrator. Born in New Brunswick, N. Y., in 1897. Pupil of P. L. Hale, A. R. James, Helena Sturtevant, Geo. Maynard and Thos. Fogarty. Member: Newport Artists' Association. Work: Author and illustrator of "Blue Magic"; "Silver Shoal Light"; "Us and the Bottleman"; "The Happy Venture." *Address*, 7 Arnold Ave., Newport, R. I.

PRICE, Eugenia. Painter. Born in Beaumont, Tex., in 1865; died in 1923. Pupil of St. Louis School of Fine Arts; Art Institute of Chicago; Julien Academy in Paris. Member: Alumni, Art Institute of Chicago; Chicago Art Club; Texas Fine Arts Society; Chicago Society of Miniature Painters.

PRICE, George. Born in England in 1826. This landscape engraver was a pupil of the Findens in London. Price came to the United States in 1853, did considerable work here, and returned to England in 1864.

PRICE, Llewellyn. Painter, who exhibited water colors at the Penna. Academy of the Fine Arts, Philadelphia, 1925. *Address*, Bryn Athyn, Penna.

PRICE, M. Elizabeth. Painter. Born in Martinsburg, West Va. Pupil of the Pennsylvania Museum; School of Industrial Art; Penna. Academy of Fine Arts. Member: Fellowship, Penna. Academy of Fine Arts; Plastic Club; National Academy of Women Painters and Sculptors; Whitney Studio Club; League of New York Artists. Director of Neighborhood Art School of Greenwich House. *Address*, 140 West 57th St., New York, N. Y.

PRICE, Margaret Evans. Painter and illustrator. Born in Chicago, Ill., in 1888. Pupil of Mass. Normal Art School, Decamp and Major. Illustrator of children's books. *Address*, 16304 Clifton Blvd., Cleveland, Ohio.

PRICE, Genl. Samuel W. Portrait painter. Born in 1828.

PRICHARD, Sidney. Painter, who exhibited water colors at the Penna. Academy of Fine Arts, Philadelphia, 1925. *Address*, Stockton Springs, Me.

PRIME, William Cowper. Painter. Born in 1825. He died in New York City in 1905.

PRITCHARD, J. Ambrose. Painter. Born in 1858. He died in Boston in 1905.

PROCTOR, A. Phimister. Sculptor and painter. Born in Ontario, Can., in 1862. Pupil of Puech and Ingalbert, Paris. Awards: Rinehart Paris scholarship; designer's medal, Chicago Exposition, 1893, where he exhibited sculptural groups; exhibited at Paris Exposition, 1900; gold medal, St. Louis Exposition, 1904; gold medal, Panama-Pacific Exposition, 1915. Represented in public parks, New York; in Denver; Zoological Park, New York; in Pittsburgh; McKinley monument, Buffalo; permanent works at St. Louis Art Gallery; Mary's Institute, St. Louis; Metropolitan Museum of Art; Princeton tigers, Princeton University. Member of Art Commission, City of New York, 1903–06. Member of National Academy, 1904; National Institute of Arts and Letters; National Sculpture Society; Canadian Art Club; American Water Color Society; Architectural League. *Address*, Los Angeles, Calif.

PRUD'HOMME, John Francis Eugene. Engraver. Born in the Island of St. Thomas, West Indies, in 1800; died in Georgetown, D. C., in 1892. His parents came to the United States in 1807 and settled in New York in 1809. About 1814 Prud'Homme was apprenticed to his brother-in-law Thomas Gimbrede to learn engraving, and was engraving over his own name in New York in 1821. He became a reputable engraver of portraits in stipple, though his best work is represented by his small plates executed for the "Annuals," about 1839. Among these "The Velvet Hat" and "Friar Puck" are to be especially admired. In 1852 Prud'Homme became interested in bank-note work, and from 1869 to 1885 he was employed by the Treasury Department at Washington, D. C. Prud'Homme was made an Academician of the National Academy of Design in 1846, and in 1834–53 he was the curator of the Academy.

PULLINGER, Herbert. Illustrator, etcher and painter. Born in Philadelphia in 1878. Pupil of Penna. Academy of Fine Arts; also known for his etchings and lithographs. *Address*, 1430 South Penn Square, Philadelphia.

PUNDERSON, L. S. This excellent engraver of portraits in stipple was working in New York in 1850–55.

PURDIE, Evelyn. Miniature painter. Born in Smyrna, Asia Minor. Pupil of Carolus-Duran and Henner in Paris. *Address*, 383 Harvard St., Cambridge, Mass.

PUREFOY, Heslope. Miniature painter. Born in Chapel Hill, N. C., 1884. Pupil of Lucia Fairchild Fuller. *Address*, 27 Charlotte St., Asheville, N. C.

PURINTON, J. Miniature painter, who flourished in 1802, Salem, Mass.

PURSELL, Henry. Engraver. In the *New York Mercury*, in 1775, Henry Pursell advertises that he has removed "from Broadway to Dock Street, near the Old Coffee House, where he carries on the engraving business in its different branches, viz., Copperplates of all kinds, Arms, crests, cyphers, etc., on plate. Ditto on watches. Ditto on seals of any metals. Types, Free Mason Medals. Gun furniture, Harness ditto, Cyphers, etc., on whips. Morning rings, Door plates, Dog Collars, etc.''

PUSHMAN, HORSEP. Painter. Pupil of Lefebvre in Paris. He received a medal from the Salon, 1921. Represented in Milwaukee and Minneapolis Art Museums. *Address*, 80 West 40th St., New York.

PUTHUFF, Hanson D. Painter. Born in Waverly, Mo., in 1875. Member of the San Francisco Art Association. Represented at Artists' Club, Denver, Col. *Address*, 161 North College Ave., Eagle Rock, Calif.

PUTNAM, Arthur. Sculptor. Born at Waveland, Mass., in 1873. Awards: Gold medal, San Francisco Exposition, 1915. Principal works: Snarling Jaguar, Metropolitan Museum of New York; Puma and Snakes, Paris Salon; The Death, Boston Museum; Sloat monument, Monterey, Calif.; etc. *Address*, 860 45th Ave., San Francisco, Calif.

PUTNAM, Brenda. Sculptor. Born in Minneapolis, Minn., in 1890. Pupil of Bela Pratt and Charles Grafly. Specialty, portrait reliefs of children. *Address*, 49 West 12th St., New York City.

PUTNAM, Stephen Greeley. Painter and wood engraver. Born in Nashua, N. H., in 1852. Pupil of H. W. Herrick, Frank French and E. J. Whitney; studied at the Brooklyn Art Association, and the Art Students' League, New York. Awards: Bronze medal for wood engravings, Paris Exposition, 1893; bronze medal, Paris Exposition, 1900; silver medal, Buffalo Exposition, 1901. *Address*, College Point, Borough of Queens, New York, N. Y.

PYLE, Howard. Painter and illustrator. Born in Wilmington, Del., 1853, he died in 1911. He was elected a member of the National Academy of Design in 1911. His illustrations are excellent, and first established his reputation. He was the author of the text and illustrations for "The Merry Adventures of Robin Hood," "The Wonder Clock"; also illustrated many books of juvenile fiction.

Q

QUANCHI, Leon W. Painter. Born in New York in 1892. Pupil of George De Forrest Brush, and of Douglas Volk. Exhibited at the National Academy of Design, New York, 1925. *Address*, 771 Lexington Ave., New York.

QUARRE, F. Engraver. He was also a lamp-shade manufacturer located in Philadelphia in 1850, and possibly earlier. The only engraved work of this man seen by the compiler is an oval of a very good imitation of lace, printed in white on a brown ground. In the center of this oval is an embossed view of New York, seemingly taken from Hoboken. Below this view is "New York," in white on the brown ground. This view was used as a magazine illustration.

QUARTLEY, Arthur. Painter. Son of the wood engraver, was born in France in 1839. He settled in New York in 1851. He painted signs, and later devoted his time to marine painting. He was elected an Associate of the National Academy in 1879 and an Academician in 1886. His most important pictures are "View of North River," "Trinity from the River," "Lofty and Lowly," and "Morning in New York Harbor." He died in New York in 1886.

QUARTLEY, Frederick William. Engraver. Born in 1808. He adopted the profession of wood engraving in England in 1852; he then came to New York where he lived his professional life and died in 1874. His best known work was "Picturesque America" and "Picturesque Europe." He was also a painter; among his pictures are "Niagara Falls," "Catskill Falls," and "Butter-Milk Falls."

QUESNAY, Alexander Marie. Portrait painter in miniature and portrait draughtsman in crayon. Numerous extended advertisements inserted in the New York newspapers during 1784, concerning his Academy for Dancing and Drawing, are reprinted in W. Kelby's "Notes on American Artists." He was active in New York City about 1784.

QUIDOR, John. Painter. Born in 1801. He studied with Inman, and was a pupil of John Wesley Jarvis in his New York studio. Chas. Loring Elliott studied with Quidor. He painted very cleverly numerous imaginative subjects, often taking his inspiration from Washington Irving's tales. He painted "Rip Van Winkle," also "Ichabod Crane." He died in 1881.

QUINLAN, Will J. Painter and etcher. Born in Brooklyn, N. Y., in 1877. Pupil of J. B. Whittaker at Adelphi College; National Academy of Design in New York, and of Maynard and Ward. Member: Chicago Society of Etchers; New York Society of Etchers; California Society of Etchers. Award: Shaw black and white prize. Work represented in New York Public Library; Oakland (Calif.) Public Museum. *Address*, 333 Warburton Ave., Yonkers, N. Y.

QUINN, Edmond T. Sculptor and painter. Born in Philadelphia, Pa. Pupil of Eakins in Philadelphia; Injalbert in Paris. Elected Associate Member of the National Academy; National Sculpture Society, 1907. Award: Silver medal, Panama-Pacific Exposition, San Francisco, 1915. Work: Statue, "John Howard," Williamsport, Pa.; statue, "Zoroaster," Brooklyn Institute of Arts and Sciences; reliefs on "Kings' Mountain (S. C.) Battle Monument"; bust of Edgar Allan Poe, Fordham, New York; "Nymph," statuette, Metropolitan Museum, New York; statue of Maj. Gen. John E. Pemberton, Vicksburg (Miss.) National Military Park; statue of Edwin Booth as "Hamlet," Gramercy Park, New York; bust of Prof. Hooper, Brooklyn Museum. *Address*, 207 East 61st St., New York, N. Y.

QUISTGAARD, J. W. Portrait painter. Born in Denmark, 1877. Painted portraits of Theodore Roosevelt, Joseph Choate, and C. M. Depew. *Address*, 80 West 40th St., New York.

R

RAAB, George. Painter and sculptor. Born in Sheboygan, Wis., in 1866. Pupil of Richard Lorenz in Milwaukee; C. Smith in Weimar; Courtois in Paris. Member of Milwaukee Art Society and Wisconsin Painters and Sculptors. Award: Medal, Milwaukee Art Institute, 1917. Work: "The Lone Pine," St. Paul Institute; "The Veil of Snow," Milwaukee Art Institute. Curator, Layton Art Gallery. *Address,* 438 Jefferson Ave., Milwaukee, Wis.

RACHMIEL, Jean. Painter. Born in Haverstraw-on-Hudson, N. Y., in 1871. Art pupil under his father; later under George de Forest Brush, New York; went to Paris, 1890; studied under Jules Lefebvre; entered École des Beaux Arts and studied with Leon Bonnat. Exhibitor in Paris Salon annually since 1898.

RADCLIFFE, C. Was a stipple-engraver of portraits and vignettes located in Philadelphia as early as 1805.

RADITZ, Lazar. Portrait painter. Born in Russia in 1887. Emigrated to America in 1903. Studied at Penna. Academy of Fine Arts. Awarded Cresson Scholarship Toppen Prize. Work: Self-portrait, Pennsylvania Academy of the Fine Arts, Philadelphia; "Dr. I. M. Hays," American Philosophical Society, Philadelphia; "Mrs. R," Reading (Pa.) Museum; "Judge Mayer Sulzberger," Dropsie College, Philadelphia; "Dr. Hobart M. Hare," University of Pennsylvania, Philadelphia; "Daniel Baugh," Baugh Institute of Anatomy, Philadelphia; "Dr. S. G. Dixon," Academy of Natural Science, Philadelphia. *Address,* 1520 Chestnut St., Philadelphia, Pa.

RADITZ, Violetta C. Painter, who exhibited water colors at the Penna. Academy of the Fine Arts, Philadelphia, 1925. *Address,* 143 North 20th St., Philadelphia.

RAE, John. Illustrator and painter. Born in Jersey City, N. J., in 1882. Pupil of Howard Pyle and of F. V. Du Mond. Member: Society of Illustrators, 1912. Illustrated "The Girl I Left Behind Me," "Historic Houses of New Jersey," "The Big Family," "Pies and Pirates," "Why," "Fables in Rhyme." Author and illustrator of "New Adventures of Alice." Represented in Library of Congress, Washington. *Address,* Cedars Road, Caldwell, N. J.

RAKEMANN, Carl. Mural painter. Born in Washington, D. C., in 1878. Studied in Europe. Was a student at the Royal Academy in Dusseldorf, Germany, for two years, after which he resided for a year in Paris, France.

Returning to Germany, he continued his studies as a student at the Royal Academy in Munich, and during the following year he returned to the United States. A close student of nature, he has not confined himself to any one medium, employing etching, water color, oil, and fresco as means of art expression. He has, however, occupied himself largely in the field of mural decoration. Represented in the Contemporary American Oil Paintings Exhibit, Corcoran Gallery of Art, Washington, D. C.; also in various private collections. Member of several art societies and clubs. *Address,* North Chevy Chase, Md.

RALEIGH, Henry. Illustrator and etcher. Born in Portland, Ore., in 1880. Pupil of Hopkins Academy, San Francisco. Member of Salmagundi Club of New York. *Address,* Westport, Conn.

RALPH, W. Line-engraver of views, etc., of little merit. He was working in Philadelphia in 1794–1808, and engraved at least one plate for the *New York Magazine.*

RAMAGE, John. English miniature painter. Born in 1763. He was living in Boston, Mass., in 1775, and in New York in 1777. He painted a miniature of George Washington. He became involved in debt and fled to Canada in 1794, where he died in 1802. He was buried in the Protestant Cemetery in Montreal. (See Strickland's Dictionary of Irish Artists.)

RAMSDELL, Fred W. Painter of landscapes and portraits. Born in 1865. Studied at Art Students' League, New York, and with Collin in Paris. He had a studio at Lyme, Conn. He died in 1915.

RAMSEY, L. A. Painter and illustrator. Born in Bridgeport, Ill., in 1873. Pupil of Laurens and of the Julien Academy in Paris. Member: Society of Utah Artists. *Address,* 255 West 6th St., N., Salt Lake City, Utah.

RAMSEY, Milne. Painter. Born in Philadelphia in 1847. Student at Penna. Academy of Fine Arts, and pupil of Bonnat in Paris. In 1878 he sent the "Bird Fanciers" to the first exhibition of the Society of American Artists in New York. He died in Philadelphia in 1915.

RAND, Ellen G. Emmet (Mrs. William Blanchard). Painter. Born in San Francisco, Calif., in 1876. Studied in New York and Paris. Member: National Association of Women Painters and Sculptors. Awards: Silver medal, St. Louis Exposition, 1904; gold medal, Panama-Pacific Exposition, San Francisco, 1915. Work: Portrait of A u g u s t u s

20

Saint Gaudens and of Benjamin Altman, Metropolitan Museum, New York. *Address*, 137 East 66th St., New York.

RAND, Henry A. Painter. Born in Philadelphia, Pa., in 1886. Pupil of Penna. Academy of Fine Arts under Chase, Anshutz and Breckenridge. Member: Philadelphia Sketch Club; Fellowship, Penna. Academy of Fine Arts. Work: "Snow Shadows," Pennsylvania Academy of the Fine Arts, Philadelphia. *Address*, Holicong, Bucks County, Pa.

RAND, Margaret A. Painter. Born in Dedham, Mass., 1868. Member of Boston Art Club, which owns her painting "Pansies." *Address*, 49 Kirkland St., Cambridge, Mass.

RANDALL, Asa Grant. Painter. Born in Waterboro, Maine, in 1863. Pupil of Arthur Dow and of the Pratt Institute. *Address*, 498 Broadway, Providence, R. I.

RANDALL, D. Ernest. Painter and illustrator. Born in Rush County, Ind. Pupil of Art Institute of Chicago. *Address*, 1736 Union St., San Francisco, Calif.

RANDALL, Paul A. Painter and illustrator. Born in Warsaw, Ind., in 1879. Pupil of William Forsyth. *Address*, 3204 Bellefontaine St., Indianapolis, Ind.

RANDOLPH, Lee F. Painter and etcher. Born at Ravenna, Ohio, in 1880. Pupil of Cincinnati Art Academy and of the Art Students' League of New York. Represented by paintings in the Luxembourg, Paris, and in the California School of Fine Arts. *Address*, Care of California School of Fine Arts, San Francisco, Calif.

RANGER, Henry W. Landscape painter. Born in Syracuse, N. Y., in 1858, he died in New York City, 1916. He studied in this country; also in France, England and Holland. He was elected an Associate of the National Academy, 1901, and Academician in 1906. Represented in Corcoran Art Gallery by the "Top of the Hill," and in the Metropolitan Museum of Art by "High Bridge" and "Spring Woods."

RANNELLS, Will. Painter and illustrator. Born at Caldwell, Ohio, in 1892. Pupil of Cincinnati Art Academy. Illustrates for *Life, Ladies' Home Journal,* etc. Specialty, drawings of dogs. *Address*, 684 Miller Ave., Columbus, Ohio.

RANNEY, William. Painter. Born in Middletown, Conn., in 1813; died, West Hoboken, New Jersey, in 1857. Represented by "Duck-Shooting" in Corcoran Art Gallery, Washington, D. C. Elected Associate Member of the National Academy in 1850. His work

is mainly connected with the life of hunters and trappers in the west.

RANSOM, Alexander. Painter. Noted in Tuckerman's "American Artist Life."

RANSOM, Caroline L. Ormes. Born in Newark, Ohio, in 1838; died in Washington, D. C., in 1910. She was taught by her mother in drawing and painting in water colors, and received some help from an itinerant portrait painter, who visited her father's home and painted portraits of the family. She afterwards went to New York, and studied landscape painting under A. B. Durand, and portrait painting under Thomas Hicks and Daniel Huntington. Visited Europe later, where she was for some time a pupil of Kaulbach, at Munich. Her first work of note was painted in her studio in Cleveland, Ohio; she afterwards worked in New York, prior to her coming to Washington, D. C., where she maintained a studio at 915 F Street, N. W., for many years. Among her works are: Portraits of Maj. Gen. McPherson, Salmon P. Chase, Senator Benjamin F. Wade, Joshua R. Giddings, Alexander Hamilton, John A. Dix, John W. Taylor, James A. Garfield, and Thomas Jefferson.

RAPHAEL, Joseph. Painter. Born in Jackson, Calif., in 1872. Pupil of San Francisco Art Association and of the Julien Academy, Paris. *Address*, 345 Sutter St., San Francisco, Calif.

RASCHEN, Carl Martin. Painter and illustrator. Born in 1882. Pupil of Rochester Athenaeum and of the Mechanics' Institute and of Gilbert Gaul. Member: Rochester Art Club; Rochester Picture Painters' Club; St. Louis Brush and Pencil Club. *Address*, 368 Alexander St., Rochester, N. Y.

RASMUSSEN, Bertrand. Painter. Born in Arendal, Norway, in 1890. Pupil of Laurens in Paris. Member: Society of Independent Artists; Brooklyn Water Color Club; League of New York Artists. *Address*, 468 60th St., Brooklyn, New York, N. Y.

RATLIFF, Blanche C. (Mrs.). Painter. Born in Texas, 1896. Pupil of O. B. Jacobson. Represented by work in University of Oklahoma. *Address*, 510 Kentucky Ave., Fort Worth, Tex.

RATTNER, Abraham. Painter. Member of Fellowship of the Penna. Academy of Fine Arts. *Address*, Care of Penna. Academy of Fine Arts, Philadelphia.

RAU, William. Painter and illustrator. Born in New York City, 1874. Pupil of Chase and Ward. Has painted mural panels. *Address*, 161 Columbus Ave., New York City.

RAUL, Harry Lewis. Sculptor. Born in Easton, Pa., in 1883. Pupil of Penna. Academy of Fine Arts, and of Chase and Grafly. Represented by "Green Mountain Statue" at Easton, Pa., and "Soldiers' Monument," West Chester, Pa. *Address,* 1807 Washington Building, Easton, Penna.

RAVENSCROFT, Ellen. Painter. Member of the National Association of Women Painters and Sculptors, who exhibited in the 33d Annual Exhibition, New York. *Address,* 51 West 16th St., New York.

RAVLIN, Grace. Painter. Born in Kaneville, Kane County, Ill. Studied at Art Institute of Chicago; Penna. Academy of Fine Arts, Philadelphia; under Simon-Menard Cour, Paris. Exhibited at the Salon, Paris. Represented in the Luxembourg Museum, Paris, and by two other pictures in the collection of the French Government. *Address,* 11 West 37th St., New York, N. Y.

RAWDON, Freeman. Engraver. Born in Tolland, Conn., in 1804. Freeman Rawdon was a pupil of his brother Ralph Rawdon, an engraver, then of Albany, N. Y. In 1828 he was the Rawdon of the New York engraving firm of Rawdon, Wright & Co., and Rawdon, Wright & Hatch, and of other combinations of a later date. These firms conducted an extensive business in general and bank-note engraving, and employed many engravers. Freeman Rawdon signed very little work.

RAWDON, Ralph. Engraver. In 1813 Ralph Rawdon was engraving in a very crude manner in Cheshire, Conn. He was associated in this work with Thomas Kensett, the father of the American artist. About 1816 Rawdon removed to Albany, N. Y., where he engraved stipple portraits over his own name, and with his brother and A. Willard he was in the bank-note and general engraving business in that city.

RAWSON, Carl W. Painter. Born in Des Moines, Ia., in 1884. Pupil of Cumming Art School; National Academy of Design; Minneapolis School of Art. *Address,* 637 Kenwood Parkway, Minneapolis, Minn.

RAY, Man. Painter, who exhibited in Philadelphia in 1921, in "Exhibition of Paintings Showing the Later Tendencies in Art." *Address,* 47 West 8th St., New York City.

RAYMOND, Frank Willoughby. Etcher and engraver. Born in Dubuque, Ia., in 1881. Pupil of Art Institute of Chicago. Member: California Society of Etchers; Chicago Society of Etchers; Palette and Chisel Club. Work: Represented in Art Institute of Chicago; Toledo Museum of Art. *Address,* 123 Fifth Ave., New York, N. Y.

RAYMOND, Grace R. Painter. Born in Mt. Vernon, Ohio. Pupil of Chicago Art Institute. Member of Washington Water Color Club. *Address,* 923 Mansfield St., Winfield, Kans.

RAYNOR, Grace H. Sculptor. Born in New York, 1884. Specialty, portrait statuettes and heads. *Address,* 159 West 56th St., New York.

REA, John L. Sculptor. Born in Beekmantown, Clinton County, N. Y., in 1882. Pupil of H. A. MacNeil and of James Earle Fraser. *Address,* Plattsburgh, Clinton County, N. Y.

READ, E. Joseph. Painter. Born in Howard, Steuben County, N. Y., in 1862. Pupil of College of Fine Arts, Syracuse University; under Fremiet in Paris. During the winter he paints in the West Indies. *Address,* 249 West Passaic Ave., Rutherford, N. J.

READ, Frank E. Painter, etcher and architect. Born in Austinburg in 1862. Pupil of W. M. Hunt. Member: Seattle Fine Arts Society. *Address,* 232 Harvard, North, Seattle, Washington.

READ, Henry. Painter. Born in Twickenham, England, in 1851. Member of Art Commission of the City and County of Denver; National Academy of Artists. Director, Denver Students' School of Art. Work: Represented in Denver Art Association. *Address,* 1311 Pearl St., Denver, Colo.

READ, Thomas Buchanan. Painter. Born in Chester County, Pa., in 1822; died in New York in 1872. He entered the studio of a sculptor in Cincinnati in 1839, but painting soon proved more attractive to him. He opened a studio in New York in 1841 and in Philadelphia in 1846. In 1850, however, he went to Europe, working and studying in Florence and Rome, finally making the latter city his home, with occasional visits to the United States. He painted both fancy pictures and portraits, and also executed a few works in sculpture, as, for instance, a bust of General Sheridan. A portrait of himself is owned by the National Gallery of Washington. D. C.

READ, William. Portrait painter. Born in 1607 in Batcombe, England. He came over in 1635 and settled in Weymouth, Mass. He lived in Boston till 1674, and died at Norwich, Conn., in 1679. In 1641 he painted the portrait of Richard Bellingham, Governor of Massachusetts. The picture is inscribed "Govr. R. Bellingham, Effigies Delin, Boston Anno Dom, 1641. Ætatis 49, W. R." This is supposed to be the earliest known portrait painted in this country.

REAM, Carducius P. Painter. Born in Lancaster, Ohio, in 1837. He died in Chicago, Ill., in 1917. He is represented in the Chicago Art Institute.

REAM, Miss Vinnie (Mrs. Hoxie). Sculptor. She modelled a statue of "Lincoln" at the Capitol as ordered by a vote of Congress. She later studied abroad. She was born in Madison, Wisconsin, in 1847. The "Lincoln" is extraordinary work for so young a girl, and has much dignity in its bowed head.

REASER, Wilbur (Aaron). Painter. Born in Hicksville, Ohio, in 1860. Pupil of Mark Hopkins Institute in San Francisco; of Constant and Lefebvre in Paris. Member: San Francisco Art Association. Awards: Gold and silver medals, California Exposition, 1894; first Hallgarten prize, National Academy of Design, 1897. Specialty, portraits. Work: "Mother and Daughter," Carnegie Gallery, Pittsburgh; "Old Man and Sleeping Child," Art Gallery, Des Moines, Ia.; portrait of "Senator W. B. Allison," U. S. Senate Lobby, Washington; "Senator C. S. Page," the Capitol, Montpelier, Vt. *Address*, 15 Arden Place, Yonkers, N. Y.

REASON, Philip H. Engraver. This very clever engraver of portraits in stipple was a negro, educated and apprenticed to an engraver by certain members of the antislavery party in New York City. He engraved a few good portraits, but race prejudice was too strong for him and he was compelled to abandon engraving for other employment early in the fifties.

REAUGH, F. Painter. Born near Jacksonville, Ill., in 1860. Pupil of St. Louis School of Fine Arts; Julien Academy in Paris under Doucet. Member: Dallas Art Association. Work: "Driving the Herd," Dallas, Tex., Art Association. Specialty, Texas cattle and western landscape. *Address*, Oak Cliff, Tex.

REBECK, Steven. Sculptor. Born in Cleveland, Ohio, in 1891. Specialty, portraits. Work: Statue of Shakespeare, Cleveland, Ohio. *Address*, 4036 Cooper Ave., Cleveland, Ohio.

REBISSO, Louis T. Sculptor. He taught modelling for years in the Art Academy of Cincinnati. His equestrian statue of Genl. McPherson is in Washington and his Genl. Grant is in Chicago.

RECCHIA, Richard H. Sculptor. Born in Quincy, Mass., in 1885. Studied at the Boston Museum of Fine Arts School, and in Paris and Italy. Member: Copley Society. Award: Bronze medal, Panama-Pacific Exposition, San Francisco, 1915. Work: Bas-relief portrait of Gov. Curtis Guild, Boston State House; "Architecture," figure panel on Boston Museum of Fine Arts. *Address*, 5 St. Botolph Studios, Boston, Mass.

RECKLESS, Stanley L. Painter. Born in Philadelphia, Pa., in 1892. Pupil of Penna. Academy of Fine Arts; and of the Julien Academy in Paris. Member of Graphic Sketch Club, Philadelphia. Awarded Cresson Traveling Scholarship, Penna. Academy of Fine Arts, 1915–16. *Address*, Lumberville, Bucks County, Pa.

REDERUS, S. F. Painter. Born in the Netherlands in 1854. Pupil of R. Wynkoop, Bridgeport, Conn. Member: Milwaukee Art Institute; Dubuque Artists' Society. Work represented in Presbyterian Church, Nortonville, Kans. *Address*, 18 South Glen Oak Ave., Dubuque, Ia.

REDFIELD, Edward Willis. Landscape painter. Born in Philadelphia, Penna., in 1869. As a youth he studied in the classes of the Penna. Academy of Fine Arts, working hard there for five years. With the idea of becoming a portrait painter he studied in Paris under Bouguereau and Robert-Fleury, and there learned to paint in the highly finished type of work for which his teachers were famous. Following his studio work in Paris, Redfield painted landscapes and trees from nature in the forest of Fontainebleau. On his return to this country he settled down on the banks of the Delaware River in Pennsylvania, the scene of some of his finest pictures. He is a most rapid painter and his amazing feat of finishing a large canvas in a day's time is often hardly believable. The brush effects are surprising; he places lumps of color on the canvas, lifted into peaks by pulling the brush away, and yet every effect is perfectly rendered. He has been awarded the gold medal, Art Club of Philadelphia, 1896; Temple gold medal, Penna. Academy of Fine Arts, Philadelphia, 1903; 2d Hallgarten prize, National Academy, 1904; Shaw Fund prize, Society of American Artists, 1904; Corcoran bronze medal, Corcoran Gallery of Art, Washington, 1907; gold medal of honor, Penna. Academy of Fine Arts, 1907; 1st Clark prize and Corcoran gold medal, Corcoran Gallery, 1908; honorable mention, Paris Salon, 1908. Represented in permanent collections of Art Institute of Chicago; Carnegie Institute, Pittsburgh; Academy of Fine Arts, Art Club, Philadelphia; Boston Art Club; New Orleans Art Association; Telfair Academy of Fine Arts, Savannah; Corcoran Gallery, Washington, D. C.; Brooklyn Institute of Arts and Sciences; John Herron Art Institute, Indianapolis; Luxembourg, Paris; Detroit Museum of Art; Metropolitan Museum of New York; Lincoln (Nebr.) Art Association; Albright Art Gallery, Buffalo, N. Y. *Address*, Center Bridge, Bucks County, Pa.

REDFIELD, Heloise G. Miniature painter. Born in Philadelphia, Pa., in 1883. Pupil of

Penna. Academy of Fine Arts under Chase and Cecilia Beaux, and under Mme. La Farge in Paris. *Address*, 121 West 40th St., New York.

REDMAN, Henry N. Painter. Exhibited a landscape at the Penna. Academy of Fine Arts, 1926. *Address*, Boston, Mass.

REDMOND, Granville. Painter. Born at Philadelphia in 1871. Educated in California Institution for Education of the Deaf, Dumb and Blind; graduated in 1890. During this same period he studied art, and received honorable mention and the W. E. Brown gold medal for best study from life at San Francisco Art Association; entered Julien Academy, Paris, and studied under Benjamin Constant and Jean Paul Laurens. Exhibited at the Paris Salon in 1894; La. Purchase Exposition, St. Louis; 1904; silver medal, Seattle Exposition, 1909; the latter picture being acquired by the Gov. of Washington, and hung in the Capitol at Olympia. *Address*, Menlo Park, Cal.

REED, Abner. Engraver. Born in East Windsor, Conn., in 1771; died in Toledo, Ohio. Abner Reed was apprenticed to a sadler and commenced engraving by working upon the engraved metal nameplates then used on saddles. In 1803 he settled in Hartford, Conn., and regularly engaged in the business of engraving, plate printing, and sign painting. In 1811 he returned to East Windsor, and became largely interested in banknote engraving for U. S. and Canadian banks. He was one of the earliest banknote engravers in this country, having engraved the plates for the Hartford Bank of 1792. Among the apprentices in his employ at East Windsor were William Mason, later a well-known wood engraver of Philadelphia, Asaph Willard, later of New York, Oliver Pelton, Alfred Daggett, Vistus Balch, Fred Bissell, Ebenezer F. Reed and Lewis Fairchild, wood engravers, and William Phelps, a plate printer.

REED, Earl H. Etcher. Born in Geneva, Ill., in 1863. Member of Chicago Society of Artists. Represented in Library of Congress, Washington, D. C.; Chicago Art Institute; New York Public Library; Milwaukee Art Instiute. *Address*, 4758 Lake Park Ave., Chicago.

REED, Helen. Boston painter, who began her professional career in that city by drawing portraits in crayon. Later she went to Florence where she studied sculpture under Preston Powers, sending to America bas-reliefs in marble which have been exhibited at the Boston Art Club and in New York.

REEVS, George M. Portrait painter. Born in Yonkers, N. Y., in 1864. Pupil of Constant, Laurens and Gerome in Paris. *Address*, 35 West 14th St., New York, N. Y.

REGESTER, Charlotte. Painter. Born in Baltimore in 1883. Pupil of Rose Clark, W. M. Chase, Buffalo Art Students' League, and of the New York Art Students' League. Member: National Association of Women Painters and Sculptors; Buffalo Artists' Society. *Address*, 439 West 23d St., Buffalo, N. Y.

REHN, Frank Knox Morton. Marine painter. Born in Philadelphia in 1848; died in Magnolia, Massachusetts, in 1914. Pupil of Pennsylvania Academy of the Fine Arts, Philadelphia. Elected Associate Member of the National Academy, 1899; National Academy, 1908; Society of American Artists, 1903; American Water Color Society; New York Water Color Club. Represented by "In the Glittering Moonlight" at the Corcoran Gallery.

REICH, Jacques. Painter and etcher. Born in Hungary, 1852; died in 1923. Studied art in Budapest; came to United States, 1873; continued studies at National Academy of Design, New York, Penna. Academy of Fine Arts, Philadelphia, and in Paris. Located in New York in 1885. Made most of pen portraits for Scribner's Cyclopaedia of Painters and Paintings, and for Appleton's Cyclopaedia of American Biography; has etched on copper a series of portraits of American and English authors; engaged in etching and publishing a series of etched portraits of famous Americans, the following of which have already appeared: Washington, Jefferson, Alexander Hamilton, Benjamin Franklin, Daniel Webster, Abraham Lincoln, Roosevelt, Cleveland, McKinley, Paul Jones, Andrew Carnegie, George William Curtis, Andrew Jackson, U. S. Grant, James Madison, John Marshall, President Taft, Gen. Robert E. Lee, Dr. Andrew D. White, James Abbott McNeill Whistler, Woodrow Wilson, etc.; among many private plates etched are portraits of Whitelaw Reid, E. H. Harriman, H. H. Rogers, John W. Mackay, Gov. Winthrop, Mark Hanna, Charles B. Alexander, Nelson Wilmarth Aldrich and Gen. Thomas Hamlin Hubbard.

REICH, John. Engraver. In 1806 John Reich was a die-sinker of considerable merit, and he was frequently employed by Robert Scot, engraver of the United States Mint in Philadelphia, to prepare the dies for National coin. He engraved the dies for several fine medals, including Washington, after Stuart; Franklin, from the Houdon bust; a Peace medal of 1783, and a Tripoli medal presented to Com. Edward Preble in 1806. John Reich was one of the founders of the Society of Artists, organized in Philadelphia in 1810, and is entered on the list of Fellows of the Society as "die-sinker at the United States Mint."

REICHE, F. This German engraver was executing crude line work in Philadelphia in 1795. He was engraving portraits on wood in 1800.

REICHMANN, (Mrs.) Josephine Lemos. Painter. Born in Louisville, Ky., in 1864. Pupil of Art Institute of Chicago; Art Students' League of New York; C. W. Hawthorne. Member: Chicago Society of Artists, and of the Chicago Art Club. *Address,* 1540 East 57th St., Chicago, Ill.

REID, Albert Turner. Illustrator. Born in Concordia, Kans., in 1873. Pupil of New York School of Art and of the Art Students' League of New York. Member: Authors', Artists' and Dramatists' League, New York. Work: Illustrations in magazines and books; "The Leavenworth Post." Owner and publisher of "The Albert T. Reid Cartoon Syndicate." *Address,* 452 Fifth Ave., New York, N. Y.

REID, Jean Arnot. Miniature painter. Born in Brooklyn, N. Y., in 1882. Pupil of Brandegee; American School of Miniature Painting; Art Students' League of New York. Member: National Association of Women Painters and Sculptors; American Society of Miniature Painters. *Address,* Care of Bankers' Trust Co., 57th St., New York, N. Y.

REID, M. C. W. Painter. Born in New York City. Pupil of J. Alden Weir, Douglas Volk, G. Wharton Edwards and F. Edwin Elwell. Member: National Academy of Women Painters and Sculptors; New York Municipal Artists' Society; College Artists' Association. Professor of Art, Hunter College, New York City. *Address,* Hunter College, 68th St., New York, N. Y.

REID, Robert. Painter. Born in Stockbridge, Mass., in 1862. Studied at Museum of Fine Arts, Boston, 1880 (for three years assistant instructor in same); Art Students' League, New York, 1885–89; Academie Julien, under Boulanger and Lefebvre. Exhibited annually in the Salon, and in the Paris Exposition, 1889; returned to New York, 1889; he was one of the New York artists who painted frescoes of the domes of the Liberal Arts Building, Chicago Exposition; formerly instructor in painting, Art Students' League and Cooper Institute. Awarded Clarke prize, 1897; 1st Hallgarten prize, 1898, National Academy of Design; gold and silver medals, Paris Exposition, 1900. He has painted mural decorations for many public and private buildings including the Library of Congress, Washington, D. C.; Appellate Court House, New York; Mass. State House, Boston; Paulist Fathers Church, New York; Fine Arts Palace, San Francisco. Represented in Metropolitan Museum of Art; Corcoran Gallery, and National Gallery of Washington, D. C.; museums of Minneapolis, Omaha, Cincinnati, Indianapolis, Brooklyn; Albright Gallery, Buffalo; Nebraska Art Association, Lincoln, Nebr.; Art Association, Richmond, Ind.; etc. National Academy, 1906; member of National Institute of

Arts and Letters, and "Ten American Painters." *Address,* Colorado Springs, Colo.

REIFFEL, Charles. Landscape painter. Born in Indianapolis, Ind. Self-taught. Member: Allied Artists' Association; Contemporary International Society Art League; Conn. Society of Artists; Conn. Academy of Fine Arts; Buffalo Society of Artists. Award: Fellowship prize, Buffalo Society of Artists, 1908; Harris silver medal, Art Institute of Chicago, 1917; honorable mention, Conn. Academy of Fine Arts, 1920. Work: "Railway Yards—Winter Evening," Corcoran Art Gallery, Washington, D. C. *Address,* Belden Hill Road, Wilton, Conn.

REINAGLE, Hugh. Landscape, genre and scene-painter. He was the son of Frank Reinagle, the lessee of the Chestnut St. Theater, Philadelphia. He was born in Philadelphia in 1790, and died in 1834, in New Orleans, La. Reinagle studied scene-painting with John J. Holland; he also painted landscapes, among which are "A View of the City of New York," "Niagara Falls," and several views on the Hudson River, N. Y. He worked in both water colors and oils.

REINDEL, William George. Painter and etcher. Born in Fraser, Macomb County, Mich., in 1871. Studied in America and Europe, but largely self-taught. Member: Cleveland Society of Artists; Chicago Society of Artists; Chicago Society of Etchers. Represented in New York Public Library. *Address,* Euclid, Ohio.

REINHART, Benjamin Franklin. Painter. Born in Penna. in 1829. He studied in the National Academy, N. Y. He was elected an Associate Member in 1871. Among his works, many of which have been engraved, are "Cleopatra," "Evangeline," "Young Franklin and Sir William Keith," and "Washington Receiving the News of Arnold's Treason." He died in 1885.

REINHART, Charles Stanley. Painter. Born in Pittsburgh, Penna., in 1844; died in 1896. Genre painter and illustrator. Studied in Paris, and at the Royal Academy, Munich, under Professors Streyhuber and Otto. Awards: Second medal, Paris Exposition, 1889; Temple gold medal, Pennsylvania Academy of the Fine Arts, 1888. Member of Art Clubs in Munich, Pittsburgh and New York. Represented at Corcoran Art Gallery, Washington, D. C.

REINHART, Stewart. Painter, sculptor and etcher. Born in Baltimore in 1897. Pupil of Edward Berge and Maxwell Miller. *Address,* 45 Washington Square, New York, N. Y.

REINHART, William Henry. Sculptor. Born in Maryland in 1825; died in Rome, Italy, in 1874. He worked with a stone cutter and studied drawing in Baltimore. In 1855 he went to Italy to study and while there executed the bas-reliefs of ''Night'' and ''Morning.'' In 1857 he opened his studio in Baltimore. His best known statues are ''Clytie'' owned by the Peabody Institute, and ''Rebecca'' in the Corcoran Art Gallery.

REISS, F. Winold. Painter, illustrator and etcher. Born in Germany. Pupil of Franz Von Stuck; Royal Academy, Munich. Member: Society of Independent Artists. Work: Appoll's Theater; South Sea Island Ballroom of Hotel Sherman, Chicago; Restaurant Crillon, Restaurant Élysée, New York City. *Address,* 4 Christopher St., New York, N. Y.

RELYEA, Charles M. Illustrator and painter. Born in Albany, N. Y., in 1863. Pupil of Penna. Academy of Fine Arts under Thomas Eakins; under F. V. Du Mond in New York. Member of Allied Artists' Association, and Players' Club, N. Y. *Address,* 2447 Morris Ave., New York, N. Y.

REMICK, Christian. Painter. An early Boston artist, born in 1726, who painted views of Boston Harbor, and of the Boston Commons at the time of the Revolution.

REMINGTON, Frederic. Sculptor, painter, etcher and illustrator. Born in Canton, N. Y., in 1861; died in Ridgefield, Conn., in 1909. Studied one year at the Yale Art School, but otherwise was self-taught. Owing to ill health he went West and, after clerking in a general store, became a cowboy and later stockman on a ranch. It was from the knowledge gained in these connections and from his own experiences that sprang the inspiration for his remarkably vivid and faithful portrayal of the life on the western plains and in the mining camps, for which he became so justly renowned. His first commission, executed in the early eighties, was an Indian picture based on ''Geronimo's Campaign.'' He produced a large number of oil paintings and about fifteen bronzes, and was the author of several books. For some years he occupied a large studio at New Rochelle, N. Y., but removed to Ridgefield about six months before his death. He received a silver medal for sculpture at the Paris Exposition in 1889; he was an Associate Member of the National Academy of Design, and a member of the National Institute of Arts and Letters.

RENAULT, J. F. Painter. The ''Surrender of Cornwallis,'' engraved by Tanner, Vallance, Kearny & Co., after a drawing by J. F. Renault, published in 1824 was sold to subscribers. It might be interesting to note that the original painting of the ''Surrender of Cornwallis'' by J. F. Renault was exhibited by him throughout the United States previous to 1824. In a prospectus published by Benjamin Tanner in the *New England Palladium & Commercial Advertiser* for February 10, 1824, we are told that ''The Engraving is exe-

cuted by Tanner, Vallance, Kearny & Co. from an Original Drawing by J. F. Renault.''

RENCH, Miss Polly. Miniature painter. Sister of Mrs. James Claypole, of Philadelphia. Nothing is known of her work, except that she was painting miniatures in Philadelphia, and in a letter written by Charles Willson Peale to his son Rembrandt in 1812, he notes her work (letter published in Sartain's ''Reminiscences'').

RENEZETTI, Aurelius. Sculptor. Executed a portrait bust of the late N. W. Ayer. *Address,* 226 Ionic St., Philadelphia, Pa.

RESLER, George Earl. Etcher. Member: Chicago Society of Etchers. Award: First prize, 1913, and second prize, 1914, Minnesota State Art Commission; bronze medal for etchings, St. Paul Institute, 1918. *Address,* 1726 Juliet St., St. Paul, Minn.

RETTIG, John. Painter. Born in Cincinnati. Pupil of Cincinnati Art School, Duveneck and Potthast; Collin, Courtois, and Prinet in Paris. Member: Cincinnati Art Club; Society of Independent Artists. *Address,* 2227 Kemper Lane, Walnut Hills, Cincinnati, Ohio.

RETZCH, Frederick August Moritz. Painter, illustrator and etcher. Born in Dresden in 1799; he died at New Dresden, N. Y., in 1857. In 1836 he was elected an honorary member of the National Academy of Design. His reputation rests upon his designs and beautiful outline etchings illustrating the works of Goethe, Schiller, etc. These prints and his ''Game of Chess'' attracted much attention in New York at the time of their issue.

REUTERDAHL, Henry. Naval painter. Born at Malmo, Sweden, in 1871. Served as correspondent during Spanish-American War; also during the first part of the European War, 1914. Contributor to leading magazines. He was attached to the Battleship Minnesota during the fleet's cruise around South America, and during the cruise to the Mediterranean, 1913. He was present during the Vera Cruz campaign, 1914. Represented in permanent collection at the United States Naval Academy, by paintings of this cruise, presented to the navy by George von L. Meyer, Sec. of Navy; also in the National Museum, Washington; Naval War Collection, Newport; Toledo Museum. Silver medal for painting, Panama-Pacific Exposition, 1915. Painted panels for steam yachts ''Noma,'' ''Vincent Astor, owner; ''Viking,'' G. F. Baker, Jr.; for schooner ''Vagrant,'' Harold S. Vanderbilt, owner. Formerly instructor of Art Students' League. Member: Architectural League; Artists' Fund Society of New York; Associate Member of United States Naval Institute; Society of Naval Architects and Marine Engravers. Club: New York Yacht. *Address,* 800 Boulevard, Weehawken, N. J.

REVERE, Paul. Engraver. Born in Boston, Mass., in 1735; died there in 1818. The father of Paul Revere came from the Island of Guernsey and established himself in Boston as a goldsmith. In this business the son was trained in Boston, and he there learned to engrave upon silver-plate.

Aside from some possible book-plates, his best known engraved plates may be noted as follows: a "Portrait of Jonathan Mahew"; "The Repeal of the Stamp Act (1766)"; the caricature of the seventeen Rescinders, and "The Landing of the British Troops" (1768); also his famous "Boston Massacre" of 1770. For the *Royal American Magazine* of 1774–75, Revere engraved a number of plates. His work is exceedingly crude in execution and is only valuable for its historical interest. See "Paul Revere and His Engraving," by William Loring Andrews.

REYNOLDS, Frederick T. Mezzotint engraver, of English birth and. training, who came to this country and settled in New York. See "Frederick Reynolds, An American Master of Mezzotint" by W. H. Nelson. See Vol. 1, "The Print Connoisseur" (List of Plates). *Address,* 154 East 38th St., New York City.

REYNOLDS, Thomas. In the *New York Daily Advertiser,* 1786, Thomas Reynolds advertises that he has established a "seal manufactory in Philadelphia; where he engraves on stone arms, crests and cyphers; searches out family arms, descents, etc.; and he likewise cuts on brass all sorts of state and public seals."

REYNOLDS, Wellington Jarard. Painter. Born in Chicago in 1866. Student of Art Institute of Chicago; Royal Academy of Munich, Bavaria; University of Munich; Julien Academy, Paris. Represented in University of Chicago; Piedmont Gallery and Golden Gate Park Museum, San Francisco; North End Woman's Club, Fritz von Frantzius' Gallery, Chicago. Instructor at Art Institute of Chicago. Member of Chicago Society of Artists. *Address,* 5 E. Ontario St., Chicago.

RHEAD, Louis John. Painter. Born in Etruria, England, in 1857. Came to United States in 1883. Painter in oil and water colors, exhibiting in America and European galleries. Gold medal, Boston, 1895, for artistic posters; gold medal, St. Louis Exposition, 1904. *Address,* 217 Ocean Ave., Brooklyn, N. Y.

RHEAD, Lois W. Sculptor, who exhibited at the National Association of Women Painters and Sculptors, New York, 1924. *Address,* Zanesville, Ohio.

RHETT, Hannah Mc C. Painter. Born in Columbia, S. C., in 1871. Pupil of Art Students' League of New York and of Laurens in Paris. *Address,* 7 Lamball St., Charleston, S. C.

RHIND, J. Massey. Sculptor. Born in Edinburgh, Scotland, in 1858. Educated at Scotch Academy and Royal Academy, London, and also under Dalau in Paris. Came to the United States in 1889, and established himself as a sculptor in New York. Member: Architectural League; National Sculpture Society; Municipal Art Society. *Address,* 208 E. 20th St., New York.

RIBCOWSKY, Dey De. Marine painter. Born in Bulgaria in 1880. Studied in Paris. *Address,* 233 South Broadway, Los Angeles, Calif.

RICCI, Ulysses A. Sculptor, who exhibited at the Penna. Academy of Fine Arts portrait study of "Miss Audrey Munson" (1915). *Address,* 335 East 46th St., New York, N. Y.

RICCIARDI, Caesare. Painter. Born in Italy in 1892. Pupil of Academy of Fine Arts, Philadelphia. *Address,* Art Alliance, 1823 Walnut St., Philadelphia.

RICE, E. A. This portrait engraver in mezzotint was working for Baltimore engravers about 1845.

RICE, James R. Engraver. Born in Syracuse, N. Y., in 1824. He studied engraving under his brother W. W. Rice, of Rawdon, Wright, Hatch & Co., of New York. He removed to Philadelphia in 1851, and as late as 1876 was engraving portraits there in connection with J. Earle.

RICE, W. W. Engraver of portraits and subject plates, who was a member of the firm of Rawdon, Wright, Hatch & Co., of New York in 1846. He was engraving over his own name as late as 1860.

RICE, William Clarke. Painter and sculptor. Born in Brooklyn, N. Y., in 1875. Pupil of George de F. Brush. Has also painted mural decorations. *Address,* 145 East 23d St., New York.

RICE, William Morton Jackson. Portrait painter. Born in Brooklyn in 1854. Studied painting in Paris under Carolus-Duran, in 1881–84. Elected an Associate Member of the National Academy in 1900. He died in 1922.

RICE, William S. Painter and illustrator. Born in 1873. Pupil of Philadelphia School of Industrial Art, and of the Drexel Institute, Philadelphia. Member: California Society of Etchers; California Miniature Painters; San Francisco Artists' Association; Oakland Artists' Association. Work: "The Oakland Estuary," California State Library; "Windswept," California School of Arts and Crafts. Specialty, wood block prints and landscape painting in oils and water colors. *Address,* 2083 Rosedale Ave., Oakland, California.

RICE-MEYROWITZ, Jenny D. Painter. Born in Arkansas. Student of St. Louis School of Fine Arts. She has painted a number of portraits. *Address*, 140 West 57th St., New York.

RICH, John H. Painter. Born in Boston, Mass., in 1876. Pupil of Art Students' League of New York; School of Boston Museum of Fine Arts. Member of California Art Club. Awarded Paige traveling scholarship from School of Boston Museum of Fine Arts, 1905–07. *Address*, 4823 Sixth Ave., Los Angeles, Calif.

RICHARDS, Ella E. Painter. Born in Virginia. Studied in Baltimore and New York, and with Lefebvre, Robert-Fleury and Collin in Paris. Awards: Medal, Omaha Exposition, 1899; bronze medal, Charleston Exposition, 1902. Work represented in "The American Society of Civil Engineers," New York; Bank of Montclair, N. J.; Norfolk National Bank, and Citizens' Bank of Norfolk, Va. *Address*, 1009 Carnegie Hall, New York, N. Y.

RICHARDS, F. De Berg. Painter and etcher, who lived for years in Philadelphia. He died there in 1903.

RICHARDS, Frederick Thompson. Painter. Born in Philadelphia in 1864. Pupil of the Penna. Academy of Fine Arts, Thomas Eakins, Edmund B. Bensell, and of the Art Students' League, New York. Exhibited at the Paris Exposition, 1900. On staff of *Life* since 1889, also *Collier's Weekly;* cartoonist for *New York Herald,* 1901–02; also for *New York Times, New York Evening Mail;* Philadelphia *Press* and the Philadelphia *North American.* Author: "The Royal Game of Golf" (series of color prints); "Color Prints from Dickens" (portfolio); and "The Blot Book." *Address*, 110 West 48th St., New York, N. Y.

RICHARDS, George M. Painter and illustrator. Born in Darien, Conn., in 1880. Pupil of Douglas John Connah, Robert Henri and Edward Penfield. Member of Whitney Studio Club. Illustrator for *Century, Collier's, Adventure, McCall's* (magazines). *Address*, 452 Fifth Ave., New York.

RICHARDS, Harriet R. Painter and illustrator. Born in Hartford, Conn. Pupil of Yale School of Fine Arts; of Frank Benson in Boston; Howard Pyle in Wilmington, Del. Member: Paint and Clay Club of New Haven. Illustrated holiday editions of books by Louisa Alcott and W. D. Howells, etc. *Address*, 227 Edwards St., New Haven, Conn.

RICHARDS, Lee Greene. Painter, sculptor and illustrator. Born in Salt Lake City in 1878. Pupil of J. T. Harwood and of Laurens and Bonnat. Member: Salon d'Automne;

Utah Society of Artists. Award: Honorable mention, Paris Salon, 1904. *Address*, 125 South 2d East, Salt Lake City, Utah.

RICHARDS, Lucy Currier (Mrs. F. P. Wilson). Sculptor. Born in Lawrence, Mass. Pupil of Boston Museum School; Kops in Dresden; Eustritz in Berlin; Julien Academy in Paris. Member: Copley Society; National Association of Women Painters and Sculptors. *Address*, 30 East 57th St., New York, N. Y.

RICHARDS, Myra R. Sculptor and painter. Born in Indianapolis in 1882. Pupil of Herron Art Institute under Otis Adams, Rudolph Schwartz and Geo. Julian Zolnay. Member of Indianapolis Sculpture Society. *Address*, 1446 North Alabama St., Indianapolis, Ind.

RICHARDS, Oren C. Painter. Born in South Boston in 1842. In 1860 he studied under George Innes at Medford, Mass. He has painted scenery at nearly all the Boston theaters, and easel-pictures of still-life in oils.

RICHARDS, T. Addison. Painter. Born in England in 1820. He came to America, his early years being passed in Georgia and the Carolinas. He painted landscapes and views of Lake George and the White Mountains. He became Secretary of the National Academy of Design and had his studio in New York. He also was well known as an author and illustrator of books on art and travel. He died at Annapolis, Md., in 1900.

RICHARDS, William Trost. Marine painter. Born in Philadelphia, Penna., in 1833; died in Newport, R. I., in 1905. Pupil of Paul Weber; later studied in Florence, Rome and Paris. Awards: Medal, Centennial Exposition, Philadelphia, 1876; Temple medal, Pennsylvania Academy of the Fine Arts, 1885; bronze medal, Paris Exposition, 1889. Member: American Water Color Society; honorary member, National Academy of Design. Represented by "On the Coast of New Jersey," painted to order for the Corcoran Art Gallery, 1883; also "On the Coast of New England," painted in 1894. See "Life of William T. Richards," by Harrison S. Morris, Philadelphia, 1912.

RICHARDSON, Andrew. This man is noted in Tuckerman's "Artist Life" as painting landscapes about 1860. The National Academy of Design elected Andrew Richardson a member in 1833. He died in 1876.

RICHARDSON, Catharine P. Portrait painter, who exhibited a portrait of Henry Nickerson, in the exhibition of the National Academy of Design, 1924. *Address*, Brookline, Mass.

RICHARDSON, Clara Virginia. Painter and etcher. Born in Philadelphia in 1855. Pupil of Ferris, Moran and Snell. Member of Plastic Club; Philadelphia Art Alliance; Alumnae of the Philadelphia School of Design for Women. *Address*, 1503 Master St., Philadelphia.

RICHARDSON, Francis Henry. Painter. Born in Boston in 1859. Pupil of William M. Hunt, Boston; Academie Julien, Paris, under Boulanger, Lefebvre, Laurens and Benjamin Constant. Exhibited at the Paris Salon, also at Munich, Berlin, London, Venice, etc.; also in all the principal exhibitions in America; represented in collections of the Boston Art Club; Lasell Seminary; Salmagundi Club, and in the Town of Braintree, Mass.; also in numerous private collections. Devotes attention largely to portrait work. Honorable mention, Paris Salon, 1899; medal, American Art Society, Philadelphia. *Address*, 110 Tremont St., Boston.

RICHARDSON, Frederick. Painter. Born in Chicago in 1862. Educated in St. Louis; received art education at St. Louis School of Fine Arts, and Academie Julien, Paris. Artist on staff of Chicago *Daily News*. Instructor at Art Institute of Chicago; in New York since 1903; illustrator for various magazines. Exhibited paintings in Paris Salon in 1889. Published ''Book of Drawings by Frederick Richardson.'' Member of American Federation of Arts; Society of Illustrators. *Address*, 7 West 43d St., New York City.

RICHARDSON, Helen Ely. Sculptor, who exhibited at the Penna. Academy of the Fine Arts, Philadelphia, 1924. *Address*, 213 Alexandrine St., Detroit, Mich.

RICHARDSON, Margaret F. Painter. Born in Winnetka, Ill. Pupil of De Camp, Tarbell and Major. Awards: Harris bronze medal, Art Institute of Chicago, 1911; Maynard portrait prize, National Academy of Design, 1913. Represented in the Pennsylvania Academy of the Fine Arts. *Address*, Fenway Studios, Boston, Mass.

RICHARDSON, Marion. Painter and etcher. Born in Brooklyn, N. Y., in 1877. Pupil of Chase, Du Mond and Senseney. Member of California Miniature Painters. *Address*, 140 West 57th St., New York, N. Y.

RICHARDSON, Mary N. Portrait painter. Born at Mt. Vernon, Me., in 1859. Pupil of Boston Museum School and of the Colarossi Academy, Paris. Represented by portrait of Prof. Charles C. Hutchins, at the Walker Art Gallery, Bowdoin College, Brunswick, Me. *Address*, 309 Fenway Studios, Boston, Mass.

RICHARDSON, S. This man was a bookplate engraver apparently working about 1795, but with no indication of locality. The one known example of his work represents a woman with left hand on an anchor, with ships in the distance. In the base is a blank tablet surmounted by an urn. On the tablet is written in ink ''I. H. Swale, 1795.'' The plate is signed ''S. Richardson Sculpsit.''

RICHARDSON, Theodore F. Landscape painter. Born in Readfield, Me., in 1855. For years he made a specialty of Alaskan scenery. He died in 1914.

RICHERT, Charles H. Painter, who exhibited water colors at the Penna. Academy of the Fine Arts, Philadelphia, 1925. *Address*, Arlington Heights, Mass.

RICHMOND, Agnes M. Painter. Born in Alton, Illinois. Member: Allied Artists of America; National Association of Women Painters and Sculptors; Society of Independent Artists, New York. Awarded Watrous prize, National Association of Women Painters and Sculptors, New York, 1911. *Address*, 439 East 52d St., New York City.

RICHTER, Wilmer S. Illustrator. Born in Philadelphia in 1891. Pupil of Industrial Art School, Philadelphia. *Address*, 608 Denckla Building, Philadelphia.

RICKETSON, Walton. Sculptor. Born in New Bedford, Mass., in 1839. Engaged as sculptor since 1870. Among his notable works are: Portrait busts of A. B. Alcott, Louisa May Alcott, Henry D. Thoreau, George William Curtis, R. W. Emerson: also intaglios, bas-reliefs; he was the designer of the Gesnold memorial tower on the Island of Cuttyhunk, Mass., in 1902. *Address*, 10 Anthony St., New Bedford, Mass.

RIDDELL, William W. Painter. Born in Chicago in 1877. Pupil of Chicago Art Institute and of Laurens in Paris. *Address*, 3211 West 62d St., Chicago, Ill.

RIDER, Alexander. Historical and miniature painter, who flourished 1810–25 in Philadelphia. Rider came to the United States with his countryman Krimmel from Germany, and in 1811 he is listed as a ''Fancy Painter,'' and in 1812 as a ''Miniature Painter.'' There was a Rider in Charleston, S. C., in 1819 but it is not certain that he was the same man.

RIDGWAY, W. This excellent engraver of historical subjects in line was working in New York in connection with Wm. Wellstood, and was engraving for New York publishers at a much later date.

RIES, Gerta. Sculptor, who exhibited a portrait of John Cotton Dana at the Annual Exhibition of the National Academy of Design, 1925. *Address,* 130 Henry St., Brooklyn, N. Y.

RIGBY, Mrs. F. G. Portrait painter, who died in New York. Her husband, also a portrait painter, is deceased.

RIGGS, Robert. Painter, who exhibited water colors at the Penna. Academy of Fine Arts, Philadelphia, 1925. *Address,* 218 Walnut St., Philadelphia, Pa.

RILEY. This name, as "Riley, Engraver," is signed to poorly engraved music and words published by J. & M. Paff, City Hotel, Broadway, New York. The date is apparently about 1800.

RILEY, Mary G. Painter, who exhibited at the Penna. Academy of Fine Arts, Philadelphia, in 1924. *Address,* 2141 Le Roy Place, Washington, D. C.

RIMMER, William. Sculptor and painter. Born in England in 1816; he died in South Milford, Mass., in 1879. He came to this country in 1818, and in 1860 modelled the "Falling Gladiator" now in the Boston Museum of Fine Arts. He painted a number of other pictures besides producing numerous works of sculpture. It is however as a teacher that Dr. Rimmer is best known.

RINEHART, William Henry. Sculptor. Born in Frederick, Md., in 1825. He was apprenticed to a stone-cutter in Baltimore in 1855, then went to Italy, studying for three years in Florence. He has executed many portrait busts; his statue of Chief Justice Taney, ordered by the State of Maryland, was unveiled at Annapolis in 1872.

RINGIUS, Carl. Painter. Born in Sweden in 1879. Pupil of Chas. N. Flagg and of Robert B. Brandegee. *Address,* 62 Vernon St., Hartford, Conn.

RIPLEY, Lucy P. (Mrs.). Sculptor. Born in Minnesota. She studied under Saint Gaudens, French and Rodin. Work: Bronze statue "The Inner Voice." *Address,* 36 West 12th St., New York.

RISQUE, Caroline E. Sculptor. Born in St. Louis, Mo., in 1886. Studied at St. Louis School of Fine Arts, and in Paris. Specialty, small bronzes. *Address,* 7623 Henderson Road, Clayton, Mo.

RISWOLD, Gilbert P. Sculptor. Born in Sioux Falls, S. D., in 1881. Pupil of Lorado Taft and of Charles Milligan. Work: "Statue of Stephen A. Douglass," Springfield, Ill.; "Mormon Pioneer Monument," Salt Lake City, Utah. *Address,* 1038 Fine Arts Building, 410 South Michigan Ave., Chicago, Ill.

RITCHIE, Alexander Hay. Born in Glasgow, Scotland, in 1822; died in 1895 in Brooklyn, N. Y. Ritchie studied drawing in Edinburgh under Sir Wm. Allan, and came to New York in 1841. He apparently learned to engrave after he reached this country; but he ultimately established an extensive general engraving business in New York, his earlier prints being issued about 1847. Ritchie himself was a very clever engraver of portraits in mezzotint, and it is claimed that he finished every plate that went out of his establishment. He also painted in oils, and began exhibiting at the Academy in 1848, and was an Associate Member in 1863, and an Academician of the National Academy of Design in 1871.

RITMAN, Louis. Painter. Born in Chicago, Ill. Honors and awards: Silver medal, Panama-Pacific International Exposition, San Francisco, 1915. Represented by "The Sunlit Window." *Address,* 1826 South Milliard Ave., Chicago, Ill.

RITSCHEL, William. Marine painter. Born in Nuremberg, Germany, in 1864. Pupil of F. Kaulbach and C. Raupp in Munich; he came to United States in 1895. Member: Associate Member of the National Academy, 1910; National Academy, 1914; New York Water Color Club; Artists' Fund Society; National Art Club. Work: "Rocks and Breakers," Pennsylvania Academy of the Fine Arts; "Across the Plains, Arizona," Ft. Worth (Tex.) Museum; "Desert Wanderers," Chicago Art Institute; "Fog and Breakers," Detroit Art Club; "Rockbound Coast," City Art Museum, St. Louis; "Evening Tide, California," Smithsonian Institution, Washington, D. C. *Address,* 58 West 57th St., New York, N. Y.

RITTASE, Roger M. Painter, who exhibited "Summer Morning" at the Penna. Academy of the Fine Arts, Philadelphia, 1924. *Address,* 225 South Sydenham St., Phila.

RITTENBERG, Henry R. Painter. Born in Libau, Russia, in 1879. Pupil of W. M. Chase at Penna. Academy of Fine Arts; of Ludwig Heterich in Munich. Member: Associate Member of the National Academy; Fellowship, Penna. Academy of Fine Arts; Phila. Art Club; National Art Club. Awards: Honorable mention, Art Club of Phila., 1906; Maynard portrait prize, National Academy of Design, 1920. Instructor at Art Students' League of New York. *Address,* 222 West 59th St., New York, N. Y.

RIX, Julian. Painter. Born in Peacham, Vt., in 1850; died in New York in 1903. Landscape painter. Self-taught. Commenced painting at the age of twenty-two, as a sign and decorative painter in San Francisco; afterward came East and settled in New York. Represented by "Pompton Plains, New Jersey," painted in 1898, at the Corcoran Gallery.

ROBB, Elizabeth B. Painter. Member: Pittsburgh Artists' Association. A w a r d s : Third prize, Artists' Association of Pittsburgh, 1914; first prize, Artists' Association of Pittsburgh, 1915. *Address*, 24 Herron Ave., Emsworth, Pa.

ROBBINS, Ellen. Painter in water colors, and pupil of the New England School of Design. Was born in 1828 and died in 1905. She is spoken of by Tuckerman in his "American Artist Life" as receiving many orders for exquisite water color paintings of flowers and autumn leaves.

ROBBINS, Frederick. Painter and etcher. Born in Oak Park, Ill., in 1893. Pupil of Carl N. Werntz; Spencer Mackey; Lee Randolph. Member: California Miniature Painters; California Society of Etchers. *Address*, 2319 Lombard St., San Francisco, Calif.

ROBBINS, Horace Wolcott. Born in Mobile, Ala., in 1842. He was elected an Associate Member of the National Academy in 1864, and an Academician in 1878, and in 1882 became recording secretary. He has worked both in oil and water colors, his pictures being chiefly landscapes of mountain and lake scenery. Among his works are "New England Elms," "Lake Katahdin, Maine," and Views of Jamaica. In 1865 he visited the West Indies with Frederick E. Church. He died in 1903.

ROBBINS, John Williams. Painter and etcher. Born in Windham, Conn., in 1856. Studied in Boston Normal Art School under Emil Carlsen; in life class under P. F. Vinton; water color under T. O. Langerfeldt; at Art Students' League of New York, under Brush and Dewing. Work represented in New York Public Library. *Address*, Farmington, Conn.

ROBERTS. Engraver. Some rather poor line book illustrations published in New York in 1841 are thus signed.

ROBERTS, Alice Mumford (Mrs. Robert Stewart Culin). Painter. Born in Philadelphia in 1875. Pupil of Joseph De Camp, Carl Newman and Robert Henri. Member: Fellowship, Penna. Academy of Fine Arts. Awards: Mary Smith prize, Penna. Academy of Fine Arts, 1906. *Address*, 296 Sterling Place, Brooklyn, New York, N. Y.

ROBERTS, B. Portrait painter and engraver, who was working in Charleston, S. C., in 1735. His advertisement appears in the *South Carolina Gazette* of May, 1735.

ROBERTS, Blanche G. Sculptor, who exhibited "Beatrice" at Penna. Academy of Fine Arts in Philadelphia, 1915. *Address*, 284 Reservoir Place, Bronx, New York.

ROBERTS, Elizabeth W. Painter. Born in Philadelphia, Pa., in 1871. Pupil of Elizabeth Bonsall and of H. R. Poore in Philadelphia; of Bouguereau, Robert-Fleury, Lefebvre and Merson in Paris. Member: Penna. Academy of Fine Arts. Awards: Mary Smith prize, Penna. Academy of Fine Arts, 1889; honorable mention, Paris Salon, 1892. Work: "The Boy with the Violin," Pennsylvania Academy, Philadelphia; "The Madonnas of 'Marks," Asilo Giovanni in Bragora, Venice, Italy; "Reflections," Public Library, Concord, Mass.; "Concord March," Fenway Court, Boston. *Address*, Concord, Mass.

ROBERTS, Howard. Sculptor. Born in Philadelphia in 1843. He studied art at the Penna. Academy of the Fine Arts. Modelled statuettes of Hawthorne's "Scarlet Letter," "Hypathia" and "Lucille," and numerous portrait busts. His statue of Robert Fulton is in the Capitol in Washington, D. C. He died in Paris in 1900.

ROBERTS, John. Painter and engraver. Born in Scotland in 1768; died in New York in 1803. He came to New York in 1793, says Wm. Dunlap. Roberts was engraving views, script, etc., in New York in 1796, and his name as an engraver appears in the directories of 1802–03. Dunlap describes him as a sort of universal genius, ready to do anything, but erratic and incapable of turning his advantages to personal account. A small mezzotint portrait by him, of Washington, exists, which is extremely rich in effect and shows fine execution. Dunlap says this was engraved by Roberts in New York, in 1799, from a miniature portrait by Benjamin Trott. Owing to some misunderstanding between the painter and the engraver Roberts deliberately destroyed the copperplate and a few proof impressions alone remain. He painted miniatures, drew portraits in crayon, and was a musician of no mean skill; but he abused his gifts, and intemperance ended his life.

ROBERTS, Mrs. Violet K. Painter and illustrator. Born in "The Dalles," Ore., in 1880. Pupil of Benson, Beck, Moscheowitz, Prellwitz. Member: Alumni, Pratt Institute. *Address*, 417 Columbia Rd., Washington, D. C.

ROBERTSON. Engraver. A large and well-engraved frontispiece, apparently intended for an edition of Cook's Voyages, of about 1815, is signed "Robertson sc." While this plate bears some indication of American origin, it may be English.

ROBERTSON, A l e x a n d e r. Miniature painter. Born in 1768. He also worked in water colors, chiefly in landscape. Like his brother Archibald he was well known as a teacher. He died in 1841.

ROBERTSON, Archibald. Painter, designer and etcher. Born in Monymusk, near Aberdeen, Scotland, in 1765; died in New York City in 1835. He studied art in Edinburgh and London from 1782 to 1791. In the latter year he came to the United States, bringing with him from his patron, the Earl of Buchan, and for presentation to General Washington, a box made of the oak that sheltered Sir William Wallace after the battle of Falkirk. At the request of the Earl of Buchan, Washington sat for his portrait to Robertson. From 1792 to 1821 he followed his profession in New York as a painter, largely in water colors, and was a teacher of drawing. He designed for engravers and the early lithographers of New York, and drew a number of large views of New York, which were engraved. A. Robertson was one of the founders and a director of the American Academy of Art.

ROBERTSON, Walter. Born in Dublin, about 1792, he afterward sailed with Gilbert Stuart for the United States. He worked in Phila. and New York, copying some of Stuart's portraits in miniature, and painting a number of miniatures of his own composition.

ROBERTSON, W. Engraver. This man was a script engraver employed in New York in 1831.

ROBESON, Edna Amelia. Miniature painter. Born in Davenport, Ia., in 1887. Pupil of Frank Phoenix and of the Art Students' League of New York. Member: Penna. Society of Miniature Painters. *Address*, Bettendort, Ia.

ROBIN, Augustus. Engraver. Born in New York of French parentage. This good engraver of portraits and subject plates was in the employ of J. C. Buttre, of New York, for nearly forty years.

ROBINS, Susan P. B. Painter. Born in Boston, 1849. Pupil of John Johnston, Ross Turner and F. Crowninshield; also of the Boston Museum School under Philip Hale. Member: Copley Society, 1894. *Address*, 95 Mt. Vernon St., Boston, Mass.

ROBINSON. Engraver. This name is signed to a number of small, wonderfully designed, but poorly engraved plates illustrating an edition of Weems' "Life of Washington," published in 1815 by Matthew Carey, of Philadelphia.

ROBINSON, Adah M. Painter. Born in Richmond, Ind., in 1882. Pupil of J. E. Bundy, George Elmer Browne and of the Art Institute of Chicago. *Address*, 1118 West 13th St., Oklahoma City, Okla.

ROBINSON, Alexander. Painter. Born in Portsmouth, N. H., in 1867. Pupil of Lowell School of Design (Boston Museum of Art); Academie Julien, Paris, under Ducet and Constant. Member: New York Water Color Club; Phila. Water Color Club; Chicago Water Color Club. Specialty, water colors. *Address*, Care Morgan, Harjes & Co., 14 Place Vendome, Paris.

ROBINSON, Alonzo Clark. Sculptor. Born in Darien, Conn., in 1876. *Address*, Rue Cardinet, Paris, France.

ROBINSON, Boardman. Painter and illustrator who exhibited at Penna. Acad. of Fine Arts, 1926. *Address*, 39th St., New York.

ROBINSON, Charles Dorman. Landscape and marine painter. Born in Vermont in 1847. Pupil of William Bradford, 1862; of Geo. Inness and M. F. H. De Haas, 1863; of Gignoux and Cropsey, Newport, Vt., 1866–67; studied under Boudin; also studied methods of Segantini, 1900, Paris. Resided in Vt., 1861–73; in Clinton, Ia.; San Francisco since 1874 (except in Paris, France, 1899–1901). Dean of Pacific Coast artists. First diploma, Mechanics' Fair, San Francisco, 1860; money award, Sacramento State Agricultural Society, 1878; gold medal, same, 1903. Spent 19 seasons in the Yosemite and the high Sierras; has 84 paintings, mostly of the Yosemite Valley, in Great Britain. Member: San Francisco Art Association.

ROBINSON, David. Painter and illustrator. Born in Poland in 1886. Studied in America and France. *Address*, 13 West 29th St., New York City.

ROBINSON, Florence Vincent. Painter. Born in Taunton, Mass., in 1874. Studied in Paris under Bouveret, Vignal and Harpignes. Specialties, water colors and illustrations. Work bought by the State, in France; Museum of Fine Arts, Boston; Harvard University; Cleveland Art School, etc. Member: American Water Color Society, Societé des Aquarellistes, Paris. *Address*, 510 Park Ave., New York City.

ROBINSON, Helen Avery. Sculptor. Born in Louisville, Kentucky. She studied under Solon H. Borglum. *Address*, 200 West 58th St., New York.

ROBINSON, John. Miniature painter. He was an English artist who settled in Phila. in 1817, where he died about 1829. He showed a miniature of West, with picture of "Christ Rejected" in the background, and said that Benj. West had sat for it. A miniature of Saml. Milligan is signed "J. R. 1819."

ROBINSON, L. S. Mona. Painter, who exhibited in the Annual Exhibition of the Penna. Academy of Fine Arts, Philadelphia, 1924. *Address*, Paoli, Penna.

ROBINSON, Nora B. Miniature painter, who exhibited at the Penna. Academy of the Fine Arts, Philadelphia, 1925. *Address*, 9 Cedar Ave., Rockville Centre, Long Island, N. Y.

ROBINSON, Theodore. Painter of landscapes and figure subjects. Born in Irasburg, Vermont, 1852; died in New York in 1896. Pupil of Carolus-Duran and of Gerome. Awarded the Webb prize, 1890; Shaw prize, 1892. Represented by "Valley of the Seine from Giverny Heights," in the Corcoran Art Gallery. See *Scribner's Magazine*, "Field of Art" by Eliot Clark.

ROBINSON, Thomas. Painter. Born in 1835. He died in 1888. The Worcester Art Museum owns his painting "Fowls in Yard." He also painted a portrait group of five dogs that attracted much attention.

ROBINSON, W. Engraver. About 1825–30 this W. Robinson etched in a fairly good style a Masonic certificate published by R. D. Desilver, of Philadelphia. This may be the "Robinson" noted above.

ROBINSON, William S. Painter. Born East Gloucester, Mass., in 1861. Studied in Boston, France and Holland. Honorable mention, Paris Exposition, 1900; Pan-American Exposition, Buffalo, 1901; gold medal, American Art Society, Philadelphia, 1902; bronze medal, St. Louis Exposition, 1904; Carnegie prize, National Academy of Design, 1910. Elected to National Academy, 1911. Member: American Water Color Society; New York Water Color Club; Boston Art Club. Painter and teacher. Studio in New York. Represented by "Monhegan Headlands," signed and dated 1911, at National Gallery, Washington, D. C. *Address*, Old Lyme, Conn.

ROBINSON, W. T. Painter. Born in Somerville, Mass., in 1852. Pupil of George N. Cass in Boston; École des Beaux Arts; École de Medecine; Gobelin Tapestry Schools; under Bouguereau and Diogene Maillart in Paris. Member: National Art Club. *Address*, Auditorium Building, Malden, Mass.

ROBUS, Hugo. Painter, who exhibited in Philadelphia, 1921, in "Exhibition of Paintings Showing the Later Tendencies in Art." *Address*, 9 East 14th St., New York City.

ROCHE. Engraver. Several of the plates of the American edition of Maynard's "Josephus," published in New York in 1791, are signed "Roche sc." No other plates are known.

ROCHE, M. Paul. Etcher and painter. Born in Ireland in 1885. Member of Brooklyn Society of Etchers. Represented in Brooklyn Museum, Chicago Art Institute, and Library of Congress. *Address*, 630 77th St., Brooklyn, N. Y.

ROCKEY, A. B. Nothing is known about this painter except that he was born in Mifflinsburg, Penna., in 1799. He moved to Philadelphia where he began painting about 1825. He worked in that city for many years painting portraits and copying pictures. The Penna. Historical Society owns several of his portraits.

ROCKWELL, Norman. Illustrator. Born in New York City in 1894. Pupil of Bridgman and Fogarty. *Address*, 40 Prospect St., New Rochelle, N. Y.

RODINA, K. Michaloff. Sculptor. Exhibited at Penna. Academy of Fine Arts, Philadelphia, in 1915. *Address*, 439 Sixteenth St., Brooklyn, N. Y.

ROECKER, Henry Leon. Painter. Born in Burlington, Ia. Pupil of Academy of Design in Chicago. *Address*, 444 East 42d Place, Hyde Park, Chicago, Ill.

ROERICH, Nicholas. Painter. Born in Russia. He came to America about 1920. Has painted Western scenes, also coast and lake views in Maine. In 1921 he organized the "Master Institute of United Arts" in New York City. *Address*, 310 Riverside Drive, New York City.

ROGERS. Miniature painter, who flourished in Salem about 1782.

ROGERS, Barksdale. Illustrator and painter. Born in Macon, Ga. Pupil of Steinlen in Paris; also studied in Munich. Work: Illustrations for *Judge, The New York Sunday World, Scribner's Magazine* and *Puck*. *Address*, Greenwich, Conn.

ROGERS, Charles. Miniature painter, who flourished in Boston about 1846.

ROGERS, Franklin Whiting. Born in Cambridge, Mass., in 1854. Pupil of J. Foxcroft Cole in 1874. He has devoted himself especially to the painting of dogs. Among his works are "The Two Friends," "Steady" and "Resignation."

ROGERS, Gretchen W. Painter, who exhibited a portrait of a "Young Girl" at the Penna. Academy of the Fine Arts, Philadelphia, 1914. *Address*, 30 Ipswich St., Boston, Mass.

ROGERS, John. Sculptor and modeller, who was born in Salem, Mass., in 1829. His well-known "Rogers' Groups" were familiar subjects connected with the Civil War. His best known group of the "Slave Auction" was done in 1859. Mr. Rogers also executed the equestrian statue of General Reynolds which stands before the City Hall in Philadelphia. He was elected a member of the National Academy of Design in 1863, and belonged to the National Sculpture Society. He died in 1904.

ROGERS, John. Engraver. Born in England about 1808; died in New York about 1888, says Mr. Samuel Hollyer. Rogers came to New York in 1850–51, and he engraved for the book publishers a large number of portraits and some subject plates. He generally worked in line and was a very good engraver.

ROGERS, Louise De Gignilliet. Painter and etcher. Born in Macon, Ga. Pupil of Steinlen, Paris; also of Robert Henri; at one time studied in Munich. Member: Brooklyn Society of Etchers; Conn. Society of Artists. Painted portraits of Ex-Vice-President Marshall; William Jennings Bryan; Senator Tillman, and others. *Address*, Greenwich, Conn.

ROGERS, Nathaniel. Painter. Born in Bridgehampton, Long Island, in 1788; died in 1844. He went to New York in 1811 and became a pupil of Joseph Wood, and soon took high rank as a painter of miniatures, among which were those of Fitz-Greene Halleck and Joseph Rodman Drake. He was one of the founders of the National Academy of Design in New York.

ROGERS, Randolph. Sculptor. Born in New York State in 1825. About 1850 he went to Italy to study, and on his return he opened his studio in New York. In 1858 he designed the bronze doors for the Capitol in Washington. He also executed portrait statues of Abraham Lincoln for Philadelphia and of William H. Seward for New York. He has resided in Italy since 1860.

ROGERS, William Allen. Painter and caricaturist. Born in Springfield, Ohio, in 1854. Member: Society of Illustrators; Century Association. On staff of the *New York Herald*. *Address*, 640 Madison Ave., New York, N. Y.

ROLLINSON, Charles. Engraver and copperplate printer, living in New York in 1808–1832, and dying in the latter year. He was probably a son, or other near relative, of William Rollinson, as his address for a considerable time was No. 28 John St., the same as that of Wm. Rollinson. The only plates found by the compiler, and signed by C. Rollinson as engraver, consist of architectural subjects, diagrams, etc.

ROLLINSON, William. Engraver. Born in Dudley, Staffordshire, England, in 1762;

died in New York in 1842. Rollinson was probably a silversmith and learned to engrave upon plate. He came to the United States prior to 1789, as he is credited with having ornamented the silver buttons on the coat worn by Washington at his inauguration as President.

His earliest work upon copperplate appears in the American edition of Brown's family Bible, published in New York in 1792. This work is crude, though his small profile of Washington—executed in 1791, according to Wm. Dunlap—is a much better piece of work. Rollinson rapidly progressed in the art of engraving, and about 1796 he changed his style to stipple and furnished some very good portrait plates for the *Analectic* and other magazines. His large plate of Alexander Hamilton is said to have been commenced in 1800 and published by Rollinson, and the painter Archibald Robertson, in 1805.

ROLPH, J. A. This reputable landscape engraver was working in New York, 1834–46, and probably later.

ROLSHOVEN, Julius. Painter. Born in Detroit in 1858. Pupil of Cooper Union, New York; Hugo Crola at Dusseldorf; Loefftz in Munich; Frank Duveneck in Florence; Robert-Fleury in Paris. Member: Societé Nationale des Beaux Arts, Paris; Detroit Fine Arts Society; International Art Congress; Paris Society. Awarded second medal, Paris Exposition, 1889; honorable mention, Paris Exposition, 1900; bronze medal, Pan-American Exposition, Buffalo, 1901; medals, Munich, Berlin, Brussels and Chicago. Work: "Chioggia Fishing Girl," Cincinnati Museum; "The Refectory of San Damaino, Assisi," Detroit Institute; represented in Minneapolis Museum, Brooklyn Museum, and Union League Club of Chicago. *Address*, Care of Athletic Club, Detroit, Mich.

ROMANO, Nicholas. Painter and sculptor. Born in Montoro, Italy, in 1889. Pupil of Albert Laessle. Represented in the Pennsylvania Academy of the Fine Arts, Philadelphia; Philadelphia Art Alliance; Graphic Sketch Club of Philadelphia. *Address*, 313 Race St., Philadelphia, Pa.

ROMANS, Bernard. Engraver. Born in Holland about 1720; died at sea in 1784. Romans was educated in England, and about 1755 he came to the American Colonies.

At the outbreak of the Revolution he entered the service of the American Colonies, and was present at Lexington and Bunker Hill, according to the statement made in connection with his published proposals for issuing his view of the Battle of Bunker Hill and his map of Boston. Romans is referred to in the *New York Mercury* of 1775 as "the most skillful draughtsman in all America," though his view of the battle of Bunker Hill is anything but artistic in its composition. He engraved this view on a large scale, and it was published by Nicholas Brooks, of Philadelphia, in September and October, 1775; "An Exact View of the Late Battle of Charlestown, June 17th, 1775" to give the plate its full title. It was re-engraved by Robert Aitken on a small scale and published in the *Pennsylvania Magazine* for 1775.

RONDONI, Romolo. Sculptor, who exhibited at the Penna. Academy of the Fine Arts, Philadelphia, 1914. *Address*, 35 East 30th St., New York City.

ROOK, Edward F. Painter. Born in New York, N. Y., in 1870. Pupil of Constant and Laurens in Paris. Member: Associate Member of National Academy, and Academician in 1924. Awarded Temple gold medal, Penna. Academy of Fine Arts, 1898; bronze medal, Pan-American Exposition, Buffalo, 1901; bronze medal, Corcoran Gallery, Washington, D. C., 1919. Work: "Deserted Street, Moonlight," Pennsylvania Academy, Phila.; "Pearl Clouds, Moonlight" and "Wisteria," Cincinnati Museum; represented in Boston Art Club and in the Lotos Club, New York; also in Portland Art Museum, Portland, Maine. *Address*, Old Lyme, Conn.

ROOS, Peter. Painter. Born in Sweden in 1850. Member: Boston Art Club. Awarded medal, Boston, 1874. Specialty, landscape. *Address*, 24 Sacramento St., Cambridge, Mass.

ROOSEVELT, S. Montgomery. Portrait painter. Born in New York City in 1864; died in 1920. Pupil of Art Students' League of New York; Academie Julien, Paris. Painted portraits of Theodore Roosevelt, Bishop James H. Darlington, Oliver Belmont, Hudson Maxim, Henry F. Shoemaker, Earl of Kintare, etc. Member: National Association of Portrait Painters; Artists' Fund Society; Chevalier Legion of Honor, France.

ROOT, Orville Hoyt. Painter, who exhibited at the Penna. Academy of Fine Arts, Philadelphia, 1914. *Address*, Paris, France.

ROOT, Robert Marshall. Painter and illustrator. Born in Shelbyville, Ill., in 1863. Pupil of Constant, Laurens and Lefebvre. Awarded State Centennial Medal, Springfield, 1918. Work: Historical painting, "Lincoln and Douglas Debate, 1858," Springfield; "Portrait Lt. Gov. Barat O'Harra," Lt. Governor's office, Springfield; "The Power, The Wisdom, The Justice of the Law" in Atty. General's office, Springfield. *Address*, Syndicate Building, Shelbyville, Ill.

ROPES, Joseph. Painter. Born in Salem, Mass., in 1812. He studied at the National Academy of Design in New York in 1847.

He was in Italy from 1865 to 1876, and exhibited landscapes in the Centennial Exposition in Philadelphia in 1876. His studio was in Germantown for ten years. He died in New York about 1885.

ROSE, George L. Painter. Born in Newport, R. I., in 1861. Pupil of John La Farge. Member of National Society of Mural Painters. *Address*, Forest Hall, 1256 Wisconsin Ave., Washington, D. C.

ROSE, Guy. Painter. Born in San Gabriel, Calif., in 1867; died in 1925. Pupil of Emil Carlsen in San Francisco; Lefebvre, Constant and Doucet in Paris. Member: California Art Club. Awarded honorable mention, Paris Salon, 1894; gold medal, Panama-California Exposition, San Diego, 1915; prize, California Art Club, 1916.

ROSE, Ruth Starr (Mrs. W. S.). Painter and sculptor. Born in Wisconsin in 1887. Pupil of Art Students' League of New York. *Address*, Pickbourne, Easton, Md.

ROSELAND, Harry. Painter. Born in Brooklyn in 1867. Pupil of Beckwith in New York. Member of Brooklyn Art Club. *Address*, 191 Clinton St., Brooklyn, N. Y.

ROSEN, Charles. Landscape painter. Born in Westmoreland County, Penna., in 1878. Studied art at National Academy of Design, and in the New York School of Art. Awarded 3d Hallgarten prize, 1910; 1st Hallgarten prize, 1912; Shaw purchase prize, Salmagundi Club, 1914; honorable mention, Carnegie Institute, Pittsburgh, 1914; silver medal, San Francisco Exposition, 1915; Inness gold medal, also Altman prize at National Academy of Design. Represented in permanent collections, including Duluth Art Association, Minneapolis Society of Fine Arts, Delgado Museum, New Orleans, Butler Art Institute, Youngstown, Ohio, and also in many private collections. Elected Associate Member of the National Academy, 1913; National Academy, 1917. *Address*, Columbus, Ohio, and Woodstock, N. Y.

ROSENBAUER, W. W. Sculptor. Born in Chambersburg, Penna., in 1890. Pupil of St. Louis School of Fine Arts. Exhibited at National Academy of Design, New York, 1925. *Address*, Philadelphia, Penna.

ROSENBERG, Henry. Painter. Born in New Brunswick, N. J., in 1858. Studied in Italy. Director of Art School, Halifax. *Address*, Halifax, N. S.

ROSENBERG, James. Painter. Born in Allegheny City, Penna., in 1874. Member of Society of Independent Artists. *Address*, 27 West 67th St., New York.

ROSENBERG, Louis C. Etcher and illustrator. Born in Portland, Ore., in 1890. Pupil of Mass. Institute of Tech. Member of Brooklyn Society of Etchers. *Address*, 100 East 42d St., New York.

ROSENBERG, Samuel. Portrait painter. Born in Philadelphia in 1896. Pupil of Volk and Collens. Member of Pittsburgh Associated Artists. *Address*, 345 Fifth Ave., New York City.

ROSENKRANZ, Clarence C. Painter. Born near Hammondsport, N. Y. Pupil of Chase and Shirlaw. Represented by "New England Winter" in Minn. Art Society. *Address*, 314 Hawthorne Road, Duluth, Minn.

ROSENMEYER, Bernard J. Illustrator and painter. Born in New York in 1870. Pupil of Art Students' League of New York, and of Constant and Laurens in Paris. *Address*, Tenafly, N. J.

ROSENTHAL, Albert. Painter and etcher. Born in Philadelphia in 1863; son of Max Rosenthal. Albert Rosenthal studied lithography under his father and was at the same time a pupil at the Pennsylvania Academy of Fine Arts. In 1884 he commenced to etch and for some years he was largely engaged in portrait work, confining himself chiefly to the reproduction of the portraits of American historical characters. In 1889–92 he studied in Paris at the École des Beaux Arts, under Gerome; upon his return to the United States in the latter year he became a portrait painter, with his studio in Philadelphia. He has painted many portraits of prominent people in his native city. *Address*, 10 South 18th St., Philadelphia, Pa.

ROSENTHAL, David. Painter and illustrator. Born in Cincinnati, Ohio, in 1876. Studied in Italy. *Address*, 30 Hurbert Block, Cincinnati, Ohio.

ROSENTHAL, Louis. Sculptor. Born in Russia. He came to America in 1907. He studied under Ephraim Keyser in Baltimore, where he won a scholarship that enabled him to study abroad. Specialty, small or miniature sculptures.

ROSENTHAL, Max. Etcher and lithographer. Born in Turck, Russian Poland, 1833; died in Philadelphia in 1918. Mr. Rosenthal studied drawing and painting in Paris. He came to Philadelphia in 1849 and there continued his studies at the Pennsylvania Academy of Fine Arts. Having been a pupil of the famous Thurwanger in Paris and in Philadelphia, in connection with his brother, Mr. Rosenthal established himself in the lithographic business in the latter city, and he made notable progress in developing the then new art of chromo-lithography in this country.
Upon retiring from the lithographing business, about 1884, Mr. Rosenthal turned his attention to etching, and in connection with his son, Albert Rosenthal, issued a series of portraits of men prominent in American history. In 1890 he took up the work of engraving in mezzotinto, and as he was already a reputable painter of portraits and historical subjects, his artistic training led him to produce mezzotinto portraits of merit.

ROSENTHAL, Michael. Painter. Born in Russia, 1885. Pupil of Robert Henri. *Address*, 1947 Broadway, New York City.

ROSENTHAL, Toby E. Painter. Born in New Haven, Conn., in 1848. Studied drawing under Henri Bacon, and painting under Fortunato Arriola, San Francisco; student at Royal Academy, Munich, under Straehuber, Carl Raupp and Carl von Piloty, 1865–72. Professionally engaged as a painter since leaving the academy, having classes in painting and composition. He paints chiefly figural compositions and genre work; has also painted many portraits in California, England and Germany. Medals at Centennial Exposition, Philadelphia, 1876; Royal Academy, Munich; International Exposition, Munich.

ROSENZWEIG, Lippa. Sculptor. Exhibited at Penna. Academy of the Fine Arts, Phila., 1926. *Address*, 1930 N 13th St., Philadelphia, Pa.

ROSS, Denman W. Painter and illustrator. Born in Cincinnati, Ohio, in 1853. He is a Trustee of the Museum of Fine Arts, Boston. His painting "The Musicians" is owned by the Museum. *Address*, 24 Craigie St., Cambridge, Mass.

ROSSE, Hermann. Painter and mural decorator. Born in Holland in 1887. *Address*, Art Institute of Chicago.

ROSSEAU, Percival L. Painter. Born in New Orleans, La., in 1869. Pupil of Lefebvre and Robert-Fleury in Paris. Awarded honorable mention, Paris Salon, 1900; third class medal, Paris Salon, 1906. His specialty is animal painting, and his pictures of hunting dogs have been much sought for. *Address*, Grassy Hill, Lyme, Conn.

ROSSITER, Thomas P. Portrait and historical painter. Born in New Haven, Conn., in 1817. Pupil of Nathaniel Jocelyn; also studied in London and Paris. In 1846 he opened his studio in New York. He was elected an Associate Member of the National Academy in 1840, and an Academician in 1849. He painted "Washington's First Cabinet," "Washington at Valley Forge" (60 in. by 92 in.), "Washington's Entry into Trenton," and a series of pictures on the "Life of Christ." He died at Cold Spring, N. Y., in 1871.

21

ROST, Christian. Engraver. Born in Germany. He studied in Paris and in London, and in the latter city he made the drawings and engraved on wood for a work describing the exhibits at the London World's Fair of 1850. It is not known when Mr. Rost came to the United States, but he was engraving very good portrait and subject plates in line in New York in 1860. In 1865 he was in the employ of George E. Perrine, and at a later date he was employed by the American Bank-Note Co. He died some years ago at Mount Vernon, N. Y.

ROTH, Ernest David. Painter and etcher. Born in Stuttgart, Germany, in 1879. Came to America when he was very young. Pupil of National Academy of Design in New York. Studied etching under James D. Smillie. Elected an Associate Member of the National Academy; also member of New York Water Color Club. Awarded third Shaw prize for black and white, bronze medal for painting and silver medal for etching, Panama-Pacific Exposition, San Francisco, 1915; J. Sanford Saltus prize, Salmagundi Club, 1917; first honorable mention, Chicago Art Institute, 1917; Shaw prize, Salmagundi Club, 1918. Prints to be found in collections of New York Public Library; Boston Museum of Art; Library of Congress, Washington, D. C.; Public Library, Newark, N. J.; Chicago Art Institute; Minneapolis Institute of Art; Uffizi Gallery, Florence, Italy. *Address*, 5 Bank St., New York, N. Y.

ROTH, F. G. R. Sculptor. Born in Brooklyn, N. Y., in 1872. Pupil of Hellman and Meyerheim in Vienna. Elected Associate Member of the National Academy, 1906; National Academy, 1906; New York Architectural League, 1902; National Sculpture Society. Awarded silver medal, St. Louis Exposition, 1904; silver medal, Buenos Aires Exposition, 1910; gold medal, Panama-Pacific Exposition, San Francisco, 1915. Represented in Metropolitan Museum, New York, and Detroit Institute of Arts. *Address*, Sherwood Place, Englewood, N. J.

ROTHERMEL, Peter F. Born in Luzerne County, Pa., in 1817. He was an eminent American historical painter, and one of the greatest colorists this country has produced, and a master of composition involving the management of large masses of figures. He began the active practice of his profession in 1840, by painting portraits in Philadelphia, having received instructions from Bass Otis; he went to Europe in 1856, spending some time in the art centers of the Continent, and painting his first historical picture. He was an active member of the Artists' Fund Society of Philadelphia, of which he was elected Vice-President in 1844, and was made a Director of the Penna. Academy of Fine Arts in 1847-55. Among his best known works are

"St. Agnes," painted in 1858, and now in Russia; "Patrick Henry before the Virginia House of Burgesses," engraved by Alfred Jones for the American Art Union of Philadelphia, 1852; "St. Paul, on Mars Hill"; "Amy Robsart interceding for Leicester," property of Mrs. Blanchard; also the colossal picture of the Battle of Gettysburg, ordered by the Legislature of Pennsylvania, and finished in 1871. The last-named picture, which has been engraved by John Sartain, is preserved in Memorial Hall, Fairmount Park, Philadelphia. He died near Pottstown, Penna., in 1895.

ROTHWELL, J. Engraver. This man was engraving book illustrations, in a crude line manner, in New York in 1841.

ROUDEBUSH, John H. Sculptor. He was awarded a medal at the Paris Exposition of 1900, and at Buffalo in 1901, for his group, "The Wrestlers."

ROUGERON, Marcel J. Painter. Born in Paris, France, 1875. Pupil of Julien, Gerome, de Datti, Vibert, in Paris. Member: Societé Royale des Artistes Belges. Awards: Officer of Public Instruction of France, 1900; Grand Croix of St. Stanislaus, 1904. *Address*, 94 Park Ave., New York, N. Y.

ROULAND, Orlando. Portrait painter. He maintained studios in London and in Marblehead, Mass. He has painted in his English studio Sir Alfred East, R. A., the Duke of Argyle and Sir Robert Morant. In this country his portraits include those of Roosevelt, Edison, John Burroughs and John Bigelow. His figure-sketch of the "Balloon Lady" and his New York City scene "When Night Comes On" are excellent pieces of painting.

ROWE, Clarence. Illustrator and etcher. Born in Philadelphia, Pa., in 1878. Pupil of Max Bohm, Penna. Academy of Fine Arts; of Bouguereau and Ferrier in Paris. Member: Salmagundi Club; Society of Illustrators; Greenwich Society of Artists; Guild of Free Lance Artists. *Address*, Cos Cob, Conn.

ROWE, J. Staples. Portrait painter. Born in 1856. He studied in Boston and New York, and painted life size portraits, and miniatures. He died in New York in 1905.

ROWELL, Mrs. Fanny. Painter. Born in Princeton, N. J., in 1865. Pupil of J. B. Whittaker in Brooklyn; Colarossi Academy in Paris; Trager at Sevres. Member: National Art Club; New York Municipal Artists' Society. *Address*, National Arts Club, 14 Gramercy Park, New York, N. Y.

ROWLAND, William. Miniature painter, who flourished about 1777 in New York. He came from Glasgow, Scotland, and settled in New York.

ROWSE, Samuel Worcester. Painter. Born in 1822 at Bath, Me. He died in 1901, at Morristown, New Jersey. After a brief period in Augusta, Maine, as an engraver, Samuel W. Rowse came to Boston in 1852 and worked for a lithographic firm. He soon after established himself as an excellent crayon portrait draughtsman. At the Studio Building where he lived in 1861, and worked for a number of years, he had as a friend Eastman Johnson. In 1872, with his friend Chauncey Wright, he visited London and was frequently the guest of Charles Eliot Norton. While in London he met Ruskin and is recorded as saying, "He wanted me to hold the brush while he painted." About 1880 he moved to New York. With his friend Eastman Johnson he again visited London in 1891. He is represented in the large portrait by Eastman Johnson, called "Two Men," now at the Metropolitan Museum and reproduced in the *World's Work*, in 1906. He finally settled in Morristown, N. J., where he died, leaving a considerable estate. His work was regularly in demand and in later years he was sometimes paid as much as four hundred dollars for his portrait drawings. Rowe's portraits are of great excellence. They are drawn in black crayon and although large in size recall in execution the work of the English pencil portrait-draughtsman, Samuel Lawrence. An obituary notice of Rowse appeared in the New York *Tribune* for May 26, 1901.

ROYCE, Elizabeth R. (Mrs. Edw.). Sculptor. Member of National Association of Women Painters and Sculptors. *Address*, 11 Greycourt, Ithaca, N. Y.

RUBINS, H. W. Etcher. Born in Buffalo, N. Y., in 1865. Pupil of Art Institute of Chicago. Member of Chicago Society of Etchers; Minneapolis Society of Fine Arts. Work represented in New York Public Library. *Address*, 1200 2d Ave., South Minneapolis, Minn.

RUCKSTUHL, F. Wellington. Sculptor. Born in Breitenbach, Alsace, in 1853. Studied art in Paris. Honorable mention, Paris Salon, 1888; grand medal, Chicago Exposition, 1893. Principal works in sculpture: "Evening," lire-size female (marble), Metropolitan Museum of New York; "Mercury Amusing Himself" (bronze), heroic group, Portland Place, St. Louis; "Victory" (bronze), heroic size, on Soldiers' and Sailors' Monument, Jamaica, L. I.; Franklin, Goethe and Macaulay, colossal granite heads, façade, Library of Congress; equestrian statue, Brig. Gen. John F. Har-

tranft, Capitol Hill, Harrisburg, Pa. *Address*, The National Arts Club, New York, N. Y.

RUDD, Emma R. Painter, who exhibited at the 33d Annual Exhibition of National Association of Women Painters and Sculptors, New York. *Address*, Lyons, New York.

RUDERSDORF, Lillian. Painter. Born in Clarkson, Nebr., in 1882. Pupil of University of Nebr.; Art Institute of Chicago. *Address*, 21 East Van Buren St., Chicago, Ill.

RUDOLPH, Pauline D. (Mrs.). Painter. Born in Chicago. Pupil of Penna. Academy of the Fine Arts and of Boulanger and Lefebvre in Paris. *Address*, Winnetka, Ill.

RUDY, Mary E. Painter. Born in Burlington, Ia., in 1861. Pupil of Art Institute of Chicago. *Address*, 4516 Lake Park Ave., Chicago, Ill.

RUGGLES, Dr. Edward. Painter of small landscapes and miniature views. He painted many studies in the White Mountains. His views and landscapes met a ready sale, where the socalled "Ruggles Gems" were in much demand.

RUGGLES, E., Jun'r. This man was a book-plate engraver, apparently working between 1790 and 1800, somewhere in New England. The only plate seen is that for Walter Lyon; in reality a label with peculiarly conventionalized peacock feathers used as borders.

RUHNKA, Roy. Painter, who exhibited water colors at the Penna. Academy of Fine Arts, Philadelphia, 1925. *Address*, 3616 Walnut St., Philadelphia.

RUMMELL, John. Painter. Born in Springville, N. Y., in 1861. Pupil of Ahrens, and of John F. Carlsen. *Address*, 68 Greenfield St., Buffalo, N. Y.

RUMMLER, Alex. J. Painter. Born in Dubuque, Ia., in 1867. Pupil of Laurens in Paris. *Address*, 21 Maple Ave., Glenbrook, Conn.

RUMSEY, Charles C. Sculptor. Born in Buffalo, N. Y., in 1879; killed in automobile accident in New York in 1922. Studied in Boston Art School and later in Paris. He worked principally in bronze, and modelled many statues of race horses.

RUNGIUS, Carl (Clemens Moritz). Painter. Born in Germany in 1869. Studied painting at Berlin Art School; School of Applied Arts; Academy of Fine Arts. Began painting in Berlin, 1889, came to the United States in 1894, and has since been engaged in his profession, making a specialty of painting American big game. He has exhibited at the Society of American Artists; National Academy of Design; Penna. Academy of the Fine Arts. Elected Member of the National Academy of Design, 1920. *Address,* 96 Fifth Ave., New York.

RUSH, Olive. Painter and illustrator. Born in Fairmount, Ind. Pupil of Art Students' League of New York under Twachtman and Mowbray; under Howard Pyle at Wilmington, Del.; Richard Miller in Paris. Exhibited at the Paris Salon and in principal cities of the United States; painted altar decoration, St. Andrew's P. E. Church, Wilmington, Del. Specialty, portraits of children and women; also paintings in oil and water color, and mural decorations. Awarded Art Association prize, 1919, and represented in permanent collection, John Herron Art Institute. Member of New York Water Color Club and Wilmington Society of Fine Arts. *Address,* State Saving & Trust Building, Indianapolis, Ind.

RUSH, William. Sculptor. Born in Philadelphia in 1756; died in that city, 1833. Apprenticed to Edward Cutbush, a carver, he gained much reputation as a maker of figureheads for ships. Notable among these were the figures "Genius of the United States" and "Nature" for the frigates "United States" and "Constellation," and of celebrities such as Rousseau, Franklin and Penn for other vessels. The figure of the "Indian Trader" for the ship "William Penn" excited great admiration in London, where carvers sketched it and made casts of the head, while the figure of a river-god, carved for the ship "Ganges," is said to have been worshipped by the Hindoos on her calls to Indian ports. His "Tragedy" and "Comedy," done for the first Chestnut Street Theater, may now be seen at the Forrest Home at Phila.; his "Leda and the Swan," originally placed before the first waterworks on the site of the City Hall, was later moved to Fairmount, where a bronze replica—he himself worked in nothing but wood and clay—has since replaced it. For the first Custom House he designed the much-admired figure of "Commerce"; for the permanent bridge at Market Street those of "Commerce" and "Agriculture"; for St. Augustine's Church a representation of the Crucifixion. Among a large number of statues executed by him the most notable was that of Washington, purchased by the city in 1814 and still on exhibition in Independence Hall, Philadelphia. He served in the Revolutionary Army.

RUSHTON, Robert. Painter, who exhibited water colors at the Penna. Academy of Fine Arts, Philadelphia, 1925. *Address,* 5238 Carlisle St., Philadelphia.

RUSSELL, Charles M. Painter, sculptor and illustrator. Born in St. Louis, Mo., in 1865. *Address,* 1219 Fourth Ave., North Great Falls, Mont.

RUSSELL, James. Painter. Born in New Albany, Ind., 1873. Member of Louisville Art League. *Address,* 201 East Market St., New Albany, Ind.

RUSSELL, M. B. Miniature painter, flourishing in Boston in 1834.

RUSSELL, W. C. Miniature painter, who flourished in New York about 1837.

RUSSELL, Walter. Painter. Born in Boston in 1871. Studied at Museum of Fine Arts, Boston; Drexel Institute, Philadelphia; Academie Julien, Paris; also pupil of Albert Munsell, Ernest Major, Howard Pyle and Jean Paul Laurens. Illustrator for New York magazines, 1890–97; artist and correspondent during Spanish-American War for *Century Magazine* and *Collier's Weekly;* now devotes entire attention to specialty of painting children's portraits and child subjects; he painted portraits of the children of President Roosevelt. and those of Ex-Gov. Ames of Mass.; also portraits of other prominent people of the United States. *Address,* 1 West 67th St., New York.

RUSSMANN, Felix. Painter. Born in New York City, 1888. Pupil of National Academy of Design, and he was awarded the third Hallgarten prize in 1918. Exhibited "Moonlight" at Carnegie Institute, Pittsburgh, 1924. *Address,* Chicago, Ill.

RUTHERFORD. He is spoken of by Tuckerman in his "American Artist Life" as a "genre painter of promise who died young."

RUYL, Louis H. Illustrator and etcher. Born in Brooklyn, N. Y., in 1870. *Address,* 171 Madison Ave., New York.

RUZICKA, Rudolph. Illustrator, etcher and wood engraver. Born in Bohemia in 1883. Pupil of Art Institute of Chicago. *Address,* 954 Lexington Ave., New York.

RYDEN, Henning. Sculptor and painter. Born in Sweden in 1869. Pupil of Art Institute of Chicago; also studied in Berlin and London. Member: Salmagundi Club, 1908. Awarded honorable mention, Panama-Pacific Exposition, San Francisco, 1915. Work represented in the American Numismatic Society. *Address,* 809 Madison Ave., New York, N. Y.

RYDER, Albert P. Painter. Born in New Bedford, Mass., in 1847; died in New York City, 1917. Pupil of William E. Marshall the engraver, and of the National Academy of Design, N. Y. Among his works, "Death on a Pale Horse," "The Pasture," "The Curfew Hour," "Pegasus," "The Flying Dutchman," "Launcelot and Elaine," and "Jonah and the Whale." He was elected a Member of the National Academy in 1906. (See *International Studio* for July, 1925.)

RYDER, Chauncey Foster. Painter. Born in Danbury, Conn., in 1868. Pupil of Art Institute of Chicago, and of Raphael Collin and Jean Paul Laurens, Paris, France. Honorable mention, Societé des Artiste Francais, Paris, 1907; silver medal, San Francisco Exposition, 1915. Represented in Isaac Delgrado Museum of Art, New Orleans; Corcoran Gallery, Washington, D. C.; Art Institute of Chicago; Engineers' Club, New York. Member of American Water Color Society. Elected Associate Member of the National Academy; also National Academy in 1920. *Address*, 171 West 12th St., New York.

RYDER, Marilla. Painter, who exhibited at Penna. Academy of Fine Arts, Philadelphia, 1924. *Address*, 2940 Washington St., Roxbury, Mass.

RYDER, Platt P. Portrait and genre painter. Born in 1821 at Brooklyn, N. Y.; died in 1896. Pupil of Bonnat in Paris, also studied in London. Elected in 1868 an Associate of the National Academy. His portrait of Geo. P. Putnam painted in 1872, is in the Metropolitan Museum; he also painted "Clean Shave," "Reading the Cup," "Spinning Wheel" and "Watching and Waiting."

RYDER, Worth. Painter and etcher. Born in Kirkwood, Ill., in 1884. Award: Silver medal for etching, Panama-Pacific, San Francisco, 1915. *Address*, Berkeley, Calif.

RYERSON, Margery (Austen). Painter and etcher. Born in Morristown, N. J., in 1886. Pupil of Robert Henri and Charles W. Hawthorne. Member of Washington Water Color Club and Brooklyn Society of Etchers. *Address*, 315 West 57th St., New York, N. Y.

RYERSON, Mary McIlvaine. Sculptor. Born in Philadelphia, Pa. Pupil of Saint Gaudens and Fraser. *Address*, 53 East 56th St., New York.

RYLAND, Robert K. Mural painter and illustrator. Born in Grenada, Miss., in 1873. Pupil of Art Students' League and of the National Academy of Design in New York. Member of Mural Painters; New York Architectural League, 1910; Salmagundi Club. Awarded Lazarus European Scholarship, 1902–05. Member of National Society of Mural Painters. *Address*, 61 Poplar St., Brooklyn.

S

SABATINI, Raphael. Painter. Exhibited "Lizza" at the Penna. Academy of Fine Arts, Philadelphia, 1924. *Address*, 1515 Arch St., Philadelphia, Pa.

SABIN, Joseph F. Etcher and illustrator. Born in 1846, he has long been a resident of New York. Member of the New York Etchers' Society. He made the illustrations for "Shakespeare's House." His "John Falstaff," after George Cruikshank, is well known. *Address*, Nassau St., New York City.

SACHEVERELL, John. Engraver. The *Pennsylvania Gazette*, Philadelphia, March 15–22, 1732–33, contains an advertisement for the sale of "a quantity of white metal, or pewter, teapots, teaspoons, etc. These are of the newest Fashion, and so very neat, as not easily to be distinguished from Silver." The importer, John Sacheverell, adds to his notice that he "performs all Sorts of Engraving or Carving in Gold, Silver, Brass, Copper or Steel, after the newest and neatest manner."

SACKS, Joseph. Painter. Born in Shavli, Russia, in 1887. Pupil of the Penna. Academy

of the Fine Arts, under Anshutz, Chase and Kendall. Member: Fellowship, Penna. Academy of the Fine Arts; Philadelphia Sketch Club; Philadelphia Art Alliance. *Address*, 1629 Chestnut St., Philadelphia, Pa.

SACKER, Amy M. Illustrator. Born in Boston in 1876. Pupil of DeCamp and of C. Howard Walker. Member: Copley Society. Award: Bronze medal for book covers, Pan-American Exposition, Buffalo, 1901. Art Director in Motion Pictures. *Address*, 739 Boylston St., Boston, Mass.

SACKETT, Clara E. Painter. Born in Westfield, N. Y. Pupil of Art Students' League of New York; of Aman-Jean and Delecluse in Paris. Member: Buffalo Society of Artists. Award: Prize, Buffalo Society of Artists. *Address*, 30 Ipswich St., Boston, Mass.

SACKS, Joseph. Painter, who exhibited a portrait, "The Red Headed Boy," at the Penna. Academy of the Fine Arts, Philadelphia, 1924. *Address*, 552 South Madison Ave., Pasadena, Calif.

SADD, H. S. Born in England. He was engraving good portraits in mezzotint in New York in 1840. He produced a number of plates in this country, but Mr. Alfred Jones says that he went to Australia after a comparatively short stay in the United States.

SAGE, Cornelia Bentley (Mrs. William). Painter and art critic. Born in Buffalo, N. Y. Pupil of Art Students' League, Buffalo; Art Students' League, New York, under James Carroll Beckwith, John H. Twachtman, Robert Reid, Irving R. Wiles and Charles Curran. Director at Buffalo Fine Arts Academy, and Albright Art Gallery. She has organized and managed many notable exhibitions. She took a course in the École du Louvre, Paris, 1914. Received medal, National Institute Social Sciences, 1914, and Societé des Beaux Arts, Paris, 1916. President of Buffalo Society of Artists, 1911; honorable president of Guild of Allied Arts, Buffalo, 1911–12. Editor: "Academy Notes"; contributor to magazines. *Address*, Buffalo Fine Arts Academy, or Albright Art Gallery, Buffalo, N. Y.

SAHLER, Helen G. Sculptor. Born at Carmel, N. Y. Studied at Art Students' League of New York and under Hermon MacNeil and Enid Yandell. Exhibited reliefs, busts and full-length figures at National Academy of Design; National Sculpture Society; Architectural League; Municipal Art Society of New York; Penna. Academy of Fine Arts; Panama-P. I. Exposition, 1915; etc. Principal works: Relief of Gov. Charles S. Whitman of New York; statue, "The Spirit of Revolt." Member: National Association of Women Painters and Sculptors. *Address*, 226 Central Park Square, New York City.

SAINT GAUDENS, Annetta Johnson (Mrs. Louis). Sculptor. Born in Flint, Ohio, in 1869. Member of National Association of Women Painters and Sculptors. Awarded McMillin prize, National Association of Women Painters and Sculptors, 1913. Her work is represented in Boston Museum of Art. Exhibited "The Hammer Thrower" at the Penna. Academy of Fine Arts, 1924. *Address*, 589 Halsey St., Brooklyn, N. Y.

SAINT GAUDENS, Augustus. Sculptor. Born in Dublin, Ireland, in 1848; died in Cornish, N. H., in 1907. He came to this country with his parents in 1848, an infant 6 months of age. The father was a shoemaker, and the conditions surrounding his boyhood made it necessary that Augustus, the third of five sons, should, as soon as possible, aid in the family support. At the age of 13 he was apprenticed to a stone cameo cutter named Avet, and at the same time he entered the night classes in drawing of the Cooper Institute. In 1864 he revolted at the ill nature of his employer and left him for employment

with another, Jules LeBrethon, and changed his art school from the Cooper Institute to the National Academy of Design, where he commenced to model from life. In 1867 he was assisted by his father to go to Paris to study. His living was earned by cutting cameos, while he pursued a course of study at the Petite École, and later at the École des Beaux Arts under Jouffroy.' During the Franco-Prussian War he was strongly in favor of joining the French Army, but was persuaded by a letter from his mother to abandon the idea, and instead of entering the army he went to Rome for further study, where for about four years his life was a series of struggles with poverty. In 1873 Saint Gaudens was located in New York City, and in a letter dated May 12, 1873, addressed to A. B. Mullett, then Supervising Architect of the Treasury, he expressed a desire to know whether the competition for the Farragut Statue had been annulled, and if another competition would be held. He was at that time anxious to compete for the Farragut Statue, and stated that he soon expected to return to Italy. In 1876 he was engaged on his portrait bust of Chief Justice Taney for the Supreme Court room. His letter of July 31, 1876, gives us a glimpse of a young sculptor deferring to the wishes of others and meekly taking orders for commissions to be executed in accordance with the suggestions of his patrons. In 1885 Saint Gaudens had tasted of success, and had tested his ability to such an extent that he prescribed terms and conditions to those who would employ him, and in a letter to Edward Clark, then Architect of the Capitol, he thanked the commission having in charge the proposed Lafayette Monument, for the honor conferred by the invitation to furnish a model for the Lafayette Statue, but stated that if the same proposal had been made to other sculptors he must decline the honor. Twelve years had made a great change in the fortunes of this sculptor. Among the prominent works of Saint Gaudens are: The Shaw Memorial, Boston; the Lincoln Statue, Chicago; the Adams Memorial and many other important works. He is represented in the permanent collections of the Metropolitan Museum; Penna. Academy of Fine Arts; Corcoran Art Gallery, and many others of the American Galleries and Museums. The Memorial Collection of casts of his works is in Cornish, N. H., presented by Mrs. Saint Gaudens to the State of New Hampshire and open to the public.

SAINT GAUDENS, Carlotta (Mrs. Homer). Miniature and water color painter. Born in Rochester, N. Y., in 1884. Pupil of Penna. Academy of Fine Arts and Art Students' League of New York. *Address*, Windsor, Vt.

SAINT GAUDENS, Louis. Sculptor. Brother of Augustus. He was born in New York in 1854. He studied in Paris, and modeled a "Faun" and "St. John" for the church of the "Incarnation," New York, and other statues. He worked in his brother's studio and assisted him with most of his work. He died in 1893.

SAINT, Lanne L. Sculptor. Member of National Sculpture Society, New York, 1907. *Address*, 161 Columbia Ave., New York, N. Y.

SAINT, Lawrence. Etcher. Born in Sharpsburg, Pa., in 1885. Pupil of Penna. Academy of Fine Arts, under Chase; Beaux; Pocre; Sergeant Kendall; also studied in Europe. Work represented in Victoria and Albert Museum, London; Carnegie Institute, Pittsburgh; Bryn Athyn Church, Bryn Athyn, Pa. Illustrator of "Stained Glass of the Middle Ages in England and France." *Address*, Bryn Athyn, Pa.

SALA, Rafael. Painter, who exhibited in Philadelphia, 1921, in "Exhibition of Paintings Showing the Later Tendencies in Art." *Address*, 216 West 50th St., New York City.

SALAZAR, Joseph D. Portrait painter, who had his studio in New Orleans about 1792. He painted a portrait of Danl. W. Coxe, which was exhibited at the Loan Exhibition of Historic Portraits at the Penna. Academy of the Fine Arts in 1887.

SALEMME, Antonio. Sculptor. Born in Italy in 1892. Student at Boston Museum of Fine Arts and afterwards abroad. Member of National Sculpture Society. Works: Bronze statue, "Prayer," Newark Public Library; Portraits, Mrs. W. A. Read, Robert Stein and Stanley Kimmel. *Address*, 53 Washington Square, New York.

SALERNO, Vincent. Sculptor. Born in Sicily, Italy, in 1893. Pupil of A. S. Calder, H. A. MacNeil. Work: "Portrait of Justice Hendrick," Supreme Court, New York, N. Y. *Address*, 119 East 23d St., New York, N. Y.

SALING, Paul E. Painter. Exhibited at Penna. Acad. of Fine Arts, 1926. *Address*, Hartford, Conn.

SALISBURY, Alta West (Mrs.). Painter. Member of National Association of Women Painters and Sculptors, New York. Exhibited in the 33d Annual Exhibition. *Address*, 75 Ellenton Ave., New Rochelle, N. Y.

SALMON, Robert W. An English marine painter, who came to this country in 1829. He was painting in Boston as late as 1840. His painting "The Wharves of Boston" hangs in the old Boston State House. "Rocks at Nahant," and a list of his paintings are preserved at the Boston Museum of Fine Arts.

SALVATORE, Victor D. Sculptor and painter. Born in Italy in 1885. Pupil of Charles Miehaus. *Address*, 8 Macdougal Alley, New York City.

SAMMONS, F. H. C. Painter. Born in England in 1838. He lived in America for many years, and was connected with the Chicago Art Institute. He was also a skillful restorer of paintings.

SAMPSON, Alden. Painter. Born in Manchester, Me., in 1853. *Address*, 168 East 51st St., New York, N. Y.

SANBORN, Earl Edward. Painter. Born in Lyme, N. H., in 1890. Pupil of Burbank, Tarbell, Benson and Paxton. Member of the Boston Art Club. Awarded Paige European traveling scholarship from the Boston Museum of Fine Arts, 1914–16. *Address*, 162 Washington St., Wellesley Hill, Mass.

SANDERSON, Charles Wesley. Painter. Born in Brandon, Vt., in 1838. He studied in Vermont, later going to Paris and studying at Julien's. On his return to this country he painted landscapes in water colors. His studio was in Boston, and he died there in 1905.

SANDHAM, Henry. Painter. Born in Montreal in 1842. He worked in Canada until 1880 when he went to England, and on his return from abroad he established his studio in Boston. His best work is done in historical painting and portraiture, and he had success with marine painting. His portraits of Dr. Duryea and Robert Swan are in Boston. He was a member of the Boston Art Club.

SANDONA, Matteo. Painter. Born in Schio, Italy, in 1881. Pupil of Nani and Bianchi. Member of the San Francisco Artists' Association. Awarded silver medal, Lewis and Clark Exposition, Portland, 1905; silver medal, Sacramento, 1917. Member: International Jury of Awards for Paintings, Panama-Pacific Exposition, San Francisco, 1915; League of New York Artists; Bohemian Club, San Francisco. Work: "Portrait of Mary Pickford," National Gallery, Washington, D. C.; "Chrysanthemums," Golden Gate Park Memorial Museum, San Francisco. *Address*, 471 Buena Vista Ave., San Francisco, Calif.

SANDOR, Mathias. Painter. Born in Hungary in 1857; died in New York City in 1920. Educated at Art Students' League of New York, 1885–86; Academie Julien, Paris, 1889–90, under Francois Flameng and Gabriel Ferrier. Came to the United States in 1881, and began making designs for commercial purposes and painting portraits. He is now a portrait, miniature and landscape painter.

Member of Artists' Fund Society, and of the American Federation of Arts. He exhibits in all important exhibitions.

SANDS, J. An engraver of music on copper, working in Baltimore about 1824. He signed his name ''J. Sands Sc.''

SANDZEN, Sven Birger. Painter and etcher. Born in Bildsberg, Sweden, in 1871. Pupil of Stockholm Artists' League under Zorn and Bergh; under Aman-Jean in Paris. He came to the United States in 1894. Professor of æsthetics and painting, Bethany College, since 1894. Awarded first Moore prize, Artists of Kansas City and vicinity, 1917. Work represented in National Museum, Stockholm; Lund Museum, Sweden; Library of Congress, Washington; Chicago Art Institute. *Address*, Bethany College, Lindsborg, Kans.

SANFORD, Edward Field. Sculptor. Born in New York in 1886. Studied at Art Students' League of New York; National Academy of Design; Julien Academy in Paris; Royal Academy in Munich. Member of New York Architectural League; National Sculpture Society; Beaux Arts Institute; National Art Club. Work: ''Pegasus,'' bronze statuette, R. I. School of Design, Providence; Charles Francis Adams Memorial, Washington and Lee University, Lexington, Va.; Commemorative Tablet, Columbia University; Core Memorial, Norfolk, Va. *Address*, 49 West 12th St., New York, N. Y.

SANFORD, Isaac. Engraver. As early as 1783 Isaac Sanford engraved a music-book entitled ''Select Harmony, containing the Necessary Rules of Psalmody, together with a Collection of Approved Psalm Tunes, Hymns and Anthems.'' By Oliver Brownson. Mr. James Terry, in referring to this book, in his ''Ex Libris Leaflet, No. 4,'' describes the title as contained in a circle of music, and the whole within an engraving of an elaborate church interior covering the entire page. The plate is signed ''I. Sanford, Sculp. 1783.''
On his business-card Sanford advertised himself as ''Miniature Painter and Engraver,'' and he was engraving and publishing fairly well-executed stipple portraits and book illustrations in Hartford, Conn., as late as 1822.

SANGER, William. Painter and etcher. Born in Berlin, Germany, in 1875. Pupil of Art Students' League of New York; Artists' and Artisans' Institute of New York. Member of Society of Independent Artists, and League of New York Artists. Represented in the Hispanic Society of America, New York. *Address*, 408 West 20th St., New York, N. Y.

SANGERNEBO, Alexander. Sculptor. Born in Russia, 1856. Member of Indiana Art Club. His work is in the Union Station and Guarantee Building, Indianapolis, Ind.

SANGERNEBO, Emma (Mrs. Alexander). Painter. Born in Pittsburgh in 1877. Pupil of William Forsyth. Member of Indianapolis Art Club. Work: Figure panels, Loew's Theater, Indianapolis. *Address*, 5 East Market St., Indianapolis, Ind.

SANSAM, Miss Edith. Painter. Born in Evanston, Ill. Studied in School of New Orleans Artists' Association. President of the ''Black and White Club.'' Won Pinckney Smith medal for sketches, and Artists' Association medal for landscape in oil.

SARG, Tony. Painter and illustrator. Born in Guatemala, Central America, in 1880. *Address*, 54 West 9th St., New York.

SARGEANT, Geneve R. Painter. Born in San Francisco, Calif., in 1868. Pupil of Emil Carlsen and W. M. Chase. Represented by ''Suma, A Japanese Girl,'' at Palace of Fine Arts, San Francisco. *Address*, 577 Duboce Ave., San Francisco, Calif.

SARGENT, Henry. Painter. Born in Gloucester, Mass., in 1770. He copied the work of Copley and other early American Artists. In 1790 Trumbull commended his work and in 1793 he went to London with letters to West, but returned to Boston in 1797. He received several military commissions. He studied in Gilbert Stuart's studio in Boston about 1806, with whom he was very friendly. Many of his paintings will be found in Boston. Colonel Sargent died in that city in 1845.

SARGENT, John Singer. Painter. Born in 1856 of American parents at Florence, Italy. He was educated in Florence, Rome, and Nice, and in 1874 at the age of eighteen he came to Paris showing promise of becoming the great painter that he eventually did. He entered the studio of Carolus-Duran then the most popular portrait painter in Paris. Here Sargent worked for five years helping his master at times with his mural pictures, yet finding time to travel in Italy and Spain. Here he studied the work of Velazquez. When leaving the studio of Carolus-Duran he painted a portrait of that painter, now considered one of his greatest pictures. His studio remained in Paris until 1884 when he moved to London, yet he spent much time in the United States, painting many of his best portraits in New York and Boston. He received commissions from the Public Library of Boston and the Boston Museum of Fine Arts to paint mural decorations for their buildings. His work was chiefly portraiture; his paintings of Henry G. Marquand and William M. Chase are in the Metropolitan Museum. The ''Daughters of Edward Boit'' is in the Boston Museum of Fine Arts and his portrait of ''Mr. and Mrs. Field'' in the Penna. Academy of Fine Arts. The Players' Club of New York owns his portraits of Edwin Booth and Joseph Jefferson, as ''Dr.

Pangloss,'' ''President Lowell'' of Harvard is owned by the University. A retrospective exhibition of his important works was held February–March, 1924, at the Grand Central Art Galleries, New York. Sargent died in London, April 15th, 1925. A memorial exhibition of his work, January–February, 1926, at the Metropolitan Museum of Art, New York, showed fifty-nine paintings in oil, and sixty-two in water colors. For biography of Sargent, see ''Sargent,'' by T. Martin Wood; and ''John S. Sargent, his Life and Works,'' by William Howe Downes (1925).

SARGENT, Margaret W. Sculptor. Born at Wellesley, Mass., in 1892. Pupil of Woodbury and Borglum. Member of National Association of Women Painters and Sculptors. *Address,* 107 West 47th St., New York.

SARGENT, Walter. Painter. Born in Worcester, Mass., in 1868. Pupil of Colarossi and Delecluse Academies in Paris. *Address,* University of Chicago, Chicago, Ill.

SARKA, Charles N. Mural painter and illustrator. Born in Chicago in 1879. *Address,* 692 Madison Ave., New York.

SARKADI, Leo S. Painter. Born in Hungary in 1879. *Address,* 1947 Broadway, N. Y.

SARONY, Napoleon. Painter. Identified with lithographic printing houses since his thirteenth year. He signed some pieces himself, executed in a graceful and smooth manner.

SARTAIN, Emily. Engraver. Born in Philadelphia in 1841. The daughter of John Sartain, she learned to engrave under the tuition of her father; she also studied art under Scheussele, in Philadelphia, and under Luminais, in Paris, in 1871–75. She engraved and signed a few mezzotint portraits. In 1881–83, Emily Sartain was the art editor of *Our Continent,* and in 1886 she became the principal of the Philadelphia School of Design for Women. Miss Sartain is also a painter of portraits and genre subjects, and exhibited at the Paris Salon in 1875 and 1883. *Address,* 1346 N. Broad St., Philadelphia.

SARTAIN, Harriet. Landscape painter. Born in Philadelphia. Pupil of Philadelphia School of Design for Women, and of Teachers' College, New York. Member of Plastic Club; National Association of Women Painters and Sculptors; Philadelphia Art Alliance, and Dean of Philadelphia School of Design for Women. *Address,* 1346 North Broad St., Philadelphia, Pa.

SARTAIN, John. Engraver. Born in London, England, in 1808; died in Philadelphia in 1897. In his ''Reminiscences,'' Mr. Sartain says that in February, 1823, he was apprenticed

to John Swain, a London engraver. The first plates of any consequence engraved by Sartain were line illustrations for ''The Early Florentine School,'' by Wm. Young Ottley, London, 1826. In 1827–28, Sartain was apprenticed to Henry Richter, of London, and while in Richter's employ he engraved his first mezzotint plate, entitled ''Omphale.'' His success with this plate induced him to engrave ''The Tight Shoe''; this plate he brought to the United States and sold, in 1830, to Mr. Littell, the Philadelphia publisher. At the termination of his apprenticeship Sartain commenced business for himself in London, and there engraved a portrait of Sir Charles Wilkins and some small Annual plates for the Ackermans.

Hearing that there were opportunities for a mezzotint engraver in the United States, Sartain in 1830 left London, with his wife, and ''in a little over eight weeks'' he landed in Philadelphia. Soon after his arrival here, and for the purpose of proving his ability as an engraver, he made a mezzotint plate after ''Old Age,'' a painting by John Neagle. This was his first mezzotint executed in the United States and his first line plate done here was ''Deer,'' in a landscape, after a painting by Thomas Doughty. Mr. Sartain soon had an abundance of work, and in 1843 he became the proprietor of *Campbell's Foreign Semi-Monthly Magazine,* and was also interested in the *Eclectic Magazine.* From 1841 to 1848 Mr. Sartain had been engraving for *Graham's Magazine,* and upon the collapse of that journal in the latter year he became half owner of *Sartain's Union Magazine,* the first number of which appeared in January, 1849; this journal was discontinued in 1852. For all of these magazines Mr. Sartain was the art manager and engraver, others doing the literary work.

After 1852 Mr. Sartain devoted himself to general engraving, and his total output of engraved plates numbers about 1500. His large portrait plates are very generally admirable examples of mezzotint work. He also painted miniatures, having received instruction from Henry Richter when he was in London. For life of Sartain see ''The Reminiscences of a Very Old Man,'' by John Sartain.

SARTAIN, Samuel. Engraver. Born in Philadelphia in 1830. Samuel Sartain studied engraving under his father, John Sartain, and became an admirable engraver of mezzotint portraits. About 1851 he commenced business on his own account in Philadelphia, and did much work for the publishers of that period. He died in 1906. His best plates were after the paintings of Peale, Sully and Neagle.

SARTAIN, William. Engraver. Born in Philadelphia in 1843. William Sartain, the son of John Sartain, studied mezzotint engraving with his father and issued and signed a few portrait plates. He then studied art in Paris, under Bonnat and at the École des Beaux Arts, and became a reputable painter of landscape.

Mr. Sartain was one of the founders of the Society of American Artists, and became an Associate Member of the National Academy of Design. He was president of the New York Art Club, and was later a teacher in the life class of the Art Students' League of New York. He died in 1924. He is represented in the Metropolitan Museum of New York, and in the Corcoran Art Gallery of Washington, D. C.

SARTELLE, Mildred E. Sculptor, who exhibited at the Penna. Academy of Fine Arts, Philadelphia, 1924. *Address*, 15 Leighton Road, Wellesley, Mass.

SATTERLEE, Walter. Born in Brooklyn, New York, in 1844. He was a pupil of the National Academy, also of Edwin White and Leon Bonnat. He was elected an Associate Member of the Academy in 1879, and in 1886 he gained the Clarke prize. Among his works are "Contemplation" owned by Smith College; "Autumn," "The Cronies," and "The Fortune-Teller." He died in 1908.

SAULNIER, H. E. A script and letter engraver working in Philadelphia in 1830–40. He engraved one of the early certificates of membership of the Franklin Institute, of that city.

SAUNDER, Kendall. Painter. Born at Templeton, Mass., in 1886. Pupil of Julien Academy under Laurens, in Paris. *Address*, 47 Fifth Ave., New York, N. Y., or Westport, Conn.

SAUNDERS, L. Pearl. Painter and illustrator. Born in Tennessee. Pupil of Art Students' League of New York and of Charles Hawthorne. *Address*, 301 The Vauxhall, Nashville, Tenn.

SAUNDERS, Sophia. Miniature painter, who flourished in 1851–52 in New York.

SAUTER, George. Painter, who exhibited at the Penna. Academy of Fine Arts, Philadelphia, 1915. *Address*, 1 Holland Park Ave., London, England.

SAVAGE, Dorothy L. Painter, who exhibited water colors at the Penna. Academy of Fine Arts, Philadelphia, 1925. *Address*, 300 Goodwood Road, Baltimore, Md.

SAVAGE, Edward. Painter. Born in Princeton, Worcester County, Mass., in 1761; died there in 1817. The father of Edward, Abraham Savage, had been driven from France, by the revocation of the Edict of Nantes. Edward Savage was originally a goldsmith, a trade that produced many of our early American engravers. As early as 1789, we find him turning his attention to portrait painting. He was only twenty-eight when he left Massachu-

setts carrying with him a letter from President Willard of Harvard College to Washington, requesting him to sit for his portrait for the University, and there it will be found today. This is the first that we know of Savage as an artist. He must have had some instruction and experience in portrait painting, however, for though his portrait of Washington was not remarkable as a work of art, still it was not painted by an absolutely inexperienced hand.

Savage moved to Philadelphia, and in 1791 sailed for London; here he studied under Benjamin West, and probably learned something of the art of engraving in stipple and in mezzotint. His engraved portraits of General Knox and of Washington were issued in London, 1791–92–93.

In 1794 Savage returned to the United States, and was married in Boston to Sarah Sever, and soon after this date he settled in Philadelphia, where his brother John Savage had established himself as a merchant. In July of 1795 he exhibited the first panorama ever shown in that city. It represented London and Westminster, and a Philadelphia newspaper of the time states that it was painted "in a circle and looks like reality."

Savage apparently remained in Philadelphia until 1801, when his name disappears from the city directory. He went to New York, and from there to Boston, and to Princeton. In New York Savage joined forces with Daniel Bowen, in the New York Museum. Dunlap in his "History of the Arts of Design" calls it "a mingled establishment, half painting gallery, half museum."

In 1795 these collections were transferred to Boston, and presented at "The Head of the Mall" as the Columbia Museum. The engraving of the Washington Family was published by Savage in 1798. David Edwin the engraver was assisting Savage at this time with his work. During the yellow fever epidemic which afflicted Philadelphia, the artist and his assistants were frightened away from the city, taking refuge in Burlington, N. J. Edwin told John Sartain, the Philadelphia engraver, an amusing story of their voyage up the Delaware in a row-boat, carrying the big painting of the Washington Family along, without taking the canvas off its stretching frame. To what extent Edwin and other engravers assisted Savage has always been more or less a question. Sartain always said "Savage drew the outlines on copper, but Edwin did a large part of the engraving." This is again corroborated in part by the portrait painter, James R. Lambdin who writes: "The Group of the Washington family by Savage was engraved by Edwin at Burlington, N. J., during the prevalence of the yellow fever in Philadelphia in 1798." Besides his portraits of Washington, Savage painted portraits of Generals Wayne and Knox; also of Robert Morris, Dr. William Handy, Benjamin Rush, and John Langdon, and many others prominent at that time.

SAVAGE, Eugene Francis. Figure and mural painter, who was born in Pittsburgh, Penna. He was elected an Associate Member of the National Academy, and to the Society of Mural Painters of New York. Awarded Clarke prize, National Academy of Design, 1923. Represented by ''Arbor Day'' at Chicago Art Institute. *Address*, 200 West 57th St., New York.

SAVAGE, Marguerite D. Painter and illustrator. Born in Bay Ridge, Long Island, in 1879. Pupil of Messer, Morse and Miller. *Address*, 41 Lancaster St., Worcester, Mass.

SAVELLI, Elena G. Painter, who exhibited at the Penna. Academy of Fine Arts, Philadelphia, 1924. *Address*, 137 West School Lane, Germantown, Philadelphia, Pa.

SAVILLE, Bruce Wilder. Sculptor. Born in Quincy, Mass., in 1893. Studied with Theo. A. Ruggles Kitson for 3 years. He opened a studio in Quincy in 1911. He exhibited at the National Academy of Design and the Gorham Gallery, New York; Copley Gallery, Boston; Boston Art League. Principal works: Memorial to Rev. Mons. Corley, Yonkers, N. Y.; public monuments to Col. Stephen G. Hicks; Col. Adolph Englemann; Col. Jonathan Richmond, in Miss.; portrait bust of Lt. Joseph Evans, of Quincy, Mass.; ideal figure, 1915; portrait bust of G. G. Saville, of Quincy, Mass.; fountain figure, ''Boy and Fish,'' at Boston; etc. Member: Copley Society; Boston Art League. *Address*, Ohio State University, Columbus, Ohio.

SAVORY. This name is appended as engraver to a somewhat crudely executed line-engraving of the ''Trinity Church, Pittsburgh, Founded A. D. 1824.'' The plate is signed ''Savory Sc. Pitt.'' There is no date, but appearances would indicate that the work was done about 1830–40.

SAWRIE, Mrs. Mary B. Miniature painter. Born in Nashville, Tenn., 1879. Pupil of Chase, Vanderpoel, Dow and Julien in Paris. *Address*, 710 Russell St., Nashville, Tenn.

SAWTELLE, A. Elizabeth. Painter. Pupil of Drexel Institute, Philadelphia, and of the Corcoran Art School of Washington. *Address*, 2102 O St., Wahington, D. C.

SAWTELLE, Mary (Mrs.). Painter. Born in Washington, D. C., in 1872. Pupil of Corcoran School of Art; Delecluse Academy in Paris; under Irving Wiles in New York. *Address*, 2102 O St., Washington, D. C.

SAWYER, Edith. Miniature painter, who exhibited at the Penna. Academy of Fine Arts, Philadelphia, 1925. *Address*, 2446 Fulton St., Brooklyn, New York.

SAWYER, Edward W. Sculptor. Born in Chicago, Ill., 1876. Specialty, medals. *Address*, 2 Broadfield Road, Folkestone, England.

SAWYER, Philip A. Painter and etcher. Born in Chicago in 1877. Pupil of Leon Bonnat. *Address*, 5 Rue Vercingetorvex, Paris, France.

SAWYER, Wells M. Painter and illustrator. Born in Iowa in 1863. Pupil of Art Institute of Chicago. *Address*, 44 Argyle Terrace, Yonkers, New York.

SAXTON, John G. Painter. Born in Troy, N. Y., in 1860. Studied in Paris under Lefebvre, Rony, Robert-Fleury and Merson. Received honorable mention, Paris Exposition, 1900; Buffalo Exposition, 1901; bronze medal, St. Louis Exposition, 1904. Specialty, landscapes. *Address*, Seaford, Long Island, New York.

SAXTON, Joseph. Born in Huntington, Pa., in 1790; died in Washington, D. C., in 1873. Saxton was not an engraver, though he devised a medal-ruling machine, among his other many inventions. While he was the constructor and curator of the standard weighing apparatus in the United States Mint, in Philadelphia, in 1842, he produced two beautifully executed portraits by means of this machine. These are portraits of Franklin Peale and of Dr. R. M. Patterson; they are inscribed ''Modelled by J. G. Chapman; electrotyped by Franklin Peale; engraved with the Medal-ruling machine by Jos. Saxton, Mint of the United States, 1842.'' They are admirable pieces of work of this type.

Previous to this date, medal-ruling had been done directly from the original medal, with the disadvantage of copying all its dents, scratches, or other imperfections, and there was the possibility of injuring a valuable medal by scratching it with the tracer; then a shellac cast of the original was copied by the machine; but this device failed owing to the shellac model being liable to puncture by the tracing-point, thus producing false lines upon the plate being engraved. To avoid these difficulties, inherent in the older methods, Saxton made an electrotype copy of the original and used that as a model in the machine. As this model was copper, it could not be punctured, and any imperfections in the original could be corrected in the model; it provided a smooth, hard and true surface for the tracing-point, and produced a perfect copy.

SAYEN, Lyman. Painter, whose work was exhibited in Philadelphia in 1921, in the ''Exhibition of Paintings Showing the Later Tendencies in Art.'' He died in 1918.

SCACKI, Francisco. Engraver. This name is signed to a large but very crudely drawn and etched view of the Battle of New Orleans. It is apparently contemporaneous with the battle in date, and the only impression known has the second state of the plate printed on the back of the first impression. It is difficult to determine, however, whether Scacki is the engraver or the publisher of the plate, or both. The form of the signature is as follows: "Francisco Scacki—Copy Right Secured."

SCALELLA, Jules. Painter. Pupil of Penna. Academy of the Fine Arts; exhibited there 1926. *Address*, Ardmore, Penna.

SCARBOROUGH, John. Painter, who flourished about 1830.

SCARPITTA, G. S. C. Sculptor. Born in Italy, 1887. He settled in New York in 1910. Represented in Milwaukee Art Institute. Exhibited in Penna. Academy of Fine Arts, Philadelphia, 1914. *Address*, 7 West 42d St., New York City.

SCHABELITZ, R. F. Illustrator. Born in Stapleton, N.Y., in 1884. *Address*, 854 West 181st St., New York.

SCHAEFFER, William G. Painter. Member of the Washington Water Color Club. *Address*, 95 Madison Ave., New York.

SCHAETTLE, Louis. Mural painter. Born in Chicago, he died in New York City in 1917. He painted mural decorations in Georgian Court, Lakewood, N. J.

SCHAFF, Anton. Sculptor. Born in Wisconsin in 1869. Pupil of Saint Gaudens. Represented by statue of Genl. Ord, in Vicksburg, and monuments at Glendale and Ridgewood, Brooklyn, N. Y. *Address*, 1931 Broadway, New York.

SCHAMBERG, Morton L. Painter. Born in Philadelphia in 1881. Pupil of Wm. M. Chase. Member: Society of Independent Artists. *Address*, Care of W. Pach, 13 East 14th St., New York City.

SCHATTENSTEIN, Nikol. Painter, who exhibited at the National Academy of Design, New York, 1925. *Address*, 33 West 67th St., New York.

SCHELL, Dorothy Root. Painter. Member: Plastic Club. *Address*, Middle City Building, Phila., or 5027 Newhall St., Germantown, Philadelphia, Pa.

SCHELL, F. Cresson. Illustrator. Born in Philadelphia in 1857. Pupil of Thomas Eakins and Thomas P. Anshutz. Member: Artists' Aid Society; Fellowship, Penna. Academy of Fine Arts; Philadelphia Art Alliance; Philadelphia Sketch Club. *Address*, 5215 Archer St., Germantown, Philadelphia, Pa.

SCHENCK, Franklin Lewis. Painter. Born in 1855. Pupil of Thomas Eakins, who founded the Philadelphia Art Students' League, and appointed Schenck as curator. Represented by paintings in Brooklyn Chamber of Commerce and in the Pratt Library. *Address*, East Northport, Long Island.

SCHETKY, Caroline. Miniature painter and water color artist, formerly flourishing in Philadelphia and Boston. She married T. M. Richardson and exhibited at the Boston Athenaeum under that name; she also painted landscapes and flowers.

SCHEVILL, W. V. Portrait painter. Born in Cincinnati, Ohio, in 1864. Pupil of Lofftz, Lindenschmidt and Gysis in Munich. Member of Century Association; Salmagundi Club. Awarded the bronze medal, St. Louis Exposition, 1904. Work: "In Love," Cincinnati Museum, Cincinnati; portrait sketch, "Prince Henry of Prussia," Herron Art Institute, Indianapolis. *Address*, 44 West 77th St., New York, N. Y.

SCHICK, Fred G. Painter and illustrator. Born in Buffalo, N. Y., in 1893. Pupil of Wilcox and M. B. Cox. Member of the Buffalo Art Club, Buffalo, N. Y. *Address*, 546 Main St., Buffalo, N. Y.

SCHIFFER, Ethel Bennett (Mrs. W. B.). Illustrator, etcher and engraver. Born in Brooklyn, N. Y., in 1879. Pupil of Yale School of Fine Arts; Art Students' League of New York. Member of Society of Independent Artists; National Association of Women Painters and Sculptors. *Address*, 357 Elm St., New Haven, Conn.

SCHILLE, Alice. Painter. Born in Columbus. Pupil of Columbus Art School; Art Students' League of New York; New York School of Art under Chase and Cox; pupil of Prinet, Collin, Courtois and of the Colarossi Academy in Paris. Member: New York Water Color Club; Boston Water Color Club; National Association of Women Painters and Sculptors; Chicago Water Color Club; Philadelphia Water Color Club. Awarded Corcoran prize, Washington Water Color Club, 1908; New York Woman's Art Club; gold medal for water colors, Panama-Pacific Exposition, San Francisco, 1915; Philadelphia Water Color prize, Penna. Academy of the Fine Arts, 1915. *Address*, 1166 Bryden Road, Columbus, Ohio.

SCHILLING, A. O. Painter and illustrator. Born in Germany in 1882. Studied in Chicago, Buffalo, Rochester; also in Germany. Member: Buffalo Art Club; Buffalo Society of Artists; Rochester Art Club. *Address*, 93 North St., Rochester, N. Y.

SCHLADERMUNDT, Herman T. Mural painter. Born in Milwaukee, Wis., in 1863.

Member: New York Architectural L e a g u e, 1893; Mural Painters. Awarded Allied Arts prize, Architectural League; medal of Columbian Exposition, Chicago, 1893. Work: Mural decorations in Flagler Memorial Church, St. Augustine, Fla.; Emigrants' Industrial Bank, New York; Mosaic Vaults, Congressional Library, Washington; Grand Jury Room, Court House, Newark, N. J.; Automobile Club of America, New York; Museum of Thomas F. Ryan, New York. *Address*, Lawrence Park, Bronxville, N. Y.

SCHLAIKJER, J. W. Painter, who exhibited in the National Academy of Design, New York, 1925. *Address*, 3201 Oxford Ave., New York.

SCHLECHT, Charles. Engraver. Born in Stuttgart, Germany, in 1843; living in New York in 1905. Charles Schlecht was brought to the United States by his parents in 1852, and was apprenticed to the American Bank Note Company in 1859; he also received instruction in his profession from Charles Bush and Alfred Jones.

Mr. Schlecht made bank-note engraving his principal occupation, working in New York City and at the Bureau of Engraving and Printing in Washington, D. C. But he also produced some admirable portrait and subject plates for the publishers. Two of his large plates, executed in pure line, are especially worthy of note. These are ''Eyes to the Blind,'' after a painting by A. F. Bellows, and ''The Wish,'' after a painting by Percy Moran.

SCHLEGELL, Gustav Von. Painter. Born in St. Louis in 1877. Pupil of Robert Koehler in Minneapolis; Carl Marr in Munich; Laurent and Laurens in Paris. Work is represented in the St. Louis Artists' Guild. *Address*, St. Louis School of Fine Arts, St. Louis, Mo.

SCHLEMMER, F. Louis. Painter. Born in Crawfordsville, Ind., in 1893. Pupil of Hawthorne. Exhibited ''Sunlight'' at the Penna. Academy of the Fine Arts, Philadelphia, 1924. *Address*, Crawfordsville, Ind.

SCHLESINGER, Louis. Sculptor. Born in Bohemia in 1874. Member of New York Architectural League. *Address*, 51 West 10th St., New York.

SCHLEY, Mathilde G. Painter. Born in Wisconsin in 1874. Pupil of Lorenz. *Address*, 322 Fifteenth St., Milwaukee, Wis.

SCHMAND, J. Phillip. Portrait painter. Born in Germania, Pa., in 1871. Pupil of Mowbray and Vonnoh. Member of National Art Club. Painted portraits of Charles S. Green, John R. Patterson and Warren C. Hubbard. *Address*, Hotel des Artistes, 1 West 67th St., New York, N. Y.

SCHMEDTGEN, William Herman. Painter. Born in Chicago in 1862. Studied at the Art Institute of Chicago. Pioneer in newspaper illustrating in Chicago; commercial art work, *Chicago Mail*, 1883; and also in St. Louis and the South; head of art department, *Chicago Record*, 1886–1901; now on staff of Chicago *Record-Herald*. Illustrator for many art books and magazine articles on outdoor sports; field artist for *Record*, in Spanish-American war, in camp before Santiago; traveled and sketched for newspaper articles in Mexico and Cuba; traveled in Spain, Italy and Northern Africa for the *Record*, 1900. *Address*, Record-Herald, Chicago, Ill.

SCHMIDT, Katherine. Painter. Born in Xenia, Ohio, in 1898. Pupil of Kenneth Hayes Miller. Member: Society of Independent Artists. *Address*, Ardsley Studios, 110 Columbia Heights, Brooklyn, N. Y.

SCHMIDT, Oscar F. Painter, who exhibited at the National Academy of Design, New York, 1925. *Address*, 301 West 24th St., New York.

SCHMITT, Albert F. Painter. Born in Boston in 1873. Member: Copley Society; Boston Art Club. Awarded silver medal, Panama-Pacific Exposition, San Francisco, 1915. Work represented in the City Art Museum, St. Louis; R. I. School of Design, Providence, R. I.; Museum of Fine Arts, Boston. *Address*, 194 Brattle St., Cambridge, Mass.

SCHMITT, Carl. Painter and etcher. Born in Trumbull County, Ohio, in 1889. Pupil of National Academy of Design under Carlsen; also studied in Florence, Italy. Work: ''The Mill,'' Butler Art Institute, Youngstown, Ohio. His mural painting of ''The Nativity'' was exhibited at the Brooklyn Exhibition of Mural Painters, of New York.

SCHMITZ, Elizabeth T. Painter. Born in Philadelphia. Pupil of Penna. Academy of Fine Arts. *Address*, 1710 Chestnut St., Philadelphia.

SCHNAKENBERG, Henry E. Painter and etcher. Born in 1892. Pupil of Kenneth Hayes Miller. Member of Art Students' League of New York. *Address*, 601 West End Ave., New York, N. Y.

SCHNEIDER, Arthur. Painter and illustrator. *Address*, 939 Eighth Ave., New York.

SCHNEIDER, Otto J. Portrait painter, etcher and illustrator. Member of Chicago Society of Etchers. Born at Atlanta, Ill., 1875. Represented in Art Institute of Chicago; also by portraits of Lincoln, McKinley, Emerson and Mark Twain. *Address*, 1259 Thorndale Ave., Chicago, Ill.

SCHNEIDER, Theophile. Painter, who exhibited the ''Golden Rocks'' at the Penna. Academy of Fine Arts, Philadelphia, 1924. *Address*, 380 Fulton St., Brooklyn, N. Y.

SCHOENER, J. Portrait painter in oils and miniature. He exhibited at the Pennsylvania Academy in 1817, and was working in Philadelphia till 1827.

SCHOENFELD, Flora. Painter, who exhibited in Philadelphia, 1921, in "Exhibition of Paintings Showing the Later Tendencies in Art." *Address,* 5024 Ellis Ave., Chicago, Ill.

SCHOFF, P. R. Engraver. An excellent portrait in pure line, that of Robert Baird, after a painting by G. P. R. Healy, is thus signed. No other work has been found signed by this man, and it is possible that the signature is a letter engraver's error for the name below.

SCHOFF, Stephen Alonzo. Engraver. Born in Danville, Vt., in 1818; died at Brandon, Vt., in 1905. When Mr. Schoff was about eight years of age his parents removed first to Bradford, on the Merrimac, and later to Newburyport, Mass. Stephen Alonzo Schoff was one of a family of six children, and when he was sixteen years old he was sent to Boston and there indentured for five years to Oliver Pelton, an engraver of that city. Dissatisfied with the progress he was making, at the end of about three years, and with the consent of Mr. Pelton, Mr. Schoff became a pupil of Joseph Andrews and to this admirable line-engraver, says Mr. Schoff in a personal letter, "I owe more than can ever be repaid."

With Mr. Andrews he went to Paris in 1840, and both young men there worked for a time in the studio of Paul Delaroche, drawing from the nude. Mr. Schoff returned to the United States in 1842, and was at once employed by a bank-note engraving company in New York.

SCHOFIELD, Louis Sartain. Engraver. Born in 1868; a grandson of John Sartain. He is an expert line-engraver and a designer of great ability, and for some years has been in the employ of the Bureau of Engraving and Printing, at Washington, D. C.

SCHOFIELD, W. Elmer. Painter. Born in Philadelphia in 1867. Pupil of the Penna. Academy of the Fine Arts, and of Bouguereau, Doucet, Ferrier in Paris. Awarded first Hallgarten prize, National Academy of Design; Sesman gold medal, Penna. Academy of Fine Arts, in 1903. Represented in permanent collection at Metropolitan Museum, New York; Buffalo Museum of Art; Penna. Academy of the Fine Arts; Corcoran Art Gallery, Washington, D. C. Elected Member of the National Academy of Design in 1907. His specialty is landscape painting. *Address,* 15 Gramercy Park, New York.

SCHONHARDT, Henri. Sculptor. Born at Providence, R. I., in 1877. Studied at Académie Julien, École des Arts, Paris; private pupil of Ernest-Dubois, Paris. Worked with Dubois on the monument of Bossuet exhibited in 1900, Exhibition at Paris; also portraits of Madame Agache and Roger de Sitivaux de Greiche, in Paris. Instructor in modeling in Rhode Island School of Design, 1903–09. Principal works: Memorial to Gov. Elisha Dyer, in St. Stephen's Church, Providence, R. I.; memorial to Col. Henry Harrison Young, in City Hall Park, Providence, R. I.; Soldiers' and Sailors' Monument, at Bristol, R. I.; "Cadmus and Clytie," in R. I. School of Design Museum; life size portrait of William Grosvenor, in marble; memorial to Col. Henry Tillinghast Sisson, at Little Compton, R. I., etc. Honorable mention, Paris Salon, 1908. *Address,* 21 Audubon Ave., Providence, R. I.

SCHONLU, W. A. Painter, who exhibited "Snow Mountain" at the Penna. Academy of the Fine Arts, Philadelphia, 1924. *Address,* 173 Pleasant St., Arlington, Mass.

SCHOOK, F. De Forest. Painter. Born in Michigan in 1872. Pupil of Art Institute of Chicago; of H. O. Tanner, Menard, and Simon in Paris. Member of Chicago Society of Artists, and Chicago Water Color Club. Instructor of illustration and composition in Chicago Art Institute. *Address,* Lombard, Ill.

SCHOONMAKER, William P. Etcher. Born in New York in 1891. Pupil of Bridgman. Member of the Philadelphia Sketch Club. *Address,* 225 South Sydenham St., Philadelphia, Pa.

SCHOONOVER, Frank E. Illustrator. Born in Oxford, N. J., in 1877. Pupil of Drexel Institute and of Howard Pyle. Specialty, American Indians and Canadian trappers. *Address,* 1616 Rodney St., Wilmington, Del.

SCHOULER, Willard C. Painter. Born in Arlington, Mass., in 1852. Represented in Boston Museum of Fine Arts by "Indians of Arizona." Specialty, Western and Arabian scenes. *Address,* 173 Pleasant St., Arlington, Mass.

SCHOYER, Raphael. A copperplate printer living in Baltimore, Md., in 1824; in 1826 he was engraving some indifferently executed portraits in New York.

SCHRAM, Anraham J. Painter. Born in Grand Rapids, Mich., in 1891. Pupil of Corcoran School of Art. *Address,* 937 M St., Washington, D. C

SCHREYVOGEL, Charles. Painter. Born in New York City in 1861; died in Hoboken, N. J., in 1912. He studied in Newark, N. J., and later in Munich. In 1901 he was elected an Associate Member of the National Academy of Design.

SCHROFF, Alfred H. Painter. Born in Springfield, Mass., in 1863. Pupil of De Camp, and of the Cowles Art School. *Address,* University of Oregon, Eugene, Oregon.

SCHULENBURG, Adele (Mrs.). Sculptor. (See Mrs. C. K. Gleeson.)

SCHULER, Hans. Sculptor. Born in Germany in 1874. Pupil of Verlet in Paris. Represented by "Ariadne" in Walters Gallery, Baltimore, Md., and by "Johns Hopkins Monument," Baltimore, Md. *Address,* 5 East Lafayette Ave., Baltimore, Md.

SCHULMAN, A. G. Painter. Born in Konigsberg, Germany, in 1881. Pupil of S. J. Woolf and of the National Academy of Design, New York. Instructor, College of the City of New York. *Address,* 24 East 59th St., New York, N. Y.

SCHULTZ, George F. Landscape painter. Born in Chicago in 1869. Awarded Tuthill prize, Art Institute of Chicago, 1918. Work: "By the Sea," Union League Club, Chicago; "Among the Birches," Cliff Dwellers, Chicago; "Twilight Shadows," Arché Club, Chicago; "Autumn Weather," City of Chicago Collection. *Address,* 4003 Greenview Ave., Chicago, Ill.

SCHUSSELE, Christian. Painter. Born in Alsace in 1824. He studied in Paris, and came to Philadelphia about 1848. He exhibited his work at the Penna. Academy of Fine Arts, and was elected Prof. of Drawing and Painting at the Academy where he served till his death in 1879. Many of his paintings were engraved by John Sartain. He painted "Benjamin Franklin before the Council, London, 1773," and other American Historical scenes; painted a number of portraits of prominent Americans.

SCHUSTER, Donna N. Painter. Pupil of Art Institute of Chicago, and of Tarbell and Chase. Member of California Art Club; Society of Independent Artists; West Coast Arts Club. Awarded gold medal, Minn. State Art Ex., 1913; prize for painting, Minn. State Art Ex., 1914; silver medal, Northwestern Exhibition, St. Paul Institute, 1915; silver medal for water colors, Panama-Pacific Exposition, San Francisco, 1915; silver medal, Panama-California Exposition, San Diego, 1915; first prize for water colors. *Address,* 1229 West 37th Drive, Los Angeles, Calif.

SCHWAB, Edith Fisher (Mrs. C.). Painter. Born in Cincinnati, Ohio, in 1862. Member of National Association of Women Painters and Sculptors. *Address,* 310 Prospect St., New Haven, Conn.

SCHWAB, Eloise M. Painter and etcher. Born in Havana, Cuba, in 1894. Pupil of Kenneth Hayes Miller; also studied in Paris.

Member of Art Alliance of America. *Address,* 549 West 113th St., New York, N. Y.

SCHWABE, H. August. Painter. Born in Oberweisbach, Germany, in 1843. Learned drawing and china decorating, and at 18 worked as painter and designer of stained glass in Stuttgart; studied in Polytechnic School, Royal Academy of Fine Arts, Munich; also in Cologne. He came to the United States in 1871, and later studied at the old Academy of Design, New York, and under William Chase; also at Munich, Paris and in the Julien Academy. He has designed and painted church windows in New York, Pittsburgh, Chicago, etc. Awarded gold medal for stained glass design and execution, St. Louis Exposition, 1904; exhibited at New York Academy of Design; Art Association. He is also a portrait figure painter. Is president of the Newark Art League, and a member of the Newark Museum Association. *Address,* 917 Broad St., Newark, N. J.

SCHWANKOVSKY, Frederick J., Jr. Painter and illustrator. Born in Detroit, Mich., in 1885. Pupil of the Penna. Academy of the Fine Arts and of the Art Students' League of New York. Member of California Art Club. He did research work for the Metropolitan Picture Corporation, and was the head of the Art Department of Manual Arts High School, Los Angeles, Calif. *Address,* 1231 West 76th St., Los Angeles, Calif.

SCHWARM, Wesley A. Painter. Born in Lafayette, Ind., in 1883. Pupil of Pratt Institute and of Henri. Member of Society of Independent Artists. *Address,* 130 East 19th St., Brooklyn, N. Y.

SCHWARCZ, D. R. Painter. Born in Brooklyn in 1893. Pupil of Kenneth Hayes Miller, C. W. Hawthorne, Jonas Lie and R. S. Bredin. Member: National Association of Women Painters and Sculptors and League of New York Artists. *Address,* 272 West 90th St., New York, N. Y.

SCHWARTZ, Andrew (Thomas). Mural painter. Born in Louisville, Ky., in 1867. Pupil of Duveneck in Cincinnati; of Art Students' League of New York under Mowbray. Member of Mural Painters of America and New York Architectural League, 1904. Awarded Lazarus scholarship to Italy, 1899–1902. Work: "Christ, the Good Shepherd," Baptist Church, South Londonderry, Vt.; also represented in Cincinnati Art Museum and Utica Public Library. *Address,* 246 Fulton St., Brooklyn, N. Y.

SCHWARTZ, C. In 1814 this stipple-engraver of portraits was working in Baltimore, Md. His signed work is rare, but his large plate of Bishop James Kemp, published in Baltimore, is a capital piece of work.

SCHWARTZ, Elizabeth (Mrs. Chas. Ney-land). Painter. Member of National Association of Women Painters and Sculptors. *Address*, 3337 North 17th St., Philadelphia, Pa.

SCHWARTZKOPF, Earl C. Painter and illustrator. Born in Ohio in 1888. Member of Toledo Tile Club. *Address*, Care of Willys-Overland Co., Toledo, Ohio.

SCHWARZ, Rudolf. Sculptor. Born in Germany, he settled in Indianapolis. In 1902 he won the competition for a statue of Governor Pingree, of Michigan.

SCHWARZBURGER, C a r l. Engraver. Born in Leipzig, Germany, in 1850. Studied in Leipzig and Berlin; came to America in 1874. Went to Australia, 1886–89, to illustrate the books "Picturesque Australia"; exhibited at Chicago; also Paris Exposition, 1900; medal, Buffalo Exposition, 1901. *Address*, 565 McDonough St., Brooklyn, N. Y.

SCHWARZOTT, Maximilian. Sculptor. He has exhibited at the National Sculpture Society.

SCHWEIZER, J. Otto. Sculptor. Born in Zurich, Switzerland, in 1863. Pupil of Tuiller in Paris and studied in Italy. Member of National Sculpture Society. Work: "Gen. Muhlenberg" and "James B. Nicholson," Philadelphia; "Gen. Steuben," Utica, N. Y., and Valley Forge, Pa.; "Abraham Lincoln" and Generals Humphrey, Geary, Hays, Pleasanton, Gregg, Pa. State Memorial; Gen. Wells Monument for State of Vermont, at Gettysburg, Pa. *Address*, 2215 West Venango St., Philadelphia, Pa.

SCOFIELD, William Bacon. Sculptor. Born in Hartford, Conn., in 1864. Pupil of Gutzon Borglum. Work: "Good and Bad Spirit" (bronze), Worcester Art Museum. Author of "Verses" and "Poems of the War"; "A Forgotten Idyl"; Sketches in Verse and Clay. *Address*, Chase Building, 42 Front St., Worcester, Mass.

SCOLES, John. This engraver of portraits and subject plates was located continuously in New York from 1793 until 1844. He probably died in the latter year, as he is then registered "John Scoles, late engraver." Scoles worked in both line and stipple, but with indifferent success. He engraved many of the views appearing in the *New York Magazine* in 1793–96.

SCOMA, Mario. Sculptor, who exhibited "The Birthday" in Annual Exhibition, 1915, of the Penna. Academy of the Fine Arts, Philadelphia. *Address*, 24 Hamburg Ave., Brooklyn, N. Y.

SCOT. Painter. Nothing is known of this artist, except the mention in the diary of Rev. Wm. Bentley, Oct. 3, 1803. "At Mr. Scot's saw several full lengths of Washington which pleased me, excepting the faces so different from those I saw. Several paintings did honor to this young painter; the head of Dr. Lathrop was complete, Mr. Adams I readly knew, Mr. Murray, the Universalist not so much, Gov. Strong too full faced."

SCOT, Robert. Engraver. Born in England. He was originally a watchmaker. He appears in Philadelphia about 1783, and in that year he engraved a frontispiece for a Masonic sermon preached by Wm. Smith, D.D., and published by Hall & Sellars. He advertised himself as "Late Engraver to the State of Virginia," and in 1785 he was paid 16 pounds for engraving done for the State of Pennsylvania. Scot engraved a few fairly well-executed line portraits, including one of Washington, over his own name. In 1793, Robert Scot was appointed engraver to the newly established United States Mint in Philadelphia, and he is credited with having made the dies for the copper cent of 1793.

SCOTT, Anna Page. Painter. Pupil of Anshutz, Arthur Dow, and of the Colarossi Academy, Paris. Represented by the "Shores of the Pacific," Carnegie Library, Dubuque. *Address*, 1212 Locust St., Dubuque.

SCOTT, Charles T. Painter and sculptor. Born in Chester County, Pa., in 1876. Pupil of Penna. Museum School of Industrial Art, Philadelphia. *Address*, 320 South Broad St., Philadelphia.

SCOTT, Colin A. Painter. Born in Ottawa, Canada, 1861. Member of Providence Art Association. *Address*, College St., South Hadley, Mass.

SCOTT, Mrs. Emily S. Flower painter. Born in Springwater, N. Y., in 1832. She studied at the Art Students' League, New York, and in Paris. She is represented by paintings in the Metropolitan Museum and in the Brooklyn Institute Museum. She died in April, 1915.

SCOTT, Jeannette. Painter. Born at Kincardine, Ont., in 1864. Studied drawing at School of Design for Women; Penna. Academy of Fine Arts; also studied in Paris, 1889–94, and at the Salon de Camps de Mars. Returned to New York, 1894; professor of painting since 1895, and head of painting department since 1902, in Syracuse University. *Address*, 1111 E. Genesee St., Syracuse, N. Y.

SCOTT, John W. A. Landscape painter. Born in Dorchester, Mass., in 1815. His best known paintings are scenes in the Catskills and White Mountains. He died in Cambridge, Mass., in 1907.

SCOTT, Joseph T. Engraver (an especially good map engraver) working in Philadelphia as early as 1795. He published an atlas of the United States, printed in Philadelphia in 1796 by Francis and Robert Bailey. Scott drew and engraved the maps.

SCOTT, Julian. Painter. Born in Vermont in 1846. He entered the army at the breaking out of the Civil War. He afterwards became a pupil of the National Academy and studied under Leutze until 1868. His work consists chiefly of pictures of Army life; ''Battle of Cedar Creek,'' ''Charge at Antietam,'' ''The Recall'' and the ''Blue and the Gray.'' He died in 1901.

SCOTT, Katharine Hall. Portrait and miniature painter. Born in Burlington, Ia., in 1871. Pupil of Vanderpoel and Chase. *Address*, Mason City, Iowa.

SCOTT, William Edouard. Painter. Born in Indianapolis in 1884. Pupil of Art Institute of Chicago and of the Julien Academy in Paris. Represented by mural paintings in Herron Art Institute, Ind., and in the Court House, Springfield, Ill. *Address*, 3160 Indiana Ave., Chicago.

SCOTT, William J. Painter, who exhibited water colors at the Penna. Academy of Fine Arts, Philadelphia, 1925. *Address*, Compo Road, Westport, Conn.

SCOTT, William Wallace. Painter in water colors. Born in 1819. His studio was for many years in New York City where he died in 1905.

SCRYMSER, Christabel. Miniature painter, who exhibited miniatures at the Penna. Academy of the Fine Arts, Philadelphia, 1925. *Address*, 34 Lewis Place, Rockville Centre, Long Island, N. Y.

SCUDDER, Janet. Sculptor. Born in Terre Haute, Ind., in 1873. Educated at Cincinnati Art Academy; Art Institute of Chicago; Vittis Academy, Colarossi's Academy. and MacMonnies Studio, Paris. Awarded bronze medal, Chicago Exposition, 1893; prize medal, St. Louis Exposition, 1904; honorable mention, Salon, Paris, 1911. Principal works: ''Frog Fountain,'' in Metropolitan Museum of Art, New York; ''Young Diana,'' in Paris Salon, 1911; ''Little Lady of the Sea,'' in Salon, Paris, 1913; ''Fighting Boys Fountain,'' Art Institute of Chicago. Represented in Musée du Luxembourg, Paris; Metropolitan Museum, Numismatic Museum, New York City; Congressional Library, Washington; Peabody Institute, Baltimore; John Herron Institute, Indianapolis; Art Institute of Chicago. *Address*, Colony Club or 46 Washington Mews, New York.

SCUDDER, Raymond. Painter. Born in New Orleans, La. Pupil of Newcomb Art School; New York School of Applied Design; also of Chase and Mora. Member: New Orleans Artists' Association. *Address*, 1631 Octavia St., New Orleans, La.

SEABURY, Mrs. Roxoli. Painter. Born in 1874. Pupil of D. W. Ross, Robt. Reid and of Knirr in Munich. Student of School of Boston Museum of Fine Arts. *Address*, Broadwater Art Academy, Colorado Springs, Colo.

SEAGER, Mrs. and Miss. Miniature painters, who flourished in New York, 1834.

SEALEY, Alfred. Engraver. Born in the United States. He is said to have died in Canada about 1862. Sealey was an admirable line-engraver and devoted himself to bank-note work in his later life. In 1856 he was apparently working in Philadelphia, but some of his signed work is dated as early as 1845. In 1860 some very good line illustrations to Cooper's novels are signed ''Sealey & Smith Sculpt.'' This work was done in New York and may be ascribed to Alfred Sealey.

SEAMAN, Charles. Portrait painter in oils and miniatures, who flourished in New York about 1834.

SEARLE, Alice T. Miniature painter. Born in Troy, N. Y., in 1869. Pupil of Art Students' League of New York and of the Colarossi Academy, Paris. Member of Brooklyn Artists' Guild. *Address*, 241 Fenimore St., Brooklyn, New York.

SEARS, Philip. Sculptor. Exhibited at the Penna. Academy of Fine Arts, 1926. *Address*, 20 Heath St., Brookline, Mass.

SEARS, Sarah Choate (Mrs. J. M.). Painter. Born in Cambridge, Mass., in 1858. Pupil of Cowles Art School and Museum of Fine Arts, Boston. Awarded William T. Evans prize, 1892; medal, Chicago Exposition, 1893; honorable mention, Paris Exposition, 1900; bronze medal, Buffalo Exposition, 1901. *Address*, 12 Arlington St., Boston, Mass.

SEARS, Taber. Mural painter. Born in Boston in 1870. Studied at Boston Museum of Fine Arts School of Art; Julien School, Paris; was a pupil of Jean Paul Laurens and Luc Olivier Merson; also studied in Florence and Rome. Mural paintings: ''The Spirit of Niagara,'' in Buffalo Historical Society, New York; ''Among the Nations,'' New York City Hall; frieze of the Apostles, Epiphany Church, Pittsburgh; stained glass windows, ''The Presentation in the Temple,'' ''The Resurrection,'' ''The Ascension,'' Plainfield, N. J., Presbyn. Church. Has exhibited in the Paris Salons; Penna. Academy of the Fine Arts; New York

Water Color Club; also in annual exhibitions in New York, Buffalo, etc. Member of Architectural League of New York; National Society of Mural Painters; Artists' Aid Society. *Address*, 96 5th Ave., New York, N. Y.

SEATON, C. H. Painter. Born in Monson, Mass., in 1865. Self-taught. Member: Washington Society of Artists; Washington Landscape Club. *Address*, Glencarlyn, Va.

SEAWELL, H. W. Painter and illustrator. Born in San Francisco. Pupil of Laurens and Constant in Paris. *Address*, 1617 California St., San Francisco, Calif.

SEBRON, H. Painter. Born in 1801; died in 1879. Painted landscapes and river views in and about New Orleans.

SEIDEL, Emory P. Painter and sculptor. *Address*, McClurg Building, Chicago, Ill.

SEIDENECK, George J. Painter. Born in Chicago, Ill., in 1885. Pupil of Walter Thor and von Marr. Member: Chicago Art Club; Chicago Society of Artists; Chicago Palette and Chisel Club. Work: "Portrait of Judge Seaman," Federal Building, Chicago. *Address*, Tree Studio Building, 4 East Ohio St., Chicago, Ill.

SEIPP, Alice. Painter and illustrator. Born in New York, N. Y., in 1889. Pupil of Douglas Volk, B. W. Clinedinst and Jane Peterson. Member: National Association of Women Painters and Sculptors; New York Water Color Club. *Address*, 188 Claremont Ave., New York, N. Y.

SEISSER, Martin B. Painter. Born in Pittsburgh, Penna., in 1845. He went to Europe in 1868 and studied in Munich. On his return he opened his studio in Pittsburgh, and painted many portraits. His picture "The Crusaders," painted in 1875, was stolen in 1878 at an auction sale in Philadelphia.

SEL, Jean B. Portrait painter in oils and miniatures, who flourished in 1820–1830, New Orleans. A portrait in oil by Sel of Gov. A. B. Roman is in the Louisiana State Museum.

SELDEN, Miss Dixie. Painter and illustrator. Born in Cincinnati, Ohio. Pupil of Cincinnati Art Academy under Duveneck; also of W. M. Chase; of H. B. Snell. Member of Cincinnati Woman's Art Club and National Association of Women Painters and Sculptors. *Address*, 5 The Deventer, McWilliam St., Cincinnati, Ohio.

SELDEN, Henry Bill. Painter, who exhibited at the National Academy of Design, New York, 1925. *Address*, New London, Conn.

SELINGER, Jean Paul. Painter. Born in 1850. His painting "The Water Seller" is in the Boston Museum of Fine Arts. He died in 1909.

SELLERS, Mary. Painter. Born in Pittsburgh in 1869. Pupil of Alexander Robinson and August Hennicott in Holland. Member of National Association of Women Painters and Sculptors. *Address*, 6216 Howe St., Pittsburgh, Penna.

SELLSTEDT, Lars Gustaf. Painter. Born in Sweden in 1819. He came to the United States in 1834 and settled in Buffalo, N. Y., in 1842. He has devoted himself chiefly to portraiture, and his works include portraits of Geo. W. Clinton, Millard Fillmore, Benjamin Fitch and Grover Cleveland. He was elected an Associate Member in 1871 of the National Academy and an Academician in 1874, and died in 1911. For his life see "From Forecastle to Academy," published in Buffalo, N. Y., in 1904.

SENAT, Prosper L. Painter. Born in Philadelphia in 1852. Studied in Philadelphia, New York, London and Paris. Specialty, landscapes in water colors. He died in Philadelphia in 1925. For years he painted on the Brittany coast and at Cornwall, England.

SENECAL, Ralph L. Painter and illustrator. Born in Bolton, Canada, in 1883. Pupil of National Academy of Design. Member of Springfield Art Club; Connecticut Society of Artists; Springfield Art League. *Address*, Three Rivers, Mass.

SENSENEY, George. Painter and etcher. Born in Wheeling, West Va., in 1874. Pupil of Corcoran Art School in Washington under Howard Helmick; under Laurens and Constant in Paris. Awarded silver medal, Panama-Pacific Exposition, San Francisco, 1915. Work represented in Library of Congress, Washington, D. C. *Address*, 55 New South St., Northampton, Mass.

SENYARD, George. Painter, who died in Ohio in 1924. He toured the country with Lincoln, and made many sketches and drawings of him during his political debates.

SEPESCHY, Zeltan L. Painter and illustrator. Born in Hungary in 1898. Studied in Munich. *Address*, 209 Pasadena Ave., Highland Park, Mich.

SERGEANT, Edgar. Painter, who exhibited at the National Academy of Design, New York, 1925. *Address*, Nutley, N. J.

SERPELL, Susan W. (Mrs.). Painter. Born in California in 1875; died in 1913. In 1912 she was elected an Associate Member of the National Academy of Design, and received many medals and awards.

SERRAO, Mrs. Luella Varney. Sculptor. Born in Angola, N. Y., in 1865. Work: "An Archbishop of Odessa," in Roman Catholic Cathedral, Odessa, Russia; "Bust of Senator Rice," State Capitol of Minnesota; "Bust of Archbishop Wigger," Seaton Hall, Newark, N. J.; busts of Mark Twain and Mr. Brett, Cleveland Public Library; "Monument of Archbishop Rappe," Catholic Cathedral, Cleveland, Ohio. *Address*, 1875 East 81st St., Cleveland, Ohio.

SERVER, J. William. Painter. Born in Philadelphia, Pa., in 1882. Pupil of Deigendesch, Chase and Colarossi. Member: Art Students' League, Philadelphia. *Address*, 43 South 18th St., Philadelphia, Pa.

SERZ, J. Engraver. Born in Saxony; died in Philadelphia about 1878, as the result of a fall. Serz came to Philadelphia about 1850; he engraved several large historical plates and furnished a number of subject plates for *Sartain's Magazine* and other publications of that city.

SETON, Ernest Thompson. Painter, author and lecturer. Born in South Shields, England, in 1860. He became official naturalist to the Government of Manitoba; published "Mammals of Manitoba," 1886, and "Birds of Manitoba," 1891; studied art in Paris; is now well known as animal painter and illustrator. He was one of the chief illustrators of the "Century Dictionary," and has illustrated many books about birds and mammals. *Address*, Greenwich, Conn.

SEVERANCE, Julia G. Sculptor and etcher. Born in Oberlin, Ohio, in 1877. Pupil of Art Students' League of New York. Member: Cleveland Woman's Art Club. Work: "Rice Memorial Tablet," Oberlin Conservatory of Music, Oberlin College, Ohio; etching in Print Department, Library of Congress, Washington, D. C.; Cobb Memorial Tablet, Warner Hall, Oberlin, Ohio; Leffingwell Tablet, St. Mary's School, Knoxville, Ill. *Address* 68 South Professor St., Oberlin, Ohio.

SEWARD, C. A. Painter, who exhibited water colors at the Penna. Academy of the Fine Arts, Philadelphia, 1925. *Address*, 1534 North Holyoke Ave., Wichita, Kans.

SEWALL, Blanche H. (Mrs. C.). Painter. Born in Fort Worth, Tex., in 1889. Pupil of Fred Wagner. *Address*, The Beaconfield, Houston, Tex.

SEWELL, Amanda Brewster. Painter. Born in Essex County, N. Y. Studied at Art Students' League of New York, and under

Julien and Carolus-Duran, Paris. Began painting in Paris in 1886; exhibited at Paris Salon, 1886, 1887, 1888; awarded Dodge prize, National Academy of Design, 1888; Clarke prize, same, 1903; bronze medal, Chicago Exposition. Principal works: Portraiture in the style and spirit of the early English masters. Elected an Associate Member of the National Academy of Design. *Address*, 33 West 67th St., New York City.

SEWELL, Helen M. Painter, who exhibited "An Old Farmer" in the Penna. Academy Exhibition of 1921, in Philadelphia. *Address*, 52 Heights Road, Ridgewood, N. J.

SEWELL, Robert Van Vorst. Painter. Born in New York in 1860; died in Italy in 1924. Studied under Lefebvre and Boulanger, Paris, 1883–87. Won 1st Hallgarten prize, National Academy of Design, 1888; silver medal, Buffalo Exposition, for exhibit of designs of mural paintings, etc. His mural painting, "The Canterbury Pilgrims," in the great hall of Georgian Court, Lakewood, and several others are widely known; he painted "The Story of Psyche," a series of lunette decorations in the Palm Room of the St. Regis Hotel, New York. Elected Associate Member of the National Academy in 1902. Member of Society of Mural Painters; Architectural League of New York.

SEYFFERT, Helen F. (Mrs. L.). Painter. Member of the Fellowship of the Penna. Academy of Fine Arts. *Address*, Care of Chicago Art Institute, Chicago, Ill.

SEYFFERT, Leopold. Painter. Born in Colorado Springs, Colo. Member: Associate Member of the National Academy of Design in 1916, and Academician in 1925; Philadelphia Art Club; Allied Artists' Association; Pittsburgh Artists' Association. Awarded Fellowship prize, Penna. Academy of the Fine Arts, 1913; honorable mention, Carnegie Institute, Pittsburgh, 1913; gold medal, Philadelphia Art Club, 1915; Beck gold medal, Penna. Academy of the Fine Arts, 1918; Altman prize gold medal, National Academy of Design, 1918; first Hallgarten prize, National Academy of Design, 1918; Temple gold medal, Penna. Academy of the Fine Arts, 1921; Proctor prize, National Academy of Design, 1921. *Address*, 222 West 59th St., New York.

SEYMOUR, Joseph H. Engraver. Joseph H. Seymour was in the employ of Isaiah Thomas, at Worcester, Mass., as early as 1791. The Bible published by Thomas in that year contains thirty-two plates by Seymour, variously signed J. H., Jos. and J. Seymour, and in the printer's advertisement Thomas writes: "These plates were engraved in his Office (Thomas's) in this town in 1791 . . . and the Editor doubts not but a proper allowance will be made for work engraved by an Artist who obtained his knowledge in this country, compared with that done by European Engravers who have settled in the United States.'' Seymour was thus evidently trained to his art in the United States and must have been really at work in Worcester previous to 1791.

SEYMOUR, Ralph F. Illustrator and etcher. Born in Milan, Ill., in 1876. Pupil of Meakin in Cincinnati, also studied in Paris. Represented by etchings in Chicago Art Institute. *Address*, 410 Michigan Blvd., Chicago.

SEYMOUR, Samuel. Engraver of portraits, located in Philadelphia in 1797-1882. In 1823, as a draftsman, he accompanied Major Stephen H. Long on his exploring expedition into the Yellowstone region, and nothing later is known of him.

SHAFER, L. A. Painter, illustrator and etcher. Born in Genesco, Ill., in 1866. Pupil of Chicago Art Institute. *Address*, 232 Liberty Ave., New Rochelle, N. Y.

SHAFTENBENG, Lewis. Miniature painter, who flourished in 1783 in Baltimore, Md.

SHALER, Frederick. Painter. Born at Findlay, Ohio, in 1880. Studied with Chase in New York and had a studio for years in that city. He died in 1916.

SHALLUS, Francis. Engraver. Born in Philadelphia in 1773. He was the son of Jacob Shallus, an officer in the Revolutionary War. As a young man Francis Shallus was prominent in local politics; and in 1805 he was captain of the First Light Infantry, of Philadelphia.

His profession is given as engraver from 1797 to 1821, but he was a poor workman. He died in Philadelphia in 1821.

SHANNON, Howard J. Painter and illustrator. Born in Jamaica, New York, in 1876. Pupil of Pratt Institute under Herbert Adams. Illustrates for *Harper's Magazine, St. Nicholas* and the *Scientific Monthly*. *Address*, 73 Union Ave., Jamaica, N. Y.

SHANNON, James Jebusa. Painter. Born in Auburn, New York, in 1862; died in 1923. He resided for many years in England. Studied at South Kensington Schools, London, under Edward Poynter. Awards: Gold medal, Paris Exposition, 1889; first class medal, Berlin; first medal, Carnegie Institute, Pittsburgh, 1897; Lippincott prize, Pennsylvania Academy of the Fine Arts, 1899; silver medal, Paris Exposition, 1900; gold medal, Pan-American Exposition, Buffalo, 1901. Elected an Associate Member of the Royal Academy, 1897; Royal Academy, 1909; Associate, National Academy, 1908. His painting ''Girl in Brown'' is in the Corcoran Art Gallery, Washington.

SHAPLEIGH, Frank Henry. Born in Boston, Mass., in 1842. He studied under Emile Lamton in Paris, and spent his professional life in Boston. His paintings include ''Yosemite Valley,'' ''Mount Washington,'' the ''White Mountains'' and the ''Old Mill in Seabrook.''

SHARMAN, John. Painter, who exhibited a ''Gray Day in Winter'' at Penna. Academy of Fine Arts, 1923. *Address*, Winchester, Mass.

SHARP, Joseph Henry. Painter. Born in Bridgeport, Ohio, in 1859. Studied in Antwerp under Charles Veriat; Munich Academy under Carl Marr; with Jean-Paul Laurens and Benjamin Constant, Paris; with Duveneck in Italy and Spain. Painter of Amer. Indian subjects. Exhibited at Paris Exposition, 1900. Instructor at Cincinnati Art Museum, 1892-1902; resigned to spend all his time in the Indian country. Eleven of his portraits of famous Indians were purchased, 1900, by the Govt., and are now in the Smithsonian Institution; collection of eighty Indian portraits and pictures was purchased in 1902 by Mrs. Phoebe Hearst, for the University of California. He spends his winters at Crow Agency, Mont., where he has a cabin and a studio at the foot of Custer battlefield; summer home and studio opposite Kit Carson's old home in Taos, N. M. Represented in Butler Museum, Youngstown, Ohio. Charter member of Cincinnati Art Club; member of California Art Club; Society of Western Artists; Salmagundi Club of New York; Print Makers' Club, Los Angeles; charter member of Taos Society of Artists. *Address*, Taos, N. M., and Crow Agency, Mont.

SHARPE, C. W. This line-engraver of portraits and book illustrations was working in Philadelphia in 1850. There are some indications that he originally came from Boston to that city.

SHARPE, Julia Graydon. Painter and designer. Born in Indianapolis, Ind. Pupil of Art Students' League of New York; Wm. M. Chase, Indiana School of Art; also pupil of J. Otis Adams, William Forsyth, H. Siddons Mowbray, and Saint Gaudens. Member: Art Students' League of New York; Indiana Society of Artists. *Address*, 1314 North Delaware St., Indianapolis, Ind.

SHARPLES, Felix T. Pastel artist. Son of James Sharples. Born in England before 1789; he died in North Carolina in 1844. The pastel portrait of Alexander Hamilton owned by the New York Historical Society is done by Felix T. Sharples after the original by his father.

SHARPLES, James. Portrait painter in pastels. Born in England in 1752; died in New York City in 1811. He came to America in 1796, and traveled through the country painting portraits chiefly in pastels on thick gray paper. A large collection of his work is in Independence Hall, Philadelphia, and in Bristol, England. In 1796 he drew his pastel portrait of Washington, which was frequently copied by his wife and sons.

SHARPLES, James, Jr. Portrait draughtsman in pastel. Born in 1789, England; died in 1839 in Bristol, England. The younger son of James Sharples. He frequently copied his father's work. He returned to England with his mother and sister after his father's death.

SHARPLES, Mrs. James (Ellen). Portrait draughtsman in pastel. Born in 1769, Birmingham, England; died in 1849 in Bristol, England. Mrs. Sharples frequently copied her husband's portraits very faithfully in the exact size. After her husband's death she returned to England and settled in Bristol. In 1845 she gave two thousand pounds for the founding of the Bristol Fine Arts Academy. In her will she left, in 1849, three thousand four hundred and sixty-five pounds more. At this institution there is today the "Sharples Collection" of ninety-seven pictures by her husband, herself, James Junior and Rolinda. Her daughter Rolinda (1794–1838) was born in New York but none of her paintings were made in this country. (See *Century Magazine*, February, 1894. Also *Magazine of American History*.)

SHATTUCK, Aaron Draper. Painter. Born in New Hampshire in 1832. In 1850 he became a pupil of Alexander Ransom in Boston. In 1852 he entered the school of the Academy of Design in New York and in 1861 was elected an Academician. Among his works are "White Mountains in October," "Cattle," "Peaceful Days," and "Granby Pastures." *Address*, Granby, Conn.

SHAVER, J. R. Painter and illustrator. Born in Evening Shade, Ark., in 1867. Pupil of St. Louis School of Fine Arts. Member: Society of Illustrators, 1910. Made weekly illustrations for *Life*. Author of "Little Shavers," a book of numerous drawings of child life.

SHAW, Annie Cornelia. Landscape painter. Born in West Troy, N. Y., in 1852. She studied in Chicago, and was elected an Associate Member of the Chicago Academy of Design in 1873. Her principal works are "On the Calumet," "In the Clearing," "Fall Ploughing," and "The Russet Year."

SHAW, Harry H. Painter. Exhibited at the Penna. Academy of the Fine Arts, Phila-

delphia, 1926. *Address*, 1809 Callowhill St., Philadelphia.

SHAW, Joshua. English landscape painter. Born in 1776. He practiced his profession in Philadelphia for many years. He came to this country in 1817, bringing with him West's picture of "Christ Healing the Sick." He died in 1860.

SHAW, Stephen William. Director and instructor at the Boston Athenaeum. He was born in 1817 and died in 1900.

SHAW, Sydney Dale. Painter. Born in Walkley, England, in 1879. He came to America, 1892. Was educated at the Art Students' League, New York; Academie Colarossi, Paris, France; École Nationale des Beaux Arts, Paris. He was principally a painter of landscapes and street scenes. Exhibited at the Society of American Artists; Penna. Academy of Fine Arts; Art Institute of Chicago; International Exhibition, Rome, 1911; International Society of Painters and Sculptors, New York; Panama P. I. Exposition, 1915. Hudnut prize, American Water Color Society, 1917. Member of American Water Color Society and of the California Art Club, Los Angeles, Calif. *Address*, 1824 Morton Ave., Pasadena, Calif.

SHEAFER, Frances B. (Mrs. Waxman). Painter. Born in Pennsylvania. Pupil of Penna. Academy of Fine Arts and Philadelphia School of Design for Women. Member of Plastic Club, and of the Copley Society, Boston. Awarded special silver medal, St. Louis Exposition, 1904. *Address*, 46 Avon Hill St., Cambridge, Mass.

SHEAFER, Frank W. Painter. Born in Pottsville, Pa., in 1867. Pupil of Penna. Academy of the Fine Arts. Exhibited "Harbor Lights" at Penna. Academy of the Fine Arts, 1915. *Address*, 908 Pine St., Philadelphia.

SHEAN, Charles M. Portrait and mural painter. Born in Brooklyn. Studied at Art Students' League of New York and in Paris. Member of National Society of Mural Painters, and Architectural League of New York. Medal for mural painting, St. Louis Exposition, 1904. Author of "A Plea for Americanism in the Decoration of Public Buildings," 1901; "Mural Painting from the American Point of View." He died in 1925.

SHEELER, Charles R., Jr. Painter. Born in Philadelphia in 1883. Pupil of Penna. Academy of the Fine Arts under Chase. *Address*, 33 West 67th St., New York, N. Y.

SHEERER, Mary G. Painter. Born in Covington, Ky., in 1867. Pupil of Cincinnati Art Academy and Penna. Academy of the Fine Arts. *Address*, 1404 Broadway, South, New Orleans.

SHEETS, Mrs. F. C. Painter. Born in Albany, Ill., in 1885. Pupil of John Carlsen and of Robert Reid. *Address*, 2810 North Walker, Oklahoma City, Okla.

SHEFFER, Glen C. Illustrator. Born in Angola, Ind., in 1881. Pupil of Art Institute of Chicago and Chicago Academy of Fine Arts. Member of Palette and Chisel Club. *Address*, 59 East Van Buren St., Chicago, Ill.

SHEFFIELD, Isaac. Painter. Born in Guilford, Conn., in 1798. He painted portraits and figure pieces in and about New London, Conn. Most of his portraits are of sea captains, very red faced, with telescope in hand, standing before a red curtain. He died in 1845.

SHEGOGUE, James Henry. Painter, who devoted himself principally to portraiture, but who did produce some landscapes and genre pieces. He first exhibited at the National Academy of Design, New York, in 1835 and became an Associate Member in 1841, and an Academician in 1843. He has painted a number of prominent men and several of his portraits are owned by the city of New York. He died in 1872.

SHELDON, Charles Mills. Painter. Born at Lawrenceburg, Ind., in 1866. Studied in Paris under Constant and Lefebvre, and at the Academie Julien, 1890–91. Traveled through the Southern States, illustrating articles for the Associated Press, 1889; illustrator on *Pall Mall Budget*, 1892–95; artist and correspondent for *Black and White*, London, in South Africa during time of Jamieson raid; through Dongola Expedition, Soudan, 1896; artist correspondent of *Frank Leslie's* and *Black and White* in Cuba, 1898.

SHELLHASE, George. Painter, who exhibited water colors at the Penna. Academy of the Fine Arts, Philadelphia, 1925. *Address*, 720 Locust St., Philadelphia.

SHEPHERD, Chester George. Illustrator. Born in Lathrop, Mich., in 1894. Pupil of Art Institute of Chicago. Member of Palette and Chisel Club and the Alumni Association of the Art Institute of Chicago. *Address*, 731 Plymouth Ct., Chicago, Ill.

SHEPHERD, J. Clinton. Sculptor. Born in Des Moines, Iowa, in 1888. He studied at the Chicago Art Institute. Work: ''The Broncho Twister''; ''The Cayuse''; ''The Maverick.'' Specialty, Western Life and Animals. *Address*, 124 Waverly Place, New York.

SHEPHERD, T. S. Miniature painter, who flourished 1845–46, New York.

SHEPPARD, Warren W. Painter. Born in Greenwich, N. J., in 1859. Made studies in marine architecture (yacht designing), navigation, seamanship. Work represented in numerous private collections; among best known are: ''The Restless Sea'' (exhibited at Chicago Exposition); ''Desdemona's Palace, Venice''; ''Zuchelli Garden''; ''Under the Southern Cross''; ''Trackless Ocean''; ''Grand Canal, Venice''; ''The Sea,'' exhibited at St. Louis Exposition, 1904. *Address*, 642 Throop Ave., Brooklyn, N. Y.

SHERIDAN, John E. Illustrator. Member: Society of Illustrators, 1912, and of the Salmagundi Club. *Address*, 119 East 34th St., New York, N. Y.

SHERINYAN, Elizabeth. Painter. Born in Armenia. Pupil of Hale; H. D. Murphy; Major; Greenwood; also student at Worcester Museum School and Mass. Normal Art School. Member of Worcester Art Students' Club; Claremont Art Club, Hartford, and Artists' Color Club. *Address*, 1 Francis St., Worcester, Mass.

SHERMAN, Ella Bennett (Mrs. John). Painter. Born in New York, N. Y. Pupil of Douglas Volk, W. M. Chase and Robert Henri. Member of Washington Water Color Club; Washington Society of Artists. *Address*, 500 Powers Bldg., Rochester, N. Y.

SHERMAN & SMITH. Engravers. This firm was designing and engraving plates for the New York *New Mirror* in 1841. In 1838–39 the firm of Stiles, Sherman & Smith was engraving in the same city. In both of these cases the Smith of the firm was probably Wm. D. Smith.

SHERRATT, Thomas. About 1870 a portrait engraver of this name was working for Detroit publishers.

SHERWOOD, Mary Clare. Painter and illustrator. Born in France in 1868. Pupil of Art Students' League of New York under Weir and Chase. *Address*, All Saints College, Vicksburg, Miss.

SHERWOOD, Rosina Emmet (Mrs.). Painter and illustrator. Born in New York in 1854. Pupil of William Chase, New York; Julien Academy, Paris. Silver medal, Paris Exposition, 1889; medal, Chicago Exposition, 1893; exhibited at Paris Exposition, 1900; two bronze medals, Buffalo Exposition, 1901; silver medal, St. Louis Exposition, 1904. Elected an Associate Member of the National Academy; also member of New York Water Color Club and American Water Color Society. *Address*, 77 East 89th St., New York, N. Y.

SHERWOOD, Ruth. Sculptor. Born in Chicago in 1889. Pupil of Art Institute of Chicago. *Address*, 3146 Lake Park Ave., Chicago.

SHERWOOD, William A. Painter and etcher. Born in Baltimore, Md., in 1875. Represented by etchings in Library of Congress, Washington, D. C.; Cleveland Public Library; Royal Library of Brussels. *Address*, 38 Rue Rembrandt, Antwerp, Belgium.

SHIELDS & HAMMOND. Engravers. This first name is signed to some good landscape plates published in New Orleans in 1845. Hammond is noticed elsewhere.

SHILLING, Alexander. Painter. Born in Chicago. Principally landscape painter and painter-etcher. Member of American Water Color Society; New York Etching Club. Gold medal, Phila. Art Club; silver medal, St. Louis Exposition, 1904; Shaw prize for etching, 1913. *Address*, Van Dyke Studios, 939 8th Ave., New York.

SHINDLER, A. Zeno. Portrait draughtsman in crayons. He was working in Philadelphia about 1855–60.

SHINN, Everett. Mural painter. Born in Woodstown, N. J., in 1873. Studied art at Penna. Academy of Fine Arts, Philadelphia. He exhibits in general exhibitions and has his own exclusive exhibitions annually at New York galleries; painted the mural decorations for The Stuyvesant Theater, New York, N. Y. *Address*, 19 East 47th St., New York City.

SHIPMAN, Charles. Engraver. In the *New York Mercury* in 1768 is the following: "Charles Shipman, Ivory and Hard Wood Turner, . . . engraves Copper Plate, Seals. etc."

SHIRK, Jeannette C. Painter, who exhibited water colors at the Penna. Academy of Fine Arts, Philadelphia, 1925. *Address*, Glenshaw, Penna.

SHIRLAW, Walter. Painter and engraver. Born in Scotland in 1838 He was brought to the United States when two years old. He studied art at the National Academy and worked at bank-note engraving for some time, but had a decided talent for painting. His "Sheep Shearing in the Bavarian Highlands" received honorable mention at the Paris Exhibition of 1878, and his "Susannah and the Elders" (a study) is owned by the Boston Museum of Fine Arts. He was elected a member of the National Academy of Design in 1888. He died in 1910.

SHONNARD, Eugenie F. Sculptor. Born in Yonkers, N. Y., in 1886. Studied in New York and in Paris under Rodin and Bourdelle. Represented in Metropolitan Museum, New York, and in the Cleveland Museum of Art. *Address*, 108 West 54th St., New York.

SHOPE, Henry B. Etcher. Born in Baltimore in 1862. Member of Brooklyn Society of Etchers. Represented by etchings in New York Public Library. *Address*, 28 East 21st St., New York.

SHORE, Henrietta M. Painter. Born in Canada. Pupil of Henri and Chase; also studied in London. Represented by "Negro Woman and Children" at National Gallery of Canada. *Address*, 152 West 57th St., New York.

SHOREY, George H. Painter and illustrator. Born at Hoosick Falls, N. Y. Pupil of Walter Shirlaw. Executed some good mural paintings. *Address*, 31 West 55th St., New York.

SHOTWELL, H. C. In 1853 this landscape engraver was working for publishers in Cincinnati, Ohio.

SHRADER, Edwin R. Landscape and figure painter, also illustrator. Born in Quincy, Ill., in 1879. Student at Chicago Art Institute, and pupil of Howard Pyle. *Address*, Ottis Art Institute, Los Angeles, Calif.

SHRADY, Henry Merwin. Sculptor. Born in New York City in 1871; died there, 1922. Elected Associate Member of the National Academy of Design in 1909. Among his works are "Grant Memorial," "Washington," and "General Lee," at Charlottesville, Va.

SHRAMM, Paul H. Sculptor and illustrator. Born in Heidenheim, Germany, in 1867. Pupil of Claudinso, Schrandolph and Jacob Grunenwald in Stuttgart; of MacNeil at Pratt Institute, Brooklyn. Member of New York Society of Cartoonists. *Address*, 671 Auburn Ave., Buffalo, N. Y.

SHULGOLD, William R. Painter and etcher. Born in Russia. Pupil of Sparks, Sotter and Hawthorne. *Address*, 1835 Centre Ave., Pittsburgh, Penna.

SHULL, Lella. Portrait painter, who exhibited portrait of Mrs. Robert Henri at Annual Exhibition, 1923, of Penna. Academy of Fine Arts. *Address*, 39 West 67th St., New York.

SHULZ, Ada Walter (Mrs. Adolph R.). Painter. Born in Terre Haute, Ind., in 1870. Pupil of Art Institute of Chicago; Vitti Academy in Paris. Member of Chicago Society of Artists and Wisconsin Painters and Sculptors. Work: "Motherhood," Milwaukee Art Institute; "Mother and Child," Art Institute of Chicago. Specialty, children. *Address*, Nashville, Brown County, Ind.

SHULZ, Adolph Robert. Landscape painter. Born in Delavan, Wis., in 1869. Pupil of Art Institute of Chicago; Art Students' League of New York; Julien Academy in Paris under Lefebvre, Constant and Laurens. Member: Chicago Society of Artists. Work: "Frost and Fog," Art Institute of Chicago. *Address*, Nashville, Brown County, Ind.

SHUMWAY, Henry C. Miniature painter. Born in Middletown, Conn., in 1808, he came to New York in 1827 and entered as a student in the National Academy of Design. He began painting professionally in 1829 and died in 1884. Among the prominent men who sat to him were Henry Clay, Daniel Webster, and Prince Napoleon (afterwards Napoleon III).

SHURTLEFF, Elizabeth. Painter. Born in Concord, N. H., in 1890. Pupil of Boston Museum School of Fine Arts. *Address*, 86 Mount Vernon St., Boston, Mass.

SHURTLEFF, Roswell Morse. Painter. Born at Rindge, N. H., in 1838; died in 1915. Graduate of Dartmouth College, 1857. He took charge of architect's office, Manchester, N. H., in 1857; worked at lithography, in Boston, drawing on wood and attending evening classes, Lowell Institute, in 1859; worked as illustrator and attended Academy of Design, New York. He was illustrator for magazines and books in New York for several years. He began to paint in oils, 1870, at first animal pictures, later landscapes, in both oils and water colors. Elected Associate Member of the National Academy of Design in 1881; National Academy, 1890; was also a member of the American Water Color Society. Among his works are "The Wolf at the Door," "A Race for Life" and "Views among the Adirondacks."

SHUSTER, William Howard. Painter and etcher. Born in Philadelphia, Pa., in 1893. Pupil of J. William Server; John Sloan. Member of Society of Independent Artists; Los Cinco Pintores; Santa Fe Arts Club. *Address*, Camino del Monte Sol, Sante Fe, N. M.

SHUTTLEWORTH, Claire. Painter. Born in Buffalo. Pupil of Buffalo Art Students' League; Du Mond and Bridgman; of Merson, Collin and Leroy in Paris. Member of Buffalo Society of Artists, and National Association of Women Painters and Sculptors. Awarded Fellowship prize, Buffalo Society of Artists, 1910. Work: "The Horse Shoe Falls From Table Rock," Arnot Art Gallery, Elmira, New York. *Address*, 370 Elmwood Ave., Buffalo, N. Y.

SIBBEL, Joseph. Sculptor of ecclesiastical statuary.

SIBONI, Emma. Miniature painter, who exhibited at the Penna. Academy of Fine Arts,

Philadelphia, 1925. *Address*, 1115 Maple St., South Pasadena, Calif.

SIEBER, Edward G. Painter. Born in Brooklyn, N. Y., in 1862. Pupil of National Academy of Design; also studied in Paris. Specialty, landscape and cattle. *Address*, 9 West 14th St., New York.

SIEBERN, E. Sculptor, who exhibited at the Annual Exhibition, 1923, Penna. Academy of Fine Arts, Philadelphia. *Address*, 99 Sixth Ave., New York.

SIEBERT, Edward S. Painter and etcher. Born in Washington, D. C., in 1856. Pupil of Baur in Weimar; of Carl Hoff in Karlsruhe; of William von Diez in Munich. Awarded honorable mention and prize, Rochester, N. Y. Work: "Flute Player," Corcoran Gallery of Art, Washington, D. C. *Address*, 37 East Ave., Rochester, N. Y.

SIEGLER, Maurice. Painter, who exhibited water colors at the Penna. Academy of Fine Arts, Philadelphia, 1925. *Address*, Care of Penna. Academy of Fine Arts, Philadelphia.

SIEVERS, F. William. Sculptor. Born in Fort Wayne, Ind., in 1872. Studied in Richmond, Va.; Royal Academy of Fine Arts, in Rome, under Ferrari; Julien Academy in Paris. Work: Equestrian statue of Gen. Lee and group at Gettysburg, Pa.; equestrian statute of Stonewall Jackson, Richmond, Va. *Address*, Forest Hill, Richmond, Va.

SILEIKA, Jonas. Painter. Born in Lithuania in 1883. Studied at Art Institute of Chicago and Royal Academy, Munich. Member of Chicago Society of Artists. Awarded Joseph N. Eisendrath prize, Art Institute of Chicago, 1920. Work: "My Home," Gallery of Vilna, Lithuania. Specialty, portraits and landscapes. *Address*, Juodagoniu K. Lekeciu V., Pastas Sakiai, Lithuania.

SILSBEE, Martha. Painter. Born in Salem, Mass., in 1858. Member: Boston Water Color Club. *Address*, 82 Chestnut St., Boston, Mass.

SILVA, Francis Augustus. Painter. Born in 1835. He worked as a sign painter until the opening of the Civil War when he entered the National Army, and at the close of the war he settled in New York and devoted himself to painting marine subjects. Among his works are "Gray Day at Cape Ann," "Sunrise in Boston Harbor," and "Near Atlantic City." He died in 1886.

SILVA, William P. Painter. Born in Savannah, Ga. Pupil of Julien Academy in Paris under Laurens and Royer; of Chauncey Ryder at Etaples, France. Awards: Silver medal, Appalachian Exposition, Knoxville, 1913; silver medal, Pan-California Exposition, San Diego, 1915; gold medal, Mississippi Art Association, 1916; second prize, California State Fair, Sacramento, 1920. Work: "Pines of Picardy," Carnegie Public Library, Chattanooga, Tenn.; "Pine and Its Shadow," Gibbes Gallery, Charleston, S. C.; "Fog Coming In, Ogunquit." *Address*, Carmel-by-the-Sea, Calif.

SILVERBERG, E. Myer. Portrait painter. Born in Russia in 1876. Studied in Royal Academy of Fine Arts, Munich. Member of Pittsburgh Artists' Association. Work in High Schools and other public institutions, Pittsburgh. *Address*, 58 West 57th St., New York, N. Y.

SIMEON, Nicholas. Painter. Born in Switzerland in 1867. *Address*, 109 West 54th St., New York City.

SIMES, Mary Jane. Miniature painter, who flourished 1826–31, Baltimore, Md.

SIMKHOWITZ, Simkha. Painter, who exhibited a portrait in the National Academy, 1925. *Address*, 70 West 126th St., New York.

SIMMONE, T. Engraver. In 1814–16 Simmone was engraving a very few, but good plates for the New York publishers, David Longworth and T. C. Fay.

SIMMONS, Edward E. Mural painter. Born in Concord, Mass., in 1852. Pupil of Boulanger and Lefebvre in Paris. Represented in Mass. State House, Boston, by "Battle of Concord"; Library of Congress, Washington, by the "Muses," and in Memorial Hall, Harvard College, Cambridge, Mass. *Address*, 16 Gramercy Park, New York.

SIMMONS, Franklin. Sculptor, of Providence, Rhode Island. Born in 1842. He executed a bust of President Lincoln, which has been put in bronze; also statues of Roger Williams and William King, for the state of Maine. He died in 1913.

SIMMONS, Joseph. Engraver. The *Pennsylvania Gazette* for Jan. 3, 1765, contains the following advertisement: "Joseph Simmons, Engraver, from London, Cuts Coats of Arms and Cyphers in Stone, Silver or Steel, for Watches. He is to be spoke with at Mr. Robert Porter's, Saddler, in Market Street, opposite the Prison. N. B. As there is no other Person of the same business on the Continent, he hopes to meet with Encouragement."
Simmons was evidently a seal-cutter; and special interest lies in his claim to be the only one then in business in the country.

SIMMONS, Will. Painter, illustrator and etcher. Born in Spain, 1884. Pupil of Julien Academy and of Alexander Harrison in Paris.

Member of Brooklyn Society of Etchers. Represented in New York Public Library. *Address*, 137 East 57th St., New York City.

SIMON, Eugene J. Painter. Born in Hungary in 1889. Pupil of Kenneth Hayes Miller. *Address*, 665 East 242d St., New York.

SIMOND, L. Designer of book plates. The engraving "Christ Blessing Children," done for an orphan asylum after his design, was engraved by Leney.

SIMONET, Sebastian. Painter and illustrator. Born in Stillwater, Minn., in 1898. Pupil of Boardman Robinson. *Address*, 391 Manhattan Ave., New York.

SIMONS, Amory C. Sculptor. Born in Charleston, S. C., in 1869. He studied at the Penna. Academy of Fine Arts, and with Rodin in Paris. Work: "The Storm" and "New York Fire Engine Horses." *Address*, 207 East 17th St., New York.

SIMPSON, Edna Huestis (Mrs.). Miniature painter, who exhibited miniatures at the Penna. Academy of Fine Arts, Philadelphia, 1925. *Address*, 151 East 21st St., New York.

SIMPSON, M. This stipple-engraver designed and engraved a portrait of Washington in the center of an elaborate script memorial. This print was published in 1855 and is signed as "Designed and Engraved by S. Simpson, New York."

SIMPSON, Maxwell S. Painter, who exhibited water colors at the Penna. Academy of Fine Arts, Philadelphia, 1925. *Address*, 431 Madison Ave., Elizabeth, N. J.

SINCLAIR, Gerritt V. Landscape painter, who exhibited at the National Academy, 1925. *Address*, Milwaukee, Wis.

SINDELAR, Thomas A. Illustrator. Born in Cleveland, Ohio, in 1867. Pupil of Mucha in Paris. *Address*, 15 Maiden Lane, New York.

SINGER, William H. Painter. Born in Pittsburgh, Penna., in 1868. In 1901 he went to France to study, and later to Norway. His specialty is landscape and winter scenes. Member: Allied Artists of America; Associated Artists of Pittsburgh. Elected an Associate Member of the National Academy of Design. Represented at Portland Museum, Maine, and Hispanic Museum of New York. *Address*, 58 West 57th St., New York.

SISSON, Frederick R. Painter, who exhibited water colors at the Penna. Academy of the Fine Arts, Philadelphia, 1925. *Address*, 39 Benevolent St., Providence, R. I.

SITZMAN, Edward R. Painter. Born in Cincinnati, Ohio, in 1873. Pupil of Duveneck. Member of Indiana Art Club. *Address*, 414 Marion Building, Indianapolis, Ind.

SKELTON, Leslie James. Painter. Born in Montreal, Can., in 1848. Studied in Paris several years. Pupil of Iwill. Landscapes in oil and pastel exhibited: Salon, Paris, 1901; Liverpool Autumn Exhibition, 1902; British and Colonial Exhibition, at time of King Edward's coronation, 1902; Royal Academy, London, 1904; National Academy of Design; Denver Artists' Club; Montreal Art Association; Colorado Springs Art Society. Represented in the permanent collections of Colorado College, Colorado Springs; in National Gallery, Ottawa, Canada. One of his most noted productions entitled "Gathering Storm in Ester Park" was reproduced in colors in *Brush and Pencil* in 1903. President of Coburn Library Book Club, Colorado Springs; Winter Night Club, 1911; Colorado Springs Art Society, 1913. *Address*, 1225 N. Tejon St., Colorado Springs, Colo.

SKEU, Sigurd. Painter, who exhibited water colors at the Penna. Academy of Fine Arts, Philadelphia, 1925. *Address*, 51 Poplar St., Brooklyn, N. Y.

SKIDMORE, Lewis P. Painter and etcher. Born in Bridgeport, Conn. Pupil of Laurens and Bonnat in Paris. *Address*, 214 Clermont Ave., Brooklyn, N. Y.

SKIDMORE, Thornton D. Painter and illustrator. Born in Brooklyn, N. Y., in 1884. Pupil of Howard Pyle and Eric Pape. Member of the Society of Illustrators. *Address*, 1947 Broadway, New York.

SKINNER, Charles. This excellent banknote engraver, in the employ of The American Bank-Note Company, was working in New York at least as early as 1867. He engraved in line a few portraits for the book-publishers.

SKODIK, Antonin. Sculptor. Pupil of Art Students' League, and sculptor of "Montana."

SKOOG, Karl F. Painter and sculptor. Born in Sweden in 1878. Pupil of Bela L. Pratt. Member of Conn. Academy of Fine Arts. Awards: Prize, Rochester, N. Y., 1908; honorable mention, Art Institute of Chicago, 1912. Work: Bust of John Ericsson, Brockton, Mass.; bronze tablet in Home for Aged Swedish People, West Newton, Mass.; Perry Monument, Forest Dale Cemetery; relief of J. A. Powers, Elks Building, Malden, Mass.; medallion of R. W. Emerson, Museum of Numismatic Society, New York. *Address*, 34 Boylston St., Cambridge, Mass.

SKOU, Sigurd. Painter, who exhibited at the National Academy of Design, New York, 1925. Address, 19 West 50th St., New York.

SLADE, C. Arnold. Painter. Born in Acushnet, Mass., in 1882. Pupil of F. V. Du Mond, Laurens, Schomer and Bachet. Member of Philadelphia Art Club; Paris Artists' Association; Allied Artists of London. Work: "Sardine Boats, Brittany," Springfield, Ill., Art Club; "Venice," Philadelphia Art Club; "The Reapers," Attleboro, Mass., Public Collection; "Village of Etaples," Fenway Court Collection. *Address*, Rue d'Assas, Paris, France.

SLADE, Cora L. (Mrs. Abbott E.). Painter. Pupil of Robert S. Dunning. Member: Providence Art Club; Newport Artists' Association; Fall River Art Club. *Address*, 863 High St., Fall River, Mass.

SLATER, Edwin C. Painter. Born in New Jersey in 1884. Pupil of William Chase, Cecilia Beaux, Thomas P. Anshutz, Hugh Brenckenridge, Birge Harrison, Charles Grafly, Herman D. Murphy and Henry R. Poore. Member of Copley Society, and Fellowship of the Penna. Academy of the Fine Arts. *Address*, 118 East 59th St., New York, N. Y.

SLEETH, L. Mac D. (Mrs. Francis V.). Painter and sculptor. Born in Croton, Iowa, in 1864. Pupil of Whistler, Mac Monies and Emil Carlsen. Member of San Francisco Artists' Association and Washington Water Color Club. Work: Portrait busts in marble of "Brig. Gen'l John M. Wilson," Corcoran Gallery of Art; "Martha Washington," Memorial Continental Hall; "Rt. Rev. Bishop Henry T. Satterlee," Cathedral Foundation; all in Washington, D. C. *Address*, Dawson Terrace, Rural Route No. 1, Virginia.

SLOAN, J. Blanding. Painter, illustrator and etcher. Born in Corsicana in 1886. Pupil of Chicago Academy of Fine Arts; B. J. O. Norfeldt; George Senseney. Member of Chicago Society of Etchers. *Address*, 17 East 14th St., New York.

SLOAN, John. Painter, illustrator and etcher. Born in Lock Haven, Pa., in 1871. Awarded honorable mention, Carnegie Institute, Pittsburgh, 1905; bronze medal for etching, Panama-Pacific Exposition, San Francisco, 1915. Work represented in New York Public Library; Newark, N. J., Public Library; Cincinnati Museum of Art; Carnegie Institute, Pittsburgh; Metropolitan Museum of Art. *Address*, 88 Washington Place, New York, N. Y.

SLOAN, Marianna. Landscape and mural painter. Born in Lock Haven, Pa. Pupil of Robert Henri and Elliott Daingerfield in Philadelphia. Member of New York Water Color Club, and Fellowship of the Penna. Academy of the Fine Arts, 1916. Awarded bronze medal, St. Louis Exposition, 1904. Work: "Landscape," St. Louis Club; "Rocky Beach," Pennsylvania Academy of the Fine Arts, Philadelphia; mural decorations, Church of the Annunciation, Philadelphia; mural decorations, St. Thomas Church, Whitemarsh, Pa. *Address*, 524 Walnut St., Philadelphia.

SLOCUM, Annette M. Sculptor. Born in Cleveland, Ohio. Studied at Penna. Academy of the Fine Arts. Her specialty is portraiture. *Address*, 250 West 154th St., New York.

SLOCUM, Victor Vaughan. Sculptor, who exhibited portraits in the Penna. Academy of the Fine Arts, 1924, Philadelphia, Pa. *Address*, 1523 Chestnut St., Philadelphia.

SLOMAN, Joseph. Painter, sculptor and illustrator. Born in Philadelphia, Pa., in 1879. Pupil of Howard Pyle, B. W. Clinedinst and Clifford Grayson. Works: Art Dome, Town Hall, West New York, N. J.; "Martin Luther," Church of St. John, West New York, N. J.; stained glass memorial in Hoboken, N. J., Temple; work in Synagogue at Athens, Ga.; also in Public Library, Hoboken, N. J. *Address*, 300 Fifth St., Union Hill, N. J.

SLOPER, Norma (Wright). Painter. Born in New Haven, Conn., in 1892. Pupil of A. E. Jones; of Lucien Simon and Rene Menard in Paris. Member of Society of Conn. Painters, and Conn. Academy of Fine Arts. *Address*, 104 Lake St., New Britain, Conn.

SLUSSER, J. Paul. Painter. Born in Wauseon, Ohio, in 1886. Pupil of Paxton, Hale and Carlsen. Member of Chicago Society of Artists. *Address*, 344 East 57th St., New York.

SLUTZ, Helen Beatrice. Painter. Born in Cleveland, Ohio, in 1886. Pupil of Cleveland School of Art. Member: Chicago Society of Miniature Painters; Chicago Art Club; Cleveland Woman's Art Club. *Address*, 7320 Paxton Ave., Chicago, Ill.

SMALLEY, Janet (Mrs. Alfred). Illustrator. Member of the Fellowship of the Penna. Academy of Fine Arts. *Address*, 223 East Washington Lane, Germantown, Pa.

SMART, Miss Anna M. Painter. Born in 1847; died in 1914 in New York City. Specialty, water colors.

SMEDLEY, Will Larymore. Painter and illustrator. Born in Sandyville, Ohio, in 1871. Member of Cleveland Water Color Society. *Address*, Chautauqua-on-the-Lake, N. Y.

SMEDLEY, William Thomas. Painter. Born in Chester County, Pa., in 1858; died in 1920. Studied engraving in Philadelphia and art in the Penna. Academy of the Fine Arts; went to New York, 1878, and later to Paris; studied under Jean Paul Laurens; opened studio, New York, 1880; has since been actively engaged as illustrator for *Harper's* and other standard periodicals. In 1882 he was engaged by publishers of *Picturesque Canada* to travel with Marquis of Lorne through West and Northwest Canada and to illustrate the work; he has since made several sketching tours in the United States, and in 1890 he went around the world. He exhibited at the Paris Salon, 1888. Several of his principal productions are: "An Indiscreet Question"; "A Thanksgiving Dinner"; "A Summer Occupation." Elected member of National Academy, 1905.

SMIBERT, John. One of the earliest of the American portrait painters. His influence may be seen in the work of many of those who immediately followed him, and it is thought that Copley may have received instruction in his studio. Born in Scotland in 1688; Smibert was first a common house-painter. Later he worked for coach painters in London and afterward copied paintings for dealers until he succeeded in gaining admittance to an art academy. Leaving London he spent three years in Italy copying Raphael and other "old masters," and in 1728 came to America with the Rev. George Berkeley. A portrait of this Rev. George Berkeley with His Family, by Smibert, signed and dated 1729, is preserved at Yale University. Smibert married and left two children, one a son, Nathaniel (1734–56), who became a portrait painter, and a portrait of John Lovell, a product of his brush, is now at Harvard University, Cambridge, Mass. John Smibert worked mostly in Providence, R. I., and in Boston after 1728 and died there in 1751.

SMIBERT, Nathaniel Painter. Born in 1734. Brother of the artist John Smibert. He died in his twenty-second year having showed a great talent for portraiture, and had his life been spared he would doubtless have achieved much success. His portrait of John Lowell is owned by Harvard. He died in 1756.

SMILLIE, George Frederick Cumming. Engraver. Born in New York City in 1854. Pupil of National Academy of Design in 1871; studied under his uncle, James Smillie (of the National Academy), an engraver in the American Bank Note Co., 1871–87; and manager of Canada Bank Note Co., Montreal, 1887; Homer Lee Bank Note Co., New York, 1888; principal engraver, United States Bureau of Engraving and Printing, 1894, and superintendent of picture engraving department in 1918. He engraved portraits and vignettes appearing on United States currency and other securities, and on postage and revenue stamps. Chief works: Silver certificates of 1895; large official portraits of the Presidents of the United States; Kenyon Cox design, "America," "Spirit of Liberty," appearing on Liberty Bonds. *Address*, 2631 Connecticut Ave., Washington, D. C.

SMILLIE, George H. Painter. A son of James Smillie, the celebrated line engraver, and brother of James D. Smillie, National Academy, George H. Smillie was born in the city of New York in 1840. He is one of the most widely known of American landscape painters, and his pictures are characterized by poetic sentiment and technical skill of a high order. He is a pupil of James M. Hart, National Academy. He has made sketching trips in the Rocky Mountains, the Yosemite Valley, and Florida, but the most popular of his subjects are those he finds in picturesque spots in the interior and along the shores of Long Island. Mr. Smillie was elected a member of the American Water Color Society in 1868, and a National Academician in 1882. He died in New York in Nov. 1921. He is represented in the Metropolitan Museum, New York; the Corcoran Art Gallery, Washington, D. C.; the Rhode Island School of Design; the Union League Club of Philadelphia.

SMILLIE, Helen Sheldon Jacobs (Mrs. George H.). Painter. Born in New York in 1854. Studied under Joseph O. Eaton and James D. Smillie. Painter of genre pictures in oils and water colors. Member of American Water Color Society. *Address*, 136 East 36th St., New York.

SMILLIE, James. Engraver. Born in Edinburgh, Scotland, in 1807; died in Poughkeepsie, N. Y., in 1885. James Smillie was the son of a silversmith and he was first apprenticed to James Johnston, a silver engraver of his native city, and he also received some instruction from Edward Mitchell, a portrait engraver. In 1821 he came with his family to Quebec, Canada, where his father and elder brother established themselves in business as jewelers, and James worked with them for some time as a general engraver. In 1827, under the patronage of Lord Dalhousie, he was sent to London and to Edinburgh for instruction in engraving, but he returned to Quebec after a short time, and in 1829 he went to New York.

His first plate to attract attention was done after Robert W. Weir's painting of the "Convent Gate"; and in 1832–36 he engraved a series of plates for the *New York Mirror* after paintings by Weir. In 1832 he was made an Associate of the National Academy, and in 1851 he became an Academician.

James Smillie was an admirable line-engraver of landscape, and worked largely from his own drawings, but from 1861 until his death he devoted himself almost solely to banknote engraving, and he did much to bring that art to its present high repute.

SMILLIE, James David. Painter and engraver. Born in New York in 1833; died in 1909. James David Smillie was a son of James Smillie, and was trained by his father as an engraver on steel. While his principal work was bank-note engraving he produced some excellent general work, including a series of illustrations for Cooper's novels, after designs by F. O. C. Darby. He was an 'excellent etcher and a founder of the New York Etching Club, and later its president.

In 1864, after a visit to Europe, James D. Smillie turned his attention to painting, and in the same year he exhibited at the Academy of Design, in New York, and was made an Associate Member of the National Academy in 1865; he was made an Academician in 1876. As a painter in oils and water colors he has obtained reputation. He was one of the founders and the president (1873–79) of the American Water Color Society; he was also president of the New York Etching Club.

SMILLIE, William Cumming. Engraver. Born in Edinburgh, Scotland, in 1813. Wm. C. Smillie was a brother of James Smillie and came to Canada with his father's family in 1821. After working at silver engraving for a time in Quebec, he came to New York in 1830. He early turned his attention to bank-note engraving and was connected with several bank-note companies, the last of which, "Edmonds, Jones & Smillie," was later absorbed by the American Bank Note Co. In 1866 he secured a contract to engrave the paper currency of the Canadian government, and for this purpose he established a bank-note engraving company in Ottawa. In 1874 he retired from this business, but in 1882 he again established an engraving company in Canada, and he was still at the head of that company in 1889.

SMILLIE, William Main. Engraver. Born in New York in 1835; died there in 1888. Wm. M. Smillie was a son of James Smillie, and was early known as an expert letter-engraver. He was long employed by one of the firms that in 1857 was merged into the old American Bank Note Co.; and he was connected with the old and the present American company until his death, having been general manager of the present organization for some years.

SMITH, A. Dunlap notes an artist of this name as having painted in New York in 1834.

SMITH, A. Cary. Marine painter, who was born in New York in 1837 and lived his professional life in that city. Pupil of M. F. H. De Haas. He exhibited frequently at the National Academy, New York, and painted many pictures of private yachts.

SMITH, Albert D. Portrait painter. Born in 1886. Exhibited portrait of "Lionel Atwill as Deburau'' at the Penna. Academy of the Fine Arts, 1925. Pupil of Chase in New York. *Address*, 58 West 57th St., New York.

SMITH, Albert E. Painter and illustrator. Born in Waterbury, Conn., in 1862. Pupil of the Yale School of Fine Arts. *Address*, ''Cherryledge,'' Cos Cob, Conn.

SMITH, Alfred E. Portrait painter. Born in Lynn, Mass., in 1863. Pupil of School of Boston Museum of Fine Arts and of the Julien Academy in Paris, under Boulanger, Lefebvre, and Constant. Member of the Copley Society, Boston. *Address*, 294 Boylston St., Boston, Mass.

SMITH, Alice Ravenal Huger. Painter and illustrator. Born in Charleston, S. C., in 1876. Specialty, water colors and wood block prints. *Address*, 69 Church St., Charleston, S. C.

SMITH, Allen. Portrait and landscape‐painter. Born in 1810. He lived in Cleveland from 1841 to 1883, painting many excellent portraits of prominent citizens. In his later years he painted landscapes. His work compares with that of Healy, Huntington and Elliott, who lived during the same period. He died in 1890.

SMITH, Anita M. Painter, who exhibited at the National Academy of Design, New York; also in Penna. Academy of Fine Arts 1923 Exhibition. *Address*, Woodstock, New York, or 123 East 53d St., New York City.

SMITH, Anne Fry. Painter. Born in Philadelphia in 1890. Pupil of Fred Wagner. Member of Philadelphia Art Alliance. *Address*, 106 Oakdale Ave., Glenside, Penna.

SMITH, C. H. In 1855–60 this capital line-engraver of portraits and book-illustrations was working in Philadelphia and in New York.

SMITH, Carl Rohl. Sculptor. Born in Germany. His studio was for years in Washington, D. C., where he designed the Sherman Monument in front of the Treasury Building. He died in Copenhagen in 1900.

SMITH, Charles L. A. Painter. Born in New York in 1871. Member of Boston Art Club; California Water Color Club. *Address*, 1861 West 10th St., Los Angeles, Calif.

SMITH, Duncan. Mural painter and illustrator. Born in Virginia, 1877. Pupil of Cox, Twachtman, and De Camp. Member of National Society of Mural Painters. Instructor in Art Students' League of New York. *Address*, 42 Washington Square, New York.

SMITH, Edward Gregory. Painter, who exhibited ''Horseshoe Hill'' at the Penna.

Academy of the Fine Arts, 1915. *Address*, Lyme, Conn.

SMITH, Ella B. Painter, who exhibited ''The Long Wharf'' at the Penna. Academy of the Fine Arts, Philadelphia, 1915. *Address*, 307 Fenway Studios, Boston, Mass.

SMITH, E. Boyd. Illustrator. Born in St. John, Can., in 1860. Studied art in Paris.

SMITH, Esther. Portrait painter. Born in Connecticut. She studied under Edwin White in New York. She resided in Hartford, Conn., and there painted portraits of Theo. D. Judah, Col. G. T. Davis, Judge T. B. Butler and many others. Her specialty was the portraiture of children.

SMITH, F. Berkeley. Illustrator. Born in Astoria, L. I., N. Y., in 1868; son of F. Hopkinson Smith. Studied architecture at Columbia University, and practised until 1896. Author and illustrator: ''The Real Latin Quarter,'' ''Budapest, the City of the Magyars,'' etc. *Address*, 16 Place de la Madeleine, Paris, France.

SMITH, F. Carl. Portrait painter. Born in Cincinnati, Ohio, in 1868. Pupil of Bouguereau, Ferrier, and Constant in Paris. Represented by portraits of Mrs. Chas. W. Fairbanks and Mrs. John E. Walker at D. A. R. Continental Hall, Washington, D. C.; also Speaker Clark, The Capitol, Washington, D. C. *Address*, 3 Westmoreland Place, Pasadena, Calif.

SMITH, Francis Drexel. Painter. Born in Chicago, Ill., in 1874. Pupil of John F. Carlsen. Awarded honorable mention, Seattle Art Society, 1923. Exhibited at the Penna. Academy of the Fine Arts, Philadelphia, 1924. *Address*, 531 N. Cascade Ave., Colorado Springs, Colo.

SMITH, F. Hopkinson. Painter and author. Born in Baltimore, 1838. Has done much landscape work in water colors, also charcoal work and illustrations. Represented in Walter's Gallery, Baltimore; Marquand collection, etc. Lecturer on art subjects. Awarded bronze medal, Buffalo Exposition, 1901; silver medal, Charleston Exposition, 1902; gold medal, Phila. Art Club, 1902; gold medal, American Art Society, 1902; Commander Order of the Mejidieh, 1898, and of the Order of Osmanieh by Sultan of Turkey, 1900. Member of the American Academy of Arts and Letters, American Society, Civil Engineers, American Water Color Society, Philadelphia Art Club and the Cincinnati Art Club. *Address*, 16 Exchange Place, New York, N. Y.

SMITH, Frank Hill. Painter. Born in Boston in 1841. He studied in Boston and later in Paris under Bonnat. He has painted portraits, figure pieces, landscapes, and mural painting. He died in 1904.

SMITH, G. This name is signed to well-executed script billheads, etc., published in 1790–1800. The work was done in New York.

SMITH, George Girdler. Born at Danvers, Mass., about the close of the eighteenth century; died in Boston about 1858. He was probably a pupil of Abel Bowen, the Boston engraver, as he was in Bowen's employ in 1815 as an engraver. Little is known about G. G. Smith until 1830, when, in connection with William B. Annin, he was in the general engraving business in Boston, working under the firm name of Annin & Smith. Mr. Smith was early interested in lithography, and visited Paris for instruction and materials, but for some reason he failed in his efforts to establish himself in that business. Later, he was engaged in the bank-note engraving business with Terry and Pelton, and when that firm was absorbed by another company, Smith resumed the general engraving business with two of his former pupils, Knight and Tappan. G. G. Smith engraved portraits chiefly, in both line and stipple, and he did some good work.

SMITH, George W. Painter and architect. Born in East Liberty, Pa., in 1879. Studied in Paris and Rome; Harvard Fine Arts School. Member: National Art Club; California Art Club. *Address*, 17 Mesa Road, Santa Barbara, Calif.

SMITH, Gertrude Roberts. Born in Cambridge, Mass. Studied in Massachusetts Normal Art School; Chase School, New York; also in Paris studios. Instructor in Newcomb School of Art; University of California Summer School. Gold medal, Art Association of New Orleans. Member of Arts and Crafts Club; Art Association of New Orleans; League of Southern Artists. Represented in Delgado Museum of Art, and in the Louisiana State Museum at New Orleans. Specialty, landscapes and designs.

SMITH, Harriet F. Painter. Born in Worcester, Mass., in 1873. Pupil of Mass. Normal Art School; Denman W. Ross; E. W. D. Hamilton; Henry B. Snell; C. H. Woodbury; Philip Hale. Member of Worcester Art Students' Club; Copley Society; Eastern Art Association; New York Water Color Club. *Address*, 120 Glenville Ave., Allston, Mass.

SMITH, Harry Knox. Painter. Born in Philadelphia in 1879. Pupil of Penna. Academy of Fine Arts; Art Students' League of New York. Member of New York Architectural League, 1910. *Address*, 601 West 151st St., New York, N. Y.

SMITH, Henry Pember. Landscape painter. Born in Waterford, Conn., in 1854. He painted New England scenes and views of Venice; these were his most frequent subjects. He was a member of the American Water Color Society and the Artists' Fund Society of New York. He died in 1907.

SMITH, Henry T. A portrait and genre painter of Philadelphia. He was a member of the Artists' Fund Society and chairman of its Ex. Committee in 1867. Was a regular exhibitor at the Phila. Academy, 1861–67. Painted portraits of Henry C. Carey at the Penna. Historical Society, and of Jos. Harrison, Philadelphia.

SMITH, Hezekiah Wright. Engraver. Born in Edinburgh, Scotland, in 1828. He disappeared from Philadelphia in 1879 and was never heard of afterward. Smith was brought to New York when about five years old, and was later apprenticed to an engraver in that city. He continued his studies under Thomas Doney and became a most meritorious engraver of portraits, both in line and in stipple. In 1850 he was associated with Joseph Andrews in Boston, and in 1870–77 he was employed in New York.

In 1877 H. W. Smith established himself in Philadelphia and did considerable work in that city, but in April, 1879, he suddenly abandoned engraving, sold all his effects and left that city and was never heard of again. Among his more important plates are the following: A full-length portrait of Daniel Webster, after the painting by Chester Harding; a three-quarter length of Edward Everett; and his head of "Washington" after the Athenaeum head, by Stuart; this latter is said to be the best engraving of this famous portrait ever made.

SMITH, Holmes. Painter. Born in Keighley, England, in 1863. Member: College Artists' Association; 2 x 4 Society. Professor of drawing and history of art in Washington University, St. Louis. Specialty, water colors. *Address*, Washington University, St. Louis, Mo.

SMITH, Howard Everett. Portrait painter. Born in West Windham, N. H., in 1885. Studied at Art Students' League of New York; pupil of Howard Pyle, Wilmington, Del., for two years. Has exhibited in leading cities of United States; represented in United States Treasury Building by portrait of William H. Osburn, ex-commissioner of internal revenue; also in many private galleries. Awarded John Wanamaker prize, Phila., 1904; Paige traveling scholarship, Museum of Art, Boston, 1911–13; bronze medal, San Francisco Exposition, 1915; first Hallgarten prize, National Academy of Design, New York, 1917. Member: American Federation of Arts; Guild of Boston Artists; Art Students' League of New York. Regular contributor of illustrations and articles to *Harper's Monthly*, 1905–13; and occasional contributor since that time. Instructor of painting at Rhode Island School of Design, Providence, R. I. Elected an Associate Member of the National Academy. *Address*, Fenway Studios, 30 Ipswich St., Boston, Mass.

SMITH, Isabel E. (Mrs. F. Carl). Miniature painter. Born in Smith's Landing, near Cincinnati, Ohio. Pupil of L'hermitte, Deliance and Callot in Paris. Member of Paris Woman's Art Club; Pasadena Fine Arts Club. *Address*, 3 Westmoreland .Place, Pasadena, Calif.

SMITH, Ishmael. Painter, sculptor and illustrator. Born in Barcelona, Spain, in 1886. Member of Salmagundi Club. Works: Monument to Pablo Torull, Caja de Ahorros de Sabadell, Catalunya; Portrait of Mila Y. Fontanals, Institut des estudie Catalans; Portrait of Alphonse Maseras and group in sculpture, Museum of Barcelona, Spain. *Address*, 260 Riverside Drive, New York, N. Y.

SMITH, J. Andre. Etcher and painter. Member of Salmagundi Club. Awarded gold medal for etching, Panama-Pacific Exposition, San Francisco, 1915. *Address*, 411 West End Ave., New York, N. Y.

SMITH, Jack W. Painter. Born in Paterson, N. J., in 1873. Studied at Cincinnati Art Academy and Art Institute of Chicago. Member of California Art Club; California Water Color Society. Awards: Silver medal, San Diego Exposition, 1915; bronze medal, San Diego Exposition, 1916; silver medals, Sacramento Exposition, 1917 and 1918; first prize, Los Angeles Liberty Exposition, 1918; Black prize, California Art Club, 1919; gold and bronze medals, Sacramento Exposition, 1919; second prize, Phoenix, Ariz., Exposition, 1920. *Address*, 602 South Alvarado St., Los Angeles, Calif.

SMITH, Jacob. Painter, who exhibited water colors at the Penna. Academy of the Fine Arts, Philadelphia, 1925. *Address*, 51 Poplar St., Brooklyn, New York.

SMITH, James P. Miniature painter. Born in 1803, and resided in Philadelphia. He died in Philadelphia in 1888. Contemporary with Thomas Sully. He attained great proficiency in his art. Sully invariably sought his approval of portraits he painted before he let them leave his studio. He painted several miniatures of Washington, after the portraits painted by Gilbert Stuart.

SMITH, Jessie Willcox. Illustrator and painter. Born in Philadelphia. Pupil of the Penna. Academy of the Fine Arts; Drexel Institute under Howard Pyle. Member of Plastic Club; Philadelphia Water Color Club; Fellowship, Penna. Academy of Fine Arts; Society of Illustrators, 1904; New York Water Color

Club. Awarded bronze medal, Charleston Exposition, 1902; Mary Smith prize, Penna. Academy of Fine Arts, 1903; silver medal, St. Louis Exposition, 1904; Beck prize, Phila. Water Color Club, 1911; silver medal, water colors, Panama-Pacific Exposition, San Francisco, 1915. Specialty, paintings and illustrations of children. *Address*, Allen Lane, Philadelphia, Pa.

SMITH, John Rubens. Engraver. Born in England about 1770; died in New York City in 1849. Tuckerman, in his ''Book of the Artists,'' says that Jno. Rubens Smith was the son of the famous English engraver John Raphael Smith (1740–1811). John R. Smith was working as an engraver in Boston in 1811, and in 1816 he was in New York, painting portraits, engraving, and conducting a drawing-school. He remained in New York until 1826, and then possibly went to Philadelphia, as he was engraving and teaching drawing in that city in 1835–37. He again appears in New York in 1845 and once more opened his school. Among his known pupils were Sully, Agate, Cummings, Leutze and Swain R. Gifford. In noting his death the Historic Annals of the National Academy of Design describes Smith as ''short in figure, with a large head, peculiar one-sided gait and an indescribable expression of countenance.'' As an engraver he worked in stipple, aquatint and mezzotint, chiefly upon portraits, and he was an experienced engraver.

SMITH, Joseph Lindon. Painter. Born in Pawtucket, R. I., in 1863. Pupil of Boston Museum School under Crowninshield and Grundmann; at Julien Academy in Paris under Boulanger and Lefebvre. Member of Mural Painters; Copley Society, 1882; Century Association. Awarded Beck prize, Phila. Water Color Club, 1905. Work: Mural paintings in Boston Public Library and in the former Horticultural Hall, Philadelphia. Made copies of paintings in Italy, Egypt, Turkey, Mexico, Guatamia, Java, India, China and Japan for Museums in the United States. Represented in Corcoran Gallery and Smithsonian Institution, Washington; Chicago Art Institute; Harvard University; Rhode Island School of Design; Gardner Collection, Boston. The Boston Museum of Fine Arts owns a large collection of his water colors. *Address*, 102 Chestnut St., Boston, Mass.

SMITH, Marcella. Painter. Born in England in 1887. Studied in London and Paris; also in Corcoran School of Art, Washington, D. C. *Address*, 1320 New Hampshire Ave., Washington, D. C.

SMITH, Marshall J. Native of New Orleans. Died in Covington, La. Studied under R. Clague. Specialty, Louisiana landscapes and portraits. Represented in Louisiana State Museum, New Orleans, La.

SMITH, Oliver P. Painter. Born in Hartford, Conn., in 1867. Pupil of National Academy of Design. Specialty, mural painting. *Address*, 550 East Lincoln Ave., Mt. Vernon, N. Y.

SMITH, R. K. Engraver. A weak stipple portrait of Rev. John Flavel is signed "Engraved by R. K. Smith from an Original." This plate appears as a frontispiece to "The Fountain of Life Opened, Etc.," by Rev. John Flavel, and it was published by Joseph Martin, Richmond, Va., 1824. No other example of the work of the engraver has been found.

SMITH, Rosamond. Painter, who exhibited at the Annual Exhibition, 1923, Penna. Academy of Fine Arts, Philadelphia. *Address*, Fenway Studios, Boston, Mass.

SMITH, Russell. Painter. Born in Glasgow, Scotland, in 1812; died at Edge Hill, Montgomery County, Penna., in 1896. Coming to this country with his parents in 1819, he afterwards studied art with James R. Lambdin, Philadelphia artist, and father of Alfred C. Lambdin, the well-known local journalist. For six years after 1834 he worked at the Chestnut and Walnut street theaters as a scene painter, but after his marriage to a fellow artist he took to landscape painting in which he met with great success. He also became noted as a scientific draughtsman, being employed by Sir Charles Lyell and other naturalists, and did similar work for the geological surveys of Pennsylvania and Virginia. When the Academy of Music was in the process of building as the foremost structure of its type in America, he was engaged to paint the scenery, and the drop curtain which he produced, with its handsome landscape, brought him many commissions of the sort from managers in this and other cities. His "Cave at Chelten-Hills" was much admired at the Centennial Exposition. He contributed regularly to the exhibitions of the Penna. Academy of the Fine Arts for more than half a century.

His wife and his daughter, both named Mary, were artists of considerable ability.

SMITH, Sidney L. Engraver, painter and etcher. Born in Foxboro, Mass., in 1845. In 1847 his father removed to Canton, Mass., which place has since been the home of the subject of this sketch. In 1863, Sidney L. Smith was placed with Reuben Carpenter, a commercial engraver, to learn that business; but in the early part of 1864 Mr. Smith enlisted in the Union army and saw some service at the close of the Civil War. Upon returning to peaceful pursuits, he entered the engraving establishment of Joseph Andrews, in Boston. Under the general supervision of Mr. Andrews, Mr. Smith and Mr. Thomas D. Kendricks reproduced on steel the original etchings, and the original woodcuts as well, issued in England for an edition of Dickens' works. As Mr. Andrews was not an etcher and had little liking for this class of work, the young men were left pretty much to their own devices in a task which occupied them for about two and one half years.

Upon the completion of this work Mr. Smith opened an engraving establishment of his own, and for some time was engaged with such work as he could secure. In 1877 Mr. John La Farge, who had previously tried to induce Mr. Smith to abandon engraving for painting, invited the latter to assist him in the decoration of Trinity Church, in New York, and as an assistant to Mr. La Farge, Mr. Smith was engaged in this work until 1883; from then on and until 1887 he was chiefly employed in the designing of stained glass windows and in work of a decorative character.

In 1887 Mr. Smith made some etchings for Mr. Clarence Cook, and finding that others desired work of a similar character he has continued etching and designing for engravers, etc., since that date. Though Mr. Smith has produced exceptionally good and artistic work as an etcher, his experience along this line was confined to the early part of his professional career, and covers a comparatively brief period.

SMITH, T. Henry. A portrait and genre painter of Philadelphia. He was a member of the Artists' Fund Society, and Chairman of its Exhibition Committee in 1867. He was a regular exhibitor in the Penna. Academy exhibitions from 1861–67.

SMITH, Thomas. Painter. A portrait of Maria Catherine Smith was painted by Captain Thomas Smith in 1693. It belongs to the Clapp family of Dorchester, Mass.

SMITH, Thomas Herbert. Painter. Member of League of American Artists. *Address*, R. F. D. 36, Wilton, Conn.

SMITH, Thomas Lochlan. Painter. Born in Scotland in 1835. He came to this country at an early age, and was a pupil of George H. Boughton in Albany, N. Y. He devoted himself chiefly to painting winter scenes. His "Deserted House" and "Eve of St. Agnes" were exhibited at the Centennial in Philadelphia, 1876. He died in 1884.

SMITH, Twigg. Painter. Born in Nelson, New Zealand, in 1882. Pupil of Art Institute of Chicago; also of Harry M. Walcott. Member of Hawaiian Society of Artists; Chicago Art Students' League. *Address*, 122 Bates St., Honolulu, Hawaii.

SMITH, Violet Thompson. Miniature painter, who exhibited miniatures at the Penna. Academy of the Fine Arts, Philadelphia, 1925. *Address*, 100 King's Highway, West Haddonfield, N. J.

SMITH, Walter Granville. Painter and illustrator. Born in Granville, N. Y., in 1870. Pupil of Art Students' League of New York; also studied abroad. Elected Associate Member of National Academy of Design in 1908, and National Academy in 1915. Represented by "Grey Day" at Smithsonian Institution, Washington, D. C. *Address,* 96 Fifth Ave., New York.

SMITH, William. Engraver. In 1840 William Smith is referred to as a partner of David McClelland, general engravers and copper-plate printers, of Washington, D. C. No signed work by William Smith is known to the compiler, and it is possible that he was only the printer of the firm.

SMITH, William D. Engraver. In 1829 this capital line-engraver was working in Newark, N. J., and he was possibly a pupil of Peter Maverick. From 1835 to 1850 Wm. D. Smith was in business as a general engraver in New York City.

SMITH, William Good. Portrait painter in oils and miniature, who flourished 1844–1846 in New York.

SMITH, W. Linford. Painter. Born in Pittsburgh, Pa., in 1869. Pupil of Chris. Walters. Member of Pittsburgh Artists' Association. *Address,* 5029 Amderson Place, Pittsburgh, Pa.

SMITH, Wuanita. Illustrator. Born in 1866. Pupil of Penna. Academy of the Fine Arts and of Howard Pyle. *Address,* 1823 Walnut St., Philadelphia, Pa.

SMITHER, James (or Jr.). Engraver. According to all data available, this engraver in line, and in a somewhat peculiar stipple manner, was born in England in 1741; he first appears in this country in Philadelphia in 1768, when he was engraving for Robert Bell, a publisher and book-seller of that city. He then advertised his business as follows in the *Pennsylvania Journal* of 1768:

"James Smither. Engraver. At the first house in Third street, from the Cross-Keys, corner of Chestnut-street, Philadelphia. Performs all manner of Engraving in gold, silver, copper, steel and all other metals: coats of arms, and seals, done in the neatest manner. Likewise cuts stamps, brands and metal cuts for printers, and ornamental tools for book-binders. He also ornaments guns and pistols, both engraving and inlaying silver, at the most reasonable rates."

This advertisement would seem to justify the tradition that he was originally an ornamenter of guns and a gunsmith, working in the Tower of London previous to his arrival in Philadelphia. He did considerable engraving for Robert Bell, mentioned above; also engraved book-

plates and bill heads, and he is credited with having engraved the plates for some of the paper money of the province of Pennsylvania, and then having counterfeited this money for the use of the enemy during the British occupation of Philadelphia. In any event, a proclamation was issued by the Supreme Executive Council of Pennsylvania, on June 25, 1778, accusing Smither and others of having "knowingly and willingly aided and assisted the enemies of this state and the United States of America," and declaring all of them "attainted with high treason." Smither evidently left Philadelphia with the British troops, as he was working for Hugh Gaine in New York in 1777, and he advertises himself as an engraver, "late of Philadelphia," in Rivington's *Royal Gazette* of May 22, 1779. He returned to Philadelphia, as in 1786 he was engraving for publishers of that city, and the name of "James Smither, engraver and seal-cutter" appears in the Philadelphia directories for 1791–1800, 1802–19 and in 1823–24. Unfortunately, there was a James Smither (3d), also an engraver, and the directories make no distinction between the father and son. The elder James Smither was certainly engraving after 1800.

SMITHER, James (3d). Engraver. Born in 1772; died in 1793. There is some difficulty in disentangling these two names. The evidence of the existence of a "James Smither, 3d" (signed Jr.), lies in the occurrence of this name among the professional members of the Philadelphia Association of Artists, organized on Dec. 28, 1794, and plates of birds so signed are among the illustrations in Dobson's edition of Rees' Encyclopedia, published in Philadelphia in 1794–1803. In the same work, however, plates almost identical in character are signed "James Smither" and "James Smither, Jr." The directories make no distinction between father and son and give no clue. James Smither the 3d son of James Smither died during the yellow fever epidemic in Philadelphia in 1793, the father outliving the son for thirty-six years, hence the confusion in the dates of their work.

The name of James Smither, Jr., as engraver, has been found by the compiler only in Dobson's Encyclopedia; the work being in line. A. James Smither was an officer in one of the Pennsylvania militia regiments during the Revolutionary War, in 1776–77.

SMITHWICK, J. G. Wood engraver, who worked for *Harper's* and *Scribner's;* he afterwards formed a partnership with Frank French.

SMYTH, Margarita Pumpelly. Painter. Born in Newburgh, N. Y., in 1873. Pupil of Abbott H. Thayer. *Address,* Belmont St., Watertown, Mass.

SMYTH, Samuel Gordon. Mural painter and illustrator. Born in Holmesburg, Penna., in 1891. *Address,* 1216 Eighteenth St., Philadelphia.

23

SNEAD, Louise W. (Mrs.). Miniature painter and illustrator. Born in Charleston, S. C. Pupil of Chase, and of the Art Students' League of New York. *Address*, Noroton, Conn.

SNELL, Florence B. Painter, who exhibited "The Cross Roads" at the Penna. Academy of the Fine Arts, 1915. *Address*, 253 West 42d St., New York.

SNELL, Henry Bayley. Painter. Born in Richmond, England, in 1858. Studied at Art Students' League of New York. Awarded gold medal, Philadelphia Art Club; 1st prize, Tennessee Centennial, Nashville, 1897; honorable mention, Paris Exposition, 1900; assistant director of Fine Arts, United States Commission, Paris Exposition, 1900; Officier de l'Academie et de l'Instruction Publique; silver medal, Buffalo Exposition, 1901; St. Louis Exposition, 1904; silver and gold medals, Panama P. I. Exposition, 1915. Elected Member of National Academy of Design in 1906; president of New York Water Color Club. Member of American Water Color Society. *Address*, New Hope, Penna.

SNVERNIZZI, Prosper. Sculptor, who exhibited in the Penna. Academy of the Fine Arts, Philadelphia, 1926. *Address*, 500 West 178th St., New York City.

SNYDER, Clarence W. Painter, who exhibited at the Annual Exhibition of 1923, Penna. Academy of Fine Arts, Philadelphia. *Address*, 1520 Chestnut St., Philadelphia.

SNYDER, Corydon G. Painter, sculptor, illustrator and etcher. Born in Atchison, Kans., in 1879. Author of course in "Fashion Illustration" published by Federal Schools of Minneapolis; "Modern Advertising Arrangement," published by Myer Booth College, Chicago; "Retouching Not Difficult." *Address*, 1161 South Ridgeland Ave., Oak Park, Ill.

SNYDER, H. W. Engraver. Snyder was engraving in New York in 1797–1805, and in 1811 he made some good stipple portraits for the "Polyanthus," of Boston. He usually signed his plates "Snyder," but one plate, published in Boston in 1807, is signed as above. As "H. W. Snyder" he also made a number of the line illustrations in "The American Builder's Companion," published in Boston in 1816.

SOBLE, Jack. Painter, who exhibited at the National Academy of Design, New York, 1925. *Address*, 1785 Fulton Ave., New York.

SODERSTON, Herman. Painter. Born in Sweden in 1862. Pupil of Royal Academy of Fine Arts, Stockholm. Member of New Haven Paint and Clay Club; Society of Independent Artists. Represented in Memorial Hall, Hartford; Sheffield Scientific Hall, New Haven, Conn. *Address*, 840 Chapel St., New Haven, Conn.

SOHIER, Alice Ruggles. Painter. Born in Quincy, Mass., in 1880. Studied in Buffalo; also in School of Boston Museum of Fine Arts under Tarbell, and in Europe. Member: Guild of Boston Artists. Awarded bronze medal, Panama-Pacific Exposition, San Francisco, 1915. *Address*, Concord, Mass.

SOKOLSKY, Sulamith. Painter. Born in New York in 1889. Pupil of Cooper Union and of the National Academy of Design, New York. *Address*, 2103 Vyse Ave., Bronx, New York, N. Y.

SOLDWEDEL, Frederic. Painter of marine and yachting subjects. His water colors of yachts are considered his best works.

SOLOMON, Harry. Painter. Born in San Francisco in 1873. Studied in Paris. Member of Salmagundi Club. Work: "Portrait of Dr. Bennett Mitchell," in Capitol Building, Des Moines, Ia.; also in Morningside University, Sioux City. *Address*, 39 West 67th St., New York, N. Y.

SOLON, Leon Victor. Portrait and mural painter; also illustrator. Born in England in 1872. Member of National Sculpture Society, and Society of Mural Painters. *Address*, 16 East 41st St., New York.

SOMERBY, J. E. Engraver. The only record of this man as an engraver is found in the "American Coast Pilot," by Capt. Lawrence Furlong, edited by Edmund M. Blunt, Newburyport, 1804. He engraved two or three maps in this work, the rest being engraved by A. M. Peasley.

SOMMERS. He painted "Westward Ho! or Crossing the Plains." It is now in the Capitol, Washington, D. C.

SONN, Albert H. Painter and illustrator. Born in Newark, N. J., in 1867. Pupil of Cooper Institute and of the National Academy of Design, N. Y. Member: Salmagundi Club, 1900; Artists' Fund Society; New York Water Color Club. *Address*, 282 Parker St., Newark, N. J.

SONNICHSEN, Yngvar. Painter, illustrator and etcher. Born in Christiania, Norway, in 1875. Studied in Antwerp; also in Brussels; at Julien's under Bouguereau and Constant, in Paris. *Address*, P. O. Box 813, Seattle, Wash.

SONTAG, William L. Landscape painter. Born near Pittsburgh, Penna., in 1822. He was elected an Associate Member of the National Academy in 1860 and an Academician **two**

years later. His principal works are "Morning in the Alleghenies"; "View on Licking River, Ky."; "Sunset in the Wilderness"; "Fog rising off Mount Adams" and "Spirit of Solitude." He died in 1900.

SOPER, J. H. Gardner. Painter. Born in Flint, Mich., in 1877. Awarded bronze medal, Louisiana Purchase Exposition, St. Louis, 1904. *Address*, 12 Gramercy Park, New York, N. Y.

SOPER, R. F. This meritorious engraver of portraits in stipple was employed by New York publishers as early as 1831; he worked largely for J. C. Buttre, of the same city, at a later period.

SORENSON-DIEMAN, Clara Leonard. Sculptor. Born in Indianapolis, Ind., in 1877. Pupil of Lorado Taft and Victor Brenner. Member: Chicago Society of Artists; Indiana Society of Artists; Alumnae, Chicago Art Institute. Work: Memorial Tablet, Shortridge High School, Indianapolis; Memorial Tablet, Y. M. C. A., Cedar Rapids, Ia.; Memorial Tablet, Art Association, Cedar Rapids, Ia. *Address*, 1800 Second Ave., Cedar Rapids, Ia.

SOTHERN, E. A. Painter. "Alpine View" was painted by the elder Sothern (actor), and presented by him to Alfred Sutliffe, editor of the *San Francisco Chronicle*.

SOTTEK, Frank. Painter, illustrator and etcher. Born in Toledo, Ohio, in 1874. Member of Toledo Federation of Artists. *Address*, 381 South Detroit Ave., Toledo, Ohio.

SOTTER, George W. Painter. Born in Pittsburgh in 1879. Pupil of Chase, Anshutz and Redfield. Member of Pittsburgh Artists' Association. Awarded silver medal, Panama-Pacific Exposition, San Francisco, 1915; first prize, Pittsburgh Association of Artists, 1920; honorable mention, Conn. Academy of Fine Arts, 1921. Work: "The Hill Road," Reading Museum, Reading, Pa.; "Pennsylvania Country," State College, State College, Pa. *Address*, Holicong, Bucks Co., Pa.

SOUTHWARD, George. Landscape, still-life, portrait and miniature painter. Born in 1803. Studied in Boston under Ames, and accompanied that artist to Rome. At one time he was a pupil of Thomas Sully. On his return from his studies abroad he settled in Salem, Mass., and died there in 1876.

SOUTHWARD, Nathaniel. Miniature painter. Born in 1806. He worked in Boston 1842–48, visited Europe and on his return lived in New York and Philadelphia. He died in 1858. (The name is sometimes spelt "Southworth.")

SOUTHWICK, Jeanie Lea. Painter. Born in Worcester, Mass. Pupil of Shurtleff, Ross Turner, Woodbury and Chase; also of Carmine Academy in Paris. Member of Worcester Art Museum; Art Students' Club. Lecturer on Arts and Crafts of Japan, Java, etc. Specialty, water colors. *Address*, 6 Home St., Worcester, Mass.

SOUTHWICK, Katherine (Mrs. Keeler). Painter and illustrator. Born in Buxton, Me., in 1887. Pupil of Chicago Academy of Fine Arts; Art Institute of Chicago. Member: Fellowship of the Penna. Academy of the Fine Arts. Awarded Cresson traveling scholarship, Penna. Academy of Fine Arts, 1911–13. *Address*, 416 West 20th St., New York City.

SOUTHWORTH, William. An American painter whose name is mentioned by writers on art in this country about 1850.

SPACKMAN, Cyril S. Painter and etcher. Born in Cleveland, Ohio, in 1887. Member of Chicago Society of Etchers, and Print Society of England. *Address*, 63 Balfour Road, Highbury, New Park, London, England.

SPADER, W. E. Painter, who exhibited at the National Academy of Design, New York, 1925.

SPAETH, Marie Houghton (Mrs.). Painter. Born at Hanover, N. H. Specialty, portraits of children. Represented at the Penna. Academy of the Fine Arts by "Apennine Village." *Address*, Edgehill St., Princeton, N. J.

SPALDING, Elisabeth. Landscape painter. Born in Erie, Pa. Pupil of Penna. Academy of the Fine Arts, and Art Students' League of New York. Represented by "The Docks" and "Rain" in the Erie Art Club, and by "Twilight Shower," Denver Art Association. *Address*, 853 Washington St., Denver, Colo.

SPALDING, Grace. Painter, who exhibited at the Penna. Academy of the Fine Arts, Philadelphia, 1924. *Address*, New York City.

SPARHAWK-JONES, Elizabeth. Painter. Born in Baltimore in 1885. Winner of long term Cresson scholarship and the first "Charles Toppen" prize, Schools of Penna. Academy of Fine Arts; also Mary Smith prize, 1908, 1912, Penna. Academy of the Fine Arts; honorable mention, Carnegie Institute, Pittsburgh, 1909. Represented in permanent collection Art Institute, Chicago. *Address*, 1104 Spruce St., Philadelphia.

SPARKS, Arthur Watson. Painter. Born in Washington, D. C., in 1870; died in 1919. Studied at Julien Academy and École des

Beaux Arts, Paris, France, under Laurens, Cormon, Bouguereau, Thaulow, Mucha, Ferrier and Courtois. Exhibited at Paris Salon; Carnegie Institute; Penna. Academy of the Fine Arts; National Academy of Design; Art Institute, Chicago; Corcoran Gallery, etc. A w a r d e d bronze medal, San Francisco Exposition, 1915; 2d prize, Associated Artists of Pittsburgh. Principal works: "The Steel Mills"; "Under the Birches"; "Grand View Arizona Canyon"; "Clemance and Cora"; "The Model at Rest"; etc. Professor of painting at Carnegie Institute. Member of Associated Artists of Pittsburgh.

SPARKS, Will. Painter and illustrator. Born in St. Louis, Mo., in 1862. Pupil of Julien Academy in Paris. He has executed murals and is represented by paintings in the Toledo Art Museum and the St. Louis Museum. *Address,* 163 Sutter St., San Francisco, Calif.

SPARROW, T. Engraver. Plates for Maryland paper money, issued in 1770–74, are conspicuously signed "T. Sparrow, Sculp." Sparrow also engraved upon copper the title-page to *The Deputy Commissary's Guide of Maryland,* published by Anne Catherine Green & Son, Annapolis, Md., 1774.

Sparrow was chiefly a wood-engraver, and thus made book-plates, head and tail-pieces, bill-heads, etc. He was located in Annapolis, Md., and Mr. Charles Dexter Allen, in his "American Book-Plates," says that he worked there between 1765–80. This same man was apparently employed in Boston at a possibly earlier date, judging solely from the period of the designer, after whom he engraved a somewhat curious advertisement for the music dealer, John Ashton, of 197 Washington St., Boston.

SPEAKMAN, Esther. A portrait painter of Philadelphia exhibiting about 1843–61. Daughter of John Speakman. She painted a portrait of John Speakman, half length. He was Treasurer of the Academy of Natural Sciences, Philadelphia, Pa.

SPEAR, Arthur P. Painter. Born in Washington, D. C., in 1879. Pupil of Laurens in Paris. Elected an Associate Member of the National Academy, New York. *Address,* Fenway Studios, 30 Ipswich St., Boston.

SPEICHER, Eugene E. Painter. Born in Buffalo, N. Y., in 1883. Studied in Buffalo, New York and Europe. Member: Associate Member of the National Academy, 1912; Portrait Painters; National Art Club; Contemporary Club. Awards: Proctor prize, National Academy of Design, 1911; Isidor portrait prize, Salmagundi Club, 1913; third Hallgarten prize, National Academy of Design, 1914; first Hallgarten prize, National Academy of Design, 1915; silver medal, Panama-Pacific Exposition, San Francisco, 1915; Beck gold medal, Penna. Academy of the Fine Arts, 1920; third class

medal, Carnegie Institute, 1921. W o r k: "Morning Light," Metropolitan Museum, New York; "Mountain Landscape," Art League, Galveston, Tex.; "Portrait of an Old Lady," Decatur, Ill., Museum. *Address,* 253 West 42d St., New York, N. Y.

SPEIGHT, Francis. Painter, who exhibited in Penna. Academy of the Fine Arts, Philadelphia, 1926. *Address,* The Penna. Academy of the Fine Arts, Philadelphia.

SPELMAN, John A. Painter, who has exhibited at the Art Institute of Chicago and the Penna. Academy of Fine Arts, Philadelphia, 1924. *Address,* 731 Woodbine Ave., Oak Park, Ill.

SPENCELEY, J. Winfred. Engraver. Born in Boston, Mass., in 1865; living there in 1905. Mr. Spenceley learned to engrave with J. A. Lowell & Co., of Boston, and was with that firm in 1882–87, doing lettering and ornamental steel and copper-plate engraving with the intention of devoting himself to bank-note work. He was at the same time attending the art school of Tomasso Juglaris, in Boston. In 1887 he went into business for himself, and while perfecting himself in freehand drawing he took up etching. In 1901–03 he was with the Western Bank-Note Co., of Chicago, and he was later associated with the bank-note company of E. Bouligny, of the city of Mexico.

While in the employ of J. A. Lowell & Co., Mr. Spenceley worked upon several book-plates, including one for Oliver Wendell Holmes. The freedom of design and the variety incidental to book-plate work appealed to him, and he later made a specialty of this branch of engraving, designing as well as engraving the plates. Among the more important book-plates made by Mr. Spenceley may be noted the following: The plate for the Boston Public Library and those for Harvard, Dartmouth, Michigan, Ohio State, and Missouri universities. In addition to these he has designed and engraved about one hundred and fifty plates for other libraries and for private individuals. A descriptive catalogue of Mr. Spenceley's book-plates has been published by W. P. Tonesdell, Boston, 1905.

SPENCER, Mrs. In Tuckerman's "Book of the American Artists" he notes that a Mrs. Spencer was painting genre subjects with decided merit.

SPENCER, Asa. Engraver. Born in New England; died in England in 1847. In 1815 Spencer was a member of the bank-note engraving firm of Murray, Draper, Fairman & Co. of Philadelphia. He invented a process for applying lathe work to bank-note engraving, made improvements in the medal-ruling machine, and introduced other devices connected with the manufacture of bank-notes. As mentioned in the note on Gideon Fairman, he accompanied Fairman and Perkins to England in 1817. But Spencer returned to Philadelphia, and later he published a few book illustrations made by his medal-ruling machine.

SPENCER, Edna Isbester. Painter, sculptor and illustrator. Born in St. John, N. B., Canada, in 1883. Pupil of Bela Pratt; also of Robert Aitken. *Address*, Studio Building, 110 Tremont St., Boston, Mass.

SPENCER, Frederick R. Painter. Born in the town of Lenox, Madison County, New York, on the 7th of June, 1806. His parents were from the New England states; his father, General Ichabod S. Spencer from Massachusetts, and his mother from Connecticut. Mr. Spencer experienced the usual boy's inclination to imitate prints, and at the age of fifteen, being with his father in Albany, saw, for the first time, a gallery of portraits. In 1825, he came to New York to study, where he drew from the casts of the American Academy, and had the favor of the President, and received instruction in the methods he was to pursue. The young painter returned home and painted at his father's house, but in 1827 commenced painting professionally at a village in the neighborhood. He painted for a time in Utica, N. Y.; but finally made the city of New York his headquarters where he continued painting until his death in 1875. Among his portraits, he painted Henry A. Ingalls; Robert Hunter Morris (Mayor of New York, painted for the city in 1846) and Frances L. Morris, painted in 1838. He was elected a member of the National Academy in 1846.

SPENCER, Howard B. Painter. Born in Plainfield, N. J. Pupil of F. V. Du Mond and of Walt Kuhn. Member of League of New York Artists. *Address*, 1947 Broadway, New York.

SPENCER, Hugh. Illustrator. Born in St. Cloud, Minn., in 1887. Pupil of Charles S. Chapman, Harvey Dunn and Arthur Covey. Member: New York Society of Craftsmen; Boston Society of Arts and Crafts; Detroit Society of Arts and Crafts; Philadelphia Art Alliance. *Address*, Chester, Conn.

SPENCER, Joseph B. Painter of fruit, flowers and animals. Born in Salisbury, Conn., in 1829. He settled in Scranton, Penna.

SPENCER, Margaret F. (Mrs. Robert). Painter. Born in Philadelphia in 1882. Pupil of Robert Spencer. *Address*, New Hope, Pa.

SPENCER, Mary. Painter. Born in Fitchburg, Mass. Pupil of Herbert Adams, Henry B. Snell, Arthur Dow, and Richard Miller; also at Pratt Institute. Member of National As-

sociation of Women Painters and Sculptors; Art Alliance of America; Brooklyn Society of Artists; Brooklyn Water Color Club. Her specialty was water color painting. She died in 1923.

SPENCER, Mary. Painter. Born in Springfield, Ohio, in 1835. Pupil of C. T. Webber in Cincinnati. Member of Cincinnati Woman's Art Club. Work: "Fruit," Cincinnati Museum. *Address*, 3612 Woodbridge Place, Cincinnati, Ohio.

SPENCER, Robert. Landscape painter. Born in Harvard, Nebr., in 1879. Student of National Academy of Design, New York, 1889–1891; New York School of Art, 1903–05. Pupil of Chase, Du Mond, Henri, Garber, Francis Jones and Louis Mora. Has exhibited at principal exhibitions in America; also in London and Toronto. Represented in permanent collections of Metropolitan Museum of New York; in Boston Art Club; Detroit Museum of Art; Art Institute of Chicago; National Arts Club, New York City. Awarded 2d Hallgarten prize, National Academy of Design, 1913; honorable mention, Art Club of Philadelphia, 1913; Jenney Sesnan gold medal, Pa. Academy of the Fine Arts, 1914; George Inness gold medal, National Academy of Design, 1914; gold medal, Boston Art Club, 1915; gold medal, Panama P. I. Exposition, 1915. Elected Associate Member of National Academy of Design, 1914; National Academy, 1920. *Address*, New Hope, Pa.

SPENCER, W. H. This engraver of landscape, in line, was working in New York in 1825.

SPERRY, Reginald T. Landscape painter and designer. Born in Hartford, Conn., in 1845. In 1874 he moved to Brooklyn, N. Y.

SPERRY, Theodore S. Landscape painter. Born in Conn. in 1822. He painted theatrical scenery, and lived for years in Hartford, Conn.

SPICER-SIMSON, Theodore. Painter and sculptor. Born in Havre, France, in 1871. Member: Associate of Societé National des Beaux Arts, 1901; Century Association; National Sculpture Society, 1911. Awards: Highest award for medals, Brussels Exposition, 1911; also in Ghent Exposition; bronze medal, P.-P. Exposition, San Francisco, 1915. Work represented in Metropolitan Museum and Numismatic Museum, New York; Chicago Art Institute; Detroit Institute; Minneapolis Museum of Art; City Museum of Art, St. Louis; the Luxembourg, Paris; Victoria and Albert Museum, London; in Holland, Belgium, Germany and Austria-Hungary. *Address*, 7 West 43d St., New York, N. Y.

SPICUZZA, Francesco J. Painter. Born in Sicily in 1883. Member of New York

Water Color Club; Painter Group of the Middle West. Awards: Bronze medal, St. Paul Institute, 1915; silver medal, St. Paul Institute, 1917; Snyder prize, Wisconsin Painters and Sculptors, 1919. Represented in St. Paul, Minn., Institute; Milwaukee, Wisc., Art Institute. *Address*, 432 Broadway, Milwaukee, Wisc.

SPIERS, Harry. Painter. Born in Selsea, Sussex, England, in 1869. Pupil of Julien Academy in Paris. Work: ''As the Sunlight Bursts,'' Boston Museum of Fine Arts; ''At the Trough'' and ''Passing of an Autumn Day,'' Ontario Government Gallery, Toronto. *Address*, 150 Cedar St., Dedham, Mass.

SPINGARN, Amy (Mrs. J. E.). Painter. Born in New York in 1883. Pupil of K. H. Miller. Member of Society of Independent Artists. *Address*, 9 West 73d St., New York, N. Y.

SPIZZIRE, Luigi. Painter, who exhibited in the National Academy of Design Exhibition, New York, 1925. *Address*, Philadelphia, Penna.

SPRAGUE, Martin. Portrait painter and engraver. He flourished during the Colonial period in Boston, Mass.

SPRAGUE-SMITH, Isabelle Dwight (Mrs. Charles). Painter. Born in Clinton, N. Y., in 1861. Pupil of Art Students' League of New York; also studied in Paris. Member of Barnard Club. Principal of Veltin School since 1900. *Address*, The Veltin School, 160 West 74th St., New York.

SPREAD, Henry Fenton. Painter. Born in Ireland in 1844. He studied and travelled in England, Germany and Australia, and in 1870 he came to the United States. He has had his studio in Chicago, where he has founded ''Spread's Art Academy.'' Among his works are ''Chicago Arising from her Ashes'' and ''Sad News.''

SPRINCHORN, Carl. Painter. Born in Sweden in 1887; came to United States in 1904. Studied in New York and Paris. Exhibited in New York and Chicago. *Address*, 600 Madison Ave., New York.

SPRING, Edward Adolphus. Sculptor. Born in New York City in 1837. He studied with Henry K. Brown and William Rimmer. He has modelled with great success many terra cotta panels. He established the Perth Amboy Terra Cotta Co. and the Eagleswood Art Pottery.

SPRINGER, Carl. Painter. Born in Fultonham, Ohio, in 1874. Member of Art Students' League of New York; Pen and Pencil Club of Columbus. Award: First prize, Columbus Art League, 1920. Represented in Columbus Gallery of Fine Arts. *Address*, Punta Gorda, Fla.

SPRINGER, Eva. Miniature painter, who exhibited at the Penna. Academy of the Fine Arts, Philadelphia, 1925. *Address*, ''The Dresden,'' Washington, D. C.

SQUIRE, Maud H. Illustrator, painter and etcher. Born in Cincinnati, Ohio. Member of Societé des Salons and the Chicago Society of Etchers. *Address*, 34 Rue St. Louis, Vernon, France.

ST. CLAIR, Gordon. Painter, who exhibited ''Pavilion on the Moon,'' Penna. Academy of the Fine Arts, 1915, Philadelphia. *Address*, 26 Studio Building, Chicago, Ill.

ST. JOHN, J. Painter and illustrator. Born in Chicago in 1872. Pupil of Art Students' League of New York under Mowbray, Beckwith and Du Mond. Member of Chicago Society of Artists. *Address*, Tree Studio Building, Chicago, Ill.

ST. JOHN, Loia Alberta. Painter. Born in Albany, Ind., in 1879. Pupil of H. R. McGinnis; at Cincinnati Art Academy under Nowottny and Meakin; under J. O. Adams and Brandt Steele at Indianapolis. Member of Indianapolis Artists' Association; Muncie Artists' Association; Alliance; Indiana Art Club. Award: Honorable mention, Muncie Artists' Association. Work: ''October Morning,'' Montpelier, Ind., Library. *Address*, Miltanna Garden, Albany, Ind.

ST. MEMIN, Charles Balthazar Julien Fevret De. Engraver. Born in Dijon, France, in 1770; died there in 1852. At the outbreak of the French Revolution he went to Switzerland; then to Canada in 1793, and soon after he came to New York.

As a means of supporting himself in this country he introduced here the engraving of portraits by means of the ''Physionotrace,'' a machine invented by Edme Queneday, of Paris, and intended to exactly reproduce, on a reduced scale, the human profile. St. Memin made some improvements upon this device, and with it he made on a tinted paper a profile a little less than life size; this he finished by hand and with crayons directly from the sitter. With this finished crayon drawing as a guide he used a pantograph of special design to still further reduce the profile so that it would go inside a circle of about two inches in diameter, faintly scratching the reduced drawing directly on the copperplate. This copper was now etched and finished in aquatint, with some assistance with the roulette. The result was a soft, pleasing print. For the original crayon, which was ready for framing, for the plate, and for twelve impressions from the plate St. Memin charged $33.

These small portraits became very popular, and St. Memin, traveling from North to South over the country, produced about 800 of them. He kept for himself two sets of proof impressions; after his death these sets were purchased from his executors and are now in the United States, one in the Corcoran Gallery in Washington, D. C., and the other was lately in the hands of a Philadelphia collector.

Besides these portraits, St. Memin etched two large views of the city of New York, a map of the siege of Savannah, published in *The Monthly Military Repository*, C. Smith, New York, 1796, and a beautiful etched business-card of Peter Mourgeon, "Copperplate printer from Paris," of New York.

STACEY, Anna Lee (Mrs. J. F.). Painter. Born in Glasgow, Mo. Student at Pritchett Institute; also studied at Art Institute of Chicago. Awarded Young Fortnightly prize, Chicago Artists' Exhibition, 1902; Martin B. Cahn prize, Exhibition by American Artists, 1902; Marshall Field prize, 1907; Clyde M. Carr prize, Chicago Artists' Exhibition, 1912. One of her pictures, "Vista from the Ponce de Leon," was purchased by the City Commissioner for the city of Chicago, 1914. Member: Chicago Society of Artists. *Address*, 6 East Ohio St., Chicago.

STACEY, John Franklin. Painter. Born in Biddeford, Me., in 1859. Graduated from Mass. Normal Art School, Boston; student of Julien Academy, Paris. Awarded bronze medal, St. Louis Exposition, 1904; bronze medal, Buenos Aires Exposition, 1910 (picture purchased by Art Museum, Santiago, Chile); Grower prize, Art Institute of Chicago, 1911. President of Chicago Society of Artists, 1907–1909. *Address*, Studio Building, Ohio St., Chicago.

STACKPOLE, Ralph. Sculptor and etcher. Born at Williams, Ore., in 1885. Member of California Society of Etchers. Work: Portrait bust of "Judge Seawell" at City Hall, San Francisco; "Prof. Flugel," Stanford University, California. *Address*, 712 Montgomery St., San Francisco, Calif.

STADELMAN, Henryette L. Painter, who exhibited "A Bit of Provincetown" at Penna. Academy of the Fine Arts, Philadelphia, 1924. *Address*, 710 Blackshire Road, Wilmington, Del.

STAFFORD, Mary. Painter, who exhibited at the National Academy of Design, 1925. *Address*, Chicago, Ill.

STAFFORD, P. Scott. Painter. Born in Brooklyn, New York. Pupil of Robert Henri. Member of Pen and Pencil Club of Columbus, Ohio. *Address*, 1947 Broadway, New York.

STAHR, Paul C. Illustrator. Born in New York, 1883. Pupil of National Academy of Design. Illustrator for *Life, Collier's Weekly, Harper's Bazaar. Address*, 362 Audubon Ave., New York.

STAIGG, Richard Morrell. Miniature painter. Born in England in 1817, he came to the United States in 1831 and settled in Newport, R. I. He was elected a member of the National Academy of Design in 1861. He died in Newport in 1881. See Tuckerman's "Book of the Artists" for general biographical details.

STALKER, E. Well-engraved vignettes so signed are found in Philadelphia publications of 1815. There was an E. Stalker engraving in London in 1801 and again in 1823; it is possible that he was located in Philadelphia for a short time. Several of the plates noted are designed by C. R. Leslie.

STAMATA, Frank. Sculptor, who exhibited at the Penna. Academy of the Fine Arts in Philadelphia, 1921 and 1924. *Address*, 1809 Callowhill St., Philadelphia, Pa.

STANCLIFF, J. W. Marine painter. Born in Chatham, Conn., in 1814. Pupil of J. B. Flagg. Later he became President of the Connecticut School of Design.

STANGE, Emile. Painter. Born in Jersey City, N. J., in 1863. Member of Salmagundi Club. *Address*, North Hackensack, N. J.

"STANLAWS, Penrhn" (Penryhn Stanley Adamson). Portrait painter. Born in Dundee, Scotland, in 1877. He came to the United States in 1891; studied art in Paris and London. Exhibited at Paris Salon, 1904; established a studio in New York, 1908; built Hotel des Artistes (largest studio building in America), 1916, and another in 1917; pres. of Hotel des Artistes, Inc. *Address*, 1 West 67th St., New York, N. Y.

STANLEY, Jane C. Painter, who exhibited water colors at the Penna. Academy of the Fine Arts, Philadelphia, 1925. *Address*, 93 Seward Ave., Detroit, Mich.

STANSON, George C. Painter and sculptor. Born in Briscut, France, in 1885. Member of Archaeological Institute of America; California Art Club. Work: Four murals in the Biological Museum of the University of California, La Jolla, California; "After the Rain" (mural) in Golden Gate Park Museum, San Francisco; "On the Trail," Museum of Archaeology, Santa Fe, N. M. *Address*, 5653 La Mirada Ave., Los Angeles, Calif.

STANTON, Elizabeth C. Painter. Born in New York, N. Y., in 1894. Pupil of F.

Luis Mora, Geo. Bridgman and Cecilia Beaux. *Address*, Gainsborough Studios, 222 West 59th St., New York.

STANTON, Gideon Townsend. Painter. Born in Morris, Minn., in 1885. Member of New Orleans Art Association. Award: Silver medal, New Orleans Art Association, 1911. *Address*, 822 Common St., New Orleans, La.

STANTON, Lucy M. Born in Atlanta, Ga., in 1875. Studied painting in New Orleans, La., when a child. In 1896 she went to Paris, France, where she studied under M. Koopman, and at the Colarossi School. In 1905 she made a second trip to Paris, where she studied under Lucien Simon and Blanche. She has exhibited at the Salon de la Societé National des Beaux Arts; also at the Pennsylvania Academy of Fine Arts. Member of the Pennsylvania Society of Miniature Painters, and the New York Society of Miniature Painters. *Address*, 98 Chestnut St., Boston, Mass.

STANWOOD, Gertrude. Painter. Born in West Newbury, Mass., in 1874. Pupil of Joseph De Camp, Ernest Major and Lasar. Member of Society of Independent Artists. *Address*, 1015 Cathedral St., Baltimore, Md.

STARK, Otto. Painter and illustrator. Born in Indianapolis in 1859. Pupil of Lefebvre, Boulanger and Cormon in Paris. Member: International Society Art League. Awarded first Holcomb prize, Herron Art Institute, 1915. In charge of art department, Manual Training High School, and art department, Technical High School, Indianapolis; instructor, Herron Art School, Indianapolis, Ind. Work: "Two Boys" and "The Indian Trail," Herron Art Institute, Indianapolis; "River, Valley and Hill," Cincinnati Art Museum; mural decoration, City Hospital, Indianapolis, and mural decorations in the public schools of Indianapolis; "Portrait of Gen. George Rogers Clark," Indiana State House. *Address*, 1722 N. Delaware St., Indianapolis, Ind.

STARKWEATHER, William E. B. Painter. Born in Edinburgh, Scotland, in 1879. Pupil of Art Students' League of New York; in Colarossi Academy in Paris; under Sorolla in Madrid, followed by three years study in Italy. Member: New Haven Painters' Color Club; Hispanic Society of America; Salmagundi Club; New York Water Color Club. Author of "Paintings and Drawings by Francisco Goya." *Address*, 26 East 23d St., New York City.

STARR, Sidney. Painter. Born in Kingston-upon-Hull, Yorkshire, England, in 1857; died in New York in 1925. Pupil of Poynter and of Legros. Awarded bronze medal, Universal Exposition, Paris, 1889. Work: Mural decorations, Grace Chapel, New York City; 24 figures in Congressional Library, Washington,

D. C. *Address*, 256 West 85th St., New York, N. Y.

STAUFFER, Edna. Painter, illustrator and etcher. Born in Phoenixville, Pa., in 1887. Pupil of Chase, Beaux, Anshutz and Dow. Member of Fellowship of Penna. Academy of the Fine Arts. *Address*, Whitney Studio Club, 10 West 8th St., New York.

STEA, Caesar. Sculptor. Born in Bari, Italy, in 1893. Studied at National Academy of Design, New York; also pupil of A. Sterling Calder. Awarded medal by Beaux Arts, 1915. *Address*, 301 East 31st St., New York.

STEARNS, Junius Brutus. Painter. Born in Vermont in 1810. Pupil of the National Academy of Design. He became an Associate in 1848, and an Academician the following year. His work is mainly portraiture but he also painted historical subjects; his five paintings representing Washington as citizen, farmer, soldier, statesman and Christian are considered his best. His "Millennium" is in the New York Academy of Design, and several of his portraits hang in the City Hall there. He died in New York City in 1885.

STEBBINS, Emma. Painter and sculptor, who was born in New York City in 1815. For years she devoted herself to painting in oil and water color. In 1857 she went to Italy and began to model under Italian masters, also with Paul Akers. She produced the figure in Central Park fountain, "Angel of the Waters"; also Statue of Horace Mann, Boston (1860). She was an intimate friend of the actress Charlotte Cushman. She died in 1882.

STEBBINS, Roland S. Painter and illustrator. Born in Boston, Mass., in 1883. Pupil of De Camp in Boston; under Hachl in Munich. Member: Boston Art Club. Illustrator of "At the King's Pleasure."

STEDMAN, Jeanette. Portrait painter. Born in 1881. She studied in Paris early in her career. Her body was found in Lake Michigan in 1925. She had lived in Chicago, Ill., for years.

STEEL, Alfred B. This engraver of subject plates was working for *Sartain's Magazine* in 1850.

STEEL, J. In 1850 J. Steel was doing very good work for *Sartain's Magazine*. He was an engraver of buildings, etc.

STEEL, James W. Engraver. Born in Philadelphia in 1799; died there in 1879. Steel was a pupil of the Philadelphia engravers Benjamin Tanner and George Murray, and for a time he was engaged in bank-note engraving for Tanner, Vallance, Kearney & Co. Later, he became an accomplished line-engraver and produced a number of portraits, landscape and *Annual* plates. Steel was working over his own name in 1820; at a later period in his professional life he was employed chiefly upon bank-note work.

STEELE, Brandt (Theodore). Painter. Born in Battle Creek, Mich., in 1870. Pupil of his father, T. C. Steele; and of Aman-Jean in Paris. Member of Indianapolis Architectural Association; also Indiana Art Club. Instructor at Herron Art Institute, Indianapolis, Ind. *Address*, 811 East Drive, Woodruff Place, Indianapolis, Ind.

STEELE, Frederic Dorr. Illustrator. Born in Marquette, Mich., in 1873. Pupil of National Academy of Design and Art Students' League in New York. Member of Society of Illustrators, 1902. Awarded bronze medal, St. Louis Exposition, 1904. Illustrated: "The Consul," by Richard Harding Davis; "Wards of Liberty," by Myra Kelly; also illustrated books for Mark Twain, F. R. Stockton, R. Kipling, Arnold Bennett, B. Tarkington, etc. *Address*, Care of The Players, 16 Gramercy Park, New York.

STEELE, T. C. Painter. Born in Owen County, Ind., in 1847. Pupil of Royal Academy in Munich under Benczur and Loefftz. Elected Associate Member of the National Academy, 1914. Awarded honorable mention, Paris Exposition, 1900; Fine Arts Corporation prize, 1910. Work: "Gordon Hill," Cincinnati Museum; "Oaks at Vernon," "Portrait of Rev. N. A. Hyde," "The River," "Winter Sunlight," Herron Art Institute, Indianapolis; "Landscape," St. Louis Museum; "Whitewater Valley," Richmond, Ind., Art Association. *Address*, Bloomington, Ind.

STEELE, Zulma. Painter. Born in Appleton, Wis., in 1881. Pupil of Pratt Institute of Brooklyn and of the Art Students' League, New York. Member of National Association of Women Painters and Sculptors. *Address*, Woodstock, Ulster Co., N. Y.

STEENE, William. Painter and sculptor. Born in Syracuse, N. Y., in 1888. Pupil of Henri and of the Art Students' League, N. Y. He chiefly painted mural panels. *Address*, 1182 Broadway, New York.

STEEPER, John. Engraver. According to an advertisement in the *Pennsylvania Gazette*, in 1762, John Steeper was engraving "in all its branches" in Philadelphia. Westcott, in his "Philadelphia," says that the first important copperplate published in Philadelphia in 1755 was "A Southeast Prospect of the Pennsylvania Hospital with the elevation of the intended plan." He goes on to say that Montgomery and Winters drew it. It was en-

graved by J. Steeper and H. Dawkins, and was printed and sold by Robert Kennedy, of Philadelphia.

STEES, Sevilla L. Painter, who exhibited water colors at the Penna. Academy of the Fine Arts, Philadelphia, 1925. *Address*, 1853 Park Ave., Philadelphia.

STEICHEN, Edward J. Painter. Born in Milwaukee, Wis., in 1879. Represented in Metropolitan Museum, New York, by "Nocturne, Temple d'Amour"; Toledo Museum by "Across the Marshes." His mural paintings are to be seen at the Luxembourg, Paris. *Address*, Care of Knoedler & Co., New York City, N. Y.

STEIGER, Harwood M. Painter, who exhibited water colors at the Penna. Academy of the Fine Arts, Philadelphia, 1925. *Address*, 16 West Church St., Fairport, New York.

STEIN. Dunlap notes that a portrait painter of that name was born in Washington, Va., but painted principally in the region beyond the Alleghenies. He was said to have skill, and in 1820 painted a number of portraits at Steubenville, Ohio. Stein died when a young man.

STEIN, Evaleen. Painter. Born in Lafayette, Ind. Studied art at Art Institute of Chicago. Became decorative designer and illuminator, and exhibited illuminated manuscripts at the Arts and Crafts Society in Chicago; also in Indianapolis, etc. Contributor of verse to Indianapolis *Journal*, 1886–1900. Contributor: Society of Decorative Art, New York and Chicago. *Address*, 708 Hitt St., Lafayette, Ind.

STELLA, Joseph. Painter, who exhibited in Philadelphia, 1921, at the "Exhibition of Paintings Showing the Later Tendencies in Art" (Penna. Academy of the Fine Arts). *Address*, 213 West 14th St., New York City.

STELLAR, Hermine J. Painter. Born in Austria. Pupil of Art Institute in Chicago; under Cox and Bellows. Head of Department of Drawing and Painting at University of Nebraska. *Address*, 1508 East Marquette Road, Chicago, Ill.

STEMLER, Otto Adolph. Painter and illustrator. Born in Cincinnati in 1872. Student of Cincinnati Art Academy. Specialty, biblical pictures. *Address*, Kennedy Ave., Cincinnati, Ohio.

STEPHENS, Alice Barber (Mrs.). Illustrator and wood engraver. Born near Salem, N. J., in 1858. Pupil of Penna. Academy of the Fine Arts. Illustrates for *Harper's, Century*, and *Scribner's*. *Address*, Moylan, Penna.

STEPHENS, Frank L. Painter. Born in Philadelphia in 1824. He spent most of his professional life in New York City. He was an illustrator and cartoonist and was known for his caricatures; he also painted in water colors. He died in 1882.

STEPHENS, George Frank. Sculptor and lecturer. Born in Rahway, N. J., in 1859. Studied art at Penna. Academy of the Fine Arts. After leaving the art school, he worked for several years on the sculptures of the City Hall, Philadelphia. He has been an instructor in modeling in several art schools; also instructor in Drexel Institute. Member of Penna. Academy of the Fine Arts. Clubs: Philadelphia Sketch; Art; Fellowship of Pennsylvania Academy of Fine Arts, Philadelphia; National Arts (New York). *Address*, Arden, Del.

STERBA, Antonin. Painter, who exhibited at the Annual Exhibition, 1923, at Penna. Academy of the Fine Arts, Philadelphia. *Address*, Art Institute of Chicago, Chicago, Ill.

STERLING, Lindsey Morris. Sculptor, who exhibited the "Water Witch Girl" and "The Awakening," in Penna. Academy of the Fine Arts Exhibition, 1915. *Address*, 160 East 81st St., New York City, N. Y.

STERLING, Lindsey Morris (Mrs.). Sculptor. Born in Mauch Chunk, Penna., in 1876. She was a pupil at the Cooper Union; also studied in Paris. *Address*, Old Wood Road, Edgewater, New Jersey.

STERN, Mildred B. Painter, who exhibited portrait of "Miss B." at Penna. Academy of the Fine Arts, Philadelphia, 1915. *Address*, 4535 Pine St., Philadelphia, Pa.

STERNE, Maurice. Painter. Born in Libau, Russia, in 1878. He came to America at the age of twelve; studied art at the National Academy of Design, New York, and in Paris and Rome. Exhibited at the Salon de Société National des Beaux Arts (Paris); the Secession (Berlin); International Society (London); also in principal cities of United States. Represented in Metropolitan Museum of New York; Carnegie Institute of Pittsburgh; Museum of Fine Arts, Boston; Royal Museum, Berlin, etc. Member of Society of American Painters, Gravers and Sculptors. *Address*, 668 Fifth Ave., New York City.

STERNER, Albert. Portrait painter. Born in London, England, in 1863. Studied at Julien's Academy and École des Beaux Arts, Paris; came to the United States in 1879. He opened a studio in New York, 1885. Honorable mention for oil painting, "The Bachelor," at Paris Salon, Champs Elysees; bronze medal, Paris Exposition, 1900; silver medals, Buffalo Exposition, 1901; gold medal for painting, "Portrait of My Son," Munich, 1905. Instructor

in Art Students' League of New York. Pres. Society of Illustrators, 1907–09; member of American Water Color Society. Illustrator of George W. Curtis' "Prue and I"; "Coppee's Tales," 1891; "Poe's Works," 1894; "Marriage of William Ashe"; "Fenwick's Career," by Mrs. Humphrey Ward, etc. Instructor in New York School of Applied Design for Women. Elected Associated Member of National Academy, 1910; pres. Painter-Gravers of America, 1918. *Address*, 1 Lexington Ave., New York City.

STETCHER, Karl. Painter. Born in Germany in 1832, he came to New York as a youth and spent most of his life in that city where he painted a number of portraits, besides staining the windows in Trinity Church, New York. He died in Wichita, Kansas, in 1924.

STETSON, Catharine B. Sculptor, who exhibited "Study of a Baby" at the Penna. Academy Exhibition, 1921, Philadelphia. *Address*, Catalina Ave., Pasdena, Calif.

STETSON, Charles Walter. Painter, who has exhibited "Twilight, Pasadena, Cal." His studio was in Boston, Mass. In 1906 he was in Rome, Italy, and he died abroad.

STETTHEIMER, Florine. Painter, who exhibited in Philadelphia, 1921, in "Exhibition of Paintings Showing the Later Tendencies in Art" (Penna. Academy of Fine Arts). *Address*, 80 West 40th St., New York City.

STEVENS, Dalton. Illustrator. Born in Goochland County in 1878. Pupil of Art Institute of Chicago; also of Blanche and Cottet in Paris. Member: Society of Illustrators. *Address*, 13 West 29th St., New York, N. Y.

STEVENS, Dorothy. Etcher and painter. Born in Toronto in 1888. Pupil of Slade School in London. Member of Chicago Society of Etchers. Awarded silver medal for etching, Panama-Pacific Exposition, San Francisco, 1915. *Address*, 2 Spadina Gardens, 145 West Wellington St., Toronto, Canada.

STEVENS, Esther (Mrs. Walter T. Barney). Painter. Born in Indianapolis, Ind., in 1885. Pupil of Robert Henri; also at Art Students' League of New York. *Address*, Pt. Loma, San Diego, Calif.

STEVENS, George W. Miniature painter, who flourished in Boston about 1842.

STEVENS, George Washington. Painter. Born in Utica, N. Y., in 1866. Pupil of J. Francis Murphy in New York. Member of Salmagundi Club; was Associate of Museum Directors. Director, Toledo Museum of Art since 1903. *Address*, Museum of Art, Toledo, Ohio.

STEVENS, Helen B. (Mrs. T. W.). Etcher. Born in Chicago in 1878. Pupil of Art Institute of Chicago; also of Frank Brangwyn in England. Member: Chicago Society of Etchers. Award: Bronze medal, Panama-Pacific Exposition, San Francisco, 1915. Instructor in etching, and Assistant Curator of Prints, Art Institute of Chicago, 1909-12. *Address*, 5542 Pocussett St., Pittsburgh, Pa.

STEVENS, Thomas Wood. Mural painter and etcher. Born in Daysville, Ill., in 1880. Pupil of Armour Institute of Tech., Chicago; also of Frank Brangwyn in London; pupil of Sorolla v. Bastida. Member of Chicago Society of Etchers; also of Pittsburgh Artists' Association. Professor in charge of drama, Carnegie Institute of Tech., Pittsburgh. *Address*, 5542 Pocussett St., Pittsburgh, Pa.

STEVENS, Will Henry. Painter and designer. Born in Vevay, Ind., in 1881. Pupil of Cincinnati Academy under Caroline Lord, Nowottny and Meakin; under Jonas Lie and Van Dearing Perrine in New York. *Address*, Newcomb School of Art, Tulane University, New Orleans, La.

STEVENS, William Charles. Landscape painter. Born in 1854; died in 1917. The Worcester Museum of Fine Arts owns several of his paintings. *Address*, 13 West 29th St., New York, N. Y.

STEVENS, William Lester. Painter. Born in Rockport, Mass., in 1888. Pupil of Parker S. Perkins, Boston Museum School. Member: Boston Art Club; Boston Water Color Club; New York Water Color Club; Brush and Chisel Club, Boston. Work: "Winter Gray Day," Boston Art Club; "Winding Road," Boston City Club. *Address*, 8a Holbrook St., Rockport, Mass.

STEVENSON, Beulah Eisle. P a i n t e r. Born in Brooklyn. Pupil of Joseph Boston, Kenyon Cox, Kenneth Hayes Miller and John Sloan. Member of National Association of Women Painters and Sculptors; also of Brooklyn Society of Artists. *Address*, 246 Fulton St., Brooklyn, N. Y.

STEVENSON, Gordon. Painter, who exhibited water colors at the Penna. Academy of Fine Arts, Philadelphia, 1925. *Address*, 1 Lexington Ave., New York.

STEWARDSON, Edmund A. Sculptor. Pupil of Penna. Academy of the Fine Arts. Elected a member of the Society of American A r t i s t s in 1891. He died in 1892, being drowned at Newport, R. I.

STEWART, Catherine T. Painter, who exhibited water colors at the Penna. Academy of the Fine Arts, Philadelphia, 1925. *Address*, 2206 Locust St., Philadelphia.

STEWART, Charles. Engraver. In 1841 Stewart engraved a small but exceedingly fine mezzotint portrait of Peter Stuyvesant, printed by A. King, who was the publisher of some of Durand's plates. A pencil memorandum on the print says that it was engraved for the New York Historical Society.

STEWART, Grace Bliss. Painter. Born in Acherson, Kans., in 1885. Member of National Association of Women Painters and Sculptors. Exhibited at 33d Annual Exhibition, New York, 1924. *Address*, 50 West 45th St., New York.

STEWART, Joseph. Painter, who was born about 1750. He graduated from Dartmouth College in 1780. His portraits of Rev. Eleazer Wheelock, first President of Dartmouth College, and of John Phillips are signed "J. Steward." He painted a portrait of John Kemble engraved by H. Houston, published in 1796. He became a Congregationalist minister and was said to have been the first instructor of S. L. Waldo.

STEWART, Julius L. Painter. Born in Philadelphia in 1855. Pupil of J. L. Gerome and of R. de Madrazo. Honorable mention, Salon, Paris, 1885; 3d class medal, Salon, 1890; gold medal, Berlin International Art Exhibition, 1891; grand gold medal, Berlin, 1895; Munich, 1897. Exhibited at Paris Exposition, 1900. Decorated with Order of Leopold of Belgium, Antwerp, 1894; Cross of Legion d'Honneur, 1895. Elected associate member of Societé Nationale des Beaux Arts, 1895; elected member of Societé des Beaux Arts, 1899; member of International Jury, Paris Exposition, 1889; member of jury of selection, Chicago Exposition, 1893; grand gold medal, Munich, 1901; promoted officer of Legion d'Honneur, 1901; member of advisory and executive committee for St. Louis Exposition, 1904. Member: Paris Society of American Painters; Societé Nationale, Berlin, 1895; Munich, 1897. Exhibited at Paris Club de France; Philadelphia Club, Philadelphia; delegate for the fine arts, United States sect., to the Liege Exhibition, 1905; member of International Jury of Recompenses in same. He died in Paris.

STEWART, Le Conte. Painter and illustrator. Born in Glenwood, Utah, in 1891. Pupil of Art Students' League of New York, and of Carlsen. Awarded second prize, landscape, Utah State Fair, 1914; first prize, landscape, Utah State Fair, 1915. Work: Represented in Utah State collection; mural decorations in the Hawaiian Temple at Laie; Cardston Temple, Cardston, Alta, Canada. *Address*, Cardston, Alta, Canada.

STICKROTH, Harry I. Mural painter. Born in 1844; died in Chicago, 1922. Instructor in mural and decorative painting in Chicago

Art Institute. He was associated with Barry Faulkner in the mural work on the Cunard Building, New York.

STILES, Samuel. Born in East Windsor, Vt., in 1796; died in New York in 1861. He served his apprenticeship as an engraver with Abner Reed at East Windsor, and in 1824 he removed to Utica, N. Y., and formed a partnership in the banknote and general engraving business with Vistus Balch. He was also a pupil of Abner Reed. In 1828 he moved to New York as a banknote engraver. He married in 1825 Charlotte Sophia Reed, the daughter of his old preceptor Abner Reed.

STIMSON, Anna K. Sculptor. Born in New York City in 1892. Pupil of Charles Grafly. Member of Philadelphia Art Alliance; Fellowship, Penna. Academy of Fine Arts; Philadelphia Water Color Club. *Address,* 3400 Pearl St., Philadelphia, Pa.

STIMSON, John Ward. Painter and illustrator. Born in Paterson, N. J., in 1850. Pupil of École des Beaux Arts in Paris under Cabanel and Jacquesson de la Chevreuse. Studied in Italy, Holland and England. Director in Metropolitan Museum School of New York, and founder of Artist-Artisan Institute, New York, and of the School of Fine and Industrial Arts, Trenton, N. J. *Address,* Corona, Calif.

STITT, H. D. Landscape painter. Born in Hot Springs, Ark., in 1880. Pupil of Howard Pyle, Robert Spencer and Fred Wagner at Penna. Academy of the Fine Arts. Member: Charcoal Club, Baltimore. Work: "Lyric," Wilmington Society of Fine Arts. *Address,* Sudbrook, Pikesville, Maryland.

STOCKBRIDGE, Dana W. Painter. Born in Haverhill, Mass., in 1881. Pupil of School of Fine Arts at Harvard University, and of the Eric Pape School of Arts. He died in 1922.

STOCKMAN, Mrs. Helen Park. Painter. Born in 1896. Pupil of Jonas Lie, Luis Mora, and Robert Henri. Member of Society of Independent Artists. *Address,* Sherwood Place, Englewood, N. J.

STODART, G. Engraver. A well-engraved portrait of David Stoner, in stipple, is signed "G. Stodart." It was apparently published about 1835, but as G. Stodart also engraved a portrait of Washington, published in London, he may have been an English engraver. David Stoner, however, seems to have been an American.

STODDARD, Alice Kent. Portrait painter. Born in Watertown, Conn. Pupil of Penna. Academy of the Fine Arts. Represented at Penna. Academy of Fine Arts, and in the Del-

gado Museum, New Orleans, La. *Address,* 524 Walnut St., Philadelphia.

STODDARD, Frederick L. Mural painter and illustrator. Born in Canada in 1861. Pupil of St. Louis School of Fine Arts, and of Constant and Laurens in Paris. Mural paintings in City Hall, St. Louis; and in Church of Transfiguration, Baltimore. *Address,* Emerson Hill, Stapleton, Staten Island, N. Y.

STOHR, Julia Collins (Mrs. P. C.). Painter. Born in Toledo, Ohio, in 1866. Pupil of Art Students' League of New York under Beckwith, Chase, Alden Weir; also with Lathrop in Paris. Member of National Association of Women Painters and Sculptors. *Address,* Conifer, Lovell, Maine.

STOHR, Julia Collins (Miss). Painter. Born in St. Paul, Minn., in 1896. Member of National Association of Women Painters and Sculptors. Exhibited in 33d Annual Exhibition, New York, 1924. *Address,* Conifer, Lovell, Me.

STOKES, Frank Wilbert. Painter. Born in Nashville, Tenn. Studied art under Thomas Eakins, at Pa. Academy of Fine Arts; under Gerome, at École des Beaux Arts, Paris, 1882; returned to the United States; again went to Paris, 1884, and studied at Colarossi's, under Raphael Collin, and at Julien's under Boulanger and Lefebvre. He completed in 1909, for the American Museum of Natural History, New York, a series of mural decorations illustrating the allegory of the Arctic night and day, and depicting the life of the Smith Sound Eskimo. Was a contributor to magazines. *Address,* 3 Washington Square, New York.

STOLL, Frederick H. Sculptor, who exhibited at the Annual Exhibition, 1923, at Penna. Academy of the Fine Arts, Philadelphia. *Address,* American Museum of Natural History, New York.

STOLTENBERG, Hans J. Painter. Born in Germany in 1879. Member: Wisconsin Painters and Sculptors. *Address,* 490 Fifth Ave., Wauwatosa, Wisc.

STONE, Frank F. Sculptor. Born in England in 1863. Represented by portrait bust, from life, of Mark Twain, also by medallion of Mark Twain. *Address,* 1036 S. Bonnie Brae St., Los Angeles, Calif.

STONE, Henry. Engraver. In 1826 this line-engraver was also doing work in Washington, D. C. He was doubtless connected with the Mr. and Mrs. W. J. Stone here referred to, possibly a son. Henry Stone drew upon stone for lithographers of Washington, D. C.

STONE, Horatio. Sculptor. Born in Jackson, Washington County, N. Y., in 1808; died in Carrara, Italy, in 1875. At an early age he attempted wood carving, a pursuit which was not encouraged by his father. Leaving home as a lad, he did not communicate with his family for many years. Instrumental in the organization of the Washington Union Art Association, he was elected its president. This organization presented a memorial to Congress requesting recognition of American artists in the decoration of the Capitol, and as a result, the Art Commission of 1859, consisting of Henry K. Brown, James R. Lambdin, and John F. Kensett, was appointed by President Buchanan. Stone visited Italy twice in the study of his work as a sculptor. In 1857 he received the medal of the Maryland Institute for his busts of Benton and Taney, and exhibited his works in the National Academy of Design in 1849 and 1869. He is also credited with models for statues of Prof. Morse, Admiral Farragut, and Dr. Harvey, the discoverer of the circulation of the blood.

STONE, J. M. Painter. Born in Dana, Mass., in 1841. He studied in Boston, and later in Munich. He spent his professional life in Boston, where he became an instructor in the school of the Museum of Fine Arts. He painted a number of portraits.

STONE, Seymour M. Painter. Born in Russia in 1877. Pupil of Zorn in Sweden. Came to New York as a young man. *Address,* 222 South Central Park, New York City.

STONE, Walter King. Painter and illustrator. Born in Barnard, N. Y., in 1875. Pupil of Pratt Institute under Arthur Dow. He is Assistant Professor of Painting at Cornell University. *Address,* Ithaca, N. Y.

STONE, William J. In 1822 this excellent engraver of portraits in stipple and etcher of buildings, etc., was located in Washington, D. C., possibly in Government employ. A map of Washington, published in 1840 by Wm. D. Morrison, is signed "Eng'd by Mrs. W. J. Stone." There is an excellent engraved portrait of Wm. J. Stone.

STONE, William Oliver. Portrait painter. Born in 1830 at Derby, Conn.; died in Newport, R. I., in 1875. Studied with Nathaniel Jocelyn at New Haven in 1851, and then removed to New York. In 1856 he was elected an Associate Member of the National Academy, and in 1859 an Academician. He painted portraits of Bishops Williams, Littlejohn and Kip. The New York Historical Society owns his portrait of Thomas J. Bryan and the Metropolitan Museum owns his portrait of Miss Rawle.

STONER, Harry. Mural painter and illustrator. Born in Springfield, Ohio, in 1880. *Address,* 18 West 37th St., New York City.

STONER, Oliver. Painter. Born in Pleasantville, Penna., in 1894. Pupil of Snell, Breckenridge, Garber and Wagner. Member of the Fellowship of Penna. Academy of the Fine Arts. *Address,* 526 Pine St., Johnstown, Pa.

STORM, G. F. Engraver. Born in England and came to Philadelphia about 1834. Storm was an admirable engraver of portraits in stipple; he was also a good etcher. Though his stay in the United States is said to have been a short one, he engraved a considerable number of American portraits.

STORRS, John. Sculptor and etcher. Born in Chicago, Ill., in 1885. Pupil of Grafly, Rodin and Bartlett. *Address,* 109 Rue du Cherche Midi, Paris, France.

STORY, George Henry. Painter. Born in New Haven, Conn., in 1835. Studied in New York and Paris. In 1875 he was elected an Associate Member of National Academy of Design, and in 1876 he received a medal at the Centennial Exposition, Philadelphia. He painted several portraits of Lincoln, and is represented at the Metropolitan Museum by "Self-portrait," and "The Young Mother." He died in New York City in 1923.

STORY, Julian. Portrait painter. Born in Walton-on-Thames, England. He was the son of W. W. Story (poet and sculptor). Pupil of Frank Duveneck, Boulanger and Lefebvre, Paris. Awards: 3d class medal and honorable mention, Paris Salon, 1889; gold medal, Berlin, 1891; silver medal, Paris Exposition, 1900; made Chevalier Legion d'Honneur, France, 1900. Elected an Associate Member of the National Academy in 1906. He died in 1919.

STORY, Thomas C. This general engraver of portraits and historical plates was in business in New York during the period 1837–44. The firm of Story & Atwood was engraving in the same city in 1843.

STORY, Waldo. Sculptor. Son of William Wetmore Story. His studio is now in Rome.

STORY, William Wetmore. Sculptor. Born in Salem, Mass., in 1815. Graduated from Harvard College in 1838, he adopted art as a profession and about 1848 went to Italy for study. His statues of "Cleopatra and the Sibyl" and his portrait statues of Josiah Quincy, Edward Everett and Colonel Shaw are well known. He died in Italy in 1895.

STOUFFER, J. Edgar. Sculptor. Member of the Charcoal Club of Baltimore. Awarded Rinehart Scholarship to Paris, 1907–11. *Address,* 1230 St. Paul St., Baltimore, Md.

STOUT, George H. Engraver. The New York directories for 1830–50, inclusive, contain this name as an "engraver of cards, seals and door-plates."

STOUT, Ida McClelland. Sculptor. Born in Decatur, Ill. Pupil of Albin P o l a s e k. Work: "Goose Girl Fountain," Mary W. French School, Decatur, Ill.; "Princess Badoura," Hillyer Gallery, Smith College. *Address*, Art Institute, Chicago, Ill.

STOUT, James D. Engraver. This man was a map engraver about 1813, and apparently living in New York.

STOUT, James V. Engraver, who was in business in New York in 1834–38, as a general engraver and die-sinker. He also engraved some good landscape plates.

STOVER, Allan James. Painter and illustrator. Born in West Point, Miss., in 1887. Pupil of Cleveland School of Art. *Address*, Corvallis, Ore.

STOWELL, M. Louise. Painter and illustrator. Born in Rochester, N. Y. Pupil of Art Students' League of New York and of Arthur W. Dow. Member: Rochester Society of Arts and Crafts; New York Water Color Club. Specialty, water color painting. *Address*, 714 Ins. Building, Main St., Rochester, N. Y.

STRAHAN, Alfred W. Painter and illustrator. Born in Baltimore, Md., in 1886. Pupil of S. Edwin Whiteman and of Harper Pennington. Member: Charcoal Club. *Address*, 214 Chamber of Commerce Building, Baltimore, Md.

STRAIN, D. J. Painter. Born in New Hampshire, he entered Julien's studio in Paris in 1877. In 1883 he opened his studio in Boston. He has painted a number of portraits; that of General N. P. Banks is perhaps his greatest achievement. *Address*, 278 Boyleston St., Boston, Mass.

STRAUS, Mitteldorfer. Painter and illustrator. Born in Richmond, Va., in 1880. Pupil of Art Students' League of Washington; also studied in Europe and Africa. Member: New York Water Color Club; Society of Independent Artists. Awarded scholarship of Art Students' League of Washington to Pratt Institute. *Address*, 96 Fifth Ave., New York, N. Y.

STRAWBRIDGE, Anne W. Painter. Born in Philadelphia, Pa., in 1883. Pupil of W. M. Chase. Member of Fellowship of Penna. Academy of Fine Arts; also of Plastic Club. *Address*, 6711 Wissahickon Ave., Philadelphia, Pa.

STREATFEILD, Josephine. Portrait painter. Born in London, England, in 1882. Pupil of Slade School in London, under Fred Brown. Member: Society of Women Artists, London; Ontario Society of Artists. Specialty, pastel portraits of children. *Address*, Wynthrope, Sydenham, London, Eng.

STREAN, Maria Judson. Painter. Born in Washington, Pa. Pupil of Art Students' League of New York under Cox and J. Alden Weir; under Prinet and Dauchez in Paris. Member: New York Water Color Club; American Society of Miniature Painters; Penna. Society of Miniature Painters; Allied Artists' Association; National Association of Women Painters and Sculptors. Awarded honorable mention, Panama-American Exposition, Buffalo, 1901. *Address*, 140 West 57th St., New York, N. Y.

STREATOR, Harold A. Painter. Born in Cleveland, Ohio. Pupil of Art Students' League of New York, and of the Boston Museum School. Member: Salmagundi Club, 1906. *Address*, Box 345, Morristown, N. J.

STREET, Robert. Painter of portraits and historical subjects, who was for many years a resident of Philadelphia, where he did much excellent work.

He was born in 1796, and exhibited in the Pennsylvania Academy of the Fine Arts during the period between 1815–1817. In 1824 his portraits were shown in Washington, D. C., where he painted several well-known men. In 1835 Dunlap records the death of Street and the artist had the most unique experience of calling the author's attention to such a grave error. Dunlap corrects his error with many apologies in the *New York Mirror* of the issue of Feb. 28, 1835. In 1840, Robert Street held an exhibition of his own work showing over two hundred oil paintings of historical subjects, landscapes and portraits.

Catalogues of this exhibition are accessible, but unfortunately they give little valuable information regarding the portraits, as they are frequently recorded as merely "A Portrait of a Lady" or "A Portrait of a Gentleman." This exhibition opened on November 18, 1840, at the Artists' Fund Hall, Philadelphia.

STRICKLAND, William. Painter and engraver. Born in Philadelphia in 1787; died in Nashville, Tenn., in 1854. Strickland studied architecture under Benjamin H. Latrobe, but in 1809 he took up portrait painting, designing for engravers and engraving in aquatint. In this manner he produced a few portraits and a number of views illustrating events in the War of 1812.

About 1820 Strickland resumed practice as an architect and among the buildings designed by him in Philadelphia were the Masonic Hall, United States Mint, Bank of the United States, the new Chestnut Street and the Arch Street theaters and the Merchants' Exchange.

STRINGFIELD, Vivian F. Painter and illustrator. Born in California. Pupil of Pratt Institute; also of Douglas Donaldson and Ralph H. Johonnot. Member of Southern California Art Teachers' Association. Awarded bronze medal, Panama-California Exposition, San Diego, 1915. *Address,* 229 South Normandie Ave., Los Angeles, Calif.

STROHL, Clifford. Painter. Born in South Bethlehem, Pa., in 1893. Pupil of Jules Dieudonne and of Orlando G. Wales; also studied in the Penna. Academy of the Fine Arts. Member of Salmagundi Club. *Address,* 416 Avenue E, Bethlehem, Pa.

STROTHER, Col. David Hunter. Portrait painter. Born in 1816; died in 1888.

STROTHMANN, Fred. Painter and illustrator. Born in New York in 1879. Studied in New York and Paris. *Address,* 562 West 190th St., New York City.

STROUD, Clara. Painter and illustrator. Born in New Orleans, La., in 1890. Pupil of Cimiotti, Mary Lantry, Otto W. Beck, Ethel F. Shaurman and Ralph Johonnot. Member: Society of Independent Artists; National Association of Women Painters and Sculptors; Brooklyn Society of Artists; Brooklyn Water Color Club. *Address,* 61 Poplar St., Brooklyn, New York, N. Y.

STROUD, (Mrs.) Ida Wells. Painter and designer. Born in New Orleans, La., in 1869. Pupil of Pratt Institute; Art Students' League of New York; also of William Chase. Member: National Association of Women Painters and Sculptors; New York Water Color Club. Instructor in painting, drawing and design at Fawcett School of Industrial Art, Newark, N. J. *Address,* 10 West 17th St., East Orange, N. J.

STRUNK, Herbert. Sculptor. Born in Shakopee, Minn., in 1891. Pupil of St. Paul Institute School of Art. Member of St. Paul Artists' Society. Awarded silver medal, St. Paul Institute, 1915. Work: "Chief Shakopee," model in St. Paul Institute Gallery. *Address,* Shakopee, Minn.

STRYCKER, Jacobus Gerritsen. Farmer, trader, magistrate and "limner." Was born at Ruinen, province of Drenthe, in the Netherlands. His wife was Ytie Huybrechts, possibly related to the lady of the same surname, whose daughter at about the same time married Titus van Rijn, the son of a greater "limner," Rembrandt. Strycker came to New Netherland in 1651, a gentleman of considerable means and decided culture, and after a successful career died in 1687. We know something of his office holding; he was Burgher in 1653 and afterwards Alderman of New Amsterdam; also Attorney General and Sheriff of the Dutch towns on Long Island up to August, 1673. Very little of his work as an artist is known. Three of his portraits have been identified. He left a son, Gerrit, who became Sheriff of King's County in 1688, and a brother, Jan, who also left descendants.

STUART, F. T. This good engraver of portraits was working in 1850; and at a much later date he was located in Boston.

STUART, Gilbert (Charles). Portrait painter. Gilbert Stuart is conceded to have occupied the highest place among American portrait painters and he is considered among the great artists of all times and countries. Born near Narragansett, R. I., in 1755, the son of a Scotchman who had established the first snuff-mill in America and who had married Elizabeth Anthony of Newport, R. I. Gilbert Stuart was educated in Newport, and early showed great artistic talent, as at an early age he painted portraits of the prominent men of Newport. In 1770 Stuart received instruction from Cosmo Alexander, a Scotch gentleman then residing in Newport. The latter remained in the Colonies about two years, and on his return to Scotland took young Stuart with him. In 1773 Stuart returned to America where he remained until 1775 when he sailed for England on the last ship that escaped detention by the British in Boston harbor. Stuart arrived in London in September with letters to Benjamin West, in whose studio he painted for several years. In 1788 he opened his own studio in London and became one of the most sought-after portrait painters in England. Benjamin West and Sir Joshua Reynolds sat to him, and his portrait of W. Grant skating in St. James Park is considered one of his finest works. Among other prominent sitters to Stuart in London at this time was John Philip Kemble the actor; he also painted Gainsborough and Copley the artists, the Duke of Northumberland, and Admiral Sir John Jarvis. Gilbert Stuart married Miss Charlotte Coats, daughter of Dr. Coats of Berkshire, England. Two years after his marriage in 1788 Stuart went to Ireland where he painted many of the prominent personages of the time. Among others were the portraits of the Duke of Leinster, Lord Fitzgibbon, Hon. John Beresford and other eminent Irish gentlemen. Stuart was hopelessly in debt during his stay in Ireland, and sailed for America in 1792, arriving in New York where he remained for some time painting portraits. In 1794 he came to Philadelphia, his object being the painting of portraits of George Washington. (For life of Gilbert Stuart and his portraits of George Washington see "Life and Works of Stuart," by Mantle Fielding, Philadelphia, 1923.) One hundred twenty-four portraits of Washington are listed as painted by Stuart. For catalogue of his other portraits see Mason's "Life and Works of Stuart"; also list of 200 portraits by Stuart not noted in Mason's list, published in the *Pennsylvania Magazine* of the Historical Society by Mantle Fielding. Gilbert Stuart is supposed to have painted at least a thousand portraits, which are now much sought after. He maintained his studio in Philadelphia until 1803 when he moved to Washington to paint the portrait of President Jefferson and other prominent men of the time. In 1805 he removed from Washington and took up his residence in Boston where he lived the remainder of his life, dying on the 27th day of July in 1828. Stuart was elected a member of the American Academy in 1795 and an honorary member of the National Academy of Design in 1827. A memorial exhibition of his portraits was held in Boston in 1880. His portraits are in the collections of many of the prominent galleries, the Pennsylvania Academy of Fine Arts owning probably the finest collection of his works.

STUART, James E. Painter. Born near Dover, Me., in 1852. Pupil of Virgil Williams and of R. D. Yelland in San Francisco. Member: Society of Independent Artists; National Art Club. Work: "Summer Glow, Mt. Takoma" and "Sacramento River," Kalamazoo (Mich.) Art Association; "Sunset Glow, Mt. Hood," Michigan State Library, Lansing; "Showers Among the Trees, New Jersey," and "Sunset Glow, Mt. Jefferson," Omaha Public Library; "Sunset, Sacramento River," Reno Arts and Crafts Club; "Showers, Napa Valley," Oakdale Public Library; "Morning, Mt. Hood," Los Angeles Museum of History, Science and Art; "Mt. Tallac, Lake Tahoe," Otis Art Institute, Los Angeles. He was the originator of a new method of painting on aluminum and wood. *Address*, 684 Commercial St., San Francisco, Calif.

STUART, Jane. Painter. Daughter of Gilbert Stuart. Born about 1812, she followed her father's profession for many years. She was a skillful copyist and reproduced many of her father's paintings, especially his portraits of Washington. She died in Newport, R. I., in 1888. She published several articles in *Scribner's Monthly Magazine* of 1877 about her father and his work.

STUBBS, Mary H. Painter and illustrator. Born in Greenville, Ohio, in 1867. Pupil of Cincinnati Art Academy; Julien Academy in Paris. Member: Cincinnati Woman's Art Club; Cincinnati Ceramic Club. Awarded honorable mention, Columbian Exposition, Chicago, 1893. *Address*, 4429 Ellis Ave., Chicago, Ill.

STUBER, Dedrick B. Painter. Born in New York in 1878. Pupil of Bridgman, Onderdonk and Peters. *Address*, Los Angeles, Calif.

STUEVER, Celia M. Etcher and painter. Pupil of St. Louis School of Fine Arts; also studied in Paris. Member of Chicago Society of Etchers. Represented by etchings in the Library of Congress and in the New York Public

Library. *Address*, 3444 Russell Ave., St. Louis, Mo.

STURDEVANT, S. A practically unknown American engraver, there being only one example of his work catalogued. It was published in Lexington, Ky., in 1822. The portrait is very crude and occurs in a privately printed volume of sermons. It is the earliest known signed portrait engraved west of the Allegheny Mountains.

STURGEON, Ruth B. Painter and etcher. Born in Sterling, Kans., in 1883. *Address*, 115 Pearl St., Council Bluffs, Ia.

STURGES, Dwight C. Painter and etcher. Born in Boston. Member of Chicago, Boston, and Canadian Society of Etchers. Represented by etchings in Boston and Chicago Museums of Fine Arts; also in New York and Congressional Libraries. *Address*, Melrose, Mass.

STURGES, Lee. Etcher. Born in Chicago, Ill., in 1865. Pupil of Art Institute of Chicago and of the Penna. Academy of Fine Arts. Member of Chicago and Brooklyn Societies of Etchers. *Address*, Elmhurst, Ill.

STURGES, Lillian B. Painter and illustrator. Born in Wilkes-Barre, Penna. Pupil of E. F. Savage. *Address*, 2956 Belrose Ave., Pittsburgh, Pa.

STURGIS, Mabel R. Painter. Born in Boston in 1865. Pupil of Boston Museum of Fine Arts. *Address*, 100 Chestnut St., Boston, Mass.

STURTEVANT, Helena. Painter. Born in Middletown, R. I., in 1872. Pupil of Boston Museum School under Tarbell; Colarossi Academy in Paris under Blanche and Simon. Member of International Society Art League. Director of School of Art Association, Newport, R. I. *Address*, Newport, R. I.

STYLES, George C. Etcher. Born in England in 1892. Pupil of Windass. *Address*, 134 West 77th St., New York, N. Y.

SUGDEN, Thomas D. Wood engraver. Pupil of T. W. Strong. He was connected for years with the engraving department of the Century Co. He wrote a volume on wood engraving, "Remarks on Wood Engraving by One-o'-them," 1904.

SULLIVAN, D. Frank. Painter and etcher. Born in 1892. Member of Pittsburgh Associated Artists. *Address*, Carnegie Institute, Pittsburgh, Pa.

SULLIVAN, Frances. Portrait painter. Born in 1861; died in 1925. Among his portraits are Thos. C. Du Pont, J. B. McLean and F. W. Woolworth.

SULLIVAN, James Amory. Painter. Born in Boston, Mass., in 1875. Pupil of Laurens and of Alexander Harrison. *Address*, 98 Chestnut St., Boston, Mass.

SULLIVANT, Thomas S. Illustrator. Born in Columbus, Ohio, in 1854. Pupil of Penna. Academy of the Fine Arts. *Address*, 1911 Pine St., Philadelphia, Pa.

SULLY, Alfred. Painter. Son of Thomas Sully, born in 1820. Graduated from West Point in 1841. He painted in water colors and his views of the western forts where he was stationed are of artistic and historic interest. He died in 1879.

SULLY, Jane. See Darley, Mrs. Wm. H. W.

SULLY, Lawrence. Miniature painter. Born in Ireland in 1769. He was the eldest brother of Thomas Sully and came to this country with his father and settled in Charleston, S. C., removing later to Virginia where he painted, first in Norfolk and then in Richmond where he died in 1803. His brother Thomas Sully married his widow.

SULLY, Robert Matthew. Portrait painter. Born in Virginia in 1803. He was a nephew of Thomas Sully and studied with him. He visited London in 1824, painting there till 1828 when he returned to Virginia. He died in Buffalo, N. Y., in 1855 as he was enroute to Madison, Wisconsin, to execute commissions for portraits. Represented in the Corcoran Art Gallery, Washington, by his portrait of Chief Justice John Marshall.

SULLY, Thomas. Portrait painter. Born at Horncastle in Lincolnshire, England, in 1783. His parents were actors who came to this country in 1792, bringing their family with them and settling at Charleston, S. C. In 1801 Thomas Sully sailed for Norfolk, Va., where he joined his elder brother Lawrence, the miniature painter, whose widow he afterwards married. In 1801 he began his professional career as a portrait painter, and in 1806 he moved to New York City where he received instructions from the painters Trumbull and Jarvis. Early in 1808 he moved from New York to Philadelphia, which he made his permanent home, although making frequent visits to all the principal cities for the practice of his profession, besides making two trips to England. Sully also received a certain amount of criticism and instruction from Gilbert Stuart, whose studio he visited in Boston in 1807 when that artist was at the height of his fame. In 1809 Sully visited London for study, and there he settled down with the Newport artist C. B. King in a course of drawing and painting. He was much impressed by the work of Sir Thomas Lawrence whose paintings he followed in many particulars. He returned to Philadelphia in 1810 and painted there many of his finest portraits, during the next quarter of the century. In 1837 he revisited London to paint the portrait of Queen Victoria for the St. George Society of Philadelphia. The painting is still owned by the society in Philadelphia, a replica being presented by the artist to the St. Andrew Society of Charleston, S. C.; another portrait of the Queen being in the Wallace collection in London. Mr. Sully was a very rapid and industrious painter, and there are over two thousand listed portraits from his brush besides miniatures, and some five hundred subject paintings. He also painted a number of historical subjects, his best known canvas being "Washington Crossing the Delaware." Thomas Sully served for fifteen years as a Director of the Pennsylvania Academy of Fine Arts. His kindness and sympathy to young artists was well known and he had many pupils and assistants. He died in Philadelphia, loved and respected, in 1872 in his ninetieth year. See "The Life and Work of Thomas Sully" by Edward Biddle and Mantle Fielding, Philadelphia, 1921.

SULLY, Thomas W. Portrait painter. Born in Philadelphia in 1811; died there in 1847. He was the fourth child of the artist Thomas Sully and followed his father's profession. His fondness for the stage caused him to paint a series of portraits of prominent actors of his day, and these were lithographed by Newsam but unfortunately lettered "Thomas Sully." Thomas Wilcocks Sully later changed his signature to "Thomas Sully, Jr."

SUMMA, Mrs. Emily B. Painter. Born in Germany in 1875. Pupil of St. Louis School of Fine Arts. Awarded Sylvester prize for landscapes at St. Louis Artists' Guild Exhibition of 1917. *Address*, 1925 Forrest Ave., St. Louis, Mo.

SUMMERS, Dudley G. Painter and illustrator. Born in England in 1892. Pupil of George Bridgman. *Address*, 143 East 21st St., New York.

SUSAN, Robert. Portrait painter. Student of the Penna. Academy of Fine Arts. Member of Penna. Academy of Fine Arts Fellowship and California Art Club. *Address*, 1520 Chestnut St., Philadelphia, Pa.

SUTTON, Harry, Jr. Painter. Born in Salem, Mass., in 1897. Pupil of School of Boston Museum of Fine Arts, and of the Julien Academy in Paris. *Address*, 162 Newbury St., Boston, Mass.

SUYDAM, Edward H. Painter, illustrator and etcher. Born in Vineland, N. J., in 1885. Illustrates for *Harper's Monthly*. *Address*, 1430 South Penn Square, Philadelphia.

24

SUYDAM, James Augustus. Landscape painter. Born in New Hampshire in 1819; he studied with Durand and Kensett. He was elected an honorary member of the National School of Design in 1858 and an Academician in 1861. He was most successful with his coast views, his "View on Long Island" and "Hook Mountain on the Hudson" are well known. He died in 1865.

SVENDSEN, Charles C. Painter. Born in Cincinnati in 1871. Pupil of Bouguereau and of the Colarossi Academy in Paris. Specialty, figure and pastoral scenes. *Address,* P. O. Box 609, Price Hill, Cincinnati, Ohio.

SWAIN, Francis W. Painter and etcher. Born in Oakland, Calif., in 1892. Pupil of Frank Duveneck. Member of California Society of Etchers. *Address,* Selvis Building, 127 East 3d St., San Francisco, Calif.

SWAIN, W. Painter. He was elected an Associate Member of the National Academy of Design in 1836. He died in New York in 1847. Self-portrait exhibited in Centennial Exhibition of National Academy, New York, 1925–26.

SWAN, Florence (Wellington). Designer. Born in Cambridge, Mass., in 1876. Pupil of Amy M. Sacker. Member of Boston Society of Arts and Crafts; American Book-plate Society. Work: Memorial tablets in Beneficent Congressional Church, Providence; St. James' Church, Salem. *Address,* 11 Mason St., Cambridge, Mass.

SWAN, Paul. Sculptor and painter. Born in Illinois. Studied drawing under John Vanderpoel and sculpture under Taft. Later he studied in New York and Paris. He has exhibited his paintings and sculptures in the National Academy of Design, New York. *Address,* Jackson Heights, New York City.

SWANSON, Bennet A. Painter. Born in 1899. Member of St. Paul Art Society. *Address,* 663 Elfelt St., St. Paul, Minn.

SWANSON, Jonathan M. Sculptor. Born in Chicago, Ill., in 1888, he studied at the Art Institute of Chicago. Specialty, medals and portraits in low relief. *Address,* 57 West 37th St., New York City.

SWETT, C. A. Engraver. As a copperplate engraver this name appears on a "Descent from the Cross," a frontispiece to "Helps to Young Christians," published in Portland in 1839. The plate is signed as "engraved by C. A. Swett, Portland." He later engraved a plan of the city of Boston, published in 1862.

SWETT, William Otis. Landscape painter. Born in Worcester, Mass. Pupil of Whistler

and H. G. Dearth; studied in Munich, Paris, Belgium and Holland. Member: Salmagundi Club, 1903; Chicago Artists' Guild; Society of Independent Artists. Specialty, marines and landscapes. *Address,* 154 West 55th St., New York, N. Y.

SWEZEY, Agnes. Painter. Exhibited at National Academy of Design, New York, 1925. *Address,* 39 West 9th St., New York.

SWIFT, Ivan. Painter and etcher. Born in Wayne, Mich., in 1873. Pupil of Art Institute of Chicago; also under Freer, Von Sulza, Ochtman and Chase. Member of National Art Club. Work: "A Michigan Home," Detroit Institute of Arts; "Indian Summer," Duffield Branch, Detroit Library; "Toward the Light" and "In the Shadow of the Hill," Detroit Library. Author of books of verse, "Fagots of Cedar" and "The Blue Crane and Shore Songs." *Address,* Chippewa Cove Woods, Harbor Springs, Mich.

SWIFT, Ted S. Illustrator and etcher. Born in Monticello in 1900. Pupil of Pedro J. Lemos and Lorenzo P. Latimer. Member of California Miniature Painters. Represented in Thomas W. Sanford Gallery; Art Institute of Chicago; Los Angeles Museum. Contributor to *School Arts Magazine. Address,* 220 Franklin St., Napa, Calif.

SWINDELL, Bertha. Miniature painter, who exhibited at the Penna. Academy of the Fine Arts, Philadelphia, 1925. *Address,* 200 Fifth Ave., New York.

SWINNERTON, James. Painter of Southwestern scenery; his specialty is the American desert lands. He was born in California, and studied in New York. Among his best known paintings are "Coming Storm, Mojave Desert," "Clouds in Monument Valley, North Arizona," and "Here Ends the Trail."

SWISHER, Allan. Portrait and figure painter. Born in Gypsum, Kans., in 1888. Pupil of Walcott and Laurens. *Address,* University of Kentucky, Lexington, Ky.

SWOPE, H. Vance. Painter. Born in southern Indiana in 1879. Pupil of Julien Academy in Paris under Constant. Member: Circle of American Painters and Sculptors; Salmagundi Club; New York Architectural League. Work represented in Public Library, Seymour, Minn. *Address,* Van Dyck Studios, 939 Eighth Ave., New York, N. Y.

SWOPE, Mrs. Kate F. Painter. Born in Louisville, Ky. Pupil of National Academy of Design, New York. Awarded gold medal, Southern Art League, 1895; highest award, Louisville Art League, 1897. Member of Louisville Art League. *Address,* 939 Eighth Ave., New York, N. Y.

SWOPE, Virginia Vance. Painter. Born in Louisville, Ky. Pupil of Du Mond, Mora, Carlson, Penfield and Bridgman. *Address,* 939 Eighth Ave., New York, N. Y.

SWORD, James Brade. Painter. Born in Philadelphia, Pa., in 1839; died in 1915. His early life was spent in Macao, China, and he engaged in art as a profession about 1863. Has served for a number of years as vice-president and director of the Art Club of Philadelphia, as president of the Philadelphia Society of Artists, and as president of the Artists' Fund Society of Philadelphia. He is represented by portraits and paintings in many public institutions. He was a founder of the Art Club of Philadelphia. He is represented by his Portrait of John W. Jones in the House of Representatives, Washington, D. C.

SYKES, Mrs. Annie G. Painter. Born in Brookline, Mass. Pupil of Boston Museum School; Cincinnati Art Academy under Duveneck. Member: Cincinnati Woman's Art Club; National Association of Women Painters and Sculptors. *Address,* 3007 Vernon Place, Vernonville, Cincinnati, Ohio.

SYKES, Charles Henry. Cartoonist. Born in Athens, Ala., in 1882. Pupil of B. West, Clinedinst and of the Drexel Institute of Phila-

delphia. Member of Philadelphia Sketch Club. *Address,* Care of Evening Public Ledger, Philadelphia, Pa.

SYLVESTER, Frederick Oakes. Mural and landscape painter. Born in Brockton, Mass., in 1869. He was a member of the Society of Western Artists. He died in St. Louis, Mo., in 1915.

SYMONS, George Gardner. Painter. Born in Chicago, Ill., in 1863. Pupil of Art Institute of Chicago; also studied in Paris, Munich and London. Elected Associate Member of the National Academy in 1910, National Academy in 1911; Royal Society of British Artists; Union Internationale des Beaux Arts et des Lettres; Salmagundi Club, 1909; National Art Club; Chicago Society of Artists; Century Association; California Art Club; Institute of Arts and Letters. Awarded Carnegie prize, National Academy of Design, 1909. Work: "The Opalescent River," Metropolitan Museum, New York; "Snow Clouds," Corcoran Art Gallery, Washington, D. C.; "Sorrow," Cincinnati Museum; "Snow-Clad Fields in Morning Light," Toledo Museum; "The Top of the Hill and Beyond" and "The Winter Sun," Art Institute of Chicago; "Through Snow-Clad Hills and Valley," City Art Museum, St. Louis. *Address,* Art Club Building, 119 East 19th St., New York.

T

TAAKE, Daisy. Sculptor. Born in St. Louis, Mo., in 1886. Pupil of Art Institute of Chicago and St. Louis School of Fine Arts; also of Lorado Taft. Member of St. Louis Art League. Winner of St. Louis Art League Fountain Competition. *Address,* Midway Studios, 6016 Ellis Ave., Chicago, Ill.

TACK, Augustus Vincent. Painter. Born in Pittsburgh, Pa., in 1870. Pupil of Mowbray and La Farge in New York; also of Merson in Paris. Member: Art Students' League of New York; Conn. Academy of Fine Arts. Painter of religious subjects. Work: "Deposition from the Cross"; "Entombment." *Address,* 7 West 43d St., New York, N. Y.

TADAMA, Fokko. Painter. Born in India in 1871. Represented in San Francisco Art Museum. *Address,* 2012 Laurelshade Ave., Seattle, Wash.

TAFT, Lorado. Sculptor. Born at Elmwood, Ill., in 1860. Studied at École des Beaux

Arts, 1880–83. Awards: Designer's medal, Chicago Exposition, 1893; silver medal, Buffalo Exposition, 1901; gold medal, St. Louis Exposition, 1904. Elected Associate Member of National Academy in 1909; National Academy, 1911; National Sculpture Society; American Federation of Arts (dir. 1914–17). Author of "The History of American Sculpture," 1903. *Address,* 6016 Ellis Ave., Chicago, Ill.

TAGGART, George H. Portrait painter. Born at Watertown, N. Y., in 1865. Pupil of Bouguereau, Ferrier, and Lefebvre in Paris. *Address,* 200 Central Park, South, New York, N. Y.

TAGGART, Lucy M. Painter. Born in Indianapolis, Ind. Pupil of Forsyth, Chase and Hawthorne; also studied in Europe. *Address,* 1 Lexington Ave., New York.

TAIT, Arthur Fitzwilliam. Painter. Born in England in 1819, he came to the United States in 1850 and was most successful with his pictures of animals. Elected an Associate of the National Academy in 1853 and an Academician in 1858. He sketched among the Adirondack Mountains. Among his works are "Duck and Her Young," "Ruffled Grouse," "Portage" and "Racquette Lake"; his "Quail and Young" is in the Corcoran Art Gallery, Washington, D. C. Many of his pictures were reproduced in lithograph by Currier & Ives. He died in 1905.

TAIT, John Robinson. Painter. Born in Cincinnati in 1834. He studied art abroad. In 1871 he returned to the United States and after 1876 resided in Baltimore, Md. Among his works are "Lake of Four Cantons," in the Cincinnati Art Museum; his "Landscape and Cattle" was exhibited in the Centennial, in Philadelphia in 1876. He died in 1908.

TALBOT, Cornelia Breckenridge (Mrs.). Painter. Born in Natrona, Penna., in 1888. Pupil of Penna. Academy of the Fine Arts. She died in 1924. *Address,* Talbot Hall, Norfolk County, Va.

TALBOT, Grace H. Sculptor, who exhibited at the National Academy of Design, New York, 1925. *Address,* Oyster Bay, Long Island, N. Y., or 14 Washington Square, New York City.

TALBOT, Henry S. Painter. Member: Boston Art Club. Work: "Morning in Mid Ocean," Minneapolis Institute of Arts. *Address,* 387 Washington St., Boston, Mass.

TALCOTT, Allen B. Landscape painter. He had a studio on the Connecticut River, near Lyme, and painted in water colors. He died recently in New York City.

TALCOTT, Sarah W. Painter. Born in West Hartford, Conn., in 1852. Pupil of Chase and Cox in New York; also of Bouguereau and Robert-Fleury in Paris. Member of Conn. Academy of Fine Arts. *Address,* Elmwood, Conn.

TALLMADGE, Thomas Eddy. Etcher. Born in Washington, D. C., in 1876. Pupil of Mass. Institute of Technology, Boston. Member: Cliff Dwellers; Chicago Society of Etchers; New York Society of Etchers. Awarded Chicago Architectural Club traveling scholarship, 1904. *Address,* 4 East Ohio St., Security Building, Chicago, Ill.

TALLMAN, M. G. (Mrs. Walter B.). Painter. Born in Lianidloes, North Wales, in 1859. Pupil of F. S. Church; of the National Academy of Design; Art Students' League of New York; studied under Mrs. Coman and Jane Peterson. Member: Pen and Brush Club; New York Water Color Club Association; National Association of Women Painters and

Sculptors. *Address,* 3609 Broadway, New York, N. Y.

TANBERG, Mrs. Ella Hotelling. Painter. Born in Janesville, Wisc. Member: West Coast Arts; Janesville Art League; Chicago Art Club; California Art Club; Laguna Beach Artists' Association. Work: "Lily Pond, Lincoln Park," owned by Janesville Art League. *Address,* Laguna Beach, Calif.

TANEJI, Moichiro Tsuchiya. Painter. Born in Ogaki City, Japan, in 1891. Studied in Japan. Member of Penguins. *Address,* 61 West 37th St., New York, N. Y.

TANNAHILL, Mary H. Painter. Born in Warrenton, N. C. Pupil of Weir, Twachtman, Cox and Mowbray in New York. Member: Pa. Society of Miniature Painters; National Association of Women Painters and Sculptors; Provincetown Artists' Association. Awarded prize for best group, National Association of Women Painters and Sculptors, autumn, 1914. *Address,* 121 Washington Place, New York, N. Y.

TANNAHILL, Sallie B. Painter. Born in New York in 1881. Pupil of Arthur W. Dow and V. Preissig. Member of National Association of Women Painters and Sculptors. Instructor, Art Department, Teachers' College, Columbia University. *Address,* 121 Washington Place, New York, N. Y.

TANNER, Benjamin. Engraver. Born in New York City in 1775; died in Baltimore, Md., in 1848. Tanner's master is unknown, but he was engraving in New York in 1792, and was possibly one of the pupils of Peter R. Maverick of that city. He remained in New York until 1805, and in that year his name first appears in the Philadelphia directories, and he remained continuously in that city until 1845, when he apparently removed to Baltimore. In 1811, with his brother Henry S. Tanner, he commenced business as a general engraver and map publisher; in 1837 he changed his business to that of "stereographer," using steel plates for the production of checks, drafts, notes and other mercantile paper. In 1816–24 he was a member of the engraving firm of Tanner, Vallance, Kearny & Co.

As an engraver Tanner worked in both line and stipple. He produced some excellent large plates of portraits and historical subjects, especially views relating to the American Revolution and the War of 1812. Tanner engraved some plates in connection with W. R. Jones.

TANNER, Henry O. Negro painter. Born in Pittsburgh, Pa., in 1859. Studied at Penna. Academy of Fine Arts, also in Paris under Laurens and Constant. He was a painter of religious subjects. *Address,* St. Jacques, Paris, France.

TANNER, Henry S. Engraver. Born in New York City in 1786; died there in 1858. In 1811 Henry S. Tanner was in business in Philadelphia as a partner of his brother Benjamin and it was about this time that he engraved outline illustrations for some of the magazines of that city, though he was chiefly engaged upon map and chart work. The "Port Folio" of 1815 credits Henry S. Tanner with having invented a process of bank-note engraving which was intended to increase the difficulties of counterfeiting. He produced effects by white lines on a black ground, very varied in form and intricate in character.

In 1843, Henry S. Tanner removed to New York and there engaged in the engraving and publishing of maps, charts, etc. He contributed geographical and statistical articles to various periodicals, and published guide-books for a half dozen sections of the United States. Tanner was made a member of the geographical societies of London and Paris, when this distinction was rare among Americans.

TAPPAN, W. H. An engraver of portraits in mezzotint about 1840; he also engraved some line plates, in conjunction with Joseph Andrew, in Boston. He was doubtless the Tappan referred to in the sketch of Geo. G. Smith, as his partner in the engraving business in Boston.

TARBELL, Edmund C. Painter. Born in West Groton, Mass., in 1862. When quite young he proceeded straight to Paris to begin his art studies, which he pursued there in the ateliers of the Academie Julien under the direction of MM. Boulanger and Lefebvre. When he returned to the United States he took a studio in Boston, and belongs to the comparatively small but able group of painters who reside in that city. He has a fine record as a prize-winner in the exhibitions in New York and other prominent cities, his list of honors including the Clarke prize at the National Academy (1890); the first Hallgarten prize at the same institution (1894); the gold medal of the Art Club of Philadelphia (1895); a medal at the World's Fair, Chicago (1893); medals at the Pennsylvania Academy of Fine Arts; also at the Carnegie Institute, Pittsburgh; and the Shaw Fund prize at the Society of American Artists. Elected an Associate Member of the National Academy, 1902, and an Academician in 1906. *Address*, Care of Corcoran Art Gallery, Washington, D. C.

TARLETON, Mary Livingston. Painter. Born in Stamford, Conn. Pupil of Childe Hassam; Charles W. Hawthorne; Art Students' League of New York. Member: National Association of Women Painters and Sculptors. *Address*, 201 Inwood Ave., Montclair, N. J.

TATNALL, Henry Lee. Painter. Born in Brandywine Village, Del., in 1829. He died in Wilmington, Del., in 1865. His work was marine and landscape painting. He was elected president of the Delaware Artists' Association.

TAUSZKY, D. Anthony. Portrait painter. Born in Cincinnati, Ohio, in 1878. Pupil of Art Students' League of New York under Blum; Julien Academy in Paris under Laurens and Constant. Member of Salmagundi Club, 1907. Work: Portrait of Emperor Franz Josef I, Criminal Court, Vienna; portrait of George W. Wingate, Wingate School, New York, N. Y. *Address*, Pasadena, Calif.

TAYLOR. Miniature painter, who flourished in Philadelphia about 1760. He copied a miniature of Oliver Cromwell among other works.

TAYLOR, Alex. H. Portrait painter, who flourished in 1849–50 in New York.

TAYLOR, Beatrice M. Painter. Member of Pittsburgh Artists' Association. *Address*, 306 South Craig St., Pittsburgh, Pa.

TAYLOR, Charles Jay. Illustrator and painter. Born in New York in 1885. Pupil of Art Students' League, National Academy of Design and Eastman Johnson in New York; also studied in London and Paris. Member: Society of Illustrators, 1910; Pittsburgh Artists' Association; Pittsburgh Architectural Club; The Players; Philadelphia Art Club. Awards: Honorable mention for drawing, Panama-American Exposition, Buffalo, 1901; bronze medal and hors concurs, Panama-Pacific Exposition, San Francisco, 1915. Represented in Carnegie Institute of Technology. Instructor in Carnegie Technical Schools, Pittsburgh, since 1911. *Address* "The Players," 16 Gramercy Park, New York, N. Y.

TAYLOR, Edgar J. Painter and illustrator. Born in Brooklyn, N. Y., in 1862. Pupil of National Academy of Design; Art Students' League of New York under Beckwith; Brooklyn Art Guild under Eakins. Member: Brooklyn Art Club; Conn. Society of Artists; Society of Independent Artists. *Address*, Westbrook, Conn.

TAYLOR, Edwin C. Painter. Born in Detroit, Mich., in 1874. Pupil of Art Students' League of New York, and of Kenyon Cox. Member: Painters and Crafts Club. *Address*, Yale School of Fine Arts, New Haven, Conn.

TAYLOR, Elizabeth. Painter. Member: Chicago Society of Artists; Society of Independent Artists; Provincetown Painters. Work: "Flowers," Detroit Institute. *Address*, 1504 East 57th St., Chicago, Ill.

TAYLOR, Emily Drayton. Miniature painter. Born in Philadelphia, Pa., in 1860.

Pupil of Cécile Ferrère in Paris; also of Penna. Academy of the Fine Arts. Member: Pa. Society of Miniature Painters; Fellowship, Penna. Academy of Fine Arts; Plastic Club; Art Alliance, Phila. Awards: Gold medal, Earl's Court Exhibition, London, 1900; gold medal for services on jury, Charleston Exposition, 1902; silver medal, Panama-Pacific Exposition, San Francisco, 1915; medal of honor, Penna. Academy of Fine Arts. Among her works are portraits of President and Mrs. William McKinley, Dr. S. Weir Mitchell, etc. *Address*, 1504 Pine St., Philadelphia, Pa.

TAYLOR, F. Walter. Painter. Born in Philadelphia in 1874; died in 1921. Studied at Penna. Academy of Fine Arts, 1896 (awarded traveling scholarship); studied independently in Paris. Established studio in Philadelphia, 1898. Member: The Fellowship of Penna. Academy of the Fine Arts; Society of Illustrators. Illustrator of various books and received medal of honor, Panama P. I. Exposition, 1915. He has contributed numerous short stories to leading magazines.

TAYLOR, Henry Fitch. Painter. Born in Cincinnati, O., in 1853. Studied art at Academie Julien, Paris. He has exhibited at London, Paris, Rome, New York, Philadelphia, Chicago and San Francisco. Member of Association of American Painters and Sculptors. Inventor of The Taylor System of Organized Color (a device for indicating harmonious color relations). He died in New York in 1925.

TAYLOR, Ralph. Painter. Exhibited at Penna. Academy at Annual Exhibitions of 1924 and 1926 in Philadelphia. *Address*, 1422 Walnut St., Philadelphia.

TAYLOR, T. Engraver. Good landscape plates, done in line and published in New York in 1860, are so designed. Taylor was possibly a bank-note engraver, as little of his signed work is seen.

TAYLOR, William Ladd. Painter and illustrator. Born in Grafton, Mass., in 1854. He studied at Art Schools in Boston and New York, and under Boulanger and Lefebvre in Paris, 1884–85. Since then he has painted and illustrated in the United States. Recent works: "Selections from Longfellow's Poems" (series of pictures illustrating the 19th century in New England); series of pictures of the "Pioneer West"; "Old Songs Series," 1908–09; "Our Home and Country," a book of pictures of American life, 1908; "Pictures from American Literature," 1910, "Pictures from the Old Testament," 1913. *Address*, Wellesley, Mass.

TAYLOR, Will S. Painter. Exhibited at the National Academy of Design, New York, 1925. *Address*, American Museum of Natural History.

TEEL, E. Engraver. Born in the United States about 1830; died in Hoboken, N. J., before 1860. Teel was an excellent line-engraver of portraits and landscape. After being employed for some time in New York, he was working for Cincinnati publishers in 1854.

TEFFT, Carl E. Sculptor. His figure of "Lake Superior" was particularly noticeable at the Buffalo Exposition.

TELLING, Elisabeth. Etcher. Born in Milwaukee in 1881. Pupil of W. P. Henderson; George Senseney; H. E. Field; also studied in Munich. Member: Chicago Society of Etchers; Chicago Society of Artists; Brooklyn Society of Etchers; California Miniature Painters. Work: "Uncle William's Creach," California State Library, Pasadena. *Address*, 2120 Lincoln Park, West, Chicago, Ill.

TEN EYCK, John A. Painter and etcher. Born in Bridgeport, Conn., in 1893. Pupil of F. Luis Mora, Kenneth Hayes Miller, Joseph Pennell and Bror J. O. Nordfeldt. Member of Whitney Studio Club. *Address*, 111, 51 West 10th St., New York, N. Y.

TENNEY. In Tuckerman's "Book of the Artists" he is noted as painting miniatures.

TERRIL, Israel. Engraver. He arranged the music, engraved the title-page and music, and printed and sold a music-book entitled "Vocal Harmony, No. 1, Calculated for the Use of Singing Schools and Worshipping Assemblies." The imprint is "Newhaven, West Society, Engrav'd Printed and Sold by the Author (Israel Terril)," and the work was copyrighted "21 Aug. in 30th year of Independence," or in 1806. For the note on this engraver the compiler is indebted to the courtesy of Mr. A. C. Bates of the Connecticut Historical Society.

TERRILL BROS. These twin brothers were mezzotint engravers and came from Canada to the United States about 1868 and returned to England about two years later. They were pupils of Simmons of London and mainly engraved large plates of fancy subjects.

TERRY, Luther. Painter. Born in Enfield, Conn., in 1813. He studied in Hartford and in 1838 he went to Italy, where he lived for years. He has painted portraits and historical compositions. He married in 1861 the widow of Thos. Crawford the sculptor. His pictures are rarely seen in his native country. He died in 1869.

TERRY, W. D. Engraver. In 1836, in connection with Oliver Pelton, Terry founded the Bank Note Company of Boston. The firm of Terry, Pelton & Co. also did general engraving in the same city. Terry himself was a bank-note engraver, and some of his early vignettes are signed at Providence, R. I.

TETLEY, Wm. Birchall. Portrait painter in oils and miniatures who flourished in New York about 1774.

TEW, David. Engraver. The Journals of the Continental Congress record that on Oct. 28th, 1788, there was due to David Tew the sum of 213 50/90 dollars for engraving three copper-plates for bills of exchange and for repairing two other plates.

TEW, Marguerite R. Sculptor. Born in Magdalena, N. M., in 1886. Pupil of Pa. Museum, School of Independent Artists; Penna. Academy of Fine Arts (under Grafly). Member: California Art Club; Fellowship of Penna. Academy of the Fine Arts; National Association of W o m e n Painters and Sculptors. Awarded Cresson European scholarship, Penna. Academy of the Fine Arts, 1913. Work: Mayan ornament on portal of South West Museum, Los Angeles. *Address*, 4122 Pasadena Ave., Los Angeles, Calif.

TEWKSBURY, Fanny W. Painter. Born in Boston, Mass. Pupil of Mass. Institute of Technology and of Ross Turner in Boston. Member of New York Water Color Club. *Address*, 86 Park St., Newton, Mass.

THACKARA. This signature as engraver is signed to a copperplate frontispiece to ''The Instructor, or Young Man's Best Companion, etc,'' by Geo. Fisher, published by Isaac Collins, Burlington, N. J., 1775. No other example has been seen of this man's work, and it is barely possible that the plate referred to was engraved by the sailor father of James Thackara. It is poor in execution.

THACKARA, James. Engraver. Born in Philadelphia in 1767; died there in 1848. James Thackara was the son of James Thackara, Sr., who settled in Philadelphia in 1764, after having served many years as a seaman in the British navy. Young James was apprenticed to James Trenchard, and he later married his preceptor's daughter.

In 1794 Thackara was a partner of John Vallance in the engraving business in Philadelphia, and Thackara's name as engraver appears in the directories from 1791 to 1833. His work was done entirely in line and was confined to subject plates. For some time after 1826 Thackara was the keeper of the Pennsylvania Academy of Fine Arts. A very good three quarter length, seated, oil portrait of James Thackara is in the possession of his grandson, James Thackara, of Lancaster, Penna.

THACKARA, William W. Engraver. Born in Philadelphia in 1791; died there in 1839. He was the son of James Thackara and a pupil of

his father, and in 1832 they constituted the firm of Thackara & Son, general engravers in Philadelphia. This firm published, in 1814, ''Thackara's Drawing Book, for the Amusement and Instruction of Young Ladies and Gentlemen.''

THALINGER, E. Oscar. Painter. Born in Alsace-Lorraine in 1885. Pupil of St. Louis School of Fine Arts under Wuerpel, Stoddard and Campbell; with Gruber in Munich. *Address*, 4522a Adelaide Ave., St. Louis, Mo.

THAYER, Abbott Henderson. Painter, who was born in Boston, Mass., August 12, 1849. He started at sixteen years of age to make painting his profession. He went to Paris and entered the atelier of Gerome, and from the studio of this rather unimaginative French Academician he passed on to the École des Beaux Arts, and there his great ability as a draftsman was recognized, for he could always draw most beautifully if he chose to do so. On his return home from Europe, he painted numerous cattle-pieces and animal studies. The backgrounds of these paintings pointed to the mastery he was to achieve later in his landscapes.

Soon after Thayer's return to America he abandoned animal painting, and dedicated himself to ideal figure pictures rather more than portraits or landscape painting. His marvelous painting of a nude is shown in his great picture ''Figure Half-Draped'' which shows well the commanding exercise of his technique. Thayer painted in 1889 the first of his ''Winged Figures,'' now owned by Smith College; following this he painted the ''Caritas'' and the ''Virgin'' in the Freer Gallery of the Smithsonian Institution of Washington; also the ''Virgin Enthroned'' together with other angel paintings.

He painted the beautiful mural decoration at Bowdoin College in which the five figures are so skillfully arranged. Thayer painted few landscapes, but in those few we see his profound knowledge of the truth of nature and his masterly skill as a painter. The ''Winter Sunrise on Monadnock,'' in the Metropolitan Museum of Art, and the ''Sketch of Cornish Headlands'' and ''Winter Dawn on Monadnock,'' in the Freer Gallery of the Smithsonian Institution of Washington, D. C., are among the finest examples of American landscapes we have. Thayer died in 1921, leaving a great heritage to American Art. In 1922 a Memorial Exhibition of his work was held at the Metropolitan Museum in New York where seventy-eight of his paintings and many of his drawings and sketches were shown.

THAYER, Emma B. (Mrs. Abbott). Painter. Born in 1850, she died in 1924. Specialty, flower studies in oil and pastel.

THAYER, Gerald H. Painter. Born in Cornwall-on-Hudson, N. Y., in 1883. Pupil of Abbott H. Thayer. Work: ''Partridge,'' Metropolitan Museum of Art; "Rabbit," Brooklyn Museum of Art. Author of "Concealing Coloration in the Animal Kingdom"; "The Nature-Camouflage Book"; "The Seven Parsons and the Small Iguanodon." *Address*, Monadnock, N. H.

THAYER, Gladys (Mrs. David Reasoner). Painter. Born in South Woodstock, Conn., in 1886. Pupil of her father, Abbott H. Thayer. *Address*, Monadnock, N. H.

THAYER, Grace. Painter. Born in Boston. Pupil of Boston Museum School; also of Mme. Hortense Richard in Paris. Member of Copley Society, 1885. *Address*, 845 Boylston St., Boston, Mass.

THAYER, Sanford. Painter of Syracuse, New York, who has painted a number of portraits, some showing decided merit.

THAYER, Theodora W. Miniature painter. Born in Milton, Mass., in 1868. Studied with Joseph De Camp in Boston. Instructor in New York School of Art, and at Art Students' League of New York. She died in 1905. Her fine portrait of Bliss Carman is considered one of the memorable achievements in American miniature painting, the work being full of character and charm.

THEISS, John William. Water color painter. Born in Zelionople, Penna., in 1863. Pupil of Lorenzo P. Latimer. *Address*, 1308 East 46th St., Los Angeles, Calif.

THEOBALD, Eliz. S. (Mrs. Saml. T.). Sculptor and painter. Born in Cleveland, Ohio, in 1876. Pupil of Chase, Mora, and Hawthorne. Member of National Association of Women Painters and Sculptors. *Address*, 50 West 60th St., New York City.

THEOBALD, Samuel. Painter. Pupil of André Castaigne. *Address*, 60 West 50th St., New York City.

THERIAT, Charles James. Painter. Born in New York in 1860; student of Jules Lefebvre and Boulanger in Paris. Honorable mention, Paris Exposition, 1889; Salon, 1896, and Paris Exposition, 1900; bronze medal, Buffalo Exposition, 1901. Member of Paris Society of American Painters. *Address*, Le Mee, Melum, Seine-et-Marne, France.

THEUERKAUFF, Carl R. Painter. Born in Germany in 1875. Member of Rochester Art Club. *Address*, Cornwall Building, Chicago, Ill.

THEUS, Jeremiah. Portrait painter, who was one of three brothers who came to South Carolina from Switzerland in 1839. In the following year he was established in a studio and painting portraits at Charleston, S. C. His work has frequently been attributed to Copley.

He died at Charleston, S. C., in 1774, after painting for about thirty-five years in that city.

THEW, Robert. Engraver. Born in England. He came to the United States about 1850, and returned to England about 1865. Robert Thew worked in New York and in Cincinnati, and was a clever engraver of landscapes.

THOM, James Crawford. Painter. Born in New York in 1835. He studied at the National Academy in 1859 and then went abroad for study and exhibited in London where he gained several medals. Among his paintings are "By the River-side," "The Monk's Walk," "Forgotten Cares," "The Old Farm House," and a number of landscapes painted along the Hudson River. He died in 1898.

THOMAS, C. H. Miniature painter, who flourished in New York in 1838–39.

THOMAS, Conrad A. Painter. Born in Germany in 1858. Has painted a number of mural pictures. *Address*, 210 Sixth Ave., Pelham, N. Y.

THOMAS, Henry. Portrait painter. Pupil of John Neagle. He worked in Philadelphia, and a portrait of the actor Junius Brutus Booth, painted by him, was exhibited in the Loan Collection of Historic Portraits, Philadelphia, 1887.

THOMAS, Isaiah. Engraver. Born in Boston in 1749; died in Worcester, Mass., in 1831. After serving as an apprentice with Zachariah Fowle, in 1770, in partnership with his former master, Thomas commenced the publication of the *Massachusetts Spy*. About this time he seems to have tried engraving on type metal. To this later well-known printer and publisher are credited some very crude cuts signed "I. T.," appearing in "The History of the Holy Jesus, etc., 15th edition, printed by I. Thomas for L. Fowle."

THOMAS, Marjorie. Painter, who exhibited at the Annual Exhibition of Penna. Academy, Philadelphia, 1924. *Address*, Scottsdale, Ariz.

THOMAS, Paul Kirk Middlebrook. Painter. Born in Philadelphia in 1875. Pupil of William M. Chase, Cecilia Beaux, Charles Grafly, and others; also student at Penna. Academy of the Fine Arts for four years. Makes specialty of portraits; received bronze medal, St. Louis Exposition, 1904. Member: American Federation of Arts; life member of Lotos Club, New York. Writer on art. *Address*, New Rochelle, N. Y.

THOMAS, Roland. Painter. Born in Kansas City, Mo., in 1883. Pupil of William

Chase, Robert Henri and Frank Vincent Du Mond. Member: Kansas City Arts and Crafts; and American Artists, Munich. Awarded landscape prize, Mo. State Art Exhibit, 1912. Work: "Autumn," Elverhoj Art Gallery, Milton, New York; "Winter Dachaön," American Artists' Club, Munich; mural decoration in Curtiss Building, Kansas City, Mo. *Address,* 409 East 10th St., Kansas City, Mo.

THOMAS, S. Seymour. Painter. Born at San Augustine, Tex., in 1868. Studied at Art Students' League, New York, 1886–88; at Julien Academy and École des Beaux Arts, Paris. Work has been principally portraiture. Honorable mention, Salon, Paris, 1895; gold medals, Salon, 1901; 2d gold medal, Hors Concours, 1904; bronze medal, Paris Exposition, 1900; gold medal, Munich, 1901; Chevalier de la Légion d'Honneur, 1905; member of International Jury of Awards, St. Louis Exposition, 1904; member of Paris Society of American Painters. Painted portraits of Hon. James Bryce, Cardinal William Henry O'Connell, Gen. Lew Wallace; also portrait of President Woodrow Wilson for the White House, and one for the State House of N. J.; "Portrait of a Lady and Dog," acquired by the Metropolitan Museum, 1915. *Address,* 11 Impasse Rousin, Paris, and 80 West 40th St., New York, N. Y.

THOMASON, Francis Q. Painter, who exhibited at the Penna. Academy of the Fine Arts, Philadelphia, 1914.

THOMPSON. Some poorly drawn and badly engraved subject plates are thus signed. They were published in New York in 1834.

THOMPSON, Albert. Painter. Born in Woburn, Mass., in 1853. He became a pupil of Wm. E. Norton in 1880–81; he also studied in Paris. His work is mainly landscapes and cattle-pieces; among his paintings are "After the Shower," "Clearing Up," "Changing Pasture," and "An October Afternoon."

THOMPSON, A. W. Painter. Born in Baltimore, Md., in 1840; died in Summit, N. J., in 1896. He studied in Paris, and his paintings cover a wide range of subjects, his landscapes having real merit. Member of National Academy of Design in 1875. The New York Historical Society owns "The Parting Guests."

THOMPSON, Arad. Painter, who graduated from Dartmouth College in 1807 and lived and painted portraits in Middleborough, Mass.

THOMPSON, Cephas G. Landscape and portrait painter who was born in Middleborough, Mass., in 1809. At 18 years of age he painted portraits in Plymouth, Mass., and afterwards in Providence, R. I. He had a studio in New York in 1837–47 and resided in Italy 1852–60, returning to New York to practise his

profession. He painted portraits of many American authors and the collection is now owned by the New York Historical Society. He died in 1888.

THOMPSON, D. G. Engraver. Born in England; died in New York about 1870. Thompson spent a considerable part of his early life in India with a brother who held some official position in that country. He was engraving in New York in 1856, working on portraits and landscapes. He was a good water color artist.

THOMPSON, Mrs. Edith Blight. Painter. Born in Philadelphia, Pa., in 1874. Pupil of F. V. Du Mond and Luis Mora. Member of Newport Artists' Association. Specialty, "interiors." *Address,* Westbury, Long Island, N. Y.

THOMPSON, Frederic Louis. Painter and sculptor. Born in Chilmark, Mass., in 1868. Pupil of George H. McCord. Member: Salmagundi Club; Societé des Beaux Arts. *Address,* 126 East 75th St., New York, N. Y.

THOMPSON, George Albert. Painter. Born in New Haven, Conn., in 1868. Pupil of Yale School of Fine Arts; also studied in Paris. *Address,* 12 Ashbey St., Mystic, Conn.

THOMPSON, Hannah. Painter and etcher. Born in Philadelphia in 1888. Pupil of William M. Chase. Member of California Art Club and Society of Etchers. *Address,* 415 Oakland Ave., Pasadena, Calif.

THOMPSON, Harry Ives. Painter. Born in West Haven, Conn., in 1840; died in West Haven, Conn., in 1906. Began his business career as a clerk in a country grocery in his native town. He first painted under the instruction of Benjamin Coe, a water colorist of local reputation in New Haven, Conn., whom he finally succeeded as an instructor in the drawing school. While his landscape and figure work was well received, his best work was that of a portrait painter. At the Fifty-second Annual Exhibition of the National Academy of Design he exhibited a large portrait of governors of Connecticut, now found in the library of the State Capitol. His portrait of Jonathan Trumbull is in the United States Capitol.

THOMPSON, J. D. In 1860 this capital line-engraver of landscapes was working in New York. He was probably a bank-note engraver.

THOMPSON, Jerome. Painter. Born in 1814. He was a brother of Cephas G. Thompson. He had no regular instruction. He painted portraits at an early age at Cape Cod and he had a studio in New York and also went to Europe in 1852 for study. He painted both landscapes and figures, and his "Land of

Beulah,'' ''Hiawatha's Journey'' and ''The Voice of the Great Spirit'' are well known. He died in 1886.

THOMPSON, John Edward. P a i n t e r. Born in Buffalo, N. Y., in 1882. Pupil of Art Students' League of New York and of Laurens, Blanche and Cottet in Paris. *Address*, 1556 High St., Denver, Colo.

THOMPSON, Juliet. Portrait p a i n t e r. Born in New York. Pupil of Corcoran Art School. *Address*, 48 West 10th St., New York.

THOMPSON, Launt. Sculptor. Born in Ireland in 1833. He came to America in 1847. Pupil of Erastus D. Palmer, he produced several portrait busts and later opened a studio in New York. Elected an Associate Member of National School of Design in 1859 and an Academician in 1862. His works are statues of Pierson, at Yale College; Bryant, at the Metropolitan Art Museum, N. Y.; Edwin Booth, as Hamlet. Launt died in 1894.

THOMPSON, Leslie P. Painter. Born in Medford, Mass., in 1880. Pupil of Boston Museum School under Tarbell. Member of the Botolph Club. Awarded bronze medal, St. Louis Exposition, 1904; third Hallgarten prize, National Academy of Design, 1911; H. S. Morris prize, Newport Artists' Association, 1914; silver medal, Panama-Pacific Exposition, San Francisco, 1915; Beck gold medal, Penna. Academy of Fine Arts, 1919. Elected Member of the National Academy of Design. *Address*, 30 Ipswich St., Boston, Mass.

THOMPSON, Mills. Painter and decorator. Born in Washington in 1875. Studied in Corcoran Art School, Washington, and Art Students' League, New York. Worked on decoration of Library of Congress, 1896; art editor, *Saturday Evening Post*, 1900. Decorated Siam Building at St. Louis Exposition. He was made Knight of the Most Honorable Order of the Crown of Siam, 5th class. Member of S. A. R., Society of Washington Artists. *Address*, Saranac Lake, N. Y.

THOMPSON, Nellie Louise. Painter and sculptor. Born in Jamaica Plains, Boston. Pupil of Sir James Linton and of the South Kensington School under Alyn Williams and Miss Ball Hughes in London; Cowles Art School in Boston under De Camp; pupil of Henry B. Snell. Studied sculpture under Roger Noble Burnham and Bela Pratt. Member of Copley Society, 1893; allied member, MacDougal Club. *Address*, 8 Adams Hall, Trinity Court, Dartmouth St., Boston, Mass.

THOMPSON, William John. Portrait painter. Born in 1771 in Savannah, Ga. He painted miniatures. In 1812 he moved to Edinburgh, Scotland, and died there in 1845.

THOMPSON, Woodman. Scene painter. Born in Pittsburgh in 1889. Pupil of Sparks, Sotter and Holmes. Member of Pittsburgh Associated Artists. *Address*, 115 West 47th St., New York City.

THOMPSON, Wordsworth. Painter. His picture ''Passing the Outpost'' is owned by the Union League Club of New York. He was elected a member of the National Academy of Design in 1875. He died in 1896.

THOMSON, George. Painter. Born in Canada in 1868. Member of Conn. Academy of Fine Arts. *Address*, 789 Elm St., New Haven, Conn.

THOMSON, Henry G. Painter. Born in New York in 1850. Pupil of National Academy of Design. *Address*, Wilton, Fairfield County, Conn.

THOMSON, Rodney. Illustrator. Born in San Francisco, Calif., 1878. *Address*, 49 Claremont Ave., New York, N. Y.

THOMSON, William T. Painter and illustrator. Born in Philadelphia in 1858. Pupil of Penna. Academy of the Fine Arts. *Address*, 1020 Chestnut St., Philadelphia.

THORNDIKE, George Quincy. Painter. Born in 1825; died in 1886. He graduated at Harvard College in 1847 and went abroad to study art. On his return to this country he settled in Newport, R. I. His work shows the French influences of his training. Elected an Associate Member of the National Academy of Design in 1861. Among his works are ''The Wayside Inn,'' ''The Lily Pond,'' ''The Dumplings'' and ''Newport, R. I.''

THORNE, William. Painter. Born in Delavan, Wis., in 1864. Pupil of Constant, Lefebvre and Laurens in Paris. Awards: Medal, National Academy of Design, 1888; honorable mention, Paris Salon, 1891; bronze medal, Pan-American Exposition, Buffalo, 1911. Elected Associate, National Academy, 1902; National Academy, 1913; Society of American Artists, 1893. Represented by ''The Terrace,'' painted in 1906, in the Corcoran Art Gallery, Washington, D. C. *Address*, 154 West 57th St., New York City.

THORNHILL. This man was a music engraver on copper, located in Charleston, S. C., early in the last century.

THORNTON, William. Born in Tortola, West Indies, about 1761; died in Philadelphia in 1827. William Thornton was educated as a physician and was living in England and Scotland from 1781–83, and soon after the latter date he came to Philadelphia, as he was elected a member of the American Philosophical Society of that city in 1787. He was a skilled architect and designed the Philadelphia library building, completed in 1790, and he later superintended the erection of the original Capitol at Washington. In 1802 Dr. Thornton was appointed the first superintendent of the United States Patent Office and he held that office until his death. He was prominently identified with the scientific investigations of his day.

Portions of Dr. Thornton's diaries, for 1780–83, are preserved in the Division of Manuscripts in the Library of Congress, and by the courtesy of Mr. Worthington C. Ford, chief of that division, extracts from these diaries have been furnished showing that Dr. Thornton, while in England, made a serious attempt at mezzotint engraving. He made various notes to this effect. On April 20, 1781, he "Began to Scrape a Mezzotinto"; on Oct. 15, 1781, he "Paid for taking off my mezzotints"; and "Paid Robinson for Engraving," etc. The last entry probably refers to engraving the legend under his mezzotint. In 1782 he sends "one of my Mezzotinto prints" to various personal friends mentioned by name in the diary.

One of these mezzotints is preserved in the Library of Congress; it is dated in 1781. It is an enlarged copy of an engraved gem representing Caesar Augustus, of full quarto size. The mezzotinto work is fairly well executed, though the hand of the amateur is apparent in the modeling of the face and in the hair. The plate is dedicated to his friend the Rev. Doctor Baldwin, of Aldingham. It is signed "Thornton" in Greek characters. He also assisted Thomas Jefferson with the plans for the University of Virginia buildings. The best account of him is to be found in a paper by Mr. A. C. Clark in the "Records of the Columbia Historical Society," Washington, D. C., 1915. A collection of his manuscripts, including personal notes, is to be found in the Library of Congress. Dr. Thornton copied the profile crayon drawing that Gilbert Stuart made of Jefferson in "Swiss Crayon." (See *McClure's Magazine*, May, 1898.)

THORPE, Freeman. Portrait p a i n t e r. Born in 1844; died in Hubert, Minn., in 1922. He painted many portraits of Government officials in Washington, D. C.

THOURON, Henry J. Painter, who studied at the Penna. Academy of the Fine Arts and later in Paris. On his return to this country he painted a number of altar pictures. He was instructor at the Penna. Academy of the Fine Arts for several years. He died in Rome in 1915.

THRASHER, Leslie. Painter and illustrator. Born in Piedmont, W. Va., in 1889. Pupil of Chase and Anshutz. *Address*, 51 West 10th St., New York.

THROOP, Daniel Scrope. Born in Exford, Chenango County, N. Y., in 1800; died at Elgin, Ill. Son of Major Dan Throop (1768–1824) of Norwich, Conn. D. S. Throop, among other plates, engraved a good stipple portrait of Lafayette in 1824, evidently made for a Lafayette badge. This plate is signed "D. S. Throop, Sc., Utica, N. Y."

THROOP, John Peter Vannes. Engraver. According to "Fielding's American Engravers," he was born in 1794. He was an engraver of portraits and was working in Baltimore, Md., in 1835. He was a brother of J. V. N. Throop.

THROOP, J. V. N. This man was an engraver of portraits, in line and stipple, who was working in New York and in Baltimore in 1835.

THROOP, O. H. In 1825 O. H. Throop, an engraver of landscape and vignettes, had his office at 172 Broadway, New York City.

THULSTRUP, Thure De. Painter. Born in Sweden in 1848. Studied drawing in Paris; then went to Canada as topographical engraver; he later moved to Boston. First illustrations for *New York Graphic*; on staff of *Graphic, Leslie's Weekly, Harper's Weekly* many years; self-taught in painting. Member: Society of Illustrators; American Water Color Society; John Ericsson Society. *Address*, 33 West 67th St., New York.

THUM, Patty Prather. Painter. Born in Louisville, Ky. Graduated from Vassar College; studied painting with Henry Van Ingen at Vassar and later at Art Students' League of New York. Honorable mention for book illustrations, Chicago Exposition, 1893. Member: Louisville Art League; Louisville Artists' League. Contributor to art magazines. *Address*, 654 4th St., Louisville, Ky.

THURBER, Caroline. Painter. Born in Oberlin, Ohio. Studied art in Italy and Germany; was also, 1897–1901, in Paris under Jean Paul Laurens and Benjamin Constant. Specialty, portraiture of children. *Address*, 320 Tappan St., Brookline, Mass.

TIEBOUT, Mademoiselle. French miniature painter, who flourished in New York about 1834.

TIEBOUT, Cornelius. Engraver, who had the distinction of having been the first American-born professional engraver to produce really meritorious work, is supposed to have died in obscurity in Kentucky about 1830. The date of his birth is equally uncertain, for while some biographers state that he was born in New York in 1777, existing plates engraved by Tiebout show that he was doing creditable work in 1789. All that is positively known is that he was descended from a Huguenot family which came to this country from Holland and held lands on the Delaware River as early as 1656;

they also owned property in Flatbush, Long Island, in 1669.

Tiebout was apprenticed to John Burger, a silversmith of New York, and in this business he first learned to engrave upon metal. He was engraving maps and subject plates for New York publishers in 1789–90, and fairly good line portraits in 1793.

In the latter year he went to London to seek instruction under abler masters than he could find in his native country. He there learned to engrave in the stipple manner and in 1794 there was published in London a large and well-executed stipple plate engraved by Tiebout after a painting by J. Green. In 1796 Tiebout published in London his quarto portrait of John Jay. This is probably the first really good portrait engraved by an American-born professional engraver (the mezzotint work of the artist Edward Savage not coming under this category).

In November, 1796, Cornelius Tiebout was again located in New York, engraving and publishing prints in connection with his brother, Andrew Tiebout. His name disappears from the New York directories in 1799. He went to Philadelphia about that time and conducted an extensive business as an engraver in that city until 1825. He is said to have made considerable money in his business, but he lost most of this in some disastrous speculation and then went to Kentucky about 1825 and died there some five years later.

TIFFANY, Louis Comfort. Painter, who was born in New York in 1848. Studied under George Inness and Samuel Coleman in New York; also pupil of Leon Bailly in Paris. He received the gold medal for Applied Arts at the Paris Exposition of 1900; elected Chevalier of the Legion of Honor of France in 1900; grand prize at Turin Exposition in 1904. Elected Associate Member of the National Academy of Design in 1871, and Academician in 1880. He has been Art Director of the Tiffany Studios, and president of the Tiffany Co. His achievements in stained glass have brought him world fame as the discoverer of new formulas for making decorative glass known as "Tiffany Favrile Glass." His paintings in oil and water colors are principally Oriental scenes—"Street Scene in Tangiers"; "Feeding the Flamingoes"; "The Cobblers at Bonfarick." He is a member of the American Water Color Society, New York. *Address*, 347 Madison Ave., New York City.

TIFFANY, Miss Mary A. Painter. Born in Hartford, Conn. Pupil of Tryon at Connecticut School of Design. She paints in both oil and water colors.

TIFFANY, William. He came from Baltimore, Md., and was known as an accomplished draughtsman whose pencil illustrations of Tennyson and Longfellow are remarkable for

truth and refined conception. His best known paintings are "Lenore" and "St. Christopher Bearing the Christ Child." He died in New York, 1907.

TILDEN, Alice F. Painter. Born in Brookline, Mass. Pupil of Boston Museum School; also of Wm. M. Chase in New York; also under Lucien Simon. Member of Copley Society, 1898. *Address*, 55 White St., Milton, Mass.

TILDEN, Douglas. Sculptor. Born in Chico, Calif., in 1860. Pupil of National Academy of Design under Ward and Flagg; Gotham Students' League under Mowbray; Choppin in Paris. Awarded hon. mention, Paris Salon, 1890; bronze medal, Paris Exposition, 1900; gold medal, Alaska-Yukon-Pacific Exposition, Seattle, 1909; commemorative gold medal, St. Louis Exposition, 1904. Work: "The Tired Boxer," Art Institute, Chicago; "Baseball Player," Golden Gate Park, San Francisco; memorial monuments at Portland, Ore., Los Angeles, San Francisco, etc. *Address*, Oakland, Calif.

TILDEN, John C. Painter. Born in Yonkers, N. Y., in 1889. Pupil of Penna. Academy of the Fine Arts. Awarded Cresson European scholarship, Penna. Academy of Fine Arts; second Toppan prize, Penna. Academy of Fine Arts, 1914. Work: "Autumn, 1918" and four portraits, University Club, Houston, Texas; "Portrait of Josiah Jackson," Penna. State University, Philadelphia. *Address*, Rice Institute, Houston, Tex.

TILLER, Robert. There were two engravers of this name in Philadelphia, father and son. As nearly as can be ascertained, the father was an engraver of landscape, working in line in 1818–25; while the son engraved portraits in stipple and subject plates in line in 1828–36.

TILLINGHAST, Mary E. Painter. Born in New York. Pupil of John La Farge in New York, and of Carolus-Duran and Henner in Paris. Specialty, designs for stained glass.

TILTON, John Rollin. Painter. Born in London, N. H., in 1828; died in Rome, Italy, in 1888. Landscape painter, largely self-taught. He settled in Rome in 1852. The *London Daily News* wrote of him, "He was the first American painter since Benjamin West to receive special commendation from the President of the Royal Academy." He was the recipient of Honorary Degrees of M.A. and Ph.D. from Dartmouth College. Represented by "Venetian Fishing Boats" at the Corcoran Art Gallery, Washington, D. C.

TILTON, Olive (Mrs. Bigelow). Painter. Born in Mountain Station, N. J., in 1886. Pupil of Collin and Delecluse in Paris; also studied in Munich and London. *Address*, 24 West 59th St., New York, N. Y.

TILYARD. Little is known of this painter. He was born in 1787 and died in 1827.

TIMMONS, Edward J. Painter. Born in Janesville, Wis., in 1882. Pupil of Art Institute of Chicago; also studied in Holland, France, Italy and Spain. Member: Chicago Society of Artists; Chicago Art Students' League. Work: Portraits in University of Chicago, University of Arkansas, etc. Instructor at Art Institute of Chicago. *Address*, 952 Lawrence Ave., Chicago, Ill.

TIMOSHENKO, Marina. Painter, who exhibited water colors at the Penna. Academy of the Fine Arts, Philadelphia, 1925. *Address*, 1620 Summer St., Philadelphia.

TINDALE, Edward Henry. Painter. Born in Hanson, Mass., in 1879. Studied at the Munich Academy under Carl Marr, Hans von Kayeck and Loeftz. *Address*, Fenway Studios, Boston, Mass.

TISCHLER, Marian Clara. Painter. Member: Cincinnati Woman's Art Club. *Address*, 453 Riddle Road, Cincinnati, Ohio.

TISDALE, Elkanah. Engraver. Born in Lebanon, Conn., about 1771. He was living there in 1834. In 1794–98 Tisdale was located in New York as an "Engraver and Miniature Painter," but about the latter year he removed to Hartford and became a member of the Graphic Co., an association of engravers, though he was the designer of vignettes rather than their engraver. Dunlap says that he remained in Hartford until 1825, and he was designing and engraving plates for Samuel F. Goodrich, of that city, in 1820.

Tisdale worked in both line and stipple, but his plates possess little merit. The earliest dated plates by Tisdale known to the writer are his full-page illustrations to Trumbull's "McFingal," published in New York in 1795.

Tisdale was a better designer than engraver, and he claimed to be a painter in his early life, though his best work was in the line of miniature portrait painting.

TITCOMB, M. Bradish. Painter and illustrator. Born in New Hampshire. Pupil of Boston Museum School under Tarbell, Benson and Hale. Member: Copley Society, 1895; New York Water Color Club; National Association of Women Painters and Sculptors; Conn. Academy of Fine Arts. Award: Honorable mention, Conn. Academy of Fine Arts, 1917. Work represented in the White House, Washington, D. C. *Address*, Fenway Studios, Ipswich St., Boston, Mass.

TITCOMB, Virginia Chandler. Painter and writer. Born in Otterville, Ill. Sculptor in bas-relief. She has exhibited at the National Academy of Design. Founder, 1884, and pres. of the Patriotic League of the Revolution. Memorialized 57th Congress for recognition of services rendered by Theodore R. Timby, the inventor of the revolving turret as used on the "Monitor" and all battleships of United States since the Civil War. Contributor to *Harper's Bazaar, Demorest's Magazine, Brooklyn Eagle*, etc. *Address*, 101 Lafayette Av., Brooklyn.

TITLOW, Harriet W. Painter. Born in Hampton, Va. Pupil of Robert Henri. Member: National Association of Women Painters and Sculptors; Society of Independent Artists; National Art Club. *Address*, 132 East 19th St., New York, N. Y.

TITSWORTH, Julia. Painter. Born in Westfield, Mass., in 1878. Pupil of Art Institute of Chicago; R. Collin in Paris. Member: National Association of Women Painters and Sculptors. *Address*, Care of Mrs. S. H. Titsworth, 26 East 49th St., New York, N. Y.

TITTLE, Walter. Painter and etcher. Born in Springfield, Ohio, in 1883. Studied art in New York under William M. Chase, Robert Henri and F. Luis Mora. Painter of portraits. Contributor to *Life, Harper's Weekly, Saturday Evening Post, Collier's, Harper's Monthly*, etc. Member: Royal Society of Arts, London; Society of Illustrators. Author and illustrator of "The First Nantucket Tea Party," 1907; "My County," 1909; "Colonial Holidays," 1910. Exhibitor at National Academy of Design, 1915–16–17; private exhibition of portrait etchings, Art Institute of Chicago, in 1918 (represented in permanent collection). Illustrator of "The Valley of Democracy," by Meredith Nicholson, serially in *Scribner's Magazine* from January to June, 1918. Also many other magazines and books. Etches dry-point portraits. *Address*, 3 Washington Square, New York, and London, Eng.

TOBIN, George Timothy. Painter. Born in Weybridge, Vt., in 1864. Studied at Art Students' League of New York, under George de Forest Brush. Portrait painter since 1898. Member of Art Students' League since 1893. *Address*, 250 Main St., New Rochelle, New York.

TODD, A. This engraver etched a small bust of Washington published for the Washington Benevolent Society, Concord, 1812. The firm of Gray & Todd engraved astronomical plates published in Philadelphia in 1817, but it can not be certainly said that the Todd is the same man in both cases.

TODD, Charles Stewart. Painter. Born in Owensboro, Ky., in 1885. Pupil of Cincinnati Art Academy; also of Albert Herter in New York. Member: Cincinnati Art Club; Cincinnati Mac Dowell Society. *Address,* Rookwood Pottery, Cincinnati, Ohio.

TODD, Henry Stanley. Portrait painter, working in New York City in 1902. He painted the portrait of Judge Emott in that year which is in the City Hall, New York.

TOERRING, Heléne. Miniature painter, who exhibited at the Penna. Academy of the Fine Arts, Philadelphia. 1925. *Address,* 6399 Woodbine Ave., Overbrook, Pa.

TOFEL, Jennings. Painter, who exhibited in Phila. in 1921, in ''Exhibition of Paintings Showing the Later Tendencies in Art.'' *Address,* 61 Colben St., Newburgh, N. Y.

TOLLES, Sophie Mapes. Painter, who began her art studies in Philadelphia in 1864 under Peter F. Rothermel. She later studied in France and Italy, and her first exhibition in America was at the National Academy in 1876 where she exhibited a portrait; in 1878 she exhibited several flower-pieces. Among her best known portraits is one of Linda Gilbert of Chicago.

TOLMAN, John. Portrait painter, living at Pembroke, Mass. He painted in Boston and Salem about 1816. He evidently travelled over the entire country as a portrait painter.

TOLMAN, Ruel P. Painter and etcher. Born in Brookfield, Vt., in 1878. Pupil of Art Students' League of New York. *Address,* 2020 G St., N. W., Washington, D. C.

TOLMAN, Stacy. Portrait painter. Born in Concord, Mass., in 1860. Pupil of Boulanger, Lefebvre and Cabanel in Paris. *Address,* 7 Thomas St., Providence, R. I.

TOLSON, Norman. Painter, illustrator and etcher. Born in England in 1883. He executed mural panels in La Salle Hotel, Chicago. *Address,* 3723 Warwick Blvd., Kansas City, Mo.

TOMKINS, Frank Hector. Painter. Born in Hector, N. Y., in 1847; died in Brookline, Mass., in 1922. He was a pupil of the Art Students' League of New York. He is represented at the Penna. Academy of the Fine Arts by ''The Penitent'' and in the Boston Museum by ''The Young Mother.''

TOMLINSON, Anna C. Painter, who exhibited water colors at the Penna. Academy of the Fine Arts, Philadelphia, 1925. *Address,* 281 Heath St., Boston, Mass.

TOMPKINS, Clementina M. G. Painter. Born in Washington, D. C. She has lived in Paris, studying under Bonnat. Her specialty is portraits and figure-pieces. She exhibited in this country in 1876–78.

TONETI, Francois Michel Louis. Sculptor. Born in Paris in 1863. He came to America in 1899. His work at the Chicago Fair in 1893 received an award. He collaborated with Saint Gaudens in work on the Congressional Library in Washington. He died in New York City in 1920.

TOPHAM. Engraver. Well-executed landscape plates published in Cincinnati in 1852 are thus signed.

TOPPAN, Charles. Engraver. Born in Newburyport, Mass., in 1796. He was living in 1868. Toppan was a pupil of Gideon Fairman and was with that engraver in Philadelphia in 1814. After doing some general engraving on his own account, on the death of Fairman in 1827 he became a partner in the bank-note company of Draper, Toppan, Longacre & Co. This firm later became Toppan, Carpenter, Casilear & Co., and in 1854 it was Toppan, Carpenter & Co. Having removed to New York, Mr. Toppan, in 1858–60, was president of the then American Bank Note Co., of that city.

TOPPING, James. Landscape p a i n t e r. Born in England, in 1879. Member of the Chicago Society of Artists. *Address,* 1006 North Lawler Ave., Chicago, Ill.; or 541 Forrest Ave., Oak Park, Ill.

TORRENS, Rosalba. Landscape painter, who was practising her art in Charleston, S. C., in 1808.

TORREY, Charles Cutler. Engraver. According to ''The Annals of Salem'' (Salem, Mass., 1849), Charles Cutler Torrey was brought to Salem by his parents as an infant. He studied engraving in Philadelphia about 1815 and in 1820 he established himself in that business in Salem. While he is said to have engraved a few portrait plates and some general illustrations for the book publishers, his most notable work of this period is a large and well-executed plate showing a ''North East View of the Several Halls of Harvard College.'' This print was published in Boston, in 1823, by Cummings, Hilliard & Co. A companion plate, showing a ''South View of the Several Halls of Harvard College,'' was engraved by Annin & Smith and published by the same Boston firm. Torrey left Salem in 1823 and removed to Nashville, Tenn., where he died of a fever in 1827.

He was a brother of Manasseh Cutler Torrey, a portrait and miniature painter of Salem.

TORREY, Elliot B. Painter. Born in East Hardwick, Vt. Member of the Boston Art Club. Represented in the Art Institute of Chicago. *Address,* 39 West 67th St., New York.

TORREY, Fred M. Sculptor. Born in Fairmount, W. Va., in 1884. Pupil of Lorado Taft. Member of Western Society of Sculptors. *Address*, 6016 Ellis Ave., Chicago, Ill.

TORREY, George Burroughs. Portrait painter. Born in New York in 1863. Exhibited at Paris Salon, 1900, and afterwards. He has painted portraits of William Howard Taft, Theodore Roosevelt, etc. He was decorated by the King of Greece with the Grecian Order of the Savior, 1904. *Address*, 27 East 35th St., New York, N. Y.

TORREY, Manasseh C. Portrait and miniature painter, who flourished about 1830–37 in New York, Philadelphia and in Salem.

TOWNSEND, Ethel Hore (Mrs.). Miniature painter. Born on Staten Island, N. Y., in 1876. Pupil of Henry Snell and Orlando Rouland in New York. *Address*, 184 North 19th St., East Orange, New Jersey.

TOWNSEND, Harry E. Painter, illustrator and etcher. Born in Wyoming, Ill., in 1879. Pupil of Art Institute of Chicago and of Howard Pyle. Member of Brooklyn Society of Etchers. *Address*, 23 East 63d St., New York.

TOWNSLEY, C. P. Painter. Born in Sedalia, Mo., in 1867. Pupil of Julien and Delecluse Academies in Paris; under Chase in New York. Member: Salmagundi Club; California Art Club. Formerly director, Chase European classes; London (Eng.) School of Art. Director, Otis Art Institute. *Address*, Care of Frank Brangwyn, Temple Lodge, London, Eng.

TRACY, Glen. Water color painter, who exhibited landscapes at the Cincinnati Museum in 1925. *Address*, Mt. Washington, Cincinnati.

TRADER, Effie Corwin. Miniature painter. Born in Xenia, Ohio, in 1874. Pupil of Cincinnati Art Academy; under T. Dube in Paris. Member of Cincinnati Woman's Art Club. *Address*, 538 Hale Ave., Avondale, Cincinnati, Ohio.

TRAVER, George A. Painter. Member: National Art Club; Salmagundi Club. Work: "Intervale," Brooklyn Institute Museum, Brooklyn, N. Y. *Address*, 109 West 11th St., New York, N. Y.

TRAVER, Marion Gray. Painter. Member of National Association of Women Painters and Sculptors, New York. *Address*, 109 West 11th St., New York, N. Y.

TRAVER, Warde. Painter. Born in Ann Arbor, Mich., in 1880. Pupil of Royal Academy, Munich, under Marr; also of Millet and

Snell. *Address*, Central Park Studios, 15 West 67th St., New York, N. Y.

TRAVIS, Olin H. Painter. Born in Dallas, Tex., in 1888. Pupil of Art Institute of Chicago. *Address*, 245 West North Ave., Chicago, Ill.

TREGO, Jonathan. Portrait painter, father of William Trego. Born in Pennsylvania. He painted many of the families of Bucks County, Penna., in a rather stiff and formal manner.

TREGO, William T. Painter. Born in Yardley, Bucks County, Penna., in 1859. He studied with his father Jonathan Trego. In 1879 he entered the schools of the Penna. Academy of the Fine Arts; he later studied in Paris under Fleury and Bouguereau. He died in North Wales, Penna., in 1909.

TRENCHARD, Edward. Painter. Born in Philadelphia in 1850. Studied with Peter Moran and at the National Academy of Design. His works include "The Passing Shower"; "The Old Wreck"; "Sea, Sand and Solitude"; "The Surf." Specialty, marine painting. He died in 1922.

TRENCHARD, E. C. Engraver. A well-executed stipple portrait of Count Rumford is signed as "Drawn and Engraved by E. C. Trenchard," and it appears as a frontispiece to "The Essays of Count Rumford," published by D. West, Boston, 1798.

There is some difficulty in exactly locating this E. C. Trenchard, who was engraving for Boston publishers in 1798. An Edward Trenchard, under date of 1794, signed an agreement in Philadelphia to establish in the United States a school or academy of architecture, sculpture, painting, etc., and among the other signers to this document were the American engravers James Trenchard, John Vallance, Gilbert Fox, Robert Field, and John Eckstein.

The biography of Capt. Edward Trenchard, a naval officer prominent in the War of 1812, says that he was born at Salem, Salem County, N. J., in 1784; studied art under the instruction of his uncle, James Trenchard, the Philadelphia engraver, and then went to England to complete his art education. But in 1800, this Edward Trenchard entered the United States Navy, as a midshipman, and, as stated, became prominent in that service. He died in Brooklyn, N. Y., in 1824. The pictorial bookplate of "Lieut. E. Trenchard, United States Navy," is described by Mr. Charles Dexter Allen, but it is unsigned by the engraver.

The signer of the Philadelphia agreement of 1794, and the Edward Trenchard who studied with his uncle before 1793—when James Trenchard left the United States—might well have been the engraver of the "Count Rumford" in 1798, so far as the dates are concerned, but the alleged date of birth of the naval officer, Edward Trenchard, is 1784, and the engraving is almost too well done to have been the work of a boy of fourteen years of age. On the other hand, this date of 1784 may be in error, and the later naval officer may have engraved not only the portrait in question, but his own book-plate.

TRENCHARD, James. Trenchard's grandson, Mr. James Thackara, of Lancaster, Pa., says that James Trenchard came to Philadelphia from Penns Neck, Salem County, N. J. He was located in that city as an engraver and seal-cutter as early as 1777, and in 1787 he was the artistic member of the firm that established the *Columbian Magazine*, in Philadelphia. In 1793 Trenchard went to England and remained there.

Dunlap says that Trenchard learned to engrave with J. Smither, in Philadelphia. He engraved a few portraits and a number of views in and about Philadelphia, but his work was poor. He was also a die-sinker, and made the dies for the medal of the Agricultural Society of Philadelphia, 1790.

James Trenchard was possibly a son or nephew of George Trenchard, of Salem, N. J., who was Attorney-General of West New Jersey in 1767.

TRENTANOVE, Gaetano. Sculptor. Born in Florence, Italy, in 1858. He was educated at the Fine Arts Academies of Florence and Rome. Knighted by the late King Humbert of Italy, he became an American citizen in 1892. Among his works are: Statue of James Marquette, Statuary Hall, United States Capitol; statue of Daniel Webster, Washington, D. C.; statue of Albert Pike, Washington, D. C.; Kosciuszko equestrian statue, Milwaukee, Wis.; The Last of the Spartans, Layton Art Gallery, Milwaukee, Wis.; Soldiers' Monument, Oshkosh, Wis.; Chief Oshkosh Statue, Oshkosh, Wis.; monument to Confederate soldiers, Springfield, Mo.; Soldiers' Monument, Appleton, Wis.; also many other works for private citizens in the United States and in Europe.

TREVITTS, J. Painter. Pupil of Penna. Academy of the Fine Arts. Member of Fellowship, Penna. Academy of the Fine Arts. Awarded Cresson traveling scholarship, Penna. Academy of the Fine Arts. *Address,* Manistee, Mich.

TRIEBEL, Frederick Ernst. Sculptor. Born in Peoria, Ill., in 1865. Professionally engaged as sculptor since 1888. Received 1st prize and silver medal for sculpture, Academy of Fine Arts, Florence, Italy, 1884–85, etc.; graduating "study" purchased by Italian Govt.; honorable mention for anatomy, 1886; received Galileo silver medal from Museo Nazionale di Antropologia, Florence, Italy, in 1889 and 1891; statue, "Mysterious Music,"

exhibited at Chicago Exposition, 1893, purchased by Japanese Govt. for Imperial Museum, Tokio; exhibited at St. Louis Exposition. Sec., jury of awards, Chicago Exposition. Elected academician of merit, for sculpture in Royal Academy of S. Luca, Rome, Italy, 1905. Member: Circolo Artistico, Florence; L'Associazione Artistica Internationale, Rome; National Sculpture Society; Architectural League, New York. Notable works: Peoria (Ill.) Soldiers' Monument; Iowa State Monument, battlefield of Shiloh, Tenn.; Miss. State Monument, Vicksburg National Military Park; Robert G. Ingersoll Statue, Peoria, Ill.; statues of the late Senator George L. Shoup of Ida., and of the late Senator Henry M. Rice of Minn., both for Statuary Hall, Washington; Otto Pastor Monument, Petrograd, Russia, etc. *Address,* College Point, L. I., New York.

TRIPLER, H. E. About 1850–52 this engraver of portraits and historical plates was working for New York publishers. In connection with John Bannister he engraved for *Sartain's Magazine,* of Philadelphia.

TRISCOTT, Samuel Peter Rolt. Painter. Born in Gosport, Eng., in 1846. Studied art in England. He came to the United States in 1871, and began to practice his profession. He is represented in the permanent exhibit of the Boston Museum of Fine Arts. He died in 1925.

TROCCOLI, Giovanni Battista. Painter. Born in Lauropoli, Italy, in 1882. Pupil of Denman Ross and the Julien Academy. Member: Copley Society; Boston Society of Arts and Crafts; Guild of Boston Artists. Awards: Honorable mention, C. I., Pittsburgh, 1911; Harris silver medal, Art Institute of Chicago, 1913; gold medal, Panama-Pacific Exposition, San Francisco, 1915. *Address,* 94 Somerset St., Boston, Mass.

TROTT. A copperplate engraver, who signed his plates "Trott, sp. Boston." The date of publication was 1800 to 1820.

TROTT, Benjamin. Miniature painter. Born in 1720. He was considered one of the greatest miniaturists of his day and with Malbone and the Peales he divided the honors of his profession. Trott was thoroughly American by training and experience, as he never studied abroad. He was a pupil of Gilbert Stuart, and also worked with Thomas Sully in Philadelphia in 1808. He is known to have been working in Baltimore in 1796. His miniatures suggest the treatment of Richard Cosway, especially in the use of clouds and blue sky for backgrounds. Miniatures by Benjamin Trott will be found in the Metropolitan Museum of New York, and in the Rhode Island School of Design in Providence, as well as in many of the collections of American miniatures throughout the country.

TROTTER, Newbold Hough. Painter. Born in Philadelphia in 1827. He studied at the Academy of the Fine Arts. He has devoted himself to painting pictures of animals, and his most important works in this class include: ''The Range of the Bison''; ''Grizzly Bears''; ''The Last Stand''; ''The Young Bull''; ''The Barnyard'' (signed and dated Philadelphia, 1866). He died at Atlantic City, N. J., in 1898.

TROUBETZKOY, Paul. Sculptor. Born in Lake Intra, Lake Maggiore, Italy, in 1866. Studied in Italy, Russia and France. Award: Grand prize, Paris Exposition, 1900. Bronzes placed in the Luxembourg in Paris; National Gallery in Rome; National Gallery in Venice; Museum of Alexander III in Petrograd; Treliakofsky Gallery in Moscow; National Gallery in Berlin; Royal Gallery in Dresden; Leipsig Gallery; Chicago Art Institute; Detroit Institute; Toledo Museum; Buffalo Fine Arts Academy; Golden Gate Park Museum; the Museum in Buenos Aires and the Brera Museum, Milan. *Address*, 15 West 67th St., New York, N. Y.

TROUBETZKOY, Pierre. Painter. Born in Milan, Italy, in 1864. Member: London Portrait Painters' Society. *Address*, 15 West 67th St., New York, N. Y.

TROWBRIDGE, Vaughan. Painter. Born in New York in 1869. Abandoned business life in 1897, and took up art studies in Paris with Jean Paul Laurens and Benj. Constant. Exhibited paintings and etchings in Paris Salons, 1900–13, and etchings printed in color at St. Louis Exposition, 1904. Illustrator: ''Paris and the Social Revolution'' (by Alvan F. Sanborn), 1905. *Address*, 15 Ave. Libert, Draveil, Seine-et-Oise, France.

TROYE, Edward. Painter. Born in Switzerland in 1808. He came to America when about 20 years old, and having landed in Philadelphia, he worked on *Sartain's Magazine* as an animal painter. As a painter of race horses he was most successful and was styled ''The Landseer of America.'' His equestrian portrait of Genl. Winfield Scott was purchased by the Government. He died in Georgetown, Ky., in 1874.

TRUE, Allen Tupper. Painter and illustrator. Born in Colorado Springs, Colo., in 1881. Pupil of Howard Pyle; of the Corcoran Art School in Washington; also under Brangwyn in London. Member of Denver Artists' Association. Assisted Frank Brangwyn with decorations for Panama-Pacific Exposition, 1915; mural decorations to be found in Wyoming State Capitol; Denver Public Library; Montana National Bank; open air Greek Theater, Civic Center, Denver. *Address*, Silt, Colo.

TRUESDELL, Gaylord Sangston. Painter. Born in Waukegan, Ill., in 1850; died in New York in 1899. Animal painter. Pupil of Pennsylvania Academy of the Fine Arts, Philadelphia; also of A. Morot and Cormon, in Paris. Awards: Bronze medal, Exposition Universelle, 1889; second class medal, Paris Salon, 1892; Hors Concours, Salon des Champs Elysées. His painting ''Going to Pasture,'' painted in 1889, is in the Corcoran Art Gallery, Washington, D. C.

TRUMBULL Gurdon. Painter. Born in Stonington, Conn., in 1841. Pupil of F. S. Jewett and of James M. Hart in New York. His specialty was painting game fish. He resided for years in Hartford, Conn., and died there in 1903.

TRUMBULL, Colonel John. Born in Lebanon, Conn., in 1756. Graduated from Harvard in 1773. His taste for drawing began while he was at college, and it was shortly after returning from college that he painted ''The Death of Paulus Emilius at Cannae,'' his first attempt at composition. At the commencement of the Revolutionary War he joined the army as adjutant. His skill as a draughtsman attracted the attention of General Washington, who induced him to act as one of his aides-de-camp. He also filled the position of military secretary under Washington, and many of the important communications to Congress and officers of the army were in the handwriting of this artist and signed by Washington. He afterwards joined the army of General Gates, as adjutant, with the rank of colonel, but in 1777, being dissatisfied with his commission as deputy adjutant-general, he resigned and resumed his art studies. When, however, in 1778, a plan was formed for the recovery of Rhode Island from the British, he joined General John Sullivan in the enterprise, as volunteer aide-de-camp. This ended his military career.

In May, 1780, he sailed for France, and from there went to London with a letter from Benjamin Franklin to Benjamin West, under whom he wished to study art, and while pursuing his studies he was arrested for treason, and confined in prison for eight months, after which he was released, on condition of leaving the kingdom; Benjamin West and John Singleton Copley acted as sureties for him.

After the war, in 1784, he was again enabled to visit London to resume his studies under Benjamin West, and it was after that period he executed his various historical paintings of ''The Declaration of Independence,'' ''The Battle of Bunker Hill,'' ''The Death of General Montgomery,'' ''The Surrender of Burgoyne,'' ''The Sortie from Gibraltar,'' etc. He also painted several portraits, from life, of General Washington.

In 1794 he went to England as secretary to Hon. John Jay, and in 1798 was appointed

25

Fifth Commissioner for carrying into execution the Seventh Article of the Treaty of 1794. (All the papers owned by the United States Government, relating to this clause in the treaty, were destroyed by the British when they captured Washington in 1814; but John Trumbull has preserved his copy of the proceedings.) Afterwards he returned to the United States where he painted many historical portraits and pictures. These not meeting with a ready sale, he was induced to enter a contract or agreement with Yale College, to present them with the collection in return for an annuity of $1,000, and today this forms the most important historical gallery in the country. His fame rests, and worthily, too, on the four historical paintings for the Capitol at Washington. These subjects decided upon were the "Declaration of Independence," the "Surrender of General Burgoyne," the "Surrender of Lord Cornwallis," and the "General Washington Resigning his Commission." The last of these paintings was scarcely finished in April 1824, and now hangs in the rotunda of the Capitol. The "Declaration of Independence" was first "placed temporarily in a room of the north wing" of the Capitol, "then used for the sittings" of the Supreme Court of the United States. The composition of this painting resulted in numerous letters to Thomas Jefferson. In one of these the artist says "You recollect the Composition, which you kindly assisted me to sketch at Chaillot:—the Committee who drew up the Declaration form the principal Group, by which means I place yourself & some other of the most eminent Characters conspicuously—the figures large as Life. The Picture will contain Portrait of at least Fortyseven Members,—for the faithful resemblance of Thirty Six I am responsible as they were done by myself from the Life, being all who survived in the year 1791.—of the remainder Nine are from pictures done by others:—One Genl Whipple of New Hampshire, is from memory,—and one Mr. B. Harrison of Virginia, from Description aided by Memory. I at first dreaded the Sire of my Work—but I have proceeded far enough to have conquered any timidity, and to be satisfied that this Picture as a mere work of Art will be superior to those which have been heretofore engraved. The universal interest which my Countrymen feel, and always must feel in an Event important above all others, must in some degree attach to the painting which will preserve the likeness of Forty-Seven of those Patriots to whom we owe that memorable act and all its glorious consequences." The painting early elicited criticism, as well as praise. In general it was well received though criticisms were made by John Quincy Adams in his diary and other prominent men on the historical correctness of the scene. In historical painting it is often impossible to make Art and History agree, and in Trumbull's picture, Art and History do not wholly agree. These paintings

were made also in smaller size (20 in. by 30 in.) and now hang in the School of the Fine Arts of Yale University. Trumbull died in New York in 1843. His works still hold their rank not only for their historical interest, but for their artistic merit. His "Death of Montgomery" is considered one of the most spirited battle-pieces ever painted. His portraits of General Washington are of the greatest interest and his portrait of Alexander Hamilton might be called his best work. He was elected President of the American Academy of the Fine Arts in 1817, and was annually reelected to the same office for years.

TRUMP, Rachel B. Painter. Member of National Association of Women Painters. Exhibited at 33d Annual Exhibition, New York. *Address*, 806 Lodi St., Syracuse, N. Y.

TRYON, Benjamin F. Painter. Born in New York City in 1824. He studied with Richard Bengough and James H. Cafferty. His subjects are chiefly landscapes. He resided for years in Boston, where he exhibited at the Boston Art Club. Among his works are "New England Scenery," "Conway Valley" and "A Quiet Nook."

TRYON, Dwight W. Landscape painter. Born in Hartford, Conn., in 1849. He studied in Paris in the atelier of Mr. Jacquesson de la Chevreuse; he also studied from nature out of doors with Daubigny and Harpignies. On his return to this country his work received immediate recognition and he received many medals; in 1886 his painting "Daybreak" received the gold medal at the Prize Fund Exhibition at the American Art Association, New York. He also received the prize at the National Academy in 1895, a gold medal at Munich in 1898 and the first prize at the Carnegie Institute in Pittsburgh. In 1891 Tryon was elected a member of the National Academy of Design, he was also a member of the Society of American Artists and of the American Water Color Society. His pictures combine poetic sentiment with sound technical methods and are distinguished and veracious in color. He died in 1925. He is represented in the Metropolitan Museum, New York, by "Moonrise at Sunset," painted in 1890; "Early Spring," painted in 1894; and "Evening, New Bedford Harbor," painted in 1895. He is also represented in the principal galleries in America and abroad. (See "American Masters of Painting" by Charles Caffin.)

TSCHUDI, Rudolf. Painter. Born in Switzerland in 1855. Member of Cincinnati Art Club. He is represented by "Surrender of Lee," and portraits of Jefferson and Lincoln. He died in Cincinnati in 1923.

TSCHUDY, Herbert B. Painter, who exhibited water colors at the Penna. Academy of the Fine Arts, Philadelphia, 1925. *Address*, 50 Livingston St., Brooklyn, N. Y.

TUCKER, Allen. Painter. Born in Brooklyn, N. Y., in 1866. He has exhibited at the Paris Salon and in exhibitions held in New York and Philadelphia. He paints landscapes and portraits; his painting "Ice Storm" was considered one of his finest landscapes. *Address*, 121 East 79th St., New York City.

TUCKER, Benj. Portrait painter. Born in 1768. He worked in Newbury, Conn.

TUCKER, Cornelia. Sculptor, who exhibited at the Penna. Academy of the Fine Arts in 1926. *Address*, Wallingford, Penna.

TUCKER, William E. Engraver. Born in Philadelphia in 1801; died there in 1857 (says Mr. Baker). Tucker was a pupil of Francis Kearny in Philadelphia and he also studied in England for a time, as we find prints signed "Engraved in London by W. E. Tucker." Tucker's name as an engraver appears continuously in the directories of Philadelphia from 1823 until 1845.

Tucker was an excellent engraver in line and in stipple, but his best signed work is found among his small *Annual* plates. Later in life he devoted himself almost entirely to banknote engraving.

TUCKERMAN, Stephen Salisbury. Painter. Born in Boston in 1830. He studied in England but returned to Boston and taught there until 1864. He is noted for his marine views, which he has exhibited in many of the galleries abroad. His painting of the "U. S. Frigate Escaping from the British Fleet in 1812" is in the Boston Museum of Fine Arts. He died in 1904.

TUDOR, Rosamond. Painter, who exhibited a portrait at the Academy of the Fine Arts, Philadelphia, 1926. *Address*, Care of Ferargil Galleries, New York.

TULLY, Christopher. E n g r a v e r. The *Pennsylvania Magazine* for 1775 contains a large copperplate of a machine for spinning wool, which the text informs us was "drawn and engraved by Christopher Tully, who first made and introduced this machine into this country." While nothing more is known to the compiler of Tully as an engraver, the above plate was evidently made in connection with the work of the Society for Promoting American Manufactures, organized in Philadelphia in 1775. To this society C. Tully and John Hague submitted models of machines for spinning wool and cotton goods; these two machines were so similar in design that the committee appointed to examine them finally decided to divide between these two inventors the prize of 30 pounds offered by the society.

TURCAS, Jules. Landscape painter. Born in Cuba in 1854; died in Boston in 1917. He exhibited in the New York and Philadelphia galleries.

TUBLE, Sarah A. Painter, who exhibited miniatures at the Penna. Academy of the Fine Arts, Philadelphia, 1925. *Address*, 2216 East Superior St., Duluth, Minn.

TURMAN, William T. Painter. Born in Graysville, Ind., in 1867. Pupil of Art Institute of Chicago; also of J. Francis Smith, A. F. Brooks, Sterba, A. T. Van Laer. Member of Terre Haute Art Association. Work represented in High School, Columbia City, Ind.; Public Library, Thorntown, Ind. Head of Art Department, Ind. State Normal School. *Address*, Terre Haute, Ind.

TURNER, Charles Yardley. Painter. Born in Baltimore, Md., in 1850. In 1872 he went to New York and entered the school of the National Academy of Design, where he studied three years and won prizes. He then went to Paris and studied under Laurens, Munkacsy and Leon Bonnat. In Holland he found the subject of his famous picture "The Grand Canal at Dordrecht." Mr. Turner was assistant director of decorations at the Columbian Exposition in Chicago in 1893. He was elected an Associate Member of the National Academy of Design in 1883, and an Academician in 1886. One of his mural paintings is to be found in the Baltimore Court House, the subject being the incident of the brig "Peggy Stuart" entering the harbor of Annapolis in 1774. He also painted many Puritan subjects. Some of his work is in the Capitol at Madison, Wis.; also in many buildings in New York. Towards the last of his life he gave much attention to etching. He died in 1918.

TURNER, Helen M. Painter and teacher. Born in Louisville, Kentucky. Pupil of Art Students' League of New York, under Cox. Awards: Elling prize for "Landscape," New York Women's Art Club, 1912; Agar prize, Association of Women Painters and Sculptors, New York, 1913; Shaw memorial prize, National Academy of Design, 1913; honorable mention, Chicago Art Institute, 1913. Elected an Associate of National Academy, 1913, and National Academy in 1921. Member: New York Water Color Club; Allied Artists of America; Association of Women Painters and Sculptors. Represented by "Girl with a Lantern," painted 1914, Corcoran Gallery, Washington, D. C. *Address*, 111 East 10th St., New York.

TURNER, James. Engraver. This name first appears in Boston, Mass., signed to a curious view of Boston which appears in *The American Magazine* for 1744. In the *Boston Evening Post* of 1745, he advertises his varied accomplishments as follows:

"James Turner, Silversmith & Engraver, near the Town-House in Cornhill Boston. Engraves all sorts of Stamps in Brass or Pewter for the common Printing Press, Coats of Arms, Crests, Cyphers, &c., on Gold, Silver, Steel, Copper, Brass, or Pewter. He likewise makes Watch Faces, makes and cuts Seals in Gold, Silver, or Steel: or makes Steel Faces for Seals, and sets them handsomely in Gold or Silver. He cuts all sorts of Steel Stamps, Brass Rolls and Stamps for Sadlers and Bookbinders, and does all sorts of work in Gold and Silver. All after the best and neatest manner and at the most Reasonable Rates.''

While in Boston Turner engraved, among other plates, the three large folding maps used in a ''Bill in the Chancery of New Jersey,'' published in New York in 1747 by James Parker. He also there engraved a fairly good portrait of the Rev. Isaac Watts.

About 1758 James Turner appears in Philadelphia as an engraver and print-dealer on Arch Street, and he was probably working there before this date, as he was the engraver of the large map of the ''Province of Pennsylvania'' published by Nicholas Scull in Philadelphia in 1759. He engraved several book-plates for residents of Philadelphia, and the Penn coat of arms which appears in the headline of *The Pennsylvania Gazette* of this period, and signed by Turner as engraver, is probably an example of the ''stamps in Brass or Pewter for the common Printing Press'' referred to in his advertisement above.

James Turner died in Philadelphia late in the year 1759, as we find in *The Pennsylvania Gazette* of December, 1759, a notice of the sale of the household effects of ''James Turner, Engraver, deceased.'' Among these effects were ''engraving Tools, a number of Copperplates and Pictures,'' the latter probably meaning prints.

TURNER, Matilda H. Miniature painter, who exhibited at the Penna. Academy of the Fine Arts, Philadelphia, 1925. *Address*, 3422 Hamilton St., Philadelphia, Pa.

TURNER, Ross Sterling. Painter and illustrator. Born in Westport, Essex County, N. Y., in 1847; died in 1915. He practised his profession as artist after 1873. He studied in Europe, mostly in Germany (Munich) and Italy, 1876–80–82. Among his pictures in oil and water colors are: ''A Small Court, Mexico''; ''El Jardin Modesto''; ''A Painted Ship''; ''The Flying Dutchman''; ''A Bermuda Wedding.'' He became professor at Normal Art School, Boston, in 1909. Author: ''Water Colors''; ''Art for the Eye''; ''School Room Decorations,'' etc. Published reproduction of the ''Golden Galleon'' picture, *Century Magazine*, 1899.

TURNER, William Green. Sculptor. Born in Newport, R. I., in 1833. He went abroad for study and spent much of his life in Italy. He exhibited in Philadelphia in 1876.

TUTHILL, W. H. Engraver. In 1825 Tuthill was designing for the early New York lithographer Imbert; in 1830–31 he was engraving portraits, landscape and book illustrations for New York publishers. The engraving firm of Tuthill & Barnard was working in New York at a later date. A small but clever etching of ''Mr. Robert as Wormwood,'' published in New York, is signed ''Tuthill fec't,'' and can be ascribed to this man.

TUTTLE, Mary McArthur Thompson. Painter and author. Born at Hillsboro, Highland County, Ohio, in 1849. She is a portrait and landscape painter, and in 1895 and after lectured on ''Color'' before schools, colleges, etc. She painted a portrait of her mother which was exhibited in W. C. T. U. exhibit, St. Louis Exposition, 1904, and in Tremont Temple, Boston; portraits of Prof. Tuttle in Historical Seminary Room, Cornell University, and Billings Library. Author of ''Chronological Chart of the Schools of Painting.''

TUTTLE, Mrs. Mildred Jordan. Painter and etcher. Born in Portland, Me., in 1874. Pupil of Yale School of Fine Arts; also under W. M. Chase. Member of New Haven Painters and Crafts Club. Work: ''Bishop Samuel Seabury,'' Yale University. *Address*, 186 St. Ronan St., New Haven, Conn.

TUTTLE, Ruel Crompton. Portrait and mural painter. Born in Windsor in 1866. Pupil of Art Students' League of New York under Mowbray and J. Alden Weir. Member: Art Students' League of New York; Conn. Academy of Fine Arts; Washington Water Color Club. *Address*, 36 Pearl St., Hartford, Conn.

TWACHTMAN, John Henry. Landscape painter. Born in Cincinnati, Ohio, in 1853; he died in Gloucester, Mass., in 1902. He was a pupil of the School of Design of Cincinnati, under Frank Duveneck; also of the National Academy of Design, New York; and later studied in Munich, and Paris at the Academie Julien under Boulanger and Lefebvre. He was awarded the Webb prize of the Society of American Artists in 1888; Temple gold medal of the Penna. Academy of the Fine Arts, 1895, and was a member of the American Art Club of Munich. In 1898 he founded the organization known as the ''Ten American Painters.'' Mr. Twachtman ranks among the greatest American landscape painters. He shows great skill in handling the elements of natural scenery, particularly in representing snow upon the branches of the trees, and he is supposed to have been the first American artist to employ blue shadows. He was a great master of values.

TWIBILL, George W. Portrait painter. Born in Lancaster County, Penna., in 1866. Pupil of Henry Inman in 1828, he was elected an Associate of the National Academy in 1832, and an Academician in 1833. He died in 1836. The New York Historical Society has his copy of the portrait of Fitz-Greene Halleck which was painted by his master Henry Inman in 1828, and the National Academy of Design has his portrait of Colonel John Trumbull in its permanent collection of paintings.

TYLER, Bayard Henry. Painter. Born in Oneida, Madison County, N. Y., in 1855. Graduated from National Academy of Design, New York, 1882; pupil of Theo. Kaufmann; also of Art Students' League, New York, under William M. Chase, 1879. Exhibitor at National Academy of Design; Society of American Artists; Penna. Academy of the Fine Arts; Chicago Exposition, 1893; Paris Exposition, etc. His work is represented in many private collections. He painted portraits of President Roosevelt, for Municipal Art Gallery, Albany; Admiral W. H. Brownson; J. J. Albright, for Albright Memorial Library, Scranton, Pa.; Alexander S. Cochran; Professor George F.. Comfort; Rev. James E. Freeman, St. Andrew's Memorial Church. *Address*, 96 Williams St., New York City.

TYLER, Carolyn D. Miniature painter. Born in Chicago. Pupil of Art Institute of Chicago under Mrs. Virginia Reynolds. Member: Chicago Society of Artists; Chicago Water Color Club; Chicago Society of Miniature Painters; Alumni, Art Institute of Chicago; Chicago Art Club; Cordon. *Address*, 1401 East 53d St., Chicago, Ill.

TYLER, Ernest F. Painter and mural decorator. Born in New Haven, Conn., in 1879. Pupil of Yale School of Fine Arts. He worked in association with Edgar W. Jenney in making decorations for main Banking Room, Sun Life Assurance Society, Montreal, Canada; ceilings in Woolworth Building, New York; Wisconsin State Capitol Building, Madison; Union Central Life Building, Cincinnati; decorations, Hibernia Bank and Trust Co., New Orleans, La.

TYLER, G. Washington. Painter. Born in 1803; died in 1833.

TYLER, Hugh C. Painter, who exhibited at the Penna. Academy of the Fine Arts, Philadelphia, 1914. *Address*, 1115 West Clinch Ave., Knoxville, Tenn.

TYLER, James Gale. Marine painter. Born in Oswego, N. Y., in 1855. Studied for marine artist with A. Cary Smith, naval architect, who was in 1871 a marine artist. Some of his prominent pictures are: ''Abandoning the Jeannette'' (painted to order for James Gordon Bennett); ''The New World''; ''Do Not Abandon Me''; ''The Constitution''; ''The Fortunes of War''; ''The Raging Main''; ''Flying from the Alabama''; ''Norman's Woe''; ''The Flying Dutchman''; ''New England on the Lee''; ''Heaving Over the Deck Load''; ''First American Shipwreck''; ''Cloud Burst.'' He has contributed illustrations and marine art studies for L. Prang, the *Harper's*, *Century*, *Truth* and other magazines. Member: Salmagundi Club; Artists' Fund Society. *Address*, Greenwich, Conn.

TYSON, Carroll S. Painter and sculptor. Born in Philadelphia, 1878. Pupil of Penna. Academy of the Fine Arts under Chase, Anshutz and Beaux; under Carl Marr and Walter Thorr in Munich. Member: Art Club of Philadelphia; Fellowship, Penna. Academy of the Fine Arts; Society of Independent Artists. Awarded Sesnan gold medal, Penna. Academy of Fine Arts, 1915. *Address*, 319 Walnut St., Philadelphia, Pa.

U

UERKVITZ, Herta. Painter. Born in Wisconsin in 1894. Work: ''Summer Sunset,'' Seattle Fine Arts. *Address*, 3030 Hoyt Ave., Everett, Wash.

UFER, Walter. Painter. Born in Louisville, Ky., in 1876. Studied in Chicago, Dresden, Munich and Paris, after which he returned to America and devoted himself to painting Mexican Indian types. He is an Associate of the National Academy, and a member of art societies in New York, Chicago, Taos, N. M., Los Angeles, Philadelphia, Boston, Washington and abroad; he has also received many prize awards, including the Altman prize from the National Academy of Design in 1921. Ufer is represented in the Chicago Art Institute; in the Springfield (Ill.) State House; in Brooklyn; the Pennsylvania Academy; the Maryland Institute; in Los Angeles, and in the Chicago municipal collection. His pictures are fascinating Indian subjects, painted in a bold, free style. *Address*, Care of Grand Central Art Galleries, New York City.

UHLE, Bernhard. Painter. Born in Chemnitz, Saxony, in 1847. He was brought by his parents to this country in 1851, and received his first instruction in art from his father. He entered the Penna. Academy as a student at the age of fifteen. He gave the greater part of his time to photography between 1867 and 1875; went to Munich in the latter year, and remained until 1877, studying in the Academy there, under Prof. F. Barth (drawing) and Prof. Alex. Wagner (painting); made a trip to Italy, visiting the principal art galleries. He opened his studio as a portrait painter in Philadelphia in 1877, and later made a second trip to Europe in 1879, which was exclusively devoted to the study of the old masters in Munich and Paris. After his return to Philadelphia in 1880, Mr. Uhle was constantly employed in painting portraits.

ULBRICHT, Elsa E. Painter. Born in Milwaukee, Wis., in 1885. Pupil of Frederick F. Fursman; Wis. School of Art; Alex. Mueller; Walter Marshall Clute; George Senseney, and of the Pratt Institute. Member: Wis. Painters and Sculptors; Milwaukee Art Institute; Wis. Society of Applied Arts. *Address*, School of Fine and Applied Arts, Milwaukee.

ULKE, Henry. Painter. Born in Frankenstein, Germany, in 1821; died in Washington, D. C., in 1910. He was educated in Berlin. Pupil of Prof. Wach, court painter at Berlin, he became associated with the revolutionary party and enlisted in the revolutionary army. He was wounded and captured, and for a time held as a prisoner in the fortress of Spandau. Upon his release he decided to emigrate to the United States and reached New York in 1849, where he found employment as an illustrator and designer, later coming to Washington, D. C., where he continued to reside during the remainder of his life. As a painter of portraits he counted among his patrons many distinguished people some of whom were: Charles Sumner, Salmon P. Chase, Chief Justice Taney, James G. Blaine, John Sherman, W. W. Corcoran, Carl Schurz, A. R. Shepherd, Secretary Stanton, Robert G. Ingersoll and Mrs. Jefferson Davis. His portraits of different Secretaries of War are in the War Department, and his portraits of the Secretaries of the Treasury in the Treasury Department. His portrait of Gen. Grant is in the collection of portraits in the White House. Over 100 portraits were produced by this artist while in Washington. As a naturalist he was very celebrated and is credited with having made the largest known collection of American beetles, now on exhibition in the museum of natural history of the Carnegie Institute, Pittsburgh.

ULLMAN, Alice Woods (Mrs. Eugene P.). Illustrator and painter. Born in Goshen, Ind. Member: National Association of Women Painters and Sculptors; National Art Club. *Address*, 39 Commercial St., Provincetown, Mass.

ULLMAN, Eugene Paul. Painter. Born in New York in 1877. Pupil of Wm. M. Chase. Member: Associate of Societé Nationale des Beaux Arts, Paris; Salmagundi Club, 1902. Awards: Bronze medal, St. Louis Exposition, 1904; first class medal, Orleans, France, 1905; second prize, Worcester, Mass., 1906; Temple gold medal, Penna. Academy of Fine Arts, 1906; silver medal, Panama-Pacific Exposition, San Francisco, 1915. Work: "Portrait of Madam Fisher" and "The Sea," Herron Art Institute, Indianapolis, Ind. *Address*, Care of The Salmagundi Club, 47 Fifth Ave., New York, N. Y.

ULLRICH, Albert H. Painter. Born in Berlin, Germany, in 1869. Pupil of Art Institute of Chicago under Chas. E. Boutwood; Frederick Freer; Gari Melchers and Duveneck; and studied in Rome, Munich and Paris. Member: Palette and Chisel Club, Chicago; Chicago Society of Artists; Chicago Art Club. *Address*, 932 Judson Ave., Evanston, Ill.

ULP, Clifford McC. Painter and illustrator. Born in Orleans, N. Y., in 1885. Pupil of Art Students' League of New York and of Wm. M. Chase. Painted murals in the National Gallery of Washington, D. C. *Address*, 64 Adams St., Rochester, N. Y.

ULREICH, Ed. Painter, who exhibited a portrait at the Academy of the Fine Arts, Philadelphia, 1914. *Address*, 1603 Summer St., Philadelphia.

ULRICH, Charles Frederic. Painter. Born in New York in 1858; died in Berlin, Germany, in 1908. He studied at the school of the National Academy of Design in New York and later with Loefftz and Lindenschmidt in Munich. In 1884 he was the first recipient of the Clark prize at the National Academy of Design, and the prize picture "In the Land of Promise (Castle Garden)" now belongs to the Corcoran Art Gallery of Washington, D. C. His painting, "The Glass Blowers of Murano," is now in the Metropolitan Museum, New York. He resided for many years in Venice, Italy. His pictures are known for their exquisite technique, their purity of color and their strength of character.

UNDERWOOD, Clarence F. Painter. Born in Jamestown, N. Y., in 1871. Studied at Art Students' League, New York, and in the Julien Academy, Paris, under Constant, Jean Paul Laurens and Bouguereau. Has executed illustrations for *Century, Studio, McClure's* and other publishers in New York and London. Illustrator for *Harper's;* illustrated *London News,* Frederick A. Stokes & Co. (New York), *Saturday Evening Post,* Philadelphia, etc. *Address*, 106 West 55th St., New York, N. Y.

UNDERWOOD, Thomas. Engraver. Born about 1795; died at Lafayette, Ind., in 1849, "age 54 years." Underwood was a good bank-note engraver working in Philadelphia in 1829. He was a member of the bank-note company of Fairman, Draper, Underwood & Co., and after 1841, of Underwood, Bald, Spencer & Hufty.

UPTON, Florence K. Painter and illustra-

tor. Born in New York; died in London in 1922. Pupil of Kenyon Cox.

USHER, Lella. Sculptor and painter. Born in Onolaska, La Crosse Co., Wis., in 1859. Student of Saint Gaudens. Bronze portraits in Harvard and Johns Hopkins Universities and in the Fogg Art Museum, Cambridge, Mass.

V

VAGIS, Polygnotos G. Sculptor. Born in Greece in 1894. He studied at Beaux Arts Institute, Greece, and with Gutzon Borglum and John Gregory in America. He has exhibited at the National Academy of Design and Penna. Academy of Fine Arts. Work: "Greek Soldier," "The Defender," and "The Dreamer." *Address*, 23 Mac Dougal Alley, New York.

VAIL, Miss A. D. Miniature painter, who flourished in New York (1838–41).

VAIL, Eugene. Marine and figure painter. Born in Saint-Servan, France, of an American father, September, 1857. Pupil of Art Students' League of New York under Beckwith and Chase; École des Beaux Arts, Paris, under Cabanel, Dagnan-Bouveret and Collin. Awards: Honorable mention, 1886, and third class gold medal, 1888, Paris Salon; first class gold medal, Paris Exposition, 1889; Grand Diploma of Honor, Berlin; second medal, Munich; first class medal, Antwerp; silver medal, St. Louis Exposition, 1904; first medal, Liege Exposition, 1905; Legion of Honor, 1894. Represented by "Ready About," painted in 1888, at the Corcoran Art Gallery, Washington, D. C.

VAILLANT, Madame. Miniature painter, working in New York in 1825.

VAILLANT, Louis David. Mural painter. Born in Cleveland, Ohio, in 1875. Studied at Art Students' League of New York under H. Siddons Mowbray; in Paris under Luc Olivier Merson; also in Florence and Rome. Principal works: Stained glass windows in meeting-house of Society of Ethical Culture, New York; medallions in ceiling of teahouse, decorations in Hotel Hermitage, New York. Second Hallgarten prize, National Academy of Design, 1910. Member: Society of Mural Painters; Architectural League; Municipal Art Society. *Address*, 152 West 55th St., New York.

VAINI, Pietro. Italian-American painter. Born in Italy in 1847. In 1872 he settled in New York, where he painted many portraits and figure-pieces.

VALDENUIT. Some of the portrait plates issued by St. Memin, previous to 1797, are signed "St. Memin & Valdenuit, No. 12 Fair St., N. York." An aquatint portrait of a man is signed "Drawn by Gimaldi, Engraved by Valdenuit, N. Y.," in Feb. 1797.

VALENTIN, Anna (Mrs.). Sculptor. Born in Cincinnati, Ohio. Pupil of Cincinnati Art Academy, and under Rodin and Bourdelle in Paris. *Address*, 3903 Georgia St., San Diego, Calif.

VALENTINE, Albert R. Painter. Born in Cincinnati in 1862. Studied in this country, and in Europe with Duveneck. Exhibited in the Paris Salon in 1900. His specialty was the painting of wild flowers, grasses, etc. He died in 1925.

VALENTINE, Edward V. Sculptor. Born in Richmond, Va., in 1838. He studied abroad and on returning to this country he opened his studio in his native city. He executed the full-length reclining figure of Genl. Robt. E. Lee in the chapel of Washington and Lee University in Lexington, Va. *Address*, 809 East Leigh St., Richmond, Va.

VALENTINE, Elias. Valentine was a copperplate printer and engraver living in New York in 1810–18, according to the directories. As an engraver he seems to have done very little work. One of his signed plates is really a worked-over plate engraved by W. S. Leney, and another also seems to be a doctored plate.

VALENTINE, Jane H. Painter. Born in Bellefonte, Pa., in 1870. Pupil of Penna. Academy of the Fine Arts. Member of Philadelphia Art Alliance. *Address*, 50 East Chestnut Ave., Chestnut Hill, Philadelphia.

VALENTINE, William. Portrait painter. Born in England in 1798; died in 1849. He visited Boston in 1826.

VALK, Ella Snowden. Miniature painter. Member of National Association of Women Painters and Sculptors, New York. *Address,* 58 West 57th St., New York.

VALLANCE, John. Engraver. Born in Scotland; died in Philadelphia in 1823, "in the 53d year of his age." Vallance apparently came to Philadelphia about 1791, as his name as an engraver appears in that city in 1791–99, and in 1811–23. It can not be stated where he was in the interval 1800–10. In 1794, as a member of the firm of Thackara & Vallance, he was engraving in Philadelphia, and Edwin ascribes to Vallance the portrait of John Howard signed by this firm. But the stipple portrait of Hugh Blair, signed by Vallance alone, is the best example of his work seen; it is an excellent engraving. Vallance engraved a large number of encyclopedia plates and other general work of this description. He was one of the founders of the Association of Artists in America, organized in Philadelphia in 1794, and in 1810 he was treasurer of the Society of Artists, of the same city. He was for a time a member of the engraving firm of Tanner, Vallance, Kearny & Co., of Philadelphia. Vallance was an excellent script engraver, and good early bank-notes bear his name.

VALLÉE, Jean Rancois. Nothing is known of this artist except that he was painting fine miniatures in New Orleans about 1815. At that time he painted a miniature of General Andrew Jackson which the general pronounced the best portrait of him extant, and he presented it to Edward Livingston. Vallée was also known for his portrait painting. In 1826 he visited Boston, and in 1828 was painting a number of portraits there.

VAN BEEST, A. Marine painter. His picture "Engagement between the Constitution and the Guerriere" was sold recently in New York City.

VAN BOSKERCK, Robert W. Landscape painter. Born in Hoboken, N. J., in 1855. Pupil of R. Swain Gifford and A. H. Wyant in New York. Elected Associate Member of the National Academy of Design in 1897. Member: National Academy, 1907; Lotos Club; Artists' Aid Society. Awards: Silver medal, Pan-American Exposition, Buffalo, 1901; silver medal, St. Louis Exposition, 1904. Represented in the Union League and Lotos Club, New York; Layton Art Gallery, Milwaukee; Hamilton Club, Brooklyn. *Address,* 53 West 57th St., New York, N. Y.

VANCE, Fred Nelson. Mural p a i n t e r. Born in Crawfordsville, Ind., in 1880. Pupil

of Art Institute of Chicago; Smith Academy in Chicago; of Julien, Colarossi and Vitti academies in Paris; under Max Bohn in Paris; pupil of E. Vedder in Rome. *Address,* corner Plumb and Jefferson Sts., Crawfordsville, Ind.

VAN DEN HENGEL, Walter. Painter, who exhibited water colors at the Penna. Academy of the Fine Arts, Philadelphia, 1925. *Address,* 2095 North 63d St., Philadelphia.

VANDERLYN, John. Portrait and history painter. Born in Kingston, N. Y., in 1775; died there in 1852. Pupil of the famous Columbian Academy of Archibald Robertson, where, for three years, he attended the classes in the evenings, while in the daytime he was employed by Thomas Barrow who was the earliest art dealer in the city. Vanderlyn had early attracted the attention of Aaron Burr who had given him encouragement to pursue his art studies. About this time Gilbert Stuart returned to his native country and among his first portraits he painted those of Aaron Burr and Egbert Benson which Vanderlyn was allowed to copy. Gilbert Stuart had then left New York for Philadelphia and Burr sent young Vanderlyn to Stuart to get from him what instruction he could and if possible gain an entrance to his studio. Vanderlyn remained there nearly a year and then returned to New York to begin his professional career by painting portraits of Citizen Adet, the French Minister; also one of Albert Gallatin and of Theodosia Burr, the daughter of his patron, a girl of thirteen, with whom he promptly fell in love. In the fall of 1796, equipped with letters from Burr, Vanderlyn went to France and became a pupil of Vincent, exhibiting in the Paris Salon for the first time in 1800 several portraits of which he writes to his brother, Doctor Peter Vanderlyn, as follows: "One of the portraits of myself is thought a very strong likeness." This interesting self-portrait hangs in the Metropolitan Museum of Art. After five years in Paris Vanderlyn returned to his native country where he remained, however, only a couple of years, returning to Europe in 1803. There he met Washington Allston with whom he travelled, living with him in Rome. Here he painted his first historical picture, "The Massacre of Miss McCrea" by the Indians, an episode in the Revolutionary War in the Wyoming Valley, which was exhibited in the Salon of 1804 and is now in the Wadsworth Athenaeum at Hartford, Conn. He next painted his "Caius Marius amidst the Ruins of Carthage," which he took to Paris and exhibited in the Salon of 1808. This was chosen by Napoleon personally for the medal of honor, which was bestowed upon the painter by Baron Denon, the Director General of the Museums of France. In Paris Vanderlyn painted what is now supposed to be his greatest painting, "Ariadne Asleep in the Island of Naxos"; this was exhibited in the Paris Salon of 1810 and was considered the finest nude yet painted by an American; it is now in the

Penna. Academy of Fine Arts. He also painted a number of portraits for the City Hall, New York, and for a number of private commissioners. His portrait of Abraham Hasbrouck is considered one of his finest canvases, it being rich in color and having superior technical qualities. He was given one of the panels in the rotunda of the Capitol at Washington to fill and he also devoted himself to the paintings and exhibitions of panoramas, that of Versailles from his own hand being preserved in his native town as a memorial to his honor. He lived and died in poverty although he received many applications for painting portraits, a number of which he refused on account of his supersensitiveness and irritable nature. His work has frequently been confused with that of his master, Stuart, whose character he resembled in many particulars.

VANDERLYN, John (2d). Painter. Nephew of the artist and named for him. He was born in 1805; died in 1876. His identified work shows him to have been of very mediocre ability and that he was not an inheritor of his uncle's talents as a painter.

VANDERLYN, Pieter. Portrait painter. Member of one of the early Dutch families in New York State. Born in 1676; died in 1778. In 1719 he painted the portrait of Johannes Van Vechten and about forty of his portraits have been recognized as those of descendants of early Dutch families in this country. He was the grandfather of John Vanderlyn (1775–1852) the noted portrait painter.

VANDERPOEL, Emily Noyes (Mrs. John A.). Painter. Born in New York. Pupil of R. Swain Gifford and Wm. Sartain. Member: New York Water Color Club; National Association of Women Painters and Sculptors; National Art Club. Award: Bronze medal, Columbian Exposition, Chicago, 1893. Author of "Color Problems"; "Chronicles of a Pioneer School." *Address*, 22 Gramercy Park, New York, N. Y.

VANDERPOOL, Matilda. Painter. Born in Holland. Pupil of Art Institute of Chicago; also of David Ericson. Member: Chicago Water Color Club; Chicago Society of Artists; Cordon Club. *Address*, 9431 Pleasant Ave., Chicago, Ill.

VAN DER VEER, Mary. Painter. Born in Amsterdam, N. Y. Pupil of National Academy of Design under Edgar M. Ward and Will H. Low; of Philadelphia Art School under Chase; under Whistler in Paris; also studied in Holland. Member: New York Water Color Club; Plastic Club; National Association of Women Painters and Sculptors. Awards: Bronze medal, St. Louis Exposition, 1904; Shaw memorial prize, National Academy of Design, 1911. *Address*, Amsterdam, N. Y.

VAN DER WEYDEN, Harry. Painter. Born in Boston, Mass., in 1868. Pupil of Laurens, Lefebvre and Constant in Paris; Fred Brown in London. Member: Institute of Oil Painters, London. Awards: Third class medal, Paris Salon, 1891; second medal, International Exposition, Antwerp, 1894; gold medal, Atlanta Exposition, 1895; bronze medal, Paris Exposition, 1900; second gold medal, Munich, 1901; gold medal, Vienna, 1902; third medal, Liege Exposition, 1905. Work: "Christmas Eve," Art Institute of Chicago; pictures purchased by French Government, 1906 and 1908. *Address*, Rye, Sussex, England.

VANDINE, Elizabeth. Engraver. The Journals of the Continental Congress for June 7th, 1776, would indicate that this woman was a counterfeiter, the first on record in the colonies. With her husband, Henry Vandine, of Morris Co., Province of New Jersey, she was arrested for an attempt to counterfeit bills of credit emitted by Congress. She confessed that "with privity of her said husband she counterfeited several bills of the Continental Currency." For this offense and for passing the same, she and her husband were confined in the Morris County jail. The report does not enter into detail of the manufacture of these bills.

VAN DRESSER, William. Illustrator. Born in Memphis, Tenn., in 1871. Pupil of F. Luis Mora and Walter Appleton Clark. Member: Society of Illustrators, 1911. *Address*, 7 Reservoir Oval, Williamsbridge, New York City.

VAN DUZEE, Kate Keith. Painter. Born in Dubuque, Ia., in 1874. Pupil of Arthur Dow, John Johansen and Charles Woodbury. Member Chicago Arts and Crafts; Dubuque Artists' Association. Awards: Medals for water colors, Iowa State Fair, 1917, 1918; honorable mention for water color, St. Paul Institute, 1918; medal for monochromes and water colors, Iowa State Fair, 1919, 1920. Work: Oil painting in Dubuque Public Library. *Address*, 1471 Main St., Dubuque Ia.

VANDYCK, James. Miniature painter, who flourished about 1806–35.

VAN ELTEN, H. D. K. Landscape painter. Born in Holland in 1829, he came to New York in 1865. He was elected to the National Academy of Design in 1883. He died in 1904.

VAN GORDER, L. Emerson. Painter and illustrator. Born in Pittsburgh, Pa., in 1861. Pupil of Chase and C. Y. Turner in New York; École des Beaux Arts in Paris under Carolus-Duran; also studied in London. Member: New York Water Color Club; Toledo Tile Club. Work: "Quai Aux Fleurs," Museum of Art, Toledo. *Address*, 504 Euclid Ave., Toledo, Ohio.

VAN INGEN, W. B. Mural painter. Born in Philadelphia in 1858. Studied under Christian Schuessele and Thomas Eakins, Penna. Academy of Fine Arts; under John La Farge, Francis Lathrop and Louis C. Tiffany, New York; with Leon Bonnat, Paris, France. Work: Panels in the Congressional Library, Washington, D. C.; United States Mint, Philadelphia; State Capitol, Harrisburg, Pa.; State Capitol, Trenton, N. J.; United States Court House and Postoffice, Indianapolis and Chicago; etc. Commissioned by late Charles T. Yerkes to make a Japanese room for his New York residence, and in consequence he visited Japan and made extensive studies in Japanese art. Member: Fellowship, Penna. Academy of Fine Arts, Philadelphia; Architectural League, New York; Society of Mural Painters; Artists' Aid Society; Artists' Fund Society. Clubs: Lotos; Fencers; New York; Art Philadelphia. Lecturer on art and landscape architecture. *Address*, 60 Washington Mews, New York, N. Y.

VAN LAER, Alexander Theobald. Painter and lecturer. Born in Auburn, N. Y., in 1857; died in 1920. Studied art at National Academy of Design, New York, and at Art Students' League with R. Swain Gifford, and with George Poggenbeek of Holland. He has exhibited at the leading American exhibitions, and received bronze medal at the Charleston Exposition. Has lectured on art history at Chautauqua, N. Y., for seven years; also in free lecture courses of New York; lectured at Brooklyn Institute and before schools and colleges and in leading cities. Member: Jury of Selection and International Jury of Awards, St. Louis Exposition, 1904. Elected Associate Member of National Academy, 1902, and National Academy, 1909. Member: American Water Color Society; New York Water Color Club. Specialty, landscapes.

VAN LAER, Belle. Miniature painter. Born in Philadelphia in 1862. Pupil of S. J. Ferris. *Address*, Johnsville, Bucks County, Penna.

VAN NESS, Beatrice W. Painter, who exhibited at the Penna. Academy of the Fine Arts, Philadelphia, 1924. *Address*, 91 Francis St., Brookline, Mass.

VAN REUTH, Edward C. Painter. Born in Holland in 1836; died near Baltimore, Md., in 1924.

VAN ROEKENS, Paule V. Painter. Born in France in 1898. Pupil of Penna. Academy of the Fine Arts. *Address*, 1628 Chestnut St., Philadelphia.

VAN SCIVER, Pearl A. Painter, who exhibited water colors at the Penna. Academy of the Fine Arts, Philadelphia, 1925. *Address*, 1406 East Willow Grove Ave., Chestnut Hill, Philadelphia.

VAN SOELEN, Theodore. Painter. Born in St. Paul, Minn., in 1890. Pupil of Penna. Academy of the Fine Arts. *Address*, Chamber of Commerce Building, Albuquerque, N. M.

VAN SOLUN, Frank J. Painter and etcher. Born in St. Paul, Minn. *Address*, 1617 California St., San Francisco, Calif.

VAN VEEN, Pieter. Painter. Born in Holland in 1875. Studied in Holland and France. *Address*, 58 West 57th St., N. Y.

VAN WART, Ames. Sculptor. Born in New York. Pupil of Hiram Powers. Member of Century Association, New York. *Address*, Care of Century Association, 7 West 43d St., New York, N. Y.

VAN WERVEKE (George). Illustrator. Born in Chicago, Ill., in 1888. Illustrates for *New York Times, Scribner's,* and *Century. Address*, Atelier Building, 33 West 67th St., New York, N. Y.

VARIAN, George Edmund. Painter. Born in Liverpool, Eng., in 1865; died in 1923. Studied at Brooklyn Art Guild and Art Students' League, New York. Illustrator for various magazines and books. Commissioned by McClure's to visit Mont Pelee at time of destruction of St. Pierre, and in company with George Kennan and Prof. Angelo Heilprin was first to reach the crater at top of the mountain; he witnessed three eruptions of the mountain and was almost destroyed by one. He accompanied Ray Stannard Baker to Europe and made illustrations for his book, "Seen in Germany"; also illustrated George Kennan's "The Tragedy of Pelee." Exhibited at Paris Salon, 1907.

VARNUM, William Harrison. Painter and educator. Born in Cambridge, Mass., in 1878. Studied at Julien Academy, Paris, France, 1901; Mass. State Normal Art School, 1903; pupil of Woodbury, De Camp, etc. Instructor of Industrial Art, public schools of Boston and Cambridge, 1898–1903; professor of fine and applied arts, James Millikin University, Decatur, Ill., 1903–12; assistant professor of drawing and design, 1912–17, and associate professor since 1918, University of Wisconsin. Exhibited paintings at Milwaukee and Madison, Wis.; Boston, Mass., etc. Member: College Art Association; Western Drawing and Manual Training Association. Author: "Industrial Arts Design," 1916; "Teaching of Manual Arts," 1917. *Address*, 419 Sterling Court, Madison, Wis.

VAUDECHAMP, Jean Joseph. Painter. Born in France, 1790; died there in 1866. He exhibited in the Salon, Paris, 1817, and afterward. He resided in New Orleans for several years during the '30s and painted many fine portraits. In 1833 he had a studio as portrait painter at 147 Royal Street, New Orleans, La.

VAWTER, John William. Newspaper and book illustrator. Born in Virginia in 1871. *Address*, Nashville, Brown Co., Ind.

VEDDER, Elihu. Painter and illustrator of Omar Khayyam's "Rubaiyat." Born in New York, 1836; died in Rome on January 29, 1923, in his eighty-seventh year.

He was a descendant of an old Dutch family. He studied art first under T. H. Mattison at Sherburne, N. Y., and when twenty years old went to Paris and studied in the atelier of Picot. He later spent some time in Florence and Rome and returned in 1861 to New York, where he remained five years. He then went back to Paris for a year and thereafter made his home in Rome, paying an occasional visit to America.

Mr. Vedder's murals include five panels in the Library of Congress in Washington and one in Bowdoin College. His "Greek Actor's Daughter" was shown at the Centennial Exhibition in Philadelphia in 1876. He is represented in the Metropolitan, Brooklyn and Boston Museums, and in the Carnegie Institute. He was made a National Academician in 1865, and was a member of the American Society of Mural Painters, the American Academy of Arts and Letters and The Century Society, N. Y.

VER BECK, Frank. Illustrator. Born in Belmont County, Ohio, in 1858. Illustrator and author of "A Short Little Tale from Bruintown"; "Timothy Turtle's Great Day"; "The Donkey Child"; "The Little Cat Who Journeyed to St. Ives"; "Ver Beck's Book of Bears"; "The Elephant Child"; "The Little Lost Lamb," etc. Designer of the Ver Beck earthenware models. *Address*, Care of Curtis Brown, Ltd., 6 Henrietta St., London, England.

VERBEEK, Gustave. Painter and etcher. Born in Nagasaki, Japan, in 1867. Pupil of Constant, Laurens, Girardot, Blanc and Brush.

VER BRYCK, Cornelius. Landscape and historical painter. Born in New Jersey on January 1, 1813. He studied under Samuel F. B. Morse, and in 1839 he visited London. In 1833 his portrait was painted by Thomas Sully. He died in 1844.

VERGER, P. C. Engraver. The only known plate of Verger is "The Triumph of Liberty," a folio plate signed "Engraved by P. C. Verger" in 1796. Mr. Baker, in describing this plate, says that Verger was an engraver in New York and the preceptor of Benjamin Tanner. But Tanner was actually engraving in New York in 1794, two years before the name of "Peter Verger, engraver on fine stone," appears in the New York directory for the one year 1796. The contention of the writer is that Verger was not a copperplate engraver and that this plate was engraved in France for an American market, and was probably brought over here by Verger and published by him in New York.

Verger was an "engraver upon fine stone," an art demanding a very different training and entirely different methods from those required in engraving upon copper. Then the plate referred to is very well engraved, consumed a long time in its execution and is evidently the work of an expert engraver. It is hardly possible that a seal-engraver should be an equally good copperplate engraver. Nagler, in his "Kunstler-Lexicon," in speaking of Claude du Verger, a landscape painter of 1780, refers to "a younger Verger" who was an engraver on precious stones, working in Paris in 1806. May not this "younger Verger" be the "Peter Verger, engraver on fine stone," who was in New York in 1796 and then disappears from this country?

VERHEYDEN, Francois. Painter and etcher. Born in Hoeylaert, Belgium, in 1880. Pupil of Royal Academy of Brussels. *Address*, Provincetown, Mass.

VERNON, T. Engraver. Born in England, he there learned to engrave and did much work for the *London Art Journal* before he came to New York, about 1853. Vernon was chiefly employed here by the bank-note engraving companies, and he returned to England in 1856–57.

VERSTILLE, William. Miniature painter. Born about 1755; he died in Boston, Mass., 1803. He painted miniatures in Philadelphia in 1782 and later in Boston and Salem, Mass. His miniatures are recognized in nearly every instance by the piercing black eyes given to his subjects.

VETTER, Mrs. Cornelia C. Painter and etcher. Born in Hartford in 1881. Pupil of Robert Henri; of Andrada in Paris and Spain. Member of Conn. Academy of Fine Arts, Hartford. *Address*, 29 Huntington St., Hartford, Conn.

VEZIN, Charles. Painter. Born in Philadelphia, Pa., in 1858. Pupil of Art Students' League of New York under Du Mond, Chase, George Elmer Browne, Helen M. Turner and John Carlsen. Member: Art Students' League of New York; Salmagundi Club, 1902; Municipal Artists' Society; Yonkers Artists' Association; Art Alliance of America; National Art Club; Century Association. Award: Honorable mention, Society Washington Artists, 1914. *Address*, 409 Palisade Ave., Yonkers, N. Y.

VIAVANT, George. Painter. Native of New Orleans. Studied in Southern Art Union under Parelli. Diploma, New Orleans Cotton Centennial Exposition, 1884. Specialized in water color sketches of native birds and animals. Represented in Louisiana State Museum. He died in 1925 in New Orleans, La.

VICE, Herman Stoddard. Painter and illustrator. Born in Jefferson, Ind., in 1884. Pupil of Chicago Academy of Fine Arts. Member of Palette and Chisel Club, Chicago, Ill. *Address,* 56 East Congress St., Chicago, Ill.

VICKERS, S. J. Painter. Born in Middlefield, Otsego County, N. Y., in 1872. Among other things he designed subway stations and ornamental elevated structures of the rapid transit system of New York. *Address,* Grand-View-on-Hudson, New York.

VICTOR, Sophie. Painter, who exhibited at the Penna. Academy of the Fine Arts, Philadelphia, 1924.

VIGNIER, A. Dunlap records him as painting landscapes in Philadelphia in 1811.

VINCENT, Harry A. Painter. Born in Chicago in 1864. He was elected an Associate Member of the National Academy of Design. Member of the New York Water Color Club. His painting ''Rockport Harbor'' is in Butler Art Institute, Youngstown, Ohio. He exhibited in the Annual Exhibition, 1925, of the National Academy, New York. *Address,* Rockport, Mass.

VINTON, Frederick P. Painter. Born in Bangor, Maine, in 1846; died in Boston, Mass., in 1911. His specialty was portraiture. He was a pupil of William Hunt and Dr. Rimmer in Boston, and of Leon Bonnat and Jean Paul Laurens in Paris. He also studied in the Royal Academy of Bavaria under Mauger and Dietz. Honorable mention in Paris Salon, 1890. Elected Member of the National Academy of Design in 1891. A memorial exhibition of his work was held after his death in 1911 at the Boston Museum of Fine Arts, of 124 of his paintings, about fifty of them being portraits. As a painter of men he was at his best and many statesmen, jurists, authors and professional men were among his sitters. For life of Frederick P. Vinton see ''New England Artists,'' by Frank T. Robinson.

VINTON, L. Hazlehurst. Painter. Born in Boston, Mass., in 1881. Pupil of S. Simi in Florence; also of R. Collin and Richard Miller in Paris. *Address,* 51 West 12th St., New York, N. Y.

VINTON-BROWN, Pamela. Painter. Born in Boston, Mass., in 1884. Pupil of Collin and Courtois in Paris; of Edwin Whiteman in Baltimore. Member: French Miniature Society; Deutsche Werkbund. Award: Honorable mention, miniature section, Exhibition American Woman's Work, Paris, 1914. *Address,* 51 West 12th St., New York, N. Y.

VIVIAN, Calthea. Painter and etcher. Born in Fayette, Mo. Pupil of Arthur Mathews; also of Lazar and Colarossi Academy in Paris.

Member: San Francisco Artists' Association; San Francisco Society of Etchers; Laguna Beach Artists' Association; California Artists' Association. Represented in Palace of Fine Arts, San Francisco; Arkansas Auditorium Gallery. *Address,* Hotel Claremont, Berkeley, Calif.

VOGNILD, Edna (Mrs. Enoch). Painter. Born in Chicago. Pupil of Art Institute of Chicago; also of Hawthorne, J. C. Johansen, H. B. Snell, and of Colarossi and Delecluse Academies in Paris. *Address,* 22 Tooker Place, Chicago, Ill.

VOGNILD, Enoch M. Painter. Born in Chicago in 1880. Pupil of Art Institute of Chicago under Johansen and Vanderpoel; in summer under Woodbury; also studied in Julien and Delecluse Academies in Paris. Member: Art Students' League of Chicago; The Round Table; Chicago Art Club; Chicago Arts and Crafts; Chicago Society of Artists. Awarded Municipal Art League prize, 1906. *Address,* 22 Tooker Place, Chicago, Ill.

VOGT, L. C. Painter. Born in Cincinnati in 1864. Pupil of H. Siddons Mowbray and Frank Duveneck. Member: Cincinnati Art Club. Represented by three water colors in Cincinnati Museum. *Address,* 141 East Fourth St., Cincinnati.

VOLK, Douglas. Painter. Born at Pittsfield, Mass., in 1856. When fourteen years of age he accompanied his parents to Rome where he became interested in painting and studied in the Saint Luke Academy. In 1873 he studied in Paris with Gerome. In 1875 his painting ''In Brittany'' was exhibited in the Salon in Paris. On his return to this country he became instructor in the Cooper Institute, New York. He has been awarded many medals and prizes. In 1898 he was elected an Associate Member of the National Academy of Design and in 1899 an Academician. Mr. Volk is a figure painter, but his landscape backgrounds of pine forests show skill in handling. He is also a member of the ''can Federation of Arts and the National Society of Portrait Painters. His painting ''With Malice Towards None'' (Portrait of Abraham Lincoln) was exhibited in the Centennial Exhibition of the National Academy of Design, 1925. He is also represented in the Metropolitan Museum by his portrait of Felix Adler. *Address,* 119 East 19th St., New York City.

VOLK, Leonard Wells. Sculptor. Born in New York State in 1828. In 1855 he was sent abroad for study. On returning in 1857 he settled in Chicago. He executed many busts and statues of prominent men. Among his works are the life-size statue of Stephen Douglass in marble, and a portrait bust of Abraham Lincoln.

VOLKERT, Edward Charles. P a i n t e r.
Born in Cincinnati, Ohio, in 1871. Pupil of
Frank Duveneck in Cincinnati and of the Art
Students' League of New York. Member of
New York Water Color Club. Elected an Asso-
ciate Member of the National Academy of De-
sign. Mr. Volkert is well known for his land-
scape painting with cattle. *Address*, Lyme,
Conn.

VOLLMERING, Jos. Born in Anholt,
Westphalia, in 1810; died in New York City in
1887. He studied in Amsterdam and in 1847
he removed to New York and opened his studio
in that city. Elected an Associate Member of
National Academy in 1853. Landscape and
Winter-Scene in the Bryan Collection, New
York Historical Society.

VOLOZON, Denis A. Landscape painter
and portrait draughtsman in crayons. Volozon
was a Frenchman who settled in Philadelphia,
exhibited at the Academy and taught drawing
there. He also made historical compositions.
His crayon of George Washington is in the
Penna. Academy of the Fine Arts. He was
working in Philadelphia in 1811-20.

VON DER LANCKEN, Frank. Painter,
sculptor and illustrator. Born in Brooklyn, N.
Y., in 1872. Pupil of Pratt Institute under
Herbert Adams and Art Students' League, N.
Y., under Mowbray. Studied in Julien Acad-
emy in Paris. Member of Rochester Art Club.
Address, 102 Aberdeen St., Rochester, N. Y.

VONDROUS, John C. Painter, illustrator
and etcher. Born in Bohemia in 1884. Pupil
of National Academy of Design, New York.
Represented in Art Institute in Chicago; New
York Public Library; Fogg Museum, Cambridge, Mass. *Address*, 179 East 79th St., New
York.

VON HOFSTEN, H. I l l u s t r a t o r and
painter. Born in Sweden in 1865. Pupil of
Royal Academy at Stockholm under M. E.
Winge, O. Aborelius and A. Larson. Organizer
of the Forestry Painters of Chicago. Awarded
first water color prize, Swedish American Artists. *Address*, Winnetka, Ill.

VONNOH, Bessie Potter. Sculptor. Born
in St. Louis, Mo., in 1872. Studied sculpture in
the Art Institute of Chicago for three years
under Lorado Taft; otherwise is self-taught.
Her specialty is statuettes of women and children. Received bronze medal, Paris Exposition
of 1900; gold medal, St. Louis World's Fair.
Member: National Sculpture Society; Associate
Member, National Academy of Design. Represented by sculptural works in Metropolitan Museum of Art, New York, and other museums.
Married Robert W. Vonnoh, portrait painter, in
1899. Represented in Capitol, Washington, D.
C., by portrait bust of James S. Sherman. *Address*, 33 West 67th St., New York.

VONNOH, Robert. Painter. Born in Hartford, Conn., in 1858. Instructor of painting,
Cowles Art School, 1884-85; principal, E. Boston Evening Drawing School; principal instructor of portrait and figure painting, Museum of Fine Arts, Boston, 1885-87; instructor
at the Penna. Academy of the Fine Arts, Philadelphia, 1891-96. Exhibitor in Paris Salon,
and in London and Munich exhibitions; Paris
Exposition, 1899-1900; Chicago Exposition,
1893; Stockholm, 1896; Buffalo Exposition,
1901; St. Louis Exposition, 1904; also in other
exhibitions in New York, Philadelphia, Pittsburgh, Boston, Chicago, etc.; lived abroad,
1907-11. Member National Jury of American
Sect., Paris, 1900; International juries, Carnegie Exposition, Pittsburgh; International
Jury of Awards, St. Louis Exposition. Received Thomas R. Proctor portrait prize, National Academy of Design; gold medal, Charleston Exposition; gold medal, Panama P. I. Exposition; medals at Boston, Buffalo, Chicago,
Paris, etc. Represented in Penna. Academy of
the Fine Arts; Mass. Historical Society; ''The
White House,'' Washington; American Philos.
Society, etc. Elected member of National
Academy, 1906. Member: Secession (Munich);
Society of American Artists; Society of American Portrait Painters; Architectural League
of America; Allied Artists, America; Society
of Independent Artists. Instructor, composition class, Penna. Academy of Fine Arts, 1918-
1919; instructor, painting life figure, 1919-20.
Address, 145 East 23d St., New York, N. Y.

VON SALTZA, Carl F. Portrait painter.
Born in Sweden in 1858. Studied in Paris. He
came to the United States in 1891, and for
years was an instructor and teacher. Later
he spent some time in Cleveland painting portraits. He died in New York in 1905.

VON SCHNEIDAU, C. Painter. Born in
Sweden in 1893. Pupil of J. Wellington Rey-
nolds; K. A. Buehr; H. M. Walcott; C. W.
Hawthorne; Richard Miller. Member: Art
Students' League of Chicago; Chicago Swedish
Art Club; California Art Club; Laguna Beach
Artists' Association; Beachcombers' Club,
Provincetown. Awards: First prize, Art In-
stitute of Chicago, 1915; John Quincy Adams
traveling scholarship, Art Institute of Chicago,
1916; second prize for portrait, Minn. State
Fair, 1916; first prize for portrait, Swedish-
American Exhibition, Chicago, 1917; gold
medal, California State Fair, 1919; second
prize, California State Fair, 1920; second prize,
Swedish Club, Chicago, 1920. *Address*, Care
of Los Angeles Athletic Club, Los Angeles,
Calif.

VON SCHOLLEY, Ruth. Painter, who exhibited at the Penna. Academy of the Fine
Arts, Philadelphia, 1924. *Address*, 132 Riverway, Boston, Mass.

VOORHEES, Clark Greenwood. Painter. Born in New York in 1871. Graduated at Yale, 1891; Columbia, 1894; studied art at Academie Julien, Paris. Has exhibited at the National Academy of Design, New York; Carnegie Institute, Pittsburgh, Pa.; Academy of Fine Arts; Art Institute of Chicago, etc. Awarded Hallgarten prize, National Academy, 1905; bronze medal, St. Louis Exposition, 1904. *Address*, Lyme, Conn.

VOS, Hubert. Painter. Born in Maastricht, Holland, in 1855. Pupil of Academy of Fine Arts in Brussels; under Cormon in Paris. Awards: Gold medals, Paris, Amsterdam, Munich, Dresden and Brussels, etc. Specialty, types of aboriginal races, portraits and interiors. *Address*, 15 West 67th St., New York, N. Y.

VREELAND, Elizabeth L. W. (Mrs. F. K.). Painter. Born in India in 1896. Studied in New York, London, Paris and Norway. *Address*, 228 Orange Road, Montclair, N. J.

VUILLEMENOT, Fred A. Painter, sculptor and illustrator. Born in France in 1890. Member of Art Alliance of America. *Address*, Artklan Studio, Meredith Building, Ontario St., Toledo, Ohio.

VYSEKAL, Edouard A. Painter, Born in Kutna Hora, Czechoslovakia, in 1890. Pupil of Harry M. Walcott; S. Macdonald Wright. Member: California Art Club; Chicago Palette and Chisel Club. Work: "The Conquest of the Desert," Barbara Worth Hotel, El Centro, Calif.; "Korean," in Mission Inn, Riverside, Calif. *Address*, 1945 Magnolia Ave., Los Angeles, Calif.

VYSEKAL, Ella Buchanan (Mrs. E. A.). Painter. Born in Le Mars, Ia. Pupil of S. Macdonald Wright, Harry M. Walcott and Ralph Clarkson. Member of California Art Club. Work: Portrait of Christian Hoffman, in State Historical Building, Topeka, Kans. *Address*, 1945 Magnolia Ave., Los Angeles, Calif.

W

WACHTEL, Elmer. Painter. Born in Baltimore in 1864. Member of "Ten Painters," of Los Angeles, Calif. *Address*, 315 West Ave. 43, Los Angeles, Calif.

WACHTEL, Marion Kavanaugh (Mrs. Elmer). Painter. Born in Milwaukee in 1875. Pupil of Art Institute of Chicago; studied under Chase. Member of "Ten Painters," of Los Angeles; New York Water Color Club. Work: "Eucalyptus at Evening," California State Building; "San Gabriel Cañon," Friday Morning Club, Los Angeles. *Address*, 315 West Ave. 43, Los Angeles, Calif.

WACK, H. W. Painter and illustrator. Born in Baltimore, Md., in 1873. Pupil of Leon Dabo, N. R. Brewer, H. Salem Hubbell and Frank Spenlove. Member of New York League of Painters. *Address*, 130 West 57th St., New York.

WACKERMAN, Dorothy. Painter. Born in Cleveland, Ohio, in 1899. Specialty, landscapes and mural paintings. *Address*, 1615 Fourth St., Minneapolis, Minn.

WADE, Caroline D. Painter. Born in Chicago. Pupil of Art Institute of Chicago; under Courtois in Paris. Member of Chicago Society of Artists. *Address*, 59 East Van Buren St., Chicago, Ill.

WADE, J. H. Portrait painter. From 1810 to 1823 he was painting in Cleveland, Ohio, and through the southern states.

WADSWORTH, Adelaide E. Painter. Born in Boston in 1844. Pupil of Wm. M. Hunt, Frank Duveneck, John Twachtman, C. H. Woodbury and Arthur Dow. Member of Copley Society, Boston, 1894.

WADSWORTH, Frank R. Painter. Born in Chicago, Ill., in 1874. Pupil of Chicago Art Institute where he won several prizes. He was a member of the Chicago Society of Artists and died in Spain in 1905, where he was painting with William Chase's summer class.

WADSWORTH, Wedworth. Landscape painter and illustrator. Born in Buffalo, N. Y., in 1846. Member: New York Water Color Club; Salmagundi Club, 1890; Brooklyn Art Club. Author and illustrator of "Leaves from an Artist's Field Book"; illustrated "The Song of the Brook," "A Winter's Walk with Cowper," "Under the Greenwood Tree with Shakespeare," "Through Wood and Field with Tennyson," etc. *Address*, Durham, Conn.

WAGENHALS, Katherine H. Painter. Born in Ebensburg, Pa., in 1883. Pupil of Art Department of Smith College; Art Students' League of New York; Academie Moderne in Paris. Award: Art Association prize, Herron Art Institute, 1916. Work: "The Visitor," Herron Art Institute, Indianapolis. *Address,* 2124 Sunset Blvd., San Diego, California.

WAGNER, Edward Q. Painter and sculptor. Born in 1855; died in Detroit, Mich., in 1922. He did much of the sculptural work at the World's Fair, Chicago, 1904, and spent five years working for the Brazilian Government in Rio de Janeiro.

WAGNER, Frank Hugh. Painter, sculptor and illustrator. Born in Milton, Wayne County, Ind., in 1870. Pupil of Freer, Vanderpoel and Von Salza. Member: Chicago Palette and Chisel Club; Indiana Artists' Association; Richmond Artists' Association; Indiana Traveling Artists' Association; Alumni Association, Art Institute of Chicago. Work: "Adoration of the Magi," St. Joseph's Chapel, West Pullman, Ill.; "Portrait C. W. Hargrave" and "Portrait of A. Kate Huron," Chapel Hall, Danville, Ind. *Address,* Care Pine Crest Inn, Saugatauk, Mich.

WAGNER, Fred. Painter. Born in Valley Forge, Pa., in 1864. Pupil of Penna. Academy of the Fine Arts. Member of the Philadelphia Water Color Club. Awarded Fellowship prize, Pa. Academy of the Fine Arts, 1914. Work: "Addingham-Winter," Penna. Academy; "Along the Canal," Philadelphia Art Club; "Winter Evening," Reading Art Museum. Instructor at Penna. Academy of the Fine Arts Summer School, Chester Springs, Pa. *Address,* 1520 Chestnut St., Philadelphia.

WAGNER, H. S. Engraver. About 1850 H. S. Wagner was engraving portraits in mezzotint and also publishing portraits in Philadelphia. These portraits were largely those of clergymen.

WAGNER, Mary North. Painter, sculptor and illustrator. Born in Milford, Ind., in 1875. Pupil of John Vanderpoel, Charles Francis Browne, Mary S. West, Louis J. Millet, C. J. Mulligan and W. M. Chase. Member: Ind. Society of Artists; Richmond Artists' Association; Alumni Association, Art Institute of Chicago; Ind. Society of Artists. Work: Four drawings for the "Second Brownie Book," by Mrs. Alpha B. Benson. *Address,* Care Pine Crest Inn, Saugatauk, Mich.

WAGNER, Rob. Painter and illustrator. Born in Detroit, Mich., in 1872. Pupil of Julien Academy in Paris. Member of California Art Club. Awarded silver medal, Alaska-Yukon Pacific Exposition, Seattle, 1909; bronze medal,

Panama-Pacific Exposition, San Francisco, 1915. *Address,* 226 Isabel St., Los Angeles, Calif.

WAGNER, William. Seal-engraver residing in York, Penna., in 1820–35. He made a few crude attempts at engraving on copper; his plates included a portrait of Rubens and a view of York Springs. He was treasurer of the New York High School in 1835.

WAGSTAFF, C. E. This engraver of portraits in stipple was working in Boston about 1840–45. He was an associate of Joseph Andrews for some time.

WAITE, Emily B. Painter. Born in Worcester, Mass., in 1887. Pupil of Art Students' League, New York; also studied abroad. Member of Concord Art Association. Specialty, portraiture. *Address,* 104 West 40th St., New York.

WAKEMAN, Robert C. Sculptor. Born in Norwalk, Conn., in 1889. He studied at the Yale School of Fine Arts. He painted a portrait of Dr. Lively.

WALCOTT, Harry M. Painter. Born in Torringford, Conn., in 1870. Pupil of National Academy of Design, New York, and of the Julien Academy under Constant in Paris. Elected an Associate Member of the National Academy of Design, N. Y. His painting "School's Out" was exhibited at the Centennial Exhibition of the National Academy in 1925.

WALDECK, Carl Gustav. Portrait painter. Born in St. Charles, Mo., in 1866. Student of St. Louis School of Fine Arts and later at Academie Julien, Paris, under Jean Paul Laurens and Benjamin Constant. He established a studio in St. Louis, 1887; organized first exhibition at Photographers' Association of America, Wshington, 1890; awarded 1st prize for black and white drawings; bronze medal, St. Louis Exposition, 1904; silver medal, Portland (Ore.) Exposition, 1905; gold medal, Mo. State Exposition, 1913; Brown prize, St. Louis Artists' Guild, 1914; Fine Arts prize, Society of Western Artists, Indianapolis, 1914; 1st prize, St. Louis Artists' League, 1915. Officier d'-Academie, Paris, France, 1904. Member: Society of Western Artists; St. Louis Artists' League; American Art Association; Society of Ozark Painters. *Address,* Marina Building, Grand and Lindell Ave., St. Louis, Mo.

WALDEN, Lionel. Painter. Born in Norwich, Conn., in 1861. Studied with Carolus-Duran, Paris. Second-class medal, Crystal Palace, London; honorable mention, Salon, Paris; silver medal, Paris Exposition, 1900; third class medal, Salon, 1903. Represented in Luxembourg Gallery, Paris; Memorial Museum, Philadelphia, and in Cardiff, Wales; silver medal, Panama-P. I. Exposition, 1915. Member: Societé Internationale de Peinture et Sculpture; Paris Society of American Painters; National Institute of Arts and Letters. Chevalier, Legion of Honor of France, 1910. *Address*, Honolulu, Hawaii.

WALDO, Samuel Lovett. Portrait painter. Born in Windham, Conn., in 1783. Studied with Stewart, a portrait painter, at Hartford, Conn., and practised his profession at Charleston, S. C. In 1806 he went to London and studied at the Royal Academy and with West and Copley. In 1809 he settled in New York and in 1812 William Jewett came to him as a pupil and later formed a partnership with him to paint portraits jointly. He is represented at the Metropolitan Museum of New York by a self-portrait; his portrait of his wife Deliverance Mapes Waldo, painted in 1826; also by his life-sketch of General Andrew Jackson, painted in 1817. He also painted George Washington Parke Custis, David C. Colden, William Steele, Joseph M. White and R. G. Livingston De Peyster. Waldo died in New York City in 1861.

WALDO & JEWETT Samuel L. Waldo. Born in 1783; died in 1861. Elected Associate Member of the National Academy. William Jewett was born in 1795 and died in 1874. They painted portraits together in New York City for eighteen consecutive years. Their work is owned by the city of New York, the Metropolitan Museum and by a number of the prominent Art Galleries throughout the country.

WALDRON, Anne A. Painter, who exhibited water colors at the Penna. Academy of the Fine Arts, Philadelphia, 1925. *Address*, Bishop Place, New Brunswick, N. J.

WALES, George C. Etcher. Born in Boston in 1868. He studied architecture and later devoted his time to the etching of sailing ships, in which he has been most successful.

WALES, James Albert. Caricaturist and engraver. Born in 1852; died in 1886. After leaving school he studied with a wood-engraver in Toledo, but being clever at portraiture he began drawing for the illustrated newspapers; some of his best work appeared in *Puck* and *Judge*. He was a founder and chief cartoonist of the latter periodical.

WALES, Orlando G. Painter. Born in Philadelphia, Pa. Pupil of Wm. M. Chase; also of Alphonse Mucha. Member: Fellowship of the Penna. Academy of the Fine Arts; Salmagundi Club, 1908. *Address*, 832 Hamilton St., Allentown, Pa.

WALES, Susan M. L. Landscape painter. Born in Boston, Mass., in 1839. Pupil of Boston Museum School; Vincente Poveda in Rome; under Bloomers in Holland. Member

of Boston Water Color Club. *Address*, 341 Marlboro St., Boston, Mass.

WALKER, A. B. Illustrator. Born in Binghamton, N. Y., in 1878. Pupil of Kenyon Cox, Bryson Burroughs, Charles Curran and F. V. Du Mond. Member: Society of Illustrators. Produced illustrations and humorous ideas for *Life, Judge, Harper's Weekly, Harper's Bazaar, Scribner's, Century*, etc. *Address*, 253 Barclay St., Flushing, N. Y.

WALKER, Charles Alvah. Painter, engraver and etcher. Born in 1848 in London, New Hampshire. He engraved on wood and steel, his plate after Daubigny being exhibited at the Paris Salon. Later he turned to painting in water color and oil. He exhibited in the Boston Art Club, and served as its vice-president. He died in Brookline, Mass., in 1925.

WALKER, Dugald Stewart. Illustrator and painter. Born in Richmond, Va. Studied under Anne Fletcher and Harriotte Taliaferro Montague in Richmond; under Graham Cootes at the Summer School of University of Virginia; at the New York School of Art; also at Art Students' League of New York. Work: Illustrated "Hans Anderson's Fairy Tales," "Stories for Pictures," "The Gentlest Giant," etc. *Address*, 30 East 57th St., New York, N. Y.

WALKER, Ferdinand G. Painter. Born in Mitchell, Ind., in 1859. Pupil of Dagnan-Bouveret, Puvis de Chavannes, Blanche and Merson in Paris. Member: Society of Indiana Artists; Louisville Artists' Association; Chicago Arts and Crafts. Portraits in Kentucky State Historical Society Collection; University of Kentucky at Lexington; Berea College; Agricultural College of Michigan; Lincoln Institute, Simpsonville, Ky.; Kentucky State Collection at Frankfort; State House, Indianapolis, Ind.; Public Library, Jefferson Davis Memorial, New Albany, Ind., and in other places; also represented by landscapes in the public galleries at New Albany, Ind., and Lexington, Ky., and by two murals in St. Peter's Church, Louisville, Ky. *Address*, 308 Commercial Building, Louisville, Ky.

WALKER, Henry Oliver. Painter. Born in Boston in 1843. He began life in commercial pursuits in that city. His sympathy with art led him to take it up finally as a life profession, and he went to Paris in the early eighties to become a pupil of M. Bonnat. Returning to the United States, he at first took a studio in Boston, and held a very successful exhibition of his work. A few years later he came to New York, and has been for a decade well known to the art public. He is a member of the Society of

American Artists and of the National Academy. At the exhibition of the latter institution in 1895 he was awarded the Clarke prize for ''A Morning Vision.'' In 1894 at the Society of American Artists he obtained the Shaw Fund prize for ''The Singers.'' These compositions, like ''The Boy and the Muse,'' another celebrated picture from his easel, are remarkable for graceful, accurate drawing, refined color quality, and beauty of ensemble. Mr. Walker, apart from his reputation as a painter of easel pictures, is well known for his important achievements in mural painting. He executed a series of compositions and single figures illustrative of lyric poetry for the Congressional Library at Washington, and has recently completed an important piece of work for the new Appellate Court building, New York. Mr. Walker received a medal and diploma for his work exhibited at the World's Fair at Chicago in 1893. He has his studio in New York. *Address*, Belmont, Mass.

WALKER, James. Painter. Born in Enggland in 1819; died in Watsonville, Calif., in 1889. He was brought to New York City as a child, where his residence remained during the larger portion of his life. When a young man he resided for one winter in the city of New Orleans. At the breaking out of the Mexican War he was a resident of the city of Mexico, where he remained hidden for six weeks after the Mexican commander had issued an edict banishing all American residents to a distance of 300 miles in the interior. Afterwards escaping to the lines of the American Army, he served as an interpreter, accompanying the Army to the city from which he had so recently fled. He was with the Army during the battle of the valley, and remained during its occupation of the Mexican capital. After an absence of eight years he returned to New York (in 1848). He subsequently visited South America, and established a studio in New York in 1850. His residence continued in that city until 1884, with exceptions of brief intervals spent in other cities. In 1857-58 he was in Washington, and again for a brief period in 1883. In 1884 he removed to San Francisco, Calif., to execute a large French battle picture for a private gallery. His work was principally large battle paintings. Among the most prominent of these are the ''Battle of Chapultepec,'' ''Battle of Lookout Mountain'' and ''Battle of Gettysburg.'' The commission for the ''Battle of Lookout Mountain'' was given by Gen. Hooker. His painting ''The Battle of Chapultepec'' is in the Capitol in Washington, D. C.

WALKER, Horatio. Painter. Born in Listowel, Ontario, Canada. He studied miniature painting under J. A. Fraser of Toronto. In 1885 he came to New York City to study

painting. He was awarded the gold medal for competitive exhibition of the American Art Galleries in 1887; Evans prize of the American Water Color Society in 1888; bronze medal, Paris Exposition, 1889; gold medal, Columbian Exposition, Chicago, 1903; medal of honor at the Penna. Academy of the Fine Arts, 1906. He was elected a member of the National Academy of Design in 1891; also a member of the American Water Color Society. He is represented in the collections of the Metropolitan Museum, New York; Corcoran Art Gallery of Washington, D. C.; City Museum, St. Louis; National Gallery, Washington; Carnegie Institute, Pittsburgh. Walker paints the peasant types on the St. Lawrence River which he portrays with rich color. In 1901 he exhibited at the Royal Academy in London, and his work was well received in England. For life of Walker, see ''American Masters of Painting,'' also ''Story of American Painting,'' by Charles Caffin. *Address*, Care of Ferargil Galleries, New York City.

WALKER, Nellie V. Sculptor. Born in Red Oak, Ia., in 1874. Pupil of Art Institute of Chicago under Lorado Taft. Member: National Sculpture Society, 1911; Chicago Society of Artists. Awards: First Chicago Municipal Art League prize, 1907; second Grower prize, Art Institute of Chicago, 1908; Shaffer prize, Art Institute of Chicago, 1911. Work: ''Stratton Memorial,'' Colorado Springs, Colo.; portrait statue of ''Senator Harlan,'' Washington; ''Her Son,'' ideal group, Art Institute of Chicago; ''Chief Keokuk,'' Keokuk, Ia. *Address*, The Midway Studios, 6016 Ellis Ave., Chicago, Ill.

WALKER, Sophia A. Painter, sculptor and etcher. Born in Rockland, Mass., in 1855. Pupil of Lefebvre in Paris; under Mowbray and Chase in New York. Member of National Art Club. Painted ''Portrait of E. B. Woodward,'' State Normal School, Bridgewater, Mass. *Address*, 70 West 49th St., New York, N. Y.

WALKER, William H. Cartoonist. Born in Pittston, Pa., in 1871. Pupil of Art Students' League of New York. Member: Society of Illustrators, 1909; Guild of Free Lance Artists. Contributor to *Life* since 1898. Specialty, political subjects. *Address*, 336 Sanford Ave., Flushing, L. I., N. Y.

WALKLEY, David B. Painter. Born in Rome, Ohio, in 1849. Pupil of Julien Academy; Penna. Academy of Fine Arts. Member of Salmagundi Club, 1903, New York. *Address*, Rock Creek, Ohio.

WALKOWITZ, Abraham. Painter and etcher. Born in Tuiemen, Siberia, Russia, in 1880. Pupil of National Academy of Design under Ward, Maynard and F. C. Jones in New

York; of Julien Academy in Paris under Laurens. Member of Paris Allied Artists' Association. *Address,* 12 Union Square, New York, N. Y.

WALL, A. Bryan. Painter. Born in Allegheny City, Penna. Member of American Art Society and Philadelphia Art Club. Exhibited "Feeding Homeward" in Carnegie Institute, Pittsburgh. *Address,* 814 Arch St., Pittsburgh, Penna.

WALL, William Allen. Painter. Born in New Bedford, Mass., in 1801. He was apprenticed to a watchmaker, but early turned his attention to painting. He studied with Thomas Sully, and went to Europe in 1831. He returned to New Bedford in 1833. About 1840 he copied Stuart's "Lansdowne Washington"; his portrait of N. P. Willis, painted in Italy, is in the New York Historical Society. He died in New Bedford, Mass., in 1885. Several of his portraits are owned by Dartmouth College, Hanover, New Hampshire.

WALL, William G. Painter. Born in Scotland in 1792. He painted landscapes in New York in 1818 where he began his career as an artist, painting views of the Hudson River. He was elected a member of the National Academy, New York, in 1826.

WALLER, Frank. Painter. Born in New York in 1842; died in 1923. Formerly engaged as architect; became a painter after 1903. Fellow of Academy of Design, New York; has been president of Art Students' League of New York, which he incorporated; was honorable sec. Egypt Exploration Fund Society and of Ur Exploration Society; honorable life fellow, Metropolitan Museum of Art. Wrote: "Report on Art Schools," 1879; also first report Art Students' League, 1886.

WALSH, Elizabeth M. Painter. Born in Lowell, Mass. Pupil of Boston Museum of Fine Arts. Member of Concord Art Association. Address, 419 Andover St., Lowell, Mass.

WALTER, Adam B. Engraver. Born in Philadelphia in 1820; died there in 1875. Walter was a pupil of Thomas B. Welch, and he was associated with Welch in the engraving business until 1848. He was an excellent engraver of portraits, chiefly executed in mezzotint.

WALTER, Christian J. Landscape painter. Born in Pittsburgh, Pa., in 1872. Member of Associated Artists of Pittsburgh. *Address,* 809 Penn Building, Pittsburgh, Pa.

WALTER, Edgar. Sculptor. Born in San Francisco, Calif., in 1877. Studied at the Mark Hopkins Institute of Art, San Francisco, and later studied in Paris. *Address,* 1803 Franklin St., San Francisco, Calif.

WALTER, Martha. Painter. Born in Philadelphia, Pa. Studied art in the Philadelphia Art School, Penna. Academy of the Fine Arts, and with William M. Chase. Studied in Paris at the Julien Academy and the Grande Chaumiere in Paris.

Miss Walter has won many prizes and was the winner of the first award of the Cresson traveling scholarship in 1908; she also studied in Germany, Holland, Italy and Spain. She had a studio in Paris, and exhibited in the Paris Salon. In 1909 she won the "Mary Smith prize" for the best work by a woman painter. Her paintings of children are particularly happy. Represented in Toledo Museum, Ohio, and in permanent collection of the Penna. Academy of Fine Arts. *Address,* Care of the Milch Galleries, New York City.

WALTER, Valerie. Sculptor. Born in Baltimore, Md. She studied at the Maryland Institute, Baltimore, Md., and in Paris. Specialty, portrait busts. *Address,* 17 East 59th St., New York City.

WALTERS, Emile. Painter. Born in 1863. Pupil of Chicago Art Institute, and of the Pennsylvania Academy of the Fine Arts. Exhibits at National Academy of Design, New York. *Address,* 47 Fifth Ave., New York, N. Y.

WALTERS, John. Miniature painter, who flourished about 1784 in Philadelphia.

WALTMAN, Harry Franklin. Painter. Born in Ohio in 1871. Pupil of Constant and Laurens in Paris. Awarded Isidor prize, Salmagundi Club, 1916. Elected Associate Member of the National Academy, 1917; Allied Artists' Association; National Art Club, N. Y. *Address,* 428 Lafayette St., New York, N. Y.

WALTON, Florence L. Painter. Born in East Orange, N. J., in 1889. Pupil of George Bellows. *Address,* 18 East 8th St., New York, N. Y.

WANDS, Alfred J. Painter, who exhibited at the Penna. Academy of the Fine Arts, Philadelphia, 1926. *Address,* 11304 Itaska Ave., Cleveland, Ohio.

WARD, Edgar Melville. Painter. Born in Ohio in 1839. He studied in the National Academy in 1870 and in Paris 1872-78. His best known paintings were "Paternal Pride," "Lace Makers," and "Brittany Washerwomen," which was shown at the Paris Salon, 1876, and in the Philadelphia Centennial. His studio was in New York. He was elected a member of the National Academy in 1915. He died in New York, 1915.

WARD, E. F. Painter and illustrator. Born in White Plains, N. Y., in 1892. Pupil of Edward Dufner, George Bridgman and

Thomas Fogarty. Member of Guild of Free Lance Artists. Made illustrations for *Saturday Evening Post, Pictorial Review, Red Book, Woman's Home Companion*. *Address,* 33½ Court St., White Plains, N. Y.

WARD, Elsie. Sculptor. Pupil of Saint Gaudens, who practices her profession in Denver, Colo.

WARD, Irving. Portrait and landscape painter. Born in 1867. Member of Baltimore Charcoal Club. He died at his home in Baltimore, Md., in 1924.

WARD, John Q. A. Sculptor. Born near Urbana, Ohio, in 1830; died in 1910. Ward at an early age showed great talent for plastic art. He studied under Henry K. Brown in Brooklyn, N. Y., remaining in his studio for six years. In 1857 he made his first sketch for "The Indian Hunter," now in Central Park, N. Y. In 1861 he opened his studio in New York. He was elected an Associate Member of the National Academy of Design in 1862 and an Academician in the following year, and president in 1874. He was the first president of the National Sculpture Society. In 1866 he executed the group of "The Good Samaritan," now in Boston. In the field of portrait statuary Mr. Ward was one of the masters of his day; his statue of Henry W. Beecher is in Brooklyn; his statue of Commodore Oliver H. Perry in Newport, R. I., and his statue of Israel Putnam at Hartford, Conn. Other noted statues were of Horace Greeley, Lafayette, President Garfield and the equestrian statue of General Thomas at Washington, D. C.

WARD, Nina B. Painter. Born in Rome, Ga. Pupil of St. Louis School of Fine Arts; New York School of Art, and Penna. Academy of Fine Arts. Member of Fellowship, Penna. Academy of Fine Arts. Awards: Cresson European scholarship, Penna. Academy of Fine Arts, 1908 and 1911; first Toppan prize, Penna. Academy of Fine Arts, 1912; Mary Smith prize, Penna. Academy of Fine Arts, 1914. *Address,* 1515 Arch St., Philadelphia, Pa.

WARD, Winifred. Sculptor. Born in Cleveland, Ohio, in 1889. Pupil of Charles Grafly. Member: Fellowship, Penna. Academy of Fine Arts; Plastic Club; National Association of Women Painters and Sculptors; Society of Independent Artists. *Address,* 2006 Mt. Vernon St., Philadelphia, Pa.

WARE, Edward Thompson, Jr. Painter. *Address,* 127 East Third St., Cincinnati, Ohio.

WAREHAM, John Hamilton D. Painter. Born in Grand Ledge, Mich. Pupil of Duveneck and Meakin. Member of Cincinnati Municipal Art Society. Awarded bronze medal, St. Louis Exposition, 1904. Decorations in Fort Pitt Hotel, Pittsburgh; Seelbach Hotel, Louisville;

Hotel Sinton, Cincinnati; Poli's Theater, Washington, D. C. *Address,* Rookwood Pottery Co., Cincinnati, Ohio.

WARNER, C. J. Engraver. The only plate of this man known to the compiler is a fairly well-executed stipple portrait of Gen. Anthony Wayne. It was published by C. Smith, New York, 1796, and probably appeared in "The Monthly Military Repository," published by Smith in that year.

WARNER, Everett L. Painter and etcher, who was born in Vinton, Iowa, in 1877. He studied art as a pupil of the Art Students' League of New York. He has been awarded many medals and has exhibited in Washington, D. C., Boston, Philadelphia and New York. His pictures of New York City, its streets and buildings, show its picturesqueness. Associate Member of National Academy of Design, N. Y. *Address,* Care of Pittsburgh, Pa. (Carnegie Institute); or Lyme, Conn.

WARNER, George D. Engraver. This name is signed to a botanical plate published in the *New York Magazine* for December, 1791. The book-plate of George Warner is signed "Warner sculpt," and is probably the work of this engraver.

WARNER, Mrs. Lily G. Painter and illustrator. Born in Hartford, Conn. Painted flower-pieces and illustrated for *St. Nicholas Magazine*.

WARNER, Mrs. Mary L. Painter. Member of the Conn. Academy of Fine Arts; also of New Haven Paint and Clay Club. *Address,* Middletown, Conn.

WARNER, Olin Levi. Sculptor. Born in Suffield, Conn., in 1844. He studied in Paris and on his return to this country opened his studio in New York. He was elected an Associate of the National Academy in 1888. His portrait busts of Gov. Wm. A. Buckingham and Wm. Lloyd Garrison and his statuettes of "Twilight" and the "Dancing Faun" are well known. He was a member of the Society of American Artists. He died in 1896.

WARNER, William. Engraver. Born in Philadelphia about 1813; died there in 1848. Warner was a portrait-painter and a self-taught engraver in mezzotint. He made comparatively few plates, but his large plates are admirable examples of mezzotint work.

WARNICKE, John G. Engraver. Died in Philadelphia in 1818. In 1811–14 and again in 1818 Warnicke was engraving in Philadelphia. The only portrait known to the compiler, that of Franklin, is a very good piece of stipple work.

WARR, John. Engraver. There were two men of this name in Philadelphia in 1821–45 working as "general engravers." The older man was seemingly engraving in 1821–28 and the younger man, John Warr, Jr., was engraving in 1825–45. Their work consisted chiefly of vignettes, business-cards, etc., but these are well engraved.

WARR, W. W. Engraver. This W. W. Warr was a script engraver working in Philadelphia about 1830. He usually signed plates in connection with John Warr as "Engraved by J. & W. W. Warr."

WARREN, A. Coolidge. Engraver. Born in Boston, Mass., in 1819; died in New York in 1904. Mr. Warren was the son of Asa Warren, a portrait and miniature painter, and was apprenticed in 1833 to Bigelow Bros., jewelers, of Boston. Showing a decided inclination toward engraving, he was placed, a little later than this, with the Boston engraver George G. Smith. At the end of his apprenticeship Warren spent another year under the tuition of Joseph Andrews and he became a reputable line-engraver of vignettes and book illustrations. For a number of years he was in the employ of the New England Bank Note Co. and the Boston publishers, Ticknor & Fields. As the result of too much night work he was compelled to abandon engraving for about five years, and in this interval he drew upon wood for other engravers. In 1863 Mr. Warren removed to New York and engraved for the Continental Bank Note Co. and book publishers. In June, 1899, he entirely lost the sight of one eye and was compelled to permanently abandon his profession. He occupied his later years in painting.

WARREN, A. W. Marine painter. Born on a farm in Coventry, N. Y. He studied under T. H. Matteson and in 1863 was elected an Associate Member of the National School of Design. His best painting is his marine work. The Brooklyn Institute owns his "Rocky Shore, Mt. Desert." He died in 1873.

WARREN, Asa. Portrait and miniature painter, who flourished about 1846–47 in Boston.

WARREN, H. Painter. In the exhibition held in 1847 at the Penna. Academy of the Fine Arts in Philadelphia, "View on the Delaware near Trenton Bridge" is noted as for sale by the artist, "H. Warren."

WARREN, Harold B. Landscape painter and illustrator. Born in Manchester, England, in 1859. Pupil of Charles H. Moore and Charles Eliot Norton at Harvard University. Member of Copley Society, 1891. Specialty, water colors. Work: "The Parthenon," "The Propyaea," "Egina from the Parthenon" and "Northwest Corner of the Parthenon," Boston Museum. Instructor in water color, Department of Architecture, Harvard University. *Address*, 8 Craigie Circle, Cambridge, Mass.

WARREN, Henry. According to an advertisement appearing in the *Virginia Gazette* for the year 1769, "Henry Warren, limner who is now at Williamsburg has had the satisfaction of pleasing most gentlemen who have employed him." (Nothing is known of the work of this artist.)

WARRICK, Meta Vaux (Mrs. Fuller). Sculptor and illustrator. Born in Philadelphia in 1877. Pupil of School of Industrial Art; Penna. Academy of Fine Arts; pupil of Collin, Carles, Colarossi Academy and of Rodin in Paris. Member of Alumni Association, Philadelphia School of Industrial Art. Represented in Cleveland Art Museum. *Address*, 7 Warren Rd., Framingham, Mass.

WARSAW, Albert. Painter and illustrator. Born in New York in 1899. Pupil of National Academy of Design, New York. *Address*, 833 Irvine St., New York, N. Y.

WARSHAWSKY, A. G. Painter. Born in Sharon, Pa., in 1883. Pupil of Mowbray and Loeb in New York and of Winslow Homer. Member of Paris Allied Artists' Association; Salon d'Automne; Cincinnati Art Club. Work: Mural decoration, "The Dance," Rorheimer and Brooks Studios, Cleveland, Ohio; represented in Cleveland Museum of Art; Minneapolis Art Institute. Has painted mural panels for the chateau of Count Centanini in Brittany. *Address*, Care of Foinet, 19 Rue Vavin, Paris, France.

WARSHAWSKY, Xander. Painter. Born in Cleveland, Ohio, in 1887. Pupil of National Academy of Design. His painting "Overlooking the Mediterranean" is in the Cleveland Museum. *Address*, 20 Rue Durantin, Paris, France.

WARWELL. "Limner." Died in Charleston, S. C., in 1767.

WARWICK, Edward. Painter. Born in Philadelphia in 1881. Pupil of J. Frank Copeland and Charles T. Scott. Member of Philadelphia Sketch Club. *Address*, School of Industrial Art, Broad and Pine Sts., Philadelphia, Pa.

WARWICK, Ethel Herrick. Painter. Born in New York, N. Y. Pupil of W. M. Chase, Fred Wagner, Hugh Breckenridge and H. B. Snell. Member: Plastic Club; Philadelphia Art Alliance; Fellowship, Penna. Academy of Fine Arts. *Address*, 5407 Chester Ave., Philadelphia, Pa.

WASHBURN, Mrs. Painter. Daughter of the miniature painter George Munger of New Haven, she inherited her father's talent and produced a few very delicate miniature portraits on ivory.

WASHBURN, Cadwallader. Painter and etcher. Pupil of Art Students' League, New York, and of H. Siddons Mowbray and William Chase. His etchings of subjects in Venice, Japan and Spain and his Norland Series of the Maine Meadows and Woods are all delightful. *Address*, Livermore Falls, Me.

WASHBURN, Mary S. Sculptor. Born in Star City, Ind. Pupil of Art Institute of Chicago; Charles Mulligan; Edwin Sawyer in Paris. Awards: Second prize, Paris Allied Artists' Association; gold medal, Panama-Pacific Exposition, San Francisco, 1915. Work: "Statue of Gen. Milroy," Milroy Park, Rensselaer, Ind.; medal in Carnegie Institute, Pittsburgh, Pa.; Memorial to Lt. Joseph Wilson, Logansport, Ind. *Address*, 1933 Howe St., Berkeley, Calif.

WASHBURN, May N. Painter. Born in Greenfield, Mass., in 1861. Pupil of D. W. Tryon. *Address*, 1206 Carnegie Studios, 7th Ave. and 56th St., New York, N. Y.

WASHINGTON, Elizabeth Fisher. Miniature painter. Born in Siegfried's Bridge, Pa. Pupil of Penna. Academy of the Fine Arts; Hugh Breckenridge; Fred Wagner. Member: Fellowship, Penna. Academy of Fine Arts; Plastic Club; Philadelphia Art Alliance; Pa. Society of Miniature Painters. Awarded Mary Smith prize, Penna. Academy of Fine Arts, 1917; Fellowship prize, Academy of Fine Arts, 1917. Represented in Penna. Academy of Fine Arts Collection; Civic Club, Philadelphia; Pierce Business College. *Address*, 1710 Chestnut St., Philadelphia, Pa.

WASSON, George Savary. Painter and author. Born in Groveland, Mass., in 1855. He began his career as a marine artist in Boston and built a house and studio at Kittery Point, Me., 1889, in order to study the sea. Author: "Cap'n Simeon's Store," 1903; "The Green Shay," 1905; "Home from the Sea," 1908. Contributor to leading magazines. *Address*, Kittery Point, Me.

WATERMAN, Marcus. Painter. Born in Providence, R. I., in 1834. Worked in New York 1857–70. Visited Algiers 1879–83. He exhibited at Centennial, Philadelphia, 1876. Principal works: "Fountain, Algiers"; "Arab Girl"; "Roc's Egg" (1886); "Journey to the City of Brass" (1888); also numerous American forest scenes and Arabian subjects.

WATERS, George W. Painter. Born in Coventry, Chenango Co., N. Y., in 1832. He studied art in New York and later in Dresden and Munich. He exhibited a landscape "Franconia Notch" in 1876 at the Centennial Exhibition. His portrait of Joseph Jefferson as "Rip Van Winkle" attracted much attention; he also painted three portraits of Walt Whitman. He was art director for many years at Elmira College, N. Y. He died in Elmira in 1912.

WATERS, Ray Kinsman. Painter, who exhibited water colors at the Penna. Academy of the Fine Arts, Philadelphia, 1922. *Address*, 380 East Town St., Columbus, Ohio.

WATKINS, Franklin. Painter, who exhibited at Penna. Academy of the Fine Arts, Philadelphia, 1924. *Address*, 324 South 7th St., Philadelphia.

WATKINS, Susan. Painter. Born in California in 1875. Pupil of Art Students' League, New York, and of Collin in Paris. She received honorable mention in the Paris Salon of 1889 and third gold medal in the Salon of 1901. Her painting entitled "The Fan" is well known.

WATKINS, W. Reginald. Illustrator. Member of the Charcoal Club of Baltimore. *Address*, 801 Williams St., Baltimore, Md.

WATROUS, Mrs. Elizabeth Snowden Nichols. Painter and writer. Wife of the painter Harry W. Watrous. She was born in New York in 1858 and studied with Henner and Carolus-Duran in Paris. She was a member of the New York Woman's Art Club; the Pen and Brush Club; Society of Women Painters and Sculptors; the Professional Women's League. She died in New York City in 1921.

WATROUS, Harry W. Painter. Born in San Francisco in 1875. Studied in Paris at Academie Julien and in the Atelier of Leon Bonnat. Well known as genre painter with specialty of small figures very highly finished. Elected an Associate Member of National Academy in 1894 and Academician in 1895. Exhibited painting "My Mother," Centennial Exhibition of the National Academy of Design in 1925. *Address*, 58 West 57th St., New York City, N. Y.

WATSON, Amelia Montague. Painter and illustrator. Born in East Windsor Hill, Conn., in 1856. Has exhibited at New York Water Color Club; American Water Color Society; Boston Art Club. She was teacher of painting at Martha's Vineyard Summer Institute for many years. She is distinctively a painter of New England and Southern scenery, working much in Florida, and in the North Carolina and Virginia mountains and on the Southern seacoast. Made illustrations in colors for Thoreau's "Cape Cod," 1896; made cover and frontispiece in colors for Margaret Warner Morley's "The Carolina Mountains," 1913; also for John Muir's "A Thousand Mile Walk to the Gulf," 1916. *Address*, "Wild Acres," Windsor Hill, Conn.

WATSON, Charles R. Painter. Born in Baltimore, Md., in 1857. He was a member of the Baltimore Water Color Club and specialized in marine painting. He died in 1923.

WATSON, Dudley Crafts. Painter. Born in Lake Geneva, Wis., in 1885. Studied art at Art Institute, Chicago; studied also in Madrid and Valencia, Spain, Paris and London; pupil of Señor Sorolla and Sir Alfred East. Teacher, water color painting, Art Institute of Chicago; director of Milwaukee Art Institute. First prize, water color painting, Art Students' League, Chicago, 1907; exhibitor of American water colors, Art Institute, Chicago. Director of Milwaukee Art Institute. Lecturer on art for University Extension Society; author and art editor of *Milwaukee Journal*, 1917; 1st Americanization pageant, Milwaukee, 1919. Instructor of drawing, Great Lakes (Ill.) Naval Training Station, 1917; originator and producer of music-picture symphonies. Member: Wisconsin Painters' and Sculptors' Society; American Pageant Association; associate member of Boston Guild Artists; Chicago Society of Artists; Chicago Water Color Club. *Address,* 704 Marshall St., Milwaukee, Wis.

WATSON, Elizabeth V. Taylor. Painter. Born in New Jersey. Pupil of Tarbell, De Camp. Member of Copley Society. Awarded bronze medal, Tennessee Centennial Exposition, Nashville, 1897. *Address,* 404 Fenway Studios, Ipswich St., Boston, Mass.

WATSON, Ernest W. Illustrator. Born in Conway, Mass., in 1884. Pupil of Mass. Normal Art School, Boston; Pratt Institute, Brooklyn. One of the founders and directors of the Berkshire Summer School of Art. *Address,* Pratt Institute, Brooklyn, N. Y.

WATSON, Mrs. Eva Auld. Painter and illustrator. Born in Texas in 1889. Pupil of M. O. Leisser; Pittsburgh School of Design; Pratt Institute, Brooklyn. Member of the Boston Society of Arts and Crafts. Awarded honorable mention, Panama-Pacific Exposition, San Francisco, 1915. *Address,* 181 Emerson Place, Brooklyn, N. Y.

WATSON, Jessie N. Painter. Born in Pontiac, Ill., in 1870. *Address,* 1004 Chemical Building, St. Louis, Mo.

WATSON, John. Painter, who came to the Colonies in 1715 from Scotland and set up his easel in the capital of New Jersey, Perth Amboy. The year in which he was born is found by the date of his death engraved on his tombstone and the age at which he died. He was born in 1685 and died in 1768. William Dunlap in his "History of the Arts of Design," Vol. 1, devotes four pages to the career of the artist John Watson. In 1731 Watson painted his portrait of Sir Peter Warren who through his marriage into the de Lancey family had connections living in Perth Amboy, the home of the artist. This portrait was exhibited at the Union League Club, New York, in 1925.

WATSON, Minnie. Painter. She was a pupil of D. W. Tryon in Hartford, Conn., in 1875. Later she studied in New York. She has painted some excellent still-life subjects true in line and color.

WATT, Barbara H. Painter and illustrator. Born in Wellesley, Mass. Pupil of Albert H. Munsel, V. L. George, J. De Camp and D. J. Connah. Member: Brush and Chisel Club; Alumni Associate of Mass. Normal Art School. Work: Mural decoration, "Pan," Mass. Normal Art School, Boston. *Address,* 25 Oakland St., Wellesley Hills, Mass.

WATT, William G. Wood engraver. Born in New York in 1867. Pupil of E. Heinemann, Emile Clement and of the National Academy of Design. Member of Salmagundi Club in 1903. Work: "The Harvest," after L'Hermitte; "The Pool," after own painting; "A Music Party," after Metsu; "The Trousseau," by C. W. Hawthorne; "Magnolia," by J. J. Shannon. Work represented in New York Public Library; Carnegie Institute, Pittsburgh; Public Library, Newark, N. J.; Metropolitan Museum Library, New York; Salmagundi Club. Elected an Associate Member of the National Academy in 1922. He died in New York in 1924.

WATTS, J. W. Engraver. About 1850 Watts was a line-engraver of landscape in Boston. He later etched some very good portraits.

WATTS, William Clothier. Painter. Born in Philadelphia, Pa. Pupil of Penna. Academy of the Fine Arts. Member: Fellowship, Penna. Academy of the Fine Arts; Philadelphia Sketch Club. *Address,* Carmel, Monterey Co., Calif.

WAUGH, Eliza. She was a miniature painter, and married the artist Samuel B. Waugh.

WAUGH, Frederick Judd. Painter. Born in Bordentown, N. J., in 1861. He was the son of Samuel B. Waugh, portrait painter, and Mary Eliza (Young). Pupil of the Penna. Academy of the Fine Arts, Philadelphia, and of the Julien Academy in Paris. He was elected an Associate Member of the National Academy in 1909 and an Academician in 1911. He resided at various places in Europe (1892–1907). Illustrated for *Graphic* and London papers, and exhibited in Salon, Paris, previous to 1892, and later in the Royal Academy in London. Represented by paintings in the Bristol Academy, England; Walker Art Gallery, Liverpool; Durban Art Gallery (Natal, South Africa); National Gallery, Washington; Metropolitan Museum, New York; Brooklyn, New York, Institute; Art Club, Philadelphia; Masonic Temple, Philadelphia; Art Institute of Chicago; Dallas and Austin, Texas; Delgado Art Museum, New Orleans; Penna. Academy of the Fine Arts, Philadelphia; Montclair Arts Club; City Art Museum, St. Louis, etc. Member of National Academy, 1909. Member of Bristol Academy of Fine Arts, Royal Academy of the West of England. His work has been chiefly marines. *Address*, Kent, Conn.

WAUGH, Ida. Painter. Born in Philadelphia; died there in 1919. Pupil of Penna. Academy of the Fine Arts, Philadelphia, and in Paris at L'Academie Julien and L'Academie Delecluse, 1888 and 1891–92. Principal painting, "Hagar and Ishmael"; received the Norman W. Dodge prize, National Academy of Design, for portrait of Dr. Paul J. Sartain, 1896; has exhibited in Paris Salon; World's Fair (Chicago), 1893; New York; Philadelphia; California; Cincinnati and other places. Was a member of Historical Society of Penna., and of the Penna. Academy of the Fine Arts.

WAUGH, Samuel B. Portrait painter. Born in Mercer, Penna., in 1814. Studied drawing while a boy under J. R. Smith, Philadelphia; also studied the works of the old masters in Italy, Paris and England, without a teacher; lived mainly in Philadelphia, where he was at one time President of the Artists' Fund Society; honorary member of the National Academy of Design, N. Y. He died in 1885.

WAY, Andrew John Henry. Painter. Born in Washington, D. C., in 1826. He studied in Baltimore. His work was portraiture and still-life, his fruit-pieces attracting special attention. Among his works are "A Christmas Memory," "Albert Grapes" and "Flora and Pomona." Several of his paintings have been lithographed. He died in 1888.

WAY, George Brevitt. Painter. Son of the artist Andrew John Henry Way. He was born in Baltimore in 1854, and educated at the United States Naval Academy. He later studied in Paris. Among his paintings are "Twilight on the Susquehanna," "On the Upper Potomac" and "Sunset."

WAY, Mary. Portrait and miniature painter of New London, Connecticut. In the *New York Evening Post*, in 1811, it notes "Takes Likenesses upon Ivory & Glass, in colors or gold. Also landscapes or views of country Seats. Paintings not approved may be returned without charge at her painting-room No. 95 Greenwich Street, New York."

WEAR, J. F. Portrait painter. The collection of historic portraits at Independence Hall, Philadelphia, has a portrait of a signer of the Declaration of Independence, painted by J. F. Wear after the portrait painted by John Trumbull.

WEAVER, P. T. Dunlap notes his painting of small portraits in oil, in a hard manner. He was an intemperate Irishman; his portrait of Alexander Hamilton attracted attention by its strong likeness. He often painted portraits in profile on wood panels, and signed several "P. T. Weaver."

WEBB, Edna Dell. Painter. Born in Cohoes, N. Y., in 1891. Pupil of National Academy of Design; Troy School of Arts and Crafts. *Address*, 9 Lansing Avenue, Troy, N. Y.

WEBB, J. Lewis. Painter, who was born in 1856. He was elected an Associate Member of National Academy of Design in 1906. *Address*, 32 East 42d St., New York, N. Y.

WEBB, Margaret Ely. Illustrator and etcher. Born in Urbana, Ill., in 1877. Pupil of Twachtman and Cox in New York. Illustrated "The House of Prayer," by F. C. Converse; "Aldine First Reader," "Under Greek Skies," etc. *Address*, Denison House, 93 Tyler St., Boston, Mass.

WEBB, Warren. Marine painter. His specialty is oil paintings of sailing ships.

WEBBER, Wesley. Painter. Born in Gardiner, Maine, in 1841. He had a studio in Boston and in New York. He painted landscapes and scenes of the Civil War. He died in Boston in 1914.

WEBER, August J. Painter. Born in Marietta, Ohio, in 1889. Pupil of Meakin and Duveneck in Cincinnati. Member of Cincinnati Art Club. *Address*, 1234 Louden Ave., Cincinnati, Ohio.

WEBER, Carl. Landscape painter. Born in Philadelphia in 1855. Son of Paul Weber. He studied in Germany, and is represented in many galleries and collections of paintings. He died in Philadelphia in 1925.

WEBER, F. Painter, sculptor and etcher. Born in Columbia, S. C., in 1883; died in 1906. Pupil of Laurens and École des Beaux Arts in Paris. Member: Art Alliance; New York Water Color Club; Brooklyn Society of Etchers. Etchings represented in the Library of Congress, Washington, D. C.

WEBER, Max. Painter. Born in Russia in 1880. Pupil of Dow; also of Laurens and Matisse in Paris. Member: Modern Artists; League of New York Artists. Author:

"Essays on Art," "Cubist Poems," etc. *Address*, Nassau Haven, New Hyde Park, L. I., N. Y.

WEBER, Paul. Landscape and animal painter. Born in Germany about 1820. Studied in Frankfort. Came to America in 1848, and settled in Philadelphia; travelled in Scotland and Germany in 1857, and returned to America for a short time; went to Darmstadt in 1858, and was appointed Court painter. His American work was generally pure landscape, of which one of the finest examples is his "Evening," in the permanent collection of the Academy of Fine Arts. The Corcoran Gallery at Washington also has "Scene in the Catskills," painted by him in 1858. His later work gives prominence to animal life.

WEBSTER, Ambrose E. Painter, who exhibited at the Penna. Academy of the Fine Arts, Philadelphia, 1924. *Address*, Provincetown, Mass.

WEBSTER, Herman Armour. Painter and etcher. Born in New York City in 1878. Graduated from Yale University in 1900 and in October of that year he went abroad to study art in Paris and entered the Julien Academy under Jean Paul Laurens. In 1905 four of his etchings were accepted at the Paris Salon. In December, 1907, Mr. Webster's name was enrolled in the Associate membership of the Royal Society of Painter-Etchers in London of which the late Sir Francis Seymour Haden was president. He is also a member of Societé Nationale des Beaux Arts, Paris. Represented in the collections of the Musee Nationale du Luxembourg, Paris; Congressional Library of Washington, D. C.; Boston Museum of Fine Arts; Art Institute of Chicago. *Address*, 11 Passage de la Visitation, Paris, France.

WEBSTER, H. Daniel. Sculptor. Pupil of Banard and Du Mond in New York. Born at Frankville, Ia. He died in 1912. Represented by "Minute Man" (bronze); Genl. W. H. Beadle (marble); the bronze doors for American National Bank Building, Austin, Texas.

WEBSTER, Mary H. Painter and sculptor. Born in Oberlin, Ohio, in 1881. Pupil of Cincinnati Art Academy under Barnhorn and Nowottny; Injalbert, Verlet and Waldmann in Paris; Hitchcock in Holland; Hawthorne in Provincetown. Member of Cleveland Woman's Art Society. *Address*, Midway Studios, 6016 Ellis Ave., Chicago, Ill.

WEDDERSPOON, R. G. Painter. Born in Red Bank, N. J., in 1889. Pupil of Daniel Garber and Henry McCarter. Member: Fellowship, Penna. Academy of Fine Arts; Chicago Society of Artists; Chicago Art Club. *Address*, 4611 Ellis Ave., Chicago, Ill.

WEEDELL, Hazel. Painter and etcher. Born in Tacoma, Wash., in 1892. Pupil of Gustav F. Goetsch, Robert Koehler and Ernest Batchelder. Member: Alumni, Minneapolis School of Art; St. Louis Arts and Crafts. *Address*, 20 Elm Ave., Glendale, Kirkwood, Mo.

WEEKS, Caroline. Portrait painter. The collection of Colonial portraits in Independence Hall, Philadelphia, has a copy by Caroline Weeks of John Trumbull's portrait of Josiah Bartlett of New Hampshire. She painted most of her pictures from 1860 to 1870.

WEEKS, Edwin Lord. Painter. Born in Boston, Mass., in 1849 died in 1903. Landscape and figure painter. Pupil of the École des Beaux Arts; also of Bonnat and Gerome in Paris. Sketched and painted in Cairo, Jerusalem, Damascus, and Tangiers, and is especially noted for pictures of Eastern life. He received honorable mention at the Paris Salon, 1884, and was subsequently awarded medals at the Salon, 1889; Paris Exposition, 1889; Art Club, Philadelphia, 1891; London Exposition, 1896; Dresden, 1897; Munich, 1897; Pan-American Exposition, Buffalo, 1901. Chevalier of the Legion of Honor, 1896; Officer, Order of St. Michael of Bavaria; member of Paris Society of American Painters, and Boston Art Club.

WEILAND, James. Painter. Born in Toledo, Ohio. Pupil of National Academy of Design; Royal Academy in Munich; of Delecluse and Colarossi Academies in Paris. Member: Allied Artists' Association; Provincetown Artists' Association. He painted the portrait of Mrs. Edna B. Carlson, exhibited in 1925. *Address*, 61 Poplar St., Brooklyn, N. Y.

WEILL, Edmund. Painter and etcher. Born in New York in 1877. Pupil of National Academy of Design under Edgar M. Ward. Member of Brooklyn Society of Artists; Brooklyn Water Color Club; Society of Independent Artists; Salmagundi Club. *Address*, 756 East 9th St., Brooklyn, New York.

WEINDORF, Arthur. Painter. Born in Long Island City in 1885. Member of Society of Independent Artists. *Address*, Woolworth Building, New York.

WEINEDEL, Carl. Miniature painter. Born in 1795. He was working in New York in 1834; in 1839 he was elected an Associate Member of the National Academy of Design. He died in 1845.

WEINMAN, Adolph Alexander. Sculptor, who was born in Karlsruhe, Germany, in 1870. He came to America in 1880 as a boy of ten and was later apprenticed to Kaldenberg a carver of wood and ivory. During his apprenticeship he attended evening classes in drawing and modeling at the Cooper Institute, New

York, and at the Art Students' League where he was awarded the prize in the modeling class. At the age of nineteen he became the pupil of Philip Martiny, and later became an assistant to Saint Gaudens, Olin Warner and D. C. French. He has been engaged professionally as a sculptor since 1891. Awarded the silver medal at the St. Louis Exposition, 1904; won competition for the Monument to General Alexander Macomb in Detroit, 1906; Maryland Union Soldiers' and Sailors' Monument in Baltimore, 1907; the Lincoln Memorials in Hodgenville, Kentucky, and in Madison, Wisconsin; also the Lincoln statue, rotunda of State Capitol, Frankfort, Ky.; the War Memorial at Forest Hills, N. Y. He designed the new dime and half dollar for 1916. In 1911 he was elected a Member of the National Academy of Design, also a member of the National Sculpture Society. Received gold medal of honor in Sculpture from the Architectural League of New York, also the Widener gold medal at the Penna. Academy of Fine Arts, 1926, for his "Narcissus." *Address*, 441 West 21st St., New York City, N. Y.

WEINERT, Albert. Sculptor. Born in Leipzig, Germany, in 1863. Pupil of École des Beaux Arts in Brussels. Member: National Sculpture Society, 1909; Society of Independent Artists. Work: "Lake George Memorial," Lake George, N. Y.; "McKinley Monument," Toledo, Ohio; "Statue of Lord Baltimore," Baltimore, Md.; marble groups in vestibule of Hall of Records, New York, N. Y.; "Stevens T. Mason Monument," Detroit, Mich.; historical tablets for Sons of the Revolution and Society of Colonial Wars; work at Panama-Pacific Exposition, San Francisco, Calif. *Address*, 256 West 55th St., New York, N. Y.

WEIR, C. E. Painter. Brother of Professor John F. Weir of New Haven, Conn. Has painted many cabinet heads as noted in an early Art-Union Exhibition; they were of careful and minute composition.

WEIR, Irene. Painter. Pupil of J. H. Twachtman; J. Alden Weir; Yale School of Fine Arts; Art Students' League of New York; Académie, Paris. Member: New York Water Color Club; National Association of Women Painters and Sculptors; Art Alliance of America. Director, School of Design and Liberal Arts and of Art Alliance of America. *Address*, Hotel Netherland, Fifth Ave., New York, N. Y.

WEIR, John Ferguson. Sculptor and painter. Born in West Point, N. Y., in 1841. Elected an Associate Member of the National Academy of Design in 1864, and Academician in 1866. He was Director of Yale School of Fine Arts, 1869–1913. Principal works in sculpture: Statues of President Woolsey and Professor Silliman, of Yale. Has executed

many portraits and other works in painting, notably the pictures "The Gun Foundry," "The Forging of the Shaft," "The Confessional," "An Artist's Studio," "Christmas Eve," "Tapping the Furnace," "Rain and Sunshine," "The Column of St. Mark's, Venice." Author of "John Trumbull and His Works," 1902. *Address*, Yale University, New Haven, Conn.

WEIR, Julian Alden. Painter and etcher. Born in West Point, N. Y., in 1852; died in 1919. Pupil of his father, Robert W. Weir, at West Point and of Gerome in Paris. Awards: Honorable mention, Paris Salon, 1882; silver medal for painting and bronze medal for drawing, Paris Exposition, 1889; American Art Association, New York; medal, Carnegie Institute, Pittsburgh, 1897; bronze medal, Paris Exposition, 1900; gold medal for paintings and silver for engravings, Buffalo, 1901; gold medal, National Academy of Design, 1906; Lippincott prize, Pennsylvania Academy of Fine Arts, 1910; Harris silver medal, Chicago Art Institute, 1912; Beck medal, Pennsylvania Academy of the Fine Arts, 1913; first Wm. A. Clark prize and Corcoran gold medal, the Corcoran Gallery of Art, 1914. Elected Associate, National Academy, 1885; National Academy, 1886, and became its President, 1915–17. Member: American Water Color Society; Ten American Painters; National Institute of Arts and Letters. Represented in Corcoran Art Gallery by "Autumn" and portrait of Miss De L. (Awarded the first William A. Clark prize accompanied by the Corcoran gold medal in 1916.) A memorial exhibition was held at the Century Club, New York, of about forty of his best known paintings.

WEIR, Robert Walter. Painter. Born in New Rochelle, N. Y., in 1803; died in New York, 1889. Pupil of Jarvis. Studied at Florence, Italy, under Benventi; also in Rome, Italy. Became a professional painter at the age of 20. In 1829 he became a Member of the National Academy of Design and in 1832 was made professor of drawing in the National Military Academy at West Point, a position occupied by him for over 40 years. Among his works are: "The Bourbons' Last March"; "Landing of Henry Hudson"; "Indian Captives"; "Christ and Nicodemus"; "Taking the Veil"; "Child's Evening Prayer"; "The Portico of the Palace of Octavia, Rome"; "Our Lord on the Mount of Olives"; and "Last Communion of Henry Clay." His "Embarkation of the Pilgrims," in the rotunda of the Capitol, Washington, was injured during the building of the new dome of the Capitol. Professor Weir repaired this injury in 1861, having a special detail from the War Department for this purpose. His portrait of General Winfield Scott is owned by the Metropolitan Museum of New York.

WEIS, John E. Painter, who exhibited at the Penna. Academy of the Fine Arts, Philadelphia, 1926. *Address*, Art Academy, Cincinnati, Ohio.

WEIS, Samuel W. Painter. Born in Natchez, Miss., in 1870. Paints in water color and pastel. Member of New Orleans Art Association. *Address*, 1938 Straus Building, Chicago, Ill.

WEISS, Mary L. Painter, who exhibited at the Penna. Academy of the Fine Arts, Philadelphia, 1924. *Address*, East Gloucester, Mass.

WEISS, William L. Painter, who exhibited at the Penna. Academy of the Fine Arts, Philadelphia, 1924. *Address*, East Gloucester, Mass.

WELCH, Mabel R. Miniature painter. Born in New Haven, Conn. Pupil of Art Students' League, New York, under Kenyon Cox; also under Courtois in Paris. Member of American Society of Miniature Painters. Her "Study of a Child" is well known and is beautifully rendered. *Address*, 939 Eighth Ave., New York City.

WELCH, Thomas B. Engraver. Born in Charleston, S. C., in 1814; died in Paris in 1874. Welch was a pupil of James B. Longacre in Philadelphia and apparently soon after his release from his apprenticeship he formed a business connection with A. B. Walter. Over his own name he produced some good portraits in stipple and some large ones in mezzotint. For the *Annuals* he engraved some admirable pure line plates. About 1861 Welch abandoned engraving and went abroad to study art; he remained in Paris for a number of years. As showing his earlier tastes in this direction, the Philadelphia directories of 1841–45 give his occupation as "portrait-painter."

WELDON, Charles D. Painter. Born in Ohio; studied art in New York at the Art Students' League; also in London; in Paris under Munkacsy. He exhibited his first pictures at the National Academy in 1883. With the exception of a visit to Japan where he painted several years, he has since been a resident of New York and identified with the art life of the metropolis. He was elected a National Academician in 1897 and a Member of the National Academy in 1897, and is a member of the American Water Color Society. Mr. Weldon's usual subjects are found in the field of domestic genre. He is also known as a painter of Japanese motives and in all of his work gives evidence of his thorough training and artistic temperament. His water colors show skilful manipulation of the medium and are attractive in color and general aspect. *Address*, 51 West 10th St., New York City.

WELFARE, Daniel. Painter. Born in 1796. He was a student of Thomas Sully who gave him letters of introduction to many artists in this country and abroad, where he travelled and studied. He afterwards settled in Salem, N. C., where he painted for years. His son was named Thomas Sully Welfare and Sully painted a self-portrait for his namesake. He died in Salem, N. C., in 1841.

WELLMORE, E. Engraver in stipple and in line. He was a pupil of James B. Longacre in Philadelphia and over his own name he engraved some of the portraits in "The National Portrait Gallery" of 1834–35. At a much later period he was engraving book illustrations in New York. He is said to have finally become a clergyman. Wellmore was also a miniature painter as we find engravings and lithographs done after portraits painted by E. Wellmore.

WELLS, Charles S. Sculptor. Born in Glasgow, Scotland, in 1872. Pupil of Karl Bitter, Augustus Saint Gaudens and George G. Barnard. Work: Fountain, Gateway Park, city of Minneapolis. *Address*, 3004 Hennepin Ave., Minneapolis, Minn.

WELLS, J. Engraver. The only information obtainable is that J. Wells was a map-engraver working in New York in 1836.

WELLS, Marion F. Sculptor of the giant figure of "Progress" which crowns the dome of the City Hall, San Francisco, Calif.

WELLS, Newton Alonzo. Painter. Born in Lisbon, N. Y., in 1852. Pupil of Academie Julien, Paris, 1886, 1896. Instructor of drawing and geometry, Union College, N. Y., in 1877–79; professor of drawing, Syracuse University; Dean of School of Art, Western Reserve University; professor of art, University of Illinois, 1899. Has exhibited at Paris Salon and at various national and municipal art exhibitions; has mural paintings in library of University of Illinois; Sangamon Co. Court House (Springfield, ill.); Colonial Theater (Boston); Englewood High School (Chicago); designed Soldiers' Monument, Tuscola, Ill. Member: Architectural League of America; Architectural League of New York; National Society of Mural Painters. Contributor on art subjects. Series of historical mural paintings in Gayoso Hotel, Memphis, Tenn. *Address*, 1630 Monroe Building, Chicago.

WELLS, Rachel. Modeler. Her work was chiefly small profile bas-reliefs in wax; the portraits were well modeled and frequently finished in color. She was a sister of Patience Wright who married Joseph Wright who painted portraits of Washington in 1790.

WELLSTOOD, James. Engraver. Born in Jersey City, N. J., in 1855; died there in 1880. James Wellstood was the son of William Wellstood and was the pupil of his father. He became a successful and promising engraver, and at the time of his death he was a member of the engraving firm of William Wellstood & Co. His principal plates were ''The Pointer'' and ''Safe in Port''; the latter after a painting by Thomas Moran.

WELLSTOOD, John Geikie. Engraver. Born in Edinburgh, Scotland, in 1813; was living in 1889. Wellstood came to New York in 1830, and was employed by Rawdon, Wright & Co., and he remained with that engraving firm until 1847 when he began business for himself. In 1858 his firm was merged into what is now the American Bank Note Company, and he was connected with this company until 1871. In the latter year he founded the Columbian Bank Note Company in Washington, D. C., and while president of that company he designed and partially engraved the backs of all the U. S. Treasury notes issued at that time. When the printing of United States notes passed into the hands of the Treasury Department, Wellstood returned to New York, and was still employed in 1889 as a script engraver by the American Bank Note Company. Wellstood made many improvements in the manufacture of bank-notes.

WELLSTOOD, William. Engraver. Born in Edinburgh, Scotland, in 1819; died in 1900. William was a brother of Jno. G. Wellstood and came to New York with his parents in 1830. He began work there as a letter engraver, but he later devoted himself to landscape and pictorial work. From 1846 to 1871 he was employed by the Western Methodist Book Concern in Cincinnati, Ohio, and by various New York firms. He was a good line-engraver and produced a large amount of work.

WELSH, B. F. Engraver. The American engraver William Chapin, in his autobiography, says that in 1824 he worked in a New York office with an engraver by that name. Welsh afterward became a prominent Baptist clergyman.

WELSH, Herbert. Painter. Born in Philadelphia in 1851. Pupil of Bonnat in Paris; F. Auguste Ortmanns in Fontainebleau; of Onorato Carlandi in Rome. Member of Fellowship, Penna. Academy of Fine Arts. *Address*, 814 Carpenter Lane, Mt. Airy Station, Philadelphia, Pa.

WELSH, H. Devitt. Illustrator, etcher and painter. Born in Philadelphia, Pa., in 1888. Pupil of Thomas Anshutz, William M. Chase, Joseph Pennell and Walter Everett. Member: Philadelphia Sketch Club; Fellowship, Penna. Academy of Fine Arts; Society of Illustrators; Philadelphia Water Color Club; Art Directors' Club. Work: Etching of Rembrandt's ''Mill,'' and ''St. Paul,'' Widener Collection, Philadelphia; etchings of the White House for President Wilson; etching of ''The Lock,'' by Constable, Elkins Collection, Philadelphia. *Address*, 1520 Chestnut St., Philadelphia, Pa.

WELSH, Roscoe. Painter. Born in Laclede, Mo., in 1895. Pupil of Eugene, California. *Address*, 445 Garfield Ave., Chicago, Ill.

WENDEL, Theodore. Painter. Member of the Guild of Boston Artists. Represented in Boston Museum of Fine Arts, and in the Penna. Academy of the Fine Arts. *Address*, Ipswich, Mass.

WENDT, Julia Bracken (Mrs. William). Sculptor. Born in Apple River, Ill., in 1871. Removed with her parents to Galena, Ill., in 1876; began art studies in Art Institute of Chicago in 1887; assisted Lorado Taft in his studio in 1887–92. Assisted with decorations for Chicago Exposition, 1892, besides assisting with decorations on grounds, and carried out several independent commissions, among them ''The Statue of Illinois Welcoming the Nations,'' afterward presented to the State by the Ill. Woman's Exposition Bd.; took 1st sculpture prize offered in Chicago, 1898; appointed on staff of sculptors, St. Louis Exposition, 1904; took 1st prize for sculpture, Municipal Art League of Chicago, 1905; gold medal, San Diego Exposition, 1915; Mrs. W. P. Harrison prize, Los Angeles, 1918. Modeled colossal group ''Art, Science and History'' in Museum of Exposition Park, Los Angeles, California. Member: Chicago Society of Artists; Municipal Art League; California Art Club; American Federation of Arts; National Arts Club, New York; Municipal Art Commission, Los Angeles. Teacher of sculpture, Otis Art Institute, Los Angeles. *Address*, 2814 North Sichel St., Los Angeles, Calif.

WENDT, William. Painter. Born in Germany in 1865. He came to America in 1880. Painted in England, France and America; exhibited in Salon, Paris; Royal Academy, London; in leading American galleries. Awarded 2d Yerkes prize, Chicago Society of Artists, 1893; Young Fortnightly prize, 1897; bronze medal, Buffalo Exposition, 1901; silver medal, St. Louis, 1904; Chan prize, Chicago, 1904; honorable mention, Chicago Society of Artists, 1905; silver medal, Wednesday Club, St. Louis, 1910; honorable mention, Autumn Exhibition, Art Institute of Chicago, 1911; fine arts prize, Society of Western Artists, 1912; silver medal, Panama-P. I. Exposition, 1915: grand prize, San Diego Exposition, 1915; Clarence S. Black prize, California Art Club, 1917. Represented in permanent collections of Art Institute; Friends of American Art; Cliff Dwellers; Union League, Chicago; Athletic Club, Los Angeles; Cincinnati Museum; Art Association, Indianapolis; Museum of History, Science and Art, Los Angeles, etc. Elected Associate Member of the National Academy of Design in 1913.

Member: American Federation of Arts; California Art Club; Society Western Artists. *Address*, 2814 N. Sichel St., Los Angeles, Calif.

WENGER, John. Painter. Born in Russia in 1886. Studied at Art Academy, Petrograd. Member: Salmagundi Club; Society of Independent Artists. *Address*, 1931 Broadway, New York, N. Y.

WENIGER, Maria P. Sculptor. Born in Germany in 1880. Studied in Munich. Member of Art Alliance of America. Work: Miniature bronzes, "Dancers." *Address*, 442 East 58th St., New York, N. Y.

WENTWORTH. Portrait painter in oils and miniature. He also made profile portraits in pencil. He was working about 1815 in Utica, New York.

WENTWORTH, Adelaide E. Etcher. Born in Wakefield, N. H. Pupil of D. W. Ross, W. S. Robinson and Arthur Dow. Member: Cincinnati Woman's Art Club; Crafters Co. *Address*, 17 The Somerset, Avondale, Cincinnati, Ohio.

WENTWORTH, Cecile De. Painter. Born in New York. Pupil of Alexander Cabanel and Edward Detaille, Paris. Exhibiting every year in the Paris Salon since 1889; medals, Paris; Lyons; Turin; 1st gold medal at the National Exhibition, Tours; exhibited at the Paris Exposition, 1900, receiving a medal for portrait of Pope Leo XIII; represented at Musée du Luxembourg, Paris; Vatican Musée, Rome; Senate Chamber, Paris; Metropolitan Museum of New York and Corcoran Gallery, Washington, D. C., etc.; has made portraits of Theodore Roosevelt, William H. Taft, Archbishop Corrigan, etc.; also of Queen Alexandra and many notable people in Europe. Officier d'Academie, Paris, 1894; Officier de l'Instruction Publique; Chevalier Legion d'Honneur, 1901.

WENTWORTH, D. F. Painter. Studied in Munich, but was largely self-taught. Member of Conn. Academy of Fine Arts. Work: "In the Lane"; "In the Forest of Allach," at the Wadsworth Athenaeum. *Address*, 904 Main St., Hartford, Conn.

WENTZ, Henry Frederick. Painter. Born in Oregon. Pupil of Art Students' League of New York. Work: "Sand Dune, Neahkahmie," Portland Art Association. *Address*, Worcester Building, Portland, Ore.

WENZELL, Albert B. Illustrator. Born in Detroit in 1864; he died in Englewood, N. J., in 1917. He painted the mural panels in the New Amsterdam Theater, New York. Wenzell was a pupil of Strahuber and Loefftz in Munich.

WENZLER, H. A. Portrait and landscape painter, also working in miniatures. He was

of Danish birth but came to the United States at an early age and settled in New York. He was elected a Member of the National Academy in 1860, and died in New York in 1871.

WERBE, Anna L. Miniature painter, who exhibited at the Penna. Academy of the Fine Arts, Philadelphia, 1925. *Address*, The Chatham, Detroit, Mich.

WERNTZ, Carl N. Painter and illustrator. Born in Sterling, Ill., in 1874. Pupil of Vanderpoel and Mucha; also studied in Paris and Rome. *Address*, 81 East Madison Ave., Chicago, Ill.

WERTMULLER, Adolph Ulric. Painter. Born in Stockholm, Sweden, about 1750. He made his first studies in art at home; went afterwards to Paris where he studied and practised painting several years; was elected member of the Royal Academies of Sculpture and Painting in Paris and Stockholm; came to Philadelphia in May, 1794. Washington is said to have given him a single sitting for the portrait which was engraved by H. B. Hall for Irving's "Life of Washington," the picture at that time being in possession of Charles Augustus Davis of New York. The artist made several copies of this picture. He remained in this country until the Autumn of 1796, when he returned to Stockholm. He came again to Philadelphia in 1800, and in the following year married a granddaughter of Hesselius, pastor of the Swedish congregation at Wilmington, Del. Shortly after his marriage, he purchased a farm below Marcus Hook on the Delaware, where he died in 1811. After his death his pictures were sold at auction, a small copy of his "Danae" bringing $500. Some time afterward, the original was sold in New York for $1,500.

WESCOTT, Sue May. Miniature painter, who exhibited portrait miniatures at the exhibition at the Penna. Academy of the Fine Arts, Philadelphia, 1922. *Address*, 5970 Woodbine Ave., Overbrook, Pa.

WESSELHOEFT, Mary F. Painter and illustrator. Born in Boston in 1873. Pupil of Boston Art Museum. *Address*, 178 Waverly Place, New York.

WEST, Benjamin. Painter. Born in Pennsylvania, in 1728, on what is now the campus of Swarthmore College, of Quaker parentage. He early showed great artistic talent in drawing and painting and is said to have been supplied with his first colors by an Indian chief. He later received some instruction and better materials from William Williams, an English artist then sojourning in Philadelphia. West went to Lancaster, and there made his first attempt at portraiture painting a likeness of his friend William Henry, and an historical scene, "The Death of Socrates." He became a pupil of Provost William Smith, graduating as a member of the class of 1757 of the University of Pennsylvania. He fell in love with Elizabeth Shewell, a charming maid whom he parted from reluctantly to accept the aid of Philadelphia patrons who sent him to Rome to study. He left our shores in 1760 at the age of nearly twenty-two, and never returned. In Italy West made a careful study of the methods employed by Titian and other great Italian painters. After three years of study at the age of twenty-five he went to England and opened a studio in London, and there met Dr. Drummond, Archbishop of York, who presented him to George III, who recognized talent in the young artist's work, and ordered a canvas depicting "The Departure of Regulus from Rome." After this West soon became historical painter to the King. In 1765 the King founded the Royal Academy, and Sir Joshua Reynolds became its first president. After his death in 1792 he was succeeded by Benjamin West, who served as president almost uninterruptedly from 1792 till 1815. He married Elizabeth Shewell, who ran away from Philadelphia and crossed the sea to her artist lover. West painted four classes of pictures: portraits, minor historical scenes, great historical scenes and religious subjects. In his painting of the death of Wolfe at Quebec he repudiated, against the advice of his friends, the traditions of the classical school, clothing his characters in the dress of the time. West said "this battle took place in the year of 1758, out in the wilds of Canada. That Indian who was there with his scalping knife and tomahawk knew nothing about a toga, and it is inappropriate." The success of the picture brought about a revolution in art. In his great picture "Christ Healing the Sick" in the British National Gallery (a replica sent by West hangs in the Pennsylvania Hospital, Philadelphia), he gives to us an artistic expression in the thought that Christ walked the wards of the hospital to relieve the pain and the suffering which war had caused which will always make a strong appeal. His large picture "Death on the Pale Horse," painted in 1817, is twenty-five feet long, fifteen feet high and hangs in the Penna. Academy of Fine Arts. His "Penn's Treaty with the Indians" is at Independence Hall, Philadelphia. The Metropolitan Museum of New York owns his self-portrait, "Hagar and Ishmael," and "Apollo and Hyacinthus"; also several others. West lived again in his pupils, as he taught Charles Willson Peale, Gilbert Stuart, Thomas Sully, Washington Allston, and Samuel Morse. He was also painted by most of them, but the most pleasing portrait is that painted as a young man by his friend Matthew Pratt (see frontispiece). Unfortunately we have no very complete life of West. "The Life and Studies of Benjamin West" by John Galt, published in 1816, was written during West's lifetime, and its title page states that it is compiled from material furnished by himself. The Pennsylvania Historical Society, in Philadelphia, have many of West's paintings and drawings besides a large collection of his letters. In 1817, after the death of his wife, West's strength began to fail, though his mental faculties remained unimpaired. He died in London on March 11, 1820, and was buried in St. Paul's Cathedral.

WEST, Peter. Animal painter. Born in England in 1833. He came to this country and maintained studios in several cities. In 1878 he was settled in Cleveland, Ohio, where he painted many of the fine horses of that section of the country; he also painted still-life and genre subjects.

WEST, William Edward. Historical painter and portrait painter in oils and miniature. Born in 1788 in Lexington, Ky. West painted miniatures several years before he studied in Philadelphia with Thomas Sully about 1807. In 1819 he went to Natchez where he stayed until 1820 when he sailed for Europe. At Leghorn he painted a portrait of Shelley taken from life. In 1824 he was in Paris. From 1825 to 1839 he was in London. During the latter year he sailed for Baltimore. In 1840 he was in New York where he lived until 1855, when he moved to Nashville where he died in 1857. See: *Century Magazine*, October, 1905; *Putnam's Magazine*, September, 1907; Tuckerman, "Book of the Artists."

WEST, Mrs. A Mrs. West painted some very good portraits about 1820 in Attleboro, Mass.

WESTERMAN, Harry J. Painter and illustrator. Born in West Virginia in 1876. Pupil of Columbus Art School. Illustrator and cartoonist for newspaper syndicate. *Address*, 1661 Franklin Park, Columbus, Ohio.

WESTFELDT, Patrick McL. Painter. Born in New York, N. Y.; died in New Orleans in 1907. Studied with Carl Hecker and William Prettyman. Specialty, landscapes, mostly in water color.

WESTOBY. Portrait painter. The portrait of Lindley Murray, published in (Longacre and Herring) National Portrait Gallery, is noted as engraved by Gimber after the portrait by Westoby.

WESTON, Frances M. Painter, who exhibited water colors at the Penna. Academy of the Fine Arts, Philadelphia, 1922. *Address*, Haddonfield, N. J.

WESTON, Henry W. Weston was engraving, in a feeble manner, maps, Bible illustrations, etc., in Philadelphia in 1803–06, for Mathew Carey, book-publisher of that city.

WESTON, Mrs. Mary. Miniature painter.

WESTON, Morris. Painter, who exhibited at the National Academy of Design, New York, 1925. *Address*, 127 East 59th St., New York.

WESTWOOD, Charles. Engraver. Born in Birmingham, England. He came to the United States in 1851 with John Rogers, the engraver. Westwood was a clever general engraver, but he was dissipated, and committed suicide about 1855.

WETHERALD, Harry H. Painter, who exhibited water colors at the Penna. Academy of the Fine Arts, Philadelphia, 1925. *Address*, Providence, R. I.

WETHERBEE, George. Painter. Born in Cincinnati in 1851. He was educated in Boston; studied at Royal Academy of Arts, Antwerp; also in London. Has travelled and resided in West Indies, France, Germany, Italy, Belgium; finally settled in London. Member: Royal Institute of Painters in Water Colors; Royal Society of Oil Painters; Royal British Colonial Society of Artists; New Gallery Society, London. *Address*, 18 Redington Road, Hampstead, N. W., London, Eng.

WETHERILL, E. Kent K. Painter, who exhibited at the National Academy of Design, New York, 1925. *Address*, 145 East 23d St., New York, N. Y.

WETHERILL, Roy. Painter. Born in New Brunswick, N. J., in 1880. Pupil of R. L. Lambdin and of Norman Tolson. *Address*, Kansas City Art Institute, Kansas City, Mo.

WETMORE, Mary Minerva. Portrait painter. Born in Canfield, Ohio. Pupil of Cleveland Art School; Art Students' League of New York under Chase and Cox; Julien Academy in Paris under Constant and Laurens; Colarossi Academy under Courtois and Primet. Member: Chicago Society of Artists; Chicago Arts and Crafts; National Association of Women Painters and Sculptors. Instructor of painting at University of Illinois. *Address*, 511 West Church St., Champaign, Ill.

WETZEL, George J. Painter. Born in New York in 1870. Pupil of Art Students' League of New York under Mowbray, Beckwith, Cox and Chase. Member: Art Students' League of New York; National Fine Arts Society. Awards: Honorable mention, Art Club of Phila.; honorable mention, Salmagundi Club. Work: "Edgar Allan Poe Cottage," Bronx Museum of Science and Art, New York. *Address*, 1624 University Ave., New York, N. Y.

WEYL, Max. Painter. Born in Germany in 1837. He came to America in 1853. He is represented in the Corcoran Art Gallery and National Art Gallery in Washington, and in many private collections. He died in 1914.

WEYRICK, Joseph Lewis. Painter. Specialty, water colors. He died in Baltimore in 1918.

WHALEN, John W. Painter. Born in Worcester, Mass., in 1891. Pupil of Chase and Eric Pape. *Address*, 29 Richards St., Worcester, Mass.

WHALEY, Edna R. (Mrs. M. S.). Painter. Born in New Orleans, La., in 1884. Pupil of Woodward at Newcomb School of Art. Member of Columbia, S. C., Art Association. Exhibited at Albright Gallery, Buffalo; Academy of Fine Arts, Hartford, Conn. *Address*, College Place, Columbia, S. C.

WHARTON, Philip Fishbourne. Painter. Born in Philadelphia in 1841. He studied at the Penna. Academy of the Fine Arts and in Paris. His best known pictures are "Perdita" which received a medal at the Centennial in 1876, "Eventide," "Uncle Jim" and "Waiting for the Parade." He died in 1880.

WHARTON, T. H. According to Dunlap this artist was painting in New York in 1834.

WHEELER, Cleora. Illustrator. Born in Austin, Minn. Pupil of Julie Gauthier. Member: American Bookplate Society; Minn. State Art Society. Award: First award in design, Minn. State Art Society, 1913. *Address*, 1376 Summit Ave., St. Paul, Minn.

WHEELER, Clifton A. Painter. Born in Hadley, Ind., in 1883. Pupil of Forsyth in Indianapolis; Henri, Miller, and Chase in New York; also studied in Europe. Work: "Twilight in January" at Herron Art Institute. He has also done mural paintings. *Address*, 5317 Lowell Ave., Indianapolis, Ind.

WHEELER, Dora (Mrs. Keith). Painter. Born in Jamaica, L. I., in 1858. She studied with Wm. M. Chase in New York, and with Bouguereau in Paris. She painted a series of portraits of English and American authors, but devoted herself largely to decorative designing. *Address*, 33 West 67th St., New York, N. Y.

WHEELER, E. Kathleen. Sculptor. Born in England in 1884; came to America in 1914. Specialty, animals. *Address*, Hillside, Wis.

WHEELER, Helen C. Painter. Born in Newark, N. J., in 1877. Pupil of John C. Johansen. Member of Art Students' League of New York. *Address*, 6 Kirk Place, Newark, N. J.

WHEELER, Janet D. Portrait painter. Born in Detroit, Mich. Pupil of the Penna. Academy of the Fine Arts, Philadelphia; and of Julien Academy and Courtois, Paris. Exhibited at the Salon, Paris, and the Penna.

Academy of the Fine Arts, Philadelphia. *Address*, 1710 Chestnut St., Philadelphia, Pa.

WHEELER, Laura B. Portrait painter and illustrator. Born at Hartford, Conn. Pupil of William Chase and Henry McCarter. *Address*, Brinton Cottage, Cheyney, Penna.

WHEELER, W. R. Portrait painter. Born in Michigan in 1832. In 1855 he moved to Hartford, Conn. His portraits are well modeled and good likenesses, but his best work was done in painting children's heads.

WHEELOCK. L a n d s c a p e painter. In "Tuckerman's American Artist Life" the water color studies of the White Mountain scenery by Wheelock are noted as skilful and true in atmosphere.

WHEELOCK, Warren. Painter and sculptor. Born in Sutton, Mass., in 1880. *Address*, 131 Macdougal St., New York.

WHELEN, Blanche. Painter. Born in Los Angeles, Calif. Pupil of Nicholas Haz. Member of California Art Club, and Whitney Studio Club. *Address*, 1812 West 24th St., Los Angeles, Calif.

WHELPLEY, P. M. About 1845 this capital engraver was located in New York. He engraved portraits in mezzotint.

WHETSEL (Mrs. Gertrude P.). Painter. Born in Kansas in 1886. Pupil of Clyde Leon Keller. She paints marines and landscapes. Member of Portland Art Association. *Address*, 585 East 27th St., North Portland, Ore.

WHISTLER, James Abbott McNeill. Painter, etcher and lithographer who was born in Lowell, Mass., on July 11, 1834; died in London, England, July 17, 1903. Whistler entered the West Point Military Academy, but his career there was not a success, though he secured prizes in French and in drawing, and in 1854 he received his discharge. He then obtained a post as draughtsman in the office of the Coast and Geodetic Survey at Washington, in which capacity he made his first etchings. If the three months which he spent under the government taught him the technicalities of etching on copper they were not wholly wasted, but he was quite unfitted for routine work and early in 1855 he gave up his position and definitely devoted himself to art. After a short visit to England he settled in Paris in 1855 and entered the studio of Gleyre, a romantic painter with whom he can have had no sympathy. Here, however, he was associated with such men as Degas, Bracquemond, Alphonse Legros and Faintin-Latour, and among his fellow-students were Sir E. J. Poynter and Mr. George Du Maurier. While in Paris he executed the "Little French Set" of etchings which were published in 1858. In 1859 Mr. Whistler

was in London, where he lived with his brother-in-law, Sir Seymour Haden, in Sloane Street. Two of his etchings were exhibited at the Academy in this year—probably two of the Thames Series, which were produced between 1859 and 1861, though not published until many years later. He afterwards shared a studio for some time with Du Maurier in Newman Street, Oxford Street, and then, after spending some months at Wapping, where he was engaged both in painting and etching, he settled in Lindsay Row, Chelsea. His first important picture, "At the Piano," was hung at the Royal Academy in 1860 and was bought by John Phillip, R.A., the well-known painter of Spanish subjects. This was followed next year by "La Mere Gerard," a picture now in the possession of Mr. A. C. Swinburne, and for several years after this paintings and etchings by Mr. Whistler appeared in the Academy Exhibitions. In 1863 "The White Girl" was sent to the Salon but rejected; it was, however, hung in the "Salon des Refuses" where it aroused great enthusiasm among the critics.

After a visit to Valparaiso in 1865–66 where he painted several pictures of the harbor and ocean, the artist again settled in Chelsea. Here he painted many pictures of the great reach of the river opposite his house in Lindsay Row, as well as "The Thames in Ice," "The Last of Old Westminster," and other famous pictures of the Thames. During this period also were painted the series of pictures in which the influence of Japanese art is predominant, chief among them being "La Princesse du Pays de la Porcelaine," "Die Lange Leizen of the Six Marks," "The Golden Screen," "The Little White Girl," the "Symphony in White No. 3" and "The Balcony."

In 1874 Mr. Whistler held the first exhibition of his work in a gallery in Pall Mall, which attracted considerable attention. Among the pictures here exhibited were the "Portrait of the Painter's Mother," which already had been hung at the Academy two years before, and the portraits of Thomas Carlyle, Miss Alexander, and of Mr. and Mrs. Leyland, which were now seen for the first time.

On the starting of the Grosvenor Gallery by Sir Coutts Lindsay in 1877, Mr. Whistler exhibited a series of "nocturnes" and other pictures, which called for a violent attack from Ruskin.

Early in 1879 he left London and went to Venice, returning towards the end of 1880 and again settling in Chelsea. The first series of Venice etchings (twelve in number) were shown at the Fine Arts Society's Gallery in December, 1880, and early next year a collection of fifty-three Venice pastels was exhibited in the same gallery. During the next few years three exhibitions of Mr. Whistler's work were held at Messrs. Dowdeswells' Gallery—namely, "Etchings and Dry Points," second series, a collection of fifty-one prints, 1883, and "Notes, Harmonies and Nocturnes," first and second series, 1884 and 1886. Meanwhile he had been exhibiting a large number of pictures at the Grosvenor Gallery, including the Portraits of Miss Rosa Corder (1879), "Connie Gilchrist Dancing" (1879), Mrs. H. B. (now Lady) Meux (1882)—one of three portraits of this lady painted at this time—and Lady Archibald Campbell (1884); also numerous nocturnes and marines.

In 1884, Mr. Whistler was elected a member of the Royal Society of British Artists, of which two years later he became President. Mr. Whistler had been working in lithography since the possibilities of that medium had been pointed out to him in 1878, and in 1887 he published his first collection of lithographs under the title of "Notes." During the next few years he executed a large number of drawings on the stone, both figure-subjects and landscape.

In 1888 a small but important collection of his pictures was got together and exhibited by Miss Gould in the rooms of the Working Women's College in Queen's Square. It included the "Mother's Portrait," the "Carlyle," the "Miss Alexander," the "Rosa Corder," the "Irving as Philip II of Spain," and other pictures.

In 1892 an important exhibition of his work was held at the Goupil's Gallery, where was brought together a collection of "Nocturnes, Marines, and Chevalet Pieces" of all periods, including several of the painter's finest works. Had anything been needed to establish the master's reputation, this exhibition, containing, as it did, only forty-three oil paintings, would have more than sufficed to do so.

Shortly after this exhibition Mr. Whistler made a tour through France and Brittany, and settled in Paris in the Rue du Bac. Many lithographs were produced during 1893–94 in Brittany, in the Luxembourg Gardens and in his own house and gardens. In 1895 he returned to England, and spent some time at Lyme Regis, where he executed a group of paintings, including "The Master Smith" and "The Rose of Lyme Regis," and a number of lithographs, chiefly of forge subjects. In December of the same year, he exhibited a collection of lithographs at the Fine Arts Society's Gallery. Mr. Whistler was again in London in 1896 and continued the production of lithographs, among which the magnificent series of the Thames Embankment done from the Savoy Hotel are the most notable. In 1898 he was elected first President of the "International Society of Sculptors, Painters, and Gravers," a position which he held until his death, which took place on July 17th, 1903. At this time he had been ailing for many months, but was at work up to the very last.

He was an Officer of the Legion of Honor of France; a member of the Societé Nationale des Artistes Francais; Commander of the Order of the Crown of Italy; Chevalier of the Order of St. Michael of Bavaria; honorary member of the Royal Academies of Bavaria, Dresden, and of St. Luke in Rome; president of the International Society of Sculptors, Painters and Gravers of England. The Metropolitan Museum of New York owns his "Nocturne in Gold and Green"; and his "Lady in Gray." See "The Art of James McNeill Whistler by T. R. Way and G. R. Dennis (1905)" and "Life and Works of James McNeill Whistler by E. R. & J. Pennell (1908)."

WHITE, Alden. Etcher. Born in Acushnet, Mass., in 1861. Pupil of V. Preissig. Member: Chicago Society of Etchers; Boston Society of Etchers; New Bedford Art Club. *Address*, Acushnet Station, New Bedford, Mass.

WHITE, Belle Cady. Painter. Born in Chatham, N. Y., in 1868. Pupil of Pratt Institute in Brooklyn; also of Snell, Woodbury, Herbert Adams and Hawthorne. Member: Brooklyn Water Color Club. Instructor in Pratt Institute. *Address*, 150 Steuben St., Brooklyn, N. Y.

WHITE, Charles Henry. Etcher and illustrator. His etchings show the picturesque qualities of the city and factory districts of New York, Boston, Pittsburgh and other American cities. He has also illustrated for *Harper's Magazine*.

WHITE, C. Scott. Landscape painter. Born in Boston, Mass., in 1872. Pupil of Charles H. Woodbury. Member of Copley Society. *Address*, Belmont, Mass.

WHITE, Edwin. Painter. Born in South Hadley, Mass., in 1817. He studied in Paris and in Dusseldorf. His studio was in New York, and he was elected to the National Academy of Design in 1849. He was best known for his American historical pictures. "Washington Resigning His Commission" was painted for the State of Maryland. He died at Saratoga Springs, N. Y., in 1877.

WHITE, Elizabeth A. Miniature painter, who exhibited at the Penna. Academy of the Fine Arts, Philadelphia, 1925. *Address*, Marlborough-Blenheim, Atlantic City, N. J.

WHITE, George F. Painter. Born in 1868 in Des Moines, Iowa. Exhibited water colors at the Penna. Academy of Fine Arts, Philadelphia, 1922. *Address*, 3 S. W. 9th St., Des Moines, Ia.

WHITE, George H. Engraver. Some fairly good portraits, engraved in a mixed manner about 1870, are thus signed.

WHITE, G. I. This good line-engraver of portraits was working about 1825–30 in this country, but none of the prints seen give any indication of locality.

WHITE, Helene Maynard. Painter. Born in Philadelphia. Pupil of Art Students'

League; Pa. Academy of Fine Arts; Drexel Institute; also studied art in Paris. Professional portrait painter since 1895. She has exhibited at all the leading art institutions, and at the St. Louis Exposition; has painted portraits of many notable people; also modeled heroic figure of ''Chingachgook'' for Mohican Lodge, Red Bank, N. J. Awarded gold medals and silver medal, etc. Member: Fellowship, Academy of Fine Arts; Plastic Club; Harmonic Society of University of Pa.; Lyceum Club, London; Historical Pageant Association. *Address*, 1530 Walnut St., Philadelphia.

WHITE, Henry C. Painter. Born in Hartford in 1861. Pupil of D. W. Tryon and Art Students' League of New York. Member: Conn. Academy of Fine Arts; New York Water Color Club; The Pastellists. *Address*, Waterford, Conn.

WHITE, John Blake. Painter. Born in Charleston, S. C., in 1782. In 1803 he went to London and studied under Benj. West. He excelled as a historical painter; he was also an author, practiced law, and was a member and director of the South Carolina Academy of Fine Arts. He died in 1859. Painted ''Genl. Marion Inviting British Officers to Dinner''; also painted ''The Battle of New Orleans'' and ''Grave Robbers.''

WHITE, Margaret Wood (Mrs.). Painter. Born in Chicago in 1893. Pupil of Bridgman. Member of National Association of Women Painters and Sculptors. *Address*, Woodmere, L. I., N. Y.

WHITE, Nelson C. Painter, who exhibited at the National Academy, New York, 1925. Born at Waterford, Conn., in 1900. *Address*, 50 West 67th St., New York, N. Y.

WHITE, Orrin A. Painter. Born in Hanover, Ill., in 1883. Member of California Art Club. Represented by ''Sierra Peaks'' at Los Angeles Museum. *Address*, 1302 Stevenson Ave., Pasadena, Calif.

WHITE, Thomas Gilbert. Portrait and mural painter. Born in Grand Rapids, Mich., in 1877. Pupil of Julien Academy under Constant and Laurens; also student of Whistler and Mac Monnies. Painted mural panels in Pan-American Building, Washington; also painted portrait of Gov. McCreary of Kentucky. *Address*, Cowmoney Lodge, Fairfield, Conn.

WHITE, Thomas Sturt. Engraver. The *New England Weekly Journal*, for July 8, 1734, contains the following notice of a possible early engraver and printer of copperplates, though no signed work is known to the writer: ''Engraver from London, not having met with such success as he expected since he came to Boston; hereby gives Notice that he

27

intends sailing for London in the Fall, unless he meets with sufficient encouragement to oblige him to stay. This therefore is to inform all Gentlemen, Goldsmiths and others, that they may have all manner of Engraving either on Gold, Silver, Copper or Pewter; likewise Rolling Press Printing, as well and cheap as is performed in London.
''N. B. The said White lives at the Second Door on the Right Hand in Williams Court, in Cornhill.''

WHITE, Walter C. L. Painter. Born in England in 1876. Pupil of Carlsen, Beck and Bridgman. *Address*, Farmer's and St. Mark's Aves., St. Albans, L. I., N. Y.

WHITE, William Fletcher. Illustrator. Illustrations for ''Half-Told Tales'' by Henry Van Dyke (*Harper's Magazine*, Dec., 1924).

WHITECHURCH, Robert. Engraver. Born in London in 1814; he was living in 1883. Mr. Baker says that Whitechurch did not commence to engrave until he was thirty years of age. He came to the United States about 1848 and lived for some years in Philadelphia. In his later professional life he worked for the Treasury Department at Washington. He was an excellent engraver of portraits in line, stipple and mezzotint.

WHITEHAM, Edna May. Painter and illustrator. Born in Nebraska. Student at Chicago Art Institute. *Address*, 9 Westmoreland Ave., Takoma Park, Md.

WHITEHEAD, Walter. Illustrator. Born in Chicago, Ill., in 1874. Pupil of Howard Pyle. Instructor at Chicago Academy of Fine Arts. *Address*, Care of Seaman Agency, 470 Fourth Ave., New York, N. Y.

WHITEHORN, James. Painter. Born in Rutland Co., Vt., in 1787. He was made a member of the National Academy. He devoted himself to portraiture, and his picture of Silas Wright is in the City Hall, New York. He also designed the well-known mezzotint engraving of ''Henry Clay Addressing the Senate'' published about 1846. He died in 1830.

WHITEHURST, Camelia. Painter. Born in Maryland. Pupil of William Chase. Member of Fellowship of Penna. Academy of the Fine Arts. *Address*, 411 North Charles St., Baltimore, Md.

WHITEMAN, S. Edwin. Landscape painter. Born in Philadelphia, Pa., in 1860; died 1922. Pupil of Boulanger, Constant and Lefebvre in Paris. Instructor at Johns Hopkins University. Member of Charcoal Club of Baltimore, Md.

WHITEFIELD, Emma M. Painter. Born in Greensboro, N. C., in 1874. Pupil of Art Students' League, New York. Portraits in Richmond, Va., State Library. *Address*, 800 Grove Ave., Richmond, Va.

WHITESIDE, Frank Reed. Landscape painter. Born in Philadelphia, Pa., in 1866. Pupil of Penna. Academy of the Fine Arts; also of Laurens and Constant in Paris. Member: Philadelphia Sketch Club; Fellowship, Penna. Academy of the Fine Arts; Philadelphia Water Color Club; Philadelphia Art Alliance. *Address*, 1010 Clinton St., Philadelphia, Pa.

WHITING, Almon Clark. Painter. Born in Worcester, Mass., in 1878. Studied at Mass. Normal Art School, Boston; Academie Julien, Paris, under Constant and Laurens. Pupil of Whistler, Paris. Director, 1901–03, Toledo Museum of Art. Mural decoration: ''The Goose Girl,'' residence of W. W. Windle, Millbury, Mass. Member: Society of Western Artists; Salmagundi Club; American Art Association, Paris. *Address*, Salmagundi Club, 47 5th Ave., New York City.

WHITING, John D. Painter and illustrator. Born in Ridgefield, Conn., in 1884. Member of New Haven Paint and Clay Club. *Address*, 345 Whitney Ave., New Haven, Conn.

WHITLOCK, Mary U. Painter. Born at Great Barrington, Mass. Pupil of Alden Weir; Museum of Art by ''Gloucester Harbor''; Association of Women Painters and Sculptors. *Address*, 120 Montague St., Brooklyn, New York.

WHITMAN, Sarah (Mrs. William). Born in Baltimore in 1842; died in Boston in 1904. Pupil of William M. Hunt of Boston and of Couture in Paris. Represented in the Boston Museum of Art by ''Gloucester Harbor''; ''Sunset''; Portrait of Martin Brimmer; ''Warm Night''; ''Edge of Evening''; ''Rhododendrons''; ''Roses.''

WHITMER, Helen C. (Mrs.). Painter. Born in Darby, Penna., in 1870. Pupil of Breckenridge, Anshutz, Henri and Vonnoh. Member of the Pittsburgh Art Association. *Address*, 2615 Shady Ave., Pittsburgh, Penna.

WHITMORE, Robert H. Painter and etcher. Born in Dayton, Ohio, in 1890. Pupil of Cincinnati Art Academy. *Address*, R. R. 1, Osborne, Ohio.

WHITNEY, Anne. Sculptor. Born in 1821. She studied abroad and on her return to this country established her studio in Boston in 1873. She has executed many portraits and ideal groups. Her statue of Harriet Martineau is at Wellesley College, and a seated statue of

Charles Sumner is in front of the law school at Harvard. Her statue of Samuel Adams is in the Capitol at Washington. She died at the age of 94, in 1915.

WHITNEY, Beatrice (Mrs.). Painter. Born in Chelsea, Mass., in 1888. Pupil of Tarbell, Benson and Hale. Awarded prize at National Academy of Design in 1914. *Address*, 91 Francis St., Brookline, Mass.

WHITNEY, Daniel Webster. Painter. Born in Maryland in 1896. Pupil of Daniel Garber and Hugh Breckenridge. Exhibited water colors at Penna. Academy of the Fine Arts, 1922. *Address*, Catonsville, Maryland.

WHITNEY, Elias. Wood engraver. He succeeded Benj. F. Childs as superintendent of engraving for the Tract Society. His engraving of the designs of the Englishman Gilbert are among his best work and can be compared to the engraving of Dalziel. He illustrated largely for Putnam & Co., New York. (See ''History of Wood Engraving in America'' by W. J. Linton.)

WHITNEY, Mrs. Harry Payne. Sculptor. Born in New York City. She studied sculpture under Henry Anderson and James E. Fraser, New York, and took a course at the Art Students' League, New York; also studied under Andrew O'Connor, Paris, France. Principal works: Aztec Fountain, in Pan-American Building, Washington, D. C.; also Titanic Memorial, for same city; El Dorado Fountain, San Francisco; 2 panels for Triumphant Arch, New York; etc. Member: American Federation of Arts; Association of Women Painters and Sculptors; National Institute of Social Sciences; International Historical Society; National Art Club. *Address*, 871 Fifth Ave., New York, N. Y.

WHITNEY, Mrs. Helen Reed. Painter. Born in Brookline, Mass., in 1878. Pupil of Boston School of Drawing and Painting under Hale, Benson and Tarbell. Member: Plastic Club; Philadelphia Art Alliance. *Address*, Moylan, Rose Valley, Pa.

WHITNEY, Isabel L. Mural painter and illustrator. Born in Brooklyn, N. Y. Pupil of Arthur Dow; Howard Pyle; Haley-Lever. Member: Brooklyn Society of Artists; National Art Club; Art Alliance of America; Society of Independent Artists. *Address*, 337 Fourth Ave., New York, N. Y.

WHITNEY, Josepha. Painter. Born in Washington, D. C., in 1872. Pupil of Messer, Perrie and Cherouzet. *Address*, 237 Church St., New Haven, Conn.

WHITNEY, Margaret Q. Sculptor. Born in Chicago, Ill., in 1900. Pupil of Charles

Grafly. Member: Philadelphia Art Alliance; Fellowship, Penna. Academy of the Fine Arts. *Address*, 147 Gates Ave., Montclair, N. J.

WHITNEY, Philip R. Painter. Born in Council Bluffs, Ia., in 1878. Pupil of Fred Wagner; Department of Art, Mass. Institute of Technology; School of Fine Arts, University of Pennsylvania. Member: Philadelphia Sketch Club; Philadelphia Art Club; Philadelphia Art Alliance. Work: "Winter," in Penna. State College. *Address*, Moylan, Rose Valley, Pa.

WHITTAKER, John Barnard. Painter. Born in 1836. A painter of decided merit. He painted several portraits of prominent men for the city of New York. Mr. Whittaker's portrait of John W. Hunter (Mayor of Brooklyn), painted in 1876, hangs in the old City Hall.

WHITTEMORE, C. Helen (Mrs. William J.). Painter. Born in England. Pupil of William M. Chase. Member of National Association of Women Painters and Sculptors. *Address*, 58 West 57th St., New York, N. Y.

WHITTEMORE, Frances D. (Mrs.). Painter. Born in Decatur, Ill. Pupil of Alden Weir and Kenyon Cox. Student of Art Institute of Chicago. Director of Mulvane Art Museum, Washburn College, Topeka, Kans.

WHITTEMORE, Mrs. Grace Connor. Painter. Born in Columbia County, Pa., in 1876. Pupil of Daingerfield and Snell. Member of New Jersey Society of Arts and Crafts. *Address*, 6 Morse Ave., East Orange, N. J.

WHITTEMORE, William John. Painter. Born in New York in 1860. Pupil of William Hart; National Academy of Design, and Art Students' League, New York; and of Jules Lefebvre and Benjamin Constant, Paris. Silver medal, Paris Exposition, 1889; bronze medal, Atlanta Exposition; Proctor prize. Elected Associate Member of the National Academy of Design in 1917. Member: American Water Color Society; New York Water Color Club; American Society of Miniature Painters. Clubs: Century, Lotos, Salmagundi. *Address*, 58 West 57th St., New York, N. Y.

WHITTREDGE, Worthington. Painter. Born in Springfield, Ohio, in 1820; died in Summit, N. J., in 1810. Studied landscape and portrait painting in Cincinnati. Going abroad in 1849, he continued his studies in London, Paris and Antwerp, and in Dusseldorf under Andreas Achenbach. Subsequently he settled in New York, making a specialty of landscapes, and actively participating in art matters. He was elected an Associate Member and, in 1862, an Academician of the National Academy of Design, of which he was president for the year 1875–76. He received a bronze medal at the Centennial Exhibition, Philadelphia, 1876; honorable mention at the Paris Exposition, 1889; silver medals at the Pan-American Exposition, 1901, and the St. Louis Exposition, 1904.

WICKER, Mary H. Painter, who exhibited at the Annual Exhibition of Penna. Academy of the Fine Arts, Philadelphia, 1926. *Address*, 139 West 54th St., New York City.

WICKEY, Helen Reed. Painter, who exhibited water colors at the Penna. Academy of the Fine Arts, Philadelphia, 1925. *Address*, 163 West 23d St., New York City.

WICKS, Hepple en Earl. Portrait painter and illustrator. Born in Le Roy, Genesee County, N. Y. Pupil of L. M. Wiles, Irving R. Wiles, C. Y. Turner; also student at Julien Academy and Beaux Arts in Paris. *Address*, 710 Carnegie Hall, 156 West 57th St., New York City.

WIEBKING, Edward. Painter. *Address*, 104 Mason St., Cincinnati, Ohio.

WIECHMANN, Margaret H. Sculptor. Born in New York in 1886. Pupil of A. Phimister Proctor; Art Students' League and National Academy of Design, New York. Specialty, small bronzes of animals. *Address*, Wainscott, L. I., N. Y.

WIECZOREK, Max. Painter. Born in Breslau, Germany, in 1863. Studied in Italy and Germany; pupil of Ferdinand Keller and Max Thedy. Member: California Art Club; Laguna Beach Artists' Association; Art Alliance; California Water Color Society. Awards: silver medal, Pan-California Exposition, San Diego, 1915; Harrison popular prize, California Art Club, 1918; merit prize, Arizona State Fair, 1920; merit prize, Laguna Beach Artists' Association, 1920; A. J. Ackerman prize, California Art Club, 1920. Work: "Portrait of George Chaffey," Library, Union Chaffey High School, Ontario, Calif.; "Head of Christ," Keotona Institute of Theosophy, Hollywood, Calif.; "The Old Sycamore," Engineers' Club, New York, N. Y.; "Foothills," Los Angeles Athletic Club. *Address*, 311 Hollingsworth Building, Los Angeles, Calif.

WIEGAND, Gustav. Painter. Born in Bremen, Germany, in 1870. Pupil of Dresden Royal Academy under Eugene Bracht; under Chase in New York. Member: Salmagundi Club; Allied Artists' Association. Awards: bronze medal, St. Louis Exposition, 1904; second Hallgarten prize, National Academy of Design, 1905. *Address*, 44 West 96th St., New York, N. Y.

WIESSLER, William. Painter. Born in 1887. Pupil of Frank Duveneck. Member of Cincinnati Art Club. *Address*, 419 East Liberty St., Cincinnati, Ohio.

WIGAND, A. Albright (Mrs. Otto). Painter. Member: National Association of Women Painters and Sculptors. Awards: New York Woman's Art Club prize, 1908; Shaw memorial prize, National Academy of Design, 1909; Simpson prize, New York Woman's Art Club, 1909; National Art Club prize, New York Woman's Art Club, 1912. *Address*, 1947 Broadway, New York, N. Y.

WIGAND, Otto Charles. Painter. Born in New York. Pupil of Art Students' League in New York; of Boulanger and Lefebvre in Paris. Member: New York Water Color Club. *Address*, 1947 Broadway, New York, N. Y.

WIGGIN, J. This is a fraudulent signature. A portrait of Benjamin Rush in line was engraved by J. Akin and published by him in Philadelphia in 1800. A later impression of this plate is found with the name of the engraver and a long dedicatory address erased; it is relettered "Engraved by J. Wiggin."

WIGGINS, Carleton. Painter. Born in Turners, N. Y., in 1848. Studied art, National Academy of Design in 1870; Paris, 1880–81; also under H. Carmiencke and George Inness. Specialty, cattle and landscapes. Exhibited in Paris Salon, 1881; Prize Fund, 1894 (gold medal); Royal Academy, London; also in other exhibitions in United States and abroad. Principal paintings: "A Holstein Bull," 1891 (Metropolitan Museum of Art); "Morning on the Hills" (Brooklyn Museum); "The Wanderers" (Hamilton Club, Brooklyn); "Ploughing in France," 1894; "Plough Horse," 1899 (Lotos Club, New York); "Sheep and Landscape" (Newark Art Museum); etc. Elected an Associate Member of the National Academy of Design, 1892; National Academy, 1906. Member: American Water Color Society; Society of Landscape Painters. *Address*, Lyme, Conn.

WIGGINS, Guy. Painter. Born in Brooklyn, N. Y., in 1883. Awarded Hartford prize, Conn. Academy, 1916; Turnbull prize, Salmagundi Club, 1916; honorable mention, Art Club, Philadelphia, 1916; Norman W. Harris bronze medal, Art Institute, Chicago, 1918; Charles N. Flagg prize, Conn. Academy, 1918; Isador prize, Salmagundi Club, 1919; etc. Represented in Metropolitan Museum of Art, New York; Brooklyn Institute of Arts and Sciences; National Gallery, Washington; Syracuse (New York) Museum; Hackley Museum, Muskegon, Mich.; and in Reading, Pa., etc. Elected an Associate Member of the National Academy of Design, 1916. Member of Conn. Academy of Fine Arts. Clubs: Lotos (life); National Arts (life); Salmagundi (New York); Philadelphia Art. *Address*, Lyme, Conn.

WIGGINS, Sidney M. Painter and etcher. Born in New Haven, N. Y. Pupil of Robert Henri. *Address*, 601 West 138th St., New York, N. Y.

WIGHT, Moses. Painter. Born in Boston, Mass., in 1827. Studied in Boston and later in Paris under Herbert and Leon Bonnat. He painted a portrait of Humbolt at the age of 82 in Berlin in 1852, now in the collection of the Boston Museum of Fine Arts. He died in 1895.

WIGHTMAN, Thomas. Engraver. "The Croaker," a writer in the *Boston Courier*, in 1849, refers to Thomas Wightman as "a young artist" who came to Boston from England about 1806. But Wightman was in New England prior to 1806 as "Dean's Analytical Guide to Penmanship" was published in Salem in 1802, illustrated by twenty-five copperplates. We are told that these same plates were "Collected by Henry Dean and correctly engraved by Thomas Wightman." Wightman also engraved some of the plates for a mathematical text-book published in 1806 by Prof. Webber, of Harvard College. In 1814 he was in the employ of the Boston engraver Abel Bowen, and he engraved for "The Naval Monument," published by Bowen in that year. The portraits executed by Wightman are fairly well done in stipple, and the publication dates of his prints would indicate that he was working until 1820. Wightman engraved some of the plates in "The American Builder's Companion," by A. Benjamin and D. Raynerd, Boston, 1806. Some book-plates bear his name as engraver.

WILCOX, Frank Nelson. Painter and etcher. Born in Cleveland, Ohio, in 1887. Represented in the Cleveland Museum by "The Old Market." *Address*, Cleveland School of Art, Cleveland, Ohio.

WILCOX, John Angel James. Engraver. Born in Portage, N. Y., in 1835; living in Boston in 1908. In 1856 Wilcox entered the office of J. C. Kellogg, of Hartford, Conn., and there learned to engrave. In 1860 he removed to Boston and remained there. Though originally taught to engrave in strict line, he worked in stipple, mezzotint and etching with equal facility. His line portraits are admirable pieces of work, but he covered the whole range of engraving in portraits, historical and subject plates and landscapes; latterly he designed book-plates and title pages. He has also worked at portrait painting.

WILCOX, Lois. Painter. Born in Pittsburgh, Penna. Pupil of Collin, Poore, Hale and Metcalf. Member of National Association of Women Painters and Sculptors, New York. *Address*, Mountain Road, Englewood, N. J.

WILCOX, Urquhart. Painter. Born in New Haven in 1876. Pupil of Art Students' League of Buffalo. Represented by paintings in Albright Art Gallery, Buffalo. *Address*, 79 Allen St., Buffalo, N. Y.

WILCOX, W. H. Landscape painter. In 1853 he painted several views of the lakes in New York State, especially of Lake Champlain.

WILDE, Hamilton G. Painter, of Boston, Mass. Studied in this country and abroad. Principally genre painter. Work: ''Girl and Doves''; ''Sultana''; ''Roman Peasant.''

WILDE, Ida M. Miniature painter, who exhibited at the Penna. Academy of the Fine Arts, Philadelphia, 1925. *Address*, 82 Lafayette Ave., Brooklyn, N. Y.

WILDE, Miss Jenny. Painter. Native of New Orleans. She was a member of the Artists' Association of New Orleans and of the Art League of New York. She did landscape, genre and portrait work, and for many years was engaged in designing tableaux and floats for the New Orleans Carnival Organization. Represented in the Louisiana State Museum.

WILDHACK, Robert. Painter and illustrator. Born in Pekin, Ill., in 1881. Pupil of Robert Henri in New York. Specialty, posters. *Address*, Box 179, Los Angeles, Calif.

WILES, Gladys (Mrs. W. R. Jepson). Painter. Born in New York. Pupil of Cox and Chase. Member of National Association of Women Painters and Sculptors. Awarded medal of French Museum. *Address*, Care of I. R. Wiles, 130 West 57th St., New York City.

WILES, Irving Ramsey. Painter. Born in Utica, N. Y., in 1862. He was the son and a pupil of the well-known artist Lemuel M. Wiles. From his father's studio he went to the Art Students' League and from there to Paris. He studied two years in Paris at the Academie Julien under M. Lefebvre and in the atelier of M. Carolus-Duran. About 1879 he began to show his pictures in the New York exhibitions and at once made his mark. He is well known as a painter of portraits, figure-pieces, genre and out-of-door scenes. In water color he displays surpassing skill, his handling of transparent washes being almost phenomenally clever. His drawing is accurate and subtle at the same time, and his color schemes show agreeable harmonies of tint. Mr. Wiles was elected a National Academician in 1897. He is a member of the Society of American Artists and the American Water Color Society. He took the third Hallgarten prize at the Academy in 1886, and the Clarke prize in 1889 for his beautiful composition ''The Sonata.'' *Address*, 130 West 57th St., New York City.

WILES, Lemuel M. Landscape painter. Born at Perry, N. Y., in 1826. Pupil of William M. Hart and of J. F. Cropsey. He was the father of Irving R. Wiles. He died in New York City in 1905.

WILEY, Cather. Painter, who exhibited at the National Academy, New York, 1925. *Address*, Knoxville, Tenn.

WILEY, Frederick J. Painter. He was awarded a bronze medal at the St. Louis Exposition of 1904. Member of Century Association. *Address*, 139 West 55th St., New York City.

WILFORD, L. F. Painter, who received honorable mention at the California Print Makers in 1922. *Address*, R. R. 29, Stamford, Conn.

WILGUS, John. Painter, of Buffalo, N. Y. He was elected an Honorary Member of the National Academy of Design in 1839. His painting of an Indian chief was exhibited in the Centennial Exhibition of the National Academy of Design in 1925.

WILHELM, Arthur L. Painter. Born in Muscatine, Ia., in 1881. Pupil of C. C. Rosenkranz and of the Art Institute of Chicago. Award: special mention, Minn. State Exhibition, 1916. *Address*, 981 Hague Ave., St. Paul, Minn.

WILIMOVSKY, Charles A. Painter and etcher. Born in Chicago, Ill., in 1885. Pupil of Art Institute of Chicago; also of J. C. Johansen and Wm. M. Chase. Member: Chicago Art Students' League; Alumni, Art Institute of Chicago; Chicago Society of Etchers. Awards: Dean prize, Kansas City Fine Arts Institute, 1916; silver medal, Oklahoma Artists, 1917; prize, Kansas City Art Institute, 1920. Represented in Lindsborg, Kans., University; Kansas City Club. *Address*, 2110 East 30th St., Kansas City, Mo.

WILKE, William H. Illustrator and etcher. Born at San Francisco, Calif. Pupil of A. F. Mathews; also of Laurens and Blanche in Paris. Member: California Society of Etchers; California Miniature Painters. Award: gold medal, Panama-Pacific Exposition, San Francisco, 1915. *Address*, 1130 Shattuck Ave., Berkeley, Calif.

WILKINSON. In Tuckerman's ''American Artists' Life'' mention is made of Wilkinson as a landscape painter.

WILL, Blanca. Sculptor and illustrator. Born in Rochester, N. Y., in 1881. Pupil of Herbert Adams; James Fraser; G. G. Barnard; Sonia Rosental; D. W. Tryon; John Alexander; of Tryon in Karlsruhe; Tuhrig in Dresden. *Address*, 340 Millville Ave., Palo Alto, Calif.

WILLARD, Asaph. Engraver. As early as 1816 A. Willard was in business in Albany, N. Y., as a member of the firm of Willard & Rawdon, bank-note and general engravers. In 1819-28 he was a member of the Graphic Co., of Hartford, Conn. He was an engraver of maps, portraits, subject plates, etc., and his plates have little merit. Willard is mentioned as having been the first preceptor of John Cheney.

WILLET, Annie Lee (Mrs. William). Painter. Born in Bristol, Pa., in 1866. Pupil of Penna. Academy of the Fine Arts; also studied in France and England. Member: St. Dunstan's Guild, Boston; Fellowship, Penna. Academy of Fine Arts; Phila. Art Alliance. Author of articles on "stained glass." Work: Designer and maker, in collaboration with William Willet, of the sanctuary and aisle windows, West Point Military Chapel; Great West Window, Post Graduate College, Princeton; Mather Memorial, Trinity Cathedral, Cleveland; Guthrie Memorial, St. John's Church, Locust Valley, L. I.; St. Paul's Cathedral, Pittsburgh; Harrison Memorial, Calvary Church, Germantown; mural paintings in St. Alvernia's Convent, Pittsburgh; Presbyterian Hospital Chapel, Pittsburgh; Thaw Memorial, Third Presbyterian Church, Pittsburgh; Buchanan Memorial, St. Nathaniel's Church, Philadelphia. *Address,* 2218 St. James Place, Philadelphia.

WILLET, William. Mural painter, craftsman, lecturer and writer. He was born in New York City in 1868, and was a pupil of Mechanics' and Tradesmen's Institute, New York; also of Van Kirk, Chase, John La Farge; studied in France and England. Member: Mural Painters; New York Architectural League, 1910; Boston Society of Arts and Crafts; St. Dunstan's Club, Boston; Fellowship of the Pennsylvania Academy of the Fine Arts; Philadelphia Art Alliance. His work included: Sanctuary Window, West Point Military Academy; window in Proctor Hall, Princeton; Mather Memorial, Trinity Cathedral, Cleveland; Guthrie Memorial, St. John's Church, Locust Valley, L. I.; St. Paul's Cathedral, Pittsburgh; Harrison Memorial, Calvary Church, Germantown; mural paintings in St. Alvernia's Convent, Pittsburgh; Presbyterian Hospital Chapel, Pittsburgh; Thaw Memorial, Third Presbyterian Church, Pittsburgh; memorial in Greenwood Cemetery Chapel, New York; Trinity Church, Syracuse; St. Paul's Church, Halifax, N. S. He was the author of "Stained Glass in Our Churches" and other articles on stained glass. He died in Philadelphia in 1921.

WILLETT, Arthur R. Mural painter. Born in England in 1868. Member: New York Architectural League, 1897; Mural Painters; Artists' Aid Society. *Address,* 489 Fifth Ave., New York.

WILLETT, J. Painter. Born in Russia in 1882. Studied in Munich and Paris and at the Imperial Academy of Art in Petrograd. *Address,* 324 East 19th St., New York, N. Y.

WILLIAMS, Alyn. Painter. Born in Wales in 1865. Pupil of Laurens and Courtois in Paris. Member: Penna. Society of Miniature Painters; Royal Cambrian Academy. Work: Miniatures of King Edward VII and Queen Alexandra, in Guildhall, London, Art Gallery. *Address,* 230 Madison Ave., New York, N. Y.

WILLIAMS, Ballard. Painter, who exhibited at the Penna. Academy of the Fine Arts, Philadelphia, 1924. *Address,* 27 West 67th St., New York, N. Y.

WILLIAMS, Caroline G. (Mrs.). Painter. Born in Fulton, N. Y., in 1855. Pupil of Cleveland School of Art. *Address,* 1858 Marloes Ave., East Cleveland, Ohio.

WILLIAMS, Charles Sneed. Painter. Born in Evansville, Ind., in 1882. Studied in Louisville, New York and London. Member: Union Internationale des Beaux Arts; Louisville Artists' Association; Washington Art Club. Award: Four-year resident scholarship at Allan-Fraser Art College, Scotland, 1902.

WILLIAMS, Clara Elsene Peck (Mrs. J. Scott). Painter and illustrator. Member: Society of Illustrators, 1912; New York Water Color Club; National Association of Women Painters and Sculptors; Fellowship of Penna. Academy of the Fine Arts. Award: Watrous prize, New York Woman's Art Club, 1912. *Address,* South Dwight Place, Englewood, N. J.

WILLIAMS, Dwight. Landscape painter. Born in Camillus, Onondaga County, N. Y., in 1856. Pupil of John C. Perry. Member: Central New York Society of Artists. Work: "Landscape," Hamilton College, N. Y.; "Landscape," Cazenovia, New York, Public Library. *Address,* 44 Albany St., Cazenovia, N. Y.

WILLIAMS, E. G., & Bro. This engraving firm was producing portraits in New York in 1880.

WILLIAMS, Frederic Allen. Sculptor, who exhibited at the Annual Exhibition of the Penna. Academy of the Fine Arts, Philadelphia, 1926. *Address,* 1931 Broadway, New York City.

WILLIAMS, Frederick Ballard. Landscape and figure painter. Born in Brooklyn in 1871. Studied under John Ward Stimson, William Hamilton Gibson, C. Y. Turner and Edgar M. Ward. Exhibitor at all important art exhibitions in the United States. His pictures hang in Metropolitan Museum of Art, New York; National Art Gallery, Washington; Brooklyn Institute of Arts and Sciences (purchased at the National Academy of Design, figure picture, 1909); also in many prominent private collections. Bronze medal, Pan-American Exposition; Inness prize, Salmagundi Club; Isador gold medal, National Academy of Design, 1909. Elected a Member of National Academy, 1909. Member: New York Water Color Club; Council of the National Academy of Design, 1910–11. *Address*, 27 West 67th St., New York, N. Y.

WILLIAMS, Frederick D. Painter. Born in Boston. He studied in his native city and later in Paris. He devotes his time to landscapes and figure-pieces. He exhibited in 1878.

WILLIAMS, George Alfred. Painter and illustrator. Born in Newark, N. J., in 1875. He began illustrating for magazines in 1899 and has illustrated many books; of late, he has devoted most of his time to painting and writing. Exhibitor at all the important art exhibitions; represented in Newark Museum by frieze of 6 paintings, interpreting the story of Tristan and Isolde in permanent collection of Art Institute of Chicago; also in many private collections. Silver medal, Panama-P. I. Exposition, 1915. Illustrated "Am. Boy's Book of Soldiers for Defense of Our Country," 1915; Robert Havell, Junior, Engraver of Audubon's "The Birds of America," 1916; Portraits of Robert Havell, Junior, 1917; Principles, 1917. Contributor to periodicals. *Address*, Kennebunkport, Maine.

WILLIAMS, Henry. Engraver and painter. Born in 1787. A few weak stipple portraits are signed as both painted and engraved by H. Williams. John Rubens Smith engraved several portraits after paintings by Henry Williams, who is referred to by Dunlap as a portrait painter working in 1812–16. The only indication of locality and date is found on his engraved portrait of Elias Smith, which was published at Portsmouth, N. H., in 1816. In 1814 Williams published in Boston "The Elements of Drawing," illustrated by twenty-six copperplate engravings. As this book has not been seen by the compiler, he cannot say whether these plates were engraved by Williams or not. As late as 1824, H. Williams advertises as a portrait and miniature painter in the *New England Palladium* with a studio at No. 6 School Street, Boston. This notice says that "He also continues to paint from the dead in his peculiar manner by Masks, etc." He died in 1830.

WILLIAMS, Isaac L. Painter. Born in Philadelphia in 1817. At fifteen he became the pupil in drawing of John R. Smith; he afterwards practiced painting with John Neagle. Lived and followed his profession in Philadelphia. He was president of the Artists' Fund Society, of which he became a member in 1860, and he also served on several exhibition committees in the Academy. Until 1844 he devoted himself to portrait painting, but later gave equal or greater attention to landscape. In 1866, at the invitation of an English gentleman,

he visited Great Britain to paint his homestead. He travelled in France and Italy, and painted historic pictures. He returned to Philadelphia and taught drawing in schools and also had private pupils; he was first preceptor of the late Henry E. Hubley. Painted a series of historic mansions of Philadelphia, now in possession of the State Historical Society. He visited Lancaster in 1854 with a commission to paint the portrait of Rev. Bernard Keenan.

WILLIAMS, John A. Illustrator. Born in Wisconsin in 1869. Pupil of Art Students' League of New York and of the Metropolitan Museum of Art School. *Address*, 47 Fifth Ave., New York City.

WILLIAMS, John Scott. Painter, etcher and illustrator. Born in England in 1877. Pupil of Art Institute of Chicago. He has done some excellent mural paintings, and exhibited water colors at the Penna. Academy of the Fine Arts, Philadelphia, 1925. *Address*, 402 West End Ave., New York City.

WILLIAMS, Kate A. Painter, who exhibited water colors at the Penna. Academy of the Fine Arts, Philadelphia, 1925. *Address*, 1264 Boston Road, New York, N. Y.

WILLIAMS, Mildred E. Painter. Born in Detroit, Mich., in 1892. Pupil of Henri and Geo. Luks; also studied abroad. Awarded prize for best figure painting, Detroit Institute, 1923. Exhibited at Penna. Academy of the Fine Arts, 1926. *Address*, 49 East 10th St., New York City.

WILLIAMS, Pauline B. Miniature painter, who exhibited at the Penna. Academy of the Fine Arts, Philadelphia, 1925. *Address*, 128 Mulberry St., Springfield, Mass.

WILLIAMS, Reed. Etcher. Born in Pittsburgh, Penna. Member of the Los Angeles Print Makers' Association. *Address*, 1111 Central Building, Los Angeles, Calif.

WILLIAMS, Walter Reid. Sculptor. Born in Indianapolis, Ind., in 1885. Pupil of Bela Pratt, and of Paul Bartlett in Paris. *Address*, 3158 North Halsted St., Chicago, Ill.

WILLIAMS, William J. Portrait painter. Born in New York in 1759. In 1792 he painted in Philadelphia a portrait from life of Washington in Masonic regalia at the request of the Masonic Lodge of Alexandria, Va. The original pastel portrait is in Alexandria, and a copy by Miss Burke is in the Masonic Hall in Philadelphia. Williams died in Charleston, S. C., in 1823, and is buried in Cedar Grove near Charleston.

WILLIAMSON, Ada C. Painter, who exhibited at the Penna. Academy of the Fine

Arts, Philadelphia, 1924, and is a member of the Fellowship. *Address*, 1921 Arch St., Philadelphia, Pa.

WILLIAMSON, J. Maynard, Jr. Painter and illustrator. Born in Pittsburgh, Pa., in 1892. Pupil of F. V. Du Mond. Member: Pittsburgh Artists' Association. Award: Prize, Pittsburgh Artists' Association, 1911. *Address*, 514 S. Linden Ave., Pittsburgh, Pa.

WILLIAMSON, John. Painter. Born in Scotland in 1826. He was brought to this country as a child. He lived in Brooklyn, N. Y. In 1861 he was elected an Associate Member of the National Academy of Design. Many of his paintings are scenes on the Hudson River or in the Catskill Mountains. He died in 1885.

WILLIAMSON, Shirley (Mrs. Edward Lincoln Williamson). Painter. Born in New York. Pupil of Arthur Dow; Art Students' League in New York; under Constant and Rodin in Paris. Member: National Association of Women Painters and Sculptors. *Address*, 425 Treehaven Apts. Berkeley, Calif.

WILLING, John Thomson. Painter. Born in Toronto, Ont., in 1860. Art manager of the Associate Sunday Magazines, and *Every Week*, New York. Associate of Royal Canadian Academy, 1884. *Address*, 25 West 43d St., New York City.

WILLIS, Albert Paul. Landscape painter. Born in Philadelphia in 1867. Pupil of Frank V. Du Mond. Member: Philadelphia Water Color Club; Philadelphia Sketch Club. *Address*, 4703 Springfield Ave., Philadelphia, Pa.

WILLOUGHBY, Alice Estelle. Painter. Born in Groton, N. Y. Pupil of Washington Art League; Corcoran Art School. Member: Washington Water Color Club; Washington Art Club. *Address*, The Rockingham, Washington, D. C.

WILLSON, James Mallery. Painter and etcher. Born in Florida in 1890. Pupil of Maynard and Henri. *Address*, 428 West 57th St., New York, N. Y.

WILLSON, Martha B. Miniature painter. Born in Providence, R. I., in 1885. Pupil of Lucia Fairchild Fuller. Member: Providence Art Club. *Address*, 88 Congdon St., Providence, R. I.

WILMARTH, Lemuel Everett. Painter. Born in Attleboro, Mass., in 1835; died in 1918. Began to study drawing in Penna. Academy of Fine Arts, Philadelphia, 1854; went to Europe, 1858; studied at Royal Academy, Munich; also at École des Beaux Arts, Paris. Married Emma B. Barrett, 1872. Professor in charge of schools of National Academy of Design, 1870–90. Among his best known pictures are "The Pick of the Orchard"; "Ingratitude"; "Left in Charge"; "Sunny Italy"; Captain Nathan Hale.

WILMER, William A. Engraver, who died about 1855. Wilmer was a pupil of James B. Longacre in Philadelphia, and engraved some excellent portrait plates in stipple for the "National Portrait Gallery."

WILSON, Alexander. Engraver. Born in Paisley, Scotland, in 1766; died in Philadelphia, Pa., in 1813. In the life of this eminent ornithologist we are told that Wilson was taught to draw, color and etch by his friend Alexander Lawson, the engraver, and he rapidly attained a marked degree of proficiency in delineating birds. For his own great work on "American Ornithology" he later etched two plates from his own drawings.

WILSON, Claggett. Painter. Born in Washington, D. C., in 1887. Pupil of F. Luis Mora, Richard Miller and Laurens in Paris. Member: Society of Independent Artists. *Address*, 111 East 62d St., New York, N. Y.

WILSON, Edward A. Illustrator. Born in Glasgow, Scotland, in 1886. Studied at Art Institute of Chicago and with Howard Pyle. Member: Society of Illustrators in 1912; Salmagundi Club; Guild of Free Lance Artists; Art Directors' Club. *Address*, 31 West 67th St., New York, N. Y.

WILSON, John T. Portrait painter, who flourished about 1844 to 1860 in New York.

WILSON, Mrs. Lucy Adams. Painter. Born in Warren, Ohio, in 1855. Pupil of Herron Art Institute, Indianapolis; Art Students' League of New York; William Forsyth and T. C. Steele. Member: Chicago Water Color Club. Represented in Herron Art Institute; Conservatory of Art and Music, Miami, Fla. *Address*, Conservatory of Art and Music, Miami, Fla.

WILLSON, Matthew. Portrait painter in oils and miniature. Born in London in 1814. He came to this country as a young man and became a pupil of Henry Inman. He first exhibited miniatures in Philadelphia. He was elected an Associate Member of the National Academy of Design in 1843. He painted portraits, and drew in pastel from 1861 to 1891. He died in February, in Hartford, Conn., in 1892.

WILSON, Mrs. Rose Cecil O'Neil. Illustrator. Born in Wilkes-Barre, Pa. Member: Societé des Beaux Arts, Paris; Society of Illustrators, 1912. Address, Bonnebrook, Day P. O., Tanney County, Mo.

WILWARTH, Lemuel Everett. Painter. He was a pupil under Gerome, and later a teacher in the New York School of Art.

WINEBRENNER, Harry F. Sculptor and illustrator. Born in West Virginia in 1884. Pupil of Taft and Mulligan. *Address,* 1354 Ashland Ave., Santa Monica, Calif.

WINGERT, Edward Oswald. P a i n t e r. Born in Philadelphia in 1864. Pupil of Hovenden, Anshutz and Porter in Philadelphia. Member: Fellowship, Penna. Academy of Fine Arts. *Address,* Oak Lane, Philadelphia, Pa.

WINKLER, John W. Painter and etcher. Member: California Miniature Painters; Chicago Society of Etchers. Awards: Logan prize, Chicago Society of Etchers, 1918; purchase prize, California Society of Etchers, 1919. Work represented in Chicago Art Institute. *Address,* 728 Pine St., San Francisco, Calif.

WINN, James H. Painter and sculptor. Born in Newburyport, Mass., in 1866. Pupil of Art Institute of Chicago. Member: Chicago Society of Artists; Chicago Water Color Club; Cliff Dwellers' Club; Alumni, Art Institute of Chicago. Awards: Arthur Heun prize, Art Institute of Chicago, 1910; first prize and gold medal, Woman's Convention Exhibition, Knoxville, Tenn., 1913. Instructor, Jewelry and Metal Work, Art Institute of Chicago. *Address,* Fine Arts Building, 410 South Michigan Ave., Chicago, Ill.

WINNER, Margaret F. Painter and illustrator. Born in Philadelphia. Pupil of Penna. Academy of the Fine Arts and of Howard Pyle. Member: Plastic Club. *Address,* 1619 Chestnut Street, Philadelphia, Pa.

WINNER, William E. A portrait and genre painter of Philadelphia. Member of the Board of Control of the Artists' Fund Society from 1843. Exhibitor at the Penna. Academy of the Fine Arts until 1881.

WINSLOW, Earle B. Painter. Born in Northville, Mich., in 1884. Pupil of Detroit Fine Arts School; Art Students' League of New York. Member: Salmagundi Club. *Address,* 21 Bennett Ave., New York, N. Y.

WINSLOW, Mrs. Eleanor C. A. Painter and illustrator. Born in Norwich, Conn., in 1877. Pupil of Art Students' League of New York; also studied in Paris. Award: Third Hallgarten prize, National Academy of Design, 1907. Member: National Association of Women Painters and Sculptors; Conn. Academy of Fine Arts; Norwich Artists' Association. *Address,* 1190 Madison Ave., New York, N. Y.

WINSLOW, Henry. Painter, etcher and engraver. Born in Boston in 1874. Pupil of Whistler in Paris. Represented in Boston Museum of Fine Arts; New York Public Library; British Museum. *Address,* 10 Fitzroy St., London, England.

WINSTANLEY, John B. Painter and illustrator. Born in Louisville, Kentucky. Pupil of Penna. Academy of the Fine Arts and New York Water Color Club. *Address,* 644 Minnesford Ave., City Island, N. Y.

WINSTANLEY, William. An English artist of good family who came to America during the last decade of the eighteenth century. He made many good copies of Gilbert Stuart's portraits of George Washington. On his return to England he exhibited in London at the British Institution, in 1806, three Virginia landscapes.

WINTER, Alice Beach. Painter. Born at Green Ridge, Mo., in 1877. Student of Art Students' League of New York, 1901. Painter and illustrator of child life. He has illustrated child-life stories and originated many cover-designs in color for magazines. Exhibited: National Academy of Design, New York; Pa. Academy of Fine Arts, Philadelphia; Carnegie Institute, Pittsburgh; St. Louis Museum of Fine Arts; Museum of History, Science and Art, Los Angeles, Calif. Member of the Society of Women Painters and Sculptors, New York. *Address,* 53 East 59th St., New York, N. Y.

WINTER, Andrew. Painter. Exhibited at National Academy of Design, New York, 1925. *Address,* 136 West 109th St., New York, N. Y.

WINTER, Charles Allan. Painter. Born in Cincinnati, 1869. Student of Art Academy of Cincinnati, 1884–94; awarded foreign scholarship and studied at Julien Academy, Paris, under Bouguereau and Gabriel Ferrier; spent 1 year in Italy, chiefly in art galleries of Rome. Teacher of St. Louis School of Fine Arts, 1898–1901; removed to New York, 1901; has done painting and illustrating for magazines. *Address,* 53 East 59th St., New York, N. Y.

WINTER, Ezra. Painter and illustrator. Born in Manistee, Mich., in 1886. Pupil of Chicago Academy of Fine Arts; also of the American Academy at Rome. Member: Palette and Chisel Co.; Chicago Mural Painters. Elected an Associate Member of the National Academy of Design. Work: Decorations in offices of Guarantee Trust Co., New York; also in Great Hall and Vestibule, Cunard Building, New York. *Address,* 15 Vanderbilt Ave., New York, N. Y.

WINTER, G. According to Dunlap this artist was painting in New York in 1834.

WINTER, Milo. Illustrator. Born in Princeton, Ill., in 1888. Pupil of Art Institute of Chicago; American Water Color Society; Cliff Dwellers, Chicago. Illustrated "Nights with Uncle Remus," "Aesop's Fables," "Alice in Wonderland," "Bill Pop-Gun," etc. *Address*, 621 Sheridan Road, Evanston, Ill.

WINTERHALDER, Louis A. Painter and pen and ink artist. Native of New Orleans. He studied at the Art Union and under Molinary, Perrelli and Buck. Exhibited at New Orleans and at the Academy of Fine Arts, Chicago. Specialty, landscapes. Represented in Louisiana State Museum.

WINTRINGHAM, Frances M. Painter. Born in Brooklyn, N. Y., in 1884. Pupil of George Bellows, Kenneth Hayes Miller, Robert Henri and Charles Hawthorne. Member: Society of Independent Artists; League of New York Artists. *Address*, 6 Charles St., New York, N. Y.

WIRTH, Anna M. Illustrator. Born in Johnstown, Pa., in 1868. Pupil of Penna. Academy of the Fine Arts; Philadelphia School of Design for Women. Illustrated "Progressive Pennsylvania," by J. M. Swank. Author and illustrator of "The King's Jester," etc. *Address*, 518 North Lake Ave., Pasadena, California.

WISE, Louise W. (Mrs. Stephen). Painter, who exhibited at the National Academy of Design, New York, 1925. *Address*, 23 West 90th St., New York, N. Y.

WISELTIER, Joseph. Painter. Born in Paris, France, 1887. Pupil of Dow, Bement and Snell. Member of Hartford Art Association. *Address*, 107 Washington Circle, West Hartford, Conn.

WISEMAN, Robert W. Painter of animals. Exhibited at the National Academy. His studio was in New Haven, Conn.

WITMAN, Joseph. Portrait painter, of Reading, Penna. He exhibited portraits at the "Columbianum," Philadelphia, 1795.

WITT, John H. Painter. Born in Dublin, Wayne County, Ind., in 1840; died in New York City in 1900. Began life as a machinist and wagon painter in a small agricultural implement factory owned by his uncles. Commenced portrait painting at an early age and finally adopted it as a profession about 1863. Was entirely self-taught. Painted portraits of a great many governors and other prominent public men of Ohio until about 1879, when he went to New York City. Was Associate Member of National Academy of Design and member of various clubs of men of his profession.

WITTERS, Neil. Painter, illustrator and etcher. Born in Michigan. Pupil of Art Institute of Chicago. Member of Penna. Academy of Fine Arts, Philadelphia. *Address*, 311 Remington St., Saginaw, Mich.

WOELFLE, Arthur W. Painter. Born in Trenton in 1873. Pupil of Art Students' League of New York under Mowbray, Beckwith, Cox, Low and C. Y. Turner. Specialty, portraits. *Address*, 261 Madison Ave., Flushing, New York.

WOISERI, J. I. Bouquet. Engraver. As early as 1803 this man was working in New Orleans. He engraved a plan and a view of New Orleans with well-executed aquatint vignettes and views of buildings, and also a large aquatint view of Boston. In the *General Advertiser* in Philadelphia in 1804 Woiseri advertises his two New Orleans plates "for $10 for both colored." He dedicates his plates "by permission to President Thomas Jefferson." He calls himself a "designer, drawer, geographer, and engineer," and says that he has resided in New Orleans for a number of years, and has there "exercised his profession of designer and engraver." He worked six years on the New Orleans plates.

WOLCOTT, Katherine. Miniature painter. Born in Chicago, Ill., in 1880. Pupil of Art Institute of Chicago. *Address*, 5222 Blackstone Ave., Chicago, Ill.

WOLF, Henry. Painter and engraver. Born in Eckwersheim, Alsace, in 1852. Pupil of Jacques Levy, artist-engraver of Strassburg. Exhibited at Paris Salon; Chicago Exposition, 1893; Paris Exposition, 1889, and in 1900 received the silver medal, Fine Arts Exposition, Rouen, France, 1903; diploma and grand medal of honor for distinguished services in promoting art of engraving, St. Louis Exposition, 1904. Member of advisory comm., and later of International Jury of Awards, St. Louis Exposition, 1904. Elected Associate Member of the National Academy in 1905; National Academy, 1908. Member: American Federation of Arts; International Society of Sculptors, Painters and Gravers; Alliance Francaise; Union Internationale des Beaux Arts et des Lettres, Paris, France. Principal works: Engravings illustrating American Artist Series, and Gilbert Stuart Series of Men and Women in *Century Magazine.* Original engravings: "The Morning Star"; "The Evening Star"; "A Duck-Pond"; "Morning Mists"; "Lower New York in a Mist"; "The Scattering of the Mists"; "Portrait of Thomas Jefferson"; "Portrait of Thomas Carlyle"; "My Mother"; "Miss Alexander, after Whistler"; "Portrait of Robert Louis Stevenson," of "William Makepeace Thackeray"; "Masterpieces of the Metropolitan Museum of Art, New York"; "Portraits of Ladies," and "American Artists Series" appearing in *Harper's Magazine*. Contributor to other magazines. See "History of Wood Engraving in America," by W. J. Linton. He died in 1916.

WOLFE, Ada A. Painter. Born in Oakland, Calif. Pupil of Minneapolis School of Fine Arts and of the New York School of Art under Wm. M. Chase. *Address*, 2007 Willow Ave., North Minneapolis, Minn.

WOLFF, Gustave. Painter. Born in Germany in 1863. He came to America when three years old. Pupil of St. Louis School of Fine Arts under Paul Cornoyer; also studied in Europe. Member: St. Louis Arts and Crafts; St. Louis 2x4 Society. Awards: silver medal, Portland, Ore., 1905; first Dolph prize, Competitive Ex., St. Louis, 1906. Work: "The Brook," City Art Museum, St. Louis. *Address*, 508 West 162d St., New York, N. Y.

WOLFF, Otto. Painter and illustrator. Born in Cologne, Germany, in 1858. Studied in Paris. Member: Chicago Society of Artists; Chicago Art Club. Award: Honorable mention, Paris Salon, 1888. *Address*, 245 West North Ave., Chicago, Ill.

WOLFSON, William. Painter, who exhibited water colors at the Penna. Academy of the Fine Arts, Philadelphia, 1925. *Address*, 5714 McIvin St., Pittsburgh, Penna.

WOLINSKI, Joseph. Painter. Born in 1873. Pupil of Royal Art Society of New South Wales; also of Colarossi in Paris. Member: Royal Art Society, New South Wales. Work: "After Life's Fitful Fever He Sleeps Well"; "An Interior," two head studies in charcoal; and "Summer" in National Art Gallery of New South Wales. *Address*, 32 Moore Park Road, Sydney, Australia.

WOLLASTON, John. An English portrait painter. He visited the Colonies in the middle of the eighteenth century. Wollaston painted a great many portraits in New York, Philadelphia and the South from 1750 to 1767. His best portraits seem to have been painted in New York between 1751 and 1757. Among his portraits were those of Martha Dandridge Custis (Mrs. Washington) and the Custis children; Sir Charles Hardy, Gov. of New York, William Allen of Claremont, and Clara Walker Allen.

WOMRATH, A. K. Painter, illustrator and designer. Born in Frankford, Philadelphia, Pa., in 1869. Pupil of Art Students' League of New York under Twachtman and J. Alden Weir; pupil of Grasset and Merson in Paris; at Westminster School of Art, London. Member: New York Architectural League, 1902; National Art Club. *Address*, Menton, Alpes-Maritimes, France.

WOOD, Edith Longstreth. Painter, who exhibited at the National Academy of Design, New York, 1925. *Address*, Philadelphia, Penna.

WOOD, E. Miriam. Painter. Born in Birmingham, Ala., in 1888. Pupil of Ellsworth Woodward, Henry McCarter, Hawthorne, Chase; also of Newcomb School of Art, New Orleans; student at Penna. Academy of Fine Arts. Work: "The Fisherman's Dory," Mississippi Art Association. *Address*, 7014 St. Charles Ave., New Orleans, La.

WOOD, Franklin T. Etcher. Member: Chicago Society of Etchers. Award: bronze medal, Panama-Pacific Exposition, San Francisco, 1915. Represented in Chicago Art Institute. *Address*, 486 Boylston St., Boston, Mass.

WOOD, George B. Painter. Born in Philadelphia in 1832. Studied at the Pennsylvania Academy of the Fine Arts. Represented in Wilstach Collection, Fairmount Park, Phila., by landscape "Winter Twilight." The Penna. Academy of the Fine Arts owns his painting of "Dr. Tyson's Library." He died in Mass., in 1910.

WOOD, Grant. Painter and sculptor. Born in Anamosa, Ia., in 1892. Pupil of Art Institute of Chicago; Minneapolis Handicraft School of Design. Work: "Democracy," mural painting, Harrison School, Cedar Rapids. Received life membership medal, bas-relief, Cedar Rapids Art Association; decoration in National Masonic Research Building, Anamosa, Iowa. *Address*, Kenwood Park, Ia.

WOOD, Jessie Porter. Painter and illustrator. Born in Syracuse, N. Y., in 1863. Pupil of J. Carroll Beckwith, George de Forest Brush, Walter Shirlaw, J. Ward Stimson, and others. *Address*, 2005 Columbia Road, Washington, D. C.

WOOD, Joseph. Miniature painter. Born in Clarkstown, N. Y., about 1778; died in Washington, D. C., in 1852. He was largely self-taught, having to earn his living with his violin in the summer, in order to study in the winter. In 1804 he formed a partnership with John Wesley Jarvis, painting miniatures. Dunlap records a visit he made with Malbone to their studio during 1805–06. Both artists received some assistance from Malbone at the time. The partnership was dissolved in 1809 and Wood had a studio at 160 Broadway during 1812–13. The latter year he went to Philadelphia and had a studio at 93 South Third Street. His name occurs in the Philadelphia directories until 1817. He exhibited at the Penna. Academy of the Fine Arts. He moved later to Washington and in 1827 had a studio on the north side of Pennsylvania Avenue between 9th and 10th Sts. An extended account of the artist appeared in "The Port-Folio," 1811.

WOOD, Katheryn Leone. Painter. Born in Kalamazoo, Mich., in 1885. Pupil of Frederick Freer, Lawton Parker and others. Work: Miniature of Mrs. J. C. Burrows, Continental Memorial Hall, Washington, D. C. *Address*, 6 Van Nest Place, New York, N. Y.

WOOD, Stan. Painter. Wood is a San Francisco water color artist who exhibited in the New York galleries in 1925

WOOD, Thomas Waterman. Painter. Born in Montpelier, Vt., in 1823. He studied portrait painting under Chester Harding in Boston, and then established his studio in New York. Wood has delineated the negro as he developed during the Civil War. He was elected an Academician in 1871 of the National Academy of Design, New York. He painted a number of portraits of prominent men in New York City. He died in 1903.

WOOD, Virginia Hargraves. Painter and etcher. Born near St. Louis, Mo. Pupil of Chase, Du Mond, Hawthorne; also studied abroad. Member: National Association of Women Painters and Sculptors. Work: Mural decorations in Broadway Café; she has illustrated several books. *Address*, 58 West 57th St., New York, N. Y.

WOOD, William R. C. Landscape painter. Born in 1875. Pupil of S. E. Whiteman in Baltimore, he was president of the water color club. He died in 1915.

WOODBURY, Chas. H. Marine painter and etcher. Born at Lynn, Mass., in 1864. Pupil of Julien Academy in Paris under Boulanger and Lefebvre. Associate Member of National Academy, 1906, and Academician, 1907. His most important pictures: "Mid-Ocean," "A Heavy Sea," "Maine Coast" and "The Ground Swell." *Address*, 132 Riverway, Boston, Mass.

WOODBURY, Marcia O. (Mrs. C. H.). Painter. Born in Maine in 1865. Student of Woman's Art Club, New York; also with Lassar in Paris. Represented in Boston Museum of Fine Arts by "Tripych," "Mother and Daughter." She died in 1913.

WOODCOCK, T. S. Engraver. Born in Manchester, England. He came to New York about 1830, and in 1836 he was working in Philadelphia. A portrait of Andrew Jackson, published in New York in 1834, is engraved with a ruling-machine and is signed by Woodcock. About 1840 Woodcock was located in Brooklyn as an engraver and print-publisher, and about this time we find some beautiful plates of butterflies engraved by Woodcock & Harvey, Brooklyn. Woodcock finally inherited some money and returned to England.

WOODRUFF, Corice (Mrs. Henry). Sculptor. Born in Ansonia, Conn., in 1878. Pupil of Art Students' League of New York. Her specialty, small sculpture, bas-reliefs and portrait busts. *Address*, 2017 Pleasant Ave., Minneapolis, Minn.

WOODRUFF, William. Engraver of portraits and landscape. He was in business in Philadelphia in 1817–24. He worked quite well in both line and stipple. After 1824 he apparently removed to Cincinnati, as we find prints by him engraved in that city.

WOODSIDE, John A. Philadelphia painter, who flourished in the middle of the last century. He painted many portraits, historical and allegorical subjects, and was noted as the decorator of the hose carriages and engines of local fire companies, and the first locomotive. He was painting in Philadelphia before 1817.

WOODVILLE, R. Caton. Painter. Born in Baltimore, Md., in 1820. He had access to the pictures of Robert Gilmore, then one of the best collections in the country, and he copied many of the figure-pieces among them. He studied at Dusseldorf until his premature death in London in 1855. His painting "Reading the News" is owned by the National Academy of Design and has been engraved.

WOODWARD, E. F. Engraver of maps and small vignettes of events in American history. In a school atlas published in Hartford, Conn., in 1839, these engravings are signed "as Engraved by E. F. Woodward."

WOODWARD, Ellsworth. Painter and teacher. Born in Bristol County, Mass., in 1861. Studied at the School of Design and in the studios of Carl Marr, Richards and Fehr, Munich, Germany. Assistant professor of art, Tulane University; professor of art, Newcombe College, Tulane University; director of Museum of Art, Industrial Institute, Lafayette, La. Member: New Orleans Art Association; La. Art Teachers' Association; Artists' Guild of Chicago; National Society of Craftsmen; Society of Craftsmen; Society of Arts and Crafts, Boston. *Address*, Newcombe College, New Orleans, La.

WOODWARD, Mabel M. Painter. Born in Providence, R. I., in 1877. Pupil of Chase and Cox in New York. She is now instructor at the Rhode Island School of Design, Providence, R. I.

WOODWARD, Robert Strong. Painter. Born at Northampton, Mass., in 1885. Awarded first prize, National Academy of Design, in 1919. *Address*, Shelburne Falls, Mass.

WOODWARD, Stanley W. Painter, illustrator and etcher. Born in Malden, Mass., in 1890. Pupil of Frank Benson, Hale, Blashfield and of the Penna. Academy of the Fine Arts. Member of Brooklyn and Chicago Society of Etchers. *Address*, 198 Dartmouth St., Boston, Mass.

WOODWARD, William. Painter and teacher of drawing. Born in Massachusetts in 1859. Student of Rhode Island School of Design; also pupil of Boulanger and Lefebvre in Paris. *Address*, Newcombe College, New Orleans, La.

WOODWELL, Joseph R. Painter. Born in Pittsburgh, Penna., in 1843; died there in 1911. He studied for four years at Barbizon and was the friend of both Millet and Jacques. In Paris he was associated with Monet, Renoir and Pissaro.

WOOLF, Saml. J. Portrait painter. Born in New York in 1880. Pupil of Art Students' League and National Academy of Design. Represented by portrait of Cardinal Logue at Catholic Club, New York, and by ''Mark Twain'' at Brook Club, N. Y. *Address*, 253 West 42d St., New York, N. Y.

WOOLLEY. An English painter who divided his time between Philadelphia and New York about 1757. He painted small portraits in oil; also signs and other pictures.

WOOLLEY, William. Engraver in mezzotint. He produced two portraits of George Washington and a companion plate of Mrs. Washington. These plates were published by David Longworth at the Shakespeare Gallery, No. 11 Park Place, New York, probably about 1800. Our interest in this engraver lies in the fact that the larger memorial plate bears the inscription ''David Longworth Direxit. Woolley —Pinxit et Sculpsit.'' While this inscription might suggest an American origin, it is more reasonable to assume that David Longworth simply suggested the design, ordered a painting and engraving made in London and then imported both and published the print, as above stated, in New York. This contention is borne out by the fact that no other plates by Woolley are known to the writer, and the majority of the Washington portraits by Woolley now in the hands of American collectors were purchased in London. They apparently had a very limited sale in this country. In an altered and reduced state the plate has been printed from in recent years.

WOOLRYCH, Bertha Hewit (Mrs. F. Humphry). Painter and illustrator. Born in Ohio in 1868. Pupil of St. Louis School of Fine Arts; also of Morot, Collin and Courtois in Paris. Member: St. Louis Arts and Crafts; St. Louis Art Students' Association. Awards: Medal, Lewis and Clark Exposition, Portland, 1905; gold and silver medals, St. Louis School of Fine Arts; silver medal, 1908, St. Louis District, General Federation of Women's Clubs. *Address*, 3855 Hartford St., St. Louis, Mo.

WOOLRYCH, E. Humphry W. Painter and illustrator. Born in Sydney, Australia. Pupil of Royal Academy, Berlin; École des Beaux Arts, Colarossi Academy, Collin, Courtois and Purvis de Chavannes in Paris. Member: Hellas Art Club, Berlin; St. Louis Arts and Crafts; Brush and Pencil Club; 2 x 4 Society; St. Louis Architectural Club. Awards: Bronze medal, Portland Exposition, 1905; medal for portrait, Mo. State Fair, Sedalia, 1913. Work: Water color in St. Louis Public Library. *Address*, 1411 International Life Building, St. Louis, Mo.

WORCESTER, Albert. Painter and etcher. Born in West Campton, N. H., in 1878. Pupil of Luc-Olivier Merson and of Jean Paul Laurens in Paris. *Address*, 467 West Canfield Avenue, Detroit, Mich.

WORDEN, Laicita Warburton. Painter, sculptor and illustrator. Born in Philadelphia in 1892. Pupil of Penna. Academy of the Fine Arts. Member: Fellowship, Penna. Academy of the Fine Arts. *Address*, 4141 North Broad St., Philadelphia, Pa.

WORES, Theodore. Painter and illustrator. Born in San Francisco, Calif., in 1860. Pupil of Alex. Wagner and Duveneck in Munich. Member: Century Association. Award: Gold medal, Alaska-Yukon Exposition, 1909. Instructor at San Francisco Art Institute, 1907–1912. *Address*, Bohemian Club, San Francisco, Calif.

WORKMAN, David Tice. Etcher. Born in Wahpeton, N. D., in 1884. Pupil of Benson and Hale in Boston; under Pyle in Wilmington; Brangwyn and Swan in London. Member: Chicago Society of Etchers; Attic Club, Minneapolis; Minneapolis Society of Artists. Award: First prize, Minnesota State Art Commission, 1914. Work: Mural decorations, Irving School, and East Side High School, Minneapolis, Minn.; Lincoln High School, Hibbing, Minn. *Address*, 1210 First Ave., North, Minneapolis, Minn.

WORRELL, James. An early Virginia portrait painter who painted a portrait of Judge John Tyler, who was a Governor of Virginia, 1808–11. The portrait is at the College of William and Mary at Williamsburg, Va.

WORSHIP. This name is signed to some rather poor line-engravings of plans, machinery, etc., published in Philadelphia in 1815–20.

WORSWICK, Lloyd. Sculptor, who exhibited in 1924 in the Annual Exhibition of the Penna. Academy of the Fine Arts, Phila. *Address*, 441 West 21st St., New York, N. Y.

WORTH, Thomas. Painter and illustrator. Born in 1834. His caricaturist work was lithographed and was well known in New York City. He also illustrated Dickens' "Old Curiosity Shop."

WRAY, Henry Russell. Painter and etcher. Born in Philadelphia, Pa., in 1864. Member: Phila. Sketch Club; Colorado Springs Art Society. *Address,* 33 West Willamette Ave., Colorado Springs, Colo.

WRENCH, Miss Mary. Miniature painter, working in Philadelphia before the Revolution, according to the recollection of Charles Willson Peale who gave her instruction in painting. She later married Willam Rush, modeler and carver.

WRENN, Charles L. Painter and illustrator. Born in Cincinnati, Ohio, in 1880. Pupil of Chase and of the Art Students' League of New York. Member: Society of Illustrators; Salmagundi Club. *Address,* 364 West 23d St., New York, N. Y.

WRIGHT, Alice Morgan. Sculptor. Born in Albany, N. Y. Member: National Association of Women Painters and Sculptors; Society of Independent Artists. *Address,* 393 State St., Albany, N. Y.

WRIGHT, Alma Brockerman. Painter. Born in Salt Lake City in 1875. Pupil of Bonnat, Laurens, École des Beaux Arts and of the Julien and Colarossi Academies in Paris. Member: Society of Utah Artists; Paris Allied Artists' Association. Awards: State prize, 1904; medal of honor, Utah Art Institute, 1905. *Address,* L. D. S. U., Salt Lake City, Utah.

WRIGHT, Bertha Stevens (Mrs. Lawrence Wright). Painter. Born in Astoria, L. I., N. Y. Self-taught. Member: Art Alliance of America; Society of Independent Artists; League of New York Artists. *Address,* Lawrence, L. I., N. Y.

WRIGHT, Catherine Morris (Mrs.). Painter. Born in Philadelphia in 1899. Pupil of Snell and Seyffert. Has held exhibitions of own paintings and exhibited at the Penna. Academy of the Fine Arts. *Address,* Green St. and School Lane, Germantown, Philadelphia.

WRIGHT, Charles Cushing. Engraver. Born in Damascota, Me.; died in New York in 1854. Wright was left an orphan at an early age and was adopted by Charles Cushing, whose name he later assumed. After some service as a soldier in the War of 1812, he settled in Utica, N. Y., and engaged in business as a watchmaker. In 1824 he was associated with A. B. Durand, in New York, doing etching, engraving, and making the dies for a number of medals awarded by the National and by State Governments. He was one of the found-ers of the National Academy of Design in New York in 1826. He was living in Savannah in 1820, and was engraving in Charleston, S. C., in 1824. Wright attempted line-engraving without much success; his best work is found among his etched portraits.

WRIGHT, Charles H. Painter and illustrator. Born in Knightstown; Ind., in 1870. Pupil of Art Students' League of New York. Member: Society of Illustrators, 1914; Salmagundi Club; New York Water Color Club; Guild of Free Lance Artists. *Address,* Room 309, 1931 Broadway, New York, N. Y.

WRIGHT, Charles Lennox. Painter and illustrator. Born in Boston, Mass., in 1876. Pupil of Art Students' League of New York; under Dagnan-Bouveret in Paris. *Address,* Bayside, L. I., N. Y.

WRIGHT, F. E. Painter. Born in South Weymouth, Mass., in 1849. He studied in Paris for some time under Bonnat and Boulanger. His professional life has been spent in Boston where his portraits are generally owned.

WRIGHT, Fred W. Painter. Born in Crawfordsville, Ind., in 1880. Pupil of Julien Academy and P. Marcel-Baroneau in Paris; J. Otis Adams. Member: Salmagundi Club; League of New York Artists. *Address,* 15 West 67th St., New York, N. Y.

WRIGHT, G. Engraver of vignettes, etc. He was working in Philadelphia in 1837. About this date the engraving firm of Wright & Balch was producing line portraits in New York. The Wright of this firm was probably the above.

WRIGHT, G. Painter, who exhibited water colors at the Penna. Academy of the Fine Arts, Philadelphia, 1925. *Address,* Westport, Conn.

WRIGHT, George Frederick. Portrait painter. Born in Washington, Conn., in 1828. Student at the National Academy, New York, and later he spent two years abroad. He painted most of his portraits in Hartford and they are remarkable for their natural flesh-tints and accuracy of likeness. He died in 1881.

WRIGHT, George H. Painter and illustrator. Born in Fox Chase, Pa., in 1872. Pupil of Penna. Academy of the Fine Arts and Spring Garden Institute. Member: Society of Illustrators, 1911; Salmagundi Club; Society of Independent Artists; Guild of Free Lance Artists. *Address,* Salmagundi Club, 47 Fifth Ave., New York, N. Y.

WRIGHT, Mrs. Gladys Yoakum. Painter. Born in Greenville, Tex. Pupil of McLeod School of Art in Los Angeles. *Address,* 606 West Third St., Fort Worth, Tex.

WRIGHT, James Henry. Portrait and landscape painter, who was born in 1813. His studio was at 835 Broadway, New York City. He died in Brooklyn in 1883. He painted a portrait of Daniel Webster, and the New York Historical Society owns his view of Donagham Manor.

WRIGHT, Joseph. Painter. Son of Joseph Wright and Patience Lovell, born in Bordentown, N. J., in 1756. After the death of his father, his mother took her family to London, where, becoming famous as a modeler in wax, she was enabled to give her son a good education. Turning his attention to portrait painting, he received advice and instruction from West and Hoppner, the latter marrying his sister, and before leaving England, Wright painted the portrait of the Prince of Wales, afterward George IV. He went to Paris in 1782, under protection of Franklin, to continue his art studies. He came to America soon after, bringing letters from Franklin to Washington. Painted the portrait of Washington who gave him several sittings at Rocky Hill, near Princeton, N. J., in 1783. He painted two other portraits of Washington about this time and in 1790 drew a profile likeness of him as he sat in church. In 1787 Wright had a studio in Pearl Street, New York, and in that city he married Miss Vandervoort. He later removed to Philadelphia and there painted portraits, modeled in clay and practised die-sinking. This latter accomplishment gained for him, shortly before his death, the appointment of die-sinker to the United States Mint. He made a design for a cent of 1792 though it is not known that this design was ever executed; but he made the dies for a Washington medal after the Houdon bust, and for a medal voted by Congress to Major Lee. His etching of Washington, though quite well executed, is the only plate by Joseph Wright on record. He died in 1793.

WRIGHT, Josephine M. Miniature painter, who exhibited miniatures at the Penna. Academy of the Fine Arts, Philadelphia, 1925. *Address*, 1010 North Stoneman Ave., Alhambra, Calif.

WRIGHT, M. Louise (Mrs. John Wright). Painter, illustrator and miniature painter. Born in Philadelphia in 1875. Pupil of Penna. Academy of the Fine Arts; Whistler and Julien Academy in Paris; F. W. Jackson in England. *Address*, 2 Cheltenham Terrace, London.

WRIGHT, S. Mac Donald. Painter, who exhibited at Penna. Academy of the Fine Arts, 1921, in ''Exhibition Showing Later Tendencies in Art.'' *Address*, Los Angeles, Calif.

WRIGHT, Patience. Born in Bordentown, N. J., in 1725, of Quaker parentage, Patience and Joseph Wright. After her husband's death the former made herself known by her small portraits in wax, chiefly profile bas-reliefs. She died in London in 1786, where for many years she was quite the ''rage.'' (See letter from Washington to Mrs. Wright of Jan. 30, 1785.)

WRIGHT, Rufus. Painter. Born in 1832. He was a pupil of the National Academy of Design. His portraits include those of Roger B. Taney, Edward M. Stanton and Wm. H. Seward; among his other works are ''The Morning Bouquet'' and ''Feeding the Birds.''

WRIGHTSON, J. Engraver. Born in England. He came to the United States about 1854. Wrightson was a reputable line-engraver of landscape and book illustrations. He worked in Boston and in New York, but soon after 1860 he returned to England and died there in 1865.

WUERMER, Carl. Painter, who exhibited at the National Academy of Design, New York, 1925, and at the Penna. Academy of the Fine Arts, Philadelphia, 1925. *Address*, Chicago, Ill., or Woodstock, Ulster Co., N. Y.

WUERPEL, Edmund Henry. Painter. Born in St. Louis in 1866. Pupil of the St. Louis School of Fine Arts; W. A. Bouguereau, Tony Robert-Fleury, Gabriel Ferrier and Edmund Aman-Jean in Paris. Formerly instructor, director since 1909, of St. Louis School of Fine Arts. Exhibited at Paris Salons. Member: St. Louis Artists' Guild; Society Western Artists. Honorable mention, American Art Association, Paris. Exhibited at Paris Exposition, 1900. Served on American Jury in Paris for Chicago Exposition, 1893; member of Jury of Selection and of International Jury of Awards, St. Louis Exposition, 1904. Represented by pictures in St. Louis Museum of Fine Arts. Indianapolis Art Museum lecturer and writer on history of art. Bronze medal, International Exposition, Buenos Aires; 1st prize, St. Louis Artists' Guild, 1914; silver medal, Seattle Exposition. Member of Jury of Selection and International Jury of Awards, Panama-P. I. Exposition, 1915. *Address*, St. Louis School of Fine Arts.

WUERTZ, Emil H. Painter. Born in Germany. He resided for years in Chicago. He died in 1898.

WUNDER, Adalbert. Portrait painter and draughtsman in crayon and ink. Born in Germany in 1827. In 1855 he opened his studio in Hartford, Conn.

WYANT, Alexander H. Landscape painter. Born in Port Washington, Ohio, in 1836; died in New York in 1892. Devoted himself in early life to painting photographs and portraits in Cincinnati. At the age of 21 years he visited George Inness whose influence is shown in many of his most important works. He was later a pupil of Hans Gude in Karlsruhe and a student of the works of Turner and Constable in London. He exhibited first at the National Academy of Design in New York in 1865. Elected a Member of the National Academy, and one of the founders of the American Water Color Society. His studio was in New York. Represented by paintings in the Metropolitan Museum; Corcoran Art Gallery; National Gallery, Washington, D. C.

WYETH, N. C. Painter and illustrator. Born in Needham, Mass., in 1882. Pupil of Howard Pyle. Member: Society of Illustrators, 1912; Philadelphia Sketch Club; Salmagundi Club, 1908; Fellowship, Penna. Academy of the Fine Arts. Awards: Beck prize, Philadelphia. Water Color Club, 1910; gold medal, Panama-Pacific Exposition, San Francisco, 1915. Mu-

rals in: Missouri State Capitol; Hotel Traymore, Atlantic City; Reading Museum of Fine Arts; Federal Reserve Bank of Boston; New York Public Library; Hotel Utica, Utica, New York. *Address*, Needham, Mass.

WYLIE, Robert. Painter. Born on the Isle of Man in 1839; died in Pont Aven, Brittany, in 1877. As a child he was brought to America by his parents who settled in Philadelphia. Genre painter. Pupil of Pennsylvania Academy of the Fine Arts, by the Directors of which he was sent in 1863 to France to study; entered the École des Beaux Arts and worked under Gerome. Awarded second class medal, Paris Salon, 1872.

Y

YAFFEE, Edith Widing. Painter. Born in Helsingfors, Finland, in 1895. Pupil of Paxton, Hale and of the Penna. Academy of the Fine Arts. Awards: Chaloner Paris-American prize, 1920; European traveling scholarship, Penna. Academy of the Fine Arts, 1921. *Address*, 91 Walker Road, Swampscott, Mass.

YALE, Dr. Leroy Milton. Painter and etcher. Born at Vineyard Haven, Mass., in 1841. He was a founder of the New York Etching Club and produced several hundred plates. His collection is in the New York Public Library. He died in 1906.

YANDELL, Enid. Sculptor. Born in Louisville, Ky., in 1870. Pupil of Philip Martiny, New York, and of Mac Monnies and Rodin in Paris. Designer's medal, Chicago Exposition, 1893; has exhibited in Paris Salon regularly since 1895; silver medal, Nashville Exposition, 1897; honorable mention, Buffalo Exposition, 1901; bronze medal, St. Louis Exposition, 1904; decorated Officier d'Academie, French Govt., 1906. Organizer of the Braustock Summer School of Art, Edgartown, Island of Marthas Vineyard, Mass., 1907. Sculptor of the Woman's Building, Chicago Exposition, 1893; Carrie Brown Memorial Fountain, Providence, 1900; Emma Willard Memorial, Albany, N. Y.; Chancellor Garland, Vanderbilt University, Nashville, Tenn.; Hogan Fountain, Louisville, Ky., 1905; Daniel Boone Monument, Louisville, Ky., 1906; Thomas Monument, Nashville, 1907; fountains for John H. Hammond, Mt. Kisco, N. Y., 1909; for J. R. Steers, Port Chester, N. Y., 1911, etc. Member: National Sculpture Society; Municipal Art So-

ciety; National Arts and Crafts Society; National Scenic and Historical Preservation Society; National Arts Club; Women's Cosmopolitan Club. Organized "Appui Aux Artistes," Paris, France, 1914. *Address*, 155 East 38th St., New York, N. Y.

YARROW, William H. K. Painter. Born at Glenside, Penna., in 1891. Pupil of Penna. Academy of the Fine Arts and of the Colarossi Academy of Paris. *Address*, Care of Daniel Gallery, 2 West 47th St., New York, N. Y.

YATES, Cullen. Painter. Born in Bryan, Ohio, in 1866. Pupil of National Academy of Design; Chase and Ochtman in New York; École des Beaux Arts, Colarossi and Julien Academies, under Laurens and Constant, in Paris. Bronze medal, St. Louis Exposition, 1904; Inness prize, Salmagundi Club, 1907. Elected an Associate Member of the National Academy, 1908; Academician in 1919. Member of the American Water Color Society; New York Water Color Club; National Arts Club. Specialty, landscapes. Studio in New York. Painted the "Rock-Bound Coast, Cape Ann," signed and dated 1909. *Address*, Shawnee, Penna.

YATES, Elizabeth M. Painter. Born in Stoke-on-Trent, Staffordshire, England, in 1888. Pupil of Pratt Institute. *Address*, 374 McKinley Parkway, Buffalo, N. Y.

YEAGER, Joseph. Engraver in line and etcher of portraits. Was working in Philadelphia from 1816 until 1845. He closely copied

Cruikshank's etchings for American editions of "Harry Lorrequer" and other English works.

YEATS, John Butler. Painter. He was born in Ireland in 1839; died in New York City in 1922. Father of the artist, Jack B. Yeats. He painted numerous portraits of well-known people. He was a member of the Society of Independent Artists.

YELLAND, Raymond. Painter. Born in England in 1848. He came to this country as a youth and studied at the National Academy; he was also a pupil of James R. Brevoort and William Page. Among his paintings are: "Half-moon Beach"; "Mount Hood"; "The Columbia River."

YENS, Karl (Julius Heinrich). Painter, illustrator and etcher. Born in Altona, Germany, in 1868. Pupil of Max Koch in Berlin; under Constant and Laurens in Paris. Member: California Art Club; California Teachers' Association; California Miniature Painters. Awards: Bronze and silver medals, Pan-California International Exposition, San Diego, 1915; second Black prize, California Art Club, 1919. Work: Mural decorations in City Hall, Altona, Germany; Country Club House, Brookline, Mass.; Duquesne Club, Pittsburgh, Pa. *Address*, Laguna Beach, Calif.

YEOMANS, Walter C. Painter and illustrator. Born in Avon, Ill., in 1882. Pupil of Art Institute of Chicago. Member: Palette and Chisel Club; Chicago Society of Etchers. *Address*, Care of Art Department, Hawtin Engraving Co., Chicago, Ill.

YEWELL, George Henry. Painter. Born in Havre-de-Grace, Md., in 1830. Pupil of Thomas Hicks, New York; student in National Academy of Design, 1851–56; studied in Paris, 1856–61, in atelier of Thomas Couture. Resided at Rome, Italy, 1867–78, and for one winter in Cairo, Egypt; since 1878 in New York. Elected Member of National Academy, 1880; patron, Metropolitan Museum of Art, New York. His work is chiefly portraiture. Among his portraits are those of Isaac Davis, Alexander Mitchell, Frederick Layton and Robert Lucas. He died in 1923.

YOHN, F. C. Illustrator. Born in Indianapolis, Ind., in 1875. Pupil of Indianapolis Art School; Art Students' League of New York, under Mowbray. Member: Society of Illustrators, 1901; Guild of Free Lance Artists. *Address*, Norwalk, Conn.

YOUNG, Arthur. Cartoonist. Born in Stephenson County, Ill., in 1866. Pupil of Julien Academy and of Bouguereau in Paris. Cartoons and illustrations in *Life, Collier's Weekly, Puck, Metropolitan Magazine, The Liberator.* *Address*, 9 East 17th St., New York, N. Y.

YOUNG, C. Jac. Painter and etcher. Born in Bavaria in 1880. Pupil of E. M. Ward and C. Y. Turner. Member: Brooklyn Society of Etchers; California Miniature Painters; Salmagundi Club. *Address*, 114 Highpoint Ave., Weehawken Heights, N. J.

YOUNG, Charles Morris. Painter. Born in Gettysburg, Penna., in 1869. Landscape painter. Pupil of Penna. Academy of the Fine Arts, Philadelphia; also of Colarossi Academy, Paris. Awards: Toppan prize, Pennsylvania Academy of the Fine Arts, 1894; honorable mention, Pan-American Exposition, Buffalo, 1901; silver medal, St. Louis Exposition, 1904; gold medal, Philadelphia Art Club, 1908; honorable mention, Carnegie Institute, Pittsburgh, 1910; silver medal, Buenos Aires Exposition, 1910; gold medal, Panama-Pacific International Exposition, 1915. Member: Philadelphia Art Club; Philadelphia Water Color Club; Associate Member of the National Academy. Represented by "The North Wind" at the Corcoran Art Gallery, Washington, D. C. *Address*, Radnor, Penna.

YOUNG, Eliza Middleton Coxe. Painter. Born in Philadelphia in 1875. Pupil of Anshutz and Charles Morris Young. Work: "Garden Study," Herron Art Institute, Indianapolis. *Address*, Radnor, Penna.

YOUNG, Eva H. Miniature painter, who exhibited at the Penna. Academy of the Fine Arts, Philadelphia, 1922. *Address*, 115 West 16th St., New York, N. Y.

YOUNG, Gladys G. Painter, who exhibited water colors at the Penna. Academy of the Fine Arts, Philadelphia, 1925. *Address*, 67 Pinckney St., Boston, Mass.

YOUNG, J. Harvey. Painter. Born in Salem in 1830. He moved his studio to Boston in 1848. His work is largely portraiture. Work: "Wm. Warren" (actor), painted in 1867; "Dr. Peabody" (Exeter Academy); "Mrs. John H. Holmes"; "Horace Mann"; "Edward Everett."

YOUNG, James H. Engraver of Philadelphia from 1817–45. At times he was a member of the firms of Kneass & Young, and of Young & Delleker, both in business in Philadelphia. The only plates found signed by Young alone are early encyclopedia plates in line.

YOUNG, Mahonri. Sculptor, etcher and painter. Born in Salt Lake City in 1877. Pupil of Art Students' League, New York; Julien, Colarossi and Delecluse Academies, Paris.

State prizes for painting and sculpture, Utah Arts Institute, 1906; Helen Foster Barnett prize, National Academy of Design, 1911; honorable mention, American Art Association, Paris, for etching, 1904; honorable mention, Buenos Aires, for sculpture, 1910; silver medal, Panama-P. I. Exposition, 1915. Teacher, Art Students' League. Elected an Associate Member of the National Academy, 1912. Member: National Sculpture Society; American Painters and Sculptors; Society of Utah Artists; Society of Etchers, Chicago; Architectural League; Society of Etchers, New York; Painter-Gravers, etc.; Numismatic Society; New York Water Color Club. *Address*, 148 Prospect St., Leonia, N. J.

YOUNG, Mary Eliza. Miniature painter, who married Samuel B. Waugh. She was the mother of Frederick J. Waugh, the painter.

YOUNG, Thomas. Painter. Native of Providence, R. I., where he produced numerous portraits. The portraits of Thomas Coles and John Matthewson Eddy by Young are in the Providence Athenaeum; he also painted a portrait of Nehemiah Knight, Governor of Rhode Island.

Z

ZEIGLER, A. Lee Woodward. Painter. Born in Baltimore in 1868. Studied at the Maryland Institute, and Art School of Charcoal Club, Baltimore. Has illustrated editions de luxe of works of Charles Kingsley, Theophile Gautier, Jane Austin and Honoré de Balzac. Has exhibited at American Water Color Society; Water Color Club; National Academy of Design, N. Y. Gold medal, exhibition of Northwestern Artists, 1915. Director of St. Paul Institute School of Art, 1910–18. *Address*, Newburgh, N. Y.

ZEITLIN, Alexandre. Sculptor, who exhibited at the Annual Exhibition at Academy of the Fine Arts, Philadelphia, 1926. *Address*, 41 Gramercy Park, New York City, N. Y.

ZELL, Ernest N. Painter. Born in Dayton, Ohio, in 1874. Pupil of Columbus Art School; Cincinnati Art Academy; Shinnecock Summer School; Summer School, Ohio State University at Columbus; under Chase in Holland. Member: Pen and Pencil Club, Columbus; Columbus Art League. *Address*, 119 Westwood Ave., Grandview, Columbus, Ohio.

ZETTLER, Emil Robert. Sculptor. Born in Chicago. Studied at Art Institute of Chicago; Royal Academy of Berlin; Julien Academy in Paris. Awards: Honorable mention, Art Institute of Chicago, 1912; medal, Chicago Society of Artists, 1915; bronze medal, Panama-Pacific Exposition, San Francisco, 1915; silver medal, Art Institute of Chicago, 1916; Logan medal, Art Institute of Chicago, 1917. Work: Municipal Art Collection, Chicago, Ill. *Address*, 4 East Ohio St., Chicago, Ill.

ZILVER, Alida. Sculptor. Exhibited in the 1924 Annual Exhibition at the Penna.

Academy of the Fine Arts. *Address*, 1947 Broadway, New York.

ZIMM, Bruno Louis. Sculptor. Born in New York in 1876. He studied under J. Q. A. Ward and Augustus Saint Gaudens. Member of National Sculpture Society. *Address*, Woodstock, N. Y.

ZIMMELE, Mrs. Margaret. Painter, sculptor and illustrator. Born in Pittsburgh, Penna., in 1872. Pupil of Chase, Shirlaw, Whittemore, Lathrop, Carlsen and Hawthorne. Member: Society of Washington Artists; Pittsburgh Artists' Association; Washington Society of Artists. *Address*, Garber Galleries, 1210 18th St., Washington, D. C.

ZIMMERMAN, Eugene. Caricaturist. Born in Basle, Switzerland, in 1862. On staff of *Puck* since 1882; *Judge* since 1884. Author of "This and That About Caricature"; "Cartoons and Caricatures"; "Home Spun Philosophy." Conducts correspondence school of caricature, cartooning and comic art. *Address*, Horseheads, Chemung County, N. Y.

ZIMMERMAN, M. W. Painter, who exhibited water colors at the Penna. Academy of the Fine Arts, Philadelphia, 1925. *Address*, 1518 Waverly St., Philadelphia.

ZOGBAUM, R. F. Naval painter and illustrator. Born in Charleston, S. C., in 1849. Pupil of Art Students' League in New York; under Bonnat in Paris. Member: American Water Color Society; Century Association. Award: medal, Columbian Exposition, Chicago, 1893. Mural decorations: "First Minnesota

Regiment at Battle of Gettysburg,'' State Capitol, St. Paul; ''Battle of Lake Erie,'' Federal Building, Cleveland; ''Hail and Farewell,'' Woolworth Building. Portraits: ''Rear Admiral Taylor,'' Naval War College, Newport; ''Dr. Henry Loomis Nelson,'' Williams College, Williamstown, Mass. Illustrations for ''Horse, Foot and Dragoons,'' ''All Hands,'' ''Ships and Sailors.'' *Address*, 125 West 87th St., New York, N. Y.

ZOLNAY, George Julian. Sculptor. Born in 1863. Pupil of Imperial Academy of Fine Arts in Vienna; National Academy of Bucharest. Member: St. Louis Arts and Crafts; Washington Art Club; Union International des Arts et Sciences, Paris; Society of Washington Artists. Awards: gold medal, St. Louis Exposition, 1904; gold medal, Portland Exposition, 1905. Decorated by the King of Roumania with the Order ''Bene Merenti'' first class. Work: ''Pierre Laclede Monument'' and Confederate monument, St. Louis, Mo.; ''Winnie Davis'' and ''Jefferson Davis'' monuments, Richmond, Va.; ''Soldiers' Monument'' and ''Sam Davis Monument,'' Nashville, Tenn.; ''Gen. Bartow'' and ''Gen. McLaws'' monuments, Savannah, Ga.; ''Soldiers' Monument,'' Owensboro, Ky.; pediment of ''Edgar Allan Poe Monument,'' University of Virginia, Charlottesville, Va.; colossal, ''Lions,'' on City Gates, University City, Mo.; main group, United States Customs House, San Francisco, Calif. *Address*, 1738 N St., N. W., Washington, D. C.

ZORACH, William. Painter. Born in Russia. He came to the United States when four years of age. Studied in National Academy of Design in New York; also in Paris. *Address*, Care of The Daniel Gallery, 2 West 47th St., New York City.

ZYLINSKI, Andrew. Painter. Born in Zaile, Lithuania, gov. Suvalki, in 1869. Pupil of Wojciech, Gerson, and Warsaw (Poland) School of Design. Member: St. Louis Art League. Work: ''Early Morning,'' Delgado Art Museum; ''Mark Twain,'' Commercial Club, Hannibal, Mo. *Address*, Box 195, Ebenezer, N. Y.

BIBLIOGRAPHY

The following list of books and publications on American Art has in many cases been consulted by the author, and he duly acknowledges his indebtedness for information contained therein.

A

Abbey, Edwin. Life and Works. By E. V. Lucas. 2 vols. London. 1921.

Addison, Julia de Wolf. The art of the National Gallery. Boston. 1909.

Addison, Julia de Wolf. The Boston Museum of Fine Arts. Boston. 1910.

A. L. A. Catalogue of American portraits published at Washington, D. C. 1906.

Allen, Charles D. Classified list of early American book-plates. To accompany an exhibition at the Grolier Club, October, 1894. New York. 1894.

Allston, Washington. Life and Letters. By Jared B. Flagg. New York. 1892.

Allston, Washington. Pictures in 1839. Record of impressions produced by the exhibition. Remarks on the progress and present state of the fine arts in the United States. In *Analectic Mag.*, vol. 6, Nov. 1815.

Allston, Washington. Correspondence. *Century Mag.*

Allston, Washington. Description of the grand historical picture of Belshazzar's Feast. Boston. 1844.

Allston, Washington. Outlines and sketches. Boston. 1850.

Allston, Washington. Exhibition of pictures at Harding's Gallery, School Street. In *No. Am. Rev.*, vol. 50, Apr. 1840.

Allston, Washington. Lectures on art and poems. New York. 1850.

Allston's lectures (review). In *New Englander*, vol. 8, Aug. 1850.

American Art News. New York. (Weekly.)

American Art Annual. Vols. 1 to 24.

American Magazine Art. (Formerly Art and Progress.) New York.

American Academy of the Fine Arts. Catalogues of annual exhibition (1st, 1816). New York. Various dates.

American Academy of the Arts. Charter and by-laws. With an account of the statues, etc., belonging to the Academy. New York. 1815.

American Sculpture Exhibition. (Catalogue.) 1923. National Sculpture Society.

Amory, Martha B. Domestic and artistic life of John Singleton Copley. Boston. 1882.

Amory, Martha B. John Singleton Copley, R. A. In *Scribner's Mo.*, vol. 21, Mar. 1881.

Andrews, William L. Essay on the portraiture of the American Revolutionary War. New York. 1896.

Andrews, William L. New Amsterdam, New Orange, New York. A chronologically arranged account of engraved views of the city from MDCLI until MDCCC. New York. 1897.

Andrews, William L. Fragments of American history illustrated solely by the works of those of our own engravers who flourished in the Eighteenth Century. New York. 1898.

Andrews, William L. Paul Revere and his engraving. New York. 1901.

Ancestral Records and Portraits. A compilation from the archives of Chapter I, Colonial Dames of America. New York. 1910. 2 vols.

Appleton, John. Alleged portrait of Rev. John Wilson, with notices of other early painters. In *M. H. S. Proc.*, 1st ser., vol. 10, 1867.

Armstrong, William. Some new Washington relics. I. From the collection of Mrs. B. W. Kennon. In *Century*, vol. 40, May 1890.

Arts (The) Monthly. New York City.

Atlee, Saml. Y. Hiram Powers, Sculptor. *Living Age*, Sept. 1854.

Audubon, Lucy. The life of John James Audubon. New York. 1869.

Avery, Samuel P. Some account of the "Gibbs-Channing" portrait of George Washington. Painted by Gilbert Stuart. New York. 1900.

B

Baker, William S. The engraved portraits of Washington, with biographical sketches of the painters. Philadelphia. 1880.

Baker, William S. American engravers and their works. Philadelphia. 1875.

Baker, William S. Medallic portraits of Washington. Philadelphia. 1885.

Baker, William S. History of a rare Washington print. In Penn. Mag., vol. 13, 1889.

Baker, William S. The first portrait of Washington. In Penn. Mag., vol. 16, 1892.

Balch, Edwin S. Art in America before the Revolution. (Society of Colonial Wars in . . . Pennsylvania, vol. 2, pt. 1.) Philadelphia. 1908.

Bartlett, Ellen S. John Trumbull, the patriot painter. In *N. E. Mag.*, vol. 13, Jan. 1896.

Bates, Albert C. An early Connecticut engraver (Richard Brunton) and his work. Hartford. 1906.

Baxter, Sylvester. "Handbook of the Boston Public Library." Boston. 1916.

Bayley, Frank W. Life and works of John Singleton Copley. Boston. 1915.

Bayley, Frank W. Little known early American portrait painters. Boston. 1915–1917. 3 vols.

Benjamin, Samuel G. W. Art in America. A critical and historical sketch. New York. 1880.

Benjamin, Samuel G. W. Fifty years of American art, 1828–1878. 3 articles. In Harper's Mag., vol. 59, 1879.

Benjamin, Samuel G. W. Early American art. In Harper's Mag., vol. 59, Nov. 1879.

Berry, Rose V. S. "John Singer Sargent: Some of His American Work." Art and Archaeology, September, 1924, pp. 83–112.

Biddle, Edward, and Charles H. Hart. Memoirs of the life and works of Jean Antoine Houdon. Philadelphia. 1911.

Bitter, Karl. Sculptor biography by F. Schevill.

Blackall, C. H. "Sargent Decorations in the Boston Museum of Fine Arts." American Architect and Architectural Review, March 29, 1922.

Blashfield, Edwin H. Mural painting in America. New York. 1913.

Bolton, Ethel S. Wax portraits and silhouettes. Boston. 1914.

Bolton, Theo. Early American miniature painters. (1921.)

Bolton, Theo. Early American portrait draftsman in crayons. (1923.)

Boston Art Club. Report of . . . memorial meeting in honor of the late Mr. Joseph Andrews (engraver). Boston. 1873.

Boston Athenaeum. Catalogue at 1st (to 50th) exhibition of paintings and sculpture at the Athenaeum gallery. Boston. 1827–1873.

Boston Public Library. List of books and magazine articles on American engraving, etching and lithography. In Boston Public Library Monthly Bulletin, vol. 9, December, 1904.

Boston Public Library. List of portraits of Benjamin Franklin owned by the Public Library of City of Boston. In Boston Public Library Bulletin, vol. 11, July, 1892.

Bowdoin College. Catalogue of art collection by Henry Johnson. Brunswick, Me. 1906.

Bowen, Clarence W. History of the Centennial Celebration of the Inauguration of George Washington. New York. 1892.

Bowen, Clarence W. The inauguration of Washington. In Century, vol. 37, Apr. 1889.

Bowles, Samuel. Chester Harding. In Atlantic, vol. 19, Apr. 1867.

Bradley, Joseph P. Saint-Memin's portrait of Marshall. In Century, vol. 38, Sept. 1889.

Breck, Joseph. Two portraits by Charles Willson Peale. In Art in Am., vol. 2, Oct. 1914.

Brewer, Thomas M. Reminiscences of John James Audubon. In Harper's Mag., vol. 61, Oct. 1880.

Brinton, Christian. Sargent and His Art. Munsey's Magazine, December, 1906.

Brinton, Christian. Modern Artists. New York. 1908.

Brooklyn Institute of Arts and Sciences. Early American paintings. Catalogue of an exhibition, February 3 to March 12, 1917. Brooklyn. 1917.

Brown, William G. List of portraits in the various buildings of Harvard University. (Harvard University Library, Bibliographical Contributions, No. 53.) Cambridge. 1898.

Bryan, Michael. Bryan's dictionary of painters and engravers. Edited by G. C. Williamson. London. 1903–1905. 5 vols.

Bryant, Lorinda M. American pictures and their painters. New York. 1917.

Burch, R. M. Color printing and color printers. New York. 1910.

Burr, Frederic M. Life and works of Alexander Anderson, M.D., the first American wood engraver. New York. 1893.

C

Caffin, Charles H. American masters of painting. New York. 1902.

Caffin, Charles H. The story of American painting. New York. 1907.

Caffin, Charles H. John S. Sargent, the Greatest Contemporary Portrait Painter. World's Work, November, 1903, pp. 4099–4116.

Caffin, Charles H. Drawings by John S. Sargent. Metropolitan Magazine, July, 1909, pp. 413–418.

Carrington, Fitzroy. Prints and their makers. Century Co. N. Y. 1912.

Carson, Hampton L. Life and Works of Benj. West.

Carson Sale. Collection of engraved portraits (belonging to Hampton L. Carson). Catalogue compiled by S. V. Henkels. Philadelphia. 1904. 4 vols.

Cary, Elizabeth L. The Gallery of National Portraiture in the Pennsylvania Academy. In Scrip, vol. 2, Aug. 1907.

Catlin, George. Catalogue descriptive and instructive of Indian cartoons. New York. 1871.

Champlin, John D., Jr., and Charles C. Perkins. Cyclopedia of painters and paintings. New York. 1886–1887. 4 vols.

Chase, Wm. M. Life and Art by Chase and Roof.

Cheney, John, and Seth Wells. Catalogue of the engraved and lithographed work by Sylvester R. Koehler. Boston. 1891.

Cheney, Ednah D. Memoir of John Cheney, engraver. Boston. 1889.

Cheney, Ednah D. Memoir of Seth W. Cheney, artist. Boston. 1881.

Clark Sale. Catalogue of the Dr. Charles E. Clark collection of American portraiture. To be sold January 15–17, 1901. Boston. 1901.

Clay Sale. Rare and valuable collection of portraits and choice engravings gathered by J. Henry Clay. To be sold December 3 and 4, 1897. Philadelphia. 1897.

Cline, I. M. Artists of New Orleans, La.

Clement, Clara Erskine. Painters, sculptors, architects, engravers and their works, 13th ed. Boston. 1895.

Clement, Clara E. Early religious painting in America. In *N. E. Mag.*, vol. 11, Dec. 1894.

Clement, Clara E., and Laurence Hutton. Artists of the nineteenth century and their works. Boston. 1880.

Cleveland, Edith R. Archibald Robertson and his portraits of the Washingtons. In *Century*, vol. 40, May, 1890.

Cleveland Museum of Art. Catalogue of the inaugural exhibition, June 6 to September 20, 1916. Cleveland. 1916.

Coad, Oral S. William Dunlap. A study. New York. 1917.

Coburn, Frederick W. The Sargent Decorations in the Boston Public Library. *American Magazine of Art*, February, 1917.

Coffin, William A. The Sargent Loan Exhibition in Boston. *New York Sun*, February 21, 1899.

Colden, Cadwallader D. Life of Robert Fulton. New York. 1817.

Conant, Samuel S. Progress of the fine arts. In First century of the Republic, pp. 399–415. New York. 1876.

Cope, Edw. R. Sale of engravings. Catalogue compiled by S. V. Henkels. Philadelphia, May, 1896.

Copley, Singleton. See Masters in Art. Pub. Boston. 1904.

Copley, Stuart, and Allston. (Exhibition at the Boston Athenaeum.) In *Old and New*, vol. 4, Dec. 1871.

Copley, John S., and Henry Pelham. Letters and papers, 1739–1776. (Massachusetts Historical Society, Collections, vol. 71. Boston. 1914.)

Copley Society, Boston. Catalogues of loan exhibitions. Boston. Various dates.

Copley, John Singleton. By Augustus Perkins.

Copley, John Singleton. By Frank W. Bayley.

Copley, John Singleton. By Martha B. Amory.

Cortissoz, Royal. Sargent the Painter of Modern Tenseness. *Scribner's Magazine*, March, 1924, pp. 345–352.

Cortissoz, Royal. John S. Sargent. *Scribner's Magazine*, November, 1903.

Cortissoz, Royal. The Field of Art. *Scribner's Magazine* (various dates).

Cox, Kenyon. Old Masters and New. New York, 1905, pp. 145, 146, 244, 255, 265.

Cox, Kenyon. Two Ways of Painting. *Scribner's Magazine*, vol. 52.

Crawford, Thomas. By Samuel Osgood. New York. 1875.

Cummings, Thomas S. Historical annals of the National Academy of Design. Philadelphia. 1865.

Cunningham, Allan. Lives of the most eminent British painters and sculptors. London. 1829–1837. 6 vols.

Cunningham, Henry W. Christian Remick, an early Boston artist. Boston. 1904.

Currier, John J. History of Newburyport, Mass., 1764–1909. (Vol. 2, Chap. 24, Authors, artists and engravers.) Newburyport. 1909. 2 vols.

Custis, George W. Parke. Recollections and private memoirs of Washington. (Chap. 27, Portraits of Washington.) New York. 1860.

D

Dalton, Charles H. Letter to Winthrop Murray Crane, with some account of Houdon's statue of Washington and of Stuart's original portrait. Cambridge. 1906.

Darrach, Charles G. Christian Gobrecht, artist and inventor. In *Penna. Mag.*, vol. 30, 1906.

Davol, Ralph. Early American artists. In *N. E. Mag.*, vol. 45, Jan. 1912.

Delaplaine, Joseph. Delaplaine's repository of the lives and portraits of distinguished American characters. Philadelphia. 1815.

Dexter, Arthur. The fine arts in Boston. In Memorial History of Boston, Justin Winsor, editor; vol. 4, pp. 383–414. Boston. 1880–1881.

Dexter, J. Richards. Notable paintings from old Salem. In *N. E. Mag.*, vol. 39, Dec. 1908.

Dickinson, H. W. Robert Fulton, engineer and artist. London. 1913.

Dodge, Pickering. Painting. Its rise and progress. Boston. 1846.

Downes, Wm. H. Winslow Homer, Life and Works. Boston. 1911.

Downes, Wm. H. John S. Sargent, Life and Works. Boston. 1925.

Downes, William H. Boston painters and paintings. 6 articles (1 and 2). In *Atlantic*, vol. 62, 1888.

Downes, William H. Stuart's portraits of Washington. In *N. E. Mag.*, vol. 9, Feb. 1894.

Downes, William Howe. Twelve Great Artists. Boston, 1900, pp. 165 et seq.

Downes, William H., and Frank T. Robinson. Our American old masters. In *N. E. Mag.*, vol. 13, Nov. 1895.

Dunlap, William. History of the rise and progress of the arts of the design in the United States. New York, 1834, 2 vols., and revised edition, 1918, 3 vols.

Dunlap, William. Address to the students of the National Academy of Design, 18th of April, 1831. New York. 1831.

Dunlap, William. Description of Dunlap's painting of Christ rejected by the high priest, elders and people. Norfolk, Va. 1820.

Durand, John. Life and times of Asher B. Durand. New York. 1894.

Durand, John. John Trumbull. In *American Art Rev.*, vol. 2, 1881.

E

Earle, Alice M. Two centuries of costume in America. New York. 1903. 2 vols.

Edes, Henry H. Chief Justice M a r t i n Howard and his portrait by Copley. In Colonial Soc. of Mass. Pubs., vol. 6, Mar. 1900.

Ehrich Galleries. One Hundred Early American Paintings. New York. 1918.

Engraved Portraits of Washington and other notable Americans. Sale catalogue compiled by S. V. Henkels. Philadelphia. 1906.

Essex Institute. H i s t o r i c a l collections. Salem. 1859–1916. 52 vols.

Etching and Etchers. By Philip Gilbert Hamerton. Boston. 1876.

Etting, Frank M. Historical account of the old State House of Pennsylvania. Boston. 1876.

Etting, Frank M. Portraiture of William Penn. In *Scribner's Mo.*, vol. 12, May, 1876.

F

Fairman, Charles E., compiler. Works of art in the United States Capitol building, including biographies of the artists. Washington. 1913.

Felt, Joseph B. Annals of Salem, 2d ed. Salem. 1845–1849. 2 vols.

Fenollosa, Ernest F. Mural Paintings in the Boston Public Library. Boston, 1896, pp. 19–28.

Fevret de Saint-Memin, Charles B. J. The St. Memin collection of portraits. New York. 1862.

Fielding, Mantle. Catalogue of the engraved works of David Edwin. Philadelphia. 1905.

Fielding, Mantle. American engravers upon copper and steel. A supplement to Stauffer's American engravers. Philadelphia. 1917.

Fielding, Mantle. Memoir and catalogue of paintings by John Neagle for Memorial Exhibition at Penna. Academy of Fine Arts. Philadelphia. 1925.

Fielding, Mantle. Edward Savage, and his Washington Family. *Penna. Magazine of History and Biography.*

Fielding, Mantle. Joseph Andrews. 2 articles. In *Penna. Mag.*, vol. 31, 1907.

Fielding, Mantle, and Edward Biddle. The Life and Works of Thomas Sully. Including catalogue of 2631 of his paintings. Philadelphia. 1921.

Flagg, Jared B. Life and letters of Washington Allston. New York. 1892.

Ford, Paul L. Some Pelham-Copley letters. In *Atlantic*, vol. 71, Apr. 1893.

Foster, Joshua J. Miniature painters, British and foreign, with some account of those who practiced in America in the eighteenth century. New York. 1903. 2 vols.

Fowler, Frank. The Work of John S. Sargent. *Bookman*, January, 1904, pp. 537–539.

Fowler, Frank. The Sully portraits at the U. S. Military Academy, West Point. In *Scribner's Mag.*, vol. 43, Jan. 1908.

Fowler, Frank. Metropolitan Museum of Art. The American School. Some early painters. In *Scribner's Mag.*, vol. 42, July, 1907.

Fraser, Charles. Catalogue of miniature portraits, landscapes, etc. Accompanied by a life of the artist. Charleston, S. C. 1857.

French, Harry W. Art and artists of Connecticut. Boston. 1879.

G

Galt, John. Life, studies, and works of Benjamin West. London. 1820.

Gilliams, E. Leslie. A Philadelphia sculptor: William Rush. In *Lippincott's Mag.*, vol. 52, Aug. 1893.

Goodwin, Daniel, Jr. Early painters of Bostonians. In Calumet Club, Chicago: Proceedings on presentation of portrait of Gen. Henry Dearborn, pp. 5–8. Chicago. 1886.

Goss, Elbridge H. Life of Colonel Paul Revere. Boston. 1891. 2 vols.

Graves, Algernon. Dictionary of artists who have exhibited works in the principal London exhibitions of oil paintings from 1769 to 1904. London. 1905–1906. 8 vols.

Green, Samuel A. John Foster, the earliest American engraver. Boston. 1909.

Green, Samuel A. Remarks on an original portrait of Rev. Increase Mather, D.D., and on some of the engravings taken from it. Cambridge. 1893.

Green, Samuel A. Remarks on *The Boston Magazine* and John Norman, engraver. Cambridge. 1904.

Green, Samuel A. John Foster, the earliest engraver in New England. In *M. H. S. Proc.*, 2d ser., vol. 19, 1905.

Greenough, Henry. Washington Allston as a painter. In *Scribner's Mag.*, vol. 11, Feb. 1892.

Greenwood, Isaac J. Remarks on the portraiture of Washington. In *Mag. Am. Hist.*, vol. 2, Jan. 1878.

Griswold, Rufus W. The Republican court; or American society in the days of Washington. New York. 1867.

Grolier Club. Exhibition of engraved portraits of Washington, December 14, 1899, to January 6, 1900. New York. 1900.

Grolier Club. Catalogue of the engraved work of Asher B. Durand exhibited April, 1895. New York. 1895.

Grolier Club. Catalogue of exhibition on lithography. 1796–1896.

H

Haddon, Rawson W. The Roger Morris house, or Jumel Mansion, New York City. 2 articles. In *Arch. Rec.*, vol. 42, 1917.

Halsey, R. T. H. Malbone and his miniatures. In *Scribner's Mag.*, vol. 47, May, 1910.

Halsey Sale. The Frederic R. Halsey collection of prints. Part I. Americana. To be sold November 1–3, 1916. New York. 1916.

Hale, Edward E. The early art of Thomas Cole. In *Art in Am.*, vol. 4, Dec. 1915.

Hardie, James. New universal biographical dictionary. New York. 1805. 4 vols.

Harding, Chester. My egotistography. Cambridge. 1866.

Harding, Chester. Artist. By M. E. White. Cambridge. 1890.

Harrison, Constance C. Washington in New York in 1789. In *Century*, vol. 37, Apr. 1889.

Harrison, C. C. Home and Haunts of Washington. *Century Mag.*, Nov. 1887.

Harrison, Constance C. Washington at Mount Vernon after the Revolution. In *Century*, vol. 37, Apr. 1889.

Hart, Charles H. Catalogue of the engraved portraits of Washington. New York. 1904.

Hart, Charles H. Anthony Wayne. Presentation of his portrait (by Henry Elouis). In *Penna. Mag.*, vol. 35, 1911.

Hart, Charles H. An etched profile portrait of Washington by Joseph Hiller, 1794. In Essex Inst. Hist. Coll., vol. 43, 1907.

Hart, Charles H. Life portraits of Andrew Jackson. In *McClure's Mag.*, vol. 9, July, 1897.

Hart, Charles H. Life portraits of Alexander Hamilton. In *McClure's Mag.*, vol. 8, Apr. 1897.

Hart, Charles H. Life portraits of Benjamin Franklin. In *McClure's Mag.*, vol. 8, Jan. 1897.

Hart, Charles H. Life portraits of Daniel Webster. In *McClure's Mag.*, vol. 8, Feb. 1897.

Hart, Charles H. Life portraits of George Washington. In *McClure's Mag.*, vol. 8, Feb. 1897.

Hart, Charles H. Original portraits of Washington. In *Century*, vol. 40, May, 1890.

Hart, Charles H. Life portraits of Thomas Jefferson. In *McClure's Mag.*, vol. 9, Sept. 1897.

Hart, Charles H. An original portrait of Dr. Franklin, painted by Joseph Wright. In *Penna. Mag.*, vol. 32, 1908.

Hart, Charles H. Portrait of Abraham Hasbrouck by John Vanderlyn. In *Art in Am.*, vol. 5, Feb. 1917.

Hart, Charles H. Original portraits of Washington. In *Century*, vol. 37, Apr. 1889.

Hart, Charles H. Portrait of Thomas Dawson, Viscount Cremorne, by Mather Brown. In *Art in Am.*, vol. 5, Oct. 1917.

Hart, Charles H. Portrait of Richard Mentor Johnson by John Neagle. In *Art in Am.*, vol. 4, Aug. 1916.

Hart, Charles H. Portrait of John Grimes by Matthew Harris Jouett. In *Art in Am.*, vol. 4, April, 1916.

Hart, Charles H. Portrait of Jean Antoine Houdon by Rembrandt Peale. In *Art in Am.*, vol. 3, Feb. 1915.

Hart, Charles H. Thomas Mifflin and Sarah Morris Mifflin, by John Singleton Copley. In *Art in Am.*, vol. 5, June, 1917.

Hart, Charles H. Portrait of Jacques Louis David by Rembrandt Peale. In *Art in Am.*, vol. 3, Aug. 1915.

Hart, Charles H. Portraits of Patrick Henry. In Numismatic and Antiquarian Soc. of Phila., Proc., 1911.

Hart, Charles H. Unknown life masks of great Americans. In *McClure's Mag.*, vol. 9, Oct. 1897.

Hart, Charles H. The Wilson portrait of Franklin. In *Penna. Mag.*, vol. 30, 1906.

Hart, Charles H. An unpublished life portrait of Washington. In *McClure's Mag.*, vol. 8, Nov. 1896.

Hart, Charles H. Jouett's Kentucky children. In *Harper's Mag.*, vol. 101, June, 1900.

Hazelton, John H. The historical value of Trumbull's "Declaration of Independence." In *Penna. Mag.*, vol. 31, 1907.

Healy, Geo. P. A. Reminiscences. Chicago. 1894.

Henderson, Helen W. The art treasures of Washington. Boston. 1912.

Hensel, William U. Jacob Eichholtz, painter. In *Penna. Mag.*, vol. 37, 1913.

Heraldic Journal. Recording the armorial bearings and genealogies of American families. Boston. 1865–1868. 4 vols.

Herrick, Francis H. Audubon the naturalist. New York. 1917. 2 vols.

Hesselius, Gustavus. The earliest painter and organ-builder in America. In *Penna. Mag.*, vol. 29, 1905.

Hind, A. M. History of Engraving and Etching. Boston. 1908.

Historical Society of Pennsylvania. *Pennsylvania Magazine of History and Biography*, Philadelphia, 1877–1917. 41 vols.

Historical Society of Pennsylvania. Philadelphia. 1872. Catalogue of paintings and other works of art.

Hitchcock, J. Ripley W. Etching in America. New York. 1886.

Hoeber, Arthur. The treasures of the Metropolitan Museum of Art. New York. 1899.

Hoeber, Arthur. The story of art in America. 4 articles (1–3). In *Bookman*, vols. 30–31, 1910.

Holden Sale. Catalogue of the collection of Americana and engravings formed by Edwin Babcock Holden. To be sold April 21 to May 5, 1910. Compiled by Robert Fridenberg. New York. 1910.

Howe, Winifred E. History of the Metropolitan Museum of Art, with a chapter on the early institutions of art in New York. New York. 1913.

Hubard, William J. A national standard for the likeness of Washington. In *Mag. Am. Hist.*, vol. 4, Feb. 1880.

Hudson-Fulton Celebration. Catalogue of art exhibition at the Metropolitan Museum, New York, 1909, by Henry W. Kent and Florence N. Levy.

Huntington, Daniel. A. B. Durand. A memorial address. New York. 1887.

I

Independence Hall, Philadelphia. Catalogue of the national portraits.

Innes, Geo. See Masters in Art, pub.

Isham, Samuel. History of American painting. New York. 1905.

J

Jackson, Henry E. Benjamin West; his life and works. Philadelphia. 1900.

Jackson, Joseph. Bass Otis, America's first lithographer. In *Penna. Mag.*, vol. 37, 1913.

Johnston, Elizabeth B. Original portraits of Washington. Boston. 1882.

K

Kepple, Frederick. The Golden Age of Engraving. New York. 1910.

Koehler, Sylvester R. Catalogue of the engraved and lithographed work of John Cheney and Seth Wells Cheney. Boston. 1891.

Koehler, Sylvester R. American Painters. London. 1883.

Koehler, Sylvester R. Painting in America. In Buxton, Harry J. W.: English painters, pp. 185–222. London. 1883.

Kip, William I. Recollections of John Vanderlyn, the artist. In *Atlantic*, vol. 19, Feb. 1867.

Kimball, Fiske. Thomas Jefferson and the first monument of the classical revival in America. 3 articles. In *Am. Inst. of Architects, Journal*, vol. 3, 1915.

Kimball, Fiske. The genesis of the White House. In *Century*, vol. 95, Feb. 1918.

L

Lamb, Martha J. The Ingham portrait of De Witt Clinton. In *Mag. Am. Hist.*, vol. 27, May, 1892.

Lamb, Martha J. Unpublished Washington portraits; some of the early artists. In *Mag. Am. Hist.*, vol. 19, Apr. 1888.

Latrobe, John H. B. The Capitol and Washington at the beginning of the present century. Baltimore. 1881.

Lee, Hannah F. Familiar sketches of sculpture and sculptors. Boston. 1854. 2 vols.

Leslie, Charles R. Autobiographical recollections. London. 1860. 2 vols.

Lester, Charles E. Artists of America. New York. 1846.

Lester, Charles E. Charles Loring Elliott. In *Harper's Mag.*, vol. 38, Dec. 1868.

Levis, Howard C. Bibliography of American books relating to prints and the art and history of engraving. London. 1910.

Lincoln, N. L. Engraved portraits of American Patriots by Saint-Memin.

Linton, William J. The masters of wood engraving. New Haven. 1889.

Linton, William J. History of wood engraving in America. Boston. 1882.

Lithography (with lithograph by T. Edwards). In *Boston Monthly Mag.*, vol. 1, Dec. 1825.

Lithography (with an original lithograph by Bass Otis). In *Analectic Mag.*, vol. 14, July, 1819.

Longacre, James B., and James Herring. National portrait gallery of distinguished Americans. New York. 1834–1839. 4 vols.

Lossing, Benson J. The National Academy of the Arts of Design, and its surviving founders. In *Harper's Mag.*, vol. 66, May, 1883.

Lossing, Benson J. Memorial of Alexander Anderson, the first engraver on wood in America. New York. 1872.

Lossing, Benson J. The home of Washington; or Mount Vernon and its associations. Hartford. 1870.

Lounsbery, Elizabeth. American miniature painters. *The Mentor*, No. 123, Jan. 15, 1917.

Low, Will H. A century of painting in America; fathers of art in America. In *McClure's Mag.*, vol. 20, Feb. 1903.

M

Macbeth Gallery, New York. Paintings by American artists. Colonial portraits. New York. 1914.

Malbone, Edward G. Biographical notice of. In *Analectic Mag.*, vol. 6, Sept. 1815.

Mason, George C. Life and Works of Gilbert Stuart. New York. 1879.

Massachusetts Historical Society. List of portraits in the hall of the Historical Society. In Mass. Historical Society, Collections, 3d ser., vol. 7, 1838.

Mather, Increase. Portraits of, by Kenneth B. Murdock.

Mc Spadden, J. Walter. Famous painters of America. New York. 1907.

Metropolitan Museum of Art. Catalogue of an exhibition of Colonial portraits, November 6 to December 31, 1911. New York. 1911.

Metropolitan Museum of Art. Catalogues. New York. Various dates.

Michigan State Library. Biographical sketches of American artists. 3d ed. Lansing. 1915.

Mitchell Sale. Unequaled collection of engraved portraits. . . belonging to James T. Mitchell. To be sold January 18, 1906, to February 27, 1908. Catalogue compiled by S. V. Henkels. Philadelphia. 1906–1908. 6 vols.

Montgomery, Walter, editor. American art and American art collections. Boston. 1889. 2 vols.

Morgan, John H. The work of M. Fevret de Saint-Memin. In *Brooklyn Museum Quarterly*, vol. 5, Jan. 1918.

Morgan, John H. Early American Painters. (In New York Historical Society.)

Morse, Samuel F. B. Letters and journals. Edited by Edward L. Morse. Boston. 1914. 2 vols.

Morris, Harrison S. Memoir of William T. Richards.

Munn, Charles A. Three types of Washington portraits. New York. 1908.

Museum of Fine Arts. Descriptive catalogue of an exhibition of early engraving in America, December 12, 1904, to February 5, 1905. Cambridge. 1904.

Museum of Fine Arts. Exhibition of the works of Washington Allston, July 18, 1881. Boston. 1881.

Museum of Fine Arts. Exhibition of portraits painted by Gilbert Stuart, May 4, 1880. Boston. 1880.

Muther, Richard. History of modern painting. New York. 1896. 4 vols. (Especially vol. 1.)

N

National Academy of Design. Catalogues of annual exhibitions (1st, 1826). New York. Various dates.

National Academy of Design. Catalogue of Centennial Exhibition, 1925.

National cyclopaedia of American biography. New York. 1898–1908. 15 vols.

New international encyclopaedia. New York. 1914–1916. 23 vols. (Redgrave, Samuel. Dictionary of artists of the English school.) London. 1874.

New York Art Commission. Catalogue of the works of art belonging to the City of New York. 1909.

New York Historical Society. Gallery of Art. Catalogue. New York. 1915.

New York Public Library. Check list of engraved views of the city of New York in the New York Public Library. In *New York Public Library, Bulletin*, vol. 5, 1901.

New York Public Library. Historical prints and early views of American cities. Catalogue of loan exhibition, April to October, 1917. New York. 1917.

Noble, Louis L. Life and works of Thomas Cole. 3d ed. New York. 1856.

O

Ord, George. Sketch of the life of Alexander Wilson. Philadelphia. 1828.

Ormsby, Waterman L. Description of the present system of bank-note engraving. New York. 1852.

P

Paine, Nathaniel. Early American engravings . . . in the library of the American Antiquarian Society. In *Antiq. Soc. Proc.*, N. S., vol. 17, Apr. 1906.

Park, Lawrence. Joseph Badger, 1708–1765, and a descriptive list of some of his works. In *M. H. S. Proc.*, vol. 51, 1918.

Parkman, Francis. Report on the alleged Sharpless portraits of Washington. In *M. H. S. Proc.*, 2d ser., vol. 3, Jan. 1887.

Parsons, Arthur J., compiler. Catalogue of the Gardiner Greene Hubbard collection of engravings, presented to the Library of Congress. Washington. 1905.

Peacock, Virginia T. Famous American belles. Philadelphia. 1901.

Peale, Charles W. Extracts from correspondence relative to establishment of the Academy of the Fine Arts, Philadelphia. In *Penna. Mag.*, vol. 9, 1885.

Peale, Charles Willson. Washington portraits by Charles H. Hart. In Am. Hist. Asso., Ann. Rept., 1896, vol. 1.

Peale Memorial Exhibition at Penna. Academy of Fine Arts. Philadelphia. 18—.

Peale, Rembrandt. Catalogue of original paintings . . . to be sold Nov. 18th, 1862. Philadelphia. 1862.

Peale, Rembrandt. Portrait of Washington (testimonials). Philadelphia. 1824.

Peale, Rembrandt. Peale's "Court of Death"; biographical sketch, and history of the painting. New York. 1845.

Peale, Rembrandt. Washington portraits. Four letters. In *Mag. Am. Hist.*, vol. 5, Aug. 1880.

Peck, Grace B. Amateur art in early New England. In *Harper's Mag.*, vol. 104, May, 1902.

Pennell, E. R. and J. Life of James McNeill Whistler. Philadelphia. 1907.

Pennell, Joseph. Adventures of an illustrator. Boston. 1925.

Pennell, Joseph. The Illustration of Books. Century Co., N. Y.

Pennsylvania Academy of the Fine Arts. Descriptive catalogue of the permanent collection, Philadelphia. Various dates.

Pennsylvania Academy of the Fine Arts Loan Exhibition Historical Portraits, 1887.

Pennsylvania Academy of the Fine Arts. Catalogues of annual exhibitions (1st, 1811), Philadelphia. Various dates.

Perkins, Augustus T. Sketch of the life of John Singleton Copley. Boston. 1873.

Perkins, Augustus T. Sketches of the artists Blackburn and Smibert. In *M. H. S. Proc.*, vol. 16, Dec. 1878.

Perkins, Augustus T. Additional notes on the portraits by Blackburn and Smibert. In *M. H. S. Proc.*, vol. 17, May, 1879.

Philadelphia Museum. Historical collection of paintings. Philadelphia. 1813.

Piers, Harry. Artists in Nova Scotia. In Nova Scotia Hist. Soc. Coll., vol. 18, 1914.

Poland, William C. Robert Feke, the early Newport painter, and the beginnings of Colonial painting. Providence. 1907.

Pousette-Dart, Nathaniel. Memoir of Robert Henri.

Pratt, Herbert L. Catalogue of American Paintings.

Pratt, Matthew. Autobiographical notes of Matthew Pratt, painter. In *Penna. Mag.*, vol. 19, 1895.

Preyer, David C. The art of the Metropolitan Museum of New York. Boston. 1909.

Price, Samuel W. Old masters of the Bluegrass. Louisville.

Prince, S. Irenaeus. Life of S. F. B. Morse. New York. 1875.

Print Collector's Quarterly. 12 vols.

Print Connoisseur. 1921–1922–1923.

R

Rathbun, Richard. The National Gallery of Art (Washington, D. C.). 2d ed. Washington. 1916.

Redgrave, Richard, and Samuel Redgrave. A century of painters of the English school. 2d ed. London. 1890.

Redwood Library, Newport. Catalogue of art collection. Newport. 1885.

Reigart, J. Franklin. Life of Robert Fulton. Philadelphia. 1856.

Richter, Emil H. Prints and their History. Boston. 1914.

Robinson, Jeanie F. J., and Henrietta C. Bartlett, editors. Genealogical records . . . from family Bibles. New York. 1917.

Robinson, Frank T. Living New England Artists. Boston. 1888.

Rogers, Edmund Law. Sale of engravings. Catalogue compiled by S. V. Henkels. Philadelphia. 1896.

Rogers, Edmund L. Some new Washington relics. II. From the collection of Edmund Law Rogers. In *Century*, vol. 40, May, 1890.

S

Sachse, Julius F. Portraits and busts in the collection of the American Philosophical Society. Philadelphia. 1898.

Sanborn, Franklin B. Thomas Leavitt and his artist friend, James Akin. In *Granite Monthly*, vol. 25, Oct. 1898.

Sanderson, John, and Robert Waln, editors. Biography of the signers of the Declaration of Independence. Philadelphia. 1823–1827. 9 vols.

Sartain, John. Reminiscences of a very old man, 1808–1897. New York. 1899.

Scharf, J. Thomas, and Thompson Westcott. History of Philadelphia, 1609–1884 (especially Chap. XXXII, Art and Artists). Philadelphia. 1884. 3 vols.

Schevill, F. Biography of Karl Bitter.

Seguier, Frederick P. Critical and commercial dictionary of the works of painters. London. 1870.

Sellers, Horace W. Charles Willson Peale, artist-soldier. In *Penna. Mag.*, vol. 38, 1914.

Shackleton, Robert. A Benvenuto of the backwoods (Chester Harding). In *Harper's Mag.*, vol. 133, July, 1916.

Sharples. Portraits of Washington. History and descriptive details of Middleton's portraits of Mary, the mother of Washington, and Mary Phillipse. Boston. 1886.

Shedd, Julia A. Famous painters and paintings. 4th ed. Boston. 1896.

Sheldon, George W. American painters, with 83 examples of their work. New York. 1879.

Slade, Denison R. Henry Pelham, the half-brother of John Singleton Copley. In Colonial Soc. of Mass. Pubs., vol. 5, Feb. 1898.

Smibert, John. Smibert-Hoffatt letters. In *M. H. S. Proc.*, vol. 49, 1915.

Smith, Alice R. Huger. Charles Frazer, the friend and contemporary of Malbone. In *Art in Am.*, vol. 3, June, 1915.

Spencer, Edwina. Story of American painting. 5 articles. In *Chautauquan*, vols. 48–49, 1907–1908.

Spooner, Shearjashub. Anecdotes of painters, engravers, sculptors and architects. New York. 1865. 3 vols. (All American material is in vol. 1.)

Spooner, Shearjashub. Biographical history of the fine arts. New York. 1865. 2 vols.

Stauffer, David McN. American engravers upon copper and steel. New York. 1907. 2 vols.

Stauffer, David McN. Lithographic portraits of Albert Newsam. 4 articles. In *Penna. Mag.*, vols. 24–26, 1900–1902.

Stuart, Gilbert C. Life and works by George C. Mason. New York. 1897.

Stuart, Gilbert C. Portraits not mentioned in Mason's life of Stuart by Mantle Fielding. In *Penna. Mag.*, vol. 38, 1914.

Stuart, Gilbert C. Portraits of George Washington by Gilbert Stuart, Mantle Fielding. Philadelphia. 1923.

Stuart, Gilbert. See Masters in Art, pub. Boston. 1906.

Stuart, Gilbert C. Catalogue of an exhibition of portraits painted by the late Gilbert Stuart. Boston. 1828.

Stuart, Gilbert C. Two portraits by Gilbert Stuart. Saml. Isham (*McClure's Mag.*, June, 1908).

Stuart, Gilbert C. Portrait of James Ward, R. A., by Gilbert Stuart. In *Art in Am.*, vol. 4, 1916.

Stuart, Jane. The Stuart portraits of Washington. In *Scribner's Mo.*, vol. 12, July, 1876.

Stuart, Jane. Anecdotes of Gilbert Stuart. In *Scribner's Mo.*, vol. 14, July, 1877.

Stuart, Jane. The youth of Gilbert Stuart. In *Scribner's Mo.*, vol. 13, Mar. 1877.

Sully, Thomas. Life and works. By Edward Biddle and Mantle Fielding.

Sully, Thomas. By Henry Budd. *Penna. Mag.*, April, 1918.

Sully, Thomas. Hints to young painters, and the process of portrait painting as practiced by the late Thomas Sully. Philadelphia. 1873.

Sweetser, M. Foster. Life of Washington Allston. Cambridge. 1876.

T

Taft, Lorado. History of American sculpture. New York. 1903.

Trowbridge, John. Samuel Finley Breese Morse. Boston. 1901.

Trumbull, John. Catalogue of the collection of studies and sketches made by Col. John Trumbull. To be sold December 14, 1896. Compiled by S. V. Henkels. Philadelphia. 1896.

Trumbull, John. Autobiography, reminiscences and letters. New York. 1841.

Trumbull, John. A historian in color by Charles C. Hyde. In *Mag. Am. Hist.*, vol. 28, Oct. 1892.

Trumbull, John. Catalogue of paintings by Colonel Trumbull, 5th ed. New Haven. 1864.

Trumbull, John. Painting of the Declaration of Independence. In *Penna. Mag.*, vol. 31, 1907.

Tuckerman, Henry T. Art in America. Its history, condition and prospects. 1858.

Tuckerman, Henry T. The character and portraits of Washington. New York. 1859.

Tuckerman, Henry T. Book of artists. American artist life . . . preceded by an historical account of the rise and progress of art in America. New York. 1867.

V

Van Dyke, John C. American Painting and Its Traditions. New York, 1919, pp. 243–270.

Van Dyke, John C. John S. Sargent, Portrait Painter. *Outlook*, May 2, 1903, pp. 31–39.

Van Dyke, John C. Text-book of the history of painting. New York. 1894.

Van Rensselaer, Mariana G. Washington Allston, Hon. N. A. D. In *Mag. of Art.*, vol. 12, 1889.

W

Walter, James. Memorials of Washington and of Mary, his mother, and Martha, his wife, from letters and papers of Robert Cary and James Sharples. New York. 1887.

Walton, William. American paintings in the Metropolitan Museum. In *Scribner's Mag.*, vol. 42, Nov. 1907.

Ware, William. Lectures on the works and genius of Washington Allston. Boston. 1852.

Ward, Townsend Alexander Lawson (Engraver). *Penna. Hist. Soc. Mag.*

Washington, George. His person as represented by the artists. By Sherwin McRae. Richmond. 1873.

Watson, John F. Annals of Philadelphia and Pennsylvania. Enlarged by Willis P. Hazard. Philadelphia. 1877–1879. 3 vols.

Wead, Charles Kasson. The portraits of St. Memin. *Appleton's Mag.*, July, 1906.

Weir, John F. Brief sketch of the life of John Trumbull, to which is added a catalogue of his works. New York. 1901.

Weir, Robert W. Catalogue of oil paintings and water colors by Robert W. Weir. Sold at auction, February 19. New York. 1891.

Weitenkampf, Frank. American graphic art. New York. 1912.

Weitenkampf, Frank. How to Appreciate Prints.

Weitenkampf, Frank. The fine arts in New York City. In Wilson, James G., editor: Memorial history of the city of New York, vol. 4, pp. 344–370. New York. 1893.

West, Benjamin. Unpublished letters of Benjamin West. *Penna. Mag.*, vol. 32, 1908.

West, Benjamin. By John Sartain. Published in *Sartain's Mag.*

West, Benjamin. By Martha J. Lamb. In *Mag. Am. Hist.*, vol. 27, Mar. 1892.

West's Gallery. Catalogue of pictures and drawings by the late Benjamin West. London. 1824.

West, Benjamin. Gallery of pictures painted by Benjamin West; engraved in outline by Henry Moses. London. 1811.

West, Benjamin. Description of picture "Death on the Pale Horse." London. 1818.

West, Benjamin. Description of the picture "Christ Healing the Sick in the Temple," by John Robinson. Philadelphia. 1818.

Wharton, Anne H. Social life in the early Republic. Philadelphia. 1902.

Wharton, Anne H. Heirlooms in miniatures. Philadelphia. 1898.

Wharton, Anne H. Salons Colonial and Republican. Philadelphia. 1900.

Whelen Sale. Important collection of engraved portraits of Washington . . . (and Franklin) belonging to Henry Whelen, Jr., to be sold April 27, 1909. Catalogue compiled by S. V. Henkels. Philadelphia. 1900.

White, Margaret E., editor. Sketch of Chester Harding, artist, drawn by his own hand. Boston. 1890.

Whitmore Sale. Catalogue of the private library of William H. Whitmore. To be sold November 11–14, 1902. Boston. 1902.

Whitmore, William H. Abel Bowen, engraver. Boston. 1884.

Whitmore, William H. The early painters and engravers of New England. In *M. H. S. Proc.*, vol. 9, May, 1866.

Whitmore, William H. Notes concerning Peter Pelham . . . and his successors. Cambridge. 1867.

Who's Who in America. Vols. 1 to 13.

Williams, George A. Robert Havell, Junior, engraver of Audubon's "The Birds of America." In *Print-Collector's Quarterly*, vol. 6, Oct. 1916.

Willing, J. Thomson. Makers of American art. *The Mentor*, No. 45, Dec. 22, 1913.

Wilson, Robert. Art and artists in provincial South Carolina. In City of Charleston, Year Book, 1899, pp. 137–147.

Wilson, Rufus R. America's first painters. In *N. E. Mag.*, vol. 26, Mar. 1902.

Winsor, Justin. Portraits of Washington. In Winsor, Justin, editor: Narrative and critical history of America, vol. 7, pp. 563–582. Boston. 1888.

Winsor, Justin. Savage's portrait of Washington. In *Harvard Graduates Mag.*, vol. 3, June, 1895.

Woolsey, Theodore S. The American Vassari (William Dunlap). In *Yale Review*, N. S., vol. 3, July, 1914.

Worcester Art Museum. Bulletin. 1910. Print Connoisseur.

Y

Yale College. Catalogue of paintings belonging to Yale College. New Haven. 1852.

Young, Stark. The Sargent Exhibition. *New Republic*, March 19, 1924.

ABBREVIATIONS used in this ADDENDUM

AA — American Academy of Fine Arts

AAAL — American Academy of Arts and Letters

AAU — American Art Union (including its original name, Apollo Association and their predecessor, the Apollo Gallery)

ALNY — Architectural League of New York

ASL — Art Students League

b. — born

BA — Boston Athenaeum

cat. — catalogue

d. — died

DAB — Dictionary of American Biography

FARL — Frick Art Reference Library

fl. — flourished

G&W — Groce & Wallace

m.c. — marked copy

MF — Mantle Fielding

MMA — Metropolitan Museum of Art

NA — National Academy of Design

NAD — National Academy of Design

NIAL — National Institute of Arts and Letters

NSS — National Sculpture Society

NYC — New York City

N-YHS — New-York Historical Society

NYPL — New York Public Library

PA — Pennsylvania Academy of the Fine Arts

PAFA — Pennsylvania Academy of the Fine Arts

months

states

countries

ACHERT, Fred.   Misindexed after Ackerson.

ACHESON, Georgina Elliott.   Misindexed after Achert.

ADAMS, Dunlap.   Also a writing master; in NYC, 1763. See G&W.

ADAMS, Herbert.   b. Jan. 28, 1858 in West Concord, Vt. per *Brookgreen Gardens,* I [MF states that this was in 1856 at Concord, Vt.]; d. 1945. He studied at the Mass. State Normal Art School, visited Italy in 1898; upon his return from Paris he came to N.Y. and was an instructor at Pratt Institute, Brooklyn for eight years. Among his works are: Pratt Memorial Angel (Emmanuel Baptist Church, Brooklyn); angel (Welch Memorial, Auburn Theological Seminary); bronze doors for the Library of Congress (finished upon the death of Olin Warner in 1896); doors for St. Bartholemew's Church, N.Y.; doors for the AAAL; doors for the Mariner's Museum (Newport News); William Ellery Channing (Boston); war memorial (Fitchburg and Winchester, Mass.); Sea Scape (Brookgreen Gardens, S.C.); Eagle (Brookgreen Gardens, S.C.); monument to Cornelius Scranton Bushnell and John Ericsson (New Haven, Conn.). He was a sculp-

tor member of the National Arts Commission. In 1915 he was awarded the medal of honor of the Architectural League of New York. He also received a medal of honor of the Panama-Pacific Exposition; the 1926 gold medal of the NIAL; the president's medal of honor from the NA in 1938; honorary MA's from Yale University and Tufts College.

ADAMS, Joseph Alexander.   b. New Germantown, N.J. in 1803; d. Sept. 16, 1880 in Morristown, N.J. He began work in NYC in 1824 and is best known for the cuts in Harper's *Illuminated Bible* of 1846. See DAB; Cowdrey, NAD; Hamilton; G&W.

AGATE, Alfred [T].   b. Feb. 14, 1812 per G&W [same date in Webster's and DAB; not 1818 as in MF]; d. Jan. 5, 1846 in Washington, D.C. He exhibited at the NA in 1831. He joined the around-the-world exploring expedition of Charles Wilkes as an artist, returning in 1842 and settling in Washington. See Hamilton, 202; DAB; Cowdrey, NAD; G&W.

AGATE, Frederick S[tyle(s)].   d. May 1, 1844 at Sparta, N.Y. He was one of the founders of the NA; he exhibited at the NA and also at the PA, the Artists' Fund Society, and the Apollo Association. See DAB; Cowdrey, NAD; Cowdrey, AA & AAU; Rutledge, PA; G&W.

AITKEN, Robert. b. in 1734 at Dalkeith, Scotland; d. July 15, 1802. See DAB; G&W.

AITKEN, Robert Ingersoll. b. May 8, 1878 in San Francisco; d. Jan. 3, 1949. He opened his own studio at 18. Returning from France to U.S. in 1907 he settled in NYC and became an instructor at the ASL and director of the Schools of the NA. Among his works are: many busts for the Hall of Fame, N.Y.U.; the Missouri and Mississippi rivers (Missouri State Capitol); Fountain of Earth and Fountain of the Arts and Sciences (Jefferson City, Mo.); Gompers Monument (Wash., D.C.); Light Dispersing Darkness (General Electric Company, Nela Park, Cleveland, Ohio); George Rogers Clark Memorial (Charlottesville, Va.); pediment of the U.S. Supreme Court Bldg. and figures at the entrance of the National Archives Bldg. at Wash., D.C.; The Marine (Parris Is., S.C.); Zeus (Brookgreen Gardens). He is a member of the NIAL, the Architectural League of N.Y. and the Union Internationale des Beaux Arts et des Lettres. He exhibited four sculptures at the 1913 Armory Show. See *Brookgreen Gardens, I;* cat. of the 1963 Armory Show; m.c. NYPL.

AKERS, Benjamin Paul. b. July 10, 1825 in Sacoarapa, Westbrook, Me.; d. May 21, 1861. See DAB; Cowdrey, NA; Rutledge, PA; G&W.

AKERS, Charles. b. Oct. 15, 1836 [or 1835] near Hollis, Me.; d. Sept. 16, 1906 in NYC. He was the brother of Benjamin Paul Akers with whom he studied in Rome *c.* 1855. See G&W.

AKIN [or AITKEN], James. Born in Charleston, S.C.; d. July 18, 1846. He worked in Salem and Newburyport, Mass. from 1804 to 1808 but spent most of his life from *c.* 1790 to 1846 in Philadelphia. He exhibited at the Artists' Fund Society in 1841 and postumously at the PA in 1853. He engraved in both copperplate and wood and was also a miniaturist, profilist and designer. See Rutledge, PA; G&W; Hamilton.

ALCOT [properly spelled Alcott], [Abigail (Abba)] May. b. July 26, 1840; d. in 1889 in Paris. She illustrated many books for her older sister, Louisa May Alcott and also did landscapes. She attended the life classes of William Morris Hunt in Boston and exhibited at the Paris Salon. She is the "Amy" in *Little Women*. See G&W; Hamilton.

ALEXANDER, Cosmo [or Cosmo John or Cosmus]. b. *c.* 1724; d. Aug. 25, 1772 in Edinburgh. See G&W.

ALEXANDER, Francis. b. Feb. 3, 1800 in Killingly, Conn.; d. March 27, 1880 in Florence, Italy. He was made an honorary member of the NA in 1840 and moved to Europe permanently in 1853. He collected Italian primitives and was the father of Esther Frances (Francesca Alexander), whom he taught. See DAB; Rutledge, PA; Cowdrey, NAD; Cowdrey, AA & AAU; G&W.

ALEXANDER, Mary L. MF spells the name of one of her teachers incorrectly. It should be Duveneck, not Duvenech. See m.c. Met 4.

ALEXANDER, Mrs. Nina. Misindexed after Allerdice.

ALLEN & GAW. See R. M. Gaw. See G&W.

ALLEN, Joel [Knott]. His birthplace, Farmington, Conn. is now called Southington. He spent most of his life in Middletown, Conn., where he died and may have cut the city seals of that town. See G&W.

ALLEN, Sarah Lockhart. b. Aug. 12, 1793; d. July 11, 1877 in Salem. See G&W.

ALLSTON, Washington. b. Nov. 5, 1779 in Georgetown, S.C. per G&W [MF states that this was in Waccanaw]; d. July 9, 1843 in Cambridgeport, Mass. per G&W but MF says in Cambridge. Graduated from Harvard in 1800. See DAB; G&W.

AMANS, Jaques [the name is correctly spelled Jacques]. He exhibited at the Salon in Paris in 1831 and 1837. See Barker; G&W.

AMATEIS, Edmond [the name is correctly spelled Edmund], [Romulus]. b. Feb. 7, 1897 at Rome, Italy. His father was Louis Amateis. He studied at the Beaux-Arts Institute of Design in 1916, at the Academie Julian with Jean Boucher and Paul Landowski, returned to the Beaux-Arts Institute and worked in the studios of Henry Shrady and John Gregory. In 1921 he won a three-year fellowship to the American Academy in Rome. Returning, he opened a studio in N.Y. For a time he was an associate in sculpture at Columbia U. Among his works are: Baltimore War Memorial; pediment and twelve metopes, Buffalo Historical Soc. Bldg.; relief, Rochester Times-Union Bldg.; panel, Kansas City Liberty Memorial; pair of griffins, Acacia Life Insurance Bldg.; spandrels and relief, Dept. of Labor and Interstate Commerce Bldg., Wash., D.C.; Eliphalet Remington in the post office at Ilion, N.Y.; reliefs, Madison Square Postal Station, N.Y.; Pastoral (Brookgreen Gardens). He is a member of the National Sculpture Society, the Architectural League of N.Y. and the NA. See *Brookgreen Gardens, I.*

AMES, Daniel F.   He also did portraits. See Cowdrey, NAD; Cowdrey, AA & AAU; G&W.

AMES, Ezra.   b. May 5, 1768 in Framingham, Mass.; d. Feb. 23, 1836 at Albany, N.Y. He was also a miniaturist, landscape, sign and fancy painter. His portrait of George Clinton was bought by the PA. See G&W.

AMES, Joseph Alexander.   b. in Roxbury, Mass. according to G&W [MF says Roxbury, N.H.]; d. Oct. 30, 1872. He went to Italy in 1848 and there painted a portrait of Pope Pius IX. He was a frequent exhibitor at the BA; he also exhibited at the Maryland Historical Soc., the NA, the PA and the Washington Art Assn. See DAB; Cowdrey, NAD; Rutledge, PA; Cowdrey AA & AAU; G&W.

AMES, Julius R[ubens].   b. Jan. 1 or May 1, 1801 at Albany, N.Y.; d. June 5, 1850 in Albany. In 1839 he wrote the abolitionist pamphlet *Liberty*, pub. by the American Anti-Slavery Society. See G&W.

AMES, [Lydia] May.   d. 1946. See m.c., NYPL.

AMES, [Mrs.] Sarah Fisher [Clampitt]. b. in Lewes per G&W but Lewis in MF, Aug. 13, 1817; d. March 8, 1901. See Rutledge, PA; G&W.

ANCORA, Pietro.   He was associated with Bell & Ancora's Art Gallery in 1819

and was a teacher of D. H. Strother. He exhibited at the PA and the Artists' Fund Society. See Rutledge, PA; G&W.

ANDERSON, Abraham Archibald.   Misindexed after Alexander Anderson.

ANDERSON, Alexander.   d. Jan., 1870 per G&W [MF says in April]. He did engravings for designers such as Wm. Morgan, Th. Matteson and E. Purcell and taught wood engraving to Garret Lansing, John H. Hall, William Morgan, and his own daughter Ann, who later married Andrew Maverick. He began engraving in wood *c.* 1793 and is the first known U.S. wood engraver. He exhibited frequently at the American Academy, the Society of Artists, and at the NA, of which he was a founder. See DAB; Cowdrey, AA & AAU; Cowdrey, NAD; Rutledge, PA; Hamilton; G&W.

ANDERSON, Hugh.   While in St. Clairsville, Ohio he met Sylvester Genin, several of whose paintings he engraved. See G&W.

ANDERSON, Karl.   b. 1874; d. 1956. He exhibited six oil paintings at the 1913 Armory Show. See the cat. of the 1963 Armory Show.

ANDERSON, W[illiam].   b. *c.* 1834 in Indiana. See G&W.

ANDERTON, G.   b. *c.* 1825 per G&W but MF says *c.* 1828; d. *c.* 1890. See G&W.

ANDREW, John.   b. 1815 at Hull, England; d. 1875. See G&W. His son John also did wood engraving.

ANDREWS, Ambrose.   Active 1824-59. He also did landscapes and was an itinerant painter. He exhibited at the AAU, the American Institute, the Royal Academy, the NA and the PA. A portrait by him of Philip Schuyler and family is owned by the NYHS. See Cowdrey, NAD; Cowdrey, AA & AAU; Rutledge, PA; G&W.

ANDREWS, Eliphalet F[razer].   b. June 11, 1835; d. March 19 or 20, 1915. He also studied in Germany at the Dusseldorf Academy; upon his return to the U.S. he settled in Washington. See Cowdrey, NAD; G&W.

ANDREWS, Joseph.   See DAB; G&W.

ANNABLE [given as Annibale in G&W], George O[liver].   d. April 22, 1887 in

Brooklyn, N.Y. He studied with Mrs. Jane (Value) Chapin and also in Europe for four years. See G&W.

ANNIN, William B.   He engraved portraits, views and maps, including the maps for Morse's *American Geography*. See G&W.

ANTHONY, Andrew Varick Stout.   b. Dec. 4, 1835; d. July 2, 1906 in West Newton, Mass. He studied engraving with T. W. Strong and occasionally designed work himself. In about 1853 he went to California and established the firm of Anthony & Baker. In 1878 he did four illustrations for Lowell's *The Rose,* Boston, 1878. See DAB; G&W; Hamilton.

APPLETON, Thomas [Gold].   b. March 31, 1812; d. April 17, 1884 in NYC. He was educated at Harvard and was also an essayist, poet and patron of art. See DAB; G&W.

ARMSTRONG, Arthur.   d. June 18, 1851. He also worked in Virginia. See G&W.

ARMSTRONG, D[avid] Maitland.   b. April 15, 1836 at Danskammer, N.Y. He was also a glass stainer. He graduated from Trinity College in 1858 and visited Europe in 1859. He was trained as a lawyer and was the U.S. Consul at Rome, 1869-73. See DAB; G&W.

ARMSTRONG. William G.   d. 1890. See G&W.

ARTER, Charles J. [should be J. Charles according to m.c., FARL].

ATHERTON, E[zra].   He was also a portraitist and wood engraver. See G&W.

AUDUBON, John James.   b. Les Cayes, Haiti, W.I. He spent most of his time between 1826 and 1839 in Great Britain and spent his last years in or near N.Y.C. His sons, John Woodhouse Audubon and Victor Gifford Audubon assisted him in his work from 1832 until his death. See Cowdrey, NAD; G&W.

AUDUBON, John Woodhouse.   b. Nov. 30, 1812 in Henderson, Ky; d. Feb. 18 or 21, 1862 near NYC. He painted portraits and wildlife and was trained by his father. He exhibited at the AA, AAU and the NA. See Cowdrey, NAD; Cowdrey, AA & AAU; G&W.

AUDUBON, Victor Gifford.   b. June 12 or 29, 1809 in Louisville, Ky.; d. Aug. 17 or 18, 1860 in NYC. He painted wildlife, landscapes and portraits and was taught by his father. He exhibited at the Royal Academy, and at the NA, the AA and the AAU. See Cowdrey, NAD; Cowdrey, AA & AAU; G&W.

AUGUR, Hezekiah.   b. Feb. 21, 1791 in New Haven, Conn. according to G&W [MF says New Hampshire]. He exhibited at the NA, PA, and BA. See DAB; Cowdrey, NAD; Rutledge, PA; G&W.

AULT, George C.   d. Dec. 30, 1948. See m.c. Met 4; m.c., NYPL.

BABCOCK, Elizabeth Jones.   d. Sept. 13, 1963. See m.c. Met 5.

BABCOCK, William P.   b. Jan. 17, 1826. He exhibited at the BA, 1853-56, 1859, 1864, 1869-70 and at the NA in 1863. Fielding describes him as a pupil of Conture in Paris; this should be Couture. See Benezit; G&W.

BACON, George.   He was also a publisher. See G&W.

BACON, Henry.   He exhibited at the BA, the NA, and the Paris Salon. See G&W.

BADGER, James W.   He was also a portraitist. See G&W.

BADGER, John C.   b. *c.* 1822 in N.H. He exhibited at the PA in 1852 and 1854. See Rutledge, PA; G&W.

BADGER, Joseph.   b. March 14, 1708; d. 1765. see DAB; Barker, p. 125; G&W.

BADGER, Thomas.   b. Dec. 25, 1792 in So. Reading (now Wakefield), Mass.; d. Feb. 3, 1868 in Cambridge, Mass. He exhibited at the BA, the NA and the AA. See Cowdrey, NAD; Cowdrey, AA & AAU; G&W.

BAER, William Jacob.   d. 1941. See m.c., FARL.

BAILLY, Joseph A[lexis].   b. Jan. 21, 1825; d. June 15, 1883 in Philadelphia. He was also a wood carver. See DAB; G&W.

BAINBOROUGH, [William].   See William Bamborough. See G&W.

BAKER, Bryant. b. July 8, 1881 in London, England. He comes from a family of builders and carvers. From 1901 to 1907 he studied at the City and Guilds Technical Institute and spent four years at the Royal Academy of Arts. He came to the U.S. in 1916. He had comprehensive exhibitions at the Corcoran Gallery of Art, Washington, D.C. in 1919 and in N.Y. in 1923. Among his works are: Edward VII (Huddersfield, Eng.); Archdeacon Hemming Robeson (Tewkesbury Abbey, Eng.); Delaware patriots (Statuary Hall, Capitol, Washington, D.C.); Grover Cleveland, Millard Fillmore (City Hall, Buffalo); Young Lincoln (Delaware Park); Gov. Reuben Fenton (Jamestown, N.Y.); monument to pioneer woman (Cherokee Strip, Okla.); Eros (art gallery, Manchester, Eng.); Memory (art gallery, Hull, Eng.); L'Apres-Midi d'un Faune (Brookgreen Gardens, S.C.). See *Brookgreen Gardens I*.

BAKER, George A[ugustus]. b. March, 1821; d. April 2, 1880. See DAB; Cowdrey, NAD; Rutledge, PA; G&W.

BAKER, Horace. b. Nov. 12, 1833; d. March 12, 1918. See G&W.

BAKER, Joseph E. He was also a lithographer and pencil portraitist. See G&W.

BAKER, William H. d. March 29, 1875, according to G&W; MF states that he died on May 29 of that year. See G&W.

BALCH, Vistus. b. Feb. 18, 1799; d. Oct. 25, 1884.

BALDWIN, William. b. *c.* 1808 in Louisiana. He was also a portraitist. See G&W.

BALL, Thomas. b. June 3, 1819; d. Dec. 11, 1911 at Montclair, N.J. He was an apprentice of Abel Bowen. See DAB; Cowdrey AA & AAU; G&W.

BALLIN, Hugo. d. Nov. 27, 1956 in Santa Monica, Cal. See m.c., NYPL.

BALLING, [Ole Peter Hansen]. b. April 13, 1828 in Christiana (now Oslo), Norway; d. May 1, 1906. See Rutledge, PA; G&W.

BAMBOROUGH, William. b. in Durham, England. He was a friend of J. J. Audubon and settled in Columbus, Ohio.

BANNERMAN, W[illiam] W. d. *c.* 1845/46. See G&W.

BANNING, William J. [or T.]. b. in Lyme, Conn. according to G&W; MF states that he was born in Lynne, Conn. See Cowdrey, NAD; G&W.

BANNISTER, E[dward] M. d. Jan. 11, 1901.

BANNISTER, James. b. 1821; d. Oct. 11, 1901 in Brooklyn, N.Y. He exhibited at the NA in 1858. See Cowdrey, NAD; G&W.

BANVARD, John. d. May 17, 1891. Panorama, landscape and portrait painter. He exhibited at the BA and the NA. See DAB; Cowdrey, NAD; G&W.

BARBEE, William R[andolph]. b. Jan. 17, 1818 near Luray, Va.; d. June 16, 1868 near Luray. See Rutledge, PA; G&W.

BARBER, Charles E. He was taught by his father William Barber, and was his assistant in the Mint. After his father's death he was appointed Chief Engraver by Rutherford B. Hayes, and held that position to 1917. While the two Barbers were in this position, they engraved heads of the presidents in office. Charles E. Barber executed the dies for American currency and also designed coinage for foreign nations. See m.c., FARL.

BARBER, John Warner. b. Feb. 2, 1798 at E. Windsor, Conn. according to G&W; MF states that he was born in Windsor, Vt.; d. June 22, 1885 at New Haven, Conn. He was also a draftsman, author, editor and publisher. He may have engraved in Hartford before settling in New Haven. See DAB.

BARBER, William. Misindexed after M. Barker. b. May 2, 1807 in London; d. Aug. 31, 1879 in Philadelphia. He was a miniature sculptor in London and came to America in 1853. In 1869 President Andrew Johnson appointed him Chief Engraver of the United States Mint in Philadelphia. See Rutledge, PA; G&W; m.c., FARL.

BARBIERE-WALBONNE [also Barbier-Walbonne and Barbierre-Walbonne; G&W do not acknowledge MF's spelling]. d.

1860 in Passy, France. He also did portraits and historical scenes. See Benezit; G&W.

BARCLAY, McClelland.   d. 1943. See m.c. Met 2.

BARNARD, George Grey.   b. May 24, 1863 in Bellefonte, Pa.; d. April 24, 1938 in NYC. As an apprentice to a jeweller he became an expert engraver. He went to Paris for twelve years, where he also studied at the Atelier Cavelier. He taught at the ASL, N.Y. from 1900 to 1903 and then took a studio at Moret-sur-Loing for eight years. Among his works are: God Pan (Columbia U., N.Y.); The Burden Bearers and Work and Brotherhood (Capitol, Harrisburg, Pa.); Lincoln (Cincinnati); Rising Woman, Adam, Eve (Rockefeller Estate, Pocantico Hills, N.Y.); Maidenhood (Brookgreen Gardens). There is a memorial collection of his work at Swarthmore, Pa. He was a member of the AAAL, the NIAL, the Independent Sculptors Society, the Association with the Societe Nationale des Beaux-Arts, Paris, and a corresponding member of the Academie des Beaux Arts, France. His collection of French Romanesque and Gothic Sculpture is built into the MMA's cloisters, Washington Heights, N.Y. He exhibited five sculptures at the 1913 Armory Show. His work is also at the Art Institute of Chicago. See *Brookgreen Gardens I; 75th Anniv. Cat., ASL!* cat. of the 1963 Armory Show.

BARNARD, W[illiam] S.   b. *c.* 1809 in Connecticut. See G&W.

BARRALET, John James.   b. Dublin, Ireland according to G&W; MF states that he was born in London; d. Jan. 16, 1815. He was also a book illustrator and drawing master. He came to the U.S. in 1795 and exhibited at the Society of Artists and the PA. See Rutledge, PA; G&W.

BARRATT, Thomas E.   b. *c.* 1814 in England. He was also a portraitist. See Rutledge, PA; G&W.

BARRY, Charles A.   b. July 14, 1830 in Boston; d. 1892. He was also a crayon portraitist and an artist for "Ballou's Pictorial." He exhibited at the BA and the NA. See Cowdrey, NAD; G&W.

BARTHOLEMEW, Edward Sheffield. b. July 8, 1822 in Colchester, Conn. He

exhibited at the PA in 1859, 1863 and 1869. See DAB; Cowdrey, NAD; Rutledge, PA; G&W.

BARTLETT, Paul Wayland.   b. Jan. 24, 1865 in New Haven, Conn.; d. Sept. 20, 1925 in Paris. He went to Paris to live with his mother at age 9; studied with Fremiet at the Jardin des Plantes and was associated with the sculptor-ceramist Jean Carries. Among his works are: bust of his grandmother, exhibited at the Paris Salon, 1880; The Bohemian Bear Tamer (MMA, N.Y.); a series of small animal bronzes (Musee de Luxembourg); fountains, exhibited at the Pan-American Exposition, Buffalo, 1901 (gold medal) and the St. Louis Exposition (grand prize); Michael Angelo (rotunda of Library of Congress); General McClellan (Philadelphia); the pediment of N.Y. Stock Exchange (as an assistant of J.Q.A. Ward); the pediment of House Wing of the Capitol, Washington; six statues for attic of NYPL facade; equestrian statue of Washington (Philadelphia); Benjamin Franklin (Waterbury, Conn.); two statues of Puritans (Hartford State Capitol); Robert Morris (Philadelphia); Pilgrim Mother (Provincetown, Mass.); Patriotism Guarding the Flag (Duluth, Minn.); Fledgling (Brookgreen Gardens); Study in Bronze, which is probably the Statuette of Adam, Sitting (Brookgreen Gardens). He was a member, Legion of Honor; an associate member of the Academie des Beaux-Arts, France and of the Academie Royale des Sciences, des Lettres et des Beaux-Arts de Belgique; and a member of the AAAL. See *Brookgreen Gardens I.*

BARTLETT, Truman H[owe].   He was a sculptor of portraits and monuments. He exhibited at the NA from 1866 to 1880. See DAB; G&W.

BATEMAN, William.   He also engraved seals. See G&W.

BAUM, Walter E.   d. July 12, 1956 in Sellersville, Pa. See m.c., NYPL.

BEACH, Chester.   b. May 23, 1881. He studied architectural modeling at the Lick Polytechnic School. He worked as a silver designer and studied drawing at the Mark Hopkins Institute. Then he went to Paris in 1904 to the Academie Julian and afterwards opened his own studio. In 1907 he opened a studio in NYC. Among his works are: The Stoker (Brooklyn Museum); The Sacred Fire (AAAL, N.Y.); Beyond (California Palace of the Legion of Honor); Surf (Newark Museum); Cloud Forms (Brooklyn Museum); The Glint of the Sea (Ball State Teachers' College, Muncie, Ind.); Fountain of the Waters (Cleveland Museum of Art); Service to the Nation (A.T.&T. Bldg., N.Y.); Torch Race (Barnard College, N.Y.); portrait bust of his wife (Art Institute of Chicago); Sylvan (Brookgreen Gardens); also ivory statuettes. He is also a member of the NIAL and exhibited four sculptures at the 1913 Armory Show. See *Brookgreen Gardens, I;* cat. of the 1963 Armory Show.

BEAL, Gifford.   b. Jan. 24, 1879; d. Feb. 5, 1956 in NYC. A student of the ASL, he was also an instructor there in 1931 and 1932, president of the League in 1916 and from 1918 to 1930, and was an Honorary Member of the League. He was a member of the NA, a fellow of the PA, and a member of the American Institute of Arts and Letters, the Architectural League of America, the National Society of Mural Painters, the National Arts Club, the Century Club, the Lotos Club, and the American Watercolor Society. He exhibited two oil paintings at the 1913 Armory Show. See 75th Anniv. Cat., ASL; m.c., NYPL; cat. of the 1963 Armory Show.

BEARD, James Henry.   b. May 20, 1812 according to Webster's, G&W, and Cowdrey; MF says he was born in 1814. He was also an animal and genre painter. He became a National Academician in 1872. See DAB; Cowdrey, NAD; Cowdrey, AA & AAU; G&W.

BEARD, William Holbrook.   b. April 13, 1824 according to Webster's, G&W, Rutledge, PA and Cowdrey; MF gives the date as 1825. See DAB; Cowdrey AA & AAU; Cowdrey, NAD; Rutledge, PA; G&W.

BEAU, John Anthony.   He was also a drawing teacher.

BEBIE, W.   He also did landscapes. See Benezit; G&W.

BECK, Augustus J.   See J. Augustus Beck; G&W.

BECK, [George].   b. 1748 or 1750 in Ellford, England; d. Dec. 14, 1812 in Lexington, Ky. according to G&W; MF states that he died in 1814. See Rutledge, PA; G&W; m.c. 2, N-YHS.

BECK, J. Augustus.   b. 1831 in Lititz, Pa; d. between 1912 and 1918. He also did landscapes and was a sculptor. He was a student of Hiram Powers and Thomas Crawford in Italy. See Rutledge, PA; G&W.

BECKER, Maurice.   b. 1889. He exhibited one charcoal drawing at the 1913 Armory Show. See the cat. of the 1963 Armory Show.

BECKWITH, Henry.   b. in England. See G&W.

BECKWITH, James Carroll.   b. 1852; d. 1917. See m.c. Met 3; m.c. 2, N-YHS.

BEEST, Albert Van.   b. June 11, 1820 in Rotterdam; d. Oct. 8, 1860 in NYC. He was also a landscapist and teacher. He exhibited at the BA in 1857 and 1861. See G&W.

BELAUME, J. [or Bellaume].   He was a general and seal engraver. See G&W.

BELCHER, Hilda.   d. April 26, 1963. See m.c., FARL.

BELKNAP, Zedekiah.   b. March 8, 1781 in Weathersfield, Vt.; d. April, 1858. See G&W.

BELLEW, Frank Henry Temple.   b. April 18, 1828 in Cawnpore, India; d. June 29, 1888 in NYC. He was a caricaturist, cartoonist and comic illustrator who came to the U.S. in 1850. See DAB; Cowdrey, NAD; Hamilton; G&W.

BELLOWS, Albert Fitch.   b. Nov. 29, 1829 in Milford, Mass. according to Webster's, G&W, Cowdrey, Rutledge and Hamilton; MF says he was born in 1830 in Milbury, Mass.; d. Nov. 24, 1883 in Auburndale, Mass. He was a landscape and genre painter in oils and watercolors and also an etcher. See DAB; Cowdrey, NAD; Rutledge, PA; Hamilton; G&W.

BELLOWS, George [Wesley].   b. Aug. 12, 1882; d. Jan. 8, 1925 according to Webster's and the ASL; MF states that he died in 1924. He also studied with K. H. Miller and Jay Hambridge. He taught at the ASL from 1910 to 1911, from 1917 to 1919 and was an Honorary Member of the League. He was one of the founders of the Society of Independent Artists. He was also a lithographer, cartoonist, landscapist and portrait painter and exhibited six oils and eight drawings at the 1913 Armory Show. Eight of his works were exhibited at the AAAL from Dec. 11, 1964 to Jan. 10, 1965. See 75th Anniv. cat., ASL; cat. of the 1963 Armory Show; the AAAL exhibition cat., *Robert Henri and His Circle*.

BENBRIDGE, Henry.   b. prob. in Nov., 1743; the date 1744 is that of his baptism on May 27. See DAB; G&W.

BENJAMIN, Samuel [Green Wheeler]. b. Feb. 13, 1837 in Argos, Greece; d. July 19, 1914. He was also an illustrator, author and diplomat. See DAB; Cowdrey, NAD; G&W.

BENNETT, William James.   b. 1787 according to G&W and Cowdrey; b. 1777 according to MF; d. May, 1844. He was also an etcher. See Cowdrey, NAD; G&W.

BENSELL, G[eorge] F[rederick].   b. 1837; d. 1879. He was also a genre and historical painter in oils. See Rutledge, PA; G&W.

BENSON, Eugene.   b. 1839 in Hyde Park, N.Y. according to G&W and Hamilton; MF states that he was born in 1840; d. 1908. He started working for the N.Y. dailies and also painted symbolic subjects. See DAB; Hamilton.

BENSON, Frank W.   d. 1951. See m.c. Met 2.

BENTON, Thomas Hart.   b. April 15, 1889 in Neosho, Mo. He studied at Art Institute of Chicago and the Academie Julian in Paris and taught at ASL from 1926 to 1935. He was Director of the Dept. of Painting, Kansas City Mo. Art Institute from 1930 to 1941 and executed the murals in the Whitney Museum of American Art, the New School for Social Research, N.Y., at the U. of Indiana, and for the State of Mo. in Jefferson City. He was a cartoonist and makes lithographs and illustrations. See 75th Anniv. Cat., ASL.

BERG, George Lewis.   b. 1869; d. July 1, 1941 at Los Gatos, Calif. He is represented in the Hinckley Art Gallery and

N.Y. Fed. of Women's Clubs. See m.c. Met 2.

BERGER, C[harles] F.   He was a landscape, portrait and miniature painter. See Rutledge, PA; G&W.

BERKAN, Otto.   b. in 1834 according to G&W, 1832 according to MF; d. Oct. 3, 1906. See G&W.

BERNINGHAUS, Oscar E.   d. April 27, 1952. See m.c., FARL.

BERRYMAN, Clifford Kennedy.   d. Dec. 11, 1949. See m.c. NYPL.

BEST, E[dward] S.   d. 1865. See G&W.

BETTS, Louis.   d. 1961. See m.c. Met 5.

BICKFORD, Nelson N.   b. 1846; d. 1943. He exhibited three sculptures at the 1913 Armory Show. See the cat. of the 1963 Armory Show.

BICKNELL, Albian [corrected to read Albion by m.c., FARL] H[arris].   See m.c., FARL.

BICKNELL, Evelyn M.   Water colors were not his specialty per Isabelle M. Bicknell. Information in m.c. FARL.

BICKNELL, Frank Alfred.   He did not die in 1905 per Isabelle M. Bicknell. Information in m.c. FARL. See m.c., FARL.

BIERSTADT, Albert.   b. Jan. 7, 1830; d. Feb. 18, 1902. He had a painting in the Hermitage, St. Petersburg, Russia. See DAB; Cowdrey, NAD; Rutledge, PA; Barker, p. 587; Hamilton; G&W.

BIESEL, Charles.   d. Aug. 5, 1945. See m.c., NYPL.

BIESTER, Anthony.   b. Aug. 26, 1840 at Cleves, Germany according to G&W; MF says he was born in 1837; d. March 26, 1917. See G&W.

BIGELOW, Daniel Folger.   b. July 22, 1823 in Peru, N.Y.; d. July, 1910. See G&W.

BIGELOW, I. W. [or James W.].

BIGGS, Walter.   b. 1866. See m.c. Met 3.

BIGOT, T[oussaint] F[rancois].   b. *c.* 1794 in Rennes, France; d. March 14, 1869 in New Orleans. He was also a historical and portrait painter and a drawing master. See G&W.

BILLINGS, E[dwin] [or Edward] T. d. Oct. 19, 1893 at Dorchester, Mass. See Cowdrey, NAD; G&W.

BINGHAM, Geo. Caleb. b. March 20, 1811 in Augusta Co., Va.; d. July 7, 1879 in Kansas City, Mo. He is said to have painted from 40 to 60 portraits in Natchez, Miss. He was a student of the PA and exhibited at the PA, NA and Washington Art Assn. See DAB; Cowdrey, NAD; Cowdrey, AA & AAU; Rutledge, PA; G&W; m.c., FARL.

BINON, [J.B.A.]. See G&W.

BIRCH. He was a line engraver. See G&W.

BIRCH, B. He was also a watchmaker. See G&W.

BIRCH, Reginald B. d. 1943. See m.c., Met 2.

BIRCH, Thomas. He was the son of William Birch. He was a marine, landscape, portrait and miniature painter. See DAB; Cowdrey, NAD; Cowdrey, AA & AAU; Rutledge, PA; G&W; Hamilton; m.c., FARL.

BIRCH, William [Russell]. b. April 9, 1755; d. Aug. 7, 1834. He was also a miniaturist and etcher. See DAB; Rutledge, PA; Cowdrey, NAD; Cowdrey, AA & AAU; G&W.

BISBING, H. Singlewood. d. at Ledyard, Conn. in 1933, not 1919 as in MF according to FARL. He painted pastoral scenes and animals, especially cattle. A native of Philadelphia, he studied at the PA and in Paris and Brussels. Among his teachers was J. H. L. de Hass. He spent most of his life in Europe, exhibiting at the Paris Salon in 1891 and 1896, and his work is in galleries in Paris and Berlin and also at the PA. He was a Chevalier of the Legion of Honor. See m.c., FARL.

BISHOP, Thomas. b. c. 1753; d. c. 1840 according to G&W and Rutledge; MF states that he flourished in 1753 and d. 1833. See Rutledge, PA; G&W.

BISSELL, George Edwin. b. Feb. 16, 1839; d. Aug. 30, 1920 at Mt. Vernon, N.Y. See DAB; G&W.

BISTRAM, Emil J. Misindexed after Edgar J. Bissell. See m.c., Met 2.

BITTER, Karl. b. Dec. 6, 1867 in Rudolfshein, Austria; d. April 10, 1915 in NYC. He worked in a stoneyard and entered the School of Applied Arts in Vienna in 1882 and later the Academy of Fine Arts. He studied with August Kuhne and Edmund von Hellmer. Among his works are: the interior carved decoration of the Collis Potter Huntington House, N.Y. and the Administration Bldg., Columbian Exposition, Chicago; pediment and terracotta reliefs, Pennsylvania Station, Philadelphia; sculptural ornament for Biltmore, the Vanderbilt estate in N.C.; three colossal stone Atlantes for the St. Paul Bldg., N.Y.; monument to Dr. William Pepper (U. of Pa.); Thanatos (Hubbard Memorial, Montpelier, Vt.); Villard Memorial (Sleepy Hollow, N.Y.); pediments for Wisconsin State Capitol; groups for the First National Bank, Cleveland; statues, Brooklyn Museum facade; monument to Carl Schurz (Morningside Drive, N.Y.); memorials to Dr. Angell and Dr. Tappan (U. of Mich.); Jefferson (U. of Va.); Boy Stealing Geese (Vanderbilt Estate); The Goose Girl (Rockefeller Estate, Pocantico Hills); Pulitzer Memorial Fountain, N.Y. (the statue topping it at Brookgreen Gardens). He was a member of the Art commission of the City of N.Y. and the NIAL. He exhibited one sculpture at the 1913 Armory Show. He was also the director of sculpture for the Buffalo, St. Louis and San Francisco Expositions. See *Brookgreen Gardens I.;* cat. of the 1963 Armory Show.

BJORKMAN, Olaf. b. 1886; d. 1946. He exhibited one sculpture at the 1913 Armory Show. See the cat. of the 1963 Armory Show.

BLACKBURN, Joseph. See DAB. See G&W.

BLACKSTONE, Harriett. d. March 16, 1939. See m.c. Met 2.

BLAKE, William S. He was in NYC from 1841 to 1850. See G&W.

BLAKELOCK, Ralph [Albert]. b. Oct. 15, 1847 in NYC; d. Aug. 9, 1919. He attended the Free Academy of the City of N.Y. (later CCNY) from 1864 to 1866 and then set out to paint and travel, first in the East, especially New England and then, from 1869, the West. He returned to NYC in the late '70's, married Corra Rebecca Bailey on Feb. 22, 1877, and raised a large family. In his earlier period he had exhibited frequently at the NA, but a change of style to the impressionistic put him out of favor and made it almost impossible for him to sell any of his works. He and his family lived in extreme poverty and on Sept. 12, 1899 he was placed in a mental institution where he spent the rest of his days; he was made an Academician of the NAD in 1916, and at about this time his paintings began to sell, though too late to help him. He was exhibited at the Centenary Exhibition in Celebration of the Centennial of CCNY—April 22 to May 29, 1947, at the Whitney Mus. of American Art, N.Y. He is represented in the collections of the National Collection of Fine Arts, Wash., D.C. and the MMA, N.Y. See Harold McCracken, *Portrait of the Old West* (N.Y. 1952) pp. 143-147.

BLANCHARD, Washington.   b. 1808. He exhibited at the BA in 1835 and 1836. See Rutledge, PA.

BLONDEL [or Blondell], Jacob D.   See Cowdrey, AA & AAU; Cowdrey, NAD; G&W.

BOARDMAN, Rosina Cox.   See also the duplicate entry after Bordley.

BODMER, Karl [or Charles].   b. Feb. 6, 1809 in Riesbach, Switzerland according to G&W, b. 1805 in Zurich according to MF. He was a lithographer and painted American Indians and landscapes. See G&W.

BOGARDUS, James.   b. March 14, 1800; d. April 13, 1874 in NYC. He was also an inventor and engraved portraits of Queen Victoria and Sir Robert Peel while in England, 1836-39. See G&W.

BOGARDUS, Mrs. William.   See William Bogardus.

BOGARDUS, William.   The only William Bogardus known to G&W was a house painter in NYC, 1844-60; the information in MF and others describing him as an engraver, miniaturist or die-sinker prob-

ably refers to James Bogardus. The same applies to Mrs. William Bogardus. See G&W.

BOGERT, George Hirst.   The information in MF is incorrect. He died in NYC on Dec. 13, 1944. See m.c., NYPL.

BOGGS, Frank M.   d. 1926. m.c., FARL.

BOGLE, James.   d. Oct. 12, 1873 in Brooklyn, N.Y. See G&W; m.c.,, FARL.

BOILEAU, Philip.   b. in Quebec, Canada. See m.c., NYPL.

BOIT, Edward Darley [or Darling].   b. 1840 in Boston according to G&W, 1843 according to MF; d. April 22, 1916 according to G&W, 1915 according to MF. See G&W.

BOLMAN [or Bollman], Miss [Caroline]. See Rutledge, PA; G&W.

BONAR, T[homas].   He was also a lithographer. See G&W.

BONFIELD, George R.   He came to the U.S. *c.* 1836. See Rutledge, PA; Cowdrey, NAD; Cowdrey, AA & AAU; G&W.

BONHAM,   Horace.   See Cowdrey, NAD; G&W.

BORDLEY.   Misindexed after Elizabeth Boott.

BOREIN, Edward.   d. May 19, 1945 Santa Barbara, Calif. See m.c., NYPL.

BORG, Carl O.   d. May 8, 1947. See m.c., FARL.

BORGLUM, Gutzon. [John Gutzon de la Mothe Borglum].   b. March 25, 1867 near Bear Lake, Idaho; d. March 6, 1941, not in 1918 as in MF. He became acquainted with Italian art while a student at St. Mary's College near Topeka, Kansas. He was apprenticed to a lithographer in Los Angeles in the early 1880's and then worked for a fresco painter and started painting in oils in his own studio. Going to San Francisco he studied painting with Virgil Williams and William Keith at the Art Association there. He returned to Los Angeles to paint while beginning to sculpt and then went east in 1890 and went to Paris, studying at the Academie Julian, the Ecole des Beaux-Arts, and with the sculptor

444

Stephan Sinding. He traveled to Holland, Belgium and Spain and returned to California after three years in Europe. He held his first important exhibition in London. His studio was on E. 38th St., N.Y. but he also had studios for a while in Raleigh, N.C. and San Antonio, Texas. He lived for a few years near Stamford, Conn. Among his works are: Jesse Benton Fremont (Los Angeles Museum); mural decorations, Queen's Hotel, Leeds and Midland Railway, Concert Hall, Manchester, Engl.; John Ruskin (MMA; Deering Library, Northwestern U., Evanston, Ill.); Mares of Diomedes (MMA; Brookgreen Gardens); John W. Mackay (School of Mines, Reno, Nevada); Lincoln (Capitol, Wash., D.C.); Henry L. Wyatt (Raleigh, N.C.); Collis P. Huntington (near the railroad station, Huntington, W. Va.); Henry Ward Beecher (near Plymouth Church, Brooklyn); memorial to James McConnell (U. of Va.); war memorial (Newark); Lee (Stone Mountain, Ga.); monument for the Trail Drivers' Assn. (San Antonio, Tex.); Alexander H. Stephens (Statuary Hall, Capitol, Wash., D.C.); heads of presidents (Mount Rushmore, S.D.); A Nation Moving Westward (Marietta, Ohio); Thomas Paine (Paris); Head of Nero (on permanent loan from Hispanic Soc. of America to Brookgreen Gardens); Theodore Lyman Wright Art Hall, (Beloit College, Beloit, Wisc.). He taught at the ASL from 1906 to 1907 and was a member of the Societe Nationale des Beaux-Arts, Paris, the Architectural League, the American Painters and Sculptors Society, and the Royal Society of British Artists. See *Brookgreen Gardens II;* 75th Anniv. Cat., ASL.

BORGLUM, Solon H[annibal].   b. Dec. 22, 1868 in Ogden, Utah; d. Jan. 31, 1922 at Stamford, Conn. He was the brother of Gutzon Borglum, from whom he received some instruction. In 1899 he visited the West, then spent a few years in N.Y. and finally moved his home and studio to "Rocky Ranch," Silvermine, Conn. He was in charge of the Dept. of Sculpture in the A.E.F. educational system. Returning to N.Y. after service in WWI he founded the School of American Sculpture. Among his works are: Lassoing Wild Horses (Detroit Institute of Arts); Winter (Cincinnati Art Museum); Stampede of Wild Horses (Cincinnati Art Museum); On the Border of White Man's Land (MMA, N.Y.); Blizzard, Snowdrift (Detroit Institute of Arts); Washington: 1753 (National Gallery of Canada, Ottowa; Iowa Memorial Union, U. of Iowa); equestrian monument to General John B. Morgan (Atlanta, Ga.); equestrian monument to Captain "Bucky" O'Neill (Prescott, Ariz.); Jacob Seisler (New Rochelle, N.Y.); Spirit of Death (Schieren Memorial, Green-Wood Cemetery); Fighting Bulls (Brookgreen Gardens; MMA, N.Y.). He was a member of the NSS and exhibited seven sculptures at the 1913 Armory Show. See *Brookgreen Gardens I;* cat. of the 1963 Armory Show.

BORIE, Adolphe.   d. in Philadelphia, May 15, 1934. See m.c. Met 2.

BOSS, Homer.   b. 1882; d. 1956. He exhibited two oils at the 1913 Armory Show. See the cat. of the 1963 Armory Show.

BOSTON, Joseph H.   d. 1954 in NYC. See m.c. Met 2.

BOTTUME, George F.   b. July, 1828; still living in 1878 in Springfield, Mass. according to G&W; d. 1846 in MF. See G&W.

BOUCHE, Louis.   b. March 18, 1896. He studied at the Grand Chaumiere and at Colarossi's in Paris and at the ASL in N.Y. He is an Active Member of the ASL and has taught there since 1934. He was a Guggenheim Fellow in 1933 and executed murals at the International Music Hall, Rockefeller Center, NYC and the Attorney General's Office and Dept. of the Interior Bldg., Washington, D.C. See 75th Anniv. Cat., ASL.

BOUGEREAU, Elizabeth [Jane] Gardinier [Gardner according to G&W].   b. in Exeter, N.H. in 1837; MF says in 1851; d. Jan., 1922 in St. Cloud, France. See G&W.

BOUGHTON, George H[enry].   b. Dec. 4, 1833 in Norwich, England according to G&W; Cowdrey, NAD and Webster's; MF has 1834; d. Jan. 19, 1905 in London; MF has 1904. He was a National Academician and also did portraits and genre painting. See Cowdrey, NAD; Cowdrey, AA & AAU; G&W.

BOULTON, Joseph L[orkowski].   b. May 26, 1896 at Fort Worth, Texas. He studied taxidermy. In 1915 he came to NYC and studied at the NAD, ASL and the Beaux-Arts Institute. He worked in the studio of Hermon MacNeil and now has a studio in Connecticut. Among his works are: a memorial tablet to Old Fort Worth (Ft. Worth, Texas); The Devil Dog (Marine Barracks, Wash., D.C.); Hop (Detroit Inst. of Arts); Dr. A. C. Morgan (Philadelphia County Medical Society); Seneca Egbert (U. of Pa.); Rabbit Nest (Brookgreen Gardens). Recently the sculptor has experimented with watercolor and oils. He is a member of many artists' associations, including the Allied Artists of America, the American Artists Professional League and the NSS. See *Brookgreen Gardens II.*

BOUNTHEAU, Henry Brintnell [or Breintall]. b. Dec. 14, 1797 in Charleston where he died, Jan. 31, 1877. He also did crayon portraits. See DAB; G&W.

BOURDON, [David]. He was also a musician and dancing master. See G&W.

BOUTELLE, De Witt Clinton. b. April 6, 1820; d. Nov. 5, 1884. See Cowdrey, NAD; Rutledge, PA; Cowdrey, AA & AAU; G&W.

BOUVE, E[lisha] W. In the text of MF for Bauve & Sharp read Bouve & Sharp.

BOWEN, Abel. b. Dec. 23, 1790; d. Mar. 11, 1850. He was self-taught; a piece of his autobiography in W. H. Whitmore's *Abel Bowen* issued as No. 2 of v. I of *The Collections of the Bostonian Society* (Boston, 1887) but not included in the 1884 issue of the monograph, claims that he introduced professional wood engraving in Boston. Among his students were Alonzo Hartwell, William Croome, the Devereux brothers, Hammatt Billings, George Loring Brown, Childs (probably Shubael D. Childs), Mallory, Kilburn, Crossman and Greenbough. See Hamilton; DAB.

BOWEN, Alexander. Misindexed after Thomas Bowen.

BOWEN, John. Misindexed after Alexander Bowen. See John Bower; see also G&W.

BOWER, John. He was an engraver of maps and portraits and a book illustrator. See G&W.

BOWERS, Edward. b. *c.* 1822 in Maryland. He also did genre and still life and was an Associate of the NA. See Rutledge, PA; Cowdrey, NAD; G&W.

BOWES, Joseph. He was also an architect. See G&W.

BOYLE, Ferdinand Thomas Lee. b. Ringwood, England; d. Dec. 2, 1906 in Brooklyn, N.Y. He served in the Union Army throughout the Civil War ("Art in America," Dec., 1933, p. 26) and was an Associate of the NA from 1849. See Cowdrey, NAD; Cowdrey, AA & AAU; G&W; m.c., FARL.

BRACKEN, Clio Hinton. b. July 25, 1870 in Rhinebeck, N.Y.; d. Feb. 12, 1925 in NYC. Her mother, Lucy (Brownson) Hinton, was a painter, sculptor and student of Carpeaux and Chapu; Clio also studied with Saint-Gaudens. In 1895 she went to Paris and studied with Louis Oury. In 1899 she returned to NYC to share a studio with her cousin Roland Hinton Perry. She also lived at Greenwich, Conn. and Boston before settling permanently in NYC in 1917. Among her works are: Chloe (Brookgreen Gardens, S.C.) and many portrait busts. See *Brookgreen Gardens II.*

BRACKET[T], Miss H. V. See G&W.

BRACKETT, Edwin E. This is corrected to read Edward A. in m.c., Met 3.

BRACKETT, Walter M. b. June 14, 1823 in Unity, Maine; d. March 8, 1919 in Boston, Mass. See Cowdrey, AA & AAU; Cowdrey, NAD; DAB; G&W.

BRACKMAN, Robert. b. 1898 in Odessa, Russia. He came to the U.S. at age 10 and studied at San Francisco Ferrer School and then at the NAD with Robert Henri and George Bellows. Since 1931 he has taught at the ASL, of which he is a Life Member. He is also a member of the NA, the Allied Artists of America, the Audubon Society of Artists, the Connecticut Academy and the American Water Color Society. See 75th Anniv. Cat., ASL.

BRADFORD, Willliam. b. April 30, 1823 at Fairhaven, near Bedford, Mass., according to G&W and Cowdrey, NAD; MF has 1830 in New Bedford); d. April 25, 1892 in NYC. He was also a photographer and lecturer and was an Associate of

446

the NA. He exhibited at the NA, the BA and the Royal Academy. See DAB; Cowdrey, NAD; G&W.

BRADISH, Alvah. b. Sept. 4, 1806 in Sherburne, N.Y.; d. April 2, 1901. He exhibited at the NA. See Cowdrey, NAD; G&W.

BRANDT, Carl L[udwig]. b. Sept. 22, 1831 in Hamburg, Germany; d. Jan. 20, 1905 in Savannah, Ga. He exhibited at the NA. See m.c., FARL; G&W.

BRANNAN, William Penn. d. Aug. 9, 1866. He was also an author and exhibited at the NA. See Cowdrey, NAD; G&W.

BREDIN, R. Sloan. d. 1933. See m.c. Met 2.

BREVOORT, James Renwick. b. July 20, 1832 in Yonkers Township, N.Y.; d. Dec. 15, 1918 in Yonkers. He exhibited at the NA and the BA. See DAB; Cowdrey, NAD; G&W; Hamilton.

BREWER, Nicholas Richard. The m.c. NYPL states that he was still living on Jan. 18, 1948 and crosses out the words, "Now deceased."

BREWSTER, Edmund. Active 1818-39. He was also a landscapist and exhibited at the PA. See Rutledge, PA; G&W.

BREWSTER, John. b. May 30/31, 1766; still living in 1846. See G&W.

BRICHER, Alfred [or Albert] T[hompson]. b. April 10, 1837; d. Sept. 30, 1908 at New Dorp, Staten Is., N.Y. He was also a landscapist and exhibited at the NA and the BA. See G&W.

BRIDGES, Fidelia. b. May 19, 1835; d. May, 1923 according to G&W and Rutledge, PA; MF says 1924. She was also a marine and nature painter and exhibited at the PA and the NA of which she was an Associate. See Cowdrey, NAD; Rutledge, PA; G&W.

BRIDGMAN, Frederic Arthur. d. Jan. 13, 1928 in Rouen, France. He became an Associate of the NA in 1874 and was made an Academician in 1881. See m.c. Met 2.

BRIDGMAN, George B. b. Nov. 5, 1864 at Bing, Monk Co., Canada; d. Dec. 16, 1943 in NYC. He studied at Paris with Gerome and Boulanger at the Ecole des Beaux-Arts and taught anatomy and life drawing at the ASL, N.Y. 1894-1900 and from 1904 into the 1940's. He also taught at the Grand Central School of Art. He was an Honorary Member of the ASL and wrote *Constructive Anatomy* and other works. He was also muralist. See 75th Anniv. Cat., ASL.

BRIDPORT, George. He was a decorative painter and drawing master. See G&W.

BRIDPORT, Hugh. d. *c.* 1868 in Philadelphia. He exhibited at the PA, the Royal Academy and the Artists' Fund Society. See Rutledge, PA; G&W.

BRINLEY, Daniel P[utnam]. d. July 30, 1963. He exhibited seven oil paintings at the 1913 Armory Show. See m.c. Met 5; cat. of the 1963 Armory Show.

BRISTOL, John Bunyan. b. April 14, 1826; d. Aug. 31, 1909 in NYC. He exhibited at the NA and was a landscapist. See DAB; Cowdrey, NAD; G&W.

BRODEAU, Anna Maria. b. 1775 in Philadelphia; d. Aug. 16, 1865 in Washington, D.C. See G&W.

BROOKS, Alden Finney. b. April 3, 1840; he was living in Chicago in 1931. See G&W.

BROOKS, Caroline Shawk. b. April 28, 1840; still living in 1900. See G&W.

BROOME, Isaac. b. May 16, 1835 in Valcartier, Quebec according to m.c. Met 4, G&W, and Rutledge, PA; 1836 according to MF. Coming to Philadelphia in 1838 he entered the studio of Hugh Cannon in 1851 and also studied at the PAFA. He was later made an Academician of the PA. A student of Etruscan pottery and an expert in ceramics, he was special commissioner for ceramics to the Paris Exposition and received a medal there and at the Philadelphia Centennial Exposition in 1876. He exhibited at the PA and the Washington Art Association and has written several books. His marble bust of Mrs. Frances Peters is at the PA. See m.c. Met. 4; Rutledge, PA; G&W.

BROWERE, Albertis [or Albertus] d[el] O[rient]. b. March 17, 1814 at Tarrytown, N.Y.; d. Feb. 17, 1887 at Catskill, N.Y. He was a landscapist, still life and genre painter and exhibited at the NA, the American Academy, the AAU, and the AA. See Cowdrey, NAD; Cowdrey, AA & AAU; G&W.

BROWERE, John Henri Isaac.   b. Nov. 18, 1790 according to G&W; MF and DAB give 1792 as the date; d. Sept. 10, 1834 in NYC. See DAB; G&W.

BROWN, Bolton Colt [corrected to read Coit in m.c., FARL].   d. Sept. 17, 1936. He exhibited one oil at the 1913 Armory Show. See m.c., FARL; cat. of the 1963 Armory Show.

BROWN, Frank.   Misindexed after George Bacon Brown.

BROWN, G. [B.].   See Cowdrey, AA & AAU; Rutledge, PA; G&W; m.c., FARL.

BROWN, George L[oring].   b. Feb. 2, 1814; d. June 25, 1889. He was a pupil of Abel Bowen and was also a miniaturist, portraitist, etcher and lithographer. He exhibited at the BA, NA, Apollo Association, AAU, PA and Artists' Fund Society. See Rutledge, PA; Cowdrey, NAD; Cowdrey, AA & AAU; G&W; Hamilton.

BROWN, Glenn Madison.   Birth date, given in MF as 1876, is corrected to read 1854 in m.c. Met 2; d. April 22, 1932. He was made an Associate of the NA in 1927. See m.c. Met 2.

BROWN, Harrison B. [sometimes Henry or Henry B.].   born Portland, Maine; d. March 10, 1915 in London. He was also a landscapist and exhibited at the NA. See G&W.

BROWN, Henry B.   The question of which Henry B. Brown this is is discussed in Hamilton. See Hamilton; G&W.

BROWN, Henry Kirke.   b. Feb. 24, 1814 in Leyden, Mass.; d. July 10, 1886 at Newburgh, N.Y. He exhibited at the NA, BA, PA and Washington Art Association. See Cowdrey, NAD; Rutledge, PA; DAB; Hamilton; G&W.

BROWN, John Appleton.   He is best known as a painter of apple orchards. See DAB; Hamilton.

BROWN, John G[eorge].   b. Nov. 11, 1831; d. Feb. 8, 1913. He exhibited at the NA, BA and PA. See DAB; G&W; Hamilton.

BROWN, John Henry.   b. Aug. 21, 1818; d. April 3, 1891. He exhibited at the PA and NA. See Rutledge, PA; Cowdrey, NAD; G&W.

BROWN, Mather.   b. Oct. 7, 1761 in Boston; d. May 25, 1831 in London. See DAB; G&W.

BROWN, Roy.   d. May 15, 1956. See m.c. Met 2.

BROWN, Uriel.   [This is corrected in m.c., FARL to read Uriah. G&W list him as Uriah but allow Uriel as an alternate name.] He was also a miniaturist. See m.c., FARL; G&W.

BROWN, William Mason.   b. 1828 according to G&W, 1830 according to MF; d. Sept. 6, 1898 in Brooklyn, N.Y. See G&W.

BROWNELL, Charles De Wolf.   He was living in Bristol, R.I. in 1878 and was a landscapist and still life painter. See Cowdrey, NAD; G&W.

BRUEN, R[obert] C.   He was an apprentice of Peter Maverick. See G&W.

BRULS, Michelson Godhart de.   See De Bruls.

BRUMIDI, Constantine.   b. July 26, 1805; d. Feb. 19, 1880. See DAB; G&W.

BRUNTON, Richard.   d. Sept. 8, 1832 at Groton, Conn. He was also a die-sinker. See G&W.

BRUSH, George De Forest.   b. Sept. 28, 1855; d. April 24, 1941 at Hanover, N.H. He taught at the ASL in 1885/86, from 1887 to 1891 and from 1892 to 1898. He was an Honorary Member of the ASL and a member of the NIAL. See 75th Anniv. Cat., ASL.

BRYANT, Henry.   d. Dec. 7, 1881 at E. Hartford, Conn. He was an engraver and daguerreotypist and exhibited at the NA. See Cowdrey, NAD; Cowdrey, AA & AAU; G&W.

BUBERL [or BUBERI], Casper [or Caspar].   b. 1834 in Bohemia; d. Aug. 22, 1899 in NYC. See Cowdrey, NAD; G&W.

BUCKLIN, William S.   d. 1928. See m.c., FARL.

BUELL, Abel.   b. Feb. 1, 1741/42 at Killingworth, Conn.; d. March 10, 1822 according to G&W, 1825 in MF, at New Haven, Conn. See DAB; G&W.

BULL, Martin. b. Dec. 3, 1744; d. March 24, 1825. See G&W.

BUNCE, William Gedney. b. Sept. 19, 1840; d. Nov. 5, 1916 at Hartford, Conn. He was also a marine painter. See DAB; G&W.

BURGIS, William. He was also a designer of views. See DAB; G&W.

BURLIN, Richard. He was also a portraitist and landscapist. See G&W.

BURROUGHS, Bryson. b. Sept. 8, 1869; d. 1934 in NYC. He studied with Merson and Puvis de Chavannes at Paris and taught in 1902/03 at the ASL, of which he was elected president in 1897. He was a Life Member of the ASL, a member of the Society of American Artists, an Associate of the NA and was Curator of Paintings at the MMA for 25 years. See 75th Anniv. Cat., ASL.

BURROUGHS, Edith Woodman [Mrs. Bryson]. b. Oct. 20, 1871 at Riverdale-on-Hudson; d. Jan. 16, 1916 in L.I. She studied drawing with Kenyon Cox and modeling with Saint-Gaudens. She spent two years at Paris under the sculptor Injalbert and the painter Luc Olivier Merson and also visited cathedral towns of Europe and saw Italy. In 1909 she returned to Paris where she was influenced by Maillol and his group. Among her works are: At the Threshhold (MMA); Bacchante (Brookgreen Gardens). She held a comprehensive show in NYC in 1915 and exhibited one sculpture at the 1913 Armory Show. She was a member of the NSS, which gave her a commemorative exhibition. See *Brookgreen Gardens I;* cat. of the 1963 Armory Show.

BURT, Charles [Kennedy]. b. Nov. 8, 1823 in Edinburgh; d. March 25, 1892 in Brooklyn, N.Y. See Cowdrey, AA & AAU; G&W.

BUSH, Joseph H[enry]. born between 1794 and 1800 according to G&W but in 1794 in MF and Rutledge; d. Jan. 11, 1865 at Lexington, Ky. He was a portraitist. See Rutledge, PA; G&W.

BUSH, Norton. b. Feb. 22, 1834; d. 1894 in San Francisco. He was president of

the Sacramento Bric-a-Brac Club and specialized in painting the scenery of the tropics. He also painted portraits. See Appleton; Hamilton; Barker; Cowdrey, NAD; G&W.

BUTLER, George Bernard. b. Feb. 8, 1838; d. May 4, 1907 at Croton Falls, N.Y. according to G&W and at Orton Falls according to MF. See Cowdrey, NAD; G&W.

BUTLER, Howard R. b. 1856; d. 1934. See m.c., FARL.

BUTLER, J[ohn] M. He was an engraver, copperplate printer and publisher. See Rutledge, PA; G&W.

BUTLER, Theodore Earl. b. 1876; d. 1937. He exhibited two oil paintings at the 1913 Armory Show. See the cat. of the 1963 Armory Show.

BYRD, [John] Henry. See G&W.

CADORIN, Ettore. d. June 18, 1952. See m.c., NYPL.

CAFFERTY, James H. b. in Albany; d. Sept. 7, 1869. He was also a landscapist and exhibited at the AA, NA, BA, Washington Art Association, and PA. See Cowdrey, NAD; Cowdrey, AA & AAU; Rutledge, PA; G&W.

CALDER, Alexander Stirling. b. Jan. 11, 1870 in Philadelphia. His father was the sculptor who designed the sculpture for the City Hall of Philadelphia. He studied with Thomas Eakins and Thomas Anshutz. Returning to the U.S. from study in France he became an instructor at the Penn. Museum School of Industrial Art. He was in Los Angeles in 1907/1908 and then moved his studio to N.Y. and taught at the ASL. Among his works are: marble sundial (Fairmount Park, Phila.); Man Cub (MMA); Fountains of Energy (Panama-Pacific Exposition); Fountain of the Rivers (Swann Memorial, Phila.); The Little Dear With the Tiny Black Swan (S.A. Lewisohn, Esq., Harrison, N.Y.); The Last Dryad (Julian R. Tinkham, Esq., Montclair, N.J.); Leif Ericsson (Reykjavik, Iceland); Nature's Dance (Brookgreen Gardens); Trajedy and Comedy (Logan Circle, Phila. and Brookgreen Gardens). Member of the NA, NSS, NIAL, and a charter member of the New Society of Artists.

CALLENDER, Benjamin [Jr.]. b. March 16, 1773; d. Feb. 22, 1856. See G&W.

CALLENDER, Joseph. b. May 6, 1751; d. Nov. 10, 1821. See G&W.

CALVERLEY, Charles. b. Nov. 1, 1833; d. Feb. 24, 1914 at Essex Falls, N.J. See also Caverley. See Cowdrey, NAD; G&W.

CALYO, Nicolino V. [V. stands for Viscount. It is not an initial of Calyo's name, according to m.c., FARL]. d. Dec. 9, 1884. He was also a landscape, historical and panoramic painter. See Cowdrey, NAD; G&W; m.c., FARL.

CANDEE, George Edward. He also did portraits and worked in watercolors and oils. See Cowdrey, NAD; G&W.

CANNON, Hugh. b. in Pennsylvania c. 1814 according to G&W but in Ireland according to MF. See Rutledge, PA; Cowdrey, AA & AAU; G&W.

CARLES, Arthur B[eecher]. b. 1882; d. June 18, 1952. He exhibited three oil paintings at the 1913 Armory Show. See the cat. of the 1963 Armory Show; m.c. Met 2.

CARLIN, John. b. June 15, 1813; d. April 23, 1891 in NYC. He was also a writer and exhibited at the NA, American Institute, AAU, Artists' Fund Society, and PA. See Cowdrey, NAD; Cowdrey, AA & AAU; Rutledge, PA; G&W.

CARLSEN, Emil. d. Jan. 2, 1932 in N.Y. See m.c. Met 2.

CARMIENCKE, John Hermann. b. Feb. 9, 1810 in Hamburg; d. June 15, 1867 in Brooklyn. He exhibited at the NA and PA. See Cowdrey, NAD; Rutledge, PA; G&W.

CARPENTER, Ellen M[aria]. b. Nov. 23, 1836 according to G&W but 1830 in MF; d. c. 1909. See G&W.

CARPENTER, Francis Bicknell. b. Aug. 6, 1830; d. May 23, 1900. He exhibited at the NA, AAU, and BA. See DAB; Benezit; Cowdrey, NAD; Cowdrey, AA & AAU; G&W.

CARROLL, John. b. Aug. 14, 1892 in Wichita, Kansas. He studied with Du-

veneck in Cincinnati, taught at the ASL 1926/27 and 1944-51 and taught at the Detroit Society of Arts and Crafts 1930-1944. He was a Guggenheim Fellow in 1927. See 75th Anniv. Cat., ASL.

CARTER, Dennis Malone. b. 1818 or 1820 [1820 also in Cowdrey, AA & AAU and Rutledge, PA; 1827 in MF and Cowdrey, NAD]; d. July 6, 1881 in NYC. He was also a figure painter. See Cowdrey, NAD; Cowdrey, AA & AAU; Rutledge, PA; G&W.

CARTOTTO, Ercole. d. Oct. 3, 1946. See m.c., NYPL.

CASILAER, John W. The last name is spelled incorrectly. See John W. Casilear.

CASILEAR, John W. b. June 25, 1811; d. Aug. 17, 1893 at Saratoga, N.Y. After 1854 he devoted most of his time to landscape painting. His name is linked with Durand, Kensett and Rossiter and he exhibited at the NA, AAU and PA. See Cowdrey, NAD; Cowdrey, AA & AAU; Rutledge, PA; DAB; G&W; Hamilton.

CASS, George N[elson]. b. 1831/32. He exhibited at the NA, AAU, and BA. See Cowdrey, NAD; Cowdrey, AA & AAU; G&W.

CASSATT, Mary. b. 1845, not 1855 as in MF; d. 1926. She exhibited two paintings at the 1913 Armory Show. See the cat. of the 1963 Armory Show.

CASSIDY, I. D. Gerald. b. 1879; d. 1934. See m.c. Met 3.

CATLIN, George. b. July 26, 1796; d. Dec. 23, 1872. He was also a miniaturist. See DAB; Rutledge, PA; Cowdrey, AA & AAU; G&W. See also Harold McCracken: George Catlin and the Old Frontier, NY, 1959.

CATTON, Charles, [Jr.]. b. Dec. 30, 1756 in London; d. April 24, 1819 in New Paltz, N.Y. He was a landscape and animal painter. See Cowdrey, AA & AAU; G&W.

CAUSICI, [Enrico]. b. Verona. See G&W.

CAVERLEY, Charles. See also Calverly.

CECERE, Gaetano. b. Nov. 26, 1894. He studied with Hermon A. MacNeil and at the Beaux-Arts Inst. of Design and also

450

studied in Rome. Among his works are: Kneeling Girl (Norton Gall. and School of Art, W. Palm Beach, Fla.); John Frank Stevens (Summit, Montana); Lincoln (Lincoln Memorial Bridge, Milwaukee); pediment, Stambaugh Auditorium, Youngstown, Ohio; war memorial, Clifton, N.J.; flagpole base, war memorial, Plainfield, N.J.; RFD Mail Carrier (Post Office Department Bldg., Washington, D.C.); Alumni medal for collaboration, Amer. Acad. in Rome; Soldier's Medal for Valor, U.S. Army; Boy and Faun, Eros and Stag (Brookgreen Gardens). He is the former director of the department of sculpture of Beaux-Arts Inst. of Design and is a member of the NA, NSS and the ALNY.

CERACCHI, Giuseppe.   b. July, 1751 in Corsica; d. Jan. 30, 1802 at Paris. See G&W.

CHAFFEE, Oliver N.   d. 1944. He exhibited three oil paintings at the 1913 Armory Show. See the cat. of the 1963 Armory Show.

CHAMPNEY, Benjamin.   b. Nov. 17, 1817 in New Ipswich, N.H.; d. Dec. 11, 1907 at Woburn, Mass. See DAB; Cowdrey, NAD; Cowdrey, AA & AAU; Rutledge, PA; G&W.

CHANDLER, Robert W.   The correct spelling is Robert W. Chanler per American Art Annual, 1930. See Robert W. Chanler.

CHANDLER, Winthrop.   b. April 6, 1747 in Woodstock, Conn.; d. July 29, 1790 at Woodstock, Conn. He also did landscapes. See G&W.

CHANLER, Robert W.   b. 1872; d. October 24, 1930 at Woodstock, N.Y. He exhibited several screens at the 1913 Armory Show. See the cat. of the 1963 Armory Show.

CHAPIN, William.   b. Oct. 17, 1802; d. Sept. 20, 1888. See Cowdrey, NAD; G&W.

CHAPMAN, Conrad Wise.   b. 1842; d. 1910. See m.c., FARL.

CHAPMAN, John Gadsby.   b. Dec. 8, 1808; d. Nov. 28, 1889 (1889 also per Webster's; G&W; Cowdrey, NAD and Cowdrey, AA & AAU; 1890 in MF). He studied in Rome and Florence and also made illustrations for Harper's *The Illuminated Bible of 1846* and his *American Drawing Book*. See DAB; Hamilton; G&W; Cowdrey, NAD; Cowdrey, AA & AAU; Rutledge, PA.

CHARLES, S[amuel] M.   m.c., FARL. See "Art in America," Oct., 1934, p. 145.

CHARLES, William.   b. 1776 in Edinburgh; d. Aug. 29, 1820. G&W say that Charles left Great Britain c. 1805 and was working in N.Y. from 1806 to 1814. MF says that he came to the U.S. in 1801 and established himself in N.Y. in 1807. See DAB; Cowdrey, AA & AAU; Cowdrey, NAD; G&W.

CHASE, Ellen Wheeler.   d. Aug. 1, 1948. See m.c., NYPL.

CHASE, William Merritt.   b. Nov. 1, 1849; d. 1916 in NYC. He taught at the ASL 1878-85, 1886-96, and 1907-12. He was an Honorary Member of the ASL and a member of the Society of American Artists, Ten American Painters, and the NIAL. He exhibited with the Munich Secession. See 75th Anniv. Cat., ASL.

CHENEY, John.   b. Oct. 20, 1801; d. Aug. 20, 1885. He was also a portrait painter. See DAB; G&W.

CHENEY, Seth Wells.   b. Nov. 26, 1810; d. Sept. 10, 1856 in S. Manchester, Conn. according to G&W but MF says in Boston. He was the brother of the engraver John Cheney. See DAB; Cowdrey, NAD; Rutledge, PA; G&W; Hamilton.

CHILD, Thomas.   d. Nov. 10, 1706. See Barker, pp. 16-20; G&W.

CHRISTY, Howard Chandler.   d. March 3, 1952. See m.c., NYPL.

CHURCH, Frederick Edwin.   b. May 4, 1826; d. April 7, 1900. He was a landscape painter. See DAB; Cowdrey, NAD; Cowdrey, AA & AAU; Rutledge, PA; G&W; Hamilton; Barker, p. 583.

CHURCHILL, Alfred Vance.   d. 1949. He exhibited one oil painting at the 1913 Armory Show. See the cat. of the 1963 Armory Show.

CIMIOTTI, Gustave, [Jr.]. He exhibited two oil paintings at the 1913 Armory Show. See the cat. of the 1963 Armory Show.

CLARK, Allan.   b. June 8, 1896. He is a graduate of Puget Sound College and studied with Robert Aitken at the ASL, NYC. He began independent work in 1917 and was an instructor at the Beaux-Arts Inst. of Design. In 1924 he traveled and studied for three years in the Far East and later went on the second Fogg Museum Expedition to China, making drawings for the Museum that were exhibited in 1930 in Cambridge and other cities. He established his studio in Santa Fe and held an exhibition of ten American Indian heads in NYC in 1930. Among his works are: stone figures, U. of Washington Library, Seattle; Nakimura Ganjiro (Honolulu Acad. of Arts); Mei Kwei (MMA); Maria of Cochiti (Seattle Art Mus.); Klah (House of Navajo Religion); Kongo Voodoo (MMA); Study for a Garden Pool (Brookgreen Gardens; Whitney Mus. of Amer. Art; Norton Gall. and School of Art, W. Palm Beach, Fla.); Arab, Gazelle (Brookgreen Gardens). He is a member of the NIAL. See Brookgreen Gardens I.

CLARK, Alvin [given as Alvan in Webster's, G&W and Cowdrey, NAD].   b. March 8, 1804; d. Aug. 19, 1887 according to Webster's, G&W and Cowdrey, NAD; it is given as 1864 in MF. See DAB; Cowdrey, NAD; Cowdrey, AA & AAU; G&W.

CLARK, James.   He was also a printer. See G&W.

CLARK, James L[ippitt].   b. Nov. 18, 1883. He worked in the designing room of the Gorham Company but later was asked to mount specimens at the American Museum of Natural History. He visited the West in 1906 and Europe and Africa in 1908. Upon returning to the U.S. he divided his attention between taxidermy and sculpture but took time to go on various expeditions to the Orient. He did the Vernay-Faunthorpe Hall of Asiatic Mammals and the Akeley African Hall at the American Museum of Natural History. Other works by him are in Nairobi; Ohio State U.; U. of Nebraska; the National Museum, Washington, D.C.; Rhode Island School of Design; and Brookgreen Gardens. He is a member of the NSS, a fellow of the American Geographical Society, and a member of the N.Y. Zoological Society. See *Brookgreen Gardens*. I.

CLARKE, Thomas.   MF says that Clarke was active in N.Y. ". . . at least as late as 1800 . . ." The m.c. Met 3 cites a print [H.279a] dated 1801. See m.c. Met 3; G&W.

CLASSEN, William M. [or H.].   He was a portrait, historical and landscape engraver. See G&W.

CLAY, Edward W[illiams].   b. April 9, 1799 according to G&W but 1792 in MF; d. Dec. 31, 1837. He was also a portrait painter. See DAB; G&W.

CLAYPOOLE, James.   1720 is given by G&W as the birth date of his father, Joseph; MF gives it as James' birth date. See G&W.

CLEMENTS, Gabrielle De Veaux.   d. March 26, 1948. See m.c., NYPL.

CLEVENGER, Shobal V[ail].   b. Oct. 22, 1812; d. Sept., 1843, at sea. See DAB; G&W.

CLINEDINST, B. West.   b. 1859 according to m.c. Met 2, but 1860 in MF; d. Sept. 12, 1931 at Pawling, N.Y. See m.c. Met 2.

CLONNEY, James Goodwyn.   b. Jan. 28, 1812 in Liverpool; d. Oct. 7, 1867 at Binghamton, N.Y. He exhibited at the NA, AA & AAU, and PA. See Cowdrey, NAD; Cowdrey, AA & AAU; Rutledge, PA; G&W.

CLOVER, Lewis P., [Jr.].   b. Feb. 20, 1819; d. Nov. 9, 1896 in NYC. He was a portrait, landscape and genre painter, and engraver. He exhibited at the NA, AA & AAU and the Artists' Fund Society. See Cowdrey, AA & AAU; Cowdrey, NAD; Rutledge, PA; G&W.

CLOVER, Philip.   b. 1832 according to G&W but 1842 in MF. See G&W.

CLUTE, Walter M[arshall].   See m.c., FARL.

CLYMER, Edwin Swift.   b. 1871. He exhibited one drawing at the 1913 Armory Show. See the cat. of the 1963 Armory Show.

COBB, Cyrus.   b. Aug. 6, 1834; d. Jan. 29, 1903 according to G&W but 1905 in MF. He was also a sculptor. See G&W.

COBB, Darius.   b. Aug. 6, 1834; d. April 23, 1919 at Newton Upper Falls, Mass. See G&W.

COBB, G[ersham].   According to the m.c. 1 of the N-YHS he was engraving in Boston in 1813. See m.c. 1, N-YHS.

COFFIN, W. Haskell.   d. 1941. See m.c. Met 2.

COGDELL, John Stephano [or Stevens]. b. Sept. 19, 1778; d. Feb. 25, 1847. See DAB; Cowdrey, NAD; Cowdrey, AA & AAU; Rutledge, PA; G&W; m.c., FARL.

COHEN, Nessa.   b. 1885. She exhibited three sculptures at the 1913 Armory Show. See the cat. of the 1963 Armory Show.

COHILL, Charles.   b. c. 1812 in Pennsylvania. See Rutledge, PA; G&W.

COLE, C[harles] O[ctavius].   b. July 1, 1814 in Newburyport, Mass. See G&W.

COLE, Mrs. Jessie [Duncan] Savage. d. Oct. 27, 1940. See m.c. 2, NYPL.

COLE, J[oseph] Foxcroft.   b. Nov. 9, 1837 in Jay, Me.; d. May 2, 1892 at Winchester, Mass. according to G&W but in Boston in MF. See DAB; Cowdrey, NAD; G&W.

COLE, Joseph Greenleaf.   b. April 10, 1806 in G&W, 1796 in Cowdrey, NAD and AA & AAU and 1803 in MF. See Cowdrey, NAD; Cowdrey, AA & AAU; G&W.

COLE, Thomas.   b. Feb. 1, 1801 in Bolton-le-Moor, Lancashire, Eng.; d. Feb. 11, or 12, 1848 at Catskill, N.Y. He was also a portrait and religious painter. See DAB; Benezit; Cowdrey, NAD; Rutledge, PA; Cowdrey, AA & AAU; G&W.

COLE, Timothy.   d. 1931. See m.c., FARL.

COLEMAN, Charles Caryl.   b. April 25, 1840; d. Dec. 4, 1928 at Capri, Italy. See DAB; Cowdrey, NAD; G&W.

COLEMAN, Glenn O.   d. May, 1932 at Long Beach, N.Y. He exhibited two drawings and one oil painting at the 1913 Armory Show. See the cat. of the 1963 Armory Show; m.c. Met 2.

COLEMAN, Ralph P.   d. 1920 in NYC. See m.c. Met 2.

COLEMAN, Samuel.   See also Colman, Samuel. d. 1920. He was well-known as a landscape painter and was the first president of the American Water Color Society. See DAB; Hamilton.

COLES, John, Jr.   b. 1776 or 1780; d. Sept. 6, 1854 in Charlestown, Mass. He also painted miniatures. See G&W; m.c., FARL.

COLLAS, Louis A[ntoine].   b. 1775 in Bordeaux, France. See Cowdrey, AA & AAU; G&W.

COLLES, J[ohn].   b. 1751; d. 1807. See G&W.

COLLIER, Charles M[yles].   d. Sept. 14, 1908 at Gloucester, Mass. according to G&W but in 1909 in MF. See G&W.

COLMAN, Samuel.   See also Samuel Coleman. b. March 4, 1832; d. March 26, 1920 in NYC. He was also an etcher, landscape and genre painter and a National Academician. See Cowdrey, NAD; G&W.

COLYER, Vincent.   b. Bloomingdale, N.Y.; d. July 12, 1888 on Contentment Island, near Darien, Conn. He was also a crayon portraitist and lithographer. See Cowdrey, NAD; Cowdrey, AA & AAU; Rutledge, PA; G&W.

COMAN, [Mrs.] Charlotte Buell.   d. Nov. 11, 1924. See Cowdrey, NAD; G&W.

COMEGYS, George H.   He was a genre, portrait and historical painter. See Cowdrey, NAD; Rutledge, PA; Cowdrey, AA & AAU; G&W.

CONANT, Alban Jasper.   b. Sept. 24, 1821; d. Feb. 3, 1915 in NYC according to G&W but MF gives 1914 as the date. He was also an archeologist. See G&W.

CONEY, John.   b. 1655 in Boston; d. 1722 in Boston. See G&W.

CONNAROE, George W.   b. 1803 in Delaware; d. 1882 or 1884. He was also a genre painter. See Cowdrey, AA & AAU; Rutledge, PA; G&W.

CONNELY, Pierce Francis.   He was a sculptor and landscape painter. See Rutledge, PA; G&W.

CONNER, Charles.   Misindexed after J. R. Conner.

CONNER, J. R.   d. Sept. 12, 1952. See m.c., NYPL.

CONROW, Wilford S.   d. Nov. 24, 1957 in NYC. See m.c., NYPL.

COOKE, George.   b. March 17, 1793; d. March 26, 1849 [1848 in Cowdrey, NAD; 1849 in G&W, Cowdrey, AA & AAU and Rutledge, PA]. He was an Associate of the NA. See Cowdrey, NAD; Rutledge, PA; Cowdrey, AA & AAU; G&W.

COOPER, Colin Campbell.   d. Nov. 6, 1937. See m.c., NYPL.

COOPER, Peregrine F.   He was also an animal painter. See Rutledge, PA; G&W.

COPELAND, Alfred Bryant.   d. Jan. 30, 1909 in Boston. He was a landscape painter. See G&W.

COPLEY, John Singleton.   b. July 3, 1738 according to Webster's and G&W but 1737 in MF; d. Sept. 9, 1815. The m.c. 1 at the N-YHS corrects the death rate of Peter Pelham, given in MF as 1851, to read 1751. See G&W; m.c. 1, N-YHS.

COPPINI, Pompeo.   d. Sept. 27, 1957 in San Antonio, Texas. See m.c., NYPL.

CORAM, Thomas.   b. April 25, 1757 according to G&W but in 1756 in MF; d. May 2, 1811 per G&W but in 1812 in MF, in Charleston, S.C. He was also a portrait and landscape painter. See G&W.

CORNE, Michaele Felice [His first name is given as Michele in Hamilton and as Michel in G&W].   b. c. 1752 on the island of Elba according to G&W or in 1752 according to the correction in m.c. Met 3, not in 1712 as in MF; d. July 10, 1845 at Newport, R.I. according to G&W but in 1832 in MF. He was also a landscape, panorama and mural painter, and he came to the U.S. in 1799. See G&W; Hamilton; m.c. Met 3; Barker, p. 289.

CORNER, Thomas C.   d. 1938. See m.c. Met 2.

CORNISH, [John].   He was English and is erroneously listed in many works as an American; the portrait of Charles Paxton, an American, done by him was painted in England. See G&W.

CORWAINE, Aaron H. [also given as Corwine in G&W; Corwyn and Corwin in Cowdrey, NAD but Carwaine in Rutledge, PA].   b. Aug. 31, 1802 near Maysville, Ky.; d. July 4, 1830. See Rutledge, PA; Cowdrey, NAD; G&W.

CORY, Kate T.   She exhibited one oil painting at the 1913 Armory Show. See the cat. of the 1963 Armory Show.

COSTAGGINI, Filippo [given as Philippo Costagni in G&W; Philippo Costagini in the American Art Annual, 1905/06]. G&W state that he was born in Italy in 1839, from the obit. in the American Art Annual 1905/06 which states that he died in 1904 aged 65, but MF says he was born in Rome in 1837; d. April 15, 1904 in Maryland according to G&W but MF gives 1907. See G&W; American Art Annual V, 1905/06.

COULON, George David.   b. c. 1823 in France; d. c. 1904 in New Orleans. See G&W.

COUTURIER, Henri [or Hendrick]. b. probably in Leyden, Holland; died in England. See G&W.

COWAN, Sarah E.   b. 1875; d. 1958. See m.c. Met 2.

COX, Kenyon.   b. Oct. 27, 1856; d. 1919 in NYC. He taught at the ASL from 1885 to 1909 and was an Honorary Member of the League. He was also a member of the Society of American Artists and of the Architectural League. See 75th Anniv. Cat., ASL.

COX, Louise.   d. Dec. 11, 1945. See m.c., NYPL.

COYLE, James.   d. July 22, 1828, perhaps in NYC. He was a founding member of the NA and was also a theatrical scene painter. See G&W.

CRANCH, Christopher Pearse.   b. March 8, 1813; d. Jan. 20, 1892. He was a portrait, landscape and still life painter. The son of Wm. Cranch, chief Justice of the U.S. circuit court of the District of Columbia, he studied divinity at Harvard and was a Unitarian minister until he turned to painting in 1842. In 1844 he published a volume of poems. See DAB; Appleton; Barker, p. 536; Cowdrey, NAD; Rutledge, PA; Cowdrey, AA & AAU; Hamilton; G&W.

CRANCH, John.   b. Feb. 2, 1807; d. Jan. 1, 1891. See Cowdrey, NAD; Cowdrey, AA & AAU; G&W.

CRANE, Ann.   d. Jan. 26, 1948. See m.c., NYPL.

CRANE, Robert Bruce.   d. 1937. See m.c. Met 2.

CRAWFORD, Thomas.   b. March 22, 1814 according to G&W but in 1813 in DAB, MF and Cowdrey, NAD; d. Oct. 10, 1857 in London according to G&W but MF says NYC. See DAB; Cowdrey, NAD; G&W.

CRAWLEY, John.   See Rutledge, PA; Cowdrey, AA & AAU; G&W.

CREIFELDS, Richard.   b. 1853. See m.c. Met 2.

CRISP, Arthur.   He exhibited one oil painting at the 1913 Armory Show. See the cat. of the 1963 Armory Show.

CROCKER, J. Denison.   b. Nov. 25, 1823. He was also a landscapist. See G&W.

CROOME, William.   b. 1790; d. 1860. He also engraved on steel and copper and designed as well. He is reputed to have been in part responsible for the freer and more artistic drawing on the block that appeared in the 1840's. See G&W; Hamilton.

CROPSEY, Jasper F[rancis].   b. Feb. 18, 1823; d. June 22, 1900. He was also an architect and designed the stations for the N.Y. Sixth Avenue Elevated Railroads. See DAB; Cowdrey, NAD; Cowdrey, AA & AAU; Rutledge, PA; G&W; Barker, p. 436.

CROSBY, Raymond Moreau.   d. Dec. 13, 1945. See m.c., NYPL.

CUMMINGS, Thomas Seir.   b. Aug. 26, 1804; d. Sept. 24, 1894 in Hackensack, N.J. according to G&W but MF says he died in Connecticut. He was a National Academician. See DAB; Cowdrey, NAD; G&W.

CUPRIEN, Frank W.   d. June 21, 1948. See m.c., NYPL.

CURRIER, Charles.   b. 1818 perhaps in Roxbury, Mass.; d. Jan. 4, 1887. See G&W.

CURRIER, J[oseph] Frank.   b. Nov. 21, 1843; d. 1909. He exhibited one oil painting at the 1913 Armory Show. See the cat. of the 1963 Armory Show; m.c.2, N-YHS.

CURRIER, Nathaniel.   b. March 27, 1813 in Roxbury, Mass.; d. Nov. 20, 1888 in NYC according to G&W; MF erroneously states that he was born in 1838 and died in 1862. See G&W; DAB.

CURTIS, Calvin.   b. July 5, 1822; d. 1893. See Cowdrey, NAD; G&W.

CURTIS, Eleanor Parke.   Misindexed after T. H. Cushman.

CURTIS, George [V.].   d. 1943. See m.c., NYPL.

CUSHMAN, George H[ewitt].   b. June 5, 1814; d. Aug. 3, 1876. He was also a portraitist. Following the designs of Darley, he engraved many plates for the novels of Cooper and Dickens. See DAB; Rutledge, PA; Hamilton; G&W.

CUSHMAN, Thomas Hastings.   b. June 6, 1815; d. Nov. 7, 1841. See G&W.

CUTLER, Carl Gordon.   d. 1945. He exhibited two oil paintings at the 1913 Armory Show. See the cat. of the 1963 Armory Show.

CUTLER, Jervis.   b. Sept. 19, 1768; d. June 25, 1846. See G&W.

DABO, Leon.   d. 1960. He exhibited four oil paintings at the 1913 Armory Show. See the cat. of the 1963 Armory Show.

DAGGETT, Alfred.   b. Sept. 30, 1799; d. Jan. 27, 1872. See G&W.

DAINGERFIELD, Elliott.   b. 1859; d. Oct. 22, 1932. m.c. Met 2.

DALLIN, Cyrus Edwin.   b. Nov. 22, 1861 in Springfield, Utah according to *Brookgreen Gardens I;* MF says Springville. He began studying in Boston in 1880 with Truman Bartlett and opened his own studio two years later, making portrait busts and statuettes. After returning to Boston from France in 1890 he spent several years in Salt Lake City, where he made an angel for the Mormon Temple, part of a monument to the pioneers of Utah, and some busts. He became an instructor at the Drexel Institute, Philadelphia and later settled in Boston as an instructor at the Mass. State Normal Art School. Among his works are: The Signal of Peace (Lincoln Park, Chicago); The Appeal to the Great Spirit (in front of the Boston Museum of Fine Arts); The Scout (Penn. Valley Park, Kansas City, Mo.); Alma Mater (Mary Institute, St. Louis); Anne Hutchinson (Boston State House); equestrian statue of Paul Revere (Boston); memorial to pioneer women of Utah (Springville, Utah); On the Warpath (Brookgreen Gardens, S.C.). He exhibited at the PA in 1915. He was a member of the NA, the NIAL, the NSS and the Royal Society of Arts, London. See *Brookgreen Gardens I*.

DALTON, E.   He also was a portraitist. See Rutledge, PA; G&W.

DANA, William Parsons Winchester.   b. Feb. 18, 1833; d. April 8, 1927 in London. See Cowdrey, NAD; Rutledge, PA; G&W.

DANFORTH, Mosely [or Moseley].   b. Dec. 7, or 11, 1800; d. Jan. 19, 1862. He also painted in oils and was a National Academician. See DAB; Cowdrey, NAD; Cowdrey, AA & AAU; G&W.

DARBY, Henry F.   See Cowdrey, NAD; G&W.

DARLEY, Edward H.   See Rutledge, PA; G&W.

DARLEY, Felix Octavius Carr.   He worked on steel plate and wood block and his work began to appear in the 1840's. Early in his career he interpreted humorous subjects. See Hamilton.

DARLEY, Jane Cooper (Sully).   b. Jan. 14, 1807 in N.Y.; d. March 3, 1877 in Philadelphia. See Rutledge, PA; Cowdrey, NAD; G&W.

DARLEY, John Clarendon.   b. *c.* 1808. See Rutledge, PA; G&W.

DARRAH, Mrs. [Ann] [Sophia] T[owne], [Mrs. Robert K.].   b. Sept. 30, 1819 in Philadelphia; d. 1881 in Boston. She was also a pastel portraitist. See Rutledge, PA; G&W.

DASBURG, Andrew.   b. May 4, 1887 in Paris, France. He studied at the ASL with Kenyon Cox, Birge Harrison and Rob-

ert Henri, taught at the ASL 1919-1921 and is represented in the collections of the Whitney Museum of American Art, Denver Art Museum, Los Angeles Museum of Art and Palace of the Legion of Honor. He lives in Taos, N.M. He exhibited three oil paintings and one sculpture at the 1913 Armory Show. See the cat. of the 1963 Armory Show; 75th Anniv. Cat., ASL.

DAVEY, Randall.   He exhibited one oil painting at the 1913 Armory Show. See the cat. of the 1963 Armory Show.

DAVIDSON, Jo.   b. March 30, 1883; d. Jan., 1952 at Tours, France. He studied at the ASL with George de Forest Brush and Hermon A. MacNeil and became the latter's assistant. He also studied briefly at the Ecole des Beaux-Arts. Among his works are: La Terre (Hackley Art Gallery, Muskegon, Mich; Whitney Mus. of Amer. Art); relief, Neighborhood Playhouse, N.Y.; Woodrow Wilson (Musee de Luxembourg); Marshal Foch, General Pershing, General Joffre (Musee des Invalides, Paris); Clemenceau (Cal. Palace of the Legion of Honor, San Francisco); John D. Rockefeller (Standard Oil Bldg., N.Y.); Marshal French (Ypres, Belgium); La Follette, Will Rogers (Capitol, Wash., D.C.; the latter also at Claremore, Oklahoma); Walt Whitman (Bear Mt. Park, N.Y.); Torso (Whitney Mus. of Amer. Art); My Niece (Brookgreen Gardens); Anatole France (Musee des Invalides); Dr. Abraham Jacobs (Mt. Sinai Hospital, NYC); Dorothy Thompson (Syracuse University); the John Purroy Mitchell Memorial (Columbia University, NYC). During the Spanish Civil War he modelled portraits of important loyalists and later went to S. America to make portrait busts of the chief executives of nine countries there. Shortly before his death he was in Israel making portraits of eminent Israelis, including Chaim Weizman, David Ben-Gurion and Moshe Sharett. Early in his career he exhibited ten drawings and eight sculptures at the 1913 Armory Show. He was a member of the NA, NIAL, NSS, Century Association, and is a Chevalier of the Legion of Honor. See 75th Anniv. Cat., ASL; Brookgreen Gardens I; cat. of the 1963 Armory Show; obituary, N.Y. Times, Jan. 4, 1952.

DAVIES, Arthur B[owen].   b. Sept. 26, 1862; d. 1928 in Florence, Italy. He also studied at the Chicago Academy of Design, the ASL, NYC and the Gotham Students School. He illustrated for St. Nicholas, the Century, and other magazines. In 1911 he exhibited at the ASL and was one of the principal organizers of the 1913 Armory Show. His works are also in the Minneapolis Institute of Art, San Francisco Art Institute, Brooklyn Museum, and the Butler Institute of Youngstown, Ohio. He exhibited four oil paintings, two pastels and one drawing at the 1913 Armory Show and six of his works were exhibited at the AAAL, Dec. 11, 1964-Jan. 10, 1965. See the cat. of the 1963 Armory Show; AAAL; *Robert Henri and His Circle;* 75th Anniv. Cat., ASL.

DAVIS, Charles Harold.   d. 1933. He exhibited one oil painting at the 1913 Armory Show. See the cat. of the 1963 Armory Show.

DAVIS, J[ohn] P[arker].   b. March 17, 1832 in Meredith Bridge, N.H.; d. Jan. 19, 1910 at Elmhurst, L.I., N.Y. He was also a landscape painter. See G&W.

DAVIS, Stuart.   b. Dec. 7, 1894 according to the 75th Anniv. Cat., ASL, but in 1892 in MF. He studied with Robert Henri at the Henri School of Art, NYC, taught at the ASL, NYC 1931/32 and has been teaching at the New School for Social Research. A retrospective exhibition of his work was held at the Museum of Modern Art in 1946. He is represented in the permanent collections of the Museum of Modern Art, Whitney Museum of American Art, Newark (N.J.) Museum, Allbright Art Gallery, PAFA, Phillips Memorial Gallery, Milwaukee Art Institute, L.A. Museum, Wichita Museum of Art and the Cranbrook Academy of Art. He was a cartoonist for "Harper's Weekly" and did murals for Radio City Music Hall, Radio Station WNYC, Indiana University and the U. of Georgia. He exhibited five watercolors at the 1913 Armory Show. See the cat. of the 1963 Armory Show; 75th Anniv. Cat., ASL.

DAWKINS, Henry.   M.c.1, N-YHS corrects MF and asserts that more than one of his portrait plates is known; m.c.2, N-YHS corrects the date 1775 to read 1755. He came to the U.S. c. 1753. See DAB; G&W.

DEAKIN, Edward.   M.c., FARL corrects the date of his birth in MF to read

1838 instead of 1840 and states that he died in 1923.

DEARBORN, Nathaniel.   Born in Mass.; d. Nov. 7, 1852 in S. Reading, Mass. according to G&W but MF says in South Roadway. He was a wood engraver and copperplate printer and was among the earliest engravers in Boston. He probably began engraving in 1812 and Hamilton discusses the question of whether or not he antedates Abel Bowen as a Boston engraver. See Hamilton; G&W.

DEAS, Charles.   d. 1867 according to m.c. Met 2. G&W states that he was made an Associate of the NA in 1839 and not in 1829 as in MF. See Cowdrey, NAD; Cowdrey, AA & AAU; Rutledge, PA; G&W.

DE BRULS, Michelson [or Michel] Godhart.   G&W state that he was in NYC 1757-1763, not 1759-1764 as in MF. See G&W.

DE FOREST, Lockwood.   d. April 4, 1932 in Santa Barbara, California. m.c. Met 2.

DE FRANCA, Manuel Joachim.   b. 1808; d. Aug. 22, 1865 at St. Louis, Mo. According to the notes in the m.c., FARL he is known by a signed and dated portrait of Judge John Meredith Read, which is signed and dated and reputedly painted in Philadelphia as early as 1836. He studied at the Academy of Arts in Lisbon until he was obliged to leave the country because of a civil war. He arrived in Philadelphia and came to be acquainted with Sully. He worked in Harrisburg, Pa. where he painted altarpieces for Roman Catholic churches and then went to St. Louis, where he painted many portraits. At one point he gave Sartain some lessons in figure painting. See G&W; Rutledge, PA; Cowdrey, AA & AAU; Cowdrey, NAD; Sartain: *Reminiscences of a Very Old Man,* 1899, pp. 145 and 175-176.

DE FRANCISCI, Anthony.   b. June 13, 1887. He studied art in Italy and came to the U.S. in 1903 where he studied at the NAD and with J. E. Fraser at the ASL. He assisted Brewster, Philip Martiny, H.A. MacNeil, Charles Niehaus, and A.A. Weinman and from 1915 taught sculpture at Columbia U. and the Beaux-Arts Institute of Design. He opened his own studio in

1917 and is especially known as a medalist. Among his works are: Independence Memorial (Union Sq., NYC); Metcalf Memorial (Orange, N.S.); Raymond Memorial, Engineering Society Bldg.; triptych (All Souls' Church, NYC); Bayadere (Cincinnati Art Mus.); panels (New U.S. Post Office Dept. Bldg., Wash., D.C.); Boys and Gazelle, Dolphins (Brookgreen Gardens); U.S. Silver Dollar, 1921; and the 12th issue, soc. of Medalists. He is a member of the NA, NSS and a fellow of the American Numismatic Society. See *Brookgreen Gardens I.*

DE GROOT, Adriaan M.   d. 1942, m.c., FARL.

DE HAAS, M[auritz] F[rederick] [Hendrik.]   d. Nov., 1895 in NYC. See Cowdrey, NAD; Hamilton; G&W.

DE HAVEN, Frank[lin].   d. Jan. 10, 1934 in NYC—m.c. Met 2.

DELANCY, Abraham, Jr.   b. 1742; d. 1795 according to G&W but MF says he was born probably in 1740 and d. *c.* 1786. He was a portrait painter. See G&W.

DELANEY, J. E.   G&W think that he may be James Delaney, portrait, historical and landscape engraver in NYC in 1846. See G&W.

DELLEKER, George.   He painted miniatures, one of which is dated 1805 and signed "G.D."—m.c. Met 2. See G&W.

DEL MAR, Francesca.   d. May 8, 1957 in NYC—m.c., NYPL.

DELNOCE, Luigi [also Louis or Lewis]. He also painted portraits, landscapes and bank-note vignettes. See Cowdrey, NAD; G&W.

DE MANCE, Henri.   d. Oct. 3, 1948. m.c., NYPL.

DEMILLIERE, [Auguste].   He was also a profilist and drawing master and came to NYC in Jan., 1797 according to G&W but MF says 1796. See G&W.

DEMING, E[dwin] W[illard].   b. Aug. 26, 1860; d. 1942. He spent 1887 in the Southwest and Oregon with Indians and made many visits to various tribes. Among his works are: paintings—murals of Indian life in the American Museum of Natural History; The Prayer of the Arrow (Mission House, Church of the Ascension, NYC); sculpture—Bear Cubs Nursing (Whitney Museum of American Art); Mutual Surprise (MMA); Bison (Brooklyn Museum); Sioux Warrior (Whitney Museum of American Art); The Fight (Brookgreen Gardens; Gibbes Memorial Art Gallery, Charleston, S.C.; MMA). He was a member of the Society of Mural Painters.

DEMUTH, Charles.   d. 1935. m.c. Met 4.

DENSLOW, Dorothea H[enrietta].   b. Dec. 14, 1900. She organized the Clay Club of NYC and has been its director. Among her works are: bronze fountain figure, Mischief (Richmond, Va.); memorial plaque, Beth Moses Hospital (Brooklyn); Pelican Rider, Playmates (Brookgreen Gardens). She is a member of the Conn. Academy of Fine Arts. See *Brookgreen Gardens I.*

DE PEYSTER, Gerard Beekman.   b. Sept. 21, 1834 in NYC; d. June 4, 1870 in NYC. He was a portraitist. See Cowdrey, NAD; G&W.

DE ROSE, Anthony Lewis.   See Cowdrey, AA & AAU; Cowdrey, NAD; G&W.

DERUJINSKY, Gleb [W.].   b. Aug. 13, 1888 in Smolensk, Russia. In 1911 he went to Paris, studied with Verlet and Injalbert and in 1913 began four years at the Imperial Academy of Art, Leningrad. He came to NYC in 1919 and in 1921 exhibited there. He taught at the Beaux-Arts Institute of Design and also at Sarah Lawrence College, Bronxville, N.Y. Among his works are: memorial to Senator Ryan (Pittsburgh Court House); figures, Carll Tucker Garden (Mt. Kisco); Four Seasons Sundial (estate of Mrs. John Hammond, Mt. Kisco); Day and Night (column in garden of Hon. Henry L. White, Lenox, Mass.); Annunciation (Fine Arts Gallery, San Diego); chapel, Cranbrook Foundation (Bloomfield Hills, Mich.); Head of an artist (MMA); medallion portraits (new P.O. Dept. Bldg., Wash., D.C.); Diana (Brookgreen Gardens); Theodore Roosevelt (Women's Roosevelt Memorial). He is a member of the NSS and the NA. See *Brookgreen Gardens I.*

DESSAR, Louis Paul.   d. Feb. 14, 1952 —m.c. Met 2.

DETWILLER, F[rederick] K.   d. Sept., 1953—m.c.2, N-YHS.

DE VEAUX, James.   b. Sept. 12, 1812;, d. April 28, 1844. See Rutledge, PA; Cowdrey, NAD; G&W.

DEWEY, S[ilas].   He was also a portraitist and engraver and according to G&W he was in Baltimore in 1810 and 1814-18 but MF says 1800-10 and 1814/15. See G&W.

DEWING, Francis.   He was a copperplate engraver and printer. See DAB; G&W.

DEWING, Thomas W.   d. Nov. 5, 1938 in NYC. He taught at the ASL, 1881-1888 and is an Honorary Member of the League and a member, Ten American Painters. See 75th Anniv. Cat., ASL.

DE WOLF, Wallace L.   d. 1930 per m.c., FARL.

DEXTER, Henry.   b. Oct. 11, 1806 in Nelson, N.Y.; d. June 23, 1876 in Boston according to G&W but Cambridge in MF. He was also a portrait painter. See DAB; Cowdrey, AA & AAU; G&W.

DICK, Alexander L.   See Archibald L. Dick.

DICK, Archibald L[ondonderry].   b. c. 1805; d. c. 1855. MF lists only an Alexander L. Dick but gives for him the information for Archibald L. Dick, the name being given thus in G&W and the exhibition records. See Cowdrey, NAD; Cowdrey, AA & AAU; G&W.

DICK, James T. [or L.].   b. NYC; d. Jan. 19, 1868 in Brooklyn. He was a son of Archibald L. Dick. See Cowdrey, NAD; G&W.

DICKINSON, Anson.   b. April 19, 1799 according to G&W [same date in Cowdrey, NAD and AA & AAU; MF gives 1780]; d. March 8, 1852 in Litchfield according to G&W [same date in Cowdrey; MF says 1847 in New Haven]. See Cowdrey, NAD; Cowdrey, AA & AAU; Rutledge, PA; DAB; G&W.

DICKINSON, Daniel.   G&W think he was alive at least until 1866 in Camden, N.J. and report that he may have died in Litchfield, Conn. See Rutledge, PA; Cowdrey, NAD; Cowdrey, AA & AAU; G&W.

DICKINSON, Preston.   b. 1891 in N.Y.; d. 1930 in Spain. He studied at the ASL, NYC and exhibited regularly at the Daniel Gallery in NYC. He is represented in the collections of the Museum of Art, Cleveland; Brooklyn Museum; Albright Gallery, Buffalo; Fogg Museum, Cambridge, Mass.; Hartford Athenaeum; Museum of Modern Art; Phillips Memorial Gallery, Wash., D.C.; Omaha Museum, Nebraska. See 75th Anniv. Cat., ASL.

DIEDERICH, [Wilhelm] Hunt.   b. May 3, 1884. He is the grandson of Boston painter Wm. Morris Hunt, with whom he came to live at 16 after having been raised in Europe. He spent two years in the West and then he entered the PA where he was a student of Manship. Among his works are: a series of silhouettes (MMA); Greyhounds (Seattle Art Museum; Whitney Mus. of Amer. Art); Jockey (Seattle Art Museum; Newark Mus.); Fighting Goats (Cleveland Mus. of Art); Spanish Horseman (Phillips Memorial Art Gallery, Wash., D.C.); Two Goats (Brookgreen Gardens). He is a member, Salon des Tuileries. See *Brookgreen Gardens I.*

DIELMAN, Frederick.   d. 1935. m.c. Met 2.

DIX, Charles T[emple].   b. 1840 according to G&W but 1838 in Cowdrey, NAD and MF. He was an Associate of the NA. See Cowdrey, NAD; G&W; Hamilton.

DIXEY, George.   Died probably 1853 or 1854. He was also a carver and the son of John Dixey, the latter is erroneously cited in MF as an Englishman in the entry on George Dixey but correctly identified in the entry for John Dixey. See Cowdrey, AA & AAU; G&W.

DIXEY, John   b. Dublin, prob. between 1760 and 1770; d. 1820 in NYC. He was also a carver. See Rutledge, PA; Cowdrey, AA & AAU; G&W.

DIXEY, John V.   In MF his father, John Dixey, is erroneously identified as English; he was Irish. See Cowdrey, NAD; Cowdrey AA & AAU; G&W.

DIXON, [Lafayette] Maynard.   d. Nov., 1946.—m.c., NYPL.

DODD, Samuel.   b. April 7, 1797; d. Aug. 1, 1862 in Bloomfield, N.J. See G&W.

DODGE, John Wood.   b. Nov. 4, 1807 in NYC; d. Dec. 16, 1893. He was also a dioramist. See Cowdrey, NAD; G&W.

DODSON, Richard W.   b. Feb. 5, 1812; d. July 25, 1867. See Rutledge, PA; Cowdrey, AA & AAU; G&W.

DOLINSKY, Nathan. .   He exhibited one oil painting in the 1913 Armory Show. His name is given as Nathaniel in *Armory Show, 50th Anniversary Exhibition, 1913-1963* and Milton W. Brown, *The Story of the Armory Show.*

DOLPH, John Henry.   b. April 18, 1835 in Fort Ann, N.Y.; d. Sept. 28, 1903 in NYC. He was also a genre painter. See Cowdrey, NAD; G&W.

DONEY, T[homas].   See Cowdrey, AA & AAU; G&W.

DONOHO, Gaines Ruger.   He exhibited three oil paintings at the 1913 Armory Show. See the cat. of the 1963 Armory Show.

DOOLITTLE, Amos.   b. May 18, 1754; d. Jan. 30, 1832. See DAB; G&W.

DOOLITTLE & MUNSON.   The partners were Curtis M. Doolittle and Samuel B. Munson. Banknote work their specialty and they were in Cincinnati, 1831-49. See G&W.

DORSEY, John Syng.   b. Dec. 23, 1783; d. Nov. 12, 1818. He was a medical artist. See DAB; G&W.

DOTY & JONES.   The partners were Warren S. Doty and George Jones. G&W place them in NYC 1844/56 but MF says *c.* 1830. See G&W.

DOUGAL, W. H.   b. Jan. 30, 1822 according to G&W but MF says *c.* 1808; d. 1895. He was also a draftsman. See G&W; m.c., FARL.

DOUGHERTY, Paul.   d. 1947. m.c. Met 2.

DOUGHTY, Thomas.   b. July 19, 1793; d. July 22, 1856. He was also a lithographer. His works are at the MMA; Penn. Acad.; Brooklyn Museum; Corcoran Gallery; Peabody Institute; N-YHS. See DAB; Cowdrey, NAD; Cowdrey, AA & AAU; G&W; Rutledge, PA.

DOUGLAS [or DOUGLASS].   Douglas painted a portrait of Richard Thomas Brownrigg near Edton, N.C., in 1823; he also painted portraits of the Brownrigg girls at the same time as well as a portrait of Henry Kulloch, pastor of the Independent Presbyterian Church, Savannah. m.c., FARL.

DOWNES, John I[reland] [Howe].   d. Oct. 16, 1933 in New Haven.—m.c., FARL.

DOYLE, Margaret Byron [Mrs. John Chorley].   She was also a miniaturist and exhibited at the BA in 1828 and 1829. See G&W.

DOYLE, William M.S.   b. 1769 according to G&W but in 1796 in MF; d. May, 1828. He was also a miniaturist, silhouettist, pastel and crayon portraitist. See G&W.

DRAYTON, J.   G&W think he is probably Joseph Drayton, q.v.

DRAYTON, J[oseph.]   He was also a portrait painter and engraver in Philadelphia in 1819. He did engravings for the "Analectic Magazine" and was one of the artists on the Wilkes Expedition. See G&W; Hamilton.

DREIER, Katherine Sophie.   See Drier.

DREXEL, Francis M[artin].   b. April 7, 1792; d. June 5, 1863. See DAB; Rutledge, PA; G&W.

DREYFOUS, Florence.   Misindexed after A. Dresher. She exhibited two water colors at the 1913 Armory Show. See the cat. of the 1963 Armory Show.

DRIER, Katherine S[ophie].   d. 1952. She exhibited two oil paintings in the 1913 Armory Show. Her name is given as Dreier in *Armory Show, 50th Anniversary Exhibition, 1913-1963* and Milton W. Brown, *The Story of the Armory Show.*

DRUCEZ, [P.J.].   He was from Antwerp, Belgium, and was a portrait and miniature painter. See G&W.

DRURY, J[ohn] H.   b. June 30, 1816 in Washington, D.C. according to G&W but MF says in Georgetown. He was a landscape, figure and cattle painter. See G&W.

DUBOIS, Guy Pene.   b. Jan. 4, 1884; d. 1958. He studied at the N.Y. School of Art, 1899-1905 and at Colarossi's, Paris, 1905/06. He taught at the ASL 1920-24,

1930-32 and 1935/36 and was a former music and art critic for the "N.Y. American," art critic for the "N.Y. Tribune" 1913/1914 and also art critic for the "N.Y. Evening Post." He lived and worked in France, 1924-1930 and was a member of the NA and the NIAL. He exhibited six oil paintings at the 1913 Armory Show. See the cat. of the 1963 Armory Show; 75th Anniv. Cat., ASL.

DUBOURJAL, Savinien Edme.　　b. Feb. 12, 1795; d. Dec. 8, 1865 according to G&W but in 1853 in MF, Cowdrey, NAD and AA & AAU and Rutledge, PA. He was a portraitist and a portrait draftsman in pencil. See Rutledge, PA; Cowdrey, NAD; Cowdrey, AA & AAU; Benezit; G&W.

DUBUFE, Claud[e] Marie.　　d. Oct., 1864 at St. Cloud, France. See G&W.

DUCHE, Thomas Spence [Jr.].　　b. Sept. 15, 1763; d. March 31, 1790 in London. He also painted allegories. See G&W.

DUCLORY, Lepelitier [given as Lepelletier Duclary or du Clary in G&W].　　b. c. 1824. See G&W.

DUDENSING, Richard.　　d. Sept. 4, 1899 in NYC according to G&W but MF states that he died in Germany. See G&W.

DUFFY, Richard H.　　d. 1953.　　He exhibited two sculptures at the 1913 Armory Show. See the cat. of the 1963 Armory Show.

DUGGAN, Peter Paul.　　d. Oct. 15, 1861. He was a portrait artist, especially in crayon but also in oils. He also designed medals and was a National Academician. See Cowdrey, NAD; Cowdrey, AA & AAU; Appleton; Hamilton; G&W.

DUMLER, M.G.　　Misindexed after P.S. Duval.

DUMMER, Jeremiah.　　b. Sept. 14, 1645 in Newbury, Mass.; d. May 25, 1718 in Boston. He was a silversmith. For a discussion of whether or not he was a portrait painter see G&W; DAB.

DUMOND, Frank Vincent.　　d. Feb. 6, 1951 in NYC. He also studied at the ASL, NYC and taught 1892-94 and 1902-1951 at the ASL, of which he was an Honorary Member. Early in his career he was an illustrator, especially for "Harper's Weekly." He was also a member of the NIAL, Society of Illustrators, Lotos Club, Century Association, Rochester Art Club and the National Arts Club. His work is in the Public Library of San Francisco, Liberty Tower, Hotel des Artistes and the National Arts Club, NYC. See 75th Anniv. Cat., ASL.

DUNLAP, William.　　b. Feb. 18, 1766; d. Sept. 28, 1839. See DAB; Cowdrey, AA & AAU; Cowdrey, NAD; G&W.

DUNNEL [also DUNNELL], E[lbridge] [G.].　　See G&W.

DUNNELL, William N.　　He was also an illustrator. See Cowdrey, NAD; G&W.

DURAND, Asher Brown.　　b. Aug. 21, 1796 in Jefferson Village [now Maplewood], N.J.; d. Sept. 17, 1886 in Maplewood according to G&W but MF says in South Orange, N.J. He painted landscapes, figures and portraits and early in his career copied English illustrations to be used by American publishers. See DAB; Cowdrey, NAD; Cowdrey, AA & AAU; Rutledge, PA; G&W; Hamilton.

DURAND, Cyrus.　　b. Feb. 27, 1787; d. Sept. 18, 1868. See G&W.

DURAND, William.　　He was probably a son of Cyrus Durand. See G&W.

DURANT, J[ohn] Waldo.　　b. at St. Croix, V.I., W.I. See G&W.

DURRIE, George H[enry].　　b. June 6, 1820 in Hartford according to G&W but MF says in New Haven; d. Oct. 15, 1863. He was a landscape, genre and portrait painter. See Cowdrey, NAD; G&W.

DU SIMITIERE, Pierre Eugene.　　He came to the U.S. in 1765. See DAB; G&W.

DUTHIE, James.　　He was an engraver on steel and copper and also a lithographer. See G&W.

DUVAL, Ambrose.　　He was also a portraitist and drawing master. See G&W.

DUVAL, P[eter] S.　　He was born in France. See G&W.

DUVENECK, Frank.　　d. 1916 in Ohio. He was a pupil of Diez in Munich, where he lived for more than a decade. He taught at the ASL 1898-1899 and later at the Academy of Fine Arts, Cincinnati. As a sculptor he did a memorial statue of Elizabeth Booth Duveneck in Florence, Italy. See 75th Anniv. Cat., ASL.

DUVIVIER and Son.   They were drawing teachers. See G&W.

DUYCKINCK, Evert 1st.   b. in Holland; d. in N.Y. See G&W.

DUYCKINCK Gerardus [1st].   Born NYC; died probably in 1746 according to G&W but MF has 1742. He was also a glazier. See G&W.

DUYCKINCK, Gerret [Gerrit in G&W]. He was the son of Evert Duyckinck 1st and was a limner, glazier and glass stainer. See G&W.

EAKINS, Thomas [Cowperthwait].   b. July 25, 1844; d. June 25, 1916. He taught at the ASL, NYC, 1886-88 and later lectured there; he also taught and lectured at the ASL, Philadelphia, the NAD, and the Drexel Institute. He sculpted the horses on the Brooklyn Arch and the reliefs on the Trenton Monument. See 75th Anniv. Cat., ASL.

EARL, James.   b. May 1, 1761 in Leicester, Mass.; d. Aug. 18, 1796. See DAB; G&W.

EARL, Ralph.   b. May 11, 1751 in Worcester Co., Mass. according to G&W but MF has Leicester; d. Aug. 16, 1801. He was a landscapist. See DAB; G&W.

EARL, Ralph E[leaser] Whiteside.   Born before 1785 according to G&W but MF says in 1788; d. Sept. 16, 1838 per G&W but in 1837 in MF. See G&W.

EARLE, James.   See James Earl.

EASTMAN, Seth.   b. Jan. 24, 1808; d. Aug. 31, 1875 in Washington, D.C. He was also a topographical draftsman. See Cowdrey, NAD; Cowdrey, AA & AAU; G&W.

EATON, Charles Warren.   d. Sept. 10, 1937—m.c., NYPL.

EATON, Joseph Oriel.   b. Feb. 8, 1829, at Newark, Ohio; d. Feb. 7, 1875. He was also a landscapist. See DAB; Cowdrey, AA & AAU; Cowdrey, NAD; Rutledge, PA; G&W; m.c., FARL.

EBERLE, Abastenia St. Leger. Sculptor. b. April 6, 1878; d. Feb. 26, 1942 in NYC. As a student she had some criticisms from Gutzon Borglum. In 1907 and 1908 she was in Italy, she was in Paris 1913, and in 1914 she established a studio on Madison St., NYC. Among her works are: Ragtime (Detroit Inst. of Arts); Girl Skating (MMA; Whitney Museum of American Art, NYC; Rhode Island School of Design); The Windy Doorstep (Brookgreen Gardens; Peabody Inst. [on loan to Baltimore Museum of Art]; Newark Museum; Carnegie Inst., Pittsburgh; Worcester Art Museum). She exhibited two sculptures at the 1913 Armory Show and was a member of the NSS and an Associate of the NA. See Brookgreen Gardens I; cat. of the 1963 Armory Show.

EDDY, Henry B.   b. 1872; d. 1935. He exhibited drawings at the 1913 Armory Show. See the cat. of the 1963 Armory Show.

EDDY, Isaac.   b. Feb. 17, 1777; d. July 25, 1847 in Waterford, N.Y. He was a copperplate engraver, printer and perhaps a portrait painter. See G&W.

EDDY, James.   b. May 29, 1806 in Providence, R.I.; d. May 18, 1888 in Providence. He was also a portrait painter and art dealer. See G&W.

EDMONDS, Francis W[illiam].   b. Nov. 22, 1806; d. Feb. 7, 1863 in NYC. He was also a portrait painter. See DAB; Cowdrey, NAD; Cowdrey, AA & AAU; Rutledge, PA; G&W.

EDWARDS, Thomas.   He was also a lithographer. See G&W.

EDWIN, David.   b. Dec., 1776; d. Feb. 22, 1841 in Philadelphia. He was a stipple engraver. See DAB; G&W.

EGGLESTON, Benjamin.   d. Feb., 1937. See m.c., FARL.

EHNINGER, John W[hetten].   b. July 22, 1827; d. Jan. 22, 1889 in Saratoga, N.Y. He was also a portraitist and studied with Leutze at Dusseldorf. See DAB; Cowdrey, NAD; Cowdrey, AA & AAU; Rutledge, PA; G&W, Hamilton.

EICHHOLTZ, Jacob.   b. Nov. 2, 1776; d. May 11, 1842 at Lancaster, Pa. See DAB; Rutledge, PA; G&W.

ELDER, John A[dams]. b. Feb. 3, 1833; d. Feb. 24, 1895. He was also a landscapist. See G&W.

ELDRIDGE, C[harles] W[illiam]. b. Nov., 1811; d. 1883. See G&W.

ELLIOTT, Benjamin F. b. Sept. 26, 1829; d. Sept. 6, 1870. See G&W.

ELLIOTT, Charles Loring. b. Oct. 12, 1812; d. Aug. 25, 1868. See DAB; Cowdrey, NAD; Cowdrey, AA & AAU; Rutledge, PA; G&W; Hamilton.

ELLIOTT, John. m.c. Met 3 contests the statement in MF that this painter is represented in the permanent collection of the MMA, saying that his work was not to be found among either the American or the European paintings in November, 1962.

ELLIS, George B. See Rutledge, PA; G&W.

ELLIS, Joseph B[ailey]. b. May 24, 1890; d. Jan. 24, 1950. He attended the Mass. Normal Art School, the Academy at Rome, the school of the Boston Museum of Fine Arts, and the Ecole des Beaux-Arts, Paris. He studied at Boston with Bela L. Pratt and in Paris with Victor Peter and Injalbert. Later he organized the Modern School of Art in Boston and in the summer directed the Sawyer's Is. Art School, Boothbay, Maine. He taught in numerous other institutions, finally becoming head of the sculpture department at the Carnegie Inst. of Technology. Among his works is: Water Buckaroo (Brookgreen Gardens). He was the president of the Associated Artists of Pittsburgh and the founder of the Sculptor's Society. See *Brookgreen Gardens II.*

ELLIS, Salathiel. He was also a sculptor and designer of medals. See Cowdrey, NAD; Cowdrey, AA & AAU; G&W.

ELLSWORTH, James S[anford]. d. in Pittsburgh. He was also a silhouettist and portraitist. See G&W.

ELOUIS, Jean Pierre Henri. b. Jan. 20, 1755; d. Dec. 23, 1840 according to G&W but MF says in 1843. See G&W.

ELY, A. He is probably the A. Ely in G&W, an engraver who was in Conn. *c.* 1800-32. See G&W.

EMMET, Lydia Field. d. Aug. 16, 1952 —m.c. Met 2.

EMMONS, Alexander H[amilton]. b. Dec. 12, 1816. He also did portraits and landscapes. See Cowdrey, NAD; G&W.

EMMONS, Nathaniel. d. May 19, 1740 in Boston. He also painted landscapes. See G&W.

ENNEKING, John Jos[eph]. d. 1916— m.c. Met 2.

ESSIG, George E.[merick]. b. Sept. 2, 1838; still living in 1925, in Atlantic City, N.J. He was also a landscapist. See G&W.

ESTE, Florence. b. 1860; d. 1925 or 1926. She exhibited two watercolors at the 1913 Armory Show. See the cat. of the 1963 Armory Show.

ETTER, David Rent. d. 1881. He was also an ornamental painter. See G&W.

EVANS, John T. He was a portraitist. See G&W.

EVENS, T.A. He is probably the Theodore A. Evens listed in G&W as an engraver who was in Cincinnati, 1859-60. See G&W.

EVERS, John. b. Aug. 17, 1797 in Newtown, L.I., N.Y.; d. May 3, 1884 in Hempstead, L.I. He was also a landscapist and a National Academician. See Cowdrey, AA & AAU; Cowdrey, NAD; G&W.

EXILIOUS, John G. He was a landscapist. See Rutledge, PA; G&W.

FAGNANI, Joseph [or Giuseppe]. b. Dec. 24, 1819; d. May 22, 1873. He was a sculptor, portrait and figure painter, crayon portraitist. See Cowdrey, NAD; Rutledge, PA; G&W.

FAIRBANKS, Avard Tennyson. b. March 2, 1897. He also studied at the Academie Colarossi and the Ecole de la Grande Chaumiere until beginning of WWI and then received further instruction from A. Phimister Proctor, Charles R. Knight, his father the painter John B. Fairbanks of Salt Lake City, and his brother J. Leo Fairbanks, Professor of Art, Oregon State College. He began his professional career in 1918; in 1920 he was assistant professor of sculpture at the U. of Mich. and in 1929 became associate professor there. He received a B.A. from Yale in 1925 and studied with Dante Sodini in Florence in 1927. Among his works are: Service Memorial (Oregon State College); bronze doors, U.S. Natl. Bank, (Portland, Ore.); tabernacle door, St. Mary's Cathedral (Eugene. Oregon); The Awakening Aphrodite (Eugene, Ore.); 91st Div. Monument (Fort Lewis, Wash.); Pioneer Mother Memorial (Vancouver, Wash.); Winter Quarters (Omaha, Neb.); New Frontiers (Salt Lake City); Ezra Meeker (U. of Oregon); Dean G. Carl Huber (U. of Mich.); Dean Meeks (Yale U.); Rain (Brookgreen Gardens). He is a member of the NSS, the ALNY, the American Numismatic Society, and the Circolo degli Artisti di Firenze. See *Brookgreen Gardens I*.

FAIRCHILD, Louis [Lewis in G&W.] b. *c.* 1801 according to G&W but in 1800 in MF. See G&W.

FAIRMAN, David.   b. 1782, probably in Fairfield Co., Conn.; d. Aug. 19, 1815. See G&W.

FAIRMAN, Gideon.   b. June 26, 1774; d. March 18, 1827. He was also a portraitist. See G&W.

FAIRMAN, Richard.   b. probably in Connecticut. See G&W.

FALCONER, John M.   b. May 22, 1820 in Edinburgh; d. March 12, 1903 in NYC. He was a landscape, genre and portrait painter and also an enamellist. See Cowdrey, AA & AAU; Cowdrey, NAD; Rutledge, PA; G&W.

FANNING, Solomon.   He was also an ornamental painter. See G&W.

FANSHAW, Samuel R[aymond].   b. Dec. 21, 1814 in NYC; d. Dec. 15, 1888 in NYC. He was also a portraitist. See Cowdrey, NAD; G&W.

FARMER, John.   b. Feb. 9, 1798; d. March 24, 1859. See G&W.

FARNHAM, Sally James.   b. Nov. 26, 1876 in Ogdensburg, N.Y.; d. April 28, 1943 in NYC. She attended Wells College, married the painter and designer of silverware for Tiffany and Co., Paulding Farnham, and lived in Great Neck, N.Y. She knew Frederic Remington and had the criticisms of Henry M. Schrady, Augustus Lukeman and Frederick Roth. Among her works are: cowboy statuette (collection of the

Remington Memorial, Ogdensburg, N.Y.); Soldiers' and Sailors' Monument (Ogdensburg, N.Y.); war memorials in cemeteries at Rochester, N.Y. and Bloomfield, N.J.; frieze, Governing Board Room, Pan-American Union (Washington, D.C.); Antonio Jose de Sucre, Hipolito Unanue (Hall of Patriots; the former also at Rio de Janeiro); Simon Bolivar (Central Park, NYC); Junipero Serra (San Francisco Mission, Cal.); WWI memorial (Fultonville, N.Y.); Senator W. A. Clark (Corcoran Gallery of Art, Wash., D.C.); The End of the Day (Brookgreen Gardens; monument to Vernon Castle, Woodlawn Cemetery). See *Brookgreen Gardens II*.

FASSETT, Mrs. Cornelia A[dele] [Strong]. b. Nov. 9, 1831 in Owasco, N.Y.; d. Jan. 4, 1898 in Washington, D.C. She was also a figure painter and miniaturist. See DAB; G&W.

FAULKNER, Herbert Waldron.   d. 1940.—m.c. Met 2.

FEKE, Robert.   b. probably between 1705 and 1710. See G&W.

FENN, Harry.   He began as a wood engraver and illustrated *Picturesque America*. He was at his best with landscapes; many of his early works depict New England. See Hamilton.

FENTON, Beatrice.   b. July 12, 1887. Among her works are: A Fairy Fountain, Seaweed Fountain (Philadelphia; the latter also at Brookgreen Gardens); Wood Music (Wilmington, Del.); Ariel sundial (Shakespeare Garden, U. of Pa.); Charles M. Schmitz (Phila. Acad. of Music); William Penn (Penn Club); Felix Schelling (U. of Pa.); limestone figures, gateway, Children's Hospital (Philadelphia). She is a member of the National Association of Women Painters and Sculptors and the NSS. See *Brookgreen Gardens I*.

FERGUSON, Henry [L.].   m.c. Met 2 says that the initial may be A. instead of L.

FERRIS, Jean Leon Gerome.   d. 1930. m.c., FARL.

FERRIS, Stephen J[ames].   b. Jan. 25 or Dec. 25, 1835; d. July 9, 1915. See Rutledge, PA; G&W.

FETTE, Henry G[erhard].   The 1871 in MF may be a misprint for 1851 which is the latest date given in G&W. See G&W.

FIELD, Robert.   d. Aug. 9, 1819. See G&W.

FINK, Frederick.   b. Dec. 28, 1817; d. Jan. 23, 1849. He was an Honorary Member, Professional, of the NA from 1840. See Cowdrey, NAD; Cowdrey, AA & AAU; Rutledge, PA; G&W.

FINN, Henry J[ames] [William].   b. June 17, 1787 in Sydney, N.S. according to G&W but MF says in 1782; d. Jan. 13, 1840. See DAB; G&W.

FISCHER, Anton Otto.   d. 1962. m.c., FARL.

FISCHER, J. F.   G&W think that he is probably Flavius J. Fisher. See G&W.

FISHER, Alvin [correctly spelled Alvan]. b. Aug. 9, 1792 in Needham, Mass.; d. Feb. 13, or 14, 1863 in Dedham, Mass. See DAB; Rutledge, PA; Cowdrey, AA & AAU; Cowdrey, NAD; G&W.

FISHER, Flavius J.   b. 1832 in Wytheville, Va.; d. May 9, 1905 in Washington, D.C. He was a portrait painter and crayon portraitist. See Rutledge, PA; G&W.

FISHER, Harrison.   d. 1934 in NYC. m.c., FARL.

FISHER, Hugh Antoine.   According to m.c., NYPL, the first name is Hugo, not Hugh.

FISHER, J. J.   G&W think that he is probably Flavius J. Fisher. See G&W.

FISKE, Charles A[lbert].   b. Alfred, Mass. according to G&W but MF says in Maine; d. May 13, 1915 in Greenwich, Conn. See G&W.

FITCH, John.   b. Jan. 21, 1743 in Windsor Township, Conn. according to G&W but MF says in South Windsor; d. July 2, 1798. See DAB; G&W.

FITCH, John Lee.   He was also a member of the Artists' Fund Society and the Century Association. See Cowdrey, NAD; Benezit; G&W.

FJELDE, Paul [correct spelling per *Who's Who in American Art*].   b. Aug. 12,

1892. He studied at the School of Fine Arts, Minneapolis and the State Normal School, Valley City, N. Dak.; also at the ASL and the Beaux-Arts Inst. of Design, NYC, the Royal Academy, Copenhagen and the Academie de la Grande Chaumiere, Paris. He taught sculpture at the Carnegie Inst. of Technology 1928-29 and was an instructor in modeling and drawing at the Pratt Institute, Brooklyn. Among his works are: John Scott Bradstreet (Minneapolis Inst. of Arts); memorial to Col. H.C. Heg (Lier, Norway; Glencoe, Ill.); W.W. Folwell (Library, U. of Minn.); reliefs, Washington School (McKeesport, Pa.); panels, Westinghouse Monument (Pittsburgh); panels, Mus. of Science & Industry (NYC); Nymph, Brookgreen Gardens). He is a member of the NSS. See *Brookgreen Gardens I*.

FJELKE, Paul.   See Fjelde, Paul.

FLAGG, George W[hiting].   b. June 26, 1816; d. Jan. 5, 1897 at Nantucket, Mass. He was also a genre painter. See DAB; Cowdrey, NAD; Cowdrey, AA & AAU; Rutledge, PA; G&W.

FLAGG, Henry C[ollins].   b. Dec. 10, 1811 according to G&W but MF has 1812; d. Aug. 23, 1862 in Jamestown, N.Y. He was also an animal painter and caricaturist. See Cowdrey, NAD; G&W.

FLAGG, Jared B[radley].   b. June 16, 1820; d. Sept. 25, 1899 in NYC. He was also a religious painter. See DAB; Cowdrey, NAD; Cowdrey, AA & AAU; G&W.

FLAGG, Josiah, Jr.   See DAB; G&W.

FLANAGAN, John F.   d. March 28, 1952. m.c. NYPL.

FLEISHBEIN, F.   See Francois Fleischbein.

FLEISHBEIN, Francois.   b. *c.* 1804 in Germany. See G&W.

FLORIMONT, Austin.   He was also a portraitist in oils and a drawing master. See G&W.

FOLEY, Margaret [F.].   b. probably in Vermont; d. Dec. 7, 1877 at Meran according to G&W, but MF has Menan, in the Austrian Tyrol. See Rutledge, PA; G&W.

FOLSOM, Mrs. C.A.   See Mrs. Elizabeth A. Folsom.

FOLSOM, Mrs. Elizabeth A.   She was probably Eliza A. (Freeman) Folsom, b. Dec. 27, 1812 in NYC; d. Feb., 1899, Westfield, N.J. See Cowdrey, NAD; G&W.

FOLWELL, Samuel.   b. c. 1765-68. See DAB; G&W.

FOOTE, Mary Hallock.   d. 1938. She exhibited one oil at the 1913 Armory Show. See the cat. of the 1963 Armory Show.

FORBES, Edwin.   d. March 6, 1895 in Brooklyn, N.Y. He was a pupil of Tait. See DAB; Cowdrey, NAD; G&W; Hamilton.

FORREST, Ion B.   [John or Ian in G&W; John in Cowdrey, AA & AAU and Rutledge, PA]. He was also a landscape and genre painter and an etcher. See Cowdrey, AA & AAU; Rutledge, PA; G&W.

FOSTER, C.   He was perhaps the Charles Foster who was an engraver in Cincinnati, 1842-50. See G&W.

FOSTER, John.   d. Sept. 9, 1681 in Dorchester, Mass. according to G&W but in Boston in MF. He was also a portrait painter. See DAB; Barker, pp. 29-30, repro. 31; G&W.

FOSTER, Will[iam] [Frederick].   m.c. 2, NYPL.

FOWLE, E. A.   Perhaps he was the Edward A. Fowle who was engraving in Boston, 1847-56. See G&W.

FOWLER.   See T. T. Fowler.

FOWLER, T. T.   He was probably Trevor Thomas Fowler; the dates given by MF for his stay in New Orleans are inaccurate. See G&W, Cowdrey, NAD; Cowdrey, AA & AAU; Rutledge, PA.

FOX, Gilbert.   b. in London, 1776; d. c. 1806. See DAB; G&W.

FRANCIS, John F.   b. c. 1808 in Philadelphia according to G&W [1808 in Rutledge, PA; c. 1810 in MF]; d. Nov. 15, 1886 in Jeffersonville, Pa. according to G&W but in 1885 in MF. He was also a silhouettist. See G&W.

FRANKENSTEIN, John P[eter].   b. 1816 or 1817 in Germany; d. April 16, 1881 in East New York, N.Y. He came to Cincinnati in 1831 and was also a portrait and historical painter. See Rutledge, PA;

Cowdrey, AA & AAU; Cowdrey, NAD; G&W.

FRANZONI.   See Carlo Franzoni and Giuseppe Franzoni.

FRANZONI, Carlo.   b. 1789 in Carrara, Italy according to G&W but MF says c. 1780; d. May 12, 1819 in Washington, D.C. See G&W.

FRANZONI, Guiseppe.   b. Carrara, Italy; d. April 6, 1815 in Washington, D.C. See G&W.

FRASER, Charles.   b. Aug. 20, 1782; d. Oct. 5, 1860. He was also a landscapist. See DAB; Cowdrey, NAD; Cowdrey, AA & AAU; G&W.

FRASER, James Earle.   b. Nov. 4, 1876; d. 1953. As a boy he traveled through the West and spent ten years on a ranch in So. Dakota. At 18 he entered the studio of Richard Bock in Chicago and later he helped Saint-Gaudens in his studio. He established himself in 1902 in his own studio in NYC. Among his works are: medal for Saint-Gaudens at Pan-American Expos., 1901; Head of a Young Artist (MMA); Basque (The Hispanic Society of America, NYC); The End of the Trail (Brookgreen Gardens; Waupun, Wisc.; Detroit Inst. of Arts; City Art Museum, St. Louis); Thomas Jefferson (State Capitol of Missouri); Lewis and Clark (Missouri); John Ericsson Monument (Wash., D.C.); decoration, Michigan Boulevard Bridge (Chicago); Victory (Bank of Montreal); Primitive Inventor of Water Power (Niagara Falls); Canadian Officer (Winnipeg); pediments, Natl. Archives Bldg. and Supreme Court Bldg. (Wash., D.C.); Benjamin Franklin (Franklin Inst., Phila.); George Washington (1939, NYC World's Fair); Theodore Roosevelt (Roosevelt Memorial, Amer. Museum of Natural History, NYC. Additional works are at Cathedral of St. John the Divine, Arlington National Cemetery and the Senate Chamber, the Capitol, Wash., D.C. He was a member of the Architectural League of N.Y.; vice-president NIAL; president of the NSS, a member of the NA, National Commission of Fine Arts, National Arts Club; Century Association; he was a Knight of the Order of Vasa (Sweden). He exhibited three sculptures at the 1913 Armory Show. See cat. of the 1963 Armory Show; 75th Anniv. Cat., ASL; *Brookgreen Gardens I.*

FRASER, Laura G[ardin].   b. Sept. 14, 1889. She studied sculpture with James E. Fraser, whom she married in 1913 and is best known as a medalist. Among her works are: Reclining Elks (Elks National Memorial Bldg., Chicago); Snuff (Wadsworth Athenaeum, Hartford, Conn.); Fair Play (Joseph E. Widener Estate, Phila.); Grape Baby Fountain (Rose Garden, Delaware Park, Buffalo); Lee and Jackson (Wyman Park, Baltimore); Baby Goat (Brookgreen Gardens) Lindbergh Congressional Medal; George Washington Bicentennial Medal; half dollars for the Alabama Centennial, Fort Vancouver Centennial, Oregon Trail; Grant Memorial gold dollar and half dollar; relief, Bide-a-Wee Home for Animals, NYC. She is a member of the NA and the NIAL. See *Brookgreen Gardens I*.

FRAZER, Oliver.   b. Feb. 4, 1808; d. Feb. 9, 1864. See DAB; G&W.

FRAZIER, Kenneth.   d. Aug. 31, 1949. He exhibited three oil paintings at the 1913 Armory Show. See the Cat. of the 1963 Armory Show—m.c., NYPL.

FREDERICK, John L.   b. *c.* 1797-1800 in Pennsylvania. See G&W.

FREDERICKS, Alfred.   He was also a landscape and figure painter who lived in NYC and exhibited at the NA in 1853 and 1856. He made comic illustrations for magazines. See G&W; Hamilton.

FREEMAN, E. O.   See Francis O. Freeman.

FREEMAN, Florence.   d. After 1876. She specialized in bas-reliefs and chimneypieces. See G&W.

FREEMAN, Francis O.   G&W give this as the correct name, correcting the mistake in Stauffer, a source upon which MF relied. See G&W.

FREEMAN, George.   b. April 21, 1789 according to G&W [1787 in MF; Cowdrey, NAD; Cowdrey, AA & AAU; *c.* 1787 in Rutledge, PA.]; d. March 7, 1868. He was also a portrait painter. See Cowdrey, NAD; Cowdrey, AA & AAU; Rutledge, PA; G&W; m.c., FARL.

FREEMAN, James Edward.   b. Indian Island, N.B. according to G&W but MF says in Nova Scotia; d. Nov. 21, 1884 in Rome. He was a genre and portrait painter. See DAB; Cowdrey, NAD; Rutledge, PA; G&W.

FRENCH, Daniel Chester.   b. April 20, 1850; d. Oct. 7, 1931. He collaborated with Edward Clark Potter while working for Chicago World Fair. Among his works are: The Angel of Death Staying the Hand of The Young Sculptor; doors of the Boston Public Library; groups representing the continents at the Custom House (NYC); Lincoln (Lincoln, Nebraska); Lincoln (in the Lincoln Memorial, Wash., D.C.); In Flanders Fields (Milton, Mass.); an angel embracing a girl, 1924 (Corcoran Gallery, Wash., D.C.); Memory, 1921 (MMA); Benediction (Brookgreen Gardens, and St. Paul's Memorial Church, Oaks, Pa.). Member of the National Arts Commission, Honorary Member of the ASL, corresponding member of the American Institute of Architects, member of the Society of American Artists, the Academy of San Luca in Rome, the National Arts Club, NY Architectural League and NIAL. See *Brookgreen Gardens I;* 75th Anniv. Cat., ASL.

FRERICHS, William C[harles] A[nthony].   b. in Belgium according to G&W but MF says Germany; d. March 16, 1905, in Tottenville, S.I., N.Y. He was a portrait painter. See Cowdrey, NAD; G&W.

FRISMUTH, Harriet W[hitney].   b. Sept. 17, 1880. She was educated in Philadelphia, Paris and Dresden, later worked in Berlin as an assistant to Cuno von Euchtritz and then continued her studies at the ASL with Hermon MacNeil. Among her works are: Jacobi (N.Y. County Medical Soc.); Extase (Wadsworth Atheneum, Hartford, Conn.); The Dancers, Slavonic Dancer (Wadsworth Atheneum, MMA); Joy of the Waters (Dayton Art Institute, John Herron Art Inst., Indianapolis; Ball State Teachers' College, Muncie, Ind.); Play Days (Dallas Mus. of Fine Arts; Norfolk Mus. of Arts & Sciences); Humoresque (Canajoharie Art Gallery); Roses of Yesterday (Hackensack, N.J.); Beyond (Bridgewater, Mass.); Aspiration (Windsorville, Conn.); Woodrow Wilson (Capitol, Richmond, Va.); Call of the Sea (Brookgreen Gardens); The Vine (Brookgreen Gardens; MMA). She is a member of the NA and the Architectural League of N.Y. See *Brookgreen Gardens I*.

467

FROLICH, Finn H.   d. 1947. m.c., FARL.

FROTHINGHAM, James.   d. Jan. 6, 1864 in Brooklyn, N.Y. See Rutledge, PA; Cowdrey, NAD; Cowdrey, AA & AAU; G&W.

FROTHINGHAM, Sarah C. [also Sarah in Cowdrey, NAD; Sara in G&W].   d. July 20, 1861 in NYC. She was an Associate of the NA. See Cowdrey, NAD; G&W.

FRY, John Henning.   d. Feb. 24, 1946. m.c., NYPL.

FRY, Sherry Edmundson.   b. Sept. 29, 1879. She worked two years at MacMonnies studio at Giverny and in 1908 was a fellow of the American Academy in Rome. Among her works are: Boy on a Dolphin (Brewster Estate, Mt. Kisco, N.Y.); Barrett Memorial Fountain (Staten Island); Captain Abbey (Enfield, Conn.); Ira Allen (U. of Vermont); crowning figures of Ceres (Missouri State Capitol); reliefs, Grant Memorial (Wash., D.C.); pediments, Frick residence (NYC); pediments, Dept. of Labor & Interstate Commerce Bldg. (Wash., D.C.); Maidenhood (Brookgreen Gardens). She is a member of the NSS and the NA. She exhibited one sculpture at the 1913 Armory Show. See the cat. of the 1963 Armory Show; Brookgreen Gardens I.

FUECHSEL, Herman [also Herman in Cowdrey, NAD and Rutledge, PA; Hermann in G&W].   b. August, 1833 in Brunswick, Germany; d. Sept. 30, 1915 in NYC. He was a landscapist. See Cowdrey, NAD; Rutledge, Pa; G&W.

FULLER, George.   b. Jan. 17, 1822; d. March 21, 1884 in Brookline, Mass. according to G&W but MF says in Boston. He was also a landscape and figure painter. See DAB; Cowdrey, AA & AAU; Cowdrey, NAD; G&W.

FULLER, Richard Henry.   He was a portraitist in oils and crayon. See G&W.

FULTON, Robert.   b. Nov. 14, 1765; d. Feb. 24, 1815. He was also a miniaturist. See DAB; G&W.

FURST, Moritz.   b. Bosing, near Presburg, Hungary according to G&W but spelled Boesing in MF. See Rutledge, PA; G&W.

GAERTNER, Carl F.   d. Nov., 1952. m.c., NYPL.

GAGE, G. W.   d. Aug. 7, 1957 in NYC. — m.c., NYPL.

GALLAUDET, Edward.   b. April 30, 1809; d. Oct. 11, 1847. See G&W.

GALLAUDET, Elisha.   d. 1805 in NYC. See G&W.

GALT, Alexander.   b. June 26, 1827; d. Jan. 19, 1863. See Rutledge, PA; Cowdrey, AA & AAU; G&W.

GANDOLFI, Mauro.   b. 1764 according to G&W but in 1771 in MF. He was also a watercolorist. See G&W.

GARBER, Daniel.   d. 1958. m.c., NYPL.

GARDEN, Francis.   He was also a drawing teacher and hearldic painter. See G&W.

GARRISON, Robert.   m.c., NYPL says he d. 1945 and corrects his address as given in MF to read Denver, Colo., not Conn.

GAUGENGIGL, Ignatz Marcel.   d. Aug. 3, 1932 in Boston. — m.c. Met 2.

GAUK, James.   G&W say that he was in the N.Y. directories, 1795-1806 but MF says 1799-1804. See G&W.

GAVIN, H.   G&W suggest that he may have been the Scottish engraver Hector Gavin who is not known to have worked in America. See G&W.

GAVIT, John E.   b. Oct. 29, 1817; d. Aug. 25, 1874. See G&W.

GAY, Edward [B.].   b. April 25, 1837. See Cowdrey, NAD; G&W.

GAY, George Howell.   d. 1931. m.c., FARL.

GAY, Walter.   d. 1937. m.c. Met. 2.

GAY, Winckworth Allan [his name is given in Rutledge, PA as Inckworth Allen Gay]. b. Aug. 18, 1821; d. Feb. 23, 1910 in West Hingham, Mass. The m.c. Met 2 corrects MF and states that he was the uncle, not the brother of Walter Gay. See Cowdrey, NAD; Rutledge, PA; G&W.

GAYLOR, [Samuel] Wood.   He exhibited two oil paintings at the 1913 Armory

Show. See the cat. of the 1963 Armory Show.

GENIN, Sylvester. b. Jan. 22, 1822 in St. Clairsville, Ohio; d. Apr. 4, 1850 at Kingston, Jamaica. He was also a portraitist. See G&W.

GENTH, Lillian [Mathilde]. b. 1876; d. March 28, 1953 in NYC. — m.c., NYPL; m.c. 2, N-YHS.

GERMAN, John D. [given as Germon in G&W, Cowdrey, NAD and Rutledge, PA]. See G&W; Cowdrey, NAD; Rutledge, PA.

GERRY, Samuel L[ancaster]. b. May 10, 1813 in Boston. He was also a genre, landscape and animal painter. See Rutledge, PA; Cowdrey, NAD; Cowdrey, AA & AAU; G&W.

GIBSON, Charles Dana. b. Sept. 14, 1867 in Roxbury, Mass.; d. Dec. 23, 1944 in NYC. He studied at the ASL and was an Honorary Member of the League and also a member of the NIAL, American Guild of Authors, League of Authors, Society of Illustrators, American Institute of Graphic Arts and the Society of Portrait Painters. As an author he wrote *Sketches in London, People in Dickens, The Education of Mr. Pipp, Sketches in Egypt, The Americans, A Widow and Her Friends*, and *The Social Ladder*. He also published books of illustrations and is known for his paintings and portraiture. See 75th Anniv. Cat., ASL.

GIBSON, Thomas. He was a miniature painter. See G&W.

GIFFORD, Robert Swain. b. Dec. 23, 1840; d. Jan. 15, 1905. He was a distant cousin of Sanford Robinson Gifford. See Rutledge, PA; Barker, p. 592; G&W; Hamilton.

GIFFORD, Sanford R[obinson] b. July 10, 1823; d. Aug. 24, 1880. He was a landscapist of the Hudson River School and portraitist. He is associated particularly with McEntee, Whittredge and Kensett. See DAB; Cowdrey, NAD; Cowdrey, AA & AAU; Rutledge, PA; G&W; Hamilton.

GIGNOUX, F. Regis [given as Regis Francois in G&W; Rutledge, PA, Cowdrey, NAD and Cowdrey, AA & AAU]. b. in Lyon, France; d. Aug. 6, 1882 in Paris. He was educated at Fribourg and studied with Paul Delaroche. At one time he had a studio in Brooklyn but in 1870 he returned to Europe where he spent the rest of his life. He was the only teacher of George Inness. See Cowdrey, NAD; Cowdrey, AA & AAU; Appleton; Rutledge, PA; G&W; Hamilton.

GILBERT, Grove Sheldon. b. Aug. 5, 1805; d. March 23, 1885. See Cowdrey, NAD; G&W.

GILDEMEISTER, Charles or [Karl]. b. Oct. 11, 1820 in Bremen, Germany; d. Feb. 8, 1869. He was also a painter and architect. See Cowdrey, AA & AAU; G&W.

GILES, Charles T. b. Aug. 25, 1827. See G&W.

GIMBER, Stephen H[enry]. b. *c.* 1806 according to G&W but 1810 in MF and 1810? in Cowdrey, NAD and Cowdrey, AA & AAU. He was also a portrait and miniature painter. See Cowdrey, NAD; Cowdrey, AA & AAU; G&W.

GIMBREDE, Thomas. d. Oct. 25, 1832. He was also a portrait painter. See Cowdrey, AA & AAU; G&W.

GIRARDET, P. See m.c. Met 3.

GIRAULT [or Giraud], [Louis] [Matthieux]. He was also a portraitist.

GIRSH, Frederick. b. March 31, 1821 in Budingen, a suburb of Darmstadt, Germany; d. Dec. 18, 1895. See DAB; G&W.

GLACKENS, William J[ames]. b. March 13, 1870; d. in NYC in 1938. He studied at the ASL and also lectured there. He was a member of the Society of American Artists, a Fellow of the PA, and a member of the Society of Illustrators, Portrait Painters Society and the Society of Independnt Artists. He exhibited with the "Eight" in 1908 and illustrated the action of the Spanish American War in Cuba for McClure's. He exhibited three oil paintings at the 1913 Armory Show. See 75th Anniv. Cat., ASL; cat. of the 1963 Armory Show.

GLASS, James W[illiam], [Jr.]. b. *c.* 1825 according to G&W but MF says 1825 and so do Cowdrey, NAD and Cowdrey, AA & AAU; d. Dec. 22, 1855 according to G&W and Cowdrey, AA & AAU; MF and Cowdrey, NAD say 1857. He was an Honorary Member of the NA. See Cowdrey, NAD; Cowdrey, AA & AAU; G&W.

GLOVER, DeWitt Clinton. d. Jan. 3, 1836. MF identified one of his brothers as D. Lloyd Glover; his correct name is De Lay Glover. See G&W.

GLOVER, D. L. He is probably De Lay or Dillaye Glover, b. c. 1823; d. c. 1863. He was an engraver and photographer and probably a brother of DeWitt Clinton Glover and Lloyd Glover.

GLOVER, Lloyd. b. July, 1826 according to G&W but MF has 1825. See G&W.

GOATER, John [H.]. He was also a designer and did work for *Vanity Fair*. See G&W; Hamilton.

GOBRECHT, Christian. b. Dec. 23, 1785; d. July 23, 1844 in Philadelphia. See DAB; Rutledge, PA; G&W.

GODDARD, Ralph Bartlett. d. April 25, 1936. m.c., NYPL.

GODWIN, Abraham. b. July 16, 1763; d. Oct. 5, 1835. See G&W.

GOLDBECK, W. D. See obit in *American Art Annual*. See m.c., FARL.

GOLDHTWAITE, Anne. b. 1875; d. 1944. She exhibited two oil paintings at the 1913 Armory Show. See the cat. of the 1963 Armory Show.

GOODALL, Albert Gallatin. b. Oct. 31, 1826; d. Feb. 19, 1887 in NYC. See G&W.

GOODING, William C. b. 1775; d. 1861. See G&W.

GOODMAN, Charles. b. 1796 according to G&W but c. 1790 in MF; d. Feb. 11, 1835 per G&W but in 1830 in MF. See DAB; G&W.

GORSON, Aaron Henry. d. Oct. 11, 1933 in NYC. m.c. Met 2.

GOULD, Thomas R[idgeway]. b. Nov. 5, 1818; d. Nov. 26, 1881 in Florence, Italy. See DAB; G&W.

GOULD, Walter. d. Jan. 18, 1893 in Florence, Italy. He was a portrait, genre and miniature painter. See Rutledge, PA; G&W.

GOVE, Elma Mary. She was also a portrait painted. See Cowdrey, NAD; Rutledge, PA; G&W.

GRAFLY, Charles. b. Dec. 3, 1862 in Philadelphia; d. May 5, 1929 in Philadelphia. He was apprenticed at 17 as a carver in Struther's Stoneyard and later studied at Spring Garden Institute and with the painters Thomas Eakins and Thomas Anschutz. In 1888 he went to Paris for four years and studied drawing with Bouguereau and Fleury at the Ecole des Beaux-Arts. In 1892 he returned to Philadelphia and became an instructor in modeling at the Drexel Institute. For many years his summer home and studio were at Lanesville, near Gloucester, Mass. and from 1917 he also taught at the Boston Museum of Fine Arts. Among his works are: Daedalus (PAFA); France, Great Britain (N.Y. Custom House); General Reynolds (Smith Memorial, Fairmount Park, Philadelphia); memorial to General George Gordon Meade (Washington, D.C.); Thomas Anscultz (PAFA); Childe Hassam (copy in Philadelphia Museum of Art); Frank Duveneck Carnegie Inst., Pittsburgh; Cincinnati Art Museum; Art Inst. of Chicago; Hall of American Artists, N.Y.U.); portrait busts of James Buchanan Eads, Jonathan Edwards and Admiral Farragut (Hall of Fame, N.Y.U.). He is a Fellow of the PA and a Member of the NA. See *Brookgreen Gardens I.*

GRAHAM, George. The earliest date on his prints is 1795.—m.c. Met. 3; see G&W.

GRAY & TODD. G&W think that Todd may be A. Todd; Gray is not known. See G&W.

GRAY, Henry Peters. b. June 23, 1819; d. Nov. 12, 1877. He was a portrait and figure painter. See DAB; Cowdrey, AA & AAU; Cowdrey, NAD; Rutledge, PA; G&W; Hamilton.

GRAYDON, Alexander. b. April 10, 1752; d. May 2, 1818 in Philadelphia. See DAB; G&W.

GREACEN, Edmund. d. Oct. 4, 1949. —m.c. Met. 2.

GREATH [or GROATH]. See G&W.

GREATOREX, [Mrs.] Eliza [Pratt]. b. Dec. 25, 1820 at Manor Hamilton, Ireland; d. Feb. 9, 1897 in Paris. She was a landscapist, a painter of cityscapes and an etcher. See Cowdrey, NAD; G&W.

GREENE, E[dward] D. E.   b. 1823 in Boston; d. June 17, 1879 in NYC. He was also a genre painter. See Cowdrey, NAD; Cowdrey, AA & AAU; Rutledge, PA; G&W.

GREENBERG, Morris.   d. June 22, 1949. m.c., NYPL.

GREENLEAF, Benjamin.   b. Sept. 25, 1786 at Haverhill, Mass.; d. Oct. 29, 1864 at Bradford, Mass. He painted portraits on glass. See DAB; G&W.

GREENOUGH, Horatio.   b. Sept. 6, 1805 in Boston, Mass.; d. Dec. 18, 1852 in Somerville, Mass. He was the brother of John and Richard S. Greenough. See DAB; Rutledge, PA; Cowdrey, AA & AAU; Cowdrey, NAD; G&W.

GREENOUGH, John.   b. Nov., 1801 in Boston. He was also a landscapist and the brother of Horatio and Richard S. Greenough. See G&W.

GREENOUGH, Richard S[altsonstall].   b. April 27, 1819; d. April 23, 1904 in Rome according to G&W and Webster's but in 1905 in MF. He was the brother of Horatio and John Greenough. See DAB; G&W.

GREGORY, John.   b. May 17, 1879 in London, Eng. He came to the U.S. at age 14 and in 1900 became a student of J. Massey Rhind, Barnard and MacNeil. He studied a year at Lambeth, Eng., and two years at Paris with Mercie. Returning to N.Y. in 1906 he was assistant to MacNeil, Gutzon Borglum and Herbert Adams and for three years from 1912 was a fellow of the American Academy in Rome. He has been an associate in modeling at Columbia U. and director of the sculpture Dept., Beaux-Art Inst. of Design. Among his works are: Wood Nymph, Bacchante (Whitney Mus. of Amer. Art); Orpheus and Dancing Panther (Schwab Estate, Loretto, Pa.); Courtship (Zeigler Estate, Noroton, Conn.); bronze floor plate, The Voyage, Cunard Bldg., NYC); panels, Henry Huntington Mausoleum (San Marino, California); panels (Folger Shakespeare Library, Washington, D.C.); pediments (Phila. Mus. of Art); Orpheus, 1 (Brookgreen Gardens); Orpheus, 2 (Brookgreen Gardens); Toy Venus (Brookgreen Gardens). Member of the Architectural League

of N.Y., the NA, the NIAL, a president of the NSS and Honorary Member of Beaux-Arts Inst. of Design. See *Brookgreen Gardens I*.

GREINER, Christopher [M.].   See Rutledge, PA; G&W.

GRIDLEY, Enoch G.   He was a portrait and general engraver. See G&W.

GRIFFIN, Walter.   d. 1935. See m.c., FARL.

GRIMES, Frances.   b. Jan. 25, 1869. She studied with Herbert Adams and became his assistant in 1894. Later she worked in Saint-Gaudens' studio, 1900-1907 and took her own studio in NYC in 1908. She also traveled in France, Italy and Greece to mature her knowledge. Among her works are: two panels of singing girls (in a private collection, Lakeville, Conn.); William Barnes (Decatur and Macon County Hospital, Decatur, Ill.); Henry Waters Taft (Town Hall, N.Y.); Charlotte Cushman, Emma Willard (N.Y.U. Hall of Fame); memorial to General Nelson A. Miles (Washington Cathedral). She is a member of the National Association of Women Painters and Sculptors and an Associate of the NA. See *Brookgreen Gardens I*.

GRIMES, John [C].   b. 1804 according to G&W and Rutledge, PA but 1799 in MF; d. Dec. 27, 1837 in Lexington, Ky. See Rutledge, PA; G&W.

GRISWOLD, Casimir Clayton.   d. June 7, 1918 in Poughkeepsie, N.Y. See Cowdrey, NAD; Rutledge, PA; G&W; Hamilton.

GROSS, Oscar.   d. Aug. 19, 1963. m.c. Met. 5.

GROSSMAN, Edwin Booth.   d. Feb. 17, 1957 in Poughkeepsie, N.Y.—m.c. NYPL.

GRUGER, Frederic R.   d. March, 1953 in NYC.—m.c., NYPL.

GRUNEWALD [or Greenwald], Gustavus. b. Dec. 10, 1805 in Gnadau, Germany; d. Aug. 1, 1878 in Gnadenburg, Germany. He was also a portraitist, lithographer and teacher of drawing. See Cowdrey, AA & AAU; Cowdrey, NAD; Rutledge, PA; G&W.

GRUPPE, Karl H[einrich]. b. March 18, 1893 in Rochester, N.Y. The son of the painter Charles Paul Gruppe, he was raised in Holland; at 12 he entered the Royal Academy at Antwerp where he spent four years, studying sculpture in the afternoons with Frans Joris. He later came to NYC and worked for Herbert Adams and Karl Bitter while studying at the ASL and after serving as a marine in WWI established his studio at 55th St., NYC and also worked for Charles Cary Rumsey. Among his works are: Mimi (Gallery of Fine Arts, Atlantic City); Fritz Leiber (Hollywood); Dean Anna A. Harvey (Adelphi College, Brooklyn); William Rufus King (Clinton, N.C.); shaft and statue, (Henry Hudson Memorial, N.Y.); Marcella Sembrich (Curtis Inst. of Music, Phila.); Joy (Brookgreen Gardens); a series of portrait medals for the N.Y. Numismatic Club. He is a fellow of the NSS and a National Academician. See *Brookgreen Gardens II*.

GSCHWINDT [also Geschwindt or Schwindt], R[obert]. He was an Austrian and also worked as a restorer of paintings. See G&W.

GUE, David John. b. Jan. 17, 1836; d. May 1, 1917. See G&W.

GUILLET, Madame or [Mrs.] J. [or Isidore]. See Cowdrey, NAD; Cowdrey, AA & AAU; G&W.

GULLAGER, Christian. b. March 1, 1759 in Copenhagen, Denmark according to G&W but MF says in 1762; d. Nov. 12, 1826 in Philadelphia. He was also a theatrical painter and modeller in plaster. See G&W.

GUSSOW, Bernard. b. 1881 according to the 1913 Armory Show cat. but in 1880 in MF; d. 1957. He exhibited two oil paintings at the 1913 Armory Show. See the cat. of the 1963 Armory Show.

GUSTIN, Paul Morgan. Misindexed after E. H. Gyer.

GUTMANN, Bernard. d. 1936. He exhibited one oil painting at the 1913 Armory Show. See the cat. of the 1963 Armory Show.

GUY, Francis. b. *c.* 1760 according to G&W, but in 1760 in MF, in Lorton, near Keswick, in England; d. Aug. 12, 1820. He came to the U.S. in 1795. See Rutledge, PA; G&W.

GUY, Seymour J[oseph]. b. Jan. 16, 1824 in Greenwich, England; d. Dec. 10, 1910 in NYC. He was a portrait and genre painter. See DAB; Cowdrey, NAD; Rutledge, PA; G&W.

HAAG, C. The m.c., FARL states that the NAD indexes this artist as a resident of Munich. See m.c., FARL.

HAIDT, John Valentine. b. Oct. 4, 1700 in Danzig, Germany; d. Jan. 18, 1780. He was also a religious painter. See G&W.

HAINES, William. b. June 21, 1788 in Bedhampton, Hampshire, England; d. July 24, 1848 in East Brixton, England. He was also a miniaturist. See G&W.

HALBERT, A[ugustus]. See Cowdrey, NAD; G&W.

HALE, Philip L. d. Feb. 2, 1931 in Boston. He exhibited two oil paintings at the 1913 Armory Show. —m.c. Met 2; see the cat. of the 1963 Armory Show.

HALE, Susan. b. 1834 or 1833 according to G&W but in 1838 in MF; d. Sept. 17, 1910 at Matunuck, R.I. See G&W

HALL, Anne [or Ann]. Misindexed after Susan Hale. b. May 26, 1792; d. Dec., 1863 in NYC. She was also a portraitist. See Cowdrey, AA & AAU; Cowdrey, NAD; G&W.

HALL, Charles Bryan. b. Aug. 18, 1840; he was living as late as 1906 according to G&W but MF says he died in 1906. G&W give the date of his apprenticeship as 1855, not 1885 as in MF. See G&W.

HALL, E. W. He is possibly the E. W. Hall who exhibited at the NA, 1860-64. See Cowdrey, NAD; G&W.

HALL, George Henry. b. Sept. 21, 1825 in Manchester, N.H. according to G&W but MF says in Boston; d. Feb. 17, 1913 in NYC. He was a portrait and genre painter. See DAB; Cowdrey, NAD; Cowdrey, AA & AAU; Rutledge, PA; G&W; Hamilton.

HALL, Henry Bryan, [Sr.].   b. May 11, 1808; d. April 25, 1884. He worked with both crayons and oils. See DAB; Cowdrey, NAD; G&W.

HALL, John H.   He was also a lithographer. He spent a year studying with Anderson in NYC and then went to Albany where he spent most of his time until 1848. In 1849 he joined the Gold Rush and died in California. See G&W; Hamilton.

HALL, Peter.   d. July 5, 1895. See G&W.

HALPERT, S[amuel].   b. 1884; d. 1930. He exhibited two oil paintings at the 1913 Armory Show. See the cat. of the 1963 Armory Show.

HALPIN, Frederick [W.].   d. Feb., 1880 in Jersey City, N.J. He was the brother of John Halpin. See Benezit; Cowdrey, NAD; G&W.

HALPIN, John.   He was in NYC at least until 1867 and exhibited at the NAD in 1850 and 1854. He also engraved bank notes, was a watercolorist and was a member, American Society of Painters in Water Colors. See G&W; Cowdrey, NAD; Hamilton.

HAMILTON, Hamilton.   d. 1928. m.c., FARL.

HAMILTON, James.   b. Oct. 1, 1819 at Entrien, near Belfast, Ireland; d. March 10, 1878 in San Francisco. See Rutledge, PA; Cowdrey, AA & AAU; Cowdrey, NAD; Appleton; Hamilton; G&W.

HAMLIN, William.   b. Oct. 15, 1772; d. Nov. 22, 1869. See DAB; G&W.

HAMM, Phineas Eldridge.   b. Jan. 31, 1861. See G&W.

HAMMER, Trygve.   b. Sept. 6, 1878 in Arendal, Norway. He studied at the Royal Arts and Trade School, Oslo, with instruction in modeling from Mathias Skeibrok and later traveled in Germany, Austria and Switzerland, coming to the U.S. in 1903. After studying with MacNeil, Calder, and Solon Borglum he opened his own studio in 1917. He worked as an interior decorator in private homes and did the Scandinavian Room, U. of Pittsburgh; Scofield Memorial Library of the Scandinavian Foundation, NYC; Norse Grill, Waldorf

Astoria Hotel, NYC; stained glass windows, Crescent Athletic Club, Brooklyn. Among his other works are: Head of a Man (Brooklyn Mus.); Baby's Head (Newark Mus.); Roosevelt Memorial (Tenafly, N.J.); decorative panels (Stewart Bldg., NYC); reredos (Zion Episcopal Church, Douglaston, L.I.); memorial to Robert W. de Forest (Cold Spring Harbor, L.I.); Hawk (Brookgreen Gardens). See *Brookgreen Gardens* I.

HAMMITT, Clawson S.   He copied many portraits in Delaware. See m.c., FARL.

HANCOCK, Nathaniel.   G&W give a different chronology for him, placing him in Salem in 1792, then in Portsmouth, N.H., in Boston in 1799 and back in Salem in 1809. See G&W.

HANCOCK, Walker.   b. June 28, 1901. In 1917 he studied at St. Louis School of Fine Arts with Victor Holm and E. H. Wuerpel; also at School of Fine Arts at Wash. U. and at the U. of Wisc. Later he studied with Charles Grafly, won a Cresson Traveling Scholarship, 1922-1923 and in 1925 went to the American Academy in Rome for three years. Returning to the U.S., he became an instructor at the PAFA and now lives at Cape Ann, Mass. Among his works are: Toivo (City Art Museum, St. Louis); Bird Charmer (Zool. Gardens, St. Louis); Seaweed, Young Lobsterman (PAFA); triton fountain (Parrish Art Mus., Southampton, L.I.); Bishop White (Gothic Chapel, Divinity School, Protestant Episcopal Church, Phila.); frieze (City Hall, Kansas City); rhytons (Girard College, Phila.); heroic groups (St. Louis Memorial Bldg.); Stephen Collins Foster (Hall of Fame, N.Y.U.); Booth Tarkington (John Herron Art. Inst., Indianapolis); expeditionary medal, U.S.M.C.; Boy and Squirrel (Brookgarden Gardens). He is a member of the NSS, NA, Architectural League of N.Y. and NIAL. See *Brookgreen Gardens* I.

HANKS, Jervis F.   He worked in Cleveland and Cincinnati in 1825 and 1826; he did silhouette-cutting and portrait painting at that time under the title of "Master." In 1838 he was in Cleveland where he remained at least until 1852. See G&W; Hamilton.

HANKS, O[wen] G. b. *c.* 1815 or 1820 according to G&W and *c.* 1815 in Cowdrey, NAD; MF gives 1838 which, according to G&W, is that date of his beginning work in NYC; d. *c.* 1865. See Cowdrey, NAD; G&W.

HANLEY, W[illiam] H. b. in Canada. He came to the U.S. in the early 1840's and also worked in oils. See Cowdrey, NAD; G&W.

HANSELL, George H. See Cowdrey, NAD; G&W.

HARDING, Chester. b. Sept. 1, 1792 in Conway, N.H. according to G&W but MF says in Mass.; d. Apr. 1, 1866 in Boston. See Cowrey, NAD; Cowdrey, AA & AAU; m.c., FARL; G&W.

HARDING, J. L. This entry is hopelessly confused, being an amalgam of facts about John L. and Jeremiah Harding. Jeremiah was dead by 1830 but John L. is not recorded as being active before *c.* 1835; m.c. 2, N-YHS erroneously identifies him as Jeremiah; the paintings referred to in MF and m.c. Met 2 are probably the work of John L. Harding. See John L. Harding. See G&W.

HARDING, J[ohn] L. He is not known to have been active before *c.* 1835, when he was working in Albany. See Rutledge, PA; G&W.

HARDY, Anna E[liza]. b. Jan. 26, 1839; d. Dec. 15, 1934 at South Orrington, Me. She was also a portraitist and was the daughter of Jeremiah Hardy. See Cowdrey, NAD; G&W.

HARDY, Jeremiah [Pearson]. b. Oct. 22, 1800 in Pelham, N.H.; d. Feb. 9, 1887 'cording to G&W, but in 1888 in MF, i.. Bangor, Me. He was also a miniature, genre, animal and still life painter and was the father of Anne E. Hardy. See G&W.

HARLEY, Charles Richard. He exhibited one drawing at the 1913 Armory Show. See the cat. of the 1963 Armory Show.

HARNETT, William M. b. 1848; d. 1892.—m. c. Met. 2.

HARNISCH, Albert E. See Rutledge, PA; G&W.

HARRIS, J[oseph] T. He came from Portland, Me. See Cowdrey, NAD; Cowdrey, AA & AAU; G&W.

HARRIS, Samuel. b. May, 1783; d. July 10, 1810 according to G&W but on July 7 in MF. He was also a portrait draftsman. See G&W.

HARRISON, Charles. His association with the American Bank Note Co. and his activity as late as 1900 probably should refer to David R. Harrison, who was probably his brother. See G&W.

HARRISON, Charles P. d. 1854 in NYC. He was the son of William Harrison, Sr. See G&W.

HARRISON, David R. He was probably a brother of Charles Harrison. See G&W.

HARRISON, Richard G. b. between 1790 and 1796 in Philadelphia according to G&W; if he was a son of William Harrison, Sr., as is suggested, and if he was born in Philadelphia, he must have been born in 1794 or later, 1794 being the date of his father's settling in Philadelphia. He was probably the father of Richard G. Harrison, Jr. and he was active as late as 1861. See G&W.

HARRISON, Richard G., Jr. He was probably the son of Richard G. Harrison above. G&W do not include the Jr. in his name; he may not have called himself so, Jr. being MF's addition and way of suggesting that he was Richard G. Harrison's son. See G&W.

HARRISON, Samuel. b. 1789. See G&W.

HARRISON, Thomas Alexander. d. 1930—m.c., NYPL.

HARRISON, William [Sr.]. d. Oct. 18, 1803. He was the father of William, Jr., Charles P. and Samuel Harrison, and also possibly of Richard G. Harrison. See G&W.

HARRISON, William F. b. *c.* 1812 in Pennsylvania. See G&W.

HART, Alfred. b. March 28, 1816; active as late as 1878. He was also a panoramist. See G&W.

HART, George O. d. 1933.—m.c. Met 2.

HART, James McDougal.　b. May 10, 1828; d. Oct. 24, 1901 in Brooklyn, N.Y. He was also an animal and portrait painter and the younger brother of William Hart. See DAB; Cowdrey, NAD; Cowdrey, AA & AAU; Rutledge, PA; G&W; Hamilton.

HART, Joel T[anner].　b. Feb. 10, 1810 near Winchester, Ky.; d. March 2, 1877 in Florence, Italy. See DAB; G&W.

HART, William M.　[neither G&W, nor Webster's, Cowdrey or Rutledge give a middle initial].　b. March 31, 1823; d. June 17, 1894. He was also a portrait and allegorical painter and older brother of James McDougal Hart. He was a member of the Hudson River school and was the first president of the Brooklyn Academy of Design. See DAB; Cowdrey, AA & AAU; Cowdrey, NAD; Rutledge, PA; G&W; Hamilton.

HARTLEY, Marsden.　b. in Lewiston, Maine; d. Sept. 2, 1943. He studied with John Semon, at the Cleveland School of Art with Cullen, Yates and Nina Waldeck, at the Chase School in 1898 with F. Luis Mora, F. V. DuMond, and W. M. Chase, and at the ASL and NAD. He exhibited in "291" (Arthur Steiglitz Gallery) in 1909, with the Blue Rider Group in Munich in 1913 and with the Forum Group, Anderson Gallery, in 1916. He also exhibited two oil paintings and six drawings at the 1913 Armory Show. See the 75th Anniv. Cat., ASL; the cat. of the 1963 Armory Show.

HARTMAN, C.　He may be Conrad Fried Hartman according to G&W. See G&W.

HARTMAN, Reber S.　Misindexed after Marsden Hartley.

HARTWELL, Alonzo.　He was a pupil of Abel Bowen. See Hamilton.

HARTWELL, George K[enneth].　d. Dec. 13, 1949.—m.c., NYPL.

HARVEY, Eli.　b. Sept. 23, 1860; d. Feb. 10, 1957 in Alhambra, Calif. He studied with Noble, Rebisso, Lefebvre, Benjamin Constant, Doucet, Delance, Callot, and Fremiet. In 1912 had a comprehensive exhibition in NYC. Among his works are: Jaguar Rampant (Newark Museum); Maternal Caress (MMA); a lioness (Cranbrook Academy of Art, Bloomfield Hills,

Mich.); Greyhound Recumbent (Cincinnati Art Museum); Adonis (Brookgreen Gardens; Los Angeles Museum of History, Science and Art); Young Lion with Rabbit (Brookgreen Gardens). He is a member of the N.Y. Zoological Society and an Associate of the Societe Nationale des Beaux-Arts, Paris.—m.c., NYPL; see *Brookgreen Gardens* I.

HARVEY, George.　b. c. 1800/01 in Tottenham, Eng.; d. 1878 in Eng. He was an Associate of the NA. See Cowdrey, NAD; Cowdrey, AA & AAU; G&W.

HASELTINE, James Henry.　b. Nov. 2, 1833; d. Nov. 9, 1907 in Rome. He was the brother of William Stanley Haseltine. See DAB; Rutledge, PA; G&W.

HASELTINE, W[illiam] Stanley.　b. June 11, 1835 in Philadelphia; d. Feb. 3, 1900 in Rome. He was a landscape and marine painter and the brother of James Henry Haseltine. See Rutledge, PA; Cowdrey, NAD; G&W.

HASSAM, Childe.　d. 1935 at Easthampton. He exhibited six oil paintings, five pastels and one drawing at the 1913 Armory Show.—m.c. Met 2; see the cat. of the 1963 Armory Show.

HASWELL, Ernest Bruce.　b. July 25, 1889 in Breckinridge County, Ky. He also studied with Victor Rousseau at the Academie Royale des Beaux-Arts. Among his works are: Nippert Athletic Memorial, U. of Cincinnati; memorial to the compiler of McGuffey Readers (Oxford, Ohio); sculptural decorations, (Times-Star Bldg., Cincinnati); six portraits for the Ohio State Bldg., Columbus; Little Lady of the Sea (Brookgreen Gardens). See *Brookgreen Gardens* I.

HATCH, George W.　See Cowdrey, NAD; Cowdrey, AA & AAU; G&W.

HAVELL, Robert, Jr.　b. Nov. 25, 1793 in Reading, England; d. Nov. 11, 1878 in Tarrytown, N.Y. He was an aquatint engraver and landscape painter. See DAB; Cowdrey, NAD; Cowdrey, AA & AAU; G&W; m.c., FARL.

HAVILAND, John.　b. 1792; d. March 28, 1853. He was a townscape artist. See Rutledge, PA; Cowdrey, NAD; G&W.

HAWTHORNE, Charles Webster. d. Nov. 29, 1930 in Baltimore, Md. He also studied with H. Siddons Mowbray at the NAD and ASL, and taught at the ASL, 1904/06 and 1924/25. He was a member of the Salmagundi Club and is represented in the collections of the MMA, Corcoran Gallery, Syracuse Museum of Fine Arts, Herron Art Institute, and the Boston Museum of Fine Arts.—m.c., FARL; see 75th Anniv. Cat., ASL.

HAY, De Witt Clinton. b. c. 1819. See G&W.

HAYS, Henry, [Sr.]. He was also a heraldist. See G&W.

HAYS, William Jacob, [Sr.]. b. Aug. 8, 1830 in NYC; d. March 13, 1875 in NYC. See DAB; Cowdrey, NAD; Cowdrey, AA & AAU; Rutledge, PA; G&W.

HAZLITT, John. b. in Marshfield, England; d. May 16, 1837 at Stockport, England. See G&W.

HEADE, Martin Johnson. b. Aug. 11, 1819 in Lumberville, Pa.; d. Sept. 4, 1904 in St. Augustine, Fla. He was also a still life painter. See Rutledge, PA; Cowdrey, NAD; Cowdrey, AA & AAU; G&W.

HEALY, G[eorge] P[eter] A(lexander). b. July 15, 1813; d. June 24, 1894. He also painted historical scenes. See DAB; Cowdrey, NAD; Cowdrey, AA & AAU; Rutledge, PA; G&W.

HEATON, Augustus. d. 1931. m.c., FARL.

HENNESSY, William J[ohn]. b. July 11, 1839 in Thomastown, County Kilkenny, Ireland; d. Dec. 26, 1917 according to G&W and also in Rutledge and Cowdrey; MF says 1900, which is incorrect—at Rudgwick, Sussex, England. He was also a landscapist. See DAB; Cowdrey, NAD; Rutledge, PA; G&W; Hamilton.

HENRI, Pierre. See Rutledge, PA; G&W.

HENRI, Robert. b. June 24, 1865; d. 1929 in NYC. Henri's real name was Robert Henry Cozad and he was the son of John Jackson Cozad, founder of Cozad, Nebraska near the 100th Meridian in the Platte Valley. The elder Cozad was forced to flee Nebraska. He changed his name to Richard H. Lee and those of his sons to Robert Henri and Frank Southern and from then on they were known as his foster sons. The elder Cozad built Lee's Pier at Atlantic City. Henri's portrait of his father is in the Sheldon Memorial Art Gallery at the University of Nebraska. He exhibited with the "Eight" in 1908. He exhibited three oils and two drawings at the 1913 Armory Show and 39 works by him exhibited at the AAAL Dec. 11, 1964-Jan. 10, 1965. He taught at the ASL 1916-1928 and also had his own school. He was an Honorary Member of the ASL, member of the NA, Fellow of the PA, a member of the Society of American Artists, NIAL, National Arts Club and the N.Y. Municipal Association. See Mari Sandoz, *Son of the Gamblin' Man*, N.Y. 1960; cat. of the 1963 Armory Show; 75th Anniv. Cat., ASL; cat. of the AAAL, *Robert Henri and His Circle*.

HENRY, Albert P. b. Jan. 8, 1836; d. Nov. 6, 1872 in Paris, Ky. See G&W.

HENRY, Edward L[amson]. b. Jan. 12, 1841; d. May 11, 1919 in Ellenville, N.Y. according to G&W but MF says in NYC. See Cowdrey, NAD; Rutledge, PA; G&W.

HERING, Elsie Ward. b. Aug. 29, 1872 on a farm near Fayette, Mo.; d. Jan. 12, 1923 in NYC. She studied art with Ida M. Stair, Samuel Richards and Henry Read. From 1896 she studied sculpture at the ASL, and also had some instructions from D. C. French and Siddons Mowbray before going to Paris in 1898. Returning to the U.S. she entered Saint-Gaudens' studio in Cornish, N.H. as an assistant and in 1910 married another of Saint-Gaudens' assistants, Henry Hering. Thereafter she did little independent work, helping out in her husband's studio in NYC. Among her works are: Boy and Frog (Brookgreen Gardens); George Rogers Clark (St. Louis); several portrait busts and reliefs. See *Brookgreen Gardens* I.

HERING, Henry. b. Feb. 15, 1874; d. Jan. 17, 1949 in NYC. He worked for Philip Martiny, became a student of Saint-Gaudens in 1900 and was associated with him until 1907. Among his works are: Civil War Memorial (Yale U.); classic figures (Field Museum, Chicago); The Defense of Fort Dearborn, The Regeneration of Chicago after the Great Fire (the south pylons of the Michigan Boulevard Bridge); pediment (Civic Opera House, Chicago); sculpture (Union Station, Chicago); Indiana State War Memorial (Indianapolis); four reliefs (Civic Centre, Indianapolis); Wood Nymph, 1 (Brookgreen Gardens); Wood Nymph, 2 (Brookgreen Gardens). He exhibited at the NSS, San Francisco, 1929. He was a member of the NA, NSS, Art Commission of N.Y. and the Architectural League of N.Y. See *Brookgreen Gardens* I.

HERRICK   Henry W.   The miniaturist and wood engraver of this name do not seem to be the same person. Bolton: *Miniature Painters,* lists Henry W. Herrick as a miniaturist at Nashville (Tenn.) in 1843. See following entry.

HERRICK, Henry W.   m.c. Met 3 corrects Nashville, Tenn. to read Nashwood, N.H. but we were unable to locate the source for this. He engraved on wood in Concord and Manchester, N.H. for several years and came to NYC *c.* 1848. He returned to Manchester in 1865. He was also a designer. See G&W; Hamilton.

HERRING, Frederick William.   d. Aug. 13, 1899 in NYC. See Cowdrey, AA & AAU; Cowdrey, NAD; G&W.

HERRING, James.   b. Jan. 12, 1794; d. Oct. 8, 1867 in Paris. He was the father of Frederick William Herring. See DAB; Cowdrey, AA & AAU; Cowdrey, NAD; G&W.

HERTER, Adele.   d.   1946.—m.c., NYPL.

HERTER, Albert.   d. Feb. 15, 1950.— m.c. Met 2.

HERVIER, Auguste.   See Augustin Jean Hervieue who this probably is.

HERVIEUE, Augustin Jean [given in G&W as Auguste Hervieu]. He was a watercolorist, painter of genre and humorous subjects. See G&W.

HERZEL, Paul.   b. Aug. 28, 1876 in Tillowitz, Silesia, Germany. He came at age seven with his family to St. Louis, Mo. He was one of the organizers of the Brush and Pencil Club and studied there. His works are mostly of animal subjects; others are Riveter (Moscow Museum of Western Arts; Brookgreen Gardens). See *Brookgreen Gardens I.*

HESSELIUS, Gustavus.   b. Falun, Dalecarlia, Sweden; d. May 25, 1755. He was the father of John Hesselius. See Barker, p. 129; DAB; G&W.

HESSELIUS, John.   d. April 9, 1778. See DAB; Barker, p. 129; G&W.

HETZEL, George.   d. 1899 according to G&W and Rutledge; MF says 1906. He was a landscapist, portraitist, still life and figure painter. See Rutledge, PA; G&W.

HEWINS, Philip.   b. July, 1806; d. May 14, 1850. He also painted religious subjects. See G&W.

HEWITT, William K[eesey].   b. 1817 in Philadelphia; d. 1893 [according to G&W, Cowdrey and Rutledge; MF gives b. 1818 in N.J. and d. 1892]. He was also a figure painter and crayon artist. See Rutledge, PA; Cowdrey, AA & AAU; G&W.

HICKS, Thomas.   b. Oct. 18, 1823 in Newtown, Pa., according to G&W, not Newton as in MF; d. Oct. 8, 1890 in Trenton Falls, N.Y. He was the cousin once removed of Edward Hicks per DAB but G&W say he was his first cousin. He was also a landscapist. See DAB (as John Hicks); Hamilton; Cowdrey, NAD; Cowdrey, AA & AAU; Rutledge, PA; G&W.

HIGGINS, Eugene.   d. 1958. He exhibited two paintings and one drawing at the 1913 Armory Show. See the cat. of the 1963 Armory Show.

HILL, John.   He was the father of John William Hill. See G&W.

HILL, John Henry.   b. West Nyack, N.Y.; d. 1922. He was also a landscapist and aquatintist and was the son of John William Hill. See Cowdrey, NAD; Rutledge, PA; G&W; Hamilton.

HILL, John William.   b. Jan. 13, 1812 in London. See G&W.

HILL, Pamela E. [Pamelia in G&W].   b. May 9, 1803 in Framingham, Mass.; d. at Framingham. See G&W.

HILL, Thomas.   b. Sept. 11, 1829 in Birmingham, England; d. June 30, 1908 in California. See DAB; Rutledge, PA; Hamilton; G&W; Barker, p. 587.

HILLER, J[oseph]. Jr.   d. Aug. 22, 1795. See G&W.

HILLIARD, William Henry.   d. 1905 in Washington, D.C. according to m.c. Met 2. He was also a portraitist. See G&W.

HILLS, J[ames] H.   b. *c.* 1814 in Connecticut. See G&W.

HILLYER, William, [Jr.].   See Cowdrey, AA & AAU; Cowdrey, NAD; G&W.

HINCKLEY, Robert.   b. 1853, not 1835, in Northampton, Mass.; d. June 1, 1941 in Rehoboth Beach, Del. He worked with John Singer Sargent in the atelier of Carolus Duran in Paris and was a graduate of the Ecole des Beaux Arts, Paris, where he lived for 17 years. Many of his portraits are at West Point and Annapolis. He was the author of a book, *Geyserland.* See G&W; m.c. 2, N-YHS.

HINCKLEY, Thomas Hewes.   b. Nov. 4, 1813; d. Feb. 15, 1896 at Milton, Mass. See Cowdrey, NAD; Cowdrey, AA & AAU; G&W; Hamilton; Appleton.

HINE, Charles.   d. July 29, 1871. He was a portrait and figure painter. See G&W.

HINMAN, D[avid] C.   See G&W.

HINSCHELWOOD [or Hinshelwood], Robert.   d. after 1875. He was also an etcher and landscape painter. See Cowdrey, NAD; G&W.

HINSDALE, Richard [Law].   b. May 8, 1826 according to G&W and Cowdrey, AA & AAU but in 1825 in MF and Cowdrey, NAD; d. 1856 in Hartford, Conn. See Cowdrey, NAD; Cowdrey, AA & AAU; G&W.

HINTON, Mrs. Howard.   d. Dec. 19, 1921. See G&W.

HIRSH, Alice Y.   b. 1888; d. 1935.—m.c. Met 2.

HITE, George H[arrison].   b. Urbana, Ohio; d. 1880. He was also a portraitist. See Cowdrey, AA & AAU; Cowdrey, NAD; G&W.

HOARD, Margaret.   b. 1879; d. 1944. She exhibited one sculpture at the 1913 Armory Show. See the cat. of the 1963 Armory Show.

HOBART, Elijah.   He was also a lithographer. See G&W.

HOFFBAUER, Charles.   d. July 26, 1957 in Boston, Mass.—m.c., NYPL.

HOFFMAN, Malvina.   b. June 15, 1887. She studied painting with John W. Alexander, studied sculpture at the ASL and in studio of Herbert Adams; and with Mestrovic in Zagreb, 1927. Among her works are: Mort Exquise; The Prayer (Art Institute of Chicago); portrait studies of Pavlova (MMA; Whitney Mus. of Amer. Art; Corcoran Gallery of Art; Carnegie Institute); The Sacrifice (Harvard U.); Paderewski (Amer. Acad. at Rome; Steinway Hall, NYC); John Keats (U. of Pittsburgh); Mestrovic (Brooklyn Museum); Martinique Woman, Senegalese Soldier (Brooklyn Museum; Amer. Mus. of Natural History); series of the ages of man (Field Museum of Natural Hist.); Pagan's Prayer (Norton Gallery, W. Palm Beach, Fla.); Boy and Panther Cub, 1915 (Brookgreen Gardens); Bali Dancer (Brookgreen Gardens); Andaman Isiander (Brookgreen Gardens; Field Museum of Natural History). She is a member of the NA, NSS and the ALNY. See *Brookgreen Gardens* I.

HOFFMAN, Wilmer.   b. 1890 or 1891 in Calonsville, Md.; d. May 21, 1954 in Charleston, S.C.—m.c., NYPL.

HOFFY, Alfred [M.].   b. *c.* 1790 in England. See Rutledge, PA; G&W.

HOFTRUP, J[ulius] Lars.   b. 1874, Sweden; d. April 11, 1954 in Elmira, N.Y.—m.c., NYPL.

HOLLAND, John Joseph.   d. Dec. 15, 1820. He was also a townscape painter. See Cowdrey, AA & AAU; G&W.

HOLLINGSWORTH, George.   d. 1882 according to G&W, but in 1892 in MF, at Milton, Mass. He was also a landscapist. See G&W.

HOLLYER, Samuel.   b. Feb. 24, 1826; d. Dec. 29, 1919. He is represented at the MMA by "Daniel Webster". He was also an etcher. See DAB; Cowdrey, NAD; G&W;—m.c. Met 3.

HOLT, Samuel.   He was still living in Hartford, Conn. in 1879 and was also a portraitist and ornamental painter. See G&W.

HOLYLAND, C. I.   He is probably the C. J. Holyland listed in G&W. See G&W.

HOMER, Winslow.   b. Feb. 24, 1836; d. Sept. 2, 1910 at Prout's Neck near Scarboro, Me. according to G&W but MF says in Scarboro. He worked both in oils and watercolors. Early in his career he illustrated for "Ballou's Pictorial Drawing-Room Companion" and "Harper's Weekly". See G&W; Hamilton.

HOOGLAND, William. b. *c.* 1795; d. Sept. 28, 1832 according to G&W but both MF and Cowdrey have him active in 1841. See Hamilton; Cowdrey, NAD; G&W.

HOOKER, William. See DAB; Cowdrey, AA & AAU; G&W.

HOOPER, Edward. b. May 24, 1829 in London, England; d. Dec. 13, 1870. He came to U.S. in the early 1850's. See G&W.

HOPE, James. b. Nov. 29, 1818/19 at Drygrange, Roxboroughshire, Scotland according to G&W but MF says England; d. at Watkins Glen, N.Y. He was a portrait, historical and landscape painter. See Cowdrey, NAD; Cowdrey, AA & AAU; Rutledge, PA; G&W.

HOPE, Thomas W. He was active 1834-65 according to G&W; MF says only 1839-45. See G&W.

HOPKIN, Robert. b. Jan. 3, 1832 at Glasgow, Scotland; d. March 21, 1909. He was also an animal, historical and scene painter. See G&W.

HOPKINSON, Charles Sydney. b. 1869, not 1860 as in MF per *Who's Who in American Art, 1962;* d. 1962. He exhibited four paintings at the 1913 Armory Show. See the cat. of the 1963 Armory Show.

HOPKINSON, Francis. b. Oct. 2, 1737 in Philadelphia; d. May 9, 1791. See DAB; G&W.

HOPPER, Edward. He exhibited one oil painting at the 1913 Armory Show. See the cat. of the 1963 Armory Show.

HOPPIN, Augustus. b. July 13, 1828; d. April 1, 1896 at Flushing, L.I., N.Y. He was the brother of Thomas Frederick Hoppin. See DAB; Hamilton, 318-324; Cowdrey, NAD; G&W.

HOPPIN, Thomas Frederick. b. Aug. 15, 1816; d. Jan. 21, 1872 in Providence, R. I. He was also a painter and was the brother of Augustus Hoppin. See Cowdrey, NAD; Cowdrey, AA & AAU; G&W.

HOPSON, William Fowler. b. Aug. 30, 1849; d. Feb. 13, 1935. He made about 200 bookplates, all designed to express the personality of the owner rather than any specific tradition of design. Perhaps his best known work is the series of 2500 blocks engraved for an edition of Webster's Unabridged Dictionary. Some of his work is in permanent exhibition in the NYPL. Mr. Hopson wrote several reviews and articles on engraving and is a member of the Grolier Club in NYC, Club of Old Volumes and Bibliophile Society in Boston, Rowfant Club in Cleveland, Elizabethan Club in New Haven, Calif. Bookplate Society, and the Sons of the American Revolution. See m.c. 2, N-YHS.

HORSFALL, R. Bruce. d. March 24, 1948.—m.c., NYPL.

HORTON. G&W think that he may be John S. Horton. See G&W.

HOSMER, Harriet [Goodhue]. b. Oct. 9, 1830 according to G&W and Webster's but in 1831 in MF; d. Feb. 21, 1908 at Watertown, Mass. See DAB; Cowdrey, NAD; G&W.

HOTCHKISS, Wales. He was still living in Northampton, Mass. in 1879. See G&W.

HOUDON, Jean Antoine. b. March 20, 1741 at Versailles, France; d. July 15, 1828 in Paris. See Benezit; G&W.

HOUSE, James. b. *c.* 1775; d. Nov. 17, 1834 in Georgetown, D.C. See G&W.

HOUSE, T[imothy]. He was also a historical and portrait engraver whose home was at Newtonville, Mass. He was active as early as 1836. See G&W; Hamilton.

HOUSTON, F.[rances] C. Lyons. For "he" read "she".—m.c. Met 2.

HOVEY, Otis. b. 1788. See G&W.

HOWARD, Cecil de Blaquiere. b. April 2, 1888 in Clifton, Canada; d. 1956. His mother was an amateur painter and his family moved to Buffalo when he was two and became American citizens. He studied at the ASL and was taught by J. E. Fraser. In 1905 he moved with his mother to Paris and entered the Academie Julian where he studied with Raoul Verlet and opened a studio of his own. In winter 1909/10 he studied animals in Antwerp and had the advice of Rembrandt Bugatti. In 1915 and 1916 he came to NYC and exhibited at Gorhams' and in 1925 at the Whitney Studio Club, NYC and the Albright Art Gallery, Buffalo. During WWII, when he had to flee France, he worked in NYC and taught at the N.Y. School of Applied Design for Women and was a visiting critic at the Rinehart School of Sculpture, Baltimore. Among his works are: war memorials at Hautot-sur-Mer and Ouville-la-Riviere, France; tomb of Herbert Aubrey, (Pixton Park, Dulverton, Somersetshire, England); Dance (Albright Art Gallery, Buffalo); mother and child and a nude (Whitney Mus. of Amer. Art); Jo Davidson (Whitney); Walter Reed (N.Y.U. Hall of Fame); Sun Bather (Musee Nationale d'Art Moderne, France); Fatigue, Knockout (Brookgreen Gardens; the latter also in the collection of Lord Howard de Walden). He exhibited one sculpture at the 1913 Armory Show and was a National Academician, president of the NSS, a member of the Legion of Honor and of the NIAL. See the cat. of the 1963 Armory Show; *Brookgreen Gardens* II.

HOWE, William H. d. 1929 in Bronxville, N.Y.—m.c. Met 2.

HOWE, Z[adoc]. b. Bolton, Conn. in 1777 according to m.c., FARL; d. in Billerica, Mass., in 1852. See Hamilton, 14, 73; G&W; m.c., FARL.

HOWES, Samuel P. He was also a landscapist. See G&W.

HOWLAND, Alfred Cornelius. b. Feb. 12, 1838; d. March 17, 1909; landscapist and genre painter. Among his other works is "The Yale Fence" at Yale U. See DAB; G&W; Hamilton.

HOWLAND, Edith. b. March 29, 1863; d. Sept. 8, 1949. She attended Vassar College, went to Paris and studied drawing at the Academie Julian. She also studied with George de Forest Brush and D. C. French. She took a studio at Neuilly, near Paris. Among her works are: bust of Maud Miller (exhib. Paris Salon, 1893); Between Yesterday and Tomorrow (honorable mention, Paris Salon, 1914); exhibited MMA, & Brooklyn Museum; at (Brookgreen Gardens); Boy and Swan (on loan to Bruce Museum, Greenwich, Conn.). She is an

Associate of the NSS. See *Brookgreen Gardens* I;—m.c., NYPL.

HOWS, John Augustus. b. 1832; d. Sept. 27, 1874 in NYC. He was a landscapist. See Cowdrey, NAD; Rutledge, PA; Hamilton, 333-334; G&W.

HOXTE, Vinner Ream. Corrected to read Hoxie in m.c. Met 4.

HOYT, Albert G. [given in G&W as Albert Gallatin Hoit and as probably Hoit in Cowdrey]. b. Dec. 13, 1809 according to G&W and Cowdrey, but in 1800 in MF; d. Dec. 18 or 19, 1856 at West Roxbury, Mass. See Cowdrey, AA & AAU; G&W.

HUBARD, William J[ames]. b. at Whitechurch, Shropshire, England according to G&W but MF and m.c., FARL both say Warwick; d. Feb. 15, 1862. He was also a silhouettist and sculptor. See Cowdrey, AA & AAU; Rutledge, PA; Cowdrey, NAD; G&W; m.c., FARL.

HUBBARD, Richard W[illiam]. b. Oct., 1816 according to G&W and Webster's but MF has 1817; d. Dec. 21, 1888 in Brooklyn, N.Y. He was also a portraitist. See DAB; Cowdrey, NAD; Cowdrey, AA & AAU; G&W.

HUBBELL, Henry Salem. d. Jan. 9, 1949.—m.c., NYPL.

HUDSON, Eric. d. Dec. 22, 1932. He became an Associate of the NA in 1926.—m.c. Met 2.

HUDSON, Julien [or Jules]. He was a miniaturist. See G&W.

HUDSON, William, Jr. b. 1787. He was also a landscapist. See Cowdrey, NAD; G&W.

HUGHES, Ball Robt. [m.c. 2, N-YHS corrects this to read Robt. Ball]. b. Jan. 19, 1806 in London, England; d. March 5, 1868 in Dorchester, Mass. He was also a wax-portraitist. See DAB; Rutledge, PA; Cowdrey, NAD; Cowdrey, AA & AAU; G&W.

HUMPHREY, [Miss] Elizabeth [Lizzie] B. See Hamilton.

HUMPHREYS, Albert. The date of death given as 1922 in *Armory Show, 50th Anniversary Exhibition, 1913-1963* and as 1925 in Milton W. Brown, *The Story of the*

Armory Show. He exhibited two sculptures, two oil paintings and six drawings in the 1913 Armory Show. See the cat. of the 1963 Armory Show.

HUMPHREYS, F[rancis].   b. *c.* 1815 in Ireland. See G&W.

HUMPHRYS, William.   d. Jan. 21, 1865 near Genoa according to G&W but MF says in Genoa. See Rutledge, PA; Cowdrey, AA & AAU; G&W.

HUNT, Samuel Valentine.   b. Feb. 14, 1803. He was also a landscapist. See Cowdrey, NAD; Cowdrey, AA & AAU; G&W.

HUNT, William Morris.   b. March 31, 1824; d. Sept. 8, 1879. He was also a genre painter and cameo portraitist. See DAB; Cowdrey, NAD; G&W.

HUNTINGTON, Anna H[yatt].   Sculptor. b. March 10, 1876, Anna Vaughn Hyatt. She studied with Henry Hudson Kitson at Boston and also at the ASL, with Hermon MacNeil. She had a retrospective exhibition at the AAAL, in 1936. Her work is at Brookgreen Gardens; Hispanic Society of America, NYC, and numerous other collections. She did the statue of Joan of Arc on Riverside Drive, NYC. She is the honorary vice-pres. of the National Association of Women Painters and Sculptors, a member of the NSS, NA, NIAL and a corresponding number of the Spanish Academia de Bellas Artes de San Fernando. See *Brookgreen Gardens I.*

HUNTINGTON, Daniel.   b. Oct. 14, 1816 in NYC; d. April 18, 1906 in NYC. He was also a historical and landscape painter. See DAB; Cowdrey, NAD; Cowdrey, AA & AAU; Rutledge, PA; G&W; Hamilton.

HUNTLEY, Samantha L.   d. June 19, 1949. See m.c., NYPL; m.c., FARL.

HUTTON, Isaac.   b. *c.* 1767; d. Sept. 8, 1855 at Stuyvesant Landing, Columbia Co., N.Y. See G&W.

IMBERT, Anthony.   d. before 1838. He was also a marine painter. The m.c. N-YHS asserts that his was not the first lithographic establishment in N.Y. as is stated in MF. See G&W.

INGHAM, Charles Cromwell.   b. 1796; d. Dec. 10, 1863 in NYC. He was also a miniaturist, and was a member of the NA, Sketch Club, and the Century Club. See DAB; Cowdrey, NAD; Cowdrey, AA & AAU; Rutledge, PA; G&W.

INMAN, Henry.   b. Oct. 28, 1801; d. Jan. 17, 1846. He was also a miniaturist and the father of J. O'Brien Inman. He was a National Academician. See DAB; Cowdrey, NAD; Cowdrey, AA & AAU; Rutledge, PA; G&W.

INMAN, J[ohn] O'Brien.   b. June 10, 1826 in NYC; d. May 28, 1896 at Fordham, N.Y. He was a portraitist and genre painter. See Cowdrey, NAD; G&W.

INNESS, George.   b. May 1, 1825; d. Aug. 3, 1894 at Bridge of Allan, Scotland. He was an Honorary Member of the ASL and a National Academician. See DAB; Cowdrey, NAD; Cowdrey, AA & AAU; Rutledge, PA; G&W; 75th Anniv. Cat., ASL.

IRVING, John Beaufain.   b. Nov. 26, 1825; d. April 20, 1877. He was also a genre painter. See DAB; Cowdrey, NAD; Rutledge, PA; G&W.

IVES, Chauncey B[radley].   b. Dec. 14, 1810 according to G&W, Webster's, Cowdrey and Rutledge, but 1812 in MF, at Hamden, Conn.; d. Aug. 2, 1894 in Rome. See DAB; Cowdrey, NAD; Cowdrey, AA & AAU; Rutledge, PA; G&W.

IVES, Neil McDowell.   d. Sept. 12, 1946.—m.c., NYPL.

JACKMAN, W[illiam] G.   —m.c., N-YHS; see G&W.

JACKSON, John Adam.   b. Nov. 5, 1825; d. Aug. 30, 1879 at Pracchia, Italy. See DAB; Cowdrey, NAD; Rutledge, PA; G&W.

JAMES, Alexander R.   d. Feb., 1941. —m.c., NYPL.

JANVIER, A[lbert] W[ilson].   He was also a portrait painter. See Rutledge, PA; G&W.

JARVIS, John Wesley.   d. Jan. 12, 1840 in NYC. He was also a miniaturist and sculptor and for a while Sully was his assistant in N.Y. In m.c. Met 2 the date 1833 is corrected to read 1814-1821. See Barker, p. 271; DAB; Rutledge, PA; Cowdrey, AA & AAU; Cowdrey, NAD; G&W; Hamilton.

JENKS, Phoebe Pickering. d. Boston. —m.c. Met 2.

JENNEWEIN, Carl Paul. b. Dec. 2, 1890 in Stuttgart, Germany. He came to the U.S. in 1907 and from 1908 to 1911 studied at ASL and then spent two years travelling in Germany, France, Italy and Egypt. He was a fellow of the American Academy in Rome 1916-1920 and opened his studio in N.Y. in 1921. Among his works are: Cupid and Crane (Wadsworth Atheneum, Hartford, Conn.; Newark Museum; California Palace, Legion of Honor, San Francisco); War Memorial (Barre, Vermont); Puritan (Plymouth, Mass.); Gov. Endicott (Boston, Mass.); panels (State Educ. Bldg., Harrisburg, Pa.); frieze (Lincoln Insurance Bldg., Fort Wayne, Indiana); Memory (PAFA); pediment (Phila. Mus. of Art); door (British Empire Bldg., Rockefeller Center); sculptural decoration (Dept. of Justice Bldg., Wash., D.C.); bas-reliefs, Painting, Sculpture (John Herron Art. Inst., Indianapolis); Indian and Eagle (Brookgreen Gardens; Ball State Teachers' College, Muncie, Ind.; Tours, France; National Collection of Fine Arts, Wash., D.C.); Nymph & Fawn (Brookgreen Gardens; Court House Square, Wash., D.C.); Cupid and Gazelle (Brookgreen Gardens; Baltimore Museum of Art; Cranbrook Acad. of Art, Bloomfield Hills, Mich. Montclair Art Mus.; MMA); Comedy (Brookgreen Gardens); The Greek Dance (Brookgreen Gardens; Fine Arts Gallery, San Diego). He is a member of the NSS, the American Institute of Architects, and the NIAL. See *Brookgreen Gardens*. I.

JENNINGS, Samuel. He was a portraitist and miniaturist and worked both in oils and crayons. See G&W.

JENNINGS, William. G&W think that he is probably William Jennys. See J. William Jennys.

JENNYS, J. William. G&W ascribe the initial J. to a misreading of his signature and identify him simply as William Jennys; he may be William Jennings in the entry above. See G&W.

JENNYS, Richard, Jr. [G&W omit the Jr.]. He was also a portrait painter. See G&W.

JEROME, Elizabeth Gilbert [Mrs. Benjamin N.]. b. Dec. 18, 1824; d. April 22, 1910 in New Haven. She was also a portraitist, miniaturist and crayon artist. See Rutledge, PA; Cowdrey, NAD; G&W.

JEWETT, Frederic[k] S[tiles]. b. Feb. 26, 1819 at Simsbury, Conn.; d. Dec. 26, 1864 in Cleveland, Ohio. He was also a landscapist and drawing teacher. See Cowdrey, NAD; G&W.

JEWETT, Maude S. d. April 17, 1953 at Southampton, L.I., N.Y.—m.c., NYPL.

JEWETT, William. b. Jan. 14, 1789/90 according to G&W but 1792 in Webster's and Cowdrey and 1795 in MF; d. March 24, 1874 in Bergen, N.J. per G&W but MF says in Bayonne. He was also a genre and landscape painter. See Cowdrey, AA & AAU; Cowdrey, NAD; DAB; G&W.

JEWETT, William S.[or Smith]. b. Aug. 6, 1812; d. Dec. 3, 1873 in Springfield, Mass. He was also religious, landscape and genre painter. See Cowdrey, NAD; Cowdrey, AA & AAU; G&W.

JOCELYN, Nathaniel. b. Jan. 31, 1796; d. Jan. 13, 1881. He was also a miniaturist and was the brother of Simeon Jocelyn. See DAB; Cowdrey, NAD; Cowdrey, AA & AAU; G&W.

JOCELYN, Simeon Smith. b. Nov. 21, 1799; d. Aug. 17, 1879. He was the brother of Nathaniel Jocelyn. See Cowdrey, NAD; G&W.

JOHNSON, [Miss] Content. d. Nov. 9, 1949.—m.c., NYPL.

JOHNSON, David. b. May 10, 1827 in NYC; d. Jan. 30, 1908 at Walden, N.Y. See Cowdrey, NAD; Cowdrey, AA & AAU; G&W.

JOHNSON, Eastman. See Jonathan Eastman Johnson.

JOHNSON, G[race] M[ott]. b. July 28, 1882. She also studied with J. E. Fraser at the ASL. Her chosen field was animal sculpture. She spent 1909 in Paris studying Percherons and upon returning to U.S. lived in Woodstock, N.Y. Since 1917 she has spent part of her time in N.M. Her work was shown at Whitney Studio Club, N.Y. in 1919 and 1935. and is in the collections at Brookgreen Gardens and the Whitney Museum of American Art. She is a member of the American Artists' Congress and exhibited four sculptures at the 1913 Armory Show. See the cat. of the 1963 Armory Show; *Brookgreen Gardens* I.

JOHNSON, Henrietta. m.c. 2, N-YHS corrects the death date, given as 1728 to read 1928 but this is probably in error. This is most likely Henrietta Johnston in the entry below.

JOHNSON, Horace C[hauncey]. b. Feb. 1, 1820 in G&W but 1824 in MF; active as late as 1886 in Waterbury, Conn. See G&W.

JOHNSON, [Jonathan] Eastman. b. Aug., 1824 in Lowell, Me. according to G&W but MF has Lovell; d. April 5, 1906 in NYC. MF erroneously states that he settled in N.Y. in 1860 and then gives the correct date, 1858. See DAB; Cowdrey, NAD; Cowdrey, AA & AAU; Rutledge, PA; G&W; Barker, p. 609; Hamilton.

JOHNSON, Marshall. d. 1915 in Boston.—m.c. Met 2.

JOHNSON, Samuel Frost. b. Nov. 9, 1835. He was a portraitist, still life, genre and religious painter. See G&W.

JOHNSTON, David Claypoole. b. March, 1799 according to G&W, Hamilton, Cowdrey and Rutledge; d. Nov. 8, 1865. See DAB; Cowdrey, AA & AAU; Cowdrey, NAD; Rutledge, PA; G&W; Hamilton.

JOHNSTON, Henrietta. Henrietta Johnston, as know to G&W was a portrait pastellist; she made a trip to N.Y. in 1725 (perhaps MF's 1755) to do some portraits and died March 9, 1728/29 in Charleston, S.C. See DAB; G&W.

JOHNSTON, John. b. 1753 according to G&W but 1752 in MF; d. June 29, 1818. He was also a pastellist and figure painter. See G&W.

JOHNSTON, Thomas. b. May 8, 1767. He was the father of John Johnston. See DAB; G&W.

JOHNSTON, Thomas Murphy. b. 1834 in Boston; d. Feb. 28, 1869 in Paris. He also worked in oils. See Rutledge, PA; G&W.

JONES, Alfred. b. April 7, 1819; d. April 28, 1900 in NYC. He was also a portrait and genre painter. See DAB; Cowdrey, NAD; Cowdrey, AA & AAU; G&W.

JONES, Fitzgerald [Fitz Edwin or Fitz Edward in G&W].

JONES, Hugh Bolton. d. 1927.—m.c., FARL.

JONES, S. K. b. Feb., 1825. See G&W.

JONES, Thomas Dow. b. Dec. 11, 1811 in Oneida Co., N.Y.; d. Feb. 27, 1881 in Columbus, Ohio. He was also a medallionist. See Cowdrey, NAD; Rutledge, PA; G&W.

JONES, William Foster. b. *c.* 1815 in Pennsylvania. He was also a historical painter and crayon artist.

JONES, William R. See Rutledge, PA; G&W.

JONGERS, Alphonse. d. Oct. 2, 1945. —m.c., NYPL.

JORDAN, Henry. See Hamilton, 394; Cowdrey, AA & AAU; G&W.

JOUETT, Matthew Harris. b. April 22, 1787/88 near Harrodsburg, Ky.; d. Aug. 10, 1827 near Lexington, Ky. according to G&W but MF says at Louisville, Ky. See DAB; G&W.

JUDSON, Alice. d. Apr. 3, 1948.— m.c., NYPL.

KANTOR, Morris. b. April 15, 1896. He came to U.S. in 1911 and from 1916 to 1918 studied with Homer Boss at ASL, of which he is an active member and where he has taught since 1936. He is a member, Society of Independent Artists, Society of American Painters, Sculptors and Gravers, and is represented in the collections of the MMA, Museum of Modern Art, Whitney Museum of American Art, Art Institute of Chicago, PAFA, Phillips Memorial Gallery and the Detroit Institute of Art. See 75th Anniv. Cat., ASL.

KARFIOL, Bernard. d. Aug. 16, 1952. He exhibited two oil paintings and six drawings at the 1913 Armory Show. See the cat. of the 1963 Armory Show.

KARST, John.   b. at Bingen, Germany.
See G&W.

KAUFMAN, Theodore [given as Theodor
Kaufmann in G&W and Theodore Kaufmann in Cowdrey, NAD].   b. Dec. 18,
1814 in Nelsen according to G&W and erroneously Nelson in MF; still living in
1887. See Cowdrey, NAD; G&W.

KEARNY, Francis [Kearney in G&W and
Rutledge, PA.].   b. July 23, 1785; d.
Sept. 1, 1837. See DAB; Rutledge, PA;
G&W.

KECK, Charles.   b. Sept. 9, 1875 in
NYC; d. April 23, 1951 according to m.c.,
NYPL. He studied at the ASL, NAD and
also with Charles Martiny; in 1893-1898
he was an assistant in Saint-Gaudens' studio
and in 1900-1904 he was at the American
Academy in Rome and continued to receive
criticisms from Saint-Gaudens. He also
studied in Greece, Florence and Paris and
established a studio in N.Y. upon his return to the U.S. Among his works are:
The Genius of Islam (facade of the Brooklyn Museum); America (Allegheny Memorial, Pittsburgh); Liberty Monument
(Ticonderoga, N.Y.); Victory (Montclair,
N.J.); Angel (Shriner's Peace Monument,
Toronto, Canada); Lewis and Clark (Charlottesville, Va.); Father Jacques (Lake
George, N.Y.); Father Duffy (Times
Square, N.Y.); reliefs (William Rockhill
Nelson Gallery of Art, Kansas City, Mo.);
equestrian statue of Andrew Jackson (Kan-
sas City, Mo.); Fauns at Play(Raskob
Estate, Centreville, Md.; Brookgreen Gar-
dens). He is a member of the NSS, Amer-
ican Numismatic Society, NA, and the
ALNY. See *Brookgreen Gardens I.*

KEENAN, William.   b. *c.* 1810 in
Charleston, S. C. He was also a lithographer. See G&W.

KEITH, William.   b. Nov. 21, 1839 at
Old Meldrum, Aberdeenshire, Scotland; d.
April 13, 1911 at Berkeley, Calif. He was
an engraver for the Harper publications and
then went in 1859 to California, where he
worked in the engraving shop of Harrison
Eastman and later with Durbin Van Vleck.
He began to paint and was popular. Murals
by him are at Leland Stanford University.
See DAB; G&W; Cowdrey, NAD; Hamilton.

KELLER, Henry G.   d. 1949. He exhibited two oil paintings at the 1913 Armory Show. See the cat. of the 1963
Armory Show.

KELLOG Miner K[ilbourne]. [given as
Kellogg in G&W, Cowdrey, NAD and Rut-
ledge, PA].   b. Aug. 22, 1814 at Man-
lius Square, N.Y. according to G&W but in
Cincinnati, Ohio in MF; d. 1889. He did
many oriental scenes and is an Honorary
Member of the NA. See Cowdrey, NAD;
Rutledge, PA; G&W.

KELLOGG, J[arvis] G[riggs].   b. Oct.
1, or 5, 1805; d. July 24, 1873. He was also
a lithographer.

KELLY, J[oseph].   See G&W.

KELLY, Thomas.   See Rutledge, PA;
G&W.

KELMAN, Benjamin.   d. 1933.—m.c.
Met 3.

KEMMELMYER, [Frederick].   MF says
that he ". . . made a sketch from life of
Washington on Oct. 2, 1794." The date is
given in G&W as Oct. 18, 1794. He was a
portraitist, miniaturist, historical painter
and teacher. See G&W.

KENNEDY, James.   See Rutledge, PA;
G&W.

KENSETT, John Frederick.   b. March
22, 1816 according to G&W, Rutledge, PA,
Webster's, and Cowdrey, AA & AAU but
in 1816 in MF and Cowdrey, NAD; d. Dec.
14, 1872. He was the son of Thomas Kensett, a member of the Hudson River School
and also an engraver. See Cowdrey, NAD;
DAB; Cowdrey, AA & AAU; Rutledge,
PA; G&W; Barker, p. 435; Hamilton.

KENSETT, Thomas.   b. Aug. 17, 1786
at Hampton Court, Middlesex, England; d.
June 16, 1829 at Cheshire, Conn. He was
the father of John Frederick Kensett. See
DAB under J.F. Kensett; G&W.

KENT, Ada Howe.   d. June 30, 1942.
—m.c. 2, NYPL.

KENT, Rockwell.   Born near N.Y.C.,
this realist artist is a graduate of Horace
Mann School in N.Y.C. and also studied
architecture at Columbia University. He first
exhibited in 1905 at the National Academy.
His first one-man exhibition was held in

1906 and was followed by others at the Knoedler and Wildenstein Galleries.

Among his many books in which he records his life, work, tarvels and philosophy are: *Wilderness: A Journal of Quiet Adventure in Alaska* (1920); *Voyaging: Southward from the Strait of Magellan* (1924); *N by E* (1930); *Rockwellkentiana* (1933); *Salamina* (1935); *This is my Own* (1940); *It's Me, O Lord* (1955); *Of Men and Mountains* (1959); and *Greenland Journal* (1963).

Mr. Kent, who has been politically and socially active all of his life and has written many other works in this vein was, in 1962, elected an honorary member of the Academy of Art of the U.S.S.R.

KEY, F[rancis] S[cott].   See G&W.

KEY, John Ross.   b. July 16, 1832 at Hagerstown, Md. according to G&W, Rutledge and PA but in 1837 in MF who says he was born in Baltimore; d. March 24, 1920. He was a landscapist and illustrator. See Rutledge, PA; Cowdrey, NAD; G&W.

KIDDER, J[ames].   He was also a landscapist and engraver. See G&W; Hamilton.

KILBURN, Laurence [Lawrence in G&W]. b. 1720; d. June 28, 1775 in NYC. He was also a miniaturist and fancy painter. See G&W.

KIMBALL, Isabel M.   Misindexed after Aaron Edward Kilpatrick and probably a duplicate on Isabel Moore Kimball.

KIMBERLY, Denison.   d. 1863. See G&W.

KIMMEL, P. K.   G&W identify him as Christopher Kimmel, b. in Germany *c.* 1830. He was also a lithographer and printer. See G&W.

KING, Charles Bird.   d. March 18, 1862. He was an Honorary Member of the NA. See Rutledge, PA; Cowdrey, NAD; Cowdrey: AA & AAU; G&W.

KING, G[eorge] B.   See G&W.

KING, John C[rookshanks].   b. Oct. 11, 1806 in Kilwinning, Ayrshire, Scotland; d. April 22, 1882. See Rutledge, PA; Cowdrey, NAD; Cowdrey, AA & AAU; G&W.

KING, Samuel.   b. Jan. 24, 1748/49; d. Dec. 30, 1819 in Newport, R.I. See DAB; G&W.

KINGSLEY, Eldridge.   This is corrected in m.c. Met 3 to read Elbridge.

KINNEY, B[enjamin] H[arris].   b. Feb. 7, 1821 in Mass.; d. Dec., 1888 in Worcester, Mass. See G&W.

KINNEY, Troy.   d. 1938.—m.c. Met 3.

KINSEY, Nathaniel.   b. *c.* 1829 in Delaware. See G&W.

KIRK, John.   b. *c.* 1823. See G&W.

KLINE, William Fair.   d. July 30, 1931 in Anniston, Ala. He became an Associate of the NA in 1901.—m.c. Met 2.

KLUMPKE, Anna Elizabeth.   d. Feb., 1942.—m.c. Met 2.

KNAPP, C[harles] W.   d. May 15, 1900. He was a landscapist. See Cowdrey, NAD; G&W.

KNEASS, William.   b. Sept. 25, 1780 according to G&W but in 1781 in MF; d. Aug. 27, 1840. See DAB; G&W.

KNEELAND.   This is perhaps Horace Kneeland, *c.* 1808-*c.* 1860. See Cowdrey, AA & AAU; Cowdrey, NAD; G&W.

KNIGHT, Charles Robert.   d. April, 1953 in NYC.—m.c., NYPL.

KNIGHT, D[aniel] Ridgeway.   b. March 15, 1840 according to G&W and Webster's but in 1839 in MF and Rutledge, PA; d. March 9, 1924. He was a genre and figure painter. See DAB; Rutledge, PA; G&W.

KNIGHT, L[ouis] Aston.   d. May 8, 1948 in NYC.—m.c., NYPL.

KNOWLTON, Helen Mary.   b. Aug. 16, 1832. See G&W.

KONTI, Isidore.   b. July 9, 1862; d. Jan. 11, 1938 in Yonkers, N.Y. He entered the Vienna Academy at age 16 and studied with Edmund von Hellmer. Later he continued his studies in the Meisterschule of Karl Kundmann. According to *Brookgreen Gardens I* he left for America in 1891 but MF says this was in 1890. He finally came to N.Y. and became as assistant in the studio of Karl Bitter. Among his works are: The Despotic Age (City Art Museum, St. Louis); relief (door of Grace Church, N.Y.); terracotta frieze, (Gainsborough Studios); capitals and panels (Pan-American

Bldg., Wash., D.C.); Beale and Carson Hailing Stockton's Flagship (National Collection of Fine Arts); Justinian, Alfred the Great (Cleveland Court House); McKinley Memorial (Philadelphia); Gov. F. T. Nicholls (Baton Rouge, La.); Hudson-Fulton Memorial (Yonkers, N.Y.); effigy of the Rev. Morgan Dix (Trinity Church, N.Y.); tomb of Bishop Horatio Potter (Cathedral of St. John The Divine, N.Y.); fountain (Audubon Park, New Orleans); The Genius of Immortality (MMA, Detroit Institute of Arts); Orpheus (on loan to the Baltimore Museum of Art from the Peabody Institute); Dying Melodies (museum, Oberlin College); dancing figures (Montclair & Newark Museums); Young Faun (Brookgreen Gardens). He is a member of the NA. See *Brookgreen Gardens I.*

KOOPMAN, John R.   d. Sept. 16, 1949. —m.c., NYPL.

KORBEL, Mario.   b. March 22, 1882 in Osik, Bohemia (Czechoslovakia) according to *Brookgreen Gardens I* but MF says in Russia. He studied sculpture in Bohemia, coming to the U.S. at age 18 but returned to Europe for further study. He finally settled in NYC but spent two years in Cuba during WWI. In the 1920's he returned to Czechoslovakia and established a studio in Prague. Among his works are: Alma Mater (Havana U.); Music, Dawn, Eve, Morning and Evening (George Booth Estate, Birmingham, Mich.); St. Theresa of the Child Jesus (Vatican); several works (Nicholas F. Brady Estate, L.I.); The Kiss (Ziegler Estate, Noroton, Conn.); The Three Graces, Atalanta (Cranbrook Acad. of Art, Bloomfield Hills, Mich.); Nocturne (National Gallery of Canada, Ottowa); bronze torso (Art Inst., Chicago); Sonata (Brookgreen Gardens); Night (Brookgreen Gardens; Art Inst. Chicago); marble torso (Whitney Mus. of Amer. Art); Vanity and Modesty (Cleveland Mus. of Art). He is a member of the ALNY, the NSS, an Associate of the NA and a member of the Legion of Honor. See *Brookgreen Gardens I.*

KOSKIUSKO, A[ndrzej] B[onawentura], [Thaddeus in Webster's; Tadeus in G&W]. b. Feb. 12, 1746 in Lithuania; d. Oct. 15, 1817 in Solthurn, Switzerland. He was an amateur portraitist in oils and crayons. See DAB; G&W.

KRIMMEL, John Lewis.   b. 1789 according to G&W and Cowdrey, AA & AAU, 1789 or 1787 in Rutledge, PA and 1787 in MF, in Ebingen, Wurttemberg, Germany; d. July 15, 1821. See DAB; Rutledge, PA; Cowdrey, AA & AAU; G&W.

KROLL, Leon.   He exhibited one oil painting at the 1913 Armory Show. See the cat. of the 1963 Armory Show.

KUHN, Walt.   b. Oct. 27, 1880 in NYC; d. July 13, 1949 in NYC according to m.c., NYPL but as July 3 in 75th Anniv. Cat., ASL. He studied in France, Germany, Holland, Italy and Spain and taught at the ASL, N.Y. in 1926-28 and at the N.Y. School of Art in 1908/09. He was one of the organizers of the 1913 Armory Show and exhibited two oil paintings, two drawings and one pastel there. See the cat. of the 1913 Armory Show; 75th Anniv. Cat.; ASL.

KUNIYOSHI, Yasuo.   b. Sept. 1, 1893; d. 1953 according to m.c. Met 2. He studied at the L.A. School of Art 1908-10, at the NAD in 1912, Independent School of Art, N.Y. 1914-16, and with K. H. Miller at the ASL, N.Y. 1916-20. He has taught at the ASL since 1933 and was a Guggenheim Fellow in 1935 and 1936. He was a Life Member of the ASL; president since 1947 of Artists Equity Association, a member of the Society of Painters, Sculptors and Gravers, the American Etchers Society and an Honorary Associate of the NIAL. See the 75th Anniv. Cat., ASL.

KUNTZE, Edward J.   d. 1910. He was trained mostly in Stockholm. See Appleton; Hamilton.

KURTZ, William.   d. Dec. 5, 1904. See G&W.

KURZ, Louis.   b. 1833 according to G&W but in 1834 in MF; d. March 21, 1921. He was also a scene painter and lithographer. See G&W.

KYLE, Joseph.   b. in Ohio; d. NYC. He was also a panoramist and figure painter. See Rutledge, PA; Cowdrey, NAD; Cowdrey, AA & AAU; G&W.

LABATUT, [Isador]. He was also a portraitist and painter of transparencies. See G&W.

LACHAISE, Gaston. b. March 19, 1882 in Paris; d. Oct. 18, 1935 in NYC. He was also a sculptor. At 13 he entered the Ecole Bernard Palissy and studied with Monet and Aube. Then he went to the Ecole des Beaux-Arts and worked in the atelier of Gabriel Jules Thomas and later worked for Rene Lalique. He came to Boston in 1906 and for seven years worked in the studio of Henry Hudson Kitson. He moved to NYC in 1912 where he worked for Manship and exhibited in 1918. He then moved to Georgetown, Me. in 1923. Among his works are: frieze (A.T.&T. Bldg., NYC); two peacocks (Deering Estate, Miami, Fla.); Dolphins (U. of Neb.; the Hackley Art Gall., Muskegon, Mich.; Whitney Mus. of Amer. Art); Seal (Whitney Mus. of Amer. Art; Phillips Memorial Art Gall., Washington, D.C.); Sea Gull (U.S. Coast Guard Memorial, Arlington National Cemetery); Panels (RCA and International Bldgs., Rockefeller Center); Aphrodite (Toledo Art Museum); Standing Woman (Whitney Mus. of Amer. Art); Walking Woman (Honolulu Academy of Arts); La Force Eternelle (Smith College Mus. of Art); Swans (Brookgreen Gardens); additional heads (Addison Gallery of American Art, Andover, Mass.; Brooklyn Mus.; Newark Mus.; Whitney Mus. of Amer. Art; Wichita Art Mus.; Lawrence Art Mus., Williams College). He exhibited one sculpture at the 1913 Armory Show. See the cat. of the 1963 Armory Show; *Brookgreen Gardens I.*

LADD, Anna Coleman. b. July 15, 1878 in Bryn Mawr, Pa. according to *Brookgreen Gardens I* but in Philadelphia in MF. Among her works are: Sun God Fountain, Leaping Sprites (Manchester-by-the-Sea, Mass.); Triton Babies (Boston Public Gardens); Studebaker Memorial (South Bend, Ind.); Aldrich Memorial (Grand Rapids, Mich.); Lotus Flower, bronze (Brookgreen Gardens; Phila. Print Club); portrait bust (Gardner Collection, Boston). She is a member of the NSS and a chevalier of the Legion of Honor. See *Brookgreen Gardens I.*

LAESSLE, Albert. Sculptor. b. March 28, 1877. He was also a pupil of Thomas Anshutz. Returning to Philadelphia from study abroad he worked with Grafly for several years and was an instructor at the PAFA 1921-1939. He is represented in the collections of Brookgreen Gardens, MMA, PAFA and others and did the monument to General Pennypacker (Logan Square, Philadelphia). He is a member of the Societe des Amis de la Medaille d'Art, Brussels and of the NA, NSS and NIAL. See *Brookgreen Gardens I.*

LA FARGE, John. b. March 31, 1835 in NYC; d. Nov. 14, 1910. He was an advisory director and honorary member of the ASL, a member, Society of American Artists, honorary president, Society of Mural Painters, member, NIAL, chevalier, French Legion of Honor and a member, American Institute of Architects, National Arts Club and the Century Association. He also painted still life and illustrated books. See 75th Anniv. Cat., ASL; G&W; Hamilton.

LAKEMAN, N[athaniel]. b. 1756; d. after 1830. See G&W.

LAKEY, [Mrs.] Emily Jane. b. June 22, 1837 at Quincy, N.Y. according to G&W but MF says in N.J.; d. Oct. 24, 1896 at Cranford, N.J. She was a genre painter. See G&W.

LAMBDIN, George C[ochran]. b. Pittsburgh according to G&W but MF says in Philadelphia; d. Jan. 28, 1896. He was a National Academician. See G&W.

LAMBDIN, James R[eid]. b. May 10, 1807; d. Jan. 31, 1889. He was also a miniaturist. See DAB; Rutledge, PA; Cowdrey, NAD; Cowdrey, AA & AAU; G&W.

LANDER, Louisa. b. Sept. 1, 1826; d. Nov. 14, 1923 in Washington, D.C. See G&W.

LANE, Thomas H[enry]. b. Feb. 24, 1815 according to G&W and Rutledge, PA but in 1814 in MF, in Philadelphia; d. Sept. 27, 1900. He was a portraitist and miniaturist. See Rutledge, PA; G&W.

LANG, George S. He was still living in Delaware Co., Pa. in 1883 [erroneously 1833 in MF]. See G&W.

LANG, Louis. b. March 29, 1814 in Wurtemberg, Germany according to G&W and Rutledge but in 1812 in MF; d. May

6, 1893 in NYC. He was also a miniaturist and genre painter. See Rutledge, PA; Cowdrey, NAD; Cowdrey, AA & AAU; G&W; m.c., FARL.

LANGTON, Berenice F.   d. 1960. m.c. Met 5.

LANMAN, Charles.   b. June 14, 1819 in Monroe, Mich.; d. March 4, 1895 in Georgetown, D.C. He was a landscapist, a pupil of Asher Durand and was for a while Daniel Webster's secretary. He published *The Private Life of Daniel Webster* and wrote and edited several other books and articles. See DAB; G&W; Hamilton; Cowdrey, AA & AAU; Cowdrey, NAD.

LATHROP, Gertrude K[atherine].   b. Dec. 24, 1896. She also studied with Charles Grafly at Gloucester. She shares a stuido in Albany with her sister, Dorothy Pulis Lathrop, who is a painter and a writer and illustrator of children's books. Her mother was a painter of landscapes and still life. Among her works are: Nancy Lee (National Collection of Fine Arts, Washington, D.C.); King Penguin—used as gateposts (Locust Valley, L.I. and Beverly, Mass.); World War Memorial (Albany); Sammy Houston (Brookgreen Gardens; Albany Public Library, Children's Room; Children's Room, Houston, Tex. Public Library); Great White Heron, Bozie, Saluki, Faun (Brookgreen Gardens). She is a member of the Ntl. Assn. of Women Painters and Sculptors, the NSS and the NA. See *Brookgreen Gardens I.*

LATILLA, Eugenio [Honorius].   b. 1808; d. Oct. 30, 1861 at Chappaqua, N.Y. He was also a figure painter. See Cowdrey, NAD; G&W.

LAUBER, Joseph.   d. Oct. 19, 1948.— m.c., NYPL.

LAUNTIZ, Robert E[berhard].   b. Nov. 4, 1806 in Riga, Latvia according to G&W but MF says in Russia; d. Dec. 13, 1870 in NYC. See DAB; Cowdrey, NAD; Cowdrey, AA & AAU; G&W.

LAURENT, Robert.   b. June 29, 1890 in Concarneau, France. He was brought to NYC when he was 12 by the painter and writer Hamilton Easter Field and in 1908 went to Rome with Field and Maurice Stern. He was instructed by them and also at the British Academy and by an apprenticeship to Giuseppe Dorati, wood carver and frame maker. He has taught at the Ogunquit School of Art, Me., the ASL, Brooklyn Inst. of Arts and Sciences, and the Corcoran Art School, Washington, D.C. Among his works are: Duck (Newark Mus., Whitney Mus. of American Art); Rabbit (Whitney Mus. of American Art); Pigeon (Vassar College); The Waves, The Bather (Brooklyn Mus.); Goose Girl (Radio City Music Hall); Thé Awakening (Whitney Mus. of American Art); relief (Federal Trade Commission Bldg., Washington, D.C.); relief (P.O., Garfield, N.J.); Spanning the Continent (Fairmount Park, Phila.); Kneeling Figure (Whitney Mus. of American Art); Goose (Brookgreen Gardens). He is a member of the American Soc. of Painters, Sculptors and Gravers, the Sculptors' Guild, Modern Artists of America, an associate of the NSS, vicepres., Salons of America and president, Hamilton Easter Field Art Foundation. See *Brookgreen Gardens I.*

LAURIE, Alexander [given as Lawrie or Lourie in G&W and Cowdrey, NAD and as LAWRIE in Rutledge, PA]. He is the Alexander Lawrie, Jr. listed by MF.

LAWMAN, Jasper Holman.   d. April 4, 1906. See G&W.

LAWRENCE, Charles B.   See Rutledge, PA; G&W.

LAWRENCE or LAURENCE, Samuel [also this way in Cowdrey, NAD; given as Laurence only in G&W and Rutledge, PA]. b. at Guildford, Surrey, England; d. Feb. 28, 1884 in London. See Cowdrey, NAD; Rutledge, PA; G&W.

LAWRENCE, William R[oderick].   b. March 3, 1829 at Hartford, Conn.; d. Oct. 9, 1856. He was a figure painter. See G&W.

LAWRIE, Alexander, Jr. [G&W, Cowdrey and Rutledge omit the Jr.].   b. Feb. 25, 1828; d. Feb. 15, 1917. He was also a landscapist and genre painter and is also listed in MF as Alexander Laurie. See DAB; Rutledge, PA; Cowdrey, NAD; G&W.

LAWSON, Alexander.   b. Dec. 18, 1773; d. Aug. 22, 1846. He was the father of Helen E. and Oscar A. Lawson. See DAB; Rutledge, PA; G&W.

LAWSON, Ernest.   d. Dec. 18, 1939. He studied at the ASL, with J. Alden Weir and John H. Twachtman and exhibited with the "Eight" and also at the Armory Show in 1913. Five of his oil paintings were exhibited at the AAAL, Dec. 11, 1964-Jan. 10, 1965. He was a member of the NIAL. See the cat. of the 1963 Armory Show; 75th Anniv. Cat., ASL; cat. of the AAAL, *Robert Henri and His Circle.*

LAWSON, Helen E.   See Rutledge, PA; G&W.

LAWSON, Oscar A.   b. Aug. 7, 1813; d. Sept. 6, 1854. He was also a portrait and landscape painter. See Rutledge, PA; G&W.

LAWSON, Thomas B[ayley].   b. Jan. 13, 1807; d. Jan. 4, 1888 in Lowell, Mass. He was also a miniaturist. See G&W.

LAZARUS, Jacob H[art].   He was also a figure painter. See Cowdrey, NAD; Rutledge, PA; G&W.

LE CLEAR, Thomas.   b. March 11, 1818; d. Nov. 26, 1882 in Rutherford Park, N.J. He was also a genre painter. See DAB; Cowdrey, NAD; Cowdrey, AA & AAU; G&W.

LEE, Arthur.   b. 1881; d. 1961. He exhibited four sets of drawings and four scultures at the 1913 Armory Show. See the cat. of the 1963 Armory Show.

LEHMAN, George.   See Rutledge, PA; G&W.

LEIGH, William Robinson.   William Robinson Leigh was born on a plantation in West Virginia, September 23, 1866. He started sketching at an early age and won a prize from the Corcoran of Washington when he was about 12 years old. He attended the Maryland Institute for three years and the Royal Academy in Munich for four years, after which he spent six years in Munich starving and painting. However, he won several medals from the Academy for work on Cycloramas. He returned to the United States in 1896, and made several western trips painting for Scribner's Magazine. In 1906 Leigh began to paint western subjects in earnest. He was an excellent draftsman, and in 1933 published a book, *The Western Pony,* in which he expressed his views on animal repre-

sentation. Leigh died March 11, 1955, shortly after a one-man show at the Grand Central Art Galleries featured one hundred of his paintings. His work can be found in the Woolaroc Museum, Bartlesville, Oklahoma, and the Gilcrease Institute at Tulsa, Oklahoma. Articles about Leigh are contained in The Mentor, Volume 3, No. 9 for July 15, 1915; The Mentor, Volume 15, No. 6 for July, 1927; Montana Magazine, Volume 6, No. 1, Winter, 1956, an article by Michael Kennedy; and Taft, *Artists and Illustrators of the Old West.*—Karl Yost.

LEIGHTON, Scott.   b. 1849.—m.c. 2, NYPL.

LEMET, L[ouis].   b. *c.* 1779; d. Sept. 30, 1832 in NYC. He was a crayon portraitist and engraver. G&W say he was a partner of St. Memin but m.c., 2, N-YHS says that he was only a "self-styled" partner. See G&W.

LENEY, William Satchwell.   b. Jan. 16, 1769; d. Dec. 26, 1831. See DAB; Cowdrey, AA & AAU; Rutledge, PA; G&W.

LENTELLI, Leo.   b. Oct. 29, 1879. He practiced his profession in Rome before coming to the U.S. in 1903. He was a studio assistant to several sculptors in NYC and worked with Calder on the Panama-Pacific Exposition, staying in San Francisco until 1918. Among his works are: ornament (Orpheum Theatre, St. Louis); architectural decorations (Straus Bank and Steinway Bldg., NYC); Bagnante, Diana and Leda for the Park Central Hotel, NYC; Cardinal Gibbons (Washington, D.C.); crowning features (Italian and International Bldgs., Rockefeller Center, NYC); Faun (Boca Raton Club and Brookgreen Gardens). There is a collection of his works at U. of Iowa. He is an Associate of the NA and a member of the ALNY. See *Brookgreen Gardens I.*

LEPELLETIER.   He is probably Michael Lepelletier. See G&W.

LESLIE, Anne.   b. 1792; d. after 1860. She was the sister of Eliza Leslie. See Cowdrey, AA & AAU; Cowdrey, NAD; Rutledge, PA; G&W.

LESLIE, Charles Robert.   b. Oct. 19, 1794; d. May 5, 1859. He was a portraitist, literary, genre and historical painter and the brother of Anne and Eliza Leslie. See

DAB; Rutledge, PA; Cowdrey, AA & AAU; Cowdrey, NAD; G&W.

LESLIE, Eliza. b. Nov. 15, 1787; d. Jan. 1, 1858. She was the sister of Charles Robert and Anne Leslie and made drawings, some of which served as illustrations for her own books. See DAB; G&W; Hamilton.

LESUEUR, Alexander Charles [given as Charles Alexander Lesueur in Webster's, Charles Alexandre Lesueur in G&W and as Charles Alexander Le Sueur in Rutledge, PA]. b. Jan. 1, 1778 at [Le] Havre de Grace, now Le Havre, France; d. Dec. 12, 1846 at Le Havre. He was also an illustrator, engraver and lithographer. See DAB; Rutledge, PA; G&W.

LEUTZE, Emanuel [Gottlieb]. b. May 24, 1816 at Gmund according to G&W but MF says in Emingen, Wurttemberg, Germay; d. July 18, 1868. He was also a portraitist and was a National Academician. See DAB; Rutledge, PA; Cowdrey, NAD; G&W; Hamilton; Barker, p. 465.

LEWIS, Edmond [Edmund in G&W, Rutledge, PA and Cowdrey, NAD] Darch. b. Oct. 17, 1835 in Philadelphia; d. Aug. 12, 1910 in Philadelphia. See DAB; Rutledge, PA; Cowdrey, NAD; G&W.

LEWIS, J[ames] O[tto]. b. Feb. 3, 1799 in Philadelphia; d. 1858 in NYC. He was also a landscapist. See G&W.

LEWIS, W[illiam]. b. 1788 in Salem. He was also a miniaturist. See G&W.

LEYENDECKER, Joseph Christian. d. July 26, 1951.—m.c., NYPL.

LIE, Jonas. d. 1940. He exhibited five oil paintings at the 1913 Armory Show. See the cat. of the 1963 Armory Show.

LINCOLN, James Sullivan. b. May 13, 1811; d. Jan. 18, 1888 in Providence, R.I. He was also an engraver. See G&W.

LINEN, George. b. Greenlaw, Scotland. See Cowdrey, NAD; Cowdrey, AA & AAU; Rutledge, PA; G&W.

LINSON, Corain K. d. 1934.—m.c., FARL.

LINTON, Frank B. d. 1944.—m.c., FARL.

LINTON, William J. He came to the U.S. in 1866 according to G&W, Webster's and Hamilton, not in 1867 as in MF. See DAB; Hamilton; G&W.

LION, Jules. b. c. 1816 in France. He was also a portraitist and miniaturist. See G&W.

LIVERMORE, Mrs. [Mary Spear (Mason)]. b. 1806. G&W say she was active in 1846 and 1847 on the basis of exhibition records but MF says in 1847 and 1848. See G&W.

LIVINGSTON, Harriet. b. 1786; d. 1824. See G&W.

LOBER, Georg J[ohn]. b. Nov. 7, 1892 according to Brookgreen Gardens I but 1891 in MF. He studied at the NA and Beaux-Arts Inst. of Design and with H. A. MacNeil, and Evelyn Longman. Among his works are: groups of medals (National Mus., Copenhagen, Denmark and Administration des Monnaies et de Medailles, Paris); Hans Christian Andersen (Odense, Denmark); baptistery (First Baptist Church, Plainfield, N.J.); St. Peter, St. Paul (Church of our Lady of Consolation, Pawtucket, R.I.); crucifix (Jefferson Davis Highway, Aquia, Va.); Eve (MMA); Faun (Brookgreen Gardens). He is a member of the NA, NSS, Allied Artists of American, ALNY and head of the sculpture department, Grand Central School of Art. See Brookgreen Gardens I.

LONDONER, A[my]. d. 1953. She exhibited four pastels at the 1913 Armory Show. See the cat. of the 1963 Armory Show.

LONGACRE, James Barton. b. Aug. 11, 1794; d. Jan. 1, 1869. See DAB; G&W.

LONGMAN, Evelyn B[eatrice]. b. Nov. 21, 1874. She came to NYC in 1900 and assisted MacNeil and Konti and also entered French's studio. Among her works are: Victory (Brookgreen Gardens; Art Inst. of Chicago; John Herron Art Inst., Indianapolis; MMA; Toledo Mus. of Art); Bacchante Head (Norton Gallery and School of Art, W. Palm Beach, Fla.; John Herron Art Inst., Indianapolis); The Future (Parthenon, Nashville, Tenn.); Electricity (top of the A.T.&T. Bldg., NYC); Edison (Deutsches Museum in Munich); John Wainwright (Hampton Inst.); Monument to pioneers of Industry (Hartford); frieze, Post Office and Federal Bldg. (Hartford); Boy and Fish Fountain (Rockefeller Estate, Pocantico Hills, N.Y.). She is a member of the Conn. Academy of Fine Arts and the American Numismatic Society. See *Brookgreen Gardens I*

LOOP, Henry A[ugustus]. b. Sept. 9, 1831 at Hillsdale, N.Y. according to G&W but MF says in Conn.; d. Oct. 20, 1895. See DAB; Cowdrey, NAD; Rutledge, PA; G&W.

LOOP, Mrs. Henry A. [Jeannette Shepherd Harrison]. b. March 5, 1840; d. April 17, 1909 at Saratoga, N.Y. according to G&W but MF says in NYC. She was also a figure painter. See G&W.

LORD, Phoebe G[riffin]. b. 1831 according to G&W but MF says 1797, in Connecticut. See G&W.

LORENZANI, Arthur E[manuel]. b. Feb. 12, 1886 according to *Brookgreen Gardens I*, but 1885 in MF, in Carrara, Italy. He attended the Reale Accademia di Belle Arti, Carrara, Instituti di Belle Arti, Rome and came to the U.S. in 1913. Among his works are: The Slinger (Gallery of Modern Art, Carrara); Golden Age (Brookgreen Gardens). He is a member of the Staten Island Art Assn. and the ALNY. See *Brookgreen Gardens I*.

LORING, Francis William. He was a landscript. See G&W.

LOSSING, Benson J[ohn]. b. Feb. 12, 1813; d. June 3, 1891. He learned wood engraving from J. A. Adams, the engraver for "The Poughkeepsie Casket" of which Lossing was the editor. He opened his own wood engraving shop in NYC in 1838 and started the work of illustrating his "Pictorial Field-Book of the Revolution" in 1848. He cut early blocks himself but later gave work to other members of the firm of Lossing and Barritt, and confined himself to drawing. See DAB; Hamilton; G&W.

LOUD, Mrs. H. C. See Rutledge, PA; G&W.

LOVETT, Robert. b. *c.* 1796-97 in NYC. See Cowdrey, AA & AAU; G&W.

LOW, Mary Fairchild. d. May 23, 1946.—m.c., NYPL.

LOW, Will H[icock]. d. 1932.—m.c. Met 2.

LUKS, George B. b. Aug. 13, 1867; d. Oct. 30, 1933 in NYC. He taught at the ASL 1920-24 and also lectured there. He is a member, Society of Portrait Painters; N.Y. Water Color Society; Boston Art Club; American Painters, Sculptors and Gravers and his work is at the MMA; Delgado Museum, New Orleans; Milwaukee Art Institute; Detroit Art Institute; Cleveland Museum; Harrison Gallery, L.A.; Phillips Memorial Gallery, Wash., D.C.; NYPL; Barnes Foundation. He designed library and murals (Neco Allen Hotel, Pottsville, Pa.). He exhibited three oil paintings and three drawings at the 1913 Armory Show and six of his works were exhibited at the AAAL, Dec. 11, 1964—Jan. 10, 1965. See 75th Anniv. Cat., ASL; cat. of the 1963 Armory Show; cat. of the AAAL, *Robert Henri and His Circle*.

LUND, F. See Theodore Lund.

LUND, H. See Theodore Lund.

LUND, Theodore. He exhibited at the NA in 1836 as H. Lund and in 1837 as F. Lund. See Cowdrey, NAD; Cowdrey, AA & AAU; G&W.

LUNDBERG, A. F. He exhibited one oil painting at the 1913 Armory Show. See the cat. of the 1963 Armory Show.

LUNGREN, Ferdinand Harvey. d. 1932.—m.c. 2, N-YHS.

LUPTON, Mrs. [Frances Platt Townsend]. She was an Associate of the NA. See G&W.

LYBRAND, J. G&W think that this may be Jacob Lybrand who was engraving in Philadelphia in 1828-29. See G&W.

LYMAN, S[ylvester] S. b. Sept. 24, 1813 in Easthampton, Mass. See G&W.

MAAS, Jacob. b. *c.* 1800 in Pennsylvania. See G&W.

McCARTAN, Edward. b. Aug. 16, 1879 in Albany; d. Sept. 20, 1947 according to the m.c., NYPL. He studied with Herbert Adams at the Pratt Institute, with George Grey Barnard and Hermon MacNeil at the ASL and with Injalbert at the Ecole des Beaux-Arts, Paris. He was also assistant to MacNeil and Adams before taking his own studio in NYC in 1913. Among his works are: The Kiss, Piping Pan (Albright Art Gallery, Buffalo); Girl Drinking from a Shell (Reading Public Mus. and Art Gallery); The Bather (PAFA); Eugene Field Memorial (Chicago); clock (N.Y. Central Bldg., NYC; panels (N.J. Telephone Co. Bldg., Newark, N.J.); pediment (Dept. of Labor and Interstate Commerce Bldg., Washington, D.C.); Dionysius (Brookgreen Gardens); Diana (Brookgreen Gardens; Fogg Art Museum, Cambridge, Mass.; Canajoharie Art Gallery; MMA). He was a member of the Concord Art Assn., the NA and the NIAL. See *Brookgreen Gardens I*.

MacCHESNEY, Clara T.   She was in London 1860-1928.—m.c., FARL.

McCLUSKEY, W[illiam].   He was a steel engraver. See G&W.

McCOMAS, Francis.   d. Dec. 28, 1938 per N.Y. Times, Dec. 29, 1938. He exhibited three oil paintings at the 1913 Armory Show. See the cat. of the 1963 Armory Show.

MacCORD, Charles William.   Misindexed after Mary MacCord.

MacCORD, Mary.   Misindexed after Robert Lee MacCameron.

MacDONALD, James Wilson Alexander. b. Aug. 25, 1824; d. Aug. 14, 1908 in Yonkers, N.Y. See DAB; G&W.

McENTEE, Jervis.   b. July 14, 1828; d. Jan. 27, 1891 at Rondout, N.Y. according to G&W, Cowdrey and Rutledge but in 1890 in MF. He was popular as a draftsman for wood engravers in the '60's and '70's. See DAB; Cowdrey, NAD; Cowdrey, AA & AAU; Rutledge, PA; G&W; Hamilton.

McFEE, Henry L.   b. April 14, 1886 in St. Louis, Mo.; d. March 21, 1953 per m.c., NYPL. He studied at the ASL in 1909 and was an Associate of the NA; member, NIAL; Society of American Painters, Sculptors and Gravers; Woodstock Art Association; associate professor at the Scripps College and at the Graduate School, Claremont, Calif. He is represented in the permanent collections of the Brooklyn Museum; Albright Art Gallery; Cleve-

land Museum of Arts; Detroit Institute of Arts; Corcoran Gallery; Whitney Museum of American Art; MMA; Museums of St. Louis, Cincinnati, Indianapolis, Toledo, San Antonio, Kansas City, Richmond. See 75th Anniv. Cat., ASL.

McGIBBON, James.   He was also a miniaturist. See G&W.

McKAY.   He was active '1785-91. See G&W.

McKENZIE, R[obert] Tait.   b. May 26, 1867 in Almonte, Ontario; d. April 28, 1938 in Philadelphia. He was trained and employed as a physician and in 1904 came to the U.S. as professor and director of the department of physical education at the U. of Pa., a post he held until 1930, when he became a research professor in physical education. He wrote several books on this subject. Among his works are: The Ice Bird (Amherst College); The Onslaught (U. of Pa.); The Flying Sphere (City Art Museum, St. Louis); The Competitor (National Gallery of Canada, Ottawa); The Joy of Effort (Stadium, Stockholm, Sweden); The Youthful Franklin (Brookgreen Gardens; U. of N.C., Chapel Hill; Newark Museum); Dean West (Princeton U:). Many of his works are in the Yale U. Art Gallery. See *Brookgreen Gardens I*.

MACKINTOSH, Miss S. B.   See Rutledge, PA; G&W.

MacKNIGHT, Dodge.   d. 1950. He exhibited four watercolors at the 1913 Armory Show. See the cat. of the 1963 Armory Show.

MacMONNIES, Frederick [William]. b. Sept. 28, 1863; d. March 22, 1937 in NYC. He also studied with Mercie. After winning the grand prize, Paris Exposition 1900, he stopped modeling for a while and painted portraits. Among his works are: Columbian Fountain (Chicago Exposition, 1893); Sir Harry Vane (Boston Public Library); Bacchante and Infant Faun (exhib. MMA, and Luxembourg, Paris); Princeton Battle Monument; Truth and Inspiration (Fountain, NYPL); Pioneer Monument to Kit Carson (Denver); Civic Virtue (City Hall Park, NYC); Monument to Battle of the Marne (near Meaux, France); two groups of Rearing Horses (Brookgreen Gardens and MMA). He is a member of the AAAL and a commander, Legion of Honor. See *Brookgreen Gardens I.*

MacNEIL, Hermon Atkins.   b. Feb. 27, 1866. He studied at the Mass. Normal Art School, Boston and then went to Paris in 1888 and studied with Chapu at the Academie Julian and with Falguiere at the Ecole des Beaux-Arts. Upon his return to the U.S. he worked with Martiny for the Columbian Exposition and settled at Chicago. He was at Rome 1896-1899 and taught in several art schools in NYC, where he also had a studio. In 1919-1920 he was at the American Academy at Rome as a visiting professor. Among his works are: A Primitive Chant (MMA); The Coming of the White Man (Portland, Ore.); a fountain (Louisiana Purchase Expos.); The Adventurous Bowman (Column, Panama-Pacific Expos.); statues (Capitol, Hartford, Conn.); Ezra Cornell (Cornell U.); frieze (Missouri State Capitol); pylons (Soldiers' and Sailors' Monument, Philadelphia); The Pilgrim Fathers (Waterbury, Conn.); statue (George Rogers Clark Memorial Vincennes, Ind.); Monument to the Confederate Defenders of Fort Sumter (Charleston, S.C.); several medals, Pan-American Expos., 1901; 1931 issue of the Society of Medalists; 1916 U.S. quarter; Sun Vow (Brookgreen Gardens; Baltimore Museum of Art; Albright Art Gallery, Buffalo; Art Institute, Chicago; Wadsworth Atheneum, Hartford; Montclair Art Museum; MMA; Museum of Arts and Sciences, Norfolk, Va.; City Art Museum, St. Louis; Corcoran Gallery of Art, Washington, D.C.). He was a member of the ALNY and the AAAL. See *Brookgreen Gardens I.*

McNULTY, William C.   b. 1884; d. 1963 per m.c. Met 5.

MacRAE, Elmer L[ivingston].   d. 1955. He exhibited four oil paintings and six pastels at the 1913 Armory Show. See the cat. of the 1963 Armory Show.

McRAE, John C.   See Cowdrey, NAD; G&W.

MAGER, Gus.   b. 1878; d. 1956. He exhibited two oil paintings at the 1913 Armory Show. See the cat. of the 1963 Armory Show.

MAGRATH, William.   b. March 20, 1838 in Cork Ireland; d. at Brighton, N.Y.

He was a landscapist and genre painter and a student of the Cork Art School. His first studio in America was in NYC and he became a member of the NA in 1876. He went to England in 1879 but returned to the U.S. in 1883 and settled in Washington, D.C. Among his works is: "On the Old Sod," painted in 1879. See G&W; Appleton; Hamilton.

MAIN, William.   b. 1796; d. in NYC. He was a National Academician. See Cowdrey, NAD; Cowdrey, AA & AAU; G&W.

MAJOR, James Parsons.   d. Oct. 17, 1900. See G&W.

MALBONE, Edward G[reene].   b. Aug., 1777. See G&W.

MALCOLM, James Peller.   b. Aug., 1767; d. April 5, 1815 in London. He was also a landscape draftsman. See DAB; G&W.

MANIGAULT, E[dward] Middleton. b. 1889 according to the cat. of the 1913 Armory Show but in 1887 in MF; d. 1922. He exhibited two oil paintings at the 1913 Armory Show. See the cat. of the 1963 Armory Show.

MANSHIP, Paul.   b. Dec. 25, 1885. He studied at the School of Fine Arts in St. Paul and got experience in the studios of Solon Borglum and Isidore Konti. He also worked at the PAFA under Charles Grafly. In 1935 he exhibited at the Tate Gallery, London. Among his works are: Playfulness (Detroit Inst. of Arts and Minneapolis Inst. of Arts); Little Brother (Detroit Inst. of Arts; Cincinnati Art Museum); Lyric Muse (Cincinnati Art Museum); Centaur and Dryad (Fogg Art Museum, Cambridge, Mass.; Detroit Inst. of Arts; MMA; Smith College; City Art Museum, St. Louis); Pauline (MMA); garden sculpture (McCormick Estate, Lake Forest, Ill.); Spirit of the Chase, Indian Hunter, Pronghorn Antelope (Pratt Estate, Glen Coe, L.I.); Infant Hercules (fountain, Amer. Acad. at Rome); Flight of Night (Detroit Inst. of Arts; Wadsworth Atheneum, Hartford, Conn.; Toledo Mus. of Art; Corcoran Gallery of Art, Wash., D.C.; Art Inst. of Chicago; Cleveland Mus. of Art; Detroit Inst. of Arts; Musee de Luxembourg, Paris; R.I. School of Design); panels (N.Y.T. & T. Bldg.); memorial to J. P.

Morgan (MMA); Spear Thrower (Dayton Art Inst.; Peabody Inst.; Yale U. Art Gallery); Prometheus Fountain (Rockefeller Center, NYC; The Cycle of Life (Phillips Acad., Andover, Mass.); Celestial Sphere (Woodrow Wilson Memorial, Geneva, Switz.); Paul Rainey Memorial Gateway (N.Y. Zoological Park); Samuel Osgood (P.O. Dept. Bldg., Wash., D.C.); Lincoln (Fort Wayne, Ind.); Hercules Upholding the Heavens (Mus. of Fine Arts, Houston, Texas); Actaeon, Diana (Brookgreen Gardens; Addison Gallery of American Art, Andover, Mass.; Ball State Teachers' College, Muncie, Ind.; Carnegie Inst., Pittsburgh; Norton Gallery and School of Art, W. Palm Beach, Fla.; Art Gallery, Toronto). There is a large collection of his works at Brookgreen Gardens. He is a member of the AAAL, the NIAL, the National Academy of Fine Arts of Argentina, Century Club, National Arts Club, a corresponding member of the Institute de France, a fellow of the American Academy in Rome and a chevalier of the Legion of Honor. See 75th Anniv. Cat., ASL; *Brookgarden Gardens* I.

MAPES, James Jay.   b. May 29, 1806 in Maspeth, L.I., N.Y.; d. Jan. 19, 1866 in NYC. He was an Honorary Member, amateur, of the NA. See DAB; Cowdrey, NAD; Rutledge, Pa; G&W.

MARCHANT, Edward D[alton].   b. Dec. 16, 1806; d. Aug. 15, 1887. He was also a miniaturist. See Cowdrey, NAD; Cowdrey, AA & AAU; G&W.

MARCHANT, G. W.   See G. W. Merchant.

MARE, John.   b. c. 1739 in NYC. See G&W.

MARIN, John.   His birth date is given as 1870 in *Armory Show, 50th Anniversary Exhibition, 1913-1963* and Milton W. Brown, *The Story of the Armory Show* but as 1875 in MF; d. 1953. He also studied at the Stevens Institute of Technology, the ASL, and in Paris. He has had one-man shows in N.Y. annually since 1909, exhibited at the MMA in 1936 and also at the 1913 Armory Show where he displayed ten watercolors. He is represented in the collections of the Museum of Modern Art; MMA; Brooklyn Museum; San Francisco Museum of Art; Phillips Memorial Gallery.

See 75th Anniv. Cat., ASL; cat. of the 1963 Armory Show.

MARKS, William.   Misindexed after Louis Mark.

MARSH, Henry.   See Hamilton.

MARSHALL, William Edgar.   b. June 30, 1837; d. Aug. 29, 1906. See DAB; G&W.

MARSIGLIA, G[h]erlando.   d. Sept. 4, 1850 in NYC. The m.c., FARL states that he did the portrait of General Von Steuben after Ralph Earl and not Robert Edge Pine as in MF. See Cowdrey, AA & AAU; Cowdrey, NAD; Rutledge, PA; G&W.

MARTIN, Charles.   b. 1820; d. April 5, 1906 in London. He was also a landscapist. See Cowdrey, NAD; G&W.

MARTIN, Homer D[odge].   b. Oct. 28, 1836; d. Feb. 12, 1897 in St. Paul, Minn. He was also an illustrator; see Cowdrey, NAD; Rutledge, PA; G&W; Hamilton.

MARTIN, J[ohn] B[lennerhasset].   b. Sept. 5, 1797 in Bandon, County Cork, Ireland; d. Oct. 22, 1857 at Richmond, Va. He was also a portraitist and miniaturist and m.c. Met 3 states that the quarto portrait by him of John Randolph is at the MMA. See G&W.

MARTIN, Robert.   b. Scotland. He was a steel engraver. See G&W.

MARTIN, William A. K.   He was also a landscapist and historical painter. See Rutledge, PA; G&W.

MASE, C[arolyn] C.   d. 1948. She exhibited one pastel at the 1913 Armory Show. See the cat. of the 1963 Armory Show.

MASON, Abraham John.   b. April 4, 1794 in London. He studied wtih Robert Branston in England. See Cowdrey, NAD; Cowdrey, AA & AAU; Rutledge, PA; G&W; Hamilton.

MASON, C. D.   d. July, 1915 at Mineola, L.I. See G&W.

MASON, George.   d. 1773 in Boston. See G&W.

MASON, Jonathan, Jr.   b. c. 1795; d. 1884. See G&W.

MASON, William G.   He was also a landscapist. See Rutledge, PA; G&W.

MATTESON, H[arrison] Tomkins. This is the correct spelling of the name according to G&W and m.c. Met 2 which says that he signed himself as H. Tomkins Matteson. b. May 9, 1813; d. Feb. 2, 1884 at Sherburne, N.Y. He also did illustrations, most of which were engraved by Anderson, and was a genre and portrait painter as well. See DAB; Barker, p. 483; G&W; Hamilton; Cowdrey, NAD; Cowdrey, AA & AAU.

MAUGH, Max.   This entry is marked as incorrect in m.c. Met. 4.

MAURER, Alfred H.   There is a second entry on him which is misindexed after Cornelia Field Maury and repeats the first. d. 1932. He exhibited four oil paintings at the 1913 Armory Show. See the cat. of the 1963 Armory Show.

MAURER, Louis.   b. Feb. 21, 1832 in Biebrich-on-the-Rhine, Germany; d. July 19, 1932 in NYC. He was also a lithographer. See G&W.

MAVERICK, Emily.   b. April 3, 1803 in NYC; d. 1850. She was an Associate of the NA and also a lithographer. See G&W.

MAVERICK, Maria A. and Emily.   See the individual entries for Maria Anne Maverick and Emily Maverick.

MAVERICK, Maria A[nn].   b. May 15, 1805 in NYC; d. Jan. 12, 1832 in NYC. She was also a lithographer and an Associate of the NA. See G&W.

MAVERICK, Peter.   b. Oct. 22, 1780; d. June 7, 1831 in NYC. He was the brother of Samuel Maverick and the father of Maria A., Peter, Jr. and Emily Maverick. He was also a National Academician. See DAB; Cowdrey, NAD; Cowdrey, AA & AAU; G&W.

MAVERICK, Peter, Jr.   b. Oct. 26, 1809; d. Sept. 6, 1845. See G&W.

MAVERICK, Peter Rushton.   b. April 11, 1755 in NYC; d. Dec. 12, 1811 in NYC according to G&W but MF says in Newark, N.J. See G&W.

MAVERICK, Samuel.   b. June 5, 1789 in NYC; d. Dec. 4, 1845 in NYC. He was the brother of Peter Maverick. See G&W.

MAY, Edward Harrison.   b. Croydon, England; d. May 17, 1887 in Paris. He was a portraitist, historical and genre painter and an Associate of the NA. See DAB; Cowdrey, NAD; Cowdrey, A & AAU; Rutledge, PA; G&W; Hamilton.

MAYER, Constant.   b. Oct. 3, 1829 according to G&W and Rutledge, PA but in 1832 in MF, at Besancon, France; d. May 12, 1911 in Paris. See DAB; Benezit; Rutledge, PA; Cowdrey, NAD; G&W.

MAYER, Frank [also Frank in Rutledge, PA but Francis in G&W] Blackwell.   b. Dec. 27, 1827; d. July 28, 1899 at Annapolis, Md. He was also a historical and ethnological painter. See Rutledge, PA; G&W.

MAYOR, Harriet Hyatt.   b. April 25, 1868. She is the sister of Anna Hyatt Huntington. She also received instruction from the painter Ernest L. Major and the watercolorist, Ross Turner. Among her works are: Shouting Boy (Mariner's Museum Park, Newport News); Admiral Goldsborough (Annapolis); her sister, Anna Hyatt Huntington (Collection of the AAAL, N.Y.); memorial tablet to Alpheus Hyatt (Marine Bio. Lab., Woods Hole, Mass.); memorial tablet to Alfred Mayor (Carnegie Inst., Washington, D.C.); tablets at Meeting House Plain and Stage Fort Park (Gloucester, Mass.); to Rev. Benjamin Bulkeley (Concord, Mass.); to Howard Crosby Warren (Princeton U.); Girl with Fish (Brookgarden Gardens); Boy and Chickens (Brookgreen Gardens). See Brookgreen Gardens I.

MAYR, Christian.   b. c. 1805; d. Oct. 19, 1851 according to G&W, Hamilton and Cowdrey but in 1850 in MF, in NYC. He was also a genre painter, designer and daguerrotypist. For a chronology different from that given in MF see G&W and Hamilton. See also Cowdrey, NAD; Cowdrey, AA & AAU.

MEADOWS, C[hristian].   b. c. 1814 in England. See G&W.

MEADOWS, R. M.   d. before 1812. See G&W.

MEAKIN, Lewis Henry.   He was also an etcher according to m.c. Met 3.

MEDAIRY & BANNERMAN. The partners were John Medairy and William Bannerman. See G&W.

MEER, John, [Sr.]. He was also a japanner, painter on glass and engraver on stone. See G&W.

MEINHAUSEN, George F. Misindexed after Violette Mege

MELCHERS, Gari. d. Nov., 1932 per m.c. Met 2.

MELLON, Eleanor M[ary]. b. Aug. 18, 1894 in Narberth, Pa. She studied with Victor Salvatore and A. A. Weinman at the ASL and also with Robert Aitken. She showed twenty four works at an exhibition at the Milch Galleries, N.Y., 1948. Among her works are: St. Christopher (Brookgreen Gardens). She is a Fellow, NSS; a member of the board of directors of the ALNY and vice-president, Municipal Art Society, N.Y. See *Brookgreen Gardens* II.

MERCER, William. The dates 1773-1850 given by MF for his flourishing are, according to G&W, his vital dates. He was also a miniaturist and historical painter. See G&W.

MERCHANT, G. W. He is also listed in MF as G. W. Marchant but Merchant is the correct spelling. See G&W.

MERYMAN, Richard S. d. 1963 per m.c. Met 5.

METCALF, Eliar [the correct spelling is Eliab]. b. Feb. 5, 1785; d. Jan. 15, 1834 in NYC. He was also a silhouette cutter. See Cowdrey, AA & AAU; Cowdrey, NAD; G&W.

METCALF, Willard. He taught at the ASL, 1891/92 and is a member, NIAL; Union Nationale des Beaux-Arts; American Water Color Society and Ten American Painters. See 75th Anniv. Cat., ASL.

MEURER, Charles A. d. Mar. 15, 1955 per NY Times.

MEYER, Christian. d. April 15, 1907. See G&W.

MEYER, Henry Hoppner. d. May 28, 1847 in London. See Rutledge, PA; G&W.

MIDDLETON, Thomas. b. in Fanclure, Scotland according to G&W but MF

says in Fanclure, S.C.; d. Sept. 27, 1863. He was an amateur portrait and topographical painter. See G&W.

MIELZINER, Leo. d. 1935 per m.c. Met 2.

MIFFLIN, J[ohn] H[ouston]. b. 1807 in Pennsylvania; d. 1888 at Columbia, Pa. He was also a portraitist. G&W support MF's statement that Mifflin painted portraits in Philadelphia in 1832 but make no reference to his ever having been in NYC. See Rutledge, PA; G&W.

MIGNOT, Louis Remy. d. Sept. 22, 1870 at Brighton acording to G&W but MF says in London, England. See DAB; Cowdrey, NAD; Cowdrey, AA & AAU; Rutledge, PA; G&W.

MILBOURNE, C. He is probably Cotton Milbourne. See G&W for a discussion of their identities.

MILES, Edward. b. Oct. 14, 1752 in Yarmouth, England; d. March 7, 1828. See DAB; Rutledge, PA; G&W.

MILLER, Alfred J[acob]. b. Jan. 2, 1810; d. June 26, 1874 in Baltimore. He was a landscapist and portraitist. See Rutledge, PA; Cowdrey, AA & AAU; G&W.

MILLER, Charles Henry. b. March 20, 1842 in NYC; d. Jan. 21, 1922 in NYC. He was also an etcher. See DAB; Cowdrey, NAD; G&W.

MILLER, Eleazer Hutchinson. d. April 4, 1921. He was also a portraitist. See G&W.

MILLER, George M. b. in Scotland; d. 1819 according to G&W but MF has 1818. He came to the U.S. in the late 1790's and was a wax portraitist. See Rutledge, PA; G&W.

MILLER, Kenneth Hayes. b. March 11, 1876; the place of birth given as Kenwood, N.Y. in MF and Oneida, N.Y. in ASL 75th Anniv. Cat.; d. 1952. He also studied with Cox at the ASL. He taught at the ASL 1911-1931, 1933-1936, 1944-1952 and was an Honorary Member, ASL; member, NA; Society of American Painters, Sculptors and Gravers; American Printmakers; Philadelphia Society of Etchers; Society of American Etchers. He exhibited four oil paintings at the 1913 Armory Show. See the cat. of the 1963 Armory Show; 75th Anniv. Cat., ASL.

MILLER, William H.   b. *c.* 1820 in England. See G&W.

MILLS, Clark.   b. Dec. 18, 1810 according to G&W, but in 1815 in MF and Webster's, near Syracuse, N.Y.; d. Jan. 12, 1883 in Washington, D.C. He was the father of Theodore A. Mills. See DAB; G&W.

MILLS, Theodore Augustus.   d. Dec., 1916 at Pittsburgh, Pa. See G&W.

MINOR, Robert C[rannell].   b. April 30, 1839 according to G&W and Webster's, but in 1840 in MF, in NYC; d. Aug. 3, 1904. See DAB; G&W.

MITCHELL, Harvey.   b. *c.* 1801 near Lynchburg, Va.; d. *c.* 1863/64. See G&W.

MITCHELL, John.   b.   Hartford, Conn.; d. NYC. See G&W.

MOELLER, Louis Charles.   d. 1930 per m.c. Met 2.

MOISE, Theodore Sydney.   d. at Natchitoches, La. He was also an animal painter. See G&W.

Brooklyn); Dawn of Glory (Highland Park, Brooklyn); Orphans (Brookgreen Gardens). He is a member of the Allied MOLARSKY, Maurice.   d. Jan. 1, 1950 per m.c., NYPL.

MOMBERGER, William.   b. June 7, 1829 in Frankfort-on-Main, Germany. He studied drawing and painting at Dusseldorf with Prof. Becker and did chronolithography and illustrations for books and newspapers. He had a studio at Morrisania, N.Y. and worked there at least until 1888. See Appleton; G&W; Hamilton.

MONACHISE, N.   He is probably Nicola Monachesi; b. 1795 at Tolentino, Italy; d. 1851 in Philadelphia. He was also a decorative painter. See G&W.

MONTANA, Pietro.   b. June 29, 1890 in Alcamo, Italy. He is also a sculptor. He came to the U.S. as a youth and studied at Cooper Union where he was instructed in modeling by George T. Brewster. Among his works are: Minute Man (E. Providence, R.I.); The Doughboy (Heiser Sq., Brooklyn); Victory with Peace (Freedom Square,

Artists of America, the NSS, and the Artists' Fellowship. See *Brookgreen Gardens I*.

MOONEY, Edward L[udlow].   b. March 25, 1813; d. June, 1887 in NYC. He was a National Academician. See Cowdrey, AA & AAU; Cowdrey, NAD; Rutledge, PA; G&W.

MOORE, C[harles] H[erbert].   b. April 10, 1840 in NYC; d. Feb. 15, 1930 at Hartfield, Hampshire, England. He was an Associate of the NA. See DAB; Cowdrey, NAD; G&W.

MOORE, Edwin A.   He was a painter of animals and d. 1925 per m.c. Met 2.

MOORE, Nelson A[ugustus].   b. Aug. 2, 1824 at Kensington, Conn. He was a landscapist and portraitist. See G&W.

MORA, F. Luis.   d. 1940 per m.c. Met 2.

MORAN, Edward.   b. Aug. 19, 1829 at Bolton, Lancashire, Eng.; d. June 9, 1901 in NYC. He was also a historical painter, the father of (Edward) Percy and (John) Leon Moran and the brother of Thomas and Peter Moran. He came to the U.S. in 1844 and was a student of Paul Webster and James Hamilton. He moved to NYC in 1872. See DAB; Cowdrey, NAD; Rutledge, PA; G&W; Hamilton.

MORAN, (Edward) Percy.   d. March 25, 1935 in N.Y. per m.c. Met 2.

MORAN (John) Leon.   d. 1941 in Watchung, N.J. per m.c., FARL.

MORAN, Peter.   b. March 4, 1841 according to G&W, Webster's and Rutledge, PA but in 1842 in MF; d. Nov. 9, 1914 in Philadelphia. His specialty was animal painting. See DAB; Rutledge, PA; G&W.

MORAN, Thomas.   b. Jan. 12, 1837 at Bolton, Lancashire, England; d. Aug. 26, 1926 at Santa Barbara, California. He was also a landscapist and was the brother of Peter Moran. His paintings, "The Grand Canyon of the Yellowstone" and "The Chasm of the Colorado" are in the Capitol, Washington, D.C. See DAB; Rutledge, PA; Barker, p. 588; G&W; Hamilton.

MOREIN, J. A[ugustus].   b. *c.* 1810 in the West Indies. See Cowdrey, NAD; G&W; m.c., FARL.

MORGAN, Louis [M.].   b. Nov. 21, 1814 at Mt. Pleasant, Pa.; d. in Montgomery Co., Tenn., autumn, 1852. G&W list him only as a portraitist, making no reference to any landscape work done by him. See Rutledge, PA; G&W.

MORGAN, William.   He was a portraitist and figure painter. See Cowdrey, NAD; G&W.

MORIN, J[ohn] F.   See G&W.

MORSE, Hazen.   Misindexed after Henry D. Morse. He was also a silversmith and was the father of Henry D. Morse. See G&W.

MORSE, Henry D[utton].   b. April 20, 1826; d. Jan. 2, 1888 at Jamaica Plain, Mass. He was also a landscapist and was the son of Hazen Morse. See DAB; G&W.

MORSE, Nathaniel.   He was also a silversmith. See G&W.

MORSE, Samuel Finley Breese.   b. April 27, 1791; d. April 2, 1872. He was also a miniaturist and historical painter and was a National Academician. See Cowdrey, NAD; Cowdrey, AA & AAU; Rutledge, PA; G&W.

MORSE & TUTTLE.   The original partners were Hazen Morse and Joseph W. Tuttle; they were later joined by Morse's son, George Hazen Morse. See G&W.

MORTON, John Ludlow.   b. 1792; d. Aug. 1, 1871 in NYC. He was also a portraitist, a painter of historical scenes and landscapist. See Cowdrey, AA & AAU; G&W; Hamilton.

MOSCHCOWITZ, Paul.   d. Jan. 4, 1942 per m.c. 2, NYPL.

MOSLER, Henry.   During the civil war he was an artist-correspondent for "Harper's Weekly." He exhibited in the Paris Salon and became a chevalier of the Legion d'Honneur. His painting, "Le Retour" was bought by the French Government for the Luxembourg and a portrait of Andrew H. Green, which he painted, hangs in City Hall, NYC—per notes in m.c., FARL from an article in the N.Y. Times, Nov., 1915.

MOTE, Alden.   b. Aug. 27, 1840; d. Jan. 13, 1917 in Richmond, Indiana. See G&W.

MOULTHROP, Reuben.   d. July 29, 1814. He was also a miniaturist. See G&W.

MOUNT, Henry Smith.   b. Oct. 9, 1802 at Stony Brok, L.I., N.Y.; d Jan. 20, 1841 at Setauket, L.I. He was a pupil of Lewis Child and teacher of W. S. Mount and also a figure, animal, landscape and still life painter who worked in oils. See Cowdrey, NAD; G&W.

MOUNT, (Shepard) Alonzo.   b. July 17, 1804 at Setauket, L.I., N.Y.; d. Sept. 18, 1868 at Setauket. He was also a landscapist, and a painter of still life and animals. He was the brother of H. S. Mount. See Cowdrey, NAD; Cowdrey, AA & AAU, G&W.

MOUNT, William Sidney.   b. Nov. 26, 1807; d. Nov. 19, 1868 at Setauket, L.L., N.Y. He painted portraits, still life, landscapes, genre and animals and was the brother of H. S. and S. A. Mount. The m.c. Met 2 says that contrary to what MF states Mount was a regular exhibitor of the NA, and that he had a studio in NYC from 1829 to 1836 and not for forty years as in MF. See Cowdrey, NAD; Cowdrey, AA & AAU; Rutledge, PA; G&W.

MOUNTFORT, Arnold.   d. Aug. 13, 1942 per m.c. 2, NYPL.

MOWBRAY, H. Siddons.   d. Jan. 13, 1928 in Washington, Conn. per m.c., Met 2.

MOWBRAY-CLARKE, John F.   b. 1869 according to the cat. of the 1913 Armory Show but 1863 in MF; d. 1953. He exhibited eleven sculptures at the 1913 Armory Show. See the cat. of the 1963 Armory Show.

MOZIER, Joseph.   b. Aug. 12, 1812; d. Oct. 3, 1870 at Faido according to G&W but Faids in MF, Switzerland. See DAB; Cowdrey, NAD; Cowdrey, AA & AAU; G&W.

MULLER, H.   He is probably the Hector B. Muler [or Muller or Mueller], portraitist, miniaturist and landscapist in NYC 1828-1853 listed by G&W. See Cowdrey, NAD; G&W.

MULLER-URY, Adolfo.   d. July 8, 1947 in NYC per m.c., FARL.

MULLIKEN, Jonathan.   d. June 19, 1782. See G&W.

MUMFORD, Edward William. b. 1812; d. 1858. He was also an oil and crayon portraitist. See Rutledge, PA; G&W; Hamilton.

MUNGER, Caroline. b. May 15, 1808 in East Cuilford, Conn.; d. Jan. 4, 1892 at Madison, Conn. See Cowdrey, NAD; G&W.

MUNGER, George. b. Feb. 17, 1781; d. July 2, 1825 according to G&W but 1824 in MF and Cowdrey, AA & AAU. He was also a portraitist. See Cowdrey, AA & AAU; G&W.

MUNSON, Samuel B. b. May 29, 1806; d. April 6, 1880. See G&W.

MURPHY, H[erman] Dudley. d. 1945. He exhibited one oil painting at the 1913 Armory Show. See the cat. of the 1963 Armory Show.

MURPHY, William D. b. March 11, 1834. See G&W.

MURRAY, George. d. July 2, 1822. See G&W.

MYERS, Datus E. Misindexed after Ethel Myers.

MYERS, Ethel. b. 1881; d. 1960. She exhibited nine sculptures at the 1913 Armory Show. See the cat. of the 1963 Armory Show.

MYERS, Jerome. b. March 20, 1867; d. 1940. He exhibited two oil paintings and fifteen drawings at the 1913 Armory Show and is a member, Pastellists; Society of American Painters, Sculptors and Gravers. His work is in the permanent collections of the Brooklyn Museum; Phillips Memorial Gallery; Harrison Gallery of L.A.; Art Institute of Chicago; Rochester Museum; Delgado Museum of New Orleans; Milwaukee Art Institute; MMA. He was one of the organizers of the 1913 Armory Show. See the 75th Anniv. Cat., ASL; cat. of the 1963 Armory Show.

NADELMAN, E[lie] [or Eli]. b. Feb. 23, 1882 in Warsaw, Poland; d. 1946. He studied at Munich and Warsaw before coming *c.* 1905 to Paris where he lived for twelve years. He was sponsored by Octave Mirabeau and associated with the Steins, Picasso and other experimenters. He wrote *Vers la Beaute Plastique*, N.Y. 1921, and made a series of drawings published as *Recherches de formes et de volumes*. Coming to the U.S. in 1917 he taught at the Beaux-Arts School of Design. He collected native crafts of many countries in the Mus. of Folk Art, now at N-YHS. Among his works are: Wounded Bull (R.I. School of Design); Wounded Stag (Detroit Inst. of Arts); Resting Stag (Brookgreen Gardens); La Mysterieuse (Brooklyn Mus.); Reverie (Detroit Inst. of Arts); Ideal Head (R.I. School of Design). A large collection of his works owned by Helena Rubenstein. He is a member of the ALNY, the NSS and Modern Artists of America. He exhibited twelve drawings and two sculptures at the 1913 Armory Show. See the cat. of the 1963 Armory Show; *Brookgreen Gardens I.*

NANKIVELL, Frank Arthur. d. 1959. He exhibited seven paintings and one etching at the 1913 Armory Show. See the cat. of the 1963 Armory Show.

NAST, Thomas. b. Sept. 27, 1840; d. Dec. 7, 1902. He studied at the NAD and also with Alfred Fredericks and Sol Eyting. He did cartoons for "Harper's Weekly" and also illustrated juveniles. See G&W; Hamilton.

NEAGLE, James. d. June 24, 1822. See G&W.

NEAGLE, John. b. Nov. 4, 1796; d. Sept. 17, 1865. See DAB; Rutledge, PA; Cowdrey, NAD; Cowdrey, AA & AAU; G&W.

NEAL, David [Dalhoff]. b. Oct. 20, 1838; d. May 2, 1915 in Munich. See DAB; G&W.

NEGUS, Caroline. See Cowdrey, NAD; DAB under Hildreth; G&W.

NEHLIG, Victor. d. 1909. He was also a portrait and genre painter. See Rutledge, PA; G&W; Hamilton.

NEWCOMBE, George W. b. Sept. 22, 1799; d. Feb. 10, 1845 in NYC. See Cowdrey, NAD; Rutledge, PA; G&W.

NEWELL, George Glenn. d. May 7, 1947 per m.c. 2, N-YHS.

NEWELL, Hugh. b. Oct. 4, 1830 near Belfast, Ireland; d. in Bloomfield, N.J. He was a portraitist, landscapist and a figure painter. See Cowdrey, NAD; Rutledge, PA; G&W.

NEWMAN, Henry R[oderick]. b. 1833 or 1843 at Easton, N.Y.; d. winter 1917/18 in Florence. See DAB; G&W.

NEWMAN, Robert L[oftin]. b. 1827 according to G&W, not in 1816 as MF would have it since he says that Newman was 11 in 1827; d. March 31, 1912 in NYC. He was a religious and literary painter. See G&W.

NEWPORT, J[ames] W. See Rutledge, PA; G&W.

NEWSAM, Albert. b. May 20, 1809; d. Nov. 20, 1864. See DAB; Rutledge, PA; G&W.

NEWTON, Gilbert Stuart. b. Sept. 20, 1794 according to G&W and Cowdrey, but 1795 in MF; d. Aug. 5, 1835. He was a portraitist and historical painter. See Cowdrey, AA & AAU; Cowdrey, NAD; G&W.

NICHOLS, Edward W. b. April 23, 1819 at Orford, N.H.; d. Sept. 21, 1871 at Peekskill, N.Y. MF refers to him as a portraitist, but G&W cite him as a landscapist. See Rutledge, PA; Cowdrey, NAD; G&W.

NICHOLS, Frederick B. d. After 1906. See G&W.

NICOLOSI, Joseph. b. Aug. 4, 1893 in Caltabellota, Sicily. He came to the U.S. in 1912 and from 1915 to 1919 studied with Solon Borglum, Edward McCartan and John Gregory. Among his works are: memorial to Dr. Marcus A. Heyman (Manhattan State Hospital); WWI Memorial (New Brighton, Pa. and Morristown, N.J.); 12 bas-reliefs (NYC high schools); Fountain of Youth (Hersloff Estate, Llewellyn Park, N.J.); eagle (City and County Bldg., Denver, Colo.); sculpture (P.O., Mercersburg, Pa.); Pioneer Teacher (DeWitt Clinton H.S., NYC); Dream (Brookgreen Gardens). He is a member of the NSS, the ALNY and the American Artists Professional League. See *Brookgreen Gardens I.*

NIEHAUS, Charles Henry. b. Jan. 24, 1855; d. June 19, 1935. He early practiced wood engraving, stone-cutting and carving in marble. Among his works are: The Scraper (Brookgreen Gardens; MMA); The Driller, Drake Monument (Titusville, Pa.); equestrian statue of General Forrest (Memphis, Tenn.); pediment of Kentucky State Capitol (Frankfort); Francis Scott Key Memorial (Baltimore, Md.). He is a member of the NIAL and a Fellow of L'Associazione della Artistica Internazionale di Roma. See *Brookgreen Gardens I.*

NISBET, Robert H. d. April 19, 1961 per obit in NY Times.

NOBLE, John. d. 1934 per m.c., NYPL.

NOGUCHI, Isamy [correctly spelled Isamu].

NORMAN, John. b. *c.* 1748; d. June, 1817. See DAB; G&W.

NORTHCOTE, Stafford Mantle. d. Nov. 15, 1949 per m.c., NYPL.

NUTTING, Benjamin F. b. in N.H.; d. 1887. He was also a landscapist. See G&W.

NYE, E. He was also a profilist. See G&W.

OAKLEY, [Frank] F. He was also a lithographer. See G&W.

OAKLEY, George. b. 1793, probably in England. He was a portraitist, landscapist and genre painter. See Cowdrey, AA & AAU; Cowdrey, NAD; G&W.

OAKLEY, Thornton. d. April, 1953 at Bryn Mawr, Pa. per m.c., NYPL.

OAKLEY, Violet. d. 1961 per m.c., FARL.

OBERTEUFFER, Henriette A. d. 1962 per m.c. Met 5.

O'BRIEN, John. b. in Ireland. He is listed as a painter in MF but as a sculptor in G&W. See G&W.

OCHTMAN, Leonard. d. 1934 per m.c. Met 2.

O'CONNOR, Andrew, Jr. d. June 9, 1941 per m.c., FARL.

ODDIE, Walter M. b. *c.* 1808; d. 1865. See Cowdrey, NAD; Cowdrey, AA & AAU; Rutledge, PA; G&W.

O'DONOVAN, William Rudolph. . m.c., FARL corrects the name Thomas Elkins to read Thomas Eakins.

OERTEL, Johannes Adam [Simon].   b. Nov. 3, 1823; d. Dec. 9, 1909 at Vienna, Va. He was also a portraitist. See DAB; Cowdrey, NAD; Cowdrey, AA & AAU; Rutledge, PA; G&W; Hamilton.

OFFICER, Thomas S.   b. *c.* 1810 according to G&W but 1820 in MF and Rutledge, PA and *c.* 1820 in Cowdrey, NAD and AA & AAU; d. 1859 according to G&W and Rutledge, PA but 1860 in MF and Cowdrey, NAD and AA & AAU, in San Francisco. He was also a portraitist. See Rutledge, PA; Cowdrey, NAD; Cowdrey, AA & AAU; G&W.

OGDEN, Henry A.   d. June 13, 1936 per m.c. 2, N-YHS.

OGILVIE, Clifton [correctly spelled Clinton].   b. 1838 according to G&W and Rutledge, PA but 1836 in MF; d. Nov. 29, 1900 in NYC. He was a landscapist. See Rutledge, PA; G&W.

O'HARA, Miss [Susan].   See Cowdrey, NAD; G&W.

O'KEEFFE, Georgia.   b. Nov. 15, 1877 in Sun Prairie, Wisc. She studied at the Art Institute of Chicago 1904/05 and at the ASL, N.Y., 1907/08. She is the wife of Alfred Steiglitz and a member of the NIAL. She exhibited at "291", NYC in 1917 and at the Anderson Galleries. Retrospective exhibitions were held at the Art Institute of Chicago, 1943 and the Museum of Modern Art, 1946. See 75th Anniv. Cat., ASL.

O'NEILL, John A.   He engraved on steel and wood. See G&W.

ORD, Joseph Biays.   b. in Philadelphia. He was also a religious and still life painter. See Rutledge, PA; Cowdrey, NAD; Cowdrey, AA & AAU; G&W.

ORDWAY, Alfred.   d. Nov. 17, 1897 in Boston. MF says that his specialty was landscapes but G&W cite him only as a portraitist. See G&W; m.c., FARL.

ORGAN, Marjorie (Mrs. Robert Henri). d. 1931. She exhibited six drawings at the 1913 Armory Show. See the cat. of the 1963 Armory Show.

ORMSBY, Waterman Lilly.   d. Nov. 1, 1883. He was also a banknote engraver. See DAB; Hamilton, 133, 467; G&W.

ORR, John William.   b. March 31, 1815; d. March 4, 1887 in Jersey City, N.J. according to G&W but MF says N.Y. See Hamilton; G&W.

OSBORN [or Osborne], Milo.   b. *c.* 1810 in Mass. See G&W.

OSGOOD, Charles.   b. Feb. 25, 1809; d. 1890 in Salem, Mass. He was also a miniaturist. See G&W.

OSGOOD, S[amuel] S[tillman].   b. June 9, 1808 perhaps in New Haven according to G&W but MF says in Boston. He was also a historical painter and was an Associate of the NA. See Cowdrey, NAD; Cowdrey, AA & AAU; Rutledge, PA; G&W.

OSTHAUS, Edmund.   d. 1928 per m.c., NYPL.

OSTRANDER, P[hilip].   See G&W.

OTIS, Bass.   b. July 17, 1784 in Bridgewater, Mass.; d. Nov. 3, 1861. See DAB; Rutledge, PA; Cowdrey, NAD; Cowdrey, AA & AAU; G&W.

OTTER, Thomas [P.].   He was also an engraver. See Rutledge, PA; Hamilton, 464; G&W.

OURDAN, Joseph James Prosper.   b. March, 1803; d. Oct. 25, 1874. See G&W.

OURDAN, Joseph Prosper.   b. Feb. 16, 1828 in NYC; d. May 10, 1881. See G&W.

OURLAC, Jean Nicolas.   d. in Paris. He was a landscapist. See G&W.

OUTBANK, Nahum B[all].   b. 1823; d. 1888. See m.c., FARL.

PACH, Walter.   d. 1958. He exhibited five oil paintings and five etchings at the 1913 Armory Show. See the cat. of the 1963 Armory Show.

PADDOCK, Josephine.   She exhibited three watercolors at the 1913 Armory Show. See the cat. of the 1963 Armory Show.

PAEFF, Bashka.   She was in NYC 1957 per Met 2 and is a member of the NA and the NSS.

PAGE, Walter Gilman.   b. 1863 per m.c., FARL; d. 1934 per m.c. Met 2.

PAGE, William. b. Jan. 23, 1811; d. Oct. 1, 1885 at Tottenville, S.I., N.Y. but MF says L.I. See DAB; Cowdrey, NAD; Cowdrey, AA & AAU; Rutledge, PA; G&W.

PAGES, Jules. d. May 22, 1946 per m.c., NYPL.

PALMER, Erastus Dow. b. April 2, 1817; d. March 9, 1904. See DAB; Cowdrey, NAD; Cowdrey, AA & AAU; Rutledge, PA; G&W.

PALMER, Frances [or Fanny] F[lora] [Bond]. b. c. 1812; d. Aug. 20, 1876. She was a landscape and townscape painter. See Cowdrey, NAD; G&W.

PALMER, Walter Launt. d. Apr. 16, 1932 in Albany, N.Y.

PAQUET, Anthony C. d. in Philadelphia. He engraved on wood, steel and copper. See Rutledge, PA; G&W.

PARADISE, John. b. Oct. 24, 1783 in Hunterdon Co., N.J.; d. Nov. 26, 1833 according to G&W but 1834 in Cowdrey, NAD and MF, in Springfield, N.J. according to G&W but in N.Y. in MF. See Cowdrey, NAD; G&W.

PARADISE, John Wesley. d. Aug. 17, 1862 in NYC. He was an Associate of the NA. See Cowdrey, NAD; G&W.

PARAMINO, John F. d. Oct. 6, 1956 in Wellesley, Mass. per m.c., NYPL.

PARISSEN [or PARISEN], Otto. b. 1723; d. Jan. 17, 1811 at New Rochelle, N.Y. He was also a miniaturist, goldsmith and hairworker and was the father of Philip Parissen. See G&W.

PARISSEN [or PARISEN[, Philip. d. 1882. He was also a silhouettist, hairworker and silversmith and was the father of William Parissen and the son of Otto Parissen. See G&W.

PARISSEN [or PARISEN or PARISIEN], William D. b. Feb., 1800 in NYC; d. April 9, 1832. He was the son of Philip Parissen and also a portraitist. There is confusion as to the spelling of the name and doubts as to the identity of the Parissens listed in the exhibition catalogues mentioned below, as many works are signed only with the last name. See Cowdrey, AA & AAU, NAD; G&W.

PARK, Asa. d. at Lexington, Ky. He also painted still life. See G&W.

PARKER, Edgar. b. in Framingham, Mass. See G&W.

PARKER, John Adams. b. Nov. 29, 1829 or Nov. 27, 1827; d. c. 1905. See Cowdrey, NAD; G&W.

PARKER, Stephen H[illis]. —m.c. Met 2.

PARKER, Thomas H. d. after 1851 according to G&W but MF says d. 1851. See G&W.

PARKHURST, Anita. m.c. 2, N-YHS corrects "He . . ." to read "She . . ."

PARKYNS, George Isham. b. c. 1749/50; d. c. 1820. He was also a landscapist and portraitist. See G&W.

PARSELL, Abraham, b. c. 1792 in N.J. G&W suppose that he is the father of John H. Parsell. See G&W.

PARSELL, J[ohn] H. See G&W.

PARSONS, Charles. b. May 8, 1821 at Rowland's Castle, Hampshire, England; d. Nov. 9, 1910 in Brooklyn, N.Y. He was also a landscapist and marine painter. He came to the U.S. at age nine and was an apprentice of George Endicott in NYC. Later he worked for "Harper's" and became head of the art department there. He was associated with Reinhart, Abbey and Pyle. See Cowdrey, NAD; Cowdrey, AA & AAU; G&W; Hamilton.

PARSONS, Edith B[arretto]. b. July 4, 1878. Among her works, which include many busts and some memorials, are: fountain to John Galloway (Memphis, Tenn.); soldiers' monument (Summit, N.J.); Turtle Baby Fountain (Cleveland Museum); The Bird Baby (grounds, Brooks Memorial Art Gallery, Memphis, Tenn.); Frog Baby, (Brookgreen Gardens; Ball State Teachers' College, Muncie, Ind.). See *Brookgreen Gardens I*.

PARTON, Ernest. d. 1933 per NY Times Sept. 16, 1933.

PASCIN, Jules. b. 1885; d. 1930. He exhibited two paintings, two engravings and eight drawings at the 1913 Armory Show. See the cat. of the 1963 Armory Show.

PATIGIAN, Haig.   b. Jan. 22, 1876. He came to the U.S. as a young man, settled in San Francisco and was largely self-taught in sculpture. Among his works are: Ancient History (Bohemian Club, San Francisco); tympanum (M.H. de Young Memorial Museum); pediment (Metropolitan Life Insurance Bldg., San Francisco); General Pershing San Francisco); Lincoln, Civic Center (San Francisco); Hoover (White House, Washington, D.C.); Thomas Starr King, Statuary Hall and Aeronautics pediment, Dept. of Commerce Bldg. (Washington, D.C.); Friendship (AAAL; Olympic County Club, San Francisco); Nereid (Brookgreen Gardens). He is a member of the NSS, NIAL, and an honorary life member of the Bohemian Club, San Farncisco. See *Brookgreen Gardens I.*

PATTERSON, Rebecca Burd Peale.   d. Sept., 1952 per m.c. Met 2.

PAUL, E[ugene].   b. *c.* 1830 in France. See G&W.

PAUL, Jeremiah, [Jr.].   d. July 13, 1820 in St. Louis, Mo. He was also a figure and animal painter. See Rutledge, PA; G&W.

PAULUS, Francis Petrus.   d. 1933 per m.c. Met 2.

PAXTON, William M.   d. May 13, 1941 in Boston per m.c. Met 2.

PEALE, Anna Claypoole.   b. March 6, 1791 in Philadelphia; d. Dec. 25, 1878 in Philadelphia. She was the granddaughter of James Claypoole. See DAB; Rutledge, PA; G&W.

PEALE, Charles Wilson.   b. April 15, 1741 in Queen Anne's Co., Md. according to G&W, not in Charlestown as in MF; d. Feb. 22, 1827. The m.c., FARL does not agree with the statement in MF that Peale was in Boston in 1768-69. It notes that, according to his journal, Peale was in Boston in 1765 but left in the same year to paint portraits in Virginia. He returned to Annapolis in 1766 and sailed for England in the spring of 1769. See G&W; m.c., FARL.

PEALE, James.   d. May 24, 1831. He aiso painted still life. See DAB; Rutledge, PA; G&W.

PEALE, James, Jr.   b. March 6, 1789 in Philadelphia; d. Oct. 27, 1876 in Philadelphia according to G&W [MF erroneously gives him the same dates as his father]. He also painted landscapes and still life. See G&W.

PEALE, Maria.   b. 1787; d. March 27, 1866 in Philadelphia. See Rutledge, PA; G&W.

PEALE, Mary Jean [Jane in G&W].   b. Feb. 16, 1827 according to G&W but 1826 in MF, in NYC; d. Nov., 1902. See G&W.

PEALE, Raphaelle.   b. Feb. 17, 1774 at Annapolis, Md.; d. March 5, 1825 in Philadelphia. See Rutledge, PA; Cowdrey, AA & AAU; G&W.

PEALE, Rembrandt.   b. Feb. 22, 1778. He was also a miniaturist and historical painter. See DAB; Cowdrey, AA & AAU; Rutledge, PA; Cowdrey, NAD; G&W.

PEALE, Rubens.   b. May 4, 1784 in Philadelphia; d. July 17, 1865. He was a still life and animal painter. See G&W.

PEALE, Sarah M[iriam].   b. May 19, 1800 in Philadelphia; d. Feb. 4, 1885 in Philadelphia. See Rutledge, PA; G&W.

PEALE, Titian [Ramsey].   b. Nov. 17, 1799 according to G&W and Webster's but 1800 in MF, in Philadelphia; d. March 13, 1885 in Philadelphia. See DAB; Rutledge, PA; G&W.

PEASE, Joseph Ives.   b. Aug. 9, 1809; d. July 2, 1883. He was also a watercolorist. See DAB; Rutledge, PA; G&W.

PEASE, Richard H.   b. Feb. 19, 1813. He was also a lithographer. See G&W.

PEBBLES, Frank M.   b. Oct. 16, 1839 in Wyoming Co., N.Y. according to G&W but MF says Wyoming, N.Y.; still active in 1905 in Oak Park, Ill. See G&W.

PECKHAM, Robert.   b. Sept. 10, 1785 probably at Westminster, Mass. according to G&W but MF says Petersham, Mass.; d. June 29, 1877 at Westminster. See G&W.

PEELE, John Thomas.   b. April 11, 1822 in Petersborough, England; d. May 19, 1897 in London. See Cowdrey, NAD; Cowdrey, AA & AAU; Rutledge, PA; G&W.

PELHAM, Henry.   b. Feb. 14, 1749. He was also a portraitist and miniaturist and was the son of Peter Pelham. See DAB; G&W.

PELHAM, Peter.   b. 1697, in London, Eng. according to G&W, not 1684 as in MF; d. Dec. 1751 in Boston. He was the father of Henry Pelham. See DAB; G&W.

PELL, Ella Ferris.   Misindexed after Agnes Pelton.

PELTON, Agnes.   d. 1961. She exhibited two oil paintings at the 1913 Armory Show. See the cat. of the 1963 Armory Show.

PELTON, Oliver.   b. Aug. 31, 1798; d. Aug. 15, 1882. See G&W.

PENDLETON, John [B.].   b. 1798 in NYC; d. March 10, 1866. See G&W.

PENNELL, Joseph.   b. July 4, 1860; d. 1926 in Brooklyn. He taught at the ASL, 1922-26 and founded what is now its graphics department. He was an Honorary Member of the League and a member of the NIAL, NA and a Fellow of the PA. He wrote *A Life of James McNeill Whistler, Etching and Etchers, Lithography and Lithographers, Pen Drawing and Pen Draftsmen,* and other works. See 75th Anniv. Cat., ASL.

PENNIMAN, John Ritto.   b. Jan. 30, 1783 in Milford, Mass. He was also a portraitist, lithographer and an ornamental painter. He taught Alvin Fisher. See Barker, p. 372; G&W; Hamilton.

PENNOYER, A. Sheldon.   d. 1957 ? per m.c., FARL.

PEPPER, Charles Hovey.   d. 1950. He exhibited five paintings at the 1913 Armory Show. See the cat. of the 1963 Armory Show.

PERARD, Victor Semon.   d. July 9, 1957 in Bellport, L.I. per m.c., NYPL.

PERCIVAL, Edwin.   He was a portrait, historical and landscape painter. See Rutledge, PA; G&W.

PERINE, George Edward.   b. July 9, 1837; d. Feb. 3, 1885. See G&W.

PERKINS, Charles C[allahan].   d. 1886. He was also an amateur painter. See G&W.

PERKINS, Granville.   b. Oct. 16, 1830; d. April 17, 1895 in NYC. See Rutledge, PA; Hamilton, 431-32; G&W; Appleton.

PERKINS, Jacob.   b. July 9, 1766; d. July 11, 1849. See G&W.

PERKINS, Joseph.   b. Aug. 19, 1788; d. April 27, 1842. See Rutledge, PA; G&W.

PERRINE, Van Dearing.   d. Dec. 10, 1955 in Stamford, Conn., per m.c., NYPL. He exhibited two oil paintings in the 1913 Armory Show. See the cat. of the 1963 Armory Show.

PERRY, Enoch Wood, [Jr.].   b. July 31, 1831; d. Dec. 14, 1915. He was also a genre and landscape painter. See DAB; Cowdrey, NAD; Rutledge, PA; G&W.

PERRY, Ione.   She was a figure painter. See G&W.

PERRY, Oswald.   Misindexed after Enoch Wood Perry.

PERRY, Roland Hinton.   b. Jan. 15, 1870; d. Oct. 27, 1941. His mother, Ione (Hinton) Perry, was a talented amateur painter and miniaturist. At sixteen he began to study drawing and painting at the ASL and three years later he went to Paris where he studied with Gerome, Chapu and Puech. He returned to NYC in 1894 via Germany and Norway, painting as he went; later he travelled again in France and Italy. He exhibited red chalk portraits in 1924. Among his works are: madallions, entrance pavilion, Library of Congress; Elk (Portland, Oregon); Lion in Love (Waldorf-Astoria Hotel, NYC); bronze doors, Buffalo Historical Society; figure of Pennsylvania, top of State Capitol dome, Harrisburg,; N.Y. Peace Memorial at Lookout Mt. near Chattanooga; George S. Greene (Gettysburg); Dr. Benjamin Rush in front of the US Naval Museum, Wash., D.C.); Primitive Man and Serpent (Brookgreen Gardens). See *Brookgreen Gardens II.*

PERSICO, Gennarino [given as Gennaro in G&W and Gennario in Rutledge, PA]. d. *c.* 1859. He was also a crayon artist. See Rutledge, PA; G&W.

PETERS, C[harles] F.   d. June 21, 1948 per m.c., NYPL.

PETTICOLAS [PETICOLAS in G&W], Edward F.   b. 1793 in Pennsylvania; d.

c. 1853. He was also a landscapist and was the son of P.A. Petticolas. The miniature of Elihu Etting referred to in MF was probably painted by P.A. Petticolas per m.c., FARL. See G&W.

PETTICOLAS [PETICOLAS in G&W], Philip(pe) Abraham.   b. Meziers, France, d. Aug., 1841 at Petersburg, Va. according to G&W but MF says 1843 at Richmond. See G&W.

PEYRAUD, Frank C.   d. May 31, 1948 per m.c., NYPL.

PHILLIPS, Charles.   See Cowdrey, NAD; G&W.

PICIRILLI, Attilio.   b. May 16, 1868 in Massa, Italy. The son of a marble-cutter, he studied 1881-88 at the Accadmia di San Luca in Rome. He worked in his father's marble-cutting studio and eventually became its head. Among his works are: Fireman's Monument (Riverside Drive, NYC); Governor Allen (State House Baton Rouge); President Monroe (Charlottesville, Va.); Indian Literature, Indian Law Giver (facade, Brooklyn Museum); pediment (Wisconsin State Capitol); lunettes (Frick residence, NYC); relief over doors, Palazzo d'Italia, 1935 Rockefeller Center, NYC); Fragilina (MMA); Un Sogno di Primavera (Richmond Academy of Arts); Laughing Boy and Goat (Brookgreen Gardens). He is a member of the NA, NSS, Accedemia dei Virtuosi del Pantheon, Rome, President, Italian-American Art Association, and a member of the ALNY. See *Brookgreen Gardens I.*

PICIRILLI, Furio.   b. March 14, 1870 in Massa, Italy. He was the brother of Attilio Picirilli and studied at the Accademia di San Luca, Rome. Among his works are: four groups of figures for the Court of the Seasons (San Francisco Expos.); sculptural decoration, Pierre Gaultier (Parliament House, Winnipeg, Canada); Murillo (Fine Arts Gallery, San Diego); Seal, black marble (Brookgreen Gardens, MMA). He is a member of the NA and an Associate of the ALNY. See *Brookgreen Gardens I.*

PIGALLE [or PIGAL].   See G&W.

PINE, Robert Edge.   b. 1730? according to G&W, 1730 in Webster's and 1742 in MF; d. Nov. 19, 1788. See DAB; G&W.

PLANTOU, Mrs. [Anthony].   She also painted landscapes and religious subjects. See Rutledge, PA; G&W.

PLASSMAN[N], Ernst.   b. June 14, 1823 at Sondern, Westphalia, Germany; d. Nov. 28, 1877. He was also a wood carver. See G&W.

PLATT, Charles A.   d. 1933 per m.c. Met 3.

PLOCHER, Jacob J.   d. Dec. 27, 1820. See G&W.

PLUMB, Henry G.   d. 1930 per m.c. Met 2.

POGANY, William A. and Willy (William Andrew) Pogany.   These are probably the same person per m.c., FARL.

POINCY, Paul.   b. March 11, 1833. He also painted religious subjects. See G&W.

POLASEK, Albin.   b. Feb. 14, 1879. He came to the U.S. in 1901 to join his brother in Minnesota. He was skilled as a wood carver and worked at an altar factory in Lacrosse, Wisc. for three years. He was a pupil of Charles Grafly. Among his works are: The Sower (Art Inst., Chicago); Man Carving His Own Destiny (Dallas Mus. of Fine Arts); Gov. Yates (Springfield, Ill.); J. G. Batterson (Hartford, Conn.); Theodore Thomas (Grant Park, Chicago); The Pilgrim (Bohemian National Cemetery, Chicago); Father Gibault (Vincennes, Ind.); Forest Idyl (Brookgreen Gardens; Ball State Teachers' College, Muncie, Ind.; Norton Gallery, W. Palm Beach, Fla.); Aspiration (Detroit Inst. of Arts); Fantasy (MMA); Unfettered (Art Inst. of Chicago). He is a member of the NA, the Assn. of Chicago Painters and Sculptors, and of the Board of Art Advisers, State of Illinois. See *Brookgreen Gardens I.*

POLK, Charles Peale.   b. March 17, 1767 in Md. See G&W.

POLLOCK, T[homas].   See G&W.

POMAREDE, Leon.   b. *c.* 1807 in Tarbes, France; d. 1892 in St. Louis, Mo. He was also a landscapist, panoramist, miniaturist, and painter of religious murals. See G&W.

POOLE, Abram.   d. 1961 per NY H-Tribune May 25, 1961.

POORE, Henry R.   d. 1940 per m.c., FARL.

PORTER, Raymond A.   d. April 2, 1949 per m.c. 2, NYPL.

POTTHAST, Edward Henry.   d. 1927 per m.c., FARL.

POUPARD, James.   He was a native of Martinique and was once an actor. See G&W; Hamilton.

POWELL, Lucien Whiting.   b. Dec. 13, 1846; d. Sept. 27, 1930 per m.c. 2, N-YHS.

POWELL, William Henry.   b. Feb. 14, 1823 in NYC according to G&W, Webster's, Cowdrey, NAD and Cowdrey, AA & AAU but 1824 in Ohio per MF; d. Oct. 6, 1879 in NYC. See DAB; Cowdrey, NAD; Cowdrey, AA & AAU; G&W.

POWERS, Hiram.   b. July 29, 1805 near Woodstock, Vt.; d. June 27, 1873 in Florence, Italy. See DAB; Rutledge, PA; Cowdrey, NAD; G&W.

PRAHAR, Renee.   d. 1962 per m.c. Met 5.

PRATT, Henry Cheeves [also Cheeves in Cowdrey, NAD; Cheever in G&W and Rutledge, PA].   b. June 13, 1803 at Orford, N.H.; d. Nov. 27, 1880 in Wakefield, Mass. He was also a portraitist, miniaturist and panoramist. See Cowdrey, NAD; Rutledge; PA; G&W.

PRATT, Matthew.   b. Sept. 23, 1734; d. Jan. 9, 1805 in Philadelphia. See G&W.

PRATT, Robert M.   d. Aug. 31, 1880 in NYC according to G&W, Cowdrey, NAD and Rutledge, PA but 1888 in MF. He was also a figure and flower painter and was a National Academician. See Cowdrey, NAD; Rutledge, PA; G&W.

PRENDERGAST, Charles E.   d. 1948 per obit in the Oct. issue of "Art News."

PRENDERGAST, Maurice B[razil].   b. 1859 according to the Armory Show and AAAL cats. but in 1861 in MF. He exhibited seven paintings at the 1913 Armory Show and six of his works were exhibited at the AAAL, Dec. 11, 1964-Jan. 10, 1965. See the AAAL cat., *Robert Henri and His Circle;* cat. of the 1963 Armory Show.

PRESTON, James.   b. 1873; d. 1962. He exhibited two oil paintings at the 1913 Armory Show. See the cat. of the 1963 Armory Show.

PRESTON, Mary Wilson.   See May Wilson Preston; May is given in *American Art Annual,* 1927; *Armory Show, 50th Anniversary Exhibition, 1913-1963;* Milton W. Brown, *The Story of the Armory Show.*

PRESTON, May Wilson.   d. 1949. She exhibited one oil painting at the 1913 Armory Show. See the cat. of the 1963 Armory Show.

PRICE, Genl. Samuel W[oodson].   b. Aug. 5, 1828 at Nicholasville, Ky.; d. Jan. 22, 1918 at St. Louis, Mo. He was also a figure painter. See G&W.

PROCTOR, A[lexander] Phimister.   b. Sept. 27, 1862 in Bozanquit, Ontario. He spent his youth in Denver, Colo. but in 1887 studied in NYC at the NA and the ASL. Among his works are: panthers on gateposts (Prospect Park, Brooklyn); Lions (McKinley Monument, Buffalo); Tigers (Nassau Hall, Princeton U.); Bison (Q Street Bridge, Washington, D.C.); The Circuit Rider (Salem, Mass.); Pioneer (U. of Oregon); Theodore Roosevelt as a Rough Rider (Portland, Ore.); equestrian statue of Sheriff "Til" Taylor (Pendleton, Ore.); On the Warpath, The Buckaroo (Denver Civic Center); Pioneer Mother (Kansas City); Robert E. Lee Memorial (Dallas, Texas); a group of 7 mustangs (U. of Texas); Trumpeting Elephant (Brookgreen Gardens); Pursued, bronze (Brookgreen Gardens); Some of his small bronzes are in the Los Angeles Museum of History, Science and Art (on loan); MMA, N.Y.; National Gallery of Canada, Ottowa; City Art Museum, St. Louis. See *Brookgreen Gardens I.*

PRUD'HOMME, John Francis Eugene. b. Oct. 4, 1800; d. June 22, 1892. See DAB; Cowdrey, NAD, Cowdrey, AA & AAU; Hamilton, 223; G&W.

PUNDERSON, L[emuel] S.   See G&W.

PUTNAM, Arthur.   d. 1930. He exhibited four sculptures at the 1913 Armory Show. See the cat. of the 1963 Armory Show.

PUTNAM, Brenda.   b. June 3, 1890. She studied 1905-07 at the Boston Museum Art School with Paxton, Hale and Mary E.

Moore. She worked in sculpture with James E. Fraser at the ASL, and studied drawing from life at the Corcoran Art School with E. C. Messer. In about 1927 she went to Florence to work with Libero Andreotti and upon returning to NYC investigated the theories of Archipenko. Among her works are: Mischievous Faun (Dallas Mus. of Fnie Arts); Pablo Casals (Hispanic Society of America); Puck (Folger Shakespeare Library, Washington, D.C.); mural, (P.O., St. Cloud, Minn.); Sundial, White Mouse, Communion (Brookgreen Gardens). She wrote a book, *The Sculptor's Way,* 1939. She is a member of the NA, N.H. Assn. of Women Painters and Sculptors and a secretary of the NSS. See *Brookgreen Gardens I.*

QUARRE, F. [Frederick or Ferdinand]. See G&W.

QUARTLEY, Arthur. b. May 24, 1839 at Paris, France; d. May 19, 1866 in NYC. See DAB; G&W.

QUARTLEY, Frederick William. b. July 5, 1808 at Bath, England; d. April 5, 1874 in NYC. See Hamilton, G&W.

QUESNAY, Alexander Marie [Alexandre-Marie in G&W]. b. Nov. 23, 1755 at Saint-Germain-en-Viry, France; d. Feb. 8, 1820 at Saint Maurice (Seine), France. See DAB; G&W.

QUIDOR, John. b. Jan. 26, 1801 at Tappan, N.Y.; d. Dec. 13, 1881 at Jersey City, N.J. He was a figure painter. See Cowdrey, NAD; Cowdrey, AA & AAU; Rutledge, PA; G&W.

QUINN, Edmond T. d. 1929 per m.c., FARL.

RALEIGH, Henry [Patrick]. d. June 8, 1945 per m.c., NYPL.

RAMAGE, John. b. *c.* 1748 according to G&W, not 1763 as in MF, in Ireland; d. Oct. 24, 1802 at Montreal, Canada. See G&W.

RAND, Ellen G. Emmet. d. Dec. 18, 1941 in Salisbury, Conn. per m.c. Met 2.

RANNEY, William [Tyler]. b. May 9, 1813; d. Nov. 18, 1857. He was a historical, portrait and genre painter. See DAB;

Cowdrey, NAD; Cowdrey, AA & AAU; Rutledge, PA; G&W.

RANSOM, Alexander. He was a portraitist. See Cowdrey, NAD; Rutledge, PA; G&W.

RANSOM, Caroline L. Ormes. d. Feb. 12, 1910. See Cowdrey, NAD; G&W.

RASCHEN, Carl Martin. d. June, 1962 per m.c., NYPL.

RASMUSSEN, Bertrand. He exhibited one oil painting at the 1913 Armory Show. See the cat. of the 1963 Armory Show.

RAWDON, Freeman. b. *c.* 1801 according to G&W but MF says 1804; d. Sept. 21, 1859 in NYC. See G&W.

RAWDON, Ralph. He was the brother of Freeman Rawdon. See G&W.

READ, Thomas Buchanan. b. March 12, 1822; d. May 11, 1872 in NYC. He also painted historical scenes. See DAB; Rutledge, PA; Cowdrey, NAD; Cowdrey, AA & AAU; G&W.

REAM, Carducius P[lantagenet]. b. *c.* 1836 according to G&W but MF says 1837; d. June 20, 1917. See G&W.

REASON, Philip H. He is identified by G&W as Patrick Henry Reason. See G&W.

REBISSO, Louis T. b. 1837 in Genoa, Italy; d. May 3, 1899 in Cincinnati, Ohio. See G&W.

RECCHIA, Richard H[enry]. b. Nov. 20, 1885. He was the son of a marble cutter, at whose shop he was apprenticed for two years. He studied modeling and anatomy with Bela Lyon Pratt, whose assistant he became and later was helped by Pratt and D. C. French to attend the Academie Julian, Paris and visit Italy, 1911-12. Among his works are: Sam Walter Foss, Robert Brown (Brown U.); Red Cross Disaster model (Red Cross Mus., Wash., D.C.); Gov. Oliver Ames (North Easton, Mass.); General George Wells (Shenandoah Valley, Va.); Youth (J. Breckenridge Speed Memorial Museum, Louisville, Ky.); Baby and Frog (Brookgreen Gardens). He is a member of the NSS, an Associate of the NA, a charter member of the Guild of Boston Artists and founder of the Boston Society of Sculptors. See *Brookgreen Gardens I.*

REED, Abner. d. Feb. 25, 1866 at Toledo, Ohio. See G&W.

REICH, John [or Johann Mathias]. b. 1768 at Furth, Bavaria, Germany; d. 1833 at Albany, N.Y. See Rutledge, PA; G&W.

REICHE, F. [or J.F.]. See Hamilton, 71, 440; G&W.

REID, Robert. d. 1929 per m.c. Met 2.

REINAGLE, Hugh. b. *c.* 1788 per G&W, Cowdrey, AA & AAU and Rutledge, PA but 1790 in MF and Cowdrey, NAD; d. May 23, 1834. He was also a historical and portrait painter and was a National Academician. See DAB (under Alexander Reinagle); Rutledge, PA; Cowdrey, NAD; Cowdrey, AA & AAU; G&W.

REINHART, Benjamin Franklin. b. Aug. 29, 1829 near Waynesburg, Pa.; d. May 3, 1885 in Philadelphia. He was also a portraitist. See DAB; Cowdrey, NAD; Rutledge, PA; G&W.

REINHART, Charles Stanley. He worked exclusively for Harper & Brothers, 1870/77. See DAB; Hamilton.

REINHART, William Henry. See William Henry Rinehart.

REMICK, Christian. b. April 8, 1726 in Eastham, Mass. See G&W.

REMINGTON, Frederic. b. Oct. 4, 1861; d. Dec. 26, 1909. He went to Montana at age nineteen, came back to the East in 1886 and settled in New Rochelle, N.Y. He studied at the ASL but after a cool reception of his oil paintings in 1892 stopped painting for about ten years and toured Russia, Germany and North Africa with Poultney Bigelow. In 1897 and 1898 he was in Cuba with Richard Harding Davis sketching incidents of the Spanish-American War. He turned to modeling when he stopped painting. He did illustrations for "Harper's Weekly" and "Outing" and for T. Roosevelt's *Ranch Life and the Hunting Trail.* Among his sculped works are: The Bronco Buster (Brookgreen Gardens; Amherst College; MMA; Remington Art Memorial, Ogdensburg, N.Y.; Philbrook Art Museum, Tulsa, Okla.); statue of a cowboy (Fairmount Park, Philadelphia). A collection of his works is in the Remington Art Memorial, Ogdensburg,

N.Y. and of his bronzes at the MMA. Other works are in the Institute of Albany; Museum of St. Louis; Museum of Arts, Toledo; National Gallery, Wash., D.C.; Corcoran Gallery. See 75th Anniv. Cat., ASL; *Brookgreen Gardens I.*

RENAULT, J[ohn] F[rancis]. He was an allegorical and historical painter. See G&W.

RETZCH, Frederick August Moritz. G&W correct an error in MF stemming from an error in T. S. Cummings, *Historic Annals,* p. 262 which states that Retzch died in the U.S. It is true that he was an Honorary Member of the NA, but he never came to the U.S. See Cowdrey, NAD; Cowdrey, AA & AAU; G&W.

REUTERDAHL, Henry. d. 1925. He exhibited one oil painting at the 1913 Armory Show. See the cat. of the 1963 Armory Show.

REVERE, Paul. b. Jan. 1, 1735; d. May 10, 1818. He was also a cartoonist and watercolorist. See G&W.

RICE, James R. He was the brother of W. W. Rice. See G&W.

RICE, W. W. He was the brother of James R. Rice. See G&W.

RICHARDS, Frederick De Berg. b. 1822; d. 1903 according to Rutledge, PA. See Cowdrey, AA & AAU; Cowdrey, NAD; Rutledge, PA; G&W.

RICHARDS, T[homas] Addison. b. Dec. 3, 1820 in London; d. June 28, 1900. He came to the U.S. in 1831 and was a landscapist, portraitist and illustrator. He was a National Academician. See DAB; Cowdrey, NAD; Rutledge, PA; G&W; Hamilton.

RICHARDS, William Trost. b. Nov. 14, 1833; d. Nov. 8, 1905. He was also a landscapist, portraitist and a still life painter. See DAB; Rutledge, PA; Cowdrey, NAD; G&W; Hamilton; Barker, p. 595.

RICHARDSON, Andrew. b. 1799 in Scotland; d. in New York. See Cowdrey, NAD; Cowdrey, AA & AAU; G&W.

RICHARDSON, Francis Henry. d. 1934 per m.c. Met 2.

RICHARDSON, Marion. d. Dec., 1952 per m.c., NYPL.

RICKETSON, Walton. b. May 27, 1839. See G&W.

RIDER, Alexander. He was also portraitist, landscapist and figure painter and came to the U.S. in 1810. See Rutledge, PA; G&W.

RIMMER, Dr. William. b. Feb. 20, 1816 in Liverpool, England; d. Aug. 20, 1879. He was also a portrait and figure painter and exhibited four drawings at the 1913 Armory Show. See DAB; cat. of the 1963 Armory Show.

RINEHART, William Henry. He is also erroneously listed as Reinhart in MF. b. Sept. 13, 1825 near Union Bridge, Md. according to G&W but MF says Frederick, Md.; d. Oct. 28, 1874 in Rome, Italy. See DAB; G&W.

RIPLEY, Lucy P. d. Sept. 5, 1949 per m.c., NYPL.

RITCHIE, Alexander Hay. b. Jan. 14, 1822; d. Sept. 19, 1895 in New Haven, Conn. according to G&W but MF says Brooklyn, N.Y. He was also a portraitist, genre and figure painter. See DAB; Cowdrey, NAD; Rutledge, PA; G&W.

ROBBINS, Horace Wolcott. b. Oct. 21, 1842; d. 1904 according to G&W, Cowdrey, NAD and Rutledge, PA but 1903 in MF. See Cowdrey, NAD; Rutledge, PA; G&W.

ROBERTS, B[ishop]. d. Oct., 1739. See G&W.

ROBERTS, John. He was also a miniaturist. See Hamilton, 86; G&W.

ROBERTSON, Alexander. b. May 13, 1772 according to G&W and Cowdrey, AA & AAU, but 1768 in MF, at Aberdeen, Scotland; d. in NYC. See Cowdrey, AA & AAU; G&W.

ROBERTSON, Archibald. b. May 8, 1765 at Moneymusk according to G&W but Monymusk in MF, Scotland; d. Dec. 6, 1835. He was also a miniaturist. See G&W.

ROBERTSON, Walter. b. c. 1750 per G&W [the 1792 reported as his birth date by MF is the date of the termination of his residence in London, prior to his coming to the U.S. in 1793]; d. 1802 in Futtehpore, India. See G&W.

ROBINSON, Boardman. b. Sept. 6, 1876 at Somerset, Nova Scotia; d. Sept. 7, 1952. He exhibited three drawings and two cartoons at the 1913 Armory Show. He studied at the Mass. Normal Art School, Academie Colarossi, and the Ecole des Beaux-Arts. He was an illustrator for various New York newspapers and magazines and taught at the ASL, 1919-1930. He was an Honorary Member, ASL and a member, Society of Illustrators. From 1930 to 1947 he was Resident Art Instructor, Fountain Valley School and Director, Colorado Springs Fine Art Center. He has illustrated books, including *The Brothers Karamazov, The Idiot, King Lear,* and *Moby Dick* and did murals in the Kaufmann Store, Pittsburgh; R.K.O. Bldg., NYC; Dept. of Justice Bldg., Wash., D.C. See 75th Anniv. Cat., ASL.

ROBINSON, John. He was also a portraitist. See Rutledge, PA; G&W.

ROBINSON, Theodore. Five of his oil paintings were exhibited at the 1913 Armory Show. See the cat. of the 1963 Armory Show.

ROBINSON, Thomas. b. Aug. 23, 1834 according to G&W but 1835 in Cowdrey, NAD and MF, in Pictou, N.S.; d. March 1, 1888 in Providence, R.I. He was also a landscape and genre painter. See Cowdrey, NAD; G&W.

ROBINSON, William S. d. 1945 per m.c., FARL.

ROCKWELL, Norman. b. Feb. 3, 1894 in NYC. He studied at the ASL, with George B. Bridgman and Thomas Fogarty and is a member of the Society of Illustrators and of the Freelance Artists of America. He is an illustrator, especially for the "Saturday Evening Post" and also for the "Ladies Home Journal," "American Magazine," "Women's Home Companion" and others. See 75th Anniv. Cat., ASL.

ROGERS, [Henry W.]. He was also a portraitist. See G&W.

ROGERS, John. b. Oct. 30, 1829; d. July 26, 1904 in New Canaan, Conn. See DAB; G&W.

ROGERS, Nathaniel. d. Dec. 6, 1844 at Bridgehampton, L.I. He was a National Academician. See Cowdrey, AA & AAU; Cowdrey, NAD; G&W.

ROGERS, Randolph.   b. July 6, 1825 at Waterloo, N.Y.; d. Jan. 15, 1892 in Rome, Italy. See DAB; G&W.

ROLLINSON, Charles.   b. *c.* 1793; d. Jan. 19, 1833 according to G&W but MF says 1832, in Boston. See G&W.

ROLLINSON, William.   b. April 15, 1762; d. Sept. 21, 1842. He came to the U.S. in 1788 and was also a miniaturist. See DAB; G&W.

ROLPH [or Rolfe], J[ohn] A.   b. 1799 in Essex, England; d. 1862. He was also a painter of portraits, historical scenes and landscapes. See Cowdrey, NAD; Cowdrey, AA & AAU; G&W.

ROLSHOVEN, Julius.   d. Dec. 7, 1930 in NYC per m.c. Met 2.

ROOK, Edward F.   d. 1960. He exhibited two oil paintings at the 1913 Armory Show. See the cat. of the 1963 Armory Show.

ROOSEVELT, S. Montgomery.   d. Aug. 19, 1920 per m.c., NYPL.

ROPES, Joseph.   d. 1885 according to G&W but MF says *c.* 1885. He was also a miniaturist and crayon artist. See Cowdrey, NAD; G&W.

ROSENTHAL, Albert.   d. 1939 per m.c. 2, N-YHS.

ROSENTHAL, Max.   b. Nov. 23, 1833; d. Aug. 8, 1918. See Rutledge, PA; G&W.

ROSENTHAL, Toby E.   d. 1917 per m.c. Met 2.

ROSSITER, Thomas P[richard].   b. Sept. 29, 1818 according to G&W, Webster's, Cowdrey, NAD and AA & AAU, and Rutledge, PA but 1817 in MF; d. May 17, 1871. He was an intimate of Durand, Casilear and Kensett. His "Washington and Lafayette at Mount Vernon" is at the MMA. See DAB; Cowdrey, NAD; Cowdrey, AA & AAU; Rutledge, PA; G&W; Hamilton; Barker, p. 469.

ROTH, F[rederick] G[eorge] R[ichard]. b. April 28, 1872; d. 1944 according to m.c., NYPL. He was chief sculptor of the Park Dept., NYC, 1934-1936 under the W.P.A. Among his works are: Polar Bear, Seal (in pottery, Whitney Museum of American Art); Balto (Central Park, NYC); Justin Morgan (Middlebury, Vt.);

equestrian statue of Kit Carson (Trinidad, Colo.); equestrian statue of Washington (Morristown, N.J.); Alice in Wonderland, Tales from Mother Goose (Central Park, NYC); Polar Bears, bronze (Brookgreen Gardens; Amherst College; Detroit Institute of Arts; AAAL, NYC). Many of his small bronzes are in the MMA. He was a member of the New Society of Artists, NSS, and the NIAL. See *Brookgreen Gardens I.*

ROTHERMEL, Peter F[rederick].   b. July 8, 1817 at Nescopeck, Pa.; d. Aug. 15, 1895 near Linfield, Pa. according to G&W but MF says Pottstown, Pa. See DAB; Cowdrey, NAD; Cowdrey, AA & AAU; Rutledge, PA; G&W; Hamilton.

ROULAND, Orlando.   d. June 26, 1945 per m.c., NYPL.

ROWSE, Samuel Worcester.   b. Jan. 29, 1822; d. May 24, 1901. He was also an engraver. See DAB; Cowdrey, NAD; G&W; Hamilton.

RUGGLES, Dr. Edward.   He was also an amateur marine painter. See Cowdrey, NAD; Cowdrey, AA & AAU; G&W.

RUMSEY, Charles C[ary].   b. Aug. 29, 1879; d. Sept. 21, 1922. He was the nephew of the sculptor Seward Cary; at fourteen he went to France to study with Paul Wayland Bartlett and returning to the U.S. he continued his studies with Bela Pratt. He received a B.A. from Harvard in 1902. He went back to Paris, studying especially with Fremiet and returned to the U.S. in 1906, settling in NYC where he exhibited in 1917. Among his works are: Dying Indian (Brooklyn Museum); frieze, The Buffalo Hunt (approach to Manhattan Bridge); frieze (Rice Memorial Playground, Pelham Bay Park, NYC); equestrian statue of Pizarro (Trujillo, Spain; Lima, Peru); Victory (Brownsville Soldiers' and Sailors' Monument, Brooklyn); Pagan Kin (Whitney Mus. of Amer. Art); Hound (a pair) (Brookgreen Gardens; Cleveland Mus. of Art). A retrospective selection of his works was exhibited at the Societe Nationale des Beaux-Arts, Paris, 1927. He exhibited three sculptures at the 1913 Armory Show. See *Brookgreen Gardens I;* cat. of the 1963 Armory Show.

RUSH, William.   b. July 4, 1756; d. Jan. 17, 1833. See DAB; Rutledge, PA; G&W.

RUSSELL, Charles M[arion].   Artist, sculptor, writer. b. March 19, 1864, at St. Louis. He left the family home, Oakhill, for Montana in 1880, and except for brief sojourns lived all his life in Montana, principally in Great Falls.

Russell was entirely self taught. His only instruction was his own empiricism and observation from living on the range as a cowboy, from the time he reached Montana until his marriage in 1896. His earliest known painting is a small postcard size water color entitled A Dream of Burlington which he made in 1883. In 1886 some of his illustrations appeared, adapted by another hand, in the Northwest Magazine, and from then until his death on October 24, 1926, at Great Falls, Russell illustrated scores of books and magazine articles.

He was extremely prolific. The exact number of paintings he produced is not known, but it would be approximately 3000. He worked in oil, water colors, and wash, and he also sketched in pen and ink and occasionally in crayon. He was a sculptor and approximately 110 examples of his bronzes are known. He was a writer. He wrote voluminously to friends and illustrated his letters with small sketches. Many of these were gathered in a posthumous volume, *Good Medicine*. His books *Rawhide Rawlins Stories* and *More Rawhides* were gathered with additions and published as *Trails Plowed Under,* which is a classic of Montana range life. Russell was also a story teller. Both Irvin S. Cobb and Will Rogers publicly stated that Russell was the greatest story teller they ever encountered.

Russell had several periods. His early work is crude, but starting in 1901 he began to render actual remembered scenes of life on the range with startling fidelity. His period from 1907 to 1914 produced such well known works as In Without Knocking, Jerked Down, Toll Collectors, and Wild Horse Hunters. It was during this period in 1912 that he painted the great mural which is in the State Capitol at Helena, Lewis and Clark Meeting Indians At Ross' Hole. Toward the end of his life Russell departed from portrayals of minute attention to details and painted virtually in an impressionistic style undoubtedly endeavoring to portray his feeling of love for the west and how the big sky country appeared to his eyes.

Russell had 28 one-man shows, chiefly in Chicago, New York and London. The largest collection of his work is in the Amon Carter Museum of Western Art at Fort Worth. There are important collections in the Montana Historical Society at Helena, the Trigg-C. M. Russell Gallery at Great Falls, Woolaroc Museum at Bartlesville, The Gilcrease Institute at Tulsa, The Norton Gallery at Shreveport, and the Buffalo Bill Center at Cody, Wyoming.

In early years Russell occasionally traded his pictures for groceries, but under the surprisingly capable management of his wife he lived to see his pictures fetch what he termed "dead man's prices." The largest commission he enjoyed was painting a mural for Doheny for $30,000. Today his pictures are almost beyond reach.

For a partial list of his works consult a bibliography of Charles M. Russell by Karl Yost and Frederick G. Renner.—Karl Yost.

RUSSELL, M[oses] B.   b. *c.* 1810 in New England; d. 1884. He was also a portrait and figure painter. See G&W.

RUSSELL, Walter.   d. May 19, 1963 per NY Times May 20, 1963.

RUSSELL, W. C.   See Cowdrey, NAD; G&W.

RUTHERFORD, [Alexander W.].   b. 1826 in Vermont; d. 1851 in London. He was also a portrait and still life painter. See Cowdrey, AA & AAU; Cowdrey, NAD; G&W.

RYDER, Albert P[inkham].   He exhibited ten oil paintings at the 1913 Armory Show. See the cat. of the 1963 Army Show.

SABIN, Joseph F.   d. 1927 per m.c., N-YHS.

SACHEVERELL, John.   See Hamilton, 48; G&W.

SACKS, Joseph.   Misindexed after John Sacheverell and repeated in the next column.

SADD, H[enry] S.   See Cowdrey, NAD; G&W.

SAINT-GAUDENS, Augustus.   b. March 1, 1848; d. Aug. 3, 1907. Among his works are: monument to Admiral

511

Farragut (Madison Square, NYC); The Puritan (Brookgreen Gardens; St.-Gaudens Memorial, Cornish, N.H.; U. of Nebraska, Lincoln; MMA; Whitney Museum, NYC; Carnegie Inst., Pittsburgh); memorial to Mrs. Henry Adams (Rock Creek Cemetery, Washington, D.C.); Peter Cooper (Cooper Union Sq., NYC); Sherman Memorial (Central Park, NYC). He was an officer of the Legion of Honor and taught at the ASL 1889-90, 1891/92 and 1893-98. See *Brookgreen Gardens I;* 75th Anniv. Cat., ASL.

SAINT GAUDENS, Carlotta.   d. 1927 per m.c. Met 2.

ST.-GAUDENS, Louis.   b. Jan. 1, 1853 according to *Brookgreen Gardens II* but 1854 in MF; d. March 8, 1913 according to *Brookgreen Gardens II.* His early training was as a cameo cutter. He joined his brother Augustus at his studio in Paris in 1878, studied at the Ecole des Beaux-Arts and then returned with his brother to NYC and helped him with his work there. 1898-1900 he lived and worked in Flint, Ohio and then moved to Cornish, N.H. where he lived a mile away from his brother's studio. Among his works are: recumbent lions (Boston Public Library); Samuel Brearley (Brearley School, NYC); Painting (City Art Museum, St. Louis); six statues (facade, Union Station, Wash., D.C.); Homer (Library of Congress); Holland, Portugal (attic, Custom House, NYC); baptismal font (Church of the Incarnation, NYC); relief of angels (Church of the Ascension, NYC); Pipes of Pan (MMA). See *Brookgreen Gardens II.*

SALMON, Robert W. [initial omitted in G&W, Rutledge, PA, and Cowdrey, AA & AAU; last name only given in Cowdrey, NAD].   b. *c.* 1775; d. *c.* 1842. He came to the U.S. in 1828 according to G&W but MF says 1829. See Cowdrey, NAD; Cowdrey, AA & AAU; Rutledge, PA; G&W.

SALVATORE, Victor D.   b. 1884 (not 1885 as in MF) in Tivoli, Italy, per *Who's Who in American Art,* 1962. He was a pupil of Charles Niehaus, not Miehaus. In 1962 his address was 108 E. 38th Street, NYC; home, Springfield Centre, N.Y. He exhibited two sculptures at the 1913 Armory Show. See the cat. of the 1963 Armory Show.

SANDERSON, Charles Wesley.   d. March 8, 1805. He also worked in oils. See G&W.

SANFORD, Edward Field, [Jr.].   b. April 6, 1886. He was a pupil of Prof. Bernhauer, travelled widely in Europe and was director of sculpture from 1923 to 1925 at the Beaux-Arts Inst. of Design. He retired due to ill health in ·1933 and was living at the James Semple House, Williamsburg, Va. Among his works are: sculptural decoration (State Capitol, Sacramento, Cal.); Inspiration (Va. Mus. of Fine Arts, Richmond); figures over the door and a finial (Alabama Power Co. Bldg., Birmingham); Victory (Payne Whitney Gymnasium, Yale U.); sculptural groups (Bronx County Courthouse); Infant Hermes (Estate of Joseph C. Baldwin, Jr., Mt. Kisco, N.Y.); Nereid (Estate of Benjamin Stern, Roslyn, L.I.); facade, Francis P. Garvan Mausoleum Woodlawn Cemetery, NYC); bronze doors (Girard College, Phila.); base panels (N.Y. State Theodore Roosevelt Memorial); Dancer (Brookgreen Gardens). See *Brookgreen Gardens I.*

SANFORD, Isaac.   d. *c.* 1842 in Philadelphia. He was also a portraitist. See G&W.

SARGENT, Henry.   d. Feb. 21, 1845. He was a portraitist, historical, genre and religious painter. See DAB; G&W.

SARONY, Napoleon.   b. March 9, 1821 in Quebec; d. Nov. 9, 1896 in NYC. He was also a photographer and charcoal portraitist. G&W make no reference to his being a painter as MF does. See G&W.

SARTAIN, John.   b. Oct. 24, 1808; d. Oct. 25, 1897. He was also a portraitist and was the father of Samuel Sartain. See DAB; Rutledge, PA; Cowdrey, NAD; Cowdrey, AA & AAU; G&W.

SARTAIN, Samuel.   b. Oct. 8, 1830; d. Dec. 20, 1906 in Philadelphia. He also painted portraits and genre subjects. See DAB; Rutledge, PA; G&W.

SAVAGE, Edward.   b. Nov. 26, 1761; d. July 6, 1817. He also painted historical subjects. See DAB; G&W.

SCARBOROUGH, John.   See "Art in America" Dec., 1933, p. 27.

SCARPITTA, G. S. C.   d. Aug. 18, 1948 per m.c., NYPL.

SCHAMBERG, Morton L.   d. 1918. He exhibited five oil paintings at the 1913 Armory Show. See the cat. of the 1963 Armory Show.

SCHETKY, Caroline [Mrs. Samuel Richardson according to G&W and Rutledge, PA; MF says she married a T. M. Richardson].   b. March 3, 1790 in Edinburgh, Scotland; d. March 14, 1852 in Boston. She also painted still life and portraits. See Rutledge, PA; G&W.

SCHNAKENBERG, Henry E.   b. Sept. 14, 1892 in New Brighton, N.Y. He taught at the ASL, 1923-25 and was its president in 1932. He is a member of the Society of American Painters, Sculptors and Gravers and is represented in the permanent collections of the Museum of Modern Art; MMA; PAFA; San Francisco Museum; Art Institute of Chicago; Addison Gallery. He painted the murals in the U.S. P.O.'s at Fort Lee, N.J. and Amsterdam, N.Y. and is a contributor to "The Arts." See 75th Anniv. Cat., ASL.

SCHOFF, Stephen Alonzo.   b. Jan. 16, 1818; d. May 6, 1904 at Norfolk, Conn. according to G&W and Cowdrey, AA & AAU and NAD but 1905 in Branden, Vt. per MF. See DAB; Cowdrey, AA & AAU; Cowdrey, NAD; G&W.

SCHOONOVER, Frank E.   b. Aug. 19, 1877 in Oxford, N.J. Entered Drexel Institute, Philadelphia in 1896 and was admitted to Howard Pyle's Composition Class in 1897. Made his first illustrations for *A Jersey Boy in the Revolution* in 1899 and moved into his first studio at 11 East 8th St. in Wilmington, Del. that same year. In 1903 he made his first trip to the Hudson's Bay Country. Moved his studio to 1616 N. Rodney St. in 1906 and is still in the same studio today. In 1911 he went to the Mississippi Bayou Country to gather material for *Lafitte, the Pirate of the Gulf* which was published in "Harpers' Magazine." In that same summer he traversed Hudson's Bay by canoe and explored the James Bay Country. During 1912-18 he wrote and illustrated for magazines and books. In 1919 he painted a series of WWI pictures for the "Ladies Home Journal." 1920-30 he illustrated many children's books including editions of *Robin Hood,* *Robinson Crusoe, Swiss Family Robinson, Kidnapped,* and *Gulliver's Travels.* In 1930 he designed the first of many stained glass windows, a series of which may be seen at Immanuel Church, Wilmington. In 1937 he began a period of landscape painting which has continued to the present time. Many of these have been done in the upper Delaware Valley and the Brandywine Valley. In 1942 he started his own school of art. A group of 61 of his works was exhibited at the Delaware Art Center Building (Wilmington, Del.) by the Wilmington Society of the Fine Arts, Oct. 5-28, 1962. Some of his paintings and illustrations are in the permanent collection of the Wilmington Society of Fine Arts.

SCHOYER, Raphael.   The MMA has album of wood engravings by him per m.c. Met 3. See G&W.

SCHUSSELE, Christian.   b. Aug. 16, 1826 or 1824; d. Aug. 21, 1879 at Merchantville, N.J. He was also a genre and landscape painter and a lithographer. Several of his paintings were reproduced in mezzotint by John and William Sartain and also in line engraving by Best and Whitechurch. See DAB; Rutledge, PA; Hamilton; G&W.

SCOTT, John W[hite] A[llen].   b. Roxbury, Mass. according to G&W but MF says Dorchester; d. March 4, 1907. He was also a portraitist, marine painter, lithographer and engraver. See G&W.

SCUDDER, Janet.   b. Oct. 27, 1873; d. June 9, 1940 in Rockport, Mass. She was a pupil of Rebisso, worked in a wood-carving factory in Chicago, and then entered Lorado Taft's studio as an assistant on his work for the Columbian Exposition. Dissatisfied with the lack of color in sculpture, she turned to painting in the latter part of her life. Among her works are: Young Diana (Harold Pratt, Glen Cove, L.I.); Shell Fountain (Mrs. Harold McCormick, Lake Forest, Ill.); Young Pan (estate of John D. Rockefeller, Pocantico Hills, N.Y.); statue of Japanese Art (facade, Brooklyn Museum); Seated Faun (Brookgreen Gardens); Frog Baby (Brookgreen Gardens; MMA); Victory (Brookgreen Gardens). She is an Associate of the NA, a member of the NSS, the Union Interalliee, Paris and a chevalier, Legion of Honor. See *Brookgreen Gardens I.*

SEAGER, Mrs. [Sarah] and Miss.   They were also portraitists and were probably mother and daughter. See Cowdrey, NAD; G&W.

SEALEY, Alfred.   b. *c*. 1815 in N.Y. State; d. *c*. 1868 according to G&W but MF says *c*. 1862 on the basis of information in Stauffer. See Cowdrey, NAD; G&W.

SEARS, Philip.   d. March, 1953 in Brookline, Mass. per m.c., NYPL.

SEARS, Taber.   d. Oct. 18, 1950 in NYC per m.c. Met 2.

SEBRON, H[yppolite] [Victor] [Valentin]. b. Aug. 21, 1801 in Candebec, France; d. Sept. 1, 1897 in Paris, France. He also painted dioramas. See Cowdrey, NAD; G&W.

SEL, Jean [or John] B.   d. Jan. 28, 1832. See G&W.

SELLSTEDT, Lars Gustaf.   b. April 30, 1819 at Sundsvall, Sweden; d. June 4, 1911 in Buffalo, N.Y. He was also a marine and landscape painter. See DAB; Cowdrey, NAD; Rutledge, PA; G&W.

SERZ, J[ohn].   b. *c* .1810 in Bavaria according to G&W but MF says Saxony. See G&W.

SEYMOUR, Joseph H.   He was probably related to Samuel Seymour. See G&W.

SEYMOUR, Samuel.   The termination of his stay in Philadelphia was 1822, not 1882 as in MF, per m.c. Met 3. He was also a landscapist and was probably related to Joseph H. Seymour. See Rutledge, PA; G&W.

SHAFTENBERG, Lewis.   The name is given as Lewis Shafteberg in G&W.

SHALER, Frederick [R.].—m.c. Met 2.

SHARPLES, Felix T[homas].   b. *c*. 1786; d. after 1824 according to G&W but MF says 1844.

SHARPLES, James.   b. *c*. 1751 according to G&W but MF says 1752, in Lancashire, England; d. Feb. 26, 1811. He also painted in oils. See DAB; G&W.

SHARPLES, James, Jr.   b. *c*. 1788 according to G&W but MF says 1789; d. Aug. 10, 1839. He was also a watercolorist and still life painter. See G&W.

SHATTUCK, Aaron Draper.   b. March 9, 1832 in Francestown, N.H.; d. July 30, 1928 near Granby, Conn. He was a landscapist, portraitist and animal painter. See DAB; Cowdrey, NAD; Rutledge, PA; G&W; Hamilton.

SHAW, Joshua.   b. *c*. 1777 according to G&W but MF says 1776, at Bellingborough, Lincolnshire, England; d. Sept. 8, 1860 at Burlington, N.J. See Rutledge, PA; Cowdrey, NAD; Cowdrey, AA & AAU; G&W.

SHAW, Stephen William.   b. Dec. 15, 1817 at Windsor, Vt.; d. Feb. 12, 1900 in San Francisco. He was a portrait painter. See G&W.

SHAW, Sydney Dale.,   The first name is given as Sidney in *Armory Show, 50th Anniversary Exhibition, 1913-1963* and Milton W. Brown, *The Story of the Armory Show;* given as Sydney in *American Art Annual,* 1927. He exhibited three oil paintings in the 1913 Armory Show. See the cat. of the 1963 Armory Show.

SHEELER, Charles R., Jr.   He exhibited six oil paintings at the 1913 Armory Show. See the cat. of the 1963 Armory Show.

SHEFFIELD, Isaac.   He was also a miniaturist. See G&W; "Art in America"; Dec., 1933, p. 27.

SHEGOGUE, James Henry [Henry is erroneous; it should be Hamilton].   b. Feb. 22, 1806 at Charleston, S.C.; d. April 7, 1872 at Warrenville, Conn. He also painted historical scenes. See Cowdrey, AA & AAU; Cowdrey, NAD; G&W.

SHEPHERD, Thomas S.   He was also a portraitist. See G&W.

SHEPPARD, Warren W.   d. 1937 per m.c., FARL.

SHERMAN & SMITH.   The partners were George E. Sherman and John Calvin Smith. See G&W.

SHERWOOD, Rosina Emmet.   d. Jan. 19, 1948 per m.c., NYPL.

SHILLING, Alexander.   b. 1859; d. 1937.—m.c. Met 2.

SHINDLER, A. Zeno.   b. *c*. 1813 in Germany. He was a pastel portraitist and landscapist. See Rutledge, PA; G&W.

SHINN, Everett.   b. Nov. 6, 1878 per ASL cat. but 1873 in MF and Webster's. Six of his works were exhibited at the AAAL, Dec. 11, 1964-Jan. 10, 1965. He taught at the ASL 1906/07 and was a member of the NA. He also exhibited with the "Eight" in 1908. See the AAAL cat., *Robert Henri and His Circle;* 75th Anniv. Cat., ASL.

SHIRLAW, Walter.   b. Aug. 6, 1838 in Paisley, Scotland; d. Dec. 26, 1909 in Madrid, Spain according to G&W, Webster's and Rutledge, PA but 1910 in MF. He was a genre painter, portraitist, muralist and illustrator. See DAB; Rutledge, PA; G&W.

SHONNARD, Eugenie F[rederica].   b. April 29, 1886. She studied with Alphonse Mucha at the N.Y. School of Applied Design for Women. A frequent exhibitor at the Paris Salons, 1912-1923 she exhibited at the Museum of N.M. in 1927 and has since been living in Santa Fe. She also is a painter and watercolorist, has carved doors and furniture and designed ironwork. Among her works are: Dinah (N.Y. Zoological Soc.); group of birds (Colorado Springs, Fine Arts Center); Head of a Breton Peasant (MMA); Mother and Child (Mrs. Frederick Taylor, Colorado Springs); Pueblo Indian Woman (Colorado Springs, Fine Arts Center); Marabou (Brookgreen Gardens); Co-Co (Brookgreen Gardens; Musee du Luxembourg). She is a member of the NSS, the Societe Nationale des Beaux-Arts and the Societe du Salon d'Automne, Paris. See *Brookgreen Gardens I.*

SHOTWELL, H. C.   He was a wood engraver. See G&W.

SHUMWAY, Henry C[olton].   b. July 4, 1807 according to G&W, Cowdrey, NAD and AA & AAU and Rutledge, PA but 1808 in MF; d. May 6, 1889 in NYC. He was also a portraitist and was a National Acedemician. See Cowdrey, NAD; Cowdrey, AA & AAU; Rutledge, PA; G&W.

SHURTLEFF, Roswell Morse.   b. June 14, 1838; d. Jan. 6, 1915 in NYC. He executed drawings on wood for John Andrew in Boston and attended classes at the Lowell Institute there. See DAB; G&W; Hamilton.

SIEBERN, E.   d. June 14, 1942 in NYC per m.c. Met 2.

SILVA, Francis Augustus [G&W give only Francis A.].   Member of the Water Color Society, 1872. See G&W.

SIMES, Mary Jane.   b. April 1, 1807 in Baltimore; d. May 16, 1872. See Rutledge, PA; G&W.

SIMMONE, T. [given as T. Simonne in G&W; MF's spelling is based on Stauffer]. See G&W.

SIMMONS, Franklin.   b. Jan. 11, 1839 at Lisbon, Me. according to G&W but 1842 in Providence, R.I. in MF; d. Dec. 6, 1913 in Rome. See DAB; G&W.

SIMONS, Amory C[offin].   b. April 5, 1866 according to *Brookgreen Gardens II* but 1869 in MF and *American Art Annual,* 1927. He studied with John J. Boyle, Charles Grafly, Denys Puech, Jean Dampt and Emmanuel Fremiet. He returned to the U.S. at the beginning of WWI, opening a studio in N.Y. but later went to California in the late '20's, living first in Hollywood and then in Santa Barbara. His specialty was the sculpture of horses. Among his works are: equestrian statue of "Buffalo Bill" Cody (Buffalo Bill Museum, Cody, Wyoming); Haute Ecole (MMA); French Mounted Guard (Musee de l'Armee, Paris); bronzes of Italian mounted guards (High Museum of Art, Atlanta, Ga.); oxen drawing a road roller and other works (Gibbes Art Gallery, Charleston, S.C.); Rearing Colt (Baltimore Mus.); models of the development of the horse (Mus. of Natural History, NYC); Lee Axworthy (Hall of Horses); Circus Horse, Horse being Shod (Public Library, Santa Barbara); animal statuettes (Santa Barbara Mus. of Art); Horse Scratching (Brookgreen Gardens, MMA); The Kicker (Brookgreen Gardens). In 1924 he had a room of his own sculpture at the Baltimore Museum's exhibition of American art and in 1947 exhibited at the Museum of Natural History, NYC, a series of statuettes representing the different breeds of dogs, made for Mrs. Irenee DuPont. He is a fellow of the NSS. See *Brookgreen Gardens II.*

SLOAN, John.   b. Aug. 2, 1871; d. 1951. He studied with Thomas Anschutz at the PAFA and taught at the ASL, 1916-24, 1926-30, 1935-37. He was an Honorary Member, ASL, of which he was president in 1931 and 1932, director, Society of Independent Artists and a member, NIAL. He exhibited two oil paintings and five etchings at the 1913 Armory Show, and six of his oil paintings were exhibited at the AAAL, Dec. 11, 1964-Jan. 10, 1965. See the AAAL Cat., *Robert Henri and His Circle;* 75th Anniv. Cat., ASL; cat. of the 1963 Armory Show.

SMIBERT, John.   b. March 24, 1688 in Edinburgh, Scotland; d. April 2, 1751. See G&W.

SMIBERT, Nathaniel.   b. Jan. 20, 1735 according to G&W but 1734 in MF, in Boston; d. Nov. 3, 1756 in Boston. See G&W.

SMILLIE, George H(enry).   b. Dec. 29, 1840; d. Nov. 10, 1921 at Bronxville, N.Y. See DAB; Rutledge, PA; G&W; Hamilton.

SMILLIE, James.   b. Nov. 23, 1807; d. Dec. 4, 1885; See DAB; Cowdrey, NAD; Cowdrey, AA & AAU; G&W.

SMILLIE, James David.   b. Jan. 16, 1833 in NYC; d. Sept. 14, 1909 in NYC. He was also a lithographer and landscapist and engraved illustrations for F.O.C. Darley [not Darby as in MF] for novels of Dickens. See DAB; Cowdrey, NAD; Rutledge, PA; Hamilton; G&W.

SMILLIE, William Cumming.   b. Sept. 23, 1813. See G&W.

SMITH, Albert D.   d. 1962 per m.c. Met 5.

SMITH, Allen, [Jr.].   b. in Rhode Island; d. Cleveland, Ohio. He was also a genre painter and was an Associate of the NA. See Cowdrey, NAD; Cowdrey, AA & AAU; G&W.

SMITH, F[rancis] Hopkinson.   b. Oct. 23, 1838; d. April 7, 1915 in NYC. He was also a portraitist. See DAB; G&W.

SMITH, George Girdler.   b. Sept. 8, 1795; d. Dec. 18, 1878 [erroneously in 1858 in MF and other sources]. See G&W.

SMITH, James P.   He was also a portraitist. See Rutledge, PA; G&W.

SMITH, John Rubens.   b. Jan. 23, 1775 in London; d. Aug. 21, 1849. He was also a miniaturist, lithographer and topographical painter. See DAB; Cowdrey, NAD; Cowdrey, AA & AAU; Rutledge, PA; G&W.

SMITH, Joseph Lindon.   d. Oct. 18, 1950 in Dublin, N.H. per m.c. Met 2.

SMITH, Russell.   b. April 26, 1812; d. Nov. 8, 1896 in Glenside, near Philadelphia according to G&W but MF says Edge Hill, Pa. He was also a panoramist and portraitist. See DAB; Rutledge, PA; Cowdrey, AA & AAU; G&W.

SMITH, Sidney L.   See Hamilton.

SMITH, Thomas Lochlan.   b. Dec. 2, 1835 in Glasgow; d. Nov. 5, 1884 in NYC. He was a landscapist and was an Associate of the NA. See Cowdrey, NAD; Rutledge, PA; G&W.

SMITH, William D.   b. *c.* 1800. See G&W.

SMITHER, James [or Jr.].   d. Sept., 1797 in Philadelphia according to G&W but MF says after 1800. See G&W.

SNELL, Florence B. [Mrs. Henry B.]. d. Jan. 20, 1946 per m.c., NYPL.

SNELL, Henry Bayley   d. Jan. 17, 1943 per m.c., NYPL.

SNYDER, H[enry] W.   See G&W.

SONTAG [or SONNTAG], William L. b. March 2, 1822; d. Jan. 22, 1900 in NYC. See Cowdrey, NAD; Cowdrey, AA & AAU; Rutledge, PA; G&W.

SOPER, R[ichard] F.   b. *c.* 1810 in England; d. *c.* 1862, See G&W.

SOUTHWARD, George.   b. April, 1803 in Salem, Mass.; d. Feb. 19, 1876. See G&W.

SOUTHWARD [given as Southworth in G&W and Rutledge, PA], Nathaniel.   b. Jan. 8, 1806 at Scituate, Mass.; d. April 25, 1858 at Dorchester, Mass. See Rutledge, PA; G&W.

SPARROW, T[homas].   b. *c.* 1746. See Hamilton, 49; G&W.

SPEAKMAN, [Miss] Esther.   She was also a copyist. See Rutledge, PA; G&W.

SPEICHER, Eugene E.   d. 1962. Six of his oil paintings were exhibited at the AAAL, Dec. 11, 1964-Jan. 10, 1965. See AAAL cat., *Robert Henri and His Circle.*

SPENCER, Asa   b. *c.* 1805 in Pennsylvania; the date of his death if not exactly known [MF says 1847]. The 1815 listed by MF for his membership in an engraving firm is erroneous; he was not active before 1825. See G&W.

SPENCER, Frederick R. b. June 7, 1806 in Lennox according to G&W but Lenox in MF, N.Y.; d. April 3, 1875 at Wampoville, N.Y. He was also a genre painter. See Cowdrey, AND; Cowdrey, AA & AAU; G&W.

SPENCER, Job B. [he is erroneously called Joseph in MF]. He was also a landscapist. See Cowdrey, NAD; French, *Art and Artists of Connecticut*, 1879, p. 141; G&W.

SPENCER, Joseph B. See Job B. Spencer.

SPENCER, [Miss] Mary. d. 1923. See G&W.

SPERRY, Theodore S. b. Bozrahville, Conn.; d. before 1878 in Hartford, Conn. See G&W.

SPRINCHORN, Carl. He exhibited three paintings and one pastel at the 1913 Armory Show. See the cat. of the 1963 Armory Show.

SPRING, Edward Adolphus. He was also a modeler. See G&W.

ST. MEMIN [given as Saint-Memin in G&W], Charles Balthazar Julien Fevret De. b. March 12, 1770; d. June 23, 1852. He was also a watercolor portraitist and landscapist. See DAB; G&W.

STAIGG, Richard Morell. b. Sept. 7, 1817 in Leeds, England; d. Oct. 11, 1881. He was also a portraitist, genre and landscape painter. See Cowdrey, NAD; G&W.

STANTON, Lucy M. d. 1931 per m.c. Met 4.

STEARNS, Junius Brutus. b. July 2, 1810 at Arlington, Vt.; d. Sept. 17, 1885 in Brooklyn, N.Y. He was also a genre painter. See Cowdrey, NAD; Cowdrey, AA & AAU; Rutledge, PA; G&W.

STEBBINS, Emma. b. Sept. 1, 1815; d. Oct. 25, 1882 in NYC. She was primarily a portraitist in stone, crayon, oils, pastel and watercolors but also a monumental sculptor. She was an Associate of the NA. See Rutledge, PA; Cowdrey, NAD; G&W.

STEEL, James W. d. June 30, 1879. See G&W.

STELLA, Joseph. b. 1880; d. 1946. He exhibited three oil paintings at the 1913 Armory Show. See the cat. of the 1963 Armory Show.

STERNE, Maurice. b. July 13, 1878. He was a student of Thomas Eakins and taught at the ASL, 1919/20 and 1921/22 and is a member of the NA, NIAL, Sculptors Guild and Commission of Fine Arts, Washington, D.C. He held a retrospective exhibition at the Museum of Modern Art, 1933. See 75th Anniv. Cat., ASL.

STILES, Samuel. b. July 15, 1796 in East Windsor, Conn. according to G&W but Vt. in MF; d. April 3, 1861 in NYC. He was also a portrait painter. See G&W.

STODARD, Frederick L. d. 1940 per m.c., FARL.

STONE, Henry. He was also a portrait painter. See G&W.

STONE, Horatio. b. Dec. 25, 1808; d. Aug. 25, 1875. See DAB; Cowdrey, NAD; G&W.

STONE, Walter King. d. June 21, 1949 per m.c., NYPL.

STONE, William Oliver. b. Sept. 26, 1830; d. Sept. 15, 1875. See DAB; Cowdrey, NAD; Rutledge, PA; G&W.

STORY, George Henry. b. Jan. 22, 1835; d. Nov. 24, 1923. He was also a genre painter. See G&W.

STORY, William Wetmore. b. Feb. 12, 1819 according to G&W and Webster's but 1815 in MF; d. Oct. 7, 1895 at Vallombrosa, Italy. See DAB; G&W.

STOUT, George H. b. 1807 in NYC; d. Jan. 26, 1852. See G&W.

STOUT, James D. He is probably James DeForrest Stout. b. July 22, 1783 in NYC; d. July 8, 1868 in NYC. He was the father of James Varick Stout. See G&W.

STOUT, James V[arick]. b. 1809 in NYC; d. April 26, 1860 in NYC. He was the son of J.D. Stout. See G&W.

STREET, Robert. b. Jan. 17, 1796 at Germantown, Pa.; d. 1865. He was also a religious and landscape painter. See Cowdrey, AA & AAU; G&W.

STRICKLAND, William. b. Nov., 1788 at Navesink, N.J. according to G&W and Rutledge, PA but 1787 in Philadelphia in MF and 1787? in Philadelphia in Webster's; d. Apr. 6, 1854. He also designed the capitol building at Nashville, where he was buried. See DAB; Rutledge, PA; G&W.

STROTHER, Col. David Hunter [Porte Crayon]. b. Sept. 26, 1816 at Martinsburg, Va. [now W. Va.]; d. March 8, 1888 at Charleston, W. Va. He was also an illustrator and landscapist. He studied abroad, returning to the U.S. in about 1844 and began drawing for magazines. Much of his work was in "Harper's New Monthly Magazine". He was a cousin of John P. Kennedy, for whom he illustrated *Swallow Barn*. See DAB; Cowdrey, NAD; Rutledge, PA; G&W; Hamilton.

STRYCKER, Jacobus Gerritsen. b. 1619. See comments in G&W about the alleged portrait of him at the MMA.

STUART, Gilbert. b. Dec. 3, 1755 in the Township of North Kingston, R.I. according to G&W but MF says Narragansett; d. July 9, 1828 per G&W but MF says July 27. See G&W.

STUART, Jane. b. in Boston; d. April 27, 1888. See Cowdrey, AA & AAU; Cowdrey, AND; Rutldege, PA; G&W.

SULLY, Alfred. b. May 22, 1820 in Philadelphia; d. April 27, 1879. See G&W.

SULLY, Lawrence. b. Dec. 28, 1769 in Kilkenny, Ireland; d. 1804 according to G&W but MF says 1803. See G&W.

SULLY, Robert Matthew. b. July 17, 1803 at Petersburg, Va.; d. Oct. 16, 1855. He was also a miniaturist. See Rutledge, PA; Cowdrey, NAD; Cowdrey, AA & AAU; G&W.

SULLY, Thomas. b. June 19, 1783; d. Nov. 5, 1872. He was also a miniaturist and figure painter. See Rutledge, PA; Cowdrey, NAD; Cowdrey, AA & AAU; G&W.

SUYDAM, James Augustus. b. March 27, 1819 in NYC according ot G&W but MF says in N.H.; d. Sept. 15, 1865 at North Conway, N.H. See Cowdrey, NAD; G&W; Hamilton.

SWAIN, W[illiam]. b. Dec. 27, 1803; d. Feb. 18, 1847 in NYC. See Belknap,

"Artists of Essex County, Mass." 1927, p. 13; Cowdrey, NAD; G&W.

SWETT, Cyrus A. See G&W.

SWORD, James Brade. b. Oct. 11, 1839; d. Dec. 1, 1915 in Philadelphia. See G&W.

TACK, Augustus Vincent. b. Nov. 9, 1870; d. July 21, 1949 in NYC. He taught at the ASL, 1906-10 and was a life member, ASL; member, International Society of Arts and Letters; Century Associations; New Haven Paint and Clay Club. He painted murals in the legislative chamber, new Parliament Bldg., Manitoba, Can.; Governor's Suite, Nebraska State Capitol; Church of St. Paul, N.Y.; Church of St. James, S. Deerfield, Mass.; Church of St. Agnes, Dalton, Mass.; Charles J. Dunlap Memorial, New Rochelle, N.Y.; Schelmerdive Memorial, Philadelphia and is represented in the collections of the MMA; Cleveland Museum; Phillips Memorial Gallery; Newark Art Museum; Snead Memorial Museum, Louisville, Ky. See 75th Anniv. Cat., ASL.

TAFT, Lorado. b. April 29, 1860; d. Oct. 30, 1936 in Chicago, Illinois. B.A. 1879 and M.A., University of Illinois. He was a pupil of Augustin Dumont, Bonnassieux and Jules Thomas in France and in 1886 returned to Chicago where he was an instructor in modeling at the Art Institute for twenty years. He also became a lecturer in Art History at the universities of Chicago and Illinois. Among his works are: Black Hawk (Oregon, Illinois); Columbus Memorial Fountain (Washington, D.C.); The Fountain of Time (Chicago); Thatcher Memorial Fountain (Denver); Alma Mater (U. of Illinois); The Pioneers (Elmwood, Ill.); Daughter of Phyrra (Brookgreen Gardens); The Patriots, The Pioneers (State Capitol, Baton Rouge). Several of his other works are at the U. of Illinois. He also wrote *Modern Tendencies in Sculpture*. See *Brookgreen Gardens I*.

TAIT, Arthur F[itzwilliam]. b. Aug. 5, 1819 at Livesey Hall, near Liverpool, England; d. April 28, 1905 at Yonkers, N.Y. He excelled in painting wild animals and also did sporting scenes. Many of his paintings were lithographed by Currier & Ives.

His studio was in NYC. See DAB; Cowdrey, NAD; Cowdrey, AA & AAU; Rutledge, PA; G&W; Hamilton.

TAIT, John Robinson.   b. Jan. 14, 1834; d. July 29, 1909 at Baltimore, Md. according to G&W and Rutledge, PA but 1908 in MF. See G&W.

TALBOT, Grace H[elen].   b. Sept. 3, 1901. She studied with Miss Frismuth and Solon Borglum and for a year in Paris. She exhibited in NYC in 1928 and has a studio in Syosset, L.I. Her statue, Adolescents, is at Brookgreen Gardens. See *Brookgreen Gardens I.*

TANNER, Benjamin.   b. March 27, 1775; d. Nov. 14, 1848. See DAB; Rutledge, PA; G&W.

TANNER, Henry O.   d. May 25, 1937 per m.c. Met 2.

TANNER, Henry S[chenck].   d. May 17, 1858. See DAB; G&W.

TARBELL, Edmund C.   d. 1938 per m.c. Met 2.

TATNALL, Henry Lee [Lea] in G&W. b. Dec. 31, 1829; d. Sept. 26, 1885 according to G&W but 1865 in MF. See G&W.

TAYLOR, Alexander H.   See Rutledge, PA; G&W.

TALYOR, Emily Drayton.   d. June 19, 1952 per m.c. Met 2.

TAYLOR, Henry Fitch.   He exhibited three oil paintings at the 1913 Armory Show. See the cat. of the 1963 Armory Show.

TAYLOR, William Ladd.   d. 1926. He exhibited one oil painting and drawings at the 1913 Armory Show. See the cat. of the 1963 Armory Show.

TEFFT, Carl [given as Charles in Brookgreen Gardens] Eugene.   b. Sept. 22, 1874 in Brewer, Maine; d. Sept. 20, 1951 at Presque Isle, Maine. He studied at the Artist-Artisan Institute, NYC with Blankenship and F. E. Ruckstall and became an instructor in modeling there in 1898. He was an apprentice of J.Q.A. Ward and was influenced by Saint-Gaudens. He was director of sculpture, Sesqui-Centennial Exposition, Philadelphia. Among his works are: fountain, N.Y. Botanical Garden; Fort Lee

Battle Monument; WWI Monument (Belleville, N.J.); William H. Maxwell (Amer. Mus. of Natural History, NYC); Hannibal Hamlin (Bangor, Maine); Peirce Memorial (Bangor, Maine); River Driver (Brookgreen Gardens). See *Brookgreen Gardens II.*

TERRY, Luther.   b. July 18, 1813. He was also a figure painter. See Cowdrey, NAD; Cowdrey, AA & AAU; G&W.

TERRY, W[illiam] D.   See G&W.

TETLEY, William Birchall.   He came from London in 1774. See G&W.

THACKARA, James.   b. March 12, 1767; d. Aug. 15, 1848. He was the father of William Thackara. See G&W.

THACKARA, William.   b. Feb. 9, 1791; d. April 19, 1839. See G&W.

THAYER, Abbot Henderson [corrected to read Handerson in m.c., FARL].

THAYER, Gerald H.   He was the son of Abbot H. Thayer.—m.c. Met 2.

THAYER, Sanford.   b. July 19, 1820 at Cato, N.Y.; d. Dec. 1880 at Syracuse, N.Y. He was also a genre painter. See Cowdrey, NAD; G&W.

THEUS, Jeremiah.   b. *c.* 1719; d. May 17, 1774. G&W say he came to the U.S. *c.* 1735; MF erroneously says 1839. He settled in Charleston in 1739. See G&W.

THOM, James Crawford.   b. NYC; d. Feb. 16, 1898 at Atlantic Highlands, N.J. He was also a portrait and genre painter. See Cowdrey, NAD; Rutledge, PA; G&W.

THOMAS, C[harles] H.   See Cowdrey, NAD; Cowdrey, AA & AAU; G&W.

THOMAS, Henry.   See Rutledge, PA; G&W.

THOMAS, Isaiah.   b. Jan. 19, 1749; d. April 4, 1831. See DAB; G&W.

THOMAS, S. Seymour.   d. Feb. 29, 1956 per m.c. Met 2.

THOMPSON, A[lfred] W[adsworth]. b. May 26, 1840; d. Aug. 28, 1896. He was also a historical and portrait painter. See DAB; Rutledge, PA; G&W.

THOMPSON, Arad.   b. Dec. 30, 1786 at Middleboro, Mass.; d. April 23, 1843 at

Middleboro. He was the uncle of Cephas G. Thompson. See G&W.

THOMPSON, Cephas G[iovanni]. b. Aug. 3, 1809; d. Jan. 5, 1888. He was also a genre painter and was an associate of the NA. See DAB; Cowdrey, NAD; Cowdrey, AA & AAU; Rutledge, PA; G&W.

THOMPSON, D. G[eorge]. See G&W.

THOMPSON, Harry Ives. b. Jan. 31, 1840. See G&W.

THOMPSON, Launt. b. Feb. 8, 1833 at Abbeyleix, County Queens, Ireland; d. Sept. 26, 1894 at Middletown, N.Y. See DAB; Cowdrey, NAD; G&W; Hamilton.

THOMPSON, William John. He was also a genre painter. See G&W.

THORNTON, William. b. May 20, 1759; d. March 28, 1828 in Washington, D.C. according to G&W but MF says in Philadelphia in 1827. See DAB; G&W.

THROOP, Daniel Scrope. See Hamilton.

THROOP, John Peter Vannes [Van Ness in G&W]. b. April 15, 1794 at Oxford, N.Y. He was also a lithographer. G&W state that he was sometimes listed as J.V. or J.V.N. Throop, suggesting that he was the J.V.N. Throop who is listed as his brother in MF. See G&W.

THROOP, J.V.N. See John Peter Vannes Throop.

TIEBOUT, Cornelius. b. c. 1773; d. at New Harmony, Ind. in 1832 according to G&W but MF reports 1830 in Kentucky. See DAB; G&W.

TIFFANY, Louis Comfort. d. Jan. 17, 1933 in NYC per m.c. Met 2.

TIFFANY, William [Shaw]. b. 1824; d. Sept. 27, 1907 in NYC. He was a portrait and landscape painter according to G&W but MF lists him as an illustrator and figure painter. See G&W.

TILTON, John Rollin. b. June 8, 1828 in Louden according to G&W but Londen in MF; N.H.; d. March 22, 1888. He was a watercolorist. See DAB; Rutledge, PA; G&W.

TILYARD, [Philip Thomas Coke]. b. Jan. 10, 1785 according to G&W but 1787 in MF at Baltimore, Md.; d. Dec. 21, 1830 according to G&W but 1827 in MF. He was a portrait painter. See G&W.

TISDALE, Elkanah. See Cowdrey, AA & AAU; G&W.

TOLMAN, John, [Jr.]. See G&W.

TOPPAN, Charles. b. Feb. 10, 1796; d. Nov. 20, 1874 in Florence, Italy. See G&W.

TORRENS, Rosalba [listed in G&W as Rosella Torrans, MF's spelling is also in Dunlap]. See G&W.

TORREY, Charles Cutler. b. July 9, 1799; d. Feb. 9, 1827. See G&W.

TORREY, Manasseh C[utler]. b. May 7, 1807 in Salem, Mass.; d. Sept. 24, 1837 in Pelham, Vt. See Cowdrey, NAD; G&W.

TREGO, Jonathan [K.]. b. March 11, 1817; d. c. 1868. He was also an animal and genre painter. See Rutledge, PA; G&W.

TRENCHARD, E[dmond] C. b. c. 1777 in Salem, N.S.; d. Nov. 3, 1824 in Brooklyn, N.Y. See Hamilton, 72; G&W.

TRENCHARD, James. b. 1747. See G&W.

TROTT, Benjamin. b. c. 1770 in Boston (erroneously 1720 in MF); d. Nov. 27, 1843 in Washington, D.C. He was also a portraitist. See DAB; Rutledge, PA; Cowdrey, AA & AAU; G&W.

TROTTER, Newbold Hough. d. Feb. 21, 1898. He was also a landscapist. See G&W.

TROUBETZKOY, Paul. b. Feb. 16, 1866; d. Feb. 12, 1938 at Suna, Lago Maggiore. He gave up formal study after a few lessons, being impatient with conventional methods, and worked on his own. He would have preferred to be a painter but his brother Pierre was already one. In 1897 he went to Russia and established himself in Moscow and served briefly as a professor at the Moscow Art Academy. In 1904 he transferred his studio to Paris. He visited America and stayed here 1914-20. In 1911 he exhibited at the American Numismatic Society. Among his works are: equestrian statue of Czar Alexander III (Leningrad); monument to General Otis (Los Angeles); Dante (San Francisco); Elephant (Brookgreen Gardens); statue of Puccini (La Scala, Milan); war memorial (Pallanza, Italy). Some works are in the collection of the Hispanic Society of America at NYC. See *Brookgreen Gardens I.*

TROWBRIDGE, Vaughan.   d. Paris, 1945 per m.c., NYPL.

TROYE, Edward.   d. July 25, 1874. He was also a portraitist and figure painter. See DAB; Rutledge, PA; Cowdrey, AA & AAU; G&W.

TRUMBULL, John.   b. June 6, 1756; d. Nov. 10, 1843 in NYC. He was also a miniaturist, landscapist and painter of religious subjects. See G&W.

TRYON, Dwight W.   d. 1925 per m.c., FARL.

TUCKER, Allen.   d. 1939. He exhibited five oil paintings at the 1913 Armory Show. See the cat. of the 1963 Armory Show.

TUCKER, Benjamin.   b. Nov. 11, 1768. See G&W.

TUCKERMAN, Stephen Salisbury.   b. Dec. 8, 1830; d. March, 1904 in Standsford, England. He was also a landscapist. See G&W.

TURNER, James.   d. Dec., 1759. See Hamilton, 12, 43; G&W.

TUTHILL, W[illiam] H.   See G&W.

TWACHTMAN, John Henry.   He taught at the ASL, NYC 1889-1902 and was an Honorary Member of the League and a member, American Art Club in Munich. He exhibited two oil paintings at the 1913 Armory Show. See the 75th Anniv. Cat., ASL; cat. of the 1963 Armory Show.

TWIBILL, George W.   b. *c.* 1806 in Lampeter, Pa. (MF erroneously says 1866); d. Feb. 15, 1836. See Cowdrey, NAD; Cowdrey, AA & AAU; G&W.

TYLER, G[eorge] Washington.   b. 1803 or 1805 in NYC; d. May 13, 1833 in NYC. He was a portraitist and an Associate of the NA. See Cowdrey, NAD; G&W.

TYLER, James Cale.   d. 1931 per m.c. Met 2.

TYSON, Carroll S.   d. March 19, 1956 per m.c. Met 2.

ULKE, Henry.   b. Jan. 29, 1821; d. Feb. 17, 1910. See G&W.

ULLMAN, Eugene Paul.   d. April 20, 1953 in Paris per m.c. Met 2.

VAIL, Miss A[ramenta] D[ianthe].   See Cowdrey, AA & AAU; Cowdrey, NAD; G&W.

VALDENUIT, [Thomas Bluget de].   b. 1763; d. 1846. He was also a crayon portraitist. The m.c. Met 2 states that the portrait plates referred to by MF were engraved in, as well as previously to, 1797 and that the address was No. 11, not 12, Fair Street. See G&W.

VALENTINE, Edward V[irginius].   b. Nov. 12, 1838; d. Oct. 19, 1930. See DAB; G&W.

VALLANCE, John.   b. *c.* 1770; d. June 14, 1823. See Hamilton, 476; G&W.

VALLEE, Jean [F]rancois [de].   See G&W.

VAN BEEST, A[lbert] [listed as Beest, Albert Van in G&W].   b. June 11, 1820 in Rotterdam, Holland; d. Oct. 8, 1860 in NYC. He was also a landscapist. See G&W.

VAN BOSKERCK, Robert W[ard].   d. Apr. 24, 1932 per m.c. Met 2.

VANDERLYN, John.   b. Oct. 15, 1775; d. Sept. 23, 1852. He was also a landscapist. See DAB; G&W.

VANDERLYN, Pieter.   b. 1687 in Holland according to G&W but 1676 in MF. See G&W.

VEDDER, Elihu.   b. Feb. 26, 1836 in NYC. He supported himself in N.Y. by making sketches for "Vanity Fair," diagrams for dumbbell exercise and the like. In 1867 he settled in Rome. See DAB; Hamilton; G&W.

VER BRYCK, Cornelius.   b. Jan. 1, 1813 at Yaugh Paugh, N.J.; d. May 31, 1844 in Brooklyn, N.Y. He was also a portraitist and was a National Academician. See Cowdrey, NAD; Cowdrey, AA & AAU; G&W.

VERNON, T[homas].   b. Staffordshire, England *c.* 1824; d. Jan. 23, 1872 in London. See Cowdrey, NAD; G&W.

VERSTILLE, William.   d. Dec. 6, 1803. He was also a portraitist. See G&W.

VIGNIER, A.   See Rutledge, PA; G&W.

VOLK, Leonard Wells.   b. Nov. 7, 1828 in Wells[town], N.Y.; d. Aug. 19, 1895 at Osceola, Wisc. He was the father of Douglas Volk. See DAB; G&W.

VOLK, [Stephen A.] Douglas.   b. Feb. 23, 1856; d. Feb. 7, 1935. Famed for three portraits of Abraham Lincoln, he was working on a fourth shortly before his death. The unfinished portrait would have portrayed an early scene in Volk's life when his father, Leonard Volk, made a bust of Lincoln, who posed with Douglas, then four years old, sitting on his lap. He taught at the ASL, organized the Minneapolis School of Fine Arts and was its director 1886-1893. He also painted still life though he was primarily a portraitist and landscapist. In the National Gallery at Washington are his portraits of King Albert of Belgium, General Pershing and Lloyd George. A portrait of Lincoln is in the Albright Gallery, Buffalo and his portraits of Generals Foster and Granger are at West Point. He is represented in the collections of the Carnegie Museum, Pittsburgh; Corcoran Gallery, Washington; Pittsfield Museum; Minnesota State Capitol; National Museum, Washington; Montclair Art Museum; MMA; National Arts Club; Rochester Memorial Art Gallery; Muskegon (Mich.) Art Museum; Omaha Art Museum; Portland (Me.) Art Society and the Brooklyn Museum. He was a member of the ALNY, Societe des Beaux-Arts et des Lettres, NIAL, and the Soc. of Mural Painters; the Century Club, and National Artists Assn.—N.Y. Times, Feb. 8, 1935.

VOLLMERING, Joseph.   b. at Anhalt, Germany according to G&W but MF has Anholt. He was also a portraitist. See Cowdrey, NAD; Cowdrey, AA & AAU; G&W.

VONNOH, Bessie Potter [Mrs. Robert]. b. Aug. 17, 1872; d. 1955. She exhibited three sculptures at the 1913 Armory Show. Among her works are: The Dance (Brooklyn Museum; Art Inst. of Chicago; AAAL; MMA; Newark Museum; Carnegie Inst., Pittsburgh; Rochester Atheneum); A Young Mother (Brooklyn Museum; Art Inst. of Chicago; Montclair Art Museum; MMA; Fine Arts Gallery, San Diego); Major General Crawford (Smith Memorial, Fairmount Park, Philadelphia); Enthroned (Brooklyn Museum; MMA; Corcoran Gallery of Art, Washington, D.C.); L'Allegresse (Detroit Inst. of Arts); bird fountain (Ormond Beach Park, Fla.); bird bath (Roosevelt Bird Sanctuary, Oyster Bay, L.I.); children for fountain to memory of Frances Hodgson Burnett (Central Park); Water Lilies (Brookgreen Gardens). She is a member of the NA and the NIAL. See Brookgreen Gardens I. cat. of the 1963 Armory Show.

VONNOH, Robert.   d. Dec. 28, 1933 per m.c. Met 2.

WAGNER, Fred.   d. 1940. He exhibited two works at the 1913 Army Show. See the cat. of the 1963 Armory Show.

WAGNER, H[enry] S.   See G&W.

WALDO, Samuel Lovett.   b. April 6, 1783; d. Feb. 16, 1861 in NYC. See DAB; Rutledge, PA; Cowdrey, AA & AAU; Cowdrey, NAD; G&W.

WALDO & JEWETT.   See Cowdrey, AA & AAU; Cowdrey, NAD; Rutledge, PA; G&W.

WALKER, Ferdinand G.   d. 1927 per m.c. Met 2.

WALKER, Henry Oliver.   d. Jan. 14, 1929 at Belmont, per m.c. Met 2.

WALKER, Horatio.   Misindexed after James Walker.

WALKER, James.   b. June 3, 1819; d. Aug. 29, 1889. See Cowdrey, NAD; G&W.

WALKOWITZ, Abraham.   He exhibited six paintings, five drawings and a color monotype at the 1913 Armory Show. See the cat. of the 1963 Armory Show.

WALL, William Allen.   b. May 19, 1801; d. Sept. 6, 1885. He was also a landscapist. See Cowdrey, NAD; G&W.

WALL, William G[uy].   d. after 1864. He was a watercolorist. See G&W.

WALTER, Adam B.   d. Oct. 14, 1875. See G&W.

WALTERS, Emile.   b. 1893 per m.c., FARL, not 1863 as in MF.

WALTERS, John.   He was also an engraver. See G&W.

WARD, Edgar Melville.   b. Feb. 24, 1839 at Urbana, Ohio; d. May 15, 1915 in NYC. He was a genre and landscape painter. See G&W.

WARD, John Q[uincy] A[dams].   b. June 29, 1830; d. May 1, 1910 in NYC. For seven years he worked in a foundry designing decorative objects suitable for precious metal, especially the gold mountings of swords. A sketch for one is in the collection of the AAAL. Among his works are: equestrian statue of Washington (Union Square, NYC); The Indian Hunter (Brookgreen Gardens); The Freedman (Boston Athenæum; Cincinnati Art Museum; AAAL); The Pilgrim, Shakespeare (Central Park, NYC); Washington (steps of Sub-Treasury Bldg., NYC); William Gilmore Simms (Charleston); General Daniel Morgan (Spartanburg); Garfield (Washington, D.C.); Horace Greely (NYC); equestrian statue of General Hancock (Philadelphia); pediment of N.Y. Stock Exchange in collaboration with Paul W. Bartlett; Naval Victory on top of arch for Admiral Dewey, NYC, 1899. He helped plan sculptural ornament for Library of Congress. He is a member of the NIAL. See DAB; G&W; *Brookgreen Gardens I.*

WARNER, William, [Jr.].   See Rutledge, PA; Cowdrey, AA & AAU; G&W.

WARNICKE, John G.   d. Dec. 29, 1818. See G&W.

WARR, John.   b. c. 1798/99 in Scotland. See G&W.

WARREN, A[sa] Coolidge.   b. March 25, 1819; d. Nov. 22, 1904 in NYC. He was also a landscapist and portraitist. See G&W.

WARREN, H[enry].   b. *c.* 1793 in England. He was a landscape, marine and figure painter. See Rutledge, PA; Cowdrey, AA & AAU; G&W.

WARSHAWSKY, Xander [also Xander in *American Art Annual,* 1927; given as Alexander L. in the Armory Show cat.].   He exhibited two oil paintings at the 1913 Armory Show. See the cat. of the 1963 Armory Show.

WARWELL.   d. May 29, 1767. See G&W.

WATERMAN, Marcus.   b. Sept. 1, 1834; d. April 2, 1914 at Moderno, Italy. He was a landscape and figure painter and was an Associate of the NA. See Cowdrey, NAD; Rutledge, PA; Appleton; G&W.

WATERS, George W.   See Cowdrey, NAD; G&W.

WATROUS, Harry W.   m.c. Met 2 states that he was born in 1857, not 1875 as in MF and died in 1940.

WATSON, John.   b. July 28, 1685 in Scotland; d. Aug. 22, 1768 in Perth Amboy, N.J. He came to the U.S. in 1714 according to G&W but MF says 1715. See "The Connoisseur," Nov., 1951, pp. 137-38; G&W.

WATTS, J[ames] W.   d. March 13, 1895 at West Medford, Mass. He was also a banknote engraver. See G&W.

WAUGH, Frederick Judd.   d. 1940 per m.c. Met 2.

WAUGH, [Mary] Eliza [Young]. Mother of Frederick Judd Waugh. See G&W.

WAUGH, Samuel B[ell].   d. Janesville, Wisc. He was also a landscapist and panoramist and was an Associate and Honorary Member, Professional, of the NA. See Rutledge, PA; Cowdrey, NAD; Cowdrey, AA & AAU; G&W.

WAY, Andrew John Henry.   b. April 27, 1826; d. Feb. 7, 1888 in Baltimore, Md. He was also a landscapist. See G&W.

WAY, [Miss] Mary.   See Cowdrey, AA & AAU; G&W.

WEBB, J. Lewis [corected to read Louis in m.c. Met 2].   b. Apr. 24, 1856 in Washington, D.C.; d. Dec. 24, 1928 in NYC.— m.c. Met 2. See "Art Digest," May 1, 1935.

WEBER, F.   m.c. Met 3 states that he had not died in 1906 as in MF but was still alive on Nov. 21, 1928.

WEBER, Max.   b. April 18, 1881 according to G&W and Webster's but 1880 in MF. He studied at the Pratt Institute and taught at the ASL 1919-21 and 1925-27. He was an Honorary Member of the

523

League and a member, American Painters, Sculptors and Gravers. He also wrote *Primitives*, 1927. See 75th Anniv. Cat., ASL.

WEBER, Paul.   b. 1823 in Darmstadt, Germany; d. 1916 in Philadelphia. He was also a portraitist. See Rutledge, PA; Cowdrey, NAD; Cowdrey, AA & AAU; G&W.

WEBSTER, Ambrose E [name given as E. Ambrose Webster in *American Art Annual*, 1927; *Armory Show, 50th Anniversary Exhibition, 1913-1963;* Milton W. Brown, *The Story of the Armory Show*]. b. 1869; d. 1935. He exhibited two oil paintings at the 1913 Armory Show. See the cat. of the 1963 Armory Show.

WEINEDEL, Carl.   d. May 11, 1845 in NYC. He was also a portraitist. See Cowdrey, NAD; G&W.

WEIMAN, Adolph Alexander.   b. Dec. 11, 1870. He also worked in the studio of Charles Niehaus and opened his own studio in 1904. Among his works are: Saltus Award of the American Numismatic Society; Colonel Vilas (Vicksburg, Miss.); panels for the Morgan Library, NYC; facade of the Municipal Bldg., (NYC); tympanum of the Madison Square Presbyterian Church (NYC); pediments, Wisconsin and Missouri capitols; sphinxes, Scottish Rite Temple (Washington, D.C.); frieze, The Terror of War, The Glory of Peace (Elks National Memorial Headquarters, Chicago); friezes, Supreme Court Room; pediments, National Archives and Post Office Bldgs.; bronze doors, AAAL; Narcissus (Brookgreen Gardens); Womboli, Pegasus, Duet, Aphrodite, Water Urchin (Brookgreen Gardens). He served on the NYC Art Commission and the National Commission of Fine Arts, 1928-1931. He was a member of the AAAL and the ALNY. See *Brookgreen Gardens I.*

WEIR, C[harles] E.   b. *c.* 1823; d. June 20, 1845 in NYC. He was a portrait and genre painter and brother of Robert W. Weir, not John F. Weir as stated in MF. See Cowdrey, NAD; Cowdrey, AA & AAU; G&W.

WEIR, John Ferguson.   d. 1926 per m.c. Met 2.

WEIR, Julian Alden.   d. in NYC. He exhibited twelve paintings and several etchings at the 1913 Armory Show. He taught at the ASL, of which he was an Honorary Member, 1885-87 and 1890-98. He was also a member of the Century Association. See the cat. of the 1963 Armory Show; 75th Anniv. Cat., ASL.

WEIR, Robert Walter.   b. June 18, 1803 in NYC according to G&W; d. May 1, 1889 in NYC. He was a landscapist, portraitist, genre painter and illustrator and was the teacher of Whistler, Lee, Grant and Sherman. He was also the father of John Ferguson Weir and Julian Alden Weir. See DAB; Cowdrey, NAD; Cowdrey, AA & AAU; Rutledge, PA; G&W; Hamilton.

WELCH, Thomas B.   d. Nov. 5, 1874. See Rutledge, PA; Cowdrey, AA & AAU; G&W.

WELFARE, Daniel.   He was a portrait and still life painter. See Rutledge, PA; G&W.

WELLMORE [or Willmore], E[dward]. He was also a portrait painter and crayon portraitist.

WELLSTOOD, James Geike.   b. Jan. 18, 1813; d. Jan. 21, 1893 at Greenwich, Conn. He was the brother of William Wellstood. See G&W.

WELLSTOOD, William.   b. Dec. 19, 1819; d. Sept. 19, 1900 in NYC. He was also an etcher. See G&W.

WENTWORTH, [Thomas Hanford].   b. March 15, 1781 in Norwalk, Conn.; d. Dec. 18, 1849 at Oswego, N.Y. He was also an engraver, lithographer and landscapist. See "Antiques," Jan., 1937, p. 10-11; ibid., June, 1937, p. 291; G&W.

WENZLER, H. A. [given as Anthon Henry Wenzler by G&W].   See Cowdrey, NAD; Cowdrey, AA & AAU; Rutledge, PA; G&W.

WERTMULLER, Adolph Ulric[h].   b. Feb. 18, 1751; d. Oct. 5, 1811. He was a member of the French Academy and painted a portrait of Marie-Antoinette which he exhibited in the Salon of 1785. In 1787 he became first court painter to King Gustaf III of Sweden—m.c., FARL. He was also a miniature, historical and figure painter. See Cowdrey, AA & AAU; Rutledge, PA; G&W.

WEST, Benjamin. b. Oct. 10, 1738 according to G&W but 1728 in MF; d. March 10, 1820 according to G&W but MF says March 11. He was also a genre and landscape painter. See G&W.

WEST, William Edward. b. Dec. 10, 1788; d. Nov. 2, 1857. See DAB; Rutledge, PA; Cowdrey, NAD; Cowdrey, AA & AAU; G&W.

WESTON, Mrs. Mary [Pillsbury]. b. Jan. 5, 1817 in Hebron, N.H.; d. May, 1894 in Lawrence, Kansas. She was also a portraitist and landscapist. See Cowdrey, NAD; G&W.

WEYL, Max. b. Dec. 1, 1837 at Muhlen-on-Neckar, Germany; d. July 6, 1914 in Washington, D.C. See G&W.

WHEELER, Janet D. d. Oct. 25, 1945 per m.c., NYPL.

WHEELER, W[illiam] R. b. Scio, Mich.; d. c. 1894. He was also a miniaturist. See G&W.

WHEELOCK, [Merrill G.]. b. 1822 in Vermont; d. 1866. In 1853 he was working in Boston as an architect and from 1858-61 he seems to have worked as a portrait painter in water colors. He illustrated *The White Hills, Their Legends, Landscape, and Poetry* by Thomas Starr King, 1860. See G&W; Hamilton.

WHELPLEY, P[hilip] M. He was also a landscapist. See Cowdrey, AA & AAU; G&W.

WHISTLER, James Abbott McNeill. b. July 10, 1834 according to G&W but MF says July 11. He exhibited four oil paintings at the 1913 Armory Show. See the cat. of the 1963 Armory Show; DAB; G&W.

WHITE, Charles Henry. b. 1878. He exhibited three etchings at the 1913 Armory Show. See the cat. of the 1963 Armory Show.

WHITE, Henry C. d. Sept. 28, 1952 per m.c., NYPL.

WHITE, John Blake. b. Sept. 2, 1781 near Eutaw Springs, S.C. according to G&W, Webster's, Cowdrey, NAD and AA & AAU; d. Aug. 24, 1859 in Charleston. He was also a portraitist and miniaturist.

See DAB; Cowdrey, NAD; Cowdrey, AA & AAU; G&W.

WHITECHURCH, Robert. d. c. 1880 according to G&W but MF says still living in 1883. See Rutledge, PA; G&W.

WHITEHORN, James. See "Art in America," Dec., 1933, p. 28.

WHITNEY, Anne. b. Sept. 2, 1821 at Watertown, Mass.; d. Jan. 23, 1915 in Boston. Her statue of Harriet Martineau was burned in 1914 per m.c., FARL. See DAB; Cowdrey, NAD; G&W.

WHITNEY, Elias [James]. b. Feb. 20, 1827. He was also a genre painter. See Cowdrey, NAD; Hamilton, 496-97; G&W.

WHITNEY, Mrs. Harry Payne [Gertrude Vanderbilt]. b. April 19, 1877 according to Brookgreen Gardens but 1877? in Webster's and 1876 in the ASL cat.; d. April 18, 1942. She started the Whitney Studio Club in her studio in 1914 and it evolved into the Whitney Museum of American Art. Among her works are: Head of a Spanish Peasant (MMA); Red Cross (Musee des Invalides, Paris); war monument (Washington Heights, NYC); Columbus Monument (Palos); war memorial (St.-Nazaire, France); Buffalo Bill (Cody, Wyoming); Peter Stuyvesant (Stuyvesant Sq., NYC); Caryatid (Brookgreen Gardens; Whitney Mus. of American Art; McGill U., Montreal). She was a member of the NSS, an Associate of the NA, an Honorary Member of the ASL, a member of the National Assn. of Women Artists, and of the Portrait painters. See *Brookgreen Gardens I;* 75th Anniv. Cat.; ASL.

WHITTAKER, John Bernard. b. in Ireland. See Cowdrey, NAD; G&W.

WHITTREDGE, [Thomas] Worthington. b. May 22, 1820; d. Feb. 25, 1910 according to G&W, erroneously 1810 in MF. While in Dusseldorf he posed for the figure of Washington in Leutze's "Washington Crossing the Delaware." He was president of the NAD in 1865 and 1874-77. See DAB; Cowdrey, NAD; Cowdrey, AA & AAU; Rutledge, PA; Hamilton; G&W; Barker, p. 439.

WIEGAND, Gustav. d. Nov. 3, 1957 in Old Chatham, N.Y. per m.c., NYPL.

WIGGINS, Carleton.   d. June 11, 1932 per m.c. Met 2.

WIGGINS, Guy.   d. 1962 per m.c., FARL.

WIGHT, Moses.   b. April 2, 1827. He was also a genre painter. See G&W.

WIGHTMAN, Thomas.   See Hamilton; G&W.

WILCOX, John Angel James.   b. Aug. 21, 1835. See G&W.

WILCOX [or WILLCOX], W. H.   b. c. 1831 in N.Y. State. Active in 1870 per m.c. Met 2. See Cowdrey, AA & AAU; Rutledge, PA; G&W.

WILDE, Hamilton G[ibbs].   b. 1827; d. 1884. He was also a portrait and landscape painter. See G&W.

WILES, Lemuel M[aynard].   b. Oct. 21, 1826; d. Jan. 28, 1905. See Rutledge; PA; G&W.

WILGUS, [William] John.   b. Jan. 28, 1819 at Troy, N.Y.; d. July 23, 1853 at Buffalo, N.Y. See G&W.

WILLARD, Asaph.   b. Dec. 24, 1786 at Wethersfield, Conn.; d. July 14, 1880 in Hartford, Conn. See Hamilton, 94; G&W.

WILLIAMS, Frederick D[ickinson].   b. 1829; d. Jan. 27, 1915 in Brookline, Mass. He was also a portraitist. See G&W.

WILLIAMS, Henry.   d. Oct. 21, 1830 in Boston. See G&W.

WILLIAMS, Isaac L.   b. June 24, 1817; d. April 23, 1895 in Philadelphia. He was also a figure painter. See Rutledge, PA; Cowdrey, NAD; Cowdrey, AA & AAU; G&W.

WILLIAMS, William J[oseph].   b. Nov. 17, 1759 in NYC; d. Nov. 30, 1823 in Newbern, N.C. according to G&W but MF says Charleston, S.C. He was also a miniaturist. See G&W.

WILLIAMSON, John.   b. April 10, 1826 in Glasgow; d. May 28, 1885 at Glenwood-on-the-Hudson. See Cowdrey, NAD; Cowdrey, AA & AAU; G&W.

WILLSON, Matthew.   See Matthew Wilson.

WILMARTH, Lemuel Everett.   b. March 11, 1835; d. July 27, 1918 in Brooklyn, N.Y. He was a genre painter and was a National Academician. See DAB; Rutledge, PA; G&W.

WILSON, Alexander.   b. July 6, 1766; d. Aug. 23, 1813. See DAB; G&W.

WILSON, Claggett.   b. 1887 according to Armory Show cat. but 1886 in MF; d. May 19, 1952 per m.c. Met 2. He exhibited two oil paintings in the 1913 Armory Show. See the cat. of the 1963 Armory Show.

WILSON [incorrectly given in MF as Willson], Matthew.   b. July 17, 1814; d. Feb. 23, 1892 in Brooklyn according to G&W but MF says Hartford, Conn. See Cowdrey, NAD; Rutledge, PA; G&W.

WINNER, William E.   b. c. 1815 in Philadelphia; d. 1883 in Philadelphia. He was also a historical and religious painter. See Rutledge, PA; Cowdrey, NAD; Cowdrey, AA & AAU; G&W; Hamilton.

WINSTANLEY, William.   fl. 1793-1806 per m.c. 2, N-YHS. See Cowdrey, AA & AAU; G&W.

WINTER, G[eorge].   b. June 10, 1810 at Portsea, England; d. Feb. 1, 1876 at Lafayette, Ind. He was also a portraitist and landscapist. See Cowdrey, NAD; "Art in America," Dec., 1933, p. 28; G&W.

WITT, John H[enry].   b. May 18, 1840; d. Sept. 13, 1901 in NYC according to G&W but MF says 1900. See G&W.

WOISERI, J. I. Bouquet [listed in G&W as J. L. Boqueta De Woiseri].   He was also a landscape painter in water colors. See G&W.

WOOD, Franklin T.   d. May 22, 1945 per m.c., NYPL.

WOOD, George B[acon], [Jr.].   He was also a genre painter and silhouettist. See Rutledge, PA; G&W.

WOOD, Grant.   d. Feb. 12, 1942 in Iowa per m.c. Met 2.

WOOD, Joseph.   d. June 15, 1830 according to G&W but MF says 1852. He was also a portraitist. See Rutledge, PA; Cowdrey, AA & AAU; G&W.

WOOD, Thomas Waterman.   b. Nov. 12, 1823; d. April 4, 1903 in NYC. He was also a genre painter. See Cowdrey, NAD; G&W.

WOODSIDE, John A[rchibald], [Sr.]. b. 1781 in Philadelphia; d. Feb. 26, 1852 in Philadelphia. He was also a still life and animal painter. See Rutledge, PA; G&W.

WOODWILLE, R[ichard] Caton. b. April 30, 1825 according to G&W but MF says 1820; d. Sept. 30, 1856 according to G&W but MF says 1855. He was a genre painter. See Cowdrey, NAD; Cowdrey, AA & AAU; Rutledge, PA; G&W.

WOOLLEY, William. He was also a portrait painter. See G&W.

WORTH, Thomas. b. Feb. 12, 1834 in NYC; d. Dec. 29, 1917. He was also a genre artist. Many of his caricatures, among which were many of negro life, were printed and published by Currier & Ives. He was also a contributor to "Yankee Notions" and other magazines. See Hamilton; G&W.

WRENCH, [Polly] Mary. See G&W.

WRENN, Charles L. d. Oct., 1952 per m.c., NYPL.

WRIGHT, Alice Morgan. b. Oct. 18, 1881. She graduated from Smith College in 1904 and studied at the ASL with Hermon MacNeil, Gutzon Borglum and James E. Fraser and at Paris at the Academie Colarossi, with criticisms from Injalbert. She had a one-man show in NYC in 1937. Among her works are: Lady Macbeth (Newark, Mus.; Folger Shakespeare Library, Washington, D.C.); Pan (Harmanus Bleecker Library, Albany; National Collection of Fine Arts, Washington, D.C.); three portrait reliefs (Smith College); "I am the captain of my soul" (Brookgreen Gardens). She is a member of the NSS. See *Brookgreen Gardens I*.

WRIGHT, Charles Cushing. b. May 1, 1796 at Damariscotta [incorrectly Damascota in MF], Me.; d. June 7, 1854 in NYC. See Cowdrey, NAD; Cowdrey, AA & AAU; G&W.

WRIGHT, George Frederick. b. Dec. 19, 1828; d. at Hartford, Conn. See Cowdrey, NAD; G&W.

WRIGHT, James Henry. He was also a marine and still life painter. See Cowdrey, NAD; Cowdrey, AA & AAU; G&W.

WRIGHT, Joseph. b. July 16, 1756; d. in Philadelphia. He was also an etcher. See DAB; Rutledge, PA; G&W.

WRIGHT, Patience [Lovell]. d. March 23, 1786. See DAB; G&W.

WRIGHT, Rufus. b. Cleveland, Ohio. He was also a figure painter. See G&W.

WUNDER, Adalbert. b. Feb. 5, 1827 in Berlin, Germany. See Cowdrey, NAD; G&W.

WYANT, Alexander H[elmwig]. b. Jan. 11, 1836 at Evans Creek, Ohio according to G&W but MF says Port Washington, Ohio; d. Nov. 29, 1892 in NYC. See DAB; Rutledge, PA; G&W.

YANDELL, Enid. d. 1934. She exhibited two sculptures at the 1913 Armory Show. See the cat. of the 1963 Armory Show.

YEAGER, Joseph. b. *c.* 1792; d. June 9, 1859 in Philadelphia. See DAB; G&W.

YEWELL, George Henry. b. Jan. 20, 1830; d. Sept. 26, 1923. He was also a genre painter. See Cowdrey, NAD; Rutledge, PA; G&W.

YOHN, F[rederick] C[offay]. d. Norwalk, 1933 per m.c., FARL.

YOUNG, Arthur [Art]. d. 1943. He exhibited seven drawings at the 1913 Armory Show. See the cat. of the 1963 Armory Show.

YOUNG, J[ames] Harvey. b. June 14, 1830; d. 1918 in Brookline, Mass. See Rutledge, PA; G&W.

YOUNG, Mahonri [Mackintosh]. b. Aug. 9, 1877; d. Nov. 2, 1957 in Norwalk, Conn. per m.c., NYPL. Among his works are: Bovet Arthur—a laborer (Newark Museum); The Rigger (Brookgreen Gardens; Newark Museum); Indian groups for the American Museum of Natural History; Breton peasant woman (Whitney Museum of American Art, NYC); Right to the Jaw (Brooklyn Museum). Other works are at the Phillips Academy, Andover, Mass.; MMA; Rhode Island School of Design; Dayton Art Inst.; Peabody Inst., Baltimore. A retrospective exhibition was held at the Addison Gallery of American Art, Andover, Mass. He wrote the article on modeling in the Encyclopedia Britannica and exhibited seven sculptures and some drawings at the 1913 Armory Show. He is a member of the NIAL and the Society of American Etchers. See the cat. of the 1963 Armory Show; *Brookgreen Gardens I;* 75th Anniv. Cat., ASL.

YOUNG, Thomas.   He also painted miniatures. See G&W.

ZEIGLER, A. Lee Woodward.   d. June 16, 1952 per m.c., NYPL.

ZETTLER, Emil Robert.   d. Jan. 10, 1946 m.c., NYPL.

ZIMMERMAN, Eugene.   d. 1935 per m.c. Met 3.

ZORACH, William.   b. Feb. 28, 1887 in Eurburg, Lithuania according to ASL cat. but in Russia in MF. He also studied at the Cleveland School of Arts and the ASL, and taught at the ASL 1929-51. He was vice-president, Society of American Painters, Sculptors and Gråvers and a member of the Board, Sculptors Guild. He did the marble statue of Benjamin Franklin, P.O. Bldg., Wash., D.C. and exhibited in the Forum Group in 1916. He also exhibited two oil paintings in the 1913 Armory Show. See the cat. of the 1963 Armory Show; 75th Anniv. Cat., ASL.

PARTIAL BIBLIOGRAPHY

Album of American battle art, 1755-1918. Washington, 1947.

Appleton's Cyclopedia of American biography, ed. by J. G. Wilson and John Fiske. 7 volumes. NY, 1887-1900.

American Art Annual, 1898 —. NY, 1899 —.

Art Index, January 1929 —, A cumulative author and subject index to a selected list of fine arts periodicals and museum bulletins. NY, 1933 —.

Barker, Virgil. *American painting, history and interpretation.* NY, 1950.

Benezit, Emmanuel. *Dictionnaire critique et documentaire de peintres, sculpteurs, dessinateurs et graveurs de tous les temps et de tous les pays . . . Nouv. ed. . . .* 8 volumes. Paris, 1948-55.

Brown, Milton W. *The Story of the Armory Show.* NY, 1963.

Cowdrey, [Mary] Bartlett. *National Academy of Design exhibition record 1826-1860.* 2 volumes. NY, 1943.

Cowdrey, Mary Bartlett. *American Academy of Fine Arts and American Art Union.* 2 volumes. NY, 1953.

Dictionary of American Biography. ed. by Allen Johnson and Dumas Malone. 11 volumes. NY, 1946.

Fielding, Mantle. *American engravers upon copper and steel; biographical sketches and check lists of engravings . . .* Philadelphia, 1917.

Groce, George C. and David H. Wallace. *The New-York Historical Society's dictionary of artists in America 1564-1860.* New Haven, 1957.

Hamilton, Sinclair. *Early American book illustrators and wood engravers 1670-1870.* Princeton, NJ, 1958.

Metropolitan Museum of Art (The) presents the 75th anniversary exhibition of painting and sculpture by 75 artists associated with the Art Students League of New York. NY, 1951.

Proske, Beatrice Gilman. *Brookgreen Gardens sculpture.* 2 volumes. Brookgreen, SC, 1943-55.

Richardson, E. P. *Painting in America, the story of 450 years.* NY, 1956.

Rutledge, Anna Wells. *Cumulative record of exhibition catalogues, the Pennsylvania Academy of the Fine Arts, 1807-1870; the Society of Artists, 1800-1814; the Artists Fund Society, 1835-1845.* Philadelphia, 1955.

Stauffer, David McNeely. *American engravers upon copper and steel.* 2 volumes. NY, 1907.

[Trovato, Joseph S.] *1913 Armory Show 50th anniversary exhibition 1963, organized by Munson-Williams-Proctor Institute, sponsored by the Henry Street Settlement, New York.* [NY, 1963].

Tuckerman, Henry T. *Book of the Artists. American artist life* . . . NY, 1867.

Webster's Biographical Dictionary. Springfield, Mass. 1943.